P9-CRA-549

Word for Word

HARRAP ADVISORY COMMITTEE

A. Walton Litz, D. Phil., Holmes Professor of Belles Lettres,
Princeton University U.S.A.

Alastair Fowler, D. Phil., D. Litt., M.A., F.B.A.,
Regius Professor of Rhetoric and English Literature,
University of Edinburgh

Douglas Gray, M.A., J.R.R. Tolkien Professor of English Literature and Language,
University of Oxford

Keith Rawson-Jones, Commander of the Order of Merit, P.P.R., B.A. (Hons),
(Secretary)

A Henry Holt/Harrap Reference

Word for Word

A Dictionary of
Synonyms

JOHN O. E. CLARK

An Owl Book

Henry Holt and Company
New York

Copyright © 1988 by Clark Robinson Limited
All rights reserved, including the right to reproduce
this book or portions thereof in any form.
First published in the United States in 1990 by
Henry Holt and Company, Inc., 115 West 18th Street,
New York, New York 10011.

Library of Congress Cataloging-in-Publication Data
Clark, John Owen Edward.
Word for word : a dictionary of synonyms / John O. E. Clark. — 1st
American ed.
p.   cm. —(A Henry Holt/Harrap reference)
"Originally published in Great Britain in 1988 by Harrap Ltd."—
Verso t.p.
"An Owl book."
ISBN 0-8050-1455-1 (pbk.: alk. paper)
1. English language—Synonyms and antonyms—Dictionaries.
I. Title.   II. Series.
PE1591.C55   1990   90-4558
423'.1—dc20   CIP

Henry Holt books are available at special discounts
for bulk purchases for sales promotions, premiums,
fund-raising, or educational use. Special editions
or book excerpts can also be created to specification.
For details contact:
Special Sales Director
Henry Holt and Company, Inc.
115 West 18th Street
New York, New York 10011

First American Edition

Printed in the United States of America
Recognizing the importance of preserving
the written word, Henry Holt and Company, Inc.,
by policy, prints all of its first editions
on acid-free paper.∞

10 9 8 7 6 5 4 3 2 1

Preface

Part of the richness of English for users of the language – and one of the difficulties encountered by learners of it – results from the existence of words with more or less the same meaning. Such synonyms are seldom exact, but can provide variety to relieve what would otherwise be a limited and ultimately boring vocabulary.

Word for Word is a dictionary of synonyms for users and learners of English. It is organized in a new and, I hope, useful way. The first part of the book contains an alphabetical listing of key English words with their synonyms. Each word's part of speech is identified, and the synonyms listed in up to three categories. First are synonyms of the literal meaning (denoted by the abbreviation *lit.*), second the figurative synonyms (*fig.*) and third, if appropriate, specialist snyonyms (*spec.*). This last category includes words from the arts, sciences and technology. Where an entry represents more than one part of speech, the following order of presentation is strictly observed:

n	noun
vb	verb
adj	adjective
adj (pa.pt)	adjective (in form a past participle of a verb)
adj (pr.pt)	adjective (in form a present participle of a verb)
adv	adverb
prn	pronoun
prp	preposition
cnj	conjunction
art	(definite or indefinite) article

This consistent order of presentation is for ease and speed of access. In many cases it does not necessarily correspond with the importance or frequency of usage within the language of the parts of speech represented by the entry. The different meanings of a headword are represented by groups of synonyms separated by semi-colons.

The second part of *Word for Word* is an index of all the significant synonyms with references to the headword or headwords under which they appear in the first part of the book. Thus, to find a synonym of a particular word, look for it first in part one. If it does not appear there, look for it in the index, which will direct you to the entries under which it does appear.

The mammoth task of selection, compilation and, above all, indexing has been done mainly by four associates, to whom I offer most grateful thanks. They are Ann and Mike Darton, Louise Bostock and Bill Hemsley.

A

a
art lit: one; any; every, per.

abandon
n lit: lack of inhibitions, recklessness, unrestraint, wildness; dash, verve.
vb lit: evacuate, leave, quit, retire from; desert, forsake, leave behind, maroon; jilt, rat on; relinquish, withdraw from; *fig*: *desist*, discontinue, give up, leave off, stop; cede, renounce, resign, waive.

abandoned
adj (pa.pt) lit: derelict, deserted, evacuated, lonely, unoccupied; discarded, dropped, rejected, thrown away; cast aside, forsaken, jilted; *fig*: reckless, uninhibited, unrestrained, wild; depraved, dissipated, dissolute, reprobate, wanton.

abasement
n lit: low bow, obeisance; humbling, lowering, demotion, dethronement, humiliation, reduction, relegation, toppling; degradation, dishonour.

abashed
adj (pa.pt) lit: chagrined, confounded, discomfited, embarrassed, mortified, put out; astounded, disconcerted.

abated
adj (pa.pt) lit: attenuated, decreased, diminished, eased, ebbed, lessened, let up, moderated, slackened, subsided, waned; blunted; halted, quelled, stopped.

abbey
n lit: convent, monastery, priory; cloister; cathedral, minster.

abbreviation
n lit: abridged version, shortened form, truncated form; curtailment, reduction, truncation; abridgement, condensation, contraction.

abduct
vb lit: carry off, elope with, run away with; kidnap, seize, snatch; *spec*: extend (in myology); separate (in surgery).

aberration
n lit: lapse, quirk, vagary; deviation, eccentricity, irregularity, straying, wandering; abnormality, anomaly, oddity, peculiarity; mutant, mutation, sport, variant; *spec*: divergence, lack of focus (in light, physics).

abet
vb lit: aid, assist, help; back, second, support, sustain; encourage, incite, prompt; be an accomplice.

abhorrent
adj lit: detestable, disgusting, distasteful, hateful, horrible, horrid, loathsome, repellent, repulsive; contrary (to), offensive (to).

abiding
adj (pr.pt) lit: continuing, enduring, lasting, persevering, persistent, tenacious; constant, firm, immutable, permanent, steadfast, unchanging.

ability
n lit: capability, capacity, facility, faculty, power; aptitude, flair, gift, knack, skill, talent; adeptness, competence, dexterity, expertise, proficiency, skill.

abject
adj lit: cringing, fawning, grovelling, low, servile, slavish; contemptible, debased, despicable, mean, sordid, worthless; humiliating, ignominious; despairing, forlorn, hopeless, wretched.

able
adj lit: capable; competent, fitted, qualified; accomplished, adept, dextrous, efficient, expert, gifted, practised, proficient, skilful, skilled, talented; allowed, authorized, empowered, facilitated, permitted, sanctioned; clever enough.

abnormal
adj lit: anomalous, atypical, exceptional, extraordinary, irregular, singular, uncommon, unusual; odd, peculiar, queer, strange; deviant, mutant, unnatural.

abolish
vb lit: do away with, eliminate, erase, get rid of, put an end to, stop, terminate, wipe out; abrogate, annul, cancel, expunge, invalidate, nullify, quash, repeal, rescind, revoke, void.

abominable
adj lit: atrocious, detestable, execrable, foul, hateful, hellish, horrible, monstrous, obnoxious, odious, outrageous, repellent, repugnant, terrible, vile, wretched; disagreeable, distasteful, unpleasant.

aboriginal
adj lit: earliest, first, original, primal, primeval, primordial; ancient, primitive; indigenous, native.

abortion
n lit: miscarriage, stillbirth; termination; *fig*: calling off, cancellation, postponement; emergency stop; freak, monster, monstrosity, travesty.

abortive
adj lit: imperfect, incomplete, rudimentarily developed, stunted; *fig*: bootless, fruitless, futile, ineffectual, unavailing, unsuccessful, useless, vain.

abound
vb lit: be plentiful, proliferate, swarm, teem; infest, overflow; flourish, thrive; be rich (in), be filled (with).

about
adv lit: almost, nearly, roughly, virtually; close by, near by; active, around, moving, stirring; here and there, to and fro; again, back, backwards.
prp lit: concerning, regarding, respecting; concerned with, dealing with, referring to, treating; adjacent, beside, close by, close to, near by, near to; around, round; all over, in, on, through, throughout, with, within.

above
n lit: aforementioned, aforesaid, foregoing.
adj lit: aforementioned, aforesaid, earlier, foregoing, preceding, previous, prior; on high, overhead.
adv lit: on high, overhead; farther up, higher, upwards; on the next level upwards; heavenwards, in heaven, to heaven.

prp lit: farther up than, higher than, over; *fig*: superior to; more than; after, beyond, past.

abrasion
n lit: graze, scrape, scuff; chafing, friction, grating, rubbing, scraping, scuffing; attrition, erosion, wearing.

abrasive
n lit: grinder, scourer.
adj lit: fricative, grating, scratchy, scuffing, wearing; *fig*: chafing, grating, rasping, rough, sharp.

abridge
vb lit: abbreviate, condense, contract, cut, reduce, shorten.

abroad
adv lit: out of the country, overseas; at large, away, being spread, circulating, current, far and wide, in circulation, publicly, widely; outdoors, outside.

abrupt
adj lit: hasty, hurried, precipitate, sudden, unexpected, unforeseen; blunt, brusque, curt, gruff, sharp, short, terse; precipitous, sheer, steep; *fig*: broken, disconnected, discontinuous, jerky, uneven; *spec*: broken off (geological stratum); sharply tapered, truncate (botanical specimen).

abscess
n lit: boil, pus-filled sac; sore, swelling.

abscond
vb lit: bolt, decamp, desert, disappear, do a bunk, do a moonlight flit, make off, run away, slip off, sneak off, vanish, vamoose.

absence
n lit: being away, non-attendance; deficiency, lack, loss, omission, want; desertion, defection; non-existence; *fig*: abstraction, inattention, preoccupation, reverie.

absent
adj lit: away, elsewhere, not present; gone, out; deficient, lacking, missing, wanting; non-existent; *fig*: abstracted, distracted, faraway, inattentive, oblivious, preoccupied, vacant.

absolute
n lit: entirety, independent entity, totality, whole.
adj lit: complete, consummate, downright, out-and-out, pure, sheer, total, unadulterated, unmitigated, utter; entire,

unlimited, whole; categorical, certain, conclusive, decisive, definite, positive, sure, unambiguous, unequivocal; autocratic, autonomous, sovereign, supreme; *spec*: constant, fixed, invariable (in physics); modifying, qualifying (in grammar).

absolutely
adv lit: completely, entirely, fully, perfectly, purely, quite, sheer, thoroughly, totally, unadulteratedly, utterly, wholly; categorically, conclusively, decisively, definitely, positively, unambiguously, undoubtedly, unequivocally; exactly, precisely; autocratically, autonomously, individually.

absolve
vb lit: acquit, clear, exculpate, exonerate, free, remit, vindicate; discharge (from), excuse, exempt, release; pardon (from), shrive.

absorbing
adj (pr.pt) lit: engrossing, fascinating, gripping, riveting, spellbinding; arresting, captivating, engaging, intriguing.

abstain
vb lit: forbear (from), keep (from), refrain (from); reject, refuse; cease, desist, stop.

abstemious
adj lit: ascetic, sparing, temperate; austere, frugal, plain, self-denying.

abstract
n lit: condensation, digest, outline, paraphrase, précis, résumé, summary, synopsis; imaginative work, non-representational piece, pattern, shape.
vb lit: appropriate, remove, steal, take; detach, isolate, separate; condense, outline, paraphrase, precis, summarize.
adj lit: conceptual, conjectural, hypothetical, imagined, notional, theoretical; fantastic, imaginative, non-representational, visionary.

abstruse
adj lit: arcane, complex, complicated, difficult, obscure, recondite; esoteric.

absurd
adj lit: farcical, frivolous, inane, irrational, jejune, laughable, ludicrous, nonsensical, puerile, ridiculous, senseless, silly; crazy, daft, drivelling, foolish, idiotic, lunatic, mad, moronic, stupid.

abundant
adj lit: ample, copious, luxuriant, overflowing, plenteous, plentiful, profuse, rich, teeming.

abuse
n lit: misapplication, misuse; ill-treatment, maltreatment, oppression; despoliation, exploitation, imposition, wrong; contumely, derision, disparagement, insults, invective, opprobrium, vilification, vituperation.
vb lit: misapply, misuse; ill-treat, maltreat, manhandle, oppress; betray, despoil, exploit, impose upon, take advantage of, wrong; deride, disparage, insult, inveigh against, malign, swear at, vilify, vilipend, vituperate against.

abusive
adj lit: derisive, disparaging, insulting, offensive, rude, scathing, vilifying, vituperative; defamatory, libellous, slanderous; brutal, cruel, exploitative, oppressive.

abysmal
adj lit: bottomless, immeasurable, unfathomable; boundless, complete, deep, profound; *fig*: execrable, extremely bad, hopeless, pathetic, terrible, very poor, worthless.

abyss
n lit: chasm, crevasse, ravine; fissure, gorge; primal chaos; hell; *spec*: trench (in the ocean).

academic
n lit: master, professor, scholar; don, fellow, lecturer, tutor; scholastic, student; man of letters, polymath.
adj lit: bookish, erudite, intellectual, learned, literary, scholarly, studious, university; abstract, conjectural, hypothetical, notional, theoretical.

accelerate
vb lit: hasten, increase speed, pick up speed, put on speed, quicken, speed up; expedite, further, hurry, speed; *spec*: change velocity (in physics).

acceleration
n lit: hastening, increase in speed, quickening, speeding up; expediting, furtherance, hurrying, speeding; *spec*: rate of change of velocity (in physics).

accent
n lit: emphasis, force, stress; sound quality, tone, voice; inflection, intonation, pronunciation; idiom, language, mode of speech; diacritical mark, feet-mark, inches-mark, minute-sign, stress-mark; *spec*: contrast, highlight (in art).
vb lit: emphasize, stress; italicize, underline; highlight.

accept
vb lit: receive, take; bow to, defer to, submit to; bear, put up with, stand; *fig*: accede to, agree to, consent to, say yes to; admit, recognize, stipulate; assume, take on, undertake; declare satisfactory, pass.

acceptable
adj lit: admissible, all right, fair, passable, satisfactory; bearable, tolerable; agreeable, gratifying, pleasing, welcome.

access
n lit: admittance, entrance, entry, means of approach, passage; entering, getting in(to); path (to), road (to), way (to); *spec*: attack, onset (of illness).

accessible
adj lit: at hand, available, convenient, get-at-able, nearby, on hand, reachable, to hand; achievable, attainable, manageable, possible; approachable, friendly, open (to).

accessory
n lit: abetter, accomplice, co-conspirator, co-plotter; assistant, associate, confederate, partner; adjunct, appendage, attachment, extra, supplement, trimming.

accident
n lit: chance, fluke, happening, luck, mischance, mistake; blow, calamity, collision, contretemps, crash, disaster, misadventure, misfortune, mishap, pile-up.

accidental
n spec: effect of light (in art); note not in the key signature (in music).
adj lit: chance, fortuitous, lucky, inadvertent, incidental, unexpected, unforeseen, unintended, unintentional, unlucky, unplanned, unpremeditated, unwitting; *spec*: phantom complementary (colour, in optics).

acclaim
n lit: applause, cheering, clapping; approbation, celebrity, commendation, glory, plaudits.
vb lit: applaud, cheer, clap; commend, eulogize, extol, hail, laud, praise.

accommodate
vb lit: board, cater for, entertain, have room for, house, lodge, put up, quarter; provide, serve, supply; help, oblige; adapt, adjust, modify; conform, reconcile, settle.

accommodation
n lit: billeting, board, digs, housing, lodgings, quarters, room to stay; berth, place, reservation, seat; capacity, freedom, room, space; provision, service, supply; adaptation, adjustment, modification; conforming, reconciliation, settlement.

accompany
vb lit: attend, be with, come with, escort, go with; be inseparable from, go together with, join with; supplement; happen with, occur with; *spec*: play for, provide the backing for (in music).

accomplish
vb lit: achieve, attain, bring about, bring off, carry out, complete, do, effect, finish, fulfil, manage, perform, realize.

accomplished
adj (pa.pt) lit: achieved, attained, complete, done, effected, fulfilled, realized; adept, expert, masterly, polished, practised, proficient, skilful, talented.

accord
n lit: concurrence, correspondence, harmony, rapport, sympathy, unanimity; agreement, entente, understanding; *fig*: motivation, volition, wish.
vb lit: agree (with), be unanimous (with), concur (with), correspond (with), harmonize (with); afford, confer, give, grant, render.

accordingly
adv lit: appropriately, correspondingly, suitably; consequently, for this reason, hence, so, therefore.

according to
adj lit: handed on by, interpreted by, relayed by, transmitted by; as asserted by, as declared by, as maintained by, as stated by.

adv lit: consistent with, corresponding to, following, in conformity with, in line with; commensurate with, in proportion to, on the basis of, taking account of, in relation to.

account
n lit: description, narration, recital, record, report, statement; explanation; history, story, tale; balance, ledger, register, statement, tally; bill, charge, inventory, invoice, reckoning, score; basis, cause, consideration, ground, regard, sake; consequence, distinction, esteem, honour, importance, note, standing, worth; advantage, profit, use; exhibition, performance.
vb lit: give an explanation (for), give a reason (for); assess (to be), believe (to be), consider (to be), deem (to be), hold (to be), reckon (to be), think (to be).

accountable
adj lit: answerable, liable, responsible; comprehensible, explicable, understandable.

accrue
vb lit: accumulate, amass, be added on, build up, collect, increase, pile up.

accumulation
n lit: accretion, aggregation, amassing, build-up, coacervation, collecting, gathering, growth, hoarding, increase, massing, piling up, stock; collection, conglomeration, heap, hoard, load, pile, stack, stockpile.

accurate
adj lit: correct, right, true; exact, precise; meticulous, scrupulous, strict, unerring.

accursed
adj (pa.pt) lit: cursed, damned, doomed, hexed, ill-fated, ill-omened; bedevilled, bewitched, jinxed; luckless, unfortunate, unlucky; damnable, execrable, hateful, hellish.

accusation
n lit: arraignment, charge, impeachment, indictment; allegation, imputation.

accuse
vb lit: arraign, bring a charge against, charge, denounce, impeach, indict; allege, blame, impute.

accustom
vb lit: acclimatize, familiarize, get used (to), habituate, inure, train.

ache
n lit: pain, pang, soreness, throbbing; anguish, suffering; longing, pining, yearning.
vb lit: be in pain, suffer; hurt, pain, put in pain, throb; feel (for), have sympathy (for); hunger (for), long (for), pine (for), yearn (for).

achievement
n lit: accomplishment, attainment, fulfilment, realization; completion, effecting, performance; deed, exploit, feat; *spec*: coat of arms, escutcheon, hatchment, shield (of a family).

acid
n lit: corrosive; *fig*: hallucinogenic drug; LSD.
adj lit: corrosive; acerbic, acescent, acrid, biting, sharp, sour, tart; pungent, vinegary; *fig*: acerbic, caustic, cutting, keen, mordant, stinging, trenchant, vitriolic; ill-natured, ill-tempered; critical, decisive; *spec*: siliceous (in geology).

acknowledge
vb lit: react to, recognize, respond to; note, notice; accept, concede, grant, profess; admit, own to; greet, hail, salute; reply to, return.

acknowledgement
n lit: notice, reaction, recognition, response; acceptance, admission, profession, realization; greeting, hail, salutation, salute; answer, reply, return; credit, gratitude, thanks.

acquaintance
n lit: associate, colleague, contact, friend of a friend, neighbour; association, familiarity, fellowship, relationship; introduction; *fig*: awareness, conversance, experience, knowledge, understanding.

acquiesce in
vb lit: accede to, bow to, comply with, conform to; keep silent about, stay quiet about; accept, give in to, submit to; be content enough with.

acquiescent
adj lit: compliant, conformist; complacent, keeping quiet; accepting,

demure, obedient, submissive; content enough, happy enough.

acquire
vb lit: come into the possession of, get, obtain, pick up, procure, secure; collect, gain, gather; buy, purchase; attain, win.

acquisition
n lit: possession, property; addition, gain, prize; buy, purchase; amassing, attainment, collection, gaining, procurement.

acquit
vb lit: absolve, clear, exculpate, exonerate, vindicate; discharge, free, liberate, release; pay off, repay, settle; bear, behave, conduct, perform.

acrid
adj lit: acid, astringent, biting, caustic, corrosive, irritant, pungent, sharp, stinging; bitter, vinegary; *fig*: acrimonious, cutting, harsh, mordant, pointed, trenchant.

across
adv lit: to the other side; crosswise; from side to side.
prp lit: over, to the other side of; on the other side of.

act
n lit: accomplishment, achievement, deed, exploit, feat, operation, performance, stroke; decree, law, measure, ordinance, statute; routine, show, turn; affectation, dissimulation, front, pose, posture, pretence, simulation.
vb lit: function, go, move, operate, perform, take effect, work; behave, conduct oneself; impersonate, play, portray, represent; counterfeit, dissimulate, feign, imitate, pose, pretend, put it on, sham.

action
n lit: effect, functioning, movement, operation, performance, working; activity, energy, liveliness, vigour; act, deed, move, stroke; gesticulation, gesture; mechanism, mode of operation, procedure, process; battle, clash, combat, conflict, engagement, fighting; plot, scenario, story; case, lawsuit, litigation, prosecution, suit; event, happening.

activate
vb lit: get going, mobilize, prompt, set going, set in motion, start, switch on, trigger, turn on; galvanize, impel, rouse; motivate; *spec*: catalyse (in chemistry); make radioactive (in physics); purify, treat (sewage).

active
adj lit: busy, doing, going, engaged, occupied, working; functioning, moving, operative, running, ticking over; animated, brisk, bustling, energetic, spirited, sprightly, vigorous, vivacious; alert, lively, quick; enterprising, enthusiastic, hardworking, industrious, militant, zealous; *spec*: subjective (form of a verb, as opposed to passive).

activity
n lit: animation, bustle, commotion, hurly-burly, life, motion, movement, stir; act, deed, work; exercise, exertion, work; hobby, interest, pastime, pursuit; endeavour, enterprise, project, scheme, venture.

actor
n lit: artiste, performer, player, Thespian; impersonator, impostor, role-player; poseur, pretender, sham; agent, executor.

actual
adj lit: authentic, genuine, literal, physical, positive, real, true; current, existing, present, prevailing.

actually
adv lit: authentically, genuinely, indeed, literally, physically, positively, really, truly; as a matter of fact, in fact.

acuity
n lit: acumen, discernment, discrimination, keenness, penetration, perception, perspicacity, sensitivity, sharpness, shrewdness; astuteness, cleverness, subtlety.

acute
adj lit: pointed, sharp; excruciating, fierce, intense, piercing, racking, severe, stabbing, violent; brief, shortlived, sudden; critical, dangerous, grave, serious, urgent, vital; discerning, discriminating, keen, observant, penetrating, perceptive, sensitive; astute, clever, shrewd, subtle; *fig*: at an angle, oblique; *spec*: less than a right-angle (geometry).

adage
n lit: aphorism, axiom, dictum, maxim, proverb, saw, saying; epigram, motto, quotation.

adamant
adj lit: flinty, hard, steely, stony, unbreakable, unyielding; *fig*: firm, immovable, inexorable, intransigent, obdurate, rigid, unbending, uncompromising, unshakable.

adapt
vb lit: acclimatize, adjust, conform; alter, change, modify, shape, tailor; fit, match, suit.

adaptation
n lit: remodelling, reworking, variation, version; acclimatization, adjustment, conforming, habituation, naturalization; alteration, changing, modification, shaping, tailoring to fit.

add
vb lit: compute, count up, find the sum of, reckon, total, tot up; affix (to), annex, append, increase by, put next (to), put on (to); continue, go on to say.

addict
n lit: dependant, junkie, user; adherent, devotee, enthusiast, fan, follower; buff, freak, nut.
vb lit: habituate, hook (on), make dependent; enslave.

additional
adj lit: extra, further, more, other, supplementary; fresh, new; appended, attached; spare.

address
n lit: location, postal direction, exact whereabouts; disquisition, dissertation, lecture, sermon, speech, talk; articulation, diplomacy, tact; adroitness, dexterity, facility, ingenuity, skill.
vb lit: direct, label for posting, write the destination on; accost, greet, hail, speak to, talk to; apply (to), bring to the attention of; deliver a speech to, give a talk to, lecture; *spec*: access, coding (on a computer); prepare to hit (a golf-ball).

adept
n lit: expert, master; ace, dab hand, whiz; mage, magus.
adj lit: able, adroit, dextrous, expert, masterly, proficient, skilled.

adequate
adj lit: enough, passable, requisite,

sufficient; fair, reasonable, satisfactory; commensurate, competent, suitable.

adhere
vb lit: attach (to), be stuck (to), remain glued (to), stick (to); cleave (to), cling (to); *fig*: be devoted (to), be faithful (to), be loyal (to), hold (to), keep (to).

adherent
n lit: devotee, disciple, follower, sectary; fan, supporter.

adjacent
adj lit: alongside, contiguous; adjoining, neighbouring, next, next-door.

adjourn
vb lit: defer, delay, postpone, put off; stay, suspend; recess; move (to), transfer (to).

adjudicate
vb lit: arbitrate, judge, referee, umpire; award, pass judgement, pronounce.

adjust
vb lit: accustom, adapt, become used, be reconciled, conform, make fit; alter, change, fix, modify, reset, retune, tune; arrange, dispose, order, position, redress, regulate; accommodate, settle.

administer
vb lit: control, direct, govern, manage, oversee, run, superintend, supervise; dispense, distribute, give, provide, tender; apply, execute, impose, mete out; *spec*: formally declare (an oath); stabilize (prices, wages).

administration
n lit: board, control, direction, management, running, superintendence, supervision; cabinet, government, ruling party; term of office; dispensing, distribution, provision; application, execution, imposition.

admiration
n lit: appreciation, esteem, regard, respect, veneration; delight, pleasure, wonder.

admire
vb lit: appreciate, esteem, hold in high regard, respect, venerate; delight in, take pleasure in, wonder at; like, love.

admission
n lit: access, admittance, allowing in, entry, introduction, passage; entrance fee, ticket price; acknowledgement, confession, disclosure, revelation.

admit
vb lit: acknowledge, confess, disclose, let out, own, reveal; accept, concede, grant, recognize; allow, permit; allow in, let in, receive; be large enough for, have room for; permit the possibility (of).

admittance
n lit: access, admission, allowing in, entry, introduction, passage.

admonish
vb lit: castigate, censure, chastise, chide, rebuke, reprimand, reprove; berate, scold, tell off; caution, forewarn; exhort, remind.

adopt
vb lit: take on, take over, take up; assume, choose, embrace, espouse, select; become a parent to, bring up, foster.

adorable
adj lit: captivating, lovable, precious; beloved, darling; alluring, attractive, charming, delightful, wonderful.

adore
vb lit: dote on, idolize, love, worship; revere, venerate; be crazy about, go wild about; prostrate oneself before.

adorn
vb lit: bedeck, deck, decorate, embellish, ornament; beautify, dress, garnish, grace; festoon, garland.

adroitness
n lit: adeptness, deftness, dexterity, expertise, mastery, proficiency, skill; craft, ingenuity, quick thinking.

adulation
n lit: flattery, fawning, sycophancy; blarney, bootlicking, crawling, flannel, servility; acclaim, applause, genuflection, obeisance, praise.

adult
n lit: grown-up, mature person, responsible citizen.
adj lit: full-grown, fully developed, grown-up, mature; ripe; *fig*: complex, erudite, intellectual; erotic, explicit, sexy.

adulterate
vb lit: dilute, thin, water down, weaken; *fig*: contaminate, debase, devalue.

advance
n lit: development, headway, progress; betterment, breakthrough, furtherance, gain, improvement, promotion, step up; credit, loan; approach, overture, proposition.
vb lit: go forward, move on, move up, proceed, progress; accelerate, further, hasten, promote, speed; bring forward, expedite; elevate, upgrade; benefit, grow, improve, thrive; credit with, lend, loan; offer, present, put forward, submit; propose, suggest.
adj lit: early, prior; forward, in front.

advantage
n lit: assistance, benefit, gain, good, help, profit, use; blessing, boon, convenience; ascendancy, dominance, edge, precedence, superiority, sway, upper hand; *spec*: one point ahead (tennis).

adventure
n lit: enterprise, exploit, undertaking; exciting experience; readiness for anything; chance, risk, speculation.
vb lit: endanger, hazard, imperil, jeopardize, risk; soldier (on).

adventurous
adj lit: daring, enterprising, intrepid, venturesome; audacious, bold, temerarious; dangerous, hazardous, risky.

adversary
n lit: antagonist, enemy, foe, foeman, opponent; Evil One, Lucifer, Satan.

adverse
adj lit: antagonistic, hostile, inimical, opposing, unfavourable, unfriendly; contrary, negative, unfortunate, unpropitious; detrimental, harmful, injurious.

advertise
vb lit: display, exhibit, flaunt, hype, make known, plug, promote, promulgate, publicize, publish, puff, push, tout; announce, emblazon, proclaim, signal; advise of, draw attention to, give notice of, inform about, warn of; put up for sale.

advertisement
n lit: commercial, display, hype, notice, plug, promotion, publicity, puff; bill, circular, classified ad, hoarding, poster, small ad.

advice
n lit: counsel, counselling, direction, feedback, gen, guidance, instruction, recommendation, suggestion, tip; information, intelligence, notice, notification, word; caution, warning.

advisable
adj lit: desirable, expedient, judicious, politic, prudent, recommended, sensible, wise.

advise
vb lit: counsel, direct, give guidance to, instruct, make a recommendation to; inform, give notice of, notify; enjoin, recommend, suggest; caution, tip off, warn.

adviser
n lit: consultant, counsellor, guide, mentor, teacher, tutor; coach, instructor, trainer; abetter, aide, assistant, henchman.

advocate
n lit: apostle, champion, proponent, supporter, upholder; counsellor, speaker, spokesperson; apologist, defender, intercessor; barrister, counsel, lawyer, solicitor.
vb lit: advise, counsel, enjoin, exhort, recommend, propose, suggest, urge; argue for, champion, plead for, speak on behalf of, support.

aeroplane
n lit: aircraft; jet; crate, flying-machine, kite; shuttle.

affable
adj lit: amiable, amicable, benign, cordial, friendly, genial, good-humoured, kindly, sociable, urbane; courteous, gracious.

affair
n lit: circumstance, episode, event, happening, incident, matter, occurrence, question, subject, topic; business, concern, dealing, enterprise, transaction, undertaking; amour, relationship, romance.

affect
vb lit: act on, concern, influence, involve, relate to, touch; alter, change, disorder, disturb, modify, upset; impress, move, stir; adopt, assume, feign, pretend, put on, simulate.

affected
adj (pa.pt) lit: concerned, in question, involved; acted on, influenced, touched; distressed, impressed, moved, stimulated, stirred, upset, wounded; damaged, impaired, injured; artificial, assumed, feigned, insincere, pretended, sham, simulated, spurious, unnatural; camp, mincing, precious.

affecting
adj (pr.pt) lit: distressing, emotive, moving, pitiable, pitiful, sad, touching, upsetting; inspiring, rousing, stimulating, stirring.

affection
n lit: attachment, fondness, friendliness, kindness, liking, love, tenderness.

affiliated
adj (pa.pt) lit: allied, associated, confederated, connected; amalgamated, annexed, combined, united.

affinity
n lit: attraction, fondness, partiality; inclination, leaning; closeness, connection, correspondence, rapport, relationship, sympathy; resemblance; *spec*: reactive towards (chem).

affirm
vb lit: assert, aver, certify, declare, state; attest, confirm, corroborate, ratify, validate, verify; maintain, reiterate, repeat; formally testify, swear.

afflict
vb lit: burden, distress, oppress, plague, trouble; grieve, hurt, pain, rack, torment, wound.

affliction
n lit: adversity, burden, cross, hardship, scourge, suffering, trial, tribulation, trouble; distress, grief, misery, pain, sorrow, torment, woe; disease, malady, plague.

affluent
adj lit: opulent, prosperous, rich, wealthy, well off; filthy rich, flush, loaded, moneyed, rolling in it, well heeled.

afford
vb lit: have the money for, be able to buy; put up with, stand, sustain, tolerate; spare; confer, furnish, give, grant, impart, provide, render, supply.

affront
n lit: insult, offence, outrage, slight; indignity, provocation; injury, wound.
vb lit: insult, offend, outrage, slight; offer provocation; abuse, injure, wound.

afraid
adj lit: alarmed, fearful, frightened, panicky, panic-stricken, petrified, scared, terrified; alarmed, in a cold sweat, jumpy, nervous, timorous, uptight; anxious, concerned, worried; browbeaten, cowed,

rattled, shaken, unnerved; cowardly, chicken, yellow.

after
adj lit: later, subsequent; following, next.
adv lit: behind, in the rear; afterwards, later, next, subsequently, thereupon.
prp lit: behind, beyond, in pursuit of, to the rear of; following, subsequent to, upon; about, concerning, with regard to; according to, copying, imitating, in the style of; identically to.
cnj lit: as soon as, once, when.

again
adv lit: afresh, anew, another time, once more, one more time; back, over; on the other hand, yet; also, besides, furthermore, moreover.

against
prp lit: in contact with, on, touching, upon; abutting, adjacent to, bordering, contiguous with, next to; contrary to, counter to, in opposition to, versus; in contrast to; in anticipation of, in preparation for; for, in return for.

age
n lit: period of existence, time of life; advanced years, elderliness, senescence; majority, maturity, ripeness; generation; aeon, century, epoch, era, historical period, time; long while, years.
vb lit: grow old, grow up, mature, mellow, put years on, ripen; decline, deteriorate, get old.

aged
adj (pa.pt) lit: elderly, grey, hoary, old; of the age of; matured, ripened; ancient, antediluvian, superannuated.

agenda
n lit: programme, schedule, timetable; layout, list, menu, plan, scheme; *spec*: good works (in theology).

agent
n lit: bailiff, factor, steward; emissary, envoy, representative; executor, operative; spy; instrument, vehicle; active ingredient, cause, effective means; *spec*: campaign manager (in party politics).

aggravate
vb lit: exacerbate, inflame, intensify, magnify, make worse, worsen; augment, heighten, increase; annoy, exasperate, irk, irritate, needle, provoke.

aggression
n lit: bellicosity, belligerence, hostility, pugnacity; force, violence; encroachment, infringement, invasion, raid; assault, attack, onslaught.

aggrieved
adj (pa.pt) lit: distressed, hurt, injured, oppressed, pained, saddened, wounded; ill-used, wronged.

agitation
n lit: oscillation, shaking, shivering, shuddering, stirring; churning, tossing, turbulence; commotion, disturbance, excitement, ferment, flurry, fluster, lather, tumult, turmoil, unrest; *fig*: altercation, argument, controversy, debate, disputation; anxiety, nervousness, worry.

ago
adv lit: back, gone by, past, since; in the past.

agonize
vb lit: be anguished, be racked, suffer; distress, harrow, pain, rack, torment; *fig*: be anxious (over), strive, struggle (over), worry (over).

agony
n lit: anguish, pangs, torment, torture; pain, suffering.

agrarian
adj lit: agricultural, agronomic, arable, farming, tilling.

agree
vb lit: be of one mind (with), concur; be consistent (with), chime, coincide, correspond, get on together, harmonize; comply, parallel, tally; assent, concede, consent, grant; *spec*: correspond in case, number or person (grammar).

agreeable
adj lit: delightful, enjoyable, pleasant, pleasurable; appropriate, compatible, consistent, fitting, suitable; amenable, consenting, well-disposed.

agreement
n lit: accord, concord, concurrence; chorus, concert, harmony, unison; correspondence, identity, match; arrangement, compact, pact, treaty, understanding; bargain, contract, deal.

agriculture
n lit: agronomics, agronomy, cultivation, farming, tillage, tilling the soil; husbandry.

ahead
adv lit: in advance (of), in front (of); forwards, on, onwards, straight on; in the lead, winning.

aid
n lit: assistance, help, support; benefit, service, use; assistant, helper, supporter; *spec*: fund, subsidy (in feudal times and for modern charities).
vb lit: assist, benefit, be of use to, help, subsidize, sustain; abet, second, serve, support; facilitate, further, promote.

ail
vb lit: afflict, be the matter with, be wrong with, distress, oppress, plague, trouble; hurt, pain, torment; be ill, flag, weaken; decrease, diminish, fade, lessen.

aim
n lit: ambition, aspiration, end, goal, intention, object, objective, target; desire, intent, wish.
vb lit: direct (at), level (at), point (at), sight (at), train (at); aspire (to), intend (to), mean (to), plan (to), purpose (to), strive (to), try (to).

aimless
adj lit: adventitious, chance, erratic, fortuitous, haphazard, irrelevant, purposeless, random, undirected, unpredictable; maundering, meandering, rambling.

air
n lit: atmosphere, ether, waves; empyrean, heavens, sky; breeze, wind; breath, puff; ambience, aura; bearing, demeanour, feeling, flavour, impression, look, mien, tone; expression, utterance; aria, melody, melody-line, tune.
vb lit: aerate, circulate, dry, freshen, hang out, ventilate; *fig*: declare, disclose, divulge, expose, express, give vent to, make public, publicize, reveal, voice.

airfield
n lit: aerodrome; airforce base; landing strip, runway.

airily
adv lit: breezily, buoyantly, jauntily; blithely, casually, nonchalantly; ethereally, gracefully, lightly.

airless
adj lit: close, heavy, muggy, oppressive, stifling, stuffy.

airport
n lit: international aerodrome; airline building, terminal.

airs
n lit: affected mannerisms; pretensions.

airy
adj lit: fresh, ventilated; breezy, draughty, gusty; light, open, spacious; diaphanous, ethereal, flimsy, insubstantial, wispy; illusory, imaginary, immaterial, unreal; high, lofty; *fig*: breezy, buoyant, jaunty; blithe, casual, nonchalant; lively, sprightly.

aisle
n lit: corridor, gangway, passage; lane, pathway, walkway.

alacrity
n lit: avidity, dispatch, expedition, liveliness, promptness, quickness, rapidity, readiness, speed, sprightliness, zeal; eagerness, enthusiasm, willingness.

alarm
n lit: apprehension, consternation, fear, fright, panic, trepidation; anxiety, nervousness, uneasiness; bell, danger signal, flare, hooter, siren, warning; *spec*: appel (in fencing).
vb lit: frighten, panic, put the wind up, scare; startle, unnerve; alert, signal, warn.

album
n lit: collection, compilation; dossier, file, scrapbook; stamp collection; visitors' book; long-playing record, LP.

alcoholic
n lit: boozer, dipsomaniac, drunkard, inebriate, lush, soak, tippler, toper, wino; meths-drinker.
adj lit: distilled, fermented, spiritous, vinous; strong (drink); inebriating, intoxicating.

alcove
n lit: aumbry, bay, corner, embrasure, niche, nook, recess.

alert
n lit: alarm; warning; lookout, watch.
vb lit: alarm, warn; inform, notify, send a signal to.
adj lit: attentive, awake, observant, on guard, on the ball, on the lookout, on

watch, ready, vigilant, wary, watchful;
brisk, lively, nimble, quick, sprightly.

alien
n lit: foreigner, outsider, stranger;
extraterrestrial, little green man,
Martian; outcast; *spec*: hybrid (plant).
adj lit: exotic, foreign, outlandish,
strange, unfamiliar.

alienate
vb lit: disaffect, estrange, set at odds, turn
against; detach, disinterest, separate;
spec: convey, sequester, transfer
ownership (in property law).

alight
vb lit: descend (from), disembark (from),
dismount (from), get down (from), get
off; come down, land, settle (on), touch
down.
adj lit: burning, ignited, incandescent,
lighted, lit, on fire; ablaze, aflame,
blazing, flaming; *fig*: aglow, bright,
illuminated, lighted up, lit up, shining.

align
vb lit: bring into line, even up, justify, line
up, order, range, straighten; *fig*: affiliate,
ally, confederate, side (with).

alike
adj lit: identical, similar, uniform; akin,
analogous, compatible, corresponding;
equal, parallel.
adv lit: identically, similarly, uniformly;
compatibly, correspondingly, in the
same way; equally, to the same
degree.

alive
adj lit: animate, breathing, conscious,
living, organic; active, extant, in
existence, operative, unextinguished;
awake (to), sensitive (to); animated,
brisk, eager, energetic, lively, spirited,
sprightly, vigorous, vital, vivacious.

all
adj lit: every; every one of; every bit of,
every part of; as much as possible,
maximum, optimum; any; nothing but,
only, solely.
adv lit: altogether, completely, entirely,
fully, totally, utterly, wholly;
exclusively.
prn lit: everyone; everything; every atom,
every bit, every part, every scrap.

allege
vb lit: assert, aver, charge, declare, state;
claim, maintain.

allegiance
n lit: adherence, devotion, faithfulness,
fealty, loyalty.

allergy
n lit: hypersensitivity, sensitivity;
anaphylaxis; *fig*: antipathy, aversion,
hostility, loathing.

alley
n lit: passage, passageway, pathway;
corridor, gangway, walkway; backstreet,
lane; rink.

alliance
n lit: coalition, confederacy,
confederation, federation, league;
marriage, partnership, union;
association, combination.

allocation
n lit: apportioning, assignment,
distribution, sharing out; allotment,
portion, quota, ration, share.

allot
vb lit: allocate, apportion, assign,
distribute, mete out, share out.

allow
vb lit: give permission, permit; authorize,
give leave, license; bear, stand, suffer;
give, grant, provide with; admit,
concede, own to; keep free, leave, spare;
take into account.

allowed
adj (pa.pt) lit: acceptable, all right, okay,
permissible; authorized, licensed,
permitted, sanctioned; left over, spare;
provided (for).

alloy
n lit: amalgam, blend, composite,
compound, mixture; combination, cross,
hybrid; *fig*: defect, impurity.
vb lit: amalgamate, blend, compound,
fuse, mix, weld together; *fig*: debase,
devalue, qualify, temper.

all right
adj lit: adequate, not bad, okay, passable,
satisfactory; average, standard;
acceptable, good enough; healthy, well;
safe, undamaged, unharmed,
unimpaired.
adv lit: adequately, passably,
satisfactorily; acceptably, well enough;
certainly, definitely, positively, without
question.

all-round
adj lit: multifaceted, multipurpose, non-specialist; encyclopaedic, wide-ranging; generalized; unlimited.

allure
n lit: appeal, attraction, seductiveness, temptation; fascination; charm.
vb lit: attract, captivate, charm, enchant, entice, fascinate, seduce, tempt.

ally
n lit: confederate, partner; acolyte, assistant, associate, collaborator, colleague, friend; helper, supporter; accomplice, catspaw, henchman, subordinate.
vb lit: confederate (with), join forces (with), unite (with); associate (with), collaborate (with), combine (with); connect (to), relate (to).

almighty
adj lit: all-powerful, omnipotent; supreme; invincible, irresistible; *fig*: awesome, enormous, indescribable, tremendous, unspeakable.

alone
adj lit: by oneself, isolated, single, solitary, unaccompanied; apart, separate; matchless, unique; abandoned, detached, forlorn, forsaken.
adv lit: by oneself, solitarily, solo; in isolation, separately; exclusively, merely, only, solely.

along
adv lit: forwards, onwards; down; as escort, in company (with), together (with); in parallel, side by side.
prp lit: by the side of; down, down the length of.

aloof
adj lit: detached, distant, remote, reserved, withdrawn; forbidding, haughty, standoffish, superior, unapproachable; chilly, cool, unsympathetic.
adv lit: apart, away, distant; detachedly, separately.

aloud
adv lit: audibly; noisily; distinctly.

already
adv lit: before then, by that time, previously; before now, by now, now, yet.

also
adv lit: additionally, in addition; likewise; besides, to boot, too; again, furthermore, moreover.

alteration
n lit: change, modification, reshaping; adjustment, amendment, correction, revision; difference, shift, variance; conversion, metamorphosis, transformation.

alternate
vb lit: happen in turns, take turns; interchange, rotate; oscillate, vary.
adj lit: every other, odd; interchanging, rotating.

alternative
n lit: choice, option, preference; other, second; substitute.
adj lit: other, second; substitute; different.

although
cnj lit: albeit, in spite of the fact that; while.

altitude
n lit: elevation, height; angle of elevation, vertical height; perpendicular; peak, summit; *fig*: celebrity, eminence, high rank, status.

altogether
n fig: birthday suit, nude.
adv lit: completely, entirely, fully, quite, thoroughly, totally, utterly, wholly; all in all, all told, as a whole, collectively, generally, in general.

altruism
n lit: disinterest, unselfishness; charity, generosity, humanitarianism, philanthropy; beneficence, consideration, public-spiritedness; self-denial.

always
adv lit: ever; all the time, constantly, continually, eternally, forever, perpetually, unceasingly; consistently, every time, invariably, repeatedly.

amateurish
adj lit: inexpert, naive, unprofessional; clumsy, inept, rude, maladroit.

amaze
vb lit: astonish, astound, bowl over, dumbfound, flabbergast, overwhelm, rock, stagger, stun, stupefy, surprise.

amazement
n *lit*: astonishment, stupefaction, surprise; wonder.

ambassador
n *lit*: emissary, envoy, plenipotentiary; diplomat, representative; consul, legate, nuncio.

ambiguous
adj *lit*: equivocal, indeterminate, unclear; cryptic, delphic, dubious, enigmatic, obscure, oracular.

ambitious
adj *lit*: aspiring, eager, hopeful; desirous, driving, enterprising; audacious, bold, challenging, demanding, difficult, exacting; ostentatious, pretentious, showy.

ambivalence
n *lit*: equivocation, indecision, indeterminacy, irresolution, vacillation; contradiction.

ambush
n *lit*: hold-up, lying in wait, stake-out, trap; mugging.
vb *lit*: bushwhack, hold up, lie in wait for, pounce on, surprise, trap, waylay.

amenable
adj *lit*: agreeable, open to persuasion, persuadable, tractable; acquiescent, docile, submissive; accountable, answerable, liable.

amend
vb *lit*: correct, fix, mend, rectify, remedy, repair; ameliorate, better, improve, revise.

amends
n *lit*: atonement, compensation, redress, reparation, restitution.

amid(st)
prp *lit*: among(st), in the middle of, surrounded by.

amiss
adj *lit*: askew, awry, defective, faulty, inaccurate, incorrect, out of order, untoward, wrong.
adv *lit*: (go) askew, awry, out of order, wrong; (take) as an insult, badly.

ammunition
n *lit*: armament, materiel, munitions; explosives, missiles, propellants, weapons; *fig*: fuel, stock, supplies; fire-power.

amnesty
n *lit*: dispensation, immunity, remission; cease-fire, peace agreement, truce.

among(st)
prp *lit*: amid(st), of; along with, in with, together with; in the middle of, surrounded by; between, to each one of; throughout.

amorous
adj *lit*: amatory, ardent, enamoured, impassioned, lovesick, passionate; affectionate, fond, loving; lecherous, lustful.

amount
n *lit*: extent, magnitude, mass, measure, number, quantity, volume; entirety, lot, sum, total, whole.
vb *lit*: add up (to), come (to).

ample
adj *lit*: broad, bulky, capacious, commodious, expansive, extensive, full, large, liberal, roomy, spacious, substantial, wide; abundant, copious, plentiful, profuse; enough and to spare, more than adequate, supersufficient.

amplify
vb *lit*: augment, boost, heighten, increase, intensify, magnify; elaborate on, enlarge on, expand, extend, flesh out, supplement.

amuse
vb *lit*: be funny, divert, entertain, make laugh, tickle; keep occupied.

amusement
n *lit*: diversion, divertissement; entertainment; enjoyment, fun, hilarity, laughter, merriment, mirth; game, pastime, recreation.

amusing
adj (*pr.pt*) *lit*: comic, diverting, droll, entertaining, funny, hilarious, humorous, merry, witty; enjoyable, interesting.

anaemic
adj *lit*: ashen, bloodless, pale, pallid, wan; feeble, frail, sickly, weak; *fig*: colourless, dull, insipid; characterless, spiritless.

analogy
n *lit*: correlation, correspondence, equivalence, likeness, parallel, resemblance, similarity; parallelism, point of comparison; *spec*: proportion (in mathematics).

analyse
vb lit: break down, dissect, resolve; consider, examine carefully, study; assay, evaluate, test; interpret.

analysis
n lit: breakdown, dissection, resolution; examination, study; assay, evaluation, results of testing; finding, interpretation; reasoning.

anarchy
n lit: lawlessness; revolution; law of the jungle, survival of the fittest; *fig*: chaos, confusion, disorder.

anathema
n lit: taboo; abomination; curse, damnation, excommunication, proscription.

anatomy
n lit: composition (of the body), structure (of the body); dismemberment, dissection; examination, investigation, science, study; analysis, interpretation.

ancestor
n lit: forebear, forefather, forerunner, progenitor; precursor; *spec*: testator (bequeathing an inheritance).

ancient
adj lit: age-old, antedeluvian, antique, archaic, hoary, old, primeval, primordial; antiquated, obsolete.

ancillary
adj lit: auxiliary, dependent, extra, supplementary; secondary, subordinate, subservient, subsidiary; assistant, serving.

and
cnj lit: as well as, in addition to, plus, together with, with; furthermore, moreover; so that; in order to, to.

anew
adv lit: again, another time, once more, over again; afresh, from the beginning.

angel
n lit: divine messenger, guardian spirit, spirit messenger; *fig*: darling, divinity, jewel, saint, treasure; *spec*: backer, sponsor (of a play); freak echo (on radar).

anger
n lit: choler, exasperation, fury, ire, passion, rage, spleen, strong displeasure, temper, wrath; resentment.

vb lit: enrage, exasperate, incense, infuriate, madden, outrage, provoke, rile, seriously displease.

angle
n lit: corner, crook, elbow, hook; bend, curve; slant, slope, tilt; *fig*: approach, outlook, perspective; point of view, standpoint; plot, scheme.
vb lit: bend, curve, tack, turn; fish; *fig*: bias, slant; fish (for), scheme (for), try (for).

angry
adj lit: beside oneself, enraged, exasperated, fuming, furious, hopping mad, incensed, infuriated, irate, livid, maddened, on the warpath, provoked, raging, riled, seething, wrathful.

anguish
n lit: agony, dolour, pain, suffering, torment, torture; distress, misery.

angular
adj lit: cornered, hooked; pointed, sharp; *fig*: bony, gaunt, lean, rangy, scrawny, skinny; awkward, clumsy, gawky, stiff.

animal
n lit: beast, creature; quadruped; *fig*: brute, monster, savage.
adj fig: brutish, instinctual, lower, sensual.

animosity
n lit: antagonism, antipathy, bad blood, dislike, enmity, hatred, hostility, ill will, loathing, malevolence, rancour.

annex
vb lit: affix, append, attach, fasten on, join on, tack on; appropriate, arrogate, seize, take over.

annihilate
vb lit: crush out of existence, destroy utterly, eliminate, eradicate, exterminate, extirpate, liquidate, obliterate, wipe out.

announce
vb lit: declare, make known, proclaim; advertise, broadcast, promulgate, publish; divulge, reveal, tell; betoken, herald, portend, presage, signal.

announcement
n lit: declaration, proclamation, statement; broadcast, bulletin, communique, notice, promulgation, publication; disclosure, revelation.

annoyance
n lit: aggravation, displeasure,
exasperation, irritation, vexation;
bother, nuisance, trouble; bind, bore,
pain, pain in the neck, pest.

annul
vb lit: abrogate, cancel, invalidate, nullify,
render void, repeal, rescind, reverse,
revoke, void.

anoint
vb lit: oil, mark with oil, perfume; daub,
smear, spread over; *fig*: consecrate,
hallow, make holy, sanctify.

anomaly
n lit: abnormality, inconsistency, oddity,
peculiarity, something strange;
deviation, eccentricity, irregularity.

anonymous
adj lit: unattested, uncredited,
unidentified, unnamed, unsigned;
nameless, unknown; bland,
characterless, colourless, nondescript,
undistinguished, unexceptional.

answer
n lit: reaction, reply, response, return;
comeback, defence, explanation,
rejoinder, retort, riposte; solution;
resolution.
vb lit: react, react to, reply, reply to,
respond, respond to; explain, rejoin,
retort, riposte; solve; resolve.

antagonize
vb lit: alienate, disaffect, make an enemy
of, offend, rub up the wrong way; anger,
annoy, irritate; counteract, neutralize,
work against.

antic
n lit: caper, frolic, gesture, jape, jest, joke,
lark, prank, stunt, trick; business.

anticipate
vb lit: await, be prepared for, expect,
foresee, foretell, look forward to, predict,
see coming, wait for; antedate, be ahead
of, forestall, precede.

antidote
n lit: countermeasure, cure, neutralizer,
remedy; antitoxin, antivenin.

antique
n lit: bygone, heirloom, relic.
adj lit: antiquarian, classic, vintage;
ancient, antiquated, obsolescent,
obsolete, old-fashioned, outdated; aged,
elderly, old.

antiquity
n lit: ancient times, olden days; age, old
age.

antiseptic
n lit: disinfectant, germicide.
adj lit: antibiotic, hygienic, sanitary,
sterile, uncontaminated, unpolluted;
aseptic.

apart
adj lit: by oneself, cut off, distant,
isolated, separated; dismantled,
disparate, dissected, divorced, in bits, in
pieces, separate.
adv lit: by oneself, independently,
isolatedly, separately, to one side;
asunder, to bits, to pieces.

apartment
n lit: chambers, flat, living quarters,
rooms, suite; bed-sit, digs, room.

apathy
n lit: disinterest, impassivity, indifference,
passivity, unconcern; lethargy, sloth,
torpor; coldness, insensitivity,
numbness.

ape
n lit: anthropoid, monkey, primate;
chimpanzee, gibbon, gorilla, orang-utan;
fig: imitator, mimic, parodist; boor,
bumpkin, clod, lout, oaf.
vb lit: copy, imitate; caricature, mimic,
parody, parrot.

aperture
n lit: cleft, crack, fissure, gap, hole,
interstice, opening, orifice, perforation,
slot; chink, embrasure, eyelet, slit.

apex
n lit: acme, crest, crown, peak, pinnacle,
point, summit, tip, top; *fig*: climax,
culmination, height, zenith.

apologetic
adj lit: contrite, penitent, regretful,
remorseful, repentant, sorry; appeasing,
conciliatory.

apology
n lit: expression of contrition, mea culpa,
regrets; *fig*: caricature (of), excuse (for),
mockery (of), parody (of), travesty (of).

apostate
n lit: heretic, recreant, schismatic;
defector, deserter, recidivist, renegade,
turncoat.

apostle
adj lit: heretical, lapsed, recanting, recreant, schismatic; backsliding, renegade, unfaithful, untrue.

apostle
n lit: evangelist, missionary, preacher; advocate, champion, herald, messenger, propagandist, proselytizer; disciple.

appalling
adj (pr.pt) lit: awful, dire, disheartening, dreadful, fearful, grim, harrowing, horrific, horrifying, shocking, terrible.

apparatus
n lit: equipment, gear, implements, machinery, tackle, tools, utensils; appliance, materials, outfit; mechanism, organs, system; *fig*: apparat, bureaucracy, infrastructure, network, organization, setup.

apparent
adj lit: clear, evident, manifest, obvious, patent, plain, visible; conspicuous, overt; ostensible, outward, seeming; superficial; optical; *spec*: angular (diameter of a heavenly body); diffracted (position seen in a medium denser than air).

apparently
adv lit: ostensibly, superficially; outwardly, overtly, seemingly; evidently, obviously, patently, plainly.

apparition
n lit: manifestation, materialization, vision; ghost, phantom, presence, shade, spectre, spirit, revenant, wraith; spook; *fig*: dreadful thing, hulking shape, terrifying form; *spec*: reappearance (after an eclipse).

appeal
n lit: entreaty, petition, plea, prayer, supplication, demand, request, allure, attraction, charm, fascination, interest; *spec*: referral to a higher court.
vb lit: apply (to), make a petition (to), plead (to), pray (to); make a request (to); be alluring (to), be attractive (to), be fascinating (to); *spec*: refer to a higher court.

appear
vb lit: be seen, come into sight, come into view, come to light, emerge, loom, manifest oneself, materialize, surface; arise, crop up, develop, occur, show up, turn up; arrive, be present, come, enter; look, seem; be clear, be evident, be manifest, be obvious, be patent, be plain; become available, be on sale, be on show, come out; act, perform.

appearance
n lit: advent, arising, arrival, being present, coming, emergence, entry, manifestation, materialization, realization, surfacing; cropping up, occurrence, showing up, turn-up; availability, being on show, performance; air, bearing, demeanour, expression, figure, look, manner, mien, outward aspect; form, guise, semblance, shape; vision, visitation.

appeasing
adj (pr.pt) lit: assuaging, conciliatory, mollifying, pacific, placatory, propitiatory, soothing; allaying, alleviating, easing, lessening, satisfying.

appendix
n lit: addendum, addition, extra, supplement; adjunct, extension, tailpiece.

appetite
n lit: hunger; desire, hankering, longing, yearning; relish, taste; room, space, stomach; *fig*: inclination, liking, readiness, willingness, zest.

appetizing
adj lit: inviting, juicy, mouthwatering, succulent, tasty, tempting; delectable, moreish, wholesome, yummy.

applause
n lit: acclaim, big hand, cheering, clapping, ovation; acclamation, accolade, plaudits, praise.

appliance
n lit: apparatus, device, gadget, instrument, machine; *spec*: fire-engine; orthopaedic brace, truss.

application
n lit: employment, exercising, implementation, performance, practising, putting into execution, operation, realization, use, utilization; appositeness, immediacy, pertinence, relevance, value; attentiveness, commitment, dedication, diligence, industry, perseverance, persistence; bringing into contact, introduction; anointing, coating, daubing on, putting on; cream, dressing, lotion, ointment, salve; claim, petition, request, suit.

apply
vb lit: bring to bear, employ, exercise, implement, practise, put into execution, operate, realize, use, utilize; appertain, be apposite, be pertinent, be relevant, be valid; commit (oneself to), dedicate (oneself to), give (oneself to), throw (oneself) in(to); appeal (to), make a petition (to), make a request (to), send in for information (to); address (to), introduce (to), put next (to); coat, daub on, put on, spread on.

appoint
vb lit: assign, commission, nominate; arrange, choose, designate, determine, establish, fix, set; decree, direct, ordain, prescribe; equip, fit out, furnish, provide.

appointment
n lit: assignation, date, engagement, meeting; consultation, interview, session; assignment, job, office, position, post situation; choice, commissioning, installation, nomination.

apposite
adj lit: appropriate, apt, fitting, suitable, suited, to the purpose; appertaining, germane, pertinent, relevant, to the point.

appraisal
n lit: examination, scrutiny, survey; assessment, estimate, evaluation, judgement, opinion; assay, rating, valuation.

appreciate
vb lit: be grateful for, be obliged for, be thankful for; cherish, enjoy, esteem, like, prize, relish, value; gain, grow, increase, rise; acknowledge, be aware of, be cognizant of, comprehend, know, perceive, realize, recognize, take account of, understand.

appreciation
n lit: gratitude, indebtedness, obligation, thanks; admiration, enjoyment, esteem, liking, relish; gain, growth, increase, rise; acknowledgement, cognizance, comprehension, knowledge, perception, realization, recognition, understanding.

apprehend
vb lit: appreciate, be aware, believe, conceive, grasp, perceive, realize, understand; capture, catch, collar,

detain, grab, seize, take; arrest, nab, nick, pinch, run in.

apprehension
n lit: anxiety, dread, fear, foreboding, misgiving, suspicion, uneasiness, worry; arrest, capture, detention, seizure; awareness, grasp, perception, realization, recognition, understanding.

apprentice
n lit: acolyte, learner, probationer, pupil, student; beginner, novice, tiro; neophyte.

approach
n lit: access, avenue, drive, entrance, pathway; advance, coming up, drawing near, nearing; course, means, method, mode, procedure, technique, way; attitude, way of thinking; application, overture, proposal, proposition, suggestion; approximation, likeness. *vb lit*: advance towards, come up to, draw near to, get close to, move towards, near; bend one's mind to, tackle; appeal to, apply to, make overtures to, sound out; approximate to, come close to, compare with, resemble.

appropriate
vb lit: annex, arrogate, commandeer, confiscate, impound, make off with, possess oneself of, seize, take over; embezzle, pocket, steal; pilfer, thieve; allocate, apportion, assign, earmark, set aside. *adj lit*: applicable, apposite, apt, fit, fitting, suitable, suited, to the purpose, well-suited; appertaining, correct, germane, pertinent, relevant, right, timely, to the point.

approval
n lit: acclaim, applause, appreciation, approbation, commendation, praise; admiration, esteem, favour, liking, regard, respect; agreement, blessing, consent, endorsement, okay, recommendation; authorization, leave, licence, permission, sanction; *spec*: sale-or-return (basis for selling).

approve
vb lit: have a high opinion (of), think very well (of); agree to, commend, consent to, endorse, okay, pass, validate; authorize, give leave for, license, permit, sanction.

approximate
vb lit: approach, be bordering on, come
close (to), come near (to), verge on; be
like, have the semblance of, resemble.
adj lit: close, estimated, loose, rough,
virtual; comparable, similar; adjacent,
bordering, near, nearby, neighbouring.

aptitude
n lit: bent, disposition, flair, gift, knack,
leaning, predilection, proclivity,
propensity, talent; ability, faculty,
quickness; appositeness,
appropriateness, fitness, pertinence,
relevance, suitability.

arbitrary
adj lit: capricious, personal, subjective,
whimsical; chance, random, unreasoned;
erratic, inconsistent; absolute,
autocratic, despotic, dictatorial,
imperious, peremptory, tyrannical.

arbitration
n lit: adjudication, determination,
judgement, settlement.

arch
n lit: span, vault; *spec*: instep (of the foot).
vb lit: arc, bend, bow, curve round; be
domed, be vaulted; build a colonnade.
adj lit: artful, coy, knowing, mischievous,
pert, roguish, saucy, waggish; cunning,
shrewd, sly, wily.

architect
n lit: designer, planner; author, builder,
creator, deviser, founder, inventor,
originator, prime mover.

architecture
n lit: art of building, construction design;
buildings; construction, design,
planning, structure, style.

archives
n lit: annals, chronicles, records, registers;
documents, papers, rolls; public records
office.

ardent
adj lit: fervent, fervid, fiery, hot-blooded,
impassioned, intense, lusty, passionate,
spirited, vehement, zealous; eager,
earnest, enthusiastic.

ardour
n lit: feeling, fervour, fieriness, fire, heat,
intensity, passion, spirit, vehemence,
warmth, zeal; eagerness, earnestness,
enthusiasm.

arduous
adj lit: backbreaking, exhausting,
fatiguing, gruelling, heavy, laborious,
onerous, punishing, severe, strenuous,
taxing, tough.

area
n lit: breadth, compass, expanse, extent,
range, scope, size, width; district,
locality, neighbourhood, patch, plot,
region, section, sector, territory, tract,
zone; department, domain, province;
field, realm, sphere; arena, court, floor,
space, yard.

arena
n lit: bowl, court, field, ground, hall, park,
pitch, ring, stadium, stage, theatre;
amphitheatre, battlefield, battleground,
lists; *fig*: proving-ground, testing-
ground; council chamber.

argue
vb lit: bandy words, dispute, fall out,
fight, have an altercation, have words,
quarrel, remonstrate, wrangle; bicker,
disagree, squabble; debate, discuss,
question, assert, claim, contend, hold,
maintain, plead; persuade (into), talk
(into); imply, suggest; demonstrate,
evince, exhibit, indicate, manifest, point
to, show.

argument
n lit: altercation, clash, dispute, falling
out, fight, quarrel, remonstration, row,
wrangle; bickering, disagreement,
squabble; debate, discussion; assertion,
case, claim, contention, line of
reasoning, plea, point; gist, plot,
storyline, theme.

arid
adj lit: dehydrated, dried up, dry,
moistureless, parched, barren, sterile,
fig: dull, empty, lifeless, uninteresting.

aridity
n lit: dehydration, drought, dryness;
barrenness, sterility; *fig*: dullness,
emptiness, lifelessness, tediousness.

arise
vb lit: ascend, come up, get up, go up; get
out of bed, stand up, wake up; climb,
mount, soar; appear, come into sight,
crop up, develop, emerge, occur, show
up, surface, turn up; emanate, issue,
originate, spring, stem; ensue, follow,
proceed, result.

aristocrat
n lit: grandee, noble, patrician, titled personage; *fig*: best of its kind.

aristocratic
adj lit: blue-blooded, high-born, lordly, noble, patrician, titled, upper-class, well-born; pedigree; courtly, dignified, polished, refined, well-bred; arrogant, haughty, lah-de-dah, proud, snobbish.

arithmetic
n lit: mathematics, sums; calculation, computation, reckoning; number theory.

arm
n lit: forelimb, upper limb; appendage, cross-piece, extension, offshoot, projection, sleeve; branch, department, division, section, sector; channel, creek, inlet, sound, strait, tributary; *fig*: authority, might, power, strength.
vb lit: equip with weapons, issue with weapons, provide materiel; activate, render active, switch on; provide with the means of attack or defence; *fig*: equip (oneself with), fortify (oneself with), protect (oneself with); *spec*: put an armature on (a magnet).

armed
adj (pa.pt) lit: fortified, furnished with weapons, primed, protected; activated, active, switched on; able to attack or defend; *fig*: accoutred, equipped, fitted out, provided, strengthened.

armistice
n lit: ceasefire, truce; peace agreement.

armour
n lit: breastplate, chain-mail, coat of mail, cuirass, helmet, mail, suit of mail; bullet-proof vest, Kevlar vest, steel plating; protection, sheathing; shield.

army
n lit: military, soldiers, soldiery, troops; battalions, brigades, legions; *fig*: horde, host, multitude, throng.

aroma
n lit: bouquet, fragrance, perfume, scent, smell; odour, whiff; redolence; *fig*: flavour, hint, suggestion.

aromatic
adj lit: balmy, fragrant, perfumed, scented; odoriferous, pungent, redolent; savoury, spicy.

around
adv lit: all over the place, everywhere, here and there; all over, throughout; in a circle; back, in the opposite direction; active, doing, moving.
prp lit: about, encircling, enclosing, encompassing, surrounding; all over the place within, scattered in; approximately, close on; on the far side of, on the other side of.

arouse
vb lit: awaken, wake up; animate, excite, inflame, kindle, rouse, stimulate, stir up; goad, incite, provoke, spur, whip up; foment, foster, incite, whet.

arrange
vb lit: array, dispose, form up, group, marshal, order, organize, position, range, set out; align, classify, file, line up, rank, sort; adjust, straighten, tidy; devise, fix up, plan, schedule; contrive, determine, settle; adapt, orchestrate, score, transcribe.

arrangement
n lit: disposition, formation, grouping, order, positioning; organization; design, plan, scheme, system; adjustment, moving; agreement, compact, deal, terms, treaty, tryst, understanding; adaptation, interpretation, orchestration, score, setting, transcription, version.

array
n lit: collection, display, exhibition, formation, muster, parade, show.
vb lit: display, exhibit, form up, muster, parade, show; align, arrange, draw up, group, marshal, organize, range; accoutre, bedeck, caparison, clothe, deck, equip, fit out, outfit.

arrest
n lit: apprehension, capture, detention, seizure; bust, cop; blockage, check, halt, obstruction, stoppage, suppression.
vb lit: apprehend, capture, catch, detain, take into custody; nab, nick, pinch, run in; block, check, halt, obstruct, stop, suppress; delay, inhibit, restrain, retard, slow; *fig*: absorb, engross, fascinate, grip, hold.

arresting
adj (pr.pt) lit: absorbing, engrossing, fascinating, gripping, holding, riveting; conspicuous, noticeable, remarkable, striking, stunning; engaging, formidable, impressive.

arrival
n lit: advent, approach, coming; appearance, entrance, entry; arising, occurrence; incomer, newcomer, visitor.

arrive
vb lit: come, show up, take one's place (at), turn up; appear, enter, make an entry, put in an appearance; *fig*: become famous, make good, make it to the top, succeed.

arrogant
adj lit: conceited, disdainful, haughty, high-handed, imperious, overbearing, presumptuous, proud, supercilious, swaggering; blustering, impudent, insolent, pretentious.

arrogate
vb lit: apportion (to), assign (to); take (to oneself); ascribe (to), attribute (to).

arrow
n lit: bolt, dart, quarrel; flight, shaft; gnomon, indicator, needle, pointer; *spec*: stem (of a plant).

arsenal
n lit: ammunition dump, armoury, arms depot, magazine, ordnance depot; *fig*: stockpile, store, supply.

art
n lit: representation; drawing, painting; craft, craftsmanship, expertise, mastery, skill, virtuosity; facility, ingenuity, knack, talent; deftness, dexterity; artifice, craftiness, duplicity, wile.

artful
adj lit: adroit, clever, ingenious, neat, resourceful, smart, subtle; cunning, designing, hoydenish, knowing, scheming, sly; deceitful, duplicitous, tricky, wily.

article
n lit: commodity, item, object, thing; essay, feature, piece, story; clause, division, heading, paragraph, part, section; *fig*: matter, subject, topic; *spec*: a or the (in grammar); count (on a charge-sheet); provision (in a contract).

articulate
vb lit: enounce, express clearly, pronounce, speak, talk; connect (with), fit together (with), hinge, joint.

adj lit: coherent, eloquent, expressive, fluent, lucid, well-spoken; clear, intelligible, meaningful; jointed, segmented.

artifice
n lit: artfulness, deftness, finesse, ingenuity, inventiveness, skill; contrivance, device, machination, stratagem, tactic; dodge, manoeuvre, ruse, trick, wile; chicanery, deception, duplicity, guile, sleight.

artificial
adj lit: man-made, synthetic; manufactured; affected, assumed, bogus, contrived, fake, false, feigned, hollow, insincere, meretricious, mock, phoney, pretended, sham, specious, spurious, unnatural.

artist
n lit: aesthete; creator; cartoonist, painter, sketcher; actor, entertainer, musician, performer, showman; architect, designer, sculptor; artisan, craftsman, expert, master, virtuoso.

artistic
adj lit: aesthetic, beautiful, elegant, exquisite, graceful; cultured, stylish, tasteful; creative, imaginative, sensitive.

as
adv lit: equally, to the same degree, to the same extent; for example, like.
prn lit: a condition that, a fact that, which is what.
prp lit: in the character of, in the part of, in the role of; in the manner of, like.
cnj lit: during the time that, when, while; in the same way that; to the same degree, to the same extent; that the result was; because, seeing that, since; though.

ascend
vb lit: climb, go up, mount, scale; drift up, float up, fly, lift off, rise, soar, take off; get up, move up, travel up; *fig*: accede to, succeed to.

ascent
n lit: climb, rise; flight, lift-off, take-off; journey up; gradient, incline, ramp, slope.

ascertain
vb lit: determine, discover, find out, learn; confirm, establish, fix, verify.

ascetic
n lit: abstainer; anchorite, coenobite,

hermit.
adj lit: abstinent, austere, disciplined, rigorous, self-denying, severe, spartan, stern; celibate.

ashamed
adj lit: conscience-stricken, embarrassed, humbled, mortified, sheepish; chagrined, crestfallen, discomfited; guilty, remorseful, sorry; bashful, shy.

ashore
adj lit: on dry land, on terra firma.
adv lit: aground, on land, on the beach; landwards, to the beach.

aside
n lit: interpolation, parenthesis; digression.
adv lit: apart, away, off, out of the way, privately, separately; in reserve.

asinine
adj lit: crazy, daft, fatuous, gormless, halfwitted, idiotic, imbecile, lunatic, moronic, senseless, stupid.

ask
vb lit: enquire, inquire, put to, quiz; seek an answer; appeal to, apply to, beg, beseech, entreat, implore, petition, request, solicit; invite; be looking for, demand, seek; call (for).

askance
adv lit: indirectly, obliquely, sideways; distrustfully, doubtfully, sceptically, suspiciously.

asleep
adj lit: dead to the world, dozing, off, napping, slumbering, snoozing; dormant, hibernating; numbed; *fig*: oblivious; inactive.

aspect
n lit: air, attitude, bearing, demeanour, look, mien; angle, outlook, point of view, viewpoint; facet, feature, side.

asperity
n lit: acerbity, brusqueness, coldness, curtness, harshness, roughness, severity, sharpness, terseness.

aspire
vb lit: be ambitious (to), be eager (to), dream one day (to), hope, long, seek, wish, yearn.

ass
n lit: donkey, jennet; burro, moke; *fig*: blockhead, chump, dolt, fathead, fool, nincompoop, nitwit, noodle, simpleton, twit.

assail
vb lit: assault, attack, beset, fall upon, lay into, set upon.

assassination
n lit: homicide, killing, murder, slaughter, slaying; butchery, destruction, elimination, extirpation, liquidation, massacre.

assault
n lit: attack, hit, onslaught; offensive, storming, strike; battery, beating, mugging, robbery with violence; sexual attack.
vb lit: assail, attack, batter, beat, beat up, fall upon, hit, lay into, mug, punch, set upon, strike, thump; invade, storm.

assemble
vb lit: bring together, collect, congregate, convene, round up; come together, flock, gather, muster, rally; accumulate, amass, build up; connect, fit together, piece together, put together.

assembly
n lit: accumulation, amassing, collection, convention, round-up; aggregation, body, company, congregation, crowd, flock, gathering, group, herd, mustering, rallying, throng; connection, fitting together, joining, piecing together, putting together.

assent
n lit: acceptance, agreement, approval, concurrence, consent, permission.
vb lit: accede (to), agree (to), subscribe (to); approve, concur, consent.

assert
vb lit: allege, aver, contend, declare, maintain, proclaim, state; press, stand upon, uphold, vindicate.

assertive
adj lit: dogmatic, emphatic, firm, forceful, insistent, positive, self-assured, strong-willed.

assess
vb lit: appraise, estimate, evaluate, gauge, judge, rate, size up, value; levy, tax; fix the value (at).

asset
n lit: fund(s), good(s), holding(s), possession(s), reserve(s), resource(s); aid, benefit, boon, help.

assign
vb lit: allocate, apportion, distribute, dole out, give out; make over (to); determine, fix, pose, set; appoint, delegate, nominate, select; accredit (to), ascribe (to), attribute (to).

assignation
n lit: meeting, rendezvous, tryst; allocation, apportioning, distribution; appointment, delegation, nomination, selection; accreditation, ascription, attribution.

assignment
n lit: charge, commission, duty, job, mission, task; allocation, apportionment, distribution; appointment, delegation, nomination, selection; accreditation, ascription, attribution.

assimilate
vb lit: absorb, imbibe, ingest; blend in, mingle, mix; *fig*: digest, learn, take in.

assist
vb lit: abet, aid, help, serve; back, further, second, support; cooperate with.

assistance
n lit: aid, help, succour; backing, furtherance, support; collaboration, cooperation.

assistant
n lit: aide, helper; abettor, accessory, accomplice, henchman; backer, partner, second, supporter; collaborator, confederate.
adj lit: associate, auxiliary, back-up, deputy, vice-; subordinate, under-.

associate
n lit: ally, collaborator, confederate, friend, partner; colleague, fellow-worker; companion, mate.
adj lit: ally, combine, confederate, join, league, unite; consort (with), fraternize (with), go around (with), mix (with). *fig*: connect (with), identify (with), link (with), relate (with).

association
n lit: alliance, combination, confederation, federation, league; club, company, group, syndicate, union; companionship, fellowship, friendship, partnership, relationship; connection, identification, link, relation.

assorted
adj lit: diverse, mixed, sundry, various; arranged, classified, graded, grouped, ranged, sorted.

assortment
n lit: diversity, medley, mixture, selection, variety; arrangement, grouping, range, selection; classification, grading, sorting.

assume
vb lit: don, put on, wear; accept, acquire, shoulder, take on, undertake; appropriate, arrogate, expropriate, seize, take over, usurp; adopt, affect, feign, simulate; *fig*: believe, guess, imagine, infer, presume, suppose, surmise, think.

assumption
n lit: acceptance, acquisition, shouldering, taking on, undertaking; appropriation, arrogation, expropriation, seizure, take-over, usurpation; adopting, affecting, feigning, simulation; *fig*: belief, conjecture, idea, inference, notion, presumption, supposition, surmise, theory; *spec*: bodily taking up (of the Virgin Mary) into heaven.

assurance
n lit: affirmation, guarantee, oath, pledge, promise, word, word of honour; certitude, confidence, conviction, poise, positivity, self-confidence; audacity, boldness, courage; insurance.

assured
adj (pa.pt) lit: confident, poised, positive, self-confident, self-possessed; certain (of), fixed, guaranteed, secure, settled, sure; audacious, bold, courageous; brazen, forward, pushy.

astonish
vb lit: amaze, astound, bowl over, dumbfound, flabbergast, stagger, startle, stun.

astonishing
adj (pr.pt) lit: amazing, astounding, dumbfounding, flabbergasting, mind-blowing, phenomenal, sensational, staggering, startling, stunning.

astonishment
n lit: amazement, disbelief, shock, speechlessness, startlement, stupefaction, wonderment.

astray
adv lit: adrift, off, off course, off target, off the straight and narrow, up the garden path, wide of the mark.

astute
adj lit: bright, canny, clever, discerning, keen, penetrating, perceptive, sharp, shrewd; cunning, subtle, wily.

asylum
n lit: refuge, retreat, sanctuary, shelter; mental institution, psychiatric hospital; funny farm, loony bin, madhouse, nuthouse.

atheist
n lit: sceptic, unbeliever; heathen, pagan; goy, infidel.

athlete
n lit: sportsman, sportswoman; gymnast, runner, track-runner; competitor, contender, contestant, player.

athletic
adj lit: agile, energetic, fit, limber, lithe, muscular, nimble, powerful, sinewy, strong, vigorous.

atmosphere
n lit: air; airiness, space; *fig*: climate, conditions; ambience, environment, feeling, mood, spirit, surroundings, tone.

atomizer
n lit: aerosol, spray; spray gun; airbrush.

atone
vb lit: answer (for), compensate (for), do penance (for), make amends (for), make expiation (for), make up (for), pay (for).

atrocious
adj lit: appalling, horrific, outrageous, shocking, terrible; barbaric, bloody, diabolical, fiendish, grisly, gruesome, inhuman, savage; evil, wicked.

atrocity
n lit: barbarity, brutality, cruelty, enormity, horror, infamy, inhumanity, outrage; great evil, wickedness.

attach
vb lit: affix, append, connect, couple, fasten, fix, glue, join on, link, secure, stick, tie, unite; affiliate (oneself with), associate (oneself with); ascribe, assign; allocate, appoint, place, put, send.

attached
adj (pa.pt) lit: bound (to), connected (to), fastened (to), joined (to), stuck (to); party (to); arrested, detained; *fig*: partial (to); devoted (to).

attack
n lit: assault, charge, invasion, offensive, onset, onslaught, raid, strike; bout, fit, paroxysm, seizure, spasm; calumny, criticism, denigration, spleen, vilification, vituperation.
vb lit: assail, assault, charge, fall upon, invade, set upon, storm; criticize, denigrate, insult, vilify.

attain
vb lit: accomplish, arrive at, bring off, fulfil, get to, obtain, reach, realize, win.

attainable
adj lit: feasible, obtainable, possible, potential, practicable, realizable, winnable.

attainment
n lit: accomplishment, achievement, feat, fulfilment, realization, triumph, victory, win; gift, skill, talent.

attempt
n lit: bash, bid, crack, effort, go, shot, try, venture.
vb lit: endeavour (to), make an effort (to), seek (to), strive (to), try (to), venture (to).

attend
vb lit: be at, be present at, frequent, go to, show up at, turn up at, visit; accompany, chaperon, escort, guard, usher; serve, wait (upon); care for, look after, nurse, take care of, tend; be attached to, be connected with, follow, result from; listen (to), pay attention (to), pay heed (to); look (to), see (to).

attendance
n lit: appearance, being present, presence; audience, house; crowd, gate, turnout.

attendant
n lit: aide, companion, helper; flunkey, lackey, menial, servant, waiter; chaperon, duenna, escort, usher; caretaker, custodian, guard, warden.
adj lit: accompanying, attached, concomitant, consequent, corresponding, related.

attention
n lit: awareness, concentration, consciousness, mind, notice, observation; heed; care, concern, consideration, thoughtfulness; civility, compliment(s), courtesy, gallantry, regard(s), respect(s).

attentive
adj lit: civil, complimentary, concerned, considerate, courteous, devoted, gallant, obliging, respectful, thoughtful; alert (to), awake (to); heedful, mindful, studious.

attest
vb lit: aver, bear out, be witness to, confirm, corroborate, demonstrate, evince, manifest, show, testify to, verify, vouch for.

attic
n lit: loft, rafters, roof-space.

attitude
n lit: pose, position, posture, stance; bearing, demeanour, manner, mien; disposition, mood; approach, outlook, perspective, viewpoint.

attract
vb lit: draw, induce, pull; allure, entice, lure; appeal to, charm, enchant, fascinate.

attraction
n lit: draw, inducement, magnetism, pull; allure, enticement, lure; appeal, charm, enchantment, fascination.

attractive
adj lit: magnetic, mesmeric; alluring, captivating, enticing, luring, seductive; appealing, charming, enchanting, fascinating; beautiful, gorgeous, handsome, lovely.

attribute
n lit: characteristic, facet, feature, point, property, quality, trait; hallmark, sign, symbol, trademark.
vb lit: ascribe, assign, charge, credit, put down (to), set down (to).

attune
vb lit: acclimatize (to), accustom (to), adjust (to), regulate (to), set (to).

auburn
adj lit: carroty, chestnut-coloured, coppery, red-brown, tawny.

audible
adj lit: detectable, discernible, distinct, perceptible, that can be heard.

audience
n lit: congregation, crowd, fans, gallery, gate, house, onlookers, spectators, turnout, viewers; market, public; consultation, interview, reception.

audit
n lit: check, examination, inspection, review; balancing.
vb lit: check, examine, inspect, review; balance.

auditorium
n lit: hall, lecture-hall, nave, school-hall, theatre.

augment
vb lit: add to, boost, enhance, extend, heighten, increase, intensify, strengthen, swell.

august
adj lit: dignified, grand, imposing, majestic, noble, princely, regal, stately.

auspicious
adj lit: cheering, encouraging, favourable, hopeful, optimistic, promising, propitious.

austere
adj lit: bleak, cold, harsh, plain, severe, spare, spartan, stark; forbidding, grim, hard, rigorous, stern, strict, unrelenting; abstemious, ascetic, economical, puritanical, self-denying, solemn, straitlaced.

austerity
n lit: bleakness, coldness, harshness, severity, simplicity, starkness; grimness, hardness, rigour, rigorousness, sternness, strictness; abstemiousness, asceticism, puritanism, self-denial, solemnity.

authentic
adj lit: actual, genuine, original, real, true, valid, veritable.

author
n lit: writer; creator, founder, generator, inventor, maker, originator, parent, prime mover, producer.

authoritarian
n lit: autocrat, despot, dictator, martinet, tyrant.
adj lit: autocratic, despotic, dictatorial, doctrinaire, tyrannical.

authoritative
adj lit: authentic, official, sanctioned; commanding, confident, decisive, definite, imperative, masterful, self-assured; dogmatic, imperious, peremptory; confirmed, factual, reliable, trustworthy, valid.

authoritarian
n lit: autocrat, despot, dictator, martinet, tyrant.
adj lit: autocratic, despotic, dictatorial, doctrinaire, tyrannical.

authoritative
adj lit: authentic, official, sanctioned; commanding, confident, decisive, definite, imperative, masterful, self-assured; dogmatic, imperious, peremptory; confirmed, factual, reliable, trustworthy, valid.

authority
n lit: government, power, rule, supremacy; administration, board, council, local government, powers that be; connoisseur, expert, master, specialist; command, control, dominion, influence, jurisdiction, prerogative; licence, permission, sanction, say-so, testimony, warrant, word; example, precedent.

authorize
vb lit: commission, empower, entitle, license, permit, sanction, warrant; approve, confirm, ratify, vouch for.

automatic
adj lit: mechanical, robot, self-activating, self-propelling, self-regulating; instinctual, involuntary, reflex, spontaneous, unconscious; inescapable, inevitable, unavoidable; *fig*: habitual, routine.

automaton
n lit: android, machine, robot; *fig*: iceberg, zombie.

autonomous
adj lit: independent, sovereign; self-determining, self-governing.

autumn
n lit: harvest-time; fall; *fig*: maturity, middle age.

auxiliary
n lit: ally, assistant, associate, partner; accessory, deputy, reserve, substitute; *spec*: colonial infantryman.
adj lit: back-up, emergency, reserve, spare, substitute; ancillary, subsidiary, supplementary.

available
adj lit: at one's disposal, on hand, on tap, to hand, usable; free, vacant; accessible, within reach; valid.

avalanche
n lit: landslide, landslip; icefall, snowslip; deluge, flood, inundation; *spec*: shower (of nuclear particles).

avarice
n lit: acquisitiveness, cupidity, greed, rapacity; meanness, miserliness, stinginess, tightness.

avaricious
adj lit: acquisitive, grasping, greedy, rapacious; mean, miserly, stingy, tight.

avenge
vb lit: repay, retaliate; get even for, take vengeance on behalf of; revenge (oneself on).

avenue
n lit: approach, driveway, pathway, walk; boulevard; road, street, thoroughfare.

aver
vb lit: affirm, assert, declare, maintain, say, state.

average
n lit: mean, medium, norm, par, run of the mill, standard.
adj lit: intermediate, medium, middle; commonplace, middling, normal, ordinary, run-of-the-mill, so-so, standard, typical, unexceptional, usual.

averse
adv lit: antipathetic (to), indisposed (to), reluctant (to), unwilling (to); hostile (to), inimical (to), opposed (to).

aversion
n lit: antipathy, disinclination, indisposition, reluctance, unwillingness; animosity, hostility, opposition.

avert
vb lit: turn away; fend off, stave off, ward off; forestall, preclude, prevent.

avid
adj lit: ardent, eager, enthusiastic, keen; fervent, intense, passionate; grasping, greedy, hungry, ravenous.

avow
vb lit: acknowledge, admit, announce, aver, declare, maintain, profess, swear.

await
vb lit: attend on, wait for; anticipate, be prepared for, be ready for, look for, look forward to.

awake
adj lit: aroused, aware, conscious; alert, vigilant, watchful.

award
n lit: conferral, endowment, presentation; gift, grant; prize, trophy.
vb lit: bestow, confer, endow, give, grant, present.

aware
adj lit: appreciative (of), apprised (of), conscious (of), informed (of), knowledgeable (of), mindful (of), sensible (of).

awareness
n lit: appreciation, consciousness, discerning, knowledge, perception, realization, recognition, sensibility, understanding.

away
adj lit: abroad, absent, not here, out; gone, off, started; distant, far.
adv lit: abroad, elsewhere, out; apart, aside; afar, hence, into the distance, off; *fig*: continuously, doggedly, incessantly, on and on, persistently, relentlessly, repeatedly.

awe
n lit: dread, respect, reverence, veneration; fear; wonder.
vb lit: daunt, impress greatly, intimidate, strike; frighten; amaze.

awesome
adj lit: daunting, dreadful, formidable, imposing, impressive, intimidating, striking; fearful, frightening; amazing, wondrous.

awful
adj lit: appalling, distressing, ghastly, horrible, nasty, ugly, unpleasant; bad, deplorable, dreadful, terrible; inadequate, poor, shoddy, wretched.

awkward
adj lit: blundering, clumsy, gawky, inelegant, inept, lumbering, ungainly; cumbersome, unmanageable, unwieldy; difficult, inconvenient, untimely; dangerous, hazardous, perilous, sticky, thorny, ticklish; compromising, embarrassing, inopportune, painful, trying, uncomfortable; disobliging, perverse, prickly, troublesome, unhelpful, unpredictable.

awning
n lit: canopy, curtain, parasol, screen, shade, shelter, sunshade, windbreak.

axe
n lit: chopper, hatchet; cleaver; pick.
vb lit: chop down, fell, hew down; *fig*: cancel, cut back, prune, wind up, dismiss, fire, lay off, sack.

axiom
n lit: aphorism, precept, principle, truism, truth.

axiomatic
adj lit: accepted, fundamental, given, granted, presupposed, self-evident, understood; aphoristic.

axle
n lit: half-shaft, pin, pivot, rod, shaft, spindle.

B

babel

n lit: bedlam, chaos, confusion, disorder, pandemonium, uproar; babble, burble, cacophony, chattering, jabbering, murmur, prattle; clamour, din, noise, racket, row.

baby

n lit: babe, infant, neonate, newborn; bairn, child; *fig*: idea, invention, pet project, plan, responsibility, scheme.

vb lit: coddle, cosset, mollycoddle, pamper, pet, spoil; *fig*: humour, indulge, spoonfeed.

adj lit: infant, newborn, young; *fig*: diminutive, little, miniature, minute, small, tiny; dwarf, midget, pygmy; childish, infantile.

babyish

adj lit: baby, childish, infantile; boyish, childlike, girlish, immature, jejune, juvenile, puerile; soft, spoiled; foolish, silly.

back

n lit: lumbar region, spine, vertebrae; hind part, hindquarters, posterior, rear; end, stern, tail; far end, other side, reverse; *fig*: effort, energy, power; *spec*: defender (in team games); keel, keelson (of a ship, boat); top, surface (of a river, the sea; of a vein of ore; of a bow in archery).

vb lit: go backwards, regress, retreat, reverse; encourage, endorse, favour, finance, second, sponsor, subsidize, support, underwrite; abet, aid, assist, come to the help of, help; bet on, gamble on; be behind, line, reinforce, strengthen; *spec*: turn, veer (of the wind).

adj lit: hind, posterior, rearward; end, hindmost, rear; distant, outlying, remote; earlier, former, old, past, previous; reverse.

adv lit: retrogressively, retrospectively; again, once more; ago, in the past.

backbiter

n lit: defamer, detractor, libeller, muck-raker, mud-slinger, scandalmonger, slanderer; snake-in-the-grass, sneak; gossip.

backbone

n lit: spinal column, spine, vertebrae, vertebral column; *fig*: axis, basis, bedrock, foundation, mainstay, support; character, determination, firmness, fortitude, grit, mettle, resolution, resolve, strength of character, tenacity, willpower; bottle, courage, nerve.

backfire

vb lit: misfire; go bang; *fig*: boomerang, go wrong, have the opposite effect, miscarry, rebound.

background

n lit: context, environment, milieu, scenario, scenery, setting, surroundings; distance, obscurity, shadow; breeding, circumstances, culture, history, past, record, track record, upbringing; credentials, experience, qualifications.

adj lit: environmental, residual, surrounding; accompanying, incidental, secondary.

backing

n lit: encouragement, endorsement, favour, seconding, support; financing, funding, investment, patronage, sponsorship, subsidizing, underwriting; aid, assistance, help; confirmation, corroboration, substantiation, verification; lining, reinforcement, strengthening; accompaniment, context, setting.

backlash

n lit: counterblast, kickback, reaction, recoil, repercussion, response; counterstrike, retaliation; anger, rage, resentment.

backslider

n lit: apostate, recidivist, relapser; sinner, trimmer.

back up

vb lit: go backwards, reverse; *fig*: affirm, bolster, confirm, corroborate, endorse, reinforce, second, stand by, substantiate, support, verify; aid, assist, be behind, come to the help of, help.

backwards
adv lit: rearwards, retrogressively; *fig*:
completely, fully, thoroughly.

bacterium
n lit: germ, microbe, micro-organism;
bacillus, coccus, schizomycete,
spirochaete.

bad
adj lit: evil, immoral, sinful, wicked,
wrong; disobedient, naughty, unruly;
damaged, defective, deficient, faulty,
imperfect, inadequate, inferior, poor,
unfavourable, unfortunate, unskilful,
unsatisfactory, worthless; erroneous,
fallacious, incorrect, invalid, spurious;
dangerous, distressing, gloomy, grave,
grim, harmful, injurious, offensive,
painful, serious, severe, unpleasant;
decayed, foetid, mouldy, off, putrescent,
rancid, rotten, sour, spoiled; adverse,
damaging, disastrous, ruinous; ailing, ill,
sick, unwell; guilty, melancholy,
remorseful, sad, sorry; distressed, upset,
wretched.

badger
vb lit: bother, chase, chivvy, harass, harry,
hound, importune, nag, pester, plague,
pursue, worry; annoy; bait, tease.

badly
adv lit: carelessly, deficiently, imperfectly,
inadequately, incorrectly, poorly,
shoddily, unfavourably, unfortunately,
unskilfully, unsatisfactorily; evilly,
immorally, sinfully, wickedly;
disobediently, improperly, naughtily,
outrageously, shamefully; acutely,
extremely, greatly, intensely, seriously;
deeply, desperately, gravely, severely.

baffle
n lit: regulator, resistance; muffle,
silencer.
vb lit: bewilder, confound, elude,
flummox, mystify, nonplus, perplex,
puzzle, stump; balk, defeat, foil,
frustrate, thwart.

bag
n lit: carrier, container, envelope, pouch,
sack; udder; *fig*: crone, hag, slag, slut,
virago, witch; interest, line, métier;
game, kill, prey, quarry.
vb lit: put into a bag; capture, catch, get,
land, take, trap; *fig*: kill, shoot; balloon,
bulge, sag, swell; book, reserve.

bail
n lit: bond, security, surety; guarantee,
pledge, warranty; cross-bar, cross-piece;
dividing pole; *spec*: curved handle; outer
court (of a castle).

bailiff
n lit: court officer, sheriff's officer; agent,
factor, steward.

bait
n lit: carrot, decoy, lure, temptation;
allurement, attraction, enticement,
inducement; loss-leader.
vb lit: decoy, set a lure; set dogs on; *fig*:
annoy, harass, irritate, needle, persecute,
provoke, torment.

bake
vb lit: cook, oven-cook, roast; dry, harden;
be cooked, be oven-cooked, be roasted;
make bread; *fig*: be very hot, scorch,
sear.

baking
n lit: cooking, oven-cooking, roasting;
drying, hardening; batch cooked.
adj (pr.pt) lit: cooking, roasting; drying,
hardening; *fig*: boiling, scorching,
searing, sizzling, sweltering, torrid, very
hot; arid, dry, parched.

balance
n lit: pair of scales, scales, weighing
machine; equilibrium, equipoise;
equality, equivalence, evenness, parity;
composure, equanimity, poise, self-
possession; stability, steadiness;
difference, remainder, residue, rest; *spec*:
regulator (in a timepiece).
vb lit: be poised, be stable, be steady;
achieve parity, be equivalent,
correspond, equal, level, match, parallel;
compensate for, counterpoise,
counterweight, equalize, offset; assess,
calculate, compute, compare, estimate,
evaluate, total, weigh, weigh up; settle,
square, tally.

balcony
n lit: stoep, verandah; gallery, upper
circle.

bald
adj lit: hairless; depilated, glabrous;
unfledged; barren, exposed, treeless; *fig*:
bare, blunt, direct, forthright, naked,
plain, simple, stark, unadorned,
undisguised, unvarnished.

bale
n lit: bundle, stack, stook; package, parcel; bucket, scoop.
vb lit: bundle up, pack, parcel up, stack up; ladle, scoop; eject, jump, parachute; *fig*: escape, quit; help, rescue.

baleful
adj lit: evil, hostile, malevolent, malignant, menacing, ominous, pernicious, sinister, venomous; lugubrious, mournful, sad; disastrous, harmful.

ball
n lit: globe, orb, sphere; bead, drop, globule, spheroid; bullet, pellet, shot, slug; dance; *spec*: delivery (in cricket); testicle.
vb lit: form a sphere, roll into a sphere; clog, entangle.

ballast
n lit: counterbalance, counterweight, deadweight, weight; stabilizer; chippings, gravel, rubble, sand; sandbags; sea-water.

balloon
n lit: airship, dirigible; sonde; bubble.
vb lit: ascend in an airship; belly, billow out, blow up, inflate, puff out; bloat, dilate, distend, expand, swell.

ban
n lit: boycott, embargo, forbidding, interdiction, prohibition, proscription; banishment, deportation, exile; anathematization, curse, excommunication; outlawry.
vb lit: bar, debar, disallow, embargo, forbid, interdict, outlaw, prohibit, proscribe, suppress; banish, deport, exile; blacklist, veto; anathematize, curse, excommunicate.

banal
adj lit: cliché-ridden, corny, hackneyed, pedestrian, platitudinous, stale, stereotyped, stock, tired, trite, unoriginal, vapid; commonplace, everyday, mundane, ordinary, trivial, unimaginative.

band
n lit: binding, ribbon, strap, strip; belt, tape; line, streak, stripe, vein; channel, frequency range, track, wavelength range; body, company, crew, gang, group, party, troop; ensemble, orchestra.

vb lit: affiliate, ally, assemble, associate, federate, group, join, league, merge, unite.

bandage
n lit: dressing, gauze, lint, plaster; band-aid, elastoplast; compress, poultice; winding-sheet.
vb lit: bind up, dress, put a plaster on; bind round, cocoon, cover, swathe, wrap.

bandit
n lit: brigand, desperado, footpad, highwayman, marauder, outlaw, pirate, robber; crook, gangster, gunman, hijacker, kidnapper, thief; con artist, exploiter, extortioner, swindler; *fig*: enemy; *spec*: fruit machine (one-armed bandit).

baneful
adj lit: destructive, disastrous, harmful, injurious, noxious, pernicious, ruinous; bad, baleful, evil, venomous; deadly, fatal, lethal, mortal.

bang
n lit: detonation, explosion, report, shot; boom, clap, clash, crash, pop, thud; blow, box, cuff, hit, knock, punch, slam, smack, thump, wallop, whack; *fig*: impetus, vigour, zest; buzz, kick, stimulus, thrill.
vb lit: bash, beat, hammer, knock, pound, pummel, rap, slam, strike, thump; clash, clatter, crash; detonate, explode, resound, thunder.
adv lit: abruptly, all at once, suddenly; hard, noisily, smack, violently; absolutely, directly, exactly, headlong, precisely, quite, right, squarely, straight.

bangle
n lit: amulet, bracelet; anklet; hoop, ring, ringlet.

banish
vb lit: cast out, deport, eject, evict, exclude, exile, expel, outlaw, transport; ban, dismiss, dispel, drive away, get rid of, oust, remove, shake off.

banisters
n lit: balusters, balustrade, handrail, rail, stair-rail.

bank
n lit: border, brink, edge, rim, riverside, shore, side, towpath; acclivity, embankment, mound, pile, rampart, ridge, rise, shelf; accumulation, heap,

mass; depository, hoard, repository, reserve, reservoir, stock, store; funds, kitty, moneybox, money exchange, pool, savings; bar, reef, shallows, shoal; camber, incline, lean, slant, slope, tilt; array, file, line, rank, row, tier; bench, settle, work-bench, work-table; *spec*: coal-face, face (in a mine); flock (of birds); ground level, pit-top, shaft-top (of a mine); manual (on an organ).

vb lit: deposit, put into the kitty, save; amass, gather, heap up, pile up, stack; count, depend, lean, rely; camber, cant, incline, lean, pitch, slant, slope, tilt, tip; embank, enclose, surround; close over, cover, extinguish.

bankrupt
n lit: debtor, defaulter.
vb lit: break, ruin; beggar, impoverish; liquidate, put into liquidation, put in the hands of a receiver.
adj lit: broke, flat broke, indebted, insolvent, ruined; destitute, failed, impoverished; bust, on the rocks, skint, washed up; *fig*: deficient, lacking, poor.

banner
n lit: standard; coat of arms, colours, crest, escutcheon, insignia; burgee, gonfalon, pennant, pennon; ensign, flag.

banquet
n lit: feast; grand dinner; meal, repast.

banter
n lit: badinage, chaffing, jesting, jokes, joking, kidding, pleasantries, quips, raillery, repartee, wisecracks; leg-pulling, mockery, ragging, ribbing, teasing.
vb lit: be flippant, chaff, jest, joke, kid, quip; be facetious, make fun of, mock, rag, rib, tease, twit.

baptise
vb lit: christen; besprinkle, dip, immerse; purify; call, dub, entitle, name; *fig*: inaugurate, initiate, introduce, launch.

baptism
n lit: christening; dipping, immersion, sprinkling; purification; *fig*: beginning, initiation, introduction; debut, inauguration, launching, naming.

bar
n lit: baton, batten, boom, paling, pole, rail, rod, shaft, stake, stick; handle, key, lever; bolt, latch; barrier, obstruction; counter; canteen, inn, pub, saloon,

taproom, tavern; bench, court, courtroom, dock, tribunal; advocates, barristers, lawyers; band, chevron, strip, stripe; block, cake, ingot, piece; bank, reef, sandbank, shallows, shoal; ridge; *fig*: ban, embargo, prohibition, proscription; deterrent, impediment, obstacle; *spec*: bride (in lace-making); measure, unit of rhythm (in musical notation); unit of pressure (in meteorology).
vb lit: bolt, latch, lock, put a bar across, secure; barricade, block, exclude, keep out, obstruct, prevent; ban, forbid, prohibit; preclude.
prp lit: but (for), except (for), excluding, save.

barb
n lit: hook, jag, prickle, spike, spur; bristle, prong, thorn, tine; *fig*: sting; cut, dig, gibe, jibe, pointed remark; affront, insult; *spec*: barbel, type of fish, whisker (on a catfish); filament, strand (on a feather).
vb lit: make jagged, make spiky; *fig*: cut, dig, gibe, prickle, spike, sting.

barbarian
n lit: brute, savage; aboriginal, foreigner, native; hooligan, lout, ruffian, thug, vandal; *fig*: boor, philistine; illiterate.
adj lit: brutish, savage, uncivilized; aboriginal, foreign, native; boorish, lowbrow, philistine; crude, primitive, uncouth, uncultured, uneducated, unsophisticated; *fig*: common, low, uncultivated, vulgar.

barbaric
adj lit: barbarous, brutal, cruel, inhuman, ruthless; neanderthal, primitive, savage, uncivilized; fierce, harsh, wild; coarse, crude, rough, rude, uncouth; *fig*: tasteless, vulgar.

barber
n lit: coiffeur, coiffeuse, haircutter, hairdresser, hair stylist.

bare
vb lit: unclothe, uncover, undress, unsheathe; disclose, expose, open, reveal; denude, strip.
adj lit: denuded, exposed, naked, nude, stripped, unclothed, uncovered, undressed, unsheathed; peeled, shorn; austere, basic, cold, hard, mere, plain, severe, simple, stark, unadorned, unvarnished; literal, sheer,

unembellished; blank, empty, open,
vacant, void; lacking, mean, poor;
barren, featureless, scrubby, treeless;
abraded, worn.

barely
adv lit: hardly, just, only just, scarcely;
austerely, plainly, severely, simply,
starkly; poorly, scantily; explicitly,
freely, openly.

bargain
n lit: agreement, arrangement, compact,
contract, deal, pact, transaction, treaty,
understanding; cheap buy, giveaway,
good deal, snip, steal.
vb lit: beat down, haggle, negotiate, wheel
and deal; barter, exchange, swap, trade,
traffic; *fig*: bank, count, depend, rely;
look (for), make allowance (for), plan
(for).

barge
n lit: canal-boat, lighter, narrow-boat,
scow; cutter, gig, launch, state boat;
pleasure-boat, sightseeing cruiser;
houseboat.
vb lit: bump (into), cannon (into), crash
(into), knock (into), push, shoulder-
charge, shove; burst (in), butt (in),
intrude, muscle (in).

bark
n lit: bay, woof, yap, yelp; casing, cortex,
covering, husk, integument, jacket, peel,
skin; sailing-ship, three-master.
vb lit: bay, yap, yelp; abrade, flay, rub,
scrape, skin; *fig*: bang, fire; bawl, cough,
shout, snap, yell.

barn
n lit: granary, grange, storehouse; silo;
depository, repository.

barometer
n lit: glass, pressure-gauge, weather-glass;
fig: indicator.

barrack
vb lit: boo, demonstrate against, give a
rough ride, heckle, hector, hiss, hoot,
howl at, jeer, protest at, taunt, whistle at.

barracks
n lit: army camp, casern, garrison,
headquarters, military establishment,
quarters; *fig*: large building, utilitarian
complex, Victorian mansion.

barrage
n lit: bar, barrier, boom, dam;
bombardment, cannonade, fusillade,
salvo, volley; *fig*: deluge, hail, onslaught,
rain, storm, torrent.

barrel
n lit: butt, cask, drum, keg, tun, vat;
firkin, hogshead; cylinder, revolving
drum, shaft, tube; chamber, piston-
chamber; *fig*: good deal, lot; *spec*:
calamus, quill (of a feather); trunk (of a
farm animal).
vb fig: drive fast, hurtle, race, speed.

barren
adj lit: desert, desolate, empty, unfruitful,
unproductive, waste; childless,
impotent, infertile, sterile; fruitless,
uninformative, unprofitable,
unresponsive, unrewarding, wasted;
boring, dull, flat, jejune, stale, trite,
unattractive, uninspiring, useless, vapid.

barrier
n lit: bar, boom, paling, pole, rail;
barricade, blockage, obstacle,
obstruction; boundary, ditch, fence,
wall; fortification, palisade, rampart,
stockade; *fig*: check, difficulty,
hindrance, hurdle, impediment,
restriction, stumbling-block; defence,
protection.

barrister
n lit: advocate, counsel, lawyer.

barter
n lit: exchange, exchanging, swapping,
trading.
vb lit: bargain, exchange, swap, trade.

base
n lit: bottom, foot, foundation; bed, dais,
pedestal, plinth, podium, rest, stand;
basis, bedrock, core, essence, floor,
grounding, heart, origin, root, source;
camp, headquarters, post, station;
centre, focal point, home, starting point;
standard; *fig*: support; least, lowest,
minimum; *spec*: alkali (in chemistry);
basis of a number system (maths), stem
(in botany, etymology, phonetics).
vb lit: build, construct, establish, found,
set up; locate, place, station; derive,
ground.
adj lit: basic, core, essential, original, root;
central, focal, home, main, primary,
principal; standard; first, starting; least,
lowest, minimum; humble, inferior,
lowly, menial, paltry, poor, servile,

shabby, subservient, vulgar, wretched; contemptible, degraded, despicable, dishonourable, ignoble, low, mean, sordid, worthless; counterfeit, fake, forged, fraudulent; adulterated, debased, impure.

baseless
adj lit: groundless, uncorroborated, unfounded, ungrounded, unjustifiable, unjustified, unsubstantiated, unsupported, unverifiable, unverified.

basement
n lit: cellar, ground floor, lower ground floor, vault.
adj lit: lining, reinforcing, supporting, underlying.

bashful
adj lit: coy, diffident, nervous, self-conscious, self-effacing, shrinking, shy, timid, timorous; embarrassed, sheepish; reserved, retiring; reticent.

basic
adj lit: core, fundamental, inherent, intrinsic, original, residual, root, underlying; standard; elementary, first, starting; least, lowest, minimum; central, essential, focal, key, main, primary, principal, vital; *spec*: alkaline (in chemistry).

basically
adv lit: firstly, fundamentally, inherently, intrinsically, originally, residually; at a minimum, at bottom, at least, at the lowest; essentially, mainly, mostly, primarily, principally.

basilica
n lit: palace; cathedral, church, minster, nave, temple; grand hall.

basin
n lit: bowl, washbasin, washbowl, washstand; bidet; dock, harbour, haven, marina, pool; delta, drainage area, flats, valley; *spec*: synclinal area (in geology).

basis
n lit: base, bottom, footing, foundation; bedrock, core, essence, floor, grounding, groundwork, heart, origin, root, source; centre, focal point, starting point; standard; essentials, fundamentals, grounds, precept, premise, principle, rationale, reason, substance.

basket
n lit: hamper, pannier, punnet; creel; wickerwork container, receptacle; *spec*: goal, net (in basketball, netball); gondola (under a balloon); grouping, linking (of currencies); ring (on a ski pole).

bastard
n lit: illegitimate child, love-child, natural child; *fig*: impostor, fake, look-alike.
adj lit: illegitimate, natural; counterfeit, fake, false, sham; adulterated, corrupt, debased; abnormal, irregular, unusual.

bastion
n lit: barbican, bulwark, defence, fortification, tower; castle, citadel, fastness, fortress, stronghold; *fig*: mainstay, prop, rock.

bat
n lit: club, stick, willow; innings, knock; lath, plank; flittermouse, pipistrelle; *fig*: pace, rate, speed; binge, carousal, drunken spree; *spec*: disc (of clay); lump, piece (of building materials); sheet (of insulation material).
vb lit: hit, rap, smack, strike, swat, whack; be a batsman, be in; blink, wink; *fig*: go, race, speed.

batch
n lit: instalment, lot, set; bunch, collection, group, pack; amount, quantity.

bath
n lit: tub, washtub; hip-bath, jacuzzi, pool, sink; ablution, dip, douche, dousing, immersion, rinse, scrub, scrubbing, soak, sponging, wash; steeping.
vb lit: clean, douse, immerse, rinse, scrub, shower, soak, soap, sponge down, wash; steep.

bathe
n lit: dip, plunge, swim.
vb lit: go swimming, swim, take a dip; cleanse, dunk, give a bath, drench, immerse, rinse, soak, steep, wash; dampen, moisten, wet; be immersed, be steeped; *fig*: cover, surround; bask, be covered.

bathing costume
n lit: bikini, swimming costume, swimsuit, trunks.

bathos
n lit: anticlimax, comedown, let-down;

insincere pathos; sentimentality.

batter

n lit: pancake mixture, sponge mixture; paste; batsman, man in; tapering slope; *spec*: damaged type (in printing).
vb lit: assault, beat, belabour, buffet, dash against, lash, paste, pelt, pound, pummel, wallop; bruise, crush, injure, mangle, maul; be thicker at the top, slope inwards.

battered

adj (pa.pt) lit: beaten up, broken, bruised, crushed, damaged, dented, dilapidated, injured, maltreated, mangled, mauled, squashed, weatherbeaten.

battery

n lit: cell, electric cell, power cell, power-pack; solar cell, voltaic cell; collection, grouping, number, sequence, series, set, suite; egg factory, intensive rearing facility; armament, artillery, cannon, fire-power, gun emplacement; beating, bruising, damaging, injury, maltreatment, mangling, mauling, squashing.

battle

n lit: action, combat, duel, engagement, fight, fighting, fray, skirmish, war, warfare; clash, conflict, contest, dispute, encounter, struggle.
vb lit: contend, fight, make war, struggle, wage war; clash, contest, dispute.

battlements

n lit: barbican, bartizan, bastion, bulwark, castle walls, crenellation, fortifications, machicolation, parapet, ramparts, tower, turret.

bawdy

adj lit: blue, indecent, lascivious, lewd, licentious, risqué, rude, salacious; coarse, gross, indelicate, ribald, suggestive; dirty, filthy, obscene, prurient, scatological; carnal, erotic, lecherous, libidinous, lustful.

bawl

n lit: bellow, holler, roar; cry, howl, shout, shriek, wail, yell; blubbering, crying, sobbing, wailing; caterwauling, clamour, squalling, vociferation.
vb lit: bellow, holler, roar; howl, shout, shriek, yell; blubber, cry, sob, wail; caterwaul, clamour, squall, vociferate.

bay

n lit: bight, cove, gulf, inlet, sound; alcove, aumbry, embrasure, niche, nook, recess; concavity, hanging valley, indentation; platform, stall, station; area, compartment, space, ward; barking, call, howl, ululation; *spec*: chestnut (horse); laurel (bush, tree).
vb lit: bark (at), bell, crý, howl, ululate; corner, trap.
adj lit: concave, recessed, semicircular; *spec*: chestnut, reddish-brown (horse); laurel (bush, tree).

bazaar

n lit: market, marketplace, souk; exchange, mart; bring-and-buy sale, fair, fête, jumble sale, rummage sale, sale of work.

be

vb lit: exist, live; abide, continue, remain, stay; last, persist, subsist, survive; befall, come about, happen, occur, take place, transpire; become, equal, represent; go; have.

beach

n lit: bank, littoral, shore, strand; sand, sands, seaside, shingle.
vb lit: drive on shore, go aground, pull on shore, run ashore; *fig*: maroon, strand.

beacon

n lit: fire, flare, lamp, light, signal, signal fire; light-buoy, lighthouse, navigation light; watchtower; radio guide-beam, radio mast; flashing light; *fig*: guiding light, indicator, landmark, pointer, sign, signpost; warning.

bead

n lit: drop, droplet, globule; blob, bubble; ball, sphere; bauble, gem, ornament, pearl, stone; *spec*: flange (on a tyre); sight (on a gun)
vb lit: form drops, form globules; string together.

beak

n lit: bill, mandible, nib, proboscis; bow, prow, ram, rostrum; spout, tip; *fig*: nose, snout; magistrate; schoolmaster; *spec*: drip-pipe, outflow, outlet (on a gutter).

beam

n lit: girder, joist, plank, spar, timber, trunk; ray, shaft, stream; emission, transmission; gleam; *fig*: broad smile, glow, grin, radiance; bottom, buttocks,

hips; *spec*: bar, cross-piece, lever (on a pair of scales); breadth, side, width (of a ship); cylinder, roller (on a loom); shank, stem (of an anchor, a plough).
vb lit: broadcast, emit, radiate, transmit; gleam, shine; aim, direct, point; *fig*: grin, smile, smile broadly.

bear
n lit: bruin, grizzly; koala, panda; *fig*: hairy giant, shaggy person; *spec*: pessimist, seller (on the stock exchange).
vb lit: bring, carry, take; convey, fetch, move, transport; drive, press, push, thrust; have, hold, possess, sustain; assume, take on; behave, conduct; entertain, harbour, support; endure, put up with, stomach, tolerate; abide, brook; admit, afford, allow, permit; experience, suffer, undergo; bring forth, bring to birth, engender, give birth to, produce, yield; affect, be relevant; go, move, tend, turn, veer; give out, render; exercise; *spec*: sell (shares).

beard
n lit: beaver, bristles, full set, stubble, whiskers; awn, tuft; *spec*: barbel (on a fish).
vb lit: brave, confront, defy, face

bearer
n lit: bringer, carrier, conveyor, messenger, porter, runner; agent, servant; holder, presenter.

bearing
n lit: air, attitude, carriage, demeanour, deportment, manner, mien, posture; compass point, direction; application, connection, import, reference, relation, relevance, significance; endurance, stomaching, toleration; *spec*: charge, device (on a coat of arms).

bear out
vb lit: affirm, back up, confirm, corroborate, endorse, substantiate, support; justify, uphold, vindicate; prove.

bear with
vb lit: be patient with, make allowances for, put up with, tolerate; stay with, wait for; hear out.

beast
n lit: animal, brute; creature; fiend, monster, ogre, savage.

beastly
adj lit: bestial, brutish, inhuman; brutal,

fiendish, monstrous, savage; *fig*: awful, irritating, mean, nasty, rotten, unpleasant; coarse, foul, vile.
adv lit: abominably, awfully, frightfully; unpleasantly.

beat
n lit: pulse, throb, vibration; drumming, percussion; accent, stress; measure, metre, rhythm, time; circuit, course, patrol, round; *spec*: interference pattern (in music and wave physics).
vb lit: bang, batter, buffet, cane, drub, flog, hit, lash, pound, strike, thrash, whip, whack; pulsate, pulse, throb, vibrate; drum, hammer, roar, thunder; fashion, forge, work; *fig*: best, conquer, defeat, overcome, vanquish; outdo, outstrip, overtake, overwhelm, surpass; be too difficult for.

beatitude
n lit: blessedness, bliss, ecstasy, felicity, holy joy; blessing.

beautiful
adj lit: bewitching, enchanting, exquisite, fair, gorgeous, graceful, handsome, lovely, magnificent, radiant, ravishing, stunning.

beauty
n lit: attractiveness, charm, good looks, grace, loveliness, prettiness, pulchritude; advantage, benefit, good feature, major attraction; charmer, corker, cracker, dish, dreamboat, goddess, good-looker, lovely, peach, stunner.

beaver
n fig: busy bee, hard worker, workaholic; beard, full set; *spec*: chin-protector (on a helmet).
vb lit: graft, hammer (away), peg (away), slave (away), slog, toil (away).

becalmed
adj lit: immobile, motionless, stranded, stuck fast.

because
cnj lit: by reason (of), on account (of); for the reason that, in that, since.

beckoning
adj (pr.pt) lit: gesticulating at, motioning, signalling, waving at; enticing, inviting, luring, tempting; gaping, open, yawning.

become

vb lit: change into, develop into, grow into, turn into; come to be, get, turn; be appropriate to, be fitting to, behove, suit; adorn, grace, set off; be the fate (of).

becoming

adj (pr.pt) lit: appropriate, compatible, fit, fitting, meet, seemly, suitable; attractive, elegant, graceful, neat, smart.

bed

n lit: berth, bunk; mattress, pallet; litter, palliasse; resting-place; bottom, floor, foundation, substratum; stratum, vein; border, garden, patch, plot, row; *fig*: marital rights, sexual relations; *spec*: layer (of farmed oysters).
vb lit: be accommodated, lodge, put up, settle (down); hit the sack, lie, sleep; have sex with, make love with, sleep with; stratify, lay down, set down; implant, insert, plant, plant out, put in.

bedevil

vb lit: confound, drive frantic, drive mad, exasperate, harass, plague, torment.

bedlam

n lit: hurly-burly, madhouse, noisy chaos, pandemonium, tumult, uproar, utter confusion.

bedraggled

adj (pa.pt) lit: drenched, saturated, soaked, sodden, straggly; dishevelled, muddy, soiled, unkempt.

beef

n lit: ox, steer; *fig*: brawn, muscle, strength, vigour; complaint, grievance, gripe, grumble, protest; argument, dispute, wrangle.
vb lit: complain, gripe, grumble, protest; argue, dispute, wrangle; *fig*: boost (up), strengthen (up).

beefy

adj fig: brawny, burly, heavy, hulking, muscular, robust, stolid, strapping, strong, vigorous.

befall

vb lit: betide, come to pass, eventuate, happen, occur, take place, transpire.

befit

vb lit: be appropriate to, be compatible with, be right for, be suitable to; become, be seemly with, suit.

before

adv lit: ahead, in front; earlier, in the past, previously; by now, sooner.
prp lit: ahead of, in front of; in the sight of; earlier than, prior to; sooner than; in preference to; superior to.

befriend

vb lit: associate with, become pally with, get in with, make friends with; assist, champion, help, stand by, support, take up the cause of.

beg

vb lit: beseech, entreat, implore, petition, plead with; ask for alms, ask for charity; *spec*: cry (off); evade, sidestep (the question).

beggar

n lit: mendicant, tramp, vagrant; supplicant; bankrupt, pauper.

begin

vb lit: commence, start; inaugurate, initiate, launch, open, set about; embark on, set out on; create, found, institute, originate; appear, come into being, emerge, spring.

beginner

n lit: acolyte, apprentice, learner, neophyte, novice, postulant, starter, student, trainee, tyro; amateur, greenhorn.

beginning

n lit: commencement, onset, start; inauguration, initiation, launch, opening; outset; birth, creation, foundation, institution, origination, root(s); appearance, arising, dawn, emergence; fountainhead, source.
adj (pr.pt) lit: first, inaugural, initial, leading, opening, original, primary; incipient, rudimentary.

begrudge

vb lit: envy, resent, take ill; give reluctantly.

beguiling

adj lit: alluring, captivating, entrancing, intriguing; amusing, diverting, entertaining, interesting; deceptive.

behalf

n lit: account, part, side.

behave

vb lit: act, conduct oneself, handle, operate, perform, work; act properly, be mannerly, be polite; react.

behaviour

n lit: activity, comportment, conduct, manners; action, handling, operation, performance; reaction, responsivity.

behind

n lit: backside, bottom, derrière, posterior, rear, seat, stern; arse, bum.
adv lit: at the back, in the rear; afterwards, farther back, following, subsequently; in detention, in reserve; late, overdue, slow; in arrears, in debt.
prp lit: at the back of, beyond, to the back of; after, following, subsequent to; later than, slower than; responsible for; backing, supporting.

being

n lit: existence, life, living; entity, essence, substance; constitution, nature; attendance, presence; creature, individual, organism.
adj (pr.pt) lit: existent; contemporaneous, continuing, present.

beleaguered

adj (pa.pt) lit: beset, besieged; *fig*: harassed, persecuted, plagued, sorely tried.

belief

n lit: confession, credo, creed, doctrine, faith, persuasion, tenet; conviction, feeling, impression, opinion, understanding, view; reliance, trust; (beyond) acceptance, (beyond) credence.

believe

vb lit: confess, have faith (in); credit; be convinced (that), hold (that); place one's trust (in), trust; consider, deem, think; conjecture, guess, imagine, presume, reckon, suppose.

believer

n lit: adherent, devotee, disciple, proselyte.

bellow

n lit: bawl, holler, howl, roar, shout, yell
vb lit: boom, bawl, holler, howl, roar, shout, thunder, yell.

belly

n lit: abdomen, corporation, gut, maw, paunch, pot, stomach, tummy.

belong

vb lit: appertain (to), attach (to), pertain (to), relate (to); be affiliated (to); be connected (with), go together (with).

belongings

n lit: gear, effects, junk, paraphernalia, possessions, stuff, things.

below

adj lit: beneath, underneath; downstairs, lower; later, subsequent; inferior, lesser.
adv lit: beneath, under, underneath; down, downstairs, lower; downstream; hereafter, later.
prp lit: beneath, lower than, under, underneath; inferior to, less than, subordinate to, unworthy of.

belt

n lit: girdle; cummerbund, sash; band, cincture; *fig*: stretch, strip, zone; layer, stratum; punch, thump, whack; nip, slug, tot.
vb lit: engirdle, fasten (on); *fig*: beat, flog, thrash, whip; punch, thump, whack; shut (up); bawl (out), roar (out), sing (out).

bemused

adj lit: bewildered, dazed, perplexed, staggered, stunned, stupefied; absorbed, daydreaming, preoccupied.

bench

n lit: form, pew, seat; counter, work-table; frame, platform, trestle-table; judiciary, magistracy, tribunal.

bend

n lit: buckle, fold, warp; angle, corner, curve, turn; stoop; fastening, knot.
vb lit: bow, buckle, fold, warp; curve, swerve, turn, veer; lean over, stoop; flex, mould, shape; *fig*: influence, persuade, sway.

beneath

adv lit: below, under, underneath; lower.
prp lit: below, lower than, under, underneath; inferior to, less than, subordinate to, unworthy of.

benefactor

n lit: patron, sponsor, subsidizer; well-wisher; backer, contributor, donor, supporter; philanthropist.

beneficial

adj lit: advantageous, gainful, helpful, profitable, useful, valuable; healthful, salutary.

benefit

n lit: advantage, gain, good, help, improvement, profit, use; dole, grant, unemployment grant, welfare; charity performance.

vb lit: be good for, do good to; advantage, aid, further, serve; be advantaged, be assisted, gain, profit.

benevolent
adj lit: beneficent, benign, charitable, considerate, generous, humane, kindly, philanthropic, well-disposed.

benign
adj lit: friendly, genial, kindly, sympathetic; advantageous, beneficial, favourable, propitious; mild, salubrious, salutary; non-malignant.

bent
n lit: bias, inclination, leaning, penchant, preference, propensity; tendency, trend; flexion, torque; ability, endurance; *spec*: type of grass.
adj lit: bowed, buckled, folded, twisted, warped; angled, curved; crooked, hunched, leaning, stooping; *fig*: determined (on), insistent (on), intent (on), resolved (on); criminal, dishonest, fraudulent, unscrupulous; gay, homosexual; deviant, kinky, perverted.

bequeath
vb lit: endow, hand down, leave (to), pass on, will (to); commit, entrust, hand over (to).

bereaved
adj (pa.pt) lit: bereft, deprived, grieving, mourning, surviving; fatherless, motherless, orphaned, widowed.

berserk
adj lit: amok, crazed, demented, deranged, frenzied, insane, maddened, maniacal, out of one's skull, uncontrollable.

berth
n lit: bed, bunk, cabin, couchette, place, seat; sleeping-place; anchorage, dock, mooring, quay, wharf; *fig*: job, position, post, situation; leeway, room, sea-room, space.

beside
adv lit: additionally, also, further, furthermore, in addition, moreover, too.
prp lit: adjoining, alongside, bordering, by the side of, contiguous with, next to; *fig*: compared to/with, in comparison with; *spec*: not pertinent to, unrelated to (the point).

besides
adv lit: additionally, also, further, furthermore, in addition, moreover, too; likewise, similarly; else, otherwise.
prp lit: as well as, in addition to, over and above; apart from, barring, excepting, other than, save.

besiege
vb lit: beset, encircle, encompass, hem in, invest, surround; *fig*: badger, beleaguer, importune, pester, plague; crowd round, mob, throng round; deluge, flood, inundate.

best
n lit: finest, flower, greatest, number one, optimum, supreme, top; elite, favourite, pick; champion, first, victor, winner; utmost.
vb lit: beat, conquer, defeat, outdo, surpass; outwit.
adj lit: finest, foremost, greatest, highest, optimum, supreme, top; favourite; champion, first, leading, victorious, winning; most advantageous; most fitting.
adv lit: most, supremely; most correctly, most efficiently, most thoroughly; most advantageously; most attractively, most fittingly.

bestial
adj lit: animal, brutal, brutish, degraded, depraved, obscene, perverted, sordid; carnal.

bet
n lit: gamble, risk, speculation, wager; ante, pledge, stake; *fig*: alternative, choice, course of action, route; belief, guess, opinion, supposition.
vb lit: gamble, punt, risk, speculate (on), stake (on), wager; *fig*: be certain, be sure.

betray
vb lit: double-cross, sell out; divulge, give away, reveal; inform on, tell on, unmask; ensnare, entrap, seduce, undo; be disloyal to, deceive; desert, forsake, leave in the lurch; *fig*: let slip, manifest, show signs of.

betrayal
n lit: double-cross, give-away, sell-out; disclosure, divulgence, unmasking; entrapment, seduction; violation; disloyalty, deception, duplicity, perfidy, treachery, treason; desertion, forsaking, ratting.

better
vb lit: ameliorate, enhance, forward, further, improve; amend, correct, rectify; beat, cap, defeat, outdo, top.
adj lit: finer, greater, higher, preferable, superior; more useful, more valuable; more apt, more suitable; more expert, more skilled; more intense; cured, healthier, progressing, recovering, stronger, well again.
adv lit: more (than); in a superior way, more advantageously, more usefully, more valuably; more aptly, more suitably; more expertly, more skilfully; more fully, more intensely.

between
prp lit: betwixt, intermediate to, in the middle of; within the range separating; connecting, joining, linking; through the combined action of; in the joint possession of.

beverage
n lit: drink, liquid refreshment; hot drink.

bewail
vb lit: cry over, grieve over, howl because of, keen over, lament, mourn, rue, ululate over, weep over.

beware
vb lit: be careful (of), be wary (of); be on one's guard (lest/that).

bewildered
adj lit: at a loss, baffled, confused, mystified, perplexed, puzzled, stunned, taken aback.

bewitched
adj lit: captivated, enchanted, entranced, fascinated, spellbound.

beyond
adv lit: at a distance, behind, farther away; past.
prp lit: across, behind, on the farther side of, over, to the farther side of; later than, past; above, besides, more than, outside; *fig*: out of the reach of, too much for the comprehension of.

bias
n lit: leaning, partiality, predilection, predisposition, prejudice; diagonal, oblique; weighting.
vb lit: influence, predispose, prejudice, slant, weight.

bid
n lit: offer, proposition, tender; *fig*:

attempt, effort, endeavour, try.
vb lit: make an offer, tender; call; greet, say, wish; ask, invite; command (to), direct (to), order (to), tell (to).

big
adj lit: colossal, enormous, gigantic, great, huge, hulking, immense, large, massive, sizable, substantial, tremendous; adult, elder, grown-up; full, loud; pregnant (with); *fig*: important, influential, powerful, prominent, valuable; altruistic, benevolent, generous, liberal, magnanimous, noble, princely; arrogant, boastful, conceited, pompous, pretentious.

bigoted
adj lit: biased, narrow-minded, opinionated, prejudiced; illiberal, intolerant.

bile
n lit: gall; *fig*: anger, choler, irascibility, peevishness, rancour, wrath.

bill
n lit: account, invoice, reckoning, score, slate, tally; advertisement, broadsheet, circular, handout, leaflet, poster; inventory, list, programme, schedule; law, measure, proposal; banknote, note; beak, neb; cleaver, pick.
vb lit: charge, invoice, put on the slate; advertise, announce, give advance warning of, stick posters up over; *spec*: touch beaks (of birds).

bind
n lit: bore, bother, drag, nuisance; dilemma, predicament, quandary, spot.
vb lit: attach, fasten, hitch, lash, rope, strap, tie up, truss; glue, stick together; confine, restrain, restrict; bandage, cover, dress, swathe; border, edge, trim; constipate, impact; *fig*: compel, constrain, necessitate, oblige, require.

binding
n lit: casing, cover, covering, jacket; border, edging, trimming; ski-fastening.
adj lit: indelible, irrevocable; compulsory, obligatory.

birch
vb lit: beat, cane, flog, thrash, whip.

bird
n lit: feathered friend, fowl; *fig*: bloke, chap, guy, person; chick, doll, girl, girlfriend; porridge, stretch, term, time; barracking, booing, raspberry.

birth

n lit: accouchement, delivery, labour, parturition; nativity; ancestry, blood, breeding, family, lineage, parentage; *fig*: beginning, creation, dawn, emergence, genesis, inauguration, origination.

biscuit

n lit: cracker, cookie, nut, savoury; crispbread.

bit

n lit: bite, chip, crumb, fragment, morsel, scrap, slice; part, piece, section, segment, small amount; coin; bore, drill; curb, mouthpiece, snaffle; *fig*: little, minute, moment, second, while.

bitch

n lit: female dog, she-wolf, vixen; *fig*: harlot, slut, tart, tramp, whore; cat, harridan, shrew, termagant, tigress, virago; back-stabber, serpent, snake-in-the-grass; beef, complaint, grievance, grouse.

bite

n lit: dentition, occlusion; grasp, grip, nip, prick, puncture, sting; morsel, mouthful, nibble, snack; *fig*: acidity, corrosiveness; kick, piquancy, punch, spice; attempt, bash, go, try; answer, reaction, response.
vb lit: chew, chomp, clench, gnaw, masticate, munch, nibble, nip; grind, grip, puncture, rend, seize, sting, tear; corrode, eat into, erode, wear away; cut, pierce; be caught, take the bait; *fig*: be effective, take effect; react, respond, snap (at); annoy, bother.

biting

adj lit: caustic, corrosive, incisive, lacerating, mordent, stinging; gnawing, rending, tearing; *fig*: sarcastic, scathing, withering; cutting, freezing, penetrating, piercing.

bitter

adj lit: acescent, acid, acrid, astringent, harsh, sour, tart; *fig*: acrimonious, hostile, rancorous, resentful, sulky, sullen; caustic, fierce, sharp, stinging, virulent; biting, freezing, intense, piercing; distressing, galling, grievous, heart-rending, painful.

bizarre

adj lit: extraordinary, fantastic, freakish, grotesque, outlandish, strange, striking, weird.

black

adj lit: dusky, ebony-coloured, jet, negroid, swart, swarthy; dark, raven, sable; dim, inky, murky, stygian; dirty, filthy, foul, grimy, soiled; *fig*: depressing, foreboding, funereal, hopeless, mournful, ominous, sombre; evil, malignant, villainous, wicked; lowering, morose, resentful, sullen, sulky; aggressive, hostile, menacing, threatening; banned, boycotted, embargoed, strike-bound.

blacken

vb lit: darken; cloud over, dim; befoul, defile, dirty, soil; *fig*: calumniate, defame, malign, slander, smear, stain, taint, tarnish.

blackmail

n lit: demanding money with menaces, extortion, intimidation; protection money.
vb lit: demand money with menaces, extort, hold to ransom, intimidate.

blackout

n lit: dizzy spell, faint, loss of consciousness, swoon; epileptic fit; electricity cut, power failure; *fig*: censorship, silence, suppression.

black sheep

n lit: disgrace, dishonour, shame; renegade, turncoat; scoundrel, villain.

blade

n lit: leaf, petal; cutting edge, edge, glaive, guillotine, knife, razor, shaft; sword, swordsman; oar, paddle, scull; *fig*: buck, dandy, gallant.

blame

n lit: accusation, censure, charge, recrimination; culpability, guilt; *fig*: fault, liability, responsibility.
vb lit: condemn (for), find fault with (for), hold responsible (for), rebuke (for), reproach (for).

bland

adj lit: balmy, calm, mild, temperate; affable, amiable, gentle, polite, smooth, suave, urbane; non-irritant, soft, soothing, weak; dull, flat, insipid, uninteresting, vapid.

blank

n lit: emptiness, space, tabula rasa, vacuity, vacuum, void; gap, hiatus; empty sheet, white page; *spec*: bullseye, inner, white (on a target).

adj lit: bare, empty, plain, pristine, unmarked, unused, white; uncut, unformed, unshaped; *fig*: bewildered, confounded, dumbfounded, nonplussed; deadpan, expressionless, impassive, lifeless, uncomprehending, vacuous.

blanket
n lit: coverlet, rug; *fig*: carpet, coat, covering, film, layer, sheet.
vb lit: carpet, coat, cover, envelop, spread oneself over; cloak, mask, obscure, veil.
adj lit: all-inclusive, comprehensive, general, universal.

blasé
adj lit: casual, indifferent, nonchalant, offhand, unexcited, world-weary; bored, sated, surfeited.

blasphemy
n lit: desecration, impiety, irreverence, profanity, sacrilege.

blast
n lit: gust, squall, storm, wind; blare, honk, hoot, peal, wail; blow, jet; bang, crash, detonation, eruption, explosion; pressure-wave; *fig*: outburst.
vb lit: blare, blow, hoot; blow up, detonate, explode, shatter; demolish, destroy, smash, wreck, zap; kill, ruin, shrivel, wither; *fig*: be scathing about, flay, pan, slate; abuse, curse, swear at, vilify; *spec*: smoke (marijuana).

blatant
adj lit: brazen, flagrant, glaring; conspicuous, obvious, overt, pronounced; clamorous, loudmouthed, noisy; garish, gaudy, loud, ostentatious.

blaze
n lit: conflagration, fire, flames; beacon, brazier; blare, brilliance, glare, glow, radiance; burst, eruption, flare-up, outburst.
vb lit: be on fire, burn, flame; be brilliant, flare, flash, glare, glow; fire (away), shoot (away); *fig*: peg (away), toil (away); explode, flare (up).

bleach
vb lit: lighten, peroxide, whiten; blanch, etiolate, fade.

bleak
adj lit: bare, barren, exposed, gaunt, open, windswept; chilly, cold, raw, windy; cheerless, colourless, depressing, discouraging, gloomy, sombre.

bleed
vb lit: lose blood, shed blood; lose sap; leak, ooze, seep, trickle; draw blood from; draw sap from; catheterize, drain, leech, siphon off, squeeze; *fig*: blackmail from, extort from; ache (for), feel (for), have pity (for); *spec*: go off the edge of the page (of illustrations).

bleeding
n lit: haemorrhage; bloodshed, discharge, emission, flow; bloodletting; infusion (into), running (into); *fig*: blasted, cursed, damned.

blemish
n lit: defect, disfigurement, fault, flaw, imperfection, mark, scar, stain; *fig*: blot, dishonour, reproach, shame, taint.
vb lit: blot, blotch, deface, disfigure, impair, mar, mark, scar, smudge, spoil, stain, taint, tarnish; *fig*: defame, slander.

blend
n lit: amalgam, combination, compound, fusion, mixture, synthesis; merging, shading; harmonization.
vb lit: amalgamate, combine, compound, fuse, mingle, mix, synthesize; merge (with); go well (with), harmonize (with).

bless
vb lit: consecrate, hallow, make holy, sanctify; commend to God's grace, invoke divine favour upon, make the sign of the cross over; make fruitful, make happy, make joyful, make prosperous; adore, extol, glorify, praise, worship.

blessing
n lit: benediction, benison; consecration, invocation; grace, thanksgiving; *fig*: approval, backing, encouragement, favour, sanction, support; benefit, gift, possession, present; boon, godsend, help, piece of luck, stroke of good fortune.

blind
n lit: louvres, shutter, slats; canopy, shade; carousal, drinking spree, pub-crawl; *fig*: cover, device, façade, feint, front, mask, ploy, pretext, pretence, ruse, screen, stratagem.
vb lit: put out the eyes of; be too bright for, dazzle; *fig*: keep in the dark, render oblivious (to), stop from seeing.

adj lit: sightless, unseeing; *fig*: dead-end;
inattentive (to), indifferent (to),
insensitive (to), oblivious (to); dark, dim,
hidden, obscured; unreasoning,
unthinking.
adv lit: ad lib, extempore, off the cuff,
straight off, unseen; through
instrumentation only.

blindly
adv lit: come what may, heedlessly, no
matter what, regardlessly; aimlessly,
haphazardly, purposelessly, randomly;
unreasoningly, unthinkingly,
unwittingly.

bliss
n lit: blessedness, felicity, heavenly joy;
ecstasy, happiness, rapture.

blister
n lit: bleb, cyst, vesicle; bubble; bulge,
swelling; vesicatory.
vb lit: cause vesicles; bubble, bulge, swell;
fig: be scathing to, crucify, pan, slate,
tear off a strip.

blizzard
n lit: drift, snow-squall, snowstorm; *fig*:
deluge, flood.

bloated
adj (pa.pt) lit: blown up, dilated,
distended, inflated, puffed up, swollen,
turgid; *spec*: salted and smoked (fish).

block
n lit: barrier, blockage, impediment,
obstacle, obstruction, stoppage; bar,
brick, cube, ingot, piece; building, site,
square; anvil, base, platform, support,
table; pulley; *fig*: group, row, set; book,
pad, ream; bonce, head.
vb lit: bar, check, halt, impede, obstruct,
stop; bung, choke, clog, plug up, stuff
up.

blockade
n lit: barricade, barrier, obstruction;
encirclement, investment, siege.
vb lit: barricade, fortify, obstruct, secure;
besiege, cut off, encircle, isolate.

blood
n lit: gore; plasma, serum; claret, cruor;
ancestry, birth, descent, extraction,
family, genealogy, lineage, pedigree,
stock, strain; kindred, relations,
relatives; *fig*: juice, sap; anger, passion,
temper; death, murder; disposition,
feeling, temperament; buck, blade,

dandy, spark; aristocracy, nobility, royal
family.
vb lit: smear with gore; *fig*: initiate (into),
introduce (into).

bloodshed
n lit: butchery, carnage, execution, killing,
slaughter, slaying.

bloom
n lit: blossom, flower; blossoming,
flowering, opening; glaucescence,
powdery surface; cloudiness, milkiness;
fig: fragrance, freshness, perfection,
prime, radiance; blush, flush, rosiness;
spec: aggregation, mass (of plankton).
vb lit: blossom, burgeon, flower, open; *fig*:
flourish, prosper, succeed, thrive; be
fragrant, be radiant.

blossom
n lit: bloom, flower; flowers, scented
petals.
vb lit: bloom, burgeon, flower; *fig*: come
into one's own, flourish, lose one's
reserve, mature, show what one can do.

blot
n lit: blotch, mark, smudge, splodge,
splurge; blemish, spot, stain; *fig*: defect,
fault, flaw.
vb lit: absorb, dry; mark, smudge,
splodge; blemish, spoil, stain; *fig*: mar,
tarnish.

blouse
n lit: chemise, shirt; blouson; bolero,
camise, camisole; bodice, smock, vest.

blow
n lit: blast, gale, gust, wind; bang, belt,
buffet, clip, clout, clump, knock, punch,
smack, sock, thump, thwack, wallop,
whack; *fig*: calamity, catastrophe,
disappointment, disaster, setback, upset;
(at a) stroke.
vb lit: fan, gust, puff, waft, whirl, whistle;
blast, buffet, sweep, whisk; breathe hard,
exhale, pant; pipe, play; blare, hoot,
sound; *fig*: exhaust, spend, squander, use
up; divulge, reveal, tell; *spec*: lose, miss
(one's chance); melt (a fuse); spout (of
whales).

blow-out
n lit: burst tyre, flat tyre, puncture;
eruption, explosion, flare-up; *fig*:
banquet, beano, feast.

blow up
vb lit: blast, burst, detonate, explode, go off; bloat, distend, inflate, pump up, swell; *fig*: appear, arise, come up; enlarge, expand; exaggerate, magnify, overstate; become incensed, be infuriated, go berserk, lose one's temper.

blue
vb lit: bleach, dye white; *fig*: exhaust, spend, squander, use up.
adj lit: aquamarine, azure, cerulean, cyan, indigo, turquoise, ultramarine; gunmetal; cold, frozen, numb; under-oxygenated; *fig*: dejected, depressed, downcast, doleful, glum, melancholy; depressing, dismal, unpromising; bawdy, erotic, indecent, obscene, smutty; *spec*: flattened, seventh (note in music).

bluff
n lit: cliff, foreland, headland, promontory, steep hill; deception, dissimulation, feint, hoax, ploy, pretence, ruse, subterfuge; bluster, boastfulness, bravado.
vb lit: deceive, defraud, hoax, make out (that), pretend (that).
adj lit: abrupt, sheer, steep, vertical; *fig*: blunt, frank, hearty, outspoken, robust.

blunder
n lit: bad mistake, boob, brick, bungle, faux pas, howler, oversight, stupid error.
vb lit: boob, make a bad mistake, slip up disastrously; flounder, stumble, wallow.

blunt
vb lit: dull, take the edge off; *fig*: dampen, deaden, muffle, soften, weaken.
adj lit: dull, flat; *fig*: bluff, forthright, frank, plain-speaking, outspoken, straightforward; explicit, forceful.

blur
n lit: blot, smear, smudge, splodge; blear, fog, haze, mist, vagueness; streak.
vb lit: blemish, blot, smear, smudge; cloud, darken, obscure, soften; unfocus; flash, streak.

blurt
vb lit: ejaculate, exclaim, get (out), retort, shoot (out), splutter; *spec*: blab, disclose, reveal (a secret).

blush
n lit: flush, glow, reddening, suffusion; bloom, rosiness.
vb lit: colour, crimson, flush, redden,

suffuse; be ashamed (at), be mortified (at).

bluster
n lit: bluffing, boasting, bombast, braggadocio, bravado.
vb lit: be windy, blow strongly; boast, brag, swagger; bully, domineer, hector; rage, rant, storm.

blustery
adj lit: boisterous, gusty, squally, stormy, windy; tempestuous, violent.

board
n lit: joist, panel, plank, timber; lath, slat; card; table; catering, food, meals, provisions; committee, council, directors, trustees; arena, platform, stage, surface.
vb lit: plank (over), shutter, timber (over); cater for, feed, provide meals for; billet, lodge, put up, quarter; enter, get on, mount.

boarder
n lit: paying guest, pensioner; live-in student, resident, invader, marauder, raider.

boarding-house
n lit: guest-house, pension; annexe, digs, hall of residence, hostel; hotel.

boast
n lit: brag, vaunt; joy, pride, pride and joy, treasure.
vb lit: brag, talk big; blow one's own trumpet, crow, vaunt; be proud of, flatter oneself on; *fig*: exhibit, have, own, possess.

boastful
adj lit: big-headed, bragging, conceited, egotistical, vaunting.

boat
n lit: craft, ship, vessel; canoe, cutter, dinghy, ketch, launch, sloop, yacht, yawl; cruiser, liner; ferry.

bob
n lit: bow, curtsey; duck, jerk, nod; pendulum, plumb, sinker, weight; topknot; racing sled.
vb lit: bow, curtsey; duck, nod; bounce, quiver, seesaw, weave, wobble.

bodily
adj lit: body, corporal, corporeal, physical; material, tangible.
adv lit: corporeally, in the flesh,

physically; completely, entirely, totally, wholly; collectively, en masse.

body
n lit: figure, form, frame; build, physique; being, human, mortal, person, soul; cadaver, corpse, mortal remains; torso, trunk; fuselage, nave; *fig*: bulk, core, main part, majority, mass; essence, matter, substance; density, firmness, fullness, opacity, solidity; band, collection, company, group, set.

bog
n lit: fen, marsh, morass, moss, quagmire, slough, swamp; *fig*: convenience, Gents, john, Ladies, latrine, lavatory, loo, privy, toilet.

bogus
adj lit: counterfeit, fake, false, imitation, phoney, sham.

boil
n lit: abscess, carbuncle, furuncle, pimple, pustule, spot, stye.
vb lit: steam, vaporize; cook, poach; evaporate; agitate, bubble, churn, foam, seethe; *fig*: be incensed, fulminate, fume, hit the roof, rage, rant.

boisterous
adj lit: blustery, gusty, rough, squally, windy; tempestuous, turbulent, violent; exuberant, loud, noisy, riotous, rollicking, rowdy, rumbustious, unruly, wild.

bold
adj lit: audacious, brave, courageous, daring, fearless, intrepid, valiant; flirtatious, forward, shameless; brash, cheeky, impudent, saucy; *fig*: bright, conspicuous, loud, showy, striking, vivid; forceful, lively, spirited.

bolster
n lit: cushion, pillow; cushioning, pad, padding; *spec*: capital (on top of a pillar).
vb lit: brace, buttress, cushion, hold (up), pillow, prop (up), support; *fig*: assist, boost, maintain, reinforce, shore (up).

bolt
n lit: bar, catch, latch, peg, pin, rod, slide; arrow, dart, quarrel; dash, runner, sprint; stroke of lightning, thunderflash; *spec*: roll (of cloth).
vb lit: bar, fasten, latch, lock, peg, pin, secure; dash, flee, fly, run for it, sprint; gobble, gorge, guzzle, stuff, wolf; *spec*: run to seed (of a plant).

bomb
n lit: explosive device, mine, shell; lava-ball; *fig*: nasty shock, unwelcome surprise; fortune, lot of money, mint; success, treat.
vb lit: blitz, blow up, bombard, detonate, shell; *fig*: fly, hurtle, race, rocket, speed.

bombard
vb lit: blitz, bomb, maintain fire upon, pound, shell, strafe; *fig*: beset, besiege, harass, harry, pester, plague.

bond
n lit: adhesivity, stickiness, tackiness; cement, glue, gum, mortar; binding, chain, cord, fastening, fetter, manacle, rope, shackle; molecular force; affinity, attachment, link, tie; agreement, contract, covenant, pledge, promise; guarantee, security, surety; debenture, promisory note; *spec*: style, technique (in bricklaying).
vb lit: cement, fasten (together), fix (together), fuse, glue, gum.

bonnet
n lit: beret, cap, glengarry; coronet, hat, mob-cap, scarf; head-dress; cover, cowl, lid; *spec*: decoy (player or bidder).

bonus
n lit: bounty, commission, dividend, extra, gratuity, honorarium, premium, reward; perk; rake-off, share of profits; prize, winnings; windfall.

book
n lit: publication, tome, volume; work; archive, chronicle, ledger, log, record; libretto, script.
vb lit: enter, insert, log, post, put down, record, register, write down; engage, line up, reserve, schedule; take the name of; check (in).

booking
n lit: charter, engagement, reservation; yellow card; motoring offence.

bookish
adj lit: academic, erudite, intellectual, learned, literary, scholarly; diligent, studious; impractical, pedantic, unworldly.

boom
n lit: arm, bar, beam, pole, strut; floating barrier; blast, burst, clap, explosion, reverberation, roar, rumble; *fig*: expansion, growth, improvement,

increase, upsurge, upturn; *spec*: cry (of
the bittern).
vb lit: blast, crash, explode, resound,
reverberate, roar, rumble; *fig*: blossom,
develop, expand, gather momentum,
grow, improve, increase, prosper, thrive.

boorish
adj lit: banausic, barbarian, clodhopping,
coarse, gross, lubberly, oafish, unrefined,
vulgar; churlish, disruptive, philistine.

boost
n lit: encouragement, furtherance, help;
expansion, hike, hoist, improvement,
increase, lift.
vb lit: advance, encourage, foster, further,
help; add to, enlarge, expand, hike up,
hoist, improve, increase, lift, promote,
support.

boot
n lit: heavy shoe, wellie, wellington; kick,
punt; luggage compartment, trunk.
vb lit: shoe; kick, punt; chuck (out), kick
(out), throw (out); avail, be of use, profit;
spec: access, insert (a computer
program).

booth
n lit: cubbyhole, niche, nook, recess;
cabin, chalet, hut; box, cabinet,
compartment; counter, office, stall;
enclosure.

border
n lit: boundary, brink, edge, frontier,
limit, margin, rim; flower-bed; edging,
fringe, hem, trimming; outskirts.
vb lit: adjoin, be adjacent to, bound,
delimit, front on, march with; edge,
fringe.

bore
n lit: hole, shaft; barrel, calibre; *fig*: drag,
nuisance, pain, pest; chore, thankless
task.
vb lit: drill, mine, penetrate (into), pierce
(into), sink a shaft (into), tunnel (into);
fig: bother, fatigue, tire, weary.

boredom
n lit: ennui, having nothing to do,
listlessness, monotony, tedium,
tediousness, tiresomeness.

boring
adj (pr.pt) lit: dismal, dull, flat,
humdrum, insipid, monotonous,
mundane, numbing, ordinary, soporific,
stale, stultifying, tedious, tiresome,
uninteresting, wearisome.

borrow
vb lit: have the use of; have, use, utilize;
adopt, appropriate, copy, derive, imitate,
pilfer, pirate, plagiarize; *spec*: make
allowance for (the terrain in golf).

bosom
n lit: breast(s), bust; chest; *fig*: emotions,
feelings, heart, sentiments; centre,
midst.
adj lit: close, dear, intimate.

boss
n lit: knob, ornament, stud; chief,
employer, foreman, gaffer, leader,
manager, master, overseer, supervisor.

bossy
adj lit: authoritarian, autocratic,
dictatorial, domineering, egotistical,
haughty, imperious, monomaniacal,
overbearing, selfish.

bother
n lit: annoyance, inconvenience, irritation,
nuisance, problem, vexation;
commotion, disturbance, fuss, to-do.
vb lit: annoy, be a nuisance,
inconvenience, irritate, pester, plague,
vex; go to the trouble (to), make the
effort (to); blast, damn.

bottle
n lit: canteen, decanter, flask, jar; *fig*:
bravery, courage, determination, guts,
nerve, pluck, resolve.

bottleneck
n lit: constriction, narrows, straits; check,
hindrance, impediment, obstruction;
congestion, jam, queue.

bottom
n lit: base, basis, floor, foundation;
underneath, underside; arse, backside,
behind, bum, posterior, rear, rump, seat;
hull, keel; *fig*: core, heart, root, source.
adj lit: base, fundamental, ground, lowest,
ultimate.

bough
n lit: branch, offshoot; shoot, stem; twig.

boulder
n lit: large rock, rounded stone.

bounce
n lit: elasticity, give, resilience,
springiness; rebound, recoil; thud,
thump; *fig*: dynamism, energy, liveliness,
pep, vivacity, zip.

vb lit: bound, glance (off), leap, rebound, recoil, ricochet; *fig*: chuck out, eject, kick out, throw out; burst (into/out of); come (back), go (back).

bound
n lit: bounce, jump, leap, skip, spring; border(s), edge(s), limit(s), margin(s); *fig*: restraint(s), restriction(s).
vb lit: bounce, jump, leap, skip, spring; border, define, delimit, terminate; *fig*: confine, restrain, restrict.
adj (pa.pt) lit: chained, pinioned, roped, secured, tied up; cased, covered, hardback, sealed, wrapped; destined (for), en route (for), making (for); certain (to), compelled (to), fated (to), obliged (to), required (to), sure (to).

boundary
n lit: border, edge, extremity, fringe, frontier, limit, line, margin, termination; *spec*: four (in cricket).

bountiful
adj lit: beneficent, generous, liberal, munificent; ample, copious, plenteous, plentiful, prolific, unstinting.

bouquet
n lit: bunch, corsage, nosegay, posy, spray; aroma, perfume, redolence, scent; *fig*: compliment(s), commendation(s), praise.

bout
n lit: contest, encounter, fight, round; period, session, spell, stint, time.

boutique
n lit: bazaar, booth, kiosk, shop, stall, stand, store.

bovine
adj lit: ox-like; ruminant; *fig*: boorish, clodhopping, dense, oafish, stolid, stupid, thick.

bow
n lit: bend, bob, inclination, kowtow, nod; curve, distortion, warp; fore, front, prow, sharp end; looped knot.
vb lit: bend (low), bob, incline, kowtow, nod; curve, distort, hunch, warp; play the violin; *fig*: defer (to), give in (to), surrender (to), yield (to); crush, oppress, subdue, weigh down.

bowl
n lit: basin, dish; container, pot, vessel; hurl, pitch, throw; ball, wood.
vb lit: fling, hurl, pitch, throw; roll.

box
n lit: carton, case, package; chest, crate, trunk; receptacle; bang, blow, buffet, clip, clout, punch, wallop; *fig*: inset, rectangle; goal area, penalty area; cabin, hut, lodge; jock, protector; *spec*: (Christmas) gratuity, tip.
vb lit: enclose, insert, pack into; confine, pen; fight, spar, trade punches; bang, buffet, clip, clout, punch, thump, wallop.

boxing
n lit: pugilism, ringcraft; fisticuffs; fighting, sparring, trading punches.

boy
n lit: adolescent, lad, son, stripling, young man, youth; bloke, chap, fellow, guy.

boycott
n lit: ban, blacking, embargo, proscription.
vb lit: ban, black, embargo, have nothing to do with, ostracize, proscribe.

bra
n lit: brassiere, bust support.

brace
n lit: caliper, frame, orthopaedic support, splint; bracket, buttress, prop, stanchion, stay, support; couple, duo, pair; drill-handle.
vb lit: bind, reinforce, splint, strap; bracket, buttress, prop, stay, support; *fig*: draw (oneself) up, steel (oneself), strengthen (oneself).

brain
n lit: central nervous system, cerebral hemispheres, cerebrum, grey matter; intellect, mind; common sense, intelligence, nous, wit; *fig*: genius, mastermind, prodigy; expert; highbrow, scholar; control system, guidance system.

brainwave
n lit: alpha wave, beta rhythm; *fig*: bright idea, innovation, inspiration, stroke of genius.

brake
n lit: check, constraint, curb, decelerator, rein; bracken, ferns, thicket, undergrowth.
vb lit: check, constrain, curb, decelerate, halt, rein in, slow, stop.

branch
n lit: bough, offshoot; shoot, stem; twig; arm, limb; *fig*: ramification; department, office, part, section, subdivision, subsidiary.

vb lit: diversify, divide, fork, ramify, spread (out); develop, expand, increase, proliferate.

brand
n lit: colophon, hallmark, label, logo, mark, sign, stamp, symbol; class, kind, make, sort, type, variety; *fig*: imputation, slur, stigma, taint.
vb lit: label, mark, sign, stamp; *fig*: call, mark down as, stigmatize as.

brandish
vb lit: flourish, swing, wave about, whirl, wield; display, exhibit, flaunt, hold (in front of).

brand-new
adj lit: fresh, new-minted, pristine, shining, spanking; state-of-the-art, up-to-the-minute.

brawn
n lit: beef, muscle, muscularity, robustness, strength, vigour.

brazen
adj lit: brass, bronze; bold, brassy, forward, immodest, saucy, shameless; blatant, open, overt.

breach
n lit: break, cleft, fissure, gap, hole, rift, split; infraction, infringement, transgression, violation; alienation, difference, division, estrangement, separation, variance; breaking of the waves, surf.
vb lit: break, crack, fracture, make an opening, rend, split; infringe, transgress against, violate.

bread
n lit: loaf; *fig*: food, livelihood, nourishment, provisions, sustenance; cash, funds, money.

breadth
n lit: latitude, span, width; beam; area, compass, extent, measure, range, scale, scope, size, spread, sweep; liberality, openness; integrity, totality.

break
n lit: crack, fracture, rupture, snap; breach, cleft, fissure, gap, hole, rent, rip, tear; alienation, divergence, estrangement, separation, split; division, parting, severance; breather, halt, intermission, interval, pause, recess, rest, stop; *fig*: chance, opportunity; piece of luck, stroke of good fortune; alteration,

change, difference; *spec*: ad lib, cadenza (in a musical performance); dawn (of day); run (of points in billiards/pool/snooker); spin (on a ball).
vb lit: come apart, crack, fracture, rupture, snap; crush, fragment, powder, shatter; breach, leave a gap in, make a hole in, rend, rip, tear; interpose, separate, split up; divide, part, sever; be intermittent; disconnect; discontinue, leave (off), stop, take a breather, take time (off); interrupt; interpolate (in), put one's oar (in); infract, infringe, transgress against; overwhelm, subdue, tame, undermine; degrade, demote, dismiss, ruin; *fig*: disclose, divulge, impart, let out, reveal, tell; appear, emerge, erupt forth; *spec*: beat, better, exceed, outdo, top (a record); cure (a habit); cushion, soften (a fall); escape from (prison); leave (cover); run (for it); spin (of a ball on bouncing); unfurl (a flag); violate (a promise, one's parole).

breakdown
n lit: failure, stoppage; disruption, interruption; collapse, exhaustion; decomposition, disintegration, dismantling, rendering, separation; analysis, cataloguing, listing.

breast
n lit: bosom, bust, chest; mammary gland; boob, bristol(s), dug, knocker(s), pap, tit; udder; nipple, teat; mound, rounded hill; *fig*: conscience, heart, mind, soul.
vb lit: reach with the chest; *fig*: confront, engage with, meet, oppose.

breath
n lit: animation, life; exhalation, inhalation, respiration; gasp, pant; breeze, flutter, puff, waft; aroma, odour, perfume, scent; *fig*: hint, suggestion, suspicion, whisper.

breathe
vb lit: exhale, inhale, respire; blow, gasp, pant, puff; *fig*: murmur, say softly, sigh, whisper; infuse (into), inject (into).

breathless
adj lit: gasping, out of breath, panting, puffing, winded; asthmatic, bronchitic, short-winded, wheezing.

breathtaking
adj lit: awe-inspiring, awesome, impressive, magnificent, splendid; exciting, sensational, thrilling.

breed
n lit: family, lineage, pedigree, stock; class, kind, race, sort, species, type, variety.
vb lit: multiply, proliferate, procreate, propagate, reproduce; cultivate, farm, raise, rear; bring up, educate, train; *fig*: beget, cause, create, generate, occasion, produce.

breeding
n lit: ancestry, family, lineage, pedigree; class, courtesy, cultivation, culture, manners, polish; farming, raising, rearing.

breeze
n lit: air current, draught, gust, puff, whiff, wind; *fig*: certainty, cinch, doddle.
vb lit: blow lightly, puff; *fig*: hurry, move briskly, sweep; *spec*: pass, sail (through) (an examination).

brew
n lit: cocktail, concoction, infusion, liquor, potion; ale, beer, lager; tea; punch.
vb lit: boil and infuse; ferment, make; *fig*: be up to, concoct, contrive, devise, hatch, plot, scheme; gather, impend, threaten.

bribe
n lit: backhander, bait, carrot, enticement, greased palm, inducement, kickback.
vb lit: buy, get at, grease the palm of, pay off, suborn.

bribery
n lit: buying off, corruption, graft, payola, subornation.

bridge
n lit: crossover, span, viaduct; flyover, overpass; catwalk, gantry; bond, connection, link; *spec*: navigation centre (on a ship); support (for the strings on a violin, for a cue, or for a pair of spectacles); top (of the nose).
vb lit: go over, lie across, span, straddle; connect, join, link.

bridle
n lit: bit, control; check, curb, restraint; recoil.
vb lit: control, govern, master; check, curb, restrain; *fig*: be indignant, bristle, get on one's high horse (at), rear (up).

brief
n lit: outline, précis, summary, synopsis; argument, contention; case, statement; summons, writ; *spec*: (papal) epistle.

vb lit: advise, bring up to date, fill in, give a rundown, inform; instruct, prime; précis, summarize.
adj lit: concise, short, succinct; outline, thumbnail; brusque, curt, sharp, terse; fleeting, momentary, short-lived, transitory.

briefs
n lit: jockey-shorts, pants, shorts, short underpants, Y-fronts.

bright
adj lit: brilliant, dazzling, effulgent, glittering, glowing, intense, luminous, resplendent, scintillating, shimmering, shining, vivid, white; clear, pellucid, translucent, transparent; blazing, cloudless, fair, sunny; *fig*: astute, clever, ingenious, intelligent, imaginative, inventive, practical, quick-witted, shrewd; cheerful, encouraging, favourable, happy, jolly, optimistic, promising; animated, lively, vivacious; glorious, illustrious, magnificent.

brilliance
n lit: brightness, dazzling effect, effulgence, intensity, luminosity, lustre, radiance, resplendence, sheen, whiteness; coruscation, glitter, scintillation, twinkle; glamour, grandeur, magnificence, splendour; *fig*: genius, greatness, ingenuity, powerful intellect, talent.

brilliant
adj lit: bright, dazzling, effulgent, intense, luminous, lustrous, radiant, resplendent, shining, very white; coruscating, glittering, scintillating, twinkling; glamorous, grand, magnificent, splendid; *fig*: excellent, expert, extremely intelligent, highly gifted, masterly, very talented; glorious, illustrious, magnificent.

brim
n lit: brink, edge, lip, margin, rim.
vb lit: be flush (with), be full up; run (over), spill (over).

bring
vb lit: carry, convey, deliver, fetch, take, transport; advance, forward, present, proffer; conduct, escort, guide, lead, steer; turn (about); cut (down), shoot (down); *fig*: induce (to), persuade (to), prevail upon (to); compel (to), force (to), oblige (to); carry (off), pull (it off); command, earn, net, sell for.

bring up
vb lit: elevate, hoist, lift, raise, weigh;
foster, nurture, rear; educate, teach,
train; broach, introduce, mention; spew
up, throw up, vomit.

brink
n lit: clifftop, edge, sheer edge; bank,
brim, riverbank, verge; *fig*: point,
threshold.

brisk
adj lit: bustling, busy, energetic, lively,
sprightly, spry, vigorous; bracing,
exhilarating, invigorating, keen, sharp;
effervescent, piquant.

bristle
n lit: hair, whisker; prickle, spine, thorn.
vb lit: horripilate, prickle, rise, stand on
end; *fig*: bridle, flare up, recoil; crawl
(with), swarm (with), teem (with).

brittle
adj lit: crisp, rigid, taut, tense, under
stress; fragile, friable; *fig*: edgy, nervous,
stiff; cool, formal, stilted; insecure,
unstable.

broach
vb lit: open, penetrate, pierce, puncture;
tap; *fig*: bring up, introduce, mention,
raise (the subject).

broad
adj lit: thick, wide; ample, free, generous,
extensive, large; capacious, open, roomy,
spacious; *fig*: comprehensive,
encyclopaedic, sweeping, universal;
liberal, permissive, progressive;
uninhibited, unrestrained; blue, coarse,
indecent, indelicate, vulgar; *spec*:
accented (dialect); clear, full
(daylight).

broadcast
n lit: programme, transmission.
vb lit: air, radio, relay, televise, transmit;
announce, circulate, noise abroad,
proclaim, publish; disperse, disseminate,
scatter, sow, seed, spread.

broad-minded
adj lit: cosmopolitan, indulgent, liberal,
permissive, progressive, tolerant.

brochure
n lit: folder, leaflet, pamphlet; literature;
programme.

brooch
n lit: cameo, clasp, clip, pendant, pin;
jewel.

brood
n lit: clutch, family, hatch, progeny,
young; children, offspring; race, type.
vb lit: hatch, incubate, sit upon; *fig*:
cogitate (on), contemplate, meditate
(on), mull (over), ponder (over), think
(upon).

brook
n lit: burn, gill, rill, rivulet, stream.
vb lit: accept, bear, endure, put up with,
stand, take, tolerate.

brothel
n lit: bordello, house of ill repute,
whorehouse; cathouse, knocking-shop.

brown
vb lit: fry, roast, sauté; seal in the stove.
adj lit: bistre, dun, sepia, tan, umber;
auburn, brunette, chestnut, hazel; dark,
dusky, tawny; bronzed, tanned;
chocolate-coloured, coffee-coloured.

browse
vb lit: crop, graze (on), nibble; flip
(through), leaf (through), scan
(through); check out, look round,
peruse.

bruise
n lit: contusion, discoloration; sore spot,
tenderness; dent, indentation.
vb lit: contuse, discolour; damage, injure,
wound; crush, pound, powder.

brush
n lit: besom, broom; bristles, hair; bushy
tail; bushes, scrub, thicket,
undergrowth; abrasion, bump, contact,
friction, glance, graze, scrape; *fig*:
confrontation, encounter, skirmish,
tussle; *spec*: (electrical) contact.
vb lit: clean, dust, sweep; paint; bump,
make contact with, glance off, scrape;
caress, flick, stroke, touch.

brusque
adj lit: abrupt, curt, sharp, short, terse;
blunt, forthright.

brutal
adj lit: bestial, callous, cruel, inhuman,
merciless, relentless, ruthless, savage,
unfeeling; harsh, repressive, rigorous,
severe, stern, strict, tyrannical; coarse,
gross, rude; carnal, sensual.

brute
n lit: animal, beast, mammal; *fig*: bully,
ruffian, sadist, savage, thug, ugly

customer; barbarian, boor, lout,
yobbo.

bubble
n lit: bead, drop, globule; blister, vesicle;
fig: lame duck, speculative venture.
vb lit: boil, effervesce, fizz, seethe; babble,
gurgle, murmur, ripple.

bubbly
n lit: champagne, sparkling wine.
adj lit: carbonated, effervescent,
tincellant, fizzy, sparkling, spumante; *fig*:
animated, chirpy, excited, lively.

buccaneer
n lit: corsair, marauder, pirate, privateer,
rover.

buckle
n lit: catch, clasp, hasp; bend, bow,
distortion, fold, kink, warp.
vb lit: do up, fasten, lace up, latch, tie up;
bend, bow, crumple, distort, fold, kink,
warp.

bud
n lit: shoot, sprout; rudimentary swelling;
gemma.
vb lit: burgeon, germinate, shoot, sprout;
develop, form.

budge
vb lit: move, shift, stir; dislodge, remove;
give way, yield.

budget
n lit: exchequer, finances, funds,
resources; allocation, cost specification,
estimate, sum set aside; financial
programme.
vb lit: allocate, cost, estimate; set aside a
sum (for); plan one's fiscal affairs.

buff
n lit: ox-hide, ox-leather; *fig*: (in the)
altogether, (in the) nude, (in the) raw;
aficionado, enthusiast, fan, freak.
vb lit: burnish (up), polish (up), rub (up).
adj lit: beige, bistre, ochre, yellowish.

bug
n lit: bed-louse, beetle, creepy-crawly,
insect, midge; bacterium, germ, micro-
organism, virus; infection; concealed
microphone; *fig*: defect, fault, gremlin,
snag; craze, fad, rage.
vb lit: plant a microphone on; eavesdrop
on, listen in to, tap; *fig*: annoy, disturb,
irk, pester, plague.

build
n lit: body-shape, figure, frame, physique.

vb lit: construct, erect, make, put up;
create, form, fashion, mould; amass,
assemble, collect, put together; base,
establish, found; augment, develop,
expand, extend, increase.

building
n lit: construction, edifice, erection,
structure; block, house.

build-up
n lit: accretion, accumulation, assembly,
collection, gathering, stacking up;
augmentation, development, expansion,
extension, formation, growth, increase;
fig: introduction, pre-publicity,
promotion.

bulb
n lit: bud, corm, tuber; rounded
protuberance, swelling; globe, orb,
sphere; electron tube, lamp, neon light.

bulge
n lit: lump, protuberance, swelling;
dilation, distension; blister, bump, cyst,
wen; broadening, expansion, thickening;
corporation, eminence, overhang,
protrusion; *fig*: fluctuation, temporary
increase, rise.
vb lit: dilate, distend, expand, project,
protrude, stick out, swell.

bulk
n lit: immensity, magnitude, size, volume;
body, majority, major proportion, mass,
most part; cargo, hold.
vb lit: expand, swell (up); amass (up), pile
(up); broaden (out), thicken (out); loom
(large), stand out (large).

bulky
adj lit: big, hulking, immense, large,
massive; cumbersome, heavy,
ponderous, unwieldy, weighty.

bull
n lit: ox; *fig*: buyer, speculator; bunkum,
nonsense, rubbish, twaddle; bullseye,
inner, target; drill, spit and polish; *spec*:
full-grown male (elephant, moose, seal,
walrus, whale, etc.); (papal) decree,
edict.

bullet
n lit: ball, pellet, shot, slug; cartridge,
casing.

bully
n lit: blackmailer, intimidator, persecutor;
oppressor; ruffian, thug, troublemaker.
vb lit: browbeat, bulldoze, domineer.

intimidate, oppress, push around, terrorize.

bump
n lit: bang, blow, collision, crash, impact, jolt, shock, thump; contusion, knob, lump, nodule; bulge, swelling.
vb lit: bang into, collide with, crash into, jolt, knock into, strike, thump; bounce, jar, rattle, shake; *fig*: run (into); kill (off).

bumper
n lit: barrier, buffer, fender, protector; drink, toast; double measure, large one.
adj lit: brim full, overflowing; immense, jumbo, mammoth, vast; abundant, excellent, super.

bumpy
adj lit: bouncy, choppy, jerky, jolting, lumpy, pitted, ridged, rough, rutted, turbulent, uneven.

bun
n lit: cake, muffin, roll, pastry, scone; coil, knot, mass.

bunch
n lit: bouquet, bundle, clump, cluster, handful, parcel, posy, sheaf, spray; batch, collection, pile; knot, tuft; band, crowd, gang, group, mob, party, team.
vb lit: assemble, cluster, concentrate, congregate, crowd together, group, pack together; clench, contract, knot.

bundle
n lit: batch, bunch, collection, group, pile, stack; bale, bolt, mass, package, parcel, roll; knot, node; *fig*: lot.
vb lit: batch up, collect together, group, pile up, stack; bale, pack up, parcel together, roll up, tie up; *fig*: hurry, hustle, push, shove, thrust.

bungle
n lit: balls-up, botch, cock-up, dog's breakfast, foul-up, mess-up.
vb lit: botch, cock up, foul up, make a mess of, muff, screw up.

bunk
n lit: bed, berth, cot, sleeping-place; balderdash, claptrap, hooey, humbug, junk, nonsense, piffle, rubbish, stuff and nonsense, tosh, twaddle; *fig*: (do a) legger, (do a) runner.

buoyant
adj lit: floating, keeping up well; *fig*: tending to rise; hopeful, optimistic;

breezy, bright, cheery, gay, jaunty, light-hearted, sunny.

burden
n lit: encumbrance, fardel, load, weight; cargo, freight; *fig*: millstone, onus, responsibility, strain, stress, worry.
vb lit: encumber, load, weigh down; saddle (with); *fig*: handicap, make difficult for, oppress, penalize, worry.

bureau
n lit: desk, escritoire, secretary, writing-table; agency, counter, department, office, service.

bureaucracy
n lit: administration, civil service, officialdom, powers that be, red tape.

burglar
n lit: housebreaker, raider, sneak thief; intruder, trespasser, robber.

burglary
n lit: breaking and entering, housebreaking, larceny, theft; break-in, robbery.

burial
n lit: interment; funeral, obsequies.

burly
adj lit: beefy, big, brawny, hefty, hulking, large, muscular, powerful, strapping, strong, sturdy.

burn
n lit: brand, scorch, singe; firing, launch, lift-off, thrust; fast ride.
vb lit: be on fire, blaze; ignite, kindle, light, set alight; glow, smoke; brand, char, cremate, incinerate, singe; oxidize; *fig*: consume, expend, use; hurt, smart, sting; be inflamed, be passionate, smoulder with desire (for), yearn (for).

burrow
n lit: hole, warren; gallery, passage, tunnel; den, lair, nest; refuge, retreat.
vb lit: dig, excavate, hollow out, tunnel.

burst
n lit: emission, outpouring, transmission; eruption, gust, rush, surge; acceleration, sprint, spurt; breach, break, rupture, split; blast, discharge, explosion, salvo, volley; display, shower.
vb lit: blow up, explode, fly apart, puncture, rupture, shatter; barge (in), rush (in); break (into), snap (into); break

(out), erupt; flood, gush, overflow, spout; implode.
adj (pa.pt) lit: flat, punctured, ruptured; blown up, exploded, shattered; breached, broken, holed.

bury
vb lit: inhume, inter, lay to rest; dig in, embed, plant, sink; *fig*: conceal, cover up, hide away; engross, immerse, preoccupy.

bus
n lit: charabanc, coach, double-decker, single-decker, tram; *fig*: banger, car, heap, wreck; aeroplane, kite; *spec*: (electrical) distributor.

bush
n lit: hedge, shrub, woody plant; forest, jungle, thicket, wilds; outback, scrub, veldt.

business
n lit: commerce, industry, manufacturing, marketing, trading; company, concern, firm, organization; craft, job, line, métier, occupation, profession, trade, work; deals, transactions; assignment, duty, function, responsibility; affair, issue, matter, topic.

businesslike
adj lit: efficient, methodical, organized, professional, systematic, well-ordered.

bust
n lit: bosom, breasts, chest, figure; head and shoulders, statue; arrest, cop, raid.
vb lit: break, burst, rupture, shatter; bankrupt, impoverish, ruin; arrest, catch, cop, raid.
adj (pa.pt) lit: broken, burst, ruptured, shattered; bankrupt, broke, impoverished, ruined; arrested, caught, raided.

bustle
n lit: ado, commotion, flurry, hurly-burly, stir; agitation, fuss.
vb lit: dash, get a move on, get one's skates on, hurry, rush, scurry, tear (about).

busy
adj lit: active, exacting, full, strenuous; engaged, engrossed, fully employed, occupied, preoccupied; hard at it, industrious, labouring, toiling away; *fig*: fussy, officious; interfering, meddlesome, prying; *spec*: over-detailed, restless (in art).

but
cnj lit: however, nevertheless, on the other hand, still, yet; except (for/that/to), save (for/that/to); unless.
adv lit: just, merely, no more than, only, simply.

butcher
n lit: slaughterer; killer, slayer; sadist, torturer.
vb lit: slaughter; carve, cut up, dress, joint; cut down, kill, slay; *fig*: botch, make an utter hash of, mutilate, travesty.

butchery
n lit: abattoir, slaughterhouse; bloodbath, bloodshed, carnage, massacre, murder.

buttocks
n lit: backside, behind, bottom, bum, derrière, gluteus maximus, posterior, seat, sit-upon.

button
n lit: boss, knop, rivet, roundel, stud; bellpush, disc, key, knob, pad; bud; *spec*: chin (in boxing).

buttonhole
n lit: bouquet, nosegay, posy; flower.
vb lit: accost, detain, take to one side, waylay; importune, lobby, petition.

buttress
n lit: abutment, pier, prop, ramp, stanchion, stay, support.
vb lit: bolster, brace, prop, shore up, support, sustain.

buy
n lit: purchase; acquisition; bargain.
vb lit: pay for, purchase; invest in; acquire, procure, secure; bribe, pay (off), square; *fig*: accept, believe, credit, grant.

buyer
n lit: emptor, purchaser; client, customer, habitué, patron; agent, purchasing manager, stock manager, supplier.

buzz
n lit: drone, hum, purr, rasp, tone, whine, whirring; sibilance; *fig*: gossip, on dit, rumour, scandal, whisper; euphoria, high, thrill.
vb lit: drone, hum, purr, rasp, whine, whir; be lively, move quickly; *fig*: resound (with), reverberate (with); call, ring, telephone; *spec*: intimidate (another aircraft).

by
adv lit: at hand; beyond, past; aside, away.
prp lit: along, alongside, beside, close to,
near; past, through, via; on, over;
because of, through the means of,
through the use of; the invention of, the
work of; in proportion to, in relation to,
with respect to; times; before, prior to;
according to; to the extent of; *spec*:
called, of, under (the name).

bypass
n lit: circumnavigation, way round;
detour; secondary route; shunt.
vb lit: circumnavigate, find one's way
round, go round; implant a shunt,
provide a short-cut; *fig*: go over the head
of; avoid, evade.

C

cab
n lit: hackney carriage, minicab, taxi, taxicab.

cabbage
n lit: brassica, Chinese leaves, kale, sprout.

cabin
n lit: bothy, but-and-ben, chalet, cottage, hovel, hut, lodge, shack, shanty, shed; berth, deckhouse, quarters, room.

cabinet
n lit: case, closet, commode, cupboard, dresser, locker; administration, assembly, council, ministry; apartment, boudoir, chamber.

cable
n lit: chain, cord, flex, line, wire; hawser, rope; telegram.

cadaverous
adj lit: ashen, blanched, colourless, corpselike, deathly, emaciated, gaunt, ghastly, haggard, pale, pallid, wan.

café
n lit: cafeteria, coffee bar, lunchroom, restaurant, snack bar, tearoom.

cage
n lit: enclosure, pen, pound.
vb lit: confine, coop up, fence in, immure, impound, incarcerate, lock up, restrain, shut up.

cag(e)y
adj lit: careful, cautious, discreet, guarded, noncommittal, shrewd, wary, wily.

cake
n lit: bar, block, cube, loaf, mass, slab.
vb lit: bake, cement, coagulate, congeal, consolidate, dry, encrust, harden, ossify, solidify, thicken.

calamity
n lit: adversity, affliction, catastrophe, disaster, downfall, hardship, misadventure, misfortune, mishap, reverse, ruin, tragedy, trial, tribulation, woe.

calculate
vb lit: adjust, compute, consider, count, determine, estimate, figure, gauge, judge, rate, reckon, value, weigh, work out; design, intend, plan.

calculating
adj (pr.pt) lit: canny, cautious, contriving, crafty, cunning, designing, devious, manipulative, scheming, sharp, shrewd, sly.

calculation
n lit: computation, estimate, estimation, figuring, forecast, judgement, reckoning; caution, circumspection, contrivance, deliberation, discretion, foresight, forethought, planning, precaution.

calibre
n lit: bore, gauge, measure; *fig*: ability, capacity, distinction, endowment, faculty, force, gifts, merit, quality, scope, stature, talent, worth.

calf
n lit: bullock, heifer, steer; foreleg, shank.

call
n lit: cry, hail, shout, signal, whoop, yell; announcement, appeal, demand, invitation, notice, plea, request, ring, summons, supplication, visit; cause, grounds, justification, occasion, reason, urge.
vb lit: announce, arouse, cry, hail, rouse, shout, waken, yell; assemble, bid, contact, convene, gather, invite, muster, phone, rally, ring up, summon; christen, describe as, designate, dub, label, name, style, term; appoint, declare, decree, ordain, order, proclaim, set apart; consider, estimate, regard, think.

calling
n lit: career, line, mission, occupation, profession, province, pursuit, trade, vocation, walk of life, work.

callous
adj lit: cold, hard-boiled, hardhearted, heartless, indifferent, insensitive, inured, obdurate, thick-skinned, torpid,

uncaring, unfeeling, unsusceptible, unsympathetic.

calm
n lit: calmness, hush, peace, quiet, repose, serenity, stillness, tranquillity.
vb lit: hush, mollify, placate, quieten, relax, soothe.
adj lit: halcyon, mild, pacific, peaceful, placid, quiet, restful, serene, smooth, still, tranquil, windless; collected, composed, cool, dispassionate, equable, impassive, imperturbable, relaxed, undisturbed, unemotional, unexcited, unflappable, unruffled.

calumny
n lit: abuse, backbiting, defamation, denigration, derogation, insult, libel, misrepresentation, revilement, slander, smear, vilification, vituperation.

cameo
n lit: intaglio, relief-carving; *fig*: outstanding performance, role.

camouflage
n lit: blind, cloak, concealment, cover, deceptive markings, disguise, front, guise, mask, mimicry, protective colouring, screen, subterfuge.
vb lit: cloak, conceal, cover, disguise, hide, mask, obfuscate, obscure, screen.

camp
n lit: bivouac, camp site, encampment, tents.
adj lit: affected, artificial, effeminate, mannered, ostentatious, posturing.

campaign
n lit: attack, drive, expedition, movement, offensive, operation, push.

can
n lit: canister, cylinder, tin, tube.

canal
n lit: ditch, irrigation channel, watercourse; duct, passage, tube.

cancel
vb lit: abolish, abrogate, annul, call off, countermand, delete, do away with, efface, eliminate, erase, expunge, obliterate, quash, repeal, repudiate, revoke; compensate for, counterbalance, make up for, neutralize, nullify, offset.

cancellation
n lit: abandonment, abolition, annulment, deletion, elimination, quashing, repeal, revocation.

cancer
n lit: blight, canker, carcinoma, growth, leukaemia, melanoma, sarcoma, tumour; *fig*: corruption, evil, malignancy, rot.

candid
adj lit: blunt, forthright, frank, guileless, impartial, ingenuous, open, outspoken, sincere, straightforward, unbiased, unprejudiced.

candidate
n lit: applicant, claimant, competitor, contender, contestant, entrant, nominee, runner, solicitant.

cane
n lit: staff, stem, stick; bamboo, rattan; walking stick.
vb lit: beat, birch, flog, give a good hiding, thrash, whack, whip.

canister
n lit: box, caddy, can; cylinder, cannon shell.

cannon
n lit: artillery piece, field gun, mortar.
vb lit: discharge a cannon; bombard, cannonade, collide, pound, shell, volley.

canon
n lit: catalogue, criterion, dictate, list, precept, principle, regulation, standard, statute, yardstick.

canopy
n lit: awning, covering, shade, tester.

cant
n lit: humbug, hypocrisy, lip service, pretentiousness, sanctimoniousness, sham; argot, jargon, lingo, vernacular.
vb lit: angle, incline, rise, slant, slope, tilt.

cantankerous
adj lit: bad-tempered, choleric, crabby, crotchety, crusty, difficult, disagreeable, grumpy, ill-humoured, irascible, irritable, peevish, quarrelsome, testy.

canteen
n lit: bar, café, dining-hall, mess, refectory, restaurant; cutlery drawer; billy-can, flask, hip-flask, water container.

canvas
n lit: sailcloth, tarpaulin; oil-painting, picture.

canvass
n lit: investigation, poll, survey, tally.

vb lit: analyse, campaign, electioneer, examine, investigate, poll, scan, scrutinize, solicit votes.

cap
n lit: cover, lid, seal, top; detonator; headdress.
vb lit: beat, better, complete, cover, crown, exceed, excel, finish, outdo, surpass, top, transcend.

capable
adj lit: able, accomplished, adept, adequate, apt, competent, efficient, experienced, gifted, proficient, qualified, skilful, susceptible.

capacious
adj lit: ample, broad, comfortable, comprehensive, expansive, extensive, generous, roomy, sizable, spacious, substantial, voluminous, wide.

capacity
n lit: amplitude, compass, extent, range, room, scope, size, space, volume; ability, aptitude, brains, capability, efficiency, faculty, power, strength; appointment, function, office, position, post, role, service, sphere.

cape
n lit: cloak; headland, peninsula, point, promontory.

caper
n lit: antic, escapade, gambol, high jinks, jape, jest, lark, mischief, prank, revel, sport, stunt.
vb lit: bounce, cavort, frisk, frolic, gambol, jump, leap, romp, skip.

capital
n lit: assets, cash, finances, funds, investment(s), means, money, property, resources, stock, wealth, wherewithal.
adj lit: cardinal, central, chief, controlling, foremost, important, leading, main, overruling, paramount, pre-eminent, prime, principal, vital; excellent, fine, first-rate, splendid, superb.

capitulate
vb lit: come to terms, give in, relent, submit, succumb, surrender, yield.

capitulation
n lit: accedence, submission, surrender, yielding.

capricious
adj lit: crotchety, erratic, fanciful, fickle, freakish, impulsive, inconstant, quirky,

unpredictable, wayward, whimsical.

capsize
vb lit: invert, keel over, overturn, tip over, turn turtle, upset.

capsule
n lit: lozenge, pill, tablet; case, pericarp, pod, receptacle, sheath, shell, vessel.

captain
n lit: boss, chief, commander, leader, master, number one, officer, (senior) pilot, skipper.

captivate
vb lit: allure, attract, beguile, charm, dazzle, enamour, enchant, enthral, fascinate, infatuate, lure, mesmerize, win.

captive
n lit: convict, detainee, hostage, internee, prisoner, slave.
adj lit: caged, confined, enslaved, imprisoned, incarcerated, locked up, restricted, subjugated.

capture
n lit: apprehension, arrest, imprisonment, seizure, taking captive, trapping.
vb lit: apprehend, arrest, bag, catch, lift, secure, seize, take into custody, take prisoner.

car
n lit: automobile, machine, motor, motorcar, vehicle; cable car, coach, (railway) carriage, van.

carafe
n lit: decanter, flagon, flask, jug, pitcher.

caravan
n lit: column, cortège, train, queue; mobile home, truck, trailer, van, wagon.

card
n lit: playing card, post card, visiting card; wire brush; *fig*: means, plan; character, crank, weirdo.

cardigan
n lit: sweater, woollen jacket, woolly.

cardinal
adj lit: capital, chief, essential, first, foremost, fundamental, important, key, leading, main, paramount, pre-eminent, prime, principal.

care

n lit: affliction, anxiety, concern, disquiet, hardship, pressure, responsibility, stress, tribulation, trouble, vexation, worry; attention, caution, circumspection, consideration, forethought, heed, meticulousness, pains, prudence, regard, vigilance; charge, custody, guardianship, management, ministration, protection, supervision, ward.
vb lit: be concerned, feel interest; like, want, wish; mind.

career

n lit: calling, life work, occupation, pursuit, vocation; course, passage, path, procedure, progress, race.
vb lit: bolt, dash, hurtle, race, rush, speed, tear.

carefree

adj lit: blithe, buoyant, careless, cheerful, easy-going, happy-go-lucky, jaunty, light-hearted, radiant, sunny, untroubled.

careful

adj lit: accurate, cautious, circumspect, conscientious, discreet, fastidious, painstaking, precise, prudent, punctilious, scrupulous, thoughtful, thrifty; alert, attentive, concerned, mindful, particular, solicitous, vigilant, wary.

careless

adj lit: absent-minded, cursory, forgetful, heedless, incautious, indiscreet, negligent, perfunctory, remiss, thoughtless, unconcerned, unmindful, unthinking; inaccurate, irresponsible, lackadaisical, neglectful, offhand, slipshod, sloppy; artless, casual, nonchalant.

caress

n lit: cuddle, embrace, fondling, hug, pat, stroke.
vb lit: cuddle, embrace, fondle, hug, kiss, nuzzle, pet, stroke.

caretaker

n lit: concierge, curator, custodian, janitor, keeper, superintendent, warden.
adj lit: holding, interim, short-term, temporary.

cargo

n lit: baggage, consignment, freight, goods, load, merchandise, shipment, tonnage, ware.

caricature

n lit: burlesque, cartoon, farce, lampoon, mimicry, parody, satire, send-up, travesty.
vb lit: burlesque, distort, lampoon, mimic, mock, parody, ridicule, satirize, send up.

carnage

n lit: blood bath, butchery, havoc, holocaust, massacre, mass murder, shambles, slaughter.

carnival

n lit: celebration, fair, festival, fête, fiesta, holiday, jamboree, jubilee, merrymaking, revelry.

carouse

vb lit: booze, drink, imbibe, make merry, quaff, roister.

carp

vb lit: cavil, censure, complain, criticize, find fault, knock, nag, quibble, reproach.

carpenter

n lit: cabinet-maker, joiner, woodworker.

carpet

n lit: carpeting, floor covering, rug.
vb lit: cover (wall to wall); *fig*: call to account, rebuke, reprimand, reprehend, summon, tell off, tick off.

carriage

n lit: conveyance, delivery, freight, transport; cab, coach, vehicle; *fig*: bearing, behaviour, conduct, demeanour, deportment, gait, manner, mien, posture.

carry

vb lit: bear, bring, convey, haul, lift, lug, move, relay, take, transport; accomplish, effect, gain, win; drive, impel, influence, motivate, spur, urge; hold up, maintain, shoulder, stand, support, sustain, uphold; broadcast, communicate, display, give, release, stock.

carry on

vb lit: continue, keep going, maintain, perpetuate, persevere, persist; administer, manage, operate, run; make a fuss, misbehave.

carry out

vb lit: accomplish, achieve, carry through, consummate, discharge, effect, fulfil, implement, realize.

cart
n lit: dray, tumbril, vehicle, wagon.
vb lit: bear, carry, heave, haul, lug.

cartilage
n lit: elastic tissue, fibre, gristle, sinew.

carton
n lit: box, case, container, pack, packet.

cartoon
n lit: animated film, animation, caricature, comic strip, drawing, lampoon, parody, sketch.
vb lit: animate, caricature, draw, lampoon, sketch.

cartridge
n lit: capsule, case, cassette, cylinder, magazine; charge, round, shell.

carve
vb lit: chip, chisel, cut, engrave, etch, fashion, grave, incise, indent, mould, sculpt, slice, whittle.

case
n lit: box, cabinet, canister, capsule, carton, cartridge, casket, chest, container, crate, holder, receptacle, suitcase, tray, trunk; casing, cover, envelope, folder, jacket, sheath, wrapping; circumstance(s), context, contingency, dilemma, event, plight, predicament, situation, state; example, instance, occasion, occurrence; *spec*: action, dispute, lawsuit, proceedings, process, suit, trial.

cash
n lit: banknotes, bullion, coinage, currency, dough, funds, money, ready money, resources, wherewithal.
vb lit: give cash, obtain cash.

cashier
n lit: accountant, bank clerk, bursar, purser, teller, treasurer.
vb lit: break, cast off, discard, discharge, dismiss, expel.

cask
n lit: barrel, keg, tun, wooden vessel.

casket
n lit: box, case, chest, coffer.

cast
n lit: fling, lob, throw, thrust, toss; air, appearance, demeanour, look, manner, semblance, stamp, style, tinge, tone; actors, company, players, troupe.

vb lit: chuck, drop, fling, hurl, launch, lob, pitch, shed, sling, throw, thrust, toss; bestow, deposit, distribute, emit, give, radiate, scatter, spread; allot, appoint, assign, choose, pick, select; add, calculate, compute, figure, forecast, reckon, total; form, found, model, mould, set, shape.

caste
n lit: class, grade, lineage, rank, social order, station, status.

castigate
vb lit: beat, cane, censure, chastise, correct, criticize, discipline, flay, flog, lash, rebuke, reprimand, scold, whip.

castle
n lit: chateau, citadel, donjon, fastness, fortress, keep, palace, peel, stronghold, tower.

casual
adj lit: accidental, chance, contingent, incidental, irregular, occasional, random, unexpected, unforeseen, unintentional; apathetic, blasé, cursory, informal, lackadaisical, nonchalant, offhand, perfunctory, unconcerned.

casualty
n lit: loss, sufferer, victim; accident, calamity, catastrophe, contingency, disaster, misadventure, misfortune, mishap.

cat
n lit: feline, grimalkin, moggy, mouser, pussy, tabby.

catalogue
n lit: directory, index, inventory, list, record, roll, roster, schedule.
vb lit: alphabetize, classify, file, index, list, register.

catapult
n lit: ballista, sling, trebuchet.
vb lit: heave, hurl, hurtle, plunge, propel, shoot, toss.

cataract
n lit: cascade, deluge, downpour, falls, rapids, torrent, waterfall; *spec*: opacity (of the eye).

catarrh
n lit: cold, inflammation; mucus, saliva.

catastrophe
n lit: adversity, affliction, blow, calamity, devastation, disaster, fiasco, mischance,

misfortune, mishap, reverse, tragedy, trial, trouble; conclusion, culmination, curtain, debacle, end, finale, termination, winding-up.

catcall
n lit: boo, gibe, hiss, jeer, raspberry, whistle.
vb lit: boo, deride, gibe, give the bird to, hiss, jeer, whistle.

catch
n lit: bolt, clasp, clip, fastener, hook, latch, sneck; disadvantage, drawback, hitch, snag, stumbling block, trap, trick.
vb lit: apprehend, arrest, capture, clutch, ensnare, entangle, entrap, grab, grasp, grip, seize, snare, snatch, take; detect, discover, expose, find out, surprise, take unawares; captivate, charm, delight, enchant, fascinate; contract, develop, go down with, succumb to, suffer from; discern, follow, hear, perceive, sense, take in.

catch on
vb lit: comprehend, find out, grasp, see, understand; become popular, find favour.

catchy
adj lit: captivating, haunting, memorable, popular.

category
n lit: class, classification, department, division, grade, grouping, heading, list, rank, section, type.

cater
vb lit: furnish, outfit, provide, provision, purvey, supply, victual.

catharsis
n lit: cleansing, lustration, purging, purification, release.

catholic
adj lit: all-embracing, broad-minded, comprehensive, eclectic, ecumenical, general, global, liberal, unbigoted, universal, unsectarian, whole, world-wide.

cattle
n lit: beasts, bovines, cows, livestock.

cause
n lit: agent, creator, genesis, mainspring, maker, originator, producer, root, source; agency, aim, basis, consideration, end, grounds, incentive, inducement, motivation, object,

purpose, reason; attempt, conviction, enterprise, ideal, movement, undertaking.
vb lit: begin, bring about, create, effect, generate, incite, induce, lead to, motivate, occasion, precipitate, provoke, result in.

caustic
adj lit: acid, acrid, alkaline, biting, burning, corrosive, mordant; acrimonious, cutting, pungent, sarcastic, scathing, stinging, trenchant, virulent.

caution
n lit: alertness, care, circumspection, deliberation, discretion, forethought, heed, prudence, vigilance; admonition, advice, counsel, injunction, warning.
vb lit: admonish, advise, tip off, urge, warn.

cautious
adj lit: alert, cagey, careful, circumspect, discreet, guarded, judicious, tentative, vigilant, wary, watchful.

cavalier
n lit: chevalier, equestrian, knight, royalist; beau, escort, gallant, gentleman.
adj lit: arrogant, condescending, disdainful, haughty, insolent, lofty, offhand, supercilious.

cave
n lit: cavern, cavity, den, grotto, hollow.
vb lit: hollow out, make into a cave.

cave in
vb lit: fall in, recede, sink, subside; cause to fall in, smash; *fig*: give in, submit, withdraw, yield.

cavernous
adj lit: concave, deep-set, hollow, sunken; echoing, resonant, reverberant.

cavil
vb lit: carp, complain, find fault, object, quibble.

cavity
n lit: crater, dent, gap, hole, hollow, pit.

cease
vb lit: break off, come to an end, conclude, culminate, discontinue, end, fail, finish, halt, leave off, refrain, stay, stop.

cede

vb lit: abandon, abdicate, allow, concede, grant, hand over, relinquish, renounce, resign, transfer, yield.

ceiling

n lit: roof; maximum altitude; peak, summit, top, upper limit.

celebrate

vb lit: commemorate, commend, eulogize, exalt, extol, honour, laud, observe, praise, proclaim, rejoice, reverence, toast.

celebration

n lit: carousal, festival, festivity, jollification, jubilee, merry-making, party, revelry; anniversary, commemoration, honouring, observance, remembrance, solemnization.

celebrity

n lit: bigwig, dignitary, luminary, name, megastar, personage, personality, superstar, VIP; distinction, fame, glory, notability, pre-eminence, prominence, renown, repute.

celestial

adj lit: angelic, divine, Elysian, eternal, ethereal, heavenly, immortal, seraphic, spiritual, sublime, supernatural.

celibate

n lit: monk, nun.
adj lit: unmarried; chaste, virginal.

cell

n lit: cavity, chamber, cubicle, cytoplasm, dungeon, stall; caucus, group, nucleus, unit.

cellar

n lit: basement, bunker, crypt, vault; salt container.

cement

n lit: adhesive, binder, concrete, glue, gum, paste, plaster, sealant.
vb lit: attach, bind, bond, combine, glue, gum, join, plaster, seal, solder, stick together, weld.

cemetery

n lit: burial ground, churchyard, graveyard, necropolis.

censor

n lit: Roman magistrate; faultfinder, monitor.
vb lit: blue-pencil, bowdlerize, cut, delete, eliminate, expurgate, gag, moralize, muzzle, quash, silence, suppress, vet.

censorship

n lit: blackout, concealment, suppression, vetting.

censure

n lit: castigation, condemnation, criticism, disapproval, dressing down, rebuke, reprehension, reprimand, reproach, stricture.
vb lit: berate, castigate, condemn, criticize, rebuke, reprehend, reprimand, reprove, upbraid.

centre

n lit: bull's-eye, crux, epicentre, focus, fulcrum, hub, middle, nub, nucleus, pivot.
vb lit: cluster, concentrate, converge, focus.

ceramics

n lit: earthenware, porcelain, pottery, terracotta.

ceremonial

n lit: ceremony, formality, rite, ritual, solemnity.
adj lit: formal, liturgical, ritual, solemn, stately.

ceremony

n lit: commemoration, function, observance, parade, service, show, solemnities; ceremonial, decorum, etiquette, form, niceties, pomp, protocol.

certain

adj lit: assured, confident, convinced, positive, satisfied, sure; conclusive, irrefutable, plain, true, undeniable, unequivocal, unmistakable, valid; bound, definite, destined, inescapable, inevitable, inexorable; decided, established, fixed, settled; constant, dependable, reliable, stable, steady, trustworthy, unquestionable; express, particular, precise, specific.

certificate

n lit: authorization, credential(s), diploma, licence, voucher, warrant.

certify

vb lit: ascertain, assure, authenticate, confirm, corroborate, endorse, guarantee, notify, testify, validate, verify, vouch.

chafe
vb lit: anger, annoy, fret, fume, grate,
incense, inflame, irritate, offend,
provoke, rub, ruffle, vex, worry.

chagrin
n lit: annoyance, discomfiture,
displeasure, disquiet, embarrassment,
humiliation, irritation, mortification,
spleen, vexation.
vb lit: annoy, discomfit, discompose,
disquiet, dissatisfy, humiliate, irk,
irritate, mortify, peeve, vex.

chain
n lit: bond, coupling, fetter, link, manacle,
union; progression, sequence, series, set,
string, succession, train.
vb lit: bind, confine, enslave, fetter,
handcuff, manacle, shackle, tether,
trammel, unite.

chair
n lit: bench, seat, sedan, throne; authority,
chairperson, office; metal socket (in
railway).

chairperson
n lit: chair, director, presider, speaker,
toastmaster.

chalet
n lit: bungalow, cabin, cottage, hut, villa.

challenge
n lit: confrontation, dare, defiance,
provocation, test, trial, ultimatum.
vb lit: accost, arouse, brave, call out,
confront, dare, defy, demand, dispute,
object to, provoke, question, require,
summon, tax, test, throw down the
gauntlet.

chamber
n lit: apartment, cavity, cubicle,
enclosure, hollow, room; assembly,
council, legislature.

champion
n lit: challenger, conqueror, defender,
nonpareil, patron, protector, title holder,
victor, vindicator, warrior, winner.
vb lit: advocate, back, defend, fight for,
support, uphold.

chance
n lit: likelihood, occasion, odds, opening,
opportunity, possibility, probability,
prospect, scope; accident, coincidence,
contingency, fate, fortuity, luck,
misfortune, providence; gamble, hazard,
jeopardy, risk, speculation, uncertainty.

vb lit: befall, betide, come to pass,
happen, occur; endanger, gamble,
hazard, jeopardize, risk, stake, venture,
wager.
adj lit: accidental, casual, contingent,
fortuitous, incidental, random,
unforeseen, unintentional.

chancy
adj lit: dangerous, dodgy, hazardous,
problematic, risky, uncertain.

change
n lit: alteration, difference, innovation,
modification, permutation, revolution,
transition, vicissitude; conversion,
exchange, substitution; break, diversion,
novelty, variety.
vb lit: alter, convert, fluctuate, modify,
reform, reorganize, shift, transform,
vacillate, vary, veer; alternate, barter,
exchange, remove, substitute, swap,
trade.

changeable
adj lit: capricious, chequered, erratic,
fickle, inconstant, irregular, labile,
mobile, shifting, uncertain,
unpredictable, unsettled, unstable,
variable, versatile, volatile, wavering.

channel
n lit: canal, conduit, duct, furrow, groove,
gutter, main, passage, strait; *fig*:
approach, avenue, course, means, path,
route, way.
vb lit: conduct, convey, direct, guide.

chant
n lit: carol, melody, psalm, song.
vb lit: carol, chorus, descant, intone,
recite, sing.

chaos
n lit: bedlam, confusion, disorganization,
lawlessness, pandemonium, tumult.

chaotic
adj lit: anarchic, confused, disordered,
purposeless, riotous, topsy-turvy,
tumultuous, uncontrolled.

chap
n lit: bloke, character, customer, fellow,
guy, individual, type.

chapel
n lit: kirk, meeting house, mission,
oratory, place of worship.

chaperon
n lit: companion, duenna, escort.

vb lit: accompany, attend, escort, protect, safeguard, watch over.

chapter
n lit: clause, episode, period, phase, section, stage.

character
n lit: attributes, calibre, complexion, disposition, individuality, nature, personality, quality, reputation, temperament, type; honour, integrity, rectitude, uprightness; eccentric, oddity, original; cipher, emblem, figure, glyph, hieroglyph, letter, pictograph, logo, rune, sign, symbol; part, portrayal, role; fellow, guy, individual, sort, type.

characteristic
n lit: attribute, feature, idiosyncrasy, peculiarity, quality, trait.
adj lit: distinctive, distinguishing, idiosyncratic, individual, singular, specific, symptomatic, typical.

characterize
vb lit: brand, distinguish, identify, indicate, mark, represent, stamp, typify.

charge
n lit: accusation, allegation, indictment; assault, attack, onslaught, rush, sortie; burden, care, custody, duty, responsibility, trust, ward; amount, cost, expenditure, expense, payment, price, rate; command, direction, exhortation, injunction, mandate, order, precept; *spec*: anion, cation, ion, unit of electricity.
vb lit: accuse, blame, impeach, incriminate, indict; assail, assault, attack, rush, storm; afflict, burden, commit, entrust; fill, instil, load, suffuse; bid, command, enjoin, exhort, instruct, require.

charitable
adj lit: benevolent, generous, lavish, philanthropic; considerate, favourable, humane, kindly, lenient, magnanimous, sympathetic, understanding.

charlatan
n lit: cheat, con man, fraud, impostor, mountebank, phoney, pretender, sham, swindler.

charm
n lit: allure, appeal, attraction, enchantment, fascination, magnetism, spell; amulet, fetish, talisman, trinket.

vb lit: allure, attract, beguile, cajole, captivate, enamour, enchant, enrapture, fascinate, please, win over.

charming
adj (pr.pt) lit: appealing, attractive, captivating, delectable, engaging, fetching, irresistible, pleasing, seductive, winning.

chart
n lit: blueprint, diagram, graph, plan, table.
vb lit: draft, graph, outline, plot, sketch.

charter
n lit: bond, contract, deed, document, franchise, licence, permit, prerogative, privilege, right.
vb lit: authorize, commission, hire, lease, rent, sanction,

chase
n lit: hunt, pursuit, race.
vb lit: drive, expel, hound, hunt, pursue, run after, track.

chasm
n lit: abyss, breach, cleft, crater, crevasse, fissure, gorge, hiatus, hollow, ravine, rift, void.

chassis
n lit: bodywork, frame, fuselage, skeleton, substructure.

chaste
adj lit: decent, decorous, innocent, modest, pure, refined, unaffected, vestal, virtuous.

chat
n lit: chatter, gossip, heart-to-heart, natter, talk.
vb lit: chatter, gossip, jaw, natter, rabbit (on), talk.

chatter
n lit: babble, chat, gab, jabber, natter, prattle, twaddle.
vb lit: babble, chat, gab, jabber, natter, prattle, twaddle.

chatterbox
n lit: chatterer, gasbag, gossip, windbag.

chauffeur
n lit: driver.

cheap
adj lit: bargain, cut-price, economical, inexpensive, low-cost, reasonable, sale; common, inferior, paltry, shoddy, tatty;

contemptible, despicable, mean, scurvy, vulgar.

cheapen
vb lit: debase, degrade, demean, derogate, discredit, lower.

cheat
n lit: deceit, deception, fraud, rip-off, swindle, trickery; charlatan, con man, dodger, double-crosser, impostor, rogue, shark, trickster.
vb lit: bamboozle, beguile, con, deceive, defraud, do, dupe, fleece, hoax, hoodwink, rip off, swindle, take in, trick; baffle, check, deprive, foil, frustrate, prevent, thwart.

check
n lit: examination, investigation, scrutiny, test; control, curb, hindrance, impediment, limitation, obstruction, restraint; blow, disappointment, frustration, reverse, set-back.
vb lit: compare, enquire into, examine, inspect, look at, make sure, note, probe, scrutinize, test, verify; arrest, bar, control, curb, delay, halt, hinder, impede, limit, obstruct, restrain, stop, thwart; blame, chide, rebuff, rebuke, reprimand, scold, tell off.

check-up
n lit: examination, inspection, physical; once-over.

cheerful
adj lit: animated, blithe, buoyant, cheery, contented, enthusiastic, happy, jaunty, jolly, merry, sparkling, sprightly, sunny.

cheer up
vb lit: brighten, buck up, comfort, encourage, enliven, perk up, rally, take heart.

chef
n lit: cook, cuisinier, head cook.

chemist
n lit: apothecary, dispenser, druggist; physicist.

chequered
adj lit: dappled, marked in squares, variegated; changing, irregular, unstable, varied.

cherish
vb lit: care for, comfort, cosset, encourage, entertain, harbour, hold dear, nurture, prize, sustain, treasure.

cherubic
adj lit: angelic, innocent, lovable, seraphic, sweet.

chest
n lit: thorax; case, casket, coffer, crate, strongbox.

chestnut
n lit: conker-tree; bay; cliché, platitude, stale joke.

chew
vb lit: bite, crunch, gnaw, grind, munch; *fig*: mull over, ponder, reflect upon, ruminate, weigh.

chic
adj lit: elegant, fashionable, modish, smart, sophisticated, stylish.

chicken
n lit: fowl, hen, rooster; coward, cowardy custard, sissy, yellow-belly; challenge, dare.
v fig: cowardly, frightened, pusillanimous, scared, timid.

chief
n lit: boss, chieftain, commander, head, leader, manager, master, ringleader, ruler, superintendent.
adj lit: capital, cardinal, especial, foremost, highest, key, leading, main, paramount, predominant, pre-eminent, prevailing, primary, principal, supreme, uppermost, vital.

child
n lit: baby, brat, infant, issue, juvenile, kid, minor, nipper, offspring, toddler, tot, youngster.

childhood
n lit: immaturity, infancy, minority, youth.

childish
adj lit: immature, infantile, juvenile, puerile, simple, young.

chill
n lit: bite, cold, coolness, crispness, nip, rawness, sharpness.
vb lit: cool, freeze, refrigerate; *fig*: dampen, deject, discourage, dishearten.
adj lit: biting, bleak, chilly, cold, freezing, raw, sharp, wintry.

chilly
adj lit: blowy, breezy, brisk, crisp, fresh, nippy, penetrating, sharp; frigid, hostile, unresponsive, unwelcoming.

chime
n lit: boom, clang, jingle, peal, ring, sound, strike, toll.

china
n lit: ceramics, crockery, porcelain, pottery, service, tableware.

chink
n lit: aperture, cleft, cranny, crevice, fissure, flaw, gap, rift.

chip
n lit: dent, flake, fragment, gash, notch, paring, scratch, shaving, sliver, wafer.
vb lit: chisel, flake, fragment, gash, nick, notch, whittle.

chips
n lit: French fries, pommes frites, sauté potatoes.

chivalrous
adj lit: bold, brave, courteous, courtly, gallant, honourable, intrepid, knightly, true, valiant.

choice
n lit: alternative, option, pick, preference, say, selection, variety.
adj lit: best, dainty, elite, exclusive, exquisite, hand-picked, precious, prime, prize, rare, special, superior, uncommon, valuable.

choir
n lit: chorus, choristers, singers, vocalists.

choke
n lit: blocking, clogging, congestion, constriction, obstruction, stoppage, suffocation; mixture.
vb lit: asphyxiate, bar, block, close, congest, constrict, dam, obstruct, smother, stifle, stop, strangle, suffocate, suppress, throttle.

choose
vb lit: adopt, designate, desire, fix on, opt for, pick, prefer, see fit, settle upon, single out, take, wish.

chop
n lit: dismissal, sacking, the axe, the boot, the sack.
vb lit: axe, cut, fell, hack, hew, lop, sever, truncate.

choppy
adj lit: blustery, rough, ruffled, squally, tempestuous.

chore
n lit: burden, duty, job, task.

chorus
n lit: choir, choristers, ensemble, singers; refrain, response, strain; accord, concert, harmony.

christen
vb lit: baptize, call, dub, name, style, term.

Christian-name
n lit: first name, initial(s), name given at baptism.

chronic
adj lit: deep-seated, incessant, incurable, ineradicable, ingrained, persistent.

chronicle
n lit: account, annals, diary, history, journal, narrative, record, register.
vb lit: enter, record, recount, register, report, set down.

chubby
adj lit: plump, podgy, portly, rotund, stout, tubby.

chuckle
n lit: cackle, chortle, giggle, glee, laughter, snigger, titter.
vb lit: cackle, chortle, giggle, laugh, snigger, titter.

chunk
n lit: block, dollop, hunk, lump, piece, portion.

church
n lit: abbey, cathedral, chapel, kirk, meeting house, minster, mission, synagogue, temple; congregation, denomination, sect.

churlish
adj lit: boorish, brusque, harsh, ill-tempered, loutish, morose, oafish, rude, uncivil, vulgar; inhospitable, mean, miserly, niggardly.

churn
vb lit: agitate, beat, foam, froth, seethe, stir up, swirl.

cigarette
n lit: ciggy, fag, gasper, smoke.

cinema
n lit: films, motion pictures, movies, picture palace.

cipher
n lit: nil, nought, zero; nobody, nonentity; character, digit, figure, numeral, symbol; code, cryptograph; device, logo, monogram.

vb lit: calculate, compute, figure out, think, work by arithmetic; put into code.

circle
n lit: band, circumference, cordon, cycle, disc, lap, loop, orb, perimeter, revolution, ring, sphere; area, bounds, circuit, compass, enclosure, orbit, range, region, scene; assembly, clique, company, fraternity, group, set, society.
vb lit: belt, circumnavigate, coil, compass, encircle, enclose, envelop, gird, revolve, ring, rotate, surround, whirl.

circuitous
adj lit: devious, indirect, meandering, periphrastic, rambling, roundabout, winding.

circulation
n lit: currency, distribution, spread, transmission; circling, flow, rotation.

circumscribe
vb lit: bound, confine, delineate, demarcate, encircle, enclose, encompass, hem in, limit, mark off, restrict, surround.

circumspect
adj lit: canny, careful, cautious, deliberate, discreet, guarded, observant, prudent, vigilant, watchful.

circumstance
n lit: condition, contingency, detail, event, fact, factor, incident, occurrence, particular, position, situation.

circus
n lit: amphitheatre; funfair, travelling show; traffic circle.

cite
vb lit: adduce, allude to, evidence, extract, mention, name, quote, specify; *spec*: call, subpoena, summon.

citizen
n lit: burgher, denizen, dweller, inhabitant, resident.

city
n lit: conurbation, metropolis, municipality.

civic
adj lit: communal, community, local, municipal.

civil
adj lit: civic, domestic, home, municipal, political; accommodating, affable,

courteous, courtly, obliging, polite, refined, urbane, well-mannered.

civilization
n lit: advancement, cultivation, culture, enlightenment, progress, refinement, sophistication; community, people, society; customs, mores, way of life.

civilized
adj lit: cultured, enlightened, humane, polite, sophisticated, urbane.

claim
n lit: affirmation, allegation, assertion, call, petition, pretension, privilege, request, requirement, right.
vb lit: allege, assert, call for, demand, exact, insist, maintain, profess, require, uphold.

clamp
n lit: bracket, fastener, grip, vice.
vb lit: brace, clinch, fasten, fix, impose, secure.

clan
n lit: band, clique, coterie, family, fraternity, group, house, race, set, tribe.

clap
n lit: acclaim, applause, cheer; bang, pat, slap, thrust, wallop, whack.
vb lit: applaud, cheer; bang, pat, slap, strike gently, thrust, thwack, wallop.

claptrap
n lit: affectation, blarney, bombast, drivel, humbug, nonsense, rubbish.

clarify
vb lit: clear up, elucidate, explain, resolve, simplify; cleanse, purify, refine.

clarity
n lit: clearness, definition, explicitness, intelligibility, lucidity, precision, simplicity.

clash
n lit: brush, collision, conflict, confrontation, disagreement, fight.
vb lit: bang, clank, clatter, crash, jar, rattle; conflict, cross swords, grapple, quarrel, war, wrangle.

clasp
n lit: brooch, buckle, clip, fastener, hook, pin, snap; embrace, grasp, hold, hug.
vb lit: clutch, connect, embrace, fasten, grapple, grasp, grip, hold, hug, press, squeeze.

class

n lit: caste, category, classification, department, division, genre, grade, group, kind, order, rank, set, sort, species, status, type, value.
vb lit: categorize, classify, codify, designate, grade, rank, rate.

classic

n lit: masterpiece, model, paradigm, prototype, standard.
adj lit: best, finest, first-rate, masterly; archetypal, definitive, exemplary, ideal, master, model, quintessential, standard; characteristic, regular, time-honoured, typical; abiding, ageless, enduring, immortal, lasting.

classify

vb lit: arrange, catalogue, categorize, codify, file, grade, rank, sort, systematize.

clause

n lit: article, chapter, paragraph, part, section; heading, item, point, provision, specification, stipulation.

claw

n lit: nail, nipper, pincer, talon, unguis.
vb lit: dig, lacerate, mangle, maul, rip, scrape, scratch.

clean

vb lit: cleanse, disinfect, dust, launder, mop, purify, rinse, scrub, sponge, sweep, wash, wipe.
adj lit: flawless, fresh, hygienic, immaculate, laundered, pure, sanitary, spotless, unblemished, unsoiled, washed; antiseptic, clarified, decontaminated, purified, sterilized, unadulterated, unpolluted; chaste, decent, good, guiltless, innocent, moral, respectable, undefiled, upright, virtuous; delicate, elegant, neat, simple, tidy, uncluttered; complete, conclusive, decisive, entire, perfect, thorough, total, unimpaired, whole.

clear

vb lit: clean, erase, purify, refine, tidy (up), wipe; break up, clarify, brighten; absolve, acquit, exuse, exonerate, vindicate; free, liberate, set free; disengage, disentangle, extricate, loosen, open, rid, unblock, unload; jump, leap, miss, pass over; earn, gain, make, reap.
adj lit: bright, cloudless, fine, halcyon, light, shining, sunny, unclouded; apparent, audible, coherent, comprehensible, conspicuous, evident, explicit, intelligible, manifest, obvious, palpable, plain, pronounced, recognizable, unambiguous, unmistakable; empty, free, open, smooth, unhindered, unimpeded, unobstructed; crystalline, glassy, pellucid, see-through, transparent; certain, decided, definite, positive, resolved, sure; clean, innocent, pure, stainless, unblemished, undefiled, untarnished.

clearing

n lit: glade; area, arena, open space.

clearly

adv lit: beyond doubt, distinctly, evidently, markedly, obviously, seemingly, undeniably.

cleft

n lit: crack, crevice, chink, fissure, split; dimple.

clergyman

n lit: chaplain, cleric, curate, father, minister, padre, parson, pastor, priest, rabbi, rector, reverend, vicar.

clerical

adj lit: ecclesiastical, pastoral, sacerdotal, theocratic; book-keeping, office, secretarial, stenographic.

clever

adj lit: able, adroit, apt, astute, bright, canny, capable, dexterous, gifted, intelligent, keen, knowledgeable, quick-witted, resourceful, shrewd, skilful, smart, talented.

click

n lit: beat, clack, tick.
vb lit: beat, clack, tick; become clear, fall into place, make sense; be compatible, feel a rapport, get on, hit it off, take to each other.

client

n lit: applicant, buyer, customer, patient, shopper.

clientele

n lit: business, clients, customers, market, regulars, trade.

cliff

n lit: crag, face, overhang, precipice, rock face, scarp.

climactic

adj lit: critical, crucial, decisive, paramount, peak.

climate
n lit: clime, region, temperature, weather;
disposition, feeling, mood, temper,
tendency.

climatic
adj lit: atmospheric, climatal, climatical,
meteorological.

climax
n lit: acme, culmination, head, height,
highlight, orgasm, peak, summit,
zenith.
vb lit: culminate, peak.

climb
n lit: ascent, rise, slope, steep part;
increase, progression.
vb lit: ascend, clamber, mount, scale;
increase, soar, top.

clinch
n lit: conclusion, confirmation, decision,
settlement, verification; bolt, clamp,
fastener, rivet; clutch, grasp, hug,
squeeze.
vb lit: assure, cap, conclude, confirm,
determine, seal, secure, settle, verify;
bolt, clamp, fasten, fix, nail, rivet;
clutch, cuddle, embrace, hug, squeeze.

clinic
n lit: medical centre, surgery; seminar,
tutorial.

cling
vb lit: adhere, attach to, be true to, clutch,
embrace, fasten, grip, stick, twine round.

clip
n lit: blow, box, clout, punch, smack,
whack; rate, speed, velocity; fastener,
holder, pin, staple.
vb lit: crop, cut, pare, prune, shear,
shorten, trim; blow, box, cuff, knock,
punch, smack, thump, wallop; attach,
fasten, fix, hold, staple.

clique
n lit: circle, coterie, faction, group, mob,
pack, set.

cloak
n lit: cape, coat, cover, mantle, wrap;
blind, front, mask, pretext, shield.
vb lit: camouflage, cover, disguise, hide,
mask, screen, veil.

clock
n lit: chronometer, repeater, timepiece,
watch; dial, gauge, meter, speedometer;
milometer, odometer; *fig*: face, kisser,
phizog.

vb lit: pace, rate, time; report (in), sign
(on); knock (off), sign (off); *fig*: look at,
see, tour, visit; punch the face of.

clog
n lit: sabot; impediment, obstruction.
vb lit: block, congest, hamper, hinder,
impede, jam, obstruct, shackle.

cloister
n lit: covered walk; convent, monastery;
den, retreat.

close
vb lit: bar, block, clog, cork, lock, plug,
seal, secure, shut, stop up; cease,
complete, conclude, discontinue, finish,
terminate, wind up; grapple (with),
wrestle (with); connect, join.
adj lit: adjacent, approaching, handy,
imminent, impending, near,
neighbouring; compact, congested,
cramped, dense, impenetrable, packed,
short, thick, tight; accurate,
conscientious, exact, literal, precise;
alert, assiduous, careful, detailed,
dogged, earnest, intense, intent, keen,
minute, painstaking, rigorous, searching,
thorough; attached, devoted, familiar,
intimate, loving; airless, heavy,
oppressive, stale, stifling, stuffy,
suffocating, unventilated; hidden,
private, reticent, secluded, secretive,
taciturn, unforthcoming; mean, miserly,
niggardly, parsimonious, stingy,
ungenerous.
adv lit: near.

closed
adj (pa.pt) lit: locked, out of service,
sealed, shut; concluded, decided,
finished, over, settled; exclusive,
restricted.

closet
n lit: cabinet, cupboard, locker; private
room.
vb lit: admit, shut.

cloth
n lit: fabric, material, textiles.

clothe
vb lit: accoutre, attire, cover, drape,
dress, equip, fit out, garb, outfit, rig,
robe.

clothes/clothing
n lit: apparel, attire, costume, dress, garb,
garments, gear, outfit, vesture,
wardrobe, wear.

cloud
n lit: billow, gloom, haze, mist, murk, nebula, vapour; dense mass, horde, multitude, swarm, throng.
vb lit: darken, dim, eclipse, obscure, overcast, shade, shadow, veil; confuse, disorient, distort, impair, muddle.

cloudburst
n lit: deluge, downburst, drizzle, monsoon, rainfall, shower.

cloudy
adj lit: blurred, confused, dim, dull, gloomy, hazy, leaden, muddy, murky, nebulous, obscure, overcast, sombre.

clout
n lit: blow, punch, slap; authority, influence, power, prestige, pull, standing, weight.
vb lit: box, hit, slap, sock, strike, thump, wallop, wham.

clown
n lit: buffoon, comedian, fool, harlequin, jester, joker, mountebank, pierrot, prankster; boor, peasant, yahoo, yokel.
vb lit: act the fool, jest, mess about.

club
n lit: bat, bludgeon, cosh, cudgel, stick, truncheon; association, circle, clique, fraternity, group, guild, lodge, order, set, society, union.
vb lit: bash, batter, beat, bludgeon, clobber, clout, cosh, pummel, strike.

clue
n lit: hint, indication, inkling, intimation, lead, sign, suspicion, tip-off, trace.

clumsy
adj lit: awkward, blundering, bungling, clownish, gauche, gawky, inept, lumbering, maladroit, uncoordinated, uncouth, ungainly, unskilful.

cluster
n lit: assemblage, batch, bunch, gathering, group, knot.
vb lit: assemble, bunch, flock, gather, group.

clutch
n lit: catch, clasp, embrace, grabbing, grasp, grip, snatch; eggs.
vb lit: catch, clasp, cling to, embrace, grab, grasp, grip, snatch.

coach
n lit: bus, carriage, vehicle; instructor, trainer, tutor.
vb lit: cram, drill, instruct, train, tutor.

coagulate
vb lit: clot, congeal, curdle, set, solidify, thicken.

coalition
n lit: affiliation, alliance, amalgamation, association, bloc, combination, confederacy, fusion, integration, league, merger, union.

coarse
adj lit: boorish, brute, gruff, loutish, rough, rude, uncivil; bawdy, earthy, improper, indelicate, offensive, ribald, smutty, vulgar; coarse-grained, crude, homespun, unpolished, unrefined.

coarseness
n lit: bawdiness, boorishness, indelicacy, offensiveness, ribaldry, roughness, smut, uncouthness.

coast
n lit: beach, coastline, littoral, seaside, shore, strand.
vb lit: cruise, drift, freewheel, get by, sail, taxi.

coat
n lit: fleece, fur, hair, hide, skin, wool; coating, covering, overlay.
vb lit: apply, cover, smear, spread.

coax
vb lit: allure, beguile, cajole, entice, persuade, prevail upon, talk into, wheedle.

cock
n lit: cockerel, rooster.
vb lit: perk up, raise, stand up.

cocky
adj lit: arrogant, brash, conceited, swaggering, vain.

cogent
adj lit: conclusive, convincing, effective, forceful, forcible, irresistible, potent, powerful, strong, urgent, weighty.

cogitate
vb lit: brood, consider, contemplate, deliberate, meditate, mull over, muse, ponder, reflect, ruminate, think.

cognac
n lit: brandy.

coherent
adj lit: articulate, comprehensible, intelligible, lucid, meaningful, rational, reasoned.

coil
n lit: convolution, curl, loop, spiral, twist.
vb lit: convolute, curl, entwine, loop, meander, snake, spiral, twist, undulate, wind.

coin
n lit: cash, change, copper, money, silver.
vb lit: issue, mint, mould; conceive, create, fabricate, forge, formulate, invent, make up, think up.

coincide
vb lit: be concurrent, occur simultaneously, synchronize; accord, harmonize, match, tally; acquiesce, concur, correspond.

coincidental
adj lit: accidental, chance, fortuitous, unintentional; coincident, concurrent, simultaneous, synchronous.

cold
n lit: chill, coldness, frigidity, frostiness, inclemency; catarrh, coryza, flu, influenza, rheum, rhinitis.
adj lit: arctic, biting, bitter, bleak, boreal, chilly, cryogenic, freezing, frosty, gelid, raw, wintry; chilled, numbed, shivery; aloof, apathetic, dead, distant, frigid, indifferent, phlegmatic, reserved, standoffish, stony, unmoved, unsympathetic.

cold-blooded
adj lit: brutal, callous, cruel, heartless, pitiless, ruthless, savage, unemotional, unmoved.

collaborate
vb lit: cooperate, join forces, participate, team up, work together; collude, conspire, fraternize.

collaborator
n lit: associate, colleague, confederate, partner, team-mate; fraternizer, quisling, traitor, turncoat.

collapse
n lit: breakdown, cave-in, disintegration, downfall, subsidence; exhaustion, failure, faint, flop.

vb lit: break down, cave in, crack up, crumble, fail, faint, fold, founder, give way, subside.

collar
vb lit: apprehend, capture, catch, grab, lay hands on, seize.

colleague
n lit: ally, associate, companion, comrade, confederate, partner, team-mate, workmate.

collect
vb lit: accumulate, aggregate, amass, gather, heap, hoard, stockpile; assemble, cluster, coacervate, congregate, convene, converge, rally; acquire, obtain, raise, secure.

collected
adj (pa.pt) lit: assembled, compiled, gathered; calm, composed, cool, placid, poised, unperturbed, unruffled.

collection
n lit: accumulation, anthology, coacervation, compilation, heap, hoard, mass, set, stockpile, store; assembly, assortment, company, congregation, crowd, gathering, group; contribution, offering.

college
n lit: body of colleagues; academy, campus, institute, polytechnic, seminary, university.

collide
vb lit: clash, conflict, crash, meet head-on.

collision
n lit: accident, bump, crash, pile-up, smash; clash, conflict, confrontation, encounter, skirmish.

collusion
n lit: complicity, connivance, conspiracy, deceit, intrigue.

colonize
vb lit: open up, pioneer, populate, settle.

colony
n lit: dependency, dominion, outpost, settlement, territory.

colour
n lit: coloration, dye, hue, paint, pigment, shade, tincture, tinge, tint; bloom, blush, brilliance, flush, glow, vividness; *fig*: appearance, disguise, façade, guise, pretence, pretext, semblance.

vb lit: dye, paint, stain, tinge, tint; *fig*:
disguise, distort, embroider, exaggerate,
falsify, garble, misrepresent, pervert,
prejudice, slant, taint; blush, burn, flush,
redden.

colourful
adj lit: bright, brilliant, intense, motley,
multicoloured, psychedelic, variegated,
vibrant, vivid; characterful, distinctive,
lively, picturesque, rich, stimulating,
unusual.

column
n lit: cavalcade, line, procession, queue,
rank, row, train; obelisk, pilaster, pillar,
post, shaft, upright.

comatose
adj lit: drowsy, drugged, lethargic, sleepy,
sluggish, soporose, stupified, torpid,
unconscious.

comb
vb lit: arrange, curry, dress, groom,
untangle; hatchel, heckle, tease, teazle;
fig: hunt, rake, ransack, rummage, scour,
search, sift, sweep.

combat
n lit: battle, conflict, contest, encounter,
engagement, fight, skirmish, warfare.
vb lit: battle, contend, contest, do battle
with, fight, oppose, resist, struggle,
withstand.

combination
n lit: amalgamation, blend, composite,
mixture; alliance, association, cartel,
coalition, compound, confederation,
consortium, merger, syndicate, union.

combine
vb lit: amalgamate, associate, bind, blend,
compound, connect, fuse, incorporate,
integrate, link, merge, put together,
synthesize, unify.

come
vb lit: appear, approach, arrive, enter,
move towards, near, occur, show up,
turn up; attain, materialize, reach; fall,
happen, take place; emanate, emerge,
flow, issue, result, turn out; be available,
be made, be produced.

comedian
n lit: clown, comic, funny man, jester,
joker, laugh, wit.

comedy
n lit: drollery, facetiousness, farce,
hilarity, humour, joking, light

entertainment, slapstick, wisecracking.

comfort
n lit: alleviation, cheer, consolation, ease,
enjoyment, help, relief, succour,
support; cosiness, opulence, snugness,
wellbeing.
vb lit: alleviate, assuage, cheer,
commiserate with, console, ease, enliven,
hearten, invigorate, reassure, relieve,
soothe, strengthen.

comfortable
adj lit: adequate, agreeable, ample,
convenient, cosy, homely, loose-fitting,
pleasant, restful, snug; contented,
happy, relaxed; affluent, prosperous,
well-off, well-to-do.

comical
adj lit: absurd, amusing, diverting, droll,
entertaining, farcical, funny, hilarious,
ludicrous, ridiculous, side-splitting.

coming
n lit: accession, advent, arrival.
adj lit: approaching, due, forthcoming,
imminent, impending, near, next;
aspiring, future, promising, up-and-
coming.

command
n lit: behest, bidding, commandment,
directive, edict, injunction, instruction,
order, precept, requirement, ultimatum;
authority, control, domination,
government, grasp, management, power,
rule, supervision, sway.
vb lit: bid, charge, compel, demand,
enjoin, require; control, dominate,
govern, head, manage, rule, supervise,
sway.

commandeer
vb lit: appropriate, confiscate, hijack,
requisition, seize, sequestrate, usurp.

commemorate
vb lit: celebrate, honour, keep, observe,
pay tribute to, remember, salute.

commend
vb lit: acclaim, applaud, compliment,
eulogize, extol, praise, recommend;
commit, consign, deliver, entrust, hand
over.

commensurate
adj lit: adequate, appropriate, compatible,
consistent, due, equivalent, fitting,
proportionate, sufficient.

comment
n lit: observation, remark, statement;
annotation, commentary, criticism,
explanation, exposition, note.
vb lit: interpose, mention, note, observe,
point out, remark, say; annotate,
criticize, elucidate, explain, interpret.

commentator
n lit: correspondent, reporter,
sportscaster; annotator, critic, expositor,
interpreter.

commerce
n lit: business, dealing, exchange, trade,
traffic; communication, intercourse,
relations.

commercial
adj lit: business, mercantile, profit-
making, trading; in demand, marketable,
popular, profitable; exploited,
mercenary, monetary, pecuniary,
venal.

commission
n lit: appointment, charge, duty,
employment, errand, function, mandate,
task, warrant; allowance, brokerage,
compensation, cut, fee, percentage;
board, commissioners, committee,
delegation, representative.
vb lit: appoint, authorize, contract,
delegate, empower, nominate, order,
send.

commit
vb lit: carry out, do, execute, perform,
perpetrate; confide, consign, deliver,
deposit, entrust, give, hand over; align,
bind, make liable, obligate, pledge, rank;
confine, imprison.

commitment
n lit: duty, liability, obligation,
responsibility; dedication, devotion,
involvement, loyalty; assurance,
guarantee, pledge, undertaking, word.

committee
n lit: board, convention, council,
delegation, panel.

common
n lit: green, heath.
adj lit: average, commonplace, customary,
daily, familiar, frequent, habitual,
humdrum, ordinary, plain, routine,
standard, stock, usual; accepted, general,
popular, prevailing, universal,
widespread; communal, community,
public, social; coarse, hackneyed,

inferior, low, pedestrian, stale,
undistinguished, vulgar.

common sense
n lit: intelligence, level-headedness, nous,
practicality, reasonableness, wit.

commotion
n lit: ado, agitation, bustle, disturbance,
excitement, fuss, hullabaloo,
perturbation, racket, rumpus, to-do,
turmoil, uproar.

communal
adj lit: collective, community, general,
joint, neighbourhood, public.

commune
n lit: community, co-operative, kibbutz.
vb lit: communicate, confer, converse,
discuss, parley; contemplate, meditate,
muse, ponder, reflect.

communicate
vb lit: acquaint, be in contact, be in touch,
convey, disclose, divulge, inform, make
known, pass on, publish, report, reveal,
ring up, spread, transmit, unfold.

communication
n lit: connection, contact, conversation,
correspondence, link, transmission;
announcement, disclosure, dispatch,
intelligence, message, news, report,
statement.

communion
n lit: accord, affinity, agreement,
closeness, concord, harmony, rapport,
sympathy, togetherness, unity; *spec*:
Eucharist, Mass, sacrament.

communiqué
n lit: announcement, bulletin, dispatch,
news flash, official communication.

community
n lit: commonwealth, general public,
people, residents, society; affinity,
identity, likeness, similarity.

compact
n lit: agreement, alliance, bargain, bond,
contract, deal, entente, pact, treaty,
understanding.
vb lit: compress, condense, cram, stuff,
lamp.
adj lit: compressed, condensed, dense,
firm, solid, thick; brief, concise, laconic,
pithy, pointed, terse, to the point.

companion
n lit: accomplice, ally, associate, colleague, comrade, crony, mate, partner; aide, assistant, attendant, chaperon, escort; counterpart, match, twin.

companionship
n lit: camaraderie, comradeship, fellowship, fraternity, rapport, togetherness.

company
n lit: assembly, band, body, circle, group, party, set, troop; association, business, concern, corporation, firm, house, partnership, syndicate; callers, guests, visitors; presence.

comparative
adj lit: approximate, by comparison, relative.

compare
vb lit: balance (with), collate (with), contrast (with), juxtapose (with); equate (to), liken (to), parallel (to); approach, approximate to, come up to, equal, match.

comparison
n lit: collation, contrast, distinction, juxtaposition; analogy, comparability, correlation, resemblance, similarity.

compartment
n lit: alcove, berth, booth, carriage, chamber, cubicle, niche, pigeonhole; category, department, section, subdivision.

compass(es)
n lit: area, bound, circle, circuit, circumference, extent, field, range, reach, scope, sphere, zone.

compassion
n lit: charity, commiseration, compunction, condolence, humanity, kindness, mercy, pity, sympathy, tenderness.

compatible
adj lit: adaptable, agreeable, congenial, congruous, consistent, harmonious, in keeping, like-minded, reconcilable, suitable.

compel
vb lit: bulldoze, coerce, drive, enforce, exact, force, hustle, impel, make, oblige, restrain, urge.

compelling
adj lit: conclusive, convincing, forceful, irrefutable, powerful, weighty; enchanting, enthralling, gripping, irresistible, mesmeric; binding, imperative, overriding, peremptory, pressing, urgent.

compensate
vb lit: atone, indemnify, make good, recompense, refund, reimburse, remunerate, repay, requite, satisfy; balance, cancel (out), counteract, make amends, make up for, offset.

compensation
n lit: amends, atonement, damages, indemnity, payment, recompense, reimbursement, remuneration, reparation, restitution, reward, satisfaction.

compete
vb lit: challenge, contend, contest, emulate, rival, strive, struggle.

competent
adj lit: able, adequate, capable, endowed, fit, proficient, qualified, sufficient, suitable.

competition
n lit: contention, contest, one-upmanship, opposition, rivalry, strife; championship, event, quiz, tournament; challengers, field, rivals.

competitor
n lit: adversary, antagonist, challenger, competition, contestant, emulator, opponent, rival.

compilation
n lit: anthology, collection, compendium, compiling, miscellany, selection.

compile
vb lit: accumulate, amass, collect, gather, marshal, organize, put together.

complacent
adj lit: contended, gratified, pleased with oneself, satisfied, self-righteous, smug, unconcerned.

complain
vb lit: bemoan, beef, carp, deplore, find fault, gripe, groan, growl, grumble, kick up a fuss, moan, whine.

complaint
n lit: accusation, criticism, dissatisfaction, fault-finding, grievance, grumble, moan, remonstrance; affliction, ailment, disease, disorder, illness, indisposition, sickness.

complement
n lit: companion, completion, counterpart, rounding-off, supplement; capacity, entirety, quota, total, totality.
vb lit: cap, complete, crown, set off.

complete
vb lit: accomplish, achieve, cap, conclude, discharge, do, execute, finalize, finish, realize, round off, settle, wrap up.
adj lit: all, entire, full, integral, unabridged, undivided, whole; accomplished, achieved, concluded, finished; absolute, consummate, perfect, thorough, total, utter.

completely
adv lit: absolutely, altogether, entirely, from beginning to end, fully, in full, quite, solidly, thoroughly, totally, utterly, wholly.

complex
n lit: network, organization, scheme, structure, system; fixation, obsession, phobia, preoccupation.
adj lit: circuitous, complicated, intricate, involved, knotty, labyrinthine, mingled, tangled, tortuous; composite, compound, heterogeneous, manifold, multiple.

complexion
n lit: colouring, hue, pigmentation, skin tone; appearance, aspect, character, countenance, guise, look, nature, stamp.

complicate
vb lit: confuse, entangle, involve, muddle, snarl up.

complicated
adj lit: complex, elaborate, interlaced, intricate, involved, labyrinthine; difficult, perplexing, problematic, puzzling.

compliment
n lit: admiration, commendation, congratulations, courtesy, eulogy, flattery, honour, praise, tribute.
vb lit: commend, congratulate, extol, felicitate, laud, praise, salute, speak highly of.

complimentary
adj lit: appreciative, commendatory, congratulatory, flattering, laudatory, panegyrical; courtesy, donated, free of charge, gratuitous, on the house.

comply
vb lit: abide by, accord, acquiesce, adhere to, agree to, consent to, defer, discharge, follow, observe, respect, satisfy, submit.

component
n lit: constituent, element, ingredient, part, unit.
adj lit: composing, inherent, intrinsic.

compose
vb lit: compound, comprise, constitute, construct, form, make, put together; contrive, create, devise, invent, produce, write; adjust, arrange, reconcile, resolve, settle; appease, assuage, calm, control, pacify, placate, quell, quiet, soothe.

composite
n lit: amalgam, compound, conglomerate, fusion, synthesis.
adj lit: blended, combined, complex, conglomerate, mixed, synthesized.

composition
n lit: arrangement, configuration, design, form, layout, make-up, organization, structure; compilation, creation, fashioning, formulation, invention, making, production; essay, exercise, opus, piece, study, work, writing; balance, concord, harmony, proportion, symmetry.

compost
n lit: combination, compound, manure, humus, mulch.

compound
n lit: alloy, blend, combination, composite, conglomerate, fusion, medley, mixture.
vb lit: amalgamate, blend, combine, concoct, fuse, intermingle, mix, unite; add to, aggravate, complicate, exacerbate, intensify, magnify, worsen; adjust, settle a dispute.
adj lit: complex, composite, intricate, multiple, not simple.

comprehension
n lit: conception, discernment, grasp, intelligence, perception, realization, understanding; compass, field, limits, range, reach, scope.

comprehensive
adj lit: all-inclusive, blanket, broad, complete, exhaustive, extensive, inclusive, sweeping, thorough, wide.

compression
n lit: condensation, consolidation, constriction, crushing, pressure, squeezing.

comprise
vb lit: comprehend, consist of, contain, include, take in; compose, constitute, form, make up.

compromise
n lit: accord, adjustment, agreement, concession, middle ground, settlement, trade-off.
vb lit: adjust, agree, arbitrate, compound, concede, meet halfway, settle; discredit, embarrass, expose, implicate, jeopardize, prejudice.

compulsion
n lit: coercion, constraint, demand, duress, obligation, pressure; drive, need, obsession, preoccupation, urge.

compulsory
adj lit: binding, imperative, mandatory, obligatory, requisite.

comrade
n lit: ally, associate, buddy, colleague, companion, compeer, confederate, crony, fellow, mate, pal, partner.

conceal
vb lit: camouflage, cover, disguise, hide, keep secret, mask, obscure, screen, secrete.

concede
vb lit: accept, admit, allow, confess, own; cede, hand over, relinquish, yield.

conceit
n lit: arrogance, complacency, egotism, narcissism, self-importance, swagger, vanity; fancy, idea, notion, opinion, thought, whim.

conceited
adj lit: arrogant, bigheaded, cocky, egotistical, immodest, puffed up, swollen-headed, vainglorious.

conceive
vb lit: appreciate, apprehend, comprehend, fancy, grasp, imagine, suppose, understand; contrive, create, design, develop, formulate, produce, think up; become pregnant.

concentrate
n lit: distillate, essence, extract.
vb lit: be engrossed in, focus attention on, put one's mind to, rack one's brains; centre, cluster, converge, focus; accumulate, collect, congregate, gather.

concentration
n lit: absorption, application, single-mindedness; centralization, compression, consolidation, convergence, intensification; accumulation, aggregation, collection, horde, mass.

conception
n lit: concept, design, idea, notion, plan; beginning, formation, inception, invention, launching, outset; appreciation, clue, comprehension, impression, inkling, understanding; fertilization, germination, insemination.

concern
n lit: affair, business, field, interest, involvement, matter, mission, responsibility, task; bearing, importance, reference, relevance; anxiety, apprehension, attention, consideration, disquiet, distress, heed, worry; company, corporation, enterprise, firm, organization.
vb lit: affect, apply to, be relevant to, involve, pertain to, regard; bother, disquiet, disturb, make uneasy, perturb, trouble, worry.

concerned
adj lit: active, implicated, involved, mixed up, privy to; anxious, bothered, distressed, troubled, uneasy, upset, worried; attentive, caring, interested, solicitous.

concerning
prp lit: about, apropos of, as to, in the matter of, on the subject of, regarding, relating to, touching, with reference to.

concert
n lit: accord, agreement, concordance, harmony, unanimity, unison; in collaboration, in league.

concerted
adj lit: agreed upon, combined, co-ordinated, joint, planned, prearranged, united.

concession
n lit: acknowledgement, admission,
assent, surrender, yielding; adjustment,
allowance, compromise, grant, permit,
privilege.

conciliatory
adj lit: appeasing, disarming, emollient,
mollifying, pacific, placatory,
propitiative.

concise
adj lit: brief, compact, compressed,
condensed, laconic, pithy, summary,
terse, to the point.

conclude
vb lit: cease, come to an end, complete,
draw to a close, finish, round off, wind
up; assume, deduce, gather, infer,
reckon, sum up, suppose; accomplish,
carry out, decide, determine, effect, fix,
pull off, settle, work out.

conclusion
n lit: close, completion, end, finish, result;
consequence, culmination, issue,
outcome, upshot; agreement, conviction,
deduction, judgement, opinion,
resolution, settlement.

concoct
vb lit: brew, contrive, cook up, design,
fabricate, hatch, invent, make up, plot,
project, think up.

concrete
n lit: cement, concretion, mortar.
adj lit: actual, explicit, factual, material,
real, specific, substantial, tangible;
calcified, compressed, consolidated,
firm, solid.

concur
vb lit: accede, acquiesce, agree, assent,
coincide, combine, consent, co-operate.

concurrence
n lit: acquiescence, agreement, assent,
consent, unanimity; coincidence,
juncture; co-operation, unison.

concussion
n lit: collision, crash, impact, jarring,
jolting, shock.

condemn
vb lit: blame, denounce, reprehend,
reproach, upbraid; convict, damn, doom,
sentence.

condense
vb lit: abbreviate, abridge, compact,
contract, curtail, epitomize, shorten,
summarize; boil down, concentrate,
precipitate, reduce, thicken.

condescending
adj lit: disdainful, lofty, patronizing,
snooty, supercilious, toffee-nosed.

condition
n lit: circumstances, plight, predicament,
situation, state of affairs; demand,
limitation, modification, prerequisite,
provision, qualification, requirement,
restriction, stipulation, terms; fettle,
fitness, health, shape, trim; ailment,
complaint, malady, problem; class,
grade, order, position, rank, status.
vb lit: accustom, adapt, prepare, ready,
tone up, train, work out.

conditional
adj lit: contingent, dependent,
provisional, qualified, subject to.

condone
vb lit: disregard, excuse, let pass, make
allowance for, overlook, pardon, turn a
blind eye to.

conduct
n lit: administration, direction,
leadership, management, organization,
running; attitude, bearing, behaviour,
demeanour, manners, ways.
vb lit: administer, control, direct, handle,
lead, manage, preside over, regulate,
supervise; accompany, attend, convey,
escort, guide, steer, usher; acquit, act,
behave, carry.

conductor
n lit: director, bandleader, maestro; guide,
host, hostess; ticket-collector; earth,
ground, lightning-rod; channel,
medium.

confer
vb lit: accord, award, bestow, give, grant,
present; consult, converse, deliberate,
discourse, parley.

conference
n lit: congress, convention, discussion,
meeting, seminar, symposium.

confess
vb lit: acknowledge, admit, blurt out,
come clean, confide, disclose, divulge,
get off one's chest, grant, own up, reveal;

affirm, assert, confirm, declare, profess,
prove.

confession
n lit: acknowledgement, admission,
disclosure, exposure, revelation.

confidence
n lit: belief, faith, reliance, trust;
assurance, boldness, courage, nerve,
self-reliance.

confident
adj lit: certain, convinced, counting on,
secure, sure; assured, bold, dauntless,
positive, self-assured.

confidential
adj lit: classified, hush-hush, intimate, off
the record, private, secret; faithful,
trusted, trustworthy.

confines
n lit: boundaries, bounds, circumference,
limits, precincts.

confirm
vb lit: assure, clinch, fix, fortify, reinforce,
strengthen; approve, authenticate, bear
out, corroborate, endorse, ratify,
sanction, substantiate, verify.

confirmation
n lit: authentication, corroboration, proof,
substantiation, validation, verification;
acceptance, approval, assent,
endorsement, ratification, sanction.

confiscate
vb lit: appropriate, commandeer,
impound, seize, sequestrate.

conflict
n lit: battle, clash, collision, combat,
contention, contest, encounter, fight,
fracas, strife, warfare; antagonism,
disagreement, discord, dissension,
friction, hostility, opposition.
vb lit: clash, collide, combat, contend,
contest, disagree, interfere, strife,
struggle.

confound
vb lit: astonish, astound, baffle, bewilder,
confuse, dumbfound, flabbergast, mix
up, perplex, surprise; annihilate,
demolish, destroy, overthrow, refute,
ruin.

confrontation
n lit: conflict, contest, encounter,
showdown.

confuse
vb lit: baffle, bemuse, bewilder, mystify,
perplex, puzzle; confound, disarrange,
disorder, mingle, mistake, mix up,
muddle, tangle; abash, addle,
demoralize, discompose, disconcert,
discountenance, disorient, embarrass,
fluster, mortify, rattle, upset.

confusion
n lit: befuddlement, bewilderment,
disorientation, perplexity, puzzlement;
bustle, chaos, clutter, commotion,
disorder, jumble, mess, muddle,
shambles, tangle, turmoil, upheaval;
abashment, chagrin, discomfiture,
distraction, embarrassment, fluster.

congenital
adj lit: constitutional, inbred, inherent,
innate; *fig*: complete, thorough, utter.

congestion
n lit: bottleneck, clogging, jam,
overcrowding, surfeit.

conglomerate
n lit: aggregate, assembly, multinational.
vb lit: accumulate, agglutinate, aggregate,
assemble, cluster, flocculate, snowball.
adj lit: amassed, clustered, composite,
heterogenous, massed.

congratulate
vb lit: compliment, felicitate, wish joy to.

congratulations
n lit: best wishes, compliments, good
wishes, greetings.

congregate
vb lit: assemble, come together,
concentrate, convene, converge, flock,
gather, mass, muster, rally, throng.

congregation
n lit: assembly, brethren, flock, host,
multitude, parishioners.

congress
n lit: assembly, conference, convention,
delegates, legislature, meeting,
parliament, representatives.

conjugal
adj lit: bridal, connubial, marital,
married, matrimonial, nuptial, wedded.

conjure
vb lit: juggle, play tricks; bewitch, charm,
enchant, fascinate, invoke, summon up;
adjure, appeal to, beseech, entreat,
implore, importune, supplicate.

connect
vb lit: affix, ally, associate, combine, join, link, unite.

connection
n lit: alliance, association, attachment, junction, link, tie, union; affinity, bond, communication, correlation, correspondence, intercourse, relationship, relevance; context, reference; acquaintance, ally, associate, contact, friend, sponsor; kin, kindred, relation, relative.

connivance
n lit: abetting, complicity, conspiring.

connoisseur
n lit: appreciator, authority, buff, devotee, expert, judge, specialist.

connotation
n lit: allusion, association, hidden meaning, implication, suggestion.

conquer
vb lit: beat, crush, defeat, humble, master, overcome, prevail, quell, rout, subdue, subjugate, surmount, vanquish; acquire, annex, occupy, seize, win.

conqueror
n lit: champion, defeater, hero, subjugator, vanquisher, victor.

conquest
n lit: defeat, overthrow, rout, triumph, victory; acquisition, annexation, appropriation, invasion, occupation, subjection, takeover; captivation, enchantment, enthralment, enticement; admirer, catch, fan, prize, supporter, worshipper.

conscience
n lit: moral sense, principles, scruples.

conscientious
adj lit: careful, diligent, exact, meticulous, painstaking, particular, punctilious, thorough; high-minded, honourable, incorruptible, just, scrupulous, strict, upright.

conscious
n lit: awareness, perception; ego, mind.
adj lit: alert, alive to, awake, aware, responsive; calculated, deliberate, intentional, rational, reasoning, responsible, wilful.

consecutive
adj lit: chronological, following, running, succeeding, successive, uninterrupted.

consent
n lit: acquiescence, approval, assent, concession, go-ahead, permission, sanction.
vb lit: accede, acquiesce, agree, assent, comply, concede, permit, yield.

consequence
n lit: effect, issue, outcome, repercussion, result; account, importance, note, portent, significance, value, weight; distinction, eminence, repute, standing, status.

consequently
adv lit: accordingly, hence, subsequently, therefore, thus.

conservative
n lit: middle-of-the-road, moderate, right-winger, Tory, traditionalist.
adj lit: cautious, conventional, die-hard, moderate, quiet, sober, traditional.

conserve
vb lit: go easy on, hoard, keep, nurse, preserve, protect, save, take care of.

consider
vb lit: cogitate, contemplate, deliberate, examine, meditate, mull over, ponder, reflect, ruminate, study, weigh; believe, deem, judge, rate, think; bear in mind, care for, reckon with, regard, remember, take into account.

considerable
adj lit: abundant, ample, comfortable, goodly, large, lavish, noticeable, plentiful, sizable, substantial, tidy; distinguished, influential, noteworthy, significant.

considerate
adj lit: attentive, concerned, kind, mindful, obliging, tactful, thoughtful, unselfish.

consideration
n lit: attention, contemplation, deliberation, examination, reflection, regard, scrutiny, thought; concern, issue, point; friendliness, kindness, respect, tact, thoughtfulness; fee, perquisite, remuneration, reward, tip.

considering
prp lit: all in all, insomuch as, in view of.

consign
vb lit: commit, deliver, entrust, hand over; deposit, send by rail, transmit.

consignment
n lit: assignment, committal, dispatch, distribution, entrusting, handing over, sending, transmittal; batch, delivery, shipment.

consist of
vb lit: be made up of, comprise, contain, include, involve.

consistent
adj lit: constant, dependable, persistent, regular, steady, undeviating; accordant, coherent, compatible, congruous, harmonious, logical.

consolation
n lit: alleviation, assuagement, comfort, ease, encouragement, help, relief, support.

consolidate
vb lit: amalgamate, cement, combine, condense, federate, fuse, harden, solidify, thicken, unite; fortify, reinforce, stabilize, strengthen.

consort
n lit: associate, companion, partner, spouse.
vb lit: associate, keep company, mingle, mix; accord, agree, square, tally.

conspicuous
adj lit: apparent, clear, evident, manifest, noticeable, obvious, perceptible, visible; distinguished, eminent, famous, outstanding, prominent, remarkable; blatant, flashy, garish, showy.

conspiracy
n lit: confederacy, frame-up, intrigue, machination, plot, treason.

conspire
vb lit: confederate, contrive, devise, intrigue, machinate, plot, scheme; combine, contribute, co-operate, tend.

constant
adj lit: continual, even, fixed, habitual, invariable, permanent, regular, stable, steady, unbroken, unvarying; ceaseless, continuous, endless, everlasting, incessant, interminable, never-ending, non-stop, persistent, relentless, sustained, uninterrupted, unrelenting; determined, dogged, persevering, resolute, unwavering; attached, devoted, faithful, staunch, true, trustworthy, unfailing.

constituent
n lit: component, element, factor, ingredient, part, unit; elector, voter.
adj lit: basic, component, elemental, essential, integral.

constitution
n lit: charter, statute; composition, establishment, formation; build, character, disposition, form, health, make-up, nature, physique, structure, temperament.

constitutional
n lit: airing, stroll, walk.
adj lit: congenital, inherent, intrinsic; chartered, statutory, vested.

construct
vb lit: assemble, build, create, design, engineer, erect, fabricate, formulate, found, make, manufacture, organize, raise, set up.

construction
n lit: building, composition, edifice, erection, fabrication, formation, shape, structure; explanation, inference, interpretation, rendering.

constructive
adj lit: helpful, practical, productive, useful.

consult
vb lit: ask advice of, consider, debate, deliberate, question, refer to, turn to; have regard for, respect, take account of.

consultant
n lit: counsel, adviser, specialist.

consultation
n lit: conference, council, deliberation, dialogue, examination, interview, meeting, session.

consume
vb lit: absorb, deplete, drain, exhaust, expend, fritter away, lavish, spend, squander, use, vanish, waste; devour, eat up, gobble, guzzle, polish off, put away; decay, demolish, destroy, devastate, ravage.

consumer
n lit: buyer, customer, purchaser, shopper.

consummate
vb lit: accomplish, achieve, carry out, complete, conclude, effectuate, finish, perform.
adj lit: absolute, accomplished, complete, finished, perfect, polished, skilled, superb, total, ultimate, unqualified, utter.

consumption
n lit: consuming, decrease, depletion, diminution, dissipation, exhaustion, expenditure, loss, using up, waste; *spec*: atrophy, phthisis, tuberculosis.

contact
n lit: association, communication; approximation, contiguity, junction, union; acquaintance, connection.
vb lit: approach, call, communicate with, get in touch with, phone, speak to, write to.

contagion
n lit: epidemic, spreading, transmission; *fig*: evil influence, moral corruption.

contagious
adj lit: catching, epidemic, infectious, spreading, transmissible.

contain
vb lit: accommodate, hold, seat; comprise, include, involve; curb, hold back, repress, restrain, stifle.

container
n lit: holder, receptacle, vessel.

contemplative
adj lit: deep in thought, meditative, musing, pensive, rapt, reflective, thoughtful.

contemporary
n lit: compeer.
adj lit: coexisting, concurrent, synchronous; current, latest, modern, newfangled, present-day, up-to-date, with it.

contempt
n lit: derision, disdain, disregard, disrespect, hauteur, mockery, scorn, slight.

contemptible
adj lit: abject, base, despicable, detestable, ignominious, low, mean, petty, shameful, small, vile.

contend
vb lit: compete, contest, grapple, jostle, skirmish, strive, struggle; affirm, argue, assert, dispute, hold, maintain.

content
n lit: comfort, contentment, ease, pleasure, satisfaction; essence, gist, meaning, substance, thoughts; capacity, size, volume.
vb lit: delight, gratify, humour, placate, please, satisfy, suffice.
adj lit: agreeable, comfortable, contented, fulfilled, satisfied.

contentious
adj lit: argumentative, bickering, controversial, cross, peevish, pugnacious, quarrelsome, wrangling.

contest
n lit: competition, game, match, tournament, trial; affray, battle, combat, conflict, discord, dispute, fight, struggle.
vb lit: compete, contend, fight, strive; argue, challenge, debate, dispute, object to, oppose.

context
n lit: background, connection, framework; ambience, circumstances, situation.

continent
n lit: landmass, mainland.
adj lit: abstinent, ascetic, celibate, chaste, self-restrained.

contingent
n lit: body, bunch, deputation, detachment, group, section, set.
adj lit: conditional on, dependent on; accidental, casual, haphazard, provisional, random.

continual
adj lit: constant, continuous, endless, frequent, incessant, perpetual, repetitive, uninterrupted.

continue
vb lit: carry on, endure, last, persist, remain, stay on, survive; go on, keep at, maintain, persevere, pursue, stick to, sustain; extend, lengthen, prolong; proceed, resume, take up.

continuous
adj lit: constant, continued, extended, prolonged, unceasing, uninterrupted.

contour
n lit: curve, form, outline, relief, shape, silhouette.

contraception
n lit: birth control, family planning.

contract
n lit: agreement, arrangement, commission, compact, covenant, deal, engagement, treaty, understanding.
vb lit: compress, condense, constrict, lessen, narrow, reduce, shrink, tighten, wither; agree, arrange, clinch, engage, enter into, negotiate, pledge; catch, develop, go down with.

contractor
n lit: hirer, lessor; boss, clerk of the works, foreman.

contradict
vb lit: contravene, counteract, deny, dispute, negate, oppose.

contradictory
adj lit: antagonistic, conflicting, discrepant, incompatible, inconsistent, irreconcilable, opposite, paradoxical.

contrary
adj lit: adverse, antagonistic, clashing, counter, inimical, opposite, paradoxical; awkward, cantankerous, difficult, froward, obstinate, wayward.

contrast
n lit: comparison, difference, disparity, dissimilarity, divergence, foil, opposition.
vb lit: compare, differentiate, distinguish, oppose, set off.

contribute
vb lit: add, bestow, chip in, donate, give, provide; be instrumental, conduce, help, tend.

contribution
n lit: addition, bestowal, donation, gift, grant, offering, subscription.

contrive
vb lit: construct, design, devise, engineer, fabricate, improvise, wangle; arrange, effect, hit upon, manage, plan, scheme.

contrived
adj lit: artificial, forced, overdone, planned, strained.

control
n lit: authority, charge, command, discipline, guidance, management, oversight, rule, supervision; check, curb, limitation, restraint.
vb lit: command, conduct, direct, manage, oversee, rule, supervise; check, constrain, curb, hold back, limit, master, restrain, subdue.

controversial
adj lit: contended, debatable, disputable, disputed.

convenience
n lit: availability, expediency, handiness, suitability, usefulness; accommodation, advantage, comfort, ease, service, use; appliance, device; chance, opportunity.

convenient
adj lit: beneficial, commodious, handy, helpful, labour-saving, opportune, suitable, useful, well-timed; accessible, at hand, nearby, within reach.

conventional
adj lit: common, customary, formal, habitual, normal, proper, regular, standard, traditional, usual; bourgeois, commonplace, hackneyed, pedestrian, routine, stereotyped.

conversation
n lit: chat, communication, dialogue, discourse, discussion, gossip, talk.

converse
n lit: antithesis, contrary, opposite, reverse.
adj lit: contrary, counter, opposite, reversed.

convert
n lit: disciple, proselyte.
vb lit: alter, change, transform, turn; adapt, apply, modify, reorganize, revise; baptize, convince, proselytize, regenerate.

convex
adj lit: bulging, outcurved, protuberant.

convict
n lit: criminal, culprit, felon, prisoner.
vb lit: condemn, find guilty, imprison, sentence.

conviction
n lit: assurance, certainty, confidence,

firmness, reliance; belief, creed, faith,
opinion, persuasion, view.

convince
vb lit: assure, persuade, prevail upon,
prove to, sway.

convulsion
n lit: agitation, commotion, disturbance,
tumult, upheaval; contortion,
contraction, fit, seizure, tremor.

cook
n lit: chef, cuisinier.
vb lit: dish up, fix, prepare; doctor, falsify,
fiddle, nobble, tamper with.

cooker
n lit: grill, hob, oven, stove.

cookery
n lit: cuisine, gastronomy.

cool
n lit: calmness, composure, poise, self-
control, temper.
vb lit: chill, freeze, refrigerate; abate,
allay, calm (down), dampen, lessen,
moderate, quiet.
adj lit: chilled, chilling, nippy, refreshing;
calm, collected, composed, level-headed,
placid, unemotional, unruffled; aloof,
apathetic, indifferent, lukewarm,
reserved, unconcerned, uninterested;
bold, brazen, cheeky, impertinent,
impudent; *fig*: cosmopolitan,
sophisticated, urbane.

co-operate
vb lit: aid, assist, collaborate, contribute,
co-ordinate, help, join forces, work
together.

co-operation
n lit: assistance, collaboration, concert,
helpfulness, participation, teamwork.

co-ordination
n lit: balance, coherence, integration,
organization, synchronization.

copious
adj lit: abundant, ample, bountiful,
extensive, generous, lavish, overflowing,
plentiful, profuse.

copper
n lit: boiler, caldron; policeman
adj lit: cupric, cuprous, of copper;
reddish-brown, copper-coloured.

copy
n lit: counterfeit, duplicate, imitation,
replica, reproduction, transcription.

vb lit: counterfeit, duplicate, photocopy,
reproduce, transcribe; ape, emulate,
follow, imitate, mimic, repeat, simulate.

cord
n lit: line, rope, string, twine; bond, link,
tie.

cordial
n lit: medicine, restorative; squash.
adj lit: affable, affectionate, agreeable,
friendly, genuine, heartfelt, hearty,
invigorating, reviving, sincere,
stimulating, strengthening, warm.

core
n lit: centre, gist, heart, kernel, medulla,
nub, pith.

cork
n lit: bark; bung, plug, stopper.

corkscrew
n lit: bottle-opener, drawer; helix, spiral.
vb lit: spin, spiral, swirl, twirl, twist.

corn
n lit: grain; maize; blister, ulcer; cliché.

corner
n lit: angle, bend, joint; cavity, cranny,
niche, nook, recess; pickle, predicament,
tight spot.
vb lit: bring to bay, trap.

corporal
adj lit: anatomical, bodily, material,
physical.

corpse
n lit: body, cadaver, carcass, remains.

corpulent
adj lit: adipose, bulky, burly, fat, large,
obese, overweight, pinguid, portly,
rotund, stout, tubby, well-covered, well-
endowed.

correspond
vb lit: accord, agree, compare, conform,
correlate, harmonize, tally; exchange
letters (with), keep in touch (with).

correspondence
n lit: agreement, comparability,
conformity, congruity, correlation,
harmony, similarity; letters, post,
postbag.

corrosive
adj lit: acid, acrid, caustic, destructive,
erosive; *fig*: cutting, incisive, trenchant,
virulent.

corrupt
vb lit: debauch, deprave, pervert; bribe, fix, nobble, square, suborn, subvert; contaminate, debase, defile, doctor, interfere with, spoil, tamper with; decay, putrefy, rot.
adj lit: debased, degenerate, depraved; bent, crooked, dishonest, unprincipled, unscrupulous; contaminated, defiled, polluted, spoiled, tainted; decayed, decaying, putrescent, putrid, rotten, rotting.

corset
n lit: bodice, foundation garment, girdle, stays; belt, truss.

cosmetic
adj lit: beautifying, decorating; concealing, hiding.

cost
n lit: charge, expense, outlay, price; damage; harm, injury, loss, penalty, sacrifice.
vb lit: be for sale at, sell at; *fig*: necessitate the loss of.

cosy
adj lit: comfortable, comfy, homely, intimate, secure, snug, warm.

cot
n lit: cradle, crib; bed, bedstead, bunk; hammock; cottage, hut, shack.

cottage
n lit: but-and-ben, cabin, chalet, hut, shack; thatched house.

couch
n lit: bed, divan, settee, settle, sofa; chaise longue; bench, seat.
vb lit: express, frame, phrase, word.

cough
n lit: bark, hack, wheeze; chill, hoarseness, huskiness.
vb lit: bark, hack, wheeze; gob (up), hawk (up), spew (up), vomit (up); *fig*: pay (up); give (up).

council
n lit: assembly, board, chamber, committee, conference, congress, diet, panel, tribunal; conclave, synod.

councillor
n lit: alderman, committee member, congressman, elder, representative, senator.

counsel
n lit: advice, direction, guidance, information, recommendations, suggestions; advocate, barrister, lawyer; adviser, consultant.
vb lit: advise, advocate, recommend, urge.

counsellor
n lit: adviser, barrister, consultant; doctor, specialist, therapist.

count
n lit: calculation, computation, reckoning; amount, sum, total; poll; charge, item, unit.
vb lit: add (up), calculate, compute, number, reckon (up), score, tally, total (up); consider, deem, judge, regard as, think; include (among); *fig*: be of account, matter, signify.

counter
n lit: bar, surface, table, top; chip, disc, tiddlywink, token; defence, parry, shield.
vb lit: answer, hit back, parry, react, reply, resist, respond, retaliate, ward off.
adj lit: adverse, contrary, opposing; against, opposed; contradictory, contrasting.
adv lit: adversely, contrarily; against, versus; in defiance of.

country
n lit: kingdom, land, nation, state, territory; area, region, zone; geography, terrain; countryside, farmland, provinces, rural areas; *fig*: electors, populace, voters.

coup
n lit: insurrection, putsch, revolt, revolution, takeover; feat, masterstroke, scoop, tour de force.

couple
n lit: brace, duet, duo, pair, twosome; one or two; few.
vb lit: clasp, connect, hitch, join, link, yoke; marry, unite; copulate, have intercourse, mate.

courage
n lit: audacity, boldness, bottle, bravery, daring, gallantry, grit, guts, nerve, pluck, valour.

course
n lit: bearing, channel, direction, heading, line, path, route, track, trajectory, way; advancement, progress, progression, sequence, succession; manner, mode,

policy, procedure; duration, elapsing, passing, term, time; classes, curriculum, lectures, programme, studies; circuit, lap, links, track; layer, stratum; *spec*: peal, set (of changes in bell-ringing).
vb lit: dash, flow, race, scud, scurry, stream, surge; chase, hunt, pursue.

court
n lit: cloister, quadrangle, square, yard; hall, manor; assizes, bar, bench, lawcourt, tribunal; attendants, cortege, entourage, retinue, suite; homage.
vb lit: date, go steady with, take out, woo; attract, draw upon oneself, invite, provoke; curry favour with, fawn upon, flatter, solicit.

courteous
adj lit: attentive, civil, courtly, gallant, gracious, polite, refined, respectful, urbane, well-bred.

cover
n lit: canopy, cap, coating, dress, envelope, jacket, lid, sheath, top, wrapper; camouflage, concealment, protection, shelter; cloak, disguise, mask, screen, veil; *fig*: indemnity, insurance.
vb lit: clothe, coat, dress, envelop, wrap up; camouflage, cloak, conceal, enshroud, hide, house, mask, obscure, screen, veil; defend, protect, shelter, shield; engulf, flood, immerse, submerge; *fig*: guarantee, indemnify, insure; comprehend, contain, embrace, encompass, include, incorporate, involve, take account of; describe, detail, recount, relate; double for, stand in for, substitute for; counterbalance, make up for; pass through, travel over.

covetous
adj lit: avaricious, envious, grasping, greedy, grudging, jealous, rapacious.

cowardly
adj lit: chicken-hearted, craven, faint-hearted, gutless, lily-livered, pusillanimous, spineless, timid, timorous, weak, yellow-bellied.

cower
vb lit: cringe, crouch, flinch, grovel, quail, quake, skulk, sneak.

coy
adj lit: arch, coquettish, flirtatious, kittenish, skittish; bashful, demure, modest, reserved, retiring, self-effacing.

crack
n lit: chink, cleft, cranny, crevice, fissure, rift, split; defect, flaw, weakness; detonation, firing, report, shot; bang, blow, clip, thump, whack; *fig*: bit of fun, jape, lark, laugh; gag, joke, quip; dig, gibe, sneer; attempt, bash, go, try; *spec*: first light (of dawn).
vb lit: chip, fracture, split; crash, make a sharp noise, snap; bang, buffet, clip, thump, whack; *fig*: give way, yield; break down, collapse, go to pieces; decipher, resolve, solve, work out; become shrill, break, falter; *spec*: break open (a safe).

cracker
n lit: biscuit, wafer, water-biscuit; banger, firework; *fig*: beauty, corker, looker, smasher.

cradle
n lit: bassinet, crib, rocker; framework, gantry, mounting, stand, support, trestle; trolley; *fig*: birthplace, fount, origin, source.
vb lit: hold in one's arms, nurse, rock; care for, look after, nurture, tend; hold up, prop up, support.

craft
n lit: art, artistry, dexterity, expertise, know-how, skill, workmanship; handiwork, work; calling, line, occupation, trade, vocation; cunning, guile, subterfuge, subtlety, trickery; aeroplane, aircraft, airship, boat, ship, spaceship, vessel.

crafty
adj lit: canny, cunning, deceitful, devious, scheming, sly, subtle, wily.

cramp
n lit: crick, muscle contraction, pain, spasm, stiffness, stitch.
vb lit: confine, cram, crowd, jam, pack, restrict, squeeze; *fig*: constrain, hamper, hinder, inhibit.

crane
n lit: boom, derrick, hoist, winch; outlet pipe; egret, heron, stork; *spec*: (camera) platform.
vb lit: raise, stretch.

crank
n lit: handle, lever, starting-handle, turning-bar; push, turn, wind; *fig*: crotchet, eccentric, obsessive, oddity, weirdo.

vb lit: turn, turn over, wind; *fig*: try to start; speed (up).

crash
n lit: bang, detonation, explosion, loud noise, thud; accident, collision, pile-up, smash; collapse, depression, disaster, failure, fiasco.
vb lit: bang, clash, detonate, explode, make a loud noise, thunder; break, fracture, shatter, shiver, smash; fall headlong (into), hurtle (into), pitch (into), plunge (into); drive (into), have an accident, plough (into), wreck; smash (through); collapse, fold up, go bust, go under; *fig*: flop (out on a bed).

crate
n lit: box, case, packing-case, tea-chest; *fig*: kite, plane; banger, heap, rust-bucket.
vb lit: box (up), encase, pack (up).

crater
n lit: basin, bowl, mouth, top; circular depression, hole, impact area.

craving
n lit: desire, hunger, longing, lust, thirst. yearning.

crawl
n lit: shuffle, slither, wriggle; dawdle, plod; *spec*: freestyle (swimming stroke).
vb lit: creep, move on all fours, shuffle, slither, wriggle; dawdle, inch along, move at a snail's pace; move furtively, move stealthily; swarm (with), teem (with); abase oneself, grovel, toady.

crazy
adj lit: demented, deranged, insane, lunatic, mad, mental, unbalanced, unhinged; bananas, barmy, bats, bonkers, certifiable, cracked, crackers, cuckoo, loony, not all there, nuts, off one's rocker, potty, round the twist, touched; absurd, asinine, bird-brained, cockeyed, half-baked, idiotic, inane, irresponsible, ludicrous, nonsensical, preposterous, scatterbrained, senseless, unworkable; bizarre, eccentric, odd, outrageous, peculiar, weird; *fig*: fanatical (about), wild (about); berserk (about), hysterical (about), spare; *spec*: asymmetrical, irregular (paving).

creak
n lit: grating, grinding; squeak, squeal.
vb lit: grate, grind, rasp; groan, squeak, squeal.

cream
n lit: milk-fat, top of the milk; emulsion; ointment, paste, salve; purée; *fig*: best, choice, élite, pick.
vb lit: off-white, yellowish; *spec*: sweet (sherry).

creamy
adj lit: buttery, milky; smooth, soft; oily; off-white, yellowish.

crease
n lit: fold, tuck; furrow, groove, wrinkle; corrugation; *spec*: (lacrosse-player's) circle; (batsman's/hockey-player's) line.
vb lit: crinkle, crumple, fold, ruck up, rumple, wrinkle; *spec*: fold (up with laughter); graze (with a bullet).

create
vb lit: bring about, bring into existence, cause, devise, dream up, form, generate, invent, make, originate, produce; constitute, dub, establish, found, set up; coin, initiate; *fig*: rant, rave.

creation
n lit: cosmos, life, nature, universe, world; formation, generation, making, origination, production; constitution, establishing, foundation, laying down, setting up; achievement, invention, mode, piece, style, work.

creative
adj lit: fertile, imaginative, ingenious, inventive, original, productive.

creature
n lit: being, living thing, organism; animal, beast, brute;

credibility
n lit: believability, plausibility, trustworthiness; integrity.

credit
n lit: belief, confidence, faith, trust; clout, influence, position, prestige, standing; esteem, regard, repute; acclaim, acknowledgement, approval, commendation, honour, merit, thanks; source of pride (to); (on) account, (on) hire-purchase; plus balance, (in) the black.
vb lit: accept, believe, buy, fall for, swallow; acknowledge (as being), honour (with being); ascribe (to), attribute (to), chalk up (to).

creditor
n lit: investor, lender, mortgagee.

creep
n lit: bootlicker, crawler, flatterer, sycophant, toady, yes-man; gradual movement; *spec*: deformation, distortion (of materials under stress).
vb lit: crawl, move on all fours, slither, squirm, wriggle; crawl, dawdle, edge, inch along; skulk, slink, sneak, steal; fawn, grovel, suck up to, toady; *spec*: deform, distort (under stress).

creepy
adj lit: eerie, ghostly, ghoulish, hair-raising, macabre, nightmarish, scary, sinister, weird.

cremate
vb lit: be consumed by fire, burn, incinerate.

crew
n lit: company, complement, hands; oarsmen; personnel, staff; band, gang, squad, team; bunch, crowd, horde, lot, mob, pack.

crib
n lit: bassinet, cot, bin, manger, rack; crate, box; pen, stall; cradle, framework, trestle; notes, translation; plagiarism.
vb lit: use notes, use a translation; pirate, plagiarize; pilfer, steal; box, cage, confine, coop up, pen, shut in.

crime
n lit: felony, malfeasance, misdeed, misdemeanour, offence, transgression; lawbreaking, misconduct, villainy; evil, sin, wickedness, wrong.

criminal
n lit: crook, felon, lawbreaker, offender, transgressor, villain; con, convict, jailbird, lag.
adj lit: bent, crooked, felonious, illegal, unlawful; *fig*: deplorable, outrageous, scandalous.

cripple
n lit: amputee, disabled person, handicapped person, hemiplegic, paralysed person, paraplegic, quadriplegic, wheelchair case.
vb lit: disable, incapacitate, lame, maim, mutilate, paralyse; *fig*: damage, impair, put out of action, spoil.

crisis
n lit: climax, crunch, crux, culmination, point of no return, turning-point; situation, emergency, exigency, extremity, plight, predicament, straits.

crisp
n lit: potato slice; crackling, scratching(s).
adj lit: brittle, crunchy; brief, brusque, incisive, succinct, terse; bracing, brisk, fresh; dapper, neat, spruce, tidy.

criterion
n lit: benchmark, gauge, norm, standard, touchstone, yardstick.

critic
n lit: commentator, pundit, reviewer; authority, connoisseur, expert; detractor, fault-finder, knocker.

critical
adj lit: climactic, dire, emergency, exigent, extreme, grave, hairy, precarious, urgent; crucial, decisive, pivotal, psychological, vital; analytical, diagnostic; derogatory, disparaging.

criticism
n lit: analysis, appreciation, assessment, commentary, critique, notice, review; censure, flak, knocking, strictures.

criticize
vb lit: analyse, appreciate, assess, comment upon, pass judgement on, review; censure, disparage, find fault with, knock, pan, pick to pieces, slate.

croak
n lit: caw, squawk, wheeze.
vb lit: caw, grunt, squawk, wheeze; *fig*: complain, grouse, grumble, moan; die, expire, kick the bucket, pass over.

crockery
n lit: ceramic wares, domestic pottery, earthenware; dishes, jars, plates, pots and pans, saucers, settings, vases.

crook
n lit: angle, bend, curve, loop; crosier, hook, shepherd's staff; *fig*: criminal, felon, swindler, thief, villain.

crooked
adj lit: bent, curved, hooked, looped, meandering, tortuous, winding; bowed, crippled, hunched; deformed, disfigured, distorted, misshapen, warped; askew, at an angle, awry, lopsided, slanting, uneven; *fig*: deceitful,

dishonest, fraudulent, treacherous, underhand, unscrupulous.

crop
n lit: fruits, harvest, produce, yield; riding whip; *spec*: craw (of certain birds); handle (of a whip).
vb lit: clip, cut, lop, mow, shear, shorten, snip, trim; browse on, graze; *fig*: come (up), pop (up), turn (up).

cross
n lit: crucifix, rood; crossing, intersection, junction; halfbreed, hybrid, mixture, mongrel; *fig*: affliction, burden, grief, trial.
vb lit: intersect, meet; bridge, extend over, pass over, span; ford, go over, get over, traverse; hybridize, interbreed, mix; foil, frustrate, impede, oppose, thwart.
adj lit: oblique, transverse; adverse, opposing; *fig*: angry, annoyed, grumpy, ill-humoured, impatient, peeved, snappish, sullen, surly, testy, waspish.

cross-eyed
adj lit: squinting, strabismal, strabismic; *fig*: myopic, short-sighted; blind.

crossroads
n lit: intersection, junction, meeting; *fig*: critical situation, crunch, point of no return, turning-point.

crowbar
n lit: hook, jemmy, lever.

crowd
n lit: army, flock, herd, host, mass, mob, multitude, pack, press, swarm, throng; bunch, clique, group, set; attendance, gate, spectators; masses, populace, public; plebs, proletariat, rabble.
vb lit: assemble, cluster, congregate, flock, muster, swarm, throng; cram, huddle, mass, press, push, surge; congest, pack, pile into, squeeze into; elbow, jostle, shove.

crowded
adj (pa.pt) lit: congested, cramped, full, packed, swarming, teeming.

crown
n lit: chaplet, coronet, diadem, tiara; monarch, sovereign; king, queen; apex, crest, pinnacle, summit, top, zenith; cranium, pate; *fig*: championship, prize, trophy; consummation, fulfilment, perfection; *spec*: corona (of a tooth, of a plant).

vb lit: make king, make queen; *fig*: invest, reward; festoon, garland; cap, consummate, fulfil, perfect, round off; cuff, hit, thump, whack.

crucial
adj lit: critical, decisive, pivotal, psychological, vital.

crucify
vb lit: fix to a cross; *fig*: torment, torture; pan, slate, tear to pieces, wipe the floor with.

cruel
adj lit: barbarous, bloodthirsty, brutal, callous, fierce, hard-hearted, harsh, heartless, implacable, inhuman, inhumane, merciless, pitiless, relentless, ruthless, sadistic, savage, unfeeling, unnatural, vicious.

cruelty
n lit: barbarity, bloodthirstiness, brutality, callousness, ferocity, fiendishness, harshness, heartlessness, inhumanity, murderousness, ruthlessness, sadism, savagery, viciousness.

cruise
n lit: boat trip, sail, pleasure-trip, voyage.
vb lit: go on a sea voyage to, sail round; coast, drift, freewheel; glide, travel smoothly.

crumb
n lit: morsel, scrap; bit, shred, snippet.

crumble
vb lit: break up, decompose, disintegrate, fall apart; crush, fragment, grind, triturate; *fig*: collapse, go to pieces.

crumple
vb lit: crease, rumple, scrumple, wrinkle; break, collapse, give way; *fig*: cave in, yield; break down, go to pieces.

crusade
n lit: campaign, drive, movement; evangelizing mission; holy war, jihad.

crush
n lit: crowd, jam, press, squash, surge, throng.
vb lit: compact, compress, crumble, crumple, grind, mangle, mash, mill, pound, squeeze; embrace, hug, press; conquer, overpower, overwhelm, rout, trounce; oppress, put down, quell, subdue, suppress; *fig*: abash, chagrin, humiliate, mortify, shame.

crust
n lit: coating, covering, skin, surface; scab; mantle; dough, pastry; *fig*: effrontery, gall, impudence, nerve.

crutch
n lit: prop, stick, support; crotch, groin.

cry
n lit: bellow, holler, scream, screech, shout, shriek, whoop, yell; bawl, weep; petition, prayer, supplication; proclamation; slogan, watchword; *spec*: call, sound (of an animal).
vb lit: bellow, call out, holler, scream, screech, shout, shriek, sing out, ululate, whoop, yell; advertise, announce, broadcast, hawk, proclaim, publish, trumpet; bawl, blubber, greet, shed tears, weep.

cuddle
n lit: embrace, hug; kiss, pet, smooch, snog.
vb lit: embrace, hug; nestle, snuggle; grope, fondle, pet, smooch, snog.

cuddly
adj lit: embraceable, huggable, lovable, soft, warm.

cudgel
n lit: billy-club, bludgeon, club, cosh, knobkerrie, nightstick, shillelagh, truncheon.
vb lit: bash, batter, bludgeon, cosh, set upon, thrash, thump; *spec*: rack (one's brains).

cuff
n lit: wristband; turn-up; box on the ear, clip, smack; *fig*: bracelet(s), handcuff(s).
vb lit: box the ears of, clip round the ear, smack one's head.

cul-de-sac
n lit: blind alley, dead end; *fig*: impasse.

culprit
n lit: guilty party, malefactor, miscreant, offender, transgressor.

cultivate
vb lit: farm, tend, till, work; grow, plant; *fig*: civilize, develop, elevate, enrich, foster, improve, refine, train; associate with, consort with, court.

cultivated
adj (pa.pt) lit: arable, planted, tilled, worked; grown, nurtured, tended; *fig*: developed, fostered, improved, trained; civilized, cultured, discriminating,
genteel, lettered, polished, refined, urbane.

culture
n lit: civilization, life-style, society, way of life; arts; education, enlightenment, erudition, polish, refinement, taste; agronomy, cultivation, farming, tillage; *spec*: growth (of bacteria etc. for experiment).

cultured
adj lit: civilized, enlightened, genteel, lettered, polished, refined; erudite, highbrow, scholarly, well-read, well-versed.

cunning
adj lit: artful, canny, crafty, devious, foxy, sharp, shrewd, smart, subtle, wily; clever, deft, dextrous, ingenious.

cup
n lit: beaker, glass, mug, teacup; chalice, goblet; trophy, vase; bra, support.

cupboard
n lit: cabinet, closet, dresser, press.

curb
n lit: chain, control, rein, strap; brake, check, restraint; *spec*: tumour (on a horse's leg).
vb lit: check, constrain, control, inhibit, muzzle, repress, restrict, suppress.

cure
n lit: antidote, medicine, remedy, specific, treatment; spiritual care; *spec*: preservation (of meats).
vb lit: correct, heal, mend, remedy, restore; *spec*: dry, pickle, salt, smoke.

curious
adj lit: enquiring, inquisitive, questioning, searching; meddling, nosy, prying; novel, quaint; bizarre, extraordinary, odd, peculiar, singular, strange, unorthodox, unusual.

curl
n lit: coil, ringlet, widow's peak; kink, twist; whorl.
vb lit: bend, coil, curve, loop, turn; entwine, ripple, spiral, twirl, twist, wind; crinkle, frizz, perm.

currency
n lit: exchange, money; circulation, exposure, popularity, vogue.

current
n lit: draught, drift, flow, stream, tide; *fig*: mood, tendency, trend.

adj lit: contemporary, ongoing, popular, present, present-day, up-to-the-minute; in, in fashion, trendy; circulating, common knowledge.

curse
n lit: execration, expletive, oath, obscenity, swear-word; anathema, evil eye, hex, jinx, malediction; affliction, calamity, disaster, misfortune, plague; *fig*: menstrual period, menstruation.
vb lit: blaspheme; swear; anathematize, damn, excommunicate; *fig*: blight, burden, plague, torment.

curt
adj lit: brusque, concise, short, succinct, terse; abrupt, blunt, sharp, summary, tart, ungracious.

curtail
vb lit: abbreviate, cut short, dock, lop, reduce, shorten, truncate.

curved
adj (pa.pt) lit: bent, bowed, hooked, humped, looping, rounded, sinuous, tortuous, winding.

cushioned
adj (pa.pt) lit: padded, protected; broken, deadened, softened.

custodian
n lit: attendant, caretaker, curator, guard, guardian, jailer, janitor, keeper, security officer, warden; bearer, owner, possessor.

custody
n lit: care, charge, guardianship, keeping, preservation, protection, ward; confinement, detention, remand; ownership, possession.

custom
n lit: convention, fashion, form, observance, practice, rule, usage; habit, routine, wont; clientele, goodwill, patrons, trade.

customary
adj lit: accepted, common, conventional, established, general, normal, ordinary, regular, routine, usual.

customer
n lit: buyer, client, patron, purchaser, shopper; habitué, regular; *fig*: character, citizen, cuss.

cut
n lit: gash, incision, laceration, nick, rip, slash, slit; chop, joint, steak; blow, knock, hit, slice; fashion, mode, shape, style;

percentage, portion, rake-off, ration, share; decrease, economy, reduction, saving; *fig*: dig, gibe, slight; *spec*: (short) way.
vb lit: gash, incise, lacerate, nick, rip, slash, slit; chop, dice; carve, chisel, engrave, saw, sculpt, whittle; clip, dock, hack, hew, lop, mow, reap, shear, trim; divide, sever, slice (through), split (off); axe, decrease, economize on, reduce, save on; abbreviate, curtail, edit out, shorten, truncate; *fig*: cold-shoulder, ignore, ostracize, send to Coventry, snub.
adj (pa.pt) lit: incised, lacerated, ripped, slit; chopped; carved, engraved, sculpted, whittled; clipped, docked, lopped, shorn, trimmed; culled, harvested, mown, reaped; cleft, divided, severed, sliced, split; axed, decreased, reduced; abridged, curtailed, edited, shortened, truncated; *fig*: cold-shouldered, ostracized, slighted, snubbed.

cutlet
n lit: chop, rib, steak; burger, schnitzel.

cut off
vb lit: excise, remove, sever; amputate; isolate, separate; disconnect, interrupt, obstruct; bring to a halt, discontinue, suspend; *fig*: disinherit, disown.

cutting
n lit: channel, excavation, gorge, open tunnel, rock passage; clipping, newspaper article; scion, shoot, slip, stem; record, recording.
adj (pr.pt) lit: arctic, biting, chill, penetrating, piercing, raw, sharp; *fig*: acid, barbed, caustic, pointed, scathing, trenchant; ironic, sarcastic.

cycle
n lit: circle, orbit, period, phases, revolution, rotation; course, series, set; alternation, recurrence; bike, trike.

cylinder
n lit: pipe, tube; drum, revolving chamber, roller; piston chamber.

cynic
n lit: misanthrope; disbeliever, sceptic; pessimist.

cynical
adj lit: misanthropic; disbelieving, distrustful, sceptical; ironic, sarcastic, sardonic, scornful; pessimistic.

D

dabble
vb lit: paddle, splash, wade; spatter, spray, sprinkle; daub; have a go (at), play (at), trifle (in).

dad
n lit: da, father, guv'nor, old man, pa, papa, pater.

daily
n lit: newspaper, paper; char, cleaner, domestic, help, maid, woman.
adj lit: diurnal, quotidian; circadian, 24-hour; day-to-day, everyday, ordinary, regular, routine.
adv lit: day by day, every day, once a day; ordinarily, regularly, routinely.

dainty
n lit: delicacy, morsel, titbit; cake, slice, sweet, tart.
adj lit: delicate, elegant, graceful, gracile, neat, petite; choosy, fastidious, fussy, particular, scrupulous; delectable, delicious, palatable, tasty.

dam
n lit: barrage, barrier, dyke, embankment, wall; reservoir, water supply; hydroelectric project.
vb lit: barricade, block up, hold back, hold in, restrain, restrict, stem.

damage
n lit: harm, hurt, impairment, injury; destruction, devastation; *fig*: cost, expense, price, sum; reparation(s).
vb lit: harm, hurt, impair, injure; mutilate, ruin, spoil, vandalize, wreck.

damaging
adj (pr.pt) lit: detrimental, harmful, injurious, ruinous.

damnable
adj lit: accursed, despicable, detestable, hateful, outrageous, pernicious, wicked.

damning
adj (pr.pt) lit: condemnatory, fatal; implicating, incriminating, indicting.

damp
n lit: clamminess, dankness, humidity, moisture; dew, fog, mist, vapour, water;

fig: chill, cold water, gloom, restraint.
vb lit: moisten, wet; water (down); *fig*: chill, deject, depress, dispirit, inhibit, restrain, stifle.
adj lit: clammy, dank, humid, moist, muggy, wet; dewy, foggy, misty; dripping, sodden, soggy, sopping.

dance
n lit: ball, dinner, disco, hop, party, social, thé-dansant; measure, step; ballet.
vb lit: take the floor, trip the light fantastic; boogie, bop, frug, jive, rock, shimmy; cavort, jig, leap, pirouette, prance, spin, sway, swing; *fig*: dart, flicker, flit, twinkle.

danger
n lit: peril; hazard, jeopardy, risk; menace, threat.

dangerous
adj lit: dicey, perilous; hairy, hazardous, precarious, risky; menacing, nasty, threatening, ugly.

dangle
vb lit: droop, flop, hang, hang down, sag, swing, trail; brandish, flaunt, flourish, wave; *fig*: follow (after), hang (around), put temptation (before).

dappled
adj lit: flecked, freckled, mottled, pied, spotted, variegated.

dare
n lit: challenge; bet, wager.
vb lit: challenge, throw down the gauntlet; be bold enough (to), have the audacity (to), risk, stake, venture.

daring
n lit: audacity, boldness, bravery, courage, dauntlessness, derring-do, grit, guts, intrepidity, nerve, spirit, temerity, valour.
adj (pr.pt) lit: audacious, bold, brave, courageous, dauntless, gritty, gutsy, intrepid, nerveless, spirited, temerarious, venturesome.

dark

adj lit: brunette, dusky, ebony, swarthy; black, night-time, nocturnal, unlit; dim, dingy, murky, overcast, threatening; bleak, drab, gloomy, grim, sombre; *fig*: doleful, morbid, mournful; cryptic, deep, enigmatic, mysterious, obscure, occult; diabolical, evil, foul, hellish, infernal, satanic, sinister, wicked; forbidding, glowering, ominous, sulky, sullen; ignorant, unenlightened, untaught.

darken

vb lit: blacken, cloud over, dim; shade, shadow; eclipse; *fig*: cast a pall over, depress, sadden; become harsh.

darling

n lit: adored, angel, apple of one's eye, beloved, chérie, dearest, light of one's life, love, precious, sweetheart, treasure; blue-eyed boy, favourite, pet.

darn

vb lit: cobble, mend, repair, sew up, stitch together.

dash

n lit: élan, flair, panache, style; dart, race, run, sprint; drop, hint, pinch, smack, suggestion, touch.
vb lit: fling, hurl, sling, throw; dart, fly, race, run, speed, sprint; shatter, shiver, smash; *fig*: blight, confound, disappoint, foil, frustrate, spoil, thwart.

dashboard

n lit: fascia, instrument panel.

dashing

adj (pr.pt) lit: dapper, debonair, elegant, flamboyant, gallant, jaunty, smart, stylish, swashbuckling.

data

n lit: facts, figures, information, statistics.

date

n lit: day, time; age, era, period; assignation, meeting, rendezvous, tryst; boyfriend, friend, girlfriend, steady; *spec*: (out of) fashion, style; (to) now; (up-to-)the-minute.
vb lit: estimate the age of, fix the period of; come (from), have existed (from), originate (from); obsolesce; go out with, go steady with.

dawn

n lit: daybreak, sunrise, sun-up; morning; *fig*: advent, birth, genesis, origin, outset, rise.
vb lit: break, brighten, lighten; *fig*: begin, develop, emerge, originate, rise; hit, strike.

dawn on

vb lit: hit, occur to, register on, strike.

day

n lit: 24 hours; date, hours of daylight, time; age, era, generation, period.

dazed

adj (pa.pt) lit: befuddled, confused, disorientated, dizzy, groggy, stunned, unstable, unsteady, woozy.

dazzle

vb lit: be blinding for, be too bright for, blind; *fig*: awe, hypnotise, overawe, overpower, overwhelm.

dead

n lit: deceased, defunct, departed; *spec*: depth, middle (of night, of winter).
adj lit: deceased, defunct, departed, perished; cold, inanimate, lifeless, still; extinct, past; barren, inactive, obsolete, sterile; *fig*: inoperative, unproductive, useless; apathetic, frigid, glazed, indifferent, numb, paralysed, soulless, wooden; shattered, spent, worn out; empty; not in play; boring, dull, flat, uninteresting; absolute, complete, total; certain, sure.

deadly

adj lit: deathly, fatal, lethal, mortal; destructive, pernicious, poisonous, venomous; *fig*: grim, implacable, relentless, ruthless; accurate, precise, unerring; boring, monotonous, tedious, uninteresting.

deaf

adj lit: hard of hearing, unable to hear; *fig*: indifferent (to), oblivious (to), unresponsive (to).

deafening

adj (pr.pt) lit: ear-splitting, penetrating, piercing, resounding, stentorian, thunderous.

deal

n lit: agreement, arrangement, contract, transaction, understanding; amount, degree, extent, portion, proportion, share; distribution.

vb lit: bargain, do business (with), trade (in), traffic (in); allot, dispense, distribute, divide, give (out), share (out); cope (with), have to do (with).

dealer
n lit: merchant, trader, wholesaler; peddler, pusher; dispenser, distributor.

dear
n lit: angel, beloved, darling, love, precious, sweetheart, treasure.
adj lit: beloved, cherished, darling, precious, treasured; close, familiar, intimate; esteemed, respected, valued; costly, expensive.
adv lit: at a high price; considerably, very much.

death
n lit: decease, demise, departure, expiration, passing, release; bereavement, loss; mortality; grim reaper; *fig*: annihilation, destruction, end, extermination, extinction, ruination, undoing; *spec*: (in at the) kill.

debacle (débâcle)
n lit: catastrophe, disaster, fiasco; defeat, rout, ruination, thrashing; reversal, setback.

debate
n lit: consideration, deliberation, meditation; dialogue, discussion, talk; argument, contention, dispute.
vb lit: consider, deliberate, meditate over; discuss, talk over; argue, contend, dispute, wrangle over.

debility
n lit: feebleness, frailty, infirmity, sickliness, weakness.

debit
n lit: debt, liability, minus entry, overdraft, owed amount.
vb lit: deduct from, draw out of, subtract from, take from.

debris
n lit: detritus, dross, fragments, litter, remains, rubble, ruins, wreckage.

debt
n lit: arrears, due, liability, obligation, owed amount; debit, overdraft; (in) the red.

decadence
n lit: decay, decline, degeneracy, degeneration, deterioration, fall, moral debasement, retrogression.

decapitate
vb lit: behead, chop off one's head, cut off one's head.

decay
n lit: atrophy, wasting, withering; decomposition, mortification, putrefaction, putrescence, rot, rotting; caries; mould; decadence, decline, degeneracy, degeneration, deterioration, disintegration.
vb lit: atrophy, waste, wither; corrode, decompose, mortify, putrefy, putresce, rot; crumble, decline, degenerate, deteriorate, disintegrate, moulder.

deceitful
adj lit: crafty, cunning, deceptive, dishonest, dissimulating, duplicitous, false, fraudulent, sly, treacherous, underhand, untrustworthy.

deceive
vb lit: bamboozle, cheat, con, double-cross, dupe, fool, hoax, lead up the garden, swindle, take in, trick.

decent
adj lit: decorous, genteel, mannerly, modest, nice, polite, presentable, proper, refined, respectable; becoming, fitting, seemly; friendly, generous, helpful, kind, obliging; adequate, ample, competent, fair, reasonable, satisfactory.

deception
n lit: cheating, chicanery, deception, dissimulation, duplicity, fraudulence, legerdemain, swindling, treachery, trickery; artifice, fake, feint, fraud, hoax, imposture, lie, pretence, ruse, stratagem, subterfuge, swindle, trick.

deceptive
adj lit: ambiguous, ambivalent, fallacious, illusory, misleading, specious, unreliable, untrustworthy.

decide
vb lit: come to a conclusion, conclude, determine, make up one's mind, resolve; adjudicate, arbitrate, choose, elect, settle.

decidedly
adv lit: clearly, definitely, distinctly, downright, firmly, positively, unashamedly, unquestionably.

decipher
vb lit: break, crack, decode, figure out, interpret, make sense of, read, translate, unravel.

decision
n lit: conclusion, resolution; arbitration, choice, judgement, settlement; ruling, verdict; firmness, finality, resolve, strength of purpose.

decisive
adj lit: conclusive, definite, definitive, final, positive; firm, forceful, resolute, strong; critical, crucial, fateful.

deck
n lit: floor, planking; level, storey; apparatus, set; *spec*: pack (of cards).
vb lit: adorn, array, beautify, dress, festoon, garland, ornament; rig (out), trick (out).

declaration
n lit: affirmation, announcement, assertion, deposition, proclamation, pronouncement, statement; *spec*: voluntary ending of an innings (in cricket).

declare
vb lit: affirm, announce, assert, depone, proclaim, pronounce, state, testify.

decline
n lit: declivity, depression, downward slope; *fig*: decrease, diminution, downturn, falling off, recession, reduction; decay, degeneration, deterioration, weakening, worsening.
vb lit: descend, dip, sink, slope downwards; *fig*: decrease, diminish, fall off, lessen, shrink, take a downturn; decay, degenerate, deteriorate, weaken, worsen; forgo, reject, say no to, turn down.

decomposition
n lit: breakdown, decay, disintegration, putrefaction, putrescence, rot, rotting.

décor
n lit: colour scheme, decoration, furnishings; stage scenery.

decoration
n lit: adornment, elaboration, embellishment, garnish, ornamentation, tinsel, trimmings; bauble, flourish, frill, ornament; award, colours, medal, order, ribbon.

decoy
n lit: bait, enticement, lure, trap.
vb lit: allure, ensnare, entice, entrap, lure, seduce.

decrease
n lit: abatement, decline, diminution, drop, easing, falling off, lessening, reduction, shrinking, slackening, subsidence, waning.
vb lit: abate, decline, diminish, drop, ease, fall off, lessen, shrink, slacken, subside, wane; make less, reduce.

decrepit
adj lit: aged, debilitated, doddery, feeble, infirm, senile, weak; battered, dilapidated, ramshackle, rickety, shaky, worn down.

dedicated
adj (pa.pt) lit: committed, consecrated, devoted, sworn; single-minded, wholehearted, zealous; purpose-built, single-function, specific.

deduce
vb lit: conclude, derive, gather, infer, understand; extrapolate.

deduct
vb lit: decrease by, remove, subtract, take away, take out, withdraw.

deduction
n lit: conclusion, corollary, extrapolation, inference, reasoning, rider; debit, decrease, reduction, subtraction, withdrawal.

deed
n lit: act, action, exploit, feat; fact, reality, truth; contract, instrument, title.

deep
adj lit: abyssal, yawning; broad, wide; *fig*: extreme, great, intense, profound; abstruse, cryptic, esoteric, mysterious, obscure; absorbed, engrossed, immersed, rapt; discerning, penetrating, sagacious, wise; erudite, learned; artful, canny, cunning, devious, knowing, shrewd; *spec*: bass, low, resonant (voice); dark, rich, strong (colour).

deer
n lit: buck, doe, fawn, hart, hind, stag.

deface
vb lit: disfigure, impair, mar, mutilate, obliterate, spoil, vandalize.

defamatory
adj lit: calumnious, damaging, denigrating, derogatory, disparaging, libellous, slanderous, vilificatory.

defaulter
n lit: bankrupt, debtor, embezzler, peculator, welsher; fraud; tax dodger; *spec*: military prisoner.

defeat
n lit: beating, overthrow, rout, thrashing, trouncing; discomfiture, failure, rebuff, repulse, reverse, setback; strategic withdrawal.
vb lit: beat, crush, overthrow, rout, thrash, trounce; confound, discomfit, foil, stop, thwart.

defect
n lit: blemish, fault, flaw, imperfection; error, inaccuracy, mistake; absence, deficiency, inadequacy, lack, weakness.
vb lit: change sides, desert, go over (to), run (to).

defective
adj lit: broken, faulty, imperfect, incomplete, inoperative, out of order; lacking, scant, short; retarded, subnormal.

defence
n lit: barricade, bastion, bulwark, fortification; cover, guard, protection, security, shelter, shield; alibi, denial, excuse, explanation, justification, rebuttal, refutation, vindication; *spec*: backs (in field games).

defend
vb lit: barricade, fortify; cover, guard, keep safe, preserve, protect, shelter, shield; champion, justify, speak up for, support, uphold, vindicate.

defensive
adj lit: covering, guarding, preserving, protective, sheltering, shielding; precautionary; hunted, wary; apologetic, explanatory, justificatory.

defer
vb lit: adjourn, hold over, postpone, put off, shelve, suspend; bow (to), give in (to), give way (to), submit (to), yield (to).

deferential
adj lit: compliant, obedient, obsequious, respectful, reverential, servile, submissive, yielding.

defiant
adj lit: contumacious, disobedient, insubordinate, mutinous, rebellious, recalcitrant, refractory, truculent, wilful; bold, challenging, daring.

deficiency
n lit: absence, deficit, inadequacy, incompleteness, insufficiency, lack, scarcity, shortage; failing, shortcoming, weakness.

deficit
n lit: shortage, shortfall; overdraft; arrears.

defile
n lit: canyon, chasm, chine, fissure, gorge, pass, ravine.
vb lit: besmirch, desecrate, dishonour, profane, taint; contaminate, dirty, foul, pollute, soil.

define
vb lit: describe, designate, explain, gloss, interpret, specify, spell out; circumscribe, delineate, limit, mark, set the parameters of.

definite
adj lit: clear, exact, explicit, express, fixed, precise; certain, positive, settled, sure.

definition
n lit: description, designation, interpretation, meaning, specification; clarification, elucidation, explanation; circumscribing, delineation, establishing, fixing; clarity, focus, register, sharpness.

deflate
vb lit: burst, collapse, flatten, go down, pop, puncture; *fig*: chasten, humble, mortify, squash, take down a peg; *spec*: depreciate, devalue (a currency).

deflect
vb lit: avert, edge, fend off, parry, ward off; glance off, ricochet; slew, swerve, turn, veer.

deformed
adj (pa.pt) lit: abnormal, disfigured, malformed, misshapen; distorted, mangled; gross, hideous, twisted, ugly, warped.

deformity
n lit: abnormality, defect, disfigurement, malformation; distortion, mutilation; ugliness.

defunct

adj lit: dead, deceased, expired; obsolete, extinct; inoperative, not in service, out of commission.

defy

vb lit: brave, challenge, confront, face; baffle, defeat, foil, frustrate, resist, thwart; be contumacious towards, be recalcitrant towards, be refractory towards, be truculent towards, disobey, flout, mutiny against, rebel against.

degenerate

vb lit: decline, decrease, lapse, regress, sink, worsen; decay, decompose, deteriorate, disintegrate.
adj lit: corrupt, debased, decadent, regressive, retrogressive; debauched, depraved, dissolute, immoral, perverted.

degrade

vb lit: cheapen, debase, demean, discredit, dishonour; disgrace, humiliate, shame; break, cashier, demote, reduce, relegate; dilute, thin, weaken; break down, decompose; erode away.

degree

n lit: extent, intensity, level, measure, quality, quantity, rate, scale, standard; division, gradation, grade, mark, point, rung, step, unit; class, position, rank, standing, status; *spec*: (university) honour, qualification.

deity

n lit: divinity, god, goddess; almighty, supreme being; immortal; fetish, idol.

dejected

adj (pa.pt) lit: blue, browned off, cheesed off, depressed, despondent, disconsolate, doleful, down, glum, in low spirits, miserable, morose.

delay

n lit: adjournment, deferment, postponement; stay, suspension; hold-up, interval, stoppage, wait.
vb lit: adjourn, defer, postpone, put off, suspend; check, detain, hold up, retard, slow, stop; dally, dawdle, linger, tarry.

delegate

n lit: agent, envoy, representative; legate, nuncio.
vb lit: accredit, authorize, commission, empower; assign, commit to, entrust, give, hand over, transfer.

delegation

n lit: commission, deputation, mission; assignment, commissioning, referral, transference.

delete

vb lit: cut out, edit out, erase, expunge, rub out; cancel, cross out, obliterate, strike out; leave out, omit.

deliberate

vb lit: consider, debate, meditate (over), mull (over), ponder (over), think (over).
adj lit: calculated, conscious, considered, intentional, premeditated, studied, voluntary; measured, methodical, prudent, unhurried.

deliberation

n lit: calculation, consideration, forethought, reflection, study, thought; calmness, coolness, reserve; debate, discussion.

delicacy

n lit: daintiness, elegance, lightness; fastidiousness, finesse, precision; subtlety; fragility, frailty, infirmity; refinement, sensibility, taste; cake, dainty, savoury, sweet, titbit.

delicate

adj lit: dainty, elegant, exquisite, fine, graceful, light; deft, expert, fastidious, precise; diplomatic, discreet, subtle, tactful; fragile, frail, sickly, squeamish, weak; discriminating, prudish, refined, sensitive; critical, difficult, ticklish, touchy; faint, muted, soft, subdued.

delicious

adj lit: appetizing, delectable, luscious, mouthwatering, scrumptious, tasty; delightful, exquisite, pleasing, pleasurable.

delight

n lit: gratification, happiness, pleasure, rapture; gem, joy, prize, treasure.
vb lit: captivate, charm, enchant, gratify, make happy, please, ravish; amuse, divert, entertain.

delightful

adj lit: agreeable, captivating, charming, enchanting, gratifying, pleasant, pleasing, pleasurable; amusing, diverting, entertaining.

delinquent
n lit: criminal, lawbreaker, offender, wrongdoer; defaulter.
adj lit: lax, neglectful, negligent, remiss, slack; behindhand, in arrears, overdue, unpaid; criminal, crooked, felonious, lawless.

delirious
adj lit: babbling, hallucinating, incoherent, rambling, raving, wandering; ecstatic; beside oneself, frenzied, hysterical, wild.

deliver
vb lit: bear, bring, carry, convey, transport; provide, supply; dispense, distribute, give out; give (to), hand over, transfer, turn over (to); cede (to), grant (to), yield (to); administer, deal, inflict; liberate, loose, release, save, set free; present, proclaim, publish, read; strike, throw.

deliverance
n lit: liberation, release, rescue; ransom, redemption.

delivery
n lit: consignment, dispatch, distribution; conveyance, transmittal; supply, transmission; ceding, surrender; liberation, release, rescue; elocution, enunciation, intonation; birth, childbirth, labour; bowl, pitch.

dell
n lit: bottom, combe, depression, dingle, glen, trough, valley.

delusion
n lit: hallucination, misapprehension, misbelief, misconception, self-deception.

demand
n lit: call, need, request, requirement; charge, claim, order, requisition.
vb lit: claim, exact, insist on, request, require; call for, necessitate, need; entail, involve.

demanding
adj (pr.pt) lit: badgering, clamorous, importunate, insistent, pressing; challenging, difficult, exacting, tough, trying.

demeanour
n lit: air, attitude, bearing, comportment, manner, mien; behaviour, conduct.

democratic
adj lit: egalitarian, populist;

proportionally represented.

demolish
vb lit: bulldoze, destroy, flatten, level, pull down, raze, tear down; *fig*: annihilate, defeat, drub, thrash, trounce; confound, overturn, totally disprove, undo; devour, gobble up, put away, stuff away.

demolition
n lit: bulldozing, destruction, levelling, pulling down, wrecking.

demonstrate
vb lit: illustrate, show, teach by example; display, evince, exhibit, make clear, manifest; march, picket, rally.

demonstration
n lit: display, exhibition, illustration, exposition, manifestation, presentation; evidence, proof, testimony; march, parade, picket line, protest.

demonstrative
adj lit: effusive, emotional, expansive, extrovert, gushing, unrestrained; characteristic, illustrative, indicative, symptomatic.

demure
adj lit: grave, prim, prudish, sedate, sober, staid; bashful, modest, retiring, shy; coquettish, coy, skittish.

den
n lit: hideaway, refuge, retreat, sanctuary, study; hideout, hole, lair, nest.

denomination
n lit: designation, name, style, title; category, class, classification, kind, sort, type; grade; size; value; communion, persuasion, religious group, sect.

denounce
vb lit: accuse, arraign, censure, impeach, indict; condemn, inveigh against.

dense
adj lit: close-knit, compact, compressed, solid; substantial, thick; *fig*: blockheaded, bovine, dim, doltish, moronic, obtuse, slow, stolid, stupid.

density
n lit: consistency; body, compactness, homogeneity; bulk, solidity, thickness; *fig*: imbecility, obtuseness, slowness, stupidity; *spec*: specific gravity.

dent
n lit: bend, buckle, concavity, depression, imprint, pit, stamp; notch.
vb lit: bend, buckle, crease, gouge, imprint, push in.

deny
vb lit: disclaim, disown, renounce, repudiate; contradict, gainsay, rebuff, refute; forbid, refuse; begrudge; negate.

depart
vb lit: blow, evaporate, exit, go, go away, leave, move out, scarper, set out, take one's leave, vamoose; disappear, vanish; retire, withdraw; deviate, diverge, stray; swerve (from), veer (from).

department
n lit: bureau, division, office, section; *fig*: business, domain, line, look-out, province, responsibility, sphere.

departure
n lit: exit, going, leaving, moving out, setting out; retiring, withdrawal; deviation, divergence, straying; change, difference, innovation, novelty; *fig*: death, decease, demise; *spec*: latitudinal distance (covered by a ship).

depend
vb lit: bank (on), count (on), lean (on), rely (on); calculate (on), reckon (on); be based (on), be contingent (upon), hinge (upon).

dependent
adj lit: conditional (on), contingent (on); based (on), calculated (on); reliant; feudal, liege.

deplorable
adj lit: disgraceful, disgusting, execrable, outrageous, reprehensible, scandalous; awful, distressing, heart-rending, lamentable, melancholy, saddening.

deposit
n lit: alluvium, dregs, lees, sediment; precipitate; loess, silt; down payment, premium, retainer, stake.
vb lit: lay, place, put, set; drop, settle; bank, lodge, pay in, put in.

depot
n lit: repository, store, warehouse; garage, station; arsenal, base, dump.

depraved
adj (pa.pt) lit: amoral, debauched, degenerate, dissolute, lascivious, licentious, perverted, wicked.

depravity
n lit: amorality, debauchery, degeneracy, lasciviousness, licentiousness, perversion, vice, wickedness.

deprecate
vb lit: lodge a protest against, object to, raise one's voice against; censure, disapprove of; try to avert, try to avoid.

depress
vb lit: lower, press down, push down; cast down, desolate, grieve, sadden; daunt, discourage, dispirit, put off; hinder, retard, slow, weaken; cheapen, debase, devalue, downgrade, reduce.

depressing
adj (pr.pt) lit: distressing, heart-rending, melancholy, saddening; daunting, discouraging, dispiriting, off-putting; retarding, weakening.

depression
n lit: basin, bowl, concavity, dell, dip, hollow, indentation; dejection, desolation, despair, despondency, hopelessness, melancholia, sadness; decline, recession, slump, stagnation.

deprivation
n lit: bereavement, confiscation, dispossession, lack, loss, removal, withdrawal; destitution, hardship, need, privation.

deprive
vb lit: bereave, dispossess, divest; rob, strip; withhold the benefit (of), withhold the use (of).

depth
n lit: breadth, drop, profundity, vertical measure, width; *fig*: intensity, strength; complexity, intricacy, involvement; insight, penetration, perception, sagacity, wisdom; erudition, learning, scholarship; (in the) middle (of), (in the) midst (of); *spec*: low pitch, profundo (of voice); darkness, richness, vibrance (of colour).

deputise
vb lit: act (for), stand in (for), take over (on behalf of); authorize, commission, delegate.

deputy
n lit: agent, delegate, locum, proxy, representative; assistant, lieutenant, second-in-command; relief, stand-in, substitute, understudy; *spec*: legislator,

member of the assembly (in certain countries); safety inspector (in a coal-mine).

deranged
adj (pa.pt) lit: confused, disordered, jumbled; *fig*: crazed, demented, insane, irrational, mentally unbalanced.

derelict
n lit: down-and-out, no-hoper, tramp, vagrant; hulk, skeleton, wreck; abandoned vessel.
adj lit: abandoned, deserted, forsaken; dilapidated, skeletal, ruined, wrecked; failing, lax, negligent, remiss.

derisory
adj lit: contemptuous, jeering, mocking, sarcastic, sardonic, scoffing, scornful; contemptible, laughable, ludicrous, ridiculous, risible; insulting, outrageous.

derivation
n lit: basis, foundation, origin, source; etymology, root; ancestry, genealogy; aetiology, cause; descent, inheritance; acquisition, extraction.

derivative
n lit: by-product, spin-off; offshoot, outgrowth; secondary form, variant; *spec*: differential coefficient (in mathematics).
adj lit: acquired, borrowed, copied, imitative, plagiarized, unoriginal.

descend
vb lit: go down, sink, subside; drop, fall, plummet, plunge; alight, climb down, dismount; pounce (upon), swoop (upon); dip, slant down, slope down; decrease, diminish, lessen, reduce; *fig*: be handed down, be passed on; be derived (from), originate (from), spring (from); lower oneself (to), stoop (to); degenerate, deteriorate, go downhill all the way.

descendants
n lit: children, grandchildren, heirs, inheritors, issue, offspring, posterity, progeny, scions, successors.

descent
n lit: coming down; drop, fall, plunge; alighting, dismount; attack (on), pounce (on), swoop (on); declivity, dip, slant, slope; decrease, diminution, lessening, reduction; *fig*: ancestry, derivation, extraction, genealogy, origin, parentage; degeneration, deterioration, regression.

describe
vb lit: delineate, draw, limn, mark out, outline; characterize, depict, detail, portray, represent; give an account of, relate, tell.

description
n lit: characterization, depiction, portrayal, representation, verbal sketch; account, narration, report, story; appearance, character, look, manner, mien, type, variety.

desert
n lit: waste, wasteland; dunes, sand; maquis, outback, pampas, scrub, veldt, wilderness; tundra; isolation, remoteness, solitude.
vb lit: abandon, forsake, walk out on; jilt, leave in the lurch, maroon, rat on, strand; leave, quit, vacate; abscond, defect, run away.

deserter
n lit: absconder, defector, runaway, truant; escapee, fugitive.

desertion
n lit: abandonment, dereliction; absconding, absence without leave, defection, going AWOL, running away, truancy.

deserve
vb lit: be worthy of, justify, merit, rate, warrant.

design
n lit: draft, drawing, elevation, outline, plan, sketch; blueprint, pattern, template; configuration, figure, form, motif; architecture, graphics, technical drawing; *fig*: aim, end, goal, intention, object, objective, target; enterprise, project, scheme, intrigue(s), machination(s).
vb lit: draft, draw, outline, plan, sketch; contrive, devise, fashion, invent; aim, intend, mean, propose, purpose.

designate
vb lit: appoint, assign, elect, nominate, pick; denote, evidence, indicate, mark out, show; call, dub, entitle, name, style, term.

designing
adj (pr.pt) lit: artful, conniving, conspiring, intriguing, scheming, sly, wily.

desirable
adj lit: alluring, seductive, sexy, tempting; advantageous, beneficial, good, preferable, profitable, useful, welcome.

desire
n lit: ambition, aspiration, hope, wish; craving, hunger, longing, yearning; lechery, libido, lust, orexis, sex drive.
vb lit: entreat, petition, request, solicit; aspire to, hope for, wish for; fancy, set one's heart on, want; crave, hunger for, long for, yearn for; lust after.

desk
n lit: bureau, escritoire, secretary, writing-table; lectern, pulpit; counter, department, kiosk, office, stall; stand.

desolate
adj lit: bare, barren, bereft, isolated, remote, solitary, uninhabited; bleak, cheerless, depressing, dismal, forlorn, gloomy, melancholy; despondent, disconsolate, miserable, unhappy, wretched.

despair
n lit: depression, hopelessness, futility, misery, utter dejection, wretchedness; great disappointment.
vb lit: be depressed, be suicidal; abandon hope (of), give up, lose hope (of).

desperate
adj lit: forlorn, hopeless, suicidal, wretched; critical, dire, drastic, urgent, well-nigh irrecoverable; dangerous, daring, hazardous, risky, wild; determined; frantic.

desperately
adv lit: forlornly, hopelessly, suicidally, wretchedly; critically, direly, drastically, urgently; dangerously, gravely, seriously, severely; *fig*: extremely, very.

despicable
adj lit: beneath contempt, contemptible, deplorable, infamous, low, mean, shameful, sordid, vile.

despise
vb lit: deride, disdain, look down on, look upon with contempt, scorn, spurn.

despite
prp lit: in spite of, notwithstanding, regardless of.

despot
n lit: absolute ruler, autocrat; dictator, oppressor, tyrant; disciplinarian, martinet.

dessert
n lit: afters, pudding, sweet; last course; blancmange, cream, fool, jelly, trifle, whip.

destination
n lit: journey's end, goal, stop, target; *fig*: aim, end, object, objective, purpose.

destined
adj (pa.pt) lit: born, intended, meant; doomed (to be), fated (to be), foreordained (to be); inescapable, inevitable, unavoidable; bound (for), en route (for), making (for).

destiny
n lit: fate, fortune, karma, kismet; doom, nemesis; providence, the gods.

destitute
adj lit: down and out, impoverished, insolvent, needy, penniless, poor, poverty-stricken; bereft (of), devoid (of), empty (of).

destroy
vb lit: abolish, annihilate, dash to pieces, demolish, dismantle, do away with, exterminate, extirpate, kill, pull down, put an end to, ravage, raze, ruin, shatter, smash, tear down, wipe out, wreck.

destruction
n lit: abolition, annihilation, demolition, dismantling, eradication, extermination, extinction, extirpation, killing, massacre, pulling down, ruin, shattering, slaughter, smashing, tearing down, undoing, wreckage.

detach
vb lit: disconnect, disengage, disunite, free, loosen, separate, sever, tear off, unfasten, unhitch; demarcate, designate, pick out, single out.

detachment
n lit: disconnection, disengagement, separation, unfastening; distance, non-involvement; aloofness, remoteness, unconcern; impartiality, neutrality, objectivity; demarcation, designation, selection; *spec*: detail, party, squad, unit (of the armed forces).

detail
n lit: particular(s), small point(s), specific(s), technicality; component, element, factor, item; nicety, trivium;

spec: detachment, party, squad, unit (of
the armed forces).
vb lit: catalogue, enumerate, itemize, list,
specify; describe, give an account,
narrate, recount; designate, detach, pick
out, single out.

detailed
adj (pa.pt) lit: blow-by-blow,
circumstantial, comprehensive,
exhaustive, itemized, minute, particular,
specific, thorough; designated, detached,
selected.

detect
vb lit: discern, distinguish, identify, make
out, notice, perceive, scent, spot, spy;
discover, find, find out, track down,
uncover; *spec*: demodulate (a signal from
its carrier wave).

detective
n lit: CID officer, investigator, plain-
clothes cop, private eye, private
investigator.

deter
vb lit: dissuade, prevent, prohibit, put off,
stop; discourage, inhibit.

detergent
n lit: cleaner, soap, soap flakes, solvent,
washing powder, washing-up liquid.

deterioration
n lit: decline, degeneration, degradation,
detriment, downturn, fall, impairment,
regression, slide, worsening.

determine
vb lit: decide, make up one's mind,
purpose, resolve; ascertain, calculate,
discover, establish, find out, learn, work
out; condition, control, dictate, govern,
regulate, rule; conclude, end, finish,
settle, terminate.

determined
adj (pa.pt) lit: dogged, persevering,
persistent, resolute, steadfast, tenacious,
tireless, unflagging; resolved (to).

detonate
vb lit: ignite, light, set off, touch off; blast,
blow up, explode.

detour
n lit: deviation, diversion;
circumnavigation, digression, excursion,
roundabout way.
vb lit: circumnavigate, deviate round,
digress, find a way round, make a
diversion.

detraction
n lit: disadvantage, drawback,
encumbrance, handicap, impediment,
restriction; belittling, defamation,
denigration, disparagement, obloquy,
slander.

devalue
vb lit: cheapen, debase, degrade;
depreciate, weaken; inflate, make
worthless.

devastating
adj (pr.pt) lit: deadly, pulverizing,
shattering, stunning; caustic, incisive,
sardonic, savage, withering;
overpowering, overwhelming.

develop
vb lit: begin, commence, establish,
generate, invent, originate, start; evolve,
form, grow, mature, progress; breed,
cultivate, foster, promote, rear; contract;
spec: elaborate on, take further (a musical
theme, a chess manoeuvre); print (a
photograph).

development
n lit: advance, evolution, growth, increase,
maturation, progress; circumstance,
event, happening, occurrence, situation;
serial expression.

deviant
n lit: pervert, weirdo; freak, misfit.

deviate
vb lit: be deflected, digress, diverge, err,
stray, turn aside; differ, vary.

device
n lit: apparatus, appliance, contraption,
gadget, instrument, tool; artifice,
contrivance, dodge, gambit, manoeuvre,
ploy, stratagem, strategy, wile; badge,
colophon, emblem, logo, motif,
trademark.

devil
n lit: Evil One; Lucifer, Old Nick, Prince
of Darkness, Satan; demon, fiend; *fig*:
beast, monster, ogre, savage; rascal,
rogue, scoundrel; bastard, beggar,
bugger, chap, sod, unfortunate.

devious
adj lit: artful, calculating, cunning,
indirect, scheming, sly, underhand, wily;
circuitous, erratic, rambling,
roundabout, twisting, winding.

devise
vb lit: contrive, design, dream up, frame, invent, plan, think up, work out; compose, write; bequeath, leave.

devoid
adj lit: barren (of), bereft (of), destitute (of), empty (of), free (of).

devote
vb lit: consecrate, dedicate, pledge; commit, give.

devoted
adj (pa.pt) lit: committed, consecrated, dedicated, pledged; ardent, caring, loving, loyal, true.

devour
vb lit: consume, eat up, get down, polish off, swallow; bolt, cram, gobble, gorge on, stuff oneself with, wolf down; *fig*: destroy, ravage, wipe out; appreciate, be absorbed by, delight in, drink in, enjoy, feast on, take in.

devout
adj lit: ardent, devoted, earnest, fervent, passionate, sincere, zealous; godly, holy, pious, religious; solemn.

dexterity
n lit: address, adroitness, artistry, deftness, expertise, facility, finesse, mastery, proficiency, skill; discrimination, perception, shrewdness.

diabolical
adj lit: devilish, fiendish, hellish, satanic; fiery, shocking; atrocious, damnable, dreadful, outrageous; excruciating.

diagnosis
n lit: analysis, determination, identification, interpretation, prognosis, pronouncement, reading, verdict; considered opinion.

diagonal
n lit: oblique, solidus, virgule.
adj lit: oblique, slanting; at 45 degrees, 45-degree.

diagram
n lit: artwork, chart, graphic, layout, outline, plan; cross-section, exploded view, representation.

dialectic
n lit: logic, ratiocination, reasoning; argumentation, debate, disputation, polemic.

dialogue
n lit: conversation, discourse, discussion; two-way communication; *fig*: lines, script, words.

diatribe
n lit: harangue, stream of abuse, tirade, verbal onslaught; denunciation.

dictate
n lit: behest, command, direction, order, precept, principle, regulation, requirement, rule.
vb lit: compose (a letter), spell out; decree, direct, ordain, prescribe, pronounce; impose, proscribe.

dictator
n lit: absolute ruler, autocrat; despot, tyrant.

dictatorial
adj lit: autocratic, despotic, tyrannical; authoritarian, disciplinarian, imperious, magisterial, oppressive, totalitarian.

diction
n lit: delivery, enunciation, pronunciation, speech; articulation, fluency; elocution, expression, phrasing, syntax, vocabulary.

die
n lit: mould, stamp, template; dice; *spec*: basis, pedestal (for a sculpture or column).
vb lit: breathe one's last, depart this life, expire, fall asleep, give up the ghost, pass away, pass over; cash in one's chips, croak, kick the bucket, peg out, pop one's clogs, snuff it; be killed, be slain, fall, lay down one's life, perish; *fig*: decline, dwindle, ebb, fade, fizzle out, lapse, pass, peter out, run down, sink, stop, subside, wane, wilt, wither; ache (for), hunger (for), long (for).

diet
n lit: fare, food, nourishment, nutriment, subsistence; controlled intake, course of regulated meals, fast, regimen.
vb lit: bant, eat to lose weight, fast, lose weight, slim.

differ
vb lit: be distinct (from), depart (from), diverge (from), vary (from); contend (with), contrast (with), demur (with), take issue (with).

difference

n lit: contrast, disparity, dissimilarity, variation; change, discrepancy, divergence; distinction, exception, particularity, singularity; clash, conflict, contention; contretemps, disagreement, dispute, squabble; balance, remainder, rest; *spec:* modification (on a coat of arms).

different

adj lit: at odds, at variance, contrasting, disparate, diverse, miscellaneous, varied, various; changed, divergent; atypical, distinctive, exceptional, particular, singular, uncommon, unique; clashing, contentious, conflicting, opposed, opposite; additional, distinct, individual, new, other, separate.

differentiate

vb lit: discriminate (between), distinguish (between), tell apart; contrast, mark off, separate; adapt, alter, change, modify; *spec:* specialize (of embryonic cells).

difficult

adj lit: complicated, demanding, intricate, involved, problematical, taxing; arduous, burdensome, hard, laborious, painstaking, strenuous; knotty, thorny, ticklish, uphill; awkward, grim, straitened, trying; fractious, obstreperous, refractory, troublesome, unmanageable; fastidious, fussy, hard to please, pedantic, tiresome.

difficulty

n lit: burden, hardship, labour, strenuousness, toil; complication, hurdle, impediment, obstacle, pitfall, stumbling-block; dilemma, enigma, intricacy, problem, predicament, quandary; fix, jam, mess, pickle, plight, spot of trouble; danger, distress, jeopardy, peril.

diffidence

n lit: doubt, fear, hesitancy, insecurity, timidity; constraint, meekness, reserve, self-consciousness, shyness, timorousness; backwardness, hesitation, reluctance.

diffusion

n lit: dispersal, dissemination, distribution, scattering, spread; homogeneity, infiltration, intermixing, pervasiveness.

dig

n lit: archaeological site, excavation; jab, poke, prod, thrust; *fig:* gibe, sarcastic remark, sneer, taunt, wisecrack.

vb lit: burrow, delve, excavate, mine, quarry, scoop, tunnel; break up, fork, hoe, spade over, till, turn over; jab, poke, prod, thrust; *fig:* go (into), probe (into), research (into); find (out), root (out); appreciate, enjoy, like, understand.

digest

n lit: abstract, condensation, paraphrase, précis, résumé, summary, synopsis.

vb lit: absorb, assimilate, metabolize; abridge, condense, paraphrase, reduce, shorten, summarize; *fig:* consider, contemplate, meditate over, ponder, take in, understand; bear, brook, endure, stand, stomach, tolerate.

digestible

adj lit: assimilable, bland, easily metabolized; *fig:* acceptable, bearable, palatable, tolerable.

digestion

n lit: absorption, assimilation, incorporation, metabolism; *fig:* consideration, contemplation, meditation, pondering; stomach, tolerance level.

digit

n lit: extremity, finger, toe; number, single figure.

dignified

adj (pa.pt) lit: august, decorous, formal, grave, imposing, noble, solemn, stately; lofty, lordly; exalted.

dignify

vb lit: distinguish, elevate, ennoble, exalt, grace, honour.

dignity

n lit: decorum, grandeur, majesty, nobility, solemnity, stateliness; hauteur, loftiness; eminence, honour, importance, rank, standing, status; pride, self-esteem.

digress

vb lit: deviate from the point, go off at a tangent, ramble, stray, wander.

dilapidated

adj (pa.pt) lit: battered, crumbling, decayed, fallen in, falling apart, in ruins, rickety, ruined, ruinous, shaky, tumbledown; neglected, shabby.

dilation

n lit: broadening, expanding, extension, spread, widening; distension, dropsy, enlargement, swelling, turgidity, turgor.

diligence

n lit: application, assiduousness, attentiveness, care, industry, sedulousness; constancy, perseverance.

dilute

vb lit: thin, water down; adulterate, cut, weaken; *fig*: attenuate, mitigate, temper; decrease, lessen, reduce.

adj lit: thin, watered down, watery; adulterated, cut, weakened; insipid, tasteless; *fig*: attenuated, mitigated, tempered; decreased, lessened, reduced.

dim

vb lit: dull, fade out, turn down; become obscure, blur, darken, obscure; tarnish.

adj lit: cloudy, grey, overcast, shadowy; blurred, dark, fuzzy, indistinct, obscure; dingy, dull, opaque, tarnished; pale, weak; *fig*: confused, hazy, vague; depressing, discouraging, gloomy, sombre; dense, obtuse, slow, stupid, thick.

dine

vb lit: eat, feed; have dinner, have lunch, have supper; banquet, feast.

dingy

adj lit: dark, dirty, drab, faded, gloomy, grimy, seedy, shabby, soiled.

dinner

n lit: lunch, supper, tea; banquet, feast, spread; meal, repast.

dip

n lit: immersion, plunge, rinse, soaking; bathe, swim; concavity, dell, depression, gulch, hollow, valley; decline, descent, fall, slip, slump; pickpocket.

vb lit: dunk, immerse, plunge, rinse, soak; bathe, duck; decline, descend, fall, lower, sink, slip, slope down, slump, subside; put a spoon (into), reach (into); bow, curtsey; *fig*: browse (in), glance (into), take a look (in); *spec*: dim (headlights).

diploma

n lit: certificate, charter, document; degree, doctorate; honour.

diplomat

n lit: ambassador, attaché, chargé d'affaires, consul, envoy, foreign office official, government spokesperson,

legate, representative, statesman; mediator, negotiator.

diplomatic

adj lit: ambassadorial, consular, governmental, official, state; politic, prudent; discreet, subtle, tactful.

dire

adj lit: appalling, awful, calamitous, catastrophic, disastrous, horrific, ruinous; dreadful, gloomy, grim, ominous; desperate, drastic, extreme, urgent.

direct

vb lit: guide, indicate how to get (to), lead, point the way (to), show (towards), usher; administer, conduct, control, govern, manage, oversee, rule, run, superintend; command, instruct, order; address, aim, level, point, train; post, route, send.

adj lit: straight, undeviating; face-to-face, head-on, immediate; nonstop, through; blunt, explicit, outspoken, plain, straightforward, unambiguous, unequivocal; candid, frank, honest, open, sincere; *spec*: quoted, verbatim (speech, words).

direction

n lit: bearing, compass-point, course, line, orientation; guidance, indication, lead; administration, control, governing, management, ruling, running, superintending, supervision; commands, instruction, orders; address, destination.

directive

n lit: command, decree, edict, instruction, law, mandate, order, rule.

directly

adv lit: straight, without deviation; face-to-face, in person; at once, immediately, instantly, promptly, right away, straight away; bluntly, plainly, straightforwardly, unambiguously, unequivocally; candidly, frankly, honestly, openly, sincerely.

director

n lit: administrator, governor, manager, member of the board, organizer, supervisor; boss, chief, controller, head, leader.

dirt

n lit: filth, grime, mud, slime; excrement, faeces, muck, prurience, scatology; earth, soil; foreign body, impurity; *fig*: concupiscence, obscenity, pornography, salacity, smut; gossip, low-down, scandal.

dirty
vb lit: befoul, defile, mess up, soil, stain.
adj lit: filthy, foul, grimy, grubby, mucky, muddy, polluted, slimy, soiled; dingy, discoloured, dusty, murky, shabby, squalid, tarnished; *fig*: blue, concupiscent, coprological, faecal, indecent, obscene, pornographic, prurient, salacious, scabrous, scatalogical, smutty; corrupt, dishonest, fraudulent, illegal; contemptible, cowardly, low, mean, treacherous; indignant, offended, resentful; lowering, rainy, squally, stormy.

disable
vb lit: cripple, debilitate, hamstring, handicap, incapacitate, put out of action, render incapable; paralyse; disqualify, invalidate.

disabled
adj (pa.pt) lit: crippled, debilitated, hamstrung, handicapped, incapacitated, out of action; bedridden, in a wheelchair; paralysed; disqualified, invalidated.

disadvantage
n lit: burden, handicap, hardship, impediment, inconvenience, liability; flaw, minus, snag, trouble, weakness; detriment, disservice, loss.
vb lit: burden, create problems for, handicap, hinder, impede, inconvenience.

disaffection
n lit: alienation, breach, divorce, estrangement, separation; antagonism, antipathy, hostility, ill will.

disagree
vb lit: be opposed, clash, conflict, contradict, differ, diverge; argue, bicker, dispute, dissent, quarrel, wrangle; cause trouble (with oneself), cause problems (with oneself); be different, be unequal, be unmatching.

disagreeable
adj lit: bad-tempered, churlish, cross, difficult, ill-natured, peevish, unfriendly, unlikable; disgusting, distasteful, nasty, obnoxious, offensive, repellent, repulsive.

disappear
vb lit: evanesce, fade out, melt away, vanish; be lost to view, go, leave, pass from one's sight; escape, flee, fly; be lost, be nowhere to be found; come to an end, die, ebb, peter out, taper off, wane.

disappearance
n lit: evanescence, evaporation, vanishing; departure, desertion, going, leaving; escape, flight; absence, eclipse, loss; end, passing, petering out, tapering off, waning.

disappoint
vb lit: chagrin, dash, dismay; fail, let one down; foil, frustrate, thwart.

disappointment
n lit: chagrin, dismay; dejection, discouragement; disillusion, letdown; frustration, mortification; misfortune, set-back.

disapprobation
n lit: deprecation, disapproval, displeasure, dissatisfaction; discontent, dislike, disfavour, odium; condemnation, rejection.

disapprove of
vb lit: deplore, deprecate, dislike, frown on, take exception to; condemn, object to.

disarming
adj (pr.pt) lit: charming, likable, winning; irresistible.

disarray
n lit: chaos, confusion, disorder, disorganization, jumble, mess, muddle, shambles; derangement, déshabillé.

disaster
n lit: calamity, cataclysm, catastrophe, ruination, tragedy; blow, misfortune, reverse, trouble.

disastrous
adj lit: calamitous, cataclysmic, catastrophic, ruinous, tragic; devastating, dire; ill-starred, unlucky.

disbelieving
adj (pr.pt) lit: doubting, dubious, incredulous, sceptical; mistrustful, suspicious; agnostic, heretical, lapsed, schismatic.

disc

n lit: circle, ring; dish, saucer; CD, record; discus, quoit; floppy; *spec*: intervertebral cartilage (in the spine).

discard

vb lit: chuck out, dispense with, dispose of, ditch, drop, dump, get rid of, jettison, throw away.

discern

vb lit: distinguish, make out, observe, perceive, recognize, see, sense; discriminate (between), judge (between), tell.

discerning

adj (pr.pt) lit: acute, astute, discriminating, perceptive, percipient, perspicacious, sensitive, shrewd; intelligent, knowing, sage, wise.

discharge

n lit: emission, flux, oozing, secretion, seepage, suppuration; emptying, evacuation, unburdening, unloading; demobilization, dismissal, ejection, release; acquittal, exoneration, freeing, liberation, remission; payment, settlement; accomplishment, execution, fulfilment, observance; blast, detonation, firing, shooting.
vb lit: emit, exude, give off, leak, ooze, secrete, seep, suppurate; empty, evacuate, unburden, unload; cashier, demobilize, dismiss, eject, expel, release, remove, sack; acquit, clear, exonerate, free, liberate, remit; pay, settle; accomplish, do, execute, fulfil, observe, perform; blast, detonate, fire, set off, shoot.

discipline

n lit: control, order, regulation; practice, regimen, training; chastisement, correction, punishment, strictness; area, branch, field, specialism, specialty; *spec*: (sports) event.
vb lit: chastise, correct, punish; be strict with, break in, control, drill, educate, exercise, regulate, train.

disclaim

vb lit: deny, disown, forswear, repudiate; abjure, reject, renounce; disavow; relinquish.

disclose

vb lit: confess, divulge, leak, reveal, tell; broadcast, make known, publish; bring to light, expose, show, uncover.

discolour

vb lit: soil, stain, tarnish; bleach, etiolate, fade, lighten, pale, yellow; darken.

discomfort

n lit: cachexia, distress, malaise; hardship, pain, soreness; inconvenience, irritation, vexation.
vb lit: annoy, cause hardship, distress, give no peace, inconvenience, irritate, nag, pain, vex; discompose, embarrass, leave uncomfortable.

discompose

vb lit: abash, agitate, discomfit, disturb, embarrass, fluster, perturb, ruffle, unnerve, take by surprise.

disconcerted

adj (pa.pt) lit: caught by surprise, fazed, flurried, flustered, nonplussed, put out, rattled, ruffled, shaken, taken aback, thrown, unsettled; foiled, frustrated, thwarted.

disconnect

vb lit: detach, disengage, put asunder, separate, take apart, uncouple, undo; free, loosen, release; cut off, switch off, turn off.

discontent

adj lit: dissatisfied, ill at ease, morose, restless, uneasy; displeased, unhappy; dog-in-the-manger, envious, grudging.

discontinue

vb lit: break off, cease, drop, give up, leave off, quit, stop, suspend; finish, put an end to, terminate.

discord

n lit: conflict, contention, disagreement, dissension, division, friction, strife; cacophony, clash, disharmony, dissonance.

discount

n lit: concession, cut, price-cut, rebate, reduction, something off.
vb lit: disbelieve, disregard, ignore, let pass, take with a pinch of salt; give a reduction, mark down, reduce.

discouraging

adj (pr.pt) lit: daunting, disheartening, dispiriting, off-putting; depressing; interruptive, obstructive.

discourtesy
n lit: impertinence, impoliteness, incivility, rudeness; slight, snub, solecism; bad manners, ill breeding.

discover
vb lit: come across, find, light upon; bring to light, dig up, reveal, turn up, uncover, unearth; ascertain, detect, discern, find out, learn; notice, perceive, realize, see, spot; conceive, devise, invent, make, originate.

discovery
n lit: digging up, finding, turning up, unearthing; ascertaining, detection, discerning, learning; noticing, perceiving, realization, seeing, spotting; conception, creation, introduction, invention, origination.

discredited
adj (pa.pt) lit: brought into disrepute, debunked, disgraced, exposed, shown up, stigmatized, undermined.

discreet
adj lit: diplomatic, tactful; judicious, politic, sensible; cautious, guarded, prudent, wary.

discretionary
adj lit: elective, open, optional, voluntary; down to oneself, up to oneself.

discriminate
vb lit: differentiate (between), distinguish (between), draw a distinction (between); act unjustly (against), be biased (against), be prejudiced (against).

discuss
vb lit: confer about, consult about, converse about, debate, go into, talk over.

discussion
n lit: conference, consultation, conversation, debate, talk; dialogue, exchange of views; negotiation, talks.

disdain
n lit: aloofness, contumely, hauteur, superciliousness, superiority; contempt, scorn; arrogance, haughtiness.
vb lit: be above, look down on, look down one's nose at, treat with contumely; scorn, spurn.

disease
n lit: ailment, complaint, disorder, illness, malady, sickness; blight, contagion, infection, infestation; condition; *fig*: failing, vice, weakness.

disembark
vb lit: alight, get down, get off (from), step down (from); land; arrive.

disfigurement
n lit: blemish, deformity, malformation, mutilation, scar; blot, blotch, mark, spot, stain.

disgrace
n lit: dishonour, ignominy, odium, opprobrium; humiliation, shame; degradation; aspersion, reproach, slur, stain, stigma.
vb lit: bring shame upon, discredit, dishonour, sully; humiliate, mortify, shame; expose, show up.

disgraceful
adj lit: appalling, contemptible, detestable, disgusting, infamous, outrageous, scandalous, shameful, shocking; dishonourable, ignominous, opprobrious, unworthy.

disguise
n lit: façade, front, imposture, semblance, simulation; costume; camouflage, cover.
vb lit: dress up (as), make up (as); camouflage, hide, mask, screen, veil; dissimulate, falsify, metamorphose.

disgust
n lit: abhorrence, aversion, detestation, distaste, loathing, nausea, repugnance, revulsion.
vb lit: fill with loathing, nauseate, offend, outrage, repel, revolt, sicken, turn one's stomach.

disgusting
adj (pr.pt) lit: detestable, distasteful, foul, loathsome, nasty, nauseating, offensive, repellent, repugnant, revolting, sickening, stomach-turning, vile.

dish
n lit: plate, platter; bowl, saucer; course, preparation, recipe.
vb lit: foil, frustrate, mess up one's chances, ruin, spoil, thwart, wreck.

dishevelled
adj (pa.pt) lit: bedraggled, deranged, déshabillé, disordered, in a mess, ruffled, rumpled, tousled, unkempt, untidy.

dishonest
adj lit: bent, corrupt, crooked, false, lying, mendacious, perfidious, treacherous, unscrupulous, untrustworthy,

untruthful; deceitful, dissimulating, economical with the truth, sham.

disillusion
n lit: disappointment, disenchantment; true perception, undeception; anticlimax.
vb lit: bring down to earth, disabuse, disenchant, open one's eyes, undeceive; disappoint, fail, let down.

disinclined
adj (pa.pt) lit: hesitant, indisposed, loath, reluctant, unwilling.

disinfectant
n lit: antiseptic, bactericide, fungicide, germicide, sterilizer; salve.

disintegration
n lit: break-up, collapse, crumbling, decomposition, destruction, falling apart, fission, fragmentation, shattering; *spec*: (radioactive) decay.

disinterested
adj (pa.pt) lit: dispassionate, equitable, impartial, neutral, unbiased, unprejudiced; detached, distant, impersonal, remote, uninvolved.

dislike
n lit: antipathy, aversion, disapproval, disfavour, distaste.
vb lit: be antipathetic towards, be averse to, be disinclined to, disapprove of, disfavour, have a distaste for, object to.

dislocate
vb lit: disarticulate, disconnect, luxate, put out, unhinge; disorder, disrupt, disturb, jumble, mess up, upset.

disloyal
adj lit: faithless, perfidious, traitorous, treacherous, unfaithful; seditious, subversive, treasonable, unpatriotic.

dismal
adj lit: bleak, cheerless, dark, depressing, discouraging, gloomy, lowering, lugubrious, sombre; boring, dreary, dull, tedious.

dismay
n lit: chagrin, disappointment, disillusion, sorrow; discouragement, sense of doom.
vb lit: appal, daunt, dishearten, disillusion, dispirit, unnerve.

dismember
vb lit: cut up, disjoint, dissect, divide up, pull apart, tear limb from limb.

dismiss
vb lit: discharge, give one's leave, send away; axe, cashier, chuck out, expel, fire, give the boot, give the sack, lay off, make redundant, remove, sack, send down, send packing; banish, dispel, shelve.

dismissal
n lit: discharge, dispatch, leave to go, marching orders, release; expulsion, laying off, notice, redundancy, removal, sacking.

disobedience
n lit: mischievousness, naughtiness; insubordination, intractability, non-compliance, recalcitrance; mutiny, revolt, revolution.

disorder
n lit: chaos, confusion, disarray, disorganization, disruption, untidiness; anarchy, lawlessness; derangement, dishevelment, dislocation.

disorganized
adj (pa.pt) lit: chaotic, confused, disordered, disrupted, untidy; all over the shop, jumbled, muddled, out of place.

disowned
adj (pa.pt) lit: abandoned, cast aside, cast off, disavowed, disclaimed, rejected, repudiated, unacknowledged, unrecognized.

dispense
vb lit: apportion, assign, deal out, disburse, distribute, dole out, measure out, mete out, provide, supply; administer, execute, implement; except (from), exempt (from), release (from); do away (with), do without, get along without.

disperse
vb lit: broadcast, diffuse, disseminate, scatter, spread, strew; break up, separate; dispel, dissipate, dissolve.

display
n lit: exhibition, parade, show; array, presentation, spectacle; façade, imposture, ostentation, pretence.
vb lit: demonstrate, evince, exhibit, parade, present, reveal, show; betray, disclose; boast, flaunt, flourish, vaunt.

displease
vb lit: annoy, be disagreeable to, exasperate, gall, irk, irritate, offend, put out, upset, vex.

disposable
adj lit: amenable, available, expendable, realizable, usable; non-returnable, throw-away; biodegradable.

disposal
n lit: command, employment, utility; assignment, bequest, dispensation; arrangement, disposition, distribution, positioning; clearance, dumping, getting rid (of), jettisoning, removal, throwing away.

dispose
vb lit: adjust, arrange, group, marshal, order, place, put, set, stand; bias (towards), condition (to), incline (to), influence (towards), move (to), prompt (to); make an end (of), free oneself (of); get rid (of), rid oneself (of).

dispute
n lit: argument, contention, debate, disagreement, dissension; altercation, conflict, discord, friction, quarrel, wrangle.
vb lit: argue with, contend with, challenge, contradict, debate, disagree with, dissent to, quarrel with, question; clash with, squabble with, wrangle with.

disqualification
n lit: disbarment, disentitlement, elimination, exclusion, expulsion; incapacitation, ineligibility.

disregard
n lit: heedlessness, ignoring, neglect, negligence; disdain, disrespect, indifference.
vb lit: discount, ignore, neglect, pass over, pay no attention to, take no notice of, turn a blind eye to; brush aside, laugh off, make light of; cut dead, snub, walk straight past.

disrespectful
adj lit: cheeky, discourteous, impertinent, impudent, insolent, rude; irreverent, sacrilegious.

disruptive
adj lit: anarchic, destructive, disorderly, distracting, obstreperous, troublesome, unruly, upsetting.

dissatisfied
adj (pa.pt) lit: discontent, disgruntled, unhappy; fed up, frustrated; disappointed, unfulfilled.

dissertation
n lit: discourse, disquisition, exposition, exegesis, sermon, treatise; thesis.

disservice
n lit: bad turn, ill turn, wrong; detriment, harm, injury, unkindness; injustice.

dissipated
adj (pa.pt) lit: abandoned, debauched, dissolute, drunken, intemperate, profligate, reprobate; dispersed, frittered away, lost, scattered, squandered.

dissolute
adj lit: abandoned, debauched, degenerate, depraved, immoral, libertine, licentious, loose, wanton, wild.

dissolution
n lit: breakdown, break-up, decomposition, disintegration, dismantling, invalidation, undoing, unmaking; evaporation, liquefaction, melting; dismemberment, separation; *fig*: adjournment, discontinuation, suspension; conclusion, end, finish, termination; death, destruction, ruin; depravity, immorality, looseness, wantonness, wildness.

dissolve
vb lit: deliquesce, liquefy, melt, thaw; break down, break up, crumble, decompose, disintegrate, disperse, dissipate, evaporate, fade away, vanish; dismantle, dismember, disunite, loose, separate; *fig*: adjourn, discontinue, suspend; annul, cancel, conclude, end, finish, terminate.

dissuade
vb lit: deter, disincline, put off; discourage.

distance
n lit: extent, range, reach, remove, separation, space, stretch; gap, interval; *fig*: coldness, coolness, reserve, restraint.
vb lit: leave behind, outrun, outstrip; dissociate (oneself from), separate (oneself from).

distant
adj lit: faraway, far-flung, far-removed, remote; apart, disparate, distinct, outlying, scattered, separate; faint,

indistinct, obscure; *fig*: cold, cool,
formal, reserved, restrained, reticent,
withdrawn.

distend
vb lit: bloat, bulge, dilate, expand, inflate,
puff out, swell.

distinct
adj lit: detached, discrete, separate,
unconnected; different, individual;
apparent, clear, evident, manifest,
marked, noticeable, patent, plain,
recognizable, unmistakable, well-
defined.

distinction
n lit: contrast, difference; differentiation,
discernment, discrimination, separation;
characteristic, idiosyncrasy,
individuality, particularity, peculiarity,
singularity, uniqueness; celebrity, credit,
eminence, fame, honour, note,
prominence, worth; award, prize.

distinctive
adj lit: different, distinguishable,
extraordinary, individual, original,
particular, peculiar, singular, special,
unique.

distinguish
vb lit: differentiate, discriminate, tell
apart; discern, make out, perceive, pick
out, recognize, see; individualize, label,
mark out, separate, single out; glorify,
make famous.

distinguished
adj (pa.pt) lit: conspicuous,
extraordinary, outstanding; celebrated,
eminent, famous, illustrious, noted,
renowned.

distort
vb lit: bend, bow, buckle, deform, twist,
warp; *fig*: misrepresent, pervert, slant.

distracted
adj (pa.pt) lit: agitated, diverted,
flustered, harassed, overwrought;
bemused, bewildered, confused; beside
oneself, demented, deranged, insane,
mad, raving.

distress
n lit: discomfort, misery, suffering,
wretchedness; anguish, grief, pain,
torment, woe; blow, calamity, difficulty,
hardship, misfortune, privation, trial.

vb lit: pain, torment, trouble, upset;
bother, disturb, harass, worry; grieve,
sadden, wound.

distribution
n lit: allocation, allotment,
apportionment, dispensing, dispersion,
dissemination, division, doling out,
giving out, handing out, measuring out,
scattering, spreading; dispersal, extent,
range, scope, spread; arrangement,
disposition, grouping; delivery,
dispatch, handling, transportation.

distributor
n lit: allocator, dispenser, disseminator,
divider, propagator; administrator,
dealer, dispatcher, transport manager,
warehouse manager, wholesaler; *spec*:
rotor arm, timing device (for a car's
spark-plugs).

distrust
n lit: chariness, doubt, scepticism,
suspicion, wariness.
vb lit: be chary of, be suspicious of, have
doubts about, suspect.

disturb
vb lit: bother, disrupt, distract,
inconvenience, interrupt, intrude on;
trouble; annoy, harass, pester, plague,
worry; discompose, distress, fluster,
perturb, ruffle, shake, unsettle; derange,
disorder, interfere with, touch.

disturbance
n lit: agitation, disorder, distraction,
upset; interruption, intrusion,
interference; barney, bother, broil,
commotion, demo, fracas, hubbub,
ruckus, ruction, rumble, rumpus,
stramash, tumult, uproar.

ditch
n lit: channel, drain, dyke, fosse, gully,
trench, verge.
vb lit: dig a channel in, drain, excavate,
irrigate; land on water; *fig*: discard, drop,
dump, get rid of, jettison; abandon,
maroon, leave in the lurch.

dive
n lit: header, plunge; drop, fall, slump; *fig*:
dump, hole, joint, shady night-club,
speakeasy.
vb lit: plunge headlong, submerge; drop,
fall, plummet, slump, swoop; dart,
jump, leap, thrust oneself.

diverge
vb lit: bifurcate, branch, divide, fork, separate, split; deviate, stray, turn aside, wander; *fig*: conflict, differ, disagree.

diverse
adj lit: differing, miscellaneous, sundry, varied, various; different, disparate, distinct, separate.

diversion
n lit: detour, deviation, digression; amusement, delectation, enjoyment, entertainment, gratification, pleasure, recreation, sport.

diversity
n lit: difference, dissimilarity, miscellaneity, multiplicity, variance, variation; assortment, medley, variety.

divert
vb lit: avert, deflect, fend off, parry, redirect, turn aside, ward off; distract (from), draw away (from), lead away (from), sidetrack; *fig*: amuse, delight, entertain, gratify.

divest
vb lit: doff, remove, strip, take off, undress; *fig*: deprive, dispossess (of), take possession (of).

divide
n lit: border, division, margin, partition; *spec*: border hills, watershed.
vb lit: bisect, halve, split in two; cut (up), disconnect, part, segregate, separate, sever, sunder; arrange, order, sort; allot, dispense, distribute, measure out, share; alienate, break up, come between, disrupt, estrange, interpose between.

divination
n lit: augury, foretelling the future, necromancy, prophecy; chiromancy, clairvoyance, dowsing, ESP, reading the tea-leaves; intuition.

divine
n lit: churchman, clergyman, cleric, minister, priest, reverend; doctor of divinity, theologian.
vb lit: apprehend, deduce, discern, infer, perceive, understand; conjecture, foretell, predict; dowse.
adj lit: godly, hallowed, holy, religious, sacred, spiritual; celestial, godlike, heavenly; beatific, mystic, numinous, transcendental; *fig*: angelic, beautiful, lovely, perfect, wonderful.

division
n lit: bisection, halving, splitting in two; disconnection, parting, segregation, separation, severing, sundering; ordering, sorting; allocation, dispensing, distribution, measuring out, sharing; alienation, break-up, disruption, divorce, estrangement, interruption.

divisive
adj lit: alienating, disruptive, estranging, inharmonious, interposing, interruptive, pernicious, unsettling, upsetting.

divorce
n lit: break, disunion, estrangement, parting, rupture, separation, splitting, sundering; annulment, decree nisi.
vb lit: dissociate, disunite, divide, part, separate, sever, split up, sunder; be separated from; have one's marriage dissolved.

dizziness
n lit: faintness, giddiness, light-headedness, shakiness, vertigo; *fig*: flightiness, frivolousness, silliness; dumbness.

dizzy
adj lit: faint, giddy, light-headed, shaky, wobbly, woozy; precipitous, steep, vertiginous; *fig*: flighty, frivolous, scatterbrained, silly; dumb; zany.

do
n lit: celebration, banquet, dance, event, feast, function, occasion, party.
vb lit: accomplish, carry out, execute, perform, render, undertake, work at; bring about, cause, effect; create, make, produce; achieve, complete, conclude, empty, exhaust, finish; cover, go, proceed, travel; journey through, look at, tour, visit; act, behave, conduct oneself; mount, play, present, put on; arrange, deal with, fix, look after, organize, prepare, see to; be responsible for, take over; bestow on, confer on, give, grant; be, get on, make out, manage; answer, be adequate, be usable, be useful, serve, suffice; figure out, resolve, solve, sort out; cook; *fig*: cheat, con, dupe, swindle, take for a ride; raid, rob; beat up, thrash; *spec*: spend time (in prison).

dock
n lit: basin, channel, harbour, quay, wharf; stump; accused's enclosure, bar, pulpit; hospital.

vb lit: berth, moor, put in, tie up; couple, hook up, join, link up; amputate, cut off; *fig*: curtail, cut short, reduce, subtract from.

doctor
n lit: consultant, general practitioner, GP, physician, specialist; casualty officer, houseman; father of the Church, theologian; don; *spec*: cook (on a ship).
vb lit: apply treatment to, treat; mend, patch up, repair; alter, change, falsify, tamper with; adulterate, dilute, nobble, spike.

dodge
n lit: feint, sidestep, swerve; *fig*: contrivance, ploy, ruse, stratagem, wile, wrinkle.
vb lit: duck, feint, sidestep, swerve; avoid, elude, evade; *fig*: escape from, get out of, shirk.

dog
n lit: hound, mutt, pooch, pup; *fig*: blackguard, cur, scoundrel, villain.
vb lit: follow, hound, pursue, shadow, tail, track, trail.

dogged
adj lit: followed, hounded, pursued, trailed; determined, indefatigable, persevering, persistent, pertinacious, steadfast, tenacious, unyielding.

dogmatic
adj lit: canonical, doctrinal, theological; assertive, authoritative, categorical, doctrinaire, emphatic, positive; imperious, overbearing, peremptory.

dole
n lit: social security, unemployment benefit, welfare; allocation, dispensation, distribution; alms, donation, gift, grant, gratuity; portion, quota, ration, share.
vb lit: apportion (out), deal (out), give (out), hand (out), mete (out), share (out).

doll
n lit: manikin, puppet; *fig*: bird, chick, filly, gal, sheila, skirt; beauty, corker, looker, smasher.

dome
n lit: cupola, hemisphere, vaulted roof; cathedral; *fig*: cranium, pate.

domestic
adj lit: indigenous, internal, national, state; domiciliary, residential; family, household, private; house, pet, trained; homely.

domesticate
vb lit: break, tame; house-train; make feel at home.

domicile
n lit: abode, dwelling, habitation, home, house, residence; habitat, nest; country, district, region, state.
vb lit: establish (oneself in), set (oneself) up (in).

dominate
vb lit: control, have the ascendancy over, lead by the nose, monopolize, prevail over, rule; be predominant in, loom over, overshadow, tower above; eclipse, outshine, upstage.

domination
n lit: ascendancy, authority, control, mastery, power, supremacy; oppression, repression, subjection, tyranny.

domineer
vb lit: be bossy (over), browbeat (over), bully (over), intimidate (over), tyrannize (over).

donate
vb lit: contribute, gift, give, present; bequeath, leave.

donation
n lit: alms, contribution, gift, present; gratuity; collection, offering.

donor
n lit: contributor, giver; benefactor, philanthropist; *spec*: source of organ(s) for transplant surgery.

doom
n lit: decree, destiny, fate, judgement, lot, verdict; catastrophe, condemnation, death, destruction, disaster, ruination; end of the world, last trump.
vb lit: destine (to be), foreordain (to be); condemn (to), consign (to), damn (to), sentence (to).

doomed
adj (pa.pt) lit: destined, fated, foreordained; ill-fated, luckless; condemned, damned.

door
n lit: entrance, entry, way in; egress, exit, ingress, way out; flap, gate, lintel, opening, port, portal, threshhold, trap.

dormant
adj lit: aestivating, hibernating, inert,

latent, quiescent; sleeping, slumbering, torpid; fallow.

dose
n lit: dosage; amount, measure, quantity; medication, medicament, medicine, placebo, tincture, treatment; *fig*: bout, session.

dot
n lit: jot, point, spot, stop; fleck, mark, speck.
vb lit: dab, fleck, spot, stipple, stud; *fig*: hit, smack; disperse, scatter, spread.

dotage
n lit: decrepitude, old age, senility; infatuation.

doting
adj (pr.pt) lit: adoring, devoted, fond, worshipping.

double
n lit: clone, doppelgänger, duplicate, lookalike, mirror image, replica, ringer, spitting image, twin.
vb lit: duplicate, grow to twice the size, increase, multiply by two; fold, plait; turn (back on oneself); act also (as), additionally perform (as/on).
adj lit: dual, duplex, duplicated, paired; twice, twofold; *fig*: insincere, perfidious, treacherous.

doubt
n lit: distrust, dubiety, lack of faith, mistrust, suspicion, uncertainty, vacillation; misgiving, qualm, reservation; ambiguity, confusion, perplexity; hesitancy, indecision, irresolution, wavering; *spec*: (without) question.
vb lit: be uncertain, distrust, have little faith in, mistrust, suspect; query, question; be hesitant, be irresolute, vacillate, waver.

doubtful
adj lit: distrustful, dubious, hesitant, irresolute, suspicious, uncertain, unconvinced, unsure; ambiguous, debatable, indeterminate, obscure, problematical, questionable, vague; disreputable, shady, suspect.

dour
adj lit: forbidding, grim, sour, sulky, sullen; austere, hard, rigorous, severe, strict, uncompromising; obstinate, stubborn, unyielding.

dowdy
adj lit: drab, frowzy, frumpy, shabby.

down
n lit: descent, drop, fall; dejection, depression, mood; failure, reversal, setback; knock-down, tackle; scrimmage, scrummage; dune, grassy undulation, hill, knoll, mound; feathers, fluff, hair.
vb lit: fell, floor, knock down, tackle, trip; drink, gulp, knock back, quaff, put away, toss off.
adv lit: to a lower position, below; to the ground; on the ground; downstairs; to the present time; to a smaller state; to a defeated state; at a disadvantage, behind; in black and white, on record; in cash, on the spot; to leeward.
prp lit: in a descent along/by/through; on/to a lower position in/on; along, with the current of.

down-to-earth
adj lit: businesslike, factual, level-headed, matter-of-fact, mundane, no-nonsense, practical, pragmatic, realistic, sensible, utilitarian.

doze
n lit: catnap, forty winks, kip, nap, siesta, snooze.
vb lit: catnap, drowse, kip, nap, snooze.

draft
n lit: outline, plan, résumé, rough, sketch; cheque, money order.
vb lit: draw up, make a rough, outline, plan, sketch out.

drag
n lit: bore, bother, burden, chore, effort, nuisance, pain; friction, resistance; trawl; scent; inhalation, pull; *spec*: (man in) woman's clothing.
vb lit: draw, haul, heave (along), pull, tow, tug; crawl, creep, dawdle, go slowly; draw (out), spin (out), stretch (out); get left behind, lag behind, straggle; *spec*: dredge, trawl (under water).

dragon
n lit: fire-breathing monster; lizard, reptile; *fig*: battleaxe, harridan, scold, Tartar, termagant, virago; paper kite.

drain
n lit: conduit, culvert, ditch, outlet, sewer; drag (on), strain (on).
vb lit: draw off, empty, evacuate, pump out; milk, tap; discharge, exude, flow (out), ooze (out), seep (out); deplete,

exhaust, sap, strain, use up.

drama
n lit: acting, stagecraft, Thespianism;
play, theatrical performance; excitement,
histrionics, scene, spectacle.

dramatic
adj lit: histrionic, theatrical, Thespian;
affecting, moving, powerful, striking;
expressive, forceful, vivid; climactic,
electrifying, exciting, sensational, tense,
thrilling.

dramatist
n lit: author, playwright; librettist,
lyricist; scriptwriter, screenplay writer;
bard.

drape
n lit: curtain, hanging; cloth, fold.
vb lit: cover, curtain, enfold, hang;
arrange in folds, pleat.

draught
n lit: breeze, current, gust, wind; drawing,
haul, pull, traction; drink, swallow, swig;
dose, measure; catch, trawl; *spec*:
displacement (of a ship).

draw
n lit: attraction, enticement, lure; dead
heat, stalemate, tie; choosing, picking,
selection.
vb lit: drag, haul, pull, tow; approach,
come, get; allure, attract, elicit, entice,
induce, invite, seduce, tempt; infuse;
extract, pull out, unsheathe;
disembowel, eviscerate; extend (out),
lengthen (out), spin (out), stretch (out);
deduce, infer, make; breathe in, inhale,
take a pull; delineate, depict, design,
map out, outline, portray, sketch;
choose, pick, select; *spec*: be biased, lean
(of a bowls wood); extrude (plastics,
wire); pull away, pull together (curtains);
pull back (a bowstring); shed, spill
(blood); write out (a cheque).

drawer
n lit: shelf; box, chest; bartender, tapster;
artist, draughtsman.

drawing
n lit: delineation, outline; illustration,
representation; pencil sketch.

drawn
adj (pa.pt) lit: gaunt, haggard, harrowed,
lined, pinched, strained, taut, worn.

dread
n lit: alarm, apprehension, dismay, fear,

fright, trepidation; awe.
vb lit: fear, quail at, shrink from, tremble
at.
adj lit: fearful, frightening, terrifying;
awesome, dire.

dreadful
adj lit: alarming, formidable, frightening,
ghastly, shocking, tragic; *fig*: abysmal,
appalling, awful, terrible, useless,
worthless.

dream
n lit: delusion, fantasy, illusion, reverie,
vision; ambition, aspiration, hope, wish;
fig: beauty, gem, joy, treasure.
vb lit: fantasize, imagine; *fig*: conceive (of),
think (of).

dreamy
adj lit: calming, lulling, relaxing, soothing;
absent, abstracted, faraway, preoccupied;
fanciful, impractical, quixotic, vague;
fantastic, intangible, misty, unreal; *fig*:
attractive, exciting.

dregs
n lit: dross, grounds, lees, residue,
sediment, settlings; *fig*: misfits, outcasts,
scum.

drench
vb lit: drown, flood, inundate, saturate,
soak, steep; dose, purge.

dress
n lit: attire, clothes, clothing, costume,
garments, get-up, outfit, rig; apparel,
garb, raiment; frock, gown, robe.
vb lit: change, put one's clothes on; clothe,
put clothes on; drape, furbish, rig out; do
(up); comb, groom; align, arrange, set,
straighten; bandage, plaster, put
medication on; garnish, season.

dressmaker
n lit: couturier, modiste, seamstress.

drift
n lit: bank, firn, heap, mound, pile;
current, flow, impetus, momentum,
movement, rush, stream; *fig*: direction,
implication, intention, meaning,
significance, tenor; *spec*: drove road,
(cattle) track; horizontal shaft (of a mine).
vb lit: coast, float; hover, waft; accumulate,
amass, bank up, pile up.

drill
n lit: auger, bit, borer, gimlet; ridge of soil;
discipline, exercise, training; *fig*: method,
procedure, routine.

vb lit: bore, make a hole in, pierce; sow in rows; discipline, exercise, instruct, train; rehearse (in), teach (in).

drink
n lit: beverage, liquid refreshment; bumper, draught, gulp, sip, snort, swallow, swig; cup, dram, glass, mouthful, mug, tot, peg; alcohol, liquor, spirits; booze, hard stuff, hooch, plonk, rotgut, vino; cocktail, brew, infusion, tipple, poison; *fig*: briny, ocean, sea.
vb lit: down, imbibe, partake of, quaff, sip, sup, swallow; gulp, guzzle, knock back, swig, swill down, toss off; booze, carouse, drown one's sorrows, hit the bottle, tope; absorb, suck up.

drip
n lit: dribble, drop, leak, trickling; *fig*: cissy, creep, softy, sop, weakling, weed, wet.
vb lit: drop, splash; dribble, trickle; filter, leak, ooze.

drive
n lit: avenue, entrance, pathway; excursion, jaunt, outing, run, spin, trip; campaign, crusade, effort, push; hit, stroke; power, transmission; *fig*: ambition, dynamism, energy, enterprise, initiative, motivation, pep, vigour, zip.
vb lit: herd, impel; compel, constrain, force, hammer, oblige, prod, spur; plunge, ram, stab; power, propel, push; hit, strike; control, direct, operate, steer; go, motor, travel; cause to become, make, send; *fig*: aim (at), get (at).

drivel
n lit: balderdash, bullshit, bunkum, codswallop, crap, gibberish, gobbledygook, nonsense, poppycock, rubbish, tosh, waffle.
vb lit: dribble, drool, slobber; babble, gibber; gab, maunder, ramble.

driver
n lit: chauffeur, motorman, navigator, pilot, steersman; cowboy, drover, herder, herdsman, shepherd; *spec*: wood (golf-club).

drizzle
n lit: haar, light rain, mist, mizzle, Scotch mist.

drone
n lit: idler, loafer, lounger, parasite, scrounger, sponger; hum, tone; burden, continuous sound, monotonous sound; remote-control decoy.

drop
n lit: bead, drip, globule; mouthful, nip, pinch, sip, taste, trace; abyss, chasm, height, precipice; fall, lowering; *fig*: decline, decrease, deterioration, downturn, reduction, slump.
vb lit: dive, fall, plummet, plunge, sink; bag, shoot; descend, droop, tumble; give birth to, lay; decline, diminish; abandon, deposit, desert, disown, omit, reject, relinquish, renounce, throw over; let (off), set down; cease, forsake, give up, quit; *spec*: send (a line, a note).

drought
n lit: dry spell; aridity, dehydration; *fig*: deficiency, inadequacy, scarcity, shortage.

drown
vb lit: engulf, flood, go under, immerse, inundate, submerge, swamp; *fig*: deaden, muffle, obliterate, overwhelm, stifle.

drubbing
n lit: beating, castigation, clobbering, cudgelling, hammering, licking, thrashing, trouncing, walloping.

drug
n lit: dose, medication, medicine; dope; narcotic; stimulant, upper; downer, sedative.
vb lit: medicate, treat; dope; anaesthetize, knock out.

drum
n lit: percussion instrument, tambour; tympanum; barrel, cylinder; pad, residence.
vb lit: beat rhythmically, tattoo, throb; *fig*: din (into), drive (into), instil (into).

drunk
adj lit: inebriated, intoxicated, maudlin; blotto, boozed up, canned, legless, paralytic, pickled, pie-eyed, pissed as a newt, plastered, stewed, stoned, tight, well-oiled.

drunkard
n lit: alcoholic, dipsomaniac, drunk, lush, soak, sot, toper, wino.

drunken
adj lit: inebriated, intoxicated, maudlin.

dry
vb lit: dehydrate, desiccate; parch; shrivel (up), wizen (up).
adj lit: arid, dehydrated, desiccated, moistureless, parched, torrid; *fig*: formal,

official; dull, monotonous, tedious; deadpan, laconic, sardonic, sharp; teetotal; brut, sugarless.

duck
n lit: drake, waterfowl; nil score, zero; dip, plunge; dodge; *fig*: love, pet, sweet.
vb lit: bob down, dodge, drop; dive, plunge, submerge; dunk, immerse; avoid, elude, evade, sidestep.

due
n lit: deserts, merits; privilege, right.
adj lit: appropriate, deserved, fitting, just, merited, rightful; adequate, enough, sufficient; outstanding, owed, payable; awaited, expected, scheduled.

dull
vb lit: cloud, dim, obscure; sully, tarnish; *fig*: alleviate, assuage, blunt, mitigate, palliate, soften; dampen, depress.
adj lit: blunt, unhoned; cloudy, dim, gloomy, overcast; drab, faded, indistinct, murky, sombre, uninteresting; dense, dim, slow, stolid, thick; apathetic, blank, indifferent, insensitive, lifeless, sluggish; boring, dreary, flat, monotonous, plain, tedious, tiresome, unimaginative.

duly
adv lit: accordingly, appropriately, fittingly, properly, rightly; punctually.

dumb
adj lit: inarticulate, mute, silent, stupid; speechless, tongue-tied.

dummy
n lit: comforter, teat; figure, form, model; counterfeit, mock-up, sample, substitute; blockhead, dimwit, dunce, numbskull.
adj lit: artificial, false, imitation, mock, simulated, trial.

dunce
n lit: ass, blockhead, cretin, dimwit, duffer, dullard, ignoramus, imbecile, moron, numbskull, thicko, twit.

dung
n lit: coprolite, droppings, faeces, guano, manure; defecation, excrement, ordure; dirt, muck.

durable
adj lit: hard-wearing, long-lasting, permanent, resistant, strong, substantial, tough; lasting, sound, stable; dogged, hardy, persevering.

duration
n lit: continuance, continuation, existence, length, persistence; period, term, time.

during
prp lit: throughout, through the entire time of; at some time in, in the course of.

dusk
n lit: eventide, gloaming, nightfall, twilight; gloom, murk, shadiness, shadow.

dusky
adj lit: dark, dark-skinned, swarthy; crepuscular, dim, gloomy, murky, nocturnal, shady, shadowy, tenebrous, twilit.

dust
n lit: ash, fluff, grains, grit, particles, powder; dirt, earth, ground, soil; cloud, fumes; *fig*: commotion, fuss, row, to-do.
vb lit: brush, brush off, clean, clear, polish, wipe; *fig*: powder, scatter, sprinkle.

dusty
adj lit: dirty, grimy, grubby; tarnished, unpolished, unswept; crumbly, friable, gritty, powdery; *fig*: dismissive, negative.

duty
n lit: allegiance, loyalty, obedience; deference, homage; charge, obligation, office, responsibility, service; assignment, function, mission, role, task; (off) operations, (off) work; *fig*: effectiveness, utility; *spec*: (customs/inland revenue) excise, impost, tax, toll.

dwarf
n lit: manikin, midget, pygmy; homunculus; gnome, goblin, sprite; *spec*: collapsed small star.
vb lit: check the growth of, retard, stunt; *fig*: dominate, make look small, overshadow, tower over.
adj lit: diminutive, midget, small, stunted, undersized; miniature, tiny.

dwell
vb lit: abide, live, lodge, reside; rest, stay, stop; *fig*: continue (on), harp (on), remain talking (on).

dye
n lit: colorant, colouring, pigment, stain.
vb lit: colour, pigment, stain, tint.

dying
adj (pr.pt) lit: declining, expiring, fading, going, passing, sinking; final, last.

dynamic

adj lit: driving, energetic, forceful, lively, self-motivating, vigorous, vivacious; *spec*: electrically recharging (data-storage system); functional (disorder of the body).

dynasty

n lit: family, house, line, succession.

E

each
adj lit: every, every single.
adv lit: apiece, individually, per capita, per person.
prn lit: every one, one and all.

ear
n lit: pinna; lug-hole; *fig*: hearing, sensitivity; attention, notice; musicality, sense of pitch.

earnest
n lit: gravity, seriousness, sincerity, solemnity; collateral, guarantee, pledge, security, surety.
adj lit: grave, serious, sincere, solemn; determined, fixed, intent, resolute, steady; ardent, devoted, eager, fervent, passionate, vehement, zealous.

earth
n lit: globe, planet, world; clay, loam, mould, soil; clod, sod.

earthquake
n lit: seismic shock, tremor; heaving, shaking; epicentre; cataclysm.

easy
adj lit: effortless, light, painless, simple, smooth, undemanding; gentle, leisurely, unhurried; carefree, comfortable, cushy, peaceful, relaxed, tranquil; affable, amiable, casual, genial, informal, natural, sociable, unpretentious; flexible, indulgent, liberal, tolerant; amenable, biddable, docile, pliant, submissive, tractable.

eat
vb lit: consume, devour, digest, ingest, swallow; bolt, chomp, masticate, munch, scoff; dine, feed; abrade (away), corrode, dissolve, erode, wear (away); *fig*: take back (one's words).

eccentricity
n lit: caprice, foible, idiosyncrasy, oddity, peculiarity, quirk; nonconformity, oddness, outlandishness, strangeness, unconventionality, weirdness; abnormality, deviation, kink, warp; divergence.

eclipse
n lit: obscuring, occultation, transit; darkening, shading; *fig*: collapse, decline, extinction, failure.
vb lit: blot out, obscure, shadow; cloak, darken, shade, shroud.

economic
adj lit: financially sound, lucrative, profitable, solvent, viable; budgetary, fiscal, monetary, pecuniary; commercial, financial, mercantile, trade; cheap, inexpensive, low-priced, reasonable.

economize
vb lit: be frugal (with), be thrifty (with), cut back (on), retrench, save.

economy
n lit: budgetary management, finance, financial organization, high finance, profit-and-loss margin, turnover; cost-efficiency, frugality, parsimony, thrift; saving.

edible
adj lit: digestible, eatable, ingestible, nutritious; harmless, non-poisonous.

edict
n lit: command, decree, law, mandate, order, ordinance, proclamation, regulation, rule, statute.

edition
n lit: impression, issue, printing; copy, volume; programme.

educate
vb lit: bring up, civilize, cultivate, enlighten, inform, rear; coach, drill, instruct, school, teach, train, tutor; indoctrination; *fig*: bring round (to), persuade (to).

education
n lit: civilizing, culture, enlightenment, informing; coaching, drill, instruction, learning, schooling, teaching, training, tuition, tutelage; indoctrination.

effect
n lit: aftermath, consequence, outcome, result; impact, importance, meaning, significance; action, force,

effective
implementation, operation; clout,
influence, power, weight; (in) fact, (in)
reality.
vb lit: accomplish, achieve, bring about,
cause, create, make, perform, produce.

effective
adj lit: active, causative, operative,
productive; compelling, consequential,
efficacious, emphatic, forceful,
important, impressive, influential,
powerful, significant, striking, telling;
able, competent, energetic, useful,
vigorous; contemporary, current, in
force, in operation.

efficient
adj lit: able, businesslike, competent,
effective, productive, proficient, skilled;
deft, dextrous, neat, tidy.

effigy
n lit: doll, dummy, guy, model, puppet;
figure, idol, representation.

effort
n lit: energy, exertion, force, pains,
power, work; strain, stress, struggle,
travail; attempt, bash, endeavour, go,
shot, stab, try.

egg
n lit: ovum, zygote; cell.
vb lit: goad (on to), lead (on to), push (on
to), spur (on to), urge (on to).

egoist
n lit: monomaniac, narcissist; bighead,
self-centred type.

eject
vb lit: boot out, chuck out, evict, expel,
get rid of, remove, throw out; discharge,
emit, spew, spout, vomit; dethrone, oust.

elaborate
vb lit: amplify, complicate, embellish,
garnish, improve (on), ornament, refine;
add more (on), embroider (on), enlarge
(on), give details (on).
adj lit: complex, detailed, intricate,
minute, thorough; complicated, fancy,
fussy, ornate, ostentatious, overdone.

elapse
vb lit: go by, pass, pass by, roll by, slip by.

elderly
adj lit: aged, old; geriatric; grey-haired,
hoary, silver-haired, white-haired;
ancient, antiquated, antique,
dilapidated, weather-beaten.

elect
n lit: chosen, élite, select, selected few.
vb lit: appoint, choose, opt for, select,
settle on, vote in.

electric
adj lit: charged, live; power; *fig*: sparkling,
stimulating, stirring, tense, thrilling.

electrify
vb lit: plug in, switch on; amplify, put a
pick-up on; *fig*: fire, galvanize, jolt,
shock, stimulate, stir, thrill.

element
n lit: component, constituent, factor,
ingredient, item, member, part, unit;
domain, field, habitat, medium; coil,
filament, resistance, wire; electrode;
rudiment(s).

elemental
adj lit: basic, fundamental, primary;
contributory, structural; rudimentary,
vestigial.

elementary
adj lit: basic, fundamental, primary;
rudimentary, vestigial; clear, easy, plain,
simple, straightforward.

elevation
n lit: altitude, height, level; hill,
mountain, rise; *fig*: advancement,
promotion, upgrading; degree, grandeur,
loftiness, rank, status; ecstasy,
exaltation; plan, scale drawing, view.

elf
n lit: brownie, fairy, fay, imp, leprechaun,
pixie.

else
adv lit: additionally, also, as well, besides,
in addition; if not, instead, otherwise.

emanation
n lit: derivation, emergence, emission;
broadcast, discharge, effusion, radiation,
transmission; aroma, beam, gas, light,
ray, scent, smell; effluent, effluvium;
ectoplasm.

embankment
n lit: bank, canal-bank, causeway, dyke,
riverside, sea-wall, wall; earthwork,
motte, mound, rampart.

embarrassment
n lit: awkwardness, bashfulness, chagrin,
discomfiture, humiliation, mortification,
shame; excess, superabundance, surfeit,

surplus; *fig*: difficulty, predicament, problem.

embassy
n lit: legation, mission; ambassador's residence, consulate; agency, ministry.

embittered
adj (pa.pt) lit: alienated, disaffected, disillusioned, resentful, soured; aggravated, exacerbated.

embrace
n lit: clasp, clinch, hug, squeeze.
vb lit: clasp, cuddle, enfold, hold, hug, squeeze; comprehend, contain, enclose, encompass, include, take in; accept, receive; *fig*: adopt, espouse, take up.

emergency
n lit: crisis, crunch, crux, exigency, extremity, matter of life and death; danger, urgency, vicissitude.

eminence
n lit: celebrity, distinction, fame, illustriousness, importance, notability, note, prominence, reputation; elevation, height, hill, rise.

emission
n lit: discharge, ejaculation, emanation, exudation, issue, radiation, transmission; escape, leak; secretion.

emit
vb lit: broadcast, diffuse, discharge, eject, ejaculate, emanate, exhale, exude, give off, give out, issue, radiate, scatter, secrete, send out, shed, throw out, transmit.

emotion
n lit: disposition, feeling, mood, sensation, sentiment; ardour, fervour, passion, vehemence.

emotive
adj lit: affecting, personal, sensitive, stirring, touching; moving, poignant, sentimental; controversial, rousing.

emphasize
vb lit: accent, accentuate, give priority to, highlight, play on, stress, underline.

employee
n lit: hand, staff-member, worker; wage-earner.

enable
vb lit: allow, capacitate, empower, facilitate, permit.

enamoured
adj (pa.pt) lit: bewitched (by), captivated (by), enraptured (by), fascinated (by), infatuated (by), in love (with), smitten (by).

enclose
vb lit: comprehend, contain, embrace, hold, include; circumscribe, encircle, encompass, hedge in, hem in, shut in; add in, insert, put in.

enclosure
n lit: cage, cell, coral, field, kraal, laager, pen, run, stall, sty, yard; bars, fence, hedge, pale, wall, wire; fencing off, privatization, walling off; addition, insertion.

end
n lit: cessation, close, closure, completion, conclusion, dénouement, expiry, finale, finish, halt, resolution, stop, termination, winding up; boundary, edge, extremity, limit, terminus, tip; death, decease, demise; abolition, annihilation, cancellation, destruction, dissolution, downfall, extinction, scrapping; aim, aspiration, goal, intention, objective, purpose; leftover, remainder, remnant, scrap; behind, bottom, bum, posterior, rear, stern; final blow, last straw, worst.
vb lit: cease, close, come to a halt, conclude, expire, finish, halt, stop, terminate, wind up; bound; decease, die, pass away; be cancelled, be destroyed, be extinguished, be scrapped; abolish, cancel, destroy, extinguish, kill, scrap.

endanger
vb lit: compromise, hazard, imperil, jeopardize, put at risk.

endearment
n lit: pet name, sweet nothing; affection, fondness, love; caress, hug, pat.

endow
vb lit: bequeath, bestow, confer, leave, make over, settle (on), will.

endure
vb lit: bear, brook, put up with, stand, stomach, swallow, take, tolerate, withstand; experience, go through, suffer, undergo; abide, continue, last, live on, persist, remain, survive.

enemy
n lit: adversary, antagonist, foe; competitor, rival; opposition, other side.

energy
n lit: animation, drive, fire, force, life, liveliness, power, stamina, strength, verve, vigour, vim, vivacity, zest, zip.

enforce
vb lit: exact, execute, implement, impose, prosecute, put into effect.

enfranchise
vb lit: emancipate, free, liberate, release; give the vote to, grant voting rights to; authorize, license.

engagement
n lit: betrothal; agreement, bond, contract, oath, pledge, understanding, vow; appointment, date, meeting, rendezvous, tryst; commission, employment, gig, job, post, situation; action, battle, conflict, encounter, fight, skirmish.

engaging
adj (pr.pt) lit: affable, agreeable, amiable, attractive, charming, fetching, genial, likable, pleasant, winning.

engineer
n lit: mechanic, physicist, technician, technologist; designer, inventor, planner.

engrave
vb lit: carve, chase, chisel, cut, etch, scribe, sculpt; imprint, print.

enigma
n lit: conundrum, mystery, puzzle, riddle, secret.

enjoy
vb lit: appreciate, delight in, like, relish, revel in, take pleasure in; experience, have, own, possess, use.

enjoyable
adj lit: amusing, delightful, entertaining, gratifying, pleasant, pleasurable; great, marvellous, super, wonderful.

enlargement
n lit: amplification, augmentation, broadening, development, diffusion, distension, elaboration, elongation, expansion, extension, growth, increase,
magnification, stretching, swelling, widening; blow-up, print.

enormity
n lit: atrocity, crime, evil, horror, outrage; depravity, monstrousness, wickedness; dimensions, immensity, magnitude, scale, size, vastness.

enough
adj lit: adequate, sufficient.
adv lit: adequately, satisfactorily, sufficiently, to a satisfactory extent.

enshrine
vb lit: consecrate, dedicate, revere, sancify, treasure.

enslave
vb lit: bring to heel, enthral, put under the yoke, subjugate, tyrannize over; *fig*: captivate, enchant, fascinate, infatuate.

ensure
vb lit: confirm, guarantee, make sure.

enter
vb lit: come into, go into, pass into, penetrate, pierce; become a member of, enlist, enrol, join, sign up for; list, log, note, record, register, take down; put forward, submit, tender.

entrance
n lit: door, doorway, ingress, way in; gate, opening, port, trap; mouth; admittance, entry; access, avenue; appearance, arrival, introduction.
vb lit: bewitch, captivate, charm, enchant, enrapture, enthral, fascinate, infatuate; hypnotize, mesmerize, spellbind.

entry
n lit: appearance, entrance, introduction; door, doorway, ingress, way in; avenue; access, admission, admittance, entrée; candidate, competitor, contestant, entrant, player; item, memo, minute, note, record; plea, submission.

envelop
vb lit: blanket, enclose, enfold, sheathe, swathe, wrap; cloak, conceal, cover, hide, obscure, veil.

envious
adj lit: covetous, green, grudging, jealous.

environment
n lit: background, context, milieu, setting, surroundings; countryside, landscape, nature; domain, habitat.

epidemic
n *lit*: outbreak, pandemic, plague, *fig*: rash, wave.
adj lit: prevalent, rampant, rife, widespread; common, general.

epilogue
n *lit*: coda, envoi, final chapter, finale, moral, postscript.

episode
n *lit*: adventure, affair, event, happening, incident, occurrence; chapter, instalment, part.

equal
n *lit*: compeer, counterpart, equivalent, fellow, match, peer.
vb lit: agree with, balance with, be level with, equate with, match, parallel, rival, tie with; amount to, come to, total.
adj lit: alike, balanced, commensurate, corresponding, even, level, like, uniform; up (to).

equalize
vb lit: balance, even up, level, square.

equally
adv lit: alike, evenly, identically, proportionately, regularly, symmetrically, uniformly; fairly, impartially, justly, squarely.

equate
vb lit: agree, balance, be equal (with), correspond, parallel, square, tally.

equivalent
n *lit*: counterpart, equal, opposite number, parallel.
adj lit: comparable (to), equal (to), tantamount (to).

erect
vb lit: build, construct, pitch, put up, raise, set up; establish, found, institute; harden, stiffen, tumesce.
adj lit: perpendicular, upright, vertical; haughty, proud; hard, ithyphallic, rigid, standing, stiff, tumescent.

erosion
n *lit*: abrasion, attrition, corrosion, disintegration, wear.

erotic
adj lit: amatory, arousing, carnal, erogenous, exciting, sensual, sexy, stimulating, titillating, voluptuous.

err
vb lit: be inaccurate, be wrong, blunder, go astray, make a mistake, misjudge; do wrong, lapse, offend, sin, transgress.

error
n *lit*: bloomer, boob, corrigendum, erratum, fault, inaccuracy, literal, mistake, slip.

especially
adv lit: expressly, mainly, markedly, notably, outstandingly, particularly, peculiarly, principally, singularly, specifically, unusually.

espionage
n *lit*: intelligence, spying; counter-intelligence; cloak-and-dagger work.

essay
n *lit*: article, composition, dissertation, paper, piece.
vb lit: attempt, have a go at, try; gauge, test, try out.

estate
n *lit*: domain, holdings, lands, property; assets, effects, possessions, wealth; condition, position, rank, standing, station, status; caste, class, order.

etcetera
prn lit: and so on, and the rest, with others similar; blah-blah.

etching
n *lit*: carving, engraving, inscription; print.

ethics
n *lit*: conscience, integrity, morality, moral values, principles, scruples, standards.

etiquette
n *lit*: courtesy, decorum, formality, manners, politeness, protocol; convention, custom, usage.

eulogize
vb lit: acclaim, commend, compliment, extol, laud, praise.

evacuate
vb lit: abandon, leave, move out of, pull out of, quit, vacate, withdraw from; defecate, empty, void.

evaporate
vb lit: vaporize; desiccate, dry up; *fig*: disappear, dissipate, dissolve, fade away, vanish.

evasion
n lit: avoidance, circumvention, cop-out, dodge, equivocation, pretext, prevarication, shift, sophistry, subterfuge, waffle.

evasive
adj lit: reserved, reticent, secretive, tight-lipped, unforthcoming; casuistical, deceitful, dissembling, elusive, equivocating, misleading, prevaricating, shifty, slippery.

eve
n lit: day before, vigil; evening, eventide.

even
vb lit: balance (up), equal (up), level (out), match (up), square (up); settle (the score).
adj lit: flat, flush, level, parallel, steady, uniform; balanced, drawn, equal, tied; constant, regular, unbroken, unwavering; calm, composed, cool, placid, serene, stable, tranquil, unruffled.
adv lit: evenly; exactly (as), just (as); indeed, nay, veritably; fully, quite, right; surprisingly; still, yet.

eventual
adj lit: ensuing, final, overall, ultimate.

ever
adv lit: at all, at any time, on any occasion; always, constantly, continually, eternally, incessantly, perpetually, unceasingly.

every
adj lit: each, each single.

everybody
prn lit: each one, each person, the world; everyone.

everyday
adj lit: daily, diurnal, quotidian; common, commonplace, conventional, familiar, habitual, informal, mundane, ordinary, routine, unexceptional.

evil
n lit: badness, immorality, iniquity, malevolence, malice, malignity, sin, sinfulness, vice, wickedness, wrongdoing; blasphemy, sacrilege, ungodliness; calamity, catastrophe, disaster, injury, misfortune, pain, sorrow, suffering.

adj lit: bad, immoral, iniquitous, malicious, malignant, sinful, wicked; blasphemous, sacrilegious, ungodly; calamitous, catastrophic, disastrous, injurious, painful, ruinous, unlucky; foul, noxious, offensive, putrescent, vile.

evolution
n lit: advancement, development, formation, growth, metamorphosis, progress, progression, transformation.

evolve
vb lit: advance, develop, form, grow, metamorphose, progress, transform.

exactly
adv lit: accurately, carefully, faithfully, faultlessly, meticulously, precisely, punctiliously, rigorously, scrupulously, specifically, unerringly.

exaggerate
vb lit: amplify, embellish, emphasize, enlarge, inflate, magnify, overstate.

exaggeration
n lit: amplification, embellishment, emphasis, enlargement, inflation, overstatement.

exalted
adj (pa.pt) lit: august, dignified, eminent, grand, high, noble; elevated, idealistic, intellectual, lofty, superior; ecstatic, elated, exhilarated, inspired, rapturous, transported.

except
vb lit: bar, exclude, leave out, omit, pass over; absolve, exempt.
prp lit: apart from, bar, barring, but, excluding, omitting, other than, save, saving; absolving, exempting.

exceptional
adj lit: abnormal, atypical, extraordinary, singular, special, strange, uncommon, unusual; excellent, outstanding, prodigious.

excerpt
n lit: clip, cutting, extract, passage, piece, sample, section, segment, scene, trailer.

excitement
n lit: activity, ado, agitation, commotion, flurry, furore; animation, elation, exaltation, fever, heat, passion; kick, thrill; impulse, stimulation, urge.

exciting
adj lit: electrifying, exhilarating, galvanizing, rousing, sensational, stimulating, thrilling.

exclamation
n lit: cry, ejaculation, interjection.

exclusive
adj lit: private, sole, unshared; chic, classy, fashionable, posh, restricted, select.

excruciating
adj lit: acute, agonizing, burning, exquisite, harrowing, intense, lancinating, painful, piercing, racking, searing, tormenting, unendurable.

execrable
adj lit: abhorrent, abominable, cursed, damned, deplorable, detestable, hateful, loathsome.

execute
vb lit: hang, kill, put to death; assassinate, murder; accomplish, carry out, complete, discharge, do, effect, fulfil, implement, perform, put into effect, realize; deliver, serve; endorse, sign, validate.

execution
n lit: capital punishment, hanging; accomplishment, carrying out, completion, discharge, doing, effecting, fulfilment, implementation, performance, realization; manner, mode, rendition, technique; delivery.

executive
n lit: administrator, manager, official; administration, directorate, government, leadership, management.

exemption
n lit: absolution, dispensation, exception, immunity.

exercise
n lit: activity, effort, exertion, movement; discipline, drill, training, work-out; employment, practice, use, utilization; problem, task, work.
vb lit: discipline, drill, practise, train, work out; apply, employ, exert, use, utilize; burden, preoccupy, provide work for.

exhaust
n lit: emission, waste; carbon monoxide.
vb lit: be emitted, discharge, escape; consume, dissipate, finish, run through, spend, use up; drain, empty, void; bankrupt, disable, fatigue, sap, tire out, weaken, wear out.

exhaustion
n lit: debilitation, fatigue, prostration, tiredness; consumption, depletion, evacuation.

exhaustive
adj lit: comprehensive, encyclopaedic, extensive, full, intensive, sweeping, thorough.

exhort
vb lit: admonish, beseech, call upon, enjoin, entreat, press, urge.

exhume
vb lit: dig up, disinter, unearth; re-examine.

exile
n lit: banishment, deportation, expatriation, expulsion; deportee, émigré, expatriate, refugee.
vb lit: banish, deport, expatriate, expel.

existence
n lit: actuality, being, life, reality; creation.

exodus
n lit: departure, evacuation, exit, flight, leaving, migration, withdrawal.

expansive
adj lit: broad, comprehensive, extensive, wide-ranging; dilating, distending, elastic, stretching; communicative, effusive, garrulous, loquacious, talkative.

expect
vb lit: anticipate, forecast, foresee, foretell, predict; contemplate, hope for, look for, watch for; demand, have to have, insist on, rely upon.

expectant
adj lit: anticipating, awaiting, gravid, pregnant; apprehensive, eager, hopeful, watchful.

expendable
adj lit: dispensable, inessential, non-essential.

expenditure
n lit: costs, expenses, outgoings, outlay, payment; application, consumption.

expense
n lit: cost, disbursement, expenditure, outlay, payment; sacrifice.

expensive
adj lit: costly, dear, exorbitant, extortionate, extravagant, overpriced, steep.

experience
n lit: familiarity, involvement, knowledge, observation, practice, trial, understanding; adventure, affair, episode, event, incident, occurrence.
vb lit: encounter, face, go through, know, meet, observe, sample, suffer, taste, try, undergo.

experienced
adj lit: adept, competent, expert, knowledgeable, practised, qualified, seasoned, trained, veteran; mature, sophisticated, worldly-wise.

explain
vb lit: clarify, elucidate, illustrate, interpret, resolve; account for, excuse, justify; rationalize.

explanation
n lit: clarification, elucidation, illustration, interpretation, resolution, solution; account, answer, excuse, justification, reason; rationalization.

exploratory
adj lit: experimental, investigative, probing, trial; expeditionary.

explore
vb lit: enquire into, examine, investigate, look into, probe, research, search; reconnoitre, scout; sightsee, tour, travel.

explosive
adj lit: unstable, volatile; *fig*: charged, electric, taut, tense; fiery, stormy, unpredictable, violent.

expose
vb lit: disclose, display, exhibit, present, reveal, show, uncover; betray, denounce, divulge, lay bare, make known, unmask; endanger, imperil, jeopardize, leave open (to).

exposure
n lit: display, exhibition, presentation, publicity, revelation, showing, uncovering; betrayal, denunciation, disclosure, unmasking; danger, jeopardy, vulnerability; acquaintance, contact, familiarity; position, setting, view; cold,
frostbite, hypothermia; negative, photograph, shutter-speed.

expressive
adj lit: eloquent, forceful, lively, moving, poignant, telling, vivid; allusive (of), indicative (of), meaningful (of), suggestive (of); pointed, pregnant, significant.

expulsion
n lit: banishment, dismissal, ejection, eviction, exclusion, removal.

exterior
adj lit: external, outer, outward, surface.

external
adj lit: exterior, outer, outward; apparent, surface, visible; alien, exotic, foreign.

extinct
adj lit: dead, defunct, vanished forever; extinguished, inactive, out, quenched; abolished, eliminated, eradicated, wiped out.

extinguish
vb lit: blow out, put out, quench, snuff out, stifle; abolish, eliminate, eradicate, expunge, extirpate, suppress, wipe out.

extortion
n lit: blackmail, coercion, ransom demand; exorbitance, overcharging.

extra
adj lit: accessory, additional, ancillary, auxiliary, fresh, more, new, supplementary; excess, redundant, spare, superfluous, surplus, unneeded, unused.

extract
vb lit: cull, draw, pluck out, pull out, take out, uproot; bring out, elicit, evoke; gather, glean, reap; distil, express, press out, squeeze out; abstract, cite, quote.

extraction
n lit: drawing, pulling, removal, taking out, uprooting; distillation, separation; ancestry, derivation, descent, lineage, parentage, pedigree.

extravagant
adj lit: excessive, lavish, profligate, wasteful; exaggerated, extreme, fanciful, fantastic, immoderate, inordinate, unreasonable, wild; flamboyant, flashy, garish, gaudy, ostentatious; costly, exorbitant, expensive, extortionate, steep.

exuberance
n lit: buoyancy, cheerfulness, ebullience, energy, excitement, high spirits, liveliness, vigour, vivacity; copiousness, lavishness, luxuriance, prodigality, profusion, richness.

exuberant
adj lit: buoyant, cheerful, ebullient, energetic, excited, high-spirited, lively, vigorous, vivacious; copious, lavish, luxuriant, prodigal, profuse, rich.

exultant
adj lit: cock-a-hoop, elated, gleeful, joyous, jubilant, transported, triumphant.

eye
n lit: orb; optic, peeper; *fig*: appreciation, discernment, discrimination, perception, vision; (keep a) watch (on).
vb lit: contemplate, gaze at, look at, regard, stare at, study, watch; leer at, ogle.

F

fable
n lit: story, tale, yarn; legend, myth; allegory, parable; fabrication, fiction, invention, smokescreen.

fabric
n lit: cloth, material, textile; composition, constituent parts, construction, infrastructure, masonry, structural elements, texture, weave; building; *fig*: framework, organization.

fabricate
vb lit: assemble, construct, contrive, devise, form, make, put together; come up with, concoct, invent, make up, trump up.

façade
n lit: exterior, face, frontage; appearance, outward form; front, mask, veneer.

face
n lit: countenance, features, physiognomy; clock, dial, kisser, mug, mush, phizog; air, appearance, expression, look; frown, girn, grimace, pout, scowl; exterior, front, obverse, outside, surface, top; façade, outward appearance; character, disposition, physical form; font, print, type; cliff-edge, edge, sheer side, wall; aspect, facet, plane; *fig*: audacity, cheek, effrontery, gall, nerve; dignity, image, prestige, status; cutting-surface; striking-surface.
vb lit: look towards, turn to; front on to, give on to, overlook; anticipate, be confronted by, have to cope with, look forward to; encounter, experience, present oneself to, stand before; brave, confront, defy, overcome, stare (down); clad, coat, cover, laminate, sheathe, veneer; edge, line, trim; *spec*: dress (stone).

facetious
adj lit: flippant, ironical, slyly humorous, tongue-in-cheek; droll, funny, witty.

facile
adj lit: simple, simplified, uncomplicated, undemanding; oversimplified; effortless, fluent, glib, quick, ready, slick, smooth; cursory, hasty, superficial; docile, easily led, submissive, yielding.

facilities
n lit: amenities, equipment, services; accommodation, buildings, rooms; arrangements, means, opportunities; resources; aid, assistance.

facility
n lit: adroitness, dexterity, efficiency, effortlessness, fluency, practised skill, smoothness; docility, pliancy.

facsimile
n lit: copy, replica, reproduction; duplicate, photocopy, print.

fact
n lit: actuality, reality, truth; act, action, circumstance, event, happening, incident, occurrence; factor.

faction
n lit: bloc, camp, claque, clique, contingent, gang, group, lobby, party, section, set, support; conflict, discord, dissension, division, strife.

factor
n lit: component, consideration, constituent, element, ingredient, part, unit; multiplicand; agent, bailiff, estate manager, steward.

factory
n lit: plant, works; makers; depot, warehouse; assembly line.

factual
adj lit: accurate, actual, authentic, detailed, exact, faithful, objective, real.

faculty
n lit: capability, function, gift, power, sense; capacity, facility, knack, talent; department, school; branch of tuition, discipline; authorization, licence, privilege.

fad
n lit: craze, cult, fashion, in thing, mode, rage, trend, vogue.

fade
vb lit: blanch, dim, discolour, dull, pale;

bleach, etiolate, wash out; decline, die, dwindle, ebb, fail, flag, wane, wilt, wither; disappear, vanish.

fail
vb lit: be unable (to), be unsuccessful (in); flub, flunk; neglect (to); be useless to; be in vain, come to nothing, fall through, flop, go wrong, miscarry; be absent, be lacking, be missing; decline, deteriorate, fade, sink, wane; cease, conk out, die, disappear, give out, give up, go out, peter out, stop; go bankrupt.

failing
n lit: blind spot, defect, fault, flaw, shortcoming, weakness; eccentricity, foible, peculiarity.

failure
n lit: unsuccessful attempt; inability (to), neglecting (to); absence, breakdown, deficiency, deterioration, lack, loss, negligence, omission; defeat, disaster, fiasco, non-starter; collapse, disintegration; bankruptcy, crash, ruin; dud, flop, incompetent, lame duck, loser, no-hoper, washout.

faint
n lit: blackout, dizzy spell, swoon, syncope.
vb lit: become dizzy, black out, flake out, keel over, lose consciousness, pass out, swoon.
adj lit: dizzy, giddy, light-headed, muzzy, woozy; exhausted, fatigued, worn to a frazzle; feeble, halfhearted, slight, weak; fearful, timid, timorous; dim, dull, faded, hazy, indistinct, light, soft, vague; distant, faltering, low, muffled, subdued.

fair
n lit: amusement park, carnival, funfair; bazaar, market; exhibition, show, trade-fair.
adj lit: blond, blonde, flaxen, light, yellow; bright, clear, cloudless, dry, sunny; beautiful, bonny, handsome, lovely, pretty; error-free, fine, legible, presentable; civil, courteous, gentle, polite; favourable, likely, promising; adequate, all right, average, moderate, not bad, okay, passable, reasonable, satisfactory; above-board, equitable, honest, impartial, judicial, judicious, just, square, unbiased, unprejudiced; open, unobstructed.

fairly
adv lit: moderately, passably, pretty, quite, rather, reasonably, satisfactorily, tolerably; equitably, honestly, impartially, justly, squarely; deservedly, meritoriously, properly, worthily.

fairy
n lit: brownie, fay, pixie, sprite; leprechaun; *fig*: gay, nancy-boy, pansy, poof, poofter, queen, queer, woofter.

fairytale
adj lit: magical, romantic, storybook; beautiful, happy, heroic, lucky, magic, sunny.

faith
n lit: belief, confidence, conviction, reliance, trust; Church, communion, creed, religion, theology, theosophy; allegiance, constancy, fidelity, loyalty.

faithful
n lit: adherents, believers, devotees, followers; Church; communicants, congregation.
adj lit: devoted, loyal, steadfast, true; dependable, reliable, trusty; accurate, actual, authentic, detailed, exact, factual, precise, truthful.

faithfulness
n lit: constancy, devotion, fidelity, loyalty; dependability, reliability; accuracy, authenticity, exactitude, precision, truth.

faithless
adj lit: disloyal, fickle, inconstant, unfaithful, unreliable; false, perfidious, traitorous, untrustworthy.

fake
n lit: copy, counterfeit, forgery, imitation, reproduction, sham, simulation; fraud, impostor; charlatan, mountebank.
vb lit: copy, counterfeit, forge, reproduce; feign, rig, sham, simulate.
adj lit: copied, counterfeit, forged, phoney, reproduced, sham, simulated; affected, assumed, false, feigned, imitation, pretended.

fall
n lit: dive, drop, plunge, slip, tumble; collapse, defeat, destruction, overthrow, ruin, surrender; death; descent, incline, slant, slope; precipitation; depth, height; *fig*: decline, decrease, dip, lessening, lowering, reduction, slump; lapse, sin, transgression; *spec*: hold, throw (in wrestling).

vb lit: dive, drop, plunge, slip, tumble; keel over, topple, trip; be defeated, be destroyed, be overthrown, collapse, surrender, yield; be lost, die, perish; descend, incline downwards, slant, slope; be precipitated, cascade, rain, shower down; *fig*: abate, be reduced, decline, decrease, diminish, dip, flag, go down, lessen, lower, slump; backslide, commit a sin, lapse, transgress; be, become, get, happen, occur, turn; be drawn (into); *spec*: be thrown (in wrestling).

fallacy
n lit: error, falsehood, flaw, inconsistency, misapprehension, misrepresentation, sophistry.

fallible
adj lit: human, liable to error, mortal, unreliable, untrustworthy.

fallow
n lit: inert, untilled, unused; *fig*: dormant, latent, undeveloped; idle, inactive.

false
adj lit: erroneous, fallacious, inaccurate, incorrect, invalid, untrue, wrong; lying, mendacious, untruthful; deceitful, dishonest, disloyal, faithless, perfidious, traitorous, unfaithful, unreliable, untrustworthy; deceiving, deceptive, misleading; artificial, counterfeit, fake, feigned, forged, sham, simulated, synthetic, trumped up; ersatz, imitation, substitute; ill-founded, misconceived; bum, off, out of tune.

falsehood
n lit: fib, lie, story, untruth; fabrication, fiction, invention; deceit, dishonesty, mendacity, untruthfulness; perjury.

falsify
vb lit: cook, doctor, forge, misrepresent, rewrite; alter, change, interfere with, tamper with.

falter
vb lit: hesitate, stumble, tremble, vacillate, waver; break, stammer, stutter; flinch, recoil; flag, slow down, tire.

faltering
adj (pr.pt) lit: diffident, hesitant, irresolute, tentative, timid, tremulous, vacillating; broken, stammering, stuttering; flagging, tiring.

fame
n lit: celebrity, distinction, eminence, illustriousness, name, note, renown, reputation, repute, stardom; infamy, notoriety.

familiar
adj lit: accustomed, beloved, intimate, known, loved, recognized, well-known; domestic, pet, tame; common, everyday, frequent, mundane, ordinary, routine; acquainted (with), at home (with), conversant (with); cordial, easy, friendly, informal, open, relaxed, unceremonious; bold, forward, presumptuous.

familiarity
n lit: closeness, fellowship, friendship, informality, intimacy, openness; acquaintance (with), experience (with); boldness, forwardness, presumption.

family
n lit: folks, household, people, relations, relatives; clan, kindred, kinsmen, tribe; children, issue, offspring, progeny; ancestry, blood, descent, genealogy, house, line, lineage, parentage, pedigree; class, genre, group, kind.

famous
adj lit: celebrated, distinguished, eminent, illustrious, legendary, noted, renowned, reputed, well-known; infamous, notorious.

fan
n lit: air conditioner, blower, vane, ventilator; aficionado, buff, devotee, enthusiast, freak, supporter.
vb lit: air-condition, blow, ventilate; *fig*: arouse, excite, kindle, provoke, stir up; *spec*: spread out (cards).

fanatic
n lit: activist, extremist, militant, zealot; addict, devotee, enthusiast.

fanatical
adj lit: burning, devoted, extreme, fervent, frenzied, militant, passionate, rabid, zealous.

fanciful
adj lit: fairytale, fantastic, imaginative; capricious, whimsical; extravagant, wild; chimerical, imaginary, unreal; imaginative, poetic, romantic.

fancy
n lit: imagination; daydream, dream, fantasy; fondness, hankering, liking, partiality, predilection, preference; caprice, humour, inclination, thought, whim; idea, notion, speculation, theory.
vb lit: conjecture, guess, imagine, reckon, suppose, think; believe, surmise, think likely; covet, crave, desire, go for, hanker after, lust after, prefer, take to, wish for, yearn for.
adj lit: decorated, elaborate, embellished, extravagant, fantastical, garish, gaudy, ornamental, ornate.

fanfare
n lit: flourish, trump, sennet, tucket; herald, introduction; hype, promotion, publicity, sales pitch, splash.

fantastic
adj lit: excellent, great, sensational, super, superb, wonderful; extreme, overwhelming, tremendous; implausible, incredible, preposterous, unbelievable; chimerical, illusory, phantasmagorical, weird, wild.

fantasy
n lit: daydream, figment of the imagination, image, mental picture, vision; nightmare; fairy story, science fiction, time story; fancy, imagination; invention, originality.

far
adj lit: distant, remote; outlying; farther, hinder, other.
adv lit: a long way, deep, distantly, remotely; considerably, definitely, much, positively.

faraway
adj lit: distant, remote; outlying; *fig*: abstracted, dreamy, preoccupied, rapt.

farce
n lit: burlesque, comedy; buffoonery, slapstick; absurdity, joke, nonsense; hollow formality, travesty.

farcical
adj lit: absurd, comic, improbable, laughable, ludicrous, nonsensical, ridiculous, silly, unbelievable.

fare
n lit: passenger, pick-up, traveller; fee, price, ticket money, transportation cost; food, provisions, rations, sustenance.

vb lit: be, do, go, get along, make out, proceed, turn out, work out; be fed, eat, feed.

farewell
n lit: adieu, goodbye, valediction; leave-taking, parting, send-off, well-wishing.

far-fetched
adj lit: hard to believe, implausible, improbable, incredible, unlikely; forced, unconvincing, unnatural.

farm
n lit: croft, homestead, plantation, ranch, smallholding; acreage, fields; battery, beds, breeding-station, piggery, stud; treatment plant, works.
vb lit: cultivate, till, work; breed, raise, rear, tend; contract (out), subcontract (out).

farmer
n lit: crofter, homesteader, rancher, smallholder; agriculturalist, agronomist; grower, planter, producer; breeder, cattleman, dairyman, shepherd, stud-owner; contractor, subcontractor.

far-sighted
adj lit: foreseeing, prescient; cautious, provident, prudent.

fascinate
vb lit: allure, attract, bewitch, captivate, enchant, enrapture, enthrall, entrance, infatuate, mesmerize, put a spell on, ravish, spellbind; interest strangely, intrigue.

fascination
n lit: allure, attraction, charm, enchantment, magic, magnetism, spell; captivation, infatuation.

fashion
n lit: convention, custom, usage; craze, fad, rage, trend, vogue; creation, cut, form, line, make, mode, pattern, shape; manner, style, way; appearance, description, kind, sort, type; high society, jet set.
vb lit: build, create, form, make, mould, knead, shape, work.

fashionable
adj lit: à la mode, chic, modish, snappy, snazzy, stylish, trendy; current, in, in vogue, latest, popular, up-to-the-minute; jetsetting, tonish, wealthy.

fast
n lit: abstinence; period of abstinence; hunger-strike.
vb lit: abstain, go hungry, refrain from eating, take no food.
adj lit: brisk, fleet, hasty, hurried, nippy, quick, rapid, swift; fixed, secure, tight; *fig*: close, firm, loyal, steadfast; dissolute, licentious, loose, promiscuous; intemperate, rash, reckless, wild; *spec*: before time, early (of a clock); permanent, unfading (colours); sound (sleep).
adv lit: briskly, hastily, hurriedly, quickly, rapidly, speedily, swiftly; fixedly, securely, tightly; *fig*: firmly, loyally, steadfastly, unflinchingly; close (by), near (by); *spec*: sound, soundly (asleep).

fasten
vb lit: attach, connect, join, link, secure, unite; bind, chain, tie; affix, bond, cement, glue; nail, rivet, tack, weld; buckle, button, do up, hook up, lace, pin (on), zip; *fig*: aim (on), concentrate (on), focus (on); latch (on to), seize (on); push (on to).

fastener
n lit: bolt, buckle, button, clasp, clip, grip, hook, knob, lace, latch, lock, nut, pin, rivet, screw, tape, zip.

fat
n lit: adipose tissue, carbohydrate; blubber, flab; grease, oil; butter, lard, margarine, polyunsaturates; *fig*: body, fullness, richness, substance.
adj lit: adipose; blubbery, corpulent, flabby, fleshy, obese, overweight, plump, portly, roly-poly, rotund, stout, tubby; greasy, oily, oleaginous; broad, bulky, enormous, great, huge, jumbo, massive, vast, wide; *fig*: fertile, fruitful, lush, rich.

fatal
adj lit: deadly, lethal, mortal; incurable, terminal; *fig*: calamitous, catastrophic, disastrous; critical, decisive, fateful, portentous.

fate
n lit: destiny, predestination, providence; lot, portion, weird; forecast, future, horoscope, stars; bad luck, ill fortune.

fated
adj lit: destined, doomed, foreordained, predestined, preordained, written.

fateful
adj lit: critical, decisive, fatal, portentous; charged, electric, emotive.

father
n lit: begetter, progenitor, sire; dad, guv'nor, old man, pa, papa, pater, pop; elder, senator, abbot, confessor, priest, prior, vicar; *fig*: author, creator, discoverer, founder, inventor, maker.
vb lit: beget, sire; engender, generate; adopt, foster; *fig*: establish, found, institute, originate.

fatherly
adj lit: parental, paternal; pastoral, priestly.

fathom
vb lit: gauge, measure, plumb, sound; comprehend, divine, grasp, understand.

fatigue
n lit: exhaustion, tiredness, weariness; debility, languor, lethargy; failure, stress, weakness.
vb lit: drain, exhaust, tire, weaken, wear out, whack.

fatten
vb lit: build (up), feed (up), force-feed, nourish, stuff.

fatuous
adj lit: asinine, brainless, idiotic, imbecile, lunatic, mindless, moronic, witless; feeble-minded, inane, vacuous.

fault
n lit: defect, deficiency, flaw; blunder, error, inaccuracy, lapse, mistake, slip; omission; blemish, imperfection; blame, culpability, guilt, responsibility; offence, sin, transgression, trespass.
vb lit: find a flaw in, pick holes in; blame.

faultless
adj lit: exemplary, flawless, immaculate, impeccable, irreproachable, perfect, spotless, unblemished.

faulty
adj lit: blemished, broken, defective, deficient, flawed, imperfect; inaccurate, incorrect, invalid, wrong; malfunctioning.

favour
n lit: approbation, approval, esteem, good books, goodwill, patronage, support; bias, partiality; good turn, kindness,

service; keepsake, kerchief, ribbon, token.
vb lit: approve of, commend, fancy, support; be biased towards, have a soft spot for, prefer, side with; grace (with), oblige (with); *fig*: look like, resemble, take after.

favourable
adj lit: approving, encouraging, positive, welcoming, well-disposed; advantageous, beneficial, good, helpful, opportune, propitious; clement, suitable.

favourite
n lit: best, choice, pick, preference; cert, certainty, cinch, hot tip, sure thing, tip.

favouritism
n lit: bias, nepotism, partiality, partisanship, preference.

fawn
adj lit: beige, buff, yellowish.

fear
n lit: anxiety, apprehension, dread, foreboding, fright, misgiving, panic, terror, timidity, trepidation, unease; horror, phobia; reverence, veneration.
vb lit: apprehend, be afraid of, be apprehensive (that), be frightened of, be terrified of, dread (that); suspect (that); be anxious (for), tremble (for); respect, revere, reverence, venerate.

fearful
adj lit: afraid, alarmed, apprehensive, frightened, intimidated, jumpy, nervous, timid; craven, cowardly, pusillanimous, timorous; appalling, atrocious, dreadful, ghastly, grim, horrendous, shocking, terrible; *fig*: awful, terrible, unpleasant.

fearless
adj lit: bold, daring, dauntless, heroic, indomitable, intrepid, unafraid, unflinching.

feasible
adj lit: achievable, possible, practicable, realizable, viable, workable.

feast
n lit: banquet, beano, blow-out, slap-up meal, spread; meal, repast; celebration, festival, saint's day; *fig*: delight, pleasure, treat.

vb lit: banquet, gorge (on), stuff, wine and dine; entertain sumptuously; *fig*: delight, gladden, gratify.

feat
n lit: accomplishment, achievement, attainment; deed, exploit, stroke.

feature
n lit: facial characteristic; aspect, attribute, idiosyncracy, mark, property, trait; attraction, highlight, specialty; article, item, piece; full-length film, movie.
vb lit: be useful (in), have a part (in), participate (in), take part (in); emphasize, highlight, play up, present, splash, star.

federal
adj lit: affiliated, allied, associated, combined, confederate, syndicated, united.

federation
n lit: alliance, association, combination, confederacy, league, syndicate, syndication.

fed up
adj fig: annoyed (with), browned off, cheesed off, dissatisfied, exasperated; bored (with).

fee
n lit: charge, cost, hire, payment, price, toll; emolument, remuneration.

feeble
adj lit: debilitated, doddering, failing, frail, puny, sickly, skinny, slight, thin, weak; delicate, effete, faint, indecisive, ineffectual, insignificant; *fig*: flimsy, inadequate, lame, poor, tame, threadbare.

feed
vb lit: cater for, provision, seat, victual; provide for, supply to; exist (on), live (on), subsist (on); devour, eat; crop, graze; *fig*: foster, fuel, nourish, strengthen; channel, duct, pipe, supply; be straight-man to, cue.

feel
vb lit: caress, finger, fondle, fumble over, grasp, grope, handle, paw, stroke, touch; be aware of, experience, notice, perceive, sense; test (out), try (out); believe (that), consider (that), hold (that), think (that); agonize (for), be sorry (for), bleed (for); have great sympathy (for).

feeling
n lit: consciousness, impression, perception, presentiment, sensation, sense; air, atmosphere, aura, mood; idea, notion, suspicion; consensus, opinion, view; affection, fondness, sentimentality, warmth; emotion, fervour, passion; compassion, empathy, sympathy, understanding.

fell
vb lit: cut down, hew down, level, raze; flatten, knock down.
adj lit: cruel, fierce, ruthless, savage, terrible; dire; deadly.

fellow
n lit: bloke, chap, customer, geezer, guy, man; colleague, comrade, member, partner; companion, equal; counterpart, like, match, mate, twin.

fellowship
n lit: association, brotherhood, club, communion, companionship, fraternity, league, order, sorority, society; amity, intimacy, sociability.

feminine
adj lit: female, womanly; girlish, ladylike; delicate, fragrant, graceful, soft, tender; buxom, curvaceous; effeminate, womanish.

fen
n lit: bog, broads, marsh, morass, swamp, water meadows.

fence
n lit: barrier, hedge, hurdle, palings, palisade, railings, stockade, wire, wire netting; receiver of stolen property.
vb lit: barricade, hedge (in), pen (in); fortify, secure, shield; dispose of stolen property; *fig*: equivocate, prevaricate.

fend off
vb lit: parry, ward off; hold off, keep at bay, resist; *fig*: avert, forestall.

ferment
n lit: barm, enzyme, leavening, mother, yeast; *fig*: agitation, commotion, excitement, frenzy, heat, stew, turmoil, upset.
vb lit: boil, bubble, foam, seethe; brew, leaven, rise; work; *fig*: agitate, excite, foment, inflame, provoke, rouse, stir up, work up.

ferocious
adj lit: dangerous, fierce, predatory, savage, wild; bloodthirsty, brutal, cruel, merciless, ruthless, vicious.

ferocity
n lit: fierceness, rapacity, savagery; bloodthirstiness, brutality, cruelty, mercilessness, ruthlessness, viciousness.

ferret
n lit: fitch, polecat.
vb lit: dig (out), get (out), nose (out), root (out), search (out); drive (out).

ferry
vb lit: chauffeur, convey, drive, escort, run, see (to), ship, transport.

fertile
adj lit: fecund, fruitful; arable, cultivable; abundant, luxuriant, productive, prolific, rich, teeming.

fertilize
vb lit: impregnate, inseminate, make pregnant; pollinate; compost, dress, manure, mulch.

fervent
adj lit: ardent, devout, earnest, enthusiastic, impassioned, vehement, zealous.

fervour
n lit: ardour, devotion, earnestness, enthusiasm, passion, vehemence, zeal.

festival
n lit: feast, saint's day; anniversary; commemoration programme, season; celebration, gala, party.

festive
adj lit: celebratory, convivial, festal, happy, holiday, jolly, joyous, merry; bright, colourful, decorative, gay.

festoon
vb lit: bedeck, beribbon, drape, garland, hang about (with), swathe.

fetch
vb lit: bring, carry, convey, deliver, get, obtain, recover, retrieve, take; escort, guide, lead; draw out, elicit; bring in, earn, make, produce, sell for.

fetching
adj lit: attractive, becoming, charming, delightful, sweet, taking, winsome.

fetish
n lit: cargo, cult object, idol, taboo, talisman; fixation, mania, obsession.

feud
n lit: grudge, hatred, rivalry, simmering resentment, vendetta, war; conflict, contention, dissension, enmity, hostility, quarrel, strife.

feudal
adj lit: liege, manorial; hierarchical.

fever
n lit: heat, high temperature; *fig*: delirium, ferment, flush, frenzy, passion.

feverish
adj lit: burning, febrile, flushed, hectic, hot, inflamed; *fig*: delirious, frenetic, frenzied, impassioned, passionate.

few
n lit: couple, handful, scattering.
adj lit: hardly any, not many; meagre, scanty, scarce, sparse.

fiancé(e)
n lit: affianced, betrothed, intended.

fiasco
n lit: catastrophe, debacle, disaster, rout, ruin.

fib
n lit: untruth, white lie; equivocation, fiction, prevarication, story.
vb lit: lie, tell an untruth; equivocate, prevaricate.

fibre
n lit: filament, strand, thread; nap, pile, texture; *fig*: being, nature, spirit, soul; (moral) strength.

fickle
adj lit: changeable, flighty, inconstant, mercurial, unfaithful, unpredictable, vacillating, variable.

fiction
n lit: narrative, story, tale, yarn; fantasy, imagination, invention; fabrication, imposture, lie, simulation, untruth.

fictitious
adj lit: imaginary, invented, made-up, unreal, untrue; imagined, make-believe; affected, assumed, counterfeit, feigned, sham, simulated.

fiddle
n lit: violin; *fig*: con, fraud, graft, ramp, rip-off, swindle.
vb lit: play the violin, scrape the strings; *fig*: fidget (with), mess about (with), play (with), tamper (with), toy (with); cheat, con, rip off, swindle.

fidelity
n lit: constancy, faithfulness, loyalty; dependability, reliability, trustworthiness; closeness, correspondence, match; exactitude, precision.

fidget
vb lit: be restless, be unable to stop moving, fiddle, mess about, play around, toy (with), trifle (with).

field
n lit: lea, meadow, pasture; acreage; *fig*: area, confines, domain, province, territory; line, sphere; bounds, limits, range, scope; department, discipline, specialty; competitors, contestants, entrants, runners; applicants, candidates.
vb lit: catch, retrieve, throw back; *fig*: cope with, deal with, handle; deflect, parry, turn aside.

fiend
n lit: demon, devil, evil spirit; brute, monster, ogre, savage, sadist, torturer; *fig*: buff, enthusiast, fanatic, freak; addict.

fierce
adj lit: dangerous, fell, feral, ferocious, murderous, predatory, savage, tigerish, untamed, wild; furious, raging, tempestuous, violent; *fig*: blazing, fiery, hot; cut-throat, intense, strong.

fiery
adj lit: ablaze, aflame, blazing, burning, flaming, glowing, heated, hot; feverish, inflamed; *fig*: ardent, fervent, fervid, passionate, spirited; irascible, short-tempered, volatile; carrot, ginger, red; acidic, acrid, bitter, pungent, raw.

fight
n lit: affray, altercation, brawl, clash, conflict, fracas, free-for-all, melee, punch-up, riot, row, scrap, scrimmage, scuffle, set-to, tussle; bout, boxing-match, contest; action, battle, engagement, skirmish, struggle, war; *fig*: aggression, belligerence, militancy; gameness, mettle, spirit.
vb lit: brawl, clash, come to blows (with), cross swords (with), do battle (with), scrap (with), scuffle (with), tussle (with), wrestle (with); box (with), spar (with); combat, engage, skirmish (with), struggle against, wage war against;

figure 133 find

bicker, squabble, wrangle; contest, dispute, oppose, resist against.

figure
n lit: digit, number, numeral; form, outline, shape; artwork, design, device, diagram, drawing, illustration, picture; body, build, frame, physique, vital statistics; *fig*: cost, price, sum, value; celebrity, character, notable, personage, personality, presence; *spec*: anomaly, eccentricity, idiosyncrasy (of speech).
vb lit: decorate, embellish, ornament; add (up), count (up), reckon (up), tot (up); act (in), appear (in), be mentioned (in), feature (in); consider, guess, imagine, reckon, suppose, think.

figurehead
n lit: cipher, front man, mouthpiece, puppet, nominal leader, token leader.

file
n lit: grater, plane, rasp, scraper; brief, case-notes, document, dossier, folder; column, crocodile, line, queue, row; rank.
vb lit: grate, plane, rasp, rub down, sand, scrape, smooth; document, enter, record, register; insert, put in place; line up, queue.

fill
vb lit: cram, crowd, pack; charge (up), replenish, restock; suffuse; supply; sate, satiate, satisfy, stuff; saturate; bung, cork, plug, seal, stop; cover, occupy, take up; *fig*: discharge, execute, fulfil; belly out, extend, inflate.

filling
n lit: stopping; contents, insides; padding, stuffing; cream, icing, jam, marzipan; *spec*: woof (in weaving).
adj (pr.pt) lit: ample, bloating, heavy, substantial.

film
n lit: coating, integument, layer; membrane, skin, tissue; dusting, powder; blur, cloud, haze, mist; celluloid, feature, movie, tape, video.
vb lit: photograph, shoot, take; blur (over), cloud (over), haze (over), mist (over).

filmy
adj lit: chiffon, diaphanous, flimsy, gauzy, gossamer, see-through, sheer, translucent, transparent; blurry, cloudy, hazy, misty.

filter
n lit: gauze, mesh, paper, sieve, strainer; tip, trap; coloured lens; lane for turning traffic.
vb lit: scree, sieve, strain; clarify, refine, purify; drip (through), leach (through), ooze (through), percolate (into).

filth
n lit: defilement, dirt, foulness, grime, mud, pollution, refuse, rubbish, slime; dung, excrement, excreta, faeces, muck, ordure, sewage, shit; indecency, obscenity, pornography, smut.

filthy
adj lit: begrimed, blackened, dirty, foul, grimy, grubby, muddy, polluted, slimy; faecal, feculent, mucky, shitty; indecent, obscene, pornographic, smutty.

final
adj lit: closing, concluding, last, terminal, terminating, ultimate; conclusive, decisive, definitive, irrevocable.

finally
adv lit: in conclusion, lastly, to end with; at last, eventually, in the end, ultimately; conclusively, decisively, definitively, irrevocably, once and for all.

finance
n lit: banking, commerce, economics, investment; bourse, money market, stock market; asset(s), backing, capital, fund(s), funding, money, resource(s).
vb lit: back, bankroll, float, fund, guarantee, put up the money for, sponsor, support, underwrite.

financial
adj lit: commercial, economic, fiscal, monetary.

find
n lit: catch, discovery; acquisition, bargain; asset, treasure.
vb lit: chance upon, come across, discover, encounter, light upon, meet, stumble on; acquire, gain, get hold of, lay one's hands on, locate, obtain, procure, run down, spot, track down, turn up, uncover; recover, regain, retrieve; bring to light, detect, reveal; furnish, provide, supply; *fig*: become aware, note, notice, observe, perceive, realize; declare, proclaim, pronounce.

finding
n lit: detection, discovery, location, recovery, retrieval, tracking down; conclusion, decision, judgement, verdict; answer, result, total.

find out
vb lit: ascertain, calculate, discover, figure out, learn, rumble, suss out, work out; observe, perceive, realize; catch out, expose, reveal, unmask.

fine
n lit: forfeit, penalty; fee, price, toll.
vb lit: mulct, penalize; compel to pay.
adj lit: admirable, attractive, beautiful, bonny, excellent, exquisite, magnificent, smart, splendid, striking, stylish; dainty, delicate, elegant, fragile, slender; slight, thin, tenuous; diaphanous, gauzy, gossamer, light, sheer; crushed, powdery, pulverized, refined; clear, pure, unadulterated, unalloyed; bright, dry, fair, sunny; agreeable, all right, good, okay, suitable; critical, discriminating, fastidious, keen, precise, sensitive, sharp; cutting, razor-edged; brilliant, polished.

finery
n lit: best clothes, embellishments, family jewels, frippery, glad rags, regalia, Sunday best, trappings.

finesse
n lit: adeptness, adroitness, artistry, craft, skill; delicacy, diplomacy, discretion, subtlety, tact; panache, savoir-faire, sophistication; guile, manoeuvre, stratagem.

finger
n lit: digit; *fig*: interest (in), share (in).
vb lit: feel, fiddle with, fondle, handle, manipulate, paw, touch, toy with; *fig*: betray, give away, identify, inform on.

finish
n lit: close, completion, conclusion, culmination, end, ending, stop, termination, winding-up; bankruptcy, liquidation, ruin; death, demolition, destruction; defeat; lustre, patina, polish, shine, surface texture; *fig*: culture, refinement, sophistication.
vb lit: accomplish, achieve, cease, close, complete, conclude, culminate (in), do, end, round off, stop, terminate, wind up; drain (off), drink (up), eat (up), use (up); destroy, ruin; kill (off); defeat; coat, face,

lacqueur, polish, texture, wax; *fig*: perfect, refine.

finite
adj lit: bounded, circumscribed, limited, qualified, restricted.

fire
n lit: combustion; blaze, conflagration, inferno; coals, embers, flames, sparks; barbecue, beacon, brazier, grate, hob, oven, stove; bombardment, fusillade, shelling, sniping; *fig*: brightness, brilliance, flare, intensity, lustre, radiance, scintillation, sparkle; ardour, fervour, force, heat, passion, zeal; animation, dash, eagerness, enthusiasm, excitement, life, spirit, verve, vigour, vivacity; creativity, inspiration; danger, hardship, ordeal, trial, tribulation.
vb lit: ignite, kindle, light, set ablaze, set alight to, set on fire; bake, roast; cauterize; detonate, explode, touch off; discharge, let off, shoot; *fig*: arouse, electrify, galvanize, inflame, inspire, rouse, stir; fuel; boot out, cashier, dismiss, give the sack, lay off; *spec*: catch, start (of a car engine).

fireworks
n lit: pyrotechnics; *fig*: paroxysms of rage, stormy scenes, tantrums, trouble.

firm
n lit: business, company, organization, outfit.
adj lit: fast, fixed, immovable, rooted, secure, solid, stable, steady, strong, sturdy, unshakable; compact, dense, hard, rigid, stiff; *fig*: adamant, inflexible, obdurate, resolute, steadfast, unfaltering, unflinching, unswerving.

firmness
n lit: fixity, immobility, security, solidity, stability, steadiness, strength, sturdiness; compactness, density, hardness, rigidity, stiffness, tensile strength; *fig*: inflexibility, obduracy, resolve, steadfastness, strength of purpose.

first
adj lit: dawn, earliest, initial, opening, original, primary, primeval; foremost, leading; chief, head, highest, prime, principal, top; basic, cardinal, elementary.
adv lit: at the outset, beforehand, initially, in the beginning, to start with; lief, rather, sooner.

first-class

adj lit: ace, crack, excellent, exceptional, first-rate, outstanding, superb, superlative, tiptop, very good.

fish

n fig: character, individual, person, type; bracket, plate, stay.
vb lit: angle (for), bait a line (for), catch, hook, net, reel in, trawl (for); dive (for); *fig*: be on the lookout (for), try (for); fumble (for), search (for).

fishy

adj lit: piscatorial; clammy, cold, scaly; *fig*: blank, expressionless, glassy, lifeless, vacant; dubious, funny, odd, peculiar, strange, suspicious, untoward.

fit

n lit: dimensions, shape, size; appropriateness, aptitude, rightness, suitability; attack, bout, convulsion, seizure, spasm; outbreak, spell; humour, mood.
vb lit: be appropriate for, be apt for, be right for, conform to, correspond to, match, suit, tally; equip (out), kit (out), rig (out); slot (in), sort (in); frame (up).
adj lit: able, adequate, competent, deserving, equipped, good enough (to), qualified (for), right, suitable, well-suited; athletic, hale, healthy, in condition, in good shape, in rude health, robust, trim, well.

fitful

adj lit: erratic, flickering, fluctuating, intermittent, spasmodic, sporadic.

fitness

n lit: appropriateness, aptitude, aptness, correspondence, eligibility, match, suitability; athleticism, good condition, health, shape.

fitting

n lit: accessory, attachment, auxiliary piece, decoration, module; measurement, trying on.
adj (pr.pt) lit: appropriate, apt, correct, proper, right, suitable; decent, desirable, seemly.

fix

n lit: exact position, location, siting; *fig*: difficulty, hole, jam, mess, pickle, predicament, quandary, spot; dose, injection, shot.

vb lit: anchor, implant, place, plant, position, set, settle; attach, bond, cement, fasten, glue, secure, stick; nail, pin, tack, tape, tie; adjust, attend to, do (up), correct, mend, patch, repair, see to, sort out; congeal, consolidate, harden, set, solidify, thicken; cook (up), get (up), make (up); *fig*: agree (on), appoint, arrange, determine, establish, name, specify; direct, focus; get even with, stop.

fixation

n lit: complex, hang-up, mania, obsession; thing.

fizzle out

vb lit: collapse, die away, fade out, flag, fold up, peter out, splutter, wane.

flabbergast

vb lit: amaze, astonish, astound, bowl over, confound, discombobulate, dumbfound, overwhelm, stagger, stun, take thoroughly aback.

flag

n lit: arms, banner, colours, ensign, jack, standard; burgee, gonfalon, pennant.
vb lit: be fatigued, droop, ebb, fade, fail, sag, slump, taper off, tire, wane, weary, wilt, wither; label, mark, tab; hail, salute, wave (down).

flagging

adj (pr.pt) lit: drooping, ebbing, fading, failing, faltering, sagging, sinking, slowing, slumping, tapering off, tiring, waning, wearying, wilting, withering; labelling, marking, tabbing; hailing, saluting, waving (down).

flagrant

adj lit: arrant, barefaced, blatant, brazen, flaunted, glaring, infamous, open, overt, shameless, undisguised.

flail

n lit: crusher, thresher.
vb lit: beat, thrash, thresh; gesticulate, whirl one's arms, windmill.

flair

n lit: ability, aptitude, feel, genius, gift, knack, talent; dash, elegance, panache, savoir-faire, style, virtuosity.

flake

n lit: chip, chipping, layer, scale, sliver; crystal; flash, spark.
vb lit: chip, peel (off), scale (off); black (out), pass (out).

flamboyant

adj lit: extravagant, florid, grandiose, ornate, ostentatious, swaggering, theatrical; garish, gaudy, loud, showy.

flame

n lit: fire; light; *fig*: amour, boyfriend, girlfriend, love, sweetheart; ardour, fervency, intensity, passion.
vb lit: blaze, burn, flare, flash, glow, shine; blush, flush, suffuse.

flaming

adj lit: ablaze, afire, alight, burning, fiery; *fig*: angry, hot, irate, raging; fervent, impassioned, vehement, violent; ginger, red; accursed, blasted, confounded, damned.

flannel

n lit: serge, twill, worsted; trouser(s); face-cloth, towelling; *fig*: bilge, blarney, bosh, prevarication, waffle; flattery.
vb fig: equivocate, hedge, prevaricate, talk bilge, waffle (on); butter up, flatter, soft-soap.

flap

n lit: apron, cover, fold, lappet, lid, tab; aerofoil, aileron; banging, beating, flailing, fluttering, swinging, threshing; *fig*: commotion, fluster, panic, state, tizzy.
vb lit: bang, beat, flail, flutter, swing, thresh, wave; *fig*: be flustered, get into a state, panic.

flare

n lit: blaze, flame, glare; beam, flash, light, ray; beacon, rocket, signal; bell, bowl, spreading, widening out.
vb lit: blaze, flame (up), glare, gleam, glow; beam, flash, flicker, light (up); belly (out), spread (out), widen (out); *fig*: burst out, erupt, fire (up).

flash

n lit: beam, blaze, burst, flare, flicker, gleam, glow, glint, glistening, scintillation, spark, sparkle; cascade, deluge, flood, spurt; *fig*: blur, streak; instant, moment, second, trice; display, exposure, show; news headline.
vb lit: beam, blaze, burst, flare, flicker, gleam, glow, glint, glisten, scintillate, spark, sparkle; *fig*: blur, shoot, streak; dash, speed, sprint, zip; display, expose, let one see, show.

flashy

adj lit: garish, gaudy, loud, ostentatious, showy; cheap, tasteless, vulgar.

flask

n lit: bottle, canteen, carafe, decanter; powder-horn; retort.

flat

n lit: apartment, room, storey; lowland, plain; marsh, swamp; shallow, shoal; backdrop, prop; *fig*: dupe, gull, john, mark.
adj lit: horizontal, level, plane, uniform; at full length, prone, prostrate, recumbent, supine; burst, collapsed, deflated, empty, punctured; *fig*: boring, colourless, dead, insipid, lifeless, stale, vapid, watery; blue, dejected, depressed, morose; absolute, categorical, fixed, positive, unequivocal, unqualified; *spec*: back, short (vowel, diphthong); below the right (musical) pitch; defunct (battery).
adv lit: horizontal, in a heap, to the ground; *fig*: absolutely, categorically, positively, unequivocally, utterly; *spec*: below the right (musical) pitch.

flatly

adv lit: absolutely, categorically, positively, unequivocally, utterly.

flatten

vb lit: even out, level, roll, smooth out; fell, knock to the ground, raze, trample over; knock back, prostrate; *spec*: lower the (musical) pitch; shorten (a vowel sound).

flatter

vb lit: be sycophantic towards, butter up, crawl to, fawn over, soft-soap, toady to, truckle to; be over-complimentary about; humour (into), wheedle (into); *fig*: become, enhance, set off, show to good advantage.

flattery

n lit: fawning, obsequiousness, servility, soft-soaping, sycophancy, toadying.

flavour

n lit: essence, piquancy, savour, smack, tang, taste; *fig*: character, feel, quality, stamp, tone; hint, suggestion, tinge, touch.
vb lit: imbue (with), infuse (with); season, spice; *fig*: add interest to, ginger up.

fleabitten

adj lit: infested, lousy, scabby, spotty; unhygienic; *fig*: grotty, grubby, low, mean, miserable, scruffy, shabby, sleazy, sordid, squalid.

flee
vb lit: beat it, bolt, fly, make off, run for it, scarper, scram, split, take a powder, take off; abscond, escape, get away; hurtle, race, speed, sprint; disappear, fade away, vanish.

fleece
n lit: coat, wool; *fig*: covering, layer, surface.
vb lit: clip, shear; *fig*: cover; cheat, con, defraud, fiddle out (of), rip off, rob, rook, swindle, take to the cleaners.

fleet
n lit: armada, flotilla, navy; company, force, squad, team.
adj lit: fast, nimble, rapid, speedy, swift; ephemeral, evanescent, fast-fading, transient.

flesh
n lit: meat, muscle, brawn, fat, gristle, tissue; food; *fig*: body, physical self; carnality, physical urges; humanity, humankind, human nature, humans, mankind.

flex
n lit: cable, connection, cord, line, wire; bend, exercise.
vb lit: bend, contract, crook, exercise; be elastic, bow, distend, give, warp.

flexible
adj lit: elastic, plastic, pliable, pliant, springy, tensile; ductile, mouldable; agile, limber, lithe, loose-limbed, nimble, supple; *fig*: adaptable, adjustable, variable; amenable, compliant, docile, responsive, tractable.

flickering
adj (pr.pt) lit: guttering, oscillating, quivering, twinkling, wavering; intermittent, irregular, spasmodic; flutter, hover.

flight
n lit: flying; air travel, flying time; collection, flock, swarm; squadron, wing; aeronautics, aviation; escape, fleeing, getaway; rout, scattering, stampede; *fig*: digression, foray, sally; staircase; salvo, volley; hurdle, jump; *spec*: feathering (on a dart or arrow).

flimsy
adj lit: delicate, frail, insubstantial, slight, chiffon, diaphanous, gauzy, gossamer, light, sheer, thin; rickety, shaky, unsteady; *fig*: feeble, implausible, shallow, trivial, unconvincing, weak.

flinch
vb lit: blanch, blench, cringe, quail, recoil, shy away, wince.

fling
n lit: heave, hurl, pitch, throw, toss; *fig*: bash, crack, go, shot, stab, try, whirl; ball, good time, spree.
vb lit: chuck, heave, hurl, pitch, sling, throw, toss.

flinty
adj lit: hard, stony, unyielding; *fig*: adamant, steely, unwavering; cruel, harsh, merciless, ruthless, unrelenting.

flip
n lit: flick, jerk, snap, toss, twist; pleasure-flight, ride, spin; boost, fillip; toddy.
vb lit: flick, jerk, snap, toss, twist; *fig*: go berserk, go mad, hit the roof; flap, get into a state, panic.

flippant
adj lit: disrespectful, facetious, frivolous, impertinent, impudent, irreverent, pert, saucy, smart-aleck.

flirt
n lit: coquette, gadabout, minx, tease; philanderer, rake.
vb lit: be coquettish (with); *fig*: play (with), toy (with), trifle (with).

flirtation
n lit: coquetry, philandering, teasing; playing (with), toying (with), trifling (with).

float
n lit: bobber, cork, quill; pontoon, raft; ballcock; blade, paddle; spatula, trowel; cart, dray, flat lorry; cash in hand, petty cash, small change.
vb lit: be buoyant, stay up; bob, drift, glide, slide; hover, levitate; *fig*: establish, launch, set up; circulate, divulge, publish; sell shares in.

flock
n lit: nap, pile, tuft, wool; colony, flight, rookery, skein; *fig*: collection, company, crowd, group, herd, mass, throng; assembly, congregation.

vb lit: assemble, collect, congregate, crowd, gather, mass, throng.

flog
vb lit: beat, flay, lash, scourge, thrash, whip; *fig*: drive, oppress, overwork, punish; *fig*: hawk, peddle, sell.

flood
n lit: deluge, inundation, spate, tide, torrent; immersion, overflow, submersion; *fig*: glut, plethora, profusion, rush.
vb lit: drown, engulf, immerse, inundate, overflow, submerge, swamp; drench, saturate, soak; flow, gush, rush, surge; *fig*: fill, glut.

floor
n lit: base, bed, bottom, ground, surface; level, storey, tier; auditorium, body; arena, theatre.
vb lit: fell, flatten, knock down, level, raze; put down, set down; *fig*: confound, defeat, discomfit, nonplus, perplex, puzzle, stump, throw.

flop
n lit: debacle, disaster, dud, failure, fiasco, lame duck, loser, non-starter.
vb lit: dangle, droop, hang (down/over), sag; collapse, fold up, go limp; reverse, turn over; *fig*: be a dud, fail, fold, founder; crash (out), sleep.

florid
adj lit: flushed, red-cheeked, rubicund; baroque, bright, colourful, elaborate, embellished, flowery, ornate, rococo, showy, sumptuous; busy, fussy, gaudy, heavy, over-elaborate.

flounder
vb lit: blunder (about), fumble, grope, stumble; struggle, thrash, thresh, wallow.

flourish
n lit: gesticulation, gesture, wave; display, parade, show; fanfare, tucket; decoration, embellishment, ornamentation; curlicue, kern, loop, sweep.
vb lit: bloom, blossom, burgeon, flower, grow, thrive; do well, get on, increase, prosper; brandish, gesture with, swish, wave, wield; display, parade, show, vaunt.

flout
vb lit: defy, spurn, treat with scorn, turn one's back on; deride, jeer at, laugh at, scoff at.

flow
n lit: circulation, current, drift, spate, stream, tide; bleeding, dripping, oozing, suppuration, trickling; effusion, emanation, emission, escape, leak; cascade, deluge, inundation, spurt.
vb lit: circulate, course, gush, pour, run, surge; bleed, drip, ooze, suppurate, trickle; be emitted, emanate, emerge, escape, issue, leak; cascade, deluge, flood, inundate, stream, teem.

flower
n lit: bloom, blossom, efflorescence; *fig*: best, cream, élite, pick.
vb lit: bloom, blossom. burgeon, effloresce, open; mature, ripen; flourish, prosper, thrive.

fluctuate
vb lit: alternate, go up and down, oscillate, seesaw, swing, undulate, vary; vacillate, waver.

fluency
n lit: articulation, ease, facility, smoothness.

fluent
adj lit: articulate, easy, idiomatic, mellifluous, natural, perfect, smooth.

fluff
n lit: down, dust, fuzz, lint, nap; *fig*: boob, botch, cock-up, foul-up, mess, muddle; (bit of) crumpet.
vb lit: puff (out), shake (out); *fig*: botch up, cock up, foul up, make a boob in, mess up, muddle up.

fluffy
adj lit: downy, hairy, fleecy, furry, fuzzy, velvety.

fluid
n lit: liquid; liquor; *spec*: gas (physics).
adj lit: flowing, gaseous, liquid; melted, moist, runny; aqueous, watery; juicy; *fig*: mellifluous, smooth, soft, tender; changeable, fluctuating, mercurial, volatile; elegant, graceful, languorous, sinuous.

flurry
n lit: agitation, commotion, ferment, flap, fluster, furore, fuss, panic, stir; blow, flutter, gust, squall; burst, rush, spell.

flush

n lit: blush, reddening, ruddiness;
freshness, prime.
vb lit: blush, burn, colour hotly, crimson,
go red, suffuse; douche, flood, rinse out,
wash; *fig*: beat (out), hunt (out), nose
(out), sniff (out).
adj lit: even, flat, level, parallel, square;
abundant, overflowing; rich, wealthy,
well-off.
adv lit: evenly (with), flush (against), level
(with), parallel (with), squarely (against).

flustered

adj (pa.pt) lit: agitated, bothered,
distracted, disturbed, excited, hurried,
nervous, perturbed, rattled, upset.

flute

n lit: fife, pipe, whistle; groove; *spec*:
shuttle (in weaving).
vb lit: pipe, whistle; sing shrilly; carve a
groove in.

flutter

n lit: agitation, palpitation, quivering,
shivering, tic, tremor, vibration, wink;
confusion, dither, flurry, fluster; *fig*: bet,
gamble, speculation, wager; *spec*:
variation (in sound reproduction).
vb lit: bat, beat, flap, ruffle; palpitate,
quiver, shiver, tremble, vibrate, wink;
bustle (about), hover.

fly

n lit: aphis, bluebottle, cleg, gnat,
housefly, insect, midge; fish-hook;
awning, flap, tent-door; trouser-buttons,
zip.
vb lit: flutter, glide, hover, sail, soar, take
wing; control, operate, pilot; have at the
masthead, hoist, raise, wave; *fig*: bolt,
dart, dash, race, shoot, speed, sprint,
tear, zip; go (at), hurl oneself (at), rush
(at); elapse, pass rapidly, roll past,
vanish.
adj lit: canny, knowing, sharp, shrewd,
smart.

foam

n lit: bubbles, froth, lather, scum, spume;
head.

focus

n lit: convergence, focal point; central
point; clarity, definition, register,
sharpness; accommodation, refraction;
fig: core, heart, hub, target.

vb lit: clarify, increase register, sharpen
(up); bring to a point, converge, join,
meet; *fig*: concentrate (on), direct (on),
home in (on).

foe

n lit: adversary, enemy.

fog

n lit: murk, smog; cloud, gloom, mist; *fig*:
bewilderment, confusion, darkness,
obscurity, perplexity, puzzlement.

foggy

adj lit: misty; cloudy, gloomy, murky;
dim, grey, obscure; *fig*: blurred,
confused, dark, hazy, indistinct,
obscure, vague.

foil

n lit: leaf metal; mercury coating,
silvering; background, contrast, setting;
button-pointed fencing sword.
vb lit: baffle, balk, circumvent, defeat,
frustrate, outwit, prevent, stop, thwart.

fold

n lit: crease, pleat, turn-over, turn-up;
furrow, wrinkle; flock of sheep, sheep-
pen; *fig*: congregation, parish.
vb lit: bend over, crease, double, pleat,
tuck, turn under; envelop (in), wrap (in);
collapse, crumple, drop in a heap, fall
over, keel over; *fig*: crash, fail, go
bankrupt, go bust.

folk

n lit: people; clan, nation, race, tribe;
family.

folksy

adj lit: affable, bucolic, friendly, good-
natured, neighbourly, rustic, sociable;
average, commonplace, everyday,
ordinary, simple, unpretentious; pseudo-
traditional.

follow

vb lit: dog, pursue, shadow, stalk, track,
trail; be after, look for, search for; be
next, come after, succeed, supersede, tag
on behind; develop, ensue, issue (from),
proceed (from), result; *fig*: copy,
emulate, imitate, model oneself on;
adhere to, be a devotee of; conform to,
keep, obey, observe; catch on,
comprehend, fathom, get, grasp, see
understand; appreciate, keep up with.

follower

n lit: adherent, believer, devotee, disciple, fan, supporter, worshipper; attendant, henchman, retainer; hanger-on, sidekick.

following

n lit: acolytes, adherents, aficionados, disciples, devotees, fans, neophytes, public, supporters; crew, entourage, retinue, staff, suite.

adj (pr.pt) lit: ensuing, later, next, subsequent, succeeding, successive.

folly

n lit: absurdity, fatuity, foolishness, idiocy, lunacy, recklessness, silliness, stupidity; artistic ruin.

fond

adj lit: enamoured (of); adoring, devoted, doting, indulgent, loving; cherished, favourite, pet.

fondle

vb lit: caress, cuddle, pet, stroke; finger, grope, handle.

fondness

n lit: affection, devotion, love; liking (for), partiality (for), predilection (for), soft spot (for), taste (for), weakness (for).

food

n lit: chow, diet, fare, grub, nosh, nourishment, pabulum, provisions, rations, sustenance, tuck, victuals; cooking, cuisine, menu; feed, fodder, provender; *fig*: energy-source, fuel.

fool

n lit: ass, blockhead, chump, clod, cretin, dolt, dunce, fathead, halfwit, idiot, imbecile, moron, nincompoop, nitwit, numbskull, simpleton, twit; butt, dupe, gull, john, mark, mug, sucker; clown, comic, jester, merryman.

vb lit: bamboozle, deceive, dupe, gull, have on, hoodwink, put one over on, take in, trick; antic (about), lark (about), mess (about); play (about with), toy (with), trifle (with).

foolhardy

adj lit: adventurous, impetuous, incautious, madcap, rash, reckless.

foolish

adj lit: asinine, barmy, batwitted, brainless, cretinous, daft, fatheaded, fatuous, half-baked, idiotic, imbecile, inane, mad, moronic, senseless, stupid;

absurd, ill-advised, imprudent, indiscreet, injudicious, unintelligent.

foolproof

adj lit: guaranteed, infallible, safe, sure; simplicity itself.

foot

n lit: arch, heel, hoof, instep, sole, toes; base, bottom, end, leg, podium, stanchion; 12 inches; *fig*: infantry, infantrymen; *spec*: metrical unit (in verse).

vb lit: pace (out), stride (out), walk; *fig*: pay, settle.

footing

n lit: basis, grip, leverage, purchase; *fig*: base, establishment, foundation; position, rank, standing, status.

footling

adj lit: fiddling, hairsplitting, insignificant, petty, pointless, trifling, trivial, unimportant.

footwear

n lit: boots, shoes; slippers; socks, stockings.

forage

vb lit: cast about (for), rummage about (for), search (for); maraud, plunder, raid, ransack.

foray

n lit: expedition, foraging trip, incursion, invasion, marauding, raid, sallying forth, sortie.

forbear

vb lit: abstain from, decline (to), hold back from, refrain from, restrain oneself from; resist temptation.

forbearance

n lit: abstinence, restraint, self-restraint; magnanimity, patience, resignation, self-control; leniency, mercy.

forbid

vb lit: ban, interdict, outlaw, prohibit, proscribe, rule out, veto.

forbidden

adj (pa.pt) lit: banned, interdicted, outlawed, out of bounds, prohibited, proscribed, ruled out, taboo, vetoed.

forbidding

adj (pr.pt) lit: dark, daunting, eerie, frightening, gloomy, grim, macabre, menacing, ominous, sinister.

force
n lit: army, body, brigade, corps, patrol, service, squad, troop; dynamism, energy, impulse, life, momentum, power, strength, vigour; coercion, compulsion, duress, pressure, violence; emphasis, fervour, intensity, vehemence; effectiveness, efficacy, punch, weight.
vb lit: compel, constrain, drive, impose (upon), oblige, pressurize; break open, prise apart, strong-arm, wrench open; extort (from), wring (from).

forceful
adj lit: dynamic, effective, effectual, potent, powerful, weighty; cogent, compelling, telling.

forceps
n lit: pincers, pliers, tongs.

forcible
adj lit: aggressive, armed, forceful, violent; *fig*: compelling, potent, powerful.

ford
n lit: shallows, watersplash.
vb lit: drive through, splash across, traverse, wade across.

fore
n lit: front, head, lead, van; bow, prow.

forebear
n lit: ancestor, forefather, predecessor, progenitor.

foreboding
n lit: anxiety, apprehension, fear, misgiving, premonition, presentiment.

forecast
n lit: haruspication, prediction, prognosis, projection, prophecy.
vb lit: augur, foresee, foretell, haruspicate, predict, prognosticate, prophesy.

forefront
n lit: foreground, front, head, lead, van.

foreground
n lit: forefront, front; centre, focus, limelight.

foreign
adj lit: alien, exotic, imported, outlandish, strange, unfamiliar; extraneous (to), irrelevant (to), unrelated (to).

foreigner
n lit: alien, immigrant, outlander, stranger.

foreman
n lit: gaffer, governor, overseer, shop steward, superintendent, supervisor; convener, spokesman.

foremost
adj lit: chief, first, front-running, head, leading, nearest, paramount, pre-eminent, principal.

forerunner
n lit: herald, precursor, predecessor; ancestor, forebear; original, prototype; augury, omen, portent, sign, token.

foresee
vb lit: anticipate, forecast, foretell, predict, prognosticate, prophesy.

foresight
n lit: anticipation, far-sightedness, forethought, preparedness, prescience.

forest
n lit: woodland, woods; copse, coppice, heath, moor, scrub, thicket, undergrowth, wilderness; national park, nature reserve, parkland.

forestall
vb lit: anticipate, avert, avoid, fend off, parry, prevent, ward off.

forestry
n lit: arboriculture, silviculture, woodcraft; dendrology.

foretell
vb lit: augur, forecast, foresee, haruspicate, predict, prognosticate, prophesy.

forever
adv lit: eternally, evermore, permanently, always, continually, incessantly, perpetually.

forewarn
vb lit: advise, alert, caution, give notice, tip off.

forfeit
n lit: fine, penalty; loss, surrendering.
vb lit: be mulcted of, be obliged to give up, have to relinquish, lose, surrender.

forge
n lit: blacksmith's, farrier's, foundry, furnace, smithy, workshop.

vb lit: fashion, form, hammer into shape, mould, shape, work; *fig:* copy, counterfeit, fake.

forgery
n lit: copy, counterfeit, fake, phoney, sham; copying, counterfeiting, faking.

forget
vb lit: fail to think of, neglect, omit, overlook; leave behind; dismiss from one's mind, put behind one.

forgetful
adj lit: absent-minded, inattentive, neglectful, oblivious, unmindful.

forgive
vb lit: absolve of, pardon for, remit; excuse of, overlook; grant pardon.

forgiveness
n lit: absolution, pardon, remission; grace, mercy.

forgo
vb lit: give up, go without, relinquish, renounce, sacrifice, waive.

forgotten
adj (pa.pt) lit: neglected, omitted, overlooked; forlorn, forsaken, left behind; behind one, dismissed from one's mind.

fork
n lit: pronged instrument; rake, trident; branch, prong, tine; bifurcation, divergence, divide, division, ramification, split; zigzag.
vb lit: impale, prong, stab; dig up, rake, turn over; bifurcate, branch, diverge, divide, ramify, split; zigzag.

forlorn
adj lit: abandoned, bereft, deserted, desolate, forgotten, forsaken, lonely, lost, neglected; desperate, hopeless, sad, unhappy, wretched.

form
n lit: mould, template; configuration, outline, pattern, shape; body, build, construction, figure, frame, physique, structure; essence, substance; framework, order, organization, plan, system; character, description, guise, mode, sort, style; fashion, manner, method, way; application, document, schedule, slip; bench, seat, settle; *fig:* condition, health, spirits, trim; behaviour, conduct, etiquette, manners,

protocol; class, grade, year; background, history, record; previous sentences.
vb lit: create, fashion, forge, make, model, mould, shape; build, construct; establish, found, set up; appear, come into being, emerge, evolve, manifest oneself, materialize, take shape; arrange, dispose, draw up, organize; *fig:* contract, cultivate, develop.

formal
adj lit: approved, conventional, correct, decorous, prescribed, punctilious, set, solemn; ceremonial, official.

formality
n lit: convention, correctness, decorum, etiquette, punctilio, punctiliousness, solemnity; ceremony, protocol; custom, matter of form, observance.

formation
n lit: compilation, composition, creation, fashioning, modelling, moulding, shaping; building, construction; development, establishment, foundation; evolution, manifestation, materialization; arrangement, configuration, disposition, form, grouping, organization.

former
adj lit: earlier, erstwhile, one-time, past, previous, prior, quondam; above, above-mentioned, aforesaid, preceding; ancient, bygone, old.

formerly
adv lit: at one time, earlier, in the past, once, previously; anciently, in days of yore.

formidable
adj lit: arduous, challenging, difficult, hard; daunting, dreadful, intimidating, terrifying; awesome, mighty, powerful, redoubtable.

formula
n lit: cipher, code; rite, rubric; menu, prescription, recipe.

formulate
vb lit: codify, couch, define, express, frame; detail, itemize, specify; come up with, devolve, invent, originate, work out.

forsake
vb lit: abandon, leave, quit; desert, leave in the lurch; disown, repudiate; forswear, relinquish, renounce, set aside.

fort
n lit: bastion, blockhouse, castle, citadel, stockade, stronghold.

forth
adv lit: away, forward, onward, out; into the open.

forthright
adj lit: blunt, candid, frank, outspoken, straightforward.

forthwith
adv lit: at once, immediately, instantly, quickly, straight away.

fortification
n lit: barbican, bulwark, buttress, defences, keep, moat, rampart, tower, turret, wall; reinforcement, strengthening.

fortify
vb lit: brace, buttress, reinforce, strengthen; prop up, shore up, support; fig: embolden, hearten, stiffen; enrich; increase the alcohol content of.

fortitude
n lit: courage, determination, grit, guts, hardihood, intrepidity, perseverance, resolution, strength of will.

fortuitously
adv lit: accidentally, adventitiously, by chance, casually, incidentally; conveniently, fortunately, luckily, opportunely.

fortunate
adj lit: favoured, lucky; convenient, opportune, timely; advantageous, favourable, felicitous.

fortune
n lit: chance, destiny, fate, luck, providence; circumstance(s), event(s), happening(s), occurrence(s); prosperity, riches, success, treasure, wealth; bomb, mint, packet, tidy sum.

forward
vb lit: dispatch, freight, remit, send, send on, ship; advance, aid, expedite, further, promote, speed on, support.
adj lit: advance, first, foremost, leading; early, precocious, premature; bold, brazen, cheeky, familiar, fresh, impudent, officious, pert, presumptuous, pushy.
adv lit: ahead, on, onward(s); into the open, into view, out; in the open, on the table.

forwardness
n lit: boldness, brazenness, cheek, familiarity, freshness, impudence, officiousness, pertness, presumption, pushiness.

foster
vb lit: bring up, raise, rear; cultivate, encourage, nurture, promote, stimulate; cherish, entertain, harbour, have, retain.

foul
n lit: breach of the rules, illegality, misdemeanour, villainy.
vb lit: contaminate, defile, dirty, pollute, smear, soil, stain; catch on, choke up, clog, entangle in, jam, obstruct, snarl up in; break the rules, commit an illegality.
adj lit: contaminated, defiled, dirty, polluted, soiled, stained; disgusting, filthy, noisome, offensive, putrescent, revolting, scabrous, squalid, stinking; disgraceful, dishonourable, iniquitous, scandalous, wicked; underhand, against the rules, illegal, unfair, unscrupulous, unsportsmanlike; blasphemous, blue, coarse, gross, indecent, obscene, scatological; blustery, rough, stormy, unfavourable, wild.

found
vb lit: base, build, embed, ground, support; establish, inaugurate, institute, originate, set up, start.
adj (pa.pt) lit: discovered, located, situated; brought to light, detected, spotted, tracked down; acquired, obtained, procured, run down.

foundation
n lit: base, basis, footing, grounding; establishment, institution, origination, setting up.

founder
n lit: architect, author, builder, constructor, designer, discoverer, initiator, inventor, originator, patriarch, patron.
vb lit: go to the bottom, sink; collapse, lurch, subside; go lame, stumble, trip; fig: break down, come to nothing, fall through.

fountain
n lit: jet, spout, spray, spring; rise, source, well-head; fig: beginning, cause, derivation, origin.

fox
n lit: dog, vixen; *fig*: crafty so-and-so, cunning devil, slyboots.
vb lit: baffle, best, defeat, foil, outsmart, outwit, thwart; discolour, stain; *fig*: befuddle, get drunk, intoxicate.

foxy
adj lit: artful, canny, crafty, cunning, guileful, knowing, shrewd, sly, vulpine, wily.

foyer
n lit: ante-room, atrium, entrance-hall, lobby, vestibule.

fracas
n lit: affray, brawl, fight, free-for-all, melee, riot, rumble, rumpus, scuffle, wrangle.

fraction
n lit: bit, fragment, part, section; chip, particle, scrap, shred, sliver; factor, multiplicand; division, sector, segment.

fractious
adj lit: captious, fretful, irritable, pettish, petulant, querulous, snappish, touchy; intractable, recalcitrant, stubborn, unruly, wilful.

fracture
n lit: break, crack, rupture, snap, splinter; breach, rent, split.
vb lit: break, crack, sever, shatter, snap, splinter; cleave, rend, split.

fragile
adj lit: breakable, brittle, delicate, fine, slight, weak; *fig*: feverish, hungover, ill, liverish, nauseous, sick.

fragment
n lit: bit, fraction, part, section; chip, particle, scrap, shard, sherd, shred, sliver.
vb lit: break up, come apart, disintegrate, shatter, shiver, splinter, split up; disperse, divide, separate, sever.

fragrance
n lit: aroma, bouquet, perfume, scent; *fig*: beauty, radiance, sweetness.

fragrant
adj lit: aromatic, perfumed, scented, sweet-smelling; *fig*: beautiful, radiant.

frail
adj lit: decrepit, delicate, feeble, flimsy, infirm, rickety, slight, unsteady, weak.

frailty
n lit: decrepitude, feebleness, flimsiness, infirmity, unsteadiness, vulnerability, weakness; defect, failing, flaw, imperfection, vice.

frame
n lit: cross-members, form, girdering, shell, skeleton, struts, system; casing, mounting, setting, surround; cradle, support, trestle; body, build, figure, morphology, physique, shape; *fig*: mood, temper.
vb lit: build (on), construct (around), fashion, form, invent, make, model, put together; case, mount, set, surround; codify, compose, couch, define, draft, express, formulate; *fig*: fit (up), fix the blame on.

framework
n lit: core, foundation, plan, shell, skeleton, structure.

franchise
n lit: authorization, charter, concession, licence; exemption, immunity; prerogative, privilege; suffrage, vote.

frank
vb lit: sign; postmark, stamp.
adj lit: blunt, candid, forthright, honest, open, outspoken, plain-spoken, sincere, straightforward, uninhibited.

frankly
adv lit: bluntly, candidly, forthrightly, honestly, openly, outspokenly, plain-spokenly, sincerely, straightforwardly, uninhibitedly.

frantic
adj lit: beside oneself, distracted, frenetic, frenzied, overwrought; feverish, headlong, hectic.

fraternity
n lit: association, brotherhood, club, company, fellowship, guild, secret order, union.

fraud
n lit: chicanery, con, deceit, deception, duplicity, forgery, hoax, swindle, trick, trickery; charlatan, con artist, counterfeit, crook, fake, forger, impostor, mountebank, phoney, quack, sham, swindler.

fraudulent
adj lit: counterfeit, crooked, deceitful, deceptive, dishonest, duplicitous, phoney, sham, spurious, swindling.

frayed
adj lit: abraded, grazed, ragged, rubbed, scuffed, tattered, threadbare, worn; *fig*: heated, strained.

freak
n lit: aberration, abnormality, anomaly, malformation, monster, mutant, sport; eccentric, oddball, weirdo; caprice, crochet, fancy, quirk, vagary, whim; *fig*: aficionado, buff, devotee, enthusiast, fanatic.
adj lit: abnormal, anomalous, bizarre, exceptional, teratological, unexpected, unheard-of, unparalleled, unrepeatable, very strange.

free
vb lit: emancipate, let go, let out, liberate, loose, redeem, release, turn loose, unleash, untie; disentangle, extricate, relieve, rescue; clear (of), rid (of).
adj lit: complimentary, for nothing, gratis, gratuitous, on the house; at large, loose, on the loose; at leisure, available, idle, spare, uncommitted, unrestricted; empty, unengaged, uninhabited, unused, vacant; casual, easy, familiar, informal, laid-back, liberal, relaxed, uninhibited; generous, lavish, munificent, open-handed, unsparing; open, unimpeded, unobstructed; allowed, permitted; at liberty, emancipated; autonomous, democratic, independent.

freedom
n lit: autonomy, independence; emancipation, liberty; release; ease, familiarity, frankness, informality, openness; laxity, licence, presumption; exemption (from), immunity (from); ability (to), discretion (to), facility (to), latitude (to), leeway (to), opportunity (to), power (to), scope (to).

freely
adv lit: cleanly, easily, readily, smoothly; candidly, frankly, openly, sincerely, straightforwardly, uninhibitedly; of one's own volition, spontaneously, voluntarily; unchallenged, unrestrainedly, unrestrictedly; abundantly, copiously, lavishly, liberally, open-handedly.

freeze
vb lit: chill, frost, ice, ice over, refrigerate; numb; *fig*: fix, peg, stiffen, stop dead, stop in one's tracks, suspend, transfix.

freezing
adj lit: arctic, bitter, chill, frosty, glacial, icy, numbing, polar.

freight
n lit: cargo, consignment, goods, load, payload, shipment; carriage, transportation.

frenzy
n lit: burst, convulsion, fit, paroxysm, seizure; delirium, passion, storm.

frequent
vb lit: be a regular at, hang out at, haunt, patronize, visit often; be most often found at.
adj lit: constant, continual, customary, familiar, habitual, persistent, recurrent, repeated.

fresh
adj lit: green, hand-picked, natural, new, verdant; raw, uncured, unprocessed; latest, modern, novel, recent, up-to-date; additional, auxiliary, different, further, supplementary; bracing, brisk, clean, crisp, invigorating, pure, spanking; blooming, glowing, healthy, rosy, wholesome; *fig*: alert, bright, energetic, invigorated, keen, lively, revived, spry, young; callow, inexperienced, untrained, youthful; bold, brazen, cheeky, familiar, impudent, pert, presumptuous, saucy.

fret
n lit: stew; ornamental network, Greek key pattern; *fig*: distressed condition, panic, state, stew; *spec*: fingerboard ridge (on a musical instrument).
vb lit: annoy, bother, disturb, irk, nag, peeve, trouble, vex; agonize, brood, distress oneself, get into a state, worry; abrade, chafe, rub, wear away.

friction
n lit: abrasion, attrition, chafing, erosion, filing, fretting, rasping, rubbing, wearing away; *fig*: antagonism, conflict, contention, discord, dissension, hostility, tension.

friend
n lit: confidant, confidante, crony, intimate; buddy, china, chum, mate, mucker, pal; ally, associate, colleague, companion, comrade, partner.

friendly
adj lit: affable, amiable, amicable, companionable, cordial, genial, kindly, matey, neighbourly, sociable, well-disposed; affectionate, attached, chummy, close, familiar, fond, intimate; benevolent, benign, generous, good, helpful, kind, sympathetic.

friendship
n lit: amity, concord, rapport, regard; affection, attachment, fondness, goodwill, love; alliance, association, companionship, comradeship, partnership.

fright
n lit: alarm, apprehension, dread, fear, panic, terror, trepidation; bad start, heart attack, scare, shock; *fig*: apparition, eyesore, mess, scarecrow, sight.

frighten
vb lit: alarm, petrify, put the wind up, scare, startle, terrify, unnerve; appal, cow, daunt, intimidate, menace, threaten; scare (away/off).

frightening
adj (pr.pt) lit: alarming, dreadful, fearsome, horrendous, petrifying, scary, startling, terrifying, unnerving; appalling, daunting, intimidatory, menacing, threatening; creepy, dark, eerie, ghastly, macabre, sinister, spooky.

frightful
adj lit: awful, dreadful, ghastly, grim, horrible, lurid, terrible; *fig*: appalling, insufferable, unpleasant, very bad.

frigid
adj lit: arctic, boreal, cold, freezing, frosty, frozen, gelid, hoary, icy, stiff with ice; *fig*: austere, chilly, forbidding, rigid, stiff, unbending; passively disinterested, unloving, unresponsive.

frigidity
n lit: coldness, frostiness, iciness; *fig*: aloofness, austerity, impassivity, rigidity; disinterest, lack of response, passivity, unapproachability.

frills
n lit: flounces, gatherings, pleats, ruches, ruffs, ruffles, tucks; *fig*: additions, decorations, embellishments, extras, frippery, trimmings; affectations, flourishes.

frilly
adj lit: flounced, pleated, ruched, ruffed, ruffled.

fringe
n lit: border, edging, trimming; tassel; edge, frieze, limits, margin, periphery, rim.
vb lit: border, edge, hem, march on, skirt.
adj lit: alternative, unconventional, unorthodox.

frisky
adj lit: coltish, high-spirited, lively, mettlesome, playful, sportive; capering, frolicsome, gamboling, leaping, romping.

frivolity
n lit: fun, irresponsibility, nonsense, silliness, triviality.

frivolous
adj lit: dizzy, flighty, fun-loving, irresponsible, nonsensical, silly, trivial; childish, insignificant, juvenile, minor, paltry, shallow, trifling, unimportant.

frock
n lit: dress, gown, robe; cassock, habit; shift, smock; petticoat, skirt; mantle, tunic.

from
prp lit: off, out of; out of the possession of; beginning at, starting at; because of, by reason of; caused by; in comparison with.

frost
n lit: freezing, hoar, rime; *fig*: chill, coldness, frigidity, hauteur; failure, flop.

frosty
adj lit: chilly, frozen, gelid, hoary, icy, wintry; *fig*: grey, white; cold, frigid, unfriendly, unapproachable.

frothy
adj lit: foaming, foamy, with a fine head; sudsy; *fig*: empty, frivolous, light, trifling, trivial, unimportant.

frown
vb lit: glare, glower, scowl; *fig*: look askance (upon).

frowsty
adj lit: close, fusty, musty, stale, stuffy.

frugal
adj lit: careful, economical, sparing, thrifty; close, meagre, miserly, parsimonious.

fruit
n lit: ovarian development; produce, product; berry, drupe, pome; grain, nut, pod, seed; crop, harvest, yield; *fig*: issue, offspring, progeny, young; advantage, benefit, profit, return; consequence, effect, outcome, result.

fruitful
adj lit: fecund, fertile; fructiferous; abundant, bountiful, copious, plentiful, productive, prolific; *fig*: advantageous, beneficial, lucrative, profitable, rewarding.

fruitless
adj lit: barren, unproductive; *fig*: abortive, bootless, futile, ineffectual, unavailing, unsuccessful, useless, vain.

fruity
adj lit: flavoursome, full, grapey, mellow; *fig*: bawdy, blue, erotic, indecent, randy, salacious, sexy, titillating.

frumpish
adj lit: dowdy, mousy, plain, shabby, unprepossessing.

frustrate
vb lit: baffle, block, bring to nothing, counter, defeat, foil, forestall, nullify, prevent, stymie, thwart; discourage, dishearten; leave unsatisfied.

frustration
n lit: bafflement, blocking, bringing to nothing, countering, defeating, foiling, forestalling, nullification, prevention, thwarting; discouragement; dissatisfaction, tension.

fuddle
vb lit: addle, bemuse, confuse, mix up, muddle, stupefy; booze, inebriate, intoxicate, tipple.

fuddy-duddy
n lit: blue-stocking, conservative, fossil, old fogy, stick-in-the-mud, stuffed shirt.
adj lit: antiquated, old-fashioned, old-fogyish, prim, stuffy; carping, censorious.

fudge
n fig: humbug, nonsense, rubbish; fib, lie, untruth; *spec*: insert, inset, stop press (in a newspaper).
vb lit: cook, fake, falsify, misrepresent; avoid, dodge, evade; bodge up, patch up, mend; equivocate, hedge, stall.

fuel
n lit: firewood, kindling, tinder; fodder, food, nourishment; fissile material, plutonium; ammunition, materiel; *fig*: encouragement, support; incitement, provocation.
vb lit: arm, charge, feed, fill up, load, prime, stoke; *fig*: encourage, intensify, provoke.

fugitive
n lit: absconder, escapee, exile, refugee, runaway.
adj lit: escaping, nomadic, roving, running, shifting; *fig*: ephemeral, fleeting, momentary, passing, temporary, transient.

fulfil
vb lit: accomplish, achieve, attain, complete, conclude, execute, keep, observe, perform, realize, satisfy.

full
adj lit: brimming, filled, loaded; chock-a-block, crammed, crowded, jammed, packed; gorged, replete, sated, satiated, satisfied; complete, entire, intact; broad, comprehensive, detailed, extensive; exhaustive, maximum, thorough; abundant, copious, plentiful; baggy, capacious, voluminous; buxom, curvaceous, rounded; deep, loud, resonant, rich.
adv lit: completely, entirely, thoroughly; to the brim; directly, straight; perfectly, very.

fully
adv lit: abundantly, amply, comprehensively, sufficiently; absolutely, completely, entirely, thoroughly, totally, utterly; altogether, perfectly.

fulminate
vb lit: blow up, crash, detonate, explode, reach flash point, roar, thunder; breathe fire and brimstone (against), inveigh (against), utter threats of violence (against).

fulsome
adj lit: excessive, immoderate, inordinate, rank; fawning, ingratiating, smarmy, sycophantic; nauseating, offensive, sickening.

fume
n lit: gas, smoke, vapour; *fig*: fury, heat, passion, rage.

vb lit: exude, smoke; *fig*: chafe, fret, rage, seethe, smoulder.

fumigate
vb lit: cleanse, disinfect, sanitize; cense, purify.

fun
n lit: amusement, diversion, enjoyment, entertainment, excitement, pleasure, recreation, sport; high jinks, japes, jocularity, jollity, larks, skylarking; buffoonery, clowning, teasing; horseplay, playfulness; (in) jest; (make) game (of), (make) sport (of).
adj lit: amusing, enjoyable, entertaining, exciting, pleasurable.

function
n lit: business, charge, duty, employment, job, mission, office, post, responsibility, role, task; activity, faculty, operation, purpose, service; equation; *fig*: affair, do, reception, party, thrash.
vb lit: go, operate, run, work.

fund
n lit: capital, exchequer, finance(s), resource(s), saving(s), treasury; kitty, pool, reserve, stock, store, vein.
vb lit: bankroll, endow, finance, float, pay for, stake.

fundamental
adj lit: basic, elementary, essential, indispensable, key, primary, underlying.

funeral
n lit: memorial service, obsequies, requiem; burial, cremation, interment.

funereal
adj lit: black, dark, dismal, gloomy, grim, melancholy, mournful, sad, slow, solemn, sombre, stately.

fungus
n lit: thallophyte; mould, mushroom, rust, toadstool, yeast; *spec*: granulation (in scars).

funnel
n lit: chimney, smoke outlet, stack; cone, filter; channel, cylinder, tube.
vb lit: channel, convey, duct, pass; filter, stream.

funny
adj lit: amusing, choice, comic, delirious, farcical, hilarious, humorous, killing, rib-tickling, riotous, side-splitting, waggish; curious, odd, peculiar, queer,

strange, suspicious, weird; eccentric, quirky; devious, tricky, underhand.

furbish
vb lit: buff (up), burnish, polish (up), rub (up); clean (up), do (up), renovate.

furious
adj lit: angry, beside oneself, boiling, enraged, fuming, incensed, livid, maddened, raging, fierce, stormy, tempestuous, tumultuous, turbulent, violent; boisterous, frenzied, unrestrained, wild.

furnish
vb lit: present, provide, supply; equip, fit out, rig out; appoint, decorate; provision, stock.

furniture
n lit: appliances, equipment, fittings, household effects, movables; accessories, accoutrements, decor, decoration, trappings.

furore
n lit: agitation, commotion, disturbance, excitement, flap, fuss, outcry, overreaction, uproar.

further
vb lit: advance, aid, assist, expedite, forward, foster, promote, speed.
adj lit: additional, extra, more, supplementary; hinder, more distant, remoter.
adv lit: additionally, again, more, more deeply; at a greater distance, to a greater distance; also, besides, moreover.

furtive
adj lit: cloak-and-dagger, secretive, shifty, skulking, slinking, sneaking, stealthy, surreptitious.

fury
n lit: anger, ire, passion, rage; ferocity. storminess, tempestuousness, turbulence, violence; frenzy, wildness.

fuse
n lit: circuit-breaker; detonating lead, touchpaper, wick.
vb lit: liquefy, melt, melt down; amalgamate, blend, join, melt together, merge, run together, solder, weld; *fig*: combine, intermingle, mix.

fuss

n lit: bother, bustle, commotion, dust, flap, flurry, fluster, furore, stir, tumult.
vb lit: be flustered, fidget, flap, fret, worry; bustle (about); create a scene (about), make a song and dance (about).

fussy

adj lit: choosy, discriminating, finicky, particular, pernickety, picky, selective; difficult, exacting, hard to please; delicate, nice, squeamish; busy, over-detailed, over-elaborate.

futile

adj lit: abortive, bootless, fruitless, ineffectual, nugatory, unprofitable, unsuccessful, vain; hopeless, pointless, useless; frivolous, trifling, trivial, worthless.

future

n lit: days to come, hereafter; outlook, way ahead.
adj lit: coming, prospective; later, subsequent; destined, eventual; unborn.

G

gab
n lit: articulation, fluency, loquaciousness; chatter, gossip; speech, talk, verbiage, verbosity; mouth.
vb lit: chatter, gossip, natter, prate, rabbit, spout, waffle, yammer.

gabble
vb lit: babble, gibber, jabber, prattle, splutter, sputter, stammer, stutter.

gad
vb lit: gallivant (around), get (about), run (around), stray, travel (around), wander (about).

gadget
n lit: appliance, contrivance, device, gizmo, implement, tool; contraption, machine.

gaff
n lit: barb, hook, spur; pole, spar; *fig*: music-hall, sideshow, theatre; *spec*: (blow the) plot, secret.

gaffe
n lit: blunder, faux pas, howler, mistake, slip, solecism.

gaffer
n lit: ancient, greybeard, old boy, old man; boss, foreman, guv'nor, manager, supervisor.

gag
n lit: curb, muzzle, silencer; heave, retch; crack, joke, one-liner, pun, wisecrack.
vb lit: curb, muzzle, silence, stifle, suppress; heave, retch; crack a joke, wisecrack.

gaily
adv lit: cheerfully, happily, joyously, light-heartedly, merrily; brightly, colourfully, flamboyantly, sportively.

gain
n lit: accretion, enlargement, growth, increase, rise; acquisition, earnings, emolument, increment, profit, return, winnings, yield; advance, advantage, benefit, headway, improvement, progress, victory, win.
vb lit: build up, enlarge, grow, increase, rise; acquire, be paid, bring in, capture, earn, get, glean, make, net, obtain, pick up, profit by, receive, secure, take, win; advance, arrive at, attain to, benefit, catch up (on), improve, make headway, progress; *spec*: stall for (time).

gait
n lit: pace, step, stride, walk; *fig*: rate, speed.

gala
n lit: carnival, festival, fête; celebration; fair, show.

gale
n lit: cyclone, hurricane, storm, tempest, tornado, typhoon; *fig*: burst, explosion, howl, outburst, peal.

gall
n lit: bile; abrasion, chafe, scrape, sore, ulcer; abscess, cyst, swelling, wen; *fig*: brass neck, cheek, effrontery, impudence, insolence, nerve; acrimony, animosity, bitterness, hostility, rancour, venom; annoyance, exasperation, harassment, pest, vexation.
vb lit: chafe, excoriate, graze, rub, scrape; *fig*: annoy, exasperate, fret, harass, irk, nettle, peeve, pester, vex.

gallant
n lit: adventurer, cavalier, daredevil, hero, Mohock, ruffler; buck, Corinthian, dandy, gentleman; admirer, beau, escort, suitor.
adj lit: audacious, bold, brave, daring, dashing, dauntless, fearless, heroic, intrepid, manly, noble, valiant; chivalrous, courteous, gentlemanly, gracious; grand, imposing, magnificent, splendid.

gallantry
n lit: audacity, boldness, bravery, courage, daring, heroism, valour; chivalry, courtesy, gentlemanliness, graciousness.

gallop
vb lit: hurry, race, run, speed; dash, fly, sprint.

gallows
n lit: gibbet, scaffold, yardarm; nubbing-cheat; hangman's rope, noose.

galore
adv lit: aplenty, everywhere, in abundance, in numbers, in quantity.

galvanize
vb lit: electrify; *fig*: fire, jerk, jolt, shock, startle.

gambit
n lit: move, opening move, ploy; sacrificial ploy.

gamble
n lit: bet, flutter, speculation, wager; chance, lottery, risk, venture.
vb lit: bet (on), have a flutter, play (at), stake, wager; chance, risk, venture.

gambol
vb lit: antic, caper, cavort, curvet, frolic, prance, skip, spring.

game
n lit: competition, contest, match, tournament; leisure activity, pastime, recreation, sport; diversion, joke, lark, romp; chase, prey, quarry; *fig*: plan, ploy, scheme, stratagem, tactic; business, line, métier; prostitution; (make) fun (of), (make) sport (of).
adj lit: brave, dogged, fearless, intrepid, persistent, spirited; prepared (for), ready (for), willing (for).

gang
n lit: band, clique, crew, group, party, ring, set, squad, team.
vb lit: combine (together), come (together), team (up).

gangling
adj lit: lanky, loosely-built, rangy, slender, spindly, tall.

gangster
n lit: bandit, brigand, desperado, hood, hoodlum, mobster, racketeer.

gap
n lit: break, discontinuity, hiatus, intermission, interstice, interval, lacuna, pause, space, vacuum, void; chink, crack, crevice, hole, opening, recess, rent, rift; *fig*: difference, disparity, divergence.

gape
vb lit: open, widen, yawn; goggle, stare.

garb
n lit: apparel, attire, clothes, clothing, costume, get-up, outfit, raiment, uniform; appearance, guise, manifestation.
vb lit: attire, clothe, dress, rig out.

garbage
n lit: debris, dross, junk, litter, offal, refuse, rubbish, scraps, slops, sweepings, trash, waste.

garble
vb lit: confuse, corrupt, distort, jumble, misinterpret, misrepresent, mix up, pervert, travesty.

gardening
n lit: cultivation, horticulture; growing, planting, sowing; landscaping.

garish
adj lit: brassy, flash, gaudy, glaring, loud, ostentatious, raffish, showy, vulgar.

garland
n lit: chaplet, coronal, lei, wreath.
vb lit: adorn, bedeck, crown, festoon, wreathe; *fig*: anthology, symposium.

garner
vb lit: accumulate, collect, gather, hoard, husband, keep, store; lay up, put by, save, treasure.

garnish
n lit: adornment, decoration, embellishment, ornament, trimming; relish.
vb lit: adorn, bedeck, decorate, embellish, ornament, trim; flavour, spice.

garret
n lit: attic, loft, roof-space; *fig*: bed-sit, digs; den, study, work-room.

garrulous
adj lit: chatty, effusive, gabby, gushing, loquacious, prolix, talkative, verbose.

gash
n lit: cut, gouge, incision, laceration, slash, slit, tear.
vb lit: cut, gouge, incise, lacerate, slash, slit, tear.

gate
n lit: barrier, boom, grill, wicket; doorway, entrance, exit, portal; channel, passage; lock, sluice, valve; *fig*:

attendance, spectators; frame, framework.
vb lit: confine, curfew, detain, keep in, restrict.

gather
vb lit: accumulate, amass, assemble, coacervate, expand, grow, heap up, increase, rise, thicken; bring together, collect, convene, group, hoard, muster, pile up, stack up, stockpile; clasp, embrace, enfold, hug; fold, pleat, ruffle, tuck; crop, cull, garner, harvest, pick, pluck, reap; *fig*: conclude, deduce, infer, presume, surmise, understand.

gauche
adj lit: graceless, ill-bred, inept, insensitive, tactless, unpolished, unsophisticated; awkward, clumsy, gawky, inelegant, maladroit.

gaudy
adj lit: bright, brilliant, clashing, colourful, florid, garish, glaring, psychedelic, vivid; adorned, ornamented.

gauge
n lit: dial, indicator, measure, meter; criterion, example, exemplar, guideline, model, pattern, sample, standard, touchstone, yardstick; bore, calibre, magnitude, span, thickness, width.
vb lit: ascertain, assess, compute, count, determine, evaluate, judge, measure, value, weigh; estimate, guess.

gaunt
adj lit: angular, bony, cadaverous, haggard, lean, pinched, scrawny, skinny, spare; bleak, desolate, forbidding, grim, harsh.

gay
n lit: homosexual; fairy, nancy-boy, pansy, pretty-boy, poof, poofter, queen, queer, woofter; bugger, catamite, sodomite.
adj lit: carefree, cheerful, festive, frolicsome, fun-loving, happy, jovial, joyous, light-hearted, merry, sportive, sunny; bright, colourful, flamboyant, flash, gaudy, showy; homoerotic, homosexual; bent, camp, effeminate, pansy, queer.

gaze
n lit: gape, look, regard, stare; contemplation.

vb lit: gape (at), look (at), look levelly (at), stare (at).

gear
n lit: cog, cogwheel; linkage, machinery, mechanism, transmission, work(s); accessories, apparatus, equipment, implements, instruments, tackle, tools; accoutrements, paraphernalia, rigging, supplies, trappings; belongings, effects, kit, stuff, things; attire, clothes, clothing, garments.
vb lit: connect, link, mesh; equip (up), fit (up), harness (up), rig (up); adapt (to), adjust (to).

gem
n lit: jewel, precious stone, stone; *fig*: flower, masterpiece, prize, treasure.

genealogy
n lit: ancestry, descent, extraction, line, stock; family tree, lineage, pedigree.

general
n lit: head, leader, officer; common, ordinary, usual.
adj lit: accepted, accustomed, common, conventional, customary, everyday, habitual, ordinary, popular, prevailing, regular, typical, universal, usual, widespread; all-inclusive, blanket, catholic, collective, comprehensive, sweeping, total; ill-defined, imprecise, indefinite, inexact, unspecific, vague.

generally
adv lit: as a rule, commonly, conventionally, customarily, habitually, largely, mainly, mostly, normally, ordinarily, predominantly, regularly, typically, universally, usually; extensively, popularly, widely.

generate
vb lit: breed, cause, create, engender, initiate, make for, originate, produce, stir up.

generation
n lit: creation, engendering, genesis, origination, procreation, production, propagation; age-group, family group; *fig*: age, day, era, period, time.

generosity
n lit: beneficence, bounty, charity, kindness, liberality, munificence; altruism, unselfishness; leniency, magnanimity.

generous
adj lit: beneficent, bounteous, bountiful, charitable, free, kind, lavish, liberal, munificent, open-handed, unstinting; abundant, ample, copious, full, rich; altruistic, unselfish; lenient, magnanimous.

genesis
n lit: beginning, conception, creation, engendering, inception, origin, root, source, start.

genetic
adj lit: hereditary, inherited; chromosomal; congenital; somatic.

genial
adj lit: affable, amiable, cheery, convivial, easygoing, friendly, hearty, jovial, smiling, warm-hearted; congenial.

genius
n lit: brain, intellect, mastermind; expert, master, natural, virtuoso; brilliance, flair; faculty, gift, knack, talent.

genteel
adj lit: civil, courteous, cultured, formal, gentlemanly, ladylike, mannerly, refined, well-bred; elegant, fashionable.

gentle
adj lit: benign, bland, meek, mild, moderate, peaceable, placid, quiet, temperate; biddable, docile, manageable, tame, tractable; compassionate, humane, lenient, merciful; calm, easy, light, low, serene, slight, soft, tender; gradual, imperceptible, muted, slow; aristocratic, noble, patrician, refined.

genuine
adj lit: authentic, bona fide, legitimate, real, true, veritable; honest, sound, sterling; natural, original, pure, unadulterated; heartfelt, sincere, unaffected, unfeigned.

germ
n lit: bacterium, microbe, micro-organism, virus; bud, corm, seed, spore; egg, gamete, nucleus, ovum; *fig*: beginning, origination.

germane
adj lit: allied (to), connected (to), related (to); apposite (to), appropriate (to), material (to), pertinent (to), relevant (to).

germinate
vb lit: bud, generate, grow, shoot, sprout.

gesticulate
vb lit: beckon, gesture anxiously, motion agitatedly, signal enthusiastically, wave wildly; mime.

gesture
n lit: gesticulation, motion, signal; action, deed, demonstration.
vb lit: beckon, gesticulate, motion, signal.

get
vb lit: acquire, come by, come into possession of, inherit, obtain, pick up, receive, succeed to; bring, fetch, procure, secure, win; earn, gain, make, net, realize; arrest, collar, entrap, grab, seize, take; hit, shoot, strike; become, come to be, grow, turn; catch, come down with, contract; contact, reach; *fig*: comprehend, follow, hear, learn, perceive, see, understand; arrange, contrive, fix, organize, wangle; induce, influence, persuade, prevail upon; arrive, come to; affect, stimulate; annoy, irritate; confound, mystify, stump; begin, start; go, leave.

get off
vb lit: alight, descend, disembark, dismount; remove, take off; *fig*: go away, scram, vamoose.

get on
vb lit: ascend, board, mount; put on, wear; *fig*: cope, make out, manage, succeed; age, become older; agree (with), be compatible (with), hit it off (with).

get round
vb lit: bypass, circumvent, evade, skirt; *fig*: cajole, persuade, talk round, wheedle.

get up
vb lit: ascend, climb, mount; arise, rise, stand; *fig*: dress; learn by heart.

ghastly
adj lit: dreadful, frightful, grim, gruesome, horrendous, horrible, terrifying; ashen, deathly pale, hideous, pallid; ghostly, spectral.

ghost
n lit: phantom, revenant, spectre, wraith; spirit; apparition, spook; pseudonymous author; second image; *fig*: glimmer, hint, merest possibility, shadow, suggestion.

vb lit: appear suddenly, flit; author, pen, write for somebody else.

ghostly
adj lit: eerie, spectral, supernatural, wraithlike; uncanny, unearthly; *fig*: blurred, dim, pale, shadowy, vague; double-image.

giant
n lit: colossus, titan; ogre; enormous person; *spec*: large star.
adj lit: colossal, enormous, gargantuan, huge, immense, mammoth, titanic, vast.

gibberish
n lit: babble, blether, drivel, gobbledegook, mumbo-jumbo, nonsense, twaddle.

giddy
adj lit: vertiginous; unsteady; *fig*: dizzy, light-headed; changeable, fickle, flighty, frivolous, inconstant, scatterbrained, unstable, volatile.

gift
n lit: contribution, donation, present; gratuity, tip; bequest, legacy; oblation, offering, sacrifice; *fig*: attribute, faculty, flair, genius, talent.

gifted
adj (pa.pt) lit: brilliant, clever, expert, masterly, superb, talented.

gig
n lit: sulky, trap; boat, cutter, dinghy; concert, engagement, jam session, performance, show; harpoon.

giggle
n lit: chortle, chuckle, snigger, titter; bit of fun, jape, joke, laugh.
vb lit: chortle, chuckle, snicker, snigger, titter.

gimmick
n lit: stunt; ploy, stratagem, trick; gambit.

ginger
vb fig: arouse, electrify, enliven, galvanize, inspirit, jolt, rouse, stimulate.

gingerly
adv lit: carefully, cautiously, charily, daintily, delicately, lightly, softly, timidly, warily.

gird
vb lit: belt, encincture, girdle; encircle, enclose, ring, surround; *fig*: arm, fortify, strengthen; ready (oneself); clothe, furnish.

girdle
n lit: belt, cincture, cummerbund, sash, suspender belt.
vb lit: bind round, encircle, encompass, ring, surround.

girl
n lit: damsel, lass, lassie, maid, maiden, wench; daughter; miss; female, lady, woman; chick, doll, bird, filly, gal, piece of crumpet, skirt.

girlish
adj lit: feminine; female, womanly; coquettish, hoydenish; adolescent, young; effeminate, smooth-cheeked.

gist
n lit: drift, idea, meaning, nub, pith, point, sense, significance.

give
n lit: bend, elasticity, flexibility, resilience, resistance.
vb lit: bestow, confer, donate, hand over, impart, issue, present; bring, deliver, fetch, let have, provide with, supply; award, contribute, pay, return; accord, cause, create, grant; administer, deal, dole out, mete out; emit, render, transmit, utter, vent; devote, entrust with, lend; demonstrate, display, evidence, furnish, manifest, show; carry out, do, make, perform; cede, relinquish, surrender, throw (in) the towel, yield; be elastic, bend; open (on to), lead (out to).

give away
vb fig: betray, divulge, leak, let slip, reveal.

glacial
adj lit: arctic, frozen, gelid, icy; *fig*: cold, freezing, frigid, frosty.

glad
adj lit: delighted, gratified, happy, pleased; willing; cheerful, cheering, gratifying, pleasing.

glamour
n lit: allure, charisma, enchantment, fascination, magic, magnetism, mysterious quality, spell; gloss, luminescence, radiance.

glance
n lit: glimpse, look, peek, peep, squinny; dekko, gander; flash, gleam, glimmer; reflection, shimmer; cannon, edge, ricochet, tip; *fig*: allusion, mention, reference.

vb lit: glimpse, look quickly, peek, peep, squint; flash, gleam, glimmer; reflect, shimmer; cannon (off), edge, ricochet (off), skim (off), tip; browse (through), leaf (through), run (over), thumb (through).

glare
n lit: dirty look, frown, gaze, glower, scowl; blaze, brilliance, brightness, dazzle; *fig*: garishness, gaudiness, loudness, showiness.
vb lit: frown, give a dirty look, gaze, glower, lower, scowl; blaze, dazzle, flare.

glaring
adj (pr.pt) lit: blazing, bright, dazzling, flaring, shining; *fig*: flashy, garish, gaudy, loud, showy; blatant, conspicuous, flagrant, gross, obvious, overt, patent, vivid.

glassy
adj lit: calm, clear, smooth, transparent, translucent, vitreous; icy, slick, slippery; blank, dazed, expressionless, glazed, lifeless.

glaze
n lit: gloss, lacquer, varnish; slip; finish, lustre, polish, shine.
vb lit: gloss, lacquer, varnish; coat, laminate; fit windows, glass; *fig*: become vacant, dull, glass over, go blank.

gleaming
adj (pr.pt) lit: bright, brilliant, coruscating, glimmering, glistening, glossy, lambent, lustrous, radiant, scintillating, shimmering, shining, sparkling.

glee
n lit: delight, elation, exultation, joy, triumph; hilarity, merriment, mirth; catch, madrigal, part-song.

glib
adj lit: fast-talking, fluent, plausible, ready, slick, smooth, suave.

glide
vb lit: plane, skate, skim, slide, slip; drift, float, sail; coast, freewheel, roll.

glimpse
n lit: glance, look, peek, peep, squinny; flash, sight, view.
vb lit: glance, look quickly, peek, peep, squint; catch sight of, espy, sight, spot.

glitter
n lit: coruscation, glistening, scintillation, shimmering, sparkle, twinkle; *fig*: display, glamour, glitz, razzamatazz, sequins, show, tinsel.
vb lit: coruscate, glisten, scintillate, shimmer, sparkle, twinkle; flash, gleam, glimmer.

globe
n lit: ball, orb, sphere; earth, planet, world; bulb, lamp-glass.

globule
n lit: bead, drop, droplet, pearl.

gloom
n lit: darkness, dimness, dusk, murk, obscurity, shadow, umbra; *fig*: dejection, depression, despair, despondency, hopelessness, low spirits, unhappiness.

gloomy
adj lit: cloudy, crepuscular, dark, dim, dusky, murky, obscure, shadowy, sombre; *fig*: blue, dejected, depressed, despondent, downcast, glum, in low spirits, morose, unhappy; black, depressing, dismal, dispiriting, doleful, joyless, pessimistic.

glorify
adj lit: adore, beatify, bless, exalt, honour, magnify, pay homage to, revere, venerate, worship; celebrate, eulogize, extol, hymn, laud, praise; beautify, illuminate, make glorious.

glorious
adj lit: beautiful, bright, brilliant, divine, excellent, fine, gorgeous, great, heavenly, marvellous, radiant, resplendent, splendid, superb, wonderful; celebrated, distinguished, eminent, honoured, illustrious, magnificent, noted, triumphant.

glory
n lit: adoration, beatification, blessing, eulogy, homage, honour, praise, reverence, veneration, worship; magnificence, majesty, pomp, splendour; distinction, eminence, illustriousness, renown; beauty, brightness, brilliance, radiance, resplendence; *fig*: aura, halo.
vb lit: delight (in), exult (in), pride oneself (in), rejoice (in), revel (in).

glow
n lit: brightness, gleam, glimmer, lambency, light, phosphorescence, radiance; *fig*: blush, flush, reddening;

ardour, fervour, heat, passion, warmth.
vb lit: gleam, glimmer, light, radiate,
shine; be red-hot, be white-hot, burn,
smoulder; be suffused, blush, colour,
flush, redden, tingle.

glue
n lit: adhesive, gum; tack; cement.
vb lit: gum, paste; affix, cement, stick,
tack.

glum
adj lit: blue, dejected, depressed,
despondent, doleful, downcast, gloomy,
in low spirits, morose, unhappy; dismal,
joyless, pessimistic.

glut
n lit: excess, saturation, superabundance,
superfluity, surfeit, surplus; cornucopia,
plethora.
vb lit: cram, fill, gorge, stuff; quench,
satiate, satisfy; deluge, flood, inundate,
overload, overwhelm, saturate.

gnawing
adj (pr.pt) lit: nibbling; fretting, nagging,
wearing, worrying.

gnome
n lit: dwarf, elf, goblin, kobold,
leprechaun, sprite, troll; banker,
hoarder.

go
n lit: attempt, bash, crack, shot, stab, try,
turn, whirl; drive, dynamism, energy,
life, spirit, verve, vigour, vivacity.
vb lit: advance, fare, move, pass, proceed,
repair, travel; depart, leave, set off,
withdraw; be spent, elapse, flow, lapse,
slip away; die, expire, pass away, perish;
break down, fail, give way; function,
operate, perform, run, work; be,
become; attend, be present; develop, fall
out, happen, result, turn out; be
acceptable, be permitted; extend
(between), lead (to), reach (to), span
(over), spread (over), stretch (to); refer
(to), take (to); contribute (towards),
serve (to), tend (towards); blend
(together), chime (together), fit
(together), harmonize (together).

goal
n lit: mark, net, target; objective; *fig*: aim,
end, object; design, intention, purpose.

god
n lit: deity, divinity; fetish, idol, image;
fig: celebrity, hero.

godforsaken
adj lit: abandoned, deserted, desolate,
lonely, neglected; backward, bleak,
remote.

godly
adj lit: devout, god-fearing, holy, pious,
religious.

godsend
n lit: blessing, boon, piece of good
fortune, stroke of luck, windfall.

go in for
vb lit: adopt, engage in, participate in,
practise, pursue, take up; compete in,
enter; apply for, make for.

gold(en)
adj lit: aureate, gilded, gilt, yellow; blond,
blonde, flaxen; *fig*: best, glorious, happy,
prosperous, rich, successful; excellent,
favourable, promising, propitious.

gone
adj (pa.pt) lit: absent, away, departed,
vanished; lost, missing; elapsed,
finished, over, past; dead, deceased,
done; exhausted, spent, used.

good
n lit: merit, morality, probity,
righteousness, virtue; advantage, benefit,
gain, profit, use, usefulness, wellbeing.
adj lit: acceptable, capital, commendable,
fine, first-rate, great, pleasing,
satisfactory, valuable, worthy; fair,
halcyon, pleasant, sunny; admirable,
beneficent, benevolent, charitable,
estimable, humane, honourable, kindly,
praiseworthy, upright, virtuous; dutiful,
mannerly, obedient, polite, proper, well-
behaved; agreeable, congenial, convivial,
enjoyable, gratifying; authentic, bona
fide, genuine, legitimate, real, true,
valid; accomplished, adept, adroit,
clever, competent, dextrous, efficient,
expert, proficient, skilled, useful;
advantageous, beneficial, favourable,
helpful, opportune, propitious; healthy,
salubrious, sound, untainted,
wholesome; adequate, ample,
considerable, extensive, large, long,
solid, substantial; (for) ever.

good-looking
adj lit: attractive, beautiful, bonny,
comely, dishy, fair, handsome, pretty;
gorgeous, ravishing.

good-natured
adj lit: benevolent, friendly, helpful, kind, kindly, obliging, well-disposed; mild, moderate, temperate.

goods
n lit: commodities, merchandise, stock, wares; belongings, chattels, effects, gear, paraphernalia, possessions, property, things.

goodwill
n lit: amity, beneficence, benevolence, favour, friendship, kindliness; *fig*: clientele, custom, popularity.

go off
vb lit: blow, decamp, depart, hop it, leave, scarper, set out, quit; discontinue, leave off; blow up, explode, fire; happen, occur, take place; expire, fade away, pass away, taper off; begin to smell, deteriorate, rot.

go on
vb lit: move ahead, pass, travel on; continue, last, persist; happen, occur, take place; chunter, manage; chatter, rabbit, waffle, witter on.

gore
n lit: blood; clotted blood, dried blood.
vb lit: impale, pierce, spike, spear, transfix.

gorge
n lit: canyon, chasm, chine, defile, fissure, ravine, rift.
vb lit: bloat, bolt, cram, feed, fill, guzzle, stuff, wolf.

gorgeous
adj lit: beautiful, dazzling, exquisite, glittering, glorious, lovely, magnificent, ravishing, resplendent, stunning; grand, opulent, sumptuous.

gossip
n lit: backbiter, busybody, chatterbox, scandalmonger; chitchat, hearsay, idle talk, scandal, tittle-tattle.
vb lit: chat, mind other people's business, prattle, tattle, tell tales.

go through
vb lit: do all of, run right through; check, examine, hunt through, search; consume, exhaust, use; bear, endure, suffer, undergo; be accepted, be approved.

govern
vb lit: administer, command, control, direct, manage, oversee, pilot, rule, steer; decide, determine, influence; check, contain, curb, discipline, master, restrain, tame.

government
n lit: administration, authority, execution, rule; assembly, congress, diet, parliament, senate; regime; command, control, direction, management.

gown
n lit: evening-dress, dress, frock; cassock, habit, robe; dressing-gown; nightie; toga; ceremonial cape.

grab
n lit: clutch, grasp, snatch; take-over bid, seizure, sequestration; scoop.
vb lit: capture, catch, clutch, grasp, grip, nab, seize, snatch.

grace
n lit: ease, elegance, finesse, panache, poise, polish, style, taste; attractiveness, charm; benevolence, charity, favour, goodwill, kindness; clemency, forgiveness, lenience, mercy, pardon; benediction, prayer, thanksgiving; divine influence, salvation; allowance, amnesty, interval, time in hand.
vb lit: adorn, bedeck, decorate, dignify, distinguish, embellish, enhance, honour, ornament.

graceful
adj lit: elegant, fine, flowing, gracile, natural, smooth, symmetrical.

gracious
adj lit: benign, civil, cordial, courteous, courtly, indulgent, kindly, well-mannered.

grade
n lit: category, class, division, level, order, quality, rank, sort; degree, mark, place, position, step; bank, incline, rise, slope.
vb lit: categorize, classify, group, order, range, rank, sort.

gradient
n lit: declivity, incline, rise, slant, slope.

gradual
n lit: antiphon, canticle, processional; antiphonal, missal.
adj lit: continuous, gentle, progressive, slow, steady.

graft
n lit: implant, scion, splice; bud, shoot; transplant, transplantation; *fig*: bribery, corruption, dishonest dealings.
vb lit: attach (on), implant, insert, splice (on), transplant.

grain
n lit: cereals, corn; kernel, seed; granule; atom, bit, crumb, morsel, ounce, particle, scrap; fibre pattern, surface texture, weave; colorative, dye; *fig*: character, disposition, temper.

grand
adj lit: august, dignified, elevated, exalted, glorious, imposing, impressive, lofty, lordly, luxurious, magnificent, majestic, opulent, palatial, splendid, stately, sumptuous; highest, main, principal, supreme.

grandiose
adj lit: imposing, impressive, magnificent, majestic, stately; affected, extravagant, over the top, pompous, pretentious.

grant
n lit: allowance, award, endowment, subsidy; allocation, donation.
vb lit: accede to, agree to, cede, concede, consent to; accord, assign, bestow, confer, convey, give, transfer, vouchsafe, yield; acknowledge, admit.

graphic
n lit: artwork, chart, cross-section, diagram, drawing, engraving, etching, line-drawing, picture, sketch, visual.
adj lit: clear, detailed, diagrammatic, explicit, pictorial, telling, vivid.

grasp
n lit: clasp, clutch, grip, hold, possession; *fig*: control, range, reach, scope; comprehension, perception, realization, understanding.
vb lit: catch, clasp, clutch, grab, grip, hold, seize; *fig*: comprehend, get, realize, see, understand.

grasping
adj (pr.pt) lit: avaricious, greedy, mean, miserly, niggardly, penny-pinching, stingy, tightfisted.

grass
n lit: greenery, herbage, pasturage, verdure; lawn, sward, turf; cannabis, ganja, hemp, marijuana, pot.

vb lit: lay out a lawn, turf; *fig*: inform (on), sneak (on), tell (on).

grate
n lit: bars, griddle, grill, grille; fireplace; mesh, screen.
vb lit: mince, shred; abrade, file, grind, rasp, rub, scrape, scratch; *fig*: chafe (on), get (on) one's nerves, jar (on).

grateful
adj lit: appreciative, thankful; obliged (to).

gratify
vb lit: delight, give pleasure, gladden, please; humour, indulge, satisfy; thrill.

gratitude
n lit: appreciation, thankfulness, thanks; obligation.

gratuitous
adj lit: free, spontaneous, unasked-for, voluntary; uncalled-for, unjustified, unmerited, unprovoked, unwarranted.

gratuity
n lit: pourboire, tip; bonus, perk, perquisite, reward.

grave
n lit: last resting-place; crypt, tomb, vault; headstone.
adj lit: grim, sedate, serious, sober, solemn, sombre; critical, dangerous, perilous, severe, threatening, urgent, weighty.

gravitate
vb lit: descend, settle, sink; *fig*: be attracted towards, be drawn towards, incline (towards), tend (towards).

gravity
n lit: force, weight; *fig*: dignity, earnestness, seriousness, sobriety, solemnity, thoughtfulness; grimness, perilousness, severity; consequence, importance, moment, significance.

graze
n lit: abrasion, scrape; scratch; cannon, glance, kiss.
vb lit: abrade, brush, chafe, scrape; cannon off, glance off, shave, skim, touch.

grease
n lit: fat, lard; lubricant, oil; lanolin; perspiration, sweat.
vb lit: lard, lubricate, oil, rub fat over, smear; *fig*: bribe with, put money in (one's palm).

greasy
adj lit: fatty, oily; slick, slippery; *fig*: fawning, ingratiating, slimy, smarmy, unctuous.

great
adj lit: big, bulky, expansive, extensive, immense, large, long, protracted, vast; considerable, decided, extreme, high, pronounced, strong; critical, crucial, grave, heavy, momentous, serious, significant, solemn; absolute, complete, positive, total; chief, grand, leading, main, principal; august, dignified, idealistic, impressive, lofty, noble; celebrated, distinguished, eminent, illustrious, notable, outstanding, prominent, remarkable; active, enthusiastic, keen; adept, adroit, expert, skilled; excellent, marvellous, terrific, tremendous, wonderful.

greed
n lit: covetousness, cupidity, desire, longing, rapacity, selfishness; esurience, gluttony, insatiability, voracity.

green
n lit: common, heath; lawn, turf; putting area.
vb lit: blooming, flourishing, grassy, leafy, verdant; immature, unripe; pliable, supple, tender, unseasoned; ill, nauseous, pallid, sick, unhealthy; environmental, environmentalist; *fig*: callow, inexperienced, new, raw, unpractised, untrained; credulous, gullible, innocent, naive, unsophisticated; envious, jealous.

greens
n lit: brassicas, cabbages, kale; leaves, salad; vegetables.

greet
vb lit: address, hail, salute, welcome; cry, shed tears, weep; *fig*: meet (with), react to (with), respond to (with).

greeting
n lit: hail, salutation, salute, welcome; compliment(s), regard(s), respect(s).

grey
adj lit: cloudy, dark, dim, dismal, drab, gloomy, murky, overcast; ashen, bloodless, pale, pallid, sallow, wan; elderly, hoary, old; *fig*: characterless, colourless, dull, neutral; indistinct, misty, vague; *spec*: white (horse).

grid
n lit: grate, grating, griddle, grill, lattice, trellis; network, system; frame, framework, rack, trestle; layout sheet, overlay, plan; chart, co-ordinates, graph-paper, squared paper.

grief
n lit: mourning, sadness, sorrow; heartache, heartbreak, misery, wretchedness; (come to) nothing, (come to) ruin.

grievance
n lit: beef, complaint, gripe, moan; grounds for complaint, hardship, wrong.

grieve
vb lit: keen, lament, mourn, sorrow, weep (for); distress, hurt, pain, sadden, wound.

grill
n lit: grate, grid, gridiron, griddle, rack; barbecue, fry-up; broilery, dining-room, kitchen, restaurant; bars, lattice, mesh.
vb lit: barbecue, broil, fry, roast, toast; *fig*: interrogate, pump, quiz

grim
adj lit: fierce, forbidding, formidable, sinister, terrible; frightful, ghastly, gruesome, hideous, horrible; harsh, implacable, merciless, ruthless, unrelenting; dark, gloomy, menacing, sullen, threatening.

grimace
n lit: frown, pout, scowl, smirk, sneer, wry face,
vb lit: girn, pull faces; frown, pout, scowl, smirk, sneer.

grime
n lit: dirt, dust, filth, mud, soot; ingrained dirt.

grind
n lit: chore, drag, drudgery, effort, labour.
vb lit: crush, granulate, grate, mill, pulverize; file, sand; hone, sharpen, whet; gnash, grit; crank, turn; *fig*: burn the midnight oil, study, work (away); force (down), oppress.

grip
n lit: clasp, clutch, grasp, hold, possession; footing, leverage, purchase; hold-all, travelling bag; clip; handle, haft; *fig*: clutches, control, influence, mastery, power; comprehension, perception, understanding.

vb lit: clasp, clutch, grasp, hold, latch on to, seize; *fig*: absorb, engross, enthral, entrance, fascinate, rivet.

gripping
adj (pr.pt) lit: absorbing, compelling, compulsive, engrossing, enthralling, exciting, fascinating, unputdownable.

grisly
adj lit: bloody, ghastly, gory, gruesome, horrible, horrific, macabre, sickening, terrible.

grit
n lit: dust particles, grains of sand, motes; chippings, gravel, sand; *fig*: backbone, doggedness, fortitude, hardihood, perseverance, spirit, tenacity.
vb lit: sand, spread gravel; gnash, grate, grind.

groan
n lit: moan, sigh.
vb lit: moan, sigh; call painfully, utter despairingly; *fig*: be burdened, be laden.

groceries
n lit: provisions, supplies, victuals; shopping.

groggy
adj lit: dazed, half-stunned, muzzy, shaky, staggering, unsteady, wobbly, woozy.

groom
n lit: stableboy, stablegirl; ostler; flunkey, manservant; bridegroom, husband.
vb lit: brush, clean, curry, rub down; dress, smarten oneself up, tidy oneself up; coach, drill, educate, prime, train.

groove
n lit: channel, cutting, furrow, rift, score, trench; *fig*: routine, rut.
vb lit: channel, flute, furrow, rifle, score.

grope
n lit: feel, fumble, scrabble; search.
vb lit: feel, flounder, fumble, scrabble; search.

gross
n lit: bulk, entirety, whole; amount before deductions; 144, twelve dozen.
vb lit: bring in, earn, make, take.
adj lit: bulky, corpulent, fat, hulking, massive, thick; coarse, crude, improper, indecent, indelicate, offensive, ribald, rude, vulgar; boorish, crass, ignorant, insensitive, unfeeling, unsophisticated; blatant, flagrant, glaring, manifest, plain,

utter; outrageous, shocking; *spec*: (earnings, income) before tax.

grotesque
adj lit: bizarre, fantastic, freakish, odd, outlandish, strange, weird.

grotto
n lit: cavern, niche, nook, recess, retreat.

ground
n lit: earth, land, soil, terra firma; arena, field, park, pitch; floor; *spec*: (electrical) earth, earthing.
vb lit: lay down, put down; base, establish, pitch, set; coach (in), educate (in), initiate (in), instruct (in), teach (in), tutor (in).
adj (pa.pt) lit: crushed, milled, powdered, pulverized; filed (down), sanded (down); eroded (away); *fig*: oppressed.

grounds
n lit: dregs, lees, sediment; domain, estate, garden, land, property, territory; area, district, zone; basis, cause, excuse, justification, motive, pretext, reason.

group
n lit: band, bunch, cluster, collection, company, gang, gathering, pack, party, set; class, category.
vb lit: assemble, associate, cluster, collect, gather, get together; arrange, assort, bracket together, classify, marshal, order, put together, sort.

grovelling
adj (pr.pt) lit: face down, kowtowing, prone; bootlicking, crawling, fawning, flattering, obsequious, servile, toadying.

grow
vb lit: develop, germinate, shoot, sprout; breed, cultivate, farm, produce, propagate; arise (from), spring (from), stem (from); augment, enlarge, expand, extend, get bigger, increase, spread, stretch, swell; advance, flourish, multiply, progress; *fig*: become, come to be, get, turn.

growl
n lit: roar, snarl; rumble.
vb lit: roar, snarl; rumble; grouse, grumble.

growth
n lit: development, germination, shoot, sprout; cultivation, propagation; evolution; augmentation, enlargement, expansion, extension, increase, spread, stretching, swelling; cancer, lump,

tumour; advance, flourishing, multiplication, progress, proliferation.

grub
n lit: caterpillar, larva, maggot; chow, eats, food, nosh, tuck.
vb lit: dig, forage, hunt (for), poke around (for), probe, rootle, rummage (for).

grudge
n lit: complaint, grievance, score; rancour, resentment.
vb lit: envy, hold against, mind, resent.

grudging
adj (pr.pt) lit: envious, rancorous, reluctant, resentful, sulky, unwilling.

gruelling
adj lit: arduous, backbreaking, demanding, exhausting, grinding, laborious, punishing, stiff, taxing.

gruesome
adj lit: bloody, ghastly, gory, grim, grisly, horrible, horrific, macabre, sickening, terrible.

guarantee
n lit: assurance, collateral, pledge, security, warranty.
vb lit: answer for, insure, pledge, promise, stand behind, vouch for, warrant.

guarantor
n lit: angel, backer, sponsor, surety, underwriter.

guard
n lit: defender, lookout, sentinel, sentry, warder, watchman; custodian, jailer, screw; escort; buffer, bumper, pad, safety screen, shield; vigilance, wariness, watchfulness.
vb lit: defend, patrol, police, protect, secure, watch over; escort, mind, tend.

guarded
adj (pa.pt) lit: careful, cautious, discreet, reserved, reticent, wary.

guardian
n lit: keeper, protector, trustee, warden; curator, custodian, escort, guard, warder.

guess
n lit: conjecture, hypothesis, speculation, supposition, surmise, theory.
vb lit: conjecture, estimate, fancy, hazard, hypothesize, imagine, reckon, surmise.

guest
n lit: caller, visitor; boarder, lodger; spec:

inquiline.

guide
n lit: beacon, key, landmark, pointer, sign, signal, signpost; directory, handbook, manual; chaperon, conductor, escort, leader, pilot, usher; fig: master, paradigm; example, inspiration.
vb lit: control, direct, handle, manoeuvre, steer; conduct, escort, lead, shepherd, usher; advise, counsel.

guile
n lit: artifice, craftiness, cunning, deception, trickery, wiliness.

guilt
n lit: blameworthiness, culpability; misconduct, wrongdoing; bad conscience, self-condemnation, shame; dishonour.

guilty
adj lit: culpable, responsible, wrong; ashamed, contrite, hang-dog, remorseful, rueful, sorry.

guinea-pig
n lit: cavy; fig: experimental subject, subject, victim.

gulf
n lit: bay, bight; chasm, cleft, rift, split, void; whirlpool; fig: gap, distance, space.

gullible
adj lit: believing, credulous, naive, susceptible, trusting, unsuspecting.

gulp
n lit: mouthful, swallow, swig; blench, gasp.
vb lit: bolt, gobble, wolf; guzzle, knock back, swallow, swig, swill, toss off; blench, gasp, recoil, swallow hard.

gun
n lit: firearm; cannon, gat, rod; pistol, revolver, rifle, shotgun; starting pistol; fig: nozzle, spray, syringe; accelerator, throttle.
vb lit: hunt (down), shoot (down); fig: hunt (for), look (for); accelerate, race, rev.

gurgle
n lit: chortle, chuckle, giggle; murmur, plash, ripple; borborygmus, rumble.
vb lit: chortle, chuckle, giggle; babble, murmur, plash, ripple; bubble, fizz; rumble.

gushing

adj (pr.pt) lit: cascading, flooding, jetting, spouting, spurting, streaming; *fig*: effusive, enthusiastic, exuberant, voluble.

gust

n lit: blast, flurry, gale, puff, squall, whiff; *fig*: burst, eruption, explosion, storm, surge.

gusto

n lit: appetite, enjoyment, enthusiasm, relish, savour, zest.

gutter

n lit: conduit, drain, pipe; ditch, groove, scuppers, trench, trough.
vb lit: flicker, smoke.

guts

n lit: bowels, intestines; entrails, tripes, viscera; *fig*: backbone, bottle, bravery, courage, fortitude, nerve, pluck, spunk; insides, machinery, works.

guy

n lit: bloke, geezer, man; chap, fellow, lad.
vb lit: caricature, make fun of, send up, take off.

guzzling

adj (pr.pt) lit: gulping, knocking back, swallowing, swigging, swilling, tossing off; gobbling, gorging, stuffing, wolfing.

gypsy

n lit: Romany, tinker, traveller; rover; vagrant.

H

habit
n lit: custom, fashion, practice, routine, rule, tendency, way; idiosyncrasy, mannerism, proclivity, trait, wont; consuetude, usage; addiction, dependence; composition, constitution, frame, make-up, nature, structure; apparel, costume, dress, garb, garment.

habitat
n lit: environment, locale, natural surroundings, scenario; abode, domicile, habitation, home.

habitual
adj lit: accustomed, constant, customary, established, frequent, inveterate, recurrent, regular, wonted; familiar, natural, normal, ordinary, routine, usual; chronic, hardened, ingrained, persistent, practised.

habituated
adj (pa.pt) lit: acclimatized, adapted, conditioned, familiarized, inured, seasoned, trained.

hack
n lit: ghost, journalist, script-writer, writer; dogsbody, drudge, gofer, slave; chop, cut, hew, slash; boot, kick; cough, rasp; bag of bones, crock, horse, jade, nag.
vb lit: chop, cut, hew, slash; mangle, mutilate; boot, kick; bark, cough, rasp; ride a horse; ad lib, extemporize; spec: access, cut into (a computer service).
adj lit: hired, mercenary; drudging, slavish.

hackneyed
adj lit: banal, bathetic, clichéd, commonplace, overworked, pedestrian, stereotyped, stock, threadbare, tired, trite, unoriginal, worn.

haemorrhage
n lit: bleeding; bruising, trauma, wound.

haggard
adj lit: care-worn, drawn, emaciated, gaunt, lean, pinched, shrunken, thin, wrinkled; aquiline.

haggle
vb lit: bargain, chaffer, dicker, negotiate, wrangle.

hail
n lit: call, cheer, greeting, shout, yell; greetings, salutation; bombardment, rain, shower, volley; fig: shouting-distance; spec: frozen rain, ice.
vb lit: address, call to, greet, shout to, yell at; accost, flag down, wave down; acclaim, applaud, glorify, honour, salute; cascade (down), pelt, pour (down), rain; come (from), have started (from), originate (from).

hair
n lit: locks, mane, mop, tresses; filament, strand, thread, villus; down, fluff, fur; fig: fraction, narrow margin, whisker; split second.

hair-raising
adj lit: bloodcurdling, creepy, frightening, horrifying, petrifying, scary, spine-chilling, terrifying.

hairy
adj lit: hirsute, shaggy, woolly; bearded, bewhiskered, stubbly, unshaven; downy, fleecy, flocculent, furry; awned, tufted; fig: chancy, dicey, hazardous, risky.

halcyon
adj lit: calm, peaceful, placid, quiet, serene, still, tranquil; happy, pleasant.

half-hearted
adj lit: lacklustre, lukewarm, perfunctory, tame, unenthusiastic.

half-way
adv lit: at the mid-point (between), in the middle (between), to the middle of the full extent; fig: in a compromise position.

hall
n lit: corridor, passageway; entrance, entry, foyer, lobby, vestibule; auditorium, chamber, meeting-place, nave, salon; dormitory, residence; manor-house, mansion.

hallucination
n lit: apparition, fantasy, illusion, vision; trip; figment of the imagination.

halo
n lit: aura, aureola, corona, nimbus.

halt
n lit: pause, standstill, stop; impasse; close, end, termination.
vb lit: draw up, hold still, pause, pull up, stop; break off, cease, desist, take a rest; arrest, check, curb, terminate; block, obstruct.
adj lit: crippled, handicapped, lame.

halting
adj (pr.pt) lit: faltering, laboured, stammering, stumbling, stuttering; awkward, clumsy, lurching.

hamlet
n lit: community, farmstead, village; cluster of houses; dorp.

hammer
n lit: gavel, mallet, striking head; clapper.
vb lit: bang, beat, hit, strike; drive; fashion, forge, make, shape; *fig*: clobber, defeat, drub, thrash, trounce; din (into), drum (into), grind (into); beaver (away at), drudge (away at), keep (on at), plug (away at), work (away at).

hamper
n lit: basket.
vb lit: delay, encumber, handicap, hinder, hold back, hold up, impede, obstruct.

hamstring
n lit: hock tendon; knee tendon.
vb fig: cripple, disable, incapacitate, lame; foil, frustrate, thwart.

hand
n lit: mitt, paw; assistance, help, support; influence, part, role, share; crewman, employee, labourer, operative, sailor, worker; clap, ovation, round of applause; artistry, deftness, dexterity, skill; calligraphy, handwriting, longhand, script, writing; *fig*: (in) order, (in) progress; (in) readiness, (in) reserve; (at) one's command, (on) tap.
vb lit: deliver, give, pass; assist, help.

handcuff
n lit: bracelet(s), manacle(s), shackle(s).
vb lit: manacle, shackle; *fig*: hinder, impede, restrain, restrict.

handful
n lit: dash, few, little, small amount or

number, smack, smidgeon, soupçon, sprinkling, touch; *fig*: effort, exertion, full-time occupation, struggle; difficulty, problem, trouble.

handicap
n lit: defect, disability, impairment; disadvantage, difficulty, drawback, encumbrance, hindrance, impediment, limitation, penalty, restriction, stumbling-block; edge, head start, odds.
vb lit: encumber, hamper, hinder, hold back, hold up, impede, limit, restrain, restrict, retard.

handicraft
n lit: artisanship, artistry, skill, workmanship.

handle
n lit: grip, haft, hilt, knob, lever, stock, switch; *fig*: agnomen, cognomen, name, nickname, praenomen, title.
vb lit: feel, fondle, grasp, hold, touch; caress, grope, maul, paw; control, direct, manage, manipulate, manoeuvre, use, wield; cope with, deal with, take care of, treat; deal in, trade in, traffic in.

hand-out
n lit: alms, charity, donation, freebie, welfare; blurb, circular, leaflet, pamphlet, press release.

handsome
adj lit: attractive, becoming, comely, fine, good-looking, personable; ample, bountiful, large, sizable; generous, liberal, magnanimous.

handy
adj lit: adept, adroit, clever, deft, dextrous, nimble, skilful; helpful, practical, serviceable, useful; accessible, available, convenient, nearby.

hang
n fig: knack, technique.
vb lit: be suspended, dangle, droop, loll, sag, trail; be poised, float, hover, swing; deck, decorate, drape, furnish; adhere, cling, stick; lynch, send to the gallows, string up, suspend; *fig*: hold (back), stay (back); loaf (around), loiter (about); wait (about).

hangdog
adj lit: browbeaten, cowed, cringing, defeated, wretched; shamefaced.

hang-up
n lit: inhibition; complex, neurosis;

fixation, obsession, preoccupation; difficulty, problem, thing.

hankering
n lit: desire, itch, longing, urge, wish, yen.

haphazardly
adv lit: arbitrarily, randomly; aimlessly, indiscriminately, unsystematically.

happen
vb lit: befall, come about, come to pass, eventuate, occur, pass, take place; fall out, turn out; be done (to), transpire (to); appear, arise, crop up, materialize.

happening
n lit: episode, event, incident, occurrence, scene; affair, experience, occasion.

happily
adv lit: cheerfully, contentedly, delightedly, gaily, gladly, joyfully, pleasurably, willingly; appropriately, suitably; felicitously, harmoniously, successfully; fortunately, luckily, providentially; blithely, casually, unwittingly

happiness
n lit: cheerfulness, contentment, delight, enjoyment, gladness, harmony, joy, joyfulness, joyousness, light-heartedness, pleasure; beatitude, blessedness, jubilation; bliss, ecstasy.

happy
adj lit: cheerful, contented, delighted, glad, gratified, joyful, joyous, pleased, sunny; blissful, ecstatic, elated, exultant, overjoyed, rapturous; over the moon, thrilled, walking on air; beatific, blessed, rapt; appropriate, apt, opportune, timely; favourable, felicitous, promising, successful; fortunate, lucky, providential; blithe, casual, unwitting.

harass
vb lit: badger, beleaguer, chivvy, harry, hassle, hound, pester, plague, trouble, vex, worry; annoy, bug, exasperate, torment.

harassment
n lit: badgering, chivvying, harrying, hassling, hounding, pestering; molestation, persecution.

harbour
n lit: anchorage, marina, port, quay, wharf, yacht-basin; *fig*: haven, mooring, shelter; asylum, refuge, retreat, sanctuary.

vb lit: accommodate, lodge, provide refuge for, shelter; conceal, hide, protect, shield; entertain, foster, hold, nurse, retain.

hard
adj lit: compact, firm, inflexible, rigid, solid, stiff, strong, tough, unyielding; bare, indisputable, physical, plain, practical, real, unvarnished; arduous, backbreaking, complex, complicated, difficult, formidable, intricate, involved, knotty, laborious, rigorous, strenuous, thorny, uphill; bad, disagreeable, distressing, grievous, harsh, painful, ugly, unpleasant; fierce, forceful, powerful, violent; cold, grim, implacable, mean, near, obdurate, pitiless, ruthless, stern, strict, stingy, unfeeling, unsparing; acrimonious, bitter, hostile, rancorous; *spec*: alcoholic (drinks); calciferous (water); penetrative (rays).
adv lit: assiduously, determinedly, diligently, energetically, forcefully, industriously, intensely, intently, keenly, persistently, powerfully, strenuously, strongly, vigorously, violently; badly, harshly, laboriously, painfully, roughly, slowly, with difficulty; completely, fully; firmly, solidly, tightly; close, near; *spec*: (frozen) fast, solid; (hold) tight.

harden
vb lit: set, solidify, stiffen; cake, congeal, freeze, gel; anneal, temper; *fig*: brace, fortify, nerve, steel, strengthen; accustom, habituate, inure, season, train; brutalize, toughen; *spec*: (share prices) rise.

hard-hitting
adj lit: aggressive, ferocious, fierce, forceful, fulsome, powerful, strong, tough, unsparing, vigorous; condemnatory, critical, damning.

hardly
adv lit: barely, just, only just, scarcely; probably not, surely not; with difficulty.

hardship
n lit: burden, difficulty, encumbrance, labour, oppression, privation, suffering, trial, tribulation, trouble.

hard up
adj lit: destitute, financially embarrassed, impecunious, impoverished, insolvent, penniless, penurious, poor, poverty-stricken; broke, cleaned out, in the red,

on one's uppers, on the breadline, skint, strapped for cash.

hardy
adj lit: enduring, hale, lusty, robust, rugged, sound, stalwart, stout, sturdy, tough; bold, daring, heroic, intrepid, manly, valiant; *spec*: all-weather (plants).

hare
n lit: jackrabbit; lagomorph; *fig*: quarry. *vb lit*: fly, race, run, speed, sprint; chase (after).

harm
n lit: damage, hurt, ill, impairment, injury; detriment, disservice, mischief. *vb lit*: damage, hurt, ill-treat, ill-use, impair, injure, maltreat, spoil.

harmful
adj lit: damaging, hurtful, impairing, injurious, noxious; baneful, deleterious, detrimental, malignant, mischievous, pernicious; destructive, ruinous.

harmless
adj lit: innocuous; not poisonous, safe; gentle, inoffensive, mild.

harmonious
adj lit: dulcet, euphonious, mellifluous, melodious, musical, symphonic; *fig*: concerted, concordant, consonant; compatible, fraternal, friendly.

harmony
n lit: euphony, mellifluousness, musicality; arrangement, chord-structure, part-writing; *fig*: accord, agreement, balance, compatibility, concord, consonance, correspondence, rapport, unanimity, unity; amicability, friendship, sympathy, understanding.

harness
n lit: gear, tack, trappings; yoke; *fig*: (back in) action. *vb lit*: hitch up, saddle; yoke; *fig*: channel, control; employ, exploit, utilize.

harp
n lit: lyre. *vb lit*: play the lyre; *fig*: dwell (on a subject), go (on), talk too much (on).

harridan
n lit: battleaxe, crone, hag, harpy, termagant, virago, witch.

harsh
adj lit: discordant, dissonant, strident; grating, jarring, rasping, raucous, rough;

brutal, cruel, dour, draconian, hard, pitiless, relentless, ruthless, stern, strict, unfeeling, unpleasant; austere, grim, severe, spartan; bleak, cold, sharp, unrelenting; acrid, astringent, bitter, pungent, sour.

harvest
n lit: gathering, gleaning, reaping; crop, produce, yield; *fig*: fruits, result, return; effect, product. *vb lit*: gather, glean, reap; pick, pluck; mow; *fig*: accumulate, amass, collect, garner, take in.

hash
n lit: hotchpotch, jumble, mess, mishmash, muddle, shambles; casserole, stew; *fig*: assortment, collection, medley, mixture, variety; *spec*: hashish; marijuana.

hassle
n lit: bother, difficulty, matter, problem, trouble; altercation, argument, disagreement, dispute, quarrel, squabble, tussle, wrangle. *vb lit*: badger, bother, harass, harry, hound, pester.

haste
n lit: dispatch, expedition, hurrying, urgency; hustle, impetuosity, rush.

hasten
vb lit: accelerate, expedite, forward, further, hurry, press, speed; goad, urge; be quick (to), go quickly (to); run, rush, scurry.

hasty
adj lit: impetuous, impulsive, precipitate, rash, thoughtless; cursory, fleeting, perfunctory, short, superficial; brusque, fiery, impatient, irascible, quick-tempered.

hatch
n lit: aperture, doorway, opening, port, trapdoor; floodgate, sluice; *spec*: brood (of incubated birds); (down the) throat. *vb lit*: brood, incubate; be born, emerge; *fig*: conceive, contrive, devise, project, think up.

hate
n lit: abhorrence, detestation, loathing, odium, repugnance, revulsion; animosity, antagonism, antipathy, dislike.

vb lit: abhor, be repelled by, detest, have
an aversion to, loathe; be antagonistic
towards, dislike intensely; be loath (to),
be sorry (to), be unwilling (to).

haul

n lit: drag, heave, pull; distance, journey,
trip; catch, harvest, yield; *fig*: booty,
loot, spoils, swag, takings.

vb lit: drag, heave, pull, tug; draw, tow,
trail; carry, hump, lug; cart, convey,
move, transport; *spec*: turn, veer (of a
sailing-ship, of the wind).

haunt

n lit: base, habitat, hangout, patch,
stamping-ground, territory; den, hidey-
hole, lair, refuge, retreat, sanctum.

vb lit: come back, frequent, return, visit;
beset, obsess, prey on, weigh on.

have

vb lit: hold, keep, own, possess, retain;
carry, stock, store; comprehend, contain,
include, take in; accept, get, obtain,
receive, secure, take; acquire, gain;
enjoy, experience, feel, meet with, suffer,
sustain, undergo; allow, consider,
endure, entertain, permit, put up with,
tolerate; be a parent of, bear, bring forth,
deliver, give birth to; be a relative of;
assert, declare, maintain; engage in,
carry on; cheat, deceive, fool, hoax,
outwit, swindle, trick; be compelled (to),
be forced (to), be obliged (to), be
required (to), ought (to); cause to, force
to, oblige to, require to; cause to be,
require to be.

have on

vb lit: be clothed in, be dressed in, wear;
fig: expect to do, need to do; deceive,
fool, mislead, tease, trick.

havoc

n lit: damage, destruction, devastation,
ravages, ruination; chaos, disorder,
disruption, mayhem, shambles.

hawk

n lit: bird of prey, falcon; *fig*: belligerent,
militant, warmonger.

vb lit: hunt with a falcon; market, peddle,
retail, sell, tout, vend; bandy (about),
bruit (about), put (about), spread
(about); clear one's throat, gargle, gob,
spit.

hazard

n lit: danger, jeopardy, peril, risk; chance,
gamble, venture; bunker, ditch, fence,

hurdle, obstacle, pitfall, stumbling-
block.

vb lit: endanger, imperil, jeopardize, risk;
bet, chance, gamble, lay odds, stake,
venture, wager.

head

n lit: brain-case, cranium, skull; block,
bonce, loaf, noddle, nut, poll; apex,
crest, crown, peak, summit, tip, top;
climax, crisis, culmination, dénouement,
turning-point; cape, foreland,
promontory; boss, captain, chief,
commander, director, leader, manager,
master, principal; fore, forefront, front,
van; beginning, origin, rise, source,
start; ability, aptitude, brains, flair,
intelligence, mentality, mind,
understanding; capacity, faculty;
division, section, subject, topic; lavatory,
toilet, WC; individual, person, soul;
spec: chuck (on a drill, a lathe); cluster
(of flowers); froth (on beer); pick-up (on
a tape-deck); pressure (of steam in a
steam-engine); (lose one's) self-control;
striking surface (of a hammer).

vb lit: be on top of, cap, crown, top; go
first of, lead; excel, outdo, outstrip; be in
charge of, command, control, direct,
govern, manage, rule, run; aim (for),
make (for), set off (for); go,
move, travel, turn; decapitate, lop, poll;
butt; cut (off), fend (off), ward (off).

heading

n lit: headline, rubric, title; division,
section; bearing, compass-point,
direction; *spec*: drift, exploratory tunnel
(in a mine), hitting a ball with one's head
(soccer), leading (a group, revolt, etc.).

headland

n lit: cape, foreland, ness, peninsula,
point, promontory.

headstrong

adj lit: heedless, impetuous, intractable,
obdurate, obstinate, perverse, pig-
headed, stubborn, wilful.

headquarters

n lit: base, barracks, camp, command
centre, home, living quarters, main
office, offices, post, residence, station.

heady

adj lit: hasty, impetuous, impulsive,
precipitate, rash, reckless; exciting,
exhilarating, thrilling; aromatic,

inebriating, intoxicating, powerful, strong.

heal
vb lit: cure, remedy, restore; knit, mend, regenerate; *fig*: patch up, reconcile, settle, smooth over.

healing
n lit: curing, officinal, remedying, restoration; knitting, mending, regeneration; *fig*: reconciliation, smoothing things over.
adj (pr.pt) lit: curative, medicinal, remedial, restorative, therapeutic; comforting, soothing.

health
n lit: condition, fitness, shape, soundness, wellbeing.

healthy
adj lit: fit, hale and hearty, in fine fettle, in good condition, in the pink, sound, well; active, flourishing, robust, strong, sturdy; beneficial, bracing, invigorating, nourishing, wholesome; hygienic, sanitary.

heap
n lit: mass, mound, pile, stack; collection, hoard, lot, store; lashing(s), load(s), ocean(s); *fig*: mess, untidy person.
vb lit: pile (up), stack (up); gather (up), hoard (up), store (up); bestow (on), load (on), shower (on).

hear
vb lit: listen to; attend to, hearken to, heed, take in; catch, pick up; attend to, hearken to, heed; be informed, be told, find, gather, learn, understand; examine, judge, try.

hearing
n lit: earshot, range; auditory perception; audience, chance to perform; performance, playing, rendition; inquiry, trial.

heart
n lit: cardiac muscle; centre, core, hub, kernel, middle, nucleus; *fig*: mind, soul; affection, love; feeling, sentiment, sympathy; disposition, nature, temperament; bottle, courage, fortitude, guts, nerve; determination, resolution, spirit; energy, enthusiasm; crux, essence,

marrow, pith, root; (by) memory, (by) rote.

heartbroken
adj lit: crushed, disconsolate, inconsolable; brokenhearted.

hearth
n lit: fireplace, fireside; brazier, furnace, grate, grid; *fig*: home; lounge, main room, sitting-room.

heartless
adj lit: brutal, callous, cold, cruel, harsh, merciless, pitiless, unfeeling.

heart-rending
adj lit: affecting, emotive, harrowing, moving, piteous, touching, tragic.

heart-warming
adj lit: affecting, cheering, gratifying, heartening, pleasing, satisfying.

hearty
adj lit: energetic, hale, hardy, lusty, robust, strong, vigorous; ebullient, effusive, enthusiastic; affable, cordial, friendly, genial, warm; genuine, sincere, whole-hearted; ample, bountiful, sizable, solid, substantial.

heat
n lit: high temperature, temperature, warmth; torridity; febrility, fever; blaze, fire, flame; *fig*: intensity, fervour, vehemence; agitation, excitement, passion; pressure; *spec*: oestrus (in female mammals); eliminator, preliminary race, qualifier.
vb lit: keep warm, make hot, warm (up); cook, microwave, put on the boil; *fig*: excite, inflame, rouse, stimulate.

heath
n lit: moor, moorland, scrub, wasteland; erica, heather, ling.

heathen
n lit: pagan, paynim, unbeliever; goy, infidel; agnostic, atheist, non-Christian; *fig*: barbarian, savage; philistine.
adj lit: godless, pagan, unbelieving, ungodly; irreligious, unchristian; atheistic; *fig*: barbarian, savage; philistine.

heave
n lit: haul, pull, tow, tug; fling, pitch, throw; convulsion, surge, swell; *spec*: dislocation, displacement (of a geological stratum).

vb lit: drag, haul, pull, tow, tug; hoist (up), lift (up); fling, hurl, pitch, throw, toss; billow, convulse, rise, surge, swell; breathe heavily, give vent to, pant, utter, wheeze; gag, retch.

heaven
n lit: garden of Eden, paradise; life to come, next world, Nirvana; Elysian fields, happy hunting-ground, place of the dead, Valhalla; firmament, sky; *fig*: bliss, ecstasy, joy, rapture.

heavenly
adj lit: beatific, blessed, paradisial, supernal; astronomical, celestial; *fig*: angelic, beautiful, divine, exquisite, lovely, ravishing, seraphic, sublime, wonderful.

heavily
adv lit: laboriously, ponderously, weightily, with difficulty; awkwardly, clumsily, sluggishly, woodenly; dully, gloomily; closely, densely, thickly, completely, decisively, thoroughly, utterly; deeply, profoundly, soundly; abundantly, copiously, excessively, much too much, profusely.

heavy
adj lit: hefty, massive, ponderous, weighty; burdened, encumbered, loaded, pregnant; bulky, portly, stout; extra-large, giant, jumbo; broad, coarse, thick; awkward, clumsy, lumbering, slow, sluggish, torpid, wooden; dull, gloomy, leaden, lowering; burdensome, difficult, hard, laborious, onerous, severe, taxing; complex, deep, grave, profound, serious; boisterous, stormy, tempestuous, turbulent, violent; abundant, copious, excessive, profuse.

heckle
vb lit: barrack, interrupt, shout down; jeer, taunt.

hectic
adj lit: excited, feverish, frantic, frenetic, frenzied; flushed, rosy; fevered; atrophied, consumptive, painfully thin, wasted.

hedge
n lit: bush, ha-ha, row of bushes, thicket; *fig*: barrier, boundary, fence, screen; cover, guarantee, protection.
vb lit: border, edge, fence; enclose (around), hem (in), put round (about), surround; *fig*: lay off, spread the load of;

be noncommittal, dodge, duck, evade, shift, sidestep.

heed
n lit: attention, care, caution, mind, notice, regard, thought.
vb lit: bear in mind, consider, listen to, mark, mind, pay attention to, take notice of.

heedless
adj lit: careless, mindless, neglectful, thoughtless, unmindful.

height
n lit: altitude, elevation; tallness; crag, fell, rocky point; hill, mountain, peak, summit; apex, crest, crown, pinnacle, top, zenith; climax, culmination, limit, maximum, ultimate; acme, embodiment, epitome; eminence, grandeur.

hell
n lit: Gehenna, Hades, infernal regions, nether world, Tartarus, underworld; abyss, bottomless pit, eternal fires, fire and brimstone, weeping and wailing and gnashing of teeth; purgatory; *fig*: agony, martyrdom, nightmare, ordeal, torment; commotion, din, uproar; deuce, dickens, heck.

helm
n lit: rudder, tiller, wheel; *fig*: controls.

help
n lit: aid, assistance, succour, support; avail, benefit, use; collaboration, cooperation; amelioration, facilitation, improvement; balm, relief, remedy; assistant, worker.
vb lit: aid, assist, lend a hand, succour, support; abet, be with, collaborate with, cooperate with; serve; ameliorate, facilitate, improve; alleviate, cure, remedy; avoid, prevent oneself from; abstain from, keep from, refrain from, resist.

helpful
adj lit: accommodating, considerate, cooperative, kind, neighbourly; beneficial, profitable, serviceable, useful; constructive, practical, productive, supportive, timely.

helpless
adj lit: defenceless, exposed, unprotected, vulnerable; feeble, incapable, weak; impotent, powerless; incompetent.

hem
n lit: border, edge; frieze, fringe, trimming.
vb lit: border, edge; enclose (in), hedge (in), shut (in).

hen
n lit: chicken; female; *fig*: girl, lady, woman.

hence
adv lit: and so, ergo, for which reason, therefore; from now, from this time; from here, from this place; from that source.

henceforth
adv lit: from now on, from this time forward, hereafter.

herald
n lit: announcer, crier, messenger; forerunner, harbinger, precursor, token; *spec*: member of the Royal College of Arms.
vb lit: pave the way, precede, presage, usher in; announce, broadcast, proclaim, publish, trumpet.

herd
n lit: collection, drove, flock, horde, multitude, swarm, throng; great unwashed, masses, mob, populace, rabble.
vb lit: assemble, collect, gather, muster; congregate, flock, rally; drive, shepherd.

hereditary
adj lit: congenital, genetic, inheritable, transmissible; ancestral, bequeathed, family, handed down, inherited, patrimonial.

heresy
n lit: blasphemy, heterodoxy, impiety, schism; apostasy; error.

heretic
n lit: schismatic; apostate; dissenter, nonconformist.

heritage
n lit: birthright, endowment, inheritance, patrimony; bequest, legacy, tradition.

hermit
n lit: anchorite, cenobite, eremite, recluse; monk; solitary.

hero
n lit: popular figure; conqueror, victor; celebrity, demigod, idol, star, superstar; champion; lead, principal character, protagonist.

heroic
adj lit: audacious, bold, brave, courageous, daring, fearless, gallant, intrepid, valiant; epic, legendary, mythological; *fig*: elaborate, exaggerated, extravagant, grandiose, inflated.

heroism
n lit: audacity, boldness, bravery, courage, daring, fearlessness, gallantry, intrepidity, valour; fortitude, perseverance.

hesitant
adj lit: reluctant, unwilling; diffident, halting, irresolute, timid, uncertain, vacillating, wavering.

hesitate
vb lit: be reluctant (to), be unwilling (to), scruple (to); delay, pause, wait; dither, falter, shillyshally, vacillate, waver.

hiatus
n lit: gap, interval, lacuna, space; blank, discontinuity, silence; break, interstice.

hidden
adj (pa.pt) lit: cloaked, concealed, covert, masked, shrouded, veiled; cryptic, occult, secret; dark, obscure; ulterior, clandestine, furtive, underhand.

hide
n lit: concealment, hiding-place.
vb lit: conceal, cover, mask, screen, shroud, veil; bury, cache; hush up, keep secret, suppress; camouflage, disguise; go to ground, go underground, hole up, lie low.

hideous
adj lit: frightful, grotesque, gruesome, horrible, monstrous, ugly, unsightly; appalling, awful, dreadful, repulsive, sickening, terrible.

hiding
n lit: beating, belting, caning, flogging, larruping, spanking, strapping, tanning, thrashing, walloping, whipping.

high
n lit: apex, peak, summit, zenith; *fig*: ecstasy, euphoria; trip; surge of adrenalin.
adj lit: lofty, tall; elevated, soaring, towering; chief, eminent, exalted, important, main, noble, prominent, ruling, superior; capital, grave, serious; extreme, great, powerful; dear, expensive, steep, stiff; extravagant,

grand, lavish, rich; arrogant, domineering, haughty, lofty, overbearing, proud; latest, most advanced; acute, piercing, sharp, shrill, soprano, treble; gamy, niffy, putrescent, rancid, slightly off, whiffy; elated, exhilarated, merry, tipsy; euphoric, freaked out, inebriated, intoxicated, legless, pissed as a newt, spaced out, stoned, turned on.
adv lit: aloft, far up, way above.

highlands
n lit: crags, fells, hills, mountains, upland; massif, plateau

highlight
n lit: climax, feature, focal point, peak; accent; light spot, reflection, reflective surface.
vb lit: accent, accentuate, emphasize, feature, play up, stress, underline; contrast, offset, set off.

high-spirited
adj lit: audacious, bold, daring, dashing, ebullient; exuberant, lively, mettlesome, spirited, vivacious.

hijack
n lit: capture, expropriation, seizure, take-over; piracy.
vb lit: capture, commandeer, expropriate, seize, take over; requisition, sequester.

hiking
n lit: backpacking, rambling, trekking, walking; marching, yomping; hitching lifts.

hilarious
adj lit: comic, droll, killing, rollicking, side-splitting, uproarious, very funny.

hill
n lit: down, fell, tor; hummock, knoll, kopje, mound; gradient, incline, rise, slope.

hindrance
n lit: check, encumbrance, handicap, impediment, limitation, restriction; barrier, hurdle, obstacle, obstruction, stumbling-block; difficulty, drawback, snag.

hinge
n lit: articulation, movable joint, pivot; *spec*: gummed paper strip (for philatelists).

vb lit: articulate, bend, pivot (on); *fig*: be contingent (on), depend (on), hang (on), turn (on).

hint
n lit: clue, intimation, pointer, suggestion, tip, whisper, word, wrinkle; implication, innuendo, insinuation; allusion, mention; dash, speck, suspicion, taste, tinge, trace, whiff.
vb lit: give a clue, suggest, tip off; imply, insinuate; allude, mention.

hire
n lit: rent, rental; charge, fee, payment, price, wages.
vb lit: charter, lease, rent; lease out, let, rent out; employ, engage, sign up, take on.

historic
adj lit: earth-shattering, epoch-making; great, important, momentous, significant; consequential, seminal; famous, illustrious.

historical
adj lit: chronicled, documented, recorded; attested, authentic, factual, verified; antiquated, archaic, old-fashioned, outmoded; of olden days.

history
n lit: ancient days, antiquity, olden days, past, yesterday; annals, archives, chronicles, records; account, recital, story; autobiography, biography.

hit
n lit: blow, buffet, impact, knock; clout, cuff, punch, rap, slap, smack, swipe, tap, thump, thwack, wallop, whack; cannon, collision; shot, stroke; *fig*: fluke, lucky chance; sensation, smash, success, triumph, winner; dig, sarcasm, thrust, witticism; assassination, murder.
vb lit: bang, bash, beat, belt, buffet, clobber, clout, cuff, knock, punch, slap, smack, strike, thump, wallop, whack; bang into, bump, cannon into, collide with, crash into, run into; damage, devastate, overwhelm; *fig*: affect, influence, leave a mark on, touch; attain, gain, reach; accomplish, achieve; come across, encounter; assassinate, murder.

hitch
n lit: catch, difficulty, drawback, problem, snag; check, delay, hindrance, stoppage; connection, coupling; knot; jerk, pull, tug.

vb lit: attach, connect, couple, harness, join, tie, yoke; marry, wed; jerk (up), pull (up), tug (up); thumb a lift.

hoard
n lit: cache, stockpile, treasure-trove; heap, mass, pile, store.
vb lit: cache, garner, lay up, put by, stash away, stockpile; amass, heap up, pile up, store.

hoarse
adj lit: croaking, grating, gruff, husky, rasping, throaty; gravelly, raucous, raw.

hoax
n lit: con, deception, dissimulation, fraud, imposture; practical joke, prank, ruse, trick.
vb lit: bamboozle, con, deceive, dissimulate, dupe, gull, hoodwink, take for a ride, take in, trick; fool, have one on, pull one's leg.

hobby
n lit: avocation, leisure activity, pastime, pursuit, sideline; amusement, entertainment.

hog
n lit: pig, swine; boar, piglet, sow; *fig*: glutton, greedy pig; selfish pig; boor; *spec*: yearling (lamb or other domestic animal).
vb lit: be a pig over, monopolize; arrogate to oneself, corner, take possession of, take over; *spec*: arch, hump (like a hog's back).

hoist
n lit: crane; dumb-waiter, lift; pulley, tackle, winch; lever; loading tailgate.
vb lit: heave up, lift, pull up, raise; lever up, prise up; draw (up), winch (up).

hold
n lit: clutch, grasp, grip; footing, leverage, purchase; *fig*: dominance, influence, power, pull, sway; *spec*: cargo space (on a ship); fermata, pause (in musical dynamics).
vb lit: clasp, cling to, clutch, grasp, grip; have, keep, retain; be in possession of, occupy, possess; bear, carry, support, sustain, take; accommodate, be large enough for, contain, seat; arrest, detain, restrain, stop; confine, imprison; *fig*: believe, consider, deem, judge, reckon, think; be in force, continue, exist, last, operate, persist, remain, stand; call, conduct, convene, convoke, organize,

run; be enough for, satisfy; adhere (to), stick (to).

hold up
vb lit: brandish, display, exhibit, lift up, present, show, wave; prop up, support, sustain; delay, detain, hinder, obstruct, retard, slow; *fig*: be maintained, endure, last, remain steady; accost, ambush, mug, rob, stick up, waylay.

hole
n lit: aperture, crack, fissure, opening, orifice, outlet, puncture, rent, tear; cavity, gap; excavation, hollow, pit, shaft; burrow, den, earth, lair, scrape, sett; *fig*: dive, dump, joint; fix, jam, mess, spot; discrepancy, fallacy, fault, flaw, inconsistency.
vb lit: sink.

holiday
n lit: break, furlough, leave, leisure-time, time off; feast, festival, saint's day; statutory day off.

hollow
n lit: basin, bowl, concavity, crater, dell, depression, dingle, hole, pit, trough; crease, dimple; palm; channel, groove.
adj lit: empty, vacant; deep-set, indented, sunken; *fig*: booming, deep, dull, resonant, sepulchral; empty, meaningless, pointless, specious, useless; artificial, false, flimsy, insincere.
adv fig: dully, resonantly, sepulchrally; falsely, insincerely; completely, thoroughly, totally, utterly.

holy
adj lit: consecrated, hallowed, sacred, sacrosanct; divine, godly, numinous; pious, religious, saintly; blessed, venerable; *fig*: awesome, dreadful, unearthly; unholy.

homage
n lit: deference, respect, reverence, veneration; honour; fealty.

home
n lit: fireside, hearth, household; abode, domicile, dwelling, habitation, place, residence; habitat, nest; base; asylum, hall of residence, institution, refuge, sanatorium; *fig*: (at) ease (in); *spec*: local win (in soccer); plate (in baseball).
vb lit: be directed (in on), be guided (in on).
adj lit: domiciliary, household, residential; own, private; familiar,

normal, usual; national; local.
adv lit: to one's domicile, to one's
household, to one's residence; to one's
country; *fig*: to one's destination, to one's
goal, to where one belongs.

homely
adj lit: domestic, familiar, friendly,
informal; comfortable, cosy, welcoming;
everyday, natural, simple, unassuming;
ordinary, plain, unprepossessing,
unpretentious.

homogeneous
adj lit: consistent, even, of constant
density, uniform; akin, cognate;
identical, unvarying.

homosexual
n lit: gay; fairy, nancy-boy, pansy, pretty-
boy, poof, poofter, queen, queer,
woofter; dyke, lesbian; bugger, catamite,
sodomite.
adj lit: gay, homoerotic; lesbian, sapphic,
bent, camp, effeminate, limp-wristed,
queer; deviant, perverted.

honest
adj lit: ethical, honourable, straight, true,
truthful, veracious; decent, law-abiding,
reputable, upright, virtuous; reliable,
trustworthy; authentic, bona fide,
genuine, real; candid, frank, open,
sincere; equitable, fair, good, just.

honesty
n lit: ethics, honour, truthfulness,
veracity; faithfulness, fidelity; decency,
integrity, legality, morality, probity,
uprightness, virtue; authenticity,
genuineness, good faith,
straightforwardness, trustworthiness;
candour, frankness, openness, sincerity;
equity, fairness, goodness, justice.

honorary
adj lit: formal, nominal, titular;
complimentary, unofficial; unpaid;
nonexecutive, sleeping.

honour
n lit: credit, esteem, fame, glory, kudos,
prestige, repute; commendation,
glorification, homage, recognition,
reverence, veneration; dignity, high
rank; decency, honesty, integrity,
morality, probity, uprightness, virtue;
chastity, modesty, purity, virginity;
compliment, grace, privilege; decoration,
distinction, title; *spec*: high trump (in
cards).

vb lit: acclaim, celebrate, glorify, pay
homage to, venerate; adore, hallow,
revere, worship; dignify, ennoble, exalt;
decorate; compliment, grace; commend,
praise; be faithful to, discharge, fulfil,
keep, perform; acknowledge, credit; *spec*:
accept, cash, clear, pass, pay (a monetary
transaction).

honourable
adj lit: decent, law-abiding, reputable,
upright, virtuous; equitable, ethical, fair,
good, honest, just, moral, principled,
reliable, trustworthy; creditable,
estimable, noble, proper, right.

hood
n lit: cope, cowl, snood; head-covering,
scarf; bonnet; cover, lid, shield, top;
gangster, gunman, hoodlum; *spec*:
blindfold, blinker (for a hawk); cowling,
diffuser, suction vent (on a chimney,
over a stove); ornamental fold (on an
academic's gown).

hook
n lit: angle, crook, loop; catch, clasp,
coupler; barb, snare; sickle.
vb lit: catch, ensnare, impale; attach,
clasp, fasten (on), fix (on); couple (on);
hit on a curve; bend, curve, veer; *spec*:
heel (in rugby).

hooligan
n lit: bully-boy, delinquent, mugger,
rowdy, ruffian, steamer, tearaway, thug,
vandal, yobbo.

hoop
n lit: band, belt, cincture, circlet, girdle,
ring; *fig*: difficulty, trial, tribulation; *spec*:
arch (in croquet).

hooter
n lit: horn, siren; steam whistle; *fig*: nose,
snout.

hop
n lit: jump, skip, step; twitch; leg, short
flight; dance, dancing party; type of
plant (used in brewing).
vb lit: jump on one leg; bound, skip,
spring; fly across, take a short flight; *fig*:
beat (it), get out of (it).

hope
n lit: desire, dream, expectancy, wish;
ambition; anticipation, expectation;
optimism; grounds for optimism,
promise.

vb lit: aspire (to), long (to), look forward (to); long (for), wait (for); be sure, earnestly wish, trust.

hopeful
adj lit: expectant, optimistic, sanguine; auspicious, encouraging, heartening, promising, propitious.

hopeless
adj lit: irreparable, irreversible; futile, impossible, impracticable, pointless, useless, vain; incompetent, inferior, worthless; despairing, desperate.

horde
n lit: crowd, host, mob, multitude, pack, swarm, throng.
n lit: skyline; line of sight; stratum; surface; *fig*: experiential expectations.

horn
n lit: antler; antenna; keratin, shell; drinking vessel; powder flask; cusp; brass instrument, bugle, trombone, trumpet; hooter, siren; *spec*: narrow piece of land (e.g., Cape Horn); point (of an anvil); stationary surface (of a hinge); tip (of a crescent).

horrible
adj lit: awful, dreadful, frightful, ghastly, grim, gruesome, hideous, repugnant, repulsive; beastly, disagreeable, mean, nasty, unkind.

horrid
adj lit: awful, beastly, disagreeable, malevolent, malignant, mean, nasty, offensive, spiteful, unpleasant.

horrify
vb lit: appal, outrage, shock; disgust, nauseate, revolt, sicken.

horror
n lit: abhorrence, disgust, nausea, repugnance, revulsion; dread, fright; *fig*: disgusting thing, loathsome creature.

hospitable
adj lit: generous, gracious, liberal, receptive, welcoming.

hospitality
n lit: welcome; reception; generosity, liberality, kindness.

host
n lit: guest-master, inviter; innkeeper, landlord, proprietor; anchor man, master of ceremonies, presenter; parasiticized object; army, horde, mass, mob,

multitude, vast number; *spec*: wafer (at communion services).
vb lit: compere, introduce, present; entertain, invite.

hostage
n lit: captive, pawn; security.

hostel
n lit: annex, hall, lodge, residence; dormitory; asylum, sanatorium.

hostile
adj lit: adverse, antagonistic, bellicose, belligerent, inimical, opposed, unfriendly.

hot
adj lit: boiling, scorching, searing, sultry, sweltering, torrid, tropical; burning, fiery, flaming, heated, roasting, scalding; curried, peppery, spicy; *fig*: ardent, fervent, intense, passionate, vehement; fierce, fiery, impetuous, lustful, stormy; approved, popular.
adv lit: close, immediately.

hotel
n lit: boarding-house, caravanserai, guest-house, hostel, rooming-house; hospice, inn; chalet, motel.

hothead
n lit: firebrand, fire-eater, madcap, rebel, tearaway; fanatic.

hound
n lit: dog, hunting-dog; *fig*: rogue, scoundrel, villain.
vb lit: chase, harry, persecute, pursue; *fig*: badger, harass, pester, provoke.

house
n lit: building, dwelling, edifice, residence; abode, domicile, home; clan, family, line, lineage; business, company, establishment, firm, organization.
vb lit: accommodate, contain, cover, harbour, keep, put up, sheathe, shelter, take in.

household
n lit: family, folks, home, ménage, people; establishment.
adj lit: domestic, family; about the house.

hovel
n lit: hole, hut, shack, shanty, slum; lean-to, shed.

hover
vb lit: be poised (over), drift, float; be suspended, hang; *fig*: hang about, loiter,

lurk, wait in the wings; alternate, oscillate, sit on the fence, vacillate, waver.

however
adv lit: by what means, how on earth, in what way; no matter how, to whatever extent.
cnj lit: all the same, at all events, but, despite this, nevertheless, nonetheless, still, yet.

hub
n lit: axle, pivot, spindle; centre, focus, middle; *fig*: heart, nerve centre.

hubbub
n lit: chatter, murmur, noise level, talking; chaos, din, hullabaloo, racket, riot, uproar.

huddle
n lit: aggregation, assembly, crowd, gathering, number; conference, consultation, discussion; jumble, mess, muddle.
vb lit: aggregate, cluster, converge, crowd, gather; curl up, hunch oneself up, nestle in a heap; cuddle, snuggle.

hug
n lit: clasp, clinch, embrace, squeeze; grip, hold.
vb lit: clasp, embrace, enfold, hold, squeeze; *fig*: cleave to, skirt, stay close to; be protective towards, cling on to, guard, hang on to, nurse.

huge
adj lit: colossal, cyclopean, enormous, gargantuan, gigantic, immense, mammoth, massive, monumental, prodigious, titanic, tremendous, vast.

hulking
adj lit: bulky, clumsy, clodhopping, lubberly, lumpish, ungainly, unwieldy.

hum
n lit: buzz, drone, murmur, purr, reverberation, rumble, susurration, thrum, tone.
vb lit: buzz, drone, murmur, purr, reverberate, rumble, thrum; stammer, stutter; *fig*: bustle, get busy, hustle, move, stir.

human
n lit: individual, man, person; mortal, soul.
adj lit: anthropoid; mortal; approachable, kindly, understanding; forgivable, natural, understandable; fallible, vulnerable.

humane
adj lit: benign, compassionate, gentle, good-natured, kindly, sympathetic, understanding; charitable, forgiving, lenient, merciful.

humanity
n lit: human race, mankind, people everywhere; benevolence, brotherly love, compassion, generosity, gentleness, kindliness, kindness, sympathy, toleration, understanding; leniency, mercy.

humble
vb lit: abase, degrade, demean, humiliate; bring down, chasten, disgrace, mortify, shame, subdue, take down a peg.
adj lit: modest, self-effacing, unassuming; deferential, obsequious, respectful, subservient; common, lowly, obscure, ordinary, simple, undistinguished, unpretentious; commonplace, insignificant, low, mean, plebeian, poor, unimportant.

humid
adj lit: muggy, steamy, sticky, sultry; damp, moist.

humiliating
adj (pr.pt) lit: embarrassing, ignominious, mortifying, shameful, shaming; degrading, demeaning.

humility
n lit: meekness, modesty, self-abasement; deference, diffidence, obsequy, respectfulness, servility, subservience; lowliness, obscurity; poverty.

humorous
adj lit: amusing, comical, funny, waggish, witty; droll, facetious, jocose, playful.

humour
n lit: mood, spirits, state of mind, temper; caprice, fancy, freak, vagary, whim; comedy, drollery, jocularity, joking, pleasantries, wit, witticisms.
vb lit: accommodate, gratify, indulge, pander to; acquiesce in, flatter.

hump
n lit: bulge, bump, lump, mound, protuberance, swelling, tump; hunch; *fig*: dumps, gripes, sulks.

vb lit: carry, haul, heave, lug; arch, bend, curve; have sex with.

hunch
n lit: feeling, impression, intuition, premonition, suspicion; hump, lump, mound.
vb lit: arch, bend, curve, tense; hunker, squat, stoop.

hunger
n lit: ravening, starvation; appetite; emptiness; craving, desire, longing, need, yearning.
vb lit: raven (for), starve (for); have an appetite (for); crave, long, lust, pine, yearn.

hungry
adj lit: ravening, starved, starving; empty, famished, peckish; *fig*: eager (for), greedy (for).

hunt
n lit: chase, pursuit; quest; search; *spec*: pack (of hounds).
vb lit: chase, harry, hound, pursue; follow, stalk, track down; forage (for), look (for), search (for), seek.

hunted
adj (pa.pt) lit: desperate, harassed, haunted, persecuted, stricken.

hurdle
n lit: barrier, fence; jump; *fig*: complication, difficulty, impediment, obstacle, snag.
vb lit: clear, jump, leap; get over, surmount.

hurl
vb lit: fling, launch, pitch, sling, throw, toss.

hurricane
n lit: cyclone, gale, storm, tempest, tornado, typhoon.

hurry
n lit: dash, rush; flurry, haste, speed; dispatch, urgency; commotion.
vb lit: dash, fly, race, run, rush; accelerate, expedite, hasten, quicken, speed; hustle, push on, spur on.

hurt
n lit: injury, lesion, sore, trauma, wound; bruise; distress, pain; damage, mischief, wrong.

vb lit: injure, wound; bruise, damage, harm, impair; ache, be sore, pain, sting, throb; *fig*: aggrieve, cut to the quick, distress, pain, sadden.
adj (pa.pt) lit: injured, wounded; bruised, damaged, harmed, impaired; in pain, sore; *fig*: aggrieved, cut to the quick, distressed, miffed, offended, pained, piqued, saddened.

husband
n lit: lord and master, man; hubby, old man; spouse.
vb lit: conserve, garner, hoard, save, store; be steward over, be thrifty with, manage carefully.

hush up
vb lit: censor, cover up, sit on, smother, suppress; keep dark, keep secret.

hussy
n lit: baggage, minx; tramp, trollop; floozy, scrubber, slut, tart.

hustle
vb lit: hasten, hurry, push, rush; force, impel, thrust; crowd, jostle; hawk, peddle, sell aggressively; solicit, walk the streets.

hut
n lit: cabin, hogan, lean-to, shack, shanty, shed.

hybrid
n lit: cross, crossbreed; mongrel, mule; amalgam, composite, mixture.

hygienic
adj lit: clean, germ-free, sanitary; aseptic, sterile; health-promoting, pure, safe.

hymn
n lit: anthem, paean, psalm, song of praise.
vb lit: sing in adoration of, sing in praise of; celebrate in song.

hype
n lit: ballyhoo, build-up, hoo-ha, pizzazz, promotion, propaganda, publicity, razzamatazz.
vb lit: build up, promote, publicize, sensationalize.

hypnotic
n lit: anaesthetic, sedative; narcotic, opiate; drug.
adj lit: mesmerizing, spellbinding, trance-inducing; narcotic, opiate; sedative, soporific.

hypocrisy
n lit: double standards, inconsistency;
cant, duplicity, insincerity, speciousness.

hypocrite
n lit: charlatan, faker, fraud, Holy Joe,
impostor, mountebank, sham.

hypothesis
n lit: postulate, premise, proposition,
supposition, theory; conjecture,
possibility, suggestion.

hypothetical
adj lit: academic, conjectural, postulated,
putative, speculative, theoretical;
proposed, supposed.

hysteria
n lit: neurosis; emotional instability;
agitation, frenzy, nervousness; panic.

hysterical
adj lit: neurotic; emotionally unstable;
agitated, distracted, distraught, frenetic,
nervous, overwrought; beside oneself,
screaming; *fig*: farcical, hilarious, killing,
uproarious.

I

icon
n lit: figure, image; holy picture, sacred statuette; shrine; *fig*: symbol; hero, idol.

icy
adj lit: arctic, biting, bitter, boreal, cryogenic, freezing, frosty, frozen, gelid, raw; glassy, slippery, slippy, wintry; *fig*: cold, distant, frigid, glacial, hostile, inimical, stony.

idea
n lit: hypothesis, suggestion, supposition, theory; design, plan, scheme; concept, conception, thought; fancy, notion, whim; belief, conviction, opinion, view, viewpoint; aim, end, intention, meaning, object, objective, purpose; import, reasoning, significance; clue, hint, inkling, suspicion; feeling, impression; essence, form, gist, nub, quality.

ideal
n lit: paragon, perfection; example, exemplar, model, paradigm, pattern; embodiment, epitome; standard(s); principle(s), value(s).
adj lit: consummate, optimal, perfect; exemplary, model; classic, compleat, quintessential, supreme; conceptual, hypothetical, imaginary, notional, paradisiacal, theoretical, unattainable, utopian.

idealistic
adj lit: optimistic, romantic; moral, principled; naive, impracticable, impractical; ambitious, hopeful; perfectionist.

identical
adj lit: alike as two peas, congruent, duplicated, exactly the same, geminate, indistinguishable, twin; corresponding, equal, equivalent, like, matching.

identify
vb lit: know, place, recognize; discern, diagnose, name, pick out, pinpoint, single out, tag; catalogue, classify, label; associate (with), categorize (with), relate (with); empathize (with), sympathize (with).

identity
n lit: name, particulars; individuality, particularity, singularity, uniqueness; equality, identicality, sameness, unity; empathy, rapport, sympathy, unanimity.

idiocy
n lit: imbecility, severe retardation; *fig*: asininity, insanity, lunacy; fatuity, inanity; stupidity; foolhardiness, rashness, recklessness.

idiom
n lit: expression, jargon, parlance, phrase, turn of phrase, usage, vernacular.

idiomatic
adj lit: everyday, fluent, native, natural, ordinary, perfect, unaccented; dialectal, vernacular; characteristic.

idiosyncratic
adj lit: characteristic, mannered, one's own special, personal, singular; eccentric, odd, peculiar.

idiot
n lit: cretin, duffer, dunce, imbecile, mental defective, moron, twerp; *fig*: blockhead, clod, dimwit, fool, halfwit, lunatic, simpleton; ass, chump, twit.

idiotic
adj lit: asinine, blockheaded, cretinous, daft, dimwitted, fatuous, feeble-minded, halfwitted, insane, lunatic, moronic, stupid, witless.

idle
vb lit: do nothing, laze, loaf, shirk, skive, slack, take it easy; fritter (away), while (away); dawdle, drift, tick over, vegetate.
adj lit: indolent, lazy, loafing, shirking, skiving, slack, slothful; inactive, inoperative, out of action, stationary, unoccupied, unused; jobless, redundant, unemployed; abortive, futile, groundless, pointless, unproductive, useless, vain, worthless; frivolous, irrelevant, trivial, unnecessary.

idleness
n lit: indolence, laziness, loafing, shirking, skiving, slacking, sloth, time-wasting;

inactivity, inertia, sluggishness, torpor; joblessness, unemployment.

idol
n lit: deity, fetish, god, icon, image, sacred figure; hero, superstar; adored, favourite.

idolatry
n lit: fetish-worship, image-worship; apotheosis, deification; *fig*: glorification, hero-worship; adoration, devotion, worship.

idolize
vb lit: bow down before, deify, reverence, worship; adore, be devoted to, love, venerate.

idyllic
adj lit: ideal, perfect, serene, sublime; arcadian, bucolic, pastoral, rural, rustic; calm, peaceful, quiet, soothing; charming, happy, innocent.

if
cnj lit: in the event that; assuming, on condition that, on the assumption that, provided, supposing; whether; admitting that, although, even though; albeit, though.

ignite
vb lit: fire, kindle, light, set alight, set fire to; burst into flames, flare up; burn.

ignominious
adj lit: abject, humiliating, mortifying, shameful; disgraced, indecorous, inglorious, sorry, undignified; dishonourable.

ignorance
n lit: lack of education, unenlightenment, unknowing; inexperience, innocence, unawareness.

ignorant
adj lit: uneducated, unlearned, unlettered, untaught, untrained; boorish, crass, gross, lumpen, uncomprehending; green, inexperienced, innocent, naive, unaware, unconscious, uninformed, unwitting.

ignore
vb lit: be oblivious to, dismiss, disregard, neglect, take no notice of, turn one's back on; overlook, turn a blind eye to; cold-shoulder, cut dead, ostracize, shun.

ill
n lit: affliction, misfortune, suffering, trial, tribulation, trouble; hurt, injury; evil, mischief, unkindness, wrong.
adj lit: indisposed, infirm, off colour, poorly, sick, unwell; damaging, detrimental, harmful; bad, evil, wicked, wrong; acrimonious, hostile, inimical, malevolent, unfriendly; inauspicious, ominous, sinister, unfavourable.
adv lit: badly, hard, poorly, unfavourably; barely, hardly, only just, scarcely; insufficiently, not really.

illegal
adj lit: criminal, felonious, illicit, prohibited, proscribed, unlawful, wrong; bootleg, unauthorized; actionable.

illegible
adj lit: indecipherable, undecipherable, unreadable; faint, impossible to make out, obscure.

illegitimate
adj lit: bastard, born out of wedlock, natural; illegal, unauthorized; inconsistent, illogical, invalid, specious, spurious, unwarranted; improper, incorrect.

ill feeling
n lit: animosity, antagonism, bad blood, enmity, hostility, rancour, resentment; mistrust, suspicion.

ill-humoured
adj lit: bad-tempered, crabby, cross, disagreeable, grumpy, irascible, irritable, morose, sulky, sullen, testy, waspish.

illiterate
adj lit: unable to read or write, unlettered; ignorant, uneducated, untaught.

illness
n lit: ailment, cachexia, complaint, disease, disorder, indisposition, infirmity, malady, sickness.

illogical
adj lit: fallacious, inconsistent, irrational, senseless; invalid, spurious, unsound; meaningless.

illuminate
vb lit: light, shed light on; brighten, light up; *fig*: clarify, elucidate, explain, make clear; *spec*: adorn, decorate (an old book).

illumination
n lit: light, lighting, lights; beam, ray; *fig*: clarification, enlightenment, insight, perception, revelation, understanding.

illusion
n lit: misapprehension, misconception, mistaken impression; apparition, daydream, figment of the imagination, magic, mirage.

illusory
adj lit: deceptive, false, unreal, untrue; figmentary, imaginary, nonexistent; erroneous, fallacious, misleading.

illustrate
vb lit: adorn with pictures, draw pictures, pictorialize, provide with visual reference, show slides; demonstrate, give examples of, exhibit.

illustration
n lit: picture; artwork, chart, drawing, figure, graphic, halftone, line-drawing, map, photo, plate, print; demonstration, example, instance, specimen; analogy, comparison.

illustrious
adj lit: celebrated, distinguished, eminent, famous, glorious, great, noted, renowned.

image
n lit: effigy, figure, likeness, picture, representation, statue, statuette; appearance, reflection; conception, idea, mental picture, notion, perception; *fig*: double, same.

imaginary
adj lit: fictitious, illusory, imagined, invented, made-up; nonexistent, unreal; hypothetical, supposed, theoretical.

imagination
n lit: conception, invention, insight, originality; creativity, ingenuity, resourcefulness, vision, wit.

imaginative
adj lit: creative, ingenious, inventive, original; fanciful, lively, vivid, witty.

imagine
vb lit: conceptualize, create, devise, dream up, invent, picture, plan, think up, visualize; believe, comprehend, realize, think; assume, deem, gather, infer, surmise; conjecture, fancy.

imitate
vb lit: copy, duplicate, echo, emulate, mirror, repeat, simulate; ape, impersonate, mimic; caricature, do, parody, take off.

imitation
n lit: copy, counterfeit, duplicate, echo, fake, forgery, impersonation, mirror-image, replica, reproduction, sham; duplication, emulation, mimicry, simulation; caricature, parody, take-off. *adj lit*: artificial, counterfeit, duplicate, ersatz, fake, forged, reproduction, sham, simulated, synthetic.

immaculate
adj lit: clean, spotless, stainless; pristine, undefiled, virgin; *fig*: faultless, flawless, perfect, untarnished; chaste, guiltless, pure, sinless, unblemished, virtuous.

immature
adj lit: adolescent, callow, childish, green, inexperienced, jejune, juvenile, young; crude, imperfect, rudimentary, undeveloped, unformed, unripe.

immediate
adj lit: direct, instant; closest, nearest; most recent; current, existing, extant, present, prevailing; urgent; *spec*: intuitive, self-evident (knowledge, in philosophy)

immediately
adv lit: at once, instantly, instantaneously, now, straight away, without delay; directly, promptly, on the spot, there and then; at first hand, from the horse's mouth.

immense
adj lit: colossal, cyclopian, enormous, gigantic, huge, mammoth, massive, monumental, prodigious, titanic, tremendous, vast.

immensity
n lit: bulk, expanse, magnitude, mass, size, vastness; boundlessness, endless vacuum, limitlessness, infinity, void.

immerse
vb lit: bath, bathe, dip, dunk, soak, steep, submerge; baptize; *fig*: absorb (in), bury (in), engage (in), engross (in), involve (in).

imminence
n lit: approach, closeness, nearness, propinquity, proximity; menace, shadow, threat.

immobile
adj lit: fixed, motionless, rigid, stationary, stiff, still, unmoving; square, stable, static, steady.

immobilize
vb lit: freeze, halt, paralyse, stop, transfix; brace, splint; cripple, disable, put out of action; withdraw from circulation.

immodest
adj lit: bold, forward, impudent, pushy, self-assertive, temerarious, unrestrained; coarse, crass, gross, rude, shameless, vulgar; bawdy, blue, indecent, indelicate, lewd, obscene.

immoral
adj lit: debauched, degenerate, depraved, indecent, lewd, licentious, obscene, pornographic, prurient, scabrous, smutty; corrupt, dishonest, evil, sinful, unethical, unprincipled, wicked, wrong; dissolute, profligate, reprobate.

immorality
n lit: debauchery, degeneracy, depravity, indecency, lewdness, licentiousness, obscenity, pornography; corruption, dishonesty, evil, sinfulness, unethical behaviour, vice, wickedness; dissoluteness, profligacy.

immortal
n lit: deity, god, goddess, hero; genius; champion, world-beater.
adj lit: deathless, eternal, everlasting, imperishable, indestructible, perpetual, timeless, undying.

immune
adj lit: insusceptible, invulnerable, resistant; proof (against), safe (against); exempt (from), free (from), not subject (to).

immunize
vb lit: inoculate, vaccinate.

impact
n lit: concussion, contact, shock; bang, blow, crash, jolt, smash; force, power; momentum; *fig*: burden, impression, thrust; brunt, weight; consequences, effects, influence, repercussions, significance.

vb lit: crash (on), hit, strike; impinge on, press together, compact, harden.

impair
vb lit: damage, harm, injure; debilitate, hinder, mar, spoil, weaken; decrease, deteriorate, lessen, reduce, worsen.

impale
vb lit: pierce, spike, spit, transfix; nail, pin; fence in, stake round; *spec*: combine (two coats of arms on one escutcheon).

impart
vb lit: communicate, disclose, divulge, pass on, relate, reveal, teach; bestow, confer, convey, give, grant.

impassable
adj lit: impenetrable, unnavigable; insurmountable, unscalable.

impassioned
adj (pa.pt) lit: ardent, emotional, fervent, fervid, fiery, heated, intense, rousing, stirring, vehement.

impatience
n lit: hastiness, impetuosity, intolerance; shortness of temper, snappishness; anxious expectancy, eagerness, restlessness; fretfulness, nervousness.

impatient
adj lit: brooking no delay, hasty, impetuous, over-eager, rash; short-tempered, snappish; anxiously expectant, eager, restless; fretful, nervous.

impeccable
adj lit: exquisite, faultless, flawless, perfect, unimpeachable; exact, precise; irreproachable, unblemished.

impel
vb lit: compel, constrain, force, oblige, require; cause, induce, inspire, instigate, move, prompt, stimulate; spur, urge; drive, propel, push.

impending
adj (pr.pt) lit: approaching, hovering, imminent, looming, menacing, near, threatening; overhanging, overshadowing; forthcoming.

impenetrable
adj lit: dense, impassable, impermeable, solid, thick; *fig*: baffling, incomprehensible, inexplicable, inscrutable, mysterious, unfathomable.

imperative
adj lit: compulsory, indispensable, obligatory, vital; crucial, essential, necessary, urgent; authoritative, commanding, exigent, imperious, insistent, peremptory.

imperceptible
adj lit: indiscernible, infinitesimal, invisible, microscopic, minute, subtle, undetectable, unnoticeable; faint, fine, tiny; gradual, ultra-slow.

imperfect
adj lit: defective, deficient, faulty, flawed, incomplete, unfinished; broken, damaged, impaired; underdeveloped; abnormal, deformed, misshapen, subnormal.

imperil
vb lit: endanger, hazard, jeopardize, put at risk, risk.

impersonal
adj lit: detached, dispassionate, formal; bureaucratic, businesslike, disinterested, neutral; cold, inhuman.

impersonate
vb lit: imitate, masquerade as, pass oneself off as, pose as; act as, mimic, play the part of, take the role of; ape, take off.

impertinence
n lit: brass neck, cheek, effrontery, impudence, insolence, sauce; nerve, presumption.

impertinent
adj lit: cheeky, fresh, impudent, insolent, saucy; brazen, pert, presumptuous, unmannerly; interfering, intrusive.

imperturbable
adj lit: composed, cool, nerveless, self-possessed, unexcitable, unflappable, unmoved, unruffled, urbane; calm, serene, tranquil; complacent; stoical.

impervious
adj lit: impermeable, sealed; *fig*: closed (to), immune (to), invulnerable (to), unreceptive (to).

impetuous
adj lit: hasty, impulsive, precipitate, rash, unthinking; eager, headlong, unrestrained.

impetus
n lit: momentum; energy, weight; *fig*: impulse, incentive, motivation, push, stimulus.

impinge
vb lit: encroach, make inroads, obtrude, overlap; collide, hit, strike; bear (upon), have an effect (on), infringe (upon), touch (upon).

impious
adj lit: blasphemous, irreligious, irreverent, profane, sacrilegious; godless, ungodly.

implacable
adj lit: inexorable, intractable, relentless, remorseless, unforgiving, unrelenting; merciless, pitiless, unbending, unyielding.

implant
n lit: graft, insert; ingrafting, insertion; infusion device, power-pack.
vb lit: embed, ingraft, insert; plant, root, sow; *fig*: inculcate, instil.

implausible
adj lit: doubtful, dubious, incredible, inconceivable, suspect, suspicious, unbelievable, unconvincing, unlikely, unreasonable.

implement
n lit: instrument, piece of equipment, tool, utensil; appliance, device.
vb lit: carry out, discharge, execute, perform, put into effect.

implementation
n lit: carrying out, discharge, execution, fulfilment, performance, putting into effect.

implicated
adj (pa.pt) lit: embroiled, entangled, involved; incriminated; connected.

implication
n lit: conclusion, corollary, inference, meaning, ramification, significance; association, connection, entanglement, involvement.

implicit
adj lit: contained, included, inherent; inferred, tacit, understood, unspoken; absolute, complete, steadfast, total, unqualified, unreserved, unshakable; *spec*: invisible (response, in psychiatry).

implore
vb lit: beg, beseech, entreat, plead with, press, urge; pray to.

imply
vb lit: hint, insinuate, intimate, suggest; connote, denote, mean, signify; entail, involve, presuppose.

impolite
adj lit: bad-mannered, discourteous, ill-mannered, rude, ungracious, unmannerly; ungentlemanly, unladylike; abusive, boorish, impudent, insolent, insulting.

impolitic
adj lit: ill-judged, imprudent, indiscreet, injudicious, untimely, unwise.

imponderable
adj lit: inconceivable, indefinable, unanswerable, unimaginable; enigmatic, inestimable, obscure, puzzling, unfathomable; immeasurable, incalculable, infinite, measureless.

import
n lit: drift, gist, meaning, sense; consequence, implication, importance, moment, significance, substance; bringing in, introduction, transporting in; immigrant, product brought in; acquisition, adoption, insertion, interpolation.
vb lit: bring in, ferry in, introduce, transport in; adopt, take on; betoken, convey, mean, portend, signify.

importance
n lit: significance, usefulness, value; consequence, distinction, mark, note, standing; concern, influence, interest; eminence, moment, substance, weight.

importunate
adj lit: badgering, bothersome, clamorous, demanding, insistent, pertinacious, pressing.

impose
vb lit: apply, enforce, establish, institute, ordain; fix (on), inflict (on), lay (on), place (on), put (on), set (on); *fig*: butt in (upon), intrude (upon), trespass (upon); play (upon), presume (upon); palm off (on); *spec*: set up (type for printing).

imposition
n lit: application, enforcement, establishment, institution, ordinance; fixing on, inflicting on, laying-on, placing on; *fig*: burden, hardship; charge, duty, tax, toll; encroachment, intrusion, presumption; deception, fraud, hoax, trick.

impossible
n lit: unattainable; inconceivable, unthinkable; insoluble, unanswerable; unendurable; unacceptable.
adj lit: impracticable, not feasible, not viable, out of the question, unattainable; inconceivable, unthinkable; insoluble, unanswerable, unworkable; god-awful, unendurable; hopelessly unsuitable, outrageous, unacceptable.

impotence
n lit: helplessness, powerlessness; inability, inadequacy, uselessness, weakness; paralysis; infertility, sterility.

impotent
adj lit: helpless, powerless; inadequate, unable, useless; incapacitated, paralysed, weak; infertile, sterile.

impound
vb lit: confine, enclose, pen, shut up; contain (in), hold (in); confiscate, repossess, retain, sequester, take into custody.

impractical
adj lit: impracticable, inoperable, not viable, unachievable, unattainable, unworkable; inapplicable, inappropriate, unrealistic, unsuitable, wrong; idealistic, romantic, visionary; all fingers and thumbs, inept, maladroit, not good with one's hands.

impracticality
n lit: impossibility, nonviability, unworkability; inapplicability, unsuitability; idealism, romanticism, unreality, wishful thinking; hopelessness, maladroitness, uselessness.

imprecation
n lit: cursing; curse, malediction, malison; *fig*: abuse, invective, swearing, vituperation; expletive, oath.

imprecise
adj lit: approximate, inexact, rough, vague; ambiguous, equivocal, indefinite, indeterminate, loose; careless, inaccurate, sloppy.

impregnable

adj lit: impenetrable, invincible, invulnerable, proof against attack, unassailable.

impress

vb lit: emboss, imprint, print, stamp; *fig*: have an effect upon, influence, make an impression on, move, reach; emphasize (on), stress (upon).

impression

n lit: brand, dent, imprint, indentation, mark, print, stamp; edition, issue, printing; *fig*: effect, impact, influence; conviction, feeling, idea, memory, notion, opinion, reaction, recollection; *spec*: model, mould (of dentition).

impressionable

adj lit: easily influenced, responsive, sensitive, suggestible, susceptible; gullible.

impressive

adj lit: affecting, commanding, imposing, moving, powerful, stirring, striking.

imprison

vb lit: confine, immure, incarcerate, intern, jail, lock up, put away, send down, shut up.

improbable

adj lit: far-fetched, implausible, unlikely; doubtful, questionable, uncertain; unforeseeable, untoward.

impromptu

adj lit: ad lib, extemporaneous, improvised, off the cuff, spontaneous, unrehearsed, unscripted.
adv lit: ad lib, extemporaneously, off the cuff, on the spur of the moment, spontaneously, without preparation.

improper

adj lit: erroneous, false, incorrect, wrong; inapposite, inappropriate, infelicitous, out of place, uncalled for, unsuitable, unwarranted; impolite, indelicate, unbecoming, unseemly, vulgar; bawdy, indecent, pornographic, rude, smutty.

impropriety

n lit: error of judgement, faux pas, gaffe, gaucherie, sin, solecism, vulgarity; crime, evil, wickedness; bawdiness, indecency, licentiousness.

improve

vb lit: ameliorate, better, enhance, make better; advance, develop, gain in strength, grow, increase, pick up, progress, rise; amend, correct, mend, polish up, rectify, reform; get better, rally, recover, recuperate.

improvement

n lit: amelioration, betterment, enhancement; advance, development, gain, growth, increase, pick-up, progress, rise; correction, emendation, polishing, rectification, reformation; rally, recovery.

improvise

vb lit: ad-lib, extemporize, make up as one goes along, play by ear; come up with, contrive, devise, throw together.

imprudent

adj lit: foolhardy, ill-advised, impolitic, improvident, incautious, irresponsible, rash, reckless, unwise.

impulse

n lit: force, impetus, momentum, pressure; push, stimulus, thrust; *fig*: drive, motivation, urge; passion, spark, spirit; fancy, inclination, whim, wish, yen.

impunity

n lit: immunity, licence; without punishment; without restriction.

impute

vb lit: ascribe, assign, attribute, credit, put down (to); charge (to).

inability

n lit: incapacity, incompetence; helplessness, impotence, powerlessness.

inaccessible

adj lit: unapproachable, unattainable, ungetatable, unreachable.

inaccurate

adj lit: erroneous, faulty, incorrect, out, wrong; imprecise, inexact; defective, unreliable.

inactive

adj lit: immobile, inert, inoperative, out of service; idle, unoccupied, unused; dormant, in abeyance, latent; indolent, lazy, lethargic, sluggish, torpid; passive, sedentary.

inadequate
adj lit: deficient, incomplete, insufficient, meagre, scanty, sparse, too few, too little; incompetent, not up to it, unfitted, unsatisfactory.

inadmissible
adj lit: banned, barred, unacceptable, unauthorized, unusable; immaterial, inappropriate.

inadvertent
adj lit: accidental, unguarded, unintentional, unwitting; careless, heedless, inattentive, thoughtless, unthinking.

inamorata
n lit: beloved, darling, love, lover, mistress, sweetheart.

inanimate
adj lit: inactive, inert, lifeless, unconscious, unmoving; dead, defunct, still; dull, soulless, spiritless, static.

inappropriate
adj lit: inapposite, inapt, incongruous, unfitting, unsuitable, unsuited; infelicitous, unbecoming, unseemly; untimely, wrong; disproportionate.

inarticulate
adj lit: dumb, silent, speechless, wordless; faltering, halting, stammering, stuttering; incoherent, incomprehensible, mumbled, unintelligible.

inattentive
adj lit: absent-minded, distrait, dreamy, preoccupied, vague; paying no heed (to).

inaudible
adj lit: silent, unheard; incomprehensible, muffled, mumbling.

inaugurate
vb lit: begin, commence, initiate, launch, open, usher in; commission, dedicate, induct, install.

inauspicious
adj lit: black, ill-omened, ominous, unfortunate, unlucky, unpromising.

incalculable
adj lit: inestimable, infinite, untold; boundless, immense, limitless, measureless, vast; countless, innumerable, numberless.

incapable
adj lit: helpless, powerless, unfit; incompetent, ineffectual, inefficient, inept; not capable (of); not admitting (of).

incapacitated
adj (pa.pt) lit: damaged, hurt, impaired, indisposed; immobilized, out of action.

incense
n lit: fumes, heady aroma, scented smoke; aroma, fragrance, perfume, scent; *fig*: homage; adulation, praise.
vb lit: anger, enrage, inflame, infuriate, madden, make one's blood boil, rile.

incentive
n lit: inducement, motivation, stimulus; bait, carrot, enticement, lure.

incessant
adj lit: ceaseless, constant, continual, continuous, endless, interminable, perpetual, persistent, unceasing, unrelenting, unremitting.

inchoate
adj lit: early, imperfect, incipient, incomplete, rudimentary, undeveloped.

incidence
n lit: distribution, range, reach, spread; frequency, occurrence, prevalence; *spec*: falling (of a ray on a surface, of a point on a line, of a line on a plane).

incident
n lit: circumstance, episode, event, happening, occasion, occurrence; action, clash, commotion, crime, disturbance, scene.

incidental
adj lit: accompanying, ancillary (to), concomitant, lesser, minor, secondary (to), subordinate (to); accidental, chance, coincidental, fortuitous, random.

incipient
adj lit: embryonic, forming, inchoate, latent, nascent; beginning, initial, primary, starting.

incision
n lit: cut; gash; slash; slicing, slitting; wound.

incite
vb lit: drive (to), foment, inflame, instigate, provoke, put up (to), rouse (to), stir up, whip up.

inclination

n lit: angle, gradient, lean, slant, slope;
heel, list; bending, bow, nod; *fig*: bent,
disposition, fondness, liking, partiality,
propensity, tendency.

incline

n lit: angle, gradient, ramp, slope.
vb lit: bend, bow, nod; lean over, stoop;
heel, list, slant, slope, tilt, tip over; *fig*:
be predisposed (to), tend (to); influence
(to), persuade (to), sway (to).

include

vb lit: contain, cover, embrace, enclose,
encompass, incorporate, take in;
comprehend, comprise, embody; add
(in), enter, insert (in); count (in), reckon
(in).

incognito

adj lit: anonymous, under an assumed
name, unknown; in disguise,
unrecognizable.
adv lit: anonymously, under an assumed
name, without being recognized; in
disguise, unrecognizably.

incoherent

adj lit: inarticulate, rambling, raving,
stammering, stuttering, unintelligible;
confused, disjointed, jumbled, wild.

income

n lit: earnings, gains, pay, proceeds,
receipts, revenue.

incompatible

adj lit: conflicting, contradictory,
irreconcilable, mutually antipathetic;
inconsistent (with); at odds,
inharmonious, unsympathetic.

inconceivable

adj lit: unimaginable, unthinkable;
incredible, mind-blowing, unbelievable;
impossible.

inconclusive

adj lit: indecisive, indeterminate;
arguable, debatable, unfinished,
unsettled.

incongruous

adj lit: different, incompatible,
inconsistent, unmatched; contradictory,
contrary; extraneous, inappropriate,
inapt, unsuited.

inconsiderate

adj lit: insensitive, self-centred, selfish,
thoughtless, unreasonable, unthinking.

inconsistent

adj lit: changeable, fickle, inconstant,
unpredictable, variable; conflicting,
contradictory, contrary, different,
incompatible, incongruous,
irreconcilable.

inconspicuous

adj lit: practically invisible, unnoticeable,
unobtrusive; unostentatious; well
camouflaged; commonplace, everyday,
ordinary.

incontinent

adj lit: excreting involuntarily, paralysed,
promiscuous, uncontrolled,
unrestrained.

inconvenience

n lit: bother, bothering, disturbance,
nuisance, putting to trouble, upset.
vb lit: bother, discommode, disrupt,
disturb, put to trouble.

incorporate

vb lit: absorb, assimilate, fuse, integrate,
merge; contain, enclose, encompass, take
in; add, insert.

incorrect

adj lit: erroneous, inaccurate, out, wrong;
defective, faulty, flawed; mistaken.

increase

n lit: addition, augmentation, extension,
gain, increment; development,
enlargement, expansion, growth;
escalation, rise, upsurge; amplification,
enhancement, intensification;
multiplication, propagation; *fig*:
offspring, progeny.
vb lit: add on to, augment, extend,
prolong; develop, enlarge, expand, gain,
grow, spread; escalate, rise, surge;
amplify, enhance, intensify; multiply,
propagate.

incredible

adj lit: beyond belief, unbelievable,
unimaginable; amazing, astonishing,
astounding, mind-boggling.

incredulous

adj lit: doubting, dubious, sceptical,
unbelieving.

incriminatory

adj lit: accusatory, blackening,

condemnatory, evidential, implicating, indicting, testificatory.

incur
vb lit: bring upon onself, draw down, evoke, invoke, provoke; earn, gain; be liable to.

incurable
adj lit: inoperable, irremediable; fatal, mortal, terminal; *fig*: incorrigible, inveterate.

indecision
n lit: doubt, hesitancy, hesitation, irresolution, vacillation.

indeed
adv lit: certainly, definitely, positively, undoubtedly, veritably; actually, in fact, really.

indefinite
adj lit: boundless, indeterminate, limitless, unbounded, unlimited; imprecise, inexact, loose, vague.

indelible
adj lit: indestructible, ineradicable, permanent.

indelicate
adj lit: immodest, improper, indecent, indecorous, near the knuckle, risqué, unseemly, vulgar.

indemnity
n lit: exemption, immunity; guarantee, hedge, insurance; compensation, reimbursement, reparation, restitution.

indent
n lit: dent, impression, notch; niche, nook, recess; demand, order, requisition; *spec*: space (at the head of a paragraph).
vb lit: cut, make an impression, nick, notch, penetrate (into); serrate, zigzag; leave space; ask (for), put in an order (for).

independence
n lit: autonomy, self-determination, self-rule, sovereignty; self-reliance, self-sufficiency; freedom, liberty; impartiality, objectivity; *fig*: private income.

independent
n spec: non-party MP, unaffiliated politician; nonconformist (cleric or congregation).

adj lit: autonomous, non-aligned, self-determining, self-governing, sovereign; self-reliant, self-sufficient; free, liberated, unaffiliated; impartial, objective.

indestructible
adj lit: imperishable, incorruptible, indissoluble, permanent, unbreakable; immortal; *fig*: durable, long-suffering, persevering.

index
n lit: forefinger; arm, gnomon, hand, indicator, needle, pointer; number, ratio, scale; *fig*: clue, indication, sign, token; *spec*: alphabetical list; power (in mathematics).

indicate
vb lit: display, point out, point to, show (to); mark, signal, single out; betoken, denote, express, reveal, signify; read, register; imply, suggest.

indication
n lit: mark, pointer, sign, signal, token; evidence, symptom; implication, inkling, suggestion; display, expression, manifestation, revelation, show; discrimination, distinguishing, pointing out.

indictment
n lit: accusation, impeachment; charge-sheet.

indifference
n lit: detachment, disinterest, unconcern; apathy, inattention, negligence; insignificance, unimportance.

indignant
adj lit: angry (at), annoyed (at), exasperated (at), full of wrath (at).

indignation
n lit: anger, annoyance, exasperation, wrath; pique, resentment.

indignity
n lit: affront, humiliation, incivility, slap in the face, slight.

indirectly
adv lit: circuitously, in a roundabout way, obliquely; deviously; at second-hand; by implication; fortuitously, incidentally.

indiscreet
adj lit: tactless, undiplomatic; ill-judged, impolitic, imprudent, incautious, injudicious; scandalous.

indiscretion
n lit: tactlessness; folly, impetuosity, imprudence; act of folly, gaffe, impropriety, peccadillo, scandal; betrayal, disclosure, leak.

indispensable
adj lit: crucial, essential, key, necessary, vital.

indisposition
n lit: ill health, illness, infirmity; ailment, complaint, sickness; disinclination, reluctance, unwillingness.

indistinct
adj lit: dim, faint, indiscernible, muffled, weak; blurred, fuzzy, hazy, ill-defined, indeterminate, misty, obscure, shadowy, vague.

individual
n lit: one, unit; being, creature; mortal, party, person, soul; character, nonconformist, one-off, original.
adj lit: discrete, distinct, particular, respective, separate, single, unique; characteristic, distinctive, idiosyncratic, peculiar, personal, singular, special.

indoctrinate
vb lit: brainwash; drill, instruct, school, train; teach.

induce
vb lit: get (to do), impel, influence, move, persuade, prompt; bring about, cause, effect, lead to, occasion; deduce, derive, infer; *spec*: produce (an electric current, radioactivity).

indulge
vb lit: cater to, gratify, pander to, satiate, satisfy; baby, cosset, humour, pamper, pet, spoil; bask (in), luxuriate (in), wallow (in); go (in) for

indulgent
adj lit: easy-going, forbearing, lenient, liberal, permissive, tolerant, understanding.

industry
n lit: commerce, manufacturing, trade; business; hard work, labour, toil; application, diligence, effort, perseverance, zeal.

inebriated
adj (pa.pt) lit: blind drunk, drunk, intoxicated, merry, tipsy; blotto, boozed up, canned, half-cut, high as a kite, legless, paralytic, pickled, pissed as a newt, plastered, smashed, sozzled, squiffy, stoned, three sheets to the wind, under the influence.

ineffectual
adj lit: bootless, futile, idle, powerless, unavailing, useless, vain; feeble, inadequate, lame, weak; incompetent.

inefficient
adj lit: wasteful; incapable, incompetent, inept, sloppy; feeble, weak.

ineligible
adj lit: disqualified, incompetent, unacceptable, unsuitable.

inept
adj lit: awkward, bumbling, clumsy, gauche, maladroit, unworkmanlike; inappropriate, infelicitous, unsuitable.

inequality
n lit: difference, disparity, irregularity, variation; disproportion; unevenness, variability; deviation.

inert
adj lit: idle, immobile, inactive, inanimate, lifeless, motionless, static, still, unconscious, unmoving; dead; passive, quiescent, unresponsive.

inertia
n lit: immobility, inactivity; passivity, unresponsiveness; apathy, idleness, indolence, lassitude, lethargy, sloth, torpor.

inestimable
adj lit: immeasurable, incalculable, invaluable.

inevitable
adj lit: automatic, inescapable, inexorable, necessary, unavoidable.

inexcusable
adj lit: indefensible, unforgivable, unjustifiable, unpardonable, unwarrantable.

inexperienced
adj lit: callow, green, immature, raw, unpractised, unschooled, untried, unversed.

inexplicable
adj lit: baffling, bewildering, confusing, incomprehensible, insoluble, mystifying, unaccountable, unfathomable.

infallible
adj lit: inability to be wrong; dependability, reliability; omniscience.

infamous
adj lit: disreputable, heinous, iniquitous, notorious, opprobrious, scandalous, shocking; disgraceful, dishonourable, outrageous.

infant
n lit: babe, baby, neonate, toddler, tot.

infantile
adj lit: babyish, childish, juvenile, puerile; *fig*: early, primary.

infatuation
n lit: crush, passion, thing; fixation, obsession.

infect
vb lit: blight, contaminate, poison, pollute, taint; affect, spread to.

infer
vb lit: conclude, deduce, derive, gather, presume, reason, surmise, take as read, understand.

inference
n lit: conclusion, corollary, deduction, presumption, reasoning, surmise, understanding.

inferior
adj lit: junior, lesser, secondary, subordinate, subsidary; lower; poor, second-rate, shoddy, substandard, worse.

infernal
adj lit: nether, Stygian, subterranean; daemonic, diabolical, hellish, satanic; *fig*: demonic, devilish, evil, fiendish.

infertile
adj lit: barren, infecund, sterile; arid, unproductive.

infiltrate
vb lit: filter through into, penetrate, percolate through, pervade; get into, pass into, slip into, sneak into.

infinite
adj lit: boundless, endless, illimitable, immeasurable, inestimable, inexhaustible, limitless, measureless, unbounded, untold; countless, numberless; eternal, everlasting, perpetual; *fig*: immense, vast.

infirm
adj lit: ailing, debilitated, decrepit, frail, weak; shaky, wobbly: indecisive, irresolute, vacillating.

inflame
vb lit: aggravate, exacerbate, intensify, worsen; excite, fire, foment, ignite, kindle, rouse; enrage, incense, infuriate, rile; *spec*: make hot and sore.

inflammatory
adj lit: aggravating, exacerbating, intensifying; explosive, fiery, incendiary, liable to lead to a breach of the peace, provocative; *spec*: causing soreness and redness.

inflate
vb lit: blow up, puff out, pump up; balloon, bloat, dilate, distend, expand, swell; *fig*: aggrandize, exaggerate; be devalued, be worth less.

inflict
vb lit: impose (upon), place (upon), visit (upon), wreak (upon); exact (upon).

influence
n lit: ascendancy, domination, spell, sway; effect, force, pressure, weight; control, direction; authority, clout, hold, leverage, power; connections, pull; *spec*: (electrostatic) induction.
vb lit: affect, dispose, incline, have an effect on, induce, lead (to), move, persuade, predispose, sway; have a bearing on; carry weight with, pull strings with.

influential
adj lit: effective, efficacious, important, significant, telling, weighty; moving, persuasive; powerful, well-connected.

inform
vb lit: advise, apprise, enlighten, let know, notify, tell; blab (on), grass (on), peach (on), sneak (on), tell (on); *spec*: animate, illuminate, permeate (in archaic senses).

informal
adj lit: casual, easy, familiar, unceremonious, unofficial; colloquial, idiomatic.

information
n lit: data, facts, gen, info; advice, intelligence, news, word; bulletin, message, printout, report.

infringe
vb lit: break, contravene, transgress, violate; encroach (upon), impinge (upon), intrude (upon).

infuriate
vb lit: enrage, incense, inflame, madden, rile.

ingratiating
adj (pr.pt) lit: bootlicking, crawling, fawning, obsequious, sycophantic, toadying; smarmy, oily, unctuous.

ingredient
n lit: component, constituent, element, factor.

inhabit
vb lit: abide in, dwell in, live in, occupy, reside in; people, populate.

inhabitant
n lit: denizen, dweller, inmate, native, occupant, occupier, resident, tenant.

inhale
vb lit: breathe in, draw breath, draw in, inspire, suck in, take in.

inherent
adj lit: basic, inborn, inbuilt, innate, intrinsic, native, natural.

inheritance
n lit: birthright, heritage; patrimony; bequest, legacy.

inhibit
vb lit: constrain, hold back, restrain; check, discourage, hinder; prevent, stop.

inhospitable
adj lit: uncongenial, unfriendly, unreceptive, unsociable, unwelcoming; barren, bleak, cheerless, desolate, forbidding, hostile, uninhabitable, uninviting.

inhuman
adj lit: barbaric, barbarous, bestial, brutal, cruel, heartless, ruthless, unfeeling; diabolical, fiendish; abnormal, subhuman; superhuman.

iniquitous
adj lit: infamous, vicious, wicked; inequitable, unfair, unjust

initial
n lit: character, letter.
vb lit: endorse, sign; countersign.
adj lit: beginning, first, inaugural, introductory, opening; early, primary, rudimentary.

initiate
n lit: beginner, learner, novice, postulant, probationer, tyro.
vb lit: begin, commence, inaugurate, launch, open, originate, pioneer, set in motion, start; induct, install.

initiative
n lit: drive, dynamism, enterprise, get-up-and-go, gumption, resourcefulness; leadership; advantage, control, dominance, lead.

inject
vb lit: jab, syringe; mainline, shoot; immunize, inoculate; infuse; *fig*: insert, introduce; throw in, toss in; force in.

injustice
n lit: inequity, wrong; bias, discrimination, inequality, prejudice, unfairness.

inn
n lit: hospice, hostel, hostelry, pub, public house, tavern; bar, boozer, local, oasis, watering-hole.

innocence
n lit: blamelessness, guiltlessness; chastity, purity, virginity, virtue; artlessness, ingenuousness, naivety, simplicity; inexperience, unsophistication, unworldliness; credulousness, gullibility; ignorance, unawareness.

innocent
adj lit: blameless, faultless, guiltless, not guilty; chaste, immaculate, pure, spotless, unblemished, virgin; artless, ingenuous, naive, open, simple; harmless, innocuous, inoffensive; inexperienced, unsophisticated, unworldly; credulous, gullible; ignorant (of), unaware (of).

innovation
n lit: creation, invention, novelty; alteration, change, introduction.

innuendo
n lit: hint, implication, inference, insinuation, overtone, suggestion, undertone.

inoffensive
adj lit: harmless, innocuous, mild, peaceable, quiet, unobtrusive, unprovocative.

inopportune
adj lit: ill-timed, inconvenient, mistimed, untimely, unhelpful, unwelcome.

inordinate
adj lit: disproportionate, excessive, exorbitant, extravagant, unwarranted; unrestrained.

inquisitive
adj lit: curious, enquiring, investigative; intrusive, nosy, prying, snooping.

insane
adj lit: certifiable, mentally disordered, not responsible for one's actions, psychopathic, psychotic; crazy, demented, deranged, lunatic, mad, mental, unbalanced, unhinged; *fig*: barking mad, barmy, bats, bonkers, crackers, cuckoo, gaga, loony, loopy, nuts, off one's rocker, raving, round the bend, round the twist; daft, foolish, idiotic, irrational, senseless, stupid.

insanitary
adj lit: contaminated, dirty, filthy, polluted, unclean, unhealthy, unhygienic.

insanity
n lit: dementia, mental derangement, mental illness; lunacy, madness; *fig*: folly, senselessness, stupidity; irresponsibility.

insatiable
adj lit: unappeasable, voracious; unquenchable.

inscribe
vb lit: carve, engrave, etch; enter, write; autograph, dedicate, sign.

insecure
adj lit: defenceless, exposed, open to attack, unprotected, unsafe, vulnerable; flimsy, precarious, rickety, rocky, shaky, unreliable, unsteady, wobbly; anxious, diffident, unsure.

insensible
adj lit: benumbed, numbed, senseless, unconscious; blind, deaf; dead, lifeless; oblivious, unaware, unmindful.

insensitive
adj lit: callous, hardened, indifferent, tough, unfeeling; indifferent, uncaring, unconcerned; dull, obtuse; dead (to), impervious (to).

insert
n lit: additional material, inset, interpolation; addendum, corrigendum; tip-in.
vb lit: implant, interpolate, interpose, introduce, put in, tuck in, work in.

inside
n lit: interior; contents; bowels, entrails, guts, innards, viscera.
adj lit: inner, interior, internal; *fig*: confidential, exclusive, private, restricted; limited, small; in prison.
adv lit: in, indoors.
prp lit: in, into, within.

insidious
adj lit: creeping, furtive, secret, sly, sneaking, stealthy, subtle, surreptitious, wily.

insight
n lit: acumen, comprehension, discernment, penetration, perspicacity, vision; understanding, wisdom; perception, realization, solution.

insignificant
adj lit: inconsequential, meaningless, negligible, nugatory, unimportant; extraneous, irrelevant; minor, paltry, petty, trifling, trivial.

insincerity
n lit: dissimulation, duplicity, hypocrisy, perfidy, pretence; dishonesty, mendacity, untruthfulness.

insipid
adj lit: bland, tasteless, watery; *fig*: banal, characterless, colourless, dull, lifeless, limp, stale, tame, trite, vapid, weak.

insist
vb lit: demand (that); maintain (that), repeat (that); stand firm (on), take a stand (on).

insistent
adj lit: compulsive, demanding, emphatic, importunate, persistent, pressing.

insolence
n lit: audacity, cheek, contumely, disrespect, effrontery, gall, impertinence, impudence, sauce.

insoluble
adj lit: undissolvable; *fig*: indecipherable, inexplicable, mystifying, unfathomable.

inspect
vb lit: examine, go over, look over, scan, scrutinize, survey, vet.

inspiration
n lit: creativity, genius, insight, muse, stimulus.

inspire
vb lit: arouse, enkindle, excite, fire, spur, stimulate, stir.

install
vb lit: lodge, place, position, settle, set up; establish, inaugurate, institute, introduce.

instance
n lit: case, example, illustration, precedent, time; phase, stage; application, plea, prompting, request.
vb lit: adduce, cite, mention, specify.

instant
n lit: flash, jiffy, moment, second, time, trice, twinkling of an eye.
adj lit: immediate, prompt, rapid; *fig*: burning, imperative, pressing; *spec*: convenience (food).

instead
adv lit: alternatively, in lieu; preferably, rather; in place (of)

instigate
vb lit: actuate, bring about, foment, kindle, prompt, provoke, stir up, whip up.

instinctive
adj lit: inborn, inherent, innate, involuntary, natural, reflex, spontaneous.

institute
n lit: academy, college, foundation, school, society; decree, doctrine, law, precept, principle, rule.

vb lit: establish, found. initiate, introduce, launch, originate, set up, start.

instruct
vb lit: coach, direct, drill, educate, school, teach, train; command, order; advise, apprise, counsel, inform, notify, tell.

instruction
n lit: coaching, direction, drill, education, schooling, teaching, training; command, order; advice, counsel, information.

instructor
n lit: coach, director, mentor, teacher, trainer; commander; adviser, counsel.

instrument
n lit: device, gadget, implement, tool, utensil; appliance, mechanism; dial, meter, read-out; agent, factor; channel, means, medium, vehicle; contract, deed, legal document, writ; *fig*: pawn, puppet.

instrumental
adj lit: contributory, helpful, influential, useful.

insubordinate
adj lit: defiant, disobedient, mutinous, rebellious, recalcitrant, refractory; unmanageable, wild.

insufferable
adj lit: insupportable, intolerable, past bearing, (altogether) too much, unbearable, unendurable; impossible.

insular
adj lit: distant, isolated, remote; limited, narrow-minded, parochial, provincial; introverted, self-centred.

insulation
n lit: cushioning, draught-proofing, lagging, padding, protection, shielding, thermal layer, wrapping.

insult
n lit: affront, incivility, offence, rudeness, scurrility, slight; abuse, invective, vituperation.
vb lit: abuse, affront, be rude to, be offensive to, call names, offend, outrage, slight.

insurance
n lit: assurance, cover, guarantee, indemnity, safeguard, security, warranty; policy; premium.

insurgent
n lit: guerrilla, mutineer, partisan, rebel, revolutionary, terrorist; hooligan, rioter.

insurrection
n lit: coup, mutiny, putsch, rebellion, revolt, revolution, uprising.

intact
adj lit: complete, entire, perfect, whole; undamaged, unharmed, unimpaired, uninjured, untouched; undefiled, unviolated, virgin.

integral
n lit: number; unit, whole.
adj lit: complete, entire, unbroken, undivided, whole; homogeneous; component, constituent, intrinsic; basic, essential, fundamental, indispensable.

integrate
vb lit: absorb, accommodate, assimilate, blend in, fuse, harmonize, incorporate, merge, mesh, mingle; connect up, put together, unify.

integrity
n lit: completeness, homogeneity, totality, unity, wholeness; *fig*: honesty, honour, incorruptibility, principle, probity, sincerity, virtue.

intellectual
n lit: thinker; academic, philosopher, scholar; highbrow.
adj lit: cerebral, mental, rational; academic, bookish, philosophical, scholarly.

intelligence
n lit: brains, grey matter, mind; acumen, discernment, discrimination, intellect, nous, perception, reason, wit; data, facts, gen, information, knowledge, news, notification, word; secret service.

intelligent
adj lit: brainy, bright, clever, discerning, discriminating, penetrating, perceptive, quick-witted, reasoning, smart, thinking.

intelligible
adj lit: comprehensible, decipherable, legible, lucid, simple, understandable.

intend
vb lit: aim (to), be determined (to), mean (to), propose (to), purpose (to); destine (for), earmark (for), have in mind (for), mean (for).

intense
adj lit: acute, concentrated, deep, extreme, great, powerful, profound, severe; burning, consuming, fanatical, fervent, impassioned, passionate, vehement; earnest, fierce, haunted, strained; bright; dense.

intensify
vb lit: aggravate, boost, concentrate, deepen, escalate, exacerbate, heighten, increase, sharpen, strengthen.

intent
n lit: aim, end, goal, object, objective, purpose.
adj lit: absorbed, engrossed, preoccupied, rapt; concentrating (on); bent (on), resolute (on), resolved (on), set (on).

intention
n lit: aim, design, idea, objective, plan, purpose, target; *spec*: concentration (of a priest in administering a sacrament); concept (in logic).

inter
vb lit: bury, lay to rest; *fig*: cover over.

interact
vb lit: be responsive (with), correspond (with), react (with), reciprocate (with), work together (with); react with each other (to), work together (to).

intercede
vb lit: interpose, intervene; arbitrate, mediate; act as advocate (for), plead (for).

intercourse
n lit: communication, contact, dealings, intercommunication, traffic; coitus, copulation, sex, sexual activity.

interest
n lit: concern, importance, moment, pertinence, relevance, significance, weight; curiosity; attention, notice, regard; activity, hobby, occupation, pastime, pursuit; claim, commitment, influence, involvement, stake; benefit, gain, profit; affair, business, matter; (in the) cause (of).
vb lit: affect, concern, involve; absorb, engross, fascinate, grab the attention of, intrigue; amuse, divert, entertain.

interesting
adj (pr.pt) lit: affecting, compelling, gripping, riveting, thought-provoking; absorbing, engrossing, fascinating,

intriguing, stimulating; amusing, diverting, entertaining, pleasing; curious, strange, unusual; funny, odd, suspicious.

interfere
vb lit: butt in, intervene, intrude, meddle, stick one's oar (in); clash (with), conflict (with); react (with); take a liberty (with).

interim
n lit: interval, meantime, meanwhile.
adj lit: provisional, stopgap, temporary.

interior
n lit: inside; centre, core, heart; heartland; contents; domestic scene.
adj lit: inside, internal, inward; inner, mental, personal, private; domestic, home.

interlude
n lit: break, breathing-space, halt, intermission, pause, respite, rest, stoppage; interim entertainment, voluntary.

intermediate
adj lit: in-between, intervening, transitional; medium, middle.

interminable
adj lit: endless, everlasting, infinite, perpetual; boring, long-drawn-out, long-winded, protracted, tedious, wearisome.

intermittent
adj lit: discontinuous, fitful, periodic, spasmodic, sporadic.

internal
adj lit: inside, interior; inner, private, secret; domestic, home; company, in-house, personnel, staff.

interpolation
n lit: insertion, interjection; addition, extra; injection.

interpose
vb lit: come (between), intercede, intervene, step in (between); inject, insert.

interpret
vb lit: decipher, decode, make sense of, translate; elucidate, explain; bring out the meaning of, render; read, understand.

interpretation
n lit: decipherment, decoding, translation; elucidation, exegesis, explanation; analysis, diagnosis, reading, understanding; performance, rendition, version; meaning.

interrogate
vb lit: cross-question, examine, grill, pump, question, quiz; ask.

interrupt
vb lit: break into, butt into, cut off, disturb, hold up, intrude into, punctuate; check, cut short, stop; break off, discontinue, suspend; interfere with, obstruct.

intersection
n lit: crossing, crossroads, junction; *spec*: common set (within groups of sets).

interval
n lit: break, distance, gap, hiatus, period, space, term, time; intermission, pause; interim, meantime, meanwhile.

interview
n lit: audience, consultation, meeting, talk; examination, interrogation.
vb lit: examine, interrogate, question, quiz.

intestines
n lit: guts, tripes, viscera; bowels, entrails, innards.

intimate
n lit: bosom friend, confidant, confidante; chum, friend, mate, pal; crony, familiar.
vb lit: hint, imply, insinuate, suggest; announce, declare, indicate, make known; advise, warn.
adj lit: close, confidential, dear, near, warm; cosy, friendly, informal, snug; personal, private; detailed, first-hand, immediate, in-depth; penetrating, thorough.

intimidate
vb lit: browbeat, bully, cow, lean on, menace, terrorize, threaten; daunt, dishearten, frighten, overawe, scare, terrify.

intolerance
n lit: impatience; dogmatism, fanaticism, illiberality, narrow-mindedness; discrimination, prejudice; chauvinism.

intolerant
adj lit: impatient, uncharitable; dogmatic,
fanatical, illiberal, narrow-minded;
discriminating, prejudiced;
chauvinistic.

intone
vb lit: chant, recite, warble; sing.

intoxication
n lit: drunkenness, inebriety; poisoning;
fig: delirium, euphoria, exaltation,
exhilaration.

intransigent
adj lit: intractable, obdurate, obstinate,
stubborn, tenacious, uncompromising,
unyielding.

intrepid
adj lit: audacious, bold, brave, daring,
dauntless, fearless, heroic, nerveless,
stout-hearted, undaunted, valiant.

intricate
adj lit: complex, complicated, elaborate,
involved, labyrinthine, tangled,
tortuous.

intrigue
n lit: complot, conspiracy, machination,
plot, scheme, stratagem, trick; amour,
liaison, romance.
vb lit: fascinate, interest; perplex, puzzle;
connive, conspire, plot, scheme.

intriguing
adj (pr.pt) lit: fascinating, interesting;
perplexing, puzzling.

introduce
vb lit: acquaint, make known, present;
bring in, establish, inaugurate, institute,
launch, pioneer, usher in; announce,
bring up, broach, lead off, preface, put
forward; add, insert, interpolate, put in;
put next to.

introduction
n lit: presentation; debut, establishment,
inauguration, institution, launching,
pioneering; foreword, opening
statement, overture, preamble, preface,
prelude, prologue; addition, insertion,
interpolation.

introverted
adj lit: indrawn, introspective; reserved,
withdrawn; self-contained; self-centred.

intruder
n lit: burglar, prowler, raider; gate-
crasher, interloper, trespasser; invader.

intrusive
adj lit: encroaching, invasive;
importunate, interfering; uncalled-for,
uninvited, unwelcome; meddlesome,
nosy; *fig*: superfluous, unnecessary.

intuition
n lit: awareness, feeling, hunch, instinct,
presentiment, sense.

intuitive
adj lit: instinctive; penetrative, percipient;
innate, instinctual, involuntary, natural,
reflex, spontaneous.

inundate
vb lit: deluge, drown, flood, immerse,
overflow, submerge.

invade
vb lit: burst in, encroach upon, infringe,
occupy, raid; infect, infest, overrun,
penetrate, permeate; assault, attack.

invalid
n lit: convalescent, patient.
adj lit: bedridden, disabled, frail, ill, sick,
sickly; inoperative, not in service, null,
void; fallacious, false, incorrect,
irrational, untrue.

invaluable
adj lit: precious, priceless; *fig*: essential,
indispensable, necessary, vital.

invariably
adv lit: always, consistently, every time,
regularly, rigidly, unfailingly.

invasion
n lit: encroachment, infringement,
intrusion, occupation, penetration,
permeation; infestation; assault, attack,
incursion, raid.

invective
n lit: abuse, execration, profanity,
vilification, vituperation; denunciation;
sarcasm.

invent
vb lit: come up with, create, construct,
devise, formulate, originate; conceive,
imagine, make up, think up; concoct,
cook up, fabricate.

invention
n lit: creativity, genius, imagination,
ingenuity, originality; construction,
devising, formulation, origination;
brainchild, creation, discovery,
innovation, novelty; fabrication, fantasy,
fiction, story; falsehood, lie, untruth.

inventive
adj lit: creative, imaginative, ingenious, original, resourceful; constructive, practical; innovative.

inversion
n lit: overturning, reversal, transposition; opposite; anastrophe.

invert
vb lit: overturn, reverse, transpose, turn inside out, turn upside down, upset; capsize, turn turtle.

invest
vb lit: authorize, empower, license; consecrate, dedicate, induct, install, ordain; endow, provide, supply; put (money in), sink (funds in); devote, lay out, spend; beset, besiege, lay siege to, surround.

investigate
vb lit: enquire into, examine, explore, go into, look into, probe, study.

inveterate
adj lit: confirmed, established, habitual, hardened, incorrigible, incurable, long-standing.

invidious
adj lit: odious, offensive, provocative, tendentious.

invigorating
adj (pr.pt) lit: bracing, exhilarating, fresh, heartening, refreshing, rejuvenating, revitalizing, stimulating.

invincible
adj lit: indestructible, indomitable, invulnerable, unassailable, unbeatable.

invisible
adj lit: imperceptible, indiscernible; inconspicuous, unseen; infinitesimal, microscopic; concealed, hidden.

invitation
n lit: call, request, suggestion; hospitality, welcome; *fig*: allurement, come-on, glad eye, inducement, temptation.

invite
vb lit: ask, bid, call, request, summon, welcome; *fig*: ask for, court, look for, provoke, tempt; attract, draw.

inviting
adj (pr.pt) lit: appealing, attractive, captivating, welcoming, winning; alluring, enticing, seductive, tempting.

invoke
vb lit: appeal to, call upon, pray to; beg, petition, supplicate; call up, conjure; apply, implement, put into effect; call in, resort to.

involuntary
adj lit: automatic, instinctual, reflex, spontaneous, uncontrolled; accidental, unintended, unintentional; reluctant, unwilling.

involve
vb lit: entail, imply, mean, necessitate; contain, cover, include, incorporate, take in; absorb, engross, grip, hold, rivet; affect, concern, touch; connect with, implicate; complicate, embroil, enmesh, entangle.

involved
adj (pa.pt) lit: complex, complicated, elaborate, intricate, labyrinthine, tangled; concerned (in), implicated (in), mixed up (in), occupied (in).

irons
n lit: chains, fetters, handcuffs, manacles, shackles.

irony
n lit: dissimulation, sarcasm; contrariness, paradox.

irrational
adj lit: absurd, crazy, illogical, insane, mindless, nonsensical, silly, senseless, unreasonable.

irregular
n lit: reservist, volunteer; part-timer, temporary.
adj lit: amorphous, asymmetrical, crooked, lopsided, lumpy, shapeless, unequal, uneven; fitful, intermittent, odd, patchy, spasmodic, sporadic, unsteady, variable; eccentric, erratic, haphazard; fluctuating, oscillating, varying; abnormal, exceptional, extraordinary, peculiar, queer, unorthodox, unusual; part-time, temporary, unauthorized, unofficial; *spec*: strong (verb).

irrelevant
adj lit: extraneous, immaterial, inappropriate, not pertinent, unconnected, unrelated; inadmissible, inapplicable.

irrepressible
adj lit: bright, bubbling, buoyant, cheery, ebullient, effervescent; cheeky, impudent, incorrigible; uncontrollable, unstoppable.

irresistible
adj lit: compelling, compulsive, overpowering, overwhelming; inescapable, inexorable; *fig*: enchanting, fascinating, ravishing.

irresponsible
adj lit: ill-advised, ill-judged, reckless, wild; undependable, unreliable, untrustworthy; feckless, flighty, giddy.

irreverent
adj lit: impious, irreligious, sacrilegious; cheeky, disrespectful, impertinent, impudent, saucy.

irrigate
vb lit: water; moisten, wet; flood, hose, spray, sprinkle.

irritate
vb lit: annoy, be trying, bother, exasperate, get on one's nerves, offend, pester, provoke, rub up the wrong way; inflame; chafe, rub; itch, tickle.

isolate
vb lit: detach, divorce, keep separate, segregate, separate; quarantine.

isolation
n lit: detachment, insularity, seclusion, segregation, separation; loneliness, solitude.

issue
n lit: child, children, offspring, progeny; delivery, dissemination, distribution, publication, supplying; edition, impression, instalment; affair, concern, matter, point, question, subject; argument, bone of contention, controversy, problem; conclusion, culmination, finale, outcome, result, upshot.
vb lit: arise, come (forth), emanate, emerge, flow, rise, spring, stem; deliver, disseminate, distribute, emit, publish, put out; announce, broadcast, circulate, release.

itch
n lit: irritation, tickling, tingling; *fig*: craving, desire, longing, lust, yearning.
vb lit: irritate, tickle, tingle; *fig*: ache, crave, long, lust, pine, yearn.

item
n lit: article, object, thing; component, detail, particular, unit; entry, matter, point, subject, topic; article, feature, notice, piece, report.

itemize
vb lit: detail, enumerate, list, number, set out, specify.

itinerant
adj lit: nomadic, roving, travelling, vagrant, wandering, wayfaring; homeless.

itinerary
n lit: programme, route, schedule, travel plan; guide-book; log.

J

jab
n lit: dig, poke, prod, stab; lunge, nudge, thrust; blow, punch; *fig*: injection, inoculation, vaccination.
vb lit: dig, poke, prod, stab; lunge, nudge, thrust; punch, straight-arm.

jack
n lit: hoist, lever, lift, lifter, winch; colours, ensign, flag; saw-horse, template; sailor; labourer, worker; *spec*: cross-piece, crosstree (on a mast); knave (in cards); (electrical) plug, socket; white ball (in bowls).
vb lit: elevate, hoist, lift, raise, winch (up); *fig*: boost, hike, increase, put (up); abandon, give (in), throw (in) the towel.

jackass
n lit: male donkey; *fig*: idiot, imbecile, moron; ass, dolt, fool, noodle, twit.

jacket
n lit: blazer, body-warmer, bolero, coat; case, casing, covering, lagging, sheath, wrapper, wrapping; outside, skin, surface; dustcover, envelope, folder.
vb lit: case, cover, lag, sheathe, wrap; enclose, enfold, envelop; *fig*: beat, drub, thrash.

jaded
adj (pa.pt) lit: dulled, glutted, gorged, sated, satiated, spent, surfeited, wearied; bored, fatigued, flagging, tired.

jagged
adj (pa.pt) lit: barbed, pointed, ragged, serrated, spiked, spiky, toothed; notched, ridged, rough, uneven; *fig*: hungover, sensitive, under the weather.

jail
n lit: lockup, prison; brig, calaboose, clink, hoosegow, jug, nick, penitentiary, stir; detention centre, remand centre; internment.
vb lit: detain, imprison, lock up, send down; confine, immure, incarcerate.

jam
n lit: conserve, preserve; crush, press, queue, squeeze, tailback, throng; blockage, congestion, obstruction; *fig*: dilemma, predicament, quandary; bit of bother, fix, hole, pickle, scrape, spot.
vb lit: cram, crush, force, pack, press, push, ram, shove, squeeze, stuff, wedge; block, clog, congest, obstruct; bring to a standstill, halt, stick fast, stop; *spec*: improvise (in jazz).

jangle
n lit: chink, chinking, clang, clanking, jingle, ringing, tinkling, tintinnabulation; cacophony, din, dissonance, racket, rattle; chiming, reverberation; clashing, grating, jarring.
vb lit: chime, chink, clang, clank, jingle, ring, tinkle, tintinnabulate; rattle, reverberate, vibrate; clash, grate, jar.

janitor
n lit: caretaker, concierge; doorkeeper, porter; attendant, custodian, warden.

jar
n lit: amphora, crock, flagon, jug, pitcher, urn, vase; pint-glass, pint-mug, tankard; container, pot, vessel; bump, jerk, jolt, knock, nudge, percussion, shock, start, vibration, wrench; clash, grating; *fig*: conflict, disagreement, quarrel.
vb lit: bump, jerk, jolt, knock, nudge, rock, shake, vibrate, wrench; clash, grate, rasp; *fig*: agitate, disturb, irritate, rattle; annoy, irk, nettle, touch on the raw; bicker, disagree, quarrel, wrangle; clash, jangle, stick out like a sore thumb.

jargon
n lit: patter, private vocabulary, technical terminology; cant, idiom, usage; *fig*: argot, patois, slang; gabbling, gibberish, gobbledegook, twittering; *spec*: creole, pidgin (in linguistics).

jaundiced
adj lit: yellowish; bilious; *fig*: cynical, sceptical; biased, preconceived, prejudiced; bitter, envious, jealous, resentful; suspicious.

jaunt
n lit: excursion, tour, trip; expedition, trek; airing, outing, promenade, ramble, stroll; ride, spin.

vb lit: go on an excursion, make a trip, tour; promenade, ramble, saunter, stroll; go for a spin, ride.

jaunty
adj lit: airy, breezy, carefree, easy, lively, perky, sprightly; dapper, smart, spruce, stylish, trim; aristocratic, arrogant, strutting, swaggering.

jaw
n lit: mandible, maxilla; pincer; *fig*: chat, chew the rag, gossip, natter; conversation, dialogue, talk; chattiness, talkativeness; scolding.
vb lit: chat, chatter, go on, gossip, natter, rabbit; censure, criticize, find fault, lecture, scold.

jealous
adj lit: covetous, envious, green-eyed; dog-in-the-manger, grudging, resentful; attentive, possessive, protective, solicitous, vigilant, zealous; anxious, mistrustful, suspicious, wary, watchful.

jealousy
n lit: covetousness, enviousness; resentment; possessiveness, protectiveness, solicitousness, vigilance, zealousness; anxiety, distrust, mistrust, suspicion, wariness, watchfulness.

jeans
n lit: casuals, denims, slacks; overalls, trousers.

jeering
n lit: barracking, boos, catcalls, gibes, heckling, hisses, mockery, obloquy, ragging, raillery, ridicule, scoffs, sneers, taunts; abuse, derision.
adj (pr.pt) lit: barracking, booing, catcalling, gibing, heckling, hissing, hooting, mocking, ridiculing, scoffing, sneering, taunting; abusive, deriding.

jejune
adj lit: adolescent, callow, immature, naive, puerile; arid, barren, dry, empty, flat; meagre, scanty; spiritless, tedious, thin, uninteresting, unsatisfying, weak.

jeopardy
n lit: danger, hazard, peril, risk; insecurity, precariousness, vulnerability.

jerk
n lit: jolt, pull, tug, tweak, twitch, wrench, yank; lurch, twist; spasm, start, tic; *fig*: louse, rat, swine, villain.

vb lit: jar, jolt, pull, tug, tweak, wrench, yank; lurch, twist, veer; go into spasm, start, twitch; bounce, bump, rattle, shake, tremble, vibrate; *fig*: force out, say brokenly, stammer, stutter; *spec*: slice and dry (meat to preserve it).

jerry-built
adj lit: badly-made, botched, defective, faulty, flimsy, rickety, slipshod; cobbled together, flung together; cheap, shabby.

jersey
n lit: cardigan, jumper, pullover, sweater; woolly.

jest
n lit: joke, pleasantry, quip, sally, wisecrack, witticism; hoax, jape, lark, prank.
vb lit: be witty, crack jokes, joke, quip, tell gags, wisecrack; hoax, jape, lark about, play tricks; kid, mock, tease.

jet
n lit: gush, spray, stream; fountain, geyser; atomizer, nozzle, rose, spout, sprinkler; aeroplane, jumbo, plane; *spec*: black lignite (stone).
vb lit: gush, issue, rush, shoot, spew, spout, spray, squirt; fly (by jet aircraft).
adj lit: black, ebony, glossy black; *fig*: moneyed, rich, wealthy.

jettison
vb lit: chuck out, discard, dump, heave over the side, throw away, throw overboard; abandon, eject, give up, reject, scrap.

jetty
n lit: mole, pier; dock, hythe, quay, wharf; harbour wall; breakwater, groyne.

jewel
n lit: gemstone, precious stone; brilliant, rock, sparkler; *fig*: gem, paragon, pearl, prize, treasure; find, marvel, rarity, wonder.
vb lit: adorn, beautify, bejewel, deck, decorate, ornament.

jewellery
n lit: gems, gemstones, precious stones; brilliants, rocks, sparklers; finery, ornaments, regalia, trinkets; bracelets, brooches, pendants, rings, tiaras; diamonds, pearls.

jib

n lit: bow-sail, foremast-sail; boom, gantry; *fig*: appearance, demeanour, face.
vb lit: balk, recoil, refuse, shrink, stop short; *spec*: gybe, tack (of a sailing-boat).

jingle

n lit: chink, chinking, clang, clanking, jangle, ringing, tinkling, tintinnabulation; chiming; catch, doggerel, simple rhyme; musical slogan; *spec*: (horse-drawn) sulky, surrey.
vb lit: chime, chink, clang, clank, jangle, ring, tinkle, tintinnabulate; rhyme, write simple verse.

jink

n lit: dodge, swerve, twist, turn; feint, pass.
vb lit: dodge, duck, elude, evade, outmanoeuvre, swerve, twist, turn, veer.

jinx

n lit: bringer of bad luck, evil omen, ill fortune, Jonah, unlucky star; curse, evil eye, hex, hoodoo, spell; black magic, voodoo.
vb lit: be unlucky for, bring misfortune to; curse, hex, illwish, put a spell on, put the evil eye on.

jittery

adj lit: jumpy, nervous, shaky; anxious, worried; agitated, flustered; fidgety, in a state.

job

n lit: appointment, assignment, calling, career, charge, duty, employment, function, livelihood, métier, occupation, office, position, post, profession, role, situation, task, vocation, work; affair, business, concern, responsibility; enterprise, piece of work, undertaking, venture; finished product, output, product; act, deed, feat; criminal act, felony; *fig*: embezzlement, fraud.
vb lit: buy and sell, deal in, trade in; hire out, let, rent.

jockey

n lit: horse-rider, rider; presenter, player; operator.
vb lit: jostle, nudge, ride against; *fig*: engineer, manage, manipulate, manoeuvre; finagle, inveigle, worm.

jocular

adj lit: amusing, cheerful, comical, droll, funny, gay, genial, good-humoured, humorous, jocose, jocund, joking, jolly,

jovial, merry, waggish, witty; facetious, flippant, jokey, mischievous, playful, roguish, teasing, tongue-in-cheek, whimsical.

jog

n lit: canter, slow run, trot; excursion, outing, short trip.
vb lit: bounce, jar, jerk, jiggle, joggle, jolt, jostle, jounce, knock, nudge, prod, push, rock, shake, vibrate; canter, lope, trot; *fig*: arouse, prompt, stimulate, stir; urge.

join

n lit: junction, seal, seam, suture, union; overlap.
vb lit: cement, combine, connect, couple, fasten together, knit, link, put together, tie together, unite, yoke together; accompany, affiliate with, associate with, converge, get together with, move to be with; adhere, stick together; add, annex, append; enlist, enrol, enter, sign; abut, border on, meet, reach, touch.

joint

n lit: articulation, hinge; connection, interface, intersection, junction, node, seam, union; section, segment; cut, roast; *fig*: dive, low dive; marijuana cigarette, reefer.
vb lit: articulate, connect, couple, fasten together, fit together, link, unite; butcher, carve, cleave, cut up, disarticulate, dismember, dissect.
adj lit: collective, combined, communal, concerted, co-operative, shared, united; mutual.

joke

n lit: gag, jest, pun, quip, wisecrack; bit of fun, jape, lark, prank; butt, laughing-stock, target; absurdity, nonsense.
vb lit: banter, be amusing, be funny, be witty, jest, quip, tell gags, wisecrack; be facetious, chaff, kid, lark about, tease.

joker

n lit: buffoon, clown, jester; comedian, comic, humorist, wag, wit; prankster, trickster; wild card; *fig*: contingency, unforeseen factor.

jolly

n lit: festivity, jollification, merriment; *fig*: flattery, gratification, humouring; *spec*: marine (soldier).
vb lit: flatter, gratify, humour; coax, wheedle; kid, tease.
adj lit: cheerful, convivial, frolicsome, gay, genial, jocund, jovial, merry,

mirthful; carefree, playful; agreeable, delightful, pleasant.
adv lit: extremely, very.

jostle
vb lit: bump, collide with, elbow, jar, jiggle, jog, joggle, press against, push against, shove, squeeze; crowd, hustle, throng.

jot
n lit: atom, bit, fraction, iota, particle, scintilla, scrap, shred, smidgeon, whit; crumb, detail, grain, mite, morsel, speck, trace, trifle, whisper.
vb lit: note (down), pen, put (down), scrawl, scribble, set (down), write (down).

journal
n lit: magazine, monthly, periodical, weekly; daybook, diary, log, record, register; newspaper.

journalist
n lit: columnist, correspondent, editor, feature-writer, hack, newspaperman, reporter, scribe, stringer, subeditor; broadcaster, commentator, newscaster; chronicler, diary-writer, record-keeper.

journey
n lit: excursion, expedition, jaunt, odyssey, outing, tour, trek, trip, voyage; pilgrimage; peregrination, ramble, travels, wanderings.
vb lit: drive, go, move, ride, tour, travel, trek, voyage, wend; ramble, roam, rove, wander; make one's way, proceed, progress.

jowls
n lit: chin, jaw; double chin; dewlap, wattle.

joy
n lit: delight, elation, exultation, felicity, gladness, happiness, pleasure, satisfaction; bliss, ecstasy, exaltation, rapture.
vb lit: delight, exult, rejoice; enrapture, gladden, please.

joyful
adj lit: delighted, elated, exultant, happy; blissful, ecstatic, exalted, enraptured, jubilant, rapturous, transported; glad, gratified, pleased, satisfied; delightful, gladdening, gratifying, pleasing, ravishing.

joyous
adj lit: beatific, ecstatic, exalted, jubilant; cheerful, joyful, rapturous; festive, gladsome, merry; elating, gladdening, heartening, pleasing.

jubilant
adj lit: elated, euphoric, exultant, joyous, triumphal, triumphant; rejoicing, shouting for joy, thrilled; cock-a-hoop, over the moon.

jubilation
n lit: celebration, elation, euphoria, exultation, festivity, joy, rejoicing, triumph; applause, cheering, clapping, ovation.

jubilee
n lit: anniversary, celebration, festival, festive occasion, festivity; season of joy, time of rejoicing.

Judas
n lit: betrayer, false friend, traitor; *spec*: peep-hole in a door.

judge
n lit: beak, bench, deemster, justice of the peace, magistrate, m'lud; appraiser, arbiter, assessor, evaluator, adjudicator, arbitrator, authority, referee, umpire; moderator.
vb lit: dispense justice, hear, sit in judgement on, try; decree, deem, declare, find, pass sentence of, pronounce sentence, rule, sentence; adjudge, appraise, assess, conclude, consider, deduce, determine, discern, estimate, evaluate, rate, suppose, think, value, weigh up; adjudicate, arbitrate, decide, distinguish, differentiate, mediate, referee, settle, umpire.

judgement
n lit: reason, reasoning; acumen, common sense, discernment, discretion, discrimination, penetration, percipience, prudence, sense, shrewdness, taste, understanding, wisdom; appraisal, assessment, conclusion, consideration, deduction, estimation, evaluation, valuation; arbitration, decision, decree, finding, opinion, view; ruling, sentence, settlement, verdict; doom, fate; punishment, retribution.

judicial
adj lit: administrative, court, judiciary, juridical, statutory; judge-like, magisterial; critical, discretionary,

discriminating; fair, impartial, objective, unbiased, unprejudiced.

judicious
adj lit: astute, discerning, discreet, discriminating, enlightened, informed, prudent, sagacious, sensible, shrewd, thoughtful, well-advised, wise; diplomatic, expedient, politic; careful, cautious, circumspect, considered, deliberate, wary; accurate, exacting.

jug
n lit: crock, ewer, pitcher; carafe, jar, urn; pot; coffee-pot; mug, tankard; *fig*: cells, jail, prison.
vb lit: boil, steam, stew; *fig*: imprison, incarcerate, jail.

juggle
vb lit: do tricks (with), throw and catch; be dextrous (with), manipulate; conjure (with), use sleight of hand; balance, carry with difficulty, tote; *fig*: alter, change, modify; cook, doctor, falsify, fix, tamper (with); play tricks (with); compare, consider, keep in the air, ponder, weigh up.

juice
n lit: sap; extract, liquor, nectar; enzyme, secretion, serum; fluid, liquid; petrol; current, electricity; *fig*: piquancy; crux, essence, nub.
vb fig: brighten (up), liven (up).

juicy
adj lit: sappy, succulent, watery, wet; *fig*: colourful, lively, racy, sensational, spicy, vivid; lurid, provocative, risqué, suggestive; lush, richly textured.

jumble
n lit: clutter, disarray, disorder, hodgepodge, hotchpotch, mess, mishmash, muddle; confusion, farrago, mixture; bric-à-brac, rummage.
vb lit: disarrange, disorder, mix, shuffle; confuse, disorganize, muddle; dishevel, entangle, tangle; be mixed, be shuffled.

jumbo
adj lit: elephantine, mammoth; extra-large, giant, outsized; colossal, enormous, gigantic, huge, immense, massive; *spec*: Boeing-747 aircraft.

jump
n lit: bound, leap, spring, vault; hop, skip; bounce, jerk, jolt, lurch, start; ditch, fence, hurdle, obstacle; break, gap,

hiatus, interval, space; boost, hike, increase, rise, upturn; *fig*: advantage.
vb lit: bound, clear, leap, spring, vault; hop, hurdle, skip; bounce, jerk, jolt, kangaroo, lurch, start; avoid, dodge, evade, get away from, leave, run away from; leave out, miss, omit, pass over; ascend, be boosted, escalate, increase, mount, rise, surge; ambush, pounce on, surprise; *fig*: agree (with), coincide (with); *spec*: raise (in poker).

jumpy
adj lit: jittery, nervous, on edge, tense; anxious, worried; agitated, fidgety, flustered, in a state, nervy; highly-strung, restless.

junction
n lit: joint, seal, seam, suture; connection, coupling, join, linking; crossing, crossroads, intersection; convergence, merging, union; contact, node; border, edge, interface.

juncture
n lit: moment, point, state of affairs, time; crisis, crux, emergency, exigency, predicament, strait; junction.

jungle
n lit: overgrowth, thicket, tropical forest, wilderness; *fig*: jumble, mass, tangle; ghetto, slums; rat-race.

junior
n lit: adolescent, child, juvenile, minor, young person; younger person; assistant, trainee; inferior, subordinate.
adj lit: younger; inferior, lesser, lower, minor, subordinate.

junk
n lit: bric-à-brac, odds and ends, rummage, scrap, trash; clutter, debris, litter, refuse, rubbish, waste; *fig*: nonsense, old rope; *spec*: Chinese vessel; drugs, narcotics; salt tack.
vb lit: scrap, throw away; abandon, discard, reject.

jurisdiction
n lit: authority, power, rule; command, control, direction, dominion, mandate, supervision, sway; district, province; area, compass, field, range, sphere, zone.

jury
n lit: adjudicators, assessors, arbitrators, examiners, judges; committee, panel, tribunal.

just

adj lit: equitable, fair, honest. impartial, right, unbiased, unprejudiced; appropriate, apt, deserved, due, fitting, merited, proper, suitable; accurate, correct, exact, precise, true; decent, good, honourable, righteous, upright; lawful, legal, legitimate.

adv lit: but, merely, only, simply, solely; barely, hardly, scarcely, with difficulty; in the immediate past, lately, recently; absolutely, entirely, exactly, perfectly, precisely, positively, quite, truly; a little, slightly.

justice

n lit: equity, fairness, honesty, impartiality, rightness; integrity, reason, rectitude, truth; judge, judiciary, law, magistrate; integrity; amends, compensation, correction, recompense, redress, reparation.

justification

n lit: grounds, rationale, reason, warrant; defence, excuse, explanation, rationalization; vindication; *spec*: alignment, ranging (lines of type); redemption, salvation (in theology).

justify

vb lit: explain, prove reasonable, validate, warrant; defend, excuse, legitimize, uphold; clear, exculpate, vindicate; *spec*: align, range (lines of type); be the salvation of, redeem (in theology); prove acceptable (in law).

jut

vb lit: overhang, project, protrude, stick out; bulge, extend, stand out.

juvenile

n lit: child; boy, girl; adolescent, minor, youth; youngster.

adj lit: young, youthful; babyish, childish, infantile, puerile; callow, immature, inexperienced, undeveloped, unsophisticated; young-looking.

K

kaput
adj lit: broken, destroyed, ruined, smashed, unserviceable, useless; dead, done, finished; outmoded, out of fashion.

keel
n lit: girder, spine, strut; ridge; *fig*: disposition; *spec*: basic longitudinal member of a ship's hull.
vb lit: collapse, faint, pass out, topple; capsize, founder, overturn, upset; careen.

keen
vb lit: bewail, lament, mourn, wail.
adj lit: avid, eager, enthusiastic, fervent, intense, zealous; ardent, devoted, impassioned, passionate; cutting, edged, honed, incisive, penetrating, piercing, pointed, sharp; biting, bitter; acute, astute, canny, clever, discerning, discriminating, perceptive, perspicacious, quick, shrewd; sensitive; *fig*: sardonic, satirical, tart, trenchant.

keep
n lit: board, livelihood, living, maintenance, subsistence; castle, donjon, fastness, fortress, stronghold, tower.
vb lit: carry, conserve, have, hold, possess, reserve, retain, stock, store, own; accumulate, heap, pile, stack; care for, defend, guard, look after, maintain, mind, preserve, protect, shelter, shield, tend, watch over; conduct, manage, operate, run; board, foster, nurture, support, sustain; arrest, constrain, detain, hold back, impede, prevent, refrain, restrain, stall; block, check, curb, delay, deter, hamper, hinder, inhibit, limit, obstruct, retard; be, carry (on), continue, endure, persevere, persist, remain, stay; last, survive; *fig*: adhere to, celebrate, commemorate, observe, perform; comply with, fulfil, honour, obey, respect.

keeper
n lit: attendant, caretaker, curator, custodian, guardian; gaoler, guard, jailer, overseer, superintendent, warden, warder; defender, preserver; owner, possessor, proprietor; *spec*: armature (of a magnet); clasp, catch, socket (of a lock).

keeping
n lit: care, charge, custody, guardianship, possession, preservation, protection, reservation, retention; accord, accordance, agreement, conformity, consistency, correspondence, harmony, proportion; adherence, celebration, commemoration, observance, performance.

keep on
vb lit: carry on, continue, last, persevere, persist; endure, remain, stay; *fig*: chatter, go on, nag, reiterate, repeat.

keepsake
n lit: memento, reminder, souvenir, token; relic, remembrance.

keep up
vb lit: continue, maintain, persevere, preserve, retain, sustain; balance, equal, match, parallel, rival, stay with; maintain, prop, support.

keg
n lit: barrel, cask, drum, tun, vat.

kerchief
n lit: headscarf, scarf; handkerchief.

kerfuffle
n lit: ado, agitation, bother, bustle, commotion, confusion, disorder, flap, fracas, furore, fuss, pandemonium, rumpus, to-do, turmoil, uproar.

kernel
n lit: core, germ, heart, marrow, pith, seed; essence, gist, nub, substance; focus, nucleus.

key
n lit: doorkey, latchkey, opener, winder; spanner, tuner; ivory, lever, note; bolt, filler, pin, wedge; capstone; character, letter; octave, register, scale, tonal system; caption, explanation, legend, scheme; answer, interpretation, solution, translation; clue, cue, hint, indicator,

lead, pointer, sign, signal; focus, hub, pivot.
vb lit: fasten, lock; adjust, loosen, tighten, tune, turn, wind up; differentiate, distinguish, encode, identify, mark, mark out, mark up; align, attune; excite, nerve, stimulate.
adj lit: controlling, crucial, deciding, decisive, essential, pivotal, vital; basic, fundamental, major, principal.

kick
n lit: boot, punt; hack, hoof; jerk, jolt, jump; *fig*: drive, force, power, punch, strength, verve, vigour, zest; opposition, resilience, resistance; potency, pungency; boost, buzz, excitement, fillip, stimulation, stimulus, thrill; enjoyment, gratification, pleasure; binge, craze, fad, phase, vogue; *spec*: recoil (of a gun).
vb lit: boot, hack, hoof, sidefoot, toe; jerk, jolt, jump, thresh; *fig*: complain, gripe, grumble, protest, rebel; abandon, break, give up, leave off, quit.

kickback
n lit: bribe, bribery, extortion, protection money; commission, interest, perks, surcharge; backlash, reaction, recoil, repercussion, ricochet.

kick-off
n lit: opening gambit, opening move; beginning, commencement, initiation, opening, outset, start.

kid
n lit: child, infant, tot, young goat, youngster; boy, girl; bairn; teenager; *spec*: goat-leather.
vb lit: bamboozle, deceive, delude, fool, hoax, hoodwink, pretend, trick; banter, joke, rag, tease.

kidnap
vb lit: abduct, hijack, hold to ransom, skyjack, take hostage; carry off, seize, steal.

kill
n lit: game, prey, quarry; death, destruction, elimination, end; *fig*: coup de grâce, end-play, final stroke.
vb lit: assassinate, butcher, dispatch, do away with, execute, extirpate, massacre, murder, put down, put to death, slaughter, slay; bump off, do in, get rid of, knock off, liquidate, neutralize, rub out, terminate with extreme prejudice, waste; annihilate, destroy, eliminate,

eradicate, exterminate, obliterate; *fig*: cancel, quash, scotch, suppress, veto; bring to an end, end, halt, stall, still, stop, terminate; quell, smother, stifle; delete, discard, reject; defeat, overcome, overwhelm, ruin, spoil; fritter away, spend, use up, waste, while away; *spec*: reduce (in metal refining).

killer
n lit: assassin, cutthroat, gunman, hitman, murderer, slayer; butcher, slaughterer; executioner; destroyer, exterminator, liquidator, neutralizer.

killing
n lit: assassination, carnage, cull, execution, extirpation, fatality, genocide, homicide, massacre, murder, slaughter, slaying; annihilation, destruction, elimination, extermination, obliteration; game, prey, quarry; *fig*: cancellation, quashing, scotching, suppression, vetoing; ending, halting, stopping, termination; bomb, coup, fortune, gain, profit.
adj lit: deadly, deathly, fatal, lethal, mortal, murderous; destructive; *fig*: arduous, debilitating, exhausting, fatiguing, gruelling, punishing, strenuous, tiring; hilarious, uproarious; fascinating, irresistible.

kin
n lit: clan, family, folks, kith, relations, relatives, stock, tribe; blood, connections; affinity, consanguinity, relationship.
adj lit: consanguine, related, tied; akin, allied, cognate.

kind
n lit: brand, category, class, make, sort, style, type, variety; breed, family, genus, ilk, race, species, strain; character, description, fashion, manner, nature, stamp; *spec*: goods, produce (in bartering).
adj lit: beneficent, benevolent, benign, charitable, generous, liberal, munificent, philanthropic; compassionate, considerate, friendly, humane, humanitarian, loving, obliging, sympathetic, tender, thoughtful, understanding; affectionate, amicable, congenial, cordial, courteous, gentle, good, gracious, indulgent.

kindle
vb lit: fire, ignite, light, set fire to; *fig*:

arouse, excite, inflame, stimulate, stir; animate, awaken, bestir, rouse; foment, incite, induce, inspire; cause, provoke, start; become excited, be roused; brighten, illuminate, light up.

kindliness
n lit: benevolence, charity, compassion, consideration, friendliness, helpfulness, humanitarianism, humanity, love, sympathy, tenderness, thoughtfulness, understanding, warmth; amiability, congeniality, cordiality, courtesy, geniality, gentility, goodness, indulgence.

kindling
n lit: firewood, tinder, wood; billets, faggots, logs; fuel.

kindly
adj lit: benevolent, charitable, compassionate, considerate, friendly, helpful, humane, humanitarian, loving, sympathetic, tender, thoughtful, understanding, warm; agreeable, amiable, amicable, congenial, cordial, courteous, genial, gentle, good, indulgent, pleasant.
adv lit: affectionately, benevolently, benignly, compassionately, congenially, considerately, helpfully, humanely, sympathetically, tenderly, thoughtfully, warmly; agreeably, genially.

kindness
n lit: altruism, beneficence, benevolence, benignity, charity, generosity, goodness, hospitality, liberality, magnanimity, munificence, philanthropy; compassion, consideration, friendliness, friendship, humanitarianism, humanity, love, sympathy, tenderness, thoughtfulness, understanding; affection, indulgence; favour, good deed, good turn, kindly act, service.

king
n lit: head of state, monarch, ruler, sovereign; emperor, overlord, prince; his majesty; *fig*: best, greatest; magnate, supremo, tycoon.

kingdom
n lit: dominion, nation, realm, state, territory; monarchy, reign, sovereignty; *fig*: area, classification, division, domain, field, province, sphere.

kink
n lit: angle, bend, coil, crimp, curve, loop, twist; cramp, crick, pinch, spasm, tweak; *fig*: complication, difficulty, hitch, knot, tangle; crotchet, eccentricity, foible, quirk, vagary, whim.
vb lit: bend, coil, crimp, curl, curve, loop, twist.

kinky
adj lit: bent, coiled, curved; crimped, curled, curly, frizzled, frizzy; *fig*: bizarre, cranky, eccentric, odd, peculiar, queer, quirky, strange, unconventional, weird, whimsical; degenerate, depraved, perverted, unnatural, twisted, warped.

kinship
n lit: affinity, blood relationship, blood ties, consanguinity; connection, relation, relationship; correspondence, resemblance, similarity.

kiosk
n lit: bookstall, booth, news-stand, stall, stand; callbox, telephone box; information bureau; ticket office.

kiss
n lit: buss, osculation; peck, smacker; greeting, salutation; *fig*: caress, contact, glance, graze, touch.
vb lit: buss, osculate; give a peck, peck; greet, salute; neck, smooch, snog; *fig*: alight on, land on; brush, caress, contact, glance off, graze, touch gently.

kit
n lit: apparatus, gear, impedimenta, outfit, paraphernalia, rig, tackle, trappings; accoutrements, effects, equipment, implements, instruments, tools, utensils; materials, parts, pieces, set; *spec*: bucket, pail, tub.
vb lit: accoutre, equip, fit, rig, tool set; furnish, provide, provision, supply.

knack
n lit: bent, facility, flair, gift, propensity, talent, trick; adeptness, aptitude, art, skill, technique, touch; ability, capacity; adroitness, dexterity.

knap
vb lit: break off, chip, flake, splinter, split; chop, hit, knock, rap, strike, tap; break up, dash, fracture, fragment, shatter; *fig*: bite, snap; nibble.

knapsack
n lit: backpack, haversack, kit-bag,
rucksack; duffel bag.

knave
n lit: blackguard, crook, deceiver,
miscreant, reprobate, rogue, scoundrel,
trickster, villain; imp, monkey,
rapscallion, rascal, scallywag, scamp,
scapegrace; *spec*: jack (in cards).

knavish
adj lit: base, crooked, deceptive,
dishonest, fraudulent, miscreant,
nefarious, reprobate, scoundrelly,
tricksy, tricky, unprincipled,
unscrupulous, villainous; impish,
naughty, rascally, roguish.

knead
vb lit: manhandle, manipulate, massage,
press, squeeze, stroke, work; form,
mould, shape; handle, knuckle; *fig*:
blend, join, mix in.

knell
n lit: chime, chiming, peal, ringing,
tolling; *fig*: death toll, funeral peal,
obituary.
vb lit: chime, peal, ring, sound, toll;
announce, herald, proclaim; call,
summon.

knickers
n lit: panties, underwear, undies;
bloomers, camiknickers, drawers, pants,
smalls.

knick-knacks
n lit: baubles, bibelots, bijouterie,
trinkets; bagatelles, gewgaws, gimcrack,
kickshaws; bric-à-brac, junk, rummage.

knife
n lit: blade, cutter, scalpel, steel; dagger,
dirk, poniard, sgian dubh, stiletto.
vb lit: cut, lacerate, pierce, slash, stab,
wound; *fig*: betray, undermine; impale,
penetrate, slice.

knit
vb lit: interlace, intertwine, link up, loop
together, tie, weave; affix, bind, cement,
connect, join, secure, unite; heal, mend;
consolidate, firm up; *fig*: crease, furrow,
wrinkle.

knob
n lit: doorhandle, handle, projection; boss,
button, stud; bump, lump, nodule,
protrusion, protuberance, swelling;
knot.

knock
n lit: blow, box, buffet, hit, punch, rap,
smack, thump; *fig*: censure, criticism;
rebuff, reversal, setback; arrest; *spec*: bat,
innings (in cricket); pinking, rattle (of an
engine).
vb lit: box, buffet, clap, clip, cuff, drive,
hammer, hit, punch, rap, smack, strike,
thump, whack; daze, stun; *fig*: belittle,
disparage, run down; censure, criticize,
condemn; *spec*: pink, rattle (of an
engine).

knock off
vb lit: decrease by, deduct, subtract, take
off; *fig*: go home, relax, rest, stop work,
take a rest; complete, conclude, finish,
terminate; build, construct, form, make,
put together; filch, nab, nick, pilfer,
pinch, purloin, shoplift, steal;
assassinate, bump off, do in, get rid of,
kill, liquidate, murder, rub out, waste.

knockout
n lit: blockbuster, coup de grâce, grand
slam, kill, KO, slam; victory; defeat; *fig*:
hit, sensation, smash, success, triumph;
beauty, cracker, dish, dream, peach,
vision.
adj lit: stunning; disqualifying; *fig*: hit,
outstanding, overwhelming, sensational,
smash, triumphant; amazing, fabulous,
unbelievable.

knoll
n lit: hillock, hummock, hump, mound,
tell, tump, tumulus.

knot
n lit: bond, bow, joint, ligature;
aggregation, assembly, band, bunch,
circle, clique, clump, cluster, collection,
company, gang, group, squad; mare's
nest, mess, tangle; complexity, focus,
node; bulge, bump, concretion, knob,
lump, swelling; *spec*: nautical mile per
hour, type of wading bird.
vb lit: bind, knit, loop, secure, tether, tie,
weave; entangle, snarl, tangle, twist;
bunch, harden, tighten.

know
vb lit: be acquainted with, be familiar
with, recognize; be assured of, be aware
of, be certain of, be informed of, be sure
of, comprehend, have learned, have
memorized, realize, understand;
apprehend, grasp, learn, perceive, see;
differentiate, discern, distinguish,
identify, make out, tell; experience, feel,

undergo; *spec*: have sexual intercourse with.

knowing
adj (pr.pt) lit: aware, conscious, deliberate, intended, intentional; competent, enlightened, expert, qualified, skilful, well-informed; acute, astute, clever, cunning, intelligent, perceptive, shrewd; eloquent, expressive, meaningful, significant.

knowledge
n lit: enlightenment, experience, learning, wisdom; education, instruction, scholarship, schooling, tuition; erudition, intelligence, science; ability, acquaintance, awareness, certainty, comprehension, consciousness, discernment, familiarity, grasp, intimacy, perception, recognition, understanding; cognizance, information, notice; *spec*: sexual intercourse.

knowledgeable
adj lit: competent, educated, enlightened, experienced, expert, familiar, qualified, skilful, well-informed; astute, clever, intelligent; aware, conversant, erudite, learned, scholarly.

known
adj (pa.pt) lit: acknowledged, admitted, avowed, overt, patent; celebrated, commonplace, famous, noted, popular, recognized, well-known; common, familiar, obvious, plain; certain, distinct, established, factual, sure; called, named.

kowtow
vb lit: abase oneself, bow down, grovel, humble oneself, prostrate oneself; *fig*: accede, acquiesce, capitulate, defer, give in, give way, knuckle under, submit, surrender, yield; be obsequious, be servile, fawn, truckle.

kudos
n lit: admiration, cachet, credit, esteem, estimation, fame, glory, honour, praise, prestige, renown, status.

L

label
n lit: marker, name-tag, tab, tag, ticket, trademark; *fig*: category, classification, description, designation, name, stamp; *spec*: codicil (to a legal document); dripstone (in architecture).
vb lit: brand, identify, mark, name, tag; *fig*: characterize, categorize, classify, describe, designate; *spec*: irradiate (in physics)

laborious
adj lit: arduous, effortful, grinding, painstaking, strenuous, taxing, toilsome; *fig*: difficult, heavy, ponderous, slow.

labour
n lit: effort, exertion, industry, toil, travail, work; employees, hands, taskforce, workers, workforce; *fig*: burden, chore, drudgery, job, task; *spec*: birth, birth pangs, childbirth, contractions, delivery (of a baby).
vb lit: plug on at, slave, strain, strive, toil, travail, work; *fig*: drudge; *spec*: make heavy weather of, pitch, roll (of a ship at sea); overdo, over-elaborate (in speech).

laboured
adj (pa.pt) lit: artificial, contrived, forced, overdone, over-elaborate, stilted, strained, wooden.

labyrinthine
adj lit: coiled, convoluted, maze-like, sinuous, tortuous, winding; *fig*: complex, complicated, entangled, intricate.

lace
n lit: braid, chiffon, crochetwork, netting, tatting; cord, string, thong, tie.
vb lit: braid, do up, entwine, fasten, interweave, string, thread, tie; *fig*: thrash; *spec*: add in, drug, fortify, mix in, nobble, spike (food or drink).

lacerate
vb lit: cut, gash, rip, slash, slice, tear, wound.

laceration
n lit: cut, gash, incision, rent, rip, slash, tear, wound.

lack
n lit: absence, dearth, deficiency, deficit, deprivation, famine, need, scarcity, shortage, shortfall, want.
vb lit: be without, do without, fail, miss, need, want.

lackadaisical
adj lit: abstracted, dreaming, dreamy, flaccid, languid, languorous, listless, spiritless; *fig*: careless, idle, indifferent, lazy, lethargic, shiftless.

lackey
n lit: attendant, dogsbody, flunkey, footman, manservant, menial, minion, servant, steward; *fig*: flatterer, sycophant, toady, tool, yes-man.

lacking
adj (pr.pt) lit: absent, defective, deficient, inadequate, missing, short, wanting.

lacklustre
adj lit: boring, drab, dull, flat, lifeless, uninspired, vapid.

laconic
adj lit: brief, concise, condensed, curt, pithy, sententious, short, succinct, terse.

lacquer
n lit: coating, shellac, varnish; glaze, gloss, sheen, veneer.
vb lit: coat, glaze, varnish; *spec*: spray (in hairdressing)

lacrimose
adj lit: crying, tearful, weepy; *fig*: grief-torn, lugubrious, maudlin, melancholy, mournful, sad.

lacuna
n lit: gap, hiatus, interval, space; *fig*: cavity, depression, dip, hole, hollow, pit; omission; *spec*: interstice (between the cells of an organism).

lad
n lit: boy, chap, fellow, guy, son, youngster, youth; *fig*: rebel, reveller, roisterer, wide boy.

laden
adj (pa.pt) lit: burdened, encumbered, full, loaded, lumbered, oppressed, weighed down.

ladylike
adj lit: effeminate, feminine, genteel; *fig*: courteous, delicate, demure, gentle, refined, soft.

lag
vb lit: dawdle, drop back, fall back, fall behind, linger, loiter, straggle, tarry, trail; *spec*: brace, insert struts, prop from inside, reinforce (a cylinder); insulate, pack round (a pipe or tank).

laggard
n lit: dawdler, lingerer, slowcoach, sluggard, snail, straggler; *fig*: idler, layabout, loafer, lounger, slacker.

lagoon
n lit: lake, pond, pool, shallows.

laid-back
adj lit: casual, relaxed, unhurried; *fig*: slow, suave, unemotional.

lair
n lit: den, nest, refuge, retreat; *fig*: base, harbour, haven, hideaway, home, sanctuary, shelter, stronghold.

lake
n lit: dam, loch, mere, pond, pool, tarn; *fig*: reservoir, store.

lambast
vb lit: beat, drub, give a thrashing, thrash; *fig*: be scathing, carpet, pan, slate, tear into.

lame
vb lit: cripple, disable, injure, maim, nobble, wound.
adj lit: crippled, disabled, game, gammy, halt, handicapped, hobbling, injured, limping, maimed, wounded; *fig*: defective, feeble, flimsy, imperfect, inadequate, insufficient, pathetic, poor, unconvincing, weak.

lament
n lit: complaint, moan; dirge, elegy, threnody, wake.
vb lit: bemoan, bewail, cry about, keen, mourn, sorrow, wail; *fig*: deplore, regret.

lamentable
adj lit: deplorable, distressing, pathetic, pitiable, pitiful, regrettable, tragic; distressed, miserable, low, meagre, poor, unfortunate, wretched.

lamentation
n lit: complaining, crying, grieving, keening, lament, moan, moaning, mourning, sorrowing, wailing, weeping.

lamp
n lit: flashlight, headlight, lantern, light, sidelight, torch; *fig*: eye.

lampoon
n lit: burlesque, caricature, parody, satire, send-up, skit, spoof, take-off.
vb lit: ape, caricature, mimic, mock, parody, pillory, ridicule, satirize, send up, spoof, take off.

land
n lit: country, district, nation, realm, region; countryside, ground, soil, terrain, tract; domain, estate, grounds, property, real estate, territory.
vb lit: alight, disembark, dock, touch down; *fig*: arrive, end up; acquire, attain, gain, get, obtain, secure, win; *spec*: get in, plant (a punch).

landlord
n lit: lease-holder, owner, proprietor; host, hotel-keeper, innkeeper.

landmark
n lit: indicator, marker, milestone, pointer, signpost; feature, monument; *fig*: event, happening, turning-point.

landslide
n lit: avalanche, landslip, rockfall.
adj fig: decisive, overwhelming, runaway.

lane
n lit: alley, passage, path, road, sidestreet, street, track; channel, course.

language
n lit: argot, dialect, jargon, lingo, patois, tongue; diction, expression, idiom, phraseology, phrasing, speech, terminology, vocabulary, wording, words; oratory, rhetoric, semantics, style; *fig*: alphabet, cipher, code, system; *spec*: gestures, indications, movements (of the body, instinctually).

languid
adj lit: faint, feeble, flagging, inert, limp, listless, slack, spiritless, torpid, weak, wearied; *fig*: apathetic, lethargic, unenthused.

languish
vb lit: decline, droop, fade, faint, flag, slacken, waste away, weaken, weary, wilt, wither; fail; endure, have a hard time, pine, suffer.

languor
n lit: ennui, inertia, lassitude, listlessness, weakness, weariness; quietness, stillness;

softness, tenderness; *fig*: apathy,
indifference, lethargy.

lank
adj lit: drooping, flabby, flaccid, limp,
straggling; gaunt, lean, scrawny, skinny,
slender, slim, thin.

lanky
adj lit: gangling, long, tall, ungainly,
weedy; lean, scrawny, skinny, thin.

lap
n lit: circuit, loop, orbit, round, tour; *fig*:
part, section, stage.
vb lit: circle, make a circuit, loop, orbit;
gently splash, ripple, slap, wash against;
lick up, suck up, sip, sup; *fig*: enjoy, love.

lapse
n lit: error, failure, fault, faux pas,
mistake, slip; indiscretion, solecism;
duration, interval, period; apostasy.
vb lit: become invalid, become void,
expire, pass, run out, stop, terminate;
decline, drop, fail, fall away, fall into
disuse, stop going, tail off; fall back, sink
back; apostasize.

lapsed
adj (pa.pt) lit: discontinued, invalid,
expired, run out, stopped, terminated;
former, past; gone, over, passed.

larceny
n lit: burglary, misappropriation,
purloining, robbery, stealing, theft,
thievery.

large
adj lit: big, colossal, cyclopean, enormous,
extensive, giant, gigantic, great, huge,
immense, massive, monumental,
substantial, vast; *fig*: expansive, grand;
spec: fair, favourable (for ships at sea).

largesse
n lit: alms, bounty, charity, generosity,
liberality, munificence, philanthropy;
donation, endowment, gift, present.

lark
n lit: antic, caper, escapade, frolic, fun,
jape, joke, prank, romp; type of bird.
vb lit: antic, be mischievous, cavort, frolic,
play, rollick, romp.

lascivious
adj lit: concupiscent, lecherous, lewd,
libidinous, lustful, wanton;
promiscuous; *fig*: erotic.

lash
n lit: blow, hit, stroke; stripe, weal; *spec*:

ferocity, force, severity (of a person's
tongue); sweep, swing, swirl, swish (of
an animal's tail).
vb lit: attach together, bind, fasten, join,
secure, tie up; beat, birch, flagellate, flog,
lay into, scourge, thrash, whip; *fig*:
castigate, censure, criticize, lambast,
rebuke, scold, upbraid; *spec*: beat down,
cascade, pour (with rain); sweep, swing,
swirl, swish (of an animal's tail).

lassitude
n lit: exhaustion, faintness, fatigue,
languor, lethargy, prostration, weakness,
weariness; *fig*: resignation.

last
n lit: concluding one, ending one, final
one, terminating one; close, conclusion,
end, final time, termination; *spec*: final
breath (at death).
vb lit: continue, endure, go on, hold out,
keep going, persist, remain, survive; be
enough, suffice.
adj lit: closing, concluding, ending,
extreme, final, latest, lattermost,
rearmost, terminal, ultimate, utmost.
adv lit: afterwards, finally, most recently,
ultimately.

last-ditch
adj lit: all-out, desperate, epic, final,
rearguard.

lasting
adj (pr.pt) lit: durable, enduring,
indelible, long-standing, perennial,
permanent, remanent, undying; abiding,
consistent, continual, continuous,
ongoing, perpetual, viable.

late
adj lit: behindhand, overdue, slow, tardy,
unpunctual; dead, deceased, departed,
erstwhile, former, last, old, past,
preceding, previous; fresh, modern,
new, recent.
adv lit: after hours, behindhand,
belatedly, dilatorily, over time, tardily,
unpunctually.

lately
adv lit: freshly, just now, newly, recently.

later
adj lit: following, next, subsequent,
succeeding, successive.
adv lit: afterwards, subsequently,
thereafter.

latest
adj lit: contemporary, current, modern,

most recent, newest, topical, up-to-date; fashionable, in, modish, trendy.

lather

n lit: bubbles, foam, froth, soapsuds, suds; *fig*: fever, flap, fluster, frenzy, state, sweat.

vb lit: foam, froth, soap; *fig*: beat, cane, drub, flog, thrash.

latitude

n lit: allowance, amplitude, compass, extent, leeway, range, reach, room, scope, space, width; freedom, laxity, liberty, licence, play; *spec*: perpendicular distance (from the equator, from the ecliptic).

lattice

n lit: grid, grille, mesh, network, tracery, trellis; *spec*: geometrical pattern (of molecules, atoms or ions in a crystal; of nuclear materials in a reactor); grid (over navigational chart); partially ordered set (in mathematics), any two elements of which have restricted bounds.

laudable

adj lit: admirable, commendable, creditable, estimable, meritorious, praiseworthy.

laugh

n lit: cackle, chortle, chuckle, giggle, guffaw, roar, titter; *fig*: bit of fun, hoot, joke, lark, scream; card, clown, comedian, comic, wag, wit.

vb lit: be amused, be convulsed, cackle, chortle, chuckle, crease up, giggle, guffaw, roar, split one's sides.

laughable

adj lit: absurd, ludicrous, nonsensical, preposterous, ridiculous; *fig*: contemptible, derisory.

laughter

n lit: cachinnation, cackling, chortling, chuckling, giggling, guffawing, hilarity, jocularity, laughing, mirth, tittering.

launch

n lit: boat, cutter, dinghy, shallop, sloop, vessel; beginning, commencement, debut, establishing, floating, flotation, inauguration, send-off, setting out, start; discharge, firing off.

vb lit: despatch, discharge, fire, fling, project, propel, push out, put forth, send off, send out, set going, throw, throw out; begin, commence, embark upon, inaugurate, initiate, open, set off, set out,

start, take off; dive, jump, rush at; *spec*: promote, publish (a new book or programme).

lavatory

n lit: bathroom, bog, cloakroom, convenience, Gents, john, Ladies, little room, loo, powder room, privy, public convenience, toilet, washroom, water closet, WC; *spec*: heads (on navy ships).

lavish

vb lit: deluge, heap, pour, shower, spare no expense with, surround with; expend, use to the full; *fig*: squander, waste.

adj lit: abundant, bountiful, copious, effusive, generous, liberal, plentiful, profuse, prolific; *fig*: exaggerated, excessive, extravagant, immoderate, improvident, intemperate, overdone, prodigal, superfluous, unrestrained, wasteful.

law

n lit: act, canon, codex, jurisprudence, ordinance, regulation, rule, statute; axiom, precept; commandment, decree, edict, order; *fig*: legal proceedings, police; *spec*: Mosaic code (of the Pentateuch); principle (in science).

law-abiding

adj lit: decent, dutiful, honest, lawful, obedient, orderly, peaceable, upright.

lawful

adj lit: allowed, authorized, constitutional, legal, legitimate, licit, permissible, permitted, rightful, sanctioned, statutory.

lawless

adj lit: anarchic, disorderly, insurgent, rebellious, riotous, seditious, ungovernable, unruly, wild; criminal, nefarious, outlawed, shady; uncontrolled, unrestrained.

lawyer

n lit: advocate, attorney, barrister, counsel, solicitor; *spec*: bramble, trailing briar; scribe (interpreter of Mosaic law).

lax

adj lit: casual, lenient, overindulgent, unfussy; careless, slipshod; flabby, loose, shapeless, slack, soft; imprecise, indefinite, non-specific, vague.

laxative

n lit: cathartic, purgative.

lay
n lit: arrangement, disposition, positioning, site; chant, hymn, lyric, poem, song; *spec*: plaiting (of a rope); (female) sexual partner.
vb lit: apply, arrange, burden, charge, cover, deposit, dispose, impose, locate, position, put, set down, spread over, station; stake, wager; *fig*: ascribe, assign, attribute, impute; contrive, design, devise, plan, plot; *spec*: bury (one deceased); exorcize; have sex with; plait (a rope); produce (an egg).
adj lit: laic, non-clerical, secular; *fig*: amateur, non-professional; *spec*: not trumps (in cards).

layabout
n lit: good-for-nothing, idler, loafer, lounger, ne'er-do-well, skiver, slacker, sponger, wastrel.

layer
n lit: bed, ply, stratum, thickness; course, row, seam; coat, coating, covering, film, mantle; *spec*: chicken, hen (of eggs); rooting shoot (of a plant).

lay in
vb lit: amass, collect, hoard, stockpile, store up.

lay off
vb lit: discharge, dismiss, make redundant, pay off, retire; *fig*: cease, desist, give up, leave alone, quit, stop; *spec*: hedge (bets); rest (between seasons, of athletes); make possible, put in the way of, set up with.

lay on
vb lit: cater for, furnish, install, provide, supply; *fig*: beat, flog, hit, strike, thrash; exaggerate, go over the top, overdo.

layout
n lit: arrangement, geography, scenario, set; display, presentation; design, draft, outline, plan.

laziness
n lit: idleness, inactivity, indolence, inertia, slackness, sloth, sluggishness, torpor.

lazy
adj lit: idle, inactive, indolent, inert, shiftless, slothful, sluggish, torpid, workshy; *spec*: extending (of tongs); weak (of heart or eye muscles).

lead
n lit: advantage, first place, front, precedence, primacy, priority; first player, principal, star, starring role, title part; clue, direction, guidance, guide, hint, suggestion; example, leadership, model, path; *spec*: channel (in ice-field); (electrical) conductor, connection, wire; first play (in cards); leash, rein, string (on a pet); lode (in mining).
vb lit: be ahead, be first, be in front, excel, outdo, outstrip, pass, precede, surpass; command, direct, govern, head, manage, preside over; conduct, convey, escort, guide, pilot, show, steer, usher; cause, draw, induce, influence, persuade, produce, prompt; begin, commence, initiate, open; *fig*: experience, go forward, go on, live, pass, spend, undergo; *spec*: take the offensive (in a game or sport).

leader
n lit: captain, chief, commander, conductor, director, guide, head, ruler, superior; first, forerunner, guide, vanguard; principal, star; *spec*: bargain offer; channel (from or in a waterway); editorial (in a periodical).

leadership
n lit: authority, captaincy, chieftancy, command, control, direction, directorship, guidance, management, organization, regulation, rule, supremacy.

leading
adj (pr.pt) lit: chief, dominant, main, primary, principal, ruling, superior; first, foremost, pre-eminent; celebrated, important, famous, noted, significant.

lead up to
vb lit: approach, broach, intimate, introduce, preface, prepare for, work round to, work towards.

leaf
n lit: blade, bract, frond, petal; *fig*: folio, page, sheet, side; *spec*: board, lath, slat (detachable from window, door or table); lamina (of gold or silver).
vb lit: flip, riffle, skim, thumb, turn; *spec*: bud, put out leaves (of trees).

league
n lit: alliance, association, cartel, compact, confederacy, confederation, federation, partnership, society, union; collaboration; category, class, group; cahoots, conspiracy.

leak

n lit: discharge, drip, emission, escape, oozing, percolation, seepage, spill, spillage; breach, crack, fissure, hole, opening, puncture; *fig*: informant, informer, mole, sneak, telltale; *spec*: urination.

vb lit: discharge, emit, exude, let out; drip out, escape, get out, issue, ooze, percolate, seep, spill, trickle out; get in, infiltrate; *fig*: admit, disclose, divulge, give away, inform, reveal, tell.

leaky

adj lit: cracked, holed, perforated, permeable, porous, punctured, riddled; discharging, dribbling, dripping, exuding, oozing, seeping; subject to infiltration.

lean

vb lit: heel, incline, list, slant, slope, tilt, tip; be supported, be propped up, rest, weigh; bend down; *fig*: favour, incline, prefer, tend; depend, rely, trust; coerce, intimidate, pressurize.

adj lit: bony, gaunt, skinny, slender, slim, thin; barren, inadequate, insufficient, meagre, mean, poor, scanty, spare, sparse, unproductive, weak; *fig*: unprofitable.

leaning

n lit: bent, bias, favouritism, inclination, partiality, penchant, predilection, preference, proclivity, taste; aptitude, propensity, tendency.

leap

n lit: bound, hop, jump, skip, spring, vault; escalation, hike, increase, rise, upsurge; *fig*: distance, journey; enterprise, undertaking; gap, interval; *spec*: jump-off point.

vb lit: bound, caper, hop, jump, skip, spring, vault; clear; cavort, frisk, gambol; escalate, increase, rise, rocket, soar, surge; *fig*: fly, hasten, hurry, run, rush; *spec*: jump (to a conclusion).

learn

vb lit: apprehend, be taught, comprehend, grasp, master, memorize, study; ascertain, be informed, be told, come to know, determine, discern, discover, find out, gather, hear, pick up.

learned

adj (pa.pt) lit: cultured, educated, erudite, lettered, literate, scholarly, well-informed, well-read; expert, skilful, skilled, well-versed.

learning

n lit: education, erudition, knowledge, letters, literacy, scholarship; culture, understanding, wisdom; expertise, lore, skill.

lease

n lit: charter, contract, franchise, hire agreement; hiring, renting, tenancy, tenure; *spec*: motivation, prospect, span (of life).

vb lit: charter, contract out, hire, let, rent.

leash

n lit: chain, lead, line, rein, strap, string, tether, thong; curb; *fig*: control, restraint; *spec*: group of three, trio (of animals, in hunting or judging).

vb lit: chain, fasten, put on a lead, secure, tether, tie up; *fig*: check, control, curb, restrain.

least

n lit: fewest, minimum, most minute, slightest, smallest, tiniest; *fig*: lowest, meanest, poorest; most feeble.

adj lit: fewest, minimal, most minute, slightest, smallest, tiniest; *fig*: lowest, meanest, poorest, most feeble.

adv lit: by the tiniest amount, minimally, to the slightest degree, to the smallest extent.

leather

n lit: hide, tanned skin; *spec*: ball (in certain games).

vb fig: beat, drub, flog, thrash.

leave

n lit: authorization, consent, dispensation, permission, sanction; freedom, holiday, liberty, time off, vacation; departure, going, parting, withdrawal; farewell, goodbye.

vb lit: depart, exit, go, move off, pull out, quit, retire from, set out, vacate, withdraw; abandon, cede, desert, evacuate, forget to take, go off without, relinquish, surrender; cease, desist, drop, give up, refrain, stop; assign, commit, give over; *spec*: bequeath to, hand on to, will to.

leave out

vb lit: forget, neglect, omit, overlook; disregard, except, exclude, ignore, reject.

leavings
n lit: debris, detritus, dregs, dross, leftovers, refuse, remains, remnants, residue, scraps, spoil, waste.

lecherous
adj lit: carnal, concupiscent, hot, libidinous, lustful, randy, rutting; lascivious, lubricious, salacious.

lecture
n lit: address, discourse, disquisition, exegesis, lesson, talk; *fig*: admonition, censure, dressing-down, rebuke, scolding, talking-to, telling-off.
vb lit: address, expound, give a talk, instruct, teach; *fig*: admonish, berate, censure, chide, reprimand, reprove, scold, tell off.

ledge
n lit: shelf, sill, step; ridge; *spec*: lode, vein (in geology).

leech
n lit: bloodsucker; *fig*: hanger-on, parasite, sponger; *spec*: doctor, physician.

leer
n lit: hot glance, smirk, stare.
vb lit: give the eye, make sheep's eyes, ogle, smirk, stare.

lees
n lit: dregs, grounds, sediment, settlings.

left
adj spec: liberal, radical, socialist.

leg
n lit: limb, member, pin; basis, brace, prop, support, upright; episode, lap, part, section, stage; *spec*: on side (in cricket); tack (in sailing).

legacy
n lit: bequest, endowment, heirloom, heritage, inheritance, patrimony; tradition; *fig*: effect, result.

legality
n lit: law, lawfulness, legitimacy; permissibility, validity.

legalize
vb lit: authorize, legitimate, legitimize, license; allow, make official, permit, sanction, validate.

legation
n lit: consulate, diplomatic mission, embassy, official residence; delegation; *spec*: papal province.

legend
n lit: fable, folklore, myth, saga, story, tale, tradition; caption, device, inscription, key, motto, table of symbols, wording; *fig*: celebrity, hero, prodigy; *spec*: hagiography.

legendary
adj lit: apocryphal, fabulous, mythical, traditional; epic, heroic, prodigious; celebrated, famous, illustrious, renowned; fictitious, untrue.

legibility
n lit: clarity, plainness, readability.

legion
n lit: army, brigade, division, force, troop; horde, host, multitude, myriad.

legislate
vb lit: enact, make a law, ordain, pass a law, rule.

legislation
n lit: enactment, lawmaking; act, bill, charter, law, measure, regulation, ruling, statute; constitution, legal code.

legislative
n lit: diet, government, judicial body, judiciary, parliament, senate.
adj lit: congressional, judicial, jurisdictive, lawmaking, parliamentary, senatorial.

legitimate
adj lit: lawful, legal, licit, statutory; authorized, official, rightful, sanctioned; authentic, correct, fair, genuine, justifiable, logical, normal, proper, real, true, valid, warranted; *spec*: by right of heredity.

leisure
n lit: freedom, holiday, liberty, spare time, time off, vacation; recreation, relaxation, rest, taking it easy.
adj lit: free, holiday, spare, unoccupied.

leisurely
adj lit: comfortable, deliberate, easy, relaxed, restful, slow, unhurried.
adv lit: comfortably, deliberately, easily, relaxedly, restfully, slowly, unhurriedly.

lend
vb lit: advance, give temporarily, let someone have for a time, loan; *fig*: afford, bestow, confer, give, impart.

length
n lit: distance, extent, measure, reach,

span; piece, portion, section, segment;
duration, period, stretch, term, time;
extensiveness, prolixity, protractedness;
spec: end-to-end distance (in rowing and
horse races); quantity (of a vowel in
phonetics).

lengthen
vb lit: draw out, elongate, extend,
increase, prolong, protract, spin out,
stretch.

lengthy
adj lit: drawn-out, extended, long, prolix,
protracted; interminable, long-drawn-
out, tedious.

lenient
adj lit: clement, compassionate,
forbearing, indulgent, merciful, tolerant;
gentle, mild.

leper
n lit: lazar; *fig*: outcast, pariah,
untouchable.

lesbian
n lit: dyke, homosexual, sapphist, tribade.

lesion
n lit: abrasion, hurt, injury, scar, sore,
ulcer, wound.

less
adj lit: lower, inferior, slighter, smaller;
not so much; minor, secondary,
subordinate.
adv lit: not so much, not so well, to a
lower degree, to a smaller extent.
prp lit: lacking, minus, sans, subtracting,
without.

lessee
n lit: lease-holder, tenant.

lessen
vb lit: abate, decrease, die away, diminish,
dwindle, ease, lighten, moderate, reduce,
slow, wind down; become smaller,
contract, erode, shrink; *fig*: belittle,
disparage, minimize.

lesser
adj lit: inferior, minor, secondary,
subordinate.

lesson
n lit: coaching, instruction, lecture, school
period, teaching, tuition; exercise,
reading, subject, study; *fig*: example,
inspiration, model, moral; admonition,
rebuke, reprimand, reproof, scolding,
warning; *spec*: reading (from the Bible).

let
n lit: hindrance, impediment,
interference, obstruction; *spec*: net, net
cord ball (in tennis).
vb lit: allow, authorize, enable, give leave,
give permission, grant, permit, sanction;
assume, suppose; contract out, hire,
lease, rent.

let down
vb lit: lower; *fig*: disappoint, disillusion,
dissatisfy, fail.

lethal
adj lit: deadly, fatal, mortal, murderous;
dangerous, devastating, poisonous,
virulent.

lethargic
adj lit: drowsy, dull, enervated, heavy,
languid, sleepy, slow, sluggish,
somnolent, torpid; apathetic, lazy.

let on
vb lit: dissemble, give the impression,
pretend, simulate; disclose, divulge,
manifest, reveal, show.

let off
vb lit: excuse, exempt, release, reprieve,
spare; absolve, forgive, pardon;
detonate, discharge, explode, fire; emit,
exude, give off, release; allow to alight.

let out
vb lit: discharge, free, liberate, release, set
free; augment, enlarge, make larger;
emit, sound, voice; betray, disclose, leak,
reveal; contract out, hire, lease, rent.

letter
n lit: character, sign, symbol;
communication, despatch, document,
epistle, message, missive, note; *fig*:
expression, language, literal meaning,
wording.

level
n lit: altitude, elevation, grade, height,
position, rank, standing, status; flat
surface, floor, layer, plane, storey,
stratum; degree, standard; *spec*: ditch,
channel (for drainage in fen country);
gallery (in a mine).
vb lit: even out, flatten, plane, smooth;
bulldoze, pull down, raze, tear down;
equalize; *fig*: aim, direct, focus, point,
train; be candid, reveal all, tell the truth;
spec: measure height (in surveying).
adj lit: even, flat, horizontal, plain, plane,
smooth, stable, steady, uniform;
balanced, commensurate, equable, equal,

equivalent, even, flush, parallel; sound;
spec: equipotential (in physics).

lever
n lit: bar, crowbar, handle, jemmy,
switch; *fig*: hold, threat.
vb lit: force, jemmy, prise.

leverage
n lit: power, purchase; *fig*: advantage,
ascendancy, clout, influence, pull,
weight.

levity
n lit: facetiousness, flippancy, frivolity,
lightheartedness, silliness, triviality;
fickleness, flightiness, giddiness,
inconstancy, instability; shallowness,
thoughtlessness; vanity.

levy
n lit: duty, imposition, impost, tax, tithe,
toll; collection, gathering; *spec*:
conscription, mobilization, mustering,
raising (of an army).
vb lit: charge, collect, exact, gather,
impose, muster, tax, tithe; *spec*: call up,
conscript, mobilize, summon (an army).

lewd
adj lit: bawdy, blue, dirty, erotic,
indecent, lascivious, libidinous,
licentious, obscene, pornographic,
salacious, smutty; debauched, lecherous,
lustful.

lewdness
n lit: bawdiness, carnality, debauchery,
depravity, indecency, lasciviousness,
lechery, licentiousness, lubricity,
obscenity, pornography, salaciousness,
smut.

liability
n lit: accountability, answerability,
responsibility; likelihood, possibility,
susceptibility, tendency; burden, debit,
debt, indebtedness, obligation, onus;
disadvantage, drawback, encumbrance,
handicap, hindrance, impediment,
millstone.

liable
adj lit: accountable, answerable, bound,
incurring, obliged, responsible; apt,
disposed, inclined, likely, prone,
tending; exposed, open, risking, subject,
susceptible, vulnerable.

liaison
n lit: bond, communication, connection,
contact, cooperation, interchange,

intercourse; go-between, intermediary,
link, middle-man; affair, entanglement,
intimacy, intrigue, romance, union; *spec*:
thickener (in soup).

liar
n lit: deceiver, fabricator, falsifier,
perjurer, storyteller; fibber, libeller,
prevaricator, slanderer; double-crosser,
fraud, impostor.

libel
n lit: calumny, defamation, smear,
vilification; slander; *spec*: accusation,
charge, complaint (in law)
vb lit: calumniate, defame, malign, smear,
traduce, vilify; slander.

libellous
adj lit: calumnious, damaging,
defamatory, false, maligning, traducing,
untrue, vilifying; slanderous.

liberal
adj lit: beneficent, bounteous, bountiful,
charitable, generous, kind, munificent,
philanthropic; abundant, ample,
copious, lavish, plentiful, profuse,
prolific; broad, easy-going, flexible, free,
general, indulgent, lenient, loose,
magnanimous, open, tolerant; broad-
minded, catholic, disinterested,
humanitarian, unbiased, unprejudiced;
progressive, radical, reformist; *spec*:
cultural, intellectual (as opposed to
practical).

liberalize
vb lit: broaden, deregulate, derestrict,
ease, extend, loosen, moderate, relax,
slacken, soften.

liberate
vb lit: deliver, emancipate, enfranchise,
free, let go, loose, release, rescue, save,
set free, turn loose, unbind, untie; *fig*:
appropriate, plunder, rob, steal, take;
spec: manumit, redeem (a slave).

liberation
n lit: deliverance, emancipation,
enfranchisement, freedom, freeing,
letting go, loosing, release, releasing,
rescue, setting free, unbinding, untying;
spec: disestablishment (of the Church);
manumission, redemption (of a slave, of
sinners); political reform, social reform
(theology)

libertine
n lit: debauchee, lecher, seducer,
voluptuary, womaniser; degenerate,

profligate, rake, reprobate, roué; *spec*: dissenter, freethinker, nonconformist.
adj lit: debauched, depraved, immoral, licentious, wanton; corrupt, decadent, degenerate, dissolute, profligate, reprobate; abandoned, uninhibited, unrestrained, unrestricted; *spec*: dissenting, freethinking, nonconformist.

liberty
n lit: emancipation, enfranchisement, freedom; autonomy, independence, power, right, self-determination; carte blanche, dispensation, exemption, immunity; authorization, franchise, leave, licence, permission, sanction; leisure, spare time; *fig*: breach of good manners, familiarity, impertinence, impropriety, impudence, insult, presumption.

licence
n lit: accreditation, certificate, charter, permit, warrant; authority, power, privilege, right; authorization, dispensation, entitlement, leave, permission, sanction; carte blanche, freedom, independence, latitude, liberty; exemption, immunity; excess, immoderation, indulgence, irresponsibility, laxity, profligacy; abandon, anarchy, debauchery, lawlessness, unruliness, wantonness.

license
vb lit: accredit, certify, warrant; authorize, commission, empower; allow, permit, sanction.

licentiousness
n lit: debauchery, immorality, lasciviousness, lechery, lewdness, lubricity, promiscuity, salaciousness, sensuality, wantonness; dissipation, dissoluteness, profligacy, self-indulgence; abandon, anarchy, lawlessness, unruliness.

lick
n lit: lap, slurp; sample, sip, taste; saliva; *fig*: bit, dab, little, speck, spot, touch; clip, pace, rate, speed, velocity; *spec*: anacrusis, intro, riff (in jazz); salt-pan.
vb lit: lap, slurp, taste, tongue; *fig*: ripple against, touch, wash; beat, conquer, defeat, rout, trounce; beat, drub, flog, spank, thrash; beat, excel, outdo, surpass; *spec*: dart, flicker, play over (of flames).

licking
n lit: beating, drubbing, flogging, spanking, thrashing; defeat, rout, trouncing.

lid
n lit: cap, cover, flap, seal, top; eyelid; *fig*: cap, hat; check, curb, restraint.

lie
n lit: deception, fabrication, falsehood, falsification, fiction, invention, perjury, story, untruth; fib, libel, prevarication, slander; arrangement, disposition, positioning, site; geography, terrain; aspect.
vb lit: deceive, fabricate, falsify, invent, perjure, tell an untruth; be economical with the truth, equivocate, fib, libel, mislead, misrepresent, prevaricate, slander, tell a story; abide, be, be arranged, be found, be located, be placed, be positioned, be prone, be recumbent, be set, be situated, extend, lean, recline, remain, repose, rest, stretch out; be constituted, consist; be buried, be interred; *spec*: be admissible, be sustainable (in law).

life
n lit: being, being alive, being awake, being conscious, breath, existence, living; biosphere, creatures, human, human being, organisms, person, soul; animation, heart, lifeblood, soul, spirit, vitality; activity, brio, energy, liveliness, verve, vigour, vivacity, zest; duration, lifetime, span, time; autobiography, biography, career, history, memoirs; *fig*: power, validity; period, term.

lifeless
adj lit: cold, dead, deceased, defunct, inanimate, inert, insensible, out cold, unconscious, unmoving; barren, desert, empty, sterile; *fig*: colourless, dull, flat, heavy, insipid, lacklustre, sluggish, static, stiff, torpid, wooden.

lift
n lit: elevation, hoisting, raising; rising; advancement, boost, fillip, progress, rise, uplift; drive, ride, transport; crane, elevator, hoist, tow-bar track; *spec*: catch (of fish); masthead rope (in sailing); upward force (in aeronautics).
vb lit: elevate, hoist, hold up, pick up, pull up, raise, support, uplift, upraise; ascend, go up, rise; advance, boost, elate, enhance, exalt, promote, upgrade;

cancel, countermand, end, relax, rescind, revoke, terminate; be dispelled, disperse; *fig*: appropriate, purloin, rob, steal, take; arrest, detain; copy, pirate, plagiarize; harvest, reap; *spec*: approach (at sea); catch (fish); mine (ore).

light
n lit: brightness, brilliance, gleam, glint, glow, illumination, incandescence, luminosity, radiance; blaze, effulgence, flash, luminescence, ray, scintillation, sparkle; dawn, daylight, daytime, morning, sun, sunshine; beacon, candle, flame, flare, lighter, match, taper; bulb, lamp, lantern, torch; lighthouse; window; *fig*: aspect, context, interpretation, slant, view; angle, approach, viewpoint; awareness, comprehension, elucidation, enlightenment, explanation, insight, understanding; example, exemplar, model; clue, hint; *spec*: traffic signal.
vb lit: brighten, illuminate, illumine, irradiate; put on, switch on, turn on; fire, ignite, kindle, set ablaze, set on fire, touch a match to; alight, come down, get off, land, perch, settle; chance, come across, encounter, happen, stumble; *fig*: clarify, expose; inflame, intoxicate; animate, cheer up.
adj lit: bright, brilliant, glowing, illuminated, luminous; sunny; fair, pale, whitish; blond; clear; delicate, easy, insubstantial, not heavy, portable, slight, thin, underweight; faint, gentle, indistinct, mild, soft, weak; unchaste; facile, frivolous, idle, inconsequential, insignificant, paltry, petty, superficial, trifling, trivial, unimportant; effortless, manageable, undemanding; amusing, entertaining, funny, pleasing, witty; agile, airy, athletic, graceful, lithe, nimble; blithe, carefree, cheerful; *fig*: dizzy, giddy, delirious; less, minus, short; *spec*: bland, digestible, frugal (diet); friable, loose, sandy (soil).

lighten
vb lit: brighten, illuminate, irradiate, shine on; become light, make paler; ease, make less weighty, unload; alleviate, assuage, lessen, mitigate, reduce, relieve; buoy up, cheer, elate, gladden, hearten, lift.

light-hearted
adj lit: blithe, carefree, cheerful, gay, jolly, jovial, merry, playful, sunny.

lightweight
adj lit: insubstantial, slight; *fig*: inconsequential, insignificant, paltry, petty, trifling, trivial, unimportant.

like
n lit: favourite, partiality, predilection, preference; match, resemblance; counterpart, equal, fellow, parallel.
vb lit: be fond of, care for, enjoy, love, relish; be partial to, choose to, fancy, prefer, select, take to; appreciate, approve of, esteem.
adj lit: alike, corresponding, equal, equivalent, identical, matching, parallel, resembling, similar.
adv lit: in the same way (as), just (as).
prp lit: similar, similar to, resembling; befitting, characteristic of; namely, such as; as much as.

likely
adj lit: anticipated, expected, probable; believable, credible, feasible, plausible, reasonable; appropriate, fitting, suitable; fair, favourite, pleasing, promising.
adv lit: doubtless, in all probability, probably.

likeness
n lit: correspondence, resemblance, similarity; appearance, form, guise, semblance, simulation; copy, facsimile, image, model, replica, representation; photo, picture, portrait.

liking
n lit: bias, inclination, partiality, penchant, predilection, preference, taste, tendency; affection, fancy, fondness, love; appreciation, approval, esteem, satisfaction, pleasure.

limb
n lit: arm, leg, member, wing; appendage, extension, extremity; bough, branch, offshoot; *fig*: projection, side-range, spur; *spec*: border, edge (in astronomy and botany).

limber
vb lit: exercise, flex, warm up.
adj lit: agile, flexible, lithe, nimble, pliant, supple.

limit
n lit: border, boundary, confines, edge, end, extent, frontier, perimeter, periphery; ceiling, maximum, termination, ultimate; restriction, stop, terminus.

vb lit: bound, circumscribe; demarcate, fix, set, specify; check, confine, hinder, ration, restrict.

limited
adj (pa.pt) lit: bounded, circumscribed, defined, fixed; cramped, confined, hampered, hemmed in, hindered, restricted; diminished, inadequate, insufficient, minimal, narrow, reduced, short, unsatisfactory; *fig*: dull, unintelligent; *spec*: assigned (in law); of restricted liability (in company law).

limp
n lit: hobble, lameness.
vb lit: drag a leg, hobble, lurch; *fig*: struggle, travel with difficulty.
adj lit: drooping, flabby, flaccid, floppy, lax, loose, slack, soft; flexible, pliable; debilitated, exhausted, spent, worn out; weak.

line
n lit: cable, cord, filament, rope, strand, string, thread, wire; bar, dash, rule, streak, stripe, stroke; crease, crow's foot, furrow, groove, score, wrinkle; column, crocodile, procession, queue, rank, row, sequence, series, succession; border, boundary, edge, limit, mark; configuration, contour, figure, outline; course, direction, path, route, trajectory; transport system; rail, track; hose, tube; *fig*: approach, method, policy, procedure; business, field, forte, interest, job, occupation, profession, specialty, trade; brand, make; card, letter, note, postcard; clue, hint, indication, lead, pointer; plot, story; accordance, correspondence, parallel.
vb lit: draw, inscribe, mark, rule; hatch; crease, furrow, score; align, form a column, range; border, fringe, hem round, skirt, surround; cover, face, fill, reinforce, stuff.

linen
n lit: cloth, drapery; bedclothes, napkins, tablecloths, towels; shirts, hand-kerchiefs; underclothes, underwear.

linger
vb lit: abide, continue, last, persist, remain, stay, wait; dawdle, delay, hang around, lag, loiter; hang on, survive.

lingering
adj (pr.pt) lit: abiding, continuing, persisting, remaining, surviving; long-drawn-out, prolonged, protracted, slow.

link
n lit: connection, contact, coupling, tie; attachment, bond, joint, relationship; *spec*: (electrical) fuse; hoop, loop, ring (of a chain).
vb lit: connect, contact, couple, join, liaise between, make contact between, tie together, unite; attach, bind, bracket, fasten, relate, yoke.

lionize
vb lit: acclaim, adulate, celebrate, exalt, fête, glorify, hero-worship, idolize, look up to; visit, go round, sightsee, tour.

lip
n lit: labium; brim, flange, rim; edge, margin, welt; *fig*: cheek, impertinence, impudence, insolence, sauce; *spec*: embouchure (in playing a wind instrument).

liquid
n lit: fluid, moisture; liquor.
adj lit: flowing, fluid, melted, moist, molten, runny, wet; aqueous, watery; juicy; *fig*: dulcet, mellifluous, smooth, soft, sweet; bright, clear, limpid, translucent; graceful; *spec*: disposable, encashable, realizable (assets).

liquidate
vb lit: discharge, dissolve, terminate; clear, pay off, settle, square, wind up; cash, encash, dispose of, realize, sell up; abolish, eliminate; *fig*: annihilate, do away with, exterminate, kill, murder, wipe out.

liquor
n lit: alcohol, grog, hard stuff, hooch, moonshine, spirits, strong drink; broth, gravy, juice, stock; infusion, solution, suspension.

list
n lit: catalogue, enumeration, inventory, record, register, roll, tally; file, print-out, schedule, tabulation; series; lean, slant, slope, tilt; *spec*: stock quotation (on the stock market).
vb lit: catalogue, enrol, enter, enumerate, inventory, itemize, note down, record, register, write down; file, schedule, tabulate; arrange in order, serialize; cant, heel, incline, lean, slant, slope, tilt, tip.

listen
vb lit: attend, be attentive, hear, hearken, pay attention; be advised, heed, mind, take notice.

listless
adj lit: apathetic, enervated, impassive, indifferent, languid, spiritless, supine, uninterested, vacant; indolent, lethargic, lifeless, limp, torpid.

literally
adv lit: accurately, exactly, faithfully, precisely, strictly, to the letter, verbatim, word for word; actually, in reality, really, truly; *fig*: as it were, in a way, virtually.

literary
adj lit: bookish, lettered, well-read; erudite, learned, scholarly; allusive, eloquent, rhetorical, oratorical; publishing.

literate
adj lit: able to read and write, educated, lettered; erudite, learned, scholarly, well-read; cultivated, cultured, knowledgeable, well-informed.

lithe
adj lit: limber, lissom, loose-limbed, pliant, supple; flexible, pliable; agile, nimble.

litigant
n lit: accuser, claimant, contender at law, disputant, plaintiff.

litigation
n lit: action, case, lawsuit, legal proceedings, prosecution, suit.

litter
n lit: debris, garbage, muck, refuse, rubbish, trash; brood, children, cubs, family, kittens, offspring, progeny, pups, young; palanquin, stretcher, travois; bed, couch, palliasse; mulch; clutter, disorder, jumble, mess.
vb lit: leave lying around, scatter, strew; make a mess; disarrange, disorder, jumble; *spec*: give birth to (a litter of animals); make a straw bed.

little
n lit: bit, bite, dab, dash, fraction, lick, modicum, morsel, pinch, small amount, spot, taste, touch, trace, trifle; short time.
adj lit: miniature, petite, short, small; diminutive, dwarf, infinitesimal, minute, tiny, wee; meagre, scant, skimpy, sparse; insignificant, minor, paltry, trifling, trivial, unimportant; mean, narrow-minded, petty, small-minded.

adv lit: barely, hardly, scarcely; rarely, seldom; only just, slightly.

live
vb lit: be, be alive, breathe, exist, have life, subsist; continue, endure, last, lead, pass, persist, remain, survive; abide, dwell, inhabit, lodge, occupy, reside, stay; be remembered; eat, feed; enjoy life, flourish, revel, thrive; *fig*: accept, put up with, tolerate.
adj lit: alive, animate, breathing, living; active, awake, alert, dynamic, energetic, vigorous; ablaze, alight, burning, connected, glowing, hot, ignited, on, switched on; contemporaneous, current, pertinent, pressing, topical, up-to-date, vital; in play; unexploded, unignited; natural, real, unquarried.

livelihood
n lit: job, living, occupation, work; employment, means, income; support.

lively
adj lit: active, brisk, energetic, quick, sprightly, spry, vigorous; agile, alert, animated, chirpy, perky, spirited, vivacious; bright, colourful, exciting, fresh, invigorating, refreshing, stimulating, stirring, vivid; bustling, busy, crowded, eventful.

liverish
adj lit: bilious, ill, nauseated, sick; *fig*: cross, disagreeable, grumpy, irascible, irritable, peevish, ratty, testy, tetchy.

livid
adj lit: anaemic, ashen, grey, leaden, pale, pallid, sallow, wan, waxen, white; black and blue, bruised, contused, discoloured, purple; angry, enraged, fuming, furious, hopping mad, incensed, infuriated, irate.

living
n lit: job, livelihood, occupation, work; employment, means, income; support; lifestyle, way of life; being, existence, life, subsistence; *spec*: benefice (for clergymen).
adj lit: alive, being, existing, live, organic, subsisting; active, contemporary, current, extant, ongoing, operative; continuing, persisting, remaining; strong, vigorous; lifelike, vivid; dwelling, lodging, occupying, residential, residing, staying.

living-room
n lit: lounge, main room, parlour, saloon, sitting-room.

load
n lit: burden, cargo, charge, weight; consignment, freight, shipment; *fig*: encumbrance, millstone, onus, pressure; affliction, busyness, trouble, worry; amount, host, lot, mass, multitude, quantity; *spec*: output (in power, of an engine); force, power, work (in physics).
vb lit: burden, charge, put in, put on, weigh down; cram, fill, heap, pack, pile on, stack, stuff; encumber; *fig*: oppress, trouble, worry; bias, prejudice, slant, weight; *spec*: adulterate, drug, fortify (wine); charge, prime (a firearm); fix, rig (dice).

loaded
adj (pa.pt) lit: burdened, charged, weighed down; crammed, filled, heaped, packed, piled, stacked, stuffed; encumbered, laden; *fig*: anxious, oppressed, troubled, worried; biased, leading, slanted, weighted; affluent, moneyed, rich, wealthy, well-heeled, well off, well-to-do; drunk, inebriated, intoxicated, legless, stoned; *spec*: adulterated, drugged, fortified (wine); charged, primed (firearm); fixed, rigged (dice).

loaf
n lit: bar, block, lump; cake, slab; *fig*: brain, common sense, head, intelligence, nous, sense; *spec*: mass (of sugar).
vb lit: idle, loll, lounge, shirk, skive, slack; be idle, do nothing; amble, dawdle, saunter.

loan
n lit: advance, credit; mortgage, overdraft; accommodation, use.
vb lit: advance, give temporarily, let someone have for a time, lend.

loathe
vb lit: abhor, abominate, be disgusted by, be repelled by, be revolted by, detest, dislike intensely, hate, hold in repugnance.

loathing
n lit: abhorrence, abomination, disgust, dislike, hate, hatred, odium, repugnance, repulsion, revulsion; antipathy, aversion.

lobby
n lit: ante-room, atrium, foyer, hall, vestibule, waiting-room; corridor, entrance; *fig*: campaigners, pressure group, supporters.
vb lit: campaign, petition, prevail on, solicit, urge; badger, exert pressure on, impress upon, lean on, pressurize, sway.

local
n lit: inhabitant, native, resident; bar, hostelry, inn, pub, tavern.
adj lit: community, district, neighbourhood, parish, parochial, provincial, regional, suburban; confined, limited, restricted; *spec*: topical (in medicine); slow (train).

locality
n lit: area, district, environs, neighbourhood, parts, region, section, vicinity, zone; location, place, scene, site, spot.

locate
vb lit: establish, fix, found, place, put, seat, set, site, situate; detect, discover, find, pin down, pinpoint, trace, track down.

lock
n lit: bolt, clasp, fastening, latch, padlock, snib; clutch, embrace, grapple, grasp, hold, hug; linkage, mesh; curl, ringlet, strand, tress; *spec*: (airtight) chamber (on a space-ship); firing mechanism (on a gun); turning-circle (on a car).
vb lit: bar, bolt, close, fasten, latch, seal, secure, shut, snib; engage, entwine, link, mesh, unite; clasp, clutch, embrace, enclose, grapple, grasp, hold, hold fast, hug, jam together, press.

lodge
n lit: cabin, chalet, cottage, house, hut, log-cabin, shelter, villa; den, haunt, lair, retreat; gatehouse, porter's room, reception; wigwam, teepee; meeting-place; *fig*: assembly, branch, chapter, club, society.
vb lit: accommodate, billet, board, harbour, put up, quarter, shelter; dwell, room, spend the night, stay, stop, temporarily reside; adhere, catch, embed, get stuck, implant, stick; deposit, file, lay, make, place, put, record, register, submit; be vested (in); *spec*: flatten (a field of grain); flush out (a deer).

lodger
n lit: boarder, paying guest, roomer,

tenant; guest, inhabitant, occupant, resident.

lodgings
n lit: accommodation, board, boarding, digs, place to stay, quarters, room, rooms, shelter; abode, dwelling, residence; harbour.

lofty
adj lit: high, soaring, tall, towering; *fig*: dignified, elevated, exalted, lordly, majestic, noble, stately, superior; grand, illustrious, sublime; arrogant, disdainful, haughty, overweening, patronizing, proud, snooty, supercilious.

log
n lit: billet, bough, branch, piece of wood, stump, trunk; account, chronicle, diary, journal, record, report, tally.
vb lit: chronicle, note, record, register, set down, tally, write up; chop, cut up, saw up; *fig*: cover, go, travel.

logic
n lit: dialectics, ratiocination, reasoning, syllogism; analysis, judgement, reason, sense, thought; coherence, connection, deduction, inference.

logical
adj lit: cogent, coherent, consecutive, consistent, deduced, proper, proven, rational, reasoned, right, sound, valid; appropriate, feasible, likely, obvious, plausible, reasonable, sensible.

loiter
vb lit: amble, dawdle, idle, loaf, stroll; hang about, skulk; delay, linger.

loll
vb lit: flop, loaf, lounge, recline, slouch, slump, sprawl; dangle, droop, hang, lean, sag.

loneliness
n lit: desolation, forsakenness, solitude; aloneness, isolation, seclusion, solitariness.

lonely
adj lit: abandoned, alone, deserted, desolate, forsaken, friendless, solitary, unaccompanied; apart, isolated, remote, secluded, single, unfrequented, uninhabited, withdrawn.

long
vb lit: crave, hunger, lust, pine, wish, yearn.
adj lit: elongated, extended, extensive,

far-reaching, lengthy, stretched; interminable, prolonged, protracted, slow, sustained; distant, remote; *spec*: accented, stressed (syllable).
adv lit: continually, through; extendedly, extensively, for years; distantly, remotely.

longing
n lit: covetousness, craving, desire, hunger, itch, lust, thirst, yearning; ambition, aspiration, urge, wish, yen.
adj lit: covetous, desirous, hungry, lustful, wishful, wistful, yearning; avid, eager.

long-suffering
adj lit: enduring, forbearing, patient, resigned, stoical, tolerant; forgiving, uncomplaining.

look
n lit: air, appearance, aspect, bearing, cast, complexion, demeanour, expression, manner, mien, semblance; examination, inspection, review, search, survey, view; gaze, observation, stare; dekko, eyeful, gander, glance, glimpse, once-over, peek, sight, squint.
vb lit: behold, contemplate, examine, gaze, inspect, observe, regard, scan, scrutinize, see, stare, study, survey, view, watch; gawp, glance, goggle; appear, seem; display, evince, exhibit, manifest, show; face, give (on to); hope.

look after
vb lit: attend, care for, mind, nurse, tend; guard, protect, supervise, watch over; attend to, take care of.

look forward to
vb lit: anticipate, await, be eager for, expect, wait for; hope for, long for, wish for, yearn for.

look into
vb lit: check, examine, go into, inspect, scrutinize, study; check out, explore, follow up, investigate, probe, research.

lookout
n lit: guard, sentinel, sentry, watchman; alert, guard, vigil, watch; crow's nest, observation post, tower, watchtower; *fig*: affair, business, concern, department, worry; outlook, prospect.

look up
vb lit: hunt for, research, search for; discover, find, trace; call in on, drop in on, go and see, visit; advance,

ameliorate, get better, improve, perk up, pick up, progress.

loom
vb lit: appear, become visible, emerge, take shape; be imminent, hang over, hover, impend, menace, overhang, overshadow, threaten, tower over.

loop
n lit: doubling, coil, convolution, curl, eyelet, hoop, noose, ring, whorl; bend, curve, spiral, twist; *spec*: antinode (in physics); closed (electrical) circuit; intra-uterine (contraceptive) device.
vb lit: circle, coil, curl, encircle; bend, curve, spiral, turn; braid, connect, double over, fold, join, knot, twist, wind round.

loophole
n lit: judas, slit, slot; *fig*: escape, let-out, pretext, way out.

loose
vb lit: detach, disconnect, disengage, free, let go, liberate, release, set free, unbind, undo, unfasten, unleash, untie; hurl, shoot, throw; relax, slacken.
adj lit: detached, disconnected, free, mobile, open, unattached, unconfined, unrestricted, unsecured, untied; flexible, free-moving, lithe, relaxed, slackened, wobbly; baggy, hanging, slack, sloppy; diffuse, ill-defined, imprecise, indefinite, inexact, vague; careless, inattentive, lax, negligent, thoughtless; *fig*: disreputable, dissolute, fast, immoral, lewd, promiscuous, wanton.

loosen
vb lit: let out, open, relax, slacken, untense, untighten; *fig*: ease up, let up, moderate, soften, weaken.

loot
n lit: booty, haul, plunder, spoils, swag; *fig*: money; prize, winnings.
vb lit: despoil, pillage, plunder, ransack, ravage, rob, sack.

lopsided
adj lit: askew, awry, crooked, tilting; asymmetrical, disproportionate, unbalanced, uneven.

lord
n lit: liege, master, owner, ruler; king, monarch, prince, sovereign; noble, nobleman, peer; commander, governor, leader, superior; *spec*: dominant planet (in astrology).

lordly
adj lit: aristocratic, dignified, grand, magnificent, noble, princely, proud, regal, stately; *fig*: arrogant, disdainful, haughty, imperious, overbearing, patronizing, supercilious; domineering, dictatorial, tyrannical.

lore
n lit: beliefs, sayings, stories, teachings, traditions, wisdom; learning, experience, knowledge, understanding; legends, myths, tales.

lose
vb lit: forget, mislay, misplace, miss; be defeated, capitulate, fail, give up, surrender, yield; default on, forfeit, pass up; be depleted by, be deprived of, be drained of, exhaust, expend, use up; be bereaved of; squander, waste; stray from, wander from; dodge, elude, escape, evade, give the slip, shake off.

loser
n lit: capitulator, defeated party, yielder; defaulter, sufferer; also-ran, dud, failure, flop, has-been, lame duck, no-hoper, nonstarter, second-rater.

loss
n lit: decrease, depletion, deprivation, diminution, reduction, shrinkage; bereavement; cost, debit, debt, expenditure, forfeiture; defeat; disappearance, forgetting, mislaying, misplacing; squandering, wastage, waste; damage, impairment, ruin, wreck.

lost
adj lit: mislaid, misplaced, missing; disappeared, vanished; adrift, astray, baffled, bewildered, clueless, disoriented, perplexed, puzzled; destroyed, ruined, wrecked; conceded, forfeited; abstracted, engrossed, entranced, preoccupied, rapt; dissipated, misapplied, misspent, misused, squandered, wasted; *fig*: dead, gone, lapsed, over, past; abandoned, depraved, dissolute, fallen, promiscuous, wanton.

lot
n lit: abundance, amount, deal, heap, host, mass, multitude, plenitude, plethora, quantity, stack; batch, bunch, collection, crowd, group, set; chance, destiny, doom, fate, hazard, kismet, portion; choice, lucky dip, random selection, selection; allocation, cut, part,

piece, quota, ration, share; plot,
property, site; *fig*: character.

lotion
n lit: application, embrocation, liniment,
solution, wash.

lottery
n lit: draw, lucky dip, prize draw, raffle,
tombola, sweepstake; chance, gamble,
matter of luck, toss-up; hazard, risk.

loud
adj lit: blaring, clamorous, deafening, ear-
splitting, forte, fortissimo, noisy,
piercing, resounding, sonorous,
stentorian, thunderous; brash, raucous,
rowdy, strident; *fig*: blatant, brassy,
coarse, crass, flashy, garish, gaudy, lurid,
obtrusive, ostentatious, showy, tasteless,
vulgar.

lounge
n lit: living-room, main room, parlour,
saloon, sitting-room.
vb lit: amble, dawdle, idle, laze, loaf,
loiter, saunter; flop, loll, recline, slouch,
slump, sprawl.

lout
n lit: barbarian, boor, brute, bully,
bumpkin, churl, oaf, yahoo, yobbo.

lovable
adj lit: adorable, appealing, captivating,
enchanting, endearing; amiable,
charming, likable, pleasing, sweet,
winsome; attractive, delightful,
engaging, fetching, winning; alluring,
desirable, fascinating, seductive.

love
n lit: adoration, affection, attachment,
devotion; adulation, infatuation; ardour,
passion; amity, fancy, fondness,
friendship, liking, regard, soft spot,
tenderness, warmth, weakness; *fig*: nil,
nought, zero; free, nothing; *spec*: angel,
beloved, darling, dear, dearest,
sweetheart.
vb lit: adore, be affectionate towards, be
attached to, be devoted to, be very fond
of, cherish, dote on, hold dear; adulate,
idolize, worship; appreciate, enjoy,
fancy, have a soft spot for, have a
weakness for, like very much, prize,
relish, savour, take great pleasure in,
treasure.

lovely
adj lit: beautiful, exquisite, gorgeous,
ravishing; captivating, delightful,

enchanting, eye-catching, fascinating,
stunning; alluring, bewitching,
desirable; appealing, attractive,
charming, engaging, fair, handsome,
lovable, pleasing, pretty, sweet, winning.

lover
n lit: friend, guy, man, mistress,
paramour, woman; admirer, beau,
boyfriend, fiancé, fianceé, girlfriend,
suitor, sweetheart; aficionado,
connoisseur, devotee, fan; adulator,
idolizer, worshipper.

low
n lit: depression, hollow; bottom level,
minimum; *spec*: depression, cyclone (in
meteorology).
vb lit: moo, ululate.
adj lit: deep, depressed, ground-level,
prone, prostrate, sunken; little, shallow,
short, small, squat, stunted; deficient,
depleted, inadequate, meagre, primitive,
reduced, scant, sparse; inferior,
insignificant, mediocre, paltry, poor,
shoddy, trifling; coarse, common,
disreputable, rough, rude, vulgar; base,
contemptible, degraded, depraved,
gross, ignoble, ill-bred, servile, sordid,
undignified; humble, mean, obscure,
plebeian; cheap, economical,
inexpensive, modest; debilitated, feeble,
frail, ill, weak; gentle, hushed, muted,
quiet, soft, subdued; blue, dejected,
depressed, despondent, disheartened,
down, forlorn, glum, miserable, morose,
sad, unhappy; *spec*: less ornate, less
rigorous, simplified (Church, or mass).
adv lit: down, short, to a depressed level,
under; to the horizon; humbly, meanly;
gently, mutedly, quietly, softly.

lower
vb lit: drop, haul down, let down, pull
down; fall, sink, submerge; depress;
abate, curtail, cut, decrease, diminish,
lessen, moderate, reduce, slash; belittle,
bring down, debase, degrade, demean,
devalue, disgrace, dishonour, humble,
humiliate; condescend, deign, stoop;
dilute, mute, quieten, soften, subdue,
tone down.
adj lit: closer to the ground; nearer
to the horizon; cut, decreased,
diminished, lessened, reduced,
slashed; inferior, lesser, minor, smaller,
subordinate.
adv lit: below, beneath, closer to the
ground, further down, further below,

further under, under, underneath; nearer to the horizon.

lowland
n lit: coastal plain, flatlands, flats, plain, plateau.

lowly
adj lit: ignoble, obscure, plebeian, poor; common, modest, ordinary, plain, simple, unpretentious; gentle, humble, meek, mild, unassuming.

loyal
adj lit: devoted, faithful, staunch, steadfast, true, trusty; attached, constant, dependable, trustworthy, unswerving; dutiful, patriotic.

loyalty
n lit: allegiance, devotion, faithfulness, fealty, fidelity, staunchness, steadfastness, trustiness; attachment, constancy, dependability, trustworthiness; patriotism, sense of duty.

lubricate
vb lit: grease, make smooth, oil; make slippery, wet; *fig*: aid, assist, expedite, smooth; bribe.

lucid
adj lit: clear, comprehensible, explicit, intelligible, perspicuous, plain, unambiguous; clear-headed, rational, reasoning, sane, sensible, sober, sound; glassy, limpid, pellucid, pure, translucent, transparent; bright, brilliant, gleaming, luminous, radiant, shining.

lucidity
n lit: clarity, clearness, coherence, explicitness, intelligibility, perspicuity, plainness; clear-headedness, rationality, sanity, sobriety; pellucidity, purity, translucency, transparency; brightness, brilliance, luminosity, radiance.

luck
n lit: chance, fortuitousness, happenstance, hazard; good fortune, serendipity; accident; destiny, fate, lot.

luckless
adj lit: ill-fated, ill-starred, unfortunate, unlucky, unpropitious; doomed, jinxed, star-crossed; hapless, unhappy, wretched.

lucky
adj lit: fortuitous, fortunate, serendipitous; blessed, charmed; auspicious, propitious.

lucrative
adj lit: gainful, paying, productive, profitable, remunerative, well-paid; advantageous, fruitful.

ludicrous
adj lit: absurd, comical, farcical, laughable, nonsensical, preposterous, ridiculous, risible; droll, funny; crazy, mad.

luggage
n lit: baggage, bags, cases, goods and chattels, impedimenta, paraphernalia, stuff, suitcases, things, trunks.

lugubrious
adj lit: dismal, doleful, gloomy, glum, hangdog, melancholy, morose, mournful, sad, sombre, sorrowful, woebegone; dreary, funereal; plaintive.

lukewarm
adj lit: tepid; *fig*: cool, half-hearted, unenthusiastic; apathetic, indifferent, uninterested.

lull
n lit: calming, let-up, interval, pause, respite, subsiding; calm, quiet, silence, stillness.
vb lit: allay, calm, pacify, soothe, still, subdue, tranquillize; hush, quieten; abate, decrease, diminish, ease off, let up, moderate, slacken, subside, wane.

lumbering
adj lit: awkward, bovine, clumsy, elephantine, heavy, hulking, ponderous, ungainly; graceless, inelegant.

luminous
adj lit: brilliant, glowing, effulgent, lit, radiant, refulgent, shining; *fig*: clear, intelligible, lucid, perspicuous, plain; enlightening.

lump
n lit: bulge, bump, growth, protrusion, protuberance, swelling, tumour; bit, chunk, clod, gobbet, hunk, mass, piece; gross, whole; deadweight, lot, mass.
vb lit: aggregate, batch, bunch, combine, conglomerate, group, mass, pool, put together; endure, put up with, stand.

lunacy
n lit: craziness, dementia, insanity, madness, mania, psychosis; *fig*: aberration, absurdity, folly, foolishness,

idiocy, imbecility, stupidity;
recklessness, wildness.

lunatic
n lit: madman, madwoman, maniac,
psychopath; loony, nutcase, nutter,
psycho; *fig*: idiot, imbecile; ass, fool,
moron; crank, eccentric, weirdo;
berserker.
adj lit: crazy, demented, deranged, insane,
mad, maniac, psychotic, raving,
unbalanced; barmy, bananas, bats,
bonkers, crackers, cuckoo, gaga, loony,
nuts, nutty, potty, round the bend,
touched, unhinged; asinine,
crackbrained, daft, foolish, idiotic,
imbecilic, inane, moronic; cranky, dotty,
eccentric, weird; berserk; reckless, wild.

lunge
n lit: jab, pass, stab, swing, swipe, thrust;
charge, pounce; lurch, plunge.
vb lit: hit out, jab, poke, stab, strike out,
swing out, swipe, thrust; bound, charge,
jump, leap, pounce; drop, fall, lurch,
plunge.

lurch
n lit: dip, drop, fall, plunge, slump; roll,
stagger.
vb lit: dip, drop, fall, plummet, plunge,
sink, slump, tumble; pitch, reel, roll,
stagger, stumble, totter, veer.

lure
n lit: bait, carrot, decoy; attraction,
enticement, inducement, temptation;
allure, charm.
vb lit: decoy, ensnare, inveigle, seduce;
attract, draw, entice, invite, lead on,
tempt; allure, charm; *spec*: recall (a
hawk).

lurid
adj lit: bloody, fiery, flaming, livid, red;
ashen, ghastly, pale, pallid, sallow, wan,
yellowish; glowering, menacing,
threatening; exaggerated, garish, gaudy,
glaring, intense, vivid; dramatic,
sensational, shocking, startling; squalid,
sordid.

lurk
vb lit: be furtive, be stealthy, creep, hide,
lie in wait, loiter with intent, prowl,
skulk, slink, steal; be hidden, lie low.

luscious
adj lit: juicy, mouth-watering, succulent;
appetizing, delicious, rich; sweet; *fig*:
voluptuous; well-proportioned; fulsome.

lush
adj lit: densely-growing, flourishing,
green, juicy, luxuriant, succulent,
tender, verdant; *fig*: lavish, luxurious,
opulent, rich, sumptuous; abundant,
prolific, teeming; extravagant, flowery,
ornate.

lust
n lit: desire, libido, passion; carnality,
concupiscence, lasciviousness, lewdness,
sensuality, wantonness; appetite,
craving, cupidity, greed, longing, thirst;
relish.
vb lit: be aroused, feel desire; crave,
hunger, long, thirst, yearn.

lustre
n lit: gleam, glistening, glitter, gloss,
sheen, shimmer, shine, sparkle;
brilliance, dazzle, radiance,
resplendence; *fig*: fame, glory, honour,
illustriousness, renown, splendour; *spec*:
glass pendant (of a chandelier); glaze (on
ceramics).

lusty
adj lit: brawny, healthy, powerful, robust,
stalwart, stout, strapping, strong, sturdy,
vigorous; manly, red-blooded, virile;
energetic, hearty.

luxuriant
adj lit: densely-growing, flourishing, lush,
prolific, rich, teeming, thriving, verdant;
fecund, fertile, fruitful; abundant,
copious, lavish, plentiful, profuse;
elaborate, excessive, extravagant, florid,
flowery, ornate, superabundant.

luxurious
adj lit: costly, expensive, grand, lavish,
magnificent, opulent, rich, sumptuous;
cushy, epicurean, pampered, self-
indulgent, sybaritic; comfortable,
palatial, plush, richly-furnished, well-
appointed.

luxury
n lit: grandeur, magnificence, richness,
sumptuousness; affluence, expense,
opulence; comfort, gratification,
indulgence, pleasure, satisfaction; extra,
extravagance, self-indulgence, treat.

lying
n lit: deceit, deception, dissimulation,
fabrication, falsehoods, falsification,
mendacity, perjury, storytelling,
untruthfulness; fibbing, libel,
prevarication, slander; fraud, imposture,
misrepresentation.

adj (pr.pt) lit: deceitful, dishonest, dissembling, double-crossing, false, mendacious, perjuring, two-faced, untruthful; devious, perfidious, treacherous; fibbing, prevaricating; fraudulent.

lyric
n lit: text, words.
adj lit: expressive, lyrical, melodic, musical; dulcet, graceful, light, mellifluous, melodious, silvery, sweet, tender; romantic, sentimental.

lyrical
adj lit: eloquent, expressive, mellifluent, poetic; ecstatic, emotional, imaginative, inspired, rapturous, romantic, sentimental; effusive, enthusiastic, impassioned.

M

macabre
adj lit: bloodcurdling, creepy, eerie, frightening, ghastly, ghostly, ghoulish, gruesome, morbid, scary, uncanny, unearthly, weird.

mace
n lit: staff, wand; club, knobkerrie, war-club; mallet; nutmeg.

macerate
vb lit: ret, soak, soften, steep; *fig*: emaciate, make gaunt.

machination
n lit: conspiracy, intrigue, plot, scheme, stratagem; artifice, dodge, gambit, move, ploy, ruse, tactic; chicanery, cunning, guile, wiliness.

machine
n lit: apparatus, appliance, device, gadget, mechanism, tool; engine, generator, motor; aeroplane, aircraft, car, motorbike, vehicle; *fig*: infrastructure, organization, set-up, system; android, automaton, robot, workaholic.
vb lit: cut, finish, heat, make, manufacture, print, saw, sew, turn.

macho
adj lit: aggressive, dominant, domineering, he-man, male, muscular, powerful, strong, strong-willed, tough, virile.

mackintosh
n lit: oilskin, raincoat, trench-coat, waterproof.

mad
adj lit: certifiable, insane, mentally disordered, not responsible for one's actions, psychopathic, psychotic; crazy, deranged, demented, lunatic, mental, unbalanced, unhinged; bananas, barmy, bats, bonkers, cracked, crackers, cuckoo, gaga, loony, loopy, not all there, nuts, off one's rocker, off one's trolley, potty, raving, round the bend, round the twist, touched; *fig*: asinine, bird-brained, cockeyed, half-baked, daft, idiotic, irrational, irresponsible, ludicrous, nonsensical, preposterous, scatterbrained, senseless, unworkable; dotty (about), fanatical (about), wild (about); agitated, excited, frantic, hectic, hysterical, riotous; berserk, furious, hysterical, incensed, spare.

maddened
adj (pa.pt) lit: driven crazy, demented, unbalanced, unhinged; driven wild, enraged, incensed, infuriated.

made
vb (pa.pt) lit: built, composed, constituted, constructed, fashioned, formed, generated, invented, manufactured, originated, produced, shaped; designed, devised, drafted, drawn up, framed, enacted, passed; appointed, elected, installed, ordained; had (one do something); added up to, amounted to, came to, totalled; earned, gained, netted, received; reckoned to be; arrived in time for, caught, got, reached; knew, recognized.

madly
adv lit: crazily, dementedly; idiotically, irrationally, irresponsibly, nonsensically, senselessly; agitatedly, excitedly, frantically, frenziedly, hectically, hysterically, recklessly, riotously, wildly; desperately, devotedly, intensely, passionately.

madness
n lit: insanity, lunacy, mental derangement, psychopathy, psychosis, dementia, irrationality; aberration, craziness, daftness, folly, recklessness, wildness; passion; rage; excitement, fever, frenzy, intoxication.

maelstrom
n lit: eddy, vortex, whirlpool; *fig*: chaos, confusion, disorder, swirl, turbulence, upheaval, whirl.

magazine
n lit: journal, monthly, paper, periodical, weekly; ammunition dump, arsenal, powder store; bandolier, clip, flask, horn, keg.

magic

n lit: black arts, necromancy, sorcery, spells, witchcraft, wizardry; paranormal, supernatural; conjuring, hocus-pocus, legerdemain, sleight of hand, trickery; *fig*: charisma, enchantment, fascination, magnetism, power; fire, life, spark.

magician

n lit: enchanter, enchantress, shaman, sorcerer, warlock, witch, wizard, wise man, wise woman; conjuror, illusionist, prestidigitator; *fig*: miracle-worker, wonder-worker; genius, expert, virtuoso.

magisterial

adj lit: authoritative, commanding, dominant, domineering, imperious, overbearing, peremptory.

magnanimity

n lit: beneficence, generosity, great-heartedness, high-mindedness, kindness, nobility, selflessness, unselfishness.

magnate

n lit: baron, big chief, big wheel, mogul, tycoon; grandee, nabob, princeling.

magnetic

adj lit: attractive; *fig*: captivating, charming, enchanting; fascinating, hypnotic, mesmerizing.

magnificence

n lit: glory, grandeur, lavishness, luxury, opulence, pomp, resplendence, splendour, sumptuousness.

magnificent

adj lit: exalted, fine, glorious, grand, grandiose, imposing, lavish, luxurious, majestic, opulent, orgulous, princely, resplendent, splendid, sumptuous, superb.

magnify

vb lit: amplify, blow up, enlarge, expand; heighten, increase, intensify; laud, praise, worship; *fig*: exaggerate, inflate, overdo, overstate.

magnitude

n lit: amplitude, capacity, dimensions, extent, immensity, measure, proportions, quantity, scale, size, volume; *fig*: consequence, eminence, importance, note, significance, weight; *spec*: brightness, brilliance (of a star).

maid

n lit: dresser, handmaiden, housemaid, servant-girl; char, daily, domestic, girl,

help, woman; damsel, lass, wench.

maiden

n lit: damsel, girl, lass, maid, virgin, wench; spinster; *fig*: corn-dolly; clothes-horse.

adj lit: spinster, unmarried, unwed, virgin; undefiled, virginal; first, inaugural; fresh, new, pristine, unused; grown from seed; *spec*: scoreless (cricketing over).

mail

n lit: correspondence, letters, post; armour, chain-link.

vb lit: dispatch, post, send.

main

n lit: might, power, strength, weight; cable, channel, duct, pipe; high seas, ocean.

adj lit: cardinal, chief, critical, essential, important, leading, pre-eminent, primary, principal, vital; extensive, great, large, strong; mere, pure, sheer.

mainly

adv lit: chiefly, for the most part, largely, mostly, predominantly, primarily, principally, substantially; generally, on the whole, usually.

maintain

vb lit: care for, foster, keep up, look after, nurture, preserve, provide for, take care of; carry on, conserve, continue, keep, retain, sustain; allege, assert, aver, claim, contend, declare, hold, insist, state; champion, defend, stand by, uphold.

maintenance

n lit: care, fostering, looking after, nurturing, preservation, provision, upkeep; conservation, continuance, retention, sustaining; defence, protection; allowance, board and lodging, grant, keep, living, support; alimony, award.

majestic

adj lit: august, dignified, exalted, grand, imperial, imposing, lofty, magnificent, princely, regal, royal, stately.

majesty

n lit: dignity, glory, grandeur, greatness, loftiness, magnificence, pomp, splendour, state, stateliness.

major

adj lit: great, important, leading, main, notable, outstanding, pre-eminent, significant, weighty; bigger, greater, higher, larger, superior; elder, senior.

majority
n lit: best part, bulk, preponderance; adulthood, maturity, seniority.

make
n lit: brand, design, form, kind, marque, model, shape, sort, style, type, variety; constitution, manufacture; build, composition.
vb lit: build, construct, create, fabricate, fashion, form, generate, invent, manufacture, originate, produce, put together, shape; design, devise, draft, draw up, frame; conclude, contract; enact, pass; convert, turn; appoint, elect, install as, ordain; have (one do something); add up to, amount to, come to, total; score; contribute, put forward; earn, gain, net, realize, receive; reckon to be; arrive in time for, catch, get, reach; know, recognize.

make do
vb lit: cope, get by, manage (with), scrape by; be content (with).

make off
vb lit: abscond, bolt, flee, fly, run for it, take to one's heels; run away (with), run off (with).

make out
vb lit: detect, discern, distinguish, perceive, see; decipher, read; comprehend, grasp, understand; allege, assert, claim, maintain, suggest; feign, pretend; complete, draft, draw up, fill out, write out; cope, fare, get by, get on, manage; prosper, succeed.

make-up
n lit: cosmetics, face, warpaint; greasepaint; composition, constitution, construction, formation, structure; layout; *fig*: character, disposition, nature, temperament.

make up
vb lit: compose, comprise, constitute, form; compensate for, complete, fill, supply; come up with, concoct, create, devise, dream up, fabricate, hatch, invent, write; atone (for), make amends (for); mend, repair; become friends again, be reconciled, make peace; make overtures (to); settle in (one's mind).

maladjusted
adj (pa.pt) lit: alienated, disturbed,

hung-up, hysterical, neurotic, unbalanced, unstable.

malaise
n lit: anxiety, disquiet, enervation, listlessness, restlessness, unease.

malcontent
n lit: grouch, grumbler; demonstrator, dissident, protester; agitator, anarchist, mischiefmaker, troublemaker.

male
n lit: boy, man; lad; boar, buck, bull, cock, dog, jack, ram, tom.
adj lit: manly, masculine, virile; butch, macho.

malefactor
n lit: criminal, crook, delinquent, felon, lawbreaker, offender, villain; evildoer, sinner, transgressor, trespasser.

malevolent
adj lit: evil-intentioned, malicious, malign, malignant, pernicious, spiteful, vicious, vindictive.

malformation
n lit: deformity, misshapenness; distension, distortion.

malfunction
n lit: breakdown, failure; defect, fault, gremlin.
vb lit: break down, conk out, fail, get stuck, go wrong, pack up, seize up, stall, stop working.

malice
n lit: evil intentions, ill will, malevolence, malignity, perniciousness, spite, spitefulness, viciousness, vindictiveness.

malignant
adj lit: evil-intentioned, malevolent, malicious, spiteful, vicious, vindictive; hostile, inimical; cancerous, dangerous, destructive, metastatic, virulent.

maltreat
vb lit: abuse, be cruel to, be rough with, bully, ill-treat; damage, hurt, injure.

man
n lit: male; person; human, individual; Homo sapiens, humanity, humankind, human race, people; gentleman; bloke, chap, cove, geezer, guy; boyfriend, husband, lover, spouse; attendant, employee, hand, retainer, servant, valet, worker; soldier; follower; team-member; *spec*: (chess/draughts) piece.
vb lit: crew, garrison, people, staff.

manage
vb lit: administer, be in charge of, control, direct, oversee, run, superintend, supervise; manipulate, operate, use, wield; carry out, cope with, do, execute, handle, perform; accomplish, bring off, effect; contrive, engineer, orchestrate; cope, fare, get by, get on, make out, survive; have time for.

manageable
adj lit: amenable, compliant, controllable, docile, submissive, tractable; achievable, attainable, possible; easy; convenient.

management
n lit: administration, board, directors; charge, control, government, handling, running, supervision; manipulation, use, wielding.

mandate
n lit: authorization, commission, directive, warrant; command, decree, edict, instruction, order.
vb lit: authorize (to), commission (to); delegate administrative power (to).

mandatory
adj lit: authorizing, commissioning; compulsory, obligatory, required.

manfully
adv lit: bravely, courageously, determinedly, gallantly, nobly, resolutely, stoutly, valiantly.

mangled
adj (pa.pt) lit: pressed, wrung; bent, broken, crooked, crushed, deformed, disfigured, distorted, lamed, maimed, mutilated, ripped, torn; *fig*: garbled, misrepresented, travestied.

mangy
adj lit: dirty, mean, scabby, scruffy, seedy, shabby, squalid.

manhandle
vb lit: haul, heave, lug, manocuvrc, pull, push, roll, shove; fondle, grope, maul, paw; abuse, knock about, rough up.

mania
n lit: elation, euphoria, violent excitement; fixation, obsession, violent enthusiasm; *fig*: craze, fad, passion.

manifest
n lit: bill of lading, cargo checklist; passenger-list.
vb lit: demonstrate, display, evince, exhibit, make evident, make visible, reveal, show; announce, declare, state publicly.
adj lit: apparent, clear, evident, obvious, patent, plain, visible.

manifestation
n lit: appearance, demonstration, display, exhibition, revelation, show; evidence, indication, sign, symptom; example, instance; apparition, materialization.

manifold
n lit: multiple exhaust inlet; carbon copy; *spec*: aggregate (in mathematics).
adj lit: abundant, many, multiple, numerous, plural; diverse, multifarious, various.

manipulation
n lit: command, control, direction, driving, guidance, handling, management, manoeuvering, piloting, steering, use, wielding; arrangement, contrivance, engineering, orchestration, organization.

manliness
n lit: machismo, maleness, masculinity, muscularity, power, strength, strength of will, toughness, virility; bravery, courage, hardihood, intrepidity, valour; chivalry, gallantry, gentlemanliness.

manner
n lit: approach, means, measures, method, mode, procedure, process, steps, way; custom, fashion, habit, practice, routine, style, usage; air, appearance, comportment, demeanour, mien, tone; attitude, behaviour; category, form, kind, nature, sort, strain, type, vein.

mannerism
n lit: characteristic, foible, habit, idiosyncrasy, quirk, trait; affectation, distortion, stiltedness.

manners
n lit: courtesy, decorum, etiquette, good form, proprieties, protocol, refinement, social graces; behaviour, conduct, mores.

manoeuvre
n lit: dodge, gambit, machination, move, ploy, scheme, stratagem, tactic; action, deployment, exercise, operation.
vb lit: command, control, deploy, direct, drive, guide, handle, locate, manage, manipulate, move, navigate, pilot, place, steer, wield; contrive, devise, engineer, orchestrate, wangle.

mantle
n lit: cape, hood; cloak, redingote; *fig*:
covering, curtain, screen, shroud, veil;
spec: incandescing mesh (in a gas lamp);
lining (of a mollusc's shell); stratum (of
rock between the earth's core and crust).
vb lit: blanket, cloak, cover, envelop,
mask, screen, shroud, veil.

manual
n lit: bible, compendium, guidebook,
handbook, instruction-book, textbook,
vade-mecum, workshop reference;
keyboard.
adj lit: hand-cranked, hand-operated.

manufacture
n lit: assembly, construction, mass-
production, production; end-product,
product.
vb lit: assemble, build, construct, make,
mass-produce, process, produce, put
together, turn out; *fig*: come up with,
concoct, devise, fabricate, make up,
think up.

manure
n lit: droppings, dung, muck; fertilizer,
mulch.

many
n lit: lots, scores, thousands.
adj lit: a large number of, countless,
innumerable, lots of, numerous, sundry,
various.

mar
vb lit: blemish, blight, blot, disfigure,
impair, scar, spoil, stain, sully, taint,
tarnish.

march
n lit: haul, hike, tramp, trek, walk, yomp;
advance, development, progress; (on the)
way; demo, demonstration, parade,
procession; military tune; border,
boundary; borderland, edge, frontier,
margin.
vb lit: hike, step out, stride out, traipse,
tramp, tread, trek, walk, yomp; abut,
adjoin, border, bound.

margin
n lit: border, boundary, edge, limit,
perimeter, periphery, verge; allowance,
elbow-room, latitude, leeway, play,
room, surplus.

marginal
adj lit: bordering, peripheral;
insignificant, minimal, negligible,
outside, slight, tiny.

marijuana
n lit: cannabis, grass, hemp, pot, smoke,
weed; hash, hashish; bhang, dagga,
ganja, kif.

marine
n lit: nautical service, navy; fleet;
maritime soldier.
adj lit: maritime, nautical, naval, ocean-
going, oceanographic, offshore, sea,
seagoing.

marital
adj lit: conjugal, connubial, married,
wedded.

maritime
adj lit: marine, nautical, naval,
oceanographic, sea; coastal, inshore,
littoral.

mark
n lit: blot, splodge, spot, stain; badge,
brand, device, emblem, logo, signature,
symbol, token; label, tag; blemish, dent,
nick, scar, scratch; footprint, sign, trace,
vestige; criterion, level, line, norm,
yardstick; aim, goal, jack, objective,
target; dupe, greenhorn, gull, innocent,
patsy, sucker; model, type; consequence,
distinction, eminence, note, standing;
point, unit.
vb lit: blot, splodge, spot, stain; sign,
write on; brand, label, tag; blemish,
dent, nick, scar, scratch; exemplify,
illustrate, register, show; attend to,
mind, note, pay heed to, watch; assess,
evaluate, grade.

marked
adj (pa.pt) lit: splodged, spotted, stained;
branded, identified, indicated, labelled,
tagged; blemished, dented, imperfect,
nicked, scarred, scratched; clear,
conspicuous, distinct, manifest, obvious,
patent, pronounced, striking; emphatic,
extreme, great, surprising, unexpected;
suspected, threatened, watched; dead,
doomed, ill-fated.

market
n lit: bazaar, mart; souk, town square;
stock exchange; buying public,
consumers, purchasers; demand.
vb lit: hawk, peddle, sell, vend; advertise,
hype, plug, promote, push.

maroon
vb lit: abandon, cast away, desert, isolate,
leave high and dry, rat on, run out on,
strand.

adj lit: chestnut, red-brown; mauve, violet.

married
adj (pa.pt) lit: hitched, spliced, wed, wedded; conjugal, connubial, marital.

marrow
n lit: core, pith, substance; *fig*: crux, heart, kernel, nub; essence, gist, spirit; best part, juice.

marry
vb lit: be wed, get hitched, get spliced, take the plunge, tie the knot, wed; ally, join, link, match, put together, unite.

marshal
n lit: officer of the royal household; law-court officer.
vb lit: arrange, array, deploy, dispose, group, line up, order; conduct, escort, guide, lead, usher.

martial
adj lit: bellicose, belligerent, warlike; military; attacking, defensive, strategic.

marvel
n lit: phenomenon, prodigy, wonder; expert, genius, virtuoso.
vb lit: be awed, gape, wonder; be astonished, be overwhelmed.

marvellous
adj lit: amazing, astonishing, astounding, phenomenal, prodigious, wonderful; fabulous, fantastic, incredible, unbelievable.

mash
vb lit: beat, crush, grind down, hash, mix, pound down, pulp, smash, whip; infuse, malt.

mask
n lit: domino; visor; *fig*: camouflage, cloak, cover, disguise, front, veil.
vb lit: camouflage, cloak, conceal, cover, disguise, screen, veil.

masquerade
n lit: masked ball; imposture, pretence, simulation; act, charade, disguise.
vb lit: be disguised (as), be dressed (as).

mass
n lit: entirety, sum, totality, whole; body, bulk, matter, substance; dimensions, magnitude, scale, size; block, chunk, lump, piece; accumulation, amount, collection, heap, load, lot, pile, quantity; crowd, horde, host, mob, multitude,

throng; majority; lower class(es); *spec*: communion service, eucharist, holy communion, the Lord's supper.
vb lit: accumulate, assemble, collect, congregate, muster, rally; concentrate (together), flock.

massacre
n lit: bloodbath, butchery, carnage, slaughter; extermination, holocaust, genocide.
vb lit: butcher, exterminate, kill, mow down, slaughter, wipe out.

massage
n lit: rub-down; manipulation, osteopathy, osteotherapy.
vb lit: knead, rub, soothe, stroke, tap; caress, fondle.

massive
adj lit: bulky, colossal, cyclopean, enormous, gigantic, hefty, huge, hulking, immense, mammoth, monumental, titanic, vast, weighty.

master
n lit: captain, chief, commander, head, lord, principal, skipper; overseer, owner; boss, director, employer; guide, instructor, teacher, tutor; guru, swami; ace, adept, expert, virtuoso; *fig*: model, mould, original, pattern.
vb lit: command, control, dominate, rule; become good at, grasp, learn; break, bridle, curb, domesticate, overpower, subdue, subjugate, tame.
adj lit: chief, foremost, grand, main, prime, principal; adept, expert, skilled, virtuoso; *fig*: model, original; *spec*: skeleton (key).

masterly
adj lit: adept, consummate, crack, expert, skilled, virtuoso; brilliant, fine, first-rate, excellent.

mastermind
n lit: brains, engineer, genius, organizer, planner.
vb lit: arrange, be the brains behind, engineer, orchestrate, organize, plan.

masterpiece
n lit: chef d'oeuvre, magnum opus, pièce de résistance, work of genius.

mastery
n lit: authority, control, domination, dominion, rule, supremacy, whip hand; triumph, victory; command, grasp,

knowledge, understanding; ability, dexterity, expertise, skill, virtuosity.

mat
n lit: carpet, cloth, floor-covering, rug; coaster, cork-tile, place-setting; mass, mess, tangle; web.

match
n lit: complement, counterpart, equal, equivalent; copy, duplicate, lookalike, replica, ringer, twin; competitor, rival; bout, competition, contest, game; alliance, marriage, pairing, partnership; light, lucifer; fuse.
vb lit: compare, equal, parallel, rival; oppose (against), pit (against); agree with, blend with, go with, harmonize with, suit; ally, couple, marry, pair, partner, put together.

matching
adj (pr.pt) lit: accompanying, complementary, coordinating, corresponding, paired, related, twinned.

matchless
adj lit: incomparable, inimitable, peerless, perfect, superior, unequalled, unique, unrivalled.

mate
n lit: partner, spouse; husband, lover, wife; buddy, china, chum, mucker, pal; associate, companion, comrade, crony; colleague, co-worker, partner; aide, assistant, henchman, second-in-command; complement, counterpart, fellow, match, twin.
vb lit: match, pair; marry, wed; breed, copulate, couple.

material
n lit: matter, substance; constituents, element(s); cloth, fabric; data, evidence, information, schema; apparatus, implement(s), instrument(s), tool(s).
adj lit: concrete, corporeal, palpable, physical, tangible; essential, important, key, significant, vital; applicable (to), germane (to), pertinent (to), relevant (to).

materialize
vb lit: appear, come into being, form, manifest oneself, take shape; arise, crop up, pop up, turn up; arrive.

materially
adv lit: considerably, fundamentally, greatly, much, seriously, substantially.

matrimonial
adj lit: conjugal, connubial, marital, marriage, nuptial, wedded.

matrimony
n lit: marriage, wedlock; nuptials, wedding.

matter
n lit: material, substance; affair, case, circumstance, concern, event, incident, occurrence, question, situation, subject, thing; argument, gist, point, purport, sense; contents, copy, text; consequence, importance, moment, significance; amount, quantity; difficulty, problem, trouble; *spec*: (discharge of) purulence, pus.
vb lit: be important, count, make a difference, signify; *spec*: suppurate (pus).

matter-of-fact
adj lit: down-to-earth, mundane, prosaic, sober, unemotional, unimaginative.

mature
vb lit: be fully developed, come of age, grow up, reach adulthood; bloom, blossom, mellow, ripen, season; *fig*: become payable, fall due.
adj lit: adult, full-grown, grown-up, of age; fully fledged, mellow, ready, ripe, seasoned; *fig*: due, payable; practical, prudent, wise.

maturity
n lit: adulthood, age of reason, majority, manhood, womanhood, years of discretion; bloom, blossoming, mellowness, ripeness; *fig*: common sense, nous, poise, practicality, prudence, wisdom.

maudlin
adj lit: emotional, mushy, sentimental, soppy, tearful; drunken, fuddled, tipsy; self-pitying.

maul
n lit: loose scrimmage, ruck.
vb lit: claw, lacerate, mangle; batter, beat, knock (about), thrash; manhandle, treat roughly; abuse, fumble, grope, molest, paw.

maundering
adj (pr.pt) lit: babbling, chattering, discursive, droning on, rabbiting, rambling, wandering, wittering on; inarticulate, muttering, stumbling; drifting, meandering, straggling.

mawkish
adj lit: emotional, maudlin, mushy, sentimental, soppy; flat, insipid, sickly, stale; disgusting, offensive; squeamish.

maxim
n lit: aphorism, guideline, obiter dictum, principle, rule, theorem; axiom, byword, proverb, saw, saying.

maximum
n lit: best, chief, greatest, highest, largest, most; apogee, ceiling, crest, height, peak, pinnacle, summit, top, zenith.

maybe
cnj lit: perchance, perhaps, possibly.

mayhem
n lit: chaos, confusion, disorder, havoc, mischief, rowdiness; injury, maiming, wounding.

maze
n lit: labyrinth; *fig*: complex, mesh, system, tangle, web; puzzle, state of bewilderment.

meadow
n lit: grass, lea, pasture; field, hayfield, paddock.

meagre
adj lit: barren, infertile, poor, unproductive; deficient, paltry, scanty, short, slight, small, sparse; bony, gaunt, lean, scrawny, skinny, thin.

meal
n lit: bite, nosh, repast, snack; banquet, blow-out, dinner, feast, lunch; flour, ground grain; powder.

mean
n lit: average, intermediate, median, medium, middle; norm, par, standard.
vb lit: betoken, connote, denote, express, indicate, signify, stand for; drive at, imply, insinuate, refer to, say, suggest; entail, involve, lead to, result in; aim (to), be resolved (to), intend (to), plan (to), propose (to), purpose (to); design (to), destine (to), fate (to), foreordain (to), make (to), predestine (to).
adj lit: average, intermediate, median, medium, middle; normal, standard; close-fisted, miserly, near, parsimonious, penny-pinching, stingy, tight; beggarly, contemptible, low, seedy, shabby, sordid, squalid, wretched; base, degenerate, degraded, dishonourable, shameful; common, humble, inferior,

low-born, menial, ordinary, plebeian, servile; *fig*: bad-tempered, cantankerous, disagreeable, ornery, rude, sour; dangerous; clever, shrewd, tricky; tasty.

meandering
adj (pr.pt) lit: convoluted, serpentine, sinuous, tortuous, wandering, winding.

meaning
n lit: connotation, import, interpretation, purport, significance; drift, gist, implication, insinuation, point, sense, substance, suggestion; force, thrust, validity, value; aim, design, intention, object, purpose.
adj lit: eloquent, expressive, pregnant, significant, speaking.

meaningless
adj lit: aimless, empty, hollow, pointless, purposeless, useless, worthless; garbled, incomprehensible, unintelligible.

means
n lit: agent, instrument, medium, method, mode, process, way; agency, instrumentality, methodology, procedure; capital, funds, income, property, resources, substance, wealth, wherewithal; (by) dint (of).

meanwhile
adv lit: at the same time, concurrently, contemporaneously, simultaneously; for the duration, for the moment, in the interim, in the meantime.

measurably
adv lit: discernibly, distinctly, materially, perceptibly, physically, quantifiably, quantitatively, visibly.

measure·
n lit: gauge, meter, rule, ruler, scale, scoop, tape; optic; benchmark, criterion, line, norm, standard, touchstone, unit, yardstick; allocation, proportion, quota, ration, share; amount, quantity; degree, extent, range, scope; dimensions, magnitude, size; column-width, page-width; action, course, manoeuvre, ploy, step; act, bill, law, resolution, statute; beat, cadence, rhythm; dance; foot, metre; *fig*: moderation, restraint; *spec*: (geological) bed(s).
vb lit: calibrate, determine, gauge, mark (off/out), quantify, value; deal (out), dole (out), mete (out).

measurement
n lit: calibration, gauging, quantifying,

valuation; amplitude, dimensions, extent, magnitude, proportions, size.

meat
n lit: flesh, viands; brawn, muscle; chow, food, grub, nourishment, provisions, rations, subsistence, victuals; *fig*: essence, heart, marrow, nub, pith, substance.

meaty
adj lit: beefy, brawny, burly, hulking, muscular, strapping; nourishing, rich; *fig*: concentrated, meaningful, pithy.

mechanical
adj lit: automated, automatic, machine-operated; emotionless, impersonal, machine-like, unfeeling; constant, habitual, mindless, monotonous, perfunctory, reflex, routine, unchanging, unthinking.

mechanism
n lit: apparatus, appliance, device, gadget, machine; action, cogs, machinery, works; functioning, operation, performance, working; means, method, procedure, system, technique.

mediate
vb lit: arbitrate, conciliate, intercede, moderate, referee, umpire; intervene (between).

mediator
n lit: arbiter, arbitrator, conciliator, go-between, intercessor, intermediary, middle-man, moderator, negotiator, peacemaker, referee, umpire.

medicinal
adj lit: curative, healing, officinal, remedial; therapeutic; medical.

medicine
n lit: medicament, medication, therapy, treatment; drug; capsule, pill, tablet; linctus; pathology; *fig*: punishment; charm, magic, spell.

mediocre
adj lit: average, commonplace, medium, ordinary, undistinguished; indifferent, less than ordinary, pedestrian, second-rate, uninspired.

mediocrity
n lit: ordinariness, undistinguished nature; lack of inspiration, pedestrianism; lightweight, nonentity, second-rater.

meditate
vb lit: cogitate (over), contemplate, deliberate (on/over), mull (over), muse (on/over), ponder (over), ruminate (over), think (over).

meditative
adj lit: contemplative, musing, pondering, reflective, ruminative, thoughtful.

medium
n lit: average, middle; compromise, midpoint; agency, channel, instrument, means, organ, vehicle; method, mode, process, way; mouthpiece, spiritist, spiritualist, transmitter; atmosphere, conditions, environment, milieu, setting.
adj lit: average, intermediate, median, middle, middling.

medley
n lit: arrangement, assortment, collection, miscellany, selection; jumble, mixture, patchwork, variety; hotch-potch, mishmash.

meek
adj lit: docile, gentle, humble, mild, submissive, unassuming; deferential, modest, peaceable; spineless, tame, weak.

meet
vb lit: come across, encounter, find, happen on, run into; greet, welcome; assemble, congregate, convene, gather, muster, rally; compete with, confront, contend against, do battle with, face, line up against; adjoin, connect, converge, join, merge, touch; *fig*: come up to, comply with, fulfil, match, measure up to, satisfy; bear, endure, experience, undergo.
adj lit: appropriate, correct, fitting, proper, right, seemly, suitable.

meeting
n lit: encounter; assignation, rendezvous, tryst; conclave, conference, convention, convocation, gathering, get-together, rally; service; concourse, confluence, conjunction, convergence, junction, merging; crossing.

melancholy
n lit: dejection, depression, despondency, sadness, sorrow, unhappiness, wretchedness.
adj lit: dejected, depressed, despondent, doleful, glum, miserable, mournful, sad, unhappy, wretched.

mellow
vb lit: age, mature, ripen, soften, sweeten.
adj lit: full, juicy, mature, rich, ripe, soft,
sweet; *fig*: mellifluous, rounded, smooth,
tuneful; elevated, expansive, happy,
jolly, merry.

melodious
adj lit: cantabile, catchy, harmonious,
musical, tuneful.

melodramatic
adj lit: exaggerated, histrionic, overdone,
sensational, stagy, theatrical.

melody
n lit: air, theme, tune; lay, song, strain;
tunefulness.

melt
vb lit: deliquesce, dissolve, fuse, liquefy,
thaw; fade (away), vanish (away); *fig*:
disarm, charm, soften.

member
n lit: associate; representative; appendage,
component, constituent, element, limb,
organ, part; *fig*: clause.

memento
n lit: keepsake, reminder, souvenir, token.

memo
n lit: agendum, circular, docket,
information-slip, note, record, reminder,
round robin, schedule; précis, summary.

memoirs
n lit: autobiography, history, life, life-
story; experiences, reminiscences;
documents, papers, records,
transactions.

memorable
adj lit: emotive, impressive, indelible,
moving, notable, remarkable, striking,
unforgettable; extraordinary, odd,
strange; historic, important; catchy,
haunting.

memory
n lit: recall, recollection; powers of
retention; remembrance, reminiscence;
commemoration, memorial; fame,
renown, reputation; data-bank, data-
base, data-store.

menace
n lit: threat; danger, hazard; *fig*: nuisance,
pain, pest.
vb lit: bully, frighten, intimidate,
terrorize, threaten; loom over,
overshadow.

mend
vb lit: fix, patch up, repair, replace;
renovate, restore; better, correct, rectify;
heal, improve, knit, recover.

menial
n lit: dogsbody, drudge, flunkey, gofer,
lackey, minion, servant, skivvy, slave,
underling.
adj lit: base, humble, ignoble, lowly,
mean, servile, subservient; boring,
monotonous, routine, unskilled.

mental
adj lit: intellectual; psychological;
internal, notional; *fig*: deranged, insane,
psychotic, unbalanced.

mentality
n lit: intellect, intelligence, IQ; integrity,
rationality; attitude, disposition,
outlook, temperament, way of thinking.

mention
n lit: acknowledgement (of), allusion,
citation, plug, reference, tribute.
vb lit: acknowledge, allude to, bring up,
cite, make known, name, refer to, say
something about, touch upon.

mercantile
adj lit: commercial, trade; industrial;
merchandising, marketing, trading.

mercenary
n lit: dog of war, freelance, hired soldier,
soldier of fortune.
adj lit: hired, paid; avaricious, greedy,
money-grubbing, venal.

merchandise
n lit: commodities, products, stock, wares;
goods.

merchant
n lit: dealer, retailer, seller, shopkeeper,
trader, tradesman, wholesaler.

merciful
adj lit: clement, compassionate, humane,
lenient, magnanimous; forgiving.

merciless
adj lit: callous, cruel, hard-hearted, harsh,
heartless, implacable, inhumane, pitiless,
ruthless; strict, unforgiving.

mercy
n lit: clemency, compassion, grace,
humanity, leniency, magnanimity, pity,
quarter; forgiveness; *fig*: blessing,
godsend, relief; (at the) disposition (of).

mere
adj lit: plain, pure, sheer, simple, stark, unadulterated, unmitigated; callow, green, young; insignificant, trifling, trivial, unimportant.

merely
adv lit: only, purely, simply, solely.

meretricious
adj lit: brash, flashy, gaudy, loud, ostentatious, showy; deceptive, illusory, specious, spurious.

merit
n lit: credit; excellence, meed, quality, value, virtue, worth; advantage, strong point.
vb lit: be worthy of, deserve, rate, warrant; earn.

merriment
n lit: conviviality, drollery, fun, hilarity, jollity, mirth, quipping, revelry, waggishness.

merry
adj lit: blithe, carefree, convivial, droll, fun, happy, jolly, waggish; *fig*: fuddled, high, mellow, sozzled, tiddly, woozy.

mesh
n lit: net, network, plexus, reticulation; lattice, web, webbing; tangle, toils.
vb lit: ensnare, entangle, net, snare, tangle; connect, coordinate, dovetail, engage, interlock; heal, knit.

mesmerize
vb lit: hypnotize, magnetize, put into a trance; dominate, fascinate, spellbind; captivate, entrance.

mess
n lit: clutter, confusion, jumble, mishmash, shambles; chaos, disarray, untidiness; blot, blotch, smear, smudge, splodge; bungle, cock-up, dog's dinner, hash; cowpat, shit, turd; *fig*: fix, jam, muddle, pickle, predicament, spot; *spec*: dining-room, refectory, sitting (in the armed forces).
vb lit: clutter (up), disorganize, jumble (up); blot, smear, smudge; cock (up), foul (up), hash (up), muck (up), muddle (up); dirty, foul, pollute, soil; fiddle (with), interfere (with), meddle (with), tinker (with); fiddle (with), play (with).

message
n lit: communiqué, dispatch, memo, news, word; import, meaning, moral, point, sense, theme.

messenger
n lit: bearer, carrier, courier, emissary, envoy, go-between.

messy
adj lit: cluttered, disorganized, jumbled, muddled; blotchy, smeared, smudged; dirty, muddied, muddy, polluted, soiled; dishevelled, matted, slovenly, tangled, unkempt.

metamorphosis
n lit: alteration, change, reformation, transformation; development.

metaphorical
adj lit: figurative, symbolic.

meteoric
adj lit: atmospheric; brilliant, dazzling, flashing, spectacular, sudden; momentary, shortlived, transient.

method
n lit: approach, fashion, manner, mode, practice, procedure, process, routine, system, technique, way; form, order, planning, structure; classification.

methodical
adj lit: businesslike, disciplined, efficient, orderly, planned, regular, systematic, tidy.

meticulous
adj lit: careful, fastidious, painstaking, particular, punctilious, scrupulous, thorough; over-exact, pedantic.

microbe
n lit: germ, micro-organism; bacillus, bacterium, virus.

microscopic
adj lit: minuscule, minute, tiny; infinitesimal.

middle
n lit: centre, midpoint; mean, medium; midriff, stomach, waist; (in the) midst (of).
adj lit: central; mean, median, medium; intermediate.

middling
adj lit: average, medium, moderate; all right, okay, passable, tolerable; indifferent, mediocre.

midget
n lit: person of restricted growth; dwarf;

homunculus, pygmy; manikin; halfpint, shrimp, titch.
adj lit: dwarf, miniature, pocket, pygmy, tiny.

mightily
adv lit: forcefully, powerfully, strongly, vigorously; exceedingly, extremely, greatly, hugely, immensely, very.

mighty
adj lit: forceful, powerful, strong, vigorous; brawny, muscular, stalwart, strapping; colossal, enormous, gigantic, huge, immense, massive, vast.

migrate
vb lit: journey, move on, shift camp, travel, trek, voyage; move elsewhere, pass (through).

mild
adj lit: easy-going, gentle, meek, peaceable, placid, serene, temperate, tender, tranquil; moderate, pleasant, warm; bland, soothing.

mildness
n lit: gentleness, meekness, placidity, serenity, temperateness, tenderness, tranquillity; moderation, warmth; blandness.

militant
n lit: activist, fanatic; terrorist; combatant, fighter, soldier; hawk, warmonger.
adj lit: active, aggressive, belligerent, combative, hawkish, pugnacious, warlike; at war, embattled.

military
n lit: armed forces, army, services, war office.
adj lit: army, service; ministry of defence, war office; soldierly.

milk
n lit: lactation; juice, sap.
vb lit: draw off, express, extract, tap; *fig*: bleed, drain, wring; exploit, impose upon, take advantage of.

milky
adj lit: clouded, fatty, opaque, white; *fig*: gentle, soft, smooth.

mill
n lit: crusher, grinder; factory, plant, processing plant, works
vb lit: crush, granulate, grind, powder, press, pulverize, punch, serrate, stamp; crowd (around), swarm (about), throng (around).

millions
n lit: astronomical figures, countless numbers, hordes, hosts, masses, vast quantities.

mimic
n lit: imitator; impersonator, impressionist; parodist.
vb lit: copy closely, duplicate, echo, imitate, look like, resemble closely, simulate; ape, caricature, impersonate, parody.

mince
vb lit: chop, cut up, dice, grind; *fig*: moderate, soften, tone down; be effeminate, pose, posture, primp, walk effeminately.

mind
n lit: brain, grey matter, intellect, intelligence, reason; consciousness, psyche, subconscious; marbles, rationality, sanity, wits; memory, recollection; thoughts; *fig*: genius, thinker; attitude, judgement, opinion, thoughts, way of thinking; imagination; attention, concentration; fancy (to), urge (to), wish (to).
vb lit: care, disapprove, feel strongly about, object, take offence; attend to, heed, listen to, mark, note; comply with, follow, obey; ensure that, make certain that, take care that; keep an eye on, look after, take care of, watch over; beware of, look out for; *fig*: recall, remember.

mindful
adj lit: aware (of), conscious (of), heedful (of), observant (of), sensible (of).

mindless
adj lit: automatic, mechanical; casual, gratuitous, incidental, indifferent, unreasoning; careless, forgetful, negligent, unmindful; asinine, batwitted, idiotic, moronic, obtuse.

mine
n lit: bomb, explosive device, shell; excavation, gallery, pit, quarry, shaft, tunnel; *fig*: fund, hoard, stock, store, wealth.
vb lit: lay a floating bomb, sink a bomb; dig (for), excavate (for), quarry (for); subvert, tunnel under.

mingle
vb lit: blend, coalesce, compound, intermix, merge, mix; associate, consort, hang around, hobnob, socialize.

minimal
adj lit: infinitesimal, minuscule, minute, tiny; invisible, virtually nonexistent; nominal, token.

minimize
vb lit: deprecate, make light of, play down, tone down; keep as small as possible, reduce as much as possible; *fig*: decrease, diminish, shrink.

minimum
n lit: least, lowest, slightest, smallest; bottom, nadir.

minister
n lit: clergyman, cleric, padre, parson, preacher, priest, vicar; cabinet/government member, consul, diplomat, envoy; agent, lieutenant, official, subordinate.
vb lit: attend to the needs of, serve, take care of.

ministry
n lit: cloth, holy orders, priesthood; bureau, government department, government office.

minor
adj lit: immature, juvenile, under-age; inconsequential, insignificant, negligible, petty, slight, trifling, trivial, unimportant; junior, subordinate; younger.

minority
n lit: lesser number, smaller group; losing voters; childhood years.

mint
n lit: coin factory, herb; *fig*: origin, source; bomb, fortune, king's ransom, packet, tidy sum.
vb lit: cast, coin, punch, stamp, strike; *fig*: come up with, create, devise, invent, make up, produce, think up.
adj lit: brand-new, fresh, perfect, undamaged, unused.

minute
n lit: agendum, memorandum, note(s), record(s); 60 seconds; *fig*: flash, instant, jiffy, moment, second, tick;
vb lit: log, make a transcript of, record, register, take notes of.
adj lit: diminutive, fine, microscopic, minuscule, tiny; insignificant, negligible, trifling, trivial, unimportant; detailed, exhaustive, meticulous, precise, punctilious, scrupulous.

minutiae
n lit: details, finer points, niceties, small type, subtleties; commonplaces, everyday matters, little things, trifles, trivia.

minx
n lit: coquette, flirt, hoyden, hussy, jade.

miracle
n lit: divine intervention, supernatural occurrence; phenomenon; magic feat, thaumaturgy, wonder; *fig*: blessing, godsend.

miraculous
adj lit: divine, providential; supernatural; extraordinary, incredible, inexplicable, phenomenal, unaccountable, unbelievable; magic, magical, thaumaturgic, wondrous.

mire
n lit: mud, ooze, quicksand, slime; bog, slough.

mirror
n lit: glass, looking-glass; double, image, likeness, reflection, twin.
vb lit: depict, display, reflect, show; echo, emulate; copy, simulate.

misadventure
n lit: accident, bad luck, ill fortune, mischance, misfortune.

misapprehension
n lit: error, false impression, misconception, misconstruction, misunderstanding.

misbehave
vb lit: act up, be disobedient, be naughty, be mischievous, be rude, get into trouble, muck about.

miscalculate
vb lit: make a mathematical error; misjudge, mistake, slip up over.

miscarriage
n lit: spontaneous abortion, stillbirth; error, failure, perversion; *fig*: botch, mismanagement.

miscellaneous
adj lit: assorted, diverse, mixed, sundry, various; jumbled, mingled, mixed up.

mischief
n lit: disobedience, misbehaviour, mucking about, naughtiness; boisterousness, devilment, horseplay, shenanigans; damage, harm, hurt,

injury, trouble; *fig*: devil, nuisance, pest, rogue, scamp.

mischievous
adj lit: badly behaved, disobedient, impish, misbehaving, mucking about, naughty, troublesome, vexatious; boisterous, careless, riotous, rough; deleterious, detrimental, malign, spiteful; destructive, evil, harmful, injurious, pernicious, wicked.

misconduct
n lit: immorality, impropriety, malpractice, unethical behaviour; disobedience, misbehaviour, naughtiness, rudeness.

misdeed
n lit: misdemeanour, offence, sin, transgression, trespass; crime.

misdemeanour
n lit: crime, infringement, misdeed, offence, transgression.

miser
n lit: hoarder, niggard, penny-pincher, Scrooge, skinflint, tightwad.

miserable
adj lit: blue, broken-hearted, dejected, depressed, desolate, despondent, dismal, doleful, down, gloomy, grief-stricken, heartbroken, melancholy, sorrowful, suffering, unhappy, wretched; bankrupt, destitute, impoverished, penniless, poor; base, deplorable, low, mean, pitiable, shabby, shameful, sordid, sorry, squalid.

miserly
adj lit: avaricious, close-fisted, grasping, mean, niggardly, parsimonious, penny-pinching, Scrooge-like, stingy, tight.

misery
n lit: dejection, depression, despair, distress, grief, melancholy, sadness, sorrow, suffering, unhappiness, wretchedness; destitution, pennilessness, penury, poverty; meanness, shabbiness, sordidness, squalor; burden, hardship, misfortune, trial, tribulation, woe.

misgiving
n lit: anxiety, apprehension, fear, qualm, reservation, scruple, suspicion, worry.

misguided
adj lit: deluded, ill-advised, led astray, misled; imprudent, injudicious, indiscreet, misplaced, unwise; mistaken.

mishap
n lit: accident, blow, contretemps, mischance, piece of bad luck, reverse, setback.

misinterpret
vb lit: misapprehend, misconstrue, misread, misunderstand; distort, falsify, garble, misrepresent, pervert, travesty.

mislaid
adj (pa.pt) lit: gone, lost, misplaced, missing, nowhere to be found, untraced, vanished.

misleading
adj (pr.pt) lit: ambiguous, confusing, deceptive, fallacious, false, inaccurate, specious, unrepresentative.

misplace
vb lit: be unable to find, lose, mislay; misattribute.

misrule
n lit: maladministration, mismanagement; anarchy, chaos, disorder, lawlessness; mischief, revelry.

miss
n lit: failure, inaccuracy; thumbs down, veto; wide berth.
vb lit: be late for, forgo, lose; fail to grasp, let slip; fail to notice, pass over, overlook; jump, leave out, neglect, omit, skip; long for, pine for, yearn for.

misshapen
adj lit: contorted, crippled, crooked, deformed, hunched, maimed, malformed, scarred, twisted, warped.

missing
adj lit: absent, gone astray, lacking, lost, mislaid, misplaced, not there, unaccounted for.

mission
n lit: assignment, charge, duty, job, quest, task, undertaking; deputation, embassy, legation; centre, church, station.

missionary
n lit: evangelist, preacher, proselytiser; preacher.

mist
n lit: fog, haar, smog, vapour; condensation, drizzle, spray.

mistake
n lit: blunder, boob, botch-up, clanger, cock-up, error, fault, gaffe, goof, howler, inaccuracy, miscalculation,

misconception, misunderstanding, oversight, slip.
vb lit: get wrong, misinterpret, misunderstand; miscalculate, misjudge; take (for).

mistaken
adj (pa.pt) lit: misguided, misinformed, wide of the mark; inaccurate, incorrect, wrong; ill-advised, ill-judged, imprudent, unwise.

mistrust
vb lit: be wary of, distrust, have doubts about, suspect.

mitigate
vb lit: alleviate, assuage, extenuate, lessen, lighten, moderate, mollify, palliate, placate, remit, soften, temper.

mix
n lit: assortment, blend, compound, medley, mixture, variety; combination, proportions, ratio; ingredients, mixture, paste.
vb lit: blend, combine, compound, diffuse, fuse, intermingle, merge, stir together; shuffle; associate (with), get on (with), hang out (with), mingle (with), socialize (with).

mixed
adj (pa.pt) lit: blended, combined, composite, fused, mingled; assorted, miscellaneous, various; crossbred, hybrid, mongrel; unisex, universal.

moan
n lit: groan, lament, sob, wail; *fig*: beef, complaint, gripe, grouse.
vb lit: groan, keen, lament, sob, whine; beef, carp, complain, gripe, grouse, grumble.

mob
n lit: crew, crowd, flock, herd, gang, group, horde, host, mass, multitude, press, set, throng; hoi polloi, masses, proles, rabble, riffraff, scum.
vb lit: crowd, jostle, surround.

mobile
adj lit: movable, portable, travelling; adaptable, changeable; itinerant, nomadic, peripatetic; ambulatory; *fig*: animated, expressive.

mobilize
vb lit: activate, call up, muster, rally, re-form.

mock
vb lit: deride, insult, jeer at, laugh at, ridicule, scoff at, sneer at, taunt; ape, burlesque, caricature, lampoon, send up, take off.
adj lit: artificial, bogus, counterfeit, ersatz, fake, false, imitation, phoney, sham, spurious.

mockery
n lit: contumely, derision, gibes, insults, ridicule, scorn; farce, travesty.

model
vb lit: archetype, example, exemplar, mould, original, pattern, prototype; copy, dummy, mock-up, replica, reproduction; design, plan, representation; kind, make, marque, sort, style, type, version; poser, sitter, subject; mannequin.
vb lit: construct, design, devise, fashion, form, mould, pattern, shape, style; display, exhibit, show off.
adj lit: facsimile, imitation; miniature, scaled-down; exemplary, ideal, perfect.

moderate
vb lit: calm, control, curb, mitigate, repress, restrain, soften, tame, tone down; chair, preside over; arbitrate (between), mediate (between).
adj lit: average, fair, medium, middling, passable, reasonable, tolerable; indifferent, mediocre, ordinary; medium-sized; equable, mild, peaceable, restrained, temperate.

modern
adj lit: contemporary, current, latest, new, novel, present-day, recent, state-of-the-art, twentieth-century, up-to-date.

modernize
vb lit: bring up to date, renovate, revamp, update.

modest
adj lit: bashful, diffident, humble, meek, reserved, retiring, self-effacing, shy; chaste, decent, demure; fair, moderate, reasonable, unpretentious.

modesty
n lit: bashfulness, diffidence, humility, meekness, reserve, reticence, self-effacement; chastity, decency, demureness; moderation, unpretentiousness.

modification
n lit: adjustment, alteration, change,

refinement; modulation; lessening, lowering, moderation, reduction.

modify
vb lit: adjust, alter, change, convert, refine, revise; modulate; lessen, lower, moderate, reduce, tone down.

modulation
n lit: adjustment, alteration, change, modification, refinement, regulation; change of key, key-change; variance in the frequency, variance in the pitch.

module
n lit: building-block, cog, component, unit; capsule; *fig*: group, set.

moist
adj lit: clammy, damp, dank, humid, sodden, soggy, sweaty, wet; rainy, watery.

moisture
n lit: damp, dampness, dankness, humidity; fluid, liquid.

molest
vb lit: abuse, fondle, grope, interfere with, maltreat, manhandle; badger, bother, harass, harry, hound, importune, pester, plague, worry; annoy, irritate, vex.

mollify
vb lit: alleviate, ease, lighten, moderate, palliate, relieve, soften, soothe, tranquillize; allay, appease, calm, pacify.

moment
n lit: instant, second, split second, twinkling of an eye; juncture, point, time; concern, consequence, historicity, importance, significance, weight; *spec*: (measure of) rotative effect.

momentary
adj lit: fleeting, instantaneous, short-lived, split-second, transitory; brief, quick, short.

momentous
adj lit: consequential, crucial, decisive, fateful, historic, important, significant, weighty.

momentum
n lit: drive, energy, force, impetus, motion, thrust.

monarch
n lit: king, queen, ruler, sovereign, supreme ruler.

monastery
n lit: abbey, friary, priory; cloister, community.

monastic
adj lit: cenobitic, cloistered, contemplative, conventual, secluded; celibate; ascetic, austere, devout, holy, pious, religious.

monetary
adj lit: cash, financial, pecuniary.

money
n lit: assets, capital, cash, currency, finances, funds, legal tender, liquidity, riches, sterling, wealth; brass, bread, dough, gelt, lolly, loot, LSD, lucre, mazuma, moolah, needful, notes, pelf, readies, shekels, wherewithal.

mongrel
n lit: cross-breed, half-breed, hybrid, mixed breed.

monitor
n lit: invigilator, overseer, supervisor, warden; prefect; alarm, detector, gauge, meter, scanner, tester; subsidiary TV screen.
vb lit: observe, oversee, supervise, watch over; keep track of, record, scan.

monkey
n lit: primate, simian; ape; *fig*: imp, jackanapes, rascal, rogue, scamp, scapegrace; (make a) fool (of); ass, laughing-stock; *fig*: £500, $500; hammer, pile-driver.
vb lit: fiddle (with), meddle (with), tamper (with); fool (about), mess (about), play (about).

monolithic
adj lit: columnar, monumental; *fig*: homogeneous, huge, imposing, massive, substantial, uniform.

monopoly
n lit: concession, exclusive possession, franchise, sole power, sole privilege, sole rights, title.

monotonous
adj lit: constant, continual, mindless, relentless, repetitious, repetitive, uniform, unvarying; boring, humdrum, soporific, tedious, wearisome.

monster
n lit: abortion, freak, mutant, obscenity; animal, beast, brute, savage; demon,

devil, fiend; colossus, giant, jumbo, mammoth, whopper.
adj lit: colossal, enormous, giant, huge, immense, jumbo, mammoth, massive, vast, whopping.

monstrosity
n lit: abortion, freak, mutant; carbuncle, eyesore, folly, fright, horror, obscenity.

monstrous
adj lit: abnormal, deformed, freakish, grotesque, malformed, mutant, obscene, teratological, unnatural; bestial, brutal, brutish, savage; cruel, demonic, diabolical, evil, fiendish, inhuman, loathsome, satanic, vicious; frightful, gruesome, hideous, horrible; colossal, enormous, giant, huge, immense, jumbo, mammoth, massive, vast, whopping.

monumental
adj lit: commemorative, memorial; columnar, monolithic, statuary; awesome, classic, epoch-making, historic, lasting, outstanding, significant; *fig*: colossal, enormous, giant, huge, immense, jumbo, mammoth, massive, vast, whopping.

mood
n lit: disposition, humour, state of mind, temper; bad temper, melancholy, moroseness, sulkiness; (not in the) right frame of mind.

moody
adj lit: capricious, changeable, erratic, fitful, mercurial, temperamental, unpredictable, volatile; bad-tempered, broody, crotchety, gloomy, ill-humoured, melancholy, morose, petulant, sulky, sullen, touchy.

mooring
n lit: anchorage, berth, buoy, capstan, jetty, marina, quayside, wharf; hawser, lashing, rope, sheet, warp.

mop
n lit: sponge, squeegee, swab; cloth, rag; brush, shock, tangle, thatch; face, grimace.
vb lit: absorb, soak (up), stem; sponge, swab, wipe (up).

mope
vb lit: be depressed, be listless, brood, hang around dejectedly, languish, sulk.

moral
n lit: lesson, message, point; envoi;

ethic(s), ideal(s), principle(s), scruple(s).
adj lit: ethical, principled; decent, good, honest, honourable, proper, upstanding, virtuous; intellectual, mental; likely, probable.

morale
n lit: confidence, heart, pride, spirit, strength of purpose.

morality
n lit: ethics, ideals, integrity, principles, standards; decency, goodness, honesty, honour, propriety, virtue.

moratorium
n lit: freeze, halt, stay, suspension; respite; deferral, delay, postponement.

morbid
adj lit: downcast, melancholy, pessimistic; brooding, gloomy, grim, sombre; ghastly, ghoulish, gruesome, macabre, sick, unhealthy; diseased, ill, infected, sickly; fatal, malignant, necrotic, terminal.

mordant
adj lit: corrosive; binding, fixative; *fig*: biting, caustic, sarcastic, scathing, cutting, incisive.

more
adj lit: additional, extra, further, supplementary; different, fresh, new, other; of greater size; of greater quantity.
adv lit: to a greater degree, to a greater extent; further; longer; additionally, again.

moreover
adv lit: additionally, also, besides, further, furthermore, in addition, likewise, too.

moribund
adj lit: dying, fading, failing, on one's deathbed, passing away, slipping away, waning; *fig*: ailing, at a standstill, on the way out, stagnant, stagnating.

mortal
n lit: human being, individual, person.
adj lit: human; corporeal, temporal; impermanent, transient, waxing and waning; deadly, fatal, lethal, terminal; deathly; to the death.

mortification
n lit: corruption, gangrene, necrosis, tissue death; discipline, flagellation, subjugation; chagrin, discomfiture, downfall, embarrassment, humiliation, loss of face, shame.

mortify
vb lit: become gangrenous, die, fester, necrose; chasten, discipline, flog, subjugate; abash, chagrin, deflate, discomfit, embarrass, humiliate, put down, put to the blush, shame.

most
adj lit: (the) greatest amount of, (the) greatest degree of, (the) greatest measure of, (the) greatest number of; nearly all, the great majority of.
adv lit: extremely; principally; to the greatest degree, to the greatest extent.

moth-eaten
adj lit: abraded, decayed, dilapidated, ragged, shabby, tattered, threadbare, worn.

mother
n lit: ma, mama, mater, mum, mummy, old lady; dam, matron, parent, protectress; abbess, prioress, superior.
vb lit: bear, engender, give birth to, produce; care for, cherish, foster, nurture, raise, rear, tend; *fig*: baby, fuss over, make a fuss of, mollycoddle, pamper.

motion
n lit: advance, movement, passage, progress, travel, way; proposal, proposition, subject, submission, theme, topic; gesticulation, gesture, signal, wave; bowel movement, defecation, evacuation.

motionless
adj lit: at rest, immobile, inert, static, stationary, still, unmoving; fixed, frozen, paralysed, stopped, transfixed; crouched, in wait, tensed.

motivate
vb lit: act as an incentive, bring (to), cause (to), drive (to), induce (to), inspire (to), instigate, prompt (to), stimulate (to), stir (to).

motivation
n lit: aim, goal, incentive, inducement, inspiration, instigation, purpose, reason, reasoning, stimulus.

motive
n lit: aim, design, intention, object, purpose, rationale, reason, reasoning, thinking; incentive, inducement, stimulus.
adj lit: activating, driving, impulsive, operative, propelling.

motor
n lit: engine, machine, works; compressor, generator; energy, power; activator, effector, operator; *fig*: car.

mottled
adj (pa.pt) lit: brindled, dappled, speckled, tabby; blotchy, patchy, variegated.

motto
n lit: catch-phrase, inscription, logo, slogan; maxim, precept, watchword; caption, headline, legend.

mould
n lit: fungus, mildew, saprophyte; dust, earth, loam, soil; die, matrix, pattern, stencil, template; cast; blancmange, jelly; *fig*: build, configuration, fashion, form, kind, shape, style, type; calibre, character, kidney, quality, stamp.
vb lit: cast, model, sculpt; create, fashion, form, shape; *fig*: control, direct, guide, influence, inform.

mound
n lit: bank, breast, hillock, knoll, tump; barrow, earthwork, rampart, tumulus; motte; heap, pile, stack.

mount
n lit: backing, frame, setting; slide; base, plinth, podium, stand; gun-carriage; horse, nag, ride, steed.
vb lit: frame, put in a frame; put on a slide; fix on a base, set; ascend, climb, go up, scale; climb on to, climb up on, get on to, get up on; accumulate, build (up), escalate, grow, increase, intensify, pile (up); organize, produce, put on, stage; deliver, launch, make, put into effect; install, place, position; *spec*: keep, stand (guard).

mountain
n lit: crag, fell, height, peak, summit; *fig*: heap, mass, pile, stack.

mountainous
adj lit: alpine, highland, upland; craggy, precipitous, rocky, serrated, sheer, soaring, towering; *fig*: enormous, giant, huge, immense, mammoth, massive, vast.

mourn
vb lit: bewail, grieve (for), lament, sorrow (for), weep for; miss; deplore, regret.

mournful
adj lit: disconsolate, grief-stricken,

heartbroken, heavy-hearted, inconsolable, melancholy, miserable, sad, sorrowul, unhappy, wretched; affecting, elegiac, piteous, plaintive, tragic.

mourning
n lit: bereavement, grief; grieving, lamentation, sorrowing, weeping; black, widow's weeds.

mousy
adj lit: murine; fig: dull brown, grey-brown, lank, limp; characterless, colourless, grey, insipid, plain, uninteresting, vapid; retiring, self-effacing, shy, timid.

mouth
n lit: jaws, lips; cake-hole, chops, gob, kisser, mandibles, trap; aperture, entrance, inlet, opening, stoma; estuary; fig: backchat, cheek, insolence, lip, sauce; chatter, gab, talk; boasting, bragging, hot air; prophet, spokesperson; grimace, pout, wry face.
vb lit: enunciate carefully, enunciate silently; declaim, orate, spout; chew; spec: train (a horse) to the bit.

move
n lit: go, play, turn; action, manoeuvre, motion, shift, stroke; gambit, initiative, ploy, strategy; change of address, relocation, transfer; campaign, plan, proposal, suggestion; (on the) road, (on the) wing.
vb lit: advance, budge, go, pass, proceed, progress, shift, travel; change address, relocate, transfer; depart (from), go away, leave, migrate (from); bring, carry, convey, fetch, take, transport, transpose; activate, drive, propel, power, push; affect, agitate, excite, stir, touch; fig: cause (to), induce (to), influence (to), inspire (to), lead (to), prompt (to), stimulate (to); advocate, propose, recommend, suggest.

movement
n lit: activity, agitation, development, progress, shift, stirring; manoeuvre, operation, progression; action, mechanism, works; exercise, gesture, motion; current, drift, flow, tendency, trend; campaign, caucus, drive, organization, party; beat, metre, pace, rhythm, tempo; spec: division, section (of a musical work).

moving
adj (pr.pt) lit: mobile; portable; powering, propelling; fig: affecting, emotive, pathetic, piteous, poignant, touching; dynamic, exciting, inspiring, motivating, stimulating.

mow
vb lit: crop, cut, reap, shear, strim; cut (down), hack (down), shoot (down).

much
n lit: a good deal, a great deal, a lot, lots, the majority.
adj lit: abundant, copious, plenteous; considerable, great, substantial.
adv lit: considerably, exceedingly, greatly; approximately, nearly; indeed, to a great degree, to a great extent.

mud
n lit: dirt, mire, ooze, slime, sludge, slush, wet; fig: calumny, defamation, libel, slander.

muddled
adj (pa.pt) lit: chaotic, confused, disordered, disorganized, jumbled, mixed, scrambled, tangled; bewildered, disoriented, perplexed, vague, woolly.

muddy
vb lit: bespatter, dirty, get mud on, smear, soil; fig: blur, cloud, confuse, obscure.
adj lit: bespattered, dirty, miry, slimy, slushy, wet; boggy, marshy, swampy; foul, impure, turbid; fig: dingy, dull, flat; blurred, cloudy, confused, obscure, vague, woolly.

muffle
vb lit: cloak, conceal, cover, envelop, hood, mask, swathe; deaden, dull, mute, quieten, silence, stifle, suppress.

muffled
adj (pa.pt) lit: deadened, dulled, faint, indistinct, muted, stifled, suppressed.

mug
n lit: beaker, cup, glass, jug, pot, tankard; fig: clock, dial, face, kisser, phizog, mush; dupe, fall guy, gull, mark, patsy, sucker; greenhorn, innocent, simpleton.
vb lit: accost, ambush, attack, jump on, pounce upon, rob, set upon; read (up), swot (up); ham up, overact.

muggy
adj lit: close, humid, oppressive, sticky, stifling, sultry.

multiple
adj lit: manifold, numerous, sundry, various; collective, compound; repeated.

multiply
vb lit: accumulate, expand, increase, spread; repeat; breed, proliferate, propagate, reproduce.

multitude
n lit: army, crowd, horde, host, legion, mass, sea, swarm, throng; herd, mob, proletariat, rabble.

mumble
n lit: muffled voice, murmur, mutter, undertone.
vb lit: mutter, stammer, stutter; swallow one's words.

mundane
adj lit: banal, commonplace, everyday, humdrum, ordinary, platitudinous, prosaic, trite; earthly, human, mortal, secular, temporal, worldly; cosmic.

municipal
adj lit: borough, civic, council, public, urban.

munificence
n lit: beneficence, bounty, generosity, liberality, philanthropy; amplitude, bounteousness, scale.

murder
n lit: assassination, homicide, killing; carnage, massacre, slaughter; *fig*: agony, hell, torture.
vb lit: assassinate, do to death, kill; bump off, do in, hit, rub out, waste; massacre, slaughter, slay; *fig*: abuse, mangle, ruin, spoil, take liberties with; drub, hammer, thrash out of sight, trounce.

murderous
adj lit: bloody, deadly, destructive, devastating, fatal, lethal, savage, withering; barbarous, bloodthirsty, cruel, sanguinary; *fig*: arduous, difficult, harrowing, strenuous.

murky
adj lit: black, dark, dim, dusky, gloomy; grey, hazy, misty; *fig*: obscure, shady.

murmuring
adj (pr.pt) lit: babbling, droning, humming, purring, rippling, rumbling, rustling, trickling, whispering; listless, muttering, restive, restless, unquiet, unsatisfied.

muscle
n lit: ligament, sinew, tendon; extensor, flexor; *fig*: brawn, power, stamina, strength; clout, force, weight.
vb lit: butt (in), elbow (in), force a way (in), thrust one's way (in).

muscular
adj lit: brawny, lusty, powerful, robust, stalwart, strapping, strong; athletic, vigorous.

muse
n lit: creativity, idea, inspiration; brown study, reverie.
vb lit: brood, cogitate, contemplate, dream, meditate, reflect, ruminate, think.

mushroom
n lit: edible fungus; toadstool, umbrella-shaped fungus; umbrella shape.
vb lit: burgeon, grow rapidly, shoot up; expand, proliferate, spread.

musical
adj lit: euphonious, harmonious, melodic, melodious, orchestral, symphonic, tuneful.

musician
n lit: bandsman, orchestra-member, performer, player, singer; arranger, composer; conductor.

must
n lit: essential, imperative, necessity, prerequisite, requirement, sine qua non; semi-fermented juice.
vb lit: be obliged to, have to; ought to, should.

musty
adj lit: damp, dampish, mildewed, moth-eaten, mouldering, mouldy, stale.

mutable
adj lit: adaptable, alterable, changeable, convertible, variable, volatile; impermanent, unstable; *fig*: fickle, inconstant.

mutation
n lit: evolution, metamorphosis, transformation; alteration, change, modification; mutant, sport, variant.

mute
vb lit: dampen, deaden, hush, muffle, silence, soften, tone down, turn down.
adj lit: aphonic, dumb, silent, speechless, voiceless; mum, unspoken, wordless.

mutilate
vb lit: cripple, damage, deform, disfigure, lame, maim, mangle; *fig*: abbreviate, abridge, butcher, censor, cut, distort, spoil.

mutiny
n lit: defiance, disobedience, insurrection, rebellion, revolt, rising, uprising.
vb lit: rebel, revolt, rise up.

mutual
adj lit: common, communal, joint, reciprocal, shared; reciprocating.

muzzle
n lit: mouth, snout; cage, clamp, guard; mouthpiece, respirator; barrel.
vb lit: curb, gag, silence; *fig*: censor, restrict, suppress.

myriad
adj lit: countless, innumerable, millions of, thousands of, untold.

mysterious
adj lit: cryptic, enigmatic, incomprehensible, inexplicable, insoluble, obscure, perplexing, puzzling, strange, uncanny, weird; furtive, secretive; concealed, covert, hidden, secret.

mystery
n lit: enigma, puzzle, riddle, secret; obscurity, secrecy; rite, ritual, sacrament.

mystical
adj lit: cabalistic, esoteric, metaphysical, occult, paranormal, preternatural, supernatural, transcendental; ritual, symbolic.

myth
n lit: folk tale, legend, story, tradition; allegory, fable, parable; fantasy, fiction, illusion, superstition.

mythical
adj lit: folkloric, legendary, traditional; allegorical, allusive; fantasy, fictitious, imaginary, invented, superstitious.

N

nab
vb lit: catch, grab, grasp, seize suddenly;
snatch away, steal; *fig*: apprehend, arrest.

nadir
n lit: bottom, depth, lowest point, rock
bottom; least, lowest, minimum.

nag
n lit: hack, horse, jade; battleaxe, harpy,
scold, shrew, tartar, termagant, virago.
vb lit: goad, henpeck, scold, upbraid;
annoy, badger, chivvy, harass, pester;
irritate, plague, provoke, vex.

nagging
adj (pr.pt) lit: bothersome, distressing,
irritating, painful, vexatious, worrisome;
continuous, persistent; scolding,
shrewish.

nail
n lit: peg, pin, tack; horn, keratin.
vb lit: pin, tack; attach, fasten, fix, join,
secure; hammer; *fig*: catch, seize.

naive
adj lit: artless, frank, guileless, ingenuous,
innocent, jejune, unsophisticated,
unworldly; childlike, natural, open,
simple, trusting; unaffected,
unpretentious; callow, credulous, green,
gullible.

name
n lit: agnomen, appellation, cognomen,
handle, moniker, sobriquet;
denomination, designation, title;
celebrity, personality; reputation;
epithet, insult, nickname.
vb lit: call, designate, dub, entitle, style,
term; baptize, christen, denominate,
label; identify, specify; cite, mention,
nominate.

named
adj (pa.pt) lit: called, designated,
dubbed, entitled, styled, termed;
baptized, christened, denominated,
labelled; identified, specified; cited,
mentioned, nominated, picked, singled
out.

nameless
adj lit: anonymous, unnamed;
undesignated, untitled; obscure,
unheard-of, unknown; indescribable,
ineffable, inexpressible, unmentionable,
unspeakable.

nap
n lit: doze, forty winks, kip, siesta, sleep,
snooze; rest; pile, shag; down, fibre; cert,
dead cert, hot tip, winner.
vb lit: doze, drop off, drowse, sleep,
snooze; tip a winner.

napkin
n lit: hand-towel, serviette; cloth,
handkerchief, tissue; bib; diaper, nappy.

narcissism
n lit: self-admiration, self-love, vanity;
conceit, egotism, pride.

narcosis
n lit: sedation; drowsiness, dullness,
lethargy, stupefaction, stupor, torpor;
anaesthesia, analgesia, insensibility,
numbness, unconsciousness.

narcotic
n lit: drug, opiate; anaesthetic, analgesic,
painkiller, sedative, tranquillizer.
adj lit: sedative; dulling, hypnotic,
soporific, stupefying; anaesthetic,
analgesic, painkilling; addictive, habit-
forming, habituating, opiate.

nark
n lit: agent, informer, insider, spy; grass,
sneak, tell-tale.
vb lit: anger, annoy, drive mad,
exasperate, irritate, peeve, rile, vex.

narrate
vb lit: recite, recount, relate, set forth, tell;
describe, detail, report; chronicle.

narrative
n lit: account, story, tale; report,
statement; caption, text, voice-over.
adj lit: anecdotal, story-telling, with a
story-line; continuous, sequential, serial.

narrator
n lit: commentator, reporter, storyteller,
voice-over; raconteur, speaker; author,
chronicler, novelist, writer.

narrow
vb lit: constrict, reduce, straiten, tighten; decrease, diminish; *fig*: limit, simplify.
adj lit: attenuated, fine, slim, thin; close, confined, constricted, tight; meagre, restricted, scanty; *fig*: biased, dogmatic, partial, prejudiced; exclusive, select; avaricious, mean, niggardly.

narrowly
adv lit: barely, by a whisker, just, only just; carefully, closely, painstakingly.

narrow-minded
adj lit: petty, illiberal, insular, short-sighted, strait-laced; biased, intolerant, prejudiced; bigoted, opinionated.

nastiness
n lit: malevolence, malice, malignity, meanness, offensiveness, spitefulness, viciousness; defilement, filth, foulness, squalor, uncleanliness, vileness; indecency, licentiousness, obscenity, pornography.

nasty
adj lit: dirty, disgusting, filthy, foul, loathsome, nauseating, objectionable, obnoxious, odious, offensive, repellent, repugnant, sickening, vile; bad, dangerous, serious, severe; abusive, despicable, disagreeable, mean, spiteful, unpleasant, vicious; gross, indecent, lewd, obscene, pornographic.

nation
n lit: country; people, population, race; community, society, state, tribe.

national
n lit: citizen, compatriot, native; inhabitant, resident, subject.
adj lit: civil, governmental, public, state; nationwide; patriotic; domestic, internal.

nationalism
n lit: patriotism; allegiance, fealty, loyalty.

nationwide
adj lit: countrywide, national; general, overall, universal.

native
n lit: aborigine, inhabitant; citizen, dweller, national, resident.
adj lit: domestic, indigenous, local, born (to); inborn, inbred, innate, intrinsic; mother, vernacular.

natter
n lit: chat, confabulation, conversation, gossip, talk; blather, chitchat, jabber.
vb lit: blather, chat, chatter, gabble, gossip, jabber, jaw on, prate, prattle, rabbit on, talk, witter on.

natty
adj lit: snappy, snazzy; chic, elegant, fashionable, stylish, well-dressed; dapper, neat, smart, spruce, trim.

natural
n lit: halfwit, simpleton; obvious choice; genius; *fig*: cert, certainty; *spec*: white note (on a piano).
adj lit: common, logical, normal, ordinary, typical, usual; characteristic, inborn, inherent, instinctive, native; artless, genuine, ingenuous, simple, spontaneous, unpretentious, unsophisticated; organic, plain, pure, unrefined, whole.

naturally
adv lit: congenitally, essentially, inherently, innately, instinctively; artlessly, genuinely, ingenuously, simply, spontaneously, unpretentiously; organically; normally, typically; *fig*: certainly, of course; absolutely.

nature
n lit: character, constitution, essence, make-up, quality; category, kind, sort, style, type, variety; cosmos, earth, environment, universe; disposition, outlook, temper, temperament; country, countryside, scenery.

naughtiness
n lit: disobedience, misbehaviour, mischievousness, roguishness, waywardness; ribaldry, vulgarity.

naughty
adj lit: bad, disobedient, misbehaving, mischievous, refractory, roguish, wayward, wicked; ribald, vulgar.

nausea
n lit: feeling sick, retching, urge to vomit; bile, gripes, hot flush, pangs; biliousness, faintness.

nauseate
vb lit: sicken, make feel ill, turn one's stomach; *fig*: disgust, offend, repel; appal, horrify.

nautical
adj lit: marine, maritime, naval, oceanographic; seafaring, seagoing.

navigate
vb lit: plot a course, steer; manoeuvre, pilot, sail; *fig*: direct, guide, skipper; find one's way (through), make one's way (to).

navigator
n lit: helmsman, mariner, pilot, steersman; co-driver, map-reader.

navy
n lit: maritime forces, seaborne troops; armada, fleet, flotilla, warships.

nay
adv lit: no; not only but also; or rather.

near
vb lit: approach, close on, draw up towards, get closer to.
adj lit: close, close by;, adjacent, adjoining, at close quarters, nigh; approaching, imminent, impending, looming, threatening; *fig*: closely-related, dear, familiar, intimate; close-fisted, mean, miserly, parsimonious, stingy, tight.
adv lit: close, nigh; into proximity, within reach; almost, close on.
prp lit: close to, nigh unto; adjacent to, alongside, not far from.

nearby
adj lit: adjacent, adjoining, neighbouring; *fig*: convenient, handy.

near by
adv lit: close by, close at hand, not far away.

nearly
adv lit: all but, almost, approximately, closely, just about, not quite, roughly, virtually.

neat
n lit: cow, heifer; ox, steer.
adj lit: accurate, fastidious, methodical, nice, orderly, precise, shipshape, smart, straight, systematic, tidy, trim; adroit, deft, dextrous, handy, nimble, skilful, stylish; pure, straight, unadulterated, undiluted.

neatness
n lit: accuracy, fastidiousness, orderliness, smartness, tidiness, trimness; adroitness, deftness, dexterity, handiness, nimbleness, preciseness, skilfulness, stylishness.

nebulosity
n lit: cloud; cloudiness, dimness, mistiness, obscurity, shadow; *fig*: ambiguity, dubiety, uncertainty.

nebulous
adj lit: amorphous, cloudlike, shapeless, unformed; *fig*: ambiguous, dim, imprecise, indistinct, misty, obscure, shadowy, uncertain, vague.

necessarily
adv lit: by definition, inescapably, inevitably, inexorably, of necessity, perforce, unavoidably, willy-nilly; certainly, without question.

necessary
adj lit: essential, imperative, indispensable, mandatory, obligatory, vital; compulsory, de rigueur, required; inevitable, unavoidable.

necessitate
vb lit: call for, demand, dictate, leave no choice but, make necessary, render indispensable, require; entail.

necessity
n lit: essential, indispensability, prerequisite, requirement, want; demand, need; compulsion, obligation; extremity, penury, privation.

need
n lit: deprivation, lack, inadequacy, insufficiency, paucity, privation, shortage, want; penury, poverty; demand, exigency, requirement, urgency.
vb lit: call for, demand, necessitate; lack, miss, require, want.

needle
n lit: point, prong, spicule, spike, tine; stylus; hypodermic syringe; gnomon, pointer; obelisk.
vb lit: aggravate, bait, goad, provoke, spur; annoy, harass, irk, nag, nettle, pester, prick, prod, ruffle, sting.

needless
adj lit: causeless, gratuitous, groundless, pointless, superfluous, uncalled-for, unnecessary, unwanted, useless.

needy
adj lit: deprived, impecunious, indigent, poor, poverty-stricken; friendless, homeless.

negate
vb lit: abrogate, annul, countermand, nullify, repeal, rescind, retract, revoke; contradict, deny, gainsay, refute.

negative
n lit: no; contradiction, denial, refusal, veto; *spec*: reversed-out image (on film). *adj lit*: contradictory, contrary, dissenting, opposing, rejecting, resisting; antagonistic, counteractive; gloomy, pessimistic, unenthusiastic, unwilling; colourless, insipid.

neglect
n lit: disregard, inattention, indifference, unconcern; default, dereliction, forgetfulness, laxity, oversight, remissness, slackness.
vb lit: disregard, ignore, overlook, pass over; evade, forget, omit, shirk, skimp.

negligence
n lit: carelessness, default, heedlessness, indifference, laxity, slackness, thoughtlessness; forgetfulness, inattention, omission, oversight.

negligible
adj lit: imperceptible, insignificant, minute, petty, trifling, trivial, unimportant.

negotiate
vb lit: bargain, deal, haggle; debate, discuss, parley, work out; get over, get past, get round, pass through.

negotiation
n lit: bargaining, dealing, haggling; debate, diplomacy, discussion, parleying, working out.

neighbour
n lit: co-resident, local; acquaintance. *vb lit*: be near, live near; abut, adjoin, border, surround.

nerve
n lit: neural tract; sinew, tendon; *fig*: bravery, courage, determination, firmness, grit, guts, intrepidity, mettle, pluck, resolution, will; audacity, brazenness, cheek, effrontery, impudence, temerity.
vb lit: brace, encourage, fortify, steel.

nerve-racking
adj lit: frightening, ghastly, grim, gripping, harrowing, heart-stopping, horrific, sickening, terrifying; formidable, stressful.

nervous
adj lit: agitated, anxious, edgy, fidgety, flustered, highly strung, jittery, jumpy, on edge, shaky, tense, uneasy, uptight.

nervousness
n lit: agitation, anxiety, edginess, jumpiness, tension, uneasiness.

nest
n lit: hatchery, home; *fig*: den, hideaway, lair; haunt, refuge, retreat; hotbed; *spec*: set (of tables).
vb lit: brood, get broody, make a home, start a family.

net
n lit: mesh, trawl; lacework, lattice, reticulum; web.
vb lit: capture, catch, enmesh, ensnare, nab, trap; *fig*: bring in, gain, earn, make, realize.
adj lit: after taxes, clear, take-home; closing, final.

network
n lit: grid, grille, mesh; organization, structure, system; circuitry, complex, labyrinth, maze, plexus, web.

neurotic
adj lit: disturbed, maladjusted, unstable; compulsive, obsessive; anxious, hysterical, nervous, overwrought.

neuter
vb lit: castrate, doctor, emasculate, geld, spay; neutralize.
adj lit: asexual, sexless; neutral.

neutral
adj lit: disinterested, even-handed, impartial, non-aligned, noncommittal, unbiased, uncommitted, uninvolved; achromatic, colourless, dull, expressionless, indistinct, toneless, undefined.

neutralize
vb lit: counteract, counterbalance, negate, nullify, offset.

nevertheless
adv lit: all the same, anyway, regardless; even so, for all that, nonetheless, notwithstanding, still, yet.

new
adj lit: fresh, latest, novel, original, pristine, unused, virgin; advanced, contemporary, current, modern, modish, recent, topical, ultra-modern, up-to-date; added, additional, extra,

supplementary; altered, different, improved, redesigned, reissued, restored; unexperienced, unexpected, unfamiliar, untried.

news
n lit: information, intelligence, tidings, word; *gen*: latest; account, bulletin, communiqué, dispatch, report, statement, story; advice, disclosure, release; gossip, hearsay, on-dit, rumour.

next
adj lit: ensuing, later, subsequent, succeeding; consequent, resulting; adjacent, closest, nearest.
adv lit: afterwards, later, subsequently, thereafter, thereupon; in turn.

nibble
n lit: bite, crumb, gobbet, morsel, peck, pinch, scrap, snack, spoonful, taste, titbit.
vb lit: bite, gnaw, peck, pick at; eat, chomp, munch.

nice
adj lit: agreeable, amiable, charming, courteous, delightful, friendly, likable, pleasant, well-mannered; dainty, neat, tidy, trim; accurate, careful, delicate, exacting, fastidious, meticulous, precise, scrupulous, subtle; cultured, respectable, well-bred.

nicety
n lit: accuracy, fastidiousness, meticulousness, precision; delicacy, distinction, subtlety; pedantry, prevarication.

niche
n lit: alcove, aumbry, hollow, nook, recess; *fig*: calling, position, slot, vocation.

nick
n lit: chip, dent, groove, mark, notch, scar, score, scratch; eleventh hour, last moment; edge, glance, snick; cells, jail, police station, prison.
vb lit: chip, damage, dent, mark, notch, scar, score, scratch; catch an edge, glance, snick; filch, nab, pilfer, pinch, steal, whip; arrest, capture, take; jail, imprison, put in the cells.

nickname
n lit: agnomen, familiar name, moniker, pet name, sobriquet; diminutive; kenning; epithet.

vb lit: address as, call, give the name, persist in addressing as, rename.

niggardly
adj lit: avaricious, grudging, mean, miserly, parsimonious, sparing; beggarly, penurious; meagre, miserable, paltry, scanty, skimpy, small.

niggle
n lit: beef, complaint, criticism, quibble; ache, gnawing, pinprick; annoyance, irritation.
vb lit: beef, carp, cavil, find fault, prevaricate; ache, gnaw away, nag; annoy, irritate, rankle.

niggling
adj (pr.pt) lit: finicky, fussy, nit-picking, petty, quibbling, trifling; insignificant, minor; irritating, nagging, persistent, troublesome.

night
n lit: dark, darkness, early hours, evening, hours of darkness, moonlight hours, night-time.
adj lit: nocturnal; after dark, late; *spec*: sleeper (train).

nightfall
n lit: dusk, evening, sundown, sunset, twilight.

nil
n lit: nought, none, no score, nothing, zero, zilch; duck; love; misère.

nimble
adj lit: agile, limber, lithe; active, brisk, lively, quick, sprightly; dextrous, proficient.

nimbus
n lit: ambience, aura, cloud, corona, glow, halo.

nincompoop
n lit: blockhead, dimwit, dunce, fool, idiot, nitwit, noodle, simpleton.

nip
n lit: dram, draught, drop, finger, mouthful, sip, taste, tot; bite, chill, frost, sharp cold.
vb lit: bite, nibble, snap; clip, grip, pinch, squeeze, tweak; *fig*: check, thwart.

nippy
adj lit: biting, chilly, sharp; agile, fast, lively, nimble, quick, spry.

nit-picking
adj (pr.pt) lit: carping, fault-finding,

finicky, hairsplitting, pedantic,
quibbling.

nobble
vb lit: disable, dope, drug, get at,
incapacitate; bribe, intimidate, suborn;
nick, pilfer, pinch, steal; grab, take.

nobility
n lit: aristocracy, high society, nobles,
upper class; dignity, excellence,
greatness, illustriousness; honour,
integrity, uprightness.

noble
n lit: aristocrat, patrician, peer.
adj lit: aristocratic, blue-blooded, high-
born, titled; dignified, eminent,
excellent, impressive, splendid;
honourable, magnanimous, upright.

nobody
n lit: lightweight, nonentity; citizen, man
in the street.
prn lit: none, no one.

nocturnal
adj lit: night, nightly, night-time.

nod
n lit: bob, bow, duck; acknowledgement,
indication, sign.
vb lit: bob, bow, duck one's head;
acknowledge, indicate, signal, silently
affirm; agree, assent, concur; doze,
droop, drop off.

node
n lit: joint, knot, knob, swelling; *spec*:
gland (in the lymphatic system).

nodule
n lit: growth, knob, lump, swelling,
tumour.

noise
n lit: sound; clamour, clatter, commotion,
din, pandemonium, racket, tumult;
babble, hubbub, outcry, uproar.

noiseless
n lit: inaudible, silent, soundless; hushed,
muted, quiet.

noisy
adj lit: clamorous, deafening, ear-
splitting, loud, piercing, tumultuous,
uproarious, vociferous; cacophonous,
strident.

nomenclature
n lit: name, naming, title; taxonomy,
terminology; vocabulary; classification,
codification.

nominal
adj lit: self-styled, so-called, titular;
formal, ostensible, supposed, theoretical;
puppet; insignificant, minimal,
symbolic, token.

nominate
vb lit: appoint, assign, choose, designate,
name, propose, recommend, select,
submit.

nominee
n lit: choice, proposal, suggestion;
aspirant, candidate, contestant, entrant,
runner.

nonaligned
adj lit: third-world; impartial, neutral,
nominally uncommitted, supposedly
independent.

nonchalance
n lit: calm, casuality, composure, cool,
imperturbability, insouciance,
offhandedness, sangfroid, unconcern;
indifference.

nonchalant
adj lit: blasé, calm, casual, composed,
cool, detached, imperturbable,
insouciant, offhand, unconcerned.

noncommittal
adj lit: cautious, circumspect, discreet,
guarded, neutral, reserved, tentative,
vague.

nondescript
adj lit: commonplace, dull, mousy,
ordinary, undistinguished,
uninteresting, unremarkable, vague.

none
adv lit: in no way, not at all, to no extent.
prn lit: nobody, no one. not any, not one;
not a bit, no part, nothing.

nonentity
n lit: nobody; extra, lightweight,
mediocrity, small fry.

nonexistent
adj lit: hypothetical, illusory, imaginary,
unreal; imagined, invented, fictitious,
supposed; legendary, mythical.

nonplus
vb lit: baffle, bewilder, confound,
discomfit, disconcert, discountenance,
dumbfound, mystify, perplex, puzzle,
take aback.

nonsense
n lit: absurdity, blather, bunk, claptrap, double Dutch, drivel, fatuity, folly, gibberish, inanity, ludicrousness, rot, rubbish, trash, twaddle, waffle.

nonsensical
adj lit: absurd, crazy, inane, irrational, ludicrous, meaningless, ridiculous.

nonstop
adj lit: direct; ceaseless, constant, continuous, endless, incessant, relentless, steady, uninterrupted, unremitting.
adv lit: ceaselessly, constantly, continuously, endlessly, incessantly, relentlessly, steadily, uninterruptedly, unremittingly.

nook
n lit: alcove, corner, cranny, crevice, niche, recess.

norm
n lit: average, mean, normal, par, rule, standard; model, pattern, yardstick.

normal
adj lit: average, common, natural, ordinary, regular, run-of-the-mill, standard, usual; rational, reasonable, well-adjusted; *spec*: volume, work; romance; narrative.
adj lit: fresh, innovative, new, original; different, rare, singular, strange, unusual.

novelty
n lit: freshness, innovation, newness, originality; oddity, strangeness, unfamiliarity; curiosity, gimmick; knick-knack, trifle, trinket; memento, souvenir.

novice
n lit: apprentice, beginner, learner, pupil, tyro; neophyte, probationer, proselyte.

now
adv lit: at once, immediately, instantly, promptly, straight away; any more, nowadays, these days; once.
cnj lit: in that, since; for, the fact is, well.

nuance
n lit: aura, innuendo, overtone, suggestion, undertone; gloss, hint, shade, tinge.

nucleus
n lit: centre, core, kernel, nub; focus.

nude
n lit: naked figure; altogether, birthday suit.
adj lit: au naturel, bare, in one's birthday suit, in the altogether, in the buff, naked, starkers, stark-naked, stripped, uncovered, undressed, with nothing on.

nudge
n lit: dig, jog, poke, prod, push, thrust.
vb lit: dig, elbow, jog, poke, prod, push, shove.

nugatory
adj lit: futile, ineffective, inoperative, useless; trifling, unimportant, worthless.

nuisance
n lit: annoyance, bore, bother, inconvenience, irritation, pest, plague, trouble, vexation.

nullify
vb lit: abrogate, annul, cancel, invalidate, negate, quash, repeal, rescind, revoke.

nullity
n lit: nothingness, nonexistence; futility, ineffectualness, invalidity, uselessness, worthlessness.

numb
adj lit: dead, frozen, immobilized, insensible, insensitive, paralysed, unfeeling; *fig*: dazed, overwhelmed, shocked, stunned.

number
n lit: digit, figure, integer, numeral, unit; amount, quantity, sum, total; company, multitude, throng; copy, edition, issue; *fig*: aria, song, tune; item, product.
vb lit: count, include in, total; classify, designate, label, rank.

numbered
adj (pa.pt) lit: categorized, classified, designated; limited, totalled.

numbness
n lit: deadness, dullness, immobilization, insensibility, insensitivity, paralysis, unfeeling; *fig*: daze, shock, torpor.

numeral
n lit: digit, figure, interger, number, unit.

numerous
adj lit: many, plentiful; abundant, copious, profuse; a myriad, countless, hosts of, multitudes of.

nurse
vb lit: care for, look after, nurture, tend, treat; cultivate, foster, garden, nourish; breast-feed, suckle.

nursery
n lit: crèche, play-room; allotment, garden, garden centre, kitchen garden, orchard, plantation.

nurture
vb lit: feed, nourish, sustain, tend; bring up, cultivate, rear.

nut
n lit: seed; drupe, kernel, stone; *fig*: bonce, head; brain, intelligence, mind; problem; buff, enthusiast, freak; crank, eccentric, lunatic; ball, bollock, testicle; *spec*: (ginger) biscuit; knob, lump (of coal); screw (to tighten bow-strings); threaded block (for a bolt).
vb lit: gather nuts; *spec*: butt, head-butt (a person); head (a ball).

nutritious
adj lit: beneficial, healthful, nourishing, sustaining, wholesome.

O

oaf

n lit: blockhead, clod, dolt, dunce, fool, halfwit, imbecile, lout, lummox, moron, nincompoop, simpleton.

oafish

adj lit: blockish, bovine, dim, dull, dumb, loutish, obtuse, slow on the uptake, stupid, thick; clumsy, lubberly, mawkish.

oar

n lit: pole, scull; blade; paddle.
vb lit: paddle, row, scull.

oasis

n lit: wadi, watering-hole; *fig*: haven, refuge, resort, resting-place; bar.

oath

n lit: promise, vow, word; bond, pledge; curse, expletive, imprecation, profanity, swearword.

obdurate

adj lit: adamant, dogged, firm, implacable, inexorable, inflexible, relentless, unrelenting, unshakable, unyielding; obstinate, pig-headed, stubborn; hard, harsh.

obedience

n lit: compliance, conformability, docility, dutifulness, submission, submissiveness, subservience, tractability; acquiescence, demureness, readiness, willingness; accordance.

obedient

adj lit: compliant, conformable, docile, dutiful, submissive, subservient, tractable; acquiescent, amenable, biddable, demure, ready, willing; law-abiding.

obelisk

n lit: column, monolith, pillar; needle.

obese

adj lit: chubby, corpulent, fat, gross, overweight, paunchy, plump, podgy, portly, roly-poly, rotund, stout, tubby.

obey

vb lit: be ruled by, bow to, serve, take orders from; comply, do what one is told, submit; act upon, carry out, discharge, execute, fulfil, perform; abide by, follow, heed, keep, mind, observe; truckle to.

obfuscate

vb lit: befog, cloud, darken, eclipse, obscure; bewilder, blur, complicate, confuse, perplex.

object

n lit: article, body, item, thing; phenomenon; fact, reality; design, intention, point, purpose; aim, end, goal, target; butt, focus.
vb lit: demur, protest; be opposed (to), take exception (to).

objection

n lit: demur, exception, opposition, protest, remonstration; counterargument.

objectionable

adj lit: disagreeable, displeasing, distasteful, obnoxious, offensive, repugnant, unpleasant, unseemly.

objective

n lit: aim, end, goal, target; aspiration, intention; design, purpose.
adj lit: detached, disinterested, dispassionate, equitable, fair, impartial, impersonal, just, unbiased, uninvolved, unprejudiced.

obligation

n lit: duty, liability, responsibility; burden, charge, commitment, requirement; must; debt, promise, trust, understanding.

obligatory

adj lit: compulsory, imperative, mandatory, necessary, required; essential, requisite, unavoidable; binding.

oblige

vb lit: do a favour, gratify, indulge, please; favour, serve; compel, constrain, force, impel, require.

obliged

adj (pa.pt) lit: beholden, grateful, indebted, thankful; appreciative, gratified, pleased; bound, compelled, forced, required.

obliging

adj (pr.pt) lit: accommodating, good-natured, helpful, willing; considerate, eager to please, generous, kind, open-hearted; agreeable, amiable, civil, courteous, friendly.

oblique

n lit: diagonal, solidus.
adj lit: angled, inclined, slanted, sloping, tilted; evasive, implied, indirect, sidelong; circuitous.

obliterate

vb lit: annihilate, destroy, efface, eliminate, eradicate, erase, extirpate, root out, wipe out; blot out, delete.

oblivion

n lit: insensibility, unawareness, unconsciousness; blackness, darkness, nothingness, vacuum, void; extinction; abstraction, forgetfulness, negligence; abeyance, limbo.

oblivious

adj lit: blithe, heedless, uncaring, unconcerned; forgetful, inattentive, negligent, unmindful, unobservant.

obnoxious

adj lit: detestable, disagreeable, insufferable, odious, repellent, unlikable, unpleasant; disgusting, foul, horrid, nasty, offensive, repugnant, repulsive, revolting, sickening.

obscene

adj lit: bawdy, blue, filthy, full-frontal, hard-core, perverted, pornographic, smutty; coarse, dirty, gross, immoral, improper, indecent, lewd, licentious, ribald, salacious, suggestive; *fig*: disgusting, horrible, sickening, vile.

obscenity

n lit: bawdiness, filthiness, perversion, pornography, smut; coarseness, dirtiness, grossness, immorality, lewdness, licentiousness, suggestiveness, vileness; expletive, four-letter word, profanity, swear-word; *fig*: atrocity, offence, outrage, vileness.

obscure

vb lit: adumbrate, blur, cloud, dim, dull, obfuscate; conceal, cover, disguise, eclipse, hide, mask, screen, shade, shroud, veil.
adj lit: abstruse, ambiguous, cryptic, enigmatic, esoteric, mysterious, opaque, recondite, vague; concealed, hidden, veiled; blurred, clouded, dim, faint, hazy, murky, shady, sombre; humble, lowly, minor, nameless, remote, undistinguished, unheard-of, unimportant, unknown.

obscurity

n lit: abstruseness, ambiguity, complexity, incomprehensibility, mysteriousness, opacity, vagueness; dimness, gloom, haziness, murkiness, shadows; insignificance, lowliness, unimportance.

obsequious

adj lit: fawning, servile, slavish, sycophantic, toadying; arse-licking, bootlicking.

observant

adj lit: alert, eagle-eyed, vigilant, wary, watchful, wide awake; attentive, insightful, penetrative, perceptive, percipient, quick on the uptake; heedful, mindful.

observation

n lit: inspection, monitoring, scrutiny, study, surveillance, watch; comment, finding, note, opinion, reflection, thought; *spec*: reading (on an instrument, dial).

observe

vb lit: espy, notice, perceive, see, spot; keep an eye on, keep under observation, look at, monitor, regard, study, view, watch, witness; comment, mention, note, remark, state; abide by, adhere to, comply with, follow, heed, obey; celebrate, commemorate, keep.

obsessed

adj (pa.pt) lit: consumed, dominated, fixated, gripped, haunted, infatuated, manic, monopolized, one-track-minded, possessed.

obsession

n lit: bee in one's bonnet, fixation, hang-up, infatuation, mania, phobia, thing; fanaticism; preoccupation, ruling passion.

obsessive
adj lit: compulsive, fixated, manic, paranoid, phobic; consuming, dominating, fanatical, haunting, passionate, overwhelming; constant, persistent.

obsolescent
adj lit: becoming old-fashioned, declining, dying out, fading, on the decline, on the way out, past one's prime, waning.

obsolete
adj lit: dead, disused, extinct, gone, no longer used, out; anachronistic, antiquated, archaic, dated, old-fashioned, old hat, outmoded, out of date, passe.

obstacle
n lit: barrier, blockage, impediment, obstruction; check, hindrance, hitch, hurdle, pitfall, stumbling-block; difficulty, snag.

obstinate
adj lit: dogged, immovable, persistent, pertinacious, steadfast, tenacious; headstrong, inflexible, intractable, mulish, pig-headed, recalcitrant, stubborn, wilful; firm, strong-minded.

obstreperous
adj lit: aggressive, belligerent, bullying, domineering, rampaging, riotous, rowdy, uncontrolled, unmanageable, unruly; boisterous, disorderly, loud, noisy, raucous; argumentative, bad-tempered, disputative, quarrelsome.

obstruct
vb lit: bar, barricade, block, prevent; check, curb, delay, hinder, hold up, impede, interfere with, interrupt, slow down, stall; hamstring, inhibit, restrict; foil, frustrate, parry, thwart; get in the way of, obscure.

obstruction
n lit: bar, barricade, barrier, blockage; check, hindrance, hold-up, impediment, stop; difficulty, snag.

obtain
vb lit: acquire, come into possession of, get, get hold of, procure; attain, gain, secure, win; catch, hold on to, possess oneself of, take; be, exist, prevail, remain, stand.

obtrude
vb lit: jut, project, protrude, stick out, thrust forward; interrupt, intrude, meddle, pry; force oneself (upon).

obtrusive
adj lit: jutting, projecting, prominent, protruding, sticking out; forward, importunate, interfering, intrusive, meddling.

obtuse
adj lit: boneheaded, stupid, thick, unintelligent; dull, dumb, insensitive, slow, stolid, uncomprehending; blunt, rounded.

obviate
vb lit: avert, forestall, preclude, prevent; get round, neutralize; intercept.

obvious
adj lit: clear, conspicuous, distinct, evident, indisputable, manifest, marked, palpable, patent, plain, pronounced, self-evident, straightforward, undeniable, unmistakable; apparent, noticeable, overt, perceptible, recognizable, visible.

occasional
adj lit: desultory, infrequent, intermittent, irregular, odd, rare, sporadic; ceremonial, formal; nonce.

occasionally
adv lit: at times, every now and then, from time to time, infrequently, intermittently, irregularly, on and off, once in a while, periodically, sometimes, sporadically.

occupant
n lit: incumbent, inhabitant, lessee, resident, tenant; addressee; denizen, inmate; occupier, squatter.

occupation
n lit: craft, employment, job, line of work, profession, trade, work; activity, pursuit; métier, vocation; incumbency, habitation, possession, residence, tenancy, tenure; conquest, domination, invasion, subjugation; sit-in, squat, take-over.

occupied
adj (pa.pt) lit: busy, hard at it, tied up, working; inhabited, lived-in; engaged, full, taken, unavailable.

occur

vb lit: befall, come to pass, eventuate, happen, pass, take place, transpire; fall out, turn out; appear, arise, be, crop up, exist, materialize, turn up; be suggested (to one), come (to one).

occurrence

n lit: episode, event, happening, incident; affair, circumstance, instance; appearance, development, eventuation, manifestation, materialization.

odd

adj lit: abnormal, bizarre, extraordinary, freakish, outlandish, peculiar, strange, unusual, weird; curious, funny, quaint, singular; exceptional, rare; mysterious, uncanny; casual, incidental, occasional, random; miscellaneous, sundry, various; alternate, uneven; leftover, remaining, single, solitary, spare, surplus.

oddity

n lit: abnormality, anomaly, eccentricity, idiosyncrasy, peculiarity, quirk, rarity; crank, eccentric, maverick, weirdo; freakishness, incongruity, oddness, strangeness, unconventionality.

odds

n lit: chances, likelihood, probability; difference, disparity, distinction; *fig*: (at) loggerheads, (at) variance.

odious

adj lit: abhorrent, detestable, execrable, hateful, horrid, loathsome, obnoxious, offensive, repulsive, revolting, unpleasant, vile.

odour

n lit: aroma, bouquet, fragrance, perfume, scent; redolence, smell, stench, stink; air, atmosphere, aura, quality, spirit.

off

adj lit: finished, unavailable; absent, on holiday, on leave; deferred, postponed; free, quiet, slack; bad, below par, poor, substandard; decomposed, mouldy, rancid, rotten.
adv lit: apart, aside, away, elsewhere, out.
prp lit: down from, from, from on top of; by means of, through the use of.

offal

n lit: entrails, giblets, guts, insides, organs, tripes; bits and pieces, dregs, scraps; garbage, refuse, rubbish.

off colour

adj lit: ill, out of sorts, poorly, under the weather, unwell; run down, washed out.

offence

n lit: crime, misdemeanour, transgression, trespass; affront, insult, slight, snub; harm, hurt, wrong; hard feelings; anger, annoyance, displeasure, indignation, pique, resentment, umbrage.

offend

vb lit: affront, insult, outrage, slight, snub; anger, annoy, disgruntle, irritate, miff, provoke, rile, upset, vex; disgust, nauseate, repel, sicken; be repugnant to, be unacceptable to; commit a crime (against), transgress (against), trespass (against).

offender

n lit: criminal, law-breaker, transgressor; sinner, wrongdoer; culprit, guilty party, malefactor, miscreant.

offensive

n lit: attack, onslaught, push; invasion; warpath.
adj lit: affronting, insulting, insolent, rude; abusive, discourteous, objectionable, unacceptable; aggressive, attacking, belligerent, intrusive, provocative; angering, enraging, infuriating, outrageous, riling; disgusting, nauseating, obnoxious, revolting, vile.

offer

n lit: bid, proposition, tender; proposal, suggestion; suit.
vb lit: display to, hold out to, make available to, present to, proffer, put to, show to; bid, tender; propose, put forward, submit, suggest; put on the market, put up for sale; come forward, volunteer (to).

offering

n lit: donation, gift, present; contribution; oblation, sacrifice.

office

n lit: capacity, function, role; appointment, employment, occupation, post, situation, station; bureau, department, section; business premises, company address, working environment; employees, staff, workers; act of worship, service.

officer
n lit: person of rank, person of authority; executive, official; agent, functionary, representative; dignitary.

official
n lit: person of authority, officer; executive; agent, functionary, representative; dignitary.
adj lit: authoritative, authorized, sanctioned; certified, endorsed, legitimate; accredited, authentic, bona fide, formal, proper.

offices
n lit: backing, help, intercession, intervention, mediation, patronage.

officiate
vb lit: arbitrate, judge, referee, umpire; invigilate, maintain order, oversee, superintend; be the chair (at), preside (over).

officious
adj lit: obtrusive, overzealous; interfering, intrusive, meddling; pedantic; bigoted, condescending, high-and-mighty, pretentious; ambitious, pushy.

off-putting
adj lit: disconcerting, dispiriting, intimidating, unnerving, unsettling.

offset
vb lit: cancel out, counteract, counterbalance, make up for.
adj lit: contrasted, highlighted; balanced, equipoised.

offspring
n lit: child, descendant, heir; children, descendants, heirs, progeny, issue, seed; successors.

often
adv lit: frequently, repeatedly, time after time; commonly, generally.

ogre
n lit: giant, monster; bogey, demon; *fig*: disciplinarian, martinet, oppressor, tyrant.

oily
adj lit: greasy, well-lubricated; sebaceous; black, inky, sticky, tarry; *fig*: fawning, smooth, slippery, unctuous.

ointment
n lit: balm, cream, lotion, salve; paste; compress, poultice.

okay
n lit: approval, assent, consent; authorization, go-ahead, green light, permission.
vb lit: agree to, approve, authorize, pass, permit, sanction.
adj lit: acceptable, adequate, all right, good enough, in order, not bad, passable, satisfactory, tolerable; correct; fine, good.
adv lit: adequately, passably, satisfactorily, well enough; correctly.

old
n lit: elderly, pensioners, senior citizens.
adj lit: of age; advanced in years, elderly, getting on, past one's prime; in one's dotage, senile; aboriginal, age-old, ancient, antediluvian, primeval, primordial; experienced, practised, veteran; customary, familiar, habitual, long-established, time-honoured, traditional; clichéd, hackneyed; antique, archaic, obsolete, out of date, unfashionable; earlier, erstwhile, ex-, former, last, original, previous; dead, empty, rejected, worn-out.

old-fashioned
adj lit: antiquated, archaic, dated, obsolescent, obsolete, outmoded, out of date, passé, unfashionable; fuddy-duddy, fusty, musty, stick-in-the-mud.

omen
n lit: augury, portent; prognostication, sign, warning.

ominous
adj lit: portentous, pregnant; inauspicious, unpromising, unpropitious; baleful, dark, glowering, lowering, menacing, sinister, threatening.

omission
n lit: exclusion, leaving out; jump, skip; gap, hiatus, interval; negligence, oversight; avoidance, inaction.

omit
vb lit: drop, exclude, leave out; delete, eliminate, erase; jump, pass over, skip; neglect, miss, overlook.

omnipotent
adj lit: almighty, supremely powerful.

omnibus
n lit: bus, coach, double-decker;
anthology, collected works, symposium.

on
adj lit: active, functioning, operative,
performing, working; available;
happening, occurring, taking place;
allowable, permissible.
adv lit: ahead, forward, further, more;
during, in, when, while; into activity,
into functioning, into operation.
prp lit: atop; adhering to, stuck to; in
regard to, with reference to; by means of,
through, with.

once
adj lit: erstwhile, former, prior, quondam,
sometime.
adv lit: at one time, formerly, in the past,
long ago, previously; on a single
occasion, just one time.
cnj lit: any time, when, whenever; if, if
ever.

one
adj lit: a, a certain, an, a single, a sole;
joined, united.
prn lit: anybody, somebody; an example, a
sample.

onerous
adj lit: backbreaking, burdensome,
exacting, exhausting, exigent, hard,
heavy, laborious, taxing, weighty.

one-sided
adj lit: biased, discriminatory,
inequitable, partial, unfair; unbalanced,
unequal.

onlooking
adj lit: observing, seeing, viewing,
watching, witnessing.

only
adj lit: lone, single, sole, unique.
adv lit: just, merely; purely; at most.

onset
n lit: beginning, commencement, start;
assault, attack, charge, onrush;
appearance, materializing, outbreak.

onslaught
n lit: assault, attack, charge, offensive; *fig*:
diatribe, harangue, tirade.

onus
n lit: burden, liability, obligation,
responsibility, task.

ooze
n lit: ebb, gentle flow, waft; dregs,
grounds, lees; alluvium, mud, silt, slime;
discharge, dribble, drip, exudation,
seepage, weeping.
vb lit: dribble, drip, exude, leak, seep,
weep; discharge, drain, emit; ebb, gently
flow, waft.

opaque
adj lit: clouded, cloudy, dim, fuzzy, hazy,
murky, obfuscated, turbid; *fig*: abstruse,
cryptic, enigmatic, obscure, unclear,
unfathomable.

open
vb lit: throw wide, uncover, unlock,
unseal; uncork, unwrap; expand, spread
out, unfold; disclose, divulge, reveal;
begin, commence, inaugurate, kick off,
launch, set in motion, start; come apart,
separate, split.
adj lit: ajar, gaping, revealed, spread out,
unclosed, unfolded, unlocked; bare,
exposed, undefended, unfortified,
unprotected; accessible, public, spacious,
sweeping, unenclosed, unfenced, wide-
open; unengaged, unoccupied, vacant;
blatant, clear, flagrant, overt, plain,
unconcealed; arguable, debatable,
undecided, unsettled; impartial,
objective, uncommitted; liable (to),
susceptible (to), vulnerable (to); candid,
frank, guileless, honest, sincere; filigree,
lacy, loose, porous, spongy; generous,
liberal, munificent.

open-ended
adj lit: free of obligation, unbounded,
undefined, unlimited, unrestricted; sine-
die.

opening
n lit: aperture, fissure, fistula, gap, hole,
orifice, perforation, rupture, slot, vent;
break, chance, opportunity, vacancy;
beginning, commencement,
inauguration, kickoff, launch, onset,
start.
adj (pr.pt) lit: commencing, first,
inaugural, initial, introductory.

openly
adv lit: candidly, forthrightly, frankly,
plainly, unreservedly; blatantly,
flagrantly, overtly, publicly.

operate
vb lit: act, function, go, perform, run,
work; be in charge of, handle, manage,
manoeuvre, use, wield; perform surgery.

operation
n lit: action, functioning, performance, running, working; activity, movement; handling, management, manipulation, manoeuvring, use, wielding; affair, campaign, exercise, procedure; deal, proceeding, undertaking; surgical procedure.

operative
n lit: employee, hand, worker; executive; shopfloorman.
adj lit: active, functioning, on, performing, running, working; effective, efficient, functional, usable, serviceable, workable; crucial, influential, key, relevant, significant.

operator
n lit: button-pusher, driver, handler, user, wielder, worker; administrator, agent, contractor, franchise-holder, representative, trader; chief, manipulator, wheeler-dealer.

opinion
n lit: assessment, estimation, impression, judgement, point of view, view; belief, conception; ideas, sentiments, thoughts; supposition, theory.

opinionated
adj lit: big-headed, bigoted, cocksure, domineering, egotistic, narcissistic, overbearing, precious, precocious, self-aggrandizing, self-assertive; biased, pig-headed, perverse, stubborn.

opponent
n lit: adversary, antagonist, challenger, co-contestant, disputant; enemy, foe, rival.

opportune
adj lit: apt, convenient, happy, timely, well-timed; felicitous, fortunate, lucky, propitious.

opportunism
n lit: making hay while the sun shines, making the most of one's chances, striking while the iron is hot; expediency, pragmatism, trimming; exploitation, gold-digging.

opportunity
n lit: break, chance, opening; convenient moment, occasion, time.

oppose
vb lit: act against, be against, counter, dispute, fight, resist, speak against, take issue with; contradict, defy, stand up to;
confront, face; bar, hinder, obstruct; contrast, counterbalance.

opposing
adj (pr.pt) lit: alternative, contesting, other, rival; confronting, facing; antipathetic, conflicting, contrary, hostile, incompatible, irreconcilable.

opposite
n lit: antithesis, contrary, converse, reverse.
adj lit: alternate, facing, other; contradictory, contrary, different, reverse; adverse, antagonistic, irreconcilable.

opposition
n lit: counteraction, defence, resistance; blocking, obstruction; antagonism, hostility; antagonist, rival; competition, opponent, other side.

oppress
vb lit: afflict, burden, depress, load down, weigh heavy on; be autocratic over, persecute, subjugate, suppress, tyrannize over.

oppressive
adj lit: burdensome, grinding, onerous, severe; despotic, overbearing, repressive, tyrannical; close, heavy, overpowering, stifling, suffocating.

oppressor
n lit: despot, dictator, persecutor, subjugator, tyrant; bully, martinet, ogre, slave-driver.

opprobrium
n lit: disgrace, disrepute, infamy; scandal, abuse, reproach, scorn.

opt for
vb lit: choose, decide on, elect, go for, plump for, prefer, select, take.

optimistic
adj lit: hopeful, inclined to look on the bright side, Micawberish; confident, positive; buoyant, cheerful.

optimum
n lit: best, ideal, most favourable, perfection.
adj lit: best, choicest, ideal, most favourable, peak, perfect, top, superlative.

option
n lit: alternative, choice; decision, preference, selection.

optional
adj lit: discretionary, noncompulsory, voluntary; additional, extra, supplementary.

opulent
adj lit: affluent, prosperous, wealthy, well-off, well-to-do; abundant, lavish, plentiful.

opus
n lit: composition, creation, oeuvre, piece, work.

oracle
n lit: prophet, seer, soothsayer; augury, divination, prediction, prognostication, prophecy; crystal-gazer, fortune-teller, guru, high priest, shaman, wizard; *fig*: authority, source; boss, chief, management.

oral
adj lit: spoken, verbal; dental, mouth.

oration
n lit: address, discourse, homily, lecture, sermon, speech; monologue.

orator
n lit: lecturer, rhetorician, speaker; politician, speech-maker; talker.

orb
n lit: ball, globe, sphere; *fig*: celestial body, celestial sphere; world; eyeball; time-cycle.

orbit
n lit: circumnavigation, encircling motion, revolution, rotation; circle, cycle; course, path; *fig*: ambit, compass, range, scope, sphere; *spec*: socket (for each eyeball). *vb lit*: circle, circumnavigate, encircle, revolve around.

orchestrate
vb lit: arrange, score; *fig*: coordinate, mastermind, organize, put together, set up, stage-manage.

ordain
vb lit: appoint, consecrate, induct, install, invest; elect, nominate; decree, dictate, lay down, prescribe, rule, will; destine, predestine, predetermine.

ordeal
n lit: labour, nightmare, torment, tribulation, uphill struggle; test, trial.

order
n lit: command, decree, directive, injunction, mandate, ordinance, rule; application, booking, request, reservation; alignment, arrangement, line, organization, regularity, symmetry, tidiness; calm, control, discipline, peace, propriety, quiet; categorization, classification, codification, grouping, progression; breed, family, genre, ilk, kind, sort, type; caste, class, grade, hierarchy, position, rank; association, brotherhood, company, fraternity, guild, league, lodge, society; (in) place, (in) sequence, (in) turn; (in) commission, (in) service; (out of) operation, (out of) repair.
vb lit: command, decree, direct, instruct, ordain, prescribe, require; apply for, book, contract for, request, reserve; adjust, align, arrange, marshal, regulate; catalogue, classify, sort out.

orderly
adj lit: methodical, neat, regular, shipshape, systematic, tidy, trim; businesslike, controlled, formal, restrained; calm, disciplined, law-abiding, quiet, well-behaved.

ordinarily
adv lit: as a rule, commonly, generally, habitually, in general, normally, usually.

ordinary
adj lit: common, everyday, habitual, humdrum, normal, regular, standard, typical, usual; common or garden, customary, familiar, household, humble, plain, prosaic, simple, unpretentious, unremarkable; average, clichéd, commonplace, hackneyed, indifferent, mediocre, pedestrian, unexceptional.

ordure
n lit: dung, excrement, filth, shit; manure, muck; dirt.

organ
n lit: implement, instrument; member, part, structural element, unit; agency, forum, journal, mouthpiece, paper, periodical, publication.

organic
adj lit: biological, biotic, living, natural; anatomical, constitutional, inherent,

integral, structural; integrated, ordered, structured, systematic.

organism
n lit: animal, being, creature, living thing; integrated structure.

organization
n lit: assembly, composition, construction, coordination, design, formation, framework, plan, planning, structure, structuring; alignment, arrangement, conformation, grouping, make-up; association, body, company, concern, consortium, corporation, group, institution, syndicate.

organize
vb lit: assemble, compose, construct, coordinate, design, form, frame, plan, structure; combine, join together, unite; align, arrange, group, line up, marshal, put in order, set up; classify, codify; be responsible for, manage, orchestrate, run, see to, take care of.

orgy
n lit: bacchanal, carousal, debauch, revelry; binge, splurge, spree; *fig*: fit, frenzy, storm.

orientation
n lit: compass bearing, direction, heading; bearings, sense of direction; adaptation, adjustment, assimilation, familiarization.

orifice
n lit: aperture, fissure, hole, mouth, opening, pore, sphincter, stoma.

origin
n lit: roots, source; beginning, commencement, outset, start; basis, creation, derivation, emergence, foundation, fount, genesis; ancestry, extraction, lineage, pedigree, provenance, stock.

original
n lit: first, master, true one; archetype, model, paradigm, pattern, prototype; *fig*: anomaly, character, eccentric, oddity, weirdo.
adj lit: early, first, initial, starting; authentic, first-hand, genuine, master, true; creative, fresh, imaginative, ingenious, innovatory, inventive, new, novel, unprecedented, unusual.

originally
adv lit: at first, first, initially, in the first place, to begin with; prehistorically, primordially; imaginatively, ingeniously, innovatively, inventively.

originate
vb lit: arise, begin, come, derive, emanate, emerge, spring, start; bring about, create, evolve, initiate, pioneer, set up.

originator
n lit: architect, author, creator, designer, deviser, founder, inventor, pioneer.

ornament
n lit: decoration, jewel, trinket; adornment, embellishment, frill, garnish, trimming; *fig*: flower, glory, pride, treasure.
vb lit: adorn, decorate, embellish, festoon, garnish, trim; *fig*: grace, honour.

ornamental
adj lit: decorative, embellishing; artistic, picturesque, scenic; extra, inessential, supplementary.

ornate
adj lit: bedecked, elaborate, florid, ornamented, showy; lavish, rich, sumptuous.

orthodox
adj lit: approved, conformist, conventional, established, official, received, traditional; customary, ordinary, usual.

orthodoxy
n lit: conformism, conformity, traditionalism; conservatism, conventionality.

oscillate
vb lit: fluctuate, undulate, vary, vibrate; swing; vacillate, waver.

ossification
n lit: calcification, hardening, sclerosis, solidifying, stiffening; *fig*: fossilization, petrifaction; crystallization, polarization.

ostensible
adj lit: apparent, evident, outward, overt, seeming, supposed, visible; alleged, professed, purported.

ostentation
n lit: affectation, flamboyance, flaunting, pretension, showing off, tinsel, window-dressing; glory, grandeur, pageantry, pomp, splendour.

ostentatious
adj lit: conspicuous, dazzling, extravagant, eye-catching, flamboyant, flash, gaudy, loud, pompous, pretentious, showy.

ostracize
vb lit: blacklist, boycott, exclude, excommunicate, expel, send to Coventry; avoid, cold-shoulder, cut dead, eschew, have nothing to do with, shun, snub.

other
adj lit: additional, ancillary, auxiliary, extra, further, more, remaining, spare, supplementary; alternative, contrasting, different, dissimilar, diverse, separate, variant.

otherwise
adj lit: different.
adv lit: alternatively, differently; apart from this, except for this.
cnj lit: if not, or else.

otiose
adj lit: idle, inactive, unoccupied; indolent, lazy, worthless; functionless, futile, valueless; superfluous, useless.

oust
vb lit: drive out, eject, force out; dispossess, evict; depose, dethrone, unseat.

out
adj lit: absent; dismissed, disqualified, eliminated; at fault, incorrect, in error, wrong; striking, on strike; exposed, in the open, public; blooming, in bloom.
adv lit: away, elsewhere, outside; not allowed, not on, unacceptable; antiquated, behind the times, dated, old-fashioned; at an end, dead, exhausted, expired, finished; completely, thoroughly, unreservedly; in society; lengthways; from a total (of), from the midst (of).
prp lit: outside.

outbreak
n lit: epidemic, upsurge; burst, eruption, explosion, flare-up, rash.

outburst
n lit: discharge, eruption, outpouring, surge; explosion, fit of temper, storm, tantrum; interpolation, interruption, intrusion.

outcast
n lit: leper, pariah, untouchable; displaced person, exile, fugitive, persona non grata, refugee; vagrant.

outcome
n lit: conclusion, consequence, end result, result, upshot; aftermath.

outcry
n lit: complaint, howl, hullabaloo, protest, screech; commotion, uproar, yell.

outdated
adj lit: antiquated, archaic, behind the times, out of date, passé, unfashionable.

outdo
vb lit: beat, excel, surpass, transcend, outstrip; get the better of, outmanoeuvre, overcome.

outer
adj lit: cortical, exterior, external, outlying, outside, peripheral, superficial.

outfit
n lit: clothes, costume, dress, get-up, suit; accoutrements, gear, trappings; clique, company, crew, group, organization, set, squad, team, unit.
vb lit: equip, fit out, kit out, stock, supply.

outgoing
adj lit: approachable, easy, extrovert, friendly, gregarious, open, sociable; departing, ex-, former, past, retiring.

outing
n lit: airing, excursion, expedition, jaunt, spin, trip.

outlaw
n lit: criminal, malefactor, miscreant; bandit, brigand, desperado, marauder; fugitive, outcast.
vb lit: ban, banish, bar, exclude, make illegal, proscribe.

outlay
n lit: cost, disbursement, expenditure, expense, outgoings.

outlet
n lit: avenue, channel, duct, opening, safety valve, vent; *fig*: market, shop, store.

outline
n lit: contour, delineation, form, profile, shape, silhouette; draft, framework, layout, plan, sketch; bare facts, rough idea, summary, synopsis, silhouette.

vb lit: delineate; draft, plan, sketch, summarize.

outlook
n lit: attitude, frame of mind, standpoint, view; expectations, forecast, prospect; aspect, panorama, scene, vista.

output
n lit: production, productivity, yield; product, turnover; data, printout; signal, transmission.

outrage
n lit: atrocity, barbarism, enormity, inhumanity; affront, insult, profanation; injury, offence, rape, violation; anger, fury, indignation, resentment.
vb lit: affront, incense, infuriate, madden, offend, shock; injure, insult; abuse, defile, maltreat, rape, ravish, violate.

outrageous
adj lit: atrocious, barbaric, infamous, monstrous, unspeakable; disgraceful, iniquitous, scandalous; exorbitant, immoderate, preposterous, shocking.

outright
adj lit: definite, direct, straightforward; absolute, arrant, complete, downright, out-and-out, thorough, total, unqualified, utter.
adv lit: absolutely, completely, explicitly, overtly, thoroughly, without hesitation; at once, immediately, instantaneously, instantly, straight away, there and then.

outset
n lit: beginning, first, inception, opening, start.

outside
n lit: cortex, exterior, façade, front, surface; topside; hide, peel, skin; extreme, most.
adj lit: exterior, external, outdoor, outer, outermost, outward, surface; extramural; extraneous; distant, marginal, negligible, slight, slim, small, unlikely.
adv lit: in the exterior, on the exterior, to the exterior.
prp lit: beyond, excluded from, the far side of; excepted from, exempt from; apart from.

outsider
n lit: alien, incomer, interloper, newcomer, nonmember, odd man out, stranger; *fig*: long shot, surprise winner.

outsize
adj lit: enormous, extra-large, giant, gigantic, jumbo, large.

outskirts
n lit: borders, boundary, edge, periphery, purlieus; suburbs.

outspoken
adj lit: blunt, candid, direct, forthright, frank, free; explicit.

outstanding
adj lit: arresting, conspicuous, eye-catching, noteworthy, prominent, striking; eminent, excellent, exceptional, great, pre-eminent, superlative; due, owing, payable, remaining, unpaid, unsettled.

outward
adj lit: exterior, external, outer, outside, surface; apparent, evident, ostensible, overt, superficial, visible.

outwardly
adv lit: apparently, as far as one can see, externally, on the face of it, ostensibly, overtly, seemingly, superficially, to all intents and purposes, visibly.

outweigh
vb lit: be more important than, be preponderant over, eclipse, have more clout than, predominate over, prevail over, take precedence over.

outwit
vb lit: get the better of, outfox, outmanoeuvre, outsmart, run rings around; cheat, deceive, defraud, dupe, swindle, take in.

oval
adj lit: egg-shaped, elliptical, ovoid.

ovation
n lit: acclaim, acclamation, applause, big hand, clapping, plaudits; enthusiastic reception, triumph.

oven
n lit: Aga, hob, stove; cooker, heater; microwave; fire, furnace, kiln; *fig*: uterus, womb.

over
adj lit: accomplished, ancient history, completed, concluded, finished, past, settled; closed, done; left, remaining, spare, surplus.
adv lit: above one, overhead; across.
prp lit: above, atop, on, on top of, superior to; exceeding, in excess of, more than.

overall
adj lit: all-embracing, complete, comprehensive, general, inclusive, long-term, total.
adv lit: generally speaking, in general, in the long term, on the whole.

overawed
adj (pa.pt) lit: cowed, daunted, intimidated, terrified; abashed, browbeaten.

overbearing
adj lit: arrogant, autocratic, bossy, dictatorial, domineering, haughty, high-handed, officious, peremptory, supercilious, superior.

overcast
adj lit: clouded, cloudy, dismal, dull, grey, leaden, lowering, threatening.

overcome
vb lit: beat, conquer, crush, defeat, get the better of, overpower, prevail over, subdue, vanquish; be victorious over, rise above, surmount; come through, survive, weather.
adj lit: affected, bowled over, overwhelmed, speechless; ecstatic, elated; horrified, terrified; awestricken; dumbstruck, flabbergasted.

overconfident
adj lit: brash, cocksure, foolhardy, hubristic, presumptuous.

overcrowded
adj (pa.pt) lit: choked, congested, crammed, full, overpopulated, packed.

overdo
vb lit: overwork at; exaggerate, overact; belabour, take to extremes, overstate; overuse.

overdue
adj lit: behind schedule, behind time, late, unpunctual; outstanding, owing.

overeat
vb lit: binge, eat like a horse, gorge, guzzle, make a pig of oneself, pack it away, pig out, stuff oneself; become bloated, get stuffed.

overflow
n lit: discharge, flood, inundation; surplus.
vb lit: flood, pour over, run over, spill over; drown, immerse, inundate, submerge, swamp.

overhang
n lit: projection, protrusion.
vb lit: bulge over, jut over, loom over, project over, protrude over, stick out over; *fig*: be imminent over, loom over, threaten.

overhaul
n lit: going-over, maintenance session, reconditioning, service; check-up, examination, inspection.
vb lit: do up, repair, service; careen, strip down; check over, examine inspect; catch up with, overtake, pass.

overheads
n lit: operating costs, running costs.

overindulgence
n lit: excess, immoderation, intemperance, surfeit.

overjoyed
adj (pa.pt) lit: delighted, ecstatic, elated, euphoric, in raptures, jubilant, over the moon, speechless with pleasure, thrilled.

overloaded
adj (pa.pt) lit: oppressed, overcharged, overtaxed, saddled with, strained, weighed down.

overlook
vb lit: command a view of, front on, look over; fail to notice, forget, miss, pass over; disregard, ignore, let one off with, let pass, omit, skip, turn a blind eye to.

overpowering
adj (pr.pt) lit: compelling, compulsive, imperative, insurmountable, irresistible, overwhelming, uncontrollable.

overrate
vb lit: assess too highly, exaggerate, make too much of, overestimate; expect too much of.

overriding
adj (pr.pt) lit: compelling, determining, dominant, final, overruling, paramount, predominant, prevailing, prime, ruling, supreme.

overrule
vb lit: countermand, disallow, override, overturn, set aside, veto; invalidate, make null and void, repeal, rescind.

overrun

vb lit: invade, occupy, overwhelm, rout, swamp; inundate, overgrow, permeate, spread like wildfire, swarm over; exceed, go beyond, overshoot.

overseas

adj lit: continental, foreign, international, transatlantic; distant, faraway, remote; out of the country.

adv lit: abroad, out of the country.

overseer

n lit: boss, chief, foreman, gaffer, manager, supervisor.

overshadow

vb lit: dominate, dwarf, eclipse, take precedence over, tower above; cloud, darken, obfuscate, obscure; blight, mar, ruin, spoil, take the edge off, temper.

overshoot

vb lit: exceed, go beyond, go past, overdo, overrun.

oversight

n lit: error, lapse, omission, slip; blunder, fault; carelessness, negligence; administration, care, direction, management, supervision, surveillance.

overt

adj lit: blatant, evident, manifest, obvious, patent, plain, public, visible.

overtake

vb lit: get past, outdistance, outdo, pass; catch unprepared, engulf, overwhelm, strike, take by surprise.

overthrow

n lit: deposing, dethronement, downfall, ejection, expulsion, ouster, removal, undoing; defeat, destruction, rout, ruin, subjugation, suppression.

vb lit: bring down, depose, dethrone, eject, expel, oust, remove, undo; defeat, destroy, rout, ruin, subdue, subjugate, suppress; abolish, do away with, demolish, overturn, put an end to, topple, raze.

overtone

n lit: association, connotation, hint,

implication, innuendo, nuance, suggestion, undercurrent.

overture

n lit: advance(s), approach, invitation, opening move, proposal, proposition; introduction, prelude.

overturn

vb lit: capsize, keel over, knock over, tip over, topple, tumble, upend; annul, countermand, invalidate, repeal, reverse; depose.

overweight

adj lit: ample, bulky, chubby, corpulent, fat, gross, heavy, hefty, massive, obese, plump, podgy, portly, stout, tubby.

overwork

n lit: overuse; fatigue, strain, stress, tiredness.

vb lit: be a hard task-master, burden, exhaust, exploit, overtax, overuse, strain, wear out; burn the midnight oil, do too much, drive oneself into the ground, go on too long.

overwrought

adj lit: agitated, in a state, keyed up, on edge, overexcited, tense, uptight, worked up, wound up; contrived, florid, fussy, overdone.

owe

vb lit: be in arrears; be under an obligation to pay, have to give, should give.

owing

adj lit: due, outstanding, unpaid, unsettled.

owing to

adv lit: as a result of, because of, due to, in consequence of, on account of.

own

vb lit: have, hold, possess, retain; acknowledge, admit (to), avow, concede (to), confess (to), go along with, grant.

adj lit: individual, personal, private.

owner

n lit: landlord, proprietor; possessor, retainer; master.

P

pace
n lit: step, stride; gait, tread, walk; momentum, motion, rate, speed, tempo, velocity.
vb lit: march, pound, stride; patrol, walk up and down; count (out), mark (out), measure (out).

pacify
vb lit: appease, conciliate, placate, propitiate; calm, quiet, smooth, tranquillize.

pack
n lit: bale, bundle; burden, load; haversack, knapsack, rucksack; band, bunch, crowd, gang, group, herd, troop; collection, deck, kit, set; application; carton, packet.
vb lit: batch, bundle, parcel up; burden, load, store, stow; cram, fill, jam, press, ram, stuff; crowd, mob, throng; compact, compress.

package
n lit: box, carton, packet, parcel; amalgamation, combination; unit, whole; deal, enterprise, transaction; product.
vb lit: batch, box, pack, parcel up, wrap up; assemble, make, manufacture, put it all together.

packed
adj (pa.pt) lit: congested, crammed, crowded, full, jammed, overloaded, seething, swarming.

pack up
vb lit: put away, tidy up; *fig*: call it a day, finish, give up; break down, fail, stall.

pact
n lit: agreement, arrangement, bargain, contract, deal, entente, treaty, understanding; alliance, coalition.

pad
n lit: buffer, cushion, guard, protection, shield, wad; block, jotter, notepad; paw, sole; apartment, flat, room; heliport, launching platform.
vb lit: cushion, fill, line, stuff; *fig*: digress, draw (out), fill (out), prevaricate.

padding
n lit: filling, packing, stuffing, wadding; *fig*: hot air, prevarication, verbiage, waffle.

paddle
n lit: oar, scull, sweep.
vb lit: oar, row, scull; dabble, dip, splash (about), wade; totter, walk unsteadily.

paddock
n lit: field, grassy expanse, meadow, pasture, turf enclosure.

pad out
vb lit: amplify, augment, eke out, fill out, inflate, protract, stretch.

padre
n lit: chaplain, reverend; minister, pastor.

pagan
n lit: heathen, paynim, unbeliever; infidel; atheist.
adj lit: godless, heathen, unbelieving; irreligious, unchristian, ungodly.

page
n lit: folio, leaf, sheet, side; attendant, boy, servant, squire; *fig*: epoch, era, period, phase, stage, time.
vb lit: call for, have called for, send to find.

pageant
n lit: floats, parade, procession; historical display; show, spectacle, tableau vivant.

pain
n lit: ache, agony, burning discomfort, pang, smarting, soreness, throb; anguish, distress, suffering, woe; grief, sadness; *fig*: bore, bother, drag, nuisance, pest.
vb lit: hurt, smart, wound; chafe, discomfort, torment; *fig*: afflict, aggrieve, agonize, distress; annoy, gall, harass, irritate, vex, worry.

painful
adj lit: aching, agonizing, excruciating, hurting, raw, smarting, sore, throbbing; abhorrent, awful, distressing, dreadful,

nasty, terrible, unpleasant; arduous, difficult, hard, tedious, trying.

painkiller
n lit: analgesic, anodyne, palliative, sedative; drug, pill, tablet.

painless
adj fig: easy, fast, no trouble, quick, simple.

painstaking
adj lit: assiduous, careful, conscientious, meticulous, punctilious, scrupulous, sedulous, thorough.

paint
n lit: colour, dye, pigment, tint, wash; emulsion, enamel; cosmetics, make-up.
vb lit: colour, dye, enamel, tint; be an artist, depict, draw, picture, portray, represent, sketch; brush (on), coat, daub, decorate, put (on), slap (on); put cosmetics on; *fig*: describe vividly, evoke.

painter
n lit: artist, drawer, sketcher; decorator, handiman; mooring-line, rope.

pair
n lit: brace, couple, doublet, duo, twosome.
vb lit: bracket, couple, match, put together, yoke; marry, mate, wed.

pal
n lit: buddy, chum, friend, mate, mucker; associate, partner.
vb lit: chum (up with), join (up with), take (up with), team (up with).

palatable
adj lit: appetizing, delicious, savoury, tasty, toothsome; *fig*: acceptable, agreeable, fair, satisfactory.

palatial
adj lit: grand, grandiose, imposing, luxurious, majestic, opulent, stately, sumptuous.

pale
vb lit: blanch, blench, go white, whiten; dim, dull, fade; *fig*: decrease, diminish, lessen.
adj lit: anaemic, ashen, bleached, faded, pallid, sallow, wan, washed-out, whitish; dim, faint, feeble, thin, weak.

paling
n lit: pole, spike, stake; fence, fencing, stockade; boundary.

pall
n lit: cloak, mantle, vestment; cloth, drape; *fig*: curtain, darkness, obscurity, veil; *spec*: chalice-cover.
vb lit: become dull, become tedious, bore, cloy, sicken, weary.

palliate
vb lit: excuse, extenuate, mitigate; alleviate, diminish, lessen, reduce.

palm
n lit: hand, paw; coconut tree, date tree; *fig*: glory, laurels, success, triumph, trophy, victory.
vb lit: conceal in one's hand; steal, thieve, walk off with; *fig*: fob (off with); pass (off as).

palpable
adj lit: real, solid, substantial, tangible; blatant, evident, obvious.

palpitation
n lit: arrhythmia, tachycardia; fluttering, pulsing, quivering, shivering; beating, pounding, throbbing.

paltry
adj lit: beggarly, derisory, despicable, insignificant, meagre, mean, miserable, petty, puny, trifling, trivial.

pampered
adj (pa.pt) lit: babied, coddled, cosseted, indulged, mollycoddled, spoilt.

pan
n lit: cooking tray, pot, vessel; toilet bowl; basin, concavity, depression, hollow; *fig*: face, features; *spec*: drum (in a steel band); floe (of ice); priming area (on a firelock).
vb lit: search (for), sift, wash; *fig*: scan, sweep, track; censure, criticize, flay, knock, slate; come (out), turn (out).

panacea
n lit: cure-all, elixir, sovereign remedy; cure, remedy.

panache
n lit: brio, dash, flair, flamboyance, style; bravado, theatricality.

pandemonium
n lit: babel, bedlam, commotion, din, hubbub, racket, tumult.

pander to
vb lit: gratify, humour, indulge, minister to; obtain for, procure for.

panel
n lit: oblong, rectangle; board, lath, plank, strip; fencing, hurdle, paling; dashboard, instrument board, switchboard; long photo, painting, picture; saddle-pad; *fig*: discussion group, jury, quiz team; *spec*: box, frame, inset, key (on a page); division, section (of a coalmine, of a hull); list (of clients, of consultants, of doctors, of jurors, of patients).

pang
n lit: gripe, pain, prick, stab, twinge; stitch; ache; *fig*: qualm, scruple.

panic
n lit: alarm, consternation, fear, fright, hysteria; red-alert, scare.
vb lit: become hysterical, go to pieces, lose one's nerve, overreact; alarm, frighten, put the wind up, scare; unnerve.

panorama
n lit: prospect, scene, view, vista; overall picture, wide view.

pant
vb lit: blow, gasp, heave, puff, wheeze; *fig*: hunger (for), long (for), pine (for), yearn (for).

pants
n lit: bloomers, briefs, drawers, knickers, panties, shorts, underpants, Y-fronts.

paper
n lit: document(s); certificate, deed, instrument; dossier(s), file(s); account(s), receipt(s); daily, journal, newspaper, organ, periodical, tabloid; article, dissertation, essay, monograph, study, thesis, treatise; examination; wrapping; (on) record.

papers
n lit: documents, dossier, file, letters; archives, records; diaries; accounts, bills, bonds, receipts, statements.

par
n lit: average, norm, standard, usual; balance, equality, equilibrium, level, parallel.

parable
n lit: allegory, fable, story with a moral.

parade
n lit: array, cavalcade, pageant, procession; march-past, military display, trooping; display, exhibition, flaunting, ostentation, show; esplanade, promenade; terraced row; *spec*: defence, parry (in fencing).
vb lit: march past, process; brandish, display, flaunt, show off, vaunt; troop.

paradigm
n lit: example, exemplar, model, pattern; conceptual framework.

paradise
n lit: garden of Eden, heaven; life to come, next world; Elysian fields, happy hunting-ground, Promised Land, Utopia; *fig*: bliss, ecstasy, joy, rapture.

paradox
n lit: ambiguity, anomaly, contradiction, enigma, inconsistency, oddity, puzzle.

paragon
n lit: ideal, perfect specimen; apotheosis, epitome, quintessence; archetype, model, paradigm.

parallel
n lit: analogy, comparison, correlation, likeness, resemblance, similarity; analogue, counterpart, duplicate, equal, equivalent, match.
vb lit: agree with, be alike with, correlate to, correspond with, equal, match; balance, complement.
adj lit: aligned, alongside, side by side; analogous, compatible, complementary, uniform.

paralyse
vb lit: anaesthetize, benumb, immobilize; cripple, debilitate, disable, lame; *fig*: arrest, halt, stop dead, transfix.

paralysis
n lit: ataxia, paresis; immobility, numbness, palsy; *fig*: disruption, shutdown, stasis, stillness, stoppage.

parameter
n lit: limitation, margin, restriction, tabulation; guideline, specification.

paramount
adj lit: chief, dominant, first, foremost, main, primary, prime, principal, supreme.

paranoid
adj lit: hysterical, neurotic; deluded, phobic.

paranormal
n lit: psychic phenomena; ESP, mental powers; supernatural.
adj lit: extra-sensory, psychic; supernatural; occult, unexplained.

paraphrase
n lit: rehash, rephrasing, restatement; rendering; abridgement, résumé, summarized version.
vb lit: rehash, rephrase, restate; render; abridge, abstract, summarize.

parasite
n lit: bloodsucker; *fig*: hanger-on, leech, scrounger, sponger; drone.

parcel
n lit: carton, package, packet; batch, bunch, bundle; company, crew, gang, pack; bit, portion, part; area, lot, plot, site.
vb lit: do (up), pack (up), wrap (up); apportion (out), deal (out), mete (out), share (out).

parched
adj lit: arid, dehydrated, desiccated, dry; thirsty; scorched, shrivelled, withered.

pardon
n lit: forgiveness; absolution, mercy, remission, reprieve; amnesty, grace; acquittal, discharge, exoneration; *spec*: (papal) indulgence.
vb lit: forgive; absolve, free, let off, release from, remit, reprieve; acquit, exculpate, excuse, overlook.

pare
vb lit: cut, peel, shave, trim; gradually reduce, nibble away at.

parent
n lit: father, mother, procreator, progenitor, sire; guardian; author, creator, generator, originator, source; derivation, prototype.

parenthesis
n lit: bracketed insertion, interpolation; aside, comment, digression, footnote, note; hiatus, interval, space.

pariah
n lit: leper, outcast, untouchable; undesirable, unperson; cur, dog.

parity
n lit: balance, equality, equilibrium, equivalence, identity, level, par, parallel, unity; conformity, congruity, correspondence; likeness, resemblance, similarity, similitude.

park
n lit: estate, garden, grounds, nature reserve, wildlife reservation, woodland; playground, playing-field, recreation ground; amusement complex, Disneyland, funfair.
vb lit: dump, leave, put down; pull up, station, stop.

parliament
n lit: assembly, congress, council, diet, government, senate; the House of Commons and the House of Lords, Westminster.

parody
n lit: burlesque, caricature, satire, send-up; apology, mockery, travesty.
vb lit: burlesque, caricature, lampoon, satirize, send up.

parrot
n lit: cockateel, cockatoo, macaw, parakeet; *fig*: copycat, imitator, mimic.
vb lit: copy, echo, imitate, mimic, repeat; recite by heart.

parry
vb lit: block, fend off, repulse, stave off, ward off; avoid, dodge, duck, shun, sidestep.

parsimonious
adj lit: close-fisted, frugal, mean, miserly, niggardly, penny-pinching, scrimping, sparing, stingy, tightfisted.

parson
n lit: clergyman, cleric, divine, minister, padre, pastor, priest, rector, reverend, vicar.

part
n lit: bit, fraction, fragment, piece, portion, scrap, section, sector, segment, share; component, constituent, element, ingredient, module, unit; limb, member, organ; area, district, region, territory, vicinity; behalf, cause, concern, interest; duty, function, involvement, say, task; character, role, voice; conduct, disposition, temperament.
vb lit: detach, disconnect, disjoin, divide, put asunder, rend, separate, sever, split, tear; break up, go separate ways, leave, quit, split up, withdraw.

partake
vb lit: engage (in), participate (in), take part (in); receive, share, take a part (of); eat.

partial
adj lit: incomplete, unfinished; biased, discriminatory, one-sided, partisan, prejudiced, unfair.

participant
n lit: contributor, member, partaker; partner, shareholder.

participate
vb lit: engage (in), have a hand (in), join (in), share (in), take part (in).

particle
n lit: atom, bit, grain, iota, jot, mite, molecule, scrap, shred, speck; crumb; prefix, suffix.

particular
n lit: circumstance(s), detail(s), fact(s), specification(s).
adj lit: choosy, fastidious, finicky, fussy, meticulous, painstaking, thorough; detailed, itemized, minute; distinct, exact, special, specific; distinctive, remarkable, singular, unusual.

particularly
adv lit: decidedly, distinctly, especially, explicitly, expressly, intimately, markedly, notably, outstandingly, specifically; individually, peculiarly, singularly, uncommonly, unusually.

partisan
n lit: adherent, devotee, follower, supporter; freedom fighter, guerrilla, nationalist, resistance fighter.
adj lit: biased, discriminatory, partial, prejudiced, tendentious; guerrilla, resistance, underground.

partition
n lit: barrier, divider, screen, septum, wall; division, segregation, separation; apportioning, distribution, rationing out; allocation, portion, ration, share.
vb lit: divide, fence (off), screen, wall (off); cut up, segment, separate, split up, subdivide; allocate, apportion.

partly
adv lit: incompletely, in part, in some measure, partially, to a degree, to some extent, up to a point.

partner
n lit: ally, associate, collaborator, colleague, co-founder, confederate; abetter, accomplice; companion, comrade, mate; helpmeet; bedfellow, consort, husband, spouse, wife.

party
n lit: bash, celebration, do, festivity, get-together, knees-up, reception, social gathering, soirée, thrash; band, body, bunch, company, detachment, group, squad, team, unit; alliance, association, clique, coalition, confederacy, faction, grouping, set, side; individual, person; contractor, defendant, litigant, plaintiff.

pass
n lit: canyon, col, defile, gap; authorization, identification, permit, safe-conduct, warrant; free ticket, voucher; advances, approach, overture; plight, predicament, situation, state of affairs; lunge, push, thrust; brandishing, gesticulation, wave; *spec*: success (in an examination).
vb lit: depart, elapse, go by, leave, move, proceed; beat, exeed, excel, outdo, surmount, surpass, transcend; get through, graduate, qualify; do, suffice; fill, occupy, spend, while away; befall, happen, occur, take place; convey, give, hand, kick, throw, transfer, transmit; accept, approve, authorize, enact, legislate, ratify, sanction, validate; declare, pronounce; disregard, ignore, miss, omit, overlook, skip; defecate, discharge, evacuate, excrete; blow over, cease, die, dwindle, ebb, expire, fade, vanish, wane; be seen (as), be taken (for).

passably
adv lit: adequately, fairly, moderately, quite, rather, reasonably, somewhat, tolerably.

passage
n lit: corridor, doorway, entrance, exit, hall, lobby, vestibule; crossing, journey, tour, trek, trip, voyage; avenue, course, lane, path, road, route, thoroughfare, way; advance, flow, passing, progress, transition; clause, excerpt, extract, piece, quotation, reading, section, text; acceptance, enactment, legislation, ratification.

passenger
n lit: fare, pillion rider, rider, ticket-holder, traveller.

passer-by
n lit: bystander, onlooker, witness; casual spectator, man in the street; pedestrian.

passing
n lit: death, decease, demise, end.
adj lit: incidental, fortuitous; casual, cursory, hasty, shallow, superficial; brief, ephemeral, fleeting, momentary, transitory.

passion
n lit: ardour, eagerness, emotion, ferocity, fervour, fire, intensity, spirit, vehemence, voracity, zeal; craving, desire, lust; enthusiasm, fondness, infatuation, love; bug, craze, mania, obsession; anger, ire, rage, resentment, wrath; frenzy, storm.

passionate
adj lit: amorous, ardent, erotic, hot, loving, lustful, sensual, sexy; aflame, eager, enthusiastic, excited, fervent, fiery, heartfelt, intense, spirited, vehement, zealous; emotional, wild; hot-headed, irascible, irritable, quick-tempered, stormy, tempestuous, violent.

passive
adj lit: inactive, inert; long-suffering, patient, resigned, submissive, unresisting; acquiescent, compliant, docile.

pass over
vb lit: disregard, ignore, leave, overlook, skip, take no notice of; forget, miss, omit.

pass up
vb lit: forgo, give a miss, ignore, let go, reject; lose, miss.

past
n lit: days gone by, former times, good old days, times past; background, experience, history, life, particulars, record.
adj lit: completed, done, extinct, finished, gone, over; ancient, bygone, old, previous; earlier, erstwhile, former, preceding, quondam.
adv lit: by, on; beyond, to the far side of; over.
prp lit: beyond, farther than, outside, over; after, subsequent to.

paste
n lit: dough, suspension, thick liquid; adhesive, glue, gum; *spec*: glass (jewellery).

vb lit: affix, cement, glue, gum, stick; *fig*: beat, hit, strike, thrash.

pastime
n lit: amusement, diversion, entertainment, hobby, leisure activity, recreation, sport.

pastor
n lit: clergyman, ecclestiastic, minister, padre, parson, priest, rector, vicar; shepherd.

pastoral
adj lit: arcadian, bucolic, rural, rustic; grassy, grazing; clerical, priestly.

pastry
n lit: dough, flour-paste, pie-crust; pie, tart; cake, slice.

pasture
n lit: grass, grazing land, meadow, paddock.

pat
n lit: dab, stroke, tap, touch; knob, portion; cake, lump.
vb lit: dab, caress, stroke, tap, touch.

patch
n lit: darn, reinforcement, replacement; bit, fragment, scrap, shred; area, ground, land, manor, stretch, vicinity; period, time; *spec*: cover, pad (over an eye); false mole (as facial decoration); overlay (in printing).
vb lit: cover over, fix (up), mend, repair; treat; put (together), reconnect (together); *fig*: make (up).

patchy
adj lit: bitty, inconsistent, intermittent, irregular, variable; sketchy, uneven, weak in places.

patent
n lit: copyright, exclusive right, title; certificate, licence.
adj lit: clear, evident, indisputable, manifest, obvious, plain, unequivocal, unmistakable; blatant, flagrant.

paternal
adj lit: fatherly, parental; benevolent, protective, solicitous; family, hereditary, patrimonial.

path
n lit: alley, footway, gangway, kerb, passage, pavement, sidewalk, track, trail, walk, walkway; course, direction, line, route, way.

pathetic
adj lit: affecting, distressing, heart-rending, moving, pitiable, sad, touching; *fig*: abysmal, feeble, lamentable, petty, weak, wet; hopeless, rubbishy, useless, worthless.

pathos
n lit: plaintiveness, poignancy, sadness.

patience
n lit: endurance, forbearance, long-suffering, perseverance, sufferance, tolerance; calmness, composure, cool; diligence, fortitude, persistence.

patient
n lit: invalid, sufferer; victim; case, client.
adj lit: enduring, forbearing, long-suffering, persevering, resigned, stoical, suffering, tolerant; calm, composed, cool; diligent, persistent; lenient, magnanimous, understanding.

patriarch
n lit: elder, father, governor, head of the family, lord, ruler; bishop, pontiff, pope, religious leader.

patrician
n lit: aristocrat, hereditary peer, member of the upper classes, noble, nobleman; bloated plutocrat.

patriotic
adj lit: loyalist, nationalist, jingoist, loyal.

patrol
n lit: policing, safeguarding, rounds, watch; guard, security man, sentinel, watchman.
vb lit: guard, inspect, keep watch over, make the rounds, police, walk the perimeter.

patron
n lit: benefactor, sponsor; angel, backer; champion, defender, guardian, protector; client, customer, shopper.

patronage
n lit: beneficence, generosity, sponsorship; backing, support; protection; guardianship, protectorate, wardship; business, custom, trade; *spec*: lordship, proprietorship.

patronize
vb lit: be condescending to, be lofty with, look down on, talk down to; fund, sponsor; back, support; be a client of, buy from, do business with, frequent, trade with.

pattern
n lit: archetype, example, model, norm, sample, specimen; diagram, guide, instructions, plan, stencil, template; arrangement, disposition, order, orderliness, positioning, sequence, system; kind, sort, style, type, variety; decoration, design, motif, ornament; *spec*: distribution (of shot on a target).
vb lit: model, mould, shape, style; decorate, ornament.

paunch
n lit: beer-belly, pot, potbelly.

pause
n lit: break, breather, delay, gap, halt, interlude, intermission, interval, lull, respite, stoppage; hesitation; interruption, suspension.
vb lit: break off, delay, halt, have a breather, rest, stop briefly; falter, hesitate, waver.

paved
adj (pa.pt) lit: asphalted, surfaced, tarred; *fig*: prepare (the way for), smooth (the way for).

paw
n lit: foot, hand; pad; claws; mitt.
vb lit: cop a feel, finger, grope, maul, molest; feel, grab, handle roughly, manhandle; *spec*: kick, strike (the ground restlessly).

pawn
n lit: collateral, deposit, pledge, security; bond, hock; cat's-paw, dupe, instrument, puppet, stooge, tool.
vb lit: deposit, hock, pledge, stake.

pay
n lit: earnings, fee, hire, remuneration, salary, stipend, wages; emolument, income, takings; reimbursement.
vb lit: cough up, foot, meet settle; clear, honour; recompense, reimburse, remunerate; be advantageous, benefit, be worthwhile, repay; bring in, return, yield; be profitable, make a return, provide a living; bestow, extend, give, present, proffer, render; *fig*: answer (for), make amends (for), suffer (for).

payable
adj lit: due, outstanding, owed; mature.

pay back
vb lit: refund, reimburse, repay, settle up, square; *fig*: get even with, have

vengeance against, retaliate against, settle a score with.

payment
n *lit*: emolument, fee, hire, remuneration, salary, stipend, wages; advance, deposit, outlay, premium; remittance, settlement.

payoff
n *lit*: discharge, settlement; bribe, buying off; *fig*: retaliation, revenge; climax, dénouement, punch-line.

peace
n *lit*: calm, hush, quiet, repose, restfulness, serenity, silence, stillness, tranquillity; amity, concord, harmony; armistice, cessation of hostilities, treaty, truce; *spec*: ease (of mind).

peaceable
adj *lit*: conciliatory, dovish, nonbelligerent, pacific; gentle, inoffensive; amicable, friendly.

peaceful
adj *lit*: calm, hushed, placid, quiet, restful, serene, silent, still, tranquil, undisturbed, unruffled; amicable, friendly, harmonious, on good terms; non-military.

peak
n *lit*: apex, crest, pinnacle, point, summit, tip, top; *fig*: climax, culmination, high point, maximum, zenith.
vb *lit*: climax, come to a head, reach a maximum.

peaky
adj *lit*: off colour, sickly, unwell; pinched, puny; sharp-featured.

peal
n *lit*: chime, chiming, clangour, resonance, reverberation, ringing, sounding, tolling; *spec*: carillon, set (of bells); grilse, sea-trout.
vb *lit*: chime, clang, resonate, resound, reverberate, ring, sound, toll.

peasant
n *lit*: countryman, rustic; bumpkin, serf, yokel.

peculiar
adj *lit*: abnormal, bizarre, freakish, funny, odd, outlandish, strange, weird; curious, extraordinary, quaint, singular, unusual; characteristic, distinctive, idiosyncratic,

individual, own, particular, private, specific, unique.

pedantic
adj *lit*: fussy, hair-splitting, particular, precise, punctilious, scrupulous; didactic, pedagogic; bookish, erudite.

peddle
vb *lit*: flog, hawk, sell, trade, vend.
n *lit*: base, dais, foot, pier, plinth, stand, support; axle-guard, pillow-block.

pedestrian
n *lit*: walker; footslogger, hiker; passer-by.
adj *lit*: on foot, walking; *fig*: dull, long-winded, prosaic, slow, tedious, trite, unimaginative.

pedigree
n *lit*: ancestry, breed, descent, extraction, genealogy, line, lineage, stock.
adj *lit*: purebred, thoroughbred.

peek
n *lit*: glance, glimpse, look, peep; dekko, gander, keek.
vb *lit*: glance, look, peep, squinny, take a look.

peel
n *lit*: rind, skin; bark; outer layer.
vb *lit*: pare, skin, strip (off); flake off.

peep
n *lit*: glance, glimpse, look, peek; cheep, chirp, chirrup, squeak, twitter.
vb *lit*: glance surreptitiously, peek, sneak a look; appear briefly, be partly visible, emerge tantalizingly; cheep, chirp, chirrup, squeak, twitter.

peer
n *lit*: aristocrat, lord, noble, nobleman; compeer, equal.
vb *lit*: gaze, look shortsightedly (at), take a close look (at); look (out), peep (out).

peerage
n *lit*: aristocracy, lords, nobility, peers.

peerless
adj *lit*: beyond compare, incomparable, matchless, second to none, superlative, unequalled, unrivalled, unsurpassed.

peeved
adj *lit*: annoyed, galled, irked, nettled, piqued, put out, upset, vexed.

peevish
adj *lit*: cantankerous, cross, crusty, fretful, grumpy, ill-tempered, irascible,

petulant, short-tempered, snappish, sulky, surly, testy, touchy, waspish.

peg
n lit: bolt, pin, stake; hook, key; dram, drink, tot; *fig*: degree, step; leg; *spec*: wooden leg.
vb lit: attach, fasten, fix, join, secure; freeze, hold, limit, set; *fig*: beaver (away at), plug (away at), work (away at).

pejorative
adj lit: deprecating, depreciating, disparaging, relegating.

pelt
n lit: fell, fur, hide, skin; (at full) speed.
vb lit: assail (with), bombard (with), pepper with), shower (with); bucket down, pour, rain cats and dogs; career, dash, race, rush, speed, tear.

pen
n lit: ballpoint, biro, felt-tip, marker, nib, quill; cage, coop, enclosure, hutch, sty; *fig*: prison; *spec*: female swan.
vb lit: be the author of, jot down, write; cage, confine (in), coop up, enclose (in), fence (in), hedge (in), shut (in).

penalize
vb lit: discipline, impose a penalty on, punish; handicap, put at a disadvantage.

penalty
n lit: punishment; fine, forfeit; disadvantage, handicap; free kick, spot kick.

penance
n lit: act of contrition, atonement, expiation, reparation; penalty, punishment; *fig*: burden, hardship, trial.

penchant
n lit: affinity, fondness, liking, partiality, propensity, taste.

pending
adj lit: hanging fire, remaining undecided, unsettled, up in the air.
prp lit: awaiting, until; during.

pendulous
adj lit: dangling, hanging down, suspended; baggy, drooping, sagging; *fig*: weeping.

penetrate
vb lit: enter, go through, perforate, pierce; get (into), infiltrate, permeate, seep, suffuse; *fig*: become clear in, get through to, impress, reach, touch; comprehend, fathom, figure out, unravel, work out.

penetrating
adj lit: biting, pervasive, piercing, pungent, sharp, shrill; *fig*: acute, astute, discerning, incisive, keen, perceptive, quick, searching, sharp, shrewd.

peninsular
adj lit: isthmian, promontorial; Iberian.

penitence
n lit: compunction, contrition, regret, remorse, repentance, self-reproach.

penitent
adj lit: contrite, regretful, remorseful, repentant; apologetic, rueful, sorry.

pennant
n lit: banner, burgee, flag, pennon, streamer.

penniless
adj lit: bankrupt, impecunious, impoverished, indigent, penurious, poverty-stricken; broke, on one's uppers, skint, stony broke, strapped for cash.

pension
n lit: allowance, benefit, old-age benefit; annuity, superannuation; *spec*: boarding-house, guest-house.

pensive
adj lit: contemplative, meditative, musing, reflective, ruminative, thoughtful, wistful; dreamy, preoccupied; serious, solemn.

pent-up
adj lit: bottled-up, constrained, curbed, held back, inhibited, repressed, stifled, suppressed.

penury
n lit: beggary, destitution, dire poverty, straitened circumstances.

people
n lit: human beings, mankind, persons; citizens, community, inhabitants, nation, population, tribe; general public, grass roots, laity, masses, mob, populace, voters; family, folks, household, kinfolk, parents; party, side, team; employees.
vb lit: inhabit, occupy, settle; populate.

pepper
n lit: capsicum, cayenne, paprika.
vb lit: flavour, season, spice; *fig*: dot, fleck, spatter, sprinkle; bombard, pelt, shower.

peppery
adj lit: fiery, hot, piquant, pungent, spicy;
fig: hot-tempered, irascible, irritable,
snappish, touchy, waspish; biting,
caustic, sarcastic, sharp, stinging.

perceive
vb lit: become aware of, discern, notice,
recognize, spot; be aware of, behold,
distinguish, observe, see; apprehend,
comprehend, conclude, deduce, gather,
get, grasp, realize, understand.

perception
n lit: apprehension, discernment, grasp,
recognition; awareness, observation,
sense; impression, notion,
understanding; consciousness, sensation.

perceptive
adj lit: acute, alert, astute, discerning,
observant, percipient, quick, sharp,
shrewd.

perch
n lit: branch, pole, resting-place, roost;
seat; bar, peg.
vb lit: alight (on), land (on), rest, settle; sit
(on); balance (on).

perchance
adv lit: by chance, maybe, perhaps,
possibly.

percussion
n lit: impact, striking; blow, bump,
concussion, jolt, knock, thump; drums.

peremptory
adj lit: absolute, categorical, final;
compelling, decisive, irrefutable,
undeniable; bossy, brusque, curt,
dogmatic, domineering, high-handed,
imperious, overbearing.

perennial
adj lit: ceaseless, eternal, everlasting,
imperishable, incessant, lasting, lifelong,
permanent, unceasing, undying;
continual, persistent, recurrent.

perfect
vb lit: complete, consummate, effect,
fulfil; accomplish, carry out, perform;
cultivate, develop, improve, polish up.
adj lit: absolute, complete, consummate,
entire, finished, unadulterated, utter,
whole; excellent, faultless, flawless,
ideal, impeccable, sublime, superb,
unblemished, untarnished; accurate,
correct, exact, precise, spot-on,

unerring; accomplished, adept, expert,
masterly, polished, skilful.

perfection
n lit: completion, consummation,
fulfilment; accomplishment,
achievement, realization; completeness,
exactness, precision; excellence,
faultlessness, sublimity; maturity;
superiority; acme, ideal, paragon.

perfidious
adj lit: deceitful, dishonest, double-
dealing, false, traitorous, treacherous,
untrustworthy.

perforate
vb lit: bore, drill, make a hole through,
pierce, puncture; honeycomb; penetrate;
rend, tear, ulcerate.

perform
vb lit: accomplish, achieve, carry out,
comply with, discharge, do, effect,
execute, pull off, transact; function,
operate, work; act, appear as, depict,
play, present, produce, put on, render,
stage.

performance
n lit: accomplishment, achievement,
carrying out, completion, discharge,
execution, exploit, feat; action,
behaviour, conduct, efficiency,
functioning, operation, practice,
working; acting, appearance, exhibition,
gig, interpretation, portrayal,
presentation, production, representation;
act, carry-on, fuss, palaver, to-do.

perfume
n lit: attar, cologne, scent; aroma, bouquet,
fragrance; redolence, smell.
vb lit: give a sweet smell to, make fragrant,
scent.

perfunctory
adj lit: cursory, offhand, sketchy,
superficial; automatic, mechanical,
routine, unthinking.

perhaps
adv lit: maybe, possibly; conceivably,
feasibly.

peril
n lit: danger, hazard, jeopardy, risk;
menace, pitfall.

period
n lit: span, spell, time, while; interval,
season, stage, stretch, term; cycle,
revolution; aeon, age, epoch, era; dot, full

stop, point; sentence, statement; *spec*:
menstruation; school lesson.

periodical
n lit: journal, magazine, paper; monthly,
quarterly, weekly.

periphery
n lit: circumference, perimeter; border,
boundary line, edge, margin; outskirts,
suburbs.

perish
vb lit: be killed, die, expire, lose one's life,
pass away; be destroyed, go under,
vanish; decay, decompose, rot, waste,
wither.

perjured
adj (pa.pt) lit: deceitful, false, forsworn,
lying, mendacious, perfidious,
treacherous, untruthful.

perky
adj lit: brisk, jaunty, pert, saucy, self-
assertive.

permanent
adj lit: fixed, immutable, imperishable,
indelible, indestructible, invariable,
lasting, perpetual, persistent, steadfast,
unchanging.

permeate
vb lit: diffuse (through), fill, filter
(through), infiltrate, penetrate, percolate
(through), pervade, seep (through), soak
(through), spread (through).

permission
n lit: approval, assent, authorization,
consent, dispensation, leave, licence,
sanction; go-ahead, green light.

permissive
adj lit: easy-going, free-living, liberal,
open; forbearing, indulgent, lax, tolerant.

permit
n lit: authorization, documentation,
licence, papers, pass, visa, warrant.
vb lit: allow, authorize, consent to,
endorse, give leave to, grant, licence,
sanction; acquiesce in, submit to,
tolerate.

pernicious
adj lit: damaging, destructive, detrimental,
harmful, injurious, noxious, potentially
fatal; deadly, poisonous, venomous; evil,
malicious, malignant, wicked.

perpendicular
adj lit: at right angles (to), on end, straight,
upright, vertical; *fig*: able to stand,
standing.

perpetrate
vb lit: bring about, carry out, commit, do,
effect, enact, execute, perform.

perpetual
adj lit: eternal, everlasting, never-ending,
undying, unending; constant, continual,
endless, incessant, interminable,
persistent, recurrent, unceasing,
uninterrupted, unremitting.

perpetuate
vb lit: keep going, keep up, maintain,
sustain; keep alive, immortalize.

perplex
vb lit: baffle, bewilder, confound, confuse,
dumbfound, puzzle, stump; complicate,
entangle, jumble, mix up, tangle.

persecute
vb lit: ill-treat, maltreat, oppress, torment,
victimize; afflict, molest; harass, hound,
hunt, pursue; *fig*: annoy, badger, bother,
pester, worry.

persevering
adj (pr.pt) lit: diligent, dogged,
indefatigable, persistent, pertinacious,
tenacious; resolute, steadfast; long-
suffering, patient.

persist
vb lit: be dogged (in), be tenacious (in),
persevere (in), stand firm (in); carry on,
continue, keep going, keep up, last,
remain.

persistent
adj lit: assiduous, dogged, indefatigable,
pertinacious, resolute, steadfast,
tenacious, tireless; immovable, obdurate,
obstinate, stubborn; constant, continual,
continuous, incessant, perpetual,
relentless, unrelenting, unremitting.

personable
adj lit: agreeable, amiable, charming, nice,
pleasant, presentable.

personage
n lit: celebrity, dignitary, personality,
public figure, somebody, VIP.

personality
n lit: character, disposition, make-up,
nature, temper, temperament; identity;
attractiveness, charisma, charm,

magnetism; dynamism; *fig*: celebrity, household name, personage, star.

personify
vb lit: embody; epitomize, exemplify, represent, symbolize, typify.

personnel
n lit: employees, members, people, staff, workers, work force.

perspicacious
adj lit: astute, discerning, observant, penetrating, percipient, perceptive, shrewd.

perspire
vb lit: sweat, swelter; drip, pour with sweat; exude, secrete.

persuade
vb lit: coax, entice, induce, influence, prevail upon; incite; convince (that), satisfy (that).

persuasion
n lit: cajolery, enticement, exhortation, inducement, wheedling; belief, conviction, creed, faith, opinion, tenet, view; cult, denomination, faction, party, school of thought, sect, side.

pert
adj lit: bold, forward, free-speaking, impudent, saucy; jaunty, stylish; in good spirits, lively.

pertinent
adj lit: admissible, applicable, appropriate, apt, fitting, material, relevant, suitable, to the point.

perturb
vb lit: agitate, alarm, bother, disconcert, disquiet, disturb, fluster, ruffle, upset, worry; confuse, disarrange, muddle, unsettle.

peruse
vb lit: browse through, con, look through, run one's eye over, scan, scrutinize.

pervasive
adj lit: diffusing, infiltrating, penetrative, percolating, permeating, spreading; common, extensive, prevalent, rife, ubiquitous, widespread.

perverse
adj lit: abnormal, depraved, deviant, immoral, unnatural; intractable, mulish, obdurate, obstinate, pig-headed, stubborn, wayward, wilful;

cantankerous, fractious, ill-tempered, peevish, refractory, sullen, surly.

pervert
n lit: debauchee, orgiast; sexual deviant; weirdo.
vb lit: distort, falsify, misinterpret, misrepresent, misuse, twist, warp; corrupt, debase, debauch, deprave, lead astray, subvert.
n lit: cynicism; dejection, depression, despair, despondency, gloom, hopelessness, melancholy.

pest
n lit: annoyance, bore, bother, irritation, nuisance, pain, thorn in one's flesh, trial; blight, curse, infection, pestilence, plague.

pester
vb lit: annoy, badger, bother, bug, disturb, drive up the wall, get at, get on someone's nerves, harass, hassle, nag, pick on, plague, worry.

pet
n lit: darling, favourite, jewel, treasure; animal; huff, rage, tantrum.
vb lit: baby, coddle, cosset, pamper, spoil; caress, fondle, pat, stroke; cuddle, kiss, neck, smooch, snog.
adj lit: cherished, dearest, favoured, particular, preferred, special; caged, domesticated, family, tame, trained.

peter out
vb lit: come to nothing, die out, dwindle, ebb, fade away, run out, taper off.

petition
n lit: appeal, application, entreaty, plea, request, suit, supplication.
vb lit: appeal to, ask, beg, beseech, call upon, entreat, plead with, solicit, supplicate; urge.

petrified
adj (pa.pt) lit: fossilized, rocklike; *fig*: frightened, numb with fright, rooted to the spot, scared stiff, terrified, terror-stricken.

petty
adj lit: contemptible, insignificant, little, measly, negligible, paltry, slight, trivial, unimportant; cheap, grudging, mean, shabby, stingy; inferior, lower, subordinate.

petulant
adj lit: captious, dog-in-the-manger, pouting, resentful, sulky; fretful, ill-humoured, irritable, peevish, snappish, waspish.

phase
n lit: juncture, period, stage, time; condition, development, state; chapter.
vb lit: carry out by stages; make regular; synchronize; get (in), gradually get (in), move (in); get (out), gradually get (out), move (out).

phenomenal
adj lit: extraordinary, fantastic, miraculous, outstanding, prodigious, remarkable, sensational, singular, unique, unparalleled.

phenomenon
n lit: circumstance, event, fact, incident, occurrence; exception, marvel, miracle, prodigy, rarity, sensation, wonder.

philanthropic
adj lit: altruistic, beneficent, benevolent, charitable, generous, munificent, public-spirited.

philistine
n lit: barbarian, boor, ignoramus, lowbrow, yahoo.
adj lit: barbarian, boorish, crass, loutish, lowbrow, uncultivated, uneducated, unrefined.

philosophical
adj lit: abstract, imponderable, learned, metaphysical, rational; calm, collected, composed, cool, imperturbable, resigned, stoical, tranquil, unruffled.

philosophy
n lit: logic, metaphysics, rationalism, reasoning, thinking, thought; attitude to life, beliefs, convictions, ideology, principles, tenets, values, viewpoint; composure, coolness, equanimity, resignation, self-possession, stoicism.

phlegmatic
adj lit: apathetic, cold, dull, frigid, heavy, impassive, lethargic, placid, sluggish, stoical, stolid, undemonstrative, unemotional.

phobia
n lit: aversion, dread, hatred, horror, irrational fear, loathing, revulsion, terror; obsession, thing.

phoney
n lit: counterfeit, fake, forgery, fraud, impostor, pretender, sham.
adj lit: affected, assumed, bogus, counterfeit, fake, forged, imitation, sham, trick.

photograph
n lit: halftone, picture, print, shot, slide, snap, snapshot, transparency.
vb lit: film, shoot, snap, take a picture of.

phrase
n lit: expression, motto, proverb, remark, saying, slogan, tag, term.
vb lit: articulate, couch, express, formulate, frame, put, say, word.

phraseology
n lit: expression, formulation, idiom, language, phrasing, style, syntax, terminology, wording.

physical
adj lit: bodily, carnal, corporeal; fleshly, profane, secular, temporal, unspiritual; material, natural, palpable, real, solid, tangible, visible.

physique
n lit: build, constitution, figure, form, frame, shape.

pick
n lit: choice, decision, option, preference, selection; choicest, crème de la crème, élite, flower, pride; axe, hammer; hook, spike.
vb lit: choose, decide upon, elect, opt for, select, settle upon, single out; instigate, provoke, start; nibble (at), peck (at); break open, crack, force, jemmy, prise open.

pick up
vb lit: hoist, lift, raise, take up; apprehend, arrest, nick, take into custody; collect, get, give a lift, go and fetch; acquire, buy, happen upon, obtain, purchase; *fig*: gain ground, get better, improve, mend, perk up, rally, recover; get the hang of, gather, grasp, learn, master.

picnic
n lit: alfresco meal, stop for tea; excursion, outing; *fig*: child's play, cinch, doddle, piece of cake, pushover.

pictorial
adj lit: graphic, illustrated; colourful, descriptive, scenic, vivid.

picture
n lit: depiction, description, image, impression, re-creation, replica, representation, reproduction; artwork, drawing, engraving, illustration, likeness, painting, photograph, portrait, print, sketch; film, motion picture, movie; *fig*: carbon copy, double, duplicate, living image, portrait, twin; archetype, embodiment, epitome, essence, personification.
vb lit: conceive of, see, visualize; depict, describe, draw, illustrate, paint, photograph, portray, render, represent, sketch.

piece
n lit: bit, chunk, division, fraction, morsel, mouthful, portion, section, segment, slice; fragment, scrap, sherd, smithereen; article, composition, creation, item, production, work of art; example, sample, specimen; fire-arm, gun; coin; *fig*: baggage, woman; entity, unity, whole; instance, occurrence, stroke; *spec*: man (in chess, draughts).
vb lit: connect (together), fit (together), fix (together), patch (together).

pied
adj lit: black-and-white; bicoloured, dappled, motley, spotted, variegated; confused, jumbled, mixed-up.

pier
n lit: breakwater, groyne, jetty, mole, quay, wharf; buttress, column, pile, pillar, upright; stand, support.

pierce
vb lit: drill, penetrate, prick, puncture, run through, spike, stab, transfix; *fig*: cut to the quick, move, pain, sting, strike, thrill, wound.

piercing
adj lit: ear-splitting, high-pitched, shattering, shrill; arctic, biting, bitter, freezing, numbing, raw; acute, agonizing, excruciating, exquisite, intense, racking, sharp, stabbing; *fig*: alert, keen, penetrating, perceptive, probing, searching, shrewd.

piety
n lit: devoutness, faith, godliness, holiness, reverence, sanctity, veneration; devotion, duty, obedience.

pig
n lit: boar, hog, piglet, porker, sow, swine; *fig*: glutton, greedy-guts, guzzler; animal, beast, brute, slob; policeman; burden, chore, hardship, problem; *spec*: ingot, mould (in an iron foundry).

pigeon
n lit: dove, squab; *fig*: dupe, john, mug, sucker, victim; business, concern, responsibility, worry.

pigeonhole
n lit: compartment, cubbyhole, niche, recess, section; category, slot.
vb lit: catalogue, classify, file, label, slot; postpone, put off, shelve.

pig-headed
adj lit: froward, intractable, mulish, obdurate, obstinate, stiff-necked, stubborn, wilful.

pile
n lit: accumulation, heap, hoard, mound, stack; building, edifice, structure; beam, column, pier, pillar, support, upright; fibre, hair, nap, shag; battery, generator, reactor; *fig*: large amount, lot, quantity; bomb, fortune, mint, packet; *spec*: haemorrhoid.
vb lit: accumulate, amass, gather, heap, hoard, stack, store; crowd, crush, flood, jam, pack, rush.

pilgrim
n lit: traveller, wayfarer; crusader, palmer; hajji; seeker.

pill
n lit: capsule, tablet; oral contraceptive; pellet; ball; *fig*: bore, drag, nuisance, pain, pest.

pillage
n lit: despoliation, looting, plundering, rapine, robbery, sack; booty, loot, plunder, spoils.
vb lit: despoil, loot, maraud, plunder, raid, ransack, ravage, rob, sack, strip.

pillar
n lit: column, pier, pilaster, support, upright; *fig*: leader, mainstay, prop, upholder.

pilot
n lit: airman, aviator; guide, helmsman, steersman; captain, coxswain, navigator.
vb lit: control, direct, drive, fly, guide, handle, navigate, operate, steer.
adj lit: experimental, initial, introductory, trial.

pin
n lit: nail, tack; needle, spike; key, peg, rod; axle, bar, cross-piece, lever, spindle, toggle; skittle; *fig*: leg; *spec*: flag (in golf).
vb lit: affix, attach, fasten, fix, secure; *fig*: hold down, immobilize, pinion, restrain.

pinch
n lit: nip, squeeze, tweak; bit, dash, speck, taste; *fig*: crisis, emergency, hardship, plight, predicament.
vb lit: nip, squeeze, tweak; chafe, confine, cramp, crush; afflict, oppress; economize, scrimp; *fig*: filch, nick, pilfer, purloin, snatch, steal; apprehend, arrest, nick, pull in, take into custody.

pinched
adj lit: drawn, gaunt, haggard, lean, thin, worn.

pine
vb lit: ache, hanker, hunger (for), long, lust, wish, yearn; grieve (for); decline, droop, dwindle, fade, languish, sicken, waste, wilt, wither.

pinnacle
n lit: acme, apex, crest, height, peak, summit, vertex, zenith; obelisk, spire, steeple.

pioneer
n lit: colonizer, frontiersman, settler; explorer, leader; deviser, discoverer, founder, innovator, inventor.
vb lit: devise, develop, discover, initiate, instigate, invent, launch, open up.

pious
adj lit: devout, God-fearing, holy, religious, reverent, saintly; *fig*: goody-goody, hypocritical, sanctimonious, unctuous.

pipe
n lit: channel, conduit, cylinder, duct, hose, tube, vessel; briar; fife, penny-whistle, whistle; *spec*: mass, vein (of ore); vent (of a volcano).
vb lit: channel, duct, convey, lead, siphon; play, whistle; *fig*: speak shrilly, trill, tweet, twitter, warble.

piquant
adj lit: pungent, savoury, seasoned, spicy, tangy, tart, tasty; *fig*: lively, provocative, scintillating, spirited, stimulating.

pique
n lit: dudgeon, hurt feelings, offence, resentment, umbrage, wounded pride.
vb lit: affront, annoy, nettle, offend, peeve, put out, vex; arouse, excite, stir, whet.

pirate
n lit: brigand, buccaneer, corsair, freebooter, raider; copyright-breaker, plagiarist.
vb lit: copy, lift, plagiarize, poach, reproduce without permission; appropriate, take over.

pit
n lit: hole, mine, shaft; abyss, chasm; crater, dent, donga, indentation, trench.
vb lit: dent, gouge, indent, nick, notch, scar; *fig*: match, oppose, set (against).

pitch
n lit: ground, playing-field, sports-field; gradient, incline, slant, slope, tilt; degree, height, level, point; modulation, sound-level, tone; *fig*: line, patter, sales talk, spiel.
vb lit: cast, chuck, fling, heave, launch, sling, throw, toss; erect, plant, put up, set up, station; flounder, lurch, plunge, wallow; dive, drop, topple, tumble.

piteously
adv lit: affectingly, distressingly, dolefully, heart-rendingly, movingly, pathetically, pitifully, wretchedly.

pitfall
n lit: danger, snare, trap; catch, difficulty, drawback, hazard, snag.

pithy
adj lit: accurate, cogent, concise, expressive, forceful, pointed, short and to the point.

pitiful
adj lit: distressing, heart-rending, pathetic, piteous, sad, wretched; abject, contemptible, despicable, miserable, shabby, sorry, worthless.

pity
n lit: compassion, empathy, feeling, sympathy; clemency, mercy; commiseration; sad thing, shame; blow, misfortune.
vb lit: be compassionate towards, bleed for, commiserate with, empathize with, feel for, sympathize with.

pivot
n lit: axle, spindle; fulcrum, hinge, hub;
centre, core, focal point, heart.
vb lit: revolve, rotate, spin, swivel, twirl;
fig: depend (on), hang (on), hinge (on),
revolve (round), turn (on).

placate
vb lit: appease, calm, conciliate, mollify,
pacify, propitiate, soothe.

place
n lit: location, position, site, spot, venue;
area, district, locality, manor,
neighbourhood, region, vicinity; town,
village; accommodation, dwelling, home,
house, pad, property, residence; chair,
reservation, seat; stead; *fig*: room, space;
affair, concern, function, prerogative,
responsibility; precedence; office, rank,
station, status; appointment,
employment, job, post.
vb lit: deposit, lay, put, rest, set, stand;
arrange, dispose, locate, position,
situate, station; allocate, appoint, assign,
commission, put out; invest; establish,
fix; classify, grade, group, order, sort;
identify, know, recognize, remember.

placid
adj lit: collected, composed, cool,
imperturbable, self-possessed, serene,
unexcitable, unruffled; calm, peaceful,
quiet, tranquil.

plague
n lit: epidemic, pandemic, pestilence;
affliction, blight, contagion, disease,
infection, infestation; *fig*: cancer, curse,
scourge, trial; aggravation, annoyance,
bother, nuisance, pain, pest.
vb lit: afflict, annoy, badger, bother, fret,
harass, hassle, persecute, pester, tease,
trouble, worry.

plain
n lit: plateau, prairie, steppe, tableland;
heath, moor, open country.
adj lit: even, flat, level, smooth; clear,
conspicuous, distinct, evident, obvious;
comprehensible, legible, unambiguous;
blunt, candid, forthright, frank,
outspoken, straightforward; common,
everyday, homely, ordinary; discreet,
modest, restrained, simple, unadorned,
unaffected, unpretentious; austere, bare,
spartan, stark; ill-favoured, unalluring,
unattractive, unprepossessing.

plaintive
adj lit: heart-rending, melancholy,
mournful, pathetic, piteous, sad, wistful,
woeful.

plan
n lit: design, draft, idea, plot, project,
proposal, proposition, scheme, strategy;
method, programme, scenario, schema;
blueprint, chart, diagram, drawing,
elevation, layout, map, sketch.
vb lit: design, devise, draft, formulate,
plot, scheme, think up; arrange,
contrive, lay out, map out, organize,
outline, project, propose; aim (to),
intend (to), mean (to), propose (to).

plane
n lit: flat, level, surface; degree, layer,
stratum; aeroplane, aircraft, jet; file,
rasp, scraper, shaver, smoother.
vb lit: glide, skate, skim; carom.
adj lit: even, flat, flush, level, smooth,
uniform.

plant
n lit: flower, vegetable, vegetation;
cutting, offshoot; *fig*: factory, foundry,
mill, works; apparatus, equipment, gear,
machinery; agent, informer, inside man,
spy, undercover agent.
vb lit: disseminate, embed, put in, scatter,
seed, sow; *fig*: establish, found, institute;
place, post, station, settle; convey,
deliver, strike; *spec*: salt (a mine).

plaque
n lit: badge, panel, plate, slab, tablet;
deposit, tartar.

plaster
n lit: gypsum, mortar, stucco; *spec*:
adhesive plaster, bandage, dressing.
vb lit: coat, cover, daub, overlay, spread;
paste over, stick on; slick down, smooth;
bombard, pepper, strafe.

plastic
n lit: nylon, polymer, synthetic
compound, vinyl.
adj lit: polymeric; synthetic; flexible,
malleable, pliable; *fig*: compliant, docile,
easily influenced, tractable; artificial,
false, phoney, sham, superficial.

plate
n lit: dish, platter; lamina, layer, panel,
sheet; badge, panel; block, mould,
stencil; brace, denture; *fig*: illustration,
print; cup, trophy; foot; *spec*: base (in

baseball); precious metal, silver; racing
horseshoe.
vb lit: coat, cover, electroplate, gild,
laminate, overlay.

plateau
n lit: massif, mesa, plain, tableland; *fig*:
levelling-off.

platform
n lit: dais, podium, rostrum, stage; basis,
raised surface; railway station; gun
mounting; oilrig; *fig*: manifesto, policy;
party programme.

platitude
n lit: banality, cliché, commonplace,
truism; inanity, triviality.

plausible
adj lit: believable, conceivable, credible,
likely, possible, reasonable, tenable; glib,
smooth, specious.

play
n lit: comedy, drama, performance, piece,
stage show, tragedy; diversion,
entertainment, fun; leisure activity,
pastime, recreation, sport; gambling,
gaming; exercise; *fig*: leeway, margin,
movement, range, room, scope, space;
(in) action, (in) function, (in) operation.
vb lit: amuse oneself, entertain oneself,
have fun; frolic, gambol, revel, romp; toy
(with), trifle (with); compete, contend
against, participate, take on, take part in,
vie with; act, impersonate, portray, take
the part of; bet on, gamble on, speculate
on, wager on; discharge (over), shower
(over), spray (over); make music with,
perform with; allow leeway, give room.

play down
vb lit: gloss over, make little of, minimize,
set no store by, soft-pedal on.

player
n lit: competitor, contestant, participant,
team member; actor, actress, entertainer,
performer; artiste, instrumentalist,
musician, virtuoso.

playful
adj lit: coy, flirtatious, frisky, frolicsome,
humorous, impish, jokey, lively, merry,
mischievous, roguish, sportive,
sprightly, vivacious, waggish.

plea
n lit: appeal, entreaty, intercession,
petition, request, supplication;

argument, claim, defence, excuse,
explanation, vindication.

plead
vb lit: appeal, ask, beg, beseech, entreat,
implore, petition, request; argue, assert,
claim, give as an excuse, maintain.

pleasant
adj lit: agreeable, delectable, delightful,
enjoyable, gratifying, pleasurable,
refreshing, satisfying, welcome; affable,
amiable, charming, cheerful, congenial,
engaging, friendly, good-humoured,
likable, nice.

please
vb lit: delight, gladden, gratify; amuse,
charm, cheer; humour, indulge, serve;
content, satisfy, suit; be inclined, choose,
like, see fit, want, wish.

pleased
adj (pa.pt) lit: delighted, gladdened,
gratified; amused, charmed, cheered;
contented, happy, satisfied; in high
spirits, over the moon, thrilled to bits,
tickled pink.

pleasure
n lit: delectation, delight, gratification;
amusement, contentment, enjoyment,
happiness, satisfaction; choice, desire,
inclination, preference, will, wish.

plebeian
adj lit: coarse, common, lower-class,
proletarian, unrefined, vulgar, working-
class.

pledge
n lit: assurance, oath, undertaking, vow,
word of honour; bail, bond, deposit,
guarantee, pawn, security; *fig*: health,
toast.
vb lit: contract, give one's word, promise,
undertake, vouch, vow; guarantee,
mortgage; *fig*: drink the health of, drink
to, toast.

plenty
n lit: ample, heaps, lots, masses, oodles,
piles, quantities, stacks; abundance,
copiousness, fruitfulness, profusion;
affluence, luxury, opulence, prosperity,
wealth.

pliable
adj lit: bendable, flexible, malleable,
plastic, pliant; limber, supple; *fig*:
adaptable, compliant, easily led,

impressionable, manageable, receptive, tractable, yielding.

plight
n lit: dilemma, hole, jam, predicament, pickle, scrape, situation, spot.

plot
n lit: conspiracy, intrigue, machination, plan, scheme; allotment, area, lot, patch, site, stretch, tract; action, gist, scenario, schema, story, story-line, thread.
vb lit: collude, conspire, intrigue, machinate, plan, scheme; calculate, chart, compute, draft, draw, map, outline; concoct, cook up, design, devise, frame; arrange for, organize, set up.

ploy
n lit: gambit, gesture, manoeuvre, stratagem, tactic; affair, enterprise, escapade, expedition, undertaking, job.

pluck
n lit: backbone, bottle, bravery, courage, grit, guts, mettle, nerve, resolution, spirit.
vb lit: cull, gather, pick, pull out; jerk, pull, snatch, tug, yank; pick, strum, thrum, twang; *fig*: fleece, rob; *spec*: de-feather, unfledge (a bird to prepare it for eating).

plug
n lit: bung, cork, spigot, stopper; cake, quid, wad; *fig*: advertisement, mention, puff, push.
vb lit: block, bung, cork, cover, pack, stop, stuff; *fig*: advertise, build up, hype, promote, publicize, push; gun down, pot, put a bullet in, shoot; drudge (away at), grind (away at), peg (away at), slog (away at).

plump
vb lit: opt (for), plunge (for), vote (for); freshen (up), shape (up).
adj lit: chubby, corpulent, podgy, portly, roly-poly, round, rotund, stout, tubby.

plunder
n lit: booty, ill-gotten gains, loot, spoils, swag.
vb lit: despoil, loot, pillage, ransack, rifle, rob, sack, steal.

plunge
n lit: dive, drop, fall, immersion, swoop.
vb lit: dive, drop, fall, lurch, nose-dive, pitch, plummet, swoop, tumble; dip,

douse, dunk, immerse, sink, submerge; *fig*: career, dash, fling oneself, hurtle.

plus
adj lit: positive; extra, supplementary.
adv lit: additionally, furthermore, moreover.
prp lit: added to, and, coupled with, with.

plush
adj lit: napped, padded, velvety; *fig*: lavish, luxurious, rich, sumptuous.

ply
vb lit: carry on, exercise, practise, pursue, work at; employ, use, utilize; handle, manipulate, wield; assail, beset, bombard, deluge, importune.

poached
adj (pa.pt) lit: appropriated, stolen; encroached upon, taken over, usurped; *spec*: boiled, steamed (egg or fish).

pocket
n lit: pouch; bag, receptacle; bunker, cavity, diverticulum, hole, hollow; *fig*: island, isolated area.
vb lit: appropriate, help oneself to, lift, pilfer, purloin, take.
adj lit: compact, concise, portable; small(-sized).

pod
n lit: husk, legume, shell; *fig*: casing, housing, socket; decompressor.

podium
n lit: dais, pedestal, platform, rostrum, stage.

poet
n lit: lyricist, rhymer, versifier; bard, troubadour, skald; *fig*: aesthete.

poetic
adj lit: aesthetic, descriptive, sensitive, sensual, sublime, vivid; affecting, ecstatic, moving; elegiac, in verse, lyrical, metrical, rhyming, rhythmical.

poignant
adj lit: acrid, piquant, pungent, sharp, tangy; *fig*: acute, penetrating, piercing, stinging; heart-rending, moving, pathetic, touching, upsetting.

point
n lit: dot, full stop, period, speck; location, place, position, site, spot; apex, end, spike, summit, tine; cape, headland, promontory; mark, score, unit; *fig*: degree, extent, stage; instant, juncture,

moment, time; aim, end, goal, intention, motive, object, purpose, reason; core, crux, essence, gist, idea, meaning, theme; aspect, detail, feature, instance, item, particular; attribute, characteristic, peculiarity, trait; *spec*: (compass) bearing; (pen) nib.
vb lit: call attention (to), direct (to); pick (out), single (out); aim (at), direct (at), level (at), train (at); sharpen, taper, whet; *spec*: arrange, set (canticles to music).

pointed
adj lit: barbed, sharp, spiky, tapering; *fig*: acute, biting, cutting, incisive, penetrating, pertinent, trenchant.

pointless
adj lit: aimless, futile, inane, irrelevant, meaningless, nonsensical, unproductive, useless, vain, worthless.

poise
n lit: balance, equilibrium; carriage, demeanour; aplomb, assurance, composure, cool, dignity, equanimity, grace, self-possession.
vb lit: balance, be suspended, hang, hover, suspend.

poison
n lit: toxin, venom; *fig*: contamination, corruption, malignancy.
vb lit: administer a lethal dose to; contaminate, pollute; *fig*: embitter, sour; corrupt, defile, mar, taint, undermine; deprave, pervert, warp.

poisonous
adj lit: toxic, venomous; corrosive; deadly, fatal, lethal, virulent; *fig*: malicious, pernicious, scathing, vicious.

poke
n lit: dig, jab, nudge, prod, thrust.
vb lit: dig, elbow, jab, nudge, prod, push, shove, thrust; rake up, riddle, stir up; jut (out), stick (out); feel (about in), grope (around in); *fig*: pry (into), snoop (into).

polarize
vb lit: crystallize, harden, set; split into opposing factions; *fig*: take on a new meaning.

pole
n lit: boom, mast, paling, post, rod, shaft, stick; electrode, terminal; *fig*: antipode, extremity.

polemic
n lit: argument, controversy, debate, dissension; controversialist.

police
n lit: constabulary, force, law; cops, fuzz, Old Bill, pigs.
vb lit: control, guard, monitor, patrol, regulate, supervise, watch.

policy
n lit: code, line, method, practice, procedure, protocol, rule; approach, custom; *fig*: discretion, prudence, shrewdness; cunning.

polish
n lit: varnish, wax; brightness, finish, gloss, lustre, sheen, sparkle; *fig*: class, finesse, panache, refinement, style.
vb lit: buff up, burnish, clean, shine, wax; *fig*: brush (up), touch (up).

polish off
vb fig: consume, down, eat up, finish up, wolf down; bump off, dispose of, do away with, eliminate, finish off, get rid of, liquidate, murder.

polite
adj lit: civil, courteous, mannerly, well-mannered; civilized, cultured, elegant, genteel, polished, well-bred.

politic
adj lit: diplomatic, discreet, expedient, in one's best interests, prudent, sensible, tactful; artful, astute, crafty, cunning, intriguing, scheming, sly.

poll
n lit: ballot, election, plebiscite, referendum, vote; census, survey; count, figures, returns, tally.
vb lit: ballot, hold a referendum, take it to a vote; canvass, register, notch up, tally; interview, question, survey.

pollute
vb lit: contaminate, dirty, foul, infect, soil, taint; *fig*: corrupt, defile, deprave, desecrate, mar, profane, sully.

pompous
adj lit: bloated, grandiose, ostentatious, portentous, pretentious, priggish, self-important, snobbish, vainglorious; boastful, bombastic, inflated, orotund, overblown, turgid.

ponder
vb lit: brood, cerebrate, cogitate, contemplate, deliberate, give thought to, mull (over), muse, puzzle (over), ruminate.

ponderous
adj lit: bulky, hefty, massive, weighty; awkward, clumsy, cumbersome, heavy-footed, lumbering; *fig*: dreary, dull, heavy, long-winded, pedantic, pedestrian, plodding, tedious, verbose.

pool
n lit: lake, pond, puddle, tarn; swimming-bath; *fig*: collective, consortium, syndicate, team; funds, jackpot, kitty, stakes.
vb lit: amalgamate, combine, merge, share.

poor
adj lit: badly off, destitute, hard up, impoverished, needy, penurious, poverty-stricken; deficient, inadequate, insufficient, meagre, niggardly, reduced, scanty, skimpy, sparse, straitened; faulty, inferior, mediocre, rotten, rubbishy, shabby, shoddy, sorry, worthless; bad, bare, barren, depleted, infertile, exhausted, infertile, unproductive; hapless, ill-fated, miserable, pathetic, unfortunate, wretched; humble, insignificant, mean, modest, paltry, trivial.

poorly
adj lit: ailing, frail, ill, indisposed, off colour, sickly, under the weather, unwell.
adv lit: badly, inadequately, incompetently, unsatisfactorily; insufficiently; meanly, shabbily.

popular
adj lit: common, conventional, general, prevailing, public, standard, stock, ubiquitous, widespread; approved, famous, fashionable, favourite, in, in demand, sought-after, well-liked.

populate
vb lit: inhabit, occupy, people, settle.

population
n lit: community, denizens, inhabitants, natives, people, residents, society.

pornographic
adj lit: blue, erotic; dirty, filthy, indecent, obscene, smutty.

port
n lit: anchorage, harbour, haven, marina, mooring, roads; door, doorway, embrasure, gate, outlet, shutter, window; larboard, left-hand side; fortified wine.

portent
n lit: augury, forewarning, harbinger, omen, premonition, presentiment, sign.

portentous
adj lit: alarming, menacing, ominous, sinister; important, momentous; *fig*: amazing, astounding, extraordinary, phenomenal, prodigious; impressive, pompous, pontifical, self-important, solemn.

portion
n lit: bit, morsel, part, piece, segment; allocation, allotment, allowance, lot, quota, ration, share; helping, serving; *fig*: destiny, fate, fortune, luck.
vb lit: dole (out), parcel (out), share (out).

portray
vb lit: draw, illustrate, paint, picture, represent, sketch; act the part of, play; describe, put in words.

pose
n lit: attitude, bearing, posture, stance; affectation, façade, front, masquerade, pretence, role.
vb lit: model, sit (for); masquerade (as), pass oneself off (as); posture, put on airs, show off, strike an attitude; arrange, position; advance, present, propound, put forward, set.

position
n lit: bearings, locale, location, place, site, situation, whereabouts; attitude, pose, stance; job, office, post; *fig*: angle, outlook, point of view, standpoint; circumstances, pass, plight, predicament, state, strait(s); caste, class, importance, prestige, rank, standing, status; capacity, function, role.
vb lit: arrange, array, lay out, place, put, set.

positive
adj lit: categorical, certain, conclusive, decisive, definitive, emphatic, express, firm, indisputable, real, unequivocal; affirmative; beneficial, constructive, efficacious, helpful, practical, progressive, useful; assured, confident, convinced, sure; absolute, complete,

consummate, thorough, unmitigated; dogmatic, emphatic, forceful; insistent, obdurate, resolute, stubborn.

positively
adv lit: absolutely, categorically, certainly, conclusively, definitely, definitively, emphatically, firmly, unequivocally, unmistakably, unquestionably.

possess
vb lit: be blessed with, enjoy, have, hold, keep, own, retain; acquire, seize, take over, usurp; *fig*: bewitch, enchant, entrance, mesmerize, obsess, put under a spell; control, dominate.

possessed
adj lit: berserk, bewitched, consumed, crazed, demented, enchanted, entranced, frenzied, haunted, obsessed.

possession
n lit: asset(s), belonging(s), effect(s), estate, property; control, custody, hold, occupancy, ownership, proprietorship, tenure, title; colony, dominion, protectorate, territory.

possessive
adj lit: acquisitive, covetous, grasping, greedy; retentive, tenacious; jealous, overprotective.

possible
adj lit: conceivable, credible, feasible, imaginable, practicable, viable; hypothetical, potential, theoretical; on, realizable, within reach.

possibly
adv lit: maybe, perhaps; at all, by any means, by some chance, in any way.

post
n lit: column, pale, pillar, pole, stake, support, upright; mail, postal service; appointment, assignment, job, office, position, situation; beat, place, station; *spec*: (winning-)line; pin (in a lock).
vb lit: assign, establish, place, position, put, station; advertise, display, publicize, publish, put up; dispatch, mail, send; advise, brief, fill in on, notify, report to.

poster
n lit: advertisement, announcement, bill, notice, placard, sticker.

posterity
n lit: children, descendants, heirs, issue, offspring, progeny.

postmortem
n lit: autopsy, dissection, examination; *fig*: analysis, enquiry, investigation.

postpone
vb lit: adjourn, defer, delay, put off, shelve, suspend.

postulate
vb lit: assume, hypothesize, posit, propose, put forward, suggest, suppose, theorize.

posture
n lit: attitude, bearing, pose, position, set, stance; *fig*: disposition, frame of mind, outlook, point of view; circumstance, mode, phase, situation, state.
vb lit: pose, put on airs, show off, strut, swagger.

pot
n lit: bowl, container, dish, jar, pan, urn, vessel; hole, cave; lavatory, toilet; cup, trophy; *fig*: kitty, pool, stakes; shot, shy, throw; paunch, potbelly; *spec*: basket, trap (for catching lobsters); cone, stack (on a chimney); large sum (of money); cannabis, marijuana.
vb lit: turn on the wheel; plant, replant; *fig*: bag, secure, shoot, win; hole, pocket.

potency
n lit: effectiveness, efficacy, force, might, power, strength; energy, vigour; capacity.

potent
adj lit: dynamic, effective, efficacious, forceful, mighty, powerful, strong, vigorous; cogent, compelling, impressive, persuasive; authoritative, commanding, dominant, influential.

potential
n lit: capacity, power, resources; ability, aptitude, capability, makings.
adj lit: budding, dormant, future, inherent, latent, possible, undeveloped.

potion
n lit: brew, concoction, draught, elixir, philtre.

pottery
n lit: ceramics, earthenware, terracotta; kiln.

pounce
n lit: dart, jump, leap, spring, swoop; ambush.
vb lit: fall (upon), jump (on), leap (on), swoop down (upon).

pour
vb lit: decant; course, flow, gush, run, spew, stream; bucket down, rain hard, sheet down; *fig*: crowd, swarm, throng.

pout
n lit: cross look, glower, grimace, moue.
vb lit: glower, grimace, look petulant, look sullen, mope, pull a long face, sulk.

poverty
n lit: beggary, destitution, insolvency, pennilessness, penury, privation; inadequacy, lack, paucity, scarcity, shortage; *fig*: aridity, barrenness, infertility, sterility.

poverty-stricken
adj lit: beggared, destitute, impecunious, impoverished, indigent, penniless, penurious, poor, strapped for cash.

powder
n lit: dust; talc; grist, meal.
vb lit: dust, spray, sprinkle; crush, grind, pestle, pound, pulverize.

power
n lit: brawn, clout, force, might, muscle, strength; ability, capability, capacity, competence, faculty, potential; energy, vigour; authority, command, control, dominance, influence, supremacy, sway; authorization, licence, prerogative, right, warrant.

powerful
adj lit: brawny, mighty, muscular, robust, stalwart, strapping, strong, sturdy; energetic, vigorous; authoritative, commanding, dominant, forceful, influential; compelling, convincing, effectual, impressive.

powerless
adj lit: defenceless, helpless, impotent, incapable, ineffectual; disabled, incapacitated, paralysed; debilitated, feeble, frail, vulnerable, weak; captive, chained, manacled, shackled.

practicable
adj lit: achievable, feasible, possible, viable, workable.

practical
adj lit: applied, functional, pragmatic, utilitarian; adept, ingenious, inventive, resourceful; businesslike, down-to-earth, factual, matter-of-fact, mundane, realistic, sensible; feasible, practicable,

serviceable, sound, workable; accomplished, efficient, experienced, proficient, skilled, working.

practically
adv lit: almost, in effect, just about, nearly, to all intents and purposes, virtually; factually, rationally, realistically, reasonably, sensibly; efficiently, ingeniously, inventively, resourcefully.

practice
n lit: custom, habit, mode, routine, rule, tradition, usage, way; application, experience, operation, use; career, profession, vocation, work; drill, exercise, rehearsal, training, work-out.

practise
vb lit: drill, exercise, prepare, rehearse, run through, train; apply, carry out, do, follow, live up to, observe; carry on, engage in, ply, pursue, work at.

practised
adj (pa.pt) *lit*: able, accomplished, adept, efficient, experienced, proficient, skilled, trained, well-rehearsed.

pragmatic
adj lit: businesslike, down-to-earth, efficient, matter-of-fact, practical, sensible, utilitarian; expedient, politic, prudent, realistic.

praise
n lit: acclaim, accolades, applause, commendation, compliments, congratulation, eulogies, panegyrics, tribute; *fig*: adoration, adulation, homage, worship.
vb lit: acclaim, applaud, commend, compliment, congratulate, eulogize, extol, honour, pay tribute to; adore, adulate, worship.

prancing
adj (pr.pt) *lit*: capering, cavorting, frisking, gambolling, leaping, romping, skipping; stalking, strutting, swaggering.

prank
n lit: antic, escapade, frolic, jape, lark, practical joke.

prattle
n lit: babble, blethering, chatter, gabble, gibbering, jabber, rabbiting on, wittering on.

vb lit: babble, blether, chatter, drone on, gabble, jabber, rabbit on, rattle on, run on, witter on.

pray
vb lit: say a prayer, say one's prayers; beg, beseech, call upon, entreat, implore, supplicate.

prayer
n lit: devotion, orison; invocation; entreaty, plea, request, supplication.

preach
vb lit: deliver a sermon, expound on the scriptures, give an address (on); orate, speak, talk; harangue, lecture; *fig*: moralize.

precarious
adj lit: chancy, dodgy, dubious, hazardous, insecure, risky, slippery, tricky, unstable, unsteady.

precaution
n lit: preventative measure, safeguard, safety measure; contingency plan; anticipation, caution, foresight, forethought, wariness.

precede
vb lit: come before, go before, herald, introduce, lead; antedate; rank before.

precedent
n lit: example, instance, model, prototype; authority, criterion, paradigm.

preceding
adj lit: above, aforementioned, earlier, former, previous, prior.

precept
n lit: commandment, decree, direction, edict, instruction, law, regulation, ruling, statute; axiom, byword, guideline, principle, saying.

precincts
n lit: district, environs, margins, neighbourhood, outskirts, surrounding area.

precious
adj lit: cherished, favourite, prized, treasured, valued; adored, beloved, dearest; costly, expensive, invaluable, priceless, valuable; *fig*: affected, artificial, camp, naff, overnice, twee.

precipice
n lit: cliff, cliff face, height, rock face, sheer drop; canyon, chasm, chine, gorge, ravine.

precipitate
n lit: solid.
vb lit: accelerate, bring on, catalyse, expedite, further, trigger; cast, fling, hurl, send forth, throw; condense, crystallize out, separate out, solidify.
adj lit: breakneck, headlong, rapid, swift; frantic, heedless, impetuous, impulsive, indiscreet, madcap, rash, reckless; abrupt, quick, sudden, unexpected, violent.

precipitous
adj lit: abrupt, falling sharply, perpendicular, sheer, steep; *fig*: heedless, hurried, impetuous, impulsive, precipitate, rash, reckless.

precise
adj lit: accurate, clear-cut, definitive, exact, express, specific; fastidious, finicky, meticulous, nice, particular, scrupulous; prim, puritanical, strict.

precision
n lit: accuracy, correctness, exactitude, fidelity, meticulousness, scrupulousness, strictness.

preclude
vb lit: debar, exclude, forestall, make impossible, obviate, prevent, prohibit, rule out.

precocious
adj lit: advanced, ahead, forward, premature, previous.

precursor
n lit: ancestor, forebear, predecessor; forerunner, harbinger, herald, messenger, vanguard; originator, pioneer.

predator
n lit: carnivore, hunter, raptor; *fig*: marauder, plunderer, vulture.

predatory
adj lit: carnivorous, rapacious, voracious, vulturine; *fig*: despoiling, destructive, marauding, plundering, raiding, ravaging.

predecessor
n lit: antecedent, forerunner, precursor; previous occupant; ancestor, forebear, forefather.

predestined
adj (pa.pt) *lit*: fated, foreordained, meant, predetermined, preordained; doomed.

predicament
n lit: corner, dilemma, jam, mess, pickle, plight, quandary, scrape, situation, spot.

predict
vb lit: augur, forecast, foresee, foretell, prophesy.

predilection
n lit: fondness, inclination, leaning, liking, penchant, preference, taste.

predisposed
adj (pa.pt) *lit*: amenable, inclined, minded, prone, susceptible, willing.

predominant
adj lit: chief, dominant, leading, main, paramount, preponderant, prime, principal, prominent, ruling, supreme.

pre-eminent
adj lit: chief, foremost, most distinguished, outstanding, paramount, predominant, supreme, unequalled, unrivalled.

preface
n lit: foreword, introduction, preamble, prelude, prologue.
vb lit: begin, introduce, lead up to, open, prefix.

prefer
vb lit: choose, favour, go for, like better, opt for, pick, plump for, select, single out; advance, elevate, promote, upgrade; *spec*: file, lodge, press (charges).

preferable
adj lit: better, eligible, favoured, more desirable, superior.

preference
n lit: choice, favourite, first choice, option, pick, selection; advantage, precedence, priority.

preferment
n lit: advancement, elevation, promotion, rise, upgrading.

pregnant
adj lit: expectant, gravid, in the family way, with child; hairy preggers, in the club, with one up the spout; *fig*: charged, expressive, meaningful, pointed, revealing, significant, telling, weighty; creative, imaginative, inventive, original;

abundant, fecund, fruitful, productive, prolific, teeming.

prejudiced
adj (pa.pt) *lit*: biased, discriminatory, influenced, jaundiced, narrow-minded, opinionated, partial, partisan, slanted, swayed, unfair.

preliminary
n lit: beginning, first round, foundation, groundwork, initiation, introduction, opening, preface, preparation, start.
adj lit: beginning, exploratory, first, initial, introductory, opening, pilot, precursory, preparatory, qualifying, trial.

prelude
n lit: curtain-raiser, foreword, intro, introduction, overture, preamble, preface, preliminary, prologue, start.

premature
adj lit: early, immature, incomplete, undeveloped, untimely; *fig*: hasty, ill-considered, ill-timed, impulsive, inopportune, precipitate, untimely.

premeditated
adj (pa.pt) *lit*: aforethought, calculated, considered, deliberate, intentional, planned, wilful.

premier
n lit: chancellor, head of government, prime minister, secretary of state.
adj lit: first, foremost, leading, main, principal, top; earliest, inaugural, initial.

premise
n lit: assumption, hypothesis, presupposition; argument, postulate, proposition.
vb lit: begin by assuming, postulate, propose, start by presupposing.

premises
n lit: building, grounds, property, site.

premium
n lit: cost, fee, instalment, price; bonus, perk, perquisite, recompense, remuneration, reward; appreciation, value.

premonition
n lit: apprehension, foreboding, intuition, misgiving, presentiment.

preoccupation
n lit: absent-mindedness, absorption, abstraction, inattentiveness, oblivion,

reverie; bee in one's bonnet, fixation, hang-up, hobbyhorse, obsession.

preoccupied
adj lit: absent-minded, absorbed, distracted, engrossed, faraway, oblivious, rapt.

preordain
vb lit: destine, fate, foreordain, predestine, predetermine; doom; foretell, prophesy.

preparation
n lit: anticipation, foresight, precaution, provision, readiness; fundamentals, groundwork, research and development; homework, revision, schoolwork, study; compound, concoction, medicine, mixture, tincture; *spec*: devotions (before a church service).

prepare
vb lit: make ready, prime, put in order; coach, equip, fit out, groom, outfit, supply, train, warm up; concoct, contrive, draw up, fix up, make, put together; brace oneself (for), fortify (oneself for), ready (oneself for), strengthen (oneself for).

prepared
adj (pa.pt) lit: all set, arranged, in order, in readiness, ready, set; able (to), disposed (to), inclined (to), of a mind (to), willing (to).

preponderant
adj lit: dominant, most important, most significant, paramount, predominant, prevailing.

preposterous
adj lit: absurd, incredible, insane, laughable, ludicrous, monstrous, nonsensical, outrageous, ridiculous, unreasonable, unthinkable.

prerequisite
n lit: condition, essential, must, necessity, precondition, requirement.
adj lit: essential, imperative, indispensable, mandatory, necessary, obligatory, vital.

prerogative
n lit: ascendancy, due, entitlement, priority, privilege, right, supremacy.

prescribe
vb lit: decree, define, direct, impose, lay down, require, rule, set, specify, stipulate.

prescription
n lit: direction, instruction, specification; formula, recipe.

presence
n lit: attendance, immediacy; company; occupancy, residence; closeness, propinquity, proximity; *fig*: air, carriage, demeanour, personality, poise, self-assurance; apparition, ghost, manifestation, spectre, spirit, wraith.

present
n lit: here and now, this moment, time being; donation, endowment, gift, gratuity.
vb lit: acquaint (with), introduce (to), make known (to); demonstrate, display, exhibit, put on, show; advance, expound, introduce, offer, produce, proffer, raise, relate, state, submit, suggest, tender; award, donate (to), endow (with), give.
adj lit: contemporary, current, existing, immediate; accounted for, at hand, available, near, ready, to hand.

presentation
n lit: award, conferral, donation, investiture, oblation, offering; arrangement, exposition, production, rendition, staging; display, performance, representation, show; *spec*: coming out, debut, introduction, launching (at court).

preserve
n lit: area, domain, realm, sphere; game reserve, reservation, sanctuary; conserve(s), jam, jelly, marmalade.
vb lit: care for, conserve, keep, protect, safeguard, save, secure, shelter, store; keep up, maintain, perpetuate, sustain, uphold.

preside over
vb lit: chair, control, direct, govern, lead, manage, officiate, run, supervise.

press
n lit: bunch, crowd, crush, mob, multitude, pack, throng; bustle, hassle, pressure, strain, stress, urgency; printing house, printing machine; bookcase, cupboard; *spec*: Fleet Street, Grub Street, journalism, newsmedia, newspapers; columnists, correspondents, journalists, newsmen, photographers, reporters.

vb lit: compress, condense, crush, jam, push, squeeze; cluster, crowd, flock, gather, mill, push, rush, seethe, swarm, throng; flatten, iron, mangle, smooth, steam; clasp, embrace, enfold, hold close, hug; compel, constrain, demand, enforce, force, insist on; beg, exhort, implore, petition, plead, pressurize, sue, supplicate, urge; afflict, assail, beset, besiege, harass, plague, trouble, vex, worry.

pressing
adj (pr.pt) lit: exigent, high-priority, imperative, important, serious, urgent, vital.

pressure
n lit: compression, crushing, force, squeezing, weight; *fig*: coercion, constraint, influence, obligation, sway; adversity, affliction, demands, distress, hassle, strain, stress.

prestige
n lit: cachet, celebrity, distinction, eminence, fame, importance, influence, kudos, renown, standing, stature, status, weight.

prestigious
adj lit: celebrated, eminent, esteemed, exalted, great, illustrious, impressive, influential, prominent, renowned.

presumably
adv lit: apparently, in all probability, most likely, one would assume, seemingly, surely.

presume
vb lit: assume, believe, conjecture, postulate, suppose, take for granted, think; dare (to), go so far as (to), have the audacity (to), make so bold as (to), venture (to); count (on), depend (on), rely (on).

presumption
n lit: audacity, boldness, cheek, effrontery, forwardness, gall, impudence, insolence, nerve, presumptuousness; assumption, hypothesis, presupposition, supposition, surmise; grounds, likelihood, probability.

presumptuous
adj lit: audacious, bold, cheeky, forward, impudent, insolent, pushy, too big for one's boots, uppish.

presupposition
n lit: assumption, preconception, prejudgement, premise, presumption, supposition, theory.

pretence
n lit: affectation, artifice, charade, cover, deceit, display, fabrication, façade, falsehood, guise, make-believe, pose, pretext, semblance, sham, show, trickery.

pretend
vb lit: affect, dissemble, fake, feign, make out, put on, sham; make believe; purport (to be); aspire (to), lay claim (to).

pretensions
n lit: aspirations, assertions, justifiable claim.

pretentious
adj lit: bombastic, conceited, exaggerated, extravagant, grandiloquent, grandiose, inflated, jumped-up, ostentatious, pompous, puffed up, snobbish, specious.

pretext
n lit: affectation, cloak, cover, device, excuse, mask, ploy, pretence.

pretty
adj lit: appealing, attractive, bonny, charming, comely, cute, good-looking, pleasing, personable; dainty, delicate, neat, nice, trim.
adv lit: fairly, moderately, quite, rather, reasonably, somewhat.

prevail
vb lit: be victorious, prove superior, triumph, win; abound, be prevalent, be widespread, obtain, predominate; use one's influence (upon).

prevalent
adj lit: dominant, governing, predominant, superior; accepted, commonplace, current, customary, everyday, frequent, rampant, rife, usual, widespread.

prevaricate
vb lit: beat about the bush, cavil, equivocate, hedge, quibble, stall, stretch the truth, waste time.

prevent
vb lit: bar, block, debar, foil, frustrate, obstruct, obviate, preclude, stop, thwart; avert, avoid, head off, inhibit, nip in the bud, stave off, ward off.

preventive

n lit: barrier, block, impediment, obstacle, obstruction; precaution, prophylactic, protection, safeguard; condom, rubber.
adj lit: blocking, counteractive, obstructive; deterrent, precautionary, protective.

previous

adj lit: anterior, earlier, erstwhile, former, past, preceding, quondam, sometime; *fig*: precipitate, premature, too early, untimely.

previously

adv lit: before, beforehand, earlier, in anticipation; formerly, in the past, once; hitherto, until now.

prey

n lit: game, quarry; *fig*: victim; mark, target.

prey on

vb lit: devour, feed on, hunt, live off; *fig*: bully, dominate, exploit, intimidate, take advantage of, victimize; burden, distress, haunt, oppress, trouble, weigh heavily.

price

n lit: bill, charge, cost, damage, expense, fee, premium, value; expenditure, outlay; estimate, evaluation; compensation, recompense, reward; odds; *fig*: consequences, penalty, toll.
vb lit: cost, estimate, evaluate, rate, value.

priceless

adj lit: invaluable, irreplaceable, precious, worth a king's ransom; immeasurable, incalculable, inestimable; *fig*: absurd, hilarious, killing, riotous, side-splitting.

prick

n lit: perforation, pinhole, puncture; cock, member, penis, phallus; *fig*: pang, prickle, smart, sting.
vb lit: drill, jab, perforate, pierce, puncture, stab; bite, prickle, smart, sting, tingle; *fig*: distress, trouble, wound.

prickly

adj lit: barbed, spiny, thorny; itchy, smarting, stinging, tingling; *fig*: bad-tempered, cantankerous, edgy, grumpy, irritable, peevish, pettish, ratty, snappish, touchy, waspish; complicated, difficult, intricate, involved, knotty, tricky, troublesome.

pride

n lit: honour, self-esteem, self-respect; arrogance, conceit, egotism, haughtiness, loftiness, presumption, pretention, self-importance; boast, prize, treasure; best, choice, élite, flower, glory; delight, gratification, joy, satisfaction.
vb lit: be proud of (oneself), congratulate (oneself), flatter (oneself).

priest

n lit: churchman, clergyman, cleric, curate, man of the cloth, minister, parson, rector, vicar; hierarch, temple official.

priggish

adj lit: goody-goody, self-righteous, smug; narrow-minded, prim, prudish, starchy, stuffy.

prim

adj lit: demure, fastidious, fussy, particular, precise, priggish, proper, prudish, schoolmarmish, stiff, straitlaced.

primarily

adv lit: above all, chiefly, for the most part, mainly, mostly, on the whole, principally; basically, essentially, fundamentally; initially, in the first place, originally.

primary

adj lit: basic, elemental, essential, fundamental, ultimate; capital, cardinal, chief, leading, main, paramount, principal, top; first, initial, introductory; elementary, rudimentary, simple; aboriginal, earliest, primal, primeval; crude, primitive, raw.

prime

n lit: best, greatest, height, heyday, peak, perfection; *fig*: beginning, opening; spring; *spec*: (musical) keynote, tonic; (musical) octave.
vb lit: coach, get ready, groom, prepare, train; charge, fuel, fill, load; brief, fill in, inform, tell; size, undercoat, whitewash.
adj lit: best, choice, excellent, first-rate, highest, perfect, superior, top-grade; basic, fundamental, original, primary, underlying; leading, main, predominant, principal; *spec*: indivisible (number).

primitive

adj lit: early, prehistoric, primeval, primordial; earliest, first; crude, elementary, rudimentary, unrefined,

unsophisticated; barbarian, savage,
uncivilized; childlike, naive, simple,
untrained.

princely
adj lit: generous, lavish, liberal, open-
handed, rich; great, large; august,
dignified, gracious, grand, high-born,
magnificent, noble, regal, royal, stately.

principal
n lit: chairperson, chief, director, head,
president; dean, director, headmaster,
headmistress, rector; guarantor, security;
culprit, ringleader; duellist; assets,
capital, money; girder, main beam,
rafter; *spec*: first violin (in an orchestra);
lead, star (of a show).
adj lit: cardinal, chief, crucial, dominant,
essential, foremost, key, leading, main,
paramount, pre-eminent, primary,
prime, vital.

principle
n lit: axiom, doctrine, dogma, golden rule,
law, maxim, precept, rule; belief, code,
creed, ethic, tenet; approach, attitude,
thesis, way of thinking; conscience, duty,
honour, integrity, morality, virtue; *fig*:
active ingredient, flavour.

print
n lit: impression; font, fount, type,
typeface; engraving; photograph,
positive, reproduction; fingerprint.
vb lit: imprint, press in, stamp; go to
press, run off.

prior
adj lit: before, earlier, previous.
adv lit: before, earlier, previously.

priority
n lit: precedence, pre-eminence,
preference, seniority, superiority,
supremacy; essential, prerequisite,
requirement, sine qua non.

prison
n lit: gaol, jail, lockup, penal institution,
penitentiary; choky, clink, jug, nick, stir.

private
n lit: squaddie, tommy; genital(s).
adj lit: exclusive, individual, intimate,
own, personal; confidential, in camera,
secret; concealed, isolated, not
overlooked, secluded, solitary;
independent, non-incorporated,
unaffiliated.

privileged
adj lit: advantaged, élite, ruling;
empowered, licensed, sanctioned; *spec*:
confidential, inside,
secret (information).

prize
n lit: award, reward, trophy; jackpot,
purse, winnings; booty, haul, loot,
pickings, plunder, swag; *fig*: aim,
ambition, desire, goal.
vb lit: appreciate, esteem, regard highly,
treasure, value.
adj lit: award-winning, champion, first-
rate, outstanding, top-class.

probable
adj lit: likely, most likely, odds-on,
plausible, presumable.

probably
adv lit: almost certainly, doubtless, in all
likelihood, most likely, presumably,
surely.

probe
n lit: gauge, hook, pick, rod; endoscope;
examination, inquest, inquiry,
investigation; unmanned capsule.
vb lit: explore, check, prod; examine, go
into, investigate, look into, query,
scrutinize, sift, test.

problem
n lit: brain-teaser, conundrum, enigma,
puzzle, riddle; difficulty, predicament,
quandary, snag, trouble; complication,
dilemma, doubt.
adj lit: delinquent, difficult,
unmanageable, unruly, wayward.

procedure
n lit: conduct, course, method, modus
operandi, plan of action, policy, practice,
process, routine, scheme, strategy, way
of working.

proceed
vb lit: carry on, continue, get on (with), go
ahead, go on, press on (with); arise
(from), come (from), derive (from),
emanate (from), issue (from), originate
(from), stem (from); ensue, follow,
result.

proceeds
n lit: earnings, gains, income, profit,
returns, revenue, takings.

process
n lit: course of action, means, measure,
method, mode, operation, practice;
action, case, suit, trial.

vb lit: deal with, handle, take care of;
alter, prepare, refine, transform, treat.

procession
n lit: cavalcade, cortège, motorcade,
parade; crocodile, file, line, queue,
sequence, series, succession; course,
cycle.

proclaim
vb lit: advertise, announce, blaze (abroad),
circulate, declare, enunciate, give out,
make known, promulgate, pronounce,
publish, trumpet.

procrastinate
vb lit: defer, delay, drag one's feet, gain
time, play for time, postpone, prolong,
put off, retard, stall.

procreate
vb lit: beget, sire, produce offspring,
reproduce; engender, generate.

procure
vb lit: acquire, come by, gain, get hold of,
lay hands on, obtain, pick up, purchase,
secure; effect, ensure.

prod
n lit: elbow, jab, nudge, poke, push,
shove; goad, poker, spur, stick; *fig*: cue,
prompt, reminder, signal.
vb lit: dig, elbow, jab, nudge, poke, push,
shove; drive, egg on, goad, incite,
motivate, prick, prompt, spur, stir, urge.

prodigal
n lit: spendthrift; squanderer, wastrel.
adj lit: extravagant, immoderate,
intemperate, profligate, reckless,
spendthrift; *fig*: bountiful, copious,
lavish, luxuriant, profuse, teeming.

prodigious
adj lit: exceptional, extraordinary,
phenomenal; astounding, fantastic,
impressive, marvellous, remarkable,
staggering, striking; colossal, immense,
massive, tremendous, vast.

prodigy
n lit: genius, precocious talent, whiz-kid,
wunderkind; exception, phenomenon;
marvel, sensation; freak, monster,
monstrosity, mutant.

produce
n lit: crop, harvest, yield; groceries,
products.
vb lit: come up with, construct, create,
devise, invent, make, manufacture, put
together, turn out; bear, bring forth,

deliver, generate; furnish, render,
supply, yield; bring about, cause, effect,
give rise to, set off, start; elongate,
extend, protract; advance, bring to light,
demonstrate, exhibit, offer, put forward,
set out; direct, do, mount, perform,
present, put on, stage.

production
n lit: assembly, construction,
manufacture, preparation; creation,
generation, origination; marketing,
presentation, supply; bringing to light,
disclosure, revelation; direction,
mounting, performance, staging.

productive
adj lit: creative, inventive; fecund, fertile,
fruitful, prolific, vigorous; *fig*:
advantageous, constructive, effective,
effectual, efficacious, helpful, profitable,
rewarding, useful, worthwhile.

profane
vb lit: blaspheme against, defile, desecrate;
abuse, violate; contaminate, pollute.
adj lit: lay, secular, temporal, worldly;
blasphemous, godless, impious,
irreverent, sacrilegious; abusive, coarse,
crude, foul, obscene, vulgar.

profess
vb lit: assert, aver, declare, maintain,
proclaim, state; acknowledge, admit,
affirm, confess, own; *fig*: claim, make
oneself out (to be), display.

profession
n lit: business, calling, line of work,
métier, occupation, vocation;
acknowledgement, affirmation, assertion,
confession, declaration, statement,
testimony; claim.

professional
n lit: business executive, career man/
woman, employee, non-amateur, wage-
earner; artist, expert, master, virtuoso;
specialist.
adj lit: career-minded, employed, full-
time, managerial, non-amateur, salaried,
wage-earning; vocational; competent,
experienced, expert, polished, proficient,
qualified, skilled, trained.

proficient
adj lit: accomplished, adept, capable,
competent, efficient, experienced, good,
qualified, skilled, trained, well-versed.

profile
n lit: contour, outline, side view, silhouette; drawing, figure, portrait, sketch; biography, cameo, character sketch, vignette; *fig*: chart, diagram, graph, table; analysis, study, survey.

profit
n lit: earnings, gains, proceeds, return, revenue, takings, yield; advantage, benefit, good, help, use, value.
vb lit: aid, benefit, gain, help, improve, serve, stand in good stead; make a killing, make money.

profitable
adj lit: commercial, cost-effective, lucrative, money-making, remunerative, rewarding; advantageous, beneficial, productive, useful, valuable, worthwhile.

profit by
vb lit: cash in on, exploit, learn from, make the most of, make use of, take advantage of, use, utilize.

profound
adj lit: deep, insightful, penetrating, philosophical, sagacious, subtle, thoughtful, wise; erudite, learned, recondite; abstruse, difficult, serious; abyssal, bottomless, cavernous, infernal, yawning; heartfelt, intense, keen, sincere; extensive, extreme, far-reaching, great, immense, vast, wide-ranging.

profuse
adj lit: abundant, copious, fulsome, generous, plentiful, prolific; extravagant, exuberant, immoderate, lavish, unstinting; excessive, prodigal.

profusion
n lit: abundance, cornucopia, multitude, plenitude, plethora, wealth; extravagance, exuberance, lavishness, luxuriance, riot, superfluity, surplus.

programme
n lit: agenda, list, order, plan, procedure, schedule, scheme, sequence, syllabus, timetable; cast-list, line-up; performance, presentation, production, show.
vb lit: arrange, bill, book, line up, schedule, organize; itemize, list, plan; order, put in sequence.

progress
n lit: advance, journey, movement, passage, way; advancement, betterment, development, growth, headway, improvement, promotion.
vb lit: advance, come on, get farther, get on, make headway, move forward, proceed, travel, work one's way up; develop, grow, improve; blossom, gain, increase.

progressive
adj lit: accelerating, advancing, developing, increasing, intensifying, worsening; continuous, ongoing; dynamic, enterprising; *fig*: advanced, avant-garde, go-ahead, radical, reformist, revolutionary; enlightened, liberal, open.

prohibited
adj (pa.pt) lit: banned, barred, embargoed, forbidden, illegal, interdicted, proscribed, outlawed; made impossible, precluded, prevented, stopped.

prohibitive
adj lit: preventive, repressive, restrictive; beyond one's means, excessive, too high, too much, too steep; outrageous, preposterous.

project
n lit: assignment, enterprise, job, plan, programme, scheme, task, undertaking, venture; proposal, proposition.
vb lit: beetle, extend forward, jut out, overhang, protrude, stick out; fling, hurl. launch, propel, throw; broadcast, radiate, transmit; estimate, forecast, foretell, predict; design, devise, draft, frame, outline, plan, scheme.

projection
n lit: bulge, extension, overhang, protrusion; jetty, pier; ledge, ridge, shelf, sill; launch, propulsion; radiation, transmission; cinematography, screening; estimate, forecast, prediction, prognosis; blueprint, outline, plan; *spec*: (astral) externalization, independence, transference; (mental) telekinesis, telepathy.

proletariat
n lit: lower classes, lower orders, masses, mob, plebs, rabble, working class.

proliferate
vb lit: breed, increase, multiply, run riot; burgeon, grow, mushroom, snowball.

prolific
adj lit: abundant, copious, profuse, rich,

teeming; fecund, fertile, generative, productive.

prolong
vb lit: extend, lengthen, make longer, produce, project, protract; carry on, continue; drag out, stretch.

promenade
n lit: esplanade, parade; pier, sea-front, terrace; amble, constitutional, saunter, stroll; *fig*: drive, ride; dance.
vb lit: amble, perambulate, saunter, stroll, take a walk; flaunt, parade, show off; *spec*: stand (at a concert).

prominence
n lit: crag, headland, height, projection, promontory, spur; bulge, hummock, lump, mound, protrusion, protuberance, rise, swelling; conspicuousness, distinctiveness, dominance, salience, visibility; distinction, precedence; celebrity, eminence, fame, importance, prestige, reputation, standing.

prominent
adj lit: beetling, jutting, protruding, protuberant; conspicuous, eye-catching, noticeable, obvious, pronounced, striking, unmistakable; celebrated, distinguished, eminent, famous, important, leading, main, outstanding, pre-eminent, renowned, top, well-known.

promiscuous
adj lit: debauched, fast, immoral, libertine, loose, of easy virtue, wanton; casual, irresponsible, random, undiscriminating; *fig*: chaotic, disordered, indiscriminate.

promise
n lit: assurance, bond, commitment, oath, pledge, undertaking, vow, word of honour; *fig*: ability, aptitude, capability, flair, potential, talent.
vb lit: assure, contract, engage, give an undertaking, give one's word, pledge, plight, take an oath, undertake, vouch; *fig*: augur, be likely (to), betoken, hint at, look like, seem to mean, suggest.

promising
adj lit: auspicious, bright, encouraging, hopeful, optimistic, propitious, reassuring, rosy; *fig*: gifted, talented; likely, rising, up-and-coming.

promontory
n lit: cape, foreland, headland, peninsula, point, spur.

promote
vb lit: advance, boost, encourage, forward, foster, further, nurture; aid, assist, help, support; elevate, exalt, raise, upgrade; advocate, back, champion, popularize, push for, recommend, sponsor; advertise, market, publicize, push, sell.

promotion
n lit: advancement, elevation, rise, upgrading; advocacy, backing, boosting, furtherance, support; advocacy, recommendation, sponsorship; advertising, marketing, media hype, plugging, publicity, sales pitch.

prompt
n lit: cue, hint, prod, reminder, spur.
vb lit: cue, jog the memory, prod, remind; cause, elicit, evoke, occasion, provoke; induce, inspire, instigate, move, spur.
adj lit: immediate, instant, instantaneous, punctual, quick, speedy, swift, timely; *fig*: alert; willing.

promptly
adv lit: at once, immediately, instantly, quickly, speedily; on the dot, punctually.

promulgate
vb lit: announce, communicate, declare, disseminate, issue, make public, proclaim, publish.

prone
adj lit: flat, horizontal, lying face down, prostrate, recumbent, supine; *fig*: apt, inclined, liable, likely, predisposed, susceptible, tending.

pronounce
vb lit: articulate, enunciate, say; accent, emphasize, stress; announce, assert, declare, decree, proclaim.

pronounced
adj (pa.pt) lit: conspicuous, distinct, evident, noticeable, obvious, striking; definite, emphatic, stressed, strong.

proof
n lit: authentication, confirmation, corroboration, substantiation, verification; evidence, testimony; *spec*: galley, ozalid, pull, slip (in publishing).

adj lit: resistant (against), sealed (against), treated (against).

prop
n lit: brace, buttress, stanchion, stay, support.
vb lit: bolster, brace, buttress, hold up, shore up, support, sustain; *fig*: lean (against), put up (against), rest (against), set (against).

propaganda
n lit: advertisement, hype, marketing, promotion, publicity, slogan; disinformation.

propagation
n lit: breeding, multiplication, proliferation, reproduction; broadcasting, diffusion, dissemination, distribution, promotion, spread, transmission.

propel
vb lit: drive, force, impel, push, shoot, shove, thrust.

proper
adj lit: decent, decorous, genteel, mannerly, polite, punctilious, refined; becoming, fitting, legitimate, right; appropriate, apt, suitable; accepted, conventional, established, formal; accurate, correct, exact, precise; characteristic, individual, own, particular, personal, specific.

property
n lit: assets, belongings, capital, effects, estate, goods, holdings, possessions, resources, wealth; building, grounds, land, premises, territory; *fig*: attribute, characteristic, feature, idiosyncrasy, peculiarity, quality, trait; *spec*: article, bit of scenery (on stage).

prophesy
vb lit: augur, foretell, predict, prognosticate; forecast, foresee.

prophet
n lit: augur, oracle, seer, sibyl, soothsayer; astrologer, clairvoyant, crystal-gazer, magus; forecaster, tipster; mouthpiece, spokesperson.

prophetic
adj lit: oracular, prescient, sibylline, visionary; clairvoyant; apocalyptic, revelatory.

propitious
adj lit: auspicious, encouraging, favourable, opportune, promising, rosy; benevolent, benign, gracious, well-disposed.

proportion
n lit: cut, division, fraction, part, percentage, quota, ration, share; dimension(s), measurement(s); distribution, ratio, relationship; (in) agreement, (in) balance, (in) correspondence.

proposal
n lit: motion, proposition, suggestion; plan, presentation, programme, project, scheme; offer, tender; conditions, terms; *spec*: request for one's hand in marriage.

propose
vb lit: advance, present, proffer, propound, put forward, submit, suggest, tender; aim, intend, mean, plan; introduce, invite, name, nominate, put up for membership, recommend; *spec*: request one's hand in marriage, pop the question.

proposition
n lit: motion, plan, project, proposal, recommendation, scheme.
vb lit: accost, make an improper suggestion to, solicit.

proprietor
n lit: freeholder, landowner, title-holder; owner, possessor; host, landlord.

propriety
n lit: decency, decorum, delicacy, etiquette, gentility, manners, politeness, punctiliousness, refinement; respectability, seemliness, virtue; appropriateness, aptness, suitability; conventionalities, formalities, protocol.

propulsion
n lit: drive, driving force, impulsion, locomotion, power, propelling force, push, thrust.

proscribe
vb lit: ban, embargo, forbid, outlaw, prohibit; banish, exclude, excommunicate, exile, ostracize.

prosecute
vb lit: bring an action against, bring to trial, indict, litigate against, prefer charges against, sue, summons, take to court; carry on, discharge, engage in,

perform, practise, work at; carry
through, continue, persevere in, persist
with, pursue, see through.

prospect
n lit: panorama, scene, sight, view, vista;
anticipation, expectation, outlook;
chance, likelihood, possibility.
vb lit: explore, look (for), pan (for),
search, sift (for) survey.

prosper
vb lit: do well, flourish, get on, get rich,
make good, make it, succeed, thrive.

prosperity
n lit: affluence, plenty, riches, success,
wealth, wellbeing.

prostitute
n lit: call girl, harlot, hooker, hustler, lady
of the night, streetwalker, tart, trollop,
whore.
vb lit: cheapen, debase, degrade, demean,
profane; pimp for, put on the game, sell.

prostitution
n lit: harlotry, streetwalking, the game,
the oldest profession, whoredom;
cheapening, debasement, degradation,
demeaning, profanity.

prostrate
vb lit: abase (oneself), cast (oneself) down
before, lay (oneself) flat; bring low,
crush, lay low, overthrow, overwhelm;
fig: drain, exhaust, sap, tire, wear out.
adj lit: flat, horizontal, on one's face,
prone; brought to one's knees,
defenceless, disarmed, impotent,
overwhelmed, paralysed, reduced; at a
low ebb, dejected, depressed, drained,
exhausted, sapped, spent, worn out.

protect
vb lit: defend, give sanctuary to, keep safe,
safeguard, shelter, shield; care for,
harbour, look after, support, take under
one's wing, watch over; conceal, hide,
keep secret; cover up for.

protection
n lit: armour, defences, guard; barrier,
cover, screen, shield; refuge, shelter;
preservation, safety, security; care,
charge, custody, guardianship, safe
keeping.

protest
n lit: complaint, demur, dissent,
objection, outcry, remonstration,
resistance.

vb lit: complain, demur, disagree, dissent,
expostulate, object, remonstrate; argue,
assert, contend, declare, insist on,
maintain, profess, testify to.

protocol
n lit: conventions, courtesies, decorum,
etiquette, formalities, propriety; accord,
draft agreement, entente, understanding;
diplomatic formula; account,
instrument, log, official note, record.

prototype
n lit: archetype, first example, original;
mock-up, model, pattern, standard.

protracted
adj lit: elongated, extended, lengthy, long
drawn-out, never-ending, prolonged,
time-consuming.

protuberant
adj lit: beetling, bulging, jutting out,
knobbly, prominent, protruding,
sticking out, swollen.

proud
adj lit: honoured; basking in the glory
(of); gratified, pleased; glorious,
gratifying, memorable, pleasing,
satisfying; august, distinguished,
eminent, grand, noble, splendid;
arrogant, boastful, conceited, haughty,
presumptuous, self-important, snobbish,
snooty, supercilious, vain; *fig*:
projecting, swelling.

prove
vb lit: confirm, corroborate, demonstrate,
establish, show, substantiate, verify; be
found (to be), turn out; *fig*: analyse,
assay, examine, experiment, put to the
test, try.

proverb
n lit: adage, axiom, maxim, saw, saying.

proverbial
adj lit: axiomatic, customary, famed,
legendary, time-honoured, traditional,
well-known.

provide
vb lit: accommodate (with), contribute,
equip (with), furnish, outfit (with), stock
up (with), supply (with); afford, give,
impart, lend, render, yield; determine,
lay down, require, specify, stipulate;
arrange (for), plan (for), prepare (for);
care (for).

provided
cnj lit: as long as, given (that), in the event (that), on condition (that), on the understanding (that).

providence
n lit: destiny, divine intervention, fate, God's will, predestination; caution, foresight, forethought, prudence.

province
n lit: colony, dependency, dominion, region, territory, zone; *fig*: area, business, duty, employment, field, function, line, responsibility, role, sphere.

provincial
n lit: country cousin, hayseed, hick.
adj lit: backwoods, parochial, remote, small-town, upcountry; uninformed, unsophisticated; insular, inward-looking, limited, narrow-minded.

provision
n lit: catering, equipping, furnishing, supplying, victualling; arrangement, plan, preparation; *fig*: agreement, clause, condition, specification, stipulation.
vb lit: stock, supply, victual; accoutre, equip.

provisional
adj lit: conditional, contingent, interim, stopgap, temporary, tentative, transitional.

proviso
n lit: condition, contingency clause, if, limitation, qualification, reservation, rider, stipulation.

provocative
adj lit: arousing, erotic, exciting, seductive, sensual, sexy, suggestive, tantalizing, titillating; aggravating, annoying, disturbing, galling, infuriating, offensive.

provoke
vb lit: bring about, cause, elicit, evoke, excite, generate, give rise to, incite, induce, inflame, instigate, lead to, occasion, precipitate, promote, prompt, rouse, stir up; annoy, enrage, exasperate, gall, get on one's nerves, incense, infuriate, irk, irritate, madden, offend, pique, rile.

prow
n lit: bows, fore; sharp end; front, head, nose.

prowess
n lit: ability, accomplishment, command, excellence, expertise, facility, mastery, skill; audacity, boldness, bravery, courage, daring, dauntlessness, intrepidity, valour.

prowl
vb lit: cruise, lurk, patrol, range, roam (around), skulk, sneak.

proximity
n lit: closeness, juxtaposition, nearness, propinquity; neighbourhood, vicinity.

proxy
n lit: agent, delegate, representative, substitute, surrogate.

prudence
n lit: care, caution, circumspection, common sense, discretion, forethought, judgement, judiciousness, precaution, sagacity, vigilance, wariness, wisdom; economy, frugality, husbandry, thrift.

prudish
adj lit: old-maidish, priggish, prim, prissy, proper, school-marmish, starchy, straitlaced, stuffy.

prune
n lit: dried plum; purple; *fig*: crone, hag, witch.
vb lit: clip, cut back, lop, pare down, reduce, shape, trim.

prying
adj (pr.pt) lit: inquisitive, nosy, snooping, spying; interfering, intrusive, meddlesome.

psalm
n lit: hymn, paean, sacred song, song of praise.

psyche
n lit: mind; innermost self; anima, persona, pneuma, spirit; self, soul.

psychiatrist
n lit: analyst, analytical psychologist, psychoanalyst, psychologist, psychotherapist, shrink.

psychic
n lit: medium; clairvoyant, dowser, sensitive; parapsychology.
adj lit: clairvoyant, ESP, extrasensory, supernatural, telekinetic, telepathic; mental, psychological; *fig*: astral.

psychological
adj lit: mental, subconscious; cognitive; emotional, psychiatric; psychosomatic.

psychotic
adj lit: certifiable, demented, deranged, insane, lunatic, mad, mental, psychopathic.

pub
n lit: bar, boozer, hospice, hostelry, inn, local, tavern.

public
n lit: citizens, community, electorate, nation, people, populace, population, society, voters; audience, buyers, clientele, market, patrons, punters, supporters, trade.
adj lit: civic, civil, national, popular, state, universal, widespread; communal, community, open to the public; accessible, unrestricted; exposed, known, open, overt, patent, plain, recognized; celebrated, important, prominent, well-known.

publication
n lit: appearance, broadcasting, declaration, disclosure, issue, printing, proclamation, promulgation; launch, marketing; book, brochure, leaflet, pamphlet, periodical.

publicize
vb lit: advertise, broadcast, highlight, hype, make known, market, plug, promote, push, spotlight.

publish
vb lit: print, produce, put out; bring out, issue, launch, market, sell; advertise, announce, broadcast, communicate, disclose, divulge, impart, leak, promulgate, publicize, spread.

puerile
adj lit: babyish, childish, immature, infantile, jejune, juvenile, petty.

puff
n lit: breath; blast, draught, gust, whiff; cloud, flurry; drag, pull; fluffy pad; *fig*: advertisement, commendation, mention, plug, review.

vb lit: blow (out), breathe, exhale, gasp, pant, wheeze; draw, inhale, pull; blow oneself (up), swell (up); *fig*: hype, plug, promote, publicize, push.

puffy
adj lit: distended, swollen, tumid; inflated; fluffy, soft.

pugilist
n lit: boxer, bruiser, fighter.

pugnacious
adj lit: aggressive, argumentative, bellicose, belligerent, combative, contentious, disputatious, quarrelsome.

pull
n lit: haul, heave, tow, tug; jerk, twitch, yank; strain, stretching; hit, stroke; row, scull; resistance; drag, inhalation, draught, swallow, swig; *fig*: ascent, climb; attraction, influence, magnetism, power; clout, influence, leverage, weight; *spec*: proof (in publishing).
vb lit: draw, haul, heave, tow, tug; jerk, twitch, yank; strain, stretch; cull, pick, pluck, strip; extract, take out; hit, knock, strike; row, scull; move, steer; drag, inhale, suck; *fig*: attract, entice, lure; arrest, catch; *spec*: hold back (a horse, a punch).

pull out
vb lit: draw, extract; drive away (from), move away (from); abandon, depart, leave, quit, retreat, withdraw.

pull up
vb lit: dig up, lift, pick, pluck, uproot; brake, rein in, screech to a halt, stop; *fig*: startle, take aback; carpet, castigate, reprimand, take to task, tell off, tick off; catch up (on), gain ground (on).

pulp
n lit: flesh, marrow, pith; mash, mush, pap.
vb lit: crush, grind, mash, mill, powder, squash.
adj lit: cheap, trashy; lurid, sensational.

pulse
n lit: heartbeat; beat, beating, rhythm, throbbing, vibration; *spec*: legume, seed vegetable (such as peas, beans or lentils).
vb lit: beat, throb, vibrate.

pulverize
vb lit: crush, granulate, grind, mill, pestle, pound; *fig*: annihilate, demolish, destroy, devastate, flatten, smash, wreck.

pump

n lit: compressor, energizer, inflater, pressurizer, siphon, syringe; dancing-shoe.

vb lit: drive, force, siphon, syringe; empty (out), inject (in); blow (up), inflate; energize, excite; *fig*: cross-examine, grill, interrogate, question, quiz; *spec*: contract (muscles).

punch

n lit: bash, blow, buffet, clout, hit, jab, knock, thump, wallop, whack; *fig*: bite, dynamism, energy, force, impact; *spec*: cold chisel; die, stamp; fruit cup; pit-prop.

vb lit: bash, box, buffet, clout, hit, jab, knock, slam, smash, strike, thump, wallop, whack; imprint, indent, stamp; bore (through), drill (through); key, type; *spec*: drive (cattle).

punctilious

adj lit: conscientious, fastidious, finicky, fussy, meticulous, particular, pedantic, precise, scrupulous, strict.

punctual

adj lit: on the dot, on time, prompt, timely.

punctuate

vb lit: mark up; *fig*: break up, interrupt; pepper, sprinkle; accentuate, emphasize, stress, underscore.

puncture

n lit: flat tyre; break, hole, rupture, slit; escape, leak.

vb lit: penetrate, perforate, pierce, prick, rupture; go down, go flat; *fig*: deflate, disillusion, humble, take down a peg.

pungent

adj lit: acrid, aromatic, bitter, peppery, piquant, sharp, spicy, strong, tart; *fig*: biting, caustic, cutting, incisive, keen, penetrating, piercing, poignant, pointed, sarcastic, scathing, stinging, trenchant.

punish

vb lit: castigate, chasten, chastise, correct, discipline, make one sorry, penalize; beat, cane, flog, spank, tan one's hide, whip; batter, hurt, injure, knock about, rough up.

punishing

adj lit: arduous, backbreaking, draining, exhausting, fatiguing, grinding, gruelling, hard, strenuous, taxing, wearing.

punishment

n lit: castigation, chastening, chastisement, correction, discipline, penalty, penance; beating, caning, flogging, spanking, tanning, whipping; battering, injury, knocking about, rough treatment.

punter

n lit: backer, better, gambler; kicker; *fig*: bloke, guy, man, person; client, customer, john, mark.

puny

adj lit: feeble, frail, pint-sized, runtish, sickly, stunted, undersized, weakly; *fig*: inconsequential, insignificant, paltry, petty, trifling, trivial.

pup

n lit: cub, whelp, young dog; *fig*: jackanapes, popinjay, whippersnapper; *spec*: (sold a) dud, dummy.

pupil

n lit: disciple, learner, schoolboy, schoolgirl, student; neophyte, novice, postulant; eye-hole.

puppet

n lit: doll, marionette; *fig*: cat's-paw, figurehead, mouthpiece, pawn, stooge.

purchase

n lit: buy; acquisition, gain, property; foothold, footing, grasp, grip, toehold; *fig*: edge, hold, influence, leverage.

vb lit: buy; acquire, come by, invest in, obtain, pick up, procure, secure, shop for.

pure

adj lit: flawless, perfect, unalloyed; straight, unmixed; authentic, genuine, natural, real, simple, true; immaculate, pristine, spotless, virgin; clean, sanitary, sterile, uncontaminated, unpolluted, untainted, wholesome; *fig*: blameless, chaste, innocent, uncorrupted, virginal, virtuous; absolute, complete, mere, sheer, total, unqualified, utter; academic, hypothetical, speculative, theoretical.

purge

n lit: aperient, cathartic, emetic, laxative; *fig*: clean-up, clear-out, sorting out, weeding out; pogrom, witch hunt.

vb lit: absolve, cleanse, expiate, forgive, pardon, purify, wash clean; evacuate, use a laxative; *fig*: clean up, clear out, sort out, weed out.

purify
vb lit: clean, cleanse, decontaminate, disinfect, fumigate, sanitize, wash clean; *fig*: absolve, shrive.

puritanical
adj lit: austere, prim, proper, prudish, severe, straitlaced, strict.

purity
n lit: flawlessness, perfection, spotlessness; clarity, cleanness, clearness, opacity; faultlessness, fineness, genuineness; simplicity; *fig*: blamelessness, chastity, innocence, virginity, virtue; piety; sincerity.

purport
n lit: bearing, drift, gist, idea, import, significance, tenor; aim, intention, objective, purpose.
vb lit: claim, declare oneself (to be), pretend, proclaim oneself (to be), profess, seem; convey, signify.

purpose
n lit: aim, design, idea, intention, object, point, reason; end, goal, objective, target; aspiration, desire, wish; determination, firmness, persistence, resolve, single-mindedness, steadfastness, tenacity, will; avail, benefit, effect, gain, outcome, profit, result, return, use.
vb lit: aim, aspire, commit oneself, determine, intend, mean, plan, propose, resolve.

purposeless
adj lit: aimless, haphazard, motiveless, random; pointless, senseless, unnecessary, useless.

purse
n lit: money-bag, pouch; exchequer, funds, money, resources, treasury; award, prize, reward; gift, present.
vb lit: draw tight, pucker, tighten.

pursue
vb lit: chase, follow, go after, hound, hunt, tail, track; *fig*: chase after, court, pay court to, woo; aim for, aspire to, seek, strive for, work towards; apply oneself to, carry on, engage in, perform, ply, practise, work at; adhere to, continue, hold to, keep on, persist in.

pursuit
n lit: chase, hunt, quest, search; activity, endeavour, hobby, interest, occupation, pastime.

push
n lit: heave, ram, shove, thrust; assault, attack, charge, offensive, onslaught; *fig*: ambition, determination, drive, dynamism, energy, enterprise, vigour; effort, go, try.
vb lit: drive, press, propel, ram, shove, thrust; elbow, jostle, shoulder, squeeze; browbeat, coerce, egg on, encourage, hurry, impel, incite, influence, oblige, persuade, urge; advertise, boost, plug, promote, publicize; hawk, peddle, market; *spec*: approach (in age).

pushed
adj (pa.pt) lit: hurried, pressed, rushed, tied up.

pushover
n lit: child's play, doddle, picnic, piece of cake, walkover; *fig*: mug, soft touch, sucker.

pushy
adj lit: aggressive, ambitious, brash, bumptious, presumptuous, self-assertive.

pusillanimous
adj lit: chicken-hearted, cowardly, craven, faint-hearted, feeble, spineless, timorous; mealy-mouthed, time-serving.

pustule
n lit: abscess, boil, pimple, spot; blister; ulcer.

put
vb lit: bring, deposit, lay, place, position, rest, set, settle, situate; push (away), thrust (away); heave, hurl, lob, pitch, throw, toss; *fig*: arrange, fix; commit, condemn, consign, doom; assign (to), constrain (to), employ (to), make (to), oblige (to), require (to); express, phrase, pose, state, word; assess (at), estimate (at); advance, bring forward, posit, present, propose, submit.

putative
adj lit: alleged, assumed, presumed, presumptive, reputed, seeming, supposed.

put off
vb lit: defer, delay, postpone, put back, reschedule; *fig*: abash, disconcert, nonplus, perturb, unsettle; discourage, dishearten, dissuade (from).

put on
vb lit: assume, don, get dressed in, slip into, wear; add, gain, increase by; do, mount, present, produce, stage; switch on, turn on; *fig*: affect, feign, simulate; bet, stake, wager.

put out
vb lit: bounce, expel, take outside; gouge out; dislocate; send out, stretch out; sail; blow out, douse, extinguish, quench, snuff; switch out, turn out; broadcast, circulate, issue, publish, release; *fig*: annoy, exasperate, irk, irritate, nettle, provoke; confound, discomfit, disconcert, discountenance, embarrass, upset; bother, impose upon, inconvenience, trouble.

putrefy
vb lit: decay, decompose, deteriorate, go bad, rot.

putrid
adj lit: bad, corrupt, decayed, decomposed, foetid, foul, off, rancid, rotten, spoiled.

put up
vb lit: build, construct, erect, raise; accommodate, board, entertain, house, lodge, take in; advance, give, invest, pledge, supply; *fig*: nominate, propose, put forward, recommend, submit; incite (to), inspire (to), instigate (to), urge (to).

put up with
vb lit: bear, endure, stand, stomach, swallow, take, tolerate; lump.

puzzle
n lit: brainteaser, conundrum, dilemma, enigma, problem, quandary, question, riddle; maze, mystery, paradox; difficulty, perplexity, uncertainty.
vb lit: baffle, beat, bewilder, mystify, nonplus, perplex, stump; brood (over), mull (over), muse (over), ponder (over), think long and hard (over); figure (out), sort (out), work (out).

puzzled
adj (pa.pt) lit: baffled, beaten, bewildered, flummoxed, mystified, perplexed, stuck, stumped.

pygmy
n lit: bushman; dwarf, homunculus, midget; *fig*: lightweight, nobody, nonentity, small fry, titch.
adj lit: diminutive, dwarf, midget, miniature, minuscule, small, stunted, undersized; elfin.

pylon
n lit: aerial, booster, mast; beacon, signalpost; gatehouse, gateway; engine support, fueltank support.

pyromaniac
n lit: arsonist, fire-raiser, incendiary.

Q

quack
n lit: cackle, honk, squawk; charlatan, con man, fraud, impostor, mountebank, shyster, swindler, trickster.
vb lit: cackle, honk, squawk.
adj lit: counterfeit, fake, fraudulent, phoney, pretended, sham.

quaff
vb lit: down, drink deeply, guzzle, imbibe, knock back.

quagmire
n lit: bog, marsh, morass, quicksand, slough, swamp; mud, ooze, slime; *fig*: difficulty, entanglement, fix, jam, pinch, predicament, quandary; imbroglio, mess, scrape.

quail
n lit: game-bird, partridge; bobwhite.
vb lit: be daunted, blanch, blench, cower, cringe, falter, flinch, quake, shrink, shudder, tremble; be afraid, bottle out, chicken out, funk, recoil in fear.

quaint
adj lit: antiquated, archaic, baroque, gothic, old-fashioned, old-world, rococo; picturesque, scenic; curious, eccentric, odd, peculiar, singular, unusual; bizarre, fantastic, grotesque, strange, whimsical.

quake
n lit: convulsion, quiver, shaking, shiver, shudder, spasm, tremor, vibration; earthquake, seismic shock.
vb lit: convulse, go into spasm, quail, quiver, shake, shiver, shudder, tremble, vibrate; flutter, palpitate, throb.

qualification
n lit: authority, capability, eligibility, power; achievements, attainments, background, certificate, experience, history, past, record; attribute, capacity, skill; distinguishing feature, distinction; caveat, exception, limitation, modification, reservation, restriction; condition, proviso.

qualify
vb lit: be accepted, be authorized, be certified, become eligible, be

empowered, be entitled, be trained; equip, fit, prepare, ready, school; limit, moderate, modify, restrict, soften, temper; abate, diminish, lessen, mitigate, reduce; characterize, describe, distinguish; have an effect upon.

quality
n lit: character, class, demeanour, description, essence, kind, make, manner, nature, sort, stamp, type; attribute, characteristic, feature, property, trait; timbre, tone; calibre, distinction, merit, standing, value, worth; position, rank, status, superiority; aristocracy, landed gentry, nobility, upper classes.

qualm
n lit: misgiving, pang of conscience, regret, scruple, twinge of conscience; disquiet, doubt, hesitation, uneasiness; gripe, pang, sick feeling, twinge.

quandary
n lit: dilemma, predicament; difficult situation, impasse, puzzle, state of doubt.

quantify
vb lit: assess, calculate, compute, evaluate, gauge, measure, total, weigh; describe.

quantity
n lit: amount, number, sum, total; aggregate, bulk, capacity, extent, magnitude, mass, measure, size, volume; dose, helping, part, portion, ration, share; *spec*: duration, length (of a musical note, of a syllable).

quarrel
n lit: altercation, argument, clash, controversy, difference of opinion, disagreement, discord, dispute, dissension, feud, row, slanging match, squabble, tiff, vendetta, wrangle; *spec*: arrow, bolt, dart (for a crossbow); (stone-mason's) chisel.
vb lit: argue, bandy words, bicker, clash, differ, disagree, dispute, dissent, fall out, feud, have words, row, squabble,

wrangle; carp, cavil, decry, demur, find fault, take exception.

quarrelsome
adj lit: antagonistic, argumentative, bellicose, belligerent, combative, disputatious, hostile, mutinous, pugnacious; choleric, cross, fractious, ill-tempered, irascible, irritable, peevish.

quarry
n lit: excavation, open-cast mine, pit; game, hunted, kill, prey, victim; *fig*: reservoir, source, well; aim, end, goal, objective.
vb lit: dig out (from), excavate; *fig*: extract.

quarter
n lit: fourth; 15 minutes; 3 months; area, district, locality, neighbourhood, place, region, side, territory, zone; compass point, direction; clemency, leniency, mercy; *fig*: authority, source; *spec*: phase (of the moon); staff, upright, vertical (in construction).
vb lit: divide into fourths; accommodate, billet, house, lodge, post, station; abide, be accommodated, board, put up, stay; range, roam; beat, search thoroughly; *fig*: compartment; impose.

quarters
n lit: accommodation, digs, lodgings, post, residence, rooms, station; barracks, camp.

quash
vb lit: annul, erase, expunge, invalidate, nullify, repeal, rescind, revoke, set aside, undo, wipe out; crush, extinguish, overthrow, put down, quell, repress, subdue, suppress.

quaver
n lit: break, shake, trembling, tremor, tremulousness; trill, vibration.
vb lit: break, quiver, shake, tremble, waver; quake; dodder.

quay
n lit: dock, hythe, jetty, landing-stage, mole, pier, wharf.

queasy
adj lit: feeling sick, nauseated, uncomfortable, uneasy, unsettled; squeamish.

queen
n lit: head of state, monarch, ruler, sovereign; consort, empress; her

majesty; *fig*: doyenne, model; idol, prima donna, star; mistress; homosexual.

queer
n lit: homosexual; catamite, sodomite; fairy, pansy, poofter.
vb lit: foil, mar, ruin, spoil, wreck; impair, jeopardize.
adj lit: abnormal, anomalous, extraordinary, odd, outlandish, peculiar, singular, strange, uncommon, unnatural, unusual, weird; curious, droll, funny, quaint; unconventional, unorthodox; dubious, fishy, questionable, suspicious; eerie, mysterious, uncanny; dizzy, faint, ill, light-headed, sick, queasy; crazy, touched; counterfeit, fake, sham.

quell
vb lit: crush, extinguish, overthrow, put down, quash, suppress; check, curb, repress, stifle, subdue; conquer, defeat, overcome; *fig*: allay, calm, mollify, pacify, quiet, soothe.

quench
vb lit: douse, drown, extinguish, put out, smother, snuff out, stifle; dip, plunge; allay, appease, cool, satiate, satisfy, slake; end, finish, stop; die down, fade out, subside.

querulous
adj lit: fretful, peevish, petulant, protesting, whining; complaining, critical, fault-finding; cantankerous, cross, grouchy, irascible, irritable, sour, testy, touchy.

query
n lit: inquiry, question; contention, controversy, debate, doubt, reservation, uncertainty; objection, problem; interrogation mark, question mark.
vb lit: ask, challenge, debate, dispute, enquire, interrogate, question; doubt, wonder.

quest
n lit: chase, expedition, hunt, pursuit, search; crusade, mission, pilgrimage; adventure, enterprise; aim, goal, objective; prey, quarry.

question
n lit: inquiry, query; contention, controversy, debate; demur, doubt, objection, problem, reservation, uncertainty; examination, interrogation; issue, motion, proposition, subject, topic.

queue
vb lit: ask, cross-examine, enquire, grill, interrogate, pump, query, quiz; challenge, debate, disbelieve, dispute, doubt, wonder about.

queue
n lit: line, line-up; crocodile, file, string; progression, series, succession; tailback, traffic jam; *spec*: pigtail.
vb lit: file, form a line, line up, stand in line; be jammed, tail back.

quibble
n lit: artifice, equivocation, evasion, irrelevance, niggle, prevarication, sophistry, subterfuge; nicety, pedantry, subtlety.
vb lit: be disputatious, cavil, equivocate, niggle, nit-pick, prevaricate, split hairs.

quick
n lit: living; flesh, sensitive part; *fig*: heart.
adj lit: express, fast, fleet, meteoric, rapid, snappy, speedy, swift; abrupt, immediate, prompt, sudden; brief, brisk, cursory, hasty, hurried, perfunctory; active, adroit, alert, animated, energetic, keen, lively, nimble, ready, sharp, spry, vivacious; adept, clever, deft, dextrous, skilful, versatile; acute, intelligent, perceptive, shrewd; excitable, irascible, touchy, volatile.
adv lit: fast, rapidly, speedily, swiftly; at once, immediately.

quicken
vb lit: accelerate, expedite, hasten, hurry up, hustle, speed up; activate, animate, arouse, awaken, excite, fire, kindle, reactivate, reanimate, rekindle, resurrect, revitalize, revive, rouse, stimulate, stir up.

quickly
adv lit: at the double, briskly, fast, flat out, rapidly, snappily, speedily, swiftly, with alacrity; abruptly, immediately, instantly, promptly, soon, smartish, suddenly; briefly, cursorily, hastily, hurriedly, perfunctorily.

quick-tempered
adj lit: choleric, fiery, hot-tempered, intolerant, irascible, mercurial, peppery, quarrelsome, temperamental, testy, touchy, volatile, waspish.

quick-witted
adj lit: acute, alert, astute, bright, clever, discerning, intelligent, perceptive, ready, sharp, shrewd.

quiescent
adj lit: dormant, inactive, latent; inert, motionless, resting, silent, still, unmoving; calm, placid, serene, tranquil.

quiet
n lit: peace, silence, stillness, tranquillity; serenity; calm, repose, rest.
vb lit: hush, silence; calm down, pacify, soothe, still.
adj lit: noiseless, silent, soundless; hushed, low, peaceful, soft; at rest, calm, motionless, placid, restful, serene, still, tranquil; dumb, mute, unresponsive; private, secluded, secret, undisturbed, unfrequented; modest, plain, restrained, sedate, sober, subdued, unobtrusive, unpretentious; gentle, inoffensive, meek, mild, reserved, retiring, shy.

quieten
vb lit: hush, silence, still; deaden, muffle, mute; appease, calm, mollify, soothe, subdue, tranquillize; allay, assuage, pacify, palliate, stop.

quietly
adv lit: noiselessly, silently, soundlessly; gently, peacefully, softly; complacently, contentedly, placidly, serenely, tranquilly; confidentially, furtively, privately, secretively, secretly; inoffensively, modestly, plainly, sedately, soberly, unobtrusively, unpretentiously; demurely, meekly, shyly.

quilt
n lit: duvet, eiderdown; padded bedspread, padded coverlet.

quintessential
adj lit: constitutional, fundamental, intrinsic; most perfect, purest; most necessary, most significant, most specific.

quip
n lit: gag, jest, joke, pleasantry, pun, riposte, wisecrack, witticism.
vb lit: banter, be facetious, be funny, jest, joke, wisecrack.

quirk
n lit: caprice, dodge, trick, twist, vagary, whim; eccentricity, foible, kink, oddity, peculiarity, singularity; flourish; *spec*: angled groove (in architecture).

quirky
adj lit: capricious, eccentric, idiosyncratic, odd, peculiar, singular, tricky, twisted, whimsical.

quit
vb lit: depart, exit, go, leave, pull out; depart from, exit from, go from, pull out from; abandon, desert, forsake, renounce; resign, retire; cease, discontinue, drop, end, halt, stop, suspend; give up, surrender, yield; pay off, repay, settle; absolve, discharge, free, remit.
adj lit: clear (of), free (of), rid (of); absolved, discharged.

quite
adv lit: fairly, moderately, rather, reasonably, relatively, somewhat; absolutely, completely, entirely, fully, perfectly, totally, wholly; indeed, exactly, precisely; actually, definitely, positively, really, truly.

quiver
n lit: palpitation, shake, shiver, shudder, spasm, tic, tremor, tremulousness, vibration; *spec*: arrow-case, arrow-holder.
vb lit: quail, quake, quaver, shake, shiver, shudder, tremble; flutter, oscillate, vibrate.

quiz
n lit: examination, interrogation, test.
vb lit: ask questions, grill, interrogate, question; examine, test.

quota
n lit: allocation, allowance, cut, helping, part, portion, proportion, ration, share, slice, whack.

quotation
n lit: allusion, excerpt, extract, passage, reference; citing, recital, repetition; *fig*: cost, estimate, price, quote, rate, tender; *spec*: company registration, share price (on the stock exchange).

quote
n lit: allusion, quotation, reference, repetition; inverted comma, quotation mark; *fig*: cost, estimate, price, rate, tender.
vb lit: adduce, allude to, cite, declaim, instance, recite, refer to, repeat the words of; put in inverted commas; *fig*: give an estimate (for), put a price (on), tender (for); *spec*: state the market price (of shares or bonds).

quotidian
adj lit: circadian, daily, once a day; commonplace, everyday, normal, ordinary, usual.

R

rabbit
n lit: bunny; hare; *fig*: greenhorn, weakling, wimp.
vb fig: chatter, gabble, gossip, jabber, prattle, talk incessantly, witter (on).

rabble
n lit: crowd, mob, throng; populace; commoners, hoi polloi, masses, proletariat, riffraff.

rabid
adj lit: hydrophobic, maddened; *fig*: berserk, crazed, frantic, frenzied, furious, mad, raging, violent; bigoted, extreme, fanatical, fervent, intemperate, intolerant, irrational, zealous.

race
n lit: chase, dash, sprint; competition, contest; blood, breed, clan, ethnic group, nation, people, stock.
vb lit: career, dart, dash, fly, gallop, hurtle, speed, tear, zip, zoom; compete (against), contest (against), run (against).

racial
adj lit: ethnic, ethnological, national, tribal.

rack
n lit: frame, stand, structure, trestle; griddle, grille; ratchet; *fig*: torment, torture.
vb lit: afflict, agonize, crucify, harrow, oppress, torture; force, pull, shake, stress, stretch, tear, wrench.

racket
n lit: ballyhoo, commotion, din, disturbance, fuss, hubbub, hullabaloo, noise, pandemonium, row, tumult, uproar; fraud, ramp, swindle; business, game, line.

racy
adj lit: animated, entertaining, exciting, exhilarating, lively, spirited, stimulating, vigorous; distinctive, piquant, spicy, strong, tangy, tasty; bawdy, blue, immodest, indecent, naughty, risqué, suggestive.

radiant
adj lit: beaming, brilliant, effulgent, gleaming, glittering, incandescent, luminous, resplendent, shining, sparkling; blissful, delighted, ecstatic, glowing, joyful, rapturous.

radiate
vb lit: diffuse, emit, give off, scatter, send out, spread; branch out, diverge, spread out; gleam, glitter, light; heat.

radical
n lit: extremist, fanatic, militant, revolutionary.
adj lit: constitutional, innate, natural, organic; basic, fundamental, profound, thoroughgoing; complete, entire, excessive, extreme, severe, sweeping, thorough; extremist, militant, revolutionary.

rag
n lit: cloth, remnant, scrap, shred, tatter; jape, lark, practical joke, prank; ragtime music; roofing-slate; *fig*: (lose one's) temper.
vb lit: abrade, become frayed, become tattered, fray; *fig*: make fun of, play jokes on, tease; scold.

rage
n lit: anger, fury, heat, ire, passion, wrath; craze, obsession; fad, latest, mode, vogue.
vb lit: be beside oneself, blow one's top, fume, rave, seethe; blow, rampage, storm, surge.

ragged
adj lit: abraded, frayed, shabby, tattered, threadbare, torn, unkempt; broken, irregular, jagged, rough, serrated, uneven; crude, unfinished; jeered, mocked, tcased.

raid
n lit: attack, incursion, invasion, onset, onslaught, sally; foray, sortie; break-in; ambush.
vb lit: assault, attack, despoil, invade, maraud, pillage, plunder, rifle, sack; break into, get into.

rail

n lit: bar, barrier, fence; balustrade, banister; line, railway track.
vb lit: enclose, fence round, hem in; rant (at), shout (at), yell (at).

railing

n lit: balustrade, barrier, enclosure, fence, palings; ranting, shouting, yelling.

rain

n lit: cloudburst, downpour, drizzle, shower; deluge, flood, torrent; cascade, fountain, spray.
vb lit: bucket down, drizzle, pour, sheet down, shower, teem; cascade, drop, fall, fountain, spray, sprinkle; *fig*: bestow, lavish.

raise

vb lit: build, construct, erect, put up, set up; heave, hoist, lift; bring up, foster, rear; breed, cultivate, develop, grow, nurture, produce, propagate; augment, boost, enlarge, escalate, heighten, increase, intensify, strengthen; elevate, exalt, promote, upgrade; activate, arouse, excite, foment, incite, instigate, motivate, provoke, stir up, whip up; bring about, cause, create, give rise to, occasion, originate, start; advance, broach, introduce, put forward, suggest; assemble, form, gather, levy, mass, muster, obtain, rally, recruit; *spec*: abandon, give up, relieve, remove (a siege).

rake

n lit: harrow, hoe; gradient, incline, slant, slope; debauchee, lecher, libertine, playboy, profligate.
vb lit: collect, gather, scrape up; break up, harrow, hoe, scour, scrape; claw, graze, scratch; comb, cover, examine, scan, scrutinize, search, sweep; *fig*: dig (up), dredge (up); scrape (together).

rake-off

n lit: commission, portion, share; bribe, protection money, slush fund.

rally

n lit: assembly, congregation, convention, gathering, mass meeting, muster; reformation, regrouping, reorganization, stand; improvement, recovery, renewal, resurgence, revival; road-race.
vb lit: assemble, convene, gather, get together, mobilize, muster, organize, round up, summon, unite; reassemble, reform, regroup, reorganize; come

round, get better, improve, perk up, recover, revive.

ram

n lit: male sheep; piston, plunger; pump; battering-ram; *spec*: beak (of a warship).
vb lit: butt, collide with, crash into, drive (home), run into; cram, drum, force, hammer, jam, pack, pound, tamp, thrust.

ramble

n lit: excursion, hike, perambulation, promenade, saunter, stroll, walk.
vb lit: amble, perambulate, roam, rove, saunter, stray, stroll, walk, wander; meander, wind, zigzag; babble, chatter, digress, maunder, rabbit on, rattle on.

rambling

adj lit: circuitous, convoluted, meandering, sinuous, tortuous, winding; digressive, disconnected, incoherent, long-winded, periphrastic, wordy; irregular, sprawling, straggling, trailing.

ramifications

n lit: developments, divisions, extensions, intricacies, offshoots, subdivisions; complexities, complications, consequences, results, sequel, upshot.

ramp

n lit: gradient, incline, rise, slope; con, fraud, swindle.

rampage

vb lit: be beside oneself, go berserk, rage, rant, rave, run amok, run riot, storm, tear.

rampant

adj lit: dominant, raging, riotous, uncontrollable, unrestrained, wild; epidemic, exuberant, profuse, rife, unchecked, widespread; erect, rearing, upright.

rampart

n lit: bastion, bulwark, defence, earthwork, embankment, fortification, parapet, wall.

ramshackle

adj lit: crumbling, derelict, dilapidated, flimsy, rickety, shabby, shoddy, tottering, tumbledown, unsteady.

rancid

adj lit: bad, foetid, foul, off, putrescent, putrid, rotten, smelly, sour, stale.

rancour

n lit: animosity, bad feeling, hostility, ill will, malice, resentment.

random

adj lit: arbitrary, casual, chance, fortuitous, haphazard, indiscriminate, unpremeditated; aimless, purposeless; spot.

range

n lit: area, bounds, compass, confines, domain, extent, limits, orbit, province, radius, reach, scope, sphere, sweep; chain, file, line, rank, row, series, string; assortment, gamut, kind, lot, selection, sort, variety.

vb lit: align, array, dispose, draw up, order; arrange, bracket, catalogue, classify, file, grade, group, rank; aim, direct, level, point, train; cruise, explore, ramble, roam, straggle, stray, stroll, wander; extend, fluctuate, go, reach, stretch, vary (between).

rank

n lit: caste, classification, division, grade, level, order, position, quality, standing, station, status, type; column, formation, group, line, row, series.

vb lit: align, arrange, array, classify, grade, line up, marshal, order, position, range, sort.

adj lit: abundant, dense, lush, productive, profuse, vigorous; bad, foetid, foul, fusty, noxious, off, offensive, pungent, rancid, stale, stinking; absolute, blatant, downright, excessive, flagrant, gross, rampant, sheer, total, unmitigated, utter; abusive, atrocious, coarse, filthy, gross, indecent, obscene, outrageous, scurrilous, vulgar.

ransack

vb lit: comb, go through, rummage through, scour, search; despoil, empty, gut, loot, pillage, plunder, raid, ravage.

ransom

n lit: redemption, surety; payment, price; blackmail, payoff.

vb lit: buy out, redeem; *fig*: liberate, rescue, set free.

rap

n lit: blow, knock, tap; *fig*: blame, punishment, rebuke, reproof; conviction, prison sentence; atom, jot, whit; *spec*: skein (of yarn).

vb lit: knock, tap, strike; censure, condemn, criticize, rebuke, reprove.

rapacious

adj lit: avaricious, extortionate, ferocious, grabbing, grasping, greedy, insatiable, predatory, ravenous, voracious.

rape

n lit: ravishment, sexual assault, violation; defilement, defloration; abuse, maltreatment; *fig*: depredation, despoliation, looting, pillage, plundering, ransacking, stripping.

vb lit: outrage, ravish, sexually assault, violate; *fig*: despoil, loot, pillage, plunder, ransack, strip.

rapid

adj lit: expeditious, express, fast, hasty, prompt, quick, speedy, swift.

rapidity

n lit: alacrity, briskness, celerity, dispatch, haste, promptitude, quickness, speed.

rapine

n lit: looting, pillage, plundering, ransacking, robbery.

rapt

adj lit: absorbed, enthralled, fascinated, gripped, intent, spellbound; blissful, captivated, charmed, delighted, enchanted, ravished, transported.

rapture

n lit: bliss, ecstasy, exaltation, happiness, joy, ravishment, trance, transport.

rare

adj lit: exceptional, infrequent, scarce, singular, sparse, sporadic, uncommon, unusual; admirable, excellent, exquisite, extreme, fine, incomparable, superb, superlative; invaluable, precious, priceless.

rarefy

vb lit: become less dense, purify, refine, thin, weaken; make subtle.

rarity

n lit: curiosity, find, gem, treasure; infrequency, paucity, scarcity, sparseness, uncommonness; excellence, exquisiteness, fineness, individual quality; preciousness, richness, value, worth.

rash
n lit: eruption, inflammation; outbreak; *fig*:
epidemic, flood, plague, series, spate,
succession.
adj lit: adventurous, audacious, brash,
foolhardy, harebrained, hasty,
headstrong, heedless, hot-headed, ill-
advised, impetuous, impulsive,
indiscreet, injudicious, madcap,
premature, reckless, thoughtless,
unthinking.

rasp
n lit: file, grater; grating, grinding, scrape.
vb lit: abrade, file, grind, rub, sand, scour,
scrape; *fig*: irk, irritate, set one's teeth on
edge, wear upon.

rate
n lit: degree, percentage, proportion, ratio,
scale; charge, cost, duty, fee, price, tariff,
tax, toll; gait, pace, speed, time, velocity.
vb lit: adjudge, appraise, assess, classify,
count, evaluate, grade, rank, reckon,
value, weigh; be worthy of, deserve,
merit; admire, respect, think highly of.

rather
adv lit: a bit, a little, fairly, pretty, quite,
relatively, slightly, somewhat, to some
extent; noticeably, significantly, very;
more preferably, sooner; instead.

ratify
vb lit: affirm, approve, authorize, bear out,
bind, confirm, consent to, corroborate,
endorse, sanction, uphold, validate.

ration
n lit: allotment, allowance, dole, helping,
portion, quota, share; provision(s),
store(s), victual(s).
vb lit: allocate (out), apportion (out), deal
(out), distribute (out), dole (out), give
(out), mete (out); budget, control, limit,
restrict.

rational
adj lit: intelligent, judicious, logical, lucid,
realistic, reasonable, sensible, sound;
cognitive, reasoning, thinking; all there,
balanced, conscious, in one's right mind,
lucid, sane.

rationale
n lit: grounds, logic, motivation,
philosophy, principle, reason, theory.

rationalize
vb lit: account for, excuse, extenuate,
justify, make allowance for, vindicate;
elucidate, reason out, resolve, think

through; cut back on, make cost-
effective, make cuts in, streamline, trim.

rattle
n lit: knock, knocking, pinking, rasp;
castanet, maraca; clatter, racket, uproar;
chatter, gossip, prattle.
vb lit: bang, clatter, jangle; bounce, jiggle,
jolt, shake, vibrate; chatter, gabble,
prattle, rabbit on, run on, witter;
disconcert, discountenance, disturb,
perturb, scare, shake, upset; reel (off),
recite (off), run (through).

raucous
adj lit: grating, harsh, hoarse, husky, loud,
noisy, rasping, rough.

raunchy
adj lit: bawdy, blue, dirty, obscene; erotic,
sexy, titillating; coarse, vulgar; shoddy.

ravage
n lit: damage, desolation, destruction,
devastation, havoc, pillage, plunder,
ruin(s), waste.
vb lit: demolish, desolate, destroy, lay
waste, loot, pillage, plunder, ransack,
raze, ruin, sack, shatter, wreck.

rave
n lit: acclaim, applause, praise;
celebration, do, party, thrash; craze,
fashion, vogue.
vb lit: babble, fume, rage, rant, roar,
seethe, splutter, thunder; be mad
(about), be wild (about), enthuse (about),
rhapsodize (over).
adj lit: acclamatory, commendatory,
ecstatic, enthusiastic, excellent,
laudatory.

ravenous
adj lit: famished, hungry, starved; *fig*:
avaricious, covetous, devouring,
ferocious, gluttonous, grasping, greedy,
rapacious, voracious.

ravine
n lit: canyon, chasm, chine, cliff, gorge,
gully, precipice, rift.

raving
adj (pr.pt) lit: berserk, crazy, delirious,
frantic, frenzied, hysterical, irrational,
out of one's mind, rabid.

ravishing
adj (pr.pt) lit: bewitching, charming,
dazzling, delightful, enchanting,
gorgeous, radiant, stunning.

raw
adj lit: bloody, fresh, uncooked,
unprepared; basic, coarse, crude, natural,
organic, rough, unrefined, untreated;
abraded, grazed, open, scratched, sore,
tender; callow, green, ignorant,
immature, inexperienced, new,
unskilled, untrained; blunt, brutal,
candid, frank, naked, plain, realistic,
unembellished; biting, bitter, bleak,
chilly, cold, freezing, harsh, piercing.

reach
n lit: capacity, compass, distance,
extension, extent, grasp, influence,
jurisdiction, power, range, scope, spread,
stretch.
vb lit: arrive at, attain, get to, make; extend
to, get hold of, grasp, stretch to, touch;
hand, hold (out), pass, stretch (out);
amount to, come to; go down to, fall to;
climb to, rise to; contact, find, get
through to, make contact with.

reaction
n lit: recoil, response; acknowledgment,
answer, feedback, reply; conservatism.

reactionary
n lit: counter-revolutionary, die-hard,
obscurantist, right-winger.
adj lit: conservative, counter-
revolutionary, rightist.

read
vb lit: look at, peruse, pore over, study;
comprehend, construe, decipher,
discover, interpret, perceive, see; deliver,
recite; display, indicate, record, register,
show.

readily
adv lit: eagerly, gladly, voluntarily,
willingly; at once, immediately,
promptly, quickly; easily, smoothly.

reading
n lit: examination, perusal, scrutiny,
study; concept, grasp, interpretation,
rendition, treatment, understanding,
version; education, erudition,
knowledge, learning, scholarship;
homily, lecture, lesson, recital, sermon.

ready
vb lit: arrange, equip, fit out, organize,
prepare, set up (for); nerve (oneself),
steel (oneself).
adj lit: arranged, fit, organized, prepared,
set; mature, ripe; agreeable, eager, game,
glad, inclined, keen, minded, prone,

willing; acute, alert, apt, astute, bright,
clever, deft, dextrous, perceptive,
prompt, quick-witted, resourceful,
sharp, skilful; about, close, near; to hand;
liable (to), likely (to).

real
adj lit: absolute, actual, authentic,
existent, factual, genuine, heartfelt,
intrinsic, legitimate, positive, rightful,
sincere, true, unfeigned, valid, veritable.

realistic
adj lit: businesslike, commonsense, down-
to-earth, level-headed, matter-of-fact,
practical, rational, sensible,
unsentimental; accurate, authentic,
lifelike, naturalistic, true-to-life.

realize
vb lit: appreciate, apprehend, become
aware of, catch on, comprehend,
conceive, grasp, recognize, take in,
understand; accomplish, bring about,
carry out, complete, consummate, do,
effect, fulfil, perform; bring in, earn,
fetch, go for, make, net, sell for.

really
adv lit: absolutely, actually, assuredly,
categorically, certainly, genuinely,
indeed, in fact, positively, truly,
undoubtedly.

realm
n lit: country, domain, dominion, land,
region, territory; area, department, field,
province, sphere, world.

reap
vb lit: gather, glean, harvest; cut, mow,
shear, trim; derive, gain, get, obtain.

rear
n lit: aft, back, back end, stern, tail;
backside, behind, bottom, bum,
posterior, seat.
vb lit: breed, bring up, care for, cultivate,
foster, grow, nurse, nurture, raise, train;
build, construct, erect; stand upright; lift
up; loom, rise, soar, tower.
adj lit: aft, back, following, hindmost, last.

rearrange
vb lit: move, realign, redeploy, redispose,
relocate, reorder, reposition; alter,
change, turn round; decorate, refurnish,
renovate; reorganize, reschedule, reset.

reason
n lit: apprehension, comprehension, intellect, logic, mentality, mind, rationality, reasoning, sanity, soundness, understanding; basis, cause, grounds, occasion, purpose; argument, defence, excuse, explanation, ground, justification, rationale, vindication; aim, end, goal, incentive, inducement, motive, object, target; moderation, propriety, sense, wisdom.
vb lit: conclude, deduce, infer, make out, think, work out; argue (with), debate (with), dispute (with), expostulate (with).

reasonable
adj lit: advisable, believable, credible, intelligent, justifiable, logical, plausible, practical, rational, sensible, sound, tenable, well-advised, wise; acceptable, equitable, fair, fit, honest, inexpensive, just, moderate, modest, proper, right, within reason.

reasoning
n lit: analysis, cogitation, deduction, logic, thinking, thought; argument, case, exposition, hypothesis, interpretation.

reassurance
n lit: backing, bolstering, boost, cheering-up, comfort, encouragement, moral support, support.

rebate
n lit: deduction, discount, reduction; refund, repayment; credit.

rebel
n lit: insurgent, mutineer, revolutionary, secessionist; dissenter, heretic, nonconformist, renegade, schismatic; anarchist; eccentric, weirdo.
vb lit: mutiny, resist, revolt, rise up, take to the streets; come out against, defy, disobey, dissent; recoil, show repugnance, shy away.

rebellious
adj lit: defiant, disloyal, insubordinate, insurgent, intractable, mutinous, revolutionary, seditious, subversive; disobedient, naughty; difficult, obstinate, recalcitrant, refractory, wilful.

rebirth
n lit: regeneration, reincarnation, renaissance, renewal, restoration, resurgence, resurrection, revival.

rebound
n lit: bounce, return; deflection, ricochet; echo, reverberation; backfire, recoil, whiplash.
vb lit: bounce, return, ricochet; echo, resound, reverberate; backfire, boomerang, recoil, whiplash.

rebuff
n lit: brush-off, cold shoulder, discouragement, refusal, rejection, repulse, slight, snub; setback.
vb lit: brush off, cut, discourage, put off, reject, repulse, snub, spurn, turn down.

rebut
vb lit: contradict, deny, dispute, refute, throw back in one's face.

rebuke
n lit: carpeting, reprimand, reproach, reproof, telling-off, ticking-off, tongue-lashing.
vb lit: castigate, censure, chide, lecture, reprimand, reproach, reprove, scold, take to task, tell off, tick off, upbraid.

recalcitrant
adj lit: defiant, difficult, disobedient, insubordinate, intractable, obstinate, refractory, stubborn, unmanageable, unruly, wayward, wilful.

recall
n lit: summons; memory, recollection, remembrance, retrieval; repeal, retraction, withdrawal.
vb lit: bring back, call back, summon; bring to mind, recollect, remember, reminisce about, revive one's memory of; renew, revive; be reminiscent of, hark back to; repeal, retract, withdraw.

recapitulate
vb lit: go over again, reiterate, repeat, run through again; paraphrase, summarize, sum up.

recede
vb lit: abate, draw back, ebb, go back, regress, retire, retreat, return, subside, withdraw; decline, diminish, dwindle, lessen, shrink, wane.

receipt
n lit: acknowledgement, counterfoil, proof of purchase; acceptance, reception; gain(s), proceed(s), profit(s), taking(s).

receive
vb lit: accept, acquire, be given, get, obtain, take; have, own, possess; accommodate, admit, entertain, incorporate, meet, take in, welcome; *fig*: sustain, undergo.

recent
adj lit: contemporary, current, late, new, present-day, up-to-date.

reception
n lit: acceptance, acquisition, receipt; greeting, recognition, response, welcome; do, function, levée, party, soirée.

receptive
adj lit: alert, enthusiastic, keen, responsive, sensitive; accessible, amenable, approachable, friendly, sympathetic, welcoming.

recess
n lit: alcove, bay, cavity, depression, indentation, niche, nook; adjournment, break, holiday, intermission, interval, respite, rest.
vb lit: set back, adjourn, take a break, take time off.

recession
n lit: decline, depression, slackening, slump; departure, fading, waning.

recipe
n lit: constituents, formula, ingredients, instructions, method, prescription, procedure, technique.

reciprocate
vb lit: exchange, interchange, requite, return the compliment, swap; do the equivalent, do the same; correspond, equal, match.

recital
n lit: account, narrative, performance, reading, relation, rendering, rendition, story, tale, telling; cataloguing, enumeration, listing.

recite
vb lit: declaim, deliver, narrate, perform, recount, relate, repeat, tell; catalogue, detail, enumerate, list.

reckless
adj lit: careless, daredevil, foolhardy, heedless, imprudent, incautious, indiscreet, madcap, mindless, negligent, precipitate, rash, thoughtless.

reckon
vb lit: add up, calculate, count, figure, number, tally, total; assess as, consider, deem, evaluate as, hold, judge, regard, think of; assume, believe, conjecture, expect, guess, imagine, suppose, surmise, think; cope (with), deal (with), settle accounts (with); bank (on), count (on), depend (on), rely (on).

recline
vb lit: be recumbent, lean, lie down, loll, lounge, repose, sprawl, stretch out.

recognize
vb lit: identify, know, make out, place, recall, remember, spot; accept, acknowledge, admit, allow, be aware of, concede, grant, own, perceive, realize, see, understand; appreciate, approve, honour, salute.

recoil
n lit: backlash, rebound.
vb lit: jerk back, react, rebound; flinch, quail, shy away; backfire, boomerang.

recommend
vb lit: approve, commend, praise, speak well of, vouch for; advise, advocate, counsel, urge; advance, propose, suggest; be in one's favour, promote.

reconcile
vb lit: accustom (oneself to), resign (oneself to); bring to terms, restore harmony between; adjust, patch up, rectify, resolve, settle, square; fit, match, suit, tally, tie in.

reconnoitre
vb lit: explore, inspect, investigate, observe, patrol, scan, scrutinize, survey.

reconstruct
vb lit: reassemble, rebuild, recreate, renovate, reorganize, restore; build up, deduce, piece together.

record
n lit: account, annals, archives, chronicle, document, entry, file, log, memorandum, minute, register, report; documentation, evidence, remembrance, testimony, trace; background, curriculum vitae, performance; best performance, best time; album, disc, platter, release, single.
vb lit: chronicle, document, enrol, enter, log, minute, note, put down, register, transcribe, write down; contain, indicate, read, say, show; cut, make a recording of, tape, video-tape.

recover

vb lit: find, get back, recapture, reclaim, recoup, regain, restore, retrieve, win back; come round, get well, heal, improve, mend, pull through, rally, regain one's strength, revive; convalesce, recuperate.

recovery

n lit: recapture, reclamation, repossession, restoration, retrieval; convalescence, healing, mending, recuperation; improvement, rehabilitation, restoration, revival, upturn.

recreation

n lit: amusement, distraction, diversion, enjoyment, entertainment, leisure activity, pastime, pleasure, relaxation.

recrimination

n lit: bickering, blaming, in-fighting, squabbling.

recruit

n lit: apprentice, beginner, convert, initiate, novice, proselyte, trainee.
vb lit: draft, enlist, enrol, levy, mobilize, muster, raise; engage, gather, obtain, procure, round up, take on; augment, build up, reinforce, replenish, restore, strengthen, supply.

rectify

vb lit: adjust, amend, correct, emend, fix, mend, put right, remedy, repair, right, square; *spec*: distil, purify, refine.

recur

vb lit: come up again, happen again, persist, repeat, return; be remembered, come back, return to mind, run through one's mind.

red

adj lit: carmine, coral, crimson, maroon, pink, ruby, scarlet, vermilion; bay, chestnut, flaming, sandy, titian; blushing, embarrassed, flushed, rubicund, shamefaced, suffused; blooming, glowing, healthy, rosy, ruddy; bloodshot, inflamed; bloodstained, gory, sanguine.

redeem

vb lit: buy back, reclaim, regain, repossess, retrieve, win back; cash (in), exchange, trade in; abide by, acquit, adhere to, carry out, discharge, fulfil, keep, meet, satisfy; absolve, rehabilitate, reinstate; atone for, compensate for, make up for, offset, redress; deliver, emancipate,

extricate, free, liberate, ransom, rescue, save, set free.

redolent

adj lit: aromatic, fragrant, odoriferous; smelling (of); *fig*: reminiscent (of), suggestive (of).

redress

n lit: aid, correction, cure, help, justice, rectification, relief, remedy, satisfaction; amends, atonement, compensation, quittance, recompense, reparation, restitution.
vb lit: compensate for, make amends for, make up for, pay for, recompense for; adjust, balance, correct, even up, mend, rectify, reform, relieve, remedy, repair.

reduce

vb lit: abate, contract, curtail, cut down, decrease, dilute, diminish, impair, lessen, slow down, truncate, weaken; bankrupt, impoverish, ruin; bring, drive, force, subdue, vanquish; lose weight, shed weight, slim; cut, discount, lower, mark down, slash; bring low, degrade, demote, downgrade, humble.

redundant

adj lit: excess, inessential, inordinate, superfluous, surplus, unnecessary, useless; diffuse, repetitious, tautological, verbose.

reel

n lit: frame, roller, spool; lurch, roll, stagger, sway; jig.
vb lit: falter, lurch, pitch, rock, stumble, totter, wobble; revolve, spin, swirl, twirl, whirl; wind (in).

refer

vb lit: allude (to); direct, guide, point, recommend; apply (to), turn (to); be directed (to), pertain (to), relate (to); attribute, credit, impute, put down (to); commit, consign, hand over, pass on, transfer.

referee

n lit: adjudicator, arbitrator, judge, umpire.
vb lit: adjudicate, arbitrate, judge, umpire.

reference

n lit: allusion (to); applicability, connection, regard, relation; credential(s), endorsement, recommendation, testimonial.

refined
adj lit: civilized, cultured, genteel, gracious, polished, sophisticated, urbane, well-mannered; discerning, discriminating, exact, fastidious, nice, precise, punctilious, subtle; clarified, distilled, filtered, pure, purified.

refinement
n lit: clarification, cleansing, distillation, filtering, processing, purification; nicety, nuance, subtlety; civility, courtesy, cultivation, delicacy, discrimination, fastidiousness, finesse, gentility, good manners, graciousness, polish, sophistication, style, taste.

reflect
vb lit: echo, imitate, mirror; cogitate, contemplate, deliberate, meditate, mull over, ponder, ruminate, think; communicate, demonstrate, display, exhibit, express, indicate, manifest, reveal.

reform
n lit: amendment, correction, improvement, rectification, rehabilitation.
vb lit: amend, better, correct, emend, mend, reconstruct, rectify, rehabilitate, renovate, reorganize, repair, restore; go straight, turn over a new leaf.

refractory
adj lit: difficult, obstinate, rebellious, recalcitrant, stubborn, unmanageable, wilful.

refrain
n lit: chorus; burden, ground; repetition.
vb lit: abstain (from), hold back (from), keep (from), withhold (from).

refreshing
adj lit: bracing, cooling, fresh, invigorating, thirst-quenching; novel, original, stimulating.

refuge
n lit: asylum, haven, hide-out, retreat, sanctuary, shelter.

refugee
n lit: émigré, exile, fugitive; outcast, stateless person.

refund
n lit: rebate, reimbursement, repayment.
vb lit: give back, reimburse, repay, restore, return.

refurbish
vb lit: do up, mend, refit, renovate, revamp, spruce up.

refuse
n lit: debris, garbage, litter, rubbish, trash, waste; offal; detritus, parings; scrap.
vb lit: decline, negate, reject, repudiate, spurn, turn down, veto, withhold.

refute
vb lit: counter, discredit, disprove, negate, prove false, rebut.

regal
adj lit: august, grand, majestic, noble, princely, royal, sovereign, stately.

regard
n lit: gaze, look, scrutiny, stare; attention, heed, notice; affection, attachment, concern, consideration, esteem, love, respect, sympathy, thought; aspect, detail, item, matter, particular, point; bearing, connection, reference, relation, relevance; best wish(es), compliment(s), greeting(s), respect(s).
vb lit: behold, gaze at, observe, scrutinize, watch; consider, esteem, hold, look upon, rate, think, view; apply to, be relevant to, have to do with, pertain to, relate to; attend, heed, listen to, mind, note, pay attention to, take notice of.

regarding
prp lit: about, apropos, as to, concerning, with regard to, in the matter of, respecting, with reference to.

regime
n lit: administration, establishment, government, leadership, reign, rule.

region
n lit: area, district, division, part, section, sector, territory, zone; locality, range, scope, vicinity; domain, field, sphere.

register
n lit: annals, archives, chronicle, file, list, memorandum, record, roll, roster, schedule.
vb lit: catalogue, check in, chronicle, enlist, enrol, enter, list, note, record, sign on, take down; display, express, indicate, manifest, record, reflect, reveal, show; *fig*: dawn on, get through, have an effect, sink in.

regress
vb lit: degenerate, deteriorate, ebb, go back, lapse, recede, retreat, retrogress, revert, wane.

regret
n lit: bitterness, compunction, contrition, disappointment, grief, remorse, repentance, ruefulness, self-reproach.
vb lit: bemoan, be upset, deplore, grieve, lament, mourn, repent, rue.

regretfully
adv lit: apologetically, remorsefully, repentantly, sadly, sorrowfully.

regrettably
adv lit: deplorably, disappointingly, distressingly, unfortunately, unhappily.

regular
adj lit: commonplace, customary, everyday, habitual, normal, ordinary, routine, typical, usual; consistent, constant, even, fixed, ordered, periodic, rhythmic, set, steady; dependable, efficient, methodical, orderly, standardized, systematic; balanced, flat, level, smooth, straight, symmetrical; approved, correct, established, formal, official, orthodox, prevailing, proper, standard, traditional.

regulate
vb lit: adjust, administer, arrange, control, direct, fit, handle, manage, moderate, monitor, organize, rule, run, supervise, systematize.

regulation
n lit: decree, dictate, edict, law, order, ordinance, procedure, requirement, rule, statute; administration, government, management, supervision; adjustment, arrangement, control, modulation.
adj lit: customary, normal, official, required, standard, usual.

rehearse
vb lit: act, drill, go over, practise, prepare, run through, train, try out.

reign
n lit: ascendancy, command, dominion, hegemony, power, rule, sovereignty, supremacy, sway.
vb lit: be sovereign (over), hold sway (over), rule (over); be rampant (over), predominate, prevail.

rein
n lit: bridle, control, curb; check, restraint, restriction.
vb lit: control, curb, steer; hold (back), hold (in).

reincarnation
n lit: metempsychosis, rebirth, transmigration of souls; recycling; *fig*: rebirth, rejuvenation, renaissance, renovation.

reinforce
vb lit: augment, bolster, buttress, fortify, harden, prop, strengthen, supplement, support, toughen.

reject
n lit: castoff, discard, second.
vb lit: ban, bar, cast aside, discard, eliminate, exclude, rebuff, repulse, scrap, spurn, throw out, turn down, veto.

rejoicing
n lit: celebration, cheer, elation, exultation, gladness, happiness, jubilation, triumph.
adj (pr.pt) lit: celebrating, elated, exalted, exultant, glad, happy, joyful, joyous, jubilant, triumphant.

rejoinder
n lit: answer, counter, response, retort, return, riposte.

relapse
n lit: backsliding, fall from grace, lapse, regression, retrogression, reversion; deterioration, recurrence, setback, worsening.
vb lit: backslide, degenerate, fail, lapse, regress, revert, slip back, weaken; deteriorate, fade, sink, worsen.

relate
vb lit: chronicle, describe, detail, impart, narrate, present, recite, report, tell; ally, associate, coordinate, correlate, join, link; be allied (to), be cognate (to), be kin (to); appertain, apply, be relevant (to), pertain, refer.

related
adj lit: accompanying, affiliated, allied, associated, connected, joint, linked; akin, cognate, consanguineous, kindred.

relationship
n lit: affair, association, bond, connection, exchange, kinship, liaison, parallel, rapport, similarity.

relative
n lit: kinsman, kinswoman, member of the family, relation.
adj lit: allied, associated, comparative, contingent, corresponding, dependent, proportionate, reciprocal, related, respective; in proportion (to), proportional (to).

relax
vb lit: abate, diminish, ease, loosen, lower, mitigate, reduce, relieve, slacken; flop, let oneself go, loosen up, rest, take it easy, unbend, unwind.

relaxation
n lit: amusement, enjoyment, entertainment, leisure, recreation, refreshment; abatement, easing, let-up, reduction, slackening, weakening.

relay
n lit: relief, shift, turn; communication, dispatch, message, transmission.
vb lit: broadcast, communicate, hand on, pass on, send, transmit.

release
n lit: acquittal, deliverance, discharge, emancipation, liberation, liberty, relief; absolution, acquittance, dispensation, exemption, exoneration, let-off; announcement, issue, proclamation, publication.
vb lit: discharge, disengage, drop, emancipate, extricate, let out, liberate, set free, turn loose, unchain, undo, unshackle, untie; absolve, acquit, dispense, excuse, exempt, exonerate, let off; break, circulate, distribute, issue, launch, make public, present, publish, put out.

relegate
vb lit: demote, downgrade, transfer downwards; leave (to the end).

relentless
adj lit: fierce, grim, harsh, implacable, inexorable, inflexible, merciless, pitiless, ruthless, uncompromising, unrelenting, unyielding; incessant, persistent, punishing, sustained, unabated, unfaltering, unremitting, unstoppable.

relevant
adj lit: admissible, applicable, appropriate, appurtenant, fitting, material, pertinent, proper, related, significant, to the point.

reliable
adj lit: dependable, faithful, predictable, regular, safe, sound, stable, true, trustworthy, upright.

relief
n lit: abatement, alleviation, comfort, cure, deliverance, easement, mitigation, release, remedy, solace; aid, assistance, help, succour, support, sustenance; break, breather, relaxation, respite, rest; distraction, diversion.

relieve
vb lit: abate, alleviate, appease, calm, comfort, console, diminish, dull, ease, mollify, palliate, salve, soften, soothe; aid, assist, help, succour, support, sustain; stand in for, substitute for, take over from; deliver, discharge, exempt, release, unburden; break, interrupt, slacken, vary.

religious
adj lit: devout, doctrinal, faithful, god-fearing, pious, reverent, sectarian, spiritual, theological; *fig*: conscientious, exact, fastidious, meticulous, punctilious, rigid, scrupulous, unswerving.

relinquish
vb lit: give up, let go, loose hold of, release; abandon, surrender; renounce, resign.

relish
n lit: appetite, appreciation, enjoyment, fondness, gusto, liking, partiality, penchant, predilection, taste, zest; flavour, piquancy, savour, smack, tang, trace; appetizer, chutney, condiment, sauce.
vb lit: appreciate, enjoy, fancy, like, like the taste of, revel in, savour.

reluctant
adj lit: averse, disinclined, grudging, hesitant, loath, recalcitrant, unenthusiastic, unwilling.

rely on
vb lit: bank on, be confident of, bet on, count on, depend on, lean on, reckon on, swear by, trust in.

remain
vb lit: continue, go on, last, persist, prevail, stand, stay, survive, wait; dwell, live, stop; be left, be over.

remainder

n lit: balance, remnant, residue, rest, surplus.

remains

n lit: crumbs, debris, fragments, leftovers, oddments, pieces, relics, remainder, residue, scraps, vestiges; bones, carcass, corpse, skeleton; hulk, ruins, shell, wreckage.

remark

n lit: aside, assertion, comment, observation, statement, utterance, word; acknowledgement, attention, consideration, heed, mention, notice, recognition, regard, thought.
vb lit: comment, mention, observe, say; espy, heed, make out, mark, notice, perceive, regard, see, take note of.

remarkable

adj lit: conspicuous, distinguished, impressive, notable, noteworthy, outstanding, pre-eminent, prominent; extraordinary, singular, striking, uncommon, unusual.

remedy

n lit: antidote, cure, medicament, medicine, panacea; corrective, countermeasure, redress, solution.
vb lit: alleviate, cure, ease, heal, palliate, relieve, restore, soothe; correct, fix, rectify, redress, repair, solve.

remember

vb lit: bear in mind, look back (on), recall, recollect, relive, reminisce, retain, think back.

reminder

n lit: alarm, bleeper; knot; memo, memorandum; keepsake, memento, souvenir.

reminiscence

n lit: echo from the past, memoir, memory, recollection, remembrance, retrospection.

reminiscent

adj lit: evocative, redolent, suggestive.

remiss

adj lit: careless, culpable, delinquent, derelict, dilatory, forgetful, inattentive, indifferent, lackadaisical, lax, neglectful, slack, slipshod, sloppy, tardy, thoughtless.

remit

n lit: authorization, brief, guidelines, instructions, orders.
vb lit: dispatch, forward, mail, post, transmit; cancel, halt, repeal, stop; abate, alleviate, decrease, diminish, dwindle, mitigate, reduce, relax, slacken, soften, wane; defer, delay, postpone, put off, suspend.

remittance

n lit: fee, payment, price; allowance, grant, stipend.

remnant

n lit: balance, leftover, remains, residue, rest; bit, fragment, piece, scrap, shred.

remonstration

n lit: argument, complaint, dispute, dissension, expostulation, objection, protest.

remorse

n lit: compunction, contrition, grief, guilt, penitence, regret, repentance, self-reproach.

remorseful

adj lit: apologetic, ashamed, conscience-stricken, contrite, guilt-ridden, penitent, regretful, repentant, rueful, self-reproachful, sorry.

remote

adj lit: distant, faraway, godforsaken, isolated, lonely, secluded; alien, extraneous, extrinsic, immaterial, irrelevant, outside, removed, unrelated; doubtful, dubious, faint, implausible, meagre, negligible, poor, slender, slight, slim, unlikely; aloof, cold, detached, indifferent, introverted, reserved, unapproachable, uninvolved, withdrawn.

remove

vb lit: abstract, delete, eliminate, extract, get rid of, throw out; amputate, take off; doff; depart, move away, quit, relocate, transfer, transport, vacate; discharge, dismiss, expel, purge, relegate; depose, dethrone, dislodge, eject, oust, unseat; *fig*: assassinate, bump off, dispose of, do away with, execute, get rid of, liquidate, murder, wipe out.

remunerate

vb lit: compensate, pay, recompense, reimburse, repay, reward.

renaissance

n lit: awakening, reappearance, rebirth,

re-emergence, renewal, restoration, resurgence, revival.

rend
vb lit: pull apart, tear, wrench; divide, remove, split.

render
vb lit: contribute, furnish, give, make available, present, provide, submit, supply, tender, yield; display, exhibit, manifest, show; exchange, return, swap, trade; cause to become, leave, make; act, depict, do, interpret, perform, play, portray; construe, explain, reproduce, transcribe, translate; cede, give up, hand over, relinquish, surrender, turn over; give back, make restitution, pay back, restore.

renewal
n lit: mending, modernization, overhaul, recreation, refit, refurbishing, renovation, repair, replenishment, restoration, revitalization, transformation.

renounce
vb lit: abandon, abdicate from, abstain from, cast off, deny, disclaim, disown, forgo, forsake, give up, leave off, quit, recant, relinquish, repudiate, resign from, spurn, throw off.

renovation
n lit: modernization, overhaul, reconditioning, refit, refurbishing, remodelling, renewal, repair, restoration, revamping.

renown
n lit: acclamation, celebrity, fame, illustriousness, notability.

rent
n lit: fee, hire, lease, payment, rental, tariff; break, chink, crack, flaw, gash, hole, rip, slash, split, tear; *fig*: breach, dissension, disunity, division, rift, rupture, schism.
vb lit: charter, hire, lease, let.

reorganize
vb lit: adapt, adjust, move, realign, rearrange, redispose, relocate; remodel, restructure, rework; reschedule; re-establish, reset.

repair
n lit: adjustment, mend, overhaul, patch, restoration; condition, fettle, form, shape, state.

vb lit: fix, heal, mend, patch, put back together, rectify, renew, renovate, restore; retrieve; compensate for, make up for, betake oneself, go, move, retire; have recourse (to), resort (to), turn (to).

repartee
n lit: badinage, banter, pleasantries, ripostes, sallies, witticisms.

repast
n lit: collation, meal; banquet, feast, spread; food, victuals.

repay
vb lit: pay back, refund, reimburse, remunerate, square; reciprocate, requite; avenge, get even with, retaliate against, revenge oneself on, settle the score with.

repeal
n lit: abolition, abrogation, annulment, cancellation, revocation, withdrawal.
vb lit: abolish, abrogate, annul, cancel, countermand, invalidate, nullify, rescind, reverse, set aside, withdraw.

repeat
n lit: duplicate, echo, recapitulation, reiteration, repetition, replay, reshowing.
vb lit: duplicate, echo, iterate, quote, recapitulate, recite, rehearse, reiterate, renew, rerun, reshow, restate.

repel
vb lit: drive off, fight off, hold off, parry, put to flight, rebuff, reject, repulse, resist, ward off; *fig*: disgust, nauseate, offend, put one off, revolt, turn one's stomach.

repentant
adj lit: apologetic, ashamed, chastened, contrite, penitent, remorseful, sorry.

repercussion
n lit: backlash, consequence, result, reverberation, side-effect.

repetition
n lit: duplication, echo, iteration, recapitulation, recital, recurrence, reiteration, renewal, repeat, restatement, return, tautology.

replace
vb lit: restock, resupply, substitute, succeed, supersede, supplant, take over from.

replenish
vb lit: make up, refill, replace, restock, restore, resupply, top up.

replica
n lit: carbon copy, copy, duplicate, facsimile, imitation, reproduction.

reply
n lit: acknowledgment, answer, comeback, counter, rejoinder, response, retort, return, riposte.
vb lit: acknowledge, answer, come back, counter, react (to), respond (to), retaliate, retort, riposte, write back.

report
n lit: account, article, broadcast, bulletin, communiqué, description, dispatch, message, piece, record, statement, story, summary; rumour; fame, reputation, repute; bang, blast, boom, crash, discharge, explosion, noise, sound.
vb lit: announce, broadcast, communicate, describe, detail, document, give an account of, inform of, notify of, pass on, publish, record, recount, relay, state, tell; appear, be present, clock in, show up, turn up.

reporter
n lit: correspondent, hack, journalist, newscaster, newshound.

repose
n lit: relaxation, respite, rest, sleep, tranquillity; serenity.
vb lit: lie, lie down, recline, relax, rest, sleep, slumber, take it easy.

reprehensible
adj lit: bad, culpable, discreditable, disgraceful, objectionable, opprobrious, shameful, unworthy.

represent
vb lit: be, correspond to, express, mean, serve as, stand for, symbolize; embody, epitomize, exemplify, personify, typify; denote, depict, describe, designate, illustrate, picture, portray, render, show, sketch; describe as, make out to be, pass off as, pretend to be; appear as, perform as.

representative
n lit: commercial traveller, rep, salesman; archetype, embodiment, epitome, exemplar, personification, type; agent, councillor, delegate, member of parliament, spokesman.

adj lit: archetypal, characteristic, evocative, exemplary, symbolic, typical; chosen, delegated, elected.

repress
vb lit: check, control, crush, curb, master, overcome, quash, quell, subdue, subjugate, suppress; bottle up, hold back, inhibit, muffle, restrain, smother, stifle, swallow.

repression
n lit: authoritarianism, censorship, coercion, constraint, control, domination, inhibition, restraint, subjugation, suppression, tyranny.

reprieve
n lit: abeyance, amnesty, deferment, pardon, postponement, remission, stay of execution.
vb lit: grant a stay of execution to, let off the hook, pardon.

reprimand
n lit: carpeting, censure, dressing-down, lecture, rebuke, reproach, reproof, scolding.
vb lit: chide, rap, rebuke, reprove, scold, take to task, tell off, tick off, upbraid.

reprisal
n lit: counterstroke, retaliation, retribution, revenge, vengeance.

reproach
n lit: censure, rebuke, reprimand, reproof; discredit (to), disgrace (to).
vb lit: censure, chide, condemn, rebuke, reprimand, scold, take to task, upbraid; be a discredit to, condemn.

reproduce
vb lit: copy, duplicate, emulate, imitate, mirror, parallel, print, recreate, replicate, represent; breed, generate, multiply, procreate, proliferate, propagate, spawn.

reproduction
n lit: copy, duplicate, facsimile, imitation, print, replica; breeding, generation, multiplication, procreation, proliferation, propagation.

repudiate
vb lit: abandon, deny, desert, discard, disown, forsake, reject, renounce, spurn.

repugnance
n lit: aversion, disgust, dislike, distaste, loathing, reluctance, revulsion.

repulsive

adj lit: disgusting, distasteful, foul, hideous, loathsome, nauseating, obnoxious, odious, offensive, revolting, sickening, vile; adverse, antagonistic, incompatible, opposed.

reputable

adj lit: creditable, estimable, honest, honourable, law-abiding, reliable, respectable, trustworthy, upright.

reputation

n lit: character, credit, distinction, fame, name, renown, repute, standing, stature.

reputedly

adv lit: allegedly, by all accounts, possibly, potentially, supposedly, traditionally.

request

n lit: appeal, application, call, demand, entreaty, petition, requisition, solicitation, suit, supplication.
vb lit: appeal for, apply for, ask for, entreat, petition, seek, solicit, sue for, supplicate.

require

vb lit: call for, demand, necessitate, take; lack, miss, need, want, wish for; bid, call upon, command, compel, constrain, instruct, oblige.

requirement

n lit: demand, need, want; essential, must, necessity, prerequisite; particular, qualification, specification.

requisition

n lit: appropriation, commandeering, demand, seizure, takeover.
vb lit: appropriate, commandeer, demand, take over; occupy, take possession of; employ, use, utilize.

rescind

vb lit: annul, cancel, countermand, invalidate, overturn, quash, repeal, retract, set aside.

rescue

n lit: extrication, liberation, recovery, relief, salvage, saving.
vb lit: deliver, extricate, free, get out, recover, release, salvage, save, set free; redeem.

research

n lit: analysis, experimentation, exploration, fact-finding, investigation, study; engineering; theoretical science.
vb lit: analyse, examine, experiment, investigate, look (into), make inquiries (into), probe (into), scrutinize, study.

resemblance

n lit: affinity, closeness, comparability, conformity, correspondence, likeness, parity, semblance, similitude.

resemble

vb lit: be like, be similar to, echo, look like, mirror, remind one of, take after.

resent

vb lit: be angry about, begrudge, be offended by, dislike, grudge, object to, take amiss, take exception to, take umbrage at.

resentment

n lit: anger, animosity, bitterness, grudge, ill feeling, indignation, irritation, pique, rancour, umbrage, vexation; envy.

reserve

n lit: capital, fund, reservoir, savings, stockpile, supply; asylum, park, reservation, sanctuary; aloofness, constraint, coolness, formality, reluctance, reservation, restraint, reticence, shyness, taciturnity.
vb lit: conserve, hoard, hold, keep back, preserve, put by, save, set aside, store, withhold; book, engage, retain, secure; defer, delay, postpone, put off.

reservoir

n lit: container, dam, store, tank, vessel, water supply; *fig*: fund, pool, stock, supply.

residence

n lit: abode, domicile, dwelling, habitation, household, lodging, home, quarters; hall, manor, mansion, palace, seat; occupancy, sojourn, stay, tenancy.

resident

n lit: citizen, denizen, inhabitant, local, lodger, occupant, tenant.
adj lit: local, neighbourhood, settled.

residue

n lit: dregs, grounds, lees; froth, scum, settlings, silt; precipitation; excess, extra, remainder, remnant, rest, surplus.

resign

vb lit: hand in one's notice; leave, quit, vacate; abandon, relinquish, surrender, yield; commit (oneself to).

resigned
adj lit: long-suffering, patient, stoical, subdued, submissive; committed (to); defeatist, fatalistic.

resilient
adj lit: bouncy, elastic, flexible, pliable, springy, supple; buoyant, hardy, irrepressible, strong, tough.

resist
vb lit: battle against, combat, contend with, counteract, curb, defy, fight back, hinder, hold out against, oppose, repel, stand up to, struggle against, thwart, weather, withstand; abstain from, avoid, forgo, leave alone, refrain from.

resistance
n lit: contention, counteraction, defiance, hindrance, impediment, intransigence, opposition.

resolute
adj lit: bold, dedicated, determined, dogged, fixed, inflexible, obstinate, persevering, purposeful, relentless, set, staunch, steadfast, stubborn, tenacious, undaunted, unflinching, unwavering.

resolution
n lit: boldness, dedication, determination, doggedness, firmness, fortitude, obstinacy, perseverance, purpose, relentlessness, stamina, steadfastness, stubbornness, tenacity, willpower; aim, intention; decision, declaration, finding, verdict; motion, proposition; settlement; answer, dénouement, outcome, solution, unravelling, working out.

resolve
n lit: conclusion, decision, design, objective, purpose, resolution, undertaking; boldness, courage, determination, firmness, resoluteness, resolution, steadfastness, willpower.
vb lit: agree, conclude, decide, design, determine, fix, intend, make up one's mind, settle, undertake; answer, clear up, crack, elucidate, fathom, work out; banish, dispel, explain, remove; analyse, break down, disentangle, disintegrate, dissolve, reduce, separate, solve, unravel; alter, convert, transform, transmute.

resort
n lit: haunt, holiday centre, retreat, spot; alternative, chance, course, expedient, possibility, recourse.

vb lit: avail oneself of, exercise, have recourse to, look to, make use of, turn to, use; frequent, haunt, head for, repair.

resounding
adj lit: booming, echoing, powerful, resonant, reverberating, ringing, sonorous, sounding, vibrant.

resourceful
adj lit: able, bright, capable, imaginative, ingenious, inventive, quick-witted, sharp, talented.

resources
n lit: assets, capital, funds, holdings, means, money, property, reserves, wealth, wherewithal.

respect
n lit: admiration, appreciation, deference, esteem, recognition, regard, reverence; aspect, characteristic, detail, facet, matter, particular, point, sense; bearing, connection, reference, relation; compliments, good wishes, greetings, regards.
vb lit: admire, adore, appreciate, defer to, honour, look up to, revere, set store by, think highly of, value, venerate; abide by, adhere to, comply with, heed, obey, observe, pay attention to, show consideration for.

respectable
adj lit: admirable, decent, decorous, estimable, honest, proper, reputable, respected, upright, worthy; ample, appreciable, considerable, fair, goodly, reasonable, sizable, substantial, tidy, tolerable.

respite
n lit: break, breather, cessation, halt, hiatus, interruption, interval, lull, pause, recess, relief, rest; adjournment, delay, moratorium, postponement, reprieve, stay, suspension.

response
n lit: acknowledgment, answer, comeback, feedback, reaction, rejoinder, reply, retort, riposte.

responsible
adj lit: in authority, in charge, in control; accountable, answerable, bound, liable, under obligation; authoritative, decision-making, executive; at fault, culpable, guilty, to blame; adult, conscientious, dependable, level-headed, mature,

rational, reliable, sensible, sober, stable, trustworthy.

responsive
adj lit: alive, awake, aware, forthcoming, open, perceptive, quick to react, sharp, susceptible, sympathetic.

rest
n lit: calm, doze, inactivity, leisure, lie-down, nap, relaxation, relief, repose, siesta, slumber, snooze, standstill, tranquillity; break, breathing space, cessation, halt, interlude, interval, lull, pause, stop, time off, vacation; haven, refuge, retreat, shelter; base, prop, stand, support, trestle; excess, leftovers, others, remainder, remains, residue, surplus.
vb lit: be at ease, doze, have a snooze, idle, laze, lie down, nap, put one's feet up, relax, sit down, sleep, slumber, take it easy; lay, lean, lie, prop, recline, repose, stretch out; break off, cease, come to a standstill, discontinue, halt, knock off, stop, take a breather; be based, be founded, depend, hang, hinge, rely; be left, go on being, keep, remain, stay.

restful
adj lit: calm, comfortable, languid, peaceful, placid, quiet, relaxed, sleepy, soothing, tranquil, undisturbed.

restitution
n lit: amends, compensation, indemnity, recompense, refund, reimbursement, remuneration, reparation, repayment, requital, restoration, return.

restless
adj lit: active, bustling, footloose, inconstant, irresolute, nomadic, roving, transient, unsettled, unsteady, wandering; agitated, anxious, edgy, fidgeting, fretful, ill at ease, jumpy, nervous, on edge, restive, troubled, uneasy, worried.

restoration
n lit: reconstruction, recovery, refurbishing, rejuvenation, renewal, renovation, repair, revival; re-establishment, reinstatement, restitution, return.

restorative
n lit: elixir, medicine, remedy, tincture, tonic.

restrained
adj (pa.pt) lit: calm, controlled,

moderate, muted, reasonable, reticent, steady, temperate, undemonstrative; discreet, quiet, unobtrusive.

restraint
n lit: coercion, compulsion, confines, control, curtailment, grip, hindrance, hold, inhibition, moderation, restriction, self-discipline, suppression; bonds, captivity, confinement, detention, fetters, imprisonment, manacles, pinions, straitjacket; ban, check, curb, embargo, limitation, rein, taboo.

restrict
vb lit: bound, confine, contain, cramp, demarcate, hamper, handicap, hem in, impede, inhibit, limit, regulate, restrain.

restriction
n lit: check, condition, confinement, constraint, control, curb, demarcation, handicap, inhibition, limitation, regulation, restraint, rule, stipulation.

result
n lit: conclusion, consequence, decision, effect, end, event, issue, outcome, reaction, sequel, termination.
vb lit: appear, arise, derive, develop, emanate, ensue, eventuate, follow, happen, issue, spring, turn out; culminate (in), end (in), terminate (in).

resume
vb lit: begin again, continue, go on, proceed, recommence, reinstitute, reopen, restart; assume again, reoccupy, take up again.

resuscitate
vb lit: bring round, bring to life, give artificial respiration to, give the kiss of life, quicken, reanimate, rescue, restore, revitalize, revive, save.

retain
vb lit: absorb, detain, grasp, grip, hang onto, hold fast, keep, maintain, preserve, reserve, save; bear in mind, keep in mind, memorize, recall, remember; commission, employ, engage, hire.

retaliate
vb lit: even the score, exact retribution, get even with, give as good as one gets, give tit for tat, make reprisal, reciprocate, strike back, take revenge, wreak vengeance.

retard
vb lit: arrest, check, clog, decelerate, defer, delay, encumber, handicap, hinder, impede, obstruct, set back, slow down, stall.

reticent
adj lit: mum, quiet, reserved, restrained, secretive, taciturn, tight-lipped, uncommunicative, unforthcoming.

retire
vb lit: be pensioned off, give up work; absent oneself, depart, exit, leave, remove, withdraw; go to bed, go to sleep, hit the sack, turn in; ebb, fall back, give ground, give way, pull out, recede, retreat.

retirement
n lit: obscurity, privacy, retreat, seclusion, withdrawal.

retiring
adj lit: bashful, coy, demure, meek, modest, quiet, reclusive, reserved, reticent, self-effacing, shy, timorous, unassuming.

retort
vb lit: answer, come back (with), fling back, give in return, rejoin, repay in kind, reply, requite, respond, say by way of repartee; *spec*: distill, purify.

retraction
n lit: pulling back, reeling in, sheathing; abjuration, denial, disavowal, recall, recantation, renouncement, repeal, repudiation, reverse, revoking, withdrawal.

retreat
n lit: departure, ebb, evacuation, flight, withdrawal; den, haunt, hideaway, privacy, resort, sanctuary, seclusion.
vb lit: back away, depart, draw back, ebb, give ground, leave, pull back, recede, retire, turn tail, withdraw.

retribution
n lit: compensation, justice, punishment, reckoning, recompense, reprisal, retaliation, revenge, vengeance.

retrieve
vb lit: fetch back, get back, recapture, recoup, recover, regain, rescue, restore, salvage, win back.

retrograde
adj lit: backward, declining, reversed, retreating, reverting.

return
n lit: homecoming, reappearance, recurrence, retreat, reversion; re-establishment, reinstatement, restoration; advantage, benefit, gain, interest, proceeds, profit, revenue, takings, yield; compensation, reciprocation, recompense, reparation, repayment, retaliation, reward; account, report, statement, summary; answer, comeback, rejoinder, reply, retort, riposte.
vb lit: come back, go back, reappear, recoil, recur, retreat, revert, turn back; convey, give back, re-establish, reinstate, remit, replace, restore, send back, transmit; pay back, reciprocate, recompense, refund, reimburse, repay, requite; bring in, earn, make, net, yield; answer, come back (with), rejoin, reply, retort; choose, pick, vote in; announce, arrive at, deliver, render, report, submit.

reveal
vb lit: announce, betray, disclose, divulge, give away, impart, leak, let out, let slip, make public, proclaim, tell; bare, display, exhibit, lay bare, manifest, show, uncover, unearth, unveil.

revel
n lit: bacchanal, carouse, celebration, debauch, festivity, merrymaking, saturnalia, spree.
vb lit: bask (in), delight (in), gloat (in), indulge (in), rejoice (in), relish (in), take pleasure (in), wallow (in); carouse, go on a spree, live it up, rave, roister, whoop it up.

revelation
n lit: announcement, betrayal, broadcasting, disclosure, discovery, expose, exposure, giveaway, leak, news, proclamation, publication, telling, uncovering, unearthing.

revenge
n lit: reprisal, requital, retaliation, retribution, vengeance, vindictiveness.
vb lit: avenge, get one's own back for, repay, requite, retaliate, take revenge for, vindicate.

revenue
n lit: gain, income, interest, proceeds, profits, returns, rewards, takings, yield.

reverberate
vb lit: echo, rebound, recoil, resound, ring, vibrate.

revere
vb lit: adore, defer to, exalt, honour, look up to, put on a pedestal, respect, reverence, venerate, worship.

reverent
adj lit: adoring, decorous, deferential, devout, humble, meek, pious, respectful, reverential, submissive.

reverse
n lit: antithesis, contradiction, contrary, converse, opposite; back, flip side, other side, rear, verso, wrong side; adversity, affliction, blow, check, defeat, disappointment, failure, misadventure, misfortune, mishap, repulse, setback, vicissitude.
vb lit: invert, transpose, turn over, turn round, upend; alter, annul, cancel, change, invalidate, negate, overrule, overthrow, quash, repeal, retract, set aside, undo; back, backtrack, go backwards, retreat.
adj lit: back to front, backward, contrary, converse, inverted, opposite.

revert
vb lit: backslide, come back, go back, lapse, recur, regress, resume, return.

review
n lit: analysis, examination, report, scrutiny, study, survey; commentary, criticism, evaluation, judgement, notice; journal, magazine, periodical; fresh look, reassessment, recapitulation, rethink, retrospect, revision; *spec*: inspection, march past, parade, procession.
vb lit: go over again, reassess, recapitulate, reconsider, re-evaluate, rethink, revise, think over; call to mind, recall, recollect, reflect on, summon up; assess, criticize, discuss, evaluate, judge, read through, scrutinize, study, weigh.

revise
vb lit: alter, amend, correct, edit, emend, modify, redo, revamp, review, rewrite, update; go over, memorize, study, swot up.

revive
vb lit: animate, awaken, bring round, cheer, come round, comfort, invigorate, quicken, rally, recover, rekindle, restore, resuscitate, revitalize, rouse.

revoke
vb lit: abolish, abrogate, annul, call back, cancel, countermand, disclaim, invalidate, negate, nullify, quash, recant, renounce, repeal, repudiate, retract, reverse, set aside, withdraw.

revolt
n lit: defection, insurgency, insurrection, mutiny, rebellion, revolution, rising, sedition, uprising.
vb lit: defect, mutiny, rebel, resist, rise, take up arms (against); give one the creeps, nauseate, offend, repel, repulse, shock, sicken, turn one's stomach.

revolting
adj lit: abhorrent, abominable, appalling, disgusting, distasteful, horrid, loathsome, nasty, nauseating, obnoxious, offensive, repellent, repugnant, repulsive, shocking, sickening.

revolution
n lit: coup d'état, insurgency, mutiny, rebellion, revolt, uprising; drastic change, innovation, metamorphosis, reformation, shift, transformation, upheaval; circle, circuit, cycle, gyration, orbit, rotation, spin, turn, whirl.

revolutionary
n lit: insurgent, insurrectionist, mutineer, rebel, revolutionist.
adj lit: extremist, insurgent, mutinous, radical, rebel, seditious, subversive; avant-garde, different, drastic, experimental, fundamental, innovative, novel, progressive, radical, thoroughgoing.

revolve
vb lit: circle, go round, gyrate, orbit, rotate, spin, twist, wheel, whirl; consider, deliberate, meditate, mull over, ponder, reflect, ruminate, think over, turn over (in one's mind).

revulsion
n lit: abhorrence, abomination, aversion, detestation, disgust, loathing, repugnance, repulsion.

reward
n lit: benefit, bonus, compensation, gain, merit, payment, premium, profit, recompense, remuneration, requital, return, wages; comeuppance, just deserts, retribution.

vb lit: compensate, honour, recompense, remunerate, repay, requite.

rhythm
n lit: accent, beat, cadence, tilt, measure, metre, movement, pattern, pulse, tempo, time.

rich
n lit: plutocracy; affluent, moneyed, opulent, wealthy, well-off.
adj lit: affluent, loaded, made of money, opulent, prosperous, wealthy, well-off, well-to-do; abounding, productive, well-provided, well-stocked, well-supplied; abundant, ample, copious, exuberant, fecund, fertile, fruitful, lush, plentiful, prolific; costly, elaborate, expensive, exquisite, lavish, precious, priceless, splendid, sumptuous, superb, valuable; creamy, fatty, full-bodied, heavy, juicy, luscious, savoury, succulent, sweet, tasty; bright, deep, intense, strong, vibrant, vivid; dulcet, full, mellifluous, mellow, resonant; amusing, funny, hilarious, humorous, ludicrous, ridiculous, side-splitting.

rid
vb lit: clear, deliver, disburden, free, purge, relieve, unburden.

riddle
n lit: brain-teaser, conundrum, enigma, mystery, problem, puzzle.

ride
n lit: drive, jaunt, lift, spin, trip, whirl.
vb lit: control, handle, manage, sit on; go, journey, move, progress, travel; dominate, enslave, grip, haunt, oppress.

ridicule
n lit: banter, chaff, derision, gibe, jeer, mockery, raillery, sarcasm, satire, scorn, sneer, taunting.
vb lit: banter, caricature, deride, humiliate, jeer, lampoon, make fun of, make one a laughing stock, mock, parody, poke fun at, pooh-pooh, satirize, scoff, sneer, taunt.

ridiculous
adj lit: absurd, contemptible, derisory, farcical, foolish, hilarious, laughable, ludicrous, outrageous, preposterous, silly, unbelievable.

rife
adj lit: common, current, numerous, prevalent, widespread; abounding, full, replete, well-supplied.

riffraff
n lit: dregs of society, rabble, scum, undesirables.

rift
n lit: break, chink, cleavage, cleft, crack, cranny, crevice, fissure, flaw, fracture, gap, opening, split; alienation, breach, difference, disagreement, estrangement, quarrel, schism, separation.

rig
n lit: accoutrements, apparatus, equipment, fittings, fixtures, gear, machinery, tackle.
vb lit: accoutre, equip, fit out, furnish, kit out, provision, supply; arrange, doctor, fake, falsify, fiddle with, fix, manipulate, tamper with, trump up.

right
n lit: authority, business, claim, due, interest, liberty, license, permission, power, prerogative, privilege; equity, good, honour, integrity, legality, morality, propriety, reason, rectitude, truth, uprightness, virtue.
vb lit: compensate for, fix, rectify, repair, settle, sort out, vindicate.
adj lit: equitable, ethical, fair, good, honourable, just, lawful, moral, proper, righteous, true, upright, virtuous; accurate, admissible, authentic, correct, exact, factual, genuine, precise, satisfactory, sound, spot-on, valid; advantageous, appropriate, becoming, deserved, done, due, fitting, ideal, opportune, propitious, rightful, seemly, suitable; all there, balanced, fit, healthy, normal, rational, reasonable, sane, unimpaired, well; conservative, reactionary, Tory; absolute, complete, out-and-out, thorough, utter.
adv lit: accurately, exactly, factually, genuinely, truly; appropriately, aptly, fittingly, properly, suitably; directly, immediately, instantly, promptly, quickly, straightaway; bang, precisely, squarely; absolutely, altogether, completely, entirely, quite, thoroughly, totally, utterly; fairly, honestly, justly, morally, virtuously; advantageously, beneficially, favourably, well.

rightful
adj lit: legal, legitimate; due, equitable, fair, just; actual, genuine, real.

rigid
adj lit: adamant, exact, fixed, harsh,

inflexible, intransigent, rigorous, set, stern, strict, stiff, stringent, unbending, uncompromising, unrelenting, unyielding.

rigorous
adj lit: austere, challenging, demanding, exacting, firm, hard, rigid, severe, tough; accurate, conscientious, meticulous, nice, precise, punctilious, scrupulous, thorough; bad, bleak, extreme, harsh, inhospitable.

rim
n lit: border, brim, brink, edge, lip, margin, verge.

rind
n lit: crust, epicarp, husk, outer layer, peel, skin.

ring
n lit: band, circle, circuit, halo, hoop, loop, round; arena, circus, rink; association, cabal, cartel, cell, clique, coterie, gang, group, mob, organization, syndicate; chime, knell, peal; buzz, phone call.
vb lit: encircle, enclose, encompass, girdle, hem in, seal off, surround; chime, clang, peal, resound, reverberate, sound, toll.

riot
n lit: anarchy, commotion, confusion, disorder, disturbance, fray, lawlessness, quarrel, row, strife, tumult, turmoil, uproar; boisterousness, excess, frolic, high jinks, jollification, merry-making, revelry, romp; display, extravaganza, show, splash.
vb lit: go on the rampage, raise an uproar, run riot, take to the streets; carouse, cut loose, frolic, go on a binge, make merry, revel, roister, romp.

rip
n lit: cut, gash, hole, rent, tear; current, overfall, rough water; cheat (off), con (off), loot (off), rifle (off), strip (off).
vb lit: cut, pull apart, rend, sunder, tear; strip, wrench, wrest; come asunder, open up, split; move fast, rush along.

ripe
adj lit: fully developed, mature, mellow, ready, ripened; accomplished, complete, finished, in readiness, perfect, prepared; auspicious, favourable, ideal, opportune, right, suitable, timely.

rise
n lit: advance, ascent, climb, improvement, increase, upsurge, upward turn; advancement, aggrandizement, progress, promotion; acclivity, elevation, hillock, incline, upward slope; increment, pay increase.
vb lit: arise, get out of bed, get up, stand up, surface; ascend, climb, go up, grow, improve, increase, lift, mount, move up, swell, wax; advance, be promoted, get on, get somewhere, go places, progress, prosper, work one's way up; appear, become apparent, crop up, emanate, emerge, happen, issue, occur, turn up; mount the barricades, mutiny, rebel, resist, revolt, take up arms.

risk
n lit: chance, gamble, hazard, jeopardy, possibility, speculation, venture.
vb lit: chance, dare, endanger, gamble, hazard, imperil, jeopardize, put in jeopardy, venture.

rite
n lit: act, ceremony, communion, custom, formality, liturgy, mystery, observance, practice, procedure, ritual, sacrament, service, usage.

ritual
n lit: ceremonial, ceremony, liturgy, observance, rite, service, solemnity; convention, custom, formality, ordinance, practice, procedure, protocol, red tape, routine, usage.
adj lit: ceremonial, ceremonious, conventional, customary, formal, habitual, procedural, routine, stereotyped.

rival
n lit: adversary, antagonist, challenger, contender, contestant, opponent; compeer, equal, equivalent, fellow, match, peer.
vb lit: be a match for, come up to, compare with, compete, contend, emulate, equal, match, measure up to, oppose, vie with.
adj lit: competing, competitive, conflicting, emulating, opposed, opposing.

river
n lit: brook, stream, watercourse, waterway; current, flow.

road
n lit: avenue, course, direction, highway,

lane, motorway, pathway, route, street, thoroughfare, track; *spec*: anchorage, roadstead.

roam
vb lit: drift, meander, prowl, ramble, range, rove, stray, stroll, walk, wander.

roar
n lit: bellow, clamour, cry, howl, rumble, shout, thunder, yell; belly laugh, guffaw, hoot.
vb lit: bawl, bay, bellow, clamour, crash, cry, howl, rumble, shout, thunder, vociferate, yell; guffaw, hoot, split one's sides.

roast
vb lit: bake, cook; burn, calcine, desiccate, prepare by heating, refine; *fig*: banter, chaff, make fun of, ridicule; criticize, reprove.

rob
vb lit: burgle, cheat, con, defraud, deprive, dispossess, hold up, loot, pillage, plunder, raid, ransack, rifle, rip off, sack, strip, swindle.

robbery
n lit: burglary, depredation, embezzlement, filching, fraud, hold-up, larceny, pillage, plunder, raid, rapine, rip-off, stealing, stick-up, swindle, theft.

robe
n lit: costume, gown, habit; bathrobe, dressing gown, wrapper; array, attire, cape, garb, mantle, vestment.
vb lit: attire, clothe, drape, dress, garb.

robot
n lit: android, automaton, clockwork, machine.

robust
adj lit: athletic, brawny, fit, hale, hardy, hearty, husky, in fine fettle, muscular, rugged, sinewy, sound, staunch, stout, strapping, strong, sturdy, tough, vigorous, well; boisterous, coarse, earthy, raw, roisterous, rollicking, rough, rude, unsubtle; common-sensical, down-to-earth, hard-headed, practical, sensible, straightforward.

rock
n lit: boulder, stone; anchor, bulwark, cornerstone, foundation, mainstay, protection, support.

vb lit: lurch, reel, roll, sway, swing, toss, wobble; astonish, astound, daze, dumbfound, jar, shake, shock, stagger, surprise.

rod
n lit: bar, baton, cane, dowel, mace, pole, sceptre, shaft, staff, stick, wand.

rogue
n lit: blackguard, charlatan, cheat, conman, crook, deceiver, fraud, mountebank, ne'er-do-well, rapscallion, rascal, reprobate, scamp, scoundrel, swindler, villain; mutant, sport, variant.
adj lit: maverick, outcast, savage, wild; breakaway, disruptive, mischievous; defective, mutant, variant.

role
n lit: character, part, portrayal, representation; capacity, duty, function, job, part, position, post, task.

roll
n lit: cycle, gyration, reel, revolution, rotation, run, spin, turn, twirl, wheel, whirl; ball, bobbin, cylinder, scroll, spool; annals, catalogue, census, chronicle, directory, index, inventory, list, record, register, schedule, table; billowing, lurching, rocking, rolling, tossing, undulation, wallowing; boom, drumming, grumble, resonance, reverberation, roar, rumble, thunder.
vb lit: elapse, flow, go past, gyrate, pass, pivot, reel, revolve, rock, rotate, run, spin, swivel, turn, twirl, undulate, wheel, whirl; coil, curl, enfold, entwine, furl, twist, wind, wrap; even, flatten, level, smooth, spread; billow, lurch, sway, swing, toss, tumble, wallow; lumber, stagger, swagger, waddle.

romance
n lit: amour, liaison, love affair; love story; courtly love; legend, myth, saga; adventure story, fiction, novel.

romantic
adj lit: amorous, lovey-dovey, mushy, passionate, sentimental, sloppy, tender; charming, exciting, fascinating, glamorous, mysterious, nostalgic; dreamy, high-flown, idealistic, starry-eyed, unrealistic, utopian, visionary, whimsical; chimerical, exaggerated, extravagant, fairy-tale, fanciful, fictitious, idyllic, imaginary, legendary, made-up, unrealistic, wild.

roof
n lit: awning, canopy, capstone, coping,
marquee, spire, steeple, thatch, upper
covering.
vb lit: cap, cover with, roof, slate, thatch,
tile, top.

room
n lit: area, capacity, compass, elbowroom,
expanse, extent, latitude, leeway,
margin, play, range, space, volume;
apartment, chamber, office; chance,
opportunity, scope.

roomy
adj lit: ample, capacious, commodious,
extensive, large, sizable, spacious, wide.

root
n lit: radicle, radix, rhizome, tuber; base,
cause, core, crux, derivation, essence,
foundation, heart, mainspring, nub,
nucleus, occasion, source, starting point;
beginnings, origins.
vb lit: anchor, become established,
entrench, fasten, fix, ground, implant,
moor, set, stick, take root.

rope
n lit: cable, cord, hawser, line, strand;
capital punishment, hanging, lynching,
noose.
vb lit: bind, fasten, hitch, lasso, moor,
pinion, tether, tie.

rosy
adj lit: pink, red, rose-coloured;
blooming, blushing, glowing, healthy-
looking, reddish, rubicund, ruddy;
auspicious, bright, cheerful,
encouraging, favourable, hopeful,
optimistic, promising, reassuring,
sunny.

rot
n lit: blight, canker, corrosion, decay,
decomposition, disintegration, mould,
putrefaction; balderdash, bosh, bunkum,
claptrap, codswallop, drivel, hogwash,
moonshine, nonsense, poppycock,
rubbish, tosh, twaddle.
vb lit: corrode, corrupt, crumble, decay,
decompose, deteriorate, disintegrate,
fester, go bad, moulder, perish, putrefy;
decline, degenerate, languish, waste
away, wither away.

rota
n lit: roster, rotation, round, routine;
supreme court.

rotary
adj lit: gyratory, revolving, rotating,
rotational, spinning, turning.

rotate
vb lit: go round, gyrate, pirouette, pivot,
reel, revolve, spin, swivel, turn, wheel;
alternate, interchange, switch, take
turns.

rotten
adj lit: bad, corroded, crumbling,
decaying, decomposed, disintegrating,
festering, fetid, foul, mouldering,
putrescent, putrid, rank, sour, unsound;
bent, corrupt, crooked, degenerate,
dishonest, disloyal, immoral, mercenary,
perfidious, treacherous, untrustworthy,
venal; base, contemptible, despicable,
dirty, disagreeable, filthy, mean, nasty,
scurrilous, vile, vicious; deplorable,
disappointing, regrettable, unfortunate,
unlucky; crummy, inadequate, inferior,
lousy, low-grade, poor, sorry,
substandard, unacceptable,
unsatisfactory; below par, ill, off colour,
poorly, ropy, rough, sick, under the
weather.

rotund
adj lit: bulbous, globular, rounded,
spherical; chubby, corpulent, fat, obese,
plump, podgy, portly, roly-poly, stout,
tubby; full, grandiloquent, orotund,
resonant, round, sonorous.

rough
n lit: draft, outline, preliminary sketch;
bruiser, bully, ruffian, thug.
vb lit: block out, draft out, outline, sketch
out; bash up, beat up, thrash up.
adj lit: broken, bumpy, craggy, jagged,
rocky, rugged, stony, uneven; bristly,
coarse, dishevelled, fuzzy, hairy, shaggy,
tangled, tousled, uncut; agitated,
boisterous, choppy, stormy,
tempestuous, turbulent, wild; bluff,
blunt, brusque, churlish, curt,
discourteous, ill-mannered, impolite,
indelicate, loutish, rude, unceremonious,
uncouth, unmannerly, unpolished,
unrefined; cruel, drastic, extreme, harsh,
nasty, severe, sharp, tough, unjust,
violent; below par, ill, off colour, poorly,
ropy, rotten, unwell, upset;
cacophonous, discordant, grating, gruff,
husky, inharmonious, jarring, rasping,
raucous; arduous, austere, hard, spartan,
uncomfortable; basic, crude, cursory,
hasty, incomplete, quick, raw,

rudimentary, sketchy, unfinished,
untutored; uncut, unprocessed,
unwrought; approximate, estimated,
foggy, general, hazy, inexact, vague.

roughly
adv lit: irregularly, unevenly;
boisterously, choppily, turbulently,
wildly; bluntly, brusquely, coarsely,
curtly, impolitely, rudely,
unceremoniously, ungraciously;
drastically, extremely, hardly, severely,
sharply, unjustly, unpleasantly,
violently; discordantly, gruffly, harshly,
raucously; arduously, toughly,
uncomfortably; basically, crudely,
hastily, imperfectly, quickly, sketchily;
approximately, generally, hazily,
inexactly, vaguely.

round
n lit: circle, disc, globe, orb, ring, sphere;
bout, cycle, sequence, series, session;
division, lap, level, period, stage; beat,
circuit, compass, course, routine,
schedule, turn; bullet, cartridge,
discharge, shot.
vb lit: bypass, circle, encircle, flank, skirt,
turn.
adj lit: annular, bowed, bulbous, circular,
curved, cylindrical, disc-shaped,
globular, orbicular, rotund, spherical;
complete, entire, solid, unbroken, whole;
ample, bountiful, considerable,
generous, large, substantial; fleshy, full,
plump, roly-poly, rounded; mellifluous,
resonant, rich, sonorous; blunt, candid,
frank, outspoken, plain, straightforward.
adv lit: in a circle, with a whirling motion;
around, in every direction, on all sides;
in circumference, in distance around; by
a longer way; from one to another;
through a round of time; about, here and
there; for all; in the opposite direction;
to the opposite opinion.
prp lit: so as to make a turn to the other
side of, so as to encircle; in all directions
from, to all parts of; about, around; on
all sides of; here and there in;
throughout; so as to rotate about.

roundabout
n lit: bypass, indirect way; jacket; traffic
circle; carousel, merry-go-round,
turntable.
adj lit: circuitous, elliptical, implicit,
indirect, not straight, oblique;
encircling, surrounding, out-of-the-way;
cut round at the bottom.

round up
vb lit: assemble, collect, drive, gather,
herd, marshal, muster, rally.

rouse
vb lit: awaken, get up, rise, wake up;
agitate, animate, bestir, disturb, excite,
exhilarate, get going, incite, instigate,
move, provoke, startle, stimulate, stir,
whip up.

rousing
adj lit: brisk, electrifying, exciting,
exhilarating, inflammatory, inspiring,
lively, moving, spirited, stimulating,
stirring, vigorous.

rout
n lit: beating, debacle, defeat, drubbing,
hiding, licking, overthrow, shambles,
thrashing, trouncing.
vb lit: beat, chase, conquer, crush, defeat,
destroy, dispel, drive off, drub, lick,
overpower, overthrow, scatter, thrash,
trounce.

route
n lit: avenue, beat, circuit, course,
direction, journey, passage, road, round,
run, way.
vb lit: convey, direct, dispatch, forward,
send.

routine
n lit: custom, formula, grind, method,
pattern, practice, procedure, usage, way,
wont; act, bit, line, performance, piece.
adj lit: conventional, customary,
everyday, familiar, normal, ordinary,
standard, typical, usual, wonted; boring,
dull, hackneyed, humdrum, run-of-the-
mill, tedious, tiresome, unimaginative,
unoriginal.

row
n lit: bank, column, file, line, queue,
range, sequence, series, string, tier;
paddle, scull; altercation, brawl,
commotion, controversy, disturbance,
fracas, fuss, quarrel, racket, rumpus,
slanging match, squabble, tiff, trouble,
uproar; castigation, dressing-down,
lecture, reprimand, rollicking, telling-
off, ticking-off.
vb lit: paddle, scull; argue, brawl, dispute,
fight, squabble, wrangle.

rowdy
adj lit: boisterous, disorderly, loutish,
noisy, rough, unruly, uproarious, wild.

rub

n lit: caress, kneading, massage, polish, stroke, wipe; catch, difficulty, drawback, hindrance, hitch, impediment, obstacle, problem, snag.

vb lit: abrade, caress, chafe, clean, grate, knead, massage, polish, scour, scrape, shine, smooth, stroke, wipe; apply, smear, spread.

rubbish

n lit: debris, dross, garbage, junk, litter, refuse, scrap, trash, waste; balderdash, bunkum, claptrap, codswallop, drivel, gibberish, moonshine, nonsense, piffle, poppycock, rot, twaddle.

vb lit: be caustic about, be scathing about, criticize severely, pan, slate.

rub out

vb lit: cancel, delete, erase, obliterate, remove, wipe out.

rude

adj lit: abrupt, abusive, blunt, brusque, churlish, curt, ill-mannered, impertinent, impudent, insolent, offhand, peremptory, unmannerly; boorish, brutish, coarse, gross, loutish, oafish, obscene, rough, scurrilous, uncouth, ungracious, vulgar; artless, crude, makeshift, primitive, roughly-made, simple; harsh, sharp, startling, sudden, unpleasant.

rudiments

n lit: basics, beginnings, elements, essentials, fundamentals.

rueful

adj lit: conscience-stricken, contrite, dismal, doleful, lugubrious, melancholy, mournful, pitiful, remorseful, repentant, sorry, woebegone, woeful.

ruffian

n lit: bruiser, brute, bully, hoodlum, hooligan, miscreant, rascal, rogue, roughneck, scoundrel, thug, villain, wretch.

ruffle

vb lit: disarrange, discompose, dishevel, mess up, rumple, tousle, wrinkle; agitate, annoy, disconcert, disturb, fluster, harass, irritate, nettle, peeve, put out, rattle, stir, trouble, unsettle, upset, vex, worry.

rug

n lit: blanket, carpet, coverlet, mackinaw, mat.

rugged

adj lit: broken, bumpy, craggy, irregular, jagged, rocky, rough, uneven; furrowed, lined, strong-featured, weathered, wrinkled; austere, dour, gruff, harsh, rude, sour, stern, surly; blunt, churlish, crude, uncouth, unpolished, unrefined; arduous, demanding, exacting, hard, laborious, rigorous, strenuous, taxing, tough, trying; beefy, brawny, burly, hardy, husky, muscular, robust, sturdy, vigorous, well-built.

ruin

n lit: bankruptcy, breakdown, collapse, crash, damage, decay, destitution, devastation, disrepair, downfall, failure, havoc, insolvency, overthrow, ruination, the end, undoing, wreckage.

vb lit: bankrupt, break, bring down, crush, defeat, demolish, devastate, impoverish, lay waste, overturn, raze, shatter, smash, wreck; botch, damage, injure, make a mess of, mangle, mar, spoil.

rule

n lit: axiom, canon, criterion, decree, guideline, law, maxim, ordinance, precept, principle, regulation, ruling, standard, tenet; administration, authority, command, control, domination, government, leadership, power, regime, reign, supremacy, sway; condition, convention, custom, habit, practice, procedure, routine, wont; course, formula, method, policy, way.

vb lit: administer, command, control, dominate, govern, lead, manage, regulate, reign; adjudicate, decide, decree, determine, establish, find, judge, pronounce, resolve, settle; be customary, hold sway, predominate, prevail.

ruler

n lit: commander, controller, governor, head of state, leader, monarch, potentate, sovereign; measure, rule, yardstick.

ruling

n lit: adjudication, decision, decree, finding, judgement, resolution, verdict.

adj lit: commanding, controlling, dominant, governing, leading, reigning, upper; chief, current, main,

predominant, pre-eminent,
preponderant, prevailing, principal,
supreme.

rumour

n lit: buzz, gossip, hearsay, report, talk,
tidings, whisper, word.
vb lit: circulate, gossip, pass around,
publish, put about, report, say, tell,
whisper.

run

n lit: dash, gallop, jog, race, rush, sprint,
spurt; drive, excursion, lift, outing, ride,
round, trip; chain, course, cycle,
passage, period, season, sequence, series,
spell, stretch, string; category, class,
kind, sort, type, variety; application,
demand, pressure; ladder, rip, snag, tear;
current, direction, drift, flow, motion,
path, stream, tendency, tide, trend,
sway; coop, enclosure, pen.
vb lit: bolt, career, dart, dash, gallop,
hasten, hotfoot, hurry, jog, leg it, race,
rush, scamper, scurry, speed, sprint;
abscond, beat it, clear out, depart,
escape, flee, make off, scarper, take off,
take to one's heels; course, glide, go,
move, pass, roll, skim; bear, carry, drive,
manoeuvre, transport; operate, ply;
function, perform, tick, work;
administer, control, direct, head, look
after, manage, mastermind, oversee,
regulate, supervise, take care of;
continue, extend, last, lie, proceed,
range, reach, stretch; cascade, discharge,
flow, gush, issue, leak, pour, spill,
stream; dissolve, fuse, liquefy, melt, turn
to liquid; be diffused, mix, spread; come
apart, ladder, tear, unravel; be current,
circulate, climb, creep, go round, trail;
display, feature, print, publish; be a
candidate, challenge, contend, stand,
take part; bootleg, deal in, smuggle,
sneak, traffic in.

run down

vb lit: crash into, knock down, run over;
cut back, decrease, reduce, trim;
debilitate, exhaust, sap, tire; belittle,
calumniate, denigrate, disparage, knock.

run into

vb lit: bump into, collide with, crash into,
hit, ram; come across, encounter, meet;
be beset by, confront, face.

runner

n lit: athlete, harrier, racer; absconder,
escapee, fugitive; race-horse; bearer,

courier; offshoot, sprig, sprout, stem,
sucker, tendril.

run out

vb lit: come to an end, dry up, end, finish,
give out, peter out; be cleaned out (of),
exhaust one's supply (of); rat (on).

run over

vb lit: crash into, knock down, run down;
overflow, spill over; check, go over,
rehearse, review, run through.

runt

n lit: dwarf, midget, miniature; last,
puniest, smallest, weakest; halfpint,
shrimp, small-fry, titch.

rupture

n lit: break, burst, fissure, fracture, rent,
split; hernia; *fig*: breach, bust-up,
disruption, estrangement, quarrel, rift,
schism.
vb lit: break, burst, cleave, fracture,
puncture, split; herniate; *fig*: break off,
sever contact.

rush

n lit: dash, hurry, race, scramble; assault,
charge, onslaught, storm; reed.
vb lit: career, dart, dash, fly, hurry, race,
run, scramble, scurry, speed; attack,
charge (at), storm.
adj lit: emergency, urgent; hasty, hurried,
quick, rapid.

rust

n lit: corrosion, oxidation; blight, fungal
disease, fungus, mildew, mould.
vb lit: corrode, oxidize; decay, deteriorate,
tarnish.

rustic

adj lit: countrified, country, inland, rural,
upcountry; homely, plain, simple,
unsophisticated; boorish, clodhopping,
coarse, crude, loutish, lumpish,
maladroit, uncouth.

rusty

adj lit: corroded, oxidized; *fig*: creaking,
croaking, hoarse; diminished, impaired,
out of practice, stiff, unpractised.

rut

n lit: furrow, gouge, groove, score,
trough; track, wheelmark; *fig*: fixed way
of doing things, pattern, routine; *spec*:
sexual excitement (in certain male
animals).

ruthless
adj lit: brutal, callous, cruel, hard-
  hearted, heartless, inhuman, merciless,
  pitiless, relentless, remorseless,
  unfeeling.

S

sabotage
n lit: damage, destruction, disruption, subversion, treachery, treason, wrecking.
vb lit: cripple, damage, destroy, disable, disrupt, incapacitate, subvert, throw a spanner in the works, undermine, vandalize, wreck.

sabre
n lit: cavalry soldier, curved sword; *spec*: skill in fencing, two-edged foil (in fencing).
vb lit: cut (with a sabre), kill (with a sabre), strike (with a sabre), wound (with a sabre).

sack
n lit: bag; bagful, unit of measure; loose-hanging coat, trail; wine; dismissal, termination of employment, the axe, the boot, the chop; *fig*: depredation, despoliation, destruction, devastation, looting, pillage, plunder, rape, rapine, ravage, ruin, waste.
vb lit: axe, discharge, dismiss, fire, give (someone) his marching orders, give (someone) the boot, kick out; *fig*: demolish, despoil, destroy, devastate, lay waste, loot, maraud, pillage, plunder, raid, ravage, rifle, ruin, spoil.

sacred
adj lit: blessed, consecrated, hallowed, holy, revered, sanctified, venerable; invulnerable, protected, sacrosanct, secure; holy, solemn.

sacrifice
n lit: burnt offering, destruction, hecatomb, immolation, loss, oblation, renunciation, surrender.
vb lit: forego, forfeit, give up, immolate, let go, lose, offer, surrender.

sacrilegious
adj lit: blasphemous, desecrating, heretical, irreverent, mocking, profane, violating.

sad
adj lit: blue, cheerless, depressed, disconsolate, dismal, doleful, down, downcast, down in the dumps, gloomy, glum, grieved, heavy-hearted, low, lugubrious, melancholy, mournful, sick at heart, sombre, wistful, woebegone; *fig*: calamitous, dark, depressing, disastrous, grievous, heart-rending, moving, pathetic, pitiful, sorry, tearful, tragic, upsetting; bad, deplorable, distressing, lamentable, miserable, regrettable, serious, unfortunate, unhappy, unsatisfactory, wretched.

saddle
vb lit: burden, charge, encumber, load, lumber, task, tax.

sadistic
adj lit: brutal, cruel, fiendish, perverse, perverted, ruthless, vicious.

sadness
n lit: bleakness, cheerlessness, depression, despondency, dolefulness, gloominess, grief, heavy heart, melancholy, misery, mournfulness, sorrowfulness, the blues, the dumps, unhappiness.

safari
n lit: hunting expedition, travellers' caravan.

safe
n lit: coffer, repository, safe-deposit box, strongbox, vault.
adj lit: guarded, impregnable, intact, out of danger, out of harm's way, protected, safe and sound, secure, unharmed, unscathed; harmless, innocuous, nonpoisonous, nontoxic, pure, unpolluted, wholesome; cautious, circumspect, conservative, dependable, discreet, prudent, realistic, reliable, sure, trustworthy, unadventurous; certain, risk-free, riskless, secure, sound.

safety
n lit: assurance, immunity, impregnability, protection, refuge, sanctuary, security, shelter.

sag
vb lit: be lopsided, droop, hang sideways, sink.

saga
n lit: narrative, story (of heroic deeds).

sagacity
n lit: acumen, acuteness, perspicacity, shrewdness, sound judgement.

sage
n lit: authority, elder, expert, guru, master, pundit, Solomon, wise man.
adj lit: acute, canny, discerning, intelligent, judicious, perspicacious, prudent, sagacious, sensible, wise.

sail
n lit: piece of canvas.
vb lit: cast anchor, embark, get under way, put to sea, set sail; captain, cruise, go by water, navigate, pilot, ride the waves, skipper, steer, voyage; *fig*: drift, float, fly, glide, shoot, skim, soar, sweep, wing.

sailor
n lit: Jack Tar, lascar, mariner, matelot, navigator, salt, sea dog, seafarer, seaman, tar.

saintly
adj lit: angelic, blessed, devout, god-fearing, godly, pious, righteous, sainted, virtuous, worthy.

sake
n lit: account, advantage, behalf, benefit, consideration, gain, good, interest, profit, regard, respect, welfare, wellbeing; *fig*: aim, cause, end, objective, purpose, reason.

salacious
adj lit: indecent, lascivious, lecherous, lewd, lustful, obscene, smutty.

salary
n lit: earnings, income, pay, remuneration, stipend.

sale
n lit: deal, disposal, selling, transaction, vending; consumers, customers, demand, market, outlet, purchasers.

salient
adj lit: arresting, conspicuous, important, marked, noticeable, outstanding, prominent, pronounced, protruding, remarkable, striking.

sallow
adj lit: anaemic, bilious, pale, pallid, sickly, unhealthy, wan, yellowish.

sally
n lit: military foray, incursion, offensive, raid, sortie, thrust; *fig*: crack, jest, joke, quip, retort, riposte, wisecrack, witticism; escapade, excursion, frolic, jaunt, trip.
vb lit: erupt, go forth, issue, rush, set out, surge.

saloon
n lit: bar, dining room, tavern; saloon car, saloon carriage, sedan.

salty
adj lit: brackish, over-salted, saline, salt, salted; *fig*: colourful, humorous, lively, piquant, pungent, racy, snappy, spicy, tangy, witty, zestful.

salutary
adj lit: advantageous, beneficial, good for one, helpful, practical, profitable, timely, useful, valuable; *fig*: healthy, salubrious.

salute
n lit: address, greeting, obeisance, recognition, salutation, tribute.
vb lit: accost, acknowledge, address, doff one's cap to, greet, hail, kiss, pay one's respects to, welcome; *fig*: honour, pay tribute to, recognize, take one's hat off to.

salvage
n lit: payment (for saving a ship), rescue (of property), saving (of waste paper).
vb lit: glean, recover, redeem, rescue, retrieve, save.

salvation
n lit: deliverance, escape, lifeline, preservation, redemption, rescue, restoration, saving.

salve
n lit: ointment, unguent; smearing tar and grease; *fig*: balm, flattery, praise, soothing words.
vb lit: anoint (wound), smear (sheep); *fig*: make good, smoothe; account for, dispose of, harmonize, vindicate; *spec*: save (cargo).

same
adj lit: aforementioned, selfsame, very; alike, corresponding, duplicate, equivalent, identical, indistinguishable, interchangeable, synonymous, twin; *fig*: consistent, constant, invariable, unaltered, unchanged, unfailing, unvarying.

sample
n lit: cross section, example, illustration, indication, instance, model, pattern, representative, sign, specimen.

vb lit: experience, inspect, partake of, taste, test, try.
adj lit: illustrative, pilot, representative, specimen, test, trial.

sanctimonious
adj lit: canting, false, goody-goody, holier-than-thou, hypocritical, pharisaical, pietistic, pious, self-righteous, smug, Tartuffian, too good to be true, unctuous.

sanction
n lit: allowance, approbation, approval, authority, authorization, backing, confirmation, endorsement, ratification, seal of approval, support; *fig*: ban, boycott, coercive measure, embargo, penalty.
vb lit: allow, approve, authorize, back, countenance, endorse, permit, support, vouch for; confirm, ratify, warrant.

sanctity
n lit: devotion, godliness, grace, holiness, piety, purity, religiousness, righteousness, sanctitude, spirituality; *fig*: inviolability, sacredness, solemnity.

sanctuary
n lit: altar, church, sanctum, shrine, temple; *fig*: asylum, haven, protection, refuge, retreat, shelter; conservation area, national park, nature reserve.

sane
adj lit: all there, in one's right mind, in possession of all one's faculties, lucid, normal, of sound mind, rational; *fig*: balanced, judicious, level-headed, moderate, reasonable, sensible, sober, sound.

sanguine
adj lit: animated, assured, buoyant, confident, hopeful, in good heart, optimistic, spirited; florid, red, ruddy.

sanitary
adj lit: clean, germ-free, hygienic, salubrious, unpolluted, wholesome.

sanity
n lit: mental health, normality, rationality, reason, right mind, saneness, stability; *fig*: common sense, good sense, judiciousness, level-headedness, sense, soundness of judgement.

sap
n lit: essence, life-blood, vital fluid; *fig*: charlie, chump, fool, jerk, nincompoop, ninny, nitwit, noddy, noodle, simpleton, twit, weakling, wet.
vb lit: bleed, deplete, drain, enervate, erode, exhaust, undermine, weaken, wear down.

sarcastic
adj lit: acerbic, acrimonious, back-handed, biting, caustic, contemptuous, cutting, cynical, derisive, disparaging, ironical, mocking, mordant, sardonic, satirical, sharp, sneering, taunting.

sardonic
adj lit: bitter, cynical, derisive, dry, ironical, jeering, malicious, malignant, mocking, mordant, sarcastic, wry.

sash
n lit: ornamental scarf; frame (for glass), sliding light (in glasshouse).

satanic
adj lit: accursed, black, demoniac, demonic, devilish, diabolic, evil, fiendish, hellish, infernal, iniquitous, malevolent, malignant, wicked.

satellite
n lit: communications satellite, moon, sputnik; *fig*: attendant, dependant, follower, hanger-on, lackey, minion, parasite, retainer, sidekick, sycophant, vassal.
adj lit: client, dependent, puppet, suborbinate, tributary, vassal.

satiated
adj (pa.pt) lit: glutted, gorged, jaded, nauseated, stuffed; sated, satisfied, surfeited.

satire
n lit: burlesque, caricature, irony, lampoon, parody, raillery, ridicule, sarcasm, send-up, spoof, travesty, wit.

satisfactory
adj lit: acceptable, adequate, all right, average, competent, fair, good enough, passable, sufficient, up to standard, up to the mark.

satisfy
vb lit: appease, assuage, content, fill, gratify, indulge, mollify, pacify, please, quench, sate, satiate, slake, surfeit; answer, be sufficient, come up to expectations, do, fulfil, meet, qualify,

serve, suffice; assure, convince, dispell
doubts, persuade, put (someone's) mind
at rest, quiet, reassure; comply with,
discharge, pay off, settle, square up; *fig*:
atone, compensate, indemnify, make
good, recompense, remunerate, requite,
reward.

satisfying
adj (pr.pt) lit: cheering, convincing,
filling, gratifying, pleasurable,
satisfactory.

saturate
vb lit: douse, drench, imbue, impregnate,
soak, souse, steep, suffuse, waterlog.

sauce
n lit: dressing, gravy, ketchup, relish;
custard, topping; *fig*: backchat, brass,
cheekiness, disrespectfulness,
impertinence, impudence, insolence, lip,
nerve, rudeness.

saucy
adj lit: cheeky, disrespectful, flippant,
forward, impertinent, impudent,
insolent, pert, presumptuous, rude; *fig*:
dashing, jaunty, natty, perky, rakish,
sporty.

saunter
n lit: airing, amble, constitutional,
promenade, ramble, stroll, turn, walk.
vb lit: amble, dally, linger, loiter, mosey,
ramble, roam, stroll, tarry, wander.

sausage
n lit: banger, chippolata, dog, frankfurter;
black pudding, salami.

savage
n lit: aboriginal, aborigine, autochthon,
heathen, indigene, native, primitive; *fig*:
barbarian, boor, roughneck, yobbo;
beast, brute, fiend, monster.
vb lit: attack, lacerate, mangle, maul, tear
into.
adj lit: feral, rough, rugged, uncivilized,
uncultivated, untamed, wild; *fig*:
barbarous, beastly, bestial, bloodthirsty, brutal, brutish, cruel, devilish,
diabolical, ferocious, fierce, inhuman,
merciless, murderous, ravening,
ruthless, sadistic, vicious; in a state of
nature, primitive, unspoilt.

save
vb lit: bail (someone) out, come to
(someone's) rescue, deliver, free,
liberate, redeem, rescue, salvage, set
free; be frugal, be thrifty, collect,

economize, hide away, hoard, hold,
husband, keep up one's sleeve, lay by,
put aside for a rainy day, put by, reserve,
set aside, store, tighten one's belt,
treasure up; *fig*: conserve, guard, keep
safe, look after, preserve, protect,
safeguard, shield, take care of; hinder,
obviate, prevent, rule out, spare.

savings
n lit: fund, nest egg, reserves, resources,
store.

saviour
n lit: defender, deliverer, friend in need,
guardian, knight in shining armour,
liberator, preserver, protector, rescuer,
salvation.

savoury
adj lit: agreeable, appetizing, dainty,
delectable, delicious, full-flavoured,
luscious, mouthwatering, palatable, rich,
scrumptious, spicy, tangy, tasty,
toothsome; *fig*: decent, honest,
reputable, respectable, wholesome.

say
n lit: crack, turn to speak, voice, vote; *fig*:
authority, influence, power, sway,
weight.
vb lit: add, affirm, announce, assert, come
out with, declare, maintain, mention,
pronounce, put into words, remark,
speak, state, utter, voice; answer,
disclose, divulge, make known, reply,
respond, reveal, tell; allege, claim, noise
abroad, put about, rumour, suggest; *fig*:
deliver, do, orate, perform, read, recite,
rehearse, render, repeat; assume,
conjecture, dare say, estimate, hazard a
guess, imagine, judge, presume,
suppose, surmise; communicate, convey,
express, imply.

saying
n lit: adage, aphorism, apophthegm,
axiom, byword, dictum, maxim,
proverb, saw.

scab
n lit: incrustation (over a wound), itch,
mange, scabies, skin-disease, fungous
plant-disease; *fig*: black-leg, worker (who
refuses to join union); rascal, scoundrel.

scabrous
adj lit: rough, scraggly, scurfy; *fig*: full of
difficulties, harsh, thorny; indelicate,
requiring tactful treatment, risqué.

scale
n lit: flake, lamina, layer, plate;
calibration, degrees, gamut, gradation,
graduation, hierarchy, ladder, pecking
order, ranking, register, sequence, series,
spectrum, spread, steps; *fig*: proportion,
ratio; degree, extent, range, reach, scope,
way.
vb lit: ascend, clamber, climb, escalade,
surmount; *fig*: adjust, proportion,
regulate.

scaly
adj lit: flaky, furfuraceous, scabrous,
scurfy, squamous, squamulose.

scamper
vb lit: dart, dash, fly, hasten, romp, run,
scoot, scurry, scuttle, sprint.

scan
vb lit: check, examine, glance over,
investigate, look one up and down, run
one's eyes over, scour, scrutinize, search,
size up, survey, sweep, take stock of.

scandalize
vb lit: affront, appal, disgust, horrify,
offend, outrage, shock.

scandalous
adj lit: atrocious, disgraceful,
disreputable, infamous, monstrous,
odious, opprobrious, outrageous,
shameful, shocking, unseemly; *fig*:
defamatory, libellous, scurrilous,
slanderous, untrue.

scanty
adj lit: bare, deficient, exiguous,
inadequate, insufficient, meagre, narrow,
poor, restricted, scant, skimpy, slender,
sparing, sparse, thin.

scar
n lit: blemish, cicatrix, injury, mark.
vb lit: brand, damage, disfigure, mark,
traumatize.

scarcely
adv lit: barely, hardly, only just; *fig*: by no
means, definitely not, hardly, not at all,
on no account, under no circumstances.

scarcity
n lit: dearth, deficiency, insufficiency,
lack, paucity, rareness, shortage,
undersupply, want.

scare
n lit: alarm, alert, fright, panic, shock,
start, terror.
vb lit: alarm, daunt, dismay, frighten, give
(someone) a turn, intimidate, panic, put
the wind up (someone), shock, startle,
terrify, terrorize.

scathing
adj lit: biting, brutal, caustic, critical,
cutting, harsh, mordant, sarcastic,
scornful, searing, trenchant, withering.

scatological
adj lit: (of) fossil dung; *fig*: filthy,
obscene.

scatter
vb lit: broadcast, diffuse, disseminate,
fling, litter, shower, spread, sprinkle,
strew; *fig*: disband, dispel, disperse,
dissipate, put to flight, separate.

scatterbrained
adj lit: bird-brained, desultory, flighty,
heedless, madcap, thoughtless.

scattering
n lit: few, handful, scatter, smattering,
sprinkling.

scavenger
n lit: animal feeding on carrion; street-
cleaner; scandal-writer.

scenario
n lit: master plan, outline, résumé,
rundown, scheme, sketch, story line,
summary, synopsis.

scene
n lit: display, exhibition, pageant,
representation, show, sight, spectacle,
tableau; area, locality, place, position,
site, situation, spot, whereabouts;
backdrop, background, set, setting; act,
division, episode, incident, part, stage;
landscape, panorama, prospect, view,
vista; *fig*: carry-on, commotion,
confrontation, fuss, row, tantrum, to-do;
arena, business, environment, field of
interest, milieu, world.

scenic
adj lit: picturesque; of the stage; affected,
dramatic, put on.

scent
n lit: aroma, bouquet, fragrance, odour,
perfume, redolence, smell; *fig*: spoor,
track, trail.

vb lit: be on the track of, detect, discern, get wind of, nose out, recognize, sense, smell, sniff, sniff out.

sceptic
n lit: agnostic, cynic, disbeliever, doubter, doubting Thomas, scoffer.

sceptical
adj lit: cynical, disbelieving, doubtful, doubting, dubious, hesitating, incredulous, mistrustful, questioning, quizzical, scoffing, unbelieving, unconvinced.

schedule
n lit: agenda, calendar, catalogue, inventory, itinerary, plan, programme, timetable.
vb lit: appoint, arrange, be due, book, organize, plan, programme, time.

scheme
n lit: contrivance, course of action, design, device, plan, programme, project, proposal, strategy, system, tactics, theory; arrangement, blueprint, chart, codification, diagram, disposition, draft, layout, outline, pattern, schedule, system; *fig*: conspiracy, dodge, game, intrigue, machinations, manoeuvre, plot, ploy, ruse, shift, stratagem, subterfuge.
vb lit: contrive, design, devise, imagine, lay plans, project, work out; *fig*: collude, conspire, intrigue, machinate, manoeuvre, plot, wheel and deal.

scheming
adj lit: artful, calculating, conniving, cunning, designing, duplicitous, foxy, Machiavellian, slippery, sly, tricky, underhand, wily.

schism
n lit: breach, break, discord, division, rift, rupture, separation, splintering, split.

scholar
n lit: academic, bookworm, intellectual, man of letters, savant; *fig*: disciple, learner, pupil, student.

scholarship
n lit: accomplishments, attainments, book-learning, education, erudition, knowledge, learning, lore; bursary, exhibition, fellowship.

school
n lit: academy, alma mater, college, department, discipline, faculty, institute, institution, seminary; *fig*: adherents, circle, class, clique, denomination, devotees, disciples, faction, followers, following, group, pupils, sect, set; creed, faith, outlook, persuasion, school of thought, stamp, way of life.
vb lit: coach, discipline, drill, educate, indoctrinate, instruct, prepare, prime, train, tutor, verse.

science
n lit: body of knowledge, branch of knowledge, discipline; *fig*: art, skill, technique.

scintillating
adj lit: animated, bright, brilliant, dazzling, ebullient, glittering, lively, sparkling, stimulating, witty.

scoff
vb lit: belittle, deride, despise, flout, gibe, jeer, knock, laugh at, make light of, mock, poke fun at, pooh-pooh, revile, ridicule, scorn, sneer, taunt, twit.

scold
n lit: nag, shrew, termagant, Xanthippe.
vb lit: berate, blame, bring (someone) to book, castigate, censure, chide, find fault with, give (someone) a dressing-down, lecture, nag, rate, rebuke, remonstrate with, reprimand, reproach, take (someone) to task, tell off, tick off, upbraid, vituperate.

scolding
n lit: dressing-down, lecture, piece of one's mind, rebuke, telling-off, ticking-off, tongue-lashing.

scoop
n lit: dipper, ladle, spoon; *fig*: exclusive, exposé, inside story, revelation, sensation.
vb lit: gather up, pick up, sweep up, take up; bail, dig, dip, excavate, gouge, hollow, ladle, scrape, shovel.

scope
n lit: area, capacity, compass, confines, elbowroom, extent, freedom, latitude, liberty, opportunity, orbit, outlook, purview, range, reach, room, space, span, sphere.

scorch

vb lit: blacken, blister, burn, char, parch, roast, sear, shrivel, singe, wither.

score

n lit: grade, mark, outcome, points, record, result, total; the facts, the setup, the situation, the truth; crowds, droves, hosts, hundreds, legions, lots, masses, millions, multitudes, myriads, swarms; *fig*: account, basis, ground, reason; a bone to pick, grievance, grudge, injury, injustice, wrong; amount due, bill, charge, debt, obligation, reckoning, tally, total.

vb lit: achieve, amass, gain, make, notch up, win; count, keep count, record, register, tally; crosshatch, cut, deface, gouge, graze, indent, mar, mark, nick, notch, scrape, scratch, slash; cross out, put a line through, strike out; gain an advantage, go down well with (someone), impress, make an impact, make a point, put oneself across, triumph; *spec*: adapt, arrange, orchestrate, set.

scorn

n lit: contempt, contemptuousness, derision, disdain, disparagement, mockery, sarcasm, scornfulness, slight, sneer.

vb lit: be above, consider beneath one, contemn, deride, disdain, flout, hold in contempt, look down on, make fun of, scoff at, slight, sneer at, spurn, turn up one's nose at.

scornful

adj lit: contemptuous, defiant, derisive, disdainful, haughty, insolent, insulting, jeering, mocking, sarcastic, sardonic, scathing, scoffing, slighting, sneering, supercilious, withering.

scotch

vb lit: crush, eradicate, nip in the bud, stamp out; foil, frustrate, prevent, thwart; cut, gash, score.

scoundrel

n lit: blackguard, criminal, crook, delinquent, villain; knave, rascal, rogue, vagabond.

scour

vb lit: abrade, rub, scrape clean, scrub; hose, play a jet over, syringe; cauterize; burnish, polish; *fig*: beat, comb, hunt through, rake through, search high and low through.

scourge

n lit: cat, lash, strap, whip; *fig*: bane, curse, misfortune, penalty, punishment; avenging angel, nemesis, terror, thorn in the flesh.

vb lit: beat, cane, flog, give a strapping, lash, thrash, welt, whip; *fig*: afflict, harass, harry, plague, terrorize, torment.

scout

n lit: advance guard, lookout, outrider, spy; patrolman; recruiter, talent spotter; agent, representative; *fig*: chap, fellow, man.

vb lit: check (out), look (around), reconnoitre (about), spy (out), take a look (around); ferret (out), hunt (for), look (for), rustle (up), search (out).

scowl

n lit: frown, glower, grimace, pout.

vb lit: frown, glower, look daggers (at), pout, snarl.

scramble

n lit: hassle, mad rush, race, rush, struggle, tussle; affray, commotion, melee, scrimmage; jumble, mess, state of confusion; hard ascent, stiff climb; *spec*: emergency take-off (by an aeroplane); (motorbike) trial.

vb lit: join the mad rush, jump, leap, race, rush, struggle; elbow one's way, jostle, push; clamber, climb, scrabble; crawl, go down on hands and knees; confuse, jumble, mix up, shuffle; encode.

scrap

n lit: bit, crumb, fragment, morsel, part, piece, shred, sliver; leaving(s), leftover(s); junk, waste; affray, battle, brawl, fight, quarrel, row, scrimmage, scuffle, set-to, skirmish, wrangle.

vb lit: abandon, discard, ditch, drop, write off; chuck out, get rid of, throw away; bicker, brawl, fight, quarrel, scuffle, wrangle.

scrape

n lit: abrasion, dent, graze, scratch, scuff-mark; rub, scouring, scrub; filing, grind, rasping; shave; depression, excavation, hollow, pit; *fig*: fix, hole, jam, mess, plight, predicament, spot of trouble; *spec*: thin layer (of butter or margarine).

vb lit: abrade, dent, graze, scratch, scuff; rub, scour, scrub; file, grind, rasp; grate, screech, squeak; shave; excavate, hollow out; *fig*: put (together), save (up); get (by), scrimp.

scrappy
adj lit: bitty, disjointed, disunited, loose, patchy, slack, uncoordinated, varying.

scratch
n lit: abrasion, graze, laceration, mark, rip, scrape, tear; (up to) standard.
vb lit: claw, etch, incise, lacerate, rip, rend, score, scrape, tear; scrawl; *fig*: cancel (out), delete, rub (out); eliminate, strike off; withdraw.
adj lit: casual, impromptu, improvised, rough.

scrawl
n lit: scratch, scribble, squiggling; script, writing; letter, message, note.
vb lit: scratch, scribble, squiggle; dash off, jot, write hurriedly.

scrawny
adj lit: bony, emaciated, gaunt, lean, scraggy, skeletal, skinny, spindly, thin, underweight.

scream
n lit: screech, shriek, wail, yell; *fig*: hoot, laugh, riot.
vb lit: cry, holler, screech, shout, shriek, wail, yell; *fig*: be conspicuous, be loud; clash, conflict, jar.

screen
n lit: divider, parclose, partition; cover, defence, hide, shield; awning, canopy, guard, shade, shelter; fence, panel, railing, wind-break; grill, mesh, raddle, sieve; grid; white surface.
vb lit: keep apart, separate; cover, protect, shelter, shield; conceal, mask, shade; filter, sieve, sift, test; examine, scan, vet; broadcast, present, project, transmit.

screw
n lit: dowel, thread; propeller; spin, twist, wind; *fig*: prison officer, warder; pay, salary, wages; jade, nag; bunk-up, fuck, leg-over, shag.
vb lit: compress, tighten, turn, twist, wind; coerce, constrain, force, pressurize; *fig*: contort, crumple, pucker; steel, summon (up); cheat, con, defraud, swindle; foul (up), mess (up), muck (up); fuck, have it off with, shag.

screwy
adj lit: crazy, insane, lunatic, mad; fishy, odd, peculiar, strange, suspicious.

script
n lit: hand, handwriting; alphabet, calligraphy, letters, writing; copy, dialogue, lines, text; libretto.

scriptural
adj lit: biblical, canonical, doctrinal, New Testament, Old Testament, rabbinical; consecrated, sacred; holy, redeeming, saving; prophetic.

scrounger
n lit: cadger, sponger; leech, parasite.

scrub
n lit: bath, clean, soaping, wash; brushwood, heath, veldt; runt.
vb lit: bath, brush, clean, rub hard, scour, soap, wash; *fig*: abandon, call off, cancel, drop, give up.

scruffy
adj lit: bedraggled, down-at-heel, messy, run-down, seedy, shabby, unkempt, untidy; disreputable, sordid, squalid.

scrum
n lit: ruck, scrimmage, scrummage; crowd, crush, press, swarm, throng; scramble, set-to, stramash, tussle.
vb lit: crowd, crush, press, swarm, throng; barge, elbow, jostle, push, shove.

scruple
n lit: doubt, hesitation, inhibition, misgiving, qualm, reluctance, squeamishness, uneasiness; demur, objection, protest.
vb lit: be loath (to), be reluctant (to), hesitate (to).

scrupulous
adj lit: accurate, conscientious, fastidious, meticulous, painstaking, pedantic, precise, strict.

scrutiny
n lit: contemplation, examination, investigation, observation, perusal, study; invigilation, refereeing, supervision.

scuff
vb lit: abrade, brush, erode, graze, rub, wear down; drag one's feet, shuffle.

scuffle
n lit: affray, brawl, fight, fray, row, rumpus, scrimmage, scrum, set-to, skirmish, tussle, wrangle; scrape, shuffle.
vb lit: brawl, fight, struggle, tussle, wrangle, wrestle; drag one's feet, shuffle.

sculpture
n lit: carving, chiselling; casting, moulding; cameo, engraving, intaglio,

relief-work; cast, bronze, statue;
modelling, statuary.
vb lit: carve, chisel, cut; cast, mould;
fashion, form, model, shape.

scum
n lit: foam, froth; dross, impurities; *fig*:
dregs, rabble, riffraff, trash.

scurrilous
adj lit: coarse, foul-mouthed, gross,
infamous, obscene, offensive, profane,
salacious, vulgar.

sea
n lit: briny, deep, main, ocean; lake;
surge, swell, tide; *fig*: expanse; host,
multitude, plethora.

seal
n lit: arms, colophon, insignia, logo, mark;
attestation, authentication, stamp; bond,
fastening, lock, weld; cap, cover, lid, top.
vb lit: close (up), make airtight, plug,
stop, waterproof; fasten (up); lock (in),
weld (in); *fig*: authenticate, ratify, stamp,
validate; conclude, consummate, finalize,
settle.

seam
n lit: closure, joint, suture; layer, stratum,
vein; furrow, line, ridge.

seamy
adj lit: laced, sewn; *fig*: disreputable,
seedy, sleazy, sordid, squalid.

search
n lit: exploration, hunt, quest; analysis,
examination, inspection, study.
vb lit: look (for); comb, examine, frisk,
rifle (through), scour; go over, inquire
in, investigate, probe; find (out), seek
(out).

searching
adj lit: discriminating, intent, keen,
minute, penetrating, probing, shrewd,
subtle, thorough.

season
n lit: division, period, term, time of year;
interval.
vb lit: flavour, pep up, spice; harden,
mature, toughen, train; *fig*: moderate,
temper.

seasoned
adj lit: hardened, mature, veteran,
weathered; *fig*: battle-scarred,
experienced, practised; well-versed.

seat
n lit: bench, chair, pew, settee, sofa, stool;
saddle; pillion; base, centre, cradle,
headquarters, site; ancestral home,
manor, residence; constituency,
incumbency, membership.
vb lit: install, place, set, settle;
accommodate, contain, sit, take.

secession
n lit: break, disaffiliation, divorce,
resignation, separation; departure,
retirement, withdrawal.

secluded
adj lit: cut off, isolated, lonely, remote,
solitary; cloistered, sheltered.

seclusion
n lit: isolation, loneliness, privacy,
remoteness, retreat, solitude,
withdrawal.

second
n lit: next, other; instant, jiffy, moment,
tick, trice; assistant, backer, supporter.
vb lit: aid, assist, back, encourage,
endorse, forward, go along with, help,
support; detach, lend, temporarily
transfer.
adj lit: following, next, succeeding;
additional, alternative, extra, further,
other; *fig*: inferior, lesser, subordinate,
supporting.

secondary
adj lit: alternative, auxiliary, relief,
reserve, supporting; inferior, lesser,
minor, second-rate, subordinate;
contingent, derivative, indirect, serial.

secret
n lit: confidence; enigma, mystery;
formula, key; (in) camera.
adj lit: private, secluded, unfrequented;
closet, covert, undisclosed; camouflaged,
concealed, disguised, hidden; classified,
hush-hush, undercover; clandestine,
furtive, stealthy; arcane, cryptic,
mysterious, recondite.

secretary
n lit: clerk, scribe, stenographer; assistant,
PA; minister, official; bureau, secretaire,
writing-desk.

secrete
vb lit: discharge, emit, exude, give off,
sweat; conceal, hide, stash, stow away.

sect
n lit: church, denomination, religion;

faction, school of thought; philosophy; class; group, party.

section
n lit: division, part, piece, portion, segment; branch, department; district, sector, zone; detachment, group, squad, team; *spec*: cutting, incision, operation (in surgery).

secular
adj lit: laic, lay, profane, temporal, worldly; age-long.

secure
vb lit: acquire, gain, get, obtain, pick up, procure; bolt, chain, fasten, fix, lock up, padlock, rivet, tie up; defend, fortify, make safe; guarantee, insure.
adj lit: defended, impregnable, invulnerable, protected, safe, unassailable; fastened, fixed, immovable, tight; confined, in custody; assured, certain, confident, sure; absolute, definite, reliable.

security
n lit: defence, protection, safety measures; asylum, safekeeping, safety, sanctuary; assurance, certainty, positivity; collateral, guarantee, pledge, stake, surety.

sedate
vb lit: drug, knock out, numb, pacify, put under, tranquillize; anaesthetize, put to sleep.
adj lit: dignified, noble, stately; composed, decorous, deliberate, grave, solemn; calm, serious.

sedative
n lit: anaesthetic, anodyne, hypnotic, narcotic, pre-med, sleeping pill, tranquillizer; downer.
adj lit: anaesthetic, anodyne, calming, hypnotic, narcotic, relaxing, soporific, tranquillizing.

sedentary
adj lit: desk-bound, immobile, inactive, stationary.

sediment
n lit: dregs, grounds, lees; loess, silt; deposit.

sedition
n lit: agitation, rabble-rousing, rebellion, revolution, subversion, treasonable activity.

seduce
vb lit: beguile, entice, lure, tempt; lead astray, lead on; deflower, introduce to sex.

seductive
adj lit: alluring, beguiling, captivating, enticing, inviting, provocative, tempting; erotic, sexy.

see
n lit: bishopric, diocese; cathedral city.
vb lit: catch sight of, discern, distinguish, espy, make out, perceive, spot; behold, have a look at, observe, view, watch, witness; look up, refer to; call in on, encounter, interview, meet, receive, speak to, visit; accompany, escort, usher; associate with, date, go out with, go steady with; *fig*: anticipate, envisage, envision, picture, visualize; be associated with, bring; experience, undergo; apprehend, fathom, get, grasp, learn, understand; appreciate, be aware of, comprehend, know, realize, recognize; deem, judge; ascertain, discover, find out, investigate; ensure, make certain, mind; consider, deliberate over, make up one's mind, reflect on, think over; accompany, escort, usher; associate with, date, go out with, go steady with.

seed
n lit: grain, kernel, spore; drupe, pip, stone; blastomere, cell; semen; *fig*: beginning, germ, source, start; descendants, heirs, issue, progeny, successors; nation, race; *spec*: top-rated player (in a tournament).
vb lit: broadcast, scatter, sow; de-pip, nip off, stone, take out; dust, powder; *spec*: classify, rate (top players in a tournament); sprinkle (dry ice on clouds).

seedy
adj lit: full of seed; gone to seed; *fig*: abraded, dilapidated, faded, old, worn; scruffy, shabby, sleazy, sordid, squalid; ill, off-colour, poorly, run-down, sickly, unwell, wan.

seek
vb lit: ask, entreat, implore, petition, request; aim for, be after, hope for, look for; hunt, pursue, search for; attempt, endeavour, strive, try.

seer
n lit: augur, foreteller, prophesier,

prophet, soothsayer; clairvoyant, dowser; fortune-teller.

seesaw
vb lit: go back and forth, go up and down, swing, teeter; *fig*: alternate, fluctuate, oscillate.

seethe
vb lit: boil, bubble, ferment, foam, froth; *fig*: be alive (with), swarm, teem; be beside oneself, be livid, fume, go berserk, rage, simmer.

see to
vb lit: arrange, be in charge of, manage, organize; attend to, do, sort out, take care of.

segregate
vb lit: isolate, seclude, separate, set apart, single out.

seize
vb lit: clasp, clutch, grab, grasp, snatch, take; apprehend, arrest, capture, take into custody; repossess, take by force; appropriate, confiscate, impound, requisition, sequester; abduct, hijack, kidnap; *fig*: clog (up), jam (up), stick fast; lash down, make fast, tie up.

seizure
n lit: apprehension, arrest, capture; repossession, retrieval; appropriation, confiscation, requisitioning, sequestration; annexation, take-over, usurpation; abduction, hijack, kidnapping; attack, convulsion, fit, spasm.

seldom
adv lit: hardly ever, infrequently, rarely, scarcely ever.

select
vb lit: choose, elect, opt for, pick out, single out, sort out.
adj lit: choice, élite, prime, superior, top-quality, top-rated; exclusive, limited; privileged.

selection
n lit: choice, election, option, pick; anthology, assortment, collection, line-up; medley; cert, certainty, hot tip, nap.

self-assertion
n lit: determination, dominance, insistence, masterfulness, positivity; pushiness, selfishness.

self-assured
adj lit: confident, poised, self-confident, self-reliant, sure of oneself.

self-centred
adj lit: egotistic, monomaniacal, narcissistic, self-absorbed, selfish.

self-conscious
adj lit: abashed, bashful, diffident, embarrassed, ill at ease, insecure, nervous, shy.

self-control
n lit: restraint, self-discipline, willpower.

self-effacing
adj lit: demure, modest, quiet, reclusive, reserved, reticent, retiring, shy, unassertive; humble, meek; timid.

self-esteem
n lit: confidence, ego, pride, self-regard, self-respect.

self-government
n lit: autonomy, home rule, independence, sovereignty.

selfish
adj lit: self-centred, self-seeking; avaricious, greedy, mean; mercenary.

selfless
adj lit: altruistic, generous, heroic, magnanimous, noble, self-denying, unselfish.

self-reliant
adj lit: able, capable, independent, practical, self-confident, self-sufficient.

self-respect
n lit: dignity, morale, pride, self-esteem, self-regard.

self-satisfied
adj lit: gratified, pleased with oneself, self-congratulatory, triumphant; complacent, overconfident, smug.

self-seeking
adj lit: calculating, mercenary, opportunistic, time-serving, trimming; out for what one can get; selfish.

sell
vb lit: deal in, hawk, peddle, retail, trade in, vend; dispose of, put up for sale; accept payment for; *fig*: market, promote, put across; convert to, convince of, get (one) hooked (on).

seller
n lit: dealer, merchant, retailer, sales

assistant, shopkeeper, tradesman; vendor; peddler, pusher.

semblance
n lit: air, appearance, aspect, atmosphere, façade, guise, image, likeness, look.

seminary
n lit: academy, boarding school, college, school; theological college.

senate
n lit: assembly, congress, diet, governing body, legislative assembly, parliament, upper house; committee of elders, council.

send
vb lit: consign, convey, dispatch, forward, have delivered, mail, post; broadcast, transmit; fling, hurl, sling, throw; fire, launch, propel, shoot; give (off); radiate (out); tell to go (away), turn (away); call (for); *fig*: excite, intoxicate, stir, thrill.

send up
vb lit: commit to prison, jail, put away, sentence; *fig*: caricature, mimic, parody, satirize, take off.

senile
adj lit: decrepit, doddering, failing, in one's dotage.

senior
adj lit: elder, older; of higher rank, superior; more advanced, upper; chief, first.

sensation
n lit: feeling; emotion; awareness, perception; effect, impression, sense; thrill; *fig*: agitation, commotion, excitement, stir; scoop; craze, fad, novelty.

sensational
adj lit: astounding, dramatic, earth-shattering, epoch-making, exciting, fantastic, galvanizing, spectacular, staggering, stupendous, thrilling; appalling, horrifying, outrageous, scandalous, shocking; excellent, exceptional, marvellous, superb, wonderful; *spec*: gutter, yellow (press).

sense
n lit: appreciation, awareness, faculty, feeling, impression; air, aura, atmosphere; intuition, premonition, presentiment; discernment, imagination, logic, nous, practicability, practicality,

reason, understanding; gist, implication, import, meaning, point, purport, significance, substance, use.
vb lit: appreciate, apprehend, be aware of, feel, get the impression, grasp, hear, perceive, realize, scent, see, taste.

senseless
adj lit: absurd, crazy, fatuous, halfwitted, idiotic, ludicrous, mindless, nonsensical, ridiculous, stupid, unreasonable; bootless, futile, meaningless, pointless; anaesthetized, deadened, insensible, knocked out, numb, unconscious.

sensibility
n lit: awareness, perception, sensitivity; emotion, feeling, sentiment; acuity, appreciation, delicacy, discernment, discrimination, taste.

sensible
adj lit: canny, down-to-earth, matter-of-fact, no-nonsense, practical, straightforward; judicious, politic, prudent, realistic; intelligent, reasonable, shrewd, sound, wise; aware (of), conscious (of), mindful (of).

sensitive
adj lit: feeling, keen, perceptive, reactive, responsive; allergic; delicate, emotional, highly-strung, impressionable, nervous, tender; thin-skinned, touchy; *fig*: controversial, hot; awkward, embarrassing; embarrassed, shame-faced.

sensual
adj lit: bodily, carnal, fleshly, physical; erotic, lascivious, lecherous, lustful, randy, sexual, voluptuous.

sensuous
adj lit: bodily, fleshly, physical; feeling, perceptive, reactive, responsive, sensory; gratifying, pleasurable.

sentence
n lit: clause, statement, thought; decision, judgement, ruling, verdict.

sententious
adj lit: aphoristic, concise, epigrammatic, laconic, pithy; canting, moralistic, pompous, sanctimonious.

sentient
adj lit: alive, aware, conscious, feeling, perceptive, responsive, sensitive.

sentiment
n lit: emotion, sensibility, tenderness;

attitude, feeling, opinion, outlook,
persuasion, view, viewpoint.

sentimental
adj lit: emotional, maudlin, nostalgic,
pathetic, simpering, sloppy, soft-
hearted, tearful, tender.

sentry
n lit: guard, lookout, picket, watch.

separate
vb lit: break off, come apart, detach,
disconnect, divide, keep apart, sever,
split; put on one side, segregate, sort out;
fig: break up, diverge, divorce, estrange,
go different ways, part company, split
up.
adj lit: detached, disconnected, disjointed,
divided, divorced, unattached; alone,
autonomous, independent, particular,
single.

separation
n lit: break, detachment, disconnection,
dissociation, division, gap, severance; *fig*:
break-up, divorce, estrangement,
parting, rift, split.

septic
adj lit: festering, infected, putrid, toxic.

sequence
n lit: course, cycle, order, progression,
succession.

sequential
adj lit: forming a sequence.

sequestered
adj lit: isolated, out-of-the-way, quiet,
remote, secluded, unfrequented.

sequestration
n lit: confiscation, seizure; seclusion,
separation, withdrawal.

seraphic
adj lit: angelic, celestial, heavenly, pure,
sublime.

serene
adj lit: calm, composed, imperturbable,
placid, unruffled; clear, cloudless,
halcyon, unclouded.

serenity
n lit: calmness, composure, peace of mind,
placidity, quietness, stillness,
tranquillity; brightness, clearness.

series
n lit: arrangement, course, order,
sequence, string, succession, train.

serious
adj lit: grave, pensive, solemn, thoughtful;
determined, earnest, genuine, resolute,
sincere; *fig*: crucial, difficult, important,
momentous, pressing, significant,
weighty; acute, critical, dangerous,
severe.

seriously
adv lit: earnestly, in all conscience, no
joking, sincerely, with a straight face; *fig*:
acutely, badly, critically, dangerously,
gravely, grievously, severely.

sermon
n lit: address, homily; *fig*: dressing-down,
harangue, talking-to.

serpentine
adj lit: like a serpent; *fig*: coiling, cunning,
meandering, sinuous, tortuous,
treacherous, writhing.

servant
n lit: attendant, domestic, help, lackey,
maid, retainer.

serve
vb lit: assist, attend to, help, minister to,
wait on, work for; act, discharge, do,
fulfil, officiate, perform; answer, be
adequate, function as, suffice, suit;
deliver, dish up, distribute, provide,
supply.

service
n lit: assistance, avail, help, supply, use,
utility; maintenance, overhaul, servicing;
duty, employment, office, work; *fig*:
ceremony, observance, worship.
vb lit: check, go over, maintain, overhaul,
repair.

serviceable
adj lit: advantageous, beneficial,
convenient, dependable, functional,
practical, profitable, useful.

servile
adj lit: of slaves, base, cringing, fawning,
grovelling, mean, slavish, yielding.

serving
n lit: helping, portion.

servitude
n lit: bondage, obedience, serfdom,
slavery, subjugation, thraldom,
vassalage.

session
n lit: assembly, discussion, meeting,
sitting, term.

set
n lit: attitude, bearing, position, posture,
turn; scene, scenery, stage setting; band,
circle, company, crew, faction, gang,
group, outfit; *fig*: assortment, batch,
collection, compendium, kit, series.
vb lit: aim, apply, direct, fix, install, lay,
locate, place, position, put, rest, situate,
stick; *fig*: agree upon, allocate, appoint,
assign, determine, establish, resolve,
schedule, settle; arrange, make ready,
prepare; adjust, coordinate, regulate,
synchronize; condense, congeal,
crystallize, solidify, thicken; allot,
impose, lay down, specify; decline,
disappear, go down, sink, vanish.
adj lit: agreed, arranged, customary,
definite, established, fixed, prearranged,
regular, settled; *fig*: conventional,
formal, routine, stock, traditional;
entrenched, firm, hardened, inflexible,
rigid, strict; bent, determined, intent.

set about
vb lit: begin, get cracking, get down to,
roll up one's sleeves, start, tackle; *fig*:
assail, attack, belabour, lambaste.

setback
n lit: bit of trouble, check,
disappointment, hitch, rebuff, reverse.

set fire to
vb lit: ignite, light, set ablaze, touch a
match to; burn, flambé.

set off
vb lit: depart, leave, sally forth, set out;
detonate, explode, light, set in motion;
bring out the highlights in, enhance,
show off.

set out
vb lit: arrange, describe, display,
elaborate, exhibit, explain, lay out,
present; *fig*: embark, get under way, hit
the road, set off, start out.

setting
n lit: background, context, frame, scene,
set, site, surroundings.

settle
vb lit: adjust, put into order, straighten
out, work out; clear up, complete,
conclude, put an end to, resolve; agree,
come to an agreement, confirm, fix;
calm, pacify, quell, quieten, reassure,
sedate, soothe; bed down, come to rest,
descend, land, make oneself comfortable;
dwell, live, make one's home, move to,
reside; colonize, found, people,
populate; acquit oneself of, clear,
liquidate, pay; decline, sink, subside.

settler
n lit: colonizer, pioneer, planter.

set-up
n lit: arrangement, conditions,
organization, regime, system.

set up
vb lit: arrange, found, initiate, install,
make provision for, organize; build up,
establish, finance, promote, subsidize;
assemble, construct, erect, put together,
raise.

sever
vb lit: break off, cut apart, part from;
divide, separate, disjoin.

several
adj lit: assorted, different, diverse, many,
some, sundry, various.

severe
adj lit: austere, Draconian, hard, harsh,
oppressive, rigid, strict, unbending;
cold, disapproving, dour, forbidding,
grim, stern, strait-laced, tight-lipped;
acute, bitter, critical, dangerous, fierce,
grinding; *fig*: ascetic, chaste, plain,
restrained, simple, Spartan,
unembellished; arduous, demanding,
exacting, punishing, rigorous, stringent,
tough; astringent, caustic, cutting,
satirical, scathing, unsparing.

sex
n lit: gender; *fig*: desire, facts of life,
libido, lust, sensuality, sexuality.

sexual intercourse
n lit: carnal knowledge, coition, coitus,
copulation, coupling, mating.

sexy
adj lit: arousing, cuddly, erotic, inviting,
naughty, provocative, seductive, sensual,
suggestive, titillating, voluptuous.

shabby
adj lit: dilapidated, faded, neglected, run-
down, scruffy, seedy, tatty, worn-out;
fig: cheap, despicable, dirty, low, mean,
rotten, shoddy.

shack
n lit: cabin, dump, hovel, hut, shanty.

shackle
n lit: bond, chain, fetter, handcuff, manacle, rope, tether.
vb lit: bind, chain, hobble, manacle, pinion, put in irons, secure, tie, trammel; *fig*: constrain, encumber, hamper, impede, inhibit, obstruct, restrict, tie (someone's) hands.

shade
n lit: dimness, dusk, gloom, shadiness, shadows; blind, canopy, cover, curtain, screen; *fig*: colour, hue, tint, tone; dash, degree, hint, nuance, semblance, suggestion, trace; apparition, ghost, manes, phantom, spectre, spirit.
vb lit: cast a shadow over, cover, darken, dim, protect, screen, shield, veil.

shadow
n lit: cover, dimness, dusk, gloom, protection, shelter; hint, suggestion, trace; *fig*: ghost, image, representation, spectre, vestige; blight, gloom, sadness.
vb lit: darken, overhang, screen, shade, shield; *fig*: dog, follow, stalk, tail.

shadowy
adj lit: crepuscular, dark, dusky, gloomy, murky, shady, tenebrous; *fig*: dim, dream-like, faint, ghostly, illusory, intangible, nebulous, spectral, unreal, vague.

shady
adj lit: cool, dim, leafy, shadowy, umbrageous; *fig*: crooked, dubious, shifty, slippery, suspicious, unscrupulous, untrustworthy.

shaft
n lit: handle, rod, stem, upright; beam, ray, streak; barb, cut, dart, sting, thrust.

shaggy
adj lit: hairy, hirsute, rough, unkempt, unshorn.

shake
n lit: agitation, convulsion, jerk, jolt, pulsation, quaking, shiver, tremor, vibration; *fig*: instant, jiffy, second, trice.
vb lit: bump, fluctuate, jar, joggle, jounce, oscillate, quake, rock, shudder, totter, tremble, wobble; brandish, wave; *fig*: agitate, churn, rouse, stir; distress, disturb, intimidate, rattle, shock, unnerve; impair, undermine, weaken.

shake off
vb lit: dislodge, get away from, get rid of, give the slip, lose, throw off.

shake up
vb lit: agitate, churn (up), mix, reorganize, stir (up), unsettle, upset.

shaky
adj lit: faltering, insecure, precarious, rickety, tottering, unstable, wobbly; *fig*: dubious, questionable, suspect, unreliable, unsound.

shallow
n lit: flat, sandbank, shelf, shoal.
adj lit: empty, flimsy, frivolous, meaningless, puerile, skin-deep, superficial, trivial, unintelligent.

sham
n lit: counterfeit, forgery, fraud, hoax, humbug, impostor, phoney, pretence, pretender.
vb lit: affect, assume, fake, feign, imitate, put on, simulate.
adj lit: artificial, bogus, counterfeit, false, imitation, mock, phoney, pseudo, spurious, synthetic.

shambles
n lit: chaos, confusion, disarray, disorder, havoc, mess, muddle.

shame
n lit: blot, contempt, derision, disgrace, disrepute, infamy, opprobrium, reproach, scandal, smear; abashment, chagrin, embarrassment, humiliation, ignominy, loss of face, mortification.
vb lit: abash, confound, disconcert, disgrace, humble, humiliate, mortify, reproach, ridicule; debase, defile, discredit, smear, stain.

shameful
adj lit: atrocious, dastardly, disgraceful, ignominious, infamous, mean, outrageous, reprehensible, unworthy, wicked; degrading, embarrassing, humiliating, mortifying.

shameless
adj lit: audacious, bare-faced, brash, brazen, depraved, flagrant, immodest, impudent, insolent, profligate, reprobate, unabashed, wanton.

shape
n lit: build, contours, figure, form, make, outline; frame, mould, pattern; *fig*: appearance, aspect, guise, likeness,

semblance; condition, fettle, health,
state.
vb lit: fashion, form, make, model, mould;
fig: adapt, define, devise, frame, modify,
plan, prepare, regulate.

shapeless
adj lit: amorphous, asymmetrical,
formless, indeterminate, irregular,
misshapen, nebulous.

share
n lit: allotment, allowance, contribution,
due, lot, portion, quota, ration, whack.
vb lit: apportion, assign, distribute, divide,
go halves, partake, participate, split.

sharp
adj lit: acute, cutting, knife-edged,
pointed, razor-sharp, serrated, spiky;
abrupt, distinct, marked, sudden; *fig*:
alert, apt, astute, bright, perceptive,
quick-witted, subtle; artful, crafty,
cunning, shrewd, sly, unscrupulous,
wily; distressing, excruciating, fierce,
piercing, sore, stabbing, stinging; clear-
cut, crisp, well-defined; chic, classy,
dressy, natty, smart, snappy, stylish;
acrimonious, biting, bitter, caustic,
harsh, hurtful, sarcastic, sardonic,
scathing, trenchant, vitriolic; acid, acrid,
burning, piquant, pungent, sour,
vinegary.
adv lit: exactly, on the dot, on time,
promptly, punctually; *fig*: abruptly,
unexpectedly, without warning.

sharply
adv lit: acutely, cuttingly, pointedly;
abruptly, suddenly; aptly, brightly,
subtly; cunningly, shrewdly; fiercely,
piercingly; smartly, stylishly; bitterly,
harshly.

shatter
vb lit: break, crack, crush to smithereens,
demolish, pulverize, smash; blast,
destroy, impair, ruin, wreck; *fig*: break
(someone's) heart, devastate,
dumbfound, upset.

shattered
adj (pa.pt) lit: broken, burst, exploded,
shivered, smashed, split; blasted,
blighted, destroyed, exhausted,
impaired, ruined.

shave
n lit: cutting off (hair); shaving, thin slice;
fig: escape, narrow miss; deception, hoax,
trick.

vb lit: crop, pare, remove hair, shear, trim;
fig: brush, graze, miss narrowly, pass
close, skirt; be hard, extort (money).

shear
vb lit: clip, cut, fleece; *fig*: deprive, strip.

sheath
n lit: case, close cover; *spec*: horny case,
skin, tissue.

shed
n lit: cover, hut, shelter; ridge, watershed.
vb lit: cause to flow, drop, let fall, pour out,
spill; cast, diffuse, emit, give forth,
radiate, scatter, throw; cast off, discard,
moult, slough.

sheen
n lit: brightness, gleam, glitter, lustre,
radiance, shine.

sheepish
adj lit: abashed, embarrassed, mortified,
shamefaced, silly, timorous.

sheer
vb lit: swerve, turn aside.
adj lit: abrupt, precipitous, steep;
absolute, complete, out-and-out, total,
unadulterated, utter; fine, pure,
seethrough, thin.

sheet
n lit: coat, film, lamina, layer, leaf, overlay,
panel, plate, surface, veneer; blanket,
covering, expanse, stretch.

shelf
n lit: board; bedrock, ledge, reef,
sandbank.

shell
n lit: case, husk, pod; frame, hull, skeleton,
structure.
vb lit: husk, shuck; barrage, blitz,
bombard, strike.

shelter
n lit: cover, guard, haven, refuge, safety,
sanctuary, screen.
vb lit: cover, defend, guard, harbour, hide,
protect, safeguard, shield.

sheltered
adj (pa.pt) lit: cloistered, isolated,
protected, reclusive, screened, secluded,
shielded, withdrawn.

shelved
adj (pa.pt) *lit*: abandoned, deferred, postponed.

shepherd
n lit: sheepminder; pastor, spiritual guide.
vb lit: guide, herd, marshal, steer, usher.

shield
n lit: buckler, escutcheon; bulwark, defence, protection, rampart, safeguard, shelter.
vb lit: cover, defend, guard, protect, screen, ward off.

shift
n lit: alteration, change, fluctuation, modification, rearrangement, shifting, switch, veering; *fig*: contrivance, craft, dodge, evasion, move, stratagem, trick, wile.
vb lit: alter, budge, displace, fluctuate, move, rearrange, remove, swerve, switch, transfer, vary, veer.

shiftless
adj lit: inefficient, lazy.

shifty
adj lit: contriving, devious, evasive, furtive, scheming, slippery, tricky, underhand, untrustworthy.

shimmering
adj lit: gleaming, glistening, scintillating, sparkling, twinkling.

shine
n lit: brightness, glare, gleam, luminosity, shimmer, sparkle; *fig*: glaze, gloss, lustre, polish, sheen.
vb lit: beam, emit light, glare, glitter, radiate, scintillate, sparkle, twinkle; *fig*: excel, stand out.

shining
adj lit: beaming, bright, effulgent, glittering, luminous, radiant, resplendent, sparkling; *fig*: brilliant, distinguished, eminent, illustrious, leading, outstanding.

shiny
adj lit: bright, burnished, glistening, glossy, lustrous, polished, satiny.

ship
n lit: boat, canoo, frigate, galley, vessel, yacht; airship, zeppelin.

shipshape
adj lit: in good order.

shirk
vb lit: avoid, dodge, duck (out of), get out of, shun, skive, slack.

shivers
n lit: shakes, trembles, quivers; fragments, smithereens, splinters.
vb lit: break, crack, fragment, shatter, smash, splinter.

shoal
n lit: sandbank, shallow, shelf.

shock
n lit: blow, breakdown, collapse, consternation, stupor, trauma, turn; clash, collision, impact, jolt.
vb lit: appal, astound, disquiet, give (someone) a turn, jar, jolt, numb, offend, outrage, scandalize, shake up, stagger, stun, stupefy, traumatize.

shocking
adj lit: abominable, atrocious, disgraceful, disgusting, dreadful, ghastly, hideous, loathsome, outrageous, repulsive, revolting, scandalous, sickening, unspeakable.

shoddy
adj lit: inferior, poor, rubbishy, second-rate, slipshod, tatty.

shoot
n lit: branch, bud, offshoot, sprig, sprout, sucker; current, rapids; chute, slide; shooting expedition, party.
vb lit: bud, burgeon, put forth new growth, sprout; bolt, dart, dash, fly, hurtle, rush, speed, tear, whisk; bag, blast, bring down, open fire, pump full of lead, zap; discharge, fire, fling, hurl, let fly.

shore
n lit: beach, coast, sands, seashore.
adj lit: littoral, waterside.

shore up
vb lit: bolster, brace, buttress, prop up, stabilize, support, underpin.

short
adj lit: abridged, compressed, concise, curtailed, laconic, pithy, summary, terse; diminutive, dumpy, petite, small; brief, fleeting, momentary; deficient, insufficient, lacking, low (on), scarce, sparse, wanting; abrupt, brusque, curt, discourteous, gruff, sharp, surly, terse, uncivil; direct, straight; crumbly (pastry).

adv lit: abruptly, by surprise, suddenly, unaware.

shortage
n lit: dearth, deficiency, lack, scarcity, shortfall, want.

shortcoming
n lit: drawback, fault, flaw, frailty, weakness.

shorten
vb lit: abbreviate, curtail, cut down, diminish, lessen, reduce, trim.

shortly
adv lit: before long, presently, soon; a short time (after or before); briefly, concisely; abruptly, curtly.

short-sighted
adj lit: myopic, near-sighted; *fig*: careless, ill-considered, imprudent, injudicious, unthinking.

short-tempered
adj lit: fiery, hot-tempered, irascible, peppery, quick-tempered, ratty, touchy.

shot
n lit: discharge, lob, pot shot; bullet, lead, pellet, projectile; marksman, shooter; *fig*: attempt, conjecture, crack, go, guess, stab, try.

shout
n lit: bellow, cry, roar, yell.
vb lit: bawl, bellow, call (out), cry (out), holler, roar, scream, yell.

shove
n lit: barge, push, thrust.
vb lit: barge, crowd, elbow, jostle, press, push, shoulder, thrust.

shovel
n lit: scoop, spade, trowel.
vb lit: dredge, heap, ladle, scoop, shift, toss.

show
n lit: demonstration, display, exhibition, exposition, fair, pageant, parade, spectacle; affectation, appearance, likeness, pretence, semblance; *spec*: entertainment, presentation, production.
vb lit: appear, display, divulge, exhibit, indicate, make known, reveal; demonstrate, explain, instruct, point out, prove; accompany, escort, guide, lead; accord, bestow, confer, grant.

showdown
n lit: clash, confrontation, crisis, exposé, moment of truth.

shower
n lit: downfall, downpour; *fig*: barrage, deluge, fusillade, torrent, volley.
vb lit: deluge, inundate, lavish, pour, spray, sprinkle.

show off
vb lit: demonstrate, display, flaunt, parade; *fig*: boast, brag, make a spectacle of oneself, swagger.

show up
vb lit: expose, highlight, pinpoint, reveal; appear, catch the eye, stand out; embarrass, mortify, put to shame, show in a bad light; arrive, come, put in an appearance, turn up.

shred
n lit: bit, fragment, piece, scrap, sliver, snippet, tatter; *fig*: grain, iota, jot, particle, trace, whit.
vb lit: cut, reduce to shreds, tear.

shrewd
adj lit: artful, calculating, canny, crafty, cunning, sly, smart, wily; discerning, far-sighted, intelligent, keen, perceptive.

shriek
n lit: howl, scream, screech, wail, yell.
vb lit: cry, scream, screech, squeal, wail, yell.

shrill
adj lit: ear-piercing, high-pitched, penetrating, screeching, sharp.

shrink
vb lit: decrease, deflate, drop off, dwindle, lessen, shrivel, wither; cower, draw back, flinch, hang back, recoil, shy away, wince.

shrivelled
adj (pa.pt) lit: desiccated, dried up, dry, shrunken, withered.

shrouded
adj (pa.pt) lit: covered, enveloped, sheeted, swathed, veiled.

shudder
n lit: quiver, spasm, trembling, tremor.
vb lit: quake, quiver, shake, shiver, tremble.

shuffle
vb lit: drag, scuffle, shamble; disarrange,

jumble, mix, shift; dodge, evade, fidget, prevaricate, pussyfoot, quibble.

shunned
adj (pa.pt) *lit*: avoided, cold-shouldered, eluded.

shut
vb lit: bar, close, fasten, seal, secure, slam.
adj lit: closed, confined, enclosed, excluded.

shut up
vb lit: box in, cage, confine, coop up, imprison, incarcerate, intern; be quiet, fall silent, hold one's tongue, hush, pipe down.

shy
vb lit: balk, draw back, flinch, rear, recoil, start, swerve, take fright.
adj lit: bashful, coy, hesitant, reserved, reticent, timid, wary.

shyness
n lit: bashfulness, lack of confidence, nervousness, reticence, timidity.

sick
adj lit: ill, nauseated, puking, queasy; ailing, indisposed, poorly, under the weather; *fig*: black, macabre, morbid; bored, fed up, tired, weary.

sicken
vb lit: nauseate, turn one's stomach; contract, fall ill, go down with, take sick.

sickening
adj lit: disgusting, distasteful, foul, loathsome, nauseating, offensive, repulsive, revolting, vile.

sickly
adj lit: ailing, bilious, delicate, faint, indisposed, in poor health, lacklustre, languid, pallid, unhealthy, weak; mawkish, nauseating, revolting, syrupy.

sickness
n lit: nausea, queasiness; ailment, bug, complaint, disease, disorder, illness, indisposition.

side
n lit: border, boundary, edge, limit, margin, periphery, rim, verge; aspect, facet, part, surface, view; *fig*: angle, opinion, point of view, position, slant, stand; camp, faction, party, team; airs, arrogance.

vb lit: ally with, associate oneself with, favour, go along with, second, support, team up with.
adj lit: flanking, lateral; *fig*: ancillary, incidental, lesser, marginal, roundabout, secondary, subsidiary.

sidekick
n lit: crony, partner.

sidelong
adj lit: covert, indirect, sideways.

sidestep
vb lit: avoid, bypass, dodge, duck, elude, evade, skip.

side-street
n lit: alley, back-street, close.

sidetrack
n lit: shunting track, siding; *fig*: distraction, diversion, interruption.
vb lit: switch to a sidetrack; *fig*: deflect, deviate, distract, divert.

sideways
adj lit: oblique, sidelong, slanted.
adv lit: edgeways, laterally, obliquely, sidewards.

sieve
n lit: colander, riddle, sifter, strainer.
vb lit: bolt, riddle, separate, sift, strain.

sift
vb lit: bolt, filter, pan, separate, sieve; *fig*: analyse, examine, go through, screen, scrutinize.

sight
n lit: eyesight, vision; appearance, eyeshot, range of vision, view, visibility; display, scene, show, spectacle, vista; *fig*: blot on the landscape, eyesore, mess, monstrosity.
vb lit: discern, make out, see, spot.

sign
n lit: evidence, gesture, hint, indication, proof, suggestion, trace; board, notice, placard; badge, device, emblem, ensign, logo, symbol; auspice, foreboding, omen, portent, warning.
vb lit: autograph, endorse, inscribe; beckon, gesture, signal, wave.

signal
n lit: beacon, cue, green light, indication, sign, token.
vb lit: beckon, gesticulate, give a sign to, indicate, motion, sign, wave.
adj lit: conspicuous, eminent,

extraordinary, memorable, noteworthy, outstanding, significant.

significance
n lit: implication(s), import, meaning, point, purport, signification; consequence, importance, matter, relevance, weight.

significant
adj lit: denoting, expressive, indicative, meaningful, suggestive; critical, important, material, momentous, serious, vital, weighty.

signify
vb lit: announce, communicate, connote, convey, express, imply, indicate, intimate, mean, portend, represent, stand for, suggest, symbolize; *fig*: carry weight, count, matter.

silence
n lit: calm, hush, lull, quiescence, stillness; dumbness, reticence, speechlessness, taciturnity.
vb lit: cut off, deaden, gag, muffle, quieten, stifle, subdue, suppress.

silent
adj lit: hushed, muted, quiet, soundless, still; dumb, mum, non-vocal, speechless, taciturn, tongue-tied, voiceless, wordless; implied, tacit, understood, unspoken.

silken
adj lit: silky, smooth, velvety.

silly
n lit: clot, ignoramus, silly-billy, twit.
adj lit: absurd, brainless, fatuous, foolhardy, frivolous, idiotic, imprudent, inane, irresponsible, meaningless, pointless, preposterous, ridiculous, senseless, stupid, witless; benumbed, dazed, groggy, stunned, stupefied.

similar
adj lit: alike, comparable, congruous, in agreement, much the same, resembling.

similarity
n lit: affinity, agreement, analogy, comparability, concordance, congruency, likeness, resemblance, sameness, similitude.

simmering
adj (pr.pt) lit: approaching boiling point, boiling gently; *fig*: agitated, angry, fuming, seething, smarting, tense, uptight.

simple
adj lit: clear, elementary, intelligible, lucid, straightforward, uncomplicated; classic, clean, natural, plain, uncluttered; pure, unalloyed, unblended, unmixed; artless, childlike, green, guileless, naive, sincere, unpretentious, unsophisticated; basic, direct, frank, honest, naked, plain, undeniable; homely, modest, rustic; brainless, dumb, feeble-minded, half-witted, moronic, silly, slow, thick.

simpleton
n lit: blockhead, dope, dunce, imbecile, jackass, moron, nincompoop, twerp.

simplicity
n lit: absence of complications, clarity, case, obviousness, straightforwardness; lack of adornment, naturalness, plainness, purity, restraint; artlessness, candour, directness, lack of sophistication, naivety, openness.

simplify
vb lit: abridge, disentangle, facilitate, streamline.

simulated
adj (pa.pt) lit: feigned, imitating, muck, pretended, put on, shamming.

simultaneous
adj lit: coincident, concurrent, contemporaneous, synchronous.

sin
n lit: crime, error, evil, misdeed, offence, transgression, trespass, unrighteousness, wrongdoing.
vb lit: err, fall, go astray, lapse, offend, transgress.

since
adv lit: continually afterwards, from then till now; at some time between then and now, later, subsequently; ago, before now.
cnj lit: after the time that, from the time when; after; because, inasmuch as, seeing that.

sincere
adj lit: artless, bona fide, earnest, genuine, heartfelt, honest, no-nonsense, open, serious, straightforward, true, unaffected.

sincerity
n lit: artlessness, bona fides, candour, frankness, genuineness, good faith, guilelessness, probity, straightforwardness, wholeheartedness.

sinful
adj lit: corrupt, depraved, erring, immoral, iniquitous, morally wrong, unrighteous, wicked.

sing
vb lit: carol, chant, chirp, croon, trill, warble, yodel; buzz, hum, purr, whistle; *fig*: blow the whistle (on), grass, inform (on), rat (on), spill the beans, squeal, turn in.

single
vb lit: choose, distinguish, fix on, pick, select, separate, winnow.
adj lit: distinct, individual, one, only, particular, singular, sole, unique; free, unattached, unmarried; exclusive, separate, unblended, undivided, unshared.

singly
adv lit: individually, one at a time, one by one.

singular
adj lit: conspicuous, exceptional, noteworthy, outstanding, prodigious, rare, remarkable, unique; curious, eccentric, extraordinary, out-of-the-way, peculiar, queer, strange; separate, single, sole.

sinister
adj lit: dire, injurious, malevolent, malignant, menacing, threatening.

sink
n lit: basin, tub; drain, sewer; marsh, pool.
vb lit: decline, descend, drop, drown, ebb, fall, founder, go down, merge, plummet, sag, submerge, subside; abate, lapse, retrogress, slump; deteriorate, die, dwindle, fade, go downhill, weaken, worsen; bore, dig, drill, excavate, lay; *fig*: defeat, destroy, finish, overwhelm, ruin; be reduced to, stoop, succumb.

sinner
n lit: miscreant, reprobate, transgressor, wrongdoer.

sip
n lit: drop, taste, thimbleful.
vb lit: sample, taste.

sit
vb lit: be seated, rest, settle, take a seat.

site
n lit: ground, place, plot, spot.
vb lit: install, place, position, situate.

situation
n lit: locality, place, position, setting, site, spot; ball game, circumstances, plight, state of affairs, status quo, the picture; rank, station, status; employment, job, office, post.

size
n lit: amount, bulk, dimensions, extent, hugeness, immensity, magnitude, mass, measurement(s), proportions, range, volume.
vb lit: arrange, classify; make of a certain size; *spec*: glaze, stiffen, treat with size.

sizzling
adj (pr.pt) lit: crackling, frizzling, spitting, sputtering.

skeletal
adj lit: bony, osteal; anorexic, emmaciated, gaunt, malnourished; infrastructural.

skeleton
n lit: bony framework; *fig*: bare bones, draft, outline, structure.

sketch
n lit: delineation, draft, drawing, outline, plan.
vb lit: delineate, depict, draft, draw, outline, plot, represent.

sketchy
adj lit: cobbled together, crude, cursory, incomplete, rough, slight, superficial, unfinished, vague.

skew
adj lit: askew, awry, slanting, twisted; bent, crooked, not symmetrical.

skewer
n lit: spit; nail, pin, stake; tent-peg.
vb lit: impale, spit, transfix; nail, pin, stake; peg.

skilful
adj lit: able, accomplished, apt, competent, dexterous, expert, handy, proficient, skilled.

skill
n lit: ability, accomplishment, aptitude, competence, dexterity, expertise, finesse, knack, proficiency, skilfulness, talent.

skimpy
adj lit: meagre, mean, niggardly, parsimonious, scanty.

skin
n lit: fell, hide, pelt; coating, crust, husk, outside, rind.
vb lit: abrade, bark, flay, graze, peel.

skinny
adj lit: emaciated, scraggy, skeletal, skin-and-bone, thin, undernourished.

skip
n lit: gait, jump, leap, spring; omission, passing over; basket, bucket, cage, wagon; *spec*: captain (in bowling).
vb lit: bounce, caper, gambol, hop, prance; eschew, give (something) a miss, leave out, omit, pass over; miss, play truant from.

skipper
n lit: captain, master.

skirmish
n lit: affray, battle, combat, conflict, encounter, fracas, incident, scrimmage, tussle.
vb lit: clash, collide, come to blows, tussle.

skirt
n lit: kilt; border, edge, fringe, margin, outskirts, periphery.
vb lit: border, edge, lie alongside; avoid, bypass, detour, evade.

skit
n lit: burlesque, parody, sketch, takeoff, travesty.

skittish
adj lit: excitable, fickle, fidgety, highly strung, jumpy, nervous.

skulk
vb lit: creep, loiter, lurk, prowl, sneak.

sky
n lit: firmament, heavens, vault of heaven; atmosphere, climate, weather.
vb lit: hit, raise, throw; hang (a painting).

slack
n lit: leeway, looseness, room.

vb lit: dodge, idle, neglect, shirk, skive, slacken.
adj lit: baggy, flexible, lax, loose, relaxed; easy-going, idle, inactive, lazy, negligent, permissive, tardy; dull, slow-moving, sluggish.

slacken
vb lit: abate, diminish, drop off, lessen, reduce, relax, slow down.

slag
n lit: dross, lava, scoria, waste ore.
vb lit: become slaglike, change into slag, form slag.

slam
n lit: bang, crash, smash, throw, thump; *spec*: gaining every trick (in bridge).
vb lit: bang, dash, fling, hurl, throw; attack, castigate, damn, lambaste, pillory, slate, vilify.

slander
n lit: backbiting, defamation, libel, misrepresentation, obloquy, scandal, smear.
vb lit: backbite, blacken (someone's) name, calumniate, defame, disparage, malign, muckrake, slur, smear, vilify.

slang
n lit: argot, cant, colloquialism, jargon, rhyming slang.
vb lit: abuse, berate, call names, hurl insults at, inveigh against, rail against, revile, vituperate.

slant
n lit: camber, incline, pitch, ramp, tilt; angle, bias, emphasis, leaning, prejudice, viewpoint.
vb lit: bend, incline, lean, list, slope, tilt; bias, twist, weight.

slap
n lit: bang, clout, smack, spank, wallop, whack; *fig*: blow, rebuff, snub.
vb lit: blow, clap, clout, cuff, hit, spank, whack; daub, spread.

slapdash
adj lit: careless, clumsy, haphazard, last-minute, perfunctory, slipshod, sloppy, slovenly.

slapstick
n lit: buffoonery, farce, horseplay.

slash
n lit: cut, gash, laceration, rip, slit.
vb lit: gash, hack, lacerate, rend, score, slit; cut (prices), lower, reduce.

slate
n lit: roofing plate; blackboard; list of candidates.
vb lit: cover with slate, roof; appoint, list, nominate; berate, castigate, criticize, lambaste, rail against, rebuke, scold.

slaughter
n lit: blood bath, bloodshed, carnage, killing, liquidation, massacre, slaying.
vb lit: butcher, do to death, exterminate, kill, massacre, murder, put to the sword, slay.

slave
n lit: drudge, serf, servant, vassal, villein.
vb lit: drudge, slog, toil.

slaver
n lit: ship used in slave-trade, slave merchant; saliva; drivel, nonsense; gross flattery.
vb lit: drool, slobber.

slavery
n lit: bondage, captivity, serfdom, servitude, thraldom, vassalage.

slavish
adj lit: abject, cringing, grovelling, low, menial, servile, sycophantic; conventional, imitative, unimaginative, uninspired.

slay
vb lit: annihilate, assassinate, destroy, eliminate, exterminate, massacre, murder, slaughter; amuse, be the death of.

sledge
n lit: sled, sleigh, toboggan; hammer.

sleek
adj lit: glossy, shiny, smooth, well-groomed.

sleep
n lit: doze, nap, rest, slumber(s), snooze.
vb lit: catnap, doze, drop off, drowse, nod off, slumber, snooze, take a nap.

sleepless
adj lit: insomniac, restless, wakeful; vigilant, watchful, wide awake.

sleepy
adj lit: drowsy, heavy, lethargic, sluggish, somnolent, torpid; dull, hypnotic, quiet, slow, slumberous, soporific.

slender
adj lit: lean, narrow, slim, sylph-like, willowy; inadequate, insufficient, meagre, scanty, small; feeble, flimsy, remote, slight, thin, weak.

slice
n lit: helping, portion, sliver, wedge.
vb lit: carve, cut, sever.

slick
vb lit: plaster down, sleek, smooth.
adj lit: glossy, smooth, soft; glib, plausible, polished, sophistical, specious; adroit, deft, sharp, skilful, sly, tricky.

slide
n lit: sliding; chute, slope, track; channel, groove, rail; avalanche, landslide; decline, downswing; sheet of glass (in microscope), photograph.
vb lit: coast, glide, skim, slip, slither, veer.

slight
n lit: affront, discourtesy, disdain, insult, rebuff, snub, (the) cold shoulder.
vb lit: affront, cold-shoulder, disparage, give offence to, scorn, snub.
adj lit: feeble, insignificant, minor, negligible, paltry, small, superficial, trivial, unimportant; delicate, fragile, lightly-built.

slim
vb lit: diet, lose weight, reduce.
adj lit: lean, narrow, sylph-like, thin, trim; faint, poor, remote, slender, slight.

slimy
adj lit: clammy, mucous, muddy, oozy, viscous; creeping, grovelling, oily, servile, smarmy, sycophantic, toadying, unctuous.

sling
n lit: strap, string; casting, hurling, throw; band, chain, loop.
vb lit: cast, chuck, fling, heave, hurl, throw, toss; dangle, hang, swing.

slip
n lit: bloomer, blunder, error, fault, indiscretion, mistake, oversight, slip of the tongue.
vb lit: glide, slide, slither; fall, lose one's footing, skid, trip (over); conceal, hide, insinuate oneself, sneak; blunder, boob, miscalculate, mistake; break free from, disappear, dodge, elude, evade, get away, outwit.

slippery
adj lit: skiddy, slippy, smooth, unsafe,
unstable, unsteady; crafty, cunning,
devious, evasive, false, shifty, sneaky,
tricky, two-faced, unreliable,
untrustworthy.

slit
n lit: cut, fissure, gash, incision, rent,
split, tear.
vb lit: cut (open), gash, knife, rip, slash,
split open.

slogan
n lit: battle cry, rallying cry; catchword,
jingle, motto.

slope
n lit: declination, descent, gradient,
inclination, ramp, scarp, slant, tilt.
vb lit: drop away, fall, incline, lean, pitch,
rise, tilt; creep, make oneself scarce,
skulk, slip.

slot
n lit: aperture, channel, groove, slit; niche,
place, space, time.
vb lit: adjust, fit in, insert, pigeonhole.

sloth
n lit: idleness, inactivity, indolence,
inertia, slackness, sluggishness, torpor.

slovenly
adj lit: careless, heedless, loose, slack,
slipshod, unkempt, untidy.

slow
vb lit: check, curb, delay, detain, hold up,
lag, reduce speed, restrict.
adj lit: creeping, dawdling, easy, laggard,
lazy, leaden, leisurely, plodding,
ponderous, slow-moving, sluggish,
unhurried; behind, delayed, dilatory,
late, tardy, unpunctual; gradual,
lingering, long-drawn-out, prolonged,
protracted; dull, inactive, quiet, sleepy,
stagnant, tedious, uneventful,
wearisome; dim, dull-witted, dumb,
obtuse, slow on the uptake, stupid, thick.

sluggish
adj lit: dull, inactive, indolent, inert,
lethargic, listless, phlegmatic, slow,
torpid, unresponsive.

slumbering
adj (pr.pt) lit: dozing, napping, reposing,
sleepy, snoozing.

slump
n lit: collapse, crash, decline, depression,
failure, fall, low, recession, reverse,
stagnation.
vb lit: collapse, crash, deteriorate, go
downhill, plummet, plunge, reach a new
low, sink; droop, hunch, loll, slouch.

slur
n lit: slurred pronunciation; *spec*: legato;
fig: affront, blot, brand, discredit,
disgrace, innuendo, insinuation,
reproach, smear, stain, stigma.
vb lit: conceal, go through hurriedly,
minimize, pass lightly over; pronounce
indistinctly; *spec*: perform legato; *fig*:
affront, disgrace, discredit, insinuate,
insult, smear, stain.

slut
n lit: slattern, sloven, trollop.

sly
adj lit: artful, clever, conniving, crafty,
cunning, devious, guileful, scheming,
shifty, stealthy, underhand, wily;
impish, mischievous, roguish.

smack
n lit: flavour, taste; dash, suggestion,
tinge, touch, trace; noisy kiss; sailing
boat; blow, crack, slap.
vb lit: box, clap, hit, pat, slap, sock, spank,
tap.
adv lit: directly, exactly, pointblank,
right, squarely, straight.

small
adj lit: diminutive, little, miniature,
minute, petite, pint-sized, puny, tiny,
undersized; insignificant, lesser, minor,
paltry, petty, trifling, trivial; inadequate,
insufficient, limited, meagre, scanty;
humble, modest, small-scale; base,
grudging, mean, narrow, selfish.

small-time
adj lit: insignificant, minor, of no account,
of no consequence, petty, unimportant.

smart
n lit: burning sensation, pang, smarting,
sting.
vb lit: burn, hurt, sting, throb, tingle.
adj lit: hard, painful, piercing, sharp,
stinging; adept, apt, astute, bright,
canny, ingenious, keen, nimble, quick-
witted, sharp, shrewd; chic, elegant,
fashionable, modish, natty, neat, snappy,
stylish, trim; impertinent, nimble-
witted, ready, saucy, witty; brisk, lively,
quick, spanking, spirited.

smarten

vb lit: brighten, improve appearance;
become clever, make alert.

smash

n lit: accident, collision, crash, pile-up;
collapse, defeat, disaster, downfall,
failure, ruin.
vb lit: break, collide, crush, demolish,
disintegrate, shatter; defeat, destroy,
overthrow, ruin, wreck.

smattering

n lit: dash, elements, modicum,
rudiments, smatter.

smear

n lit: blot, blotch, daub, smudge, splotch;
defamation, libel, mud-slinging, slander,
vilification.
vb lit: bedaub, blur, cover, dirty, rub on,
smudge, spread over, stain; asperse,
blacken, calumniate, malign, sully,
tarnish, vilify.

smell

n lit: aroma, bouquet, fragrance, odour,
redolence, scent, whiff; fetor, pong,
stench, stink.
vb lit: get a whiff of, scent, sniff; be
malodorous, pong, reek, stink to high
heaven.

smelly

adj lit: evil-smelling, foul, malodorous,
mephitic, noisome, pongy, putrid,
reeking, stinking, strong-smelling.

smiling

adj (pr.pt) lit: agreeable, amused, kind,
pleased; cheerful, grinning, pleasant.

smooth

vb lit: flatten, iron, polish, press; allay,
alleviate, calm, extenuate, facilitate,
mitigate, mollify, palliate, soften.
adj lit: even, flat, flush, level, unwrinkled;
glossy, shiny, silky, soft, velvety; calm,
equable, peaceful, serene, tranquil,
unruffled; agreeable, mellow, mild,
soothing; glib, ingratiating, persuasive,
slick, smarmy, suave, unctuous; easy,
effortless, flowing, fluent, regular,
rhythmic, unbroken, uninterrupted,
well-ordered.

smothered

adj (pa.pt) lit: choked, stifled, strangled,
suffocated; concealed, muffled,
suppressed; cocooned, inundated,
overwhelmed, showered.

smouldering

adj (pr.pt) lit: boiling, festering, fuming,
seething, simmering.

smug

adj lit: complacent, conceited, priggish,
self-opinionated, self-righteous, self-
satisfied.

snack

n lit: bite to eat, break, elevenses, nibble,
refreshments.

snag

n lit: catch, complication, disadvantage,
drawback, hitch, problem, stumbling
block.
vb lit: catch, rip, tear.

snap

n lit: crackle, fillip, flick, pop; bite, grab,
nip; energy, go, liveliness, vigour, zip.
vb lit: break, crack, give way, separate;
bite, catch, grip, nip, snatch; bark, flare
out, flash, lash out at, retort, snarl; click,
crackle, pop.
adj lit: abrupt, immediate, instant, on-
the-spot, sudden.

snare

n lit: catch, net, noose, pitfall, trap, wire.
vb lit: catch, entrap, net, seize, springe,
wire.

snarl

vb lit: growl, grumble, mumble, murmur,
show its teeth; complicate, embroil,
enmesh, entangle, entwine, muddle,
ravel.

snatch

n lit: bit, fragment, piece, smattering,
snippet, spell.
vb lit: clutch, grab, grasp, grip, make off
with, pluck, pull, seize, wrench, wrest.

sneak

n lit: informer, telltale.
vb lit: cower, lurk, sidle, skulk, slip,
smuggle, spirit; grass on, inform on, tell
on.
adj lit: clandestine, furtive, secret,
stealthy.

sneer

n lit: derision, disdain, gibe, jeer,
mockery, ridicule, scorn.
vb lit: deride, disdain, gibe, jeer, laugh,
mock, ridicule, scoff, sniff at, snigger,
turn up one's nose.

snivel
vb lit: blubber, cry, moan, sniffle, snuffle, whimper, whine.

snobbish
adj lit: arrogant, condescending, hoity-toity, patronizing, pretentious, snooty, toffee-nosed, uppish.

snoop
vb lit: interfere, pry, spy.

snooze
n lit: catnap, doze, nap, siesta.
vb lit: catnap, doze, drop off, nap, nod off.

snort
n lit: neigh, sniff, snigger, whinny; *fig*: dram, nip, tot.
vb lit: neigh, sniff, snigger, whinny.

snub
n lit: affront, brushoff, insult, put-down.
vb lit: cold-shoulder, cut dead, humble, humiliate, mortify, rebuff, slight.

snug
adj lit: comfortable, cosy, homely, sheltered, warm; compact, neat, trim.

snuggle
vb lit: cuddle, nestle, nuzzle.

so
adv lit: as shown, in that way, in the same way; as stated; to that degree, to this degree; in such a way, to such a degree; very; very much; accordingly, for that reason, therefore; also, likewise.
cnj lit: in order that, with the result that; with the intention that; if, on the condition that.
interj lit: well; all right, let it be that way; is that true?

soak
vb lit: damp, drench, immerse, moisten, penetrate, permeate, saturate, wet; absorb, assimilate, suck in, take in.

soar
vb lit: ascend, fly, hover, mount, tower, wing; escalate, rise, rocket, shoot up.

sob
n lit: catching breath, crying, gasp, snivelling, weeping.
vb lit: bawl, blubber, cry, howl, shed tears, weep.

sober
vb lit: bring back to earth, calm down, clear one's head, come to one's senses.
adj lit: abstinent, moderate, temperate; calm, clear-headed, composed, cool, level-headed, rational, reasonable, sedate, serious, sound, steady, unruffled; dark, quiet, sombre, subdued.

sobriety
n lit: abstinence, moderation, self-restraint, soberness, temperance; calmness, composure, coolness, gravity, level-headedness, restraint, seriousness, solemnity, steadiness.

sociable
adj lit: affable, approachable, convivial, cordial, friendly, genial, gregarious, neighbourly, warm.

social
adj lit: common, communal, group, public; companionable, friendly, neighbourly, sociable.

socialize
vb lit: be a good mixer, entertain, get together, go out, mix.

society
n lit: community, humanity, mankind, people, social order, the public; companionship, company, fellowship; association, circle, club, corporation, fraternity, group, guild, institute, league, organization, union; élite, gentry, high society, nobs, smart set, top drawer, upper crust.

sodden
adj lit: boggy, drenched, marshy, saturated, soaked, soggy, waterlogged.

so far
adv lit: to that point, until now, until then.

soft
adj lit: creamy, doughy, pulpy, quaggy, spongy, squashy, yielding; bendable, elastic, flexible, malleable, plastic, pliable, supple; downy, fleecy, furry, silky, smooth, velvety; delicate, diffuse, dimmed, faint, low, mellow, melodious, murmured, pale, pastel, shaded, soothing, subdued, temperate, understated, whispered; compassionate, gentle, sensitive, sympathetic, tender; easy-going, lax, lenient, overindulgent, permissive, weak; comfortable, easy, undemanding; effeminate, flabby, namby-pamby, overindulged, pampered, podgy; daft, feeble-minded, foolish, silly, soft in the head.

soften
vb lit: allay, alleviate, appease, calm, diminish, lessen, melt, mitigate, modify, muffle, palliate, quell, relax, soothe, subdue, tone down.

soft-hearted
adj lit: charitable, compassionate, generous, kind, sentimental, sympathetic, tender, warm-hearted.

soil
n lit: clay, dust, earth, ground; country, land, region.
vb lit: besmirch, defile, foul, pollute, spatter, stain, tarnish.

sojourn
n lit: stay, stopover, visit.
vb lit: abide, dwell, reside, rest, stay, stop, tarry.

sole
n lit: undersurface of foot; bottom of shoe; flatfish.
adj lit: alone, one, only, single, solitary.

solemn
adj lit: earnest, glum, portentous, serious, sober, thoughtful; august, ceremonious, dignified, grand, grave, imposing, momentous, stately; devotional, reverential, ritual, sacred, venerable.

solemnity
n lit: earnestness, grandeur, gravity, momentousness, portentousness, sanctity, seriousness; ceremonial, formalities, observance, proceedings, rite.

solicit
vb lit: ask, beseech, crave, entreat, implore, importune, petition, plead for, seek, supplicate.

solicitor
n lit: advocate, attorney, canvasser, lawyer.

solicitous
adj lit: anxious, attentive, caring, concerned, eager, troubled, worried, zealous.

solid
n lit: block, lump, mass.
adj lit: compact, dense, firm, stable, strong, sturdy, substantial; genuine, pure, real, sound; complete, unalloyed, unanimous, unbroken, united, unmixed; decent, dependable, level-headed,

reliable, sensible, sober, trusty, upright, worthy.

solidarity
n lit: accord, cohesion, concordance, harmony, like-mindedness, stability, team spirit, unanimity, unity.

solitary
adj lit: desolate, isolated, lonely, remote, secluded, unfrequented; alone, lone, sole; cloistered, hermitical, lonesome, reclusive, unsociable.

solitude
n lit: isolation, loneliness, privacy, reclusiveness, seclusion; emptiness, waste, wilderness.

solution
n lit: answer, clarification, explanation, key, resolution, solving, unravelling; blend, emulsion, mix, solvent, suspension; dissolution, melting.

solve
vb lit: clarify, clear up, crack, decipher, disentangle, elucidate, explain, expound, interpret, unfold, unravel, work out.

sombre
adj lit: dark, dim, doleful, drab, dull, funereal, gloomy, grave, melancholy, mournful, sad, shadowy, shady.

somebody
n lit: bigwig, celebrity, heavyweight, household name, public figure, V.I.P.
prn lit: anybody, anyone, one, someone.

sometimes
adv lit: at times, every now and then, from time to time, now and again, now and then, occasionally, off and on, once in a while.

somewhat
adv lit: in some degree, slightly, to some extent.

song
n lit: air, anthem, ballad, canticle, carol, chant, ditty, hymn, melody, pop song, psalm, shanty, tune.

sonorous
adj lit: deep-sounding, loud, resonant; high-sounding, imposing.

soon
adv lit: before long, in a little while, in a minute, presently, shortly; promptly, quickly; lief, readily, willingly.

soothing
adj (pr.pt) lit: calming, demulcent, emollient, lenitive, palliative, relaxing, restful.

soothsayer
n lit: augur, diviner, prophet, seer.

sophisticated
adj lit: blasé, cosmopolitan, cultivated, refined, urbane, worldly-wise; advanced, complicated, elaborate, intricate, multifaceted, subtle.

sophistication
n lit: finesse, poise, savoir-faire, urbanity, worldly wisdom.

sophistry
n lit: casuistry, fallacy, misleading argument, quibble, unsound reasoning.

soporific
n lit: anaesthetic, narcotic, opiate, sedative, tranquillizer.
adj lit: hypnotic, sedative, sleep-inducing, somnolent, tranquillizing.

sorcery
n lit: black magic, charm, divination, incantation, necromancy, spell, witchcraft, wizardry.

sordid
adj lit: dirty, filthy, foul, scamy, seedy, sleazy, squalid; backstreet, base, debauched, disreputable, shabby, vile; avaricious, covetous, grasping, mercenary, niggardly, selfish, venal.

sore
n lit: abscess, boil, inflammation, ulcer.
adj lit: burning, chafed, inflamed, irritated, raw, smarting, tender; annoying, distressing, grievous, sharp, troublesome; acute, critical, dire, extreme, pressing, urgent; afflicted, aggrieved, angry, hurt, irked, peeved, resentful, vexed.

sorrow
n lit: affliction, anguish, distress, grief, heartache, mourning, sadness, woe; blow, hardship, misfortune, trial, tribulation, trouble, worry.
vb lit: agonize, bemoan, grieve, moan, mourn.

sorrowful
adj lit: affecting, afflicted, depressed, distressing, grievous, heartbroken, lugubrious, melancholy, mournful, piteous, sad, sorry, unhappy.

sorry
adj lit: apologetic, conscience-stricken, contrite, penitent, remorseful, repentant, self-reproachful; disconsolate, distressed, grieved, melancholy, sad, sorrowful; compassionate, moved, pitying, sympathetic; abject, base, deplorable, dismal, mean, miserable, paltry, pathetic, piteous, shabby, wretched.

sort
n lit: brand, breed, category, character, class, description, genus, ilk, kind, make, nature, order, species, style, type, variety.
vb lit: arrange, assort, categorize, choose, classify, distribute, divide, grade, put in order, rank, select, separate.

soul
n lit: life, mind, psyche, reason, spirit, vital force; being, body, individual, mortal, person; embodiment, essence, personification, quintessence, type; ardour, courage, energy, feeling, fervour, inspiration, vitality.

sound
n lit: din, noise, report, resonance, reverberation, tone; drift, idea, impression, look, tenor; earshot, hearing, range.
vb lit: echo, resonate, resound, reverberate; appear, give the impression of, look, seem; announce, articulate, enunciate, express, signal; fathom, probe; examine, investigate, test.
adj lit: complete, entire, fit, hale, healthy, intact, perfect, robust, sturdy, substantial, unimpaired, vigorous, whole; fair, just, level-headed, logical, proper, prudent, reasonable, reliable, right, sensible, true, valid, well-founded; established, proven, recognized, reputable, safe, secure, solvent, stable; peaceful, unbroken, undisturbed.

soup
n lit: broth, consommé; mixture of chemicals; heavy fog; horsepower; foam, froth; *spec*: prosecution brief.
vb lit: boost (up), hot (up).

sour
vb lit: alienate, disenchant, embitter, exacerbate, exasperate, turn off.
adj lit: acid, bitter, sharp, tart; bad, fermented, gone off, rancid, turned; acrimonious, churlish, cynical,

disagreeable, embittered, grudging, ill-tempered, peevish, waspish.

source
n lit: author, beginning, cause, derivation, origin, originator, spring; authority, informant.

souvenir
n lit: keepsake, memento, reminder, token.

sovereign
n lit: autocrat, monarch, ruler.
adj lit: absolute, chief, dominant, monarchal, paramount, predominant, principal, regal, ruling, supreme; effectual, efficient, excellent.

sow
n lit: female hog; main trough.
vb lit: disseminate, implant, inseminate, plant, scatter, seed.

space
n lit: capacity, elbowroom, expanse, extent, leeway, margin, room, scope, volume; blank, distance, gap, lacuna; duration, interval, period, span, time; accommodation, berth, place.
vb lit: divide into spaces, fix the spaces of.

spacious
adj lit: ample, broad, capacious, commodious, expansive, extensive, large, roomy, sizable, vast.

span
n lit: distance, extent, reach, spread, stretch; duration, period, spell.
vb lit: arch across, bridge, extend across, link, traverse, vault.

spar
n lit: pole (in ship); crystalline mineral; boxing-match, cock-fight, sparring motion; *fig*: bandying words, dispute.
vb lit: furnish (ship) with a par; box, exchange blows, fight (with spurs); *fig*: argue, bandy words, bicker, dispute, fall out, squabble, wrangle.

spare
n lit: extra, guest room, spare part, surplus.
vb lit: afford, dispense with, do without, give, let (someone) have, manage without, part with; deal leniently with, go easy on, have mercy on, let off, pardon, refrain from, relieve from, save from.

sparing
adj (pr.pt) lit: careful, economical, frugal, prudent, thrifty.

spark
n lit: flare, flash, flicker, glint; atom, hint, jot, trace, vestige.
vb lit: excite, inspire, kindle, precipitate, set off, start, stir, trigger (off).

sparkle
n lit: brilliance, dazzle, flash, flicker, glint, spark, twinkle; animation, flash, life, panache, spirit, vim, vivacity, zip.
vb lit: beam, flash, gleam, glint, glitter, scintillate, shine, twinkle, wink; bubble, effervesce, fizz.

sparse
adj lit: few and far between, meagre, scanty, scarce.

spartan
adj lit: abstemious, ascetic, bleak, disciplined, extreme, plain, rigorous, severe, strict, stringent; bold, courageous, daring, dauntless, hardy, heroic, intrepid, unflinching.

spasm
n lit: contraction, paroxysm, twitch; burst, eruption, fit, frenzy, outburst, seizure.

spasmodic
adj lit: convulsive, fitful, intermittent, jerky, sporadic.

spastic
n lit: cerebral palsy sufferer.
adj lit: caused by spasm(s), subject to spasm(s); brief, fitful, intermittent, irregular, sudden; *fig*: choppy, disjointed, showing bursts of excitement.

spate
n lit: deluge, flood, flow, outpouring, rush; *fig*: great quantity, large number.

spatter
vb lit: bespatter, fall in drops, scatter, splash, splatter; *fig*: smear, stain.

speak
vb lit: articulate, converse, discourse, express, make known, pronounce, say, state, tell, utter, voice; address, declaim,

deliver an address, harangue, lecture, plead.

spear
n lit: javelin, lance, pike; shoot, sprout.
vb lit: penetrate, pierce, stab; germinate, shoot, sprout.

special
adj lit: distinguished, exceptional, extraordinary, festive, gala, important, memorable, momentous, red-letter, significant, unique; certain, characteristic, especial, individual, particular, peculiar, specific; chief, main, major, primary.

specialist
n lit: authority, connoisseur, consultant, expert, master.

species
n lit: breed, category, class, group, kind, sort, type, variety.

specific
adj lit: clear-cut, definite, exact, explicit, express, particular, precise, unambiguous; characteristic, distinguishing, peculiar, special.

specifications
n lit: details, items, particulars, requirements, stipulations.

specify
vb lit: cite, define, detail, enumerate, indicate, itemize, mention, name, spell out, stipulate.

specimen
n lit: copy, example, exemplar, exhibit, instance, model, pattern, proof, sample, type.

specious
adj lit: deceptive, fallacious, misleading, plausible, sophistic, unsound.

speck
n lit: blemish, blot, defect, fault, flaw, fleck, mark, speckle, spot, stain; atom, bit, dot, grain, iota, mite, modicum, particle, shred, whit.

speckled
adj lit: brindled, dappled, dotted, freckled, mottled, spotted, spotty, stippled.

spectacle
n lit: display, event, extravaganza, pageant, performance, show; curiosity, laughing stock, marvel, phenomenon, scene, sight.

spectacular
n lit: display, extravaganza, show, spectacle.
adj lit: breathtaking, dazzling, dramatic, fantastic, impressive, magnificent, sensational, splendid, striking, stunning.

spectator
n lit: beholder, eye-witness, observer, onlooker, viewer, watcher.

spectre
n lit: apparition, ghost, phantom, presence, spirit, vision, wraith.

speculate
vb lit: cogitate, conjecture, contemplate, deliberate, hypothesize, meditate, scheme, surmise, theorize; gamble, have a flutter, hazard, risk, venture.

speculative
adj lit: abstract, academic, conjectural, hypothetical, notional, tentative, theoretical; chancy, hazardous, risky, unpredictable.

speech
n lit: conversation, dialogue, discussion, talk; address, discourse, disquisition, harangue, lecture, oration; articulation, dialect, diction, idiom, jargon, language, parlance, tongue.

speed
n lit: acceleration, celerity, expedition, fleetness, momentum, pace, precipitation, quickness, rapidity, swiftness, velocity.
vb lit: belt (along), career, expedite, flash, get a move on, hurry, make haste, press on, race, rush, tear, zoom; advance, boost, facilitate, further, help, promote.

speedy
adj lit: expeditious, express, fast, hasty, headlong, immediate, precipitate, prompt, quick, rapid, summary, swift.

spell
n lit: bout, interval, period, season, stint, stretch, term, time, turn; charm, conjuration, exorcism, incantation, sorcery; allure, enchantment, fascination, magic, trance.
vb lit: amount to, herald, imply, indicate, point to, portend, promise, signify, suggest.

spellbind
vb lit: bemuse, captivate, charm, enthrall, fascinate, grip, mesmerize, possess, transfix, transport.

spell out
vb lit: clarify, elucidate, make plain, specify; discern, make out.

spend
vb lit: disburse, expend, lay out, pay out, splash out; consume, dissipate, drain, empty, exhaust, fritter away, squander, waste; bestow, devote, lavish, put in; fill, occupy, pass, while away.

spendthrift
n lit: big spender, prodigal, profligate, squanderer, waster.
adj lit: extravagant, improvident, prodigal, wasteful.

spent
adj (pa.pt) lit: debilitated, drained, exhausted, knackered, shattered, tired out, weary, worn out; consumed, expended, finished, gone.

sphere
n lit: circle, globe, globule, orb; capacity, domain, field, function, range, scope, stratum, territory, walk of life.

spicy
adj lit: aromatic, flavoured, fragrant, savoury, tangy; *fig*: improper, indelicate, keen, lively, piquant, pungent, salacious, showy, smart, spirited,

spike
n lit: point, prong, spine.
vb lit: impale, spear, stick; block, foil, frustrate, thwart.

spill
n lit: spillage, spilling; downpour (of rain); candle-lighter, spindle, splinter, sliver; bung, spigot, spile, stopper; *fig*: accident, fall, tumble.
vb lit: discharge, overflow, overturn, scatter, shed, slop over, run over, throw off, upset.

spin
n lit: gyration, revolution, roll, whirl; drive, joy ride, turn.
vb lit: gyrate, pirouette, revolve, rotate, twirl, twist; concoct, invent, recount, relate, tell, unfold; be giddy, grow dizzy, reel, swim.

spine
n lit: backbone, spinal column, vertebrae; barb, quill, ray, spike, spur.

spineless
adj lit: faint-hearted, feeble, gutless, ineffective, irresolute, lily-livered, soft, squeamish, submissive, vacillating, weak, yellow.

spindly
adj lit: attenuated, slender, spindling, thin.

spiral
n lit: coil, corkscrew, helix, volute, whorl.
adj lit: circular, coiled, helical, scrolled, voluted, whorled, winding.

spirit
n lit: air, breath, life force, psyche, soul; attitude, disposition, essence, humour, outlook, temper, temperament; ardour, backbone, courage, dauntlessness, energy, enthusiasm, force, grit, guts, life, mettle, sparkle, vigour, zest; motivation, resolution, willpower; atmosphere, feeling, gist, tenor, tone; intent, meaning, purport, sense, substance; apparition, ghost, phantom, spectre, spook, sprite, vision.
vb lit: carry (away), convey (off), steal (away), whisk (off).

spirited
adj lit: animated, ardent, bold, energetic, high-spirited, mettlesome, plucky, sprightly, vivacious.

spiritual
n lit: religious song.
adj lit: devotional, ethereal, ghostly, immaterial, non-material, otherworldly, religious, sacred.

spit
n lit: dribble, drool, saliva, spittle.
vb lit: eject, expectorate, spew, splutter, throw out.

spite
n lit: animosity, bitchiness, grudge, ill will, malevolence, malice, pique, rancour, spitefulness, spleen, venom.
vb lit: annoy, gall, harm, hurt, needle, nettle, offend, pique, put out, vex.

splash
n lit: burst, dash, spattering, splodge, touch; effect, impact, splurge, stir.
vb lit: slop, spatter, spray, sprinkle, squirt, wet; bathe, paddle, wade, wallow;

batter, dash, strike, surge, wash; blazon, flaunt, publicize, tout, trumpet.

splendid
adj lit: admirable, exceptional, glorious, illustrious, magnificent, outstanding, remarkable, renowned, sublime, superb; costly, gorgeous, impressive, lavish, luxurious, rich, sumptuous; excellent, fantastic, fine, great, marvellous, wonderful; beaming, brilliant, glittering, lustrous, radiant.

splendour
n lit: brightness, brilliance, dazzle, glory, grandeur, lustre, magnificence, pomp, renown, resplendence, solemnity, spectacle, stateliness.

splinter
n lit: chip, flake, paring, shaving, sliver.
vb lit: break into smithereens, disintegrate, fracture, shiver, split.

split
n lit: breach, crack, division, fissure, gap, rent, rip, slash, slit, tear; break-up, discord, disruption, dissension, divergence, estrangement, partition, rift, schism.
vb lit: branch, break, burst, come apart, come undone, crack, disband, diverge, fork, give way, go separate ways, part, rend, rip, separate, slit, snap, splinter; allocate, allot, distribute, dole out, halve, partition, share out; grass on, inform on, squeal on.
adj lit: ambivalent, bisected, broken, cracked, divided, fractured, ruptured.

spoil
n lit: refuse, slag.
vb lit: blemish, damage, harm, impair, mess up, ruin, upset, wreck; cosset, indulge, mollycoddle, overindulge, pamper; curdle, decay, go bad, go off, rot, turn.

sponsor
n lit: backer, guarantor, patron, promoter.
vb lit: back, finance, fund, guarantee, patronize, promote.

spoof
n lit: hoax, humbug, joke, mockery, parody, swindle, trick.

spot
n lit: blemish, blot, daub, flaw, mark, pimple, smudge, speck, stain; location, place, point, position, site; bit, little,

morsel; mess, plight, predicament, quandary, trouble.
vb lit: catch sight of, descry, detect, identify, make out, pick out, recognize, see, sight; blot, dot, fleck, mottle, soil, spatter, splodge, stain, taint, tarnish.

sprawl
vb lit: flop, lounge, ramble, slouch, slump, spread, straggle.

spray
n lit: drizzle, droplets, moisture; aerosol, sprinkler; bough, branch, shoot, sprig.
vb lit: scatter, shower, sprinkle.

spread
n lit: advancement, dispersion, escalation, expansion, increase, proliferation, spreading; extent, period, span, stretch, sweep; array, feast, repast.
vb lit: broaden, expand, fan out, sprawl, stretch, unfold, widen; escalate, multiply, mushroom, proliferate; advertise, circulate, cover, distribute, make known, promulgate, propagate, publicize, scatter, shed, transmit; arrange, array, lay, prepare.

spring
n lit: hop, jump, leap, vault; bounce, buoyancy, elasticity, flexibility, give, resilience; cause, origin, root, source, well.
vb lit: bound, hop, jump, leap, rebound, recoil, vault; derive, descend, emanate, emerge, grow, originate, start, stem; burgeon, mushroom, shoot up.

sprinkling
n lit: dash, few, handful, scatter, smattering, sprinkle.

sprite
n lit: dryad, elf, fairy, goblin, imp, leprechaun, nymph, pixie, sylph.

sprout
n lit: shoot; Brussels sprout.
vb lit: bud, germinate, grow, push, shoot, spring.

spry
adj lit: agile, brisk, nimble, quick, sprightly, supple.

spur
n lit: goad, prick, rowel; impetus, impulse, incentive, motive, stimulus.
vb lit: drive, goad, impel, incite, press, prod, prompt, stimulate, urge.

spurious
adj lit: artificial, bogus, contrived, counterfeit, fake, false, imitation, mock, phoney, pseudo, sham, simulated.

spurt
n lit: burst, rush, spate, surge.
vb lit: burst, erupt, gush, jet, spew, squirt, surge.

spy
n lit: agent, mole.
vb lit: keep under surveillance, shadow, tail, trail, watch; catch sight of, glimpse, notice, spot.

squad
n lit: band, crew, force, group, team, troop.

squalor
n lit: decay, filth, foulness, sleaziness, squalidness.

squander
vb lit: blow, dissipate, fritter away, lavish, misuse, run through, spend, waste.

square
n lit: equilateral rectangle; number multiplied by itself; *fig*: antediluvian, die-hard, fuddy-duddy, old buffer.
vb lit: agree, conform, fit, match, reconcile, tally; balance, clear up, liquidate, pay off, satisfy, settle; adapt, align, even up, level, regulate, suit, tailor; bribe, buy off, fix, rig.
adj lit: decent, equitable, ethical, fair, genuine, honest, just, straight; behind the times, conventional, old-fashioned, strait-laced, stuffy.

squash
n lit: crushed mass; gourd; beverage; squash tennis.
vb lit: compress, crush, mash, pound, press, pulp, smash, trample down; annihilate, humiliate, put down, quash, quell, silence.

squeak
n lit: peep, pipe, squeal, whine.
vb lit: peep, pipe, shrill, squeal, whine.

squeal
n lit: scream, screech, shriek, wail, yell.
vb lit: scream, screech, shout, shriek, shrill, wail, yelp; betray, blab, grass, inform on; complain, kick up a fuss, protest.

squeamish
adj lit: delicate, fastidious, finicky, particular, punctilious, scrupulous, strait-laced; nauseous, qualmish, queasy, queer, sick.

squeeze
n lit: cuddle, embrace, hold, hug; congestion, crowd, crush, jam, jostle, press, squash, thrust.
vb lit: clutch, compress, crush, grip, pinch, squash, wring; cram, crowd, force, jam, jostle, pack, ram, thrust, wedge; clasp, cuddle, embrace, hold tight, hug; bleed, extort, lean on, pressurize, put the screws on, wrest.

stab
n lit: gash, incision, jab, thrust; pang, prick, twinge; *fig*: attempt, crack, endeavour, go, try.
vb lit: cut, gore, jab, knife, pierce, puncture, run through, stick, thrust, transfix; *fig*: deceive, double-cross, let down, sell.

stable
n lit: barn, shed, stall; string, stud.
adj lit: constant, deep-rooted, enduring, established, firm, fixed, lasting, permanent, reliable, secure, sound, steady, sure, unwavering, well-founded.

staff
n lit: employees, organization, personnel, team, work-force; cane, pole, rod, stave, wand.

stage
n lit: arena, theatre; dais, platform, scaffold; jetty, pier, quay; division, juncture, lap, leg, level, phase, point.
vb lit: arrange, do, engineer, lay on, orchestrate, organize, perform, play, present, produce, put on.

stagger
vb lit: falter, lurch, reel, sway, totter, vacillate, waver, wobble; amaze, astonish, astound, bowl over, dumbfound, flabbergast, overwhelm, shake, shock, stun, stupefy, surprise, take (someone) aback; alternate, overlap, zigzag.

stagnant
adj lit: brackish, sluggish, stale, standing, still.

stagnate
vb lit: decay, deteriorate, fester, go to

seed, idle, lie fallow, rot, rust, stand still, vegetate.

stain
n lit: blemish, blot, discoloration, dye, spot, tint; disgrace, dishonour, infamy, shame, slur, stigma.
vb lit: blemish, blot, colour, discolour, dye, mark, soil, tarnish, tinge; blacken, corrupt, defile, deprave, disgrace, drag through the mud, sully, taint.

stake
n lit: paling, picket, pole, post, spike, stave, stick; bet, chance, pledge, risk, wager; claim, investment, involvement, share.
vb lit: brace, prop, support, tether, tie up; mark out, outline; bet, chance, gamble, imperil, jeopardize, pledge, put on, venture, wager.

stale
adj lit: dry, fetid, flat, fusty, musty, old, sour, stagnant; antiquated, banal, cliché-ridden, common, drab, flat, hackneyed, insipid, platitudinous, stereotyped, trite, worn-out.

stall
n lit: compartment (in stable); booth (in bazaar); orchestra seat; stalling, standstill; delay, pretense, pretext, prevarication.
vb lit: confine (in a stall); become stuck, stop; beat about the bush, block, delay, hedge, obstruct, play for time, prevaricate.

stamina
n lit: energy, force, grit, indefatigability, resilience, staying power, vigour.

stammer
n lit: faltering, stammering, stutter.
vb lit: falter, hesitate, pause, splutter, stumble, stutter.

stamp
n lit: cast, hallmark, imprint, mark, mould; breed, character, form, kind, sort, type.
vb lit: crush, trample; engrave, impress, imprint, inscribe, mark, mould; brand, categorize, identify, label, mark, pronounce, typecast.

stance
n lit: bearing, carriage, posture; attitude, position, standpoint, viewpoint.

stand
n lit: rest, standstill, stay, stopover;

attitude, opinion, position, stance, standpoint; base, booth, dais, grandstand, platform, rack, stage, stall, support.
vb lit: be upright, mount, place, position, put, set; be valid, continue, exist, halt, pause, rest, stay, stop; bear, cope with, countenance, endure, handle, put up with, stomach, sustain, take, tolerate, withstand.

standard
n lit: average, criterion, example, gauge, guide, measure, model, norm, pattern, rule, specification, type, yardstick; ethics, ideals, moral principles; banner, colours, ensign, flag, pennant.
adj lit: accepted, basic, customary, normal, orthodox, popular, regular, set, staple, stock, typical, usual.

stand by
vb lit: back, defend, stick up for, support, uphold; be prepared, wait.

stand for
vb lit: denote, exemplify, mean, represent, signify, symbolize; bear, endure, put up with, suffer, tolerate.

standing
n lit: credit, estimation, footing, rank, reputation, station, status; duration, existence, experience.
adj lit: fixed, lasting, permanent, perpetual, repeated; erect, perpendicular, upright, vertical.

star
n lit: celestial body, sun; asterisk, pentacle; *fig*: celebrity, idol, lead, name.
vb lit: bespangle, ornament with stars; perform the leading part.
adj lit: brilliant, celebrated, leading, major, principal, prominent, well-known.

stare
vb lit: gape, gawk, gaze, goggle, rubberneck.

start
n lit: beginning, commencement, dawn, foundation, inauguration, initiation, kickoff, onset, opening; advantage, head start, lead; break, chance, introduction, opportunity; convulsion, jar, spasm, twitch.
vb lit: begin, commence, get under way, go ahead, leave, set off, set out; initiate, instigate, kick off, originate, set in

motion, take the plunge; create, found, institute, launch, pioneer, set up; flinch, jerk, jump, recoil, twitch.

startling
adj lit: alarming, astounding, shocking, staggering, surprising, unforeseen.

starving
adj lit: famished, hungry, ravenous, starved.

state
n lit: circumstances, condition, pass, plight, position, predicament, situation; attitude, frame of mind, mood; glory, grandeur, pomp, splendour, style; bother, flap, panic, tizzy; country, federation, land, nation.
vb lit: affirm, articulate, assert, declare, enumerate, explain, expound, express, present, put, specify, voice.

stately
adj lit: august, ceremonious, dignified, grand, imposing, impressive, lofty, pompous, solemn.

static
n lit: electrical discharge, interference, white noise.
adj lit: constant, fixed, immobile, inert, stationary, still, unvarying.

station
n lit: depot, headquarters, location, place, position, situation; appointment, calling, grade, position, post, rank, situation, standing, status.
vb lit: assign, fix, garrison, install, post, set.

status
n lit: condition, distinction, eminence, grade, position, prestige, standing.

stay
n lit: sojourn, stopover, visit; delay, halt, pause, postponement, remission, reprieve, suspension.
vb lit: continue, delay, halt, hang around, linger, pause, remain, settle, sojourn, stay put, stop, tarry; lodge, put up at, visit; adjourn, defer, put off, suspend.

steady
vb lit: balance, brace, secure, support; compose oneself, cool down, sober (up).
adj lit: firm, fixed, stable, uniform; balanced, calm, dependable, level-headed, reliable, sensible, settled, sober, steadfast; ceaseless, consistent, constant,

faithful, habitual, persistent, regular, rhythmic, unbroken, unfaltering, uninterrupted, unwavering.

steal
vb lit: appropriate, embezzle, lift, misappropriate, nick, pilfer, pinch, pirate, plagiarize, poach, purloin, thieve, make off with; creep, slip, sneak, tiptoe.

stealthy
adj lit: clandestine, covert, furtive, secretive, skulking, sly, sneaky, surreptitious.

steep
vb lit: damp, drench, immerse, moisten, soak, submerge; fill, infuse, permeate, pervade, saturate, suffuse.
adj lit: abrupt, precipitous, sheer; excessive, extortionate, overpriced, stiff, uncalled-for, unreasonable.

steer
vb lit: conduct, control, govern, guide, pilot.

stem
n lit: axis, peduncle, stalk, stock, trunk.
vb lit: arise (from), derive (from), emanate (from), issue (from), originate; check, contain, curb, dam, hold back, resist, restrain, stop, withstand.

stench
n lit: fetor, pong, reek, stink.

step
n lit: footstep, gait, pace, stride, trace, track; action, deed, expedient, means, measure, move, procedure; advancement, phase, point, progression; degree, level, rank; doorstep, stair, tread.
vb lit: move, pace, tread, walk.

sterile
adj lit: barren, dry, fruitless, infecund, unproductive, unprofitable; antiseptic, disinfected, germ-free, sterilized.

stern
n lit: rear (of ship); buttocks, rump, tail.
adj lit: austere, forbidding, grim, harsh, rigid, serious, severe, strict, unsparing.

stick
n lit: baton, cane, rod, staff, stake, twig, wand; *fig*: fuddy-duddy, (old) fogy, pain, prig; blame, criticism, flak, hostility.
vb lit: adhere, affix, bind, cling, fasten, hold on, join, paste; insert, jab, pierce, prod, puncture, stab, transfix; bulge, jut, poke, protrude; fix, lay, place, position,

put, set; clog, come to a standstill, jam,
snag, stop; linger, remain, stay; endure,
get on with, stand, stomach, take,
tolerate; last out, put up with; stand up
for, support.

sticky
adj lit: adhesive, clinging, glutinous,
gooey, gummy, tacky, tenacious,
viscous; awkward, difficult,
embarrassing, nasty, thorny, tricky;
clammy, humid, muggy, oppressive,
sweltering.

stiff
adj lit: firm, hardened, inflexible, rigid,
solid, taut, tense, tight, unbending;
austere, chilly, constrained, formal,
laboured, pompous, prim, punctilious,
starchy, uneasy; awkward, clumsy,
crude, graceless, jerky, ungainly;
arduous, exacting, formidable, hard,
tough, trying, uphill; cruel, drastic,
extreme, harsh, oppressive, pitiless,
rigorous, severe, strict, stringent; brisk,
powerful, strong, vigorous.

stifle
vb lit: asphyxiate, choke, smother,
strangle, suffocate; check, curb,
extinguish, hush, muffle, restrain, stop,
suppress.

still
n lit: frame, photograph, picture;
distilling-apparatus; peace, quiet,
stillness, tranquillity.
vb lit: distill; allay, alleviate, calm, hush,
lull, quieten, settle, silence, smooth,
soothe, tranquillize.
adj lit: calm, hushed, inert, motionless,
peaceful, placid, quiet, restful, silent,
smooth, tranquil, undisturbed,
unruffled.
adv lit: even, yet; nevertheless; at that
time, at this time; even to that time, even
to this time; quietly, without moving.
cnj lit: but, for all that, however,
notwithstanding.

stilted
adj lit: artificial, constrained, forced,
laboured, pedantic, pompous,
pretentious, stiff, unnatural.

stimulate
vb lit: arouse, encourage, fan, foment,
goad, incite, inflame, instigate, provoke,
rouse, spur, turn on, urge.

stink
n lit: fetor, pong, stench; *fig*: complaint,
criticism.
vb lit: pong, stench, stink to high heaven;
be in disfavour, have a bad reputation.

stipulation
n lit: agreement, clause, precondition,
prerequisite, provision, requirement,
restriction, specification, term.

stir
n lit: ado, agitation, commotion,
disturbance, excitement, flurry, fuss,
to-do, uproar.
vb lit: agitate, disturb, move, quiver,
rustle, shake; arouse, excite, instigate,
provoke, raise, urge; affect, inspire,
thrill, touch; be up and about, budge, get
a move on, look lively.

stirring
adj lit: emotive, exciting, exhilarating,
lively, moving, spirited, stimulating,
thrilling.

stock
n lit: array, assortment, cache,
commodities, fund, hoard, inventory,
merchandise, range, stockpile, store,
supply, variety; cattle, horses, livestock,
sheep; breed, descent, extraction,
forebears, lineage, parentage, pedigree;
capital, funds, investment, property.
vb lit: deal in, handle, keep, sell, supply,
trade in; accumulate, buy up, hoard,
replenish, store up; equip, fit out,
furnish, kit out, provide with, provision.
adj lit: banal, basic, conventional,
customary, hackneyed, overused,
regular, routine, set, standard, staple,
stereotyped, trite, usual, worn-out.

stoical
adj lit: calm, cool, impassive,
imperturbable, long-suffering,
phlegmatic, resigned, stoic.

stolid
adj lit: apathetic, dull, heavy, obtuse,
slow, unemotional.

stomach
n lit: abdomen, belly, paunch, tummy;
appetite, inclination, mind, taste.
vb lit: bear, endure, put up with, resign
oneself to, suffer, take, tolerate.

stoop
n lit: droop, sag, slouch, slump.
vb lit: bend, crouch, duck, hunch, incline,

lean, squat; condescend, deign, demean oneself, resort, sink.

stop
n lit: cessation, conclusion, end, finish, halt, standstill; sojourn, stay, stopover, visit; bar, block, break, check, hindrance, impediment, stoppage; depot, destination, station, terminus.
vb lit: be over, break off, come to a standstill, call it a day, cease, conclude, cut short, discontinue, end, finish, leave off, peter out, pull up, quit, refrain, stall, terminate; arrest, bar, block, check, forestall, frustrate, hinder, hold back, impede, intercept, prevent, restrain, silence, stem, suspend; break one's journey, lodge, sojourn, stay, tarry.

stoppage
n lit: arrest, closure, cutoff, discontinuance, lay-off, shutdown, standstill; blockage, check, curtailment, obstruction.

store
n lit: accumulation, cache, hoard, mine, provision, reserve, stock, supply; chain store, department store, emporium, outlet, shop, supermarket; depository, storeroom, warehouse.
vb lit: accumulate, deposit, hoard, keep, lay by, put aside, reserve, salt away, save, stock.

storm
n lit: blizzard, cyclone, gale, gust, hurricane, tempest, tornado, whirlwind; assault, attack, blitz, offensive, onslaught; *fig*: agitation, commotion, disturbance, hubbub, outburst, outcry, row, rumpus, strife, turmoil.
vb lit: assail, assault, beset, charge, take by storm; complain, fume, rage, rant, scold, thunder; flounce, rush, stalk.

stormy
adj lit: blustery, gusty, rough, tempestuous, turbulent, windy.

story
n lit: account, anecdote, chronicle, history, legend, narrative, novel, recital, romance, tale, yarn; fib, fiction, lie, untruth; article, feature, news item, report.

stout
n lit: beer.
adj lit: big, bulky, burly, corpulent, obese, overweight, portly, rotund, tubby;

athletic, beefy, brawny, hulking, muscular, robust, strapping, sturdy, tough; bold, brave, dauntless, gallant, intrepid, plucky, resolute, valiant.

straddling
prp lit: across, astride, athwart, over, spanning.

straight
adj lit: direct, undeviating, unswerving; aligned, erect, horizontal, level, perpendicular, upright, vertical; blunt, forthright, frank, outright, point-blank, straightforward, unqualified; above board, accurate, equitable, fair, honest, law-abiding, reliable, trustworthy; arranged, neat, orderly, organized, shipshape, tidy; continuous, nonstop, solid, sustained, uninterrupted; conventional, orthodox, traditional; pure, unadulterated, undiluted.
adv lit: as the crow flies; at once, directly, immediately, instantly; frankly, honestly, point-blank, pulling no punches.

straight away
adv lit: at once, directly, immediately, instantly, now, right away, this minute, without any delay.

strain
n lit: effort, exertion, force, injury, struggle, tension, wrench; anxiety, burden, pressure, stress; air, melody, theme, tune; ancestry, descent, extraction, lineage, pedigree, stock; suggestion, tendency, trace, trait; manner, style, temper, tone, vein.
vb lit: draw tight, extend, stretch, tighten; exert, fatigue, injure, overwork, sprain, tax, tire, twist, wrench; endeavour, strive, struggle; filter, percolate, separate, sieve, sift.

strained
adj (pa.pt) lit: artificial, awkward, constrained, difficult, forced, laboured, put on, stiff, tense, uneasy, unnatural.

strait(s)
n lit: difficulty, dilemma, distress, embarrassment, extremity, hardship, mess, pass, plight, predicament; channel, narrows, sound.

strand
n lit: fibre, length, rope, string, thread, tress; beach, coast, shore.
vb lit: be grounded, be marooned, be

wrecked, run aground; be high and dry,
be left in the lurch.

strange
adj lit: abnormal, bizarre, curious,
extraordinary, fantastic, odd, peculiar,
perplexing, queer, rare, singular,
uncanny, weird; alien, foreign, novel,
unfamiliar, untried; a stranger to, new
to, unaccustomed to, unused to;
awkward, bewildered, ill at ease, lost,
out of place.

strangle
vb lit: asphyxiate, choke, smother,
strangulate, throttle; gag, inhibit, stifle,
suppress.

strap
n lit: belt, leash, tie.
vb lit: bind, buckle, fasten, secure, tie,
truss; beat, belt, flog, lash, whip.

strategic
adj lit: cardinal, crucial, decisive, vital;
calculated, diplomatic, planned,
political.

stray
n lit: lost animal, wanderer.
vb lit: deviate, diverge, get sidetracked,
ramble; be abandoned, drift, err, go
astray, meander, roam, rove, straggle,
wander.
adj lit: abandoned, lost, roaming;
accidental, chance, freak, odd, random.

stream
n lit: beck, brook, current, river, rivulet,
torrent, tributary.
vb lit: cascade, course, flow, gush, run,
shed, spout.

street
n lit: avenue, boulevard, lane, road,
terrace, thoroughfare.

strength
n lit: backbone, brawn, firmness, might,
robustness, stamina, sturdiness,
toughness; efficacy, energy, force,
potency, vehemence, vigour; asset,
mainstay, strong point, succour.

strenuous
adj lit: arduous, demanding, exhausting,
hard, taxing, tough, uphill; active,
determined, eager, energetic, persistent,
resolute, strong, vigorous, zealous.

stress
n lit: emphasis, importance, significance,
weight; anxiety, hassle, pressure, strain,
tension, trauma, worry; accent,
accentuation, beat.
vb lit: accentuate, dwell on, emphasize,
harp on, repeat, rub in, underline.

stretch
n lit: distance, expanse, extent, spread,
tract; period, run, space, spell, stint,
time.
vb lit: cover, extend, reach, spread; draw
out, elongate, expand, pull, rack,
tighten.

strict
adj lit: austere, firm, harsh, no-nonsense,
rigorous, stern, stringent; accurate,
exact, meticulous, particular, precise,
scrupulous; absolute, complete, utter.

stride
n lit: gait, step.
vb lit: bestride, straddle, walk with long
steps.

strident
adj lit: clashing, discordant, grating,
harsh, rasping, raucous, screeching,
shrill, stridulant.

strife
n lit: animosity, bickering, clash, conflict,
contention, controversy, discord,
friction, squabbling, wrangling.

strike
n lit: bang, blow, clout, hit, knock, slap,
smack, wallop; stoppage, walk-out.
vb lit: bang, beat, chastise, clobber, clout,
hit, knock, pound, smack, smite, thump,
wallop; clash, collide with, run into,
smash into; drive, force, thrust; come to
the mind, dawn upon, occur to, register;
chance upon, discover, find, stumble
upon, unearth; assail, assault, attack, fall
upon, set upon; achieve, arrive at, reach;
down tools, walk out.

striking
adj lit: astonishing, dazzling,
extraordinary, impressive, noticeable,
outstanding, stunning.

string
n lit: cord, fibre, twine; chain, line, queue,
sequence, series, strand, succession.
vb lit: hang, link, loop, stretch, suspend,
thread; fan out, space out, spread out.

strip
n lit: belt, bit, fillet, piece, shred, slip,

swathe.
vb lit: bare, deprive, dismantle, empty, loot, pillage, plunder, ransack, rob, spoil; disrobe, unclothe, undress.

striped
adj lit: banded, barred, striated, stripy.

strive
vb lit: attempt, contend, do one's utmost, endeavour, exert oneself, go all out, make every effort, strain, struggle, toil, try.

stroke
n lit: achievement, blow, feat, hit, knock, movement, pat, rap, thump; apoplexy, attack, fit, seizure, shock.
vb lit: caress, fondle, pat, pet.

stroll
n lit: breath of air, constitutional, excursion, promenade, ramble, walk.
vb lit: amble, make one's way, mosey, promenade, ramble, saunter, stretch one's legs, toddle, wander.

strong
adj lit: athletic, beefy, burly, hale, hardy, muscular, robust, sound, stalwart, strapping, sturdy, tough, virile; brave, courageous, determined, high-powered, plucky, resilient, resourceful, steadfast, tenacious, unyielding; acute, dedicated, deep-rooted, eager, fervent, firm, intense, keen, staunch, vehement, zealous; clear-cut, cogent, compelling, distinct, formidable, marked, persuasive, potent, telling, unmistakable, weighty, well-founded; drastic, extreme, forceful, severe; durable, hard-wearing, heavy-duty, reinforced, substantial, well-built, well-protected; bold, bright, dazzling, glaring, loud; biting, heady, highly-flavoured, hot, intoxicating, piquant, pure, spicy, undiluted.

structure
n lit: arrangement, conformation, design, form, interrelation of parts, make-up, organization; building, construction, edifice, erection.
vb lit: arrange, assemble, build up, design, put together, shape.

struggle
n lit: effort, exertion, grind, long haul, scramble, toil; battle, brush, clash, conflict, contest, encounter, skirmish, strife, tussle.

vb lit: exert oneself, go all out, strain, strive, toil, work; battle, compete, contend, fight, grapple, scuffle.

strut
n lit: brace, support; bluff, boasting; pompous gait, prancing, swagger.
vb lit: brace, support; bluff, boast; parade, prance, stalk, swagger.

stubborn
adj lit: bull-headed, dogged, headstrong, intractable, obstinate, persistent, pig-headed, recalcitrant, stiff-necked, tenacious, unshakable, wilful.

stuck
adj (pa.pt) lit: cemented, fastened, fixed, glued, joined; *fig*: at a loss, baffled, nonplussed, up against a brick wall; hung up on, infatuated, keen, mad, obsessed with.

stud
n lit: boss, head of a nail, knob; cross-piece (in chain-cable), rivet; two-headed button; pin, socket; ornament, spangle; stallion; studfarm.
vb lit: frame, support; bespangle, ornament, scatter, spangle, speckle, spot.

student
n lit: apprentice, disciple, observer, pupil, scholar, undergraduate.

studious
adj lit: assiduous, attentive, bookish, diligent, eager, hard-working, meditative, reflective, serious, thoughtful.

study
n lit: academic work, research, swotting; analysis, attention, contemplation, inquiry, investigation, scrutiny, survey; drawing, sketch; library, study.
vb lit: apply oneself to, contemplate, examine, go into, meditate, ponder, read; analyse, deliberate, investigate, look into, peruse, research, survey.

stuff
n lit: belongings, effects, equipment, gear, kit, paraphernalia, possessions, tackle, trappings; cloth, fabric, material, textile; essence, matter, quintessence, substance; balderdash, bunkum, claptrap, humbug, nonsense, poppycock, rot, rubbish, tripe, twaddle, verbiage.

vb lit: compress, cram, fill, jam, load, pad, ram, shove, squeeze, wedge; gobble, guzzle, make a pig of oneself, overindulge.

stuffy
adj lit: airless, fetid, fuggy, heavy, oppressive, stifling, suffocating, unventilated; conventional, dreary, dull, musty, old-fogyish, priggish, prim, stodgy, strait-laced.

stumble
vb lit: fall, falter, flounder, lose one's balance, lurch, reel, slip, stagger, trip; blunder upon, chance upon, happen upon, light upon; falter, stammer, stutter.

stump
vb lit: baffle, bewilder, confound, confuse, dumbfound, foil, mystify, perplex, puzzle; clomp, clump, lumber, stomp, trudge; *fig*: cough (up), pay (up).

stung
adj (pa.pt) lit: angered, exasperated, hurt, incensed, nettled, piqued, wounded.

stunning
adj lit: beautiful, dazzling, devastating, gorgeous, great, lovely, marvellous, ravishing, sensational, smashing, spectacular, striking.

stunted
adj (pa.pt) lit: diminutive, dwarfed, small, tiny, undersized.

stupefy
vb lit: amaze, astound, confound, dumbfound, shock, stagger, stun.

stupendous
adj lit: amazing, astounding, breathtaking, enormous, fabulous, fantastic, huge, mind-boggling, phenomenal, prodigious, staggering, stunning, superb, tremendous, vast.

stupidity
n lit: asininity, brainlessness, dimness, feeble-mindedness, imbecility, naivety, slowness, thick-headedness; absurdity, folly, foolhardiness, indiscretion, ineptitude, irresponsibility, ludicrousness, lunacy, rashness, senselessness, silliness.

sturdy
adj lit: athletic, brawny, durable, firm, hardy, hearty, muscular, robust, secure, stalwart, staunch, steadfast, vigorous, well-built.

style
n lit: cut, design, form, manner, technique; fashion, mode, rage, trend, vogue; approach, custom, manner, way; chic, dash, elegance, flair, panache, smartness, sophistication, stylishness, taste; affluence, comfort, grandeur, luxury; category, characteristic, genre, kind, sort, spirit, tenor, tone, type; diction, expression, phraseology, turn of phrase, vein, wording.
vb lit: adapt, cut, design, dress, fashion, tailor; address, call, dub, entitle, label, name, term.

suave
adj lit: affable, agreeable, charming, courteous, diplomatic, obliging, polite, smooth, sophisticated, svelte, urbane.

subdued
adj lit: chastened, dejected, downcast, grave, restrained, sad, serious, solemn; hushed, low-key, muted, quiet, sober, soft, subtle, toned down.

subject
n lit: affair, business, field of inquiry, issue, matter, object, point, question, theme, topic; case, guinea pig, participant, patient; citizen, dependant, national, vassal.
vb lit: expose, lay open, put through, submit, treat.
adj lit: at the mercy of, exposed, liable, open, prone, susceptible, vulnerable; conditional, contingent, dependent; answerable, bound by, inferior, obedient, satellite, subjugated, subordinate.

submit
vb lit: acquiesce, agree, bend, capitulate, comply, defer, give in, knuckle under, put up with, resign oneself, succumb, surrender, toe the line, tolerate, yield; commit, hand in, proffer, put forward, refer, tender; advance, argue, assert, contend, move, propose, propound, put, state, suggest.

subordinate
n lit: aide, assistant, attendant, junior, second, subaltern.
vb lit: make inferior (to), make junior (to),

make subject (to), make subsidiary (to), subjugate (to).
adj lit: inferior, junior, lesser, lower, minor, secondary, subject, subservient; ancillary, auxiliary, subsidiary, supplementary.

subsequently
adv lit: afterwards, at a later date, consequently, in the end, later.

subside
vb lit: abate, decrease, diminish, dwindle, ebb, lessen, level off, peter out, quieten, recede, slacken, wane; cave in, collapse, decline, drop, settle, sink.

subsidize
vb lit: finance, fund, sponsor, support, underwrite.

substance
n lit: body, fabric, material, stuff, texture; burden, gist, import, meaning, pith, significance, subject, theme; actuality, entity, force, reality; affluence, assets, estate, means, resources.

substitute
n lit: agent, deputy, expedient, locum, proxy, relief, replacement, reserve, stand-by, surrogate, temp.
vb lit: change, exchange, replace, swap, switch; act for, cover for, deputize, fill in for, stand in for.
adj lit: acting, additional, proxy, replacement, reserve, surrogate, temporary.

subtle
adj lit: delicate, ingenious, nice, penetrating, profound, refined, sophisticated; faint, implied, insinuated, slight, understated; artful, crafty, cunning, devious, intriguing, Machiavellian, scheming, shrewd, sly, wily.

subtract
vb lit: deduct, detract, remove, take off, withdraw.

subversive
n lit: deviationist, dissident, fifth columnist, saboteur, seditionary, terrorist, traitor.
adj lit: destructive, inflammatory, insurrectionary, perversive, riotous, seditious, treasonous, underground.

succeed
vb lit: be successful, do all right for oneself, flourish, make good, prosper, thrive, turn out well; be subsequent, come next, ensue, follow.

successful
adj lit: acknowledged, best-selling, booming, efficacious, flourishing, lucky, lucrative, profitable, prosperous, thriving, top.

succinct
adj lit: brief, compact, compendious, concise, condensed, laconic, pithy, summary, terse, to the point.

succumb
vb lit: capitulate, fall victim to, give way, knuckle under, submit, surrender, yield.

sudden
adj lit: abrupt, hasty, hurried, quick, rapid, rash, swift, unforseen.

sue
vb lit: charge, indict, prefer charges against (someone), prosecute, summon, take (someone) to court; appeal for, beseech, entreat, petition, plead, solicit, supplicate.

suffer
vb lit: ache, be in pain, feel wretched, grieve, hurt; bear, endure, experience, go through, put up with, sustain, undergo; be impaired, deteriorate, fall off, show to disadvantage; allow, let, permit.

sufficient
adj lit: adequate, competent, enough, satisfactory.

sugary
adj lit: saccharine, sickly sweet; cloying, over-refined.

suggest
vb lit: advise, advocate, move, propose, put forward, recommend; bring to mind, connote, evoke; hint, imply, indicate, insinuate, intimate, lead one to believe.

suggestion
n lit: motion, proposal, proposition, recommendation; hint, indication, insinuation, intimation, suspicion, trace.

suggestive
adj lit: evocative, indicative, reminiscent; bawdy, blue, improper, indecent, provocative, ribald, risqué, rude, smutty, spicy, titillating.

suit
n lit: appeal, attentions, courtship, entreaty, petition, request; costume, dress, habit, outfit; *spec*: action, case, lawsuit, proceeding, prosecution, trial.
vb lit: agree, answer, be acceptable to, become, befit, be seemly, conform to, do, go with, match, satisfy, tally; accommodate, adjust, fashion, fit, tailor.

suitable
adj lit: acceptable, applicable, appropriate, apt, becoming, befitting, convenient, fitting, in character, in keeping, pertinent, proper, relevant, right, satisfactory, seemly, suited.

suite
n lit: apartment, furniture, rooms, series, set; attendants, entourage, followers, retinue, train.

sulky
adj lit: aloof, churlish, disgruntled, moody, morose, petulant, put out, querulous, sullen, vexed.

sullenness
n lit: glumness, ill humour, moodiness, moroseness, sulkiness, sulks.

sultry
adj lit: hot, humid, oppressive, sticky, stifling, stuffy; passionate, provocative, seductive, sensual, sexy, voluptuous.

sum
n lit: aggregate, amount, quantity, reckoning, score, tally, total, whole.

summary
n lit: abridgment, abstract, compendium, digest, epitome, essence, extract, outline, résumé, review, rundown, summing-up, synopsis.
adj lit: arbitrary, compact, compendious, concise, condensed, cursory, hasty, perfunctory, pithy.

summit
n lit: acme, apex, crowning point, culmination, height, peak, pinnacle, top, zenith.

summon
vb lit: assemble, bid, call together, convene, invite, rally, send for; call into action, draw on, gather, muster.

sundry
adj lit: assorted, miscellaneous, several, some, varied, various.

sunken
adj lit: drawn, haggard, hollowed; at a lower level, buried, depressed, immersed, recessed, submerged.

sunny
adj lit: bright, clear, luminous, radiant, sunlit, unclouded; beaming, buoyant, cheery, genial, joyful, light-hearted, optimistic, pleasant.

sunrise
n lit: aurora, dawn, daybreak, daylight.

superb
adj lit: admirable, breathtaking, choice, exquisite, first-rate, gorgeous, magnificent, splendid, superior.

supercilious
adj lit: arrogant, condescending, contemptuous, disdainful, haughty, hoity-toity, imperious, insolent, lofty, overbearing, patronizing, snooty, toffee-nosed, vainglorious.

superficial
adj lit: exterior, external, peripheral, shallow, skin-deep, slight; casual, cosmetic, cursory, desultory, nodding, passing, perfunctory, sketchy; empty-headed, frivolous, lightweight, trivial; apparent, evident, ostensible, outward, seeming.

superfluous
adj lit: excess, excessive, extra, left over, needless, redundant, residuary, spare, supernumerary, surplus, uncalled-for, unnecessary, unrequired.

superintend
vb lit: administer, control, direct, look after, manage, oversee, run, supervise.

superior
n lit: boss, chief, director, manager, principal, senior, supervisor.
adj lit: better, greater, higher, more advanced, predominant, preferred, prevailing, surpassing; admirable, choice, de luxe, distinguished, excellent, exclusive, first-class, first-rate, good quality, high calibre, high-class; airy,

condescending, haughty, lofty, patronizing, pretentious, snobbish, supercilious.

supernatural
adj lit: abnormal, hidden, miraculous, mystic, occult, paranormal, psychic, spectral, uncanny, unearthly, unnatural.

supersede
vb lit: annul, displace, oust, remove, replace, set aside, supplant, suspend, take over, usurp.

supervision
n lit: administration, auspices, care, charge, control, guidance, management, oversight, surveillance.

supine
adj lit: flat, inclining backwards, recumbent, sloping backwards, supinated; inactive, indolent, inert, languid, lazy, listless, passive.

supplant
vb lit: displace, oust, overthrow, replace, supersede, take over, undermine, unseat.

supple
adj lit: elastic, flexible, limber, lithe, plastic, pliable.

supplementary
adj lit: accompanying, additional, auxiliary, complementary, extra, secondary.

supplication
n lit: appeal, entreaty, petition, plea, request, solicitation, suit.

supply
n lit: cache, fund, hoard, reserve, reservoir, source, stockpile, store; foodstuff, items, materials, necessities, provisions, rations, stores.
vb lit: afford, cater for, contribute, endow, furnish, give, grant, produce, provide, purvey, replenish, stock, store, victual.

support
n lit: back, brace, foundation, pillar, post, prop, stanchion, stay, underpinning; aid, assistance, backing, blessing, encouragement, furtherance, help, moral support, patronage, protection, relief, sustenance; keep, livelihood, maintenance, subsistence; backbone, backer, mainstay, supporter, tower of strength.

vb lit: bear, bolster, brace, buttress, hold up, prop, reinforce, sustain, underpin, uphold; cherish, finance, foster, fund, keep, look after, maintain, provide for, strengthen, subsidize, succour, take care of, underwrite; advocate, aid, assist, back, champion, defend, forward, go along with, promote, second, side with, stand behind, stick up for, take (someone's) part; attest to, authenticate, bear out, confirm, corroborate, endorse, substantiate, verify; countenance, endure, put up with, stand (for), submit, suffer, tolerate, undergo.

suppose
vb lit: assume, conjecture, dare say, expect, imagine, presume, surmise, take for granted, think; believe, conceive, conclude, consider, fancy, postulate, pretend.

supposed
adj lit: alleged, assumed, hypothetical, presumed, presupposed, professed, reputed, rumoured; meant (to), obliged (to), ought (to), required (to).

supposition
n lit: conjecture, guess, hypothesis, idea, notion, presumption, speculation, theory.

suppress
vb lit: check, conquer, crack down on, crush, drive underground, extinguish, overthrow, quash, quench, stamp out, subdue, trample on; censor, conceal, cover up, curb, hold back, keep secret, muffle, repress, restrain, silence, smother, withhold.

supreme
adj lit: cardinal, chief, culminating, extreme, first, foremost, greatest, leading, paramount, predominant, pre-eminent, prime, principal, superlative, surpassing, top, ultimate, utmost.

surcharge
n lit: additional mark (on postage stamps), extra charge; additional supply, excessive load; omission (in account).
vb lit: charge extra, overcharge; oppress, overburden, overload, overwhelm; weigh down; print a surcharge (on postage stamps); show an omission (in account).

sure
adj lit: assured, clear, confident, decided, definite, positive, satisfied; accurate,

dependable, foolproof, honest,
indisputable, infallible, precise, reliable,
trusty, undeniable, undoubted,
unmistakable; bound, guaranteed,
inescapable, inevitable, irrevocable; fast,
firm, fixed, safe, secure, solid, stable,
steady.

surface
n lit: exterior, façade, facet, outside, skin,
top, veneer.
vb lit: appear, come to light, crop up,
emerge, rise, transpire.
adj lit: apparent, exterior, external,
outward, superficial.

surfeit
n lit: excess, glut, plethora, satiety,
superfluity.
vb lit: cram, fill, glut, gorge, overfeed,
stuff.

surge
n lit: billow, efflux, flood, flow, gush,
intensification, rush, swell, upsurge,
wave.
vb lit: billow, eddy, gush, heave, rise,
rush, swell, swirl, undulate.

surly
adj lit: brusque, churlish, crusty, gruff,
ill-natured, morose, sullen, testy,
uncivil.

surmise
n lit: assumption, conclusion, deduction,
guess, hypothesis, inference, notion,
possibility, presumption, speculation,
supposition, thought.
vb lit: conclude, conjecture, consider,
deduce, fancy, hazard a guess, imagine,
infer, presume, speculate, suppose.

surpass
vb lit: beat, exceed, excel, outdo, outshine,
overshadow, top, tower over, transcend.

surplus
n lit: balance, excess, remainder, residue,
superfluity, surfeit.
adj lit: excess, extra, odd, remaining,
spare, superfluous.

surprise
n lit: amazement, astonishment,
bewilderment, incredulity; bombshell,
eye-opener, revelation, shock.
vb lit: amaze, astonish, astound, bewilder,
disconcert, flabbergast, stun, take aback;
catch off-guard, catch red-handed,
discover, startle.

surrender
n lit: capitulation, delivery,
relinquishment, renunciation,
resignation, submission.
vb lit: abandon, concede, forego, give up,
part with, relinquish, renounce, resign,
waive, yield; capitulate, give oneself up,
give way, quit, submit, succumb.

surreptitious
adj lit: clandestine, covert, fraudulent,
secret, sly, sneaking, stealthy,
underhand.

surround
vb lit: close in on, encircle, enclose,
encompass, fence in, hem in, ring; *spec*:
besiege, lay siege to.

surroundings
n lit: environment, location, milieu,
neighbourhood, setting.

survey
n lit: examination, inquiry, inspection,
review, scrutiny, study.
vb lit: contemplate, examine, inspect, look
over, reconnoitre, research, review, scan,
scrutinize, study, view.

survive
vb lit: endure, hold out, last, live, pull
through, remain alive, subsist.

susceptible
adj lit: disposed, inclined, liable, open,
prone, vulnerable; alive to,
impressionable, receptive, responsive,
sensitive, suggestible.

suspect
n lit: supposed offender.
vb lit: distrust, have one's doubts about,
mistrust, smell the rat; believe,
conjecture, consider, feel, hazard a
guess, speculate, suppose, surmise, think
probable.
adj lit: doubtful, dubious, fishy,
questionable.

suspend
vb lit: attach, dangle, hang, swing;
adjourn, cease, cut short, defer, delay,
hold off, interrupt, lay aside, postpone,
put off, shelve, stay, withhold.

suspense
n lit: anticipation, anxiety, apprehension,
doubt, expectation, indecision, tension,
uncertainty, wavering.

suspicion

n lit: bad vibes, distrust, doubt, funny feeling, misgiving, mistrust, qualm, scepticism, wariness; conjecture, guess, hunch, impression, notion, supposition, surmise; glimmer, hint, shadow, strain, suggestion, tinge, touch, trace.

sustain

vb lit: bear, carry, keep up, support, uphold; endure, experience, feel, suffer, undergo, withstand; aid, assist, foster, help, keep alive, nourish, nurture, provide for; approve, confirm, continue, keep up, maintain, protract, ratify; endorse, uphold, validate, verify.

sustenance

n lit: daily bread, food, nourishment, provisions, rations, refreshments, victuals; livelihood, maintenance, subsistence.

swallow

n lit: gulp, mouthful; gullet, throat; appetite; martin, swift.
vb lit: absorb, consume, devour, down, gulp, swill, wash down; use up, waste; choke back, repress; believe, buy, fall for.

swamp

n lit: bog, fen, marsh, mire, morass, quagmire, slough.
vb lit: capsize, engulf, flood, inundate, sink, submerge, swallow up, upset, waterlog; besiege, deluge, overload, overwhelm.

swap

n lit: barter, exchange, trade.
vb lit: bandy, barter, exchange, interchange, switch, trade, traffic.

swarm

n lit: army, bevy, crowd, drove, flock, host, mass, multitude, myriad, throng.
vb lit: congregate, crowd, flock, mass, stream, throng; crawl (with), teem (with).

sway

n lit: ascendancy, authority, control, influence, jurisdiction, power, predominance, rule, sovereignty.
vb lit: fluctuate, incline, lean, oscillate, rock, swing, wave; affect, control, dominate, guide, induce, influence, persuade, win over.

swear

vb lit: affirm, assert, attest, declare, give one's word, pledge oneself, promise, take an oath, testify, vow, warrant; be foul-mouthed, curse, imprecate, turn the air blue.

swearing

n lit: bad language, blasphemy, cursing, foul language, imprecations, profanity.

sweat

n lit: diaphoresis, exudation, perspiration; *fig*: agitation, anxiety, distress, strain, worry; chore, drudgery, effort.
vb lit: break out in a sweat, glow, perspire; *fig*: agonize, be on tenterhooks, chafe, fret, worry; stick it out.

sweep

n lit: arc, curve, gesture, movement, stroke, swing; compass, extend, range, scope, span, stretch, vista.
vb lit: brush, clean, clear; career, fly, glide, hurtle, sail, skim, tear, zoom.

sweeping

adj (pr.pt) lit: all-embracing, bird's-eye, broad, extensive, radical, thoroughgoing, wide-ranging; across-the-board, exaggerated, indiscriminate, unqualified, wholesale.

sweet

n lit: dessert, pudding, sweet course; confectionery, sweet-meats.
adj lit: cloying, honeyed, saccharine, sugary, syrupy, toothsome; affectionate, agreeable, amiable, attractive, charming, delightful, engaging, gentle, kind, sweet-tempered, taking, tender, winsome; beloved, darling, dear, pet, precious; aromatic, fragrant, fresh, perfumed, redolent, sweet-smelling; euphonic, harmonious, mellow, silvery, soft, tuneful; gone on, keen on.

sweetheart

n lit: admirer, beloved, darling, dear, flame, love, suitor, truelove, valentine.

swell

n lit: billow, rise, surge, wave; beau, dandy, fashion plate, nob.
vb lit: balloon, be inflated, billow, bloat, bulge, dilate, enlarge, expand, extend, increase, protrude, puff up; add to, aggravate, augment, enhance, intensify, mount, surge.
adj lit: de luxe, fashionable, plush, posh, smart, stylish.

swelling
n lit: blister, bruise, bump, dilation, enlargement, inflammation, lump, protuberance, puffiness.

swerve
vb lit: bend, deflect, deviate, diverge, incline, shift, stray, swing, turn, veer, wind.

swiftly
adv lit: double-quick, fast, hotfoot, hurriedly, posthaste, promptly, rapidly, speedily.

swig
n lit: drink.
vb lit: drink greedily.

swindle
n lit: con trick, deception, double-dealing, fiddle, fraud, racket, rip-off, sharp practice, trickery.
vb lit: bamboozle, cheat, con, deceive, defraud, dupe, fleece, overcharge, pull a sharp one (on someone), rip (someone) off, take (someone) for a ride, take to the cleaners, trick.

swindler
n lit: charlatan, cheat, con man, fraud, impostor, rascal, rogue, shark, trickster.

swing
n lit: fluctuation, oscillation, stroke, sway, vibration.
vb lit: be pendent, dangle, hang, suspend; fluctuate, oscillate, rock, sway, vary, veer, vibrate, wave; swivel (round), turn (round), wheel (round).

switch
n lit: riding whip, stick; blow, lash, stroke; bunch, coil (of hair); lever, plug; pair of movable rails; *fig*: about-turn, alteration, change of direction, exchange, reversal, shift, substitution, swap.
vb lit: lash, strike, swish, whip; jerk, swing, twitch, wave, whisk; connect, disconnect, turn off, turn on; shift, shunt; *fig*: change course, deviate, divert, exchange, rearrange, substitute, swap, trade.

swoop
n lit: descent, lunge, plunge, pounce, stoop, sweep.
vb lit: descend, dive, pounce, rush, stoop, sweep.

sword
n lit: blade, cutlass, rapier, sabre, scimitar;

fig: aggression, arms, massacre, military might, violence, war.

sycophant
n lit: fawner, flatterer, lickspittle, parasite, toady.

symbol
n lit: badge, emblem, logo, mark, sign, token, type.

symbolize
vb lit: betoken, connote, denote, exemplify, mean, represent, signify, stand for, typify.

sympathetic
adj lit: affectionate, caring, compassionate, concerned, kindly, understanding, warm-hearted; favourably disposed (to), in sympathy with, pro; agreeable, appreciative, compatible, congenial, like-minded.

sympathize
vb lit: bleed for, commiserate, condole, feel for, have compassion, pity; agree, be in accord, go along with, side with, understand.

sympathy
n lit: commiseration, compassion, condolence(s), empathy, pity, thoughtfulness, understanding; affinity, agreement, correspondence, harmony, rapport, union, warmth.

symptom
n lit: indication, mark, sign, syndrome, warning.

synopsis
n lit: digest, summary.

synthesize
vb lit: combine, come together, put together; form, manufacture, produce, treat.

synthetic
adj lit: artificial, fake, man-made, manufactured, mock.

system
n lit: arrangement, classification, combination, coordination, organization, scheme, setup, structure; fixed order, practice, procedure, routine, technique, theory, usage; logical process, method, orderliness, regularity, systematization.

systematic
adj lit: businesslike, efficient, methodical, organized, precise, standardized, systematized.

T

tab

n lit: flap, hook, loop, strap, tag; label, marker; chevron, epaulette, stripe; finger-protector, mitt; stage-curtain; *fig*: bill, reckoning, tally.

table

n lit: bar, counter, stand, surface; board, fare, food; flats, mesa, plain, plateau; *fig*: chart, diagram, graph, index, key, list, schedule, tabulation.

vb lit: introduce, move, propose, put forward; catalogue, chart, list, tabulate.

tableau

n lit: freeze-frame image, picture, scenario, scene, set, still-life.

tablet

n lit: block, note-pad, pad, writing-pad; capsule, lozenge, pill; sheet, slab.

taciturn

adj lit: distant, reserved, reticent, silent, tight-lipped, uncommunicative, withdrawn; antisocial, sulky, sullen, surly.

tack

n lit: drawing-pin, nail, pin; gear, harness, riding equipment, saddle; darn, temporary stitch; adhesiveness, bond, glueyness; bearing, course, heading; angle, dog-leg, zigzag; *fig*: approach, method, procedure, way.

vb lit: nail, pin; darn loosely, stitch temporarily; bond, glue, gum, paste, stick; change direction, veer, zigzag; *fig*: annex (to), append (on to), attach (on to).

tackle

n lit: accoutrements, equipment, gear, outfit, rig, trappings; attack, block, bringing down, ruck.

vb lit: apply oneself to, attack, get to grips with, grapple with, have a go at, set about, take on, undertake, wrestle with; block, bring down, fell, grab, halt, hold, pounce on, stop.

tact

n lit: address, decorousness, delicacy, diplomacy, discretion, finesse, sensitivity; judgement, sense, wisdom.

tactful

adj lit: decorous, delicate, diplomatic, discreet; judicious, politic, prudent; canny, subtle.

tactic

n lit: gambit, manoeuvre, move, ploy, stratagem, strategy; line, method, plan, policy, scheme, way.

tactical

adj lit: diplomatic, politic, strategic; canny, cunning, shrewd, subtle.

tactician

n lit: field-marshal, general, mastermind, orchestrator, schemer, strategist.

tactless

adj lit: boorish, clumsy, inconsiderate, indelicate, inept, insensitive, thoughtless, unkind; imprudent, incautious, indiscreet, undiplomatic; discourteous, impolite, rude, uncivil.

tail

n lit: appendage, end, extremity; backside, behind, bottom, bum, posterior, rear, rump, seat, stern; file, line, queue, train; coda, conclusion, finale; shadower, stalker, tracker, watcher.

vb lit: dog, follow, shadow, trace, track, trail; die (away), drop (off), fade (away), taper (off).

tailor

n lit: clothier, outfitter; couturier, dressmaker, seamstress.

vb lit: accommodate (to), adapt (to), adjust (to), alter (to), cut (to), fit (to), modify (to), style (to).

tainted

adj (pa.pt) lit: blighted, contaminated, dirty, foul, infected, poisoned, polluted, soiled; blackened, blemished, branded, disgraced, dishonoured, ruined, stigmatized, sullied, tarnished.

take

vb lit: carry (away), collect, gain possession of, get, get hold of, grasp, grip, have, hold, receive, win; bear, bring, convey, ferry, fetch, haul, lug, transport; accompany, conduct, escort, guide, lead,

usher; acquire, come into possession of,
obtain, procure, secure; marry, wed;
arrest, capture, entrap, seize; fell, hit,
kill, tackle; abduct, hijack, kidnap, run
off with; abstract, liberate,
misappropriate, nick, pinch, purloin,
steal, swipe; deduct, remove, subtract;
consume, drink, eat, ingest;
accommodate, contain, have room for;
fig: do, effect, execute, make, perform;
indulge in; accept, adopt, assume, be
guided by, comply with, obey; call for,
demand, need, require; spend, use (up);
book, engage, hire, lease, rent, reserve;
buy, purchase; choose, pick, select;
brook, endure, go through, put up with,
stand, stomach, swallow, tolerate,
withstand; bilk, cheat, con, dupe,
swindle; catch, go by, travel in; believe,
consider, interpret, perceive, presume,
regard, see; be attractive, charm,
enchant, please; learn, study; lecture in,
teach; photograph, shoot, snap; *spec*: (a
procedure/process may) be effective,
operate, work.

take back

vb lit: convey back, escort back, ferry back;
get back, recapture, recover, regain,
repossess; accept back, exchange; *fig*:
disclaim, renounce, retract, withdraw.

take down

vb lit: drop, let down, lower, pull down,
strip off; demolish, dismantle, level, raze,
tear down; jot down, minute, note,
record, write down.

take in

vb lit: accept, admit, let in, receive,
welcome; absorb, assimilate, contain,
encompass, include; fill up with;
contract, shorten, tighten; comprehend,
grasp, twig, understand; cheat, con,
dupe, fool, hoodwink, swindle, trick.

take off

vb lit: discard, divest oneself of, peel off,
strip off; become airborne, lift off;
decamp, disappear, leave, run away, set
out, vanish; caricature, imitate, lampoon,
mimic, parody, send up, travesty.

take on

vb lit: employ, engage, enrol, hire, put on
the payroll; acquire, adopt, assume, put
on; accept, get to grips with, have a go at,
tackle, undertake; compete against,
confront, face, fight, vie with; *fig*: become

emotional, cause a scene, create, get
upset, make a fuss.

take over

vb lit: convey across, escort across, ferry
across; inherit, succeed to; assume
control of, gain power over, take
command of.

take to

vb lit: convey to, escort to, ferry to; resort
to, retreat to; flee to, head for, run for; *fig*:
become friendly with, get on well with,
like, warm to.

takings

n lit: earnings, gate, income, proceeds,
profits, receipts, returns, revenue,
turnover.

tale

n lit: account, anecdote, fable, legend,
saga, story, yarn; fib, rigmarole, spiel;
rumour, scandal, secret.

talent

n lit: ability, aptitude, faculty, flair, forte,
gift, knack.

talisman

n lit: amulet, charm, fetish, mascot, token.

talk

n lit: address, dissertation, lecture,
oration, sermon, speech; chat, chitchat,
conversation, gab, gossip, natter;
confabulation, conference, consultation,
dialogue, discussion, parley; words.
vb lit: speak; chat, chatter, converse,
gossip, natter, prattle, rabbit, witter;
confabulate, confer, consult, discuss,
parley; negotiate (about); blab, grass,
spill the beans, sing, squeal.

tall

adj lit: big, high, lanky, lofty, towering; *fig*:
daunting, demanding, formidable, hard;
absurd, far-fetched, implausible,
incredible, ludicrous, preposterous,
ridiculous.

tally

n lit: count, mark, record, score, slate;
counterfoil, stub; match, mate, twin.
vb lit: agree, coincide, concur, correspond,
square; keep score, log, reckon up,
register.

tamper

vb lit: fiddle (with), fool about (with),
interfere (with), meddle (with), muck
about (with), tinker (with).

tan
n lit: sunburn; tannin.
vb lit: burn, sunburn; *fig*: beat, flog,
thrash, whip.
adj lit: beige, buff, khaki, yellow-brown.

tangible
adj lit: concrete, material, palpable,
physical, solid, substantial, tactile;
actual, evident, manifest, real.

tangle
n lit: coil, knot, mass, mesh, mess, snarl,
twist; imbroglio, mix-up; labyrinth,
maze.
vb lit: coil, interlace, intertwine, knot, mat,
mesh, snarl, twist; embroil (in), involve
(in); *fig*: contend (with), cross swords
(with), lock horns (with), mess (with).

tank
n lit: cistern, container, reservoir, vessel;
lake, pool; armoured vehicle.

tantalize
vb lit: entice, frustrate, lead on, provoke,
tease, tempt.

tantrum
n lit: flare-up, outburst, paddy, paroxysm,
rage, storm, temper.

tap
n lit: bung, plug, stopper; bug, listening
device; knock, pat, rap, touch; faucet,
spout, stopcock; (on) draught; *fig*: (on)
hand.
vb lit: bug, listen in on; knock, pat, rap,
touch; broach, draw off, open, siphon off;
exploit, make use of, milk, mine, use,
utilize; thread.

tape
n lit: band, film, ribbon, strip; binding;
finishing-line.
vb lit: bind, secure, tie (up); record, video.

taper
n lit: lighter, long match, spill, wax match.
vb lit: come to a point, narrow; die (off),
dwindle, fade, wane.

tardy
adj lit: behind, behindhand, late;
unpunctual; dilatory, slow, sluggish.

target
n lit: butt, inner; bullseye, goal, mark,
objective, quarry; prey, victim; *fig*: aim,
ambition, intention, objective.

task
n lit: assignment, charge, chore, duty, job,
mission, occupation, work.

taste
n lit: flavour, relish, savour, tang; bite,
morsel, mouthful, nip, sip, snatch,
swallow; appetite, fancy, fondness,
inclination, liking, palate, partiality,
predilection, preference; culture,
discrimination, grace, judgement,
refinement.
vb lit: have a flavour (of), savour (of);
discern, distinguish, sense; nibble,
sample, sip, take a bite of, try; *fig*:
encounter, experience, feel, know.

tasty
adj lit: appetizing, delicious, juicy,
luscious, palatable, savoury,
scrumptious, succulent, toothsome.

taunt
n lit: dig, gibe, insult, snide remark;
provocation.
vb lit: deride, insult, jeer at, mock, sneer
at, tease; provoke.

taut
adj lit: flexed, strained, stressed, stretched,
tense, tight; neat, orderly, shipshape,
tidy, trim.

tax
n lit: customs, duty, excise, impost, levy,
rate, tariff, toll; inland revenue, national
insurance; assessment, contribution;
burden, drain, load, stress, weight.
vb lit: exact a toll from, impose a levy on,
levy a rate on; burden, exhaust, load
down, sap, strain, try, weaken, weigh
upon; charge (with), reprove (with).

teach
vb lit: educate, enlighten, impart,
inculcate, inform; give lessons in, lecture,
tutor; coach, discipline, drill, instruct,
school, train; demonstrate (how), show
(how).

teacher
n lit: dominie, guru, lecturer, master,
mentor, mistress, professor, tutor; coach,
instructor, trainer; demonstrator.

teachings
n lit: commandments, doctrine,
instructions, laws, parables, precepts,
principles, sayings, tenets, wisdom,
words.

team

n lit: band, brigade, company, crew, gang, set, side, squad, troop, troupe; pair, span, yoke.
vb lit: cooperate (with), join (up with), link (up with), unite (with).

tearful

adj lit: blubbing, crying, lachrymose, weeping, weepy; distressing, pathetic, pitiable, poignant, sad.

teasing

n lit: aggravation, badgering, baiting, gibes, mockery, needling, provocation, ragging, ridicule, taunts; carding, combing out, shredding.

technical

adj lit: methodological, professional, specialist, trade; esoteric, in.

technique

n lit: art, craft, execution, knack, knowhow, proficiency, skill; manner, means, method, procedure, system, way.

tedium

n lit: banality, boredom, dreariness, dullness, ennui, monotony.

teeming

adj lit: alive (with), brimming (with), bristling (with), bursting (with), crawling (with), overflowing (with), swarming (with), thick (with); fecund, fertile, fruitful, multiplying; chucking it (down), pouring (down), sheeting (down).

teeth

n lit: dentition, dentures, occlusion; canines, incisors, molars, premolars; fangs, tusks; cogs, projections, prongs, serrations, tines; *fig*: bite, force, power.

telephone

n lit: handset, phone, receiver; blower; line.
vb lit: buzz, call, call up, dial, get on the blower to, give one a bell, give one a call, give one a ring, phone, ring.

telescope

n lit: glass, spyglass.
vb lit: concertina, flex, fold; compact, crush, squash; *fig*: compress, condense, contract, curtail, shorten, truncate.

tell

vb lit: acquaint of, apprise of, communicate to, divulge to, impart to, inform of, let know, make known to, mention to, notify of, say to; blab, grass, squeal; announce, proclaim, publish; depict, describe, narrate, recount, relate; command (to), direct (to), instruct (to), order (to); differentiate, discern, distinguish, identify, make out, see, understand; count, have an effect, register, weigh heavily.

teller

n lit: cashier, clerk; calculator, counter; psephologist, vote-counter; narrator, reciter.

temerity

n lit: audacity, brashness, foolhardiness, forwardness, heedlessness, rashness, recklessness.

temper

n lit: consistency, density, homogeneity; disposition, frame of mind, humour, mood, nature; (lose one's) composure, cool, equanimity, self-control; fury, heat, passion, rage, tantrum.
vb lit: mix, mould, work; moderate, soften; harden; check, curb, restrain; adjust the pitch of, tune.

temperament

n lit: character, disposition, frame of mind, humour, make-up, nature, outlook, personality, stamp; excitability, hot-headedness, impatience, moods, volatility; tuning, variation in pitch.

temperamental

adj lit: congenital, constitutional, inborn, innate, natural; idiosyncratic, individual; emotional, erratic, excitable, highly-strung, impatient, mercurial, moody, passionate, unpredictable, volatile.

temperance

n lit: moderation, restraint, self-control, self-discipline; abstinence, continence, sobriety, teetotalism.

temperate

adj lit: agreeable, clement, fair, mild, moderate, pleasant; balmy, cool, soft; calm, composed, equable, even-tempered, self-controlled, self-restrained, stable; abstinent, continent, sober, teetotal.

tempest

n lit: cyclone, gale, hurricane, storm, typhoon; *fig*: agitation, commotion, furore, riot, tumult, turbulence, uproar.

tempestuous

adj lit: blustery, boisterous, gusty, raging,

stormy, turbulent; emotional, excited,
feverish, furious, impassioned, intense,
uncontrolled, violent, wild.

temporal
adj lit: periodical, seasonal, timed;
chronological, historical; civil, laic,
profane, secular, worldly; *spec*: time
(travel/warp).

temporary
adj lit: bridging, impermanent, interim;
casual, lump (labour), passing, stand-in,
substitute, transient, transitory.

tempt
vb lit: allure, attract, decoy, draw, entice,
inveigle, lead on, lure, seduce, tantalize,
tease; dare, fly in the face of; test.

temptation
n lit: allure, attraction, enticement, lure,
pull, seduction, tantalization; bait,
carrot, decoy, draw, invitation, loss-
leader.

tenable
adj lit: arguable, defensible, justifiable,
plausible, rational, solid, viable;
impregnable, invulnerable, unassailable.

tenacious
adj lit: clinging, grasping, gripping,
retaining, retentive; clenched, fast, tight;
adhesive, gluey, sticky; *fig*: obdurate,
persistent, steadfast, stubborn;
determined, resolute; unforgetting.

tenacity
n lit: grasp, grip; retention; adhesiveness,
bond, tack; *fig*: firmness, obduracy,
persistence, steadfastness, stubbornness;
determination, resolve; power of recall.

tend
vb lit: attend, care for, feed, keep, look
after, maintain, nurse, see to, serve, wait
upon; guard, protect, watch over; aim
(towards), go (towards), lead (towards),
move (towards), point (towards); be
biased (towards), be inclined (towards),
gravitate (towards), incline (towards).

tendency
n lit: disposition, inclination, leaning,
partiality, proclivity, propensity; drift,
heading, movement, trend.

tender
n lit: bid, offer, proposal; coinage,
currency, money, payment; supply-
vehicle.
vb lit: give, offer, present, proffer, submit,

volunteer.
adj lit: delicate, fragile, frail, weak; callow,
green, immature, new, unripe, young;
affectionate, amorous, fond, kind,
loving, sentimental, soft-hearted,
sympathetic; compassionate, gentle,
merciful; emotional, moving, romantic,
touching; aching, inflamed, painful, raw,
red, sensitive, sore.

tenderness
n lit: delicacy, fragility, frailty, weakness;
greenness, immaturity, unripeness,
youth; affection, fondness, kindness,
love, sentiment, soft-heartedness,
sympathy; compassion, gentleness,
mercy; inflammation, painfulness,
rawness, sensitivity, soreness.

tense
vb lit: clench, contract, flex, stiffen,
tauten, tighten.
adj lit: strained, stretched, taut, tight; *fig*:
apprehensive, edgy, jittery, jumpy,
keyed up, nervous, restless, strung up,
wound up; nerve-racking, stressful.

tension
n lit: rigidity, tautness, tightness, torque;
apprehension, edginess, nervousness,
pressure, strain, stress, suspense.

tentative
adj lit: conjectural, hypothetical,
provisional, speculative, theoretical,
unconfirmed; cautious, diffident, timid,
uncertain, unsure.

tenuous
adj lit: delicate, fine, slim, stretched, thin;
dubious, flimsy, insubstantial, nebulous,
shaky, weak.

tenure
n lit: freehold, leasehold, occupation,
possession, residence; administration,
office.

tepid
adj lit: cool, lukewarm, warmish; *fig*:
apathetic, half-hearted, unenthusiastic.

term
n lit: appellation, designation, expression,
name, nickname, phrase, title, word;
duration, period, spell, time, while;
semester, session; denominator,
numerator; predicate, subject; *spec*:
completion, culmination, end (of a
pregnancy, of a period of grace).
vb lit: call, christen, designate, dub,
entitle, label, name, nickname, style.

terminal
n *lit*: airport, airport building; station, stop, terminus.
adj *lit*: concluding, final, last, ultimate; endmost, hindmost, rear; fatal, incurable, lethal, mortal.

terminate
vb *lit*: come to an end, complete, conclude, end, finish, stop; bring to an end, close, cut off, discontinue, wind up; expire, lapse, run out.

terminology
n *lit*: language, phraseology, vernacular, vocabulary; cant, dialect, jargon.

terrain
n *lit*: area, ground, land, pitch; arena, field, theatre; geography, natural features, surface features; geology, stratigraphy.

terrible
adj *lit*: bad, grave, serious, severe; appalling, awful, dreadful, frightful, horrifying; hopeless, poor, rotten, useless.

terribly
adv *lit*: awfully, badly, desperately, dreadfully, extremely, gravely, seriously, severely.

terrific
adj *lit*: enormous, extreme, great, intense, serious, severe, tremendous; excellent, fantastic, fine, magnificent, outstanding, superb, wonderful.

terrify
vb *lit*: appal, awe, frighten, horrify, intimidate, petrify, terrorize.

territory
n *lit*: area, country, district, domain, land, manor, realm, region, tract, zone.

terror
n *lit*: dread, fear, fright, panic; alarm, awe, consternation, shock; *fig*: devil, fiend, monster; scoundrel, villain; rascal, rogue, scamp.

test
n *lit*: examination; check-up; analysis, assessment, evaluation, investigation; measure, proof.
vb *lit*: analyse, assess, check up on, examine, gauge, investigate, measure, try, try out, verify.

testify
vb *lit*: attest, bear witness, give testimony, swear; assert, declare, depose.

testimonial
n *lit*: character reference, commendation, reference; honorarium, memorial gift; charity match.

testimony
n *lit*: evidence, submission, witness; affidavit, confession, deposition, statement; demonstration, indication, manifestation, proof, verification.

tête-à-tête
n *lit*: colloquy, conversation, dialogue, discussion; chat, chinwag, confab, gossip, natter, talk.

tether
vb *lit*: lash, rope, secure, tie up; moor; attach, bind, truss.

text
n *lit*: contents, matter, words; crib, reference work, source; passage, verse; motif, subject, theme, topic.

texture
n *lit*: composition, consistency, quality, structure, surface; fabric, grain, weave.

thankful
adj *lit*: appreciative, beholden, grateful, indebted, obliged.

thanks
n *lit*: bless you, cheers, much obliged, ta; appreciation, gratefulness, gratitude; acknowledgement, mention, recognition; due (to), owing (to).

theme
n *lit*: argument, idea, subject matter, thesis, topic; motif, melody, subject, tune.

then
adj *lit*: concurrent, contemporary, existing.
adv *lit*: at that time; afterwards, later, presently, soon, thereafter; next, subsequently; also, besides; accordingly, consequently, in that case.

theorem
n *lit*: axiom, formula, maxim, principle, proposition, rule.

theorize
vb *lit*: conjecture, estimate, guess, hypothesize, reckon, speculate.

theory
n lit: assumption, conjecture, estimate, explanation, guess, hypothesis, speculation, supposition; classification, philosophy, system.

therapeutic
adj lit: corrective, curative, healing, remedial, restorative; beneficial, healthy; rehabilitative.

therapy
n lit: corrective treatment, cure, healing, remedial treatment; manipulation, massage; rehabilitation; alternative medicine.

therefore
adv lit: accordingly, consequently, for that reason, hence, resultantly, so, thus.

thesis
n lit: disquisition, dissertation, monograph, paper; contention, hypothesis, postulate, premise, proposition, theory, view.

thick
n lit: centre, midst.
adj lit: broad, deep, fat, substantial, wide; compact, concentrated, condensed, dense, impenetrable, opaque; crowded, jammed, packed; bristling, covered, crawling, swarming, teeming; *fig*: guttural, hoarse, husky, throaty; distinct, marked, pronounced, strong; friendly, inseparable, intimate; batwitted, dim, dull, moronic, obtuse, slow, stupid.

thicken
vb lit: clot, coagulate, concentrate, condense, congeal, set; broaden, deepen, widen.

thick-skinned
adj fig: impassive, insensitive, unfeeling; callous, detached, indifferent; long-suffering, magnanimous, patient, stoical.

thief
n lit: burglar, housebreaker, mugger, pickpocket, robber; embezzler, fraud, swindler; kleptomaniac, shoplifter; pirate, plagiarizer, rip-off merchant.

thin
vb lit: adulterate, attenuate, dilute, water down, weaken; prune back, trim; rarefy, refine; constrict, fine down, narrow, taper.
adj lit: attenuated, fine, narrow; bony, emaciated, lanky, scraggy, scrawny,

skeletal, skinny, slender, slim, spindly; meagre, scanty, scarce, sparse; diaphanous, filmy, flimsy, see-through, sheer, skimpy, transparent, wispy; adulterated, dilute, insipid, watered down, watery, weak; rarefied, refined; *fig*: feeble, inadequate, lame, poor, superficial, unconvincing.

thing
n lit: article, fact, item, object; affair, matter, subject, theme, topic; idea, importance, point, significance, thought; attribute, property, quality; event, incident, occasion, occurrence, phenomenon, proceedings; act, action, deed, feat, turn; apparatus, device, implement, instrument, machine, tool; belonging(s), effect(s), possession(s); *fig*: animal, creature, person; bag, hobby, pastime, preoccupation; fixation, hang-up, obsession.

think
vb lit: brood, cogitate, contemplate, deliberate, meditate, mull, muse, ponder, reflect, ruminate; call to mind, consider, recall, recollect, remember; believe, conceive (of), hold, suppose; conclude, decide, deem, judge; assume, gather, guess, imagine, reckon, surmise; envisage, expect, presume, suspect; intend (to), plan (to).

think better of
vb lit: decide against, have second thoughts about, reconsider.

think nothing of
vb lit: be accustomed to, consider easy, find routine; consider silly, find footling, ignore.

thin-skinned
adj fig: over-sensitive, prickly, responsive, sensitive, touchy; emotional, highly-strung, jumpy, nervous, tense.

thirsty
adj lit: dehydrated, dry, parched; arid; *fig*: avid (for), eager (for), greedy (for), hungry (for), longing (for), yearning (for).

thorny
adj lit: barbed, prickly, spiky, spiny; *fig*: dicey, difficult, nasty, problematic, ticklish, tough, tricky, trying, worrying.

thorough
adj lit: careful, conscientious, efficient, meticulous, painstaking, scrupulous;

complete, comprehensive, exhaustive, full; intensive; arrant, out-and-out, sheer, total, unmitigated, utter.

though
adv lit: for all that, however, nevertheless, nonetheless.
cnj lit: although, despite the fact that, notwithstanding the fact that, while; albeit, yet; (as) if.

thoughtful
adj lit: caring, considerate, helpful, kind, solicitous; contemplative, deliberative, introspective, introverted, meditative, pensive, reflective, ruminative, studious; careful, provident, prudent.

thread
n lit: fibre, filament, strand; cotton, string, yarn; *fig*: drift, plot, story-line, train of thought, way.
vb lit: string; wind; meander (through), squeeze (through).

threat
n lit: intimidation, menace, warning; blackmail; danger, peril, risk.

thresh
vb lit: sift, winnow; *fig*: gesticulate with, thrash (about), windmill; convulse, squirm, writhe.

threshold
n lit: door, doorstep, doorway, entrance, gateway; minimum; *fig*: brink, edge, verge; beginning, dawn, opening, outset.

thriving
adj (pr.pt) lit: blooming, blossoming, booming, doing very well, flourishing, healthy, prosperous, successful.

throttle
n lit: bottleneck, constriction, *fig*: accelerator; acceleration, power, revs.
vb lit: choke, garotte, strangle; herniate, strangulate; gag, muzzle, silence, stifle; *fig*: accelerate, rev, speed (up); decelerate, slow (down).

through
adj lit: fast, intercity, non-stop; arterial, linking, major; completed, done, finished; breaking up, separating, severing connections; bust, washed up; exhausted, spent, whacked.
adv lit: in and straight on out; from beginning to end, from one side to the other; all the way, directly, non-stop; to the skin.

prp lit: in and straight on out of; from beginning to end of, from one side to the other of; during the whole of, throughout; around, in, on, via; because of, by reason of, owing to; as a result of, by means of, by way of, with; done with, finished with.

throw
n lit: bung, cast, fling, heave, hurl, lob, put, shy, sling, spin, toss; fall; attempt, bash, go, try, turn, venture; *fig*: article, item, unit.
vb lit: bung, cast, chuck, fling, heave, hurl, lob, put, shy, sling, spin, toss; launch, propel; fell, floor, overturn, unseat; *fig*: catch unawares, confound, disconcert, put off altogether, screw.

throwaway
adj lit: casual, offhand; apparently extemporaneous.

thumb
vb lit: hitch, hitchhike; bend, finger, mark, wear; flip (through), leaf (through), riffle (through), skip (through).

thunder
n lit: crashing, detonations, peals, rumbling; din, resonance, reverberation, roar.
vb lit: blast, boom, crack, crash, explode, peal, rumble; resound, reverberate, roar; *fig*: bellow, shout, trumpet, yell.

thunderous
adj lit: deafening, ear-splitting, reverberating, resounding, roaring; booming, crashing, pealing, rumbling; *fig*: dark, glowering, lowering, menacing, threatening.

thus
adv lit: as follows, in this way; so; accordingly, consequently, hence, therefore, understandably.

ticket
n lit: pass; card, coupon, voucher; docket, slip, tab; label, tag; parking fine, speeding fine.

tide
n lit: current, drift, ebb, flow, stream; *fig*: movement, tendency, trend.

tight
adj lit: fast, firm, fixed, secure; close-fitting, hermetic, sealed; constricted, cramped, jammed, stuck; clenched,

rigid, stiff, stretched, taut, tense;
impervious, proof; *fig*: neat, trim, well-
built; close, even, well-matched; austere,
rigorous, severe, strict, stringent;
difficult, hazardous, precarious, sticky,
thorny, ticklish, tricky; hard to come by,
scarce; grasping, mean, miserly,
parsimonious, stingy; blotto, drunk,
inebriated, intoxicated, legless, pickled,
plastered, smashed, stoned.

till
n lit: cash-register; cashbox, cash drawer,
moneybox; float; *spec*: (glacial) clay,
drift, scree.
vb lit: cultivate, plough, work; dig,
harvest.

timber
n lit: forest, trees, woods; lumber, wood;
beams, boards, joists, planks.

time
n lit: duration, interval, period, space,
span, spell, term, while; age, date, epoch,
era; day, generation, heyday, hour,
season; life, lifetime, life-span; juncture,
moment, point, stage; beat, metre,
rhythm, tempo; pace, rate, speed; *fig*:
chance, opportunity.
vb lit: clock, pace, rate; schedule.

timeless
adj lit: ageless, changeless, deathless,
eternal, immortal, imperishable,
undying.

tingling
n lit: goose pimples, itching, tickle; pins
and needles, prickling.

tint
n lit: colour, hue, shade, tone; dye, rinse,
stain, wash.
vb lit: colour, dye, rinse, stain, tinge.

tip
n lit: dump, refuse area, rubbish pile;
apex, crest, crown, peak, point, top; cap,
end, ferrule; bonus, extra, gratuity; cut,
glance, snick; hint, suggestion, wrinkle.
vb lit: cant, incline, lean, list, slant, tilt;
bung, chuck, dump, empty out, pour,
unload; leave a gratuity for, reward; cut,
glance, snick; glue (in), paste (in).

tipple
n lit: drink, poison; booze, liquor.
vb lit: booze, drink, imbibe, tope; carouse.

tired
adj (pa.pt) lit: all in, dead on one's feet,

done in, drained, drooping, exhausted,
fagged, fatigued, knackered, shattered,
spent, whacked, worn out; sick (of),
weary (of); *fig*: clichéd, corny,
hackneyed, stale, trite.

tireless
adj lit: diligent, energetic, indefatigable,
industrious, persevering, unflagging,
untiring; constant, continual, persistent.

tissue
n lit: cells, structure, texture; chain, mesh,
network, system, web; fabric, gauze,
nylon, weave; paper handkerchief;
lavatory paper, toilet roll; wrapping-
paper.

titbit
n lit: dainty, delicacy, goody; bite, morsel,
snack; revelation, tasty bit of gossip.

titillating
adj lit: arousing, exciting, provoking,
stimulating; erotic, full-frontal, lewd,
provocative, suggestive.

titivate
vb lit: doll (oneself) up, dress up, make
up, smarten (oneself) up, tart (oneself)
up, touch up.

titter
vb lit: giggle, snicker, snigger; laugh.

titular
adj lit: nominal, theoretical; so-called;
puppet; false, putative, supposed.

toast
vb lit: brown, grill, heat, roast; drink the
health of, drink to, salute.

together
adv lit: as a body, as one, collectively,
cooperatively, in unison, jointly,
mutually; at once, en masse, in unison,
simultaneously; continuously, non-stop.

toilet
n lit: bathroom, bog, closet, convenience,
gents, ladies, latrine, lavatory, loo,
powder room, privy, washroom, WC;
ablutions, grooming, titivation, toilette.

token
n lit: badge, mark, sign, symbol; keepsake,
memento, memorial, remembrance,
souvenir; evidence, expression,
indication, manifestation, proof,
representation.

tolerable
adj lit: acceptable, adequate, fair, good

enough, middling, not bad, passable;
bearable, endurable, supportable.

tolerance
n lit: forbearance, indulgence, patience,
sufferance; fortitude, resilience,
resistance, stamina, staying power;
leeway, play, swing, variation.

tolerant
adj lit: broad-minded, complaisant,
easygoing, forbearing, indulgent, liberal,
lenient, long-suffering, patient,
permissive.

tolerate
vb lit: bear, endure, put up with, stand,
stomach, suffer, swallow, take; accept,
allow, condone, let go, let pass, permit.

toll
n lit: charge, duty, fee, payment, tariff,
tax; cost, levy, loss; chime, clang, ding,
ring.
vb lit: chime, knell, peal, ring, sound.

tomb
n lit: burial chamber, crypt, grave,
sepulchre, vault; barrow, burial mound,
catacomb, cave, chamber, pyramid;
sarcophagus; shrine.

tone
n lit: air, aspect, character, effect, feel,
mood, spirit, temper, tenor; emphasis,
inflection, intonation, stress;
modulation, pitch, timbre; note; health,
strength, vigour; colour, hue, shade, tint.
vb lit: blend (in), fit (in) well; play (down),
soften (down), temper (down); brighten
(up), strengthen (up).

toneless
adj lit: even, level, unaccented,
unemphasized, uninflected; colourless,
flat.

tongue-in-cheek
adv lit: coy, facetious, flippant, jocular,
jokey, mocking, sly, wry.

tonic
n lit: bracer, cordial, corpse-reviver, pick-
me-up, restorative; boost, fillip, shot in
the arm, stimulant; doh, keynote.

top brass
n lit: big guns, heavyweights, leadership,
masters, nobs, seniors, upper crust,
VIPs.

topical
adj lit: contemporary, current, up-to-date;
local, surficial; thematic.

top up
vb lit: fill, refill, replenish.

torch
n lit: flashlight, pocket-lamp; firebrand,
sconce; arc-lamp, flame, oxy-acetylene
welder; *fig*: beacon, illumination, light.
vb lit: burn, ignite, set ablaze, set on fire.

torpid
adj lit: apathetic, indolent, languorous,
lazy, lethargic, passive, slothful,
somnolent; dormant, inactive, inert;
numb, paralysed.

torrid
adj lit: blazing, burning, parching,
roasting, scorching; *fig*: emotional,
highly-charged, passionate, searing,
violent.

torture
n lit: agony, anguish, pain, suffering,
torment; cruelty, sadism.
vb lit: hurt, put on the rack, torment; *fig*:
crucify, give hell, persecute.

tot
n lit: baby, infant, mite, toddler; dram,
finger, measure, nip, shot.
vb lit: add (up), count (up), reckon (up),
sum (up); pick out, recover, retrieve, sort
over.

total
n lit: aggregate, amount, bottom line,
sum, whole.
vb lit: add up, reckon up, tot up; amount
to, come to, work out at; *fig*: crash,
wreck, write off.
adj lit: complete, comprehensive, entire,
full, out-and-out, perfect, thorough,
unconditional, undivided, utter, whole.

totalitarian
adj lit: authoritarian, autocratic,
dictatorial, one-party, tyrannical.

tottering
adj (pr.pt) lit: lurching, reeling, rocking,
staggering, stumbling, teetering,
toppling; *fig*: vacillating, wavering.

touch
n lit: feel, feeling, physical sensation;
brush, palpation, pat, stroke, tap;
pressure; *fig*: effect, hand, influence;
handiwork, method, style, technique;
artistry, command, facility, knack, skill;
acquaintance, contact, rapport; dash,
hint, pinch, smattering, spot, suggestion,
tinge, trace; *spec*: sidelines (in rugby).

touch up (cont.)

vb lit: brush, caress, feel, finger, fondle, handle, palpate, pat, press, stroke, tap; lay hands upon; adjoin, be contiguous with, border, converge, meet, merge with, overlap; arrive at, come up to; come (down), stop over (at); *fig*: disturb, impress, move, stir, strike; affect, be pertinent to, concern, have to do with; be party to, get involved in, use; come near, compare with, equal, hold a candle to, match, rival; attain, peak at, reach; have a word (on), say something (on), speak (on); ask (for) a loan of; set (off), spark (off), trigger (off).

touch up

vb lit: finish off, perfect, put in the last details; brush up, enhance, patch up, polish, retouch, titivate; excite, indulge in frottage, stimulate manually, tumesce.

tough

adj lit: all-weather, dense, durable, hard, resilient, resistant, rugged, solid, stiff, strong, sturdy, thick; brawny, hardy, iron, seasoned, stout, strapping; hardnosed, inflexible, obdurate, obstinate, resolute, stern, stubborn, unyielding; demanding, exacting, unforgiving; aggressive, refractory, rough, violent; arduous, difficult, exhausting, knotty, laborious, strenuous, thorny, uphill; baffling, confounding, perplexing, puzzling; *fig*: bad luck, hard luck, too bad, unlucky.

tour

n lit: excursion, jaunt, outing, trip; round-trip, sightseeing-trip; circuit, course.
vb lit: do, go round, journey in, see, sightsee, travel round, visit; go on the road, play.

tourist

n lit: holiday-maker, sightseer, traveller, voyager.

tournament

n lit: joust, tourney; bout, competition, contest, event, match, series.

towards

prp lit: facing, in the direction of, to; about, concerning, regarding, with regard to, with reference to; almost, approaching, close on, coming up to, getting on for, just before, nearly, nigh on.

tower

n lit: barbican, bastion, citadel, fortress, turret, watch-tower; belfry, dome, minaret, spire, steeple; condominium, high-riser, skyscraper.
vb lit: loom, rear, rise, soar.

track

n lit: footprints, footsteps, mark, path, scent, spoor, trace, trail; wake; course, flight-path, line, orbit, trajectory; alley, bridle-path, footpath, lane, road; lines, rails, railway; (keep) sight (of), (lose) sight (of).
vb lit: dog, follow, pursue, shadow, stalk, tail, trace, trail; hunt (down).

tract

n lit: acreage, area, expanse, plot, stretch; dissertation, essay, homily, monograph, treatise; booklet, leaflet, literature.

traction

n lit: draught, drawing, haulage; extension, pulling, stretching, torque; adhesion, grip, leverage, purchase.

tradition

n lit: convention, custom, folklore, institution, practice, usage.

traditional

adj lit: age-old, ancestral, conventional, customary, established, folkloric, historic, old, time-honoured, unwritten.

traffic

n lit: vehicles; transport, transportation; freight, passengers; business, commerce, dealing, exchange, trade; hawking, peddling, selling.
vb lit: deal (in), trade (in).

tragedy

n lit: death; calamity, catastrophe, disaster.

tragic

adj lit: deadly, fatal; appalling, calamitous, catastrophic, disastrous, heart-rending, ill-starred, sad, shocking.

train

n lit: locomotive, rail, railway service; caravan, column, convoy, crocodile, file; cortege, entourage, followers, retinue, suite; chain, order, progression, sequence, series, succession.

trainee

n lit: apprentice, learner, pupil, scholar, student, tyro.

trample
vb lit: crush, flatten, squash, stamp (on), tread (on).

trance
n lit: coma, hypnotic state, spell; suggestibility; dream, reverie, stupor.

transaction
n lit: affair, coup, deal, negotiation; event, matter, occurrence; annal(s), enterprise(s), minute(s), proceeding(s), record(s).

transcend
vb lit: exceed, excel, go beyond, outdo, outstrip, rise above, surpass.

transcribe
vb lit: copy out, reproduce, rewrite, transfer, write out; interpret; translate, transliterate; dub, re-record, retape.

transit
n lit: carriage, passage, portage, shipment, transportation; eclipse, occultation; change, conversion, transition.
vb lit: cross, traverse; go, move, travel.

transition
n lit: changeover, turnaround; alteration, change, conversion, evolution, metamorphosis, progression, transmutation.

transmit
vb lit: carry, communicate, convey, forward, impart, pass on, send, transport; broadcast, radio, relay, send out, telecast, televise.

transparent
adj lit: clear, limpid, pellucid, see-through, sheer, translucent; *fig*: apparent, manifest, obvious, patent, plain unambiguous, visible; candid, frank, open, straightforward.

transport
n lit: conveyance, vehicle; carriage, postage, shipment, transportation; *fig*: ecstasy, euphoria, rapture.
vb lit: bring, carry, convey, ferry, fetch, haul, move, ship, take, transfer; banish, exile; *fig*: captivate, enchant, enrapture, entrance.

transposition
n lit: changeover, exchange, interchange, relocation, reordering, switch, transfer.

transverse
adj lit: crossover, crossways; diagonal, oblique; *spec*: (flute) with the mouthpiece on the side.

trap
n lit: gin, pitfall, snare; ambush; ruse, subterfuge, trick.
vb lit: catch, corner, ensnare, snare; ambush; dupe, trick.

trauma
n lit: harm, hurt, pain, wound; damage, impairment, injury; shock, upset; harrowing experience; psychological disturbance.

traumatic
adj lit: harmful, hurtful, painful, wounding; damaging, injurious, scarring; shocking, upsetting; harrowing, distressing, disturbing.

traverse
vb lit: bridge, cross, go across, go over, intersect, span; cover, range, roam, wander; climb diagonally, ski diagonally; move crabwise, move sideways; *fig*: counter, hinder, oppose, thwart.

tread
n lit: footfall, footstep, step, stride, walk; sole; *spec*: depth, gauge, pattern (on a tyre).
vb lit: plod, stamp, step, stride, tramp, trudge, walk; crush, flatten, trample.

treasury
n lit: bank, coffers, repository, vault; cache, hoard, store; capital, finances, funds, money; assets, resources.

treat
n lit: gift, present, reward; delight, pleasure, surprise, thrill.
vb lit: behave towards, deal with, handle; apply medication to, care for, minister to, nurse, tend; denature, process, purify, recycle, refine; be concerned with, discuss, examine; bargain, negotiate, parley; lay on for, pay for, stand (to).

treatment
n lit: care, medication, medicine, remedy, surgery, therapy; handling (of), management (of), reception (of), usage (of).

treaty
n lit: agreement, alliance, bond, contract, convention, deal, entente, pact.

tremble
vb lit: quake, quiver, shake, shudder; judder, oscillate, vibrate, wobble.

tremor
n lit: earthquake, quake, shock; quiver, shake, shiver, tic, trembling, vibration, wobble.

trench
n lit: channel, cutting, ditch, drain, drill, fosse, furrow, gutter, trough.

tresses
n lit: braids, curls, hair, locks, pigtails, plaits.

trial
n lit: court, hearing, tribunal; experiment, proof, test; attempt, effort, go, shot, stab, try; adversity, affliction, hardship, misery, tribulation; bane, bother, nuisance, pest.
adj lit: experimental, pilot, provisional.

tribe
n lit: caste, clan, dynasty, family; race, stock.

trim
n lit: clipping, crop, cut, shave; border, edging, frill, fringe, piping; array, decor, dress, gear, trappings, upholstery, woodwork; condition, form, health, order, shape; attitude, buoyancy, draught, horizontality.
vb lit: clip, crop, cut, dock, lop, pare, prune, shave, tidy; adjust, balance, distribute, order; adorn, bedeck, decorate, embellish, garnish, ornament; adapt, change, convert, metamorphose, renege.
adj lit: dapper, natty, neat, orderly, shipshape, smart, spruce, tidy; fit, sleek, slender, slim, sylph-like.

trinity
n lit: triad, trio, triplet, triumvirate; God.

trip
n lit: excursion, jaunt, outing, run, tour, voyage; slip, stumble; tackle; canter, jig, skip, trot; catch, cog, latch, mechanism; euphoria, freak-out, psychedelic experience.
vb lit: slip (up), stumble; catch out, trap; caper, dance, gambol, skip, spring; activate, set off, switch on, trigger; *fig*: be stoned, get high, freak out, turn on.

trophy
n lit: award, cup, prize.

trouble
n lit: anxiety, disquiet, distress, pain, suffering, tribulation, vexation, worry, bother, commotion, disorder, disturbance, row, unrest; ailment, complaint, disability, upset; care, effort, labour, pains; difficulty, hot water, pickle, predicament, scrape.
vb lit: afflict, annoy, bother, disconcert, disquiet, distress, disturb, fret, incommode, inconvenience, pain, plague, upset; exert (oneself).

truce
n lit: armistice, ceasefire, cessation of hostilities, moratorium, peace, treaty; arbitration, dialogue, negotiation, talks.

true
adj lit: factual, valid, veritable; authentic, genuine, natural, pure, real; accurate, correct, exact, precise, unerring; confirmed, dedicated, faithful, firm, loyal, sincere, staunch, trustworthy, upright; reliable, sure; lawful, rightful.

truly
adv lit: accurately, correctly, exactly, precisely; authentically, factually, genuinely, really, veritably; devotedly, faithfully, honestly, loyally, sincerely, steadily; extremely, very.

trumpet
n lit: bugle, horn; clarino, clarion; *fig*: bay, bellow, cry.
vb fig: blaze, blare, broadcast, proclaim, publish; bay, bellow, cry, shout, yell.

trunk
n lit: body, thorax, torso; bole, shaft, stem, stock; nose, proboscis, snout; box, chest, coffer, locker, portmanteau.
adj lit: chief, main, principal, through.

trying
adj lit: aggravating, annoying, bothersome, exasperating, irritating; boring, tedious, tiresome, wearisome.

tumble
n lit: fall, plunge, spill, toss, trip.
vb lit: fall, plunge, stumble, trip; roll, turn over.

tumour
n lit: cancer, carcinoma, excrescence, growth, lump, malignancy, melanoma, neoplasm, sarcoma.

tunnel
n lit: cave, corridor, gallery, hole, passage, shaft, subway, tube.

vb lit: burrow, dig, drive a shaft, excavate, mine.

turbid
adj lit: cloudy, dark, dense, dirty, opaque, muddy, thick; *fig*: confused, disordered, swirling.

turgid
adj lit: bloated, distended, gross, puffed out, swollen; *fig*: bombastic, grandiloquent, inflated, pompous.

turn
n lit: angle, bend, corner, curve, deviation; coil, gyration, loop, revolution, rotation, spin, twist, whirl; change, deflection, shift; drive, excursion, outing, ride; constitutional, jaunt, saunter, stroll, walk; *fig*: go, round, spell, stint, time, try; aptitude, flair, gift, knack, propensity, talent; action, deed, gesture, service; act, performance; fright, shock, start; attack, bout, dizzy spell; cast, form, mould, shape.
vb lit: arc, bend, corner, curve, deviate, go round, swerve, veer; tack, zigzag; coil, gyrate, loop, revolve, rotate, spin, twist, wheel, whirl; recoil, reverse; change direction, deflect, shift; aim, direct, point; construct, fashion, form, make, mould, shape; employ, make use of, utilize; *fig*: become, get; alter (into), change (into), convert (into), render, transform (into), translate (into); go bad, go off, sour; sicken, upset; distract, unsettle; persuade, prevail upon, subvert.

turn in
vb lit: go to bed, go to sleep, hit the hay, hit the sack, retire; deliver, give in, hand in, return, submit.

turn off
vb lit: branch off, deviate, take a left, take a right; shut down, switch off; alienate, disenchant, offend, put off, repel.

turn on
vb lit: ignite, start, switch on; assault, attack, fall on, pounce on, round on; be contingent upon, centre on, depend on, focus on, hinge on, pivot round; put on, show; arouse, attract, excite, stimulate, titillate; freak out, get high, trip.

turn out
vb lit: shut down, switch off; cast out, dispossess, evict, expel, get rid of, kick out, turf out; clean out, clear, empty; bring out, make, manufacture, produce, supply; clothe, dress, fit out, rig out; appear, attend, come, gather, go, show up; come about, develop, end up, eventuate, happen, transpire, work out.

tweak
n lit: nip, pinch, squeeze; twinge.
vb lit: nip, pinch, squeeze; pull; turn, twiddle, twist.

twine
n lit: string, thread, yarn; coil, loop; knot, snarl, tangle.
vb lit: braid, coil, loop, plait, spiral, twist (round), wind (round), wrap (round).

twinkling
n lit: flash, flicker, glimmer, glitter, scintillation, shimmer, sparkle; *fig*: blink, blinking, wink; instant, moment, second, trice.
adj (pr.pt) lit: flashing, flickering, glimmering, glistening, glittering, scintillating, shimmering, shining, sparkling; dancing, pitter-pattering; humorous, laughing.

twisted
adj lit: bent, curled, twined, wound (round); sinuous, tortuous; snarled up, tangled; pulled, ricked, sprained, turned, wrenched; contorted, crooked, deformed, distorted, kinked, screwed-up, warped; falsified, garbled, misrepresented.

twitch
n lit: convulsion, jerk, jump, spasm, tic; blink.
vb lit: convulse, flutter, jerk, jump; blink; pluck, snatch, yank.

typify
vb lit: be representative of, embody, epitomize, exemplify, personify.

tyranny
n lit: authoritarianism, autocracy, despotism, dictatorship, one-party rule, totalitarianism; oppression.

tyrant
n lit: authoritarian, autocrat, despot, dictator; oppressor; bully, martinet, slave-driver.

U

ugly
adj lit: frumpish, ill-favoured, plain, unattractive, unprepossessing, unsightly; frightful, hideous, horrible, offensive, repugnant, repulsive, revolting, stomach-churning; black, dark, evil, malevolent, malign, nasty, surly; dangerous, menacing, ominous, sinister, threatening.

ulcer
n lit: lesion, open wound, sore; erosion, perforation, rent, split, tear.

ulterior
adj lit: underlying; concealed, covert, hidden, undisclosed, veiled.

ultimate
adj lit: conclusive, final, last, terminal; finite, limiting; extreme, greatest, highest, superlative, supreme; most important, most significant; basic, fundamental, primary.

ululate
vb lit: hoot, howl, keen, screech, wail; chant; lament, mourn.

umpire
n lit: adjudicator, arbiter, arbitrator, judge, linesman, referee, scorer.
vb lit: adjudicate, arbitrate, referee; chair, moderate, preside over.

umpteen
adj lit: any number of, countless, lots of, many, n, zillions of.

unable
adj lit: helpless (to), powerless (to); unqualified (to); incapable, not up to it.

unabridged
adj lit: complete, full-length, uncut, unexpurgated.

unacceptable
adj lit: impermissible, inadequate, inadmissible, insupportable, intolerable, unsatisfactory.

unaccountable
adj lit: incomprehensible, inexplicable, puzzling; extraordinary, odd, unheard-of; not answerable (to).

unaccustomed
adj lit: unused (to); uncommon, unusual, unwonted.

unaided
adv lit: all by oneself, alone, by oneself, independently, unassisted, unattended, unsupported, without any help.

unanimous
adj lit: common, communal, concerted, of one mind, united.

unanswerable
adj lit: insoluble, unsolvable; conclusive, incontestable, incontrovertible, indisputable, unassailable, undeniable; unaccountable (to).

unappetizing
adj lit: insipid, unappealing, unattractive, uninviting; sordid, unsavoury.

unasked
adj lit: uninvited, unsought, unwanted; gratuitous, spontaneous, unexpected.
adv lit: of one's own accord, voluntarily; gratuitously, spontaneously, unexpectedly.

unattainable
adj lit: impossible, inaccessible, unreachable; inconceivable, unimaginable, unthinkable.

unauthorized
adj lit: unapproved, unofficial, unwarranted; illegal, unconstitutional; behind-the-scenes, kangaroo, private, wildcat; informal, personal.

unavailing
adj lit: abortive, fruitless, futile, hopeless, ineffectual, unproductive, unsuccessful, useless.

unaware
adj lit: ignorant (of), unconscious (of), uninformed (of), unmindful (of); uncomprehending, untaught.

unbearable
adj lit: intolerable, unendurable;
insupportable, unacceptable;
insufferable, unspeakable.

unbending
adj lit: aloof, distant, formal, haughty,
remote, rigid, stiff; inflexible,
intractable, severe, strict,
uncompromising, unrelenting,
unyielding.

unborn
adj lit: embryonic, expected, gestating;
coming, future, posterior, subsequent.

unbounded
adj lit: boundless, endless, infinite,
measureless, unbridled, unchecked,
unconfined, uncontrolled, unrestrained.

unbridled
adj lit: intemperate, rampant, riotous,
unchecked, uncontrolled, unrestrained,
unruly, violent, wild.

unbroken
adj lit: homogeneous, intact, solid,
undivided, uniform, unimpaired, whole;
deep, fast, profound, sound; constant,
continual, continuous, incessant,
uninterrupted; monotonous, relentless,
unremitting; unbowed, undomesticated,
untamed, wild.

unbusinesslike
adj lit: careless, disorderly, disorganized,
inefficient, sloppy, unprofessional,
unsystematic, untidy; uncommercial.

uncalled-for
adj lit: gratuitous, needless, unjustified,
unnecessary, unprovoked, unwarranted;
uninvited, unsought, unwelcome.

uncertain
adj lit: doubtful, indefinite,
indeterminate, speculative,
undetermined, unpredictable; dubious,
irresolute, unclear, undecided,
unresolved, unsure, vague as to; erratic,
fitful, precarious, unreliable, vacillating,
variable; inconstant, interrupted,
varying; hazy, indefinite, indistinct,
vague.

uncharacteristic
adj lit: atypical, eccentric, extraordinary,
foreign, unaccustomed, unexpected,
unnatural, untypical, unusual,
unwonted.

uncharitable
adj lit: harsh, mean, severe, strict,
unfeeling, unfriendly, unkind,
unsympathetic; inflexible, rigid,
unbending.

unclear
adj lit: clouded, opaque; indistinct,
obscure, uncertain, vague.

uncomfortable
adj lit: crammed, cramped, hard, ill-
fitting, lumpy, painful, rough;
discomfited, distressed, disturbed,
pained; fig: diffident, ill at ease, restless,
self-conscious, uneasy.

uncommon
adj lit: infrequent, novel, rare, scarce,
unusual; curious, odd, peculiar, strange,
untoward; amazing, exceptional,
extraordinary, outstanding, remarkable,
singular, special, surprising.

uncommonly
adv lit: infrequently, occasionally, rarely,
seldom; curiously, oddly, peculiarly,
strangely; amazingly, exceptionally,
extraordinarily, outstandingly,
remarkably, singularly, specially,
surprisingly.

uncommunicative
adj lit: close, dumb, guarded, mute, quiet,
reserved, reticent, secretive, silent,
taciturn, tight-lipped, unforthcoming,
withdrawn.

unconcerned
adj lit: carefree, nonchalant, relaxed,
serene, unperturbed, unruffled,
untroubled; detached, dispassionate,
uninvolved, unmoved; apathetic,
incurious, indifferent, uninterested.

unconditional
adj lit: abject, complete, full, total,
unlimited, unqualified, unrestricted.

unconfirmed
adj lit: bald, bare, unauthorized,
uncorroborated, unofficial, unsupported,
unverified.

unconscionable
adj lit: amoral, unethical, unprincipled,
unscrupulous; excessive, immoderate,
inordinate, unreasonable.

unconscious
adj lit: comatose, fainting, insensible,
knocked out, out, out cold, stunned;
anaesthetized; accidental, automatic,

inadvertent, instinctive, involuntary, reflex, unintentional, unpremeditated, unwitting; latent, repressed, subliminal, suppressed; ignorant (of), unaware (of), unmindful (of).

unconventional
adj lit: eccentric, individual, irregular, nonconformist, odd, offbeat, original, unorthodox, unusual, way-out.

uncouth
adj lit: boorish, coarse, crude, gross, impolite, loutish, lubberly, oafish, profane, rude, uncivilized, vulgar; awkward, blundering, clodhopping, clumsy, elephantine.

undecided
adj lit: inconclusive, indefinite, in the balance, unresolved, unsettled; ambivalent, dithering, in two minds, irresolute, shilly-shallying, uncertain, tentative, vacillating, wavering; debatable, moot, open.

undemonstrative
adj lit: cold, contained, detached, dispassionate, formal, impassive, reserved, reticent, unemotional, unresponsive, withdrawn.

undeniably
adv lit: beyond doubt, certainly, evidently, incontestably, incontrovertibly, indisputably, indubitably, manifestly, obviously, patently, undoubtedly, unquestionably.

under
adj lit: inferior, junior, lesser, lower, minor, subordinate; minus, short.
adv lit: below, beneath, beneath the surface; down, lower; below par.
prp lit: below, beneath; inferior to, junior to, lesser than, lower than, subject to, subordinate to; as, beneath the heading, within; less than, short of; *spec*: in (the circumstances); (a field) supporting a crop of.

undercut
vb lit: dig away the bottom of, erode the base of, tunnel under; *fig*: undermine, weaken; sell for less than, sell more cheaply than; *spec*: give (a ball) backspin.

underdone
adj lit: bloody, rare, raw, red, uncooked; low-key, not brought out, played down, subtle, under-emphasized, understated.

underestimate
vb lit: rate too low, sell short, set too little store by, underrate, undervalue.

undergo
vb lit: bear, endure, experience, go through, pass through, stand, suffer.

underground
n lit: metro, subway, tube; *fig*: maquis, resistance.
adj lit: buried, interred; subterranean; *fig*: covert, secret, undercover; alternative, avant-garde, radical, revolutionary.
adv lit: into concealment, into hiding.

undergrowth
n lit: bracken, briars, brush, scrub; jungle, wilderness.

underhand
adj lit: crafty, crooked, deceptive, devious, dishonest, furtive, sly, sneaky.

underline
vb lit: underscore; accentuate, emphasize, highlight, italicize, stress.

underlying
adj lit: basic, elementary, fundamental, primary, root; concealed, latent, ulterior.

underneath
adj lit: lower, under; below, beneath.
adv lit: below, beneath, down below; next to the skin, under the skin.
prp lit: below, beneath; inferior to, junior to, lesser than, lower than, subject to, subordinate to.

underprivileged
adj lit: deprived, disadvantaged, needy, poor; third-world.

underrated
adj (pa.pt) lit: discounted, misjudged, sold short, underestimated, undervalued.

understand
vb lit: comprehend, fathom, follow, get, grasp, realize, twig; apprehend, catch on, discern, perceive, see; be informed, believe, conclude, think; assume, gather, suppose; appreciate, know, sympathize with; interpret, speak, translate.

understanding
n lit: appreciation, comprehension, grasp, knowledge; apprising, insight, perception; belief, conclusion, view; assumption, supposition; sympathies; accord, agreement, entente, pact.

adj lit: compassionate, considerate, insightful, kindly, perceptive, sensitive, sympathetic; charitable, forbearing, forgiving, magnanimous, tolerant.

understood
vb lit: accepted, appreciated, assumed, axiomatic, preceptual, recognized, taken for granted; comprehended, implicit, implied, unspoken.

understudy
n lit: replacement, reserve, stand-in, substitute.
vb lit: deputize (for), fill in (for), replace, stand in (for), substitute (for), take over (for).

undertake
vb lit: agree (to), commit oneself (to), engage (to), promise (to); attempt, embark on, endeavour (to), set about, tackle, take on, try.

undertone
n lit: murmur, mutter; air, atmosphere, aura, feeling, overtone, undercurrent.

underwear
n lit: lingerie, smalls, underclothes, undies.

underweight
adj lit: anorexic, gaunt, lean, scrawny, skinny; malnourished, starving, undernourished.

underworld
n lit: inferno, nether regions, place of the dead; *fig*: criminal fraternity, gangland, organized crime.

underwrite
vb lit: back, finance, fund, guarantee, indemnify, insure; approve, countersign, endorse, initial, okay, sign.

undesirable
adj lit: deleterious, disagreeable, potentially harmful, unacceptable, unpleasant, unwanted, unwelcome; antisocial, obnoxious, shabby, squalid, unattractive, unsavoury, unsuitable.

undignified
adj lit: indecorous, inelegant, unbecoming, unseemly; embarrassing, humiliating, ludicrous, ridiculous, risible, mortifying.

undisciplined
adj lit: boisterous, disobedient, naughty, obstreperous, selfish, uncontrollable, unmanageable, unruly, unschooled, untrained, wayward, wild, wilful.

undisclosed
adj lit: classified, private, secret, unknown, unrevealed; confidential, hush-hush.

undisguised
adj lit: evident, frank, genuine, manifest, obvious, open, plain, transparent, unconcealed, unfeigned, unmistakable.

undisturbed
adj lit: placid, serene, tranquil; unruffled; uninterrupted; untouched.

undo
vb lit: loose, loosen, open, unfasten, untie; annul, cancel, invalidate, overturn, quash, reverse; defeat, destroy, ruin, wreck.

undone
adj (pa.pt) lit: loosened, opened, unfastened, untied; annulled, cancelled, invalidated, overturned, quashed, reversed; defeated, destroyed, ruined, wrecked; incomplete, neglected, omitted, outstanding, unfinished.

undoubtedly
adv lit: certainly, definitely, naturally, of course, surely, unmistakably, unquestionably.

undress
n lit: déshabillé, disarray, dishevelment, disorder; semi-nudity; nakedness, nudity; casual clothes, informal wear.
vb lit: disrobe, strip, take off one's clothes; peel off, strip off.

undulating
adj (pr.pt) lit: rising and falling, rolling, wavy; fluctuating, oscillating, seesawing; wave-like.

unduly
adv lit: disproportionately, excessively, exaggeratedly, inordinately, overly, too much, unnecessarily, superfluously.

uneconomic
adj lit: non-profit-making; loss-making, unprofitable, unviable.

unemployed
adj lit: idle, jobless, laid off, on the dole, out of work, redundant; between jobs, resting.

unenthusiastic
adj lit: casual, half-hearted, lukewarm, take-it-or-leave-it, wishy-washy; indifferent.

unequal
adj lit: different, disparate, dissimilar, unlike, various; lopsided, one-sided, unbalanced, uneven, unfair; irregular; not up (to), unsuited (to).

unerringly
adv lit: accurately, exactly, infallibly, precisely, specifically.

unethical
adj lit: dishonourable, immoral, unprincipled, unscrupulous; dishonest, shady, underhand.

uneven
adj lit: broken, bumpy, corrugated, lumpy, ridged, rough, undulating; fluctuating, irregular, patchy, variable, varying; asymmetrical, lopsided, top-heavy, unbalanced; one-sided, unequal, unfair.

unexpected
adj lit: abrupt, startling, sudden, surprising; surprise, unforeseen; unasked, uninvited, unsought.

unfair
adj lit: biased, discriminatory, inequitable, partial, prejudiced, unjust; dishonest, unethical, unprincipled, unsporting.

unfaithful
adj lit: adulterous, deceitful, disloyal, promiscuous, two-timing; perfidious, traitorous, treacherous; *fig*: distorted, imperfect, inaccurate, unreliable; dissimilar (to).

unfamiliar
adj lit: alien, different, new, novel, strange, unknown; unacquainted (with), unconversant (with).

unfashionable
adj lit: antediluvian, antiquated, dated, démodé, dowdy, frumpish, fuddy-duddy, old-fashioned, old hat, outmoded, out of date, passé, unchic.

unfavourable
adj lit: adverse, bad, negative, poor; contrary, hostile, inclement, stormy; inauspicious, unlucky, unpromising, unpropitious; inopportune, untimely.

unfinished
adj lit: imperfect, incomplete, uncompleted; crude, raw, rough, unpolished, unprocessed, unvarnished.

unfit
adj lit: inadequate (for), inappropriate (for), unsuitable (for), useless (for); ineligible (to), not cut out (to), physically unable (to), unprepared (to), unqualified (to); flabby, in poor condition, out of shape, unhealthy.

unflattering
adj lit: bluntly realistic, brutally frank; refreshingly honest; severe, uncomplimentary.

unfortunate
adj lit: hapless, luckless, out of luck, unlucky; inauspicious, inopportune, unfavourable, unpropitious; deplorable, infelicitous, regrettable.

unfortunately
adv lit: unhappily, unluckily; inauspiciously, infelicitously; deplorably, regrettably.

unfounded
adj lit: baseless, false, groundless, spurious, trumped-up, unjustifiable, unjustified, unwarranted; illogical, irrational.

unfriendly
adj lit: cold, disagreeable, inhospitable, reserved, uncongenial, unsociable; aggressive, antagonistic, belligerent, hostile, inimical, surly; alien, bleak, chilly, inclement, stormy; inauspicious, unfavourable, unpropitious.

ungainly
adj lit: awkward, blundering, bulky, clodhopping, clumsy, elephantine, gawky, lumbering, ungraceful.

ungovernable
adj lit: mutinous, rebellious, refractory, uncontrollable, unruly, untamable, wild.

ungracious
adj lit: bad-mannered, boorish, curt, discourteous, impolite, loutish, offhand, rude, unmannerly.

ungrateful
adj lit: begrudging, indifferent, presumptuous, selfish, unappreciative; disagreeable, distasteful, irksome, unpleasant.

unguarded
adj lit: defenceless, open, undefended, unprotected, vulnerable; *fig*: careless, hasty, impolitic, imprudent, incautious, indiscreet, rash, thoughtless, unthinking; candid, frank.

unhappily
adv lit: unfortunately, unluckily; dejectedly, despondently, disconsolately, gloomily, miserably, mournfully, sadly, wretchedly; awkwardly, badly, infelicitously, injudiciously.

unhappy
adj lit: hapless, luckless, unfortunate, unlucky; dejected, depressed, despondent, disconsolate, gloomy, miserable, mournful, sad, wretched; awkward, inept, infelicitous, injudicious, tactless.

unharmed
adj lit: intact, safe and sound, scatheless, undamaged, unhurt, unimpaired, uninjured, unscathed, without a scratch.

unhealthy
adj lit: delicate, feeble, frail, puny, sickly, thin, weak; dirty, insanitary, unhygienic; corrupting, demoralizing, perverted, sick, warped.

unheard-of
adj lit: inconceivable, undiscovered, undreamed-of, unknown; obscure, unfamiliar, unsung; novel, singular, unprecedented; outrageous, preposterous, unacceptable, unthinkable.

unhelpful
adj lit: begrudging, bolshie, obstructive, recalcitrant, uncooperative, unwilling, useless; apathetic, indifferent.

unhesitating
adj lit: immediate, instant, prompt, ready; resolute, steadfast, unfaltering, unswerving, unwavering.

unholy
adj lit: blasphemous, evil, irreligious, sinful, ungodly, wicked; profane; immoral, iniquitous; *fig*: appalling, dreadful, outrageous, unconscionable, unearthly, unreasonable.

unidentified
adj lit: anonymous, nameless, unknown, unnamed; plain, unmarked.

uniform
n lit: costume, dress, outfit, suit; regalia; livery.
adj lit: consistent, even, homogeneous, regular, smooth, unbroken, unvarying; alike, equal, identical, the same.

unify
vb lit: bond, combine, fuse, join, weld; amalgamate, confederate, merge; marry, wed; unite.

unimaginative
adj lit: boring, dull, colourless, hackneyed, insipid, lifeless, pedestrian, tame, uninspired, unoriginal, vapid; derivative, plagiaristic.

unimpeachable
adj lit: blameless, immaculate, impeccable, irreproachable, perfect, unblemished, unexceptionable; infallible.

unimpressed
adj lit: apathetic, blasé, bored, impassive, indifferent, left cold, uninterested, unmoved, unperturbed, unruffled, unsurprised.

uninhabited
adj lit: barren, desolate, empty, vacant, waste; deserted, unoccupied, unpopulated, untenanted.

uninhibited
adj lit: free, liberated, natural, spontaneous, unselfconscious; open, unconstrained, unrepressed, unrestricted; unchecked, uncontrolled.

unintelligent
adj lit: dense, dull, gormless, obtuse, slow, stupid, thick, unthinking; cretinous, imbecile, moronic; *spec*: lower (life forms).

unintelligible
adj lit: inarticulate, inaudible, incoherent, indistinct, jumbled; illegible, indecipherable, unreadable.

unintentional
adj lit: accidental, inadvertent, unintended, unpremeditated, unthinking; involuntary, reflex; unwitting.

uninviting
adj lit: disagreeable, off-putting, repellent, repugnant, unappealing, unappetizing, unattractive, unpleasant;

depressing, dismal, dreary; daunting, formidable, ominous, sinister.

union
n lit: bond, combination, coupling, fusion, joining, linkage, suture, synthesis, weld; affiliation, alliance, amalgamation, association, coalition, confederacy, confederation, league, merger; marriage, wedlock; brotherhood, fraternity, trade organization.

unique
adj lit: isolated, single, sole; incomparable, unequalled, unmatched, unparalleled, unrivalled; never-to-be-repeated, unrepeatable; *fig*: ecstatic, magic, special; characteristic, idiosyncratic.

unit
n lit: degree, figure, grade, integer, measure, measurement; component, constituent, element, item, member, module, part, piece; detachment, group, section, set, troop; entity, whole.

unite
vb lit: bond, combine, connect, couple, fasten together, fuse, join, link, suture, weld; affiliate, ally, amalgamate, associate, confederate, merge; join together in holy matrimony, marry, wed; club together, pool; unify.

unity
n lit: bond, homogeneity, integration, solidarity, unanimity; concord, consensus, harmony.

universal
adj lit: blanket, catholic, common, comprehensive, general, unlimited, unrestricted, worldwide; ecumenical; adaptable, flexible, versatile.

universally
adv lit: always, in every case, in every instance, uniformly, without exception; everywhere, generally.

universe
n lit: cosmos, macrocosm; world.

unkind
adj lit: harsh, inconsiderate, insensitive, mean, unfeeling, unfriendly, ungracious, unpleasant; cruel, malicious, nasty, spiteful.

unknown
n lit: anonymity, nobody, nonentity; enigma, mystery, puzzle; dark, mysterious, unexplored.
adj lit: anonymous, nameless, unidentified, unnamed; obscure, unfamiliar, unheard-of, unrecognized, unsung; alien, dark, mysterious, new, strange, unexplored.

unless
cnj lit: but for if, except if, save that if.

unlike
adj lit: different, dissimilar, distinct, diverse, incompatible, unequal, unrelated.
prp lit: different from, dissimilar to, distinct from, incompatible with, unequal to, unrelated to.

unlikely
adj lit: implausible, improbable, incredible, unbelievable; not expected (to), not likely (to); unconvincing; faint, remote, slight.

unload
vb lit: discharge, dump, lighten, unburden, unpack; relieve oneself of, unburden oneself of; *spec*: dispose of, sell off (old stock); remove the charge from (a firearm).

unmask
vb lit: expose, lay bare, reveal, uncover, unveil.

unmentionable
adj lit: forbidden, frowned-on, taboo; secret; indescribable, unspeakable; immoral, indecent, rude.

unnatural
adj lit: anomalous, odd, strange, unusual; bizarre, extraordinary, freakish, outlandish, peculiar, weird; abnormal, perverse, perverted, warped; appalling, brutish, callous, cruel, heartless, inhuman, monstrous, shocking, unfeeling; artificial, assumed, contrived, false, forced, laboured, self-conscious, stiff, stilted, strained.

unnecessary
adj lit: inessential, needless, redundant, superfluous, surplus; pointless, useless, wasteful.

unnerved
adj (pa.pt) lit: demoralized, discouraged, disheartened, dismayed, intimidated, put off, rattled, shaken, unmanned, upset.

unpaid
adj lit: due, outstanding, overdue, owing, payable; honorary, unsalaried; free, voluntary.

unpleasant
adj lit: disagreeable, distasteful, irksome, objectionable, obnoxious, unattractive, unpalatable; disgusting, horrible, nasty, offensive, repellent, repugnant, repulsive, unlikable.

unpopular
adj lit: avoided, disliked, ostracized, shunned, unwanted, unwelcome; antisocial, friendless, independent, unfriendly; difficult, inopportune, unfortunate, untimely.

unpredictable
adj lit: chance, random, unforeseeable; changeable, erratic, inconstant, unreliable, variable; iffy, precarious, tricky.

unprepared
adj lit: unready (for); caught on the hop, taken off guard; ill-considered, not thought through, unfinished, unpolished; ad lib, extemporaneous, improvised, spontaneous.

unprofitable
adj lit: loss-making, uneconomic, unviable; bootless, fruitless, futile, unproductive, unremunerative, unrewarding, useless, valueless.

unqualified
adj lit: incompetent (to), ineligible (to), not up (to), unfit (to); categorical, complete, outright, total, unconditional, unreserved, unrestricted.

unquestioned
adj lit: accepted, established, full, known, taken for granted, trusted; unexamined, unscrutinized, unvetted; conclusive, definite, incontestable, incontrovertible, irrefutable, undeniable, unquestionable.

unravel
vb lit: disentangle, free, straighten, undo, untangle, unwind; *fig*: clear up, explain, make out, resolve, solve, work out.

unreal
adj lit: immaterial, insubstantial, intangible, nebulous; dream, fictitious, illusory, imaginary, make-believe; artificial, false, insincere.

unrealistic
adj lit: artificial, contrived, false, laboured, stilted, unlifelike, unnatural; implausible, impracticable, impractical, improbable, unworkable; hopeful, idealistic, romantic, sentimental, wishful.

unreasonable
adj lit: illogical, irrational, nonsensical, senseless, silly; unfair, unjust, unwarranted; disproportionate, immoderate, uncalled-for, undue; capricious, erratic, inconstant, inconsistent.

unreasoning
adj lit: abject, blind, headlong, instinctual, involuntary, mad, precipitate, wild; arbitrary, biased, blinkered, discriminatory, opinionated, prejudiced.

unreliable
adj lit: irresponsible, untrustworthy; disloyal, treacherous; deceptive, uncertain, unconvincing; erratic, fallible, unsound.

unrepeatable
adj lit: never-to-be-repeated, once-and-for-all, one-off, unique; scabrous, solecistic, unmentionable.

unrepentant
adj lit: impenitent, incorrigible, shameless, supercilious, unruffled; callous, hard-bitten, indifferent, obdurate.

unreservedly
adv lit: absolutely, completely, freely, fully, totally, unconditionally, unrestrainedly, utterly, wholeheartedly.

unrest
n lit: agitation, demonstration, dissension, mutiny, rebellion, riotousness, sedition; affray, commotion, disturbance, hurly-burly, tumult, turmoil; disquiet, distress, uneasiness, worry.

unripe
adj lit: green, immature, new, raw, sharp; unready, unprepared.

unsafe
adj lit: dangerous, hazardous, perilous, precarious, risky, treacherous, unsound, unstable; unclean, unhygienic; exposed, open, pregnable, vulnerable.

unseemly
adj lit: discreditable, immodest, improper, indecorous, indelicate, tasteless, unbecoming, unworthy, vulgar; inappropriate, out of place, unsuitable.

unselfish
adj lit: altruistic, generous, kind, magnanimous, noble, philanthropic, selfless; devoted, faithful, loyal.

unsettled
adj (pa.pt) lit: agitated, disordered, disturbed, flurried, listless, restive, restless, tense, uneasy; insecure, loose, shaky, unstable, unsteady; changeable, inconstant, uncertain, variable; due, outstanding, payable, unpaid; debatable, moot, undecided, unresolved; deserted, empty, uninhabited, unoccupied, unpopulated, vacant.

unshakable
adj lit: blind, complete, firm, fixed, staunch, steadfast, total, unassailable, unswerving, unwavering.

unskilled
adj lit: inexperienced, unqualified, untrained; amateur.

unsolicited
adj lit: free, gratuitous, spontaneous, unforced, unsought, volunteered; voluntary; uncalled-for, unwelcome.

unspoilt
adj lit: genuine, intact, natural, preserved, real, unblemished, undamaged, unimpaired, untouched, wild; everyday, matter-of-fact, ordinary, unaffected, unassuming, unpretentious.

unspoken
adj lit: implicit, implied, taken for granted, understood, unsaid, unstated, unuttered; silent, unvoiced.

unsporting
adj lit: against the rules, below the belt, dishonest, inequitable, not cricket, unethical, unfair, unjust.

unsure
adj lit: diffident, insecure, irresolute, uncertain, undecided; distrustful, sceptical, suspicious.

unsuspecting
adj lit: confiding, ingenuous, innocent, naive, trusting, unwary; credulous, green, gullible; oblivious, unaware, unwitting.

untamed
adj lit: feral, ferocious, fierce, savage, unbroken, uncontrollable, wild.

untenable
adj lit: indefensible, insupportable, shaky, unsound, unsustainable, vulnerable, weak.

unthinking
adj lit: careless, inconsiderate, insensitive, tactless, thoughtless, undiplomatic; inadvertent, mechanical, unconscious, vacant; impulsive, rash, reckless.

untried
adj lit: alien, new, probationary, unfamiliar, untested; unexamined, unstretched.

untrue
adj lit: erroneous, inaccurate, incorrect, lying, wrong; deceptive, dishonest, false, misleading, spurious; disloyal, perfidious, unfaithful; treacherous, untrustworthy; bowed, distended, distorted, not straight, off, warped, wide.

untruthful
adj lit: deceitful, dishonest, false, lying, mendacious.

unusual
adj lit: abnormal, atypical, exceptional, rare, singular, uncommon, unconventional; bizarre, curious, extraordinary, queer, remarkable, surprising; fishy, odd, peculiar, strange, suspicious; characteristic, distinctive, special.

unutterably
adv lit: extremely, indescribably, ineffably, overwhelmingly, unimaginably, unspeakably.

unwanted
adj lit: extra, spare, superfluous, surplus; outcast, rejected; unasked, uninvited, unsolicited, unwelcome.

unwell
adj lit: bedridden, ill, out of sorts, poorly, sick, under the weather; ailing, indisposed, sickly, under doctor's orders.

unwholesome
adj lit: fast, instant, junk, packet; deleterious, noxious, unhealthy; corrupting, demoralizing, depraving, perverting; ailing, pale, pallid, sickly, wan.

unwieldy
adj lit: awkward, bulky, clumsy, cumbersome, hefty, ponderous, ungainly, unhandy.

unwilling
adj lit: averse, disinclined, indisposed, loath, reluctant.

unwise
adj lit: foolish, ill-advised, ill-judged, inadvisable, irresponsible, silly, stupid; impolitic, imprudent, indiscreet, injudicious, rash, reckless.

unwittingly
adv lit: accidentally, inadvertently, innocently, involuntarily, unconsciously, unintentionally, unknowingly.

unworldly
adj lit: idealistic, inexperienced, naive, romantic, sentimental, unsophisticated; abstract, metaphysical; ethereal, extraterrestrial; religious, spiritual, transcendental.

unworthy
adj lit: ineligible (to), undeserving (of), unfit (to); beneath the dignity (of), disappointing (of), uncharacteristic (of); contemptible, discreditable, dishonourable, ignoble, shameful.

upbraid
vb lit: carpet, censure, chasten, chide, lecture, rebuke, reprehend, reprimand, reproach, reprove, scold, take to task, tell off, tick off.

upbringing
n lit: fostering, raising, rearing; education; background.

upheaval
n lit: agitation, commotion, disorder, disruption, disturbance, perturbation, revolution, upset.

uphill
adj lit: ascending, climbing; *fig*: daunting, difficult, formidable, gruelling, hard, laborious, strenuous, taxing.

uphold
vb lit: advocate, champion, promote, support; defend, endorse, stand by, sustain; justify, vindicate.

upkeep
n lit: maintenance, preservation, subsistence; management, running, supervision; expenditure, expenses, overheads, running expenses.

uppish
adj lit: affected, arrogant, conceited, hoity-toity, presumptuous, snobbish, stuck-up.

upright
n lit: post, shaft, vertical; perpendicular.
adj lit: erect, perpendicular, straight, vertical; *fig*: ethical, good, honest, honourable, law-abiding, principled, trustworthy, virtuous.

uprising
n lit: insurrection, mutiny, putsch, rebellion, revolt, revolution.

uproar
n lit: babel, bedlam, clamour, commotion, din, furore, hullabaloo, outcry, pandemonium, racket, riot, ruckus, rumpus, turmoil.

uproarious
adj lit: loud, noisy, riotous, tumultuous; boisterous, rollicking; hilarious, hysterical, killing, side-splitting.

upset
n lit: defeat, reversal, reverse, setback; discomposure, distress, disturbance, shock; gastric trouble, indisposition, queasiness, sickness, stomach bug.
vb lit: knock over, overturn, spill, topple over, turn over; confuse, disorder, disorganize, jumble, mix up, undo, untidy; agitate, annoy, bother, distress, disturb, fluster; best, defeat, overcome.
adj lit: capsized, overturned, spilt, toppled, upside down; chaotic, confused, disordered, disorganized, jumbled, mixed up, untidy; agitated, annoyed, bothered, distressed, disturbed, flustered, hurt, put out, worried; queasy, sick.

upshot
n lit: conclusion, consequence, end, final result, outcome, product, result.

upside down
adj lit: capsized, inverted, overturned, upset, wrong side up.

upstart
n lit: parvenu, social climber; nobody, nonentity.
adj lit: presumptuous, pretentious, vulgar; nouveau-riche; officious, pompous, self-assertive.

uptight
adj lit: apprehensive, fearful, nervous, restless, tense, uneasy, worried; annoyed, displeased, exasperated, irked, vexed.

up to date
adj lit: au fait, current, in the swim; modern, most recent, new; fashionable, modish, stylish, trendy.

urban
adj lit: city, civic, metropolitan, municipal, town.

urbane
adj lit: civilized, cultivated, mannerly, polished, refined, sophisticated, suave; smooth-talking.

urge
n lit: compulsion, desire, drive, impulse, wish.
vb lit: constrain (to), drive, egg (on to), goad (to), incite, induce, press, push (to), spur (to); beseech, entreat, exhort, implore, petition; advise, advocate, counsel, recommend; back, champion, speak up for.

urgency
n lit: constraint, exigency, need for action; importunity, pressure.

urgent
adj lit: compelling, compulsive, crucial, emergency, essential, exigent, imperative, necessary, pressing, priority, vital; imploring, importunate, insistent.

urinate
vb lit: micturate, pass water, relieve oneself; have a pee, spend a penny; pee, piddle, piss, wee, widdle.

usage
n lit: handling, management, treatment, use; convention, custom, form, mode, practice, procedure, rule, tradition; language, idiom, syntax, vernacular, vocabulary.

use
n lit: application, employment, operation; custom, practice, treatment, usage, way; advantage, avail, benefit, good, help, object, point, profit, service, value.
vb lit: apply, employ, exercise, ply, utilize, wield; exploit, take advantage of, turn to one's account; behave towards, treat; consume, expend, spend, take (up).

used
adj lit: second-hand; cast-off, nearly-new, shop-soiled, worn; gumless, not mint, postmarked.

useful
adj lit: advantageous, beneficial, effective, good, helpful, profitable, serviceable, valuable, worthwhile; adaptable, general-purpose, practical, versatile.

usher
n lit: attendant, escort, guide, official, sidesman.
vb lit: conduct, escort, guide, lead, show; bring (in).

usual
adj lit: common, customary, everyday, familiar, general, habitual, ordinary, regular, routine, standard, stock, typical.

Utopian
adj lit: arcadian, beatific, heavenly, ideal, paradisial, perfect; idealistic, quixotic, romantic, visionary; chimerical, dream, illusory, impractical, unattainable.

utter
vb lit: announce, enunciate, pronounce, say, speak, voice; emit, give, give forth, give vent to, send up, vent; proclaim, promulgate, publish; *spec*: use (a forged note, a dud cheque).
adj lit: absolute, arrant, complete, out-and-out, sheer, total, unmitigated; *spec*: outer (darkness).

utterly
adv lit: absolutely, completely, entirely, fully, one-hundred-per-cent, quite, thoroughly, totally.

V

vacancy
n lit: job opportunity, position, post,
situation; gap, room, space; emptiness,
vacuum, void.

vacant
adj lit: available, free, idle, not in use,
unengaged, unoccupied; blank, empty,
expressionless, inane, incomprehending,
incurious, unthinking, vacuous.

vacate
vb lit: depart from, exit from, go from,
leave from, pull out from, quit; empty,
evacuate, leave free.

vaccination
n lit: immunization, inoculation.

vacuum
n lit: airlessness, nothingness, space, void;
fig: gap, hiatus, interval.
vb lit: clean, hoover.

vagrant
n lit: itinerant; beggar, tramp, vagabond;
bum, hobo; nomad, wanderer; tinker,
traveller.

vague
adj lit: blurred, dim, fuzzy, hazy, ill-
defined, indeterminate, indistinct, loose,
obscure, shadowy, unclear, unspecified,
woolly; doubtful, uncertain; aimless,
purposeless, random.

vaguely
adv lit: faintly, in a way, rather,
somewhat; dimly, fuzzily, hazily,
indistinctly, loosely, obscurely;
doubtfully, uncertainly; aimlessly,
purposelessly, randomly.

vain
adj lit: affected, bigheaded, conceited,
narcissistic, ostentatious, overweening,
pretentious, self-important, stuck-up,
swollen-headed; arrogant, cocky,
egotistical, haughty, proud, swaggering;
abortive, bootless, fruitless, futile,
hollow, idle, ineffectual, unavailing,
unproductive, unprofitable,
unsuccessful, useless, wasted; empty,
pointless, worthless.

valiant
adj lit: audacious, bold, brave,
courageous, daring, dauntless, doughty,
heroic, indomitable, intrepid, lion-
hearted, stout-hearted, unflinching.

valid
adj lit: binding, in force, operative;
authentic, genuine, legal, legitimate,
official; conclusive, fair, good, just,
logical, sound; cogent, effective.

valley
n lit: basin, combe, dale, flats, glen, strath,
vale; dell, depression, dingle, hollow;
drainage area; canyon, gorge, gulch; *fig*:
gutter, trough.

valour
n lit: audacity, boldness, bravery, courage,
daring, dauntlessness, doughtiness,
heroism, indomitability, intrepidity;
derring-do, fearlessness, spirit.

valuable
adj lit: costly, expensive, precious, worth
a lot; beneficial, estimable, helpful,
important, profitable, useful,
worthwhile; cherished, dear, prized,
treasured.

valuation
n lit: assessment, estimate, evaluation,
rating; appraisal, calculation,
computation, quantification, reckoning.

value
n lit: cost, price; evaluation, rating, worth;
benefit, help, merit, profit, use,
usefulness; effect, force, meaning; *spec*:
duration (of a musical note); tone (in
light or dark shades).
vb lit: assess, estimate, evaluate, rate;
appraise, calculate, compute, quantify,
reckon; appreciate, cherish, esteem, hold
dear, prize, respect, think highly of,
treasure.

vanish
vb lit: become invisible, disappear; be lost
to sight, dissolve, evanesce, evaporate,
fade out, melt away.

vanity
n lit: airs, bigheadedness, conceit, narcissism, ostentation, pretension, self-importance; arrogance, cockiness, egotism, haughtiness, pride; frivolity, inanity, triviality; emptiness, futility, hollowness, pointlessness, uselessness, worthlessness.

variable
adj lit: changeable, fickle, fitful, mercurial, temperamental; changing, fluctuating, inconstant, shifting, unstable, vacillating, wavering; *spec*: eclipsing, pulsating (stars).

variant
n lit: alternative, derived form, development, modified form, sport, version.

variation
n lit: adapted form, development, modified form, reworking, revised form, version; alteration, change, deviation, difference, modification; divergence, diversity.

variety
n lit: alteration, change, difference, diversity, multiplicity; assortment, medley, miscellany, mixture, range; brand, category, kind, make, order, sort, type; breed, class, species, strain, subspecies.

various
adj lit: assorted, different, differing, divers, diverse, miscellaneous, sundry; divergent, separate; several, many.

varnish
n lit: glaze, gloss, lacquer, shellac; *fig*: adornment, decoration, embellishment, polish; display, outward appearance, show.
vb lit: glaze, gloss, lacquer, shellac; *fig*: adorn, decorate, embellish, polish; disguise.

vary
vb lit: alternate, be changeable, be inconstant, be temperamental, fluctuate, vacillate, waver; alter, be inconsistent, change, differ, diversify, modify, reorder, shift, transform.

vast
adj lit: colossal, enormous, gigantic, huge, immense, mammoth, massive, monumental; boundless, immeasurable,

limitless, unbounded; astronomical, unlimited.

vat
n lit: tank, vessel; urn; barrel, cask, keg.

vault
n lit: catacomb, cellar, crypt, tomb; depository, safe, strongroom; arch, span; ceiling, roof; jump, leap; curvet.
vb lit: hurdle, jump, leap, spring; curvet.

vaulted
adj (pa.pt) lit: arched, domed; colonnaded, porticoed.

vaunted
adj (pa.pt) lit: advertised, displayed, exhibited, exposed, flaunted, paraded, publicised, shown off; infamous, much-boasted, notorious; famous.

vehicle
n lit: conveyance, mode of transport; means, medium; *fig*: apparatus, mechanism, organ; channel, wave.

veil
n lit: kerchief, scarf, shawl; chador; wimple; bridal head-dress; velum; film, curtain, screen; *fig*: cloak, concealment, disguise, mantle, mask; conventual vows, life of seclusion.
vb lit: cloak, conceal, cover, curtain off, hide, mantle, mask, obscure, screen, shroud; *spec*: darken (in photography).

veiled
adj (pa.pt) lit: concealed, covered, curtained off, hidden, mantled, masked, screened, shrouded; covert, hinted, implied, obscure.

vein
n lit: blood vessel; lode, seam, stratum; band, streak, stripe; *fig*: attitude, humour, mode, mood, strain, temper, tenor, tone; *spec*: rib (on a leaf, in an insect's wing).

venal
adj lit: bent, corrupt, for sale, mercenary, open to bribes, rapacious; crooked, dishonest.

vend
vb lit: offer for sale, sell; hawk, peddle; market.

veneer
n lit: covering layer, surface; ply; *fig*: façade, front, mask, outward appearance, pretence, show.

vb lit: cover, face, surface; *fig*: cover, mask, veil.

venerable
adj lit: august, esteemed, honoured, respected; hallowed, revered, sanctified.

venerate
vb lit: honour, revere, reverence; hallow, regard as holy; esteem, hold in high regard.

vengeance
n lit: avenging, reprisal, retaliation, retribution, revenge, settling of scores; punishment; force, fury, severity, vehemence, violence.

vengeful
adj lit: resentful, vindictive; demanding punishment, retaliatory, retributive, seeking revenge.

venial
adj lit: excusable, forgivable, pardonable; allowable, permissible; insignificant, minor, trivial.

venom
n lit: poison, toxin; bane; *fig*: acrimony, ill will, malevolence, malice, malignity, spite, virulence; acerbity, poignancy, sharpness; sting.

venomous
adj lit: poisonous, toxic; baneful; fatal, harmful, lethal, noxious; *fig*: acerbic, acidic, acrimonious, hostile, malevolent, malign, rancorous, sharp, spiteful, stinging, vindictive, virulent.

vent
n lit: escape, outflow, outlet; air-duct, air intake; aperture, opening, orifice; *spec*: anus (of birds); touch-hole (in a gun-barrel).
vb lit: air, express, give expression to, pour out, utter, voice; emit, issue.

venture
n lit: attempt, endeavour, enterprise, project, undertaking; chance, fling, gamble, hazard, risk; proposition, speculation.
vb lit: advance (forward), plunge (into), sally (forth); attempt (to), endeavour (to), propose (to), undertake (to), volunteer (to); chance, gamble, hazard, risk, stake, wager; endanger, imperil, jeopardize; dare say, guess, suggest.

venue
n lit: location, rendezvous, trysting-place, site; arena, field, pitch; scene of the crime; *spec*: hit, lunge, thrust (in fencing).

verbal
adj lit: oral, spoken, word-of-mouth; literal, word-for-word; using words, worded; *spec*: of a verb.

verbose
adj lit: garrulous, long-winded, loquacious, prolix, rambling, wordy; diffuse, periphrastic, pleonastic.

verdict
n lit: adjudication, decision, finding, judgement, ruling; conclusion, opinion.

verge
n lit: edge, fringe, margin, roadside, side; border, brim, brink, lip, threshold; *spec*: eaves, overhang (of a roof); shaft (of a pillar); staff of office.
vb lit: be side (on to), border (on), edge (on to).

verity
n lit: truth; axiom, fact, law, precept, principle, truism; actuality, reality.

versatile
adj lit: adaptable, flexible, reversible; handy, many-sided, resourceful; multifarious, multipurpose.

version
n lit: form, kind, style, type; model, variant; adaptation, interpretation, reading, rendition, translation.

vertical
adj lit: perpendicular, upright; erect; apical, at the zenith; lengthways; *spec*: harmonic (in music).

vertigo
n lit: dizziness, faintness, giddiness; altitude sickness.

very
adj lit: actual, express; exact, precise; identical, same, self-same; real, true; mere, pure, sheer.
adv lit: awfully, exceedingly, extremely, greatly, highly, really, terribly, terrifically, truly; acutely, deeply, profoundly.

vessel

n lit: boat, craft, ship; container, tank; receptacle; canal, channel, duct, tube; *fig*: medium, mouthpiece, spokesperson, transmitter.

vestige

n lit: evidence, indication, mark, sign, token, trace, track; remains, residual form; *fig*: glimmer, hint, suspicion.

vestigial

adj lit: rudimentary, undeveloped; atrophied, nonfunctional.

vet

n lit: animal doctor, animal surgeon, pet doctor; zoologist.
vb lit: check out, examine, review, scan, scrutinize; assess, appraise, size up, weigh up.

veteran

n lit: old hand, professional; ex-serviceman.
adj lit: long-serving, old, seasoned; battle-scarred, campaign-hardened.

veto

n lit: negation, negative, refusal, rejection, thumbs-down; embargo, prohibition.
vb lit: give the thumbs-down, negate, refuse, reject; interdict, rule out, turn down; ban, embargo, forbid, prohibit.

vex

vb lit: annoy, bother, displease, disturb, exasperate, nettle, peeve, put out, rile, upset; agitate, distress, fret, nag, worry.

vexatious

adj lit: annoying, bothersome, displeasing, disturbing, exasperating, nettling, peeving, riling, upsetting; agitating, distressing, nagging, worrisome, worrying; *spec*: malicious, provocative (litigation).

viable

adj lit: developing, functioning independently, self-supporting; *fig*: feasible, practicable, workable; applicable, usable; manageable, possible.

vibrant

adj lit: oscillating, quivering, shivering, trembling; pulsating, resonant, resounding, thrilling, throbbing; *fig*: animated, dynamic, lively, sparkling, spirited, vivacious.

vibrate

vb lit: oscillate, quiver, shake, shiver, tremble; pulsate, thrill, throb; resonate, reverberate; *spec*: transmit waves of (emotion).

vicar

n lit: canon, minister, padre, parish priest, parson, pastor, rector; chaplain, dean; pope.

vice

n lit: evil, iniquity, sin, wickedness; depravity, immorality, prostitution; defect, failing, fault, shortcoming; blemish, imperfection.

vicinity

n lit: environs, locality, neighbourhood; area, district, region.

vicious

adj lit: aggressive, cruel, dangerous, diabolical, ferocious, fiendish, fierce, malevolent, malicious, malignant, mean, savage, spiteful, venomous, vindictive, violent; brutal, painful, severe; *spec*: (circle) of increasing aggravation.

victim

n lit: prey, sufferer; casualty, injured party; fatality, martyr; butt, quarry, target; dupe, gull, john, patsy, sucker; fall guy, scapegoat.

victimize

vb lit: discriminate against, persecute, pick on; be malevolent towards, be vindictive towards; cheat, con, defraud, dupe, exploit, swindle.

victor

n lit: conqueror, vanquisher, winner; champion, prizewinner; best, first.

victorious

adj lit: conquering, successful, triumphant, vanquishing, winning; champion, prizewinning; best.

victory

n lit: win; success, triumph; laurels, palm, prize, trophy; conquest, supremacy.

view

n lit: outlook, panorama, prospect, scene, sight, vista; field of vision; display, exhibition, show; *fig*: aspect, conception, idea, impression, picture; attitude, judgement, notion, opinion, way of thinking; expectation; consideration.

viewpoint
vb lit: behold, eye, look at, observe, regard, scan, see, survey, watch, witness; examine, inspect, scrutinize; fig: deem (as), look on (as), think of (as).

viewpoint
n lit: position, stance, vantage point; angle, perspective; fig: attitude, slant, way of thinking.

vigorous
adj lit: active, brisk, energetic, lively, spirited, strenuous; dynamic, forceful, powerful, robust, strong; flourishing, healthy, lusty, sound, virile.

vigour
n lit: dynamism, energy, force, liveliness, pep, power, punch, snap, spirit, strength, verve, vim, vitality, zip; health, robustness, virility.

vile
adj lit: disgusting, foul, loathsome, nauseating, offensive, repellent, repugnant, repulsive, revolting, sickening; appalling, contemptible, despicable, disgraceful, worthless; evil, immoral, perverted, shocking, sinful, wicked; abject, base, coarse, debased, low, mean, vulgar, wretched.

vilification
n lit: aspersion, bad-mouthing, calumny, defamation, denigration, slander, smear; abuse, disparagement, vituperation.

villain
n lit: evildoer, malefactor, miscreant; convict, criminal, old lag, blackguard, scoundrel; libertine, rake, roué; antihero, baddie; fig: devil, monkey, rapscallion, rogue, scamp.

villainous
adj lit: evil, heinous, nefarious, wicked; criminal, infamous; cruel, diabolical, fiendish, inhuman, vicious; bad, degenerate, depraved, mean, ruffianly, vile.

vindicate
vb lit: clear, exculpate, exonerate; absolve, excuse, justify, uphold.

vindication
n lit: exculpation, exoneration, freeing from blame; excuse, explanation, justification; defence, plea.

violate
vb lit: break, contravene, infringe, transgress against; disobey, disregard; assault, defile, desecrate, dishonour, invade; abuse, debauch, deflower, outrage, rape, ravish.

violation
n lit: breach, contravention, infringement, transgression; assault, defilement, desecration, dishonouring, invasion, profanation, sacrilege; abuse, debauching, defloration, outrage, rape, ravishment.

violence
n lit: ferocity, fervour, fierceness, force, intensity, passion, power, severity, strength, vehemence; brutality, roughness, savagery, thuggery, wildness; boisterousness, storminess, turbulence; bloodshed, cruelty; harm, injury.

violent
adj lit: fervent, fierce, forceful, intense, passionate, powerful, severe, strong, vehement; brutal, rough, savage, thuggish, wild; blustery, boisterous, stormy, tempestuous, turbulent; berserk, bloody, cruel, ferocious, maniacal, murderous; dangerous, harmful, injurious; agonizing, excruciating, sharp.

virgin
n lit: maiden; damsel, young girl; spinster; madonna; spec: inexperienced boy. adj lit: chaste, maidenly; undefiled, . unsullied, untouched; fig: immaculate, pure; fresh, new, pristine, unused.

virile
adj lit: male, manly, masculine, potent, red-blooded; lusty, macho, robust, strong, vigorous.

virtually
adv lit: all but, almost, effectually, essentially, nearly, practically, pretty well.

virtue
n lit: chastity, purity; goodness, integrity, morality, probity, rectitude, righteousness, worthiness; good point, merit, plus, strength; advantage, effectiveness, efficacy, potency.

virtuosity
n lit: expertise, mastery, skill; brilliance, flair, panache.

virtuous
adj lit: chaste, clean-living, pure; ethical,

exemplary, good, honourable, moral, righteous, upright, worthy.

virulent
adj lit: poisonous, toxic, venomous; infective, malignant; deadly, lethal; harmful, injurious, noxious; *fig*: hostile, malevolent, malicious, spiteful, vicious, vindictive; acrimonious, bitter, rancorous, resentful.

visible
adj lit: apparent, clearly seen, discernible, evident, in sight, manifest, noticeable, obvious, patent, plain, unmistakable; distinct, distinguishable; *fig*: approachable by appointment, ready for visitors; *spec*: goods (in economics).

vision
n lit: eyesight, seeing, sight; eyes, view; apparition, hallucination, illusion, revelation; spectacle; *fig*: far-sightedness, foresight, imagination, prescience; insight, understanding; concept, conception, idea, image, mental picture; daydream, dream, fantasy; perfect picture, sight for sore eyes.

visit
n lit: call; sojourn, stay, stop; excursion, trip.
vb lit: call in on, go to see, look up, pop in on; be a guest of, stay with, stop at; go on an excursion to, sightsee, take a trip to, tour; *fig*: afflict, assail, attack, trouble; impose (upon), inflict (upon), wreak (upon).

visitors
n lit: callers, guests; company; foreigners, tourists, transients.

visualize
vb lit: conceive, envisage, imagine, mentally see, picture; draw up, realize.

vital
adj lit: cardiopulmonary, living, survival; alive, dynamic, energetic, lively, spirited, vibrant, vivacious; *fig*: cardinal, critical, crucial, essential, fundamental, indispensable, key, necessary, requisite.

vitriolic
adj lit: acerbic, acidic, biting, caustic, scathing, sharp, trenchant, virulent; malevolent, malicious, malignant.

vituperative
adj lit: abusive, censorious, derogatory, opprobrious, pejorative, reviling, vilificatory.

vivacious
adj lit: animated, bubbling, ebullient, effervescent, energetic, jaunty, lively, scintillating, spirited, sprightly, vibrant.

vivacity
n lit: animation, ebullience, energy, jauntiness, liveliness, pep, quickness, sparkle, spirit, sprightliness, vibrance, zip.

vivid
adj lit: brilliant, colourful, rich; bright, clear, distinct, graphic, lifelike, realistic, three-dimensional, true-to-life; dramatic, powerful, sharp, strong, telling.

vocabulary
n lit: words; jargon, language, terminology; glossary; dictionary, lexicon; *fig*: repertoire, stock, store.

vocal
adj lit: articulated, oral, spoken, sung, uttered, voiced; clamorous, eloquent, loquacious, noisy, strident, vociferous.

vocation
n lit: calling, métier, mission; life's work; profession.

vociferous
adj lit: bawling, clamorous, loud, noisy, rowdy, shouting, strident, yelling; heated, vehement.

vogue
n lit: custom, fashion, mode, style; craze, fad, rage, trend; currency, fashionability, favour, popularity, usage; acceptance, approval.
adj lit: fashionable, in, modish, popular, trendy.

voice
n lit: power of speech; sound, timbre, tone; *fig*: expression, view, vote; decision; agency, medium, spokesperson, vehicle; *spec*: (part-singing) part, singer; verb-form (in grammar).
vb lit: air, articulate, come out with, declare, express, say; resonate; accent, emphasize, stress.

void

n lit: chaos; blankness, emptiness, space, vacuum; blank, gap, hiatus, opening; absence, lack, want.
vb lit: discharge, eliminate, emit, evacuate, spew, throw up, vomit; drain, empty; annul, cancel, invalidate, nullify.
adj lit: drained, emptied; deserted, unoccupied, vacant; bare, clear, empty, free; dead, ineffectual, inoperative, invalid, useless, worthless.

volatile

adj lit: evaporative, vaporizing; explosive, mercurial, unstable; changeable, erratic, fickle, flighty, inconstant, unsettled, variable; short-lived, transient.

volley

n lit: barrage, bombardment, fusillade, hail, salvo, shower; burst, outburst, staccato rattle; *spec*: (on the) full, full toss (in cricket, tennis and football).
vb lit: discharge together, fire together, sound together; *spec*: strike before (the ball) bounces.

voluble

adj lit: articulate, fluent, garrulous, glib, loquacious, talkative; *spec*: twining, twisting (in botany).

volume

n lit: capacity, cubic capacity; amount, bulk, mass, quantity; book, tome, work; loudness, noise, sound.

voluminous

adj lit: billowing, bulky, capacious, large, roomy; layered, stratified; convoluted, in coils, in folds, pleated; prolific.

voluntary

n lit: extempore piece, improvised piece; musical prelude; musical postlude.
adj lit: discretionary, optional, spontaneous; free, unforced; honorary, unpaid; intentional, willing; independent, unaffiliated; consciously controlled, willed.

voluptuous

adj lit: hedonistic, self-indulgent; sensual; buxom, curvaceous, enticing, full-bosomed, seductive, top-heavy, well stacked.

vomit

vb lit: be sick, bring up, chuck up, heave, puke, spew, throw up; belch forth, disgorge, emit.

voracious

adj lit: devouring, greedy, hungry, insatiable, rapacious, ravening, unquenchable; *fig*: engulfing, swallowing.

vote

n lit: ballot, plebiscite, poll, referendum; suffrage; voice; choice, decision, verdict.
vb lit: ballot, go to the polling station; declare (for), opt (for); propose, recommend, suggest.

vouchsafe

vb lit: accord, confer, grant; promise; be so good as (to).

vow

n lit: oath; asseveration, pledge, promise, solemn undertaking; resolve.
vb lit: pledge, promise, swear, undertake; firmly resolve, intend specifically.

voyage

n lit: journey, passage, trip; cruise, excursion, trip; round trip, travels.

vulgar

adj lit: cheap, common, commonplace, ill-bred, low, plebeian; boorish, coarse, crude, gaudy, indelicate, tasteless, tawdry, uncouth, unmannerly; debased, degraded, ignoble; native, vernacular.

vulgarity

n lit: cliché, commonplace; crudity, ribaldry; coarseness, crudeness, indecorum, indelicacy, tastelessness, tawdriness, uncouthness.

vulnerable

adj lit: assailable, exposed, sensitive, susceptible, tender, weak; defenceless, thin-skinned, unprotected; liable, open, prone; gullible, persuadable.

vulpine

adj lit: foxlike; *fig*: artful, canny, crafty, cunning, devious, foxy, sharp, sly, wily.

W

wade
vb lit: paddle (through), splash (through), walk (through); ford; *fig*: labour (through), plod (through), plough (through), toil (through); get stuck (into), light (into), tear (into).

waffle
n lit: blather, jabber, prattle, verbiage; padding, prevarication; gibberish, gobbledegook, nonsense; *spec*: pastry, wafer-cake.
vb lit: blather, chunder, jabber, prattle, rabbit (on), witter (on); pad out, prevaricate; gibber, talk nonsense.

waft
n lit: breath, breeze, current, draught, puff.
vb lit: carry lightly, convey, transport; drift, float; breathe, blow gently, puff.

wag
n lit: shake, wave; comedian, humorist, jester, joker, wit.
vb lit: shake, wave; flutter, oscillate, rock, vibrate, wiggle; *fig*: go (on), move (on).

wage
n lit: emolument, fee, pay, payment, remuneration, salary, stipend.
vb lit: carry on, conduct, engage in, prosecute, pursue, undertake.

wager
n lit: bet, flutter, gamble; pledge, stake.
vb lit: bet, gamble, lay, stake; chance, hazard, risk, venture.

wail
n lit: howl, ululation, yowl; cry, moan, sob; clamour, drone, scream, whine.
vb lit: bemoan, cry, howl, keen, moan, sob, ululate, weep, yowl; clamour, drone, scream, whine.

wait
n lit: delay, halt, hold-up, pause, rest, stop; hiatus, interval, space; ambush; carol-singer.
vb lit: bide one's time, halt, hold back, hold on, pause, rest, stop, tarry; be delayed, remain, stay; attend (on), serve (at).

waiter
n lit: attendant, assistant, steward; *fig*: lift, tray, trolley.

waive
vb lit: defer, dispense with, disregard, forgo, relinquish, remit, renounce, set aside.

waiver
n lit: disclaimer, dispensation, moratorium, renunciation, setting aside.

wake
n lit: vigil, watch; funeral party, memorial function; backwash, track, trail, wash; *spec*: consecration anniversary (of a church).
vb lit: awaken, be roused, come to, get up, stir; activate, arouse, reanimate, revive; *fig*: enliven, excite, galvanize, kindle, stimulate; evoke, fire, provoke.

walk
n lit: constitutional, hike, perambulation, promenade, ramble, tramp; amble, saunter, stroll, traipse, trek, trudge; gait, pace, step, stride; aisle, alley, avenue, lane, path; pathway, trail; enclosure, pen, run; *fig*: activity, area, field, sphere; *spec*: flock (of wagtails).
vb lit: amble, hike, perambulate, promenade, ramble, saunter, stroll, traipse, tramp, trek, trudge; foot it, hoof it, march, step it out, stride out, yomp; inspect, pace out; advance, go, move, travel; go away, move off, withdraw; accompany, escort, take; exercise, lead.

wall
n lit: brickwork; divider, panel, partition, screen; barricade, bulwark, fortification, palisade, rampart; barrier, fence; cliff, precipice; *fig*: obstacle, obstruction; defence; *spec*: membrane (covering or lining a body organ, or a cell).
vb lit: partition (off), screen (off), separate; enclose, surround; fortify; immure; *spec*: roll, squint (of eyes).

wallop
n lit: bash, blow, buffet, hit, punch, smack, thump, whack; *fig*: force, power, strength; ale, beer, bitter.

vb lit: bash, buffet, hit, punch, smack, thump, whack; beat, defeat, trounce.

wallow
vb lit: flounder (in), lie (in), roll about (in), wade (in); lurch, stagger, stumble; heave, surge; *fig*: glory (in), indulge oneself (in), revel (in); bask (in), immerse oneself (in), luxuriate (in).

wally
n lit: berk, prat, sap, twit; cretin, idiot, imbecile, moron; ass, clown, dolt, fool, noodle.

wan
adj lit: anaemic, ashen, ghastly, pale, pallid, pasty, sickly, waxen, white; colourless; dim, faint, feeble, weak.

wand
n lit: baton, rod; caduceus, staff; cane, shoot, sprig, twig; *spec*: mark (for shooting at in archery).

wander
n lit: meander, perambulation, peregrination, promenade, ramble, roam.
vb lit: drift, meander, perambulate, peregrinate, promenade, ramble, range, roam, rove, travel; deviate, digress, diverge, go astray, straggle, stray, veer off; *fig*: be led astray, err, lapse.

wandering
adj (pr.pt) lit: circuitous, convoluted, meandering, rambling, ranging, roaming, sinuous, tortuous, winding; drifting, itinerant, nomadic, peripatetic, travelling, vagrant, wayfaring.

wane
n lit: atrophy, decline, decay, dwindling, ebb, fading, falling off, shrinking, sinking, subsiding, withering; decrease, diminution, fall, lessening, lowering, tapering off, winding down.
vb lit: abate, atrophy, decline, decay, dwindle, ebb, fade, fall off, get smaller, shrink, sink, subside, wither; decrease, diminish, fall, lessen, lower; die away, draw to a close, taper off, wear off, wind down.

wangle
n lit: bit of cunning, contrivance, device, dodge, fiddle, ploy, scheme, trick; careful management, manipulation.
vb lit: contrive, fiddle; manipulate.

want
n lit: absence, default, demand, lack,

need, requirement; craving, desire, longing, wish, yearning, yen; appetite, hunger, thirst; dearth, deficiency, insufficiency, paucity, poverty, privation, scarcity, shortage.
vb lit: desire, need, require, wish; crave, hanker for, hunger for, long for, pine for, thirst for, yearn for; be deficient in, be short of, lack, miss; seek.

war
n lit: battle, conflict, fighting, hostilities, strife, struggle; *fig*: contention, enmity, hostility; competition, rivalry; campaign.
vb lit: battle, combat, fight, struggle; *fig*: campaign (against).

warble
n lit: birdsong, chirrup, melody, tremolo, trilling; falsetto, quavering, yodel; babble, murmur, ripple; *spec*: gall (on a horse).
vb lit: cheep, chirp, trill, tweet; quaver, yodel; babble, murmur, ripple.

ward
n lit: dependant, protégé; charge; care, custody, guardianship, keeping, protection; district, division, hundred, precinct, wapentake, zone; *spec*: clinic, (hospital) dormitory, room, sanatorium; notch, slot (on a key); parry (in fencing); section (in a prison).
vb lit: guard, have custody of, keep, protect; deflect (away), fend (off), parry (off).

warden
n lit: curator, executive officer, keeper, ranger, superintendent; caretaker, janitor, watchman; administrator, custodian, guardian.

warder
n lit: guard, sentinel, sentry, watchman; jailer, keeper, prison officer, screw; beefeater, yeoman of the guard; *spec*: baton, staff of authority.

wardrobe
n lit: closet, cupboard, garderobe; attire, clothing, clothes, kit, outfits.

wares
n lit: commodities, goods, merchandise, products, stock.

warily
adv lit: cautiously, charily, gingerly, vigilantly, watchfully; circumspectly, guardedly; alertly, carefully, leerily.

warlike
adj lit: bellicose, combative, hawkish, hostile, martial, pugnacious; aggressive, belligerent, inimical, unfriendly; military.

warm
vb lit: heat (up); melt, thaw; microwave, reheat; hot (up); *fig*: limber (up); become more friendly (to), become more sympathetic (to); excite, interest, stimulate, stir (up).
adj lit: pleasantly hot; unpleasantly hot; radiating; *fig*: affable, affectionate, cordial, friendly, hearty, kind, kindly, loving, tender; lively, severe, strenuous, vigorous; ardent, earnest, enthusiastic, fervent, keen, passionate; excited, stimulated; emotional, intense; fresh, strong, vivid; irascible, sensitive, touchy; dangerous, hazardous, perilous; *spec*: close, near (in a game); rich, wealthy.

warm-hearted
adj lit: compassionate, kindly, sympathetic, tender-hearted; affectionate, loving; generous, open; amiable, cordial, hearty.

warmth
n lit: heat, temperature; radiance, radiation, sunshine; blaze, fire, flame; *fig*: ardour, emotion, enthusiasm, feeling, fervour, intensity, passion; animation, excitement, spirit, vigour, zeal; affection, kindliness, love, tenderness; cordiality, heartiness; asperity, curtness, ferocity, sharpness.

warn
vb lit: alert, caution, give notice, make aware, tip off; advise, inform, notify.

warning
n lit: alarm, alert, caution, notice, tip, tip-off; shot across the bows, threat; advice, notification, word; augury, omen, premonition, presage, sign; beacon, signal; beware.
adj (pr.pt) lit: cautionary; threatening; ominous, premonitory; *spec*: aposematic (of the coloration of organisms).

warp
n lit: bend, distortion, twist; loop; *fig*: bias; defect, kink; perversion.
vb lit: bend, be twisted, curve, distort, twist; haul, heave, hoist, winch; *fig*: misinterpret, misrepresent; pervert; *spec*: block, choke (a waterway); flood (for soil renewal).

warrant
n lit: authorization, commission, licence, permit, sanction; authority, permission; guarantee.
vb lit: affirm, assure, attest, certify, pledge, stand security for, underwrite, vouch for; call for, demand, justify, necessitate, require, sanction; entitle, excuse, permit.

warrior
n lit: fighter; man-at-arms, soldier; brave, tribesman; janissary; champion, combatant, gladiator.

wary
adj lit: alert, careful, cautious, chary, leery, vigilant, watchful; circumspect, guarded.

wash
n lit: ablution, bath, rinse, scrub, shampoo, shower; cleansing, laundering; surf, surge, swell, undertow; attrition, erosion, wear; coating, film, stain; coat, layer, suffusion; lotion, medication.
vb lit: bath, bathe, launder, rinse, scrub, shampoo, shower; moisten, steep, wet; baptise, clean, cleanse; erode (away), sweep (away); *fig*: be convincing, be plausible, hold up, hold water, stick, work.

washout
n lit: disappointment, failure, flop; disaster, fiasco.

waspish
adj lit: stinging; *fig*: crabbed, malignant, malevolent, spiteful, virulent; cross, irascible, peevish, peppery, snappish, testy, touchy.

waste
n lit: debris, dross, garbage, leavings, litter, offal, refuse, rubbish, scrap, sweepings, trash; dissipation, extravagance, loss, misuse, prodigality, profligacy, squandering; desert, outback, veldt, wilds, wilderness; destruction, devastation, havoc, ravage, ruin; *spec*: silt (in rivers); excrement, excreta, faeces, stools; urine.
vb lit: be prodigal with, blow, dissipate, fritter away, misuse, squander, throw away; atrophy, corrode, crumble, decay, diminish, dwindle, eat (away), erode, fade (away), wear (away), wither; be spent, be used up; *fig*: assassinate, kill, murder.

adj *lit*: extra, leftover, over, superfluous, unused; scrap, rejected, thrown away, unwanted; bare, barren, desolate, empty, uninhabited, wild; devastated, ravaged, ruined, unproductive.

wasteful
adj *lit*: extravagant, improvident, prodigal, profligate, spendthrift, thriftless, uneconomic.

wastrel
n *lit*: prodigal, profligate, spendthrift, squanderer; good-for-nothing, idler, layabout, loafer.

watch
n *lit*: chronometer, timepiece; lookout, sentry-go; eye, observation, surveillance; guard, vigil; period.
vb *lit*: eye, look at, mark, note, observe, pay attention to, stare at, survey, view; be on the alert, be vigilant, be wary of, look out (for), take heed of; guard, keep, look after, mind, protect, superintend, supervise; keep vigil.

watchful
adj *lit*: alert, attentive, observant, on guard, on the lookout, vigilant, wary; circumspect, guarded; heedful, mindful.

water
n *lit*: Adam's ale, H_2O; lake, ocean, river, sea; tide; rain; *fig*: amniotic fluid, blood serum, saliva, tears; urine; class, grade, quality; *spec*: clarity, lustre, transparency (of a diamond).
vb *lit*: damp, dampen, douse, drench, flood, hose, irrigate, moisten, ret, soak, souse, spray, sprinkle, steep; adulterate, dilute, thin, weaken; give a drink; *fig*: lacrimate, salivate.

waterfall
n *lit*: cascade, cataract, force; rapids, weir.

waterworks
n *lit*: pumping station; fountain, ornamental cascade; drains, pipes, plumbing; *fig*: lacrimal apparatus; urinary apparatus.

watery
adj *lit*: aqueous, fluid, liquid, wet; damp, humid, moist; boggy, marshy, soggy; adulterated, diluted, insipid, pale, runny, thin, vapid, weak, wishy-washy; lachrymose, rheumy, tearful; rainy.

wave
n *lit*: flourish, flutter, gesticulation, gesture, shake, swing; billow, breaker, roller, undulation; oscillation, sine curve; perm; *fig*: current, flood, movement, stream, surge, swell, upsurge; epidemic, outbreak, rash, trend.
vb *lit*: brandish, flap, flourish, shake, stir, swing, undulate, wag; beckon, direct, gesticulate, gesture, indicate, make a sign, signal.

waver
vb *lit*: be indecisive, be unable to make up one's mind, dither, falter, hesitate; become unsteady; flicker, gutter, fluctuate, oscillate, seesaw, vacillate, vary; reel, sway, teeter, totter, tremble, wobble.

wax
n *lit*: beeswax, candle-wax; paraffin wax; *fig*: celluloid; clay, modelling clay, plasticene, putty.
vb *lit*: polish, buff up; develop, enlarge, expand, get bigger, grow, increase, swell; become, get, turn.

way
n *lit*: avenue, channel, course, direction, lane, path, pathway, road, route, street, track; distance, journey, length; room, space; motion, movement, passage, progress; approach, course of action, means, method, mode, procedure, system, technique; custom, fashion, habit, idiosyncrasy, manner, practice, style, trait, usage, wont; aspect, feature, respect, sense; aim, desire, goal, will, wish; circumstance, condition, shape, state.
adv *lit*: far; considerably, severely.

waylay
vb *lit*: accost, ambush, intercept, lie in wait for; attack, hold up, pounce upon, surprise.

wayward
adj *lit*: contrary, disobedient, headstrong, mulish, obdurate, obstinate, self-willed, stubborn, wilful; capricious, changeable, flighty, refractory, unmanageable, unpredictable; erratic, inconstant, irregular, perverse, unsteady.

weak
adj *lit*: debilitated, delicate, effete, feeble, flimsy, frail, puny; defenceless, exposed, helpless, impotent, unprotected,

vulnerable; cowardly, ineffectual, irresolute, powerless, soft, spineless; inadequate, lacking, poor, substandard; distant, dull, faint, low, muffled, quiet, slight; *fig*: invalid, lame, pathetic, unconvincing; diluted, thin, watery, wishy-washy; *spec*: fluctuating (stock market prices); regular (verb declension); unstressed (syllable).

weaken
vb lit: fail, flag, give way, sap, soften up, temper, undermine, wane; abate, decrease, diminish, dwindle, fade, lessen, moderate; *fig*: adulterate, dilute, thin, water down; cut, debase.

weakling
n lit: milksop, mouse, shrimp, softy, titch, weed, wet, wimp; invalid.

wealth
n lit: affluence, means, money, opulence, prosperity, riches, substance; fortune, lucre, pelf, property; resources; *fig*: abundance, copiousness, luxuriance, plenitude, plethora, profusion.

wealthy
adj lit: affluent, comfortable, comfortably off, moneyed, opulent, prosperous, rich, well-to-do; filthy rich, loaded, rolling in it, stinking rich, well-heeled.

wear
n lit: abrasion, attrition, depreciation, deterioration, erosion, friction damage; use; mileage, service, utility.
vb lit: be dressed in, dress in, have on, sport; display, exhibit; abrade, depreciate, deteriorate, erode, fray, grind, rub; *fig*: bear up, endure, hold up, last; annoy, exasperate, fatigue, irk, tire (out), try, vex, weary; bring gradually (in); pass (on); accept, buy, credit, take on trust.

wearing
adj (pr.pt) lit: annoying, exasperating, fatiguing, irksome, taxing, tiring, trying, vexing, wearying.

wearisome
adj lit: annoying, boring, burdensome, dull, exhausting, irksome, monotonous, oppressive, tedious, trying, uninteresting, vexatious.

weary
vb lit: drain, fag, fatigue, jade, take it out of, tax, tire, wear out; annoy, bore, burden, exasperate, harass, irk, pester,

plague.
adj lit: all in, dead beat, dog tired, done in, drained, exhausted, fagged, fatigued, jaded, knackered, spent, taxed, tired out, whacked, worn out; annoyed, bored, exasperated, irked, plagued.

weather
n lit: atmospheric conditions, climate, elements; *fig*: normal, par; influence.
vb lit: expose, season; harden, toughen; be discoloured, be worn; *fig*: come through, get through, last, make it, ride, ride out, surmount, survive, withstand.

weave
vb lit: braid, entwine, interlace, plait; criss-cross, intertwine, mesh; *fig*: create, make, spin, work; blend, combine; twist and turn, zigzag.

wed
vb lit: be married, espouse, get hitched, get married, marry, tie the knot; *fig*: ally with, combine with, join (to), unite with; be devoted to.

wedding
n lit: marriage, matrimony, nuptials, solemnization of matrimony; *fig*: alliance, combination, joining, merger, union.

weed
n lit: darnel, tare; *fig*: milksop, shrimp, wet, wimp; runt, weakling; cigar, cigarette; cannabis, grass, marijuana, pot.
vb lit: uproot; clear; *fig*: remove, sort out.

weekly
adj lit: hebdomadal; once-a-week.
adv lit: hebdomadally; every week; once a week, every seven days.

weep
vb lit: blub, blubber, cry, shed tears; greet; snivel, sob; grieve (for), mourn (for); *fig*: drip, leak, ooze; exude, suppurate.

weigh
vb lit: have a weight of, tip the scales at; bear down, burden, load; apportion (out), dole (out), measure (out); balance, hold in the balance; *fig*: be influential, count, matter, tell; consider, contemplate, evaluate, mull over, ponder, think over; insert (in), interpolate (in); get stuck (in), lay (into); *spec*: hoist up (the anchor).

weight

n lit: heaviness; ballast, burden, load, mass; poundage, tonnage; counterpoise; lead, sinker; pendulum; dumbbell; *fig*: millstone, pressure, strain; onus, preponderance; authority, clout, importance, influence, moment, power, substance; emphasis, impact, value; force, tension; impetus; *spec*: bias (in bowls, in statistics); handicap (in horse-racing).
vb lit: ballast, charge, load, make heavier; burden, handicap, weigh down; *fig*: add to, bias.

weighty

adj lit: heavy, hefty, massive; burdensome, cumbersome, ponderous; *fig*: authoritative, consequential, important, influential, momentous, portentous, powerful, serious, significant, substantial; emphatic, forceful; demanding, exacting, exigent, onerous, taxing.

weird

adj lit: abnormal, bizarre, grotesque, odd, outlandish, peculiar, strange; creepy, eerie, ghostly, mysterious, spooky, uncanny, unearthly; freakish, unnatural; fantastic, wild.

welcome

n lit: greeting, reception, salutation; entertainment, hospitality.
vb lit: give a reception to, go to meet, greet, offer hospitality to, receive, usher in; accept with pleasure, take gladly; please come in.
adj lit: acceptable, agreeable, appreciated, desirable, gratifying, pleasing, pleasurable; *spec*: free of obligation.

weld

n lit: joint, seam, union; bond.
vb lit: forge, melt; anneal, sinter; force together; *fig*: bond, join, unite; ally, combine, put together.

welfare

n lit: health, wellbeing; benefit, good, prosperity; *fig*: dole, social security, social services.

well

n lit: bore, hole, shaft; pool, spring; compartment, hollow, niche, pit; *fig*: fount, source; repository, store; mine.
vb lit: arise, rise, spring; seep, spout, trickle; flow, gush, pour, run, spurt, stream; billow, surge.

adj lit: fine, fit, hale, healthy, robust, sound; all right, okay; fortunate, lucky; advisable, prudent; useful.
adv lit: ably, accurately, adeptly, correctly, efficiently, expertly, proficiently, properly, rightly, skilfully, suitably; carefully, closely; comfortably, more than satisfactorily; abundantly, amply, considerably, deeply, fully, greatly, heartily, highly, profoundly, substantially, thoroughly; easily, readily; approvingly, favourably, glowingly, kindly, warmly.

well-bred

adj lit: aristocratic, highborn, noble, patrician, pedigree; courteous, courtly, cultured, mannerly, polished, polite, refined.

wet

n lit: dampness, moisture, water; drizzle, rain, storm; clamminess, condensation, damp, humidity; *fig*: drip, weakling, weed, wimp.
vb lit: damp, dampen, douse, drench, flood, moisten, ret, rinse, soak, souse, spray, sprinkle, steep; baptise, dip; urinate in; *fig*: drink the health of, toast.
adj lit: damp, dank, drenched, dripping, moist, saturated, soaked, soaking, sodden, soggy, sopping, waterlogged, watery, wringing; fluid, liquid; clammy, humid; rainy, showery; *fig*: effete, ineffectual, soft, spineless, weak, wimpish; mawkish, sentimental, soppy.

wheedle

vb lit: cajole, charm, coax, draw, entice, inveigle, talk (into); blandish, butter up, flatter; cheat (out of).

wheel

n lit: hub, tyre; helm, steering column; circle, disc; change of direction, rotation, turn; *fig*: cog, part of the machinery.
vb lit: gyrate, pivot, rotate, spin, swing, swivel, turn; circle, loop, spin round, whirl round; drive, push along, take, transport.

wheeze

n lit: gag, gasp, heave, rasp, whistle; cough; *fig*: ploy, ruse, scheme; jape, lark, stunt; gag, joke; chestnut, old joke.
vb lit: breathe harshly, gag, gasp, heave, hiss, rasp, whistle; cough.

wherewithal

n lit: ability, capability, capacity, means,

power, resources, supplies; *fig*: assets, capital, cash, funds, money, ready.

whet
vb lit: file, grind, hone, sharpen, strop; *fig*: arouse, awaken, kindle, pique, quicken, rouse, stimulate, stir; augment, increase.

whiff
n lit: breath, puff; scent, smell, sniff; aroma, odour, reek, stench, stink; honk, niff, pong; *fig*: hint, trace, vestige; glimpse.

while
n lit: period, time; duration, meantime; time and effort.
cnj lit: contemporaneously as, during the time that, simultaneously as; as long as; although, whereas.

whim
n lit: caprice, conceit, fancy, humour, impulse, notion, vagary; eccentricity, quirk; *spec*: horse-drawn capstan, horse-drawn winch.

whimper
n lit: moan, sob, whine; broken cry.
vb lit: moan, sob, whine; blub, blubber, cry, weep; plead querulously, snivel, whinge.

whimsical
adj lit: capricious, fanciful, fantastical, impulsive; eccentric, freakish, funny, quirky, singular.

whine
n lit: moan, wail; drone, noise, tone; nasal timbre.
vb lit: moan, wail; complain, grouse, grumble; beef, bellyache, gripe, grizzle, whinge, yowl.

whip
n lit: cat-o'-nine-tails, crop, knout, lash, rawhide, scourge, switch, thong; *fig*: party manager; coachman, driver; *spec*: armature (in an electrical circuit); block and tackle, pulley.
vb lit: beat, flagellate, flog, lash, scourge, strap, switch, thrash; birch, cane, leather, tan; hammer, lick; conquer, defeat, drub, overcome, overpower, rout, trounce; compel, drive, goad, incite, prick, prod, provoke, spur; force, jerk, pull, seize, snatch; dart, dash, dive, flash, fly, tear; mix, stir, whisk; appropriate, nab, nick, steal, thieve, walk off with.

whirl
n lit: gyration, pirouette, revolution, rotation, spin, swirl, twirl; dizziness, giddiness; daze, dither; agitation, bustle, commotion, flurry, hurly-burly, stir; round, series, succession.
vb lit: circle, gyrate, pirouette, revolve, rotate, spin, swirl, turn, twirl; reel; wheel.

whirlwind
n lit: dust-devil, eddy, vortex; cyclone, tornado.
adj lit: instant, lightning; hasty, rapid, speedy, swift; headlong, impetuous, impulsive.

whisk
n lit: beater, mixer; swat; brush, flick, sweep, whip.
vb lit: beat, fluff up, mix, stiffen, whip; swat; brush, flick, sweep, wipe; hurry, race, rush, speed.

whisper
n lit: low voice, murmur, undertone; rustle, sighing, susurration, swish; white sound; *fig*: breath, hint, shadow, suggestion, trace, whiff; buzz, rumour, word.
vb lit: breathe, murmur, say softly; rustle, sigh, susurrate, swish; *fig*: gossip, spread a rumour.

white
n lit: Caucasian; light wine; *spec*: albumen (of an egg); inner (on a target); sclera (of the eye).
adj lit: alabaster, chalky, cream, floury, ivory, milky, pearly, snowy; colourless, transparent; ashen, bloodless, ghastly, pale, pallid, pasty, waxen; bright, light; clean, immaculate, pure, spotless, unblemished; fair, platinum blonde; *fig*: honest, reliable, trustworthy; innocent; *spec*: benign, good (magic); grey (horse).

whitewash
n lit: undercoat, whiting; *fig*: cover-up, prevarication; easy victory, shut-out, walkover.
vb lit: cover over, paint over; *fig*: camouflage, conceal, cover up, gloss over, put a good appearance on; beat easily, thrash all hands down.

whole
n lit: lot, sum, total; entirety, totality; aggregate, complete system, ensemble, total combination, unity.

adj lit: complete, entire, full, integral, total; intact, perfect, sound, unbroken, undamaged, unscathed; unabridged, uncut; better, cured, healed, healthy; all at once, in one piece.

wholehearted
adj lit: committed, dedicated, devoted, earnest, enthusiastic, heartfelt, sincere, unqualified, unreserved, unstinting, zealous; cordial, generous, hearty, warm.

wholesome
adj lit: healthful, nourishing, nutritious; beneficial, hygienic; *fig*: clean, decent, edifying, good, moral, nice, respectable, uplifting, virtuous.

wholly
adv lit: all, altogether, completely, entirely, fully, thoroughly, totally, utterly; unreservedly, unstintingly.

whoop
n lit: cry, halloo, holler, hooray, hoot, hurrah, screech, yell; war cry; gasp, wheeze.
vb lit: cheer, halloo, holler, hoot, screech, yell, yip; gasp, wheeze.

whore
n lit: harlot, loose woman, strumpet, trollop; call girl, courtesan, lady of the night; hooker, hustler, prostitute, slag, slut, streetwalker, tart, tramp.
vb lit: be promiscuous, fornicate, sleep around, womanize; be a prostitute, be on the game, sell one's body, solicit, walk the streets.

wicked
adj lit: bad, evil, impious, iniquitous, irreligious, sinful, ungodly, wrong; amoral, blackhearted, cruel, devilish, fiendish, inhuman, malevolent, malicious, malign, satanic, spiteful, vicious; abandoned, corrupt, debased, depraved, heinous, immoral, nefarious, villainous; *fig*: arch, impish, incorrigible, mischievous, naughty, roguish, sly.

wide
adj lit: ample, broad, expansive, extensive, great, large, thick, vast; dilated, distended, outspread, outstretched; capacious, commodious, full, loose, roomy, spacious; comprehensive, encyclopaedic, sweeping; badly-aimed, inaccurate, off-target; *spec*: protein-reduced (animal feed).

adv lit: as much as possible, fully; distantly, far, expansively, extensively, remotely; aside, astray, inaccurately, off, off-target.

widen
vb lit: broaden, enlarge, expand, spread, stretch; dilate, flare, open, throw open; generalize, popularize; bulk up, inflate, pad out.

widespread
adj lit: extensive, outstretched; far-flung, scattered; common, general, popular, prevalent, rife, sweeping, ubiquitous, universal, wholesale.

width
n lit: breadth, bulk, compass, diameter, girth, span, thickness; extent, reach; depth, latitude, range, scope, sweep.

wield
vb lit: apply, control, employ, exercise, handle, have at one's disposal, maintain, make use of, ply, put to use, use, utilize; brandish, flourish, hold, retain.

wife
n lit: bride, partner, spouse, woman; better half, little woman, old girl, old lady, old woman, missus, trouble and strife.

wild
n lit: natural habitat; state of nature; backwoods, desert, outback, vastness, veldt, wasteland.
adj lit: desert, desolate, empty, natural, uncivilized, uncultivated, uninhabited, unpopulated, virgin, waste; feral, unbroken, undomesticated, untamed; barbarous, brutish, primitive, rude; boisterous, disorderly, lawless, noisy, passionate, riotous, rowdy, turbulent, unbridled, uncontrolled, undisciplined, ungovernable, unmanageable, unruly, violent, wayward; berserk, crazed, demented, distracted, frenzied, hysterical, incoherent, irrational, mad, maniacal, possessed, rabid, raving; extravagant, fantastic, impracticable, irresponsible, madcap, preposterous, rash, reckless, unreasoned; dishevelled, scruffy, tousled, unkempt, windblown, windswept; blustery, choppy, ferocious, fierce, howling, intense, raging, rough, tempestuous; avid, batty, crazy, eager, enthusiastic, excited, fanatical, nuts,

potty; *spec*: arbitrary, unassigned, unlimited (playing-card).
adv lit: freely, unchecked, unrestrainedly.

wilderness
n lit: jungle, wasteland, wilds; desert, desolation, waste; *fig*: bewildering mass, confusion, jumble, maze, tangle.

wilful
adj lit: conscious, deliberate, intentional, volitional, voluntary; determined, headstrong, intransigent, mulish, obdurate, obstinate, pig-headed, single-minded, stubborn, uncompromising; intractable, perverse, refractory, unmanageable.

will
n lit: volition; choice, decision, discretion; desire, inclination, preference, wish; intention, mind, purpose, resolve; attitude, disposition, feeling; *spec*: last wishes, testament.
vb lit: aim to, be going to, intend to, mean to; be determined to, be resolved to; choose, elect, opt, prefer, want, wish; command, desire, determine, direct, ordain; bequeath, endow, hand on, leave, pass on.

willing
adj lit: agreeable, amenable, content, disposed, game, prepared, ready; eager, enthusiastic, glad, happy, keen, pleased; voluntary.

willingly
adv lit: by choice, freely, readily, voluntarily; eagerly, enthusiastically, gladly, happily, with pleasure.

willpower
n lit: determination, strength of purpose, resolution, resolve, single-mindedness; self-control, self-discipline.

wilt
vb lit: become limp, droop, sag; dry up, shrivel, wither; *fig*: dwindle, fade, flag, wane; falter, waver, weaken.

wily
adj lit: beguiling, cunning, duplicitous, fly, foxy, sly, tricky, underhand; artful, canny, crafty, devious, sharp, shrewd.

win
n lit: success, triumph, victory.
vb lit: be victorious, come first, prevail, succeed, triumph; attain, earn, gain, make, net, reach, secure; achieve, get,

obtain, receive; charm, convert, induce, persuade; *spec*: mine (coal or ore).

wince
n lit: flinch, shiver, shudder, start.
vb lit: blanch, blench, flinch, quail, recoil, shiver, shrink, shudder, start back.

wind
n lit: air, blow, breeze, draught, gale, gust; breath, puff; respiration; flatulence, flatus, gas; scent, smell; *fig*: blather, bluster, empty talk, hot air; clue, hint, inkling, intimation, rumour, suggestion, whisper; near future, offing, pipeline; *spec*: brass and woodwind (in an orchestra).
vb lit: have the breath knocked out of, puff out; scent, smell, sniff; blow, sound.

wind
n lit: angle, bend, corner, curve, meander, spiral, turn, twist, wiggle.
vb lit: bend, curve, meander, snake, spiral, turn, twist, wiggle, worm, writhe; coil, curl, encircle, loop, spiral, twine (around), twist, wreathe (around); fold (around), wrap (around); key, set; roll into a ball; reel (in), winch; *fig*: excite, make tense.

windfall
n lit: bonus, find, manna from heaven, piece of good fortune, stroke of luck; godsend, lucky break.

winding
adj (pr.pt) lit: circuitous, convoluted, crooked, curling, helical, looping, meandering, roundabout, serpentine, sinuous, spiral, tortuous, twisting.

wind up
vb lit: reel in, winch; key, re-key, reset, set; *fig*: excite, make nervous, make tense, provoke, tease, work up; be left, end up, finish up; close down, conclude, discontinue, end, finalize, finish, liquidate, put in the hands of a receiver, terminate, wrap up; cease, come to an end, halt, shut up shop, stop.

winning
adj (pr.pt) lit: conquering, successful, triumphant, unbeaten, victorious; *fig*: alluring, attractive, bonny, captivating, charming, disarming, enchanting, engaging, fascinating, fetching, pleasing, sweet, taking; influential, persuasive.

winnings

n lit: gains, haul, proceeds, profits, takings; booty, loot, plunder, prize, spoils.

winnow

vb lit: blow off, fan off, separate the wheat from the chaff, sift; *fig*: diffuse, divide, screen, separate, sort out; flutter, waft away.

wintry

adj lit: arctic, bleak, chilly, cold, dark, freezing, frosty, icy, piercing, raw, snowy; *fig*: distant, frozen, unfriendly.

wipe

n lit: brush, rub, swab; lick.
vb lit: brush, mop, rub, sponge, swab; clean (off), erase, expunge; dry; *fig*: snuff (out), stamp (out); *spec*: solder.

wiry

adj lit: bristly, kinky, spiky, stiff; lean, lithe, sinewy, sparc.

wisdom

n lit: acumen, discernment, discrimination, enlightenment, insight, judgement, knowledge, learning, penetration, percipience, prudence, sagacity, sense, understanding.

wise

adj lit: discerning, discriminating, enlightened, erudite, knowledgeable, learned, penetrating, percipient, sagacious, sage, understanding; judicious, politic, prudent, sensible, shrewd; aware, conscious, informed; clever, intelligent.

wish

n lit: aspiration, hankering, hope, inclination; desire, longing, want, yearning; whim, will; bidding, entreaty, request.
vb lit: hanker, hope; crave (for), desire, long, want, yearn; bid, express a hope (for, to); will; *fig*: foist (on), pass (on).

wishful

adj lit: hopeful, optimistic; ambitious, avid, desirous, eager, keen, longing, wanting, yearning.

wistful

adj lit: dreamy, hopeful, longing, wishful, yearning; contemplative, meditative, musing, pensive, reflective, thoughtful; disconsolate, forlorn, mournful.

wit

n lit: acumen, comprehension, discernment, intelligence, judgement, perception, penetration, percipience, understanding, wisdom; ingenuity, practicality, sense; humour, quips, repartee, sense of humour, wordplay; comedian, humorist, punster, wag.

witchcraft

n lit: black arts, magic, sorcery, spells; enchantment, supernatural power.

withdraw

vb lit: depart, fall back, go away, leave, retire, retreat; resign, scratch; disengage, draw back, pull out; debit, draw out, extract, remove, take out; recall, retract, take back, unsay.

withdrawal

n lit: departure, exodus, going, leaving, resignation, retirement, retreat; disengagement, separation; extraction, pulling out, removal; recall, retraction, revocation; *spec*: deprivation (of drugs).

withdrawn

adj (pa.pt) lit: discontinued, suspended, taken out of service; *fig*: detached, distant, introverted, uncommunicative; autistic; quiet, reserved, retiring, shy, taciturn, unforthcoming; isolated, remote, secluded, solitary.

wither

vb lit: decay, desiccate, droop, dry out, fade, shrink, shrivel, waste, wilt; blast, blight, wizen; *fig*: decline, languish; abash, humble, humiliate, mortify, shame; crush, devastate, scorch, sear.

withering

adj (pr.pt) lit: blasting, blighting, crushing, devastating, scorching, searing, trenchant; deadly, lethal, murderous; *fig*: humiliating, mortifying, scornful, shaming.

withhold

vb lit: detain, hold back, keep back, reserve, restrain, retain, sit on; deduct, keep; deny, repress, suppress; forbear (from), refrain (from).

within

adv lit: in, inside; inwardly; indoors.
prp lit: in, inside; to the nearest; closer than, less than.

without

adv lit: outside; outwardly.

prp lit: free from, lacking, not having, with no; failing, missing, neglecting; beyond, outside.
cnj lit: except, unless.

withstand
vb lit: hold out against, remain firm against, stand fast against, take; bear, cope with, endure, put up with, tolerate, weather.

witness
n lit: beholder, bystander, onlooker; spectator, viewer, watcher; deponent, testifier; corroboration, evidence, testimony, verification.
vb lit: behold, look on at, observe, see, view, watch; attest to, corroborate, depone, give evidence, testify, verify; authenticate, countersign, endorse.

wits
n lit: acumen, brains, intelligence, percipience; ingenuity, practicality, sense; consciousness, faculties, senses.

witticism
n lit: bon mot, pun, quip, riposte.

witty
adj lit: ingenious, lively, original, pointed, topical, waggish; clever; amusing, droll, funny.

wizard
n lit: enchanter, magician, magus, male witch, sorcerer, warlock; shaman, thaumaturge; adept, expert, maestro, master, virtuoso, whiz.
adj lit: beezer, dandy, jolly good, spiffing, splendid, tophole.

woe
n lit: anguish, dejection, depression, distress, gloom, grief, heartbreak, melancholy, misery, sorrow, suffering, tribulation, unhappiness, wretchedness; adversity, burden, hardship, misfortune, trial.

woeful
adj lit: anguished, dejected, depressed, disconsolate, doleful, gloomy, melancholy, miserable, mournful, plaintive, sorrowful, tragic, unhappy, wretched; appalling, awful, deplorable, dreadful, pitiful, shocking, sorry, terrible.

wolf
n lit: hunter, wild dog; *fig*: killer, pirate, predator, shark; devil, fiend; Casanova, Don Juan, lady-killer, Lothario,

philanderer, seducer, womanizer; *spec*: dissonance (in musical sound).
vb lit: bolt, gobble, pack away, scoff, stuff.

woman
n lit: bride, lady, mistress, wife; female, girl, lass, lassie, maiden, miss; bird, chick, dame, doll, gal, girlfriend; char, domestic, female servant, housekeeper, maid, maidservant.

womanly
adj lit: female, feminine; matronly, motherly, tender; buxom, curvaceous, pneumatic; elegant, ladylike; effeminate.

wonder
n lit: curiosity, marvel, miracle, phenomenon, prodigy, rarity, spectacle; admiration, awe, fascination.
vb lit: be curious, be inquisitive, inquire, query, question; conjecture, speculate, theorize, think; meditate, ponder, puzzle; be amazed, be awed, be fascinated, be flabbergasted, boggle, marvel.

wonderful
adj lit: awesome, incredible, magnificent, marvellous, miraculous, outstanding, phenomenal, remarkable, staggering, superb; brilliant, excellent, fantastic, great, magnificent, sensational, stupendous, super, terrific, tremendous.

wonted
adj lit: accustomed, customary, familiar, habitual, normal, regular, usual.

woo
vb lit: court, pay one's addresses to, press one's suit with; *fig*: chase, cultivate, pursue, seek.

wood
n lit: xylem; forest, trees; coppice, copse, grove; planking, timber; branches, logs; *fig*: barrel, cask, keg; *spec*: bowl (in the game of bowls); club (in golf).

wooden
adj lit: ligneous, log, planking, slatted, timber; *fig*: awkward, clumsy, gawky, inelegant, rigid, stiff, ungainly; inflexible, obstinate, unbending, unyielding; blank, deadpan, emotionless, expressionless, unemotional, unresponsive; dull, muffled.

woods
n lit: forest, trees, woodland; coppice, copse, grove; *fig*: danger, insecurity, tribulation.

woolly

n lit: cardigan, jersey, jumper, pullover, sweater.
adj lit: fleecy, flocculent, woollen; hairy, shaggy; *fig*: blurred, cloudy, confused, fuzzy, hazy, indistinct, obscure, vague; rough, uncivilized.

word

n lit: expression, term, vocable; speech, utterance; comment, declaration, remark, statement; chat, colloquy, consultation, conversation, discussion, talk; account, information, intelligence, news; command, go-ahead, green light, order, signal; countersign; decree, edict; assurance, guarantee, oath, pledge, promise, vow; *spec*: unit of meaning (for computers).
vb lit: couch, express, phrase, put, say.

words

n lit: libretto, lyrics; captions, text; altercation, argument, disagreement, dispute, quarrel, row.

wordy

adj lit: garrulous, long-winded, loquacious, prolix, verbose, voluble; discursive, sententious; officious, pompous.

work

n lit: employment, job, occupation, profession; business, craft, line, livelihood, métier, trade; assignment, chore, commission, duty, task, undertaking; achievement, composition, creation, oeuvre, opus, performance, piece, product, production; drudgery, effort, exertion, industry, labour, slog, toil, travail; fortification; *fig*: fuss, trouble; *spec*: froth (in fermentation processes); spin (on a cricket ball).
vb lit: drudge away, labour, slave, slog, sweat, toil, travail; be employed, be in a profession, earn a living, have a job; do enough to be worth, earn; control, direct, drive, handle, manage, move, operate, ply, use, wield; cultivate, farm, till; fashion, form, knead, manipulate, mould, process, shape; accomplish, achieve, carry out, effect, execute, implement, perform; force (in), infiltrate, insinuate, inveigle, worm, wriggle; arrange, contrive, fix, pull off, swing; function, go, run, tick; *spec*: beat to windward (in sailing); ferment.

worker

n lit: employee, hand, labourer, wage-earner; tradesman; mechanic, technician; artisan, craftsman; *spec*: electrotype plate (in printing).

working

n lit: action, functioning, mode of operation, operation, running; dig, excavation, mine, pit, quarry, shaft; *spec*: fermentation.
adj (pr.pt) lit: active, functioning, going, on, operative, running, ticking over; busy, employed, occupied; operational, practical, viable; *spec*: fermenting.

workmanship

n lit: artistry, craft, craftsmanship, expertise, skill.

work out

vb lit: calculate, deduce, find out, puzzle out, solve; add up (to), amount (to), come (to); contrive, devise, evolve, form, formulate; be effective, develop, go, happen, result, turn out; exercise, practise, train.

works

n lit: factory, mill, plant; acts, deeds, doings; compositions, creations, oeuvre, output, pieces, productions, writings; action, guts, insides, machinery, mechanism, moving parts.

work up

vb lit: agitate, arouse, excite, incite, inflame, move, rouse, spur, stir up, wind up; animate, foment, stir; cause, do enough to cause, generate; make nervous, make tense; add to, improve.

world

n lit: earth, planet earth, spaceship earth; cosmos, creation, universe; moon, planet, satellite, star, sun; existence, life, nature; everybody, everyone, humanity, humankind, man, mankind; public at large; *fig*: area, domain, field, province, realm, sphere; age, era.

worldly

adj lit: lay, profane, secular, temporal; carnal, earthly, earthy, fleshly, mundane, physical; experienced, knowing, politic, sophisticated, urbane; cosmopolitan; *fig*: avaricious, grasping, greedy, materialistic, selfish.

worldwide

adj lit: global, universal; international; general, ubiquitous.

worn

adj (pa.pt) lit: frayed, ragged, tattered, threadbare; *fig*: drawn, haggard, lined; fatigued, spent, tired, wearied; hackneyed, trite.

worn out

adj lit: frayed, ragged, tattered, threadbare; broken down, clapped out, decrepit, run down, used up; *fig*: all in, dead on one's feet, dog-tired, done in, exhausted, knackered, played out, shattered, tired out.

worried

adj (pa.pt) lit: anxious, apprehensive, bothered, concerned, nervous, perturbed, troubled, uneasy; afraid, fearful, fretful, frightened.

worry

n lit: anxiety, apprehension, care, concern, misgiving, perturbation, unease; pest, plague, problem, trial, trouble.
vb lit: agonize, be anxious, be apprehensive, be concerned, be nervous, be perturbed, be uneasy, brood; be afraid, be fearful, be fretful, be frightened, fear, fret; annoy, badger, bother, distress, disturb, harass, harry, hassle, hector, importune, perturb, pester, plague, tease, unsettle, upset; attack, bite, savage.

worse

adj lit: less well, more ill; less good, more evil; more harmful, more painful, more unfavourable, more unpleasant; more incorrect; more ill-advised, more unsuitable; inferior, of lower quality, worth less; less fortunate.
adv lit: more severely; more evilly; more harmfully, more painfully, more unfavourably, more unpleasantly; more incorrectly; more ill-advisedly, more unsuitably.

worship

n lit: devotion, glorification, homage, honour, praise, prayers; adoration, adulation, love; reverence.
vb lit: glorify, honour, laud, praise, pray to, venerate; abase oneself to, make oblation to, prostrate oneself before, sacrifice to; attend church, go to the mosque, go to the synagogue, participate in a service, praise God, praise the Lord, say devotions; adore, adulate, love; deify, idolize, put on a pedestal.

worst

n lit: least well, most ill; least good, most evil; most harmful, most painful, most unfavourable, most unpleasant; most incorrect, most ill-advised, most unsuitable; most inferior.
vb lit: beat, best, conquer, defeat, gain an advantage over, get the better of, master, overcome, overpower, vanquish.
adj lit: least well, most ill; least good, most evil; most harmful, most painful, most unfavourable, most unpleasant; most incorrect, most ill-advised, most unsuitable; most inferior, of the lowest quality; least fortunate.
adv lit: most severely; most evilly; most harmfully, most painfully, most unfavourably, most unpleasantly; most incorrectly, most ill-advisedly, most unsuitably.

worth

n lit: benefit, usefulness, utility, value; importance, quality; excellence, goodness, merit, virtue; cost, price, valuation.
adj lit: deserving of, meriting, meritorious of; of a value of; at a cost of, at a price of, valued at.

worthless

adj lit: futile, ineffectual, of no use, pointless, unavailing; insignificant, paltry, rubbishy, trashy, trifling, trivial, unimportant, valueless; unusable, useless; contemptible, despicable, ignoble.

worthwhile

adj lit: constructive, gainful, good, meaningful, not a waste of time, positive, significant, usable; beneficial, helpful, potentially profitable, productive, useful, valuable.

worthy

n lit: dignitary, luminary, notable, personage; character; celebrity.
adj lit: deserving (of), meritorious (of); admirable, commendable, creditable, estimable, honourable, laudable, praiseworthy; decent, respectable, upright, virtuous.

wound

n lit: abrasion, cut, gash, graze, incision, injury, laceration, lesion, scrape, slash; *fig*: hurt, offence, shock, slight, sting, trauma.

vb *lit*: cut, gash, graze, injure, lacerate, pierce, scrape, slash, wing; damage, harm, hurt; *fig*: cut to the quick, grieve, mortify, offend, pain, shock.

adj *(pa.pt)* *lit*: coiled, curled, looped, spiralled, turned (around), twined, twisted; folded (around), wrapped (around); keyed up, set up; *fig*: excited, nervous, tense.

wrangle

n *lit*: altercation, argument, disagreement, dispute, quarrel, row, squabble, tiff; affray, argy-bargy, barney, brawl, clash, dust-up, punch-up, set-to, shoving-match.

vb *lit*: argue, bicker, disagree, dispute, fall out, have words, quarrel, row, squabble; brawl, clash, fight, scrap; *spec*: herd, tend (horses or cattle).

wrap

n *lit*: scarf, shawl, stole; fur; cape, cloak, mantle.

vb *lit*: cloak, cover, encase, enclose, enfold, envelop, sheathe, shroud, surround, swathe; bind, pack, package, parcel up, roll up.

wrath

n *lit*: choler, ire, passion, temper; anger, fury, rage.

wrathful

adj *lit*: choleric; angry, enraged, furious, incensed, infuriated, raging; resentful.

wreathed

adj *(pa.pt)* *lit*: adorned, crowned, encircled, entwined, enveloped, festooned, surrounded; *fig*: covered; creased, lined.

wreck

n *lit*: hulk, sunken vessel; derelict, empty shell, husk, skeleton; destruction, ruin; *fig*: confounding, devastation, disruption, spoiling, undoing.

vb *lit*: lure on to the rocks, run aground, strand; break up, demolish, destroy, ravage, ruin, shatter, smash, spoil.

wreckage

n *lit*: bits, debris, flotsam, fragments, pieces, remains, rubble, ruin; derelict, empty shell, hulk, husk, skeleton.

wrench

n *lit*: heave, jerk, pull, rip, tug, twist, yank; rick, sprain, strain; adjustable spanner, spanner; *fig*: heartache, pain, shock, upheaval, uprooting.

vb *lit*: force, heave, jerk, pull, rip, tear, tug, twist, wrest, yank; rick, sprain, strain.

wrestle

vb *lit*: grapple, scrum, scuffle; fight, struggle (with); *fig*: contend (with), strive (with); labour, toil.

wretch

n *lit*: miserable creature, pathetic creature, poor thing, unfortunate; outcast, vagabond, worm; blackguard, miscreant, scoundrel, villain.

wretched

adj *lit*: brokenhearted, dejected, disconsolate, doleful, forlorn, gloomy, hopeless, miserable, pitiable, sorry, unhappy, woebegone, woeful; abject, hapless, pitiful, poor, unfortunate; contemptible, despicable, low, mean, shabby, shameful, worthless.

wriggle

n *lit*: squirm, turn, twist, waggle, wiggle; jerk, jiggle, shake, shiver, shudder, spasm; oscillation, S-bend, zigzag.

vb *lit*: snake, squirm, twist and turn, wiggle, worm, writhe; crawl on one's stomach; *fig*: dodge (out of), get (out of), sneak (out of), talk one's way (out of).

wring

vb *lit*: screw, squeeze, twist, wrench; dry, put through the mangle; extract (from), force (from), wrest (from); *fig*: coerce (from), extort (from); pain, pierce, rack, rend, tear at, wound; *spec*: clasp (hands) firmly, shake (hands) warmly.

wrinkle

n *lit*: corrugation, crease, crinkle, crow's foot, fold, furrow, line, pucker, ridge; *fig*: device, dodge, easy method, gimmick, ploy, short cut, technique, trick; hint, tip; difficulty, problem.

vb *lit*: corrugate, crease, crinkle, crumple, fold, furrow, line, ruck, ruckle, rumple.

write

vb *lit*: inscribe, pen, put down, scribble, set down; author, compose, publish; draft, draw up, jot down, record, take down, transcribe; letter, print, spell; correspond, send a note; endorse, sign; *fig*: display, exhibit, show.

write off

vb *lit*: give up as beyond recovery; disregard, forget about; *fig*: cancel, shelve; crash, damage irreparably, demolish, destroy, smash up, total, wreck.

writer
n lit: author, penpusher, scribbler, wordsmith; columnist, hack, journalist, scribe; essayist, novelist, playwright, poet; littérateur, man of letters; *spec*: lawyer (in Scotland).

writing
n lit: characters, glyphs, hieroglyphs, ideograms, letters, script, symbols; calligraphy, hand, lettering, scrawl, scribble; print, type; belles-lettres, literature; book, publication, work; scripture; authorship, composition, literary style; compilation, keying, penning, putting together, setting down, typing.

wrong
n lit: injury, misdeed, offence; evil, sin, sinfulness, transgression, wickedness; grievance, injustice, trespass.

vb lit: aggrieve, harm, ill-treat, ill-use, injure, offend, oppress; be evil to, sin against; deflower, seduce; cheat, defraud, do out of a right; calumniate, malign; misrepresent.

adj lit: erroneous, fallacious, false, inaccurate, incorrect, mistaken, untrue; bad, dishonourable, evil, immoral, improper, iniquitous, reprehensible, sinful, unethical, unjust, wicked; criminal, crooked, dishonest, felonious, illegal, illicit, unlawful; inappropriate, inapt, infelicitous, unsuitable; amiss, askew, astray, awry, not right; defective, faulty, out of order; *spec*: inner, reverse, under (side, surface).

adv lit: amiss, astray, awry, badly, inaccurately; erroneously, incorrectly, mistakenly.

wry
adj lit: askew, aslant, twisted; contorted, crooked, uneven; dry, ironic, sardonic; distorted, perverse.

X

xenophobic
adj lit: racialist, racist; chauvinist; insular,
isolationist.

Xerox
n lit: copy, facsimile, photocopy,
reproduction.

vb lit: copy, photocopy, reproduce.

xyloid
adj lit: ligneous, woody; pithy, wood-like.

Y

yacht
n lit: ketch, sailing-boat, sailing-dinghy, skiff, smack; clipper, schooner, yawl; motor launch, pleasure-boat; luxury cruiser; ship.

yap
vb lit: bark, snap, yelp, yip; *fig*: chatter, gabble, jabber, prattle, rabbit, yak.

yardstick
n lit: benchmark, criterion, standard, touchstone; gauge, measure.

yarn
n lit: filament, fibre, strand, string, thread; *fig*: fairy tale, fisherman's tale, narration, rigmarole, story, tale, tall story.
vb lit: tell stories, tell tall tales.

yawning
adj (pr.pt) lit: drowsy, falling asleep; *fig*: agape, bottomless, cavernous, deep, fathomless, gaping, open, wide-open.

yearly
adj lit: annual, once-a-year; annual, 365-day, year-long; annual, for one year, per annum, year's.
adv lit: annually, once a year; annually, for one year at a time.

yearn
vb lit: ache, crave, hanker, hunger, long, lust, pant, pine, thirst, wish.

yearning
n lit: aching, craving, desire, hunger, longing, lust, thirst, wish.

yeast
n lit: fermenting agent, leaven, raising agent; *fig*: aerator, catalyst.
vb lit: ferment, leaven, raise; *fig*: aerate, bubble, foam, froth.

yell
n lit: cry, holler, howl, scream, screech, shout, shriek; bellow, roar, wail, whoop.
vb lit: cry, holler, howl, scream, screech, shout, shriek; bawl, bellow, roar, wail, whoop; clamour, halloo.

yellow
adj lit: buttercup, canary, gold, golden, honey-coloured, lemon, ochre, primrose, saffron, sandy, sulphur; Far Eastern; jaundiced, sallow; *fig*: chicken, cowardly, craven, gutless, timid.

yes
adv lit: affirmative, all right, okay, roger; certainly, definitely, positively, surely; indeed so, quite so, really, that's true; affirmatively; furthermore, moreover.

yes-man
n lit: bootlicker, crawler, lackey, sycophant, toady; lapdog, minion, serf, thrall, underling.

yet
adv lit: by now, hitherto, so far, thus far, till now, to date, until now, up to now; already, now, so soon; even, still; additionally, besides, further, to boot.
cnj lit: all the same, but, however, nevertheless, nonetheless.

yield
n lit: crop, harvest, produce; output, product; earnings, gain, income, profit, return, revenue, takings.
vb lit: afford, bear, bring in, deliver, furnish, give, grant, produce, provide, render, supply; earn, generate, net, pay, return; accede, acquiesce, back down, bow, capitulate, cede, comply, give in, give up, relinquish, resign, submit, surrender; admit, concede, give way; bend, be pliant, flex, loosen, slacken.

yielding
adj (pr.pt) lit: accommodating, acquiescent, complacent, compliant, docile, malleable, submissive, tractable; elastic, flexible, plastic, pliable, soft, spongy, springy.

yob
n lit: bully, delinquent, hooligan, layabout, lout, ruffian, thug, tough, troublemaker, vandal, yobbo.

yoke
n lit: coupling, frame, harness; crossbar, cross-piece; *fig*: bond, link, tie; burden,

oppression; bondage, repression, serfdom, servitude, slavery; *spec*: pair (of oxen).

vb lit: couple, harness, hitch up; *fig*: attach, bracket, connect, join, link, tie, unite; oppress; enslave, set to work.

yokel
n lit: bumpkin, hick, peasant, rustic; countryman, villager.

young
n lit: babes, children, girls and boys, juveniles, kids, youth; babies, brood, cubs, infants, issue, litter, offspring, pups, progeny, sons and daughters.
adj lit: adolescent, growing, immature, infant, junior, pubescent; coltish, juvenile, youthful; *fig*: fledgling, new, recently-established; green, inexperienced, raw.

youngster
n lit: adolescent, boy, child, cub, gamin, gamine, girl, kid, lad, lassie, minor, nipper, pup, teenager, urchin, younker, youth; *spec*: midshipman.

youth
n lit: adolescence, boyhood, girlhood, immaturity, schooldays, teens; heyday, prime; boy, lad, stripling, teenager, youngster; teenagers, young, young generation, young people; juvenility, youthfulness.

Yule
n lit: Christmastide, festive season, Xmas; midwinter, winter solstice.

yuppies
n lit: bourgeoisie, intelligentsia, managerial types, professional classes, salaried personnel, self-employed, white-collar workers.

Z

zany
n lit: buffoon, clown, jester, joker; fool, simpleton.
adj lit: clownish, crazy, frenetic, hilarious, idiotic, mad, outrageous.

zap
n lit: force, pep, potency, power, strength, vitality, zip.
vb lit: blast, blow up, explode, gun down, shoot; destroy, hit, kill, strike; dart, dash, hurtle, race, speed, streak, zoom.

zeal
n lit: ardour, fanaticism, fervour, militancy, passion, readiness, spirit, verve; commitment, dedication, devotion, earnestness, enthusiasm, keenness.

zealot
n lit: extremist, fanatic, militant, partisan; buff, enthusiast, fiend, maniac.

zealous
adj lit: ardent, burning, fanatical, fervent, impassioned, militant, passionate, rabid, spirited; avid, committed, dedicated, devoted, earnest, enthusiastic, keen, unreserved, unstinting; card-carrying.

zenith
n fig: apex, height, peak, pinnacle, summit, top, vertex; acme, climax, culmination, maximum.

zero
n lit: cipher, nil, nothing, nought, o; lowest point, minimum, nadir, rock bottom; least permissible.
vb lit: calibrate; home (in on), target (in on).

zest
n lit: citrus peel; flavour, piquancy, pungency, savour, tang, taste; *fig*: excitement, spice, spirit, zeal, zing; appetite, enjoyment, enthusiasm, gusto, relish; charm, interest.

zip
n lit: brio, drive, energy, life, liveliness, pep, spirit, verve, vigour, vim, vitality, zest, zing; zip-fastener.
vb lit: dart, dash, hurtle, race, shoot, speed, streak, tear, whiz, zoom; do (up), fasten, undo, unfasten.

zither
n lit: autoharp; cimbalom, dulcimer.

zombie
n lit: dybbuk, reanimated corpse; *fig*: idiot, imbecile, moron; plodder, slowcoach.

zone
n lit: area, district, region; band, belt, section, sector; field, sphere.
vb lit: divide into areas, parcel out, partition, segment, section; encircle.

zucchini
n lit: courgette, marrow, squash; gourd.

Index

The index is designed to enable a reader to find synonyms of many more words than are presented alphabetically as the main entries in the first part of this book.

Indexed words refer to the headword or headwords under which they appear. By following this reference, a collection of other related synonyms will be found.

A

about: concerning, ready, regarding, round, towards
about the house: household
about-turn: switch
above: beyond, former, over, preceding
above all: primarily
above board: fair, straight
above-mentioned: former
abrade: bark, fret, grate, graze, rag, rasp, rub, scour, scrape, scuff, skin, wear
abrade (away): eat
abraded: bare, frayed, moth-eaten, ragged, raw, seedy
abrasion: brush, erosion, friction, gall, graze, lesion, scrape, scratch, wear, wound
abridge: digest, condense, mutilate, paraphrase, simplify
abridged: cut, short
abridgement: paraphrase, summary
abroad: away, overseas
abrogate: cancel, negate, nullify, repeal, revoke
abrogation: repeal
abrupt: bluff, brusque, curt, precipitate, precipitous, quick, rude, sharp, sheer, short, snap, steep, sudden, unexpected
abruptly: bang, quickly, sharp, sharply, short, shortly
abscess: boil, gall, pustule, sore
abscond: desert, flee, make off, run
absconder: deserter, fugitive, runner
absconding: desertion
absence: defect, deficiency, disappearance, failure, lack, void, want
absent: away, dreamy, gone, lacking, missing, off, out
absent-minded:

careless, forgetful, inattentive, preoccupied
absent-mindedness: preoccupation
absolute: complete, consummate, dead, flat, great, implicit, outright, peremptory, perfect, positive, pure, rank, real, right, secure, sheer, sovereign, strict, utter
absolutely: bang, completely, flat, flatly, fully, just, naturally, outright, positively, quite, really, right, unreservedly, utterly
absolute ruler: despot, dictator
absolution: exemption, forgiveness, pardon, release
absolve: clear, except, forgive, let off, pardon, purge, purify, quit, redeem, release, vindicate
absolved: quit
absolving: except
absorb: assimilate, blot, consume, digest, drink, grip, incorporate, integrate, interest, involve, mop, retain, soak, swallow, take in
absorbed: bemused, deep, intent, preoccupied, rapt
absorb (in): immerse
absorbing: gripping, interesting, concentration, digestion
absorption: preoccupation
abstain: fast
abstainer: ascetic
abstain from: forbear, help, resist, refrain, renounce
abstemious: austere, spartan
abstemiousness: austerity
abstinence: fast, forbearance, sobriety, temperance
abstinent: ascetic, continent, sober, temperate
abstract: digest,

extract, notional, paraphrase, remove, speculative, summary, take, unworldly
abstracted: dreamy, faraway, lackadaisical, lost
abstraction: oblivion, preoccupation
abstruse: deep, obscure, opaque, profound
abstruseness: obscurity
absurd: comical, crazy, farcical, foolish, irrational, ludicrous, nonsensical, preposterous, priceless, ridiculous, senseless, silly, tall
absurdity: farce, folly, joke, lunacy, nonsense, stupidity
abundance: lot, plenty, profusion, wealth
abundant: bumper, considerable, copious, fertile, flush, fruitful, full, generous, heavy, lavish, liberal, lush, luxuriant, manifold, much, numerous, opulent, pregnant, profuse, prolific, rank, rich
abundantly: freely, fully, heavily, well
abuse: blast, calumny, imprecation, insult, invective, jeering, maltreat, manhandle, maul, molest, murder, opprobrium, outrage, profane, rape, slang, vilification, violate, violation
abusive: impolite, jeering, nasty, offensive, profane, rank, rude, vituperative
abut: join, march, neighbour
abutment: buttress
abysmal: dreadful, pathetic
abyss: chasm, drop, hell, pit
abyssal: deep, profound
academic: bookish,

hypothetical, intellectual, pure, scholar, speculative
academy: college, institute, school, seminary
accede: concur, consent, kowtow, yield
accede to: assent, grant
accedence: capitulation
accelerate: gun, hasten, hurry, precipitate, quicken, throttle
accelerating: progressive
acceleration: burst, speed, throttle
accelerator: gun, throttle
accent: beat, emphasize, highlight, pronounce, rhythm, stress, voice
accented: broad, long
accentuate: emphasize, highlight, punctuate, stress, underline
accentuation: stress
accept: assume, brook, buy, concede, credit, embrace, have, honour, live, pass, receive, recognize, take, take in, take on, tolerate, wear
acceptable: digestible, good, okay, palatable, reasonable, satisfactory, suitable, tolerable, welcome
acceptance: assent, assumption, confirmation, passage, receipt, reception, vogue
accept back: take back
accepted: axiomatic, common, customary, general, prevalent, proper, standard, understood, unquestioned
accept payment for: sell
accept with pleasure: welcome
access: boot, entrance, entry, hack
accessible: available,

convenient, handy, open, public, receptive
accession: catalogue, coming
accessories: furniture, gear
accessory: assistant, auxiliary, extra, fitting
accident: casualty, chance, collision, crash, luck, misadventure, mishap, smash, spill
accidental: casual, chance, coincidental, contingent, inadvertent, incidental, involuntary, stray, unconscious, unintentional
accidentally: fortuitously, unwittingly
acclaim: clap, commend, credit, eulogize, hail, honour, lionize, ovation, praise, rave
acclaimed: noted
acclamation: ovation, renown
acclamatory: rave
acclimatize (to): attune
acclimatized: habituated
acclivity: bank, rise
accolade: praise
accommodate: contain, harbour, hold, house, humour, integrate, lodge, put up, quarter, receive, seat, suit, take
accommodate (to): tailor
accommodate (with): provide
accommodating: civil, helpful, obliging, yielding
accommodation: convenience, facilities, focus, loan, lodgings, place, quarters, space
accompaniment: backing
accompany: attend, chaperon, conduct, join, see, show, take, walk
accompanying:

attendant, background, incidental, matching, related, supplementary
accomplice: assistant, companion, partner
accomplish: attain, carry out, complete, conclude, consummate, discharge, do, effect, execute, finish, fulfil, hit, manage, perfect, perform, realize, work
accomplished: capable, complete, consummate, good, over, perfect, practical, practised, proficient, ripe, skilful
accomplishment: attainment, discharge, execution, feat, performance, prowess, skill, perfection, scholarship
accord: chorus, coincide, communion, comply, compromise, concert, confer, consort, correspond, give, grant, harmony, keeping, protocol, show, solidarity, understanding, vouchsafe
accordance: keeping, line, obedience
accordant: consistent
according to: by
accordingly: consequently, duly, so, then, therefore, thus
accost: buttonhole, challenge, hail, hold up, mug, proposition, salute, waylay
accouchement: birth
account: behalf, bill, chronicle, consequence, description, explanation, history, log, narrative, news, protocol, record, report, return, sake, score, tale, word, recital, story
account for: explain, rationalize, salve
accountability: liability

accountable: liable, responsible
accountant: cashier
accoutre: clothe, kit, provision, rig
accoutrements: equipment, furniture, gear, kit, outfit, rig, tackle
accredit: assign, delegate, license
accreditation: assignation, assignment, licence
accredited: official
accretion: build-up, gain
accumulate: assemble, collect, compile, concentrate, conglomerate, drift, garner, gather, harvest, keep, mass, mount, multiply, pile, stock, store
accumulation: assembly, bank, build-up, collection, concentration, mass, pile, store
accuracy: faithfulness, neatness, nicety, precision
accurate: careful, close, deadly, factual, faithful, judicious, just, neat, nice, perfect, pithy, precise, proper, realistic, right, rigorous, scrupulous, straight, strict, sure, true
accurately: exactly, literally, right, truly, unerringly, well
accursed: damnable, flaming, satanic
accusation: blame, charge, complaint, indictment, libel
accusatory: incriminatory
accuse: charge, denounce, libel
accuser: litigant
accustom: attune, condition, harden, reconcile
accustomed: familiar, general, habitual, wonted
ace: first-class, master
acerbic: sarcastic, venomous, vitriolic
acerbity: asperity,

venom
ache: hurt, itch, niggle, pain, pang, pine, suffer, yearn
ache (for): bleed, die
achievable: feasible, manageable, practicable
achieve: carry out, complete, consummate, do, effect, finish, fulfil, hit, perform, score, strike, win, work
achieve parity: balance
achievement: attainment, creation, feat, perfection, performance, qualification, stroke, work
aching: painful, tender, yearning
achromatic: neutral
acid: corrosive, cutting, sharp, sour
acidic: fiery, venomous, vitriolic
acidity: bite
acknowledge: avow, confess, grant, honour, mention, nod, own, profess, recognize, reply, salute
acknowledged: known, successful
acknowledgement: credit, concession, confession, mention, nod, profession, reaction, receipt, remark, reply, response, thanks
acme: climax, height, perfection, pinnacle, summit, zenith
acquaint: communicate, introduce
acquaintance: connection, contact, exposure, familiarity, knowledge, neighbour, touch
acquainted: familiar
acquiesce: coincide, comply, concur, consent, kowtow, submit, yield
acquiescence: concurrence, consent, obedience
acquiescent: obedient, passive,

yielding
acquiesce in:
  humour, permit
acquire: assume, buy,
  collect, conquer, find,
  gain, get, have, land,
  obtain, pick up,
  possess, procure,
  purchase, receive,
  secure, take, take on
acquired: derivative,
  found
acquisition:
  assumption, buy,
  conquest, derivation,
  gain, import,
  purchase, find,
  reception
acquisitive:
  avaricious, possessive
acquisitiveness:
  avarice
acquit: clear, conduct,
  discharge, pardon,
  redeem, release
acquittal: discharge,
  pardon, release
acquittance: release
acreage: farm, field,
  tract
acrid: bitter, caustic,
  corrosive, fiery,
  harsh, poignant,
  pungent, sharp
acrimonious: bitter,
  caustic, hard, ill,
  sarcastic, sharp, sour,
  venomous, virulent
acrimony: gall,
  venom
across: beyond,
  straddling, over
across-the-board:
  sweeping
act: behave, conduct,
  deed, do, fact, job,
  law, legislation,
  masquerade, measure,
  operate, perform,
  performance, play,
  render, rite, routine,
  scene, serve, thing,
  turn
act against: oppose
act also (as): double
act as: impersonate
**act as advocate
  (for):** intercede
act as an incentive:
  motivate
act for: substitute
act (for): deputise
act (in): figure
acting: drama,
  performance,
  substitute

action: battle,
  behaviour, case, deed,
  effect, engagement,
  fact, fight, gesture,
  incident, litigation,
  manoeuvre, measure,
  mechanism, move,
  movement, operation,
  performance, plot,
  process, step, suit,
  thing, turn, working,
  works
actionable: illegal
activate: mobilize,
  move, quicken, raise,
  trip, wake
activating: motive
activator: motor
active ingredient:
  principle
active: busy,
  concerned, effective,
  great, healthy, live,
  lively, living, militant,
  nimble, on, operative,
  quick, restless,
  strenuous, vigorous,
  working
activist: fanatic,
  militant
activity: behaviour,
  excitement, exercise,
  function, interest,
  life, movement,
  occupation,
  operation, pursuit,
  walk
act of contrition:
  penance
act of folly:
  indiscretion
act of worship: office
act properly: behave
act the fool: clown
act the part of:
  portray
**act unjustly
  (against):**
  discriminate
act up: misbehave
act upon: obey
actor: artist, player
actors: cast
actress: player
acts: works
actual: authentic,
  concrete, factual,
  faithful, real, rightful,
  tangible
actuality: existence,
  fact, substance, verity
actually: indeed,
  literally, quite, really
actuate: instigate
acuity: sensibility
acumen: insight,

intelligence,
  judgement, sagacity,
  wisdom, wit
acute: excruciating,
  high, intense, keen,
  knowing, penetrating,
  perceptive, piercing,
  poignant, pointed,
  quick, quick-witted,
  ready, sage, serious,
  severe, sharp, strong,
  sore
acutely: badly,
  seriously, sharply,
  very
acuteness: sagacity
ad lib: blind, break,
  hack, impromptu,
  unprepared,
  improvise
adage: proverb,
  saying
Adam's ale: water
adamant: firm, flinty,
  obdurate, rigid
adapt: condition,
  convert, differentiate,
  reorganize, shape,
  square, style, trim
adapt (to): gear, tailor
adaptable:
  compatible, flexible,
  mobile, mutable,
  pliable, universal,
  useful, versatile
adaptation:
  orientation, version
adapted: habituated
adapted form:
  variation
add: augment, boost,
  compound,
  contribute, count,
  figure, incorporate,
  increase, introduce,
  join, make, put on,
  reckon, say, swell, tot,
  total, weight, work up
added: new
added up to: made,
  plus
addendum: insert
addict: fanatic, fiend
addiction: habit
addictive: narcotic
addition:
  contribution,
  enclosure, increase,
  insert, interpolation,
  introduction,
  surcharge
additional: different,
  extra, fresh, further,
  more, new, optional,
  other, second, spare,
  substitute,

supplementary
additionally: beside,
  besides, else, further,
  more, moreover, plus,
  yet
additions: frills
addle: confuse, fuddle
address: dexterity,
  direct, direction,
  greet, hail, lecture,
  nickname, oration,
  salute, sermon, speak,
  speech, style, tact,
  talk
addressee: occupant
adduce: cite, instance,
  quote
adept: capable,
  experienced, good,
  great, handy, master,
  masterly, perfect,
  practical, practised,
  proficient, quick,
  smart, wizard
adeptly: well
adeptness: knack,
  finesse
adequate: capable,
  comfortable,
  commensurate,
  competent, decent,
  due, enough, fair, fit,
  good, okay,
  satisfactory,
  sufficient, tolerable
adequately: enough,
  okay, passably
adhere: cling, hang,
  join, lodge, stick
adherence: keeping
adherent: believer,
  follower, partisan
adherents: faithful,
  following, school
adhere to: hold,
  comply, follow, keep,
  observe, pursue,
  redeem, respect
adhering to: on
adhesion: traction
adhesive: cement,
  glue, paste, plaster,
  sticky, tenacious
adhesiveness: tack,
  tenacity
adhesivity: bond
adieu: farewell
adipose: fat
adjacent: close, near,
  nearby, next
adjoin: border,
  march, meet,
  neighbour, touch
adjoining: beside,
  near, nearby
adjourn: defer, delay,

dissolve, recess, stay, postpone, suspend
adjournment: delay, dissolution, recess, respite
adjudge: judge, rate
adjudicate: decide, judge, referee, rule, umpire
adjudication: ruling, verdict
adjudicator: judge, referee, umpire
adjudicators: jury
adjure: conjure
adjust: attune, calculate, compose, compound, compromise, dispose, fix, gear, key, modify, order, reconcile, rectify, redress, regulate, reorganize, scale, set, settle, slot, suit, tailor, temper, trim
adjustable: flexible
adjustment: compromise, concession, modification, modulation, orientation, regulation, repair
administer: carry on, conduct, deliver, direct, dispense, give, govern, rule, run, superintend, manage, regulate
administration: authority, bureaucracy, cabinet, conduct, direction, executive, government, management, oversight, regime, regulation, rule, supervision, tenure
administrative: judicial
administrator: director, distributor, executive, operator, warden
admirable: fine, good, rare, respectable, splendid, superb, superior, worthy
admiration: compliment, kudos, respect, wonder
admire: rate, respect
admirer: conquest,

gallant, lover, sweetheart
admissible: relevant, right
admission: concession, confession, entry
admit: avow, bear, closet, concede, confess, grant, profess, receive, recognize, take in, yield
admit (to): own
admittance: entrance, entry
admitted: known
admitting that: if
admonish: caution, exhort, lecture
admonition: caution, lecture, lesson
ado: bustle, commotion, excitement, kerfuffle, stir
adolescence: youth
adolescent: boy, girlish, immature, junior, juvenile, young, youngster
adopt: assume, borrow, choose, father, go in for, import, take, take on
adopting: assumption
adoption: import
adorable: lovable
adoration: glory, idolatry, love, praise, worship
adore: bless, glorify, honour, idolize, love, praise, respect, revere, worship
adored: darling, idol, precious
adoring: doting, fond, reverent
adorn: become, deck, garland, garnish, grace, illuminate, illustrate, jewel, ornament, trim, varnish
adorned: gaudy, wreathed
adornment: decoration, garnish, ornament, varnish
adrift: astray, lost
adroit: clever, good, great, handy, neat, slick
adroitness: dexterity, facility, finesse,

knack, neatness
adulate: lionize, love, praise, worship
adulation: idolatry, incense, love, praise, worship
adulator: lover
adult: big, mature, responsible
adulterate: dilute, doctor, load, thin, water, weaken
adulterated: base, bastard, dilute, loaded, thin, watery
adulterous: unfaithful
adulthood: majority, maturity
adumbrate: obscure
advance: boost, bring, development, evolve, forward, further, gain, go, grow, growth, improve, improvement, lend, lift, loan, look up, march, motion, move, passage, payment, pose, prefer, present, produce, progress, promote, propose, put, put up, raise, recommend, rise, speed, submit, walk
advanced: new, progressive, precocious, sophisticated
advanced in years: old
advance (forward): venture
advance guard: scout
advancement: civilization, course, elevation, evolution, lift, preferment, progress, promotion, rise, spread, step
advance(s): overture, pass
advancing: progressive
advantage: beauty, benefit, convenience, fruit, gain, good, initiative, jump, lead, leverage, merit, preference, profit, return, sake, start, use, virtue
advantaged: privileged
advantageous: beneficial, benign,

desirable, favourable, fortunate, fruitful, good, lucrative, productive, profitable, right, salutary, serviceable, useful
advantageously: right
advent: coming, dawn
adventure: episode, experience, quest
adventure story: romance
adventurer: gallant
adventurous: foolhardy, rash
adversary: competitor, enemy, foe, rival, opponent
adverse: bad, contrary, counter, cross, hostile, opposite, repulsive, unfavourable
adversely: counter
adversity: calamity, catastrophe, pressure, reverse, trial, woe
advertise: bill, cry, market, plug, post, proclaim, promote, publicize, publish, push, spread
advertised: vaunted
advertisement: bill, notice, plug, poster, propaganda, puff
advertising: promotion
advice: caution, counsel, information, instruction, news, notice, notification, warning
advisable: reasonable, well
advise: brief, caution, counsel, forewarn, guide, inform, instruct, intimate, notify, post, recommend, suggest, urge, warn
adviser: consultant, counsel, counsellor, instructor
advocacy: promotion
advocate: barrister, champion, counsel, lawyer, move, promote, recommend, solicitor, suggest, support, uphold, urge
advocates: bar
aeon: period

aerate: yeast
aerator: yeast
aerial: pylon
aerofoil: flap
aeronautics: flight
aeroplane: bus, craft,
jet, machine, plane
aerosol: atomizer,
spray
aesthete: artist, poet
aesthetic: artistic,
poetic
aetiology: derivation
afar: away
affable: bland, civil,
cordial, easy,
engaging, folksy,
genial, hearty,
pleasant, sociable,
suave, warm
affair: business,
concern, episode,
experience, function,
happening, interest,
issue, job, liaison,
lookout, matter,
occurrence,
operation, place, ploy,
relationship, subject,
thing, transaction
affect: assume, bear,
concern, get, hit,
infect, influence,
interest, involve,
move, pretend, put
on, sham, stir, sway,
touch
affectation: claptrap,
frills, mannerism,
ostentation, pose,
pretence, pretext,
show
affected: artificial,
camp, fake, fictitious,
grandiose, overcome,
phoney, precious,
scenic, uppish, vain
affecting: assumption,
dramatic, emotive,
heart-rending, heart-
warming, impressive,
interesting, mournful,
moving, pathetic,
poetic, sorrowful
affectingly: piteously
affection:
endearment, feeling,
fondness, friendship,
heart, kindness,
liking, love, regard,
tenderness, warmth
affectionate: cordial,
friendly, kind, sweet,
sympathetic, tender,
warm, warm-hearted
affectionately: kindly

affianced: fiancé
affidavit: testimony
affiliate: attach, band,
join, unite
affiliated: federal,
related
affiliation: coalition,
union
affinity: bond,
communion,
community,
connection, kin,
kinship, penchant,
resemblance,
similarity, sympathy
affirm: aver, back up,
bear out, confess,
contend, declare,
profess, ratify, say,
state, swear, warrant
affirmation:
assurance, claim,
declaration,
profession
affirmative: positive,
yes
affirmatively: yes
affix: attach, connect,
fasten, glue, knit,
paste, pin, stick
afflict: charge,
oppress, pain,
persecute, pinch,
plague, press, rack,
scourge, trouble, visit
afflicted: sore,
sorrowful
affliction: calamity,
care, catastrophe,
complaint, cross,
curse, ill, load,
plague, pressure,
reverse, sorrow, trial
affluence: luxury,
plenty, prosperity,
style, substance,
wealth
affluent: comfortable,
loaded, opulent, rich,
wealthy
afford: bear, lend,
provide, spare, supply,
yield
affray: contest, fight,
fracas, scramble,
scrap, scuffle,
skirmish, unrest,
wrangle
affront: barb,
indignity, insult,
offence, offend,
outrage, pique,
scandalize, slight,
slur, snub
affronting: offensive
aficionado: buff, fan,

freak, lover
afire: flaming
aflame: fiery,
passionate
aforementioned:
same, preceding
aforesaid: former
aforethought:
premeditated
afraid: fearful,
worried
aft: rear
after: behind, past,
since
after dark: night
after hours: late
aftermath: effect,
outcome
afters: dessert
afterwards: behind,
last, later, next,
subsequently, then
Aga: oven
again: back, further,
more
against: counter
against the rules:
foul, unsporting
agape: yawning
age: date, day,
generation, get on,
mellow, period, time,
world
aged: decrepit, elderly
age-group:
generation
ageless: classic,
timeless
agency: bureau,
cause, embassy,
means, medium,
organ, voice
agenda: programme,
schedule
agendum: minute,
memo
agent: bailiff, bearer,
buyer, cause,
delegate, deputy,
factor, means,
minister, nark, officer,
official, operator,
plant, proxy,
representative, scout,
spy, substitute
age-old: old,
traditional
aggrandize: inflate
aggrandizement:
rise
aggravate:
compound, inflame,
intensify, needle,
swell
aggravated:
embittered

aggravating:
inflammatory, plague,
provocative, trying
aggravation: teasing
aggreeable: engaging
aggregate: collect,
conglomerate,
huddle, lump,
quantity, sum, total,
whole
**aggregate (in
mathematics):**
manifold
aggregation:
assembly, bloom,
concentration,
huddle, knot
aggression: fight,
sword
aggressive: black,
forcible, hard-hitting,
macho, militant,
obstreperous,
offensive, pugnacious,
pushy, tough,
unfriendly, vicious,
warlike
aggrieve: hurt, pain,
wrong
aggrieved: hurt, sore
agile: athletic, flexible,
light, limber, lithe,
lively, nimble, nippy,
spry
agitate: boil, churn,
discompose, ferment,
jar, move, perturb,
rouse, ruffle, shake,
shake up, stir, upset,
vex, work up
agitated: distracted,
flustered, hysterical,
jittery, jumpy, mad,
nervous,
overwrought, restless,
rough, simmering,
unsettled, upset
agitatedly: madly
agitating: vexatious
agitation: bustle,
commotion,
convulsion,
disturbance,
excitement, ferment,
flurry, flutter, furore,
heat, hysteria,
kerfuffle, movement,
nervousness, sedition,
sensation, shake, stir,
storm, sweat,
tempest, unrest,
upheaval, whirl
agitator: malcontent
agnomen: handle,
name, nickname
agnostic:

disbelieving, sceptic
ago: back, since
agonize: fret, pain,
rack, sorrow, sweat,
worry
agonizing:
excruciating, painful,
piercing, violent
agony: hell, murder,
pain, torture
agree: assent, comply,
compromise, concur,
consent, contract,
correspond, equal,
equate, fix, get on,
grant, jump, match,
nod, okay, parallel,
resolve, set, settle,
square, submit, suit,
sympathize, tally,
undertake
agreeable:
comfortable,
compatible, content,
cordial, fine, good,
jolly, kindly, nice,
obliging, palatable,
personable, pleasant,
ready, savoury,
smiling, smooth,
suave, sweet,
sympathetic,
temperate, welcome,
willing
agreed upon:
concerted
agreed: set
agreement: assent,
bargain, bond,
communion,
compact,
compromise, concert,
conclusion,
concurrence,
contract,
correspondence, deal,
engagement,
harmony, keeping,
pact, provision,
similarity, stipulation,
sympathy, treaty,
understanding
agriculturalist:
farmer
agronomist: farmer
agronomy: culture
aground: ashore
ahead: before,
forward, on,
precocious
ahead of: before
aid: asset, assist,
assistance, back,
backing, back up,
benefit, cooperate,
facilities, forward,

further, help,
lubricate, profit,
promote, redress,
relief, relieve, second,
support, sustain
aide: assistant,
attendant,
companion, mate,
subordinate
aileron: flap
ailing: bad, infirm,
moribund, poorly,
sick, sickly, unwell,
unwholesome
ailment: complaint,
condition, disease,
illness, indisposition,
sickness, trouble
aim: beam, cause,
design, destination,
direct, drive, end,
fasten, goal, head,
idea, intend, intent,
intention, level, mark,
mean, meaning,
motivation, motive,
object, objective,
point, plan, prize,
propose, purport,
purpose, pursue,
quarry, quest, range,
reason, resolution,
sake, seek, set, target,
tend, turn, way, will
aimless: meaningless,
pointless,
purposeless, random,
vague
aimlessly: blindly,
haphazardly, vaguely
air: aspect,
atmosphere, bearing,
broadcast, cast,
demeanour, face,
feeling, look, manner,
melody, odour,
presence, semblance,
sense, song, spirit,
strain, tone,
undertone, vent,
voice, wind
airbrush: atomizer
air-condition: fan
air conditioner: fan
aircraft: machine,
plane
air current: breeze
air-duct: vent
airiness: atmosphere
airing: constitutional,
jaunt, outing, saunter
air intake: vent
airless: close, stuffy
airlessness: vacuum
airman: pilot
airport: terminal

airs: side, vanity
airship: balloon, ship
air travel: flight
airy: jaunty, light,
superior
aisle: walk
ajar: open
akin: homogeneous,
kin, related
alabaster: white
alacrity: rapidity
alarm: dread, fright,
frighten, monitor,
panic, perturb,
reminder, scare,
terror, warning
alarmed: fearful
alarming: dreadful,
frightening,
portentous, startling
albeit: if, though
album: record
albumen (of an egg):
white
alcohol: drink, liquor
alcoholic (drinks):
hard, drunkard
alcove: bay,
compartment, niche,
nook, recess
alderman: councillor
ale: brew, wallop
alert: attentive,
awake, careful,
cautious, close,
conscious, forewarn,
fresh, live, lively,
lookout, observant,
perceptive, piercing,
prompt, quick, quick-
witted, ready,
receptive, scare,
sharp, warn, warning,
wary, watchful
alertly: warily
alertness: caution
alfresco meal: picnic
alibi: defence
alien: external,
foreign, foreigner,
outsider, remote,
strange, unfamiliar,
unfriendly, unknown,
untried
alienate: divide, sour,
turn off
alienated: embittered,
maladjusted
alienating: divisive
alienation: breach,
break, disaffection,
division, rift
alight: descend,
disembark, get off,
kiss, land, light, live,
perch

alighting: descent
align: commit, dress,
justify, key, line,
order, organize,
range, rank, square
aligned: parallel,
straight
alignment:
justification, order,
organization
alike: equal, equally,
like, same, similar,
uniform
alike as two peas:
identical
alimony: maintenance
alive: live, living,
responsive, sentient,
susceptible, teeming,
vital
**alkali (in
chemistry):** base
**alkaline (in
chemistry):** basic
all: complete, wholly
all at once: bang,
whole
all but: nearly,
virtually
all by oneself:
unaided
all-embracing:
catholic, overall,
sweeping
**all fingers and
thumbs:** impractical
all in: tired, weary,
worn out
all in all: considering
all-inclusive: blanket,
comprehensive,
general
all-out: last-ditch
all over the shop:
disorganized
all right: fair, fine,
middling, okay,
satisfactory, so, well,
yes
all set: prepared
all the same:
however,
nevertheless, yet
all the way: through
all there: rational,
right, sane
all-weather: hardy,
tough
allay: cool, lull,
mollify, quell,
quench, quieten,
smooth, soften, still
allegation: charge,
claim
allege: assert, claim,
maintain, make out,

say
alleged: ostensible, putative, supposed
allegedly: reputedly
allegiance: duty, faith, loyalty, nationalism
allegorical: mythical
allegory: fable, myth, parable
allergic: sensitive
alleviate: comfort, dull, help, lighten, mitigate, mollify, palliate, relieve, remedy, remit, smooth, soften, still
alleviation: comfort, consolation, relief
alley: lane, path, side-street, track, walk
alliance: association, coalition, combination, compact, connection, federation, friendship, league, match, pact, party, treaty, union, wedding
allied: federal, kin, related, relative
allied (to): germane
allocate: assign, attach, budget, partition, place, ration, set, split
allocation: assignation, assignment, budget, distribution, division, dole, grant, lot, measure, partition, portion, quota
allocator: distributor
allot: cast, deal, divide, set, split
allotment: distribution, nursery, plot, ration, share, portion
allow: bear, cede, concede, enable, have, legalize, let, let off, license, permit, recognize, sanction, suffer, tolerate
allowable: on, venial
allowance: commission, concession, grace, grant, latitude, maintenance, margin, pension, portion, quota, ration, remittance, sanction,

share
allowed: free, lawful
alloy: compound
allude: coax, cite, hint, attract, attraction, captivate, charm, decoy, draw, fascination, lure, mention, quote, spell, tempt, temptation
allurement: bait, invitation
alluring: attractive, beguiling, desirable, inviting, lovable, lovely, seductive, winning
allusion: connotation, glance, hint, mention, quotation, quote, reference
allusive: expressive, literary, mythical
alluvium: deposit, ooze
ally: associate, auxiliary, band, colleague, companion, comrade, connect, connection, friend, marry, match, partner, relate, side, unite, wed, weld
alma mater: school
almighty: deity, omnipotent
almost: near, nearly, practically, probably, towards, virtually
alms: dole, donation, hand-out
aloft: high
alone: lonely, separate, sole, solitary, unaided
aloneness: loneliness
along: by, down
alongside: beside, by, near, parallel
aloof: cold, cool, remote, sulky, unbending
aloofness: detachment, disdain, frigidity, reserve
alphabet: language, notation, script
alphabetical list: index
alphabetize: catalogue
alpha wave: brainwave
alpine: mountainous
already: yet
also: beside, besides,

else, further, moreover, so, then
also-ran: loser
altar: sanctuary
alter: change, convert, differentiate, doctor, falsify, juggle, modify, process, rearrange, resolve, reverse, revise, shift, turn, tailor, vary
alterable: mutable
alteration: break, change, innovation, metamorphosis, modification, modulation, mutation, shift, switch, transition, variation, variety
altercation: dispute, fight, hassle, quarrel, row, words, wrangle
altered: new
alternate: change, fluctuate, hover, odd, opposite, rotate, seesaw, stagger, vary
alternation: cycle
alternative: bet, choice, fringe, opposing, option, other, resort, second, secondary, underground, variant
alternatively: instead, otherwise
alternative medicine: therapy
although: if, notwithstanding, though, while
altitude: elevation, height, level
altogether: buff, completely, fully, nude, right, wholly
altruism: generosity, kindness
altruistic: big, generous, philanthropic, selfless, unselfish
always: ever, forever, invariably, universally
amalgam: blend, composite, hybrid
amalgamate: blend, combine, compound, consolidate, fuse, pool, unify, unite
amalgamation: coalition, combination, package, union

amass: assemble, bank, build, bulk, collect, compile, drift, gather, harvest, hoard, lay in, pile, score
amassed: conglomerate
amassing: assembly
amateur: beginner, lay, unskilled
amatory: erotic
amaze: astonish, awe, flabbergast, stagger, stupefy, surprise
amazement: astonishment, surprise
amazing: astonishing, awesome, incredible, knockout, marvellous, portentous, stupendous, uncommon
amazingly: uncommonly
ambassador: diplomat
ambassadorial: diplomatic
ambassador's residence: embassy
ambience: atmosphere, context, nimbus
ambiguity: nebulosity, paradox, doubt, obscurity
ambiguous: deceptive, doubtful, imprecise, misleading, nebulous, obscure
ambit: orbit
ambition: desire, dream, drive, hope, longing, prize, push, target
ambitious: idealistic, officious, pushy, wishful
ambivalent: deceptive, split, undecided
amble: loaf, loiter, lounge, promenade, ramble, saunter, stroll, walk
ambulatory: mobile
ambush: hold up, jump, mug, pounce, raid, trap, wait, waylay
ameliorate: better, help, improve, look up

amelioration: help,
improvement
amenable:
disposable, easy,
flexible, manageable,
obedient,
predisposed,
receptive, willing
amend: better,
improve, rectify,
reform, revise
amends:
compensation, justice,
redress, restitution
amenities: facilities
amiability: kindliness
amiable: bland, easy,
engaging, friendly,
genial, kindly,
lovable, nice,
obliging, personable,
pleasant, sweet,
warm-hearted
amicability: harmony
amicable: friendly,
kind, kindly,
peaceable, peaceful
amiss: wrong
amity: fellowship,
friendship, goodwill,
love, peace
ammunition: fuel
ammunition dump:
magazine
amnesty: grace,
pardon, reprieve
amniotic fluid: water
amok: berserk
amoral: depraved,
unconscionable,
wicked
amorality: depravity
amorous: passionate,
romantic, tender
amorphous:
irregular, nebulous,
shapeless
amount: batch,
charge, count, deal,
dose, load, lot, mass,
matter, measure,
number, quantity,
score, size, sum, total,
volume
amount to: equal,
make, reach, spell,
total, work out
amounted to: made
amour: flame,
intrigue, romance
amphitheatre: circus
amphora: jar
ample: bountiful,
broad, capacious,
comfortable,
considerable, copious,

decent, filling,
generous, good,
handsome, hearty,
liberal, overweight,
plenty, respectable,
rich, roomy, round,
spacious, wide
amplification:
enlargement,
exaggeration, increase
amplify: elaborate,
electrify, exaggerate,
increase, magnify,
pad out
amplitude: capacity,
latitude, magnitude,
measurement,
munificence
amply: fully, well
amputate: cut off,
dock, remove
amputee: cripple
amulet: charm,
talisman
amuse: delight,
divert, interest, play,
please, slay
amused: pleased,
smiling
amusement:
diversion, fun, hobby,
pastime, pleasure,
recreation, relaxation
**amusement
complex:** park
amusement park:
fair
amusing: beguiling,
comical, delightful,
enjoyable, fun, funny,
humorous,
interesting, jocular,
light, rich, witty
an: one
anachronistic:
obsolete
anacrusis: lick
anaemic: livid, pale,
sallow, wan
anaesthesia: narcosis
anaesthetic:
hypnotic, narcotic,
sedative, soporific
anaesthetize: drug,
paralyse, sedate
anaesthetized:
senseless,
unconscious
analgesia: narcosis
analgesic: narcotic,
painkiller
analogous: parallel
analogue: parallel
analogy: comparison,
illustration, parallel,
similarity

analyse: canvass,
criticize, prove,
research, resolve, sift,
study, test
analysis: breakdown,
criticism, diagnosis,
interpretation, logic,
postmortem, profile,
reasoning, research,
review, search, study,
test
analyst: psychiatrist
analytical: critical
anarchic: chaotic,
disruptive, lawless
anarchist:
malcontent, rebel
anarchy: disorder,
licence,
licentiousness,
misrule, riot
anastrophe: inversion
anathema: curse
anathematization:
ban
anathematize: ban,
curse
anatomical: organic,
corporal
ancestor: forebear,
forerunner,
predecessor,
precursor
ancestral home: seat
ancestral: hereditary,
traditional
ancestry: birth,
blood, breeding,
derivation, descent,
extraction, family,
genealogy, origin,
pedigree, strain
anchor: fix, rock, root
anchor man: host
anchorage: berth,
harbour, mooring,
port, road
anchorite: hermit,
ascetic
ancient: elderly,
former, gaffer, old,
past
ancient history: over
anciently: formerly
ancillary: auxiliary,
extra, incidental,
other, side,
subordinate
and: plus
and so: hence
and so on: etcetera
and the rest: etcetera
android: automaton,
machine, robot
anecdotal: narrative
anecdote: tale, story

angel: darling, dear,
guarantor, love,
patron
angelic: celestial,
cherubic, divine,
heavenly, saintly,
seraphic
anger: backlash, bile,
blood, chafe, fury,
incense, nark, offence,
offend, outrage,
passion, rage,
resentment, wrath
angered: stung
angering: offensive
angle: aspect, bend,
cant, corner, crook,
hook, inclination,
incline, kink, light,
position, side, slant,
tack, turn, viewpoint,
wind
**angled groove (in
architecture):** quirk
angled: bent, oblique
angle (for): fish
angry: cross, flaming,
livid, simmering,
sore, wrathful
anguish: distress,
pain, sorrow, torture,
woe
anguished: woeful
angular: gaunt
anima: psyche
animal: beast, bestial,
brute, creature,
monster, organism,
pet, pig, thing
animal doctor: vet
animal surgeon: vet
animate: cartoon,
inform, kindle, light,
live, quicken, revive,
rouse, work up
animated: bright,
bubbly, lively,
mobile, quick, racy,
sanguine,
scintillating, spirited,
vibrant, vivacious,
cheerful
animated film:
cartoon
animation: breath,
cartoon, energy,
excitement, fire, life,
sparkle, vivacity,
warmth
animosity: aversion,
hate, ill feeling,
rancour, resentment,
spite, strife, gall
anklet: bangle
annals: chronicle,
history, record,

register, roll,
transaction
anneal: harden, weld
annex: conquer,
hostel, join, tack
annexation:
conquest, seizure
annexe: boarding-
house
annihilate: confound,
demolish, destroy,
kill, liquidate,
obliterate, pulverize,
slay, squash
annihilation: death,
destruction, end,
killing
anniversary:
celebration, festival,
jubilee
annotate: comment
annotation: comment
annotator:
commentator
announce: avow, bill,
broadcast, call, cry,
declare, herald,
intimate, introduce,
issue, knell, manifest,
notify, proclaim,
promulgate,
pronounce, publish,
report, return, reveal,
say, signify, sound,
tell, utter
announcement: call,
communication,
declaration, notice,
notification, poster,
release, revelation,
communiqué
announcer: herald
annoy: badger, bait,
bite, bother, bug,
chafe, discomfort,
displease, disturb,
fret, gall, get, harass,
irritate, jar, molest,
nag, nark, needle,
niggle, offend, pain,
persecute, pester,
pique, plague,
provoke, put out,
ruffle, spite, trouble,
upset, vex, wear,
weary, worry
annoyance: bother,
chagrin, gall,
indignation, niggle,
nuisance, offence,
pest, plague
annoyed: cross, fed
up, indignant,
peeved, upset,
uptight, weary
annoying:

provocative, sore,
trying, wearing,
wearisome, vexatious
annual: yearly
annually: yearly
annuity: pension
annul: cancel,
dissolve, negate,
nullify, overturn,
quash, repeal,
rescind, reverse,
revoke, supersede,
undo, void
annular: round
annulet: bangle
annulled: undone
annulment:
cancellation, divorce,
repeal
anodyne: painkiller,
sedative
anoint (wound):
salve
anomalous: freak,
queer, unnatural
anomaly: figure,
freak, oddity,
original, paradox
anonymity: unknown
anonymous:
incognito, nameless,
unidentified,
unknown
anonymously:
incognito
anorexic: skeletal,
underweight
answer: atone, bite,
counter, do,
explanation, finding,
guarantee, key, pay,
reaction, rejoinder,
reply, resolution,
resolve, response,
retort, return, satisfy,
say, serve, solution,
suit
answerability:
liability
answerable: liable,
responsible, subject
antagonism: conflict,
disaffection, friction,
hate, ill feeling,
opposition
antagonist:
competitor, enemy,
opponent, opposition,
rival
antagonistic:
contradictory,
contrary, hostile,
negative, opposite,
quarrelsome,
repulsive, unfriendly
ante-room: foyer,

lobby
ante: bet
antecedent:
predecessor
antediluvian: old,
square, unfashionable
antenna: horn
anterior: previous
anthem: hymn, song
anthology: collection,
compilation, garland,
omnibus, selection
anthropoid: human
antic (about): fool
antic: caper, gambol,
lark, prank
anticipate: await,
expect, face, foresee,
forestall, see, look
forward to
anticipated: likely
anticipating:
expectant
anticipation:
foresight, hope,
precaution,
preparation, prospect,
suspense
anticlimax: bathos,
disillusion
antidote: cure,
remedy
antihero: villain
**antinode (in
physics):** loop
antipathetic: averse,
opposing
antipathy: aversion,
disaffection, dislike,
hate, loathing
antiphon: gradual
antiphonal: gradual
antipode: pole
antiquated: elderly,
fuddy-duddy,
historical, obsolete,
old-fashioned, out,
outdated, quaint,
stale, unfashionable
antique: elderly, old
antiquity: history
antiseptic: clean,
disinfectant, sterile
antisocial: taciturn,
undesirable,
unpopular
antithesis: converse,
opposite, reverse
antler: horn
anus: vent
anvil: block
anxiety: care,
concern, fear,
foreboding, jealousy,
malaise, misgiving,
nervousness, strain,

stress, suspense,
sweat, trouble, worry
anxious: concerned,
insecure, jealous,
jittery, jumpy,
loaded, nervous,
neurotic, restless,
solicitous, worried
anxious expectancy:
impatience
anxiously expectant:
impatient
anybody: one,
somebody
anyone: somebody
anyway: nevertheless
apart from: besides,
except, otherwise,
outside
apart: aside, away,
disconnect, distant,
lonely, off
apartment: cabinet,
chamber, flat, pad,
room, suite
apathetic: callous,
casual, cold, cool,
dead, dull, languid,
lethargic, listless,
lukewarm,
phlegmatic, stolid,
tepid, unconcerned,
unhelpful,
unimpressed, torpid
apathy: indifference,
inertia, languor
ape: copy, imitate,
impersonate,
lampoon, mimic,
mock, monkey
aperient: chink,
hatch, hole, mouth,
opening, orifice,
purge, slot, vent
apex: crown, head,
height, high, peak,
pinnacle, point,
summit, tip, zenith
aphonic: mute
aphorism: axiom,
maxim, saying
aphoristic: axiomatic,
sententious
apical: vertical
apiece: each
aplenty: galore
aplomb: poise
apocalyptic:
prophetic
apocryphal:
legendary
apogee: maximum
apologetic: defensive,
penitent, remorseful,
repentant, sorry
apologetically:

regretfully
apology: parody
apophthegm: saying
apoplexy: stroke
aposematic: warning
apostasize: lapse
apostasy: heresy,
lapse
apostate: backslider,
heretic
apothecary: chemist
apotheosis: idolatry,
paragon
appal: dismay,
frighten, horrify,
nauseate, scandalize,
shock, terrify
appalling: atrocious,
awful, dire,
disgraceful, dreadful,
fearful, frightening,
frightful, hideous,
revolting, sensational,
terrible, tragic,
unholy, unnatural,
vile, woeful
apparatus: deck,
device, gear, kit,
machine, material,
mechanism, plant,
rig, thing, vehicle
apparel: dress, garb,
habit, clothes/
clothing
apparent: clear,
conspicuous, distinct,
external, manifest,
obvious, ostensible,
outward, superficial,
surface, transparent,
visible
apparently:
outwardly,
presumably
apparition: fright,
ghost, hallucination,
illusion,
manifestation,
presence, shade,
spectre, spirit, vision
appeal: ask, attract,
attraction, call,
charm, conjure,
invoke, petition, plea,
plead, request, sue,
suit, supplication
appealing: attractive,
charming, inviting,
lovable, lovely, pretty
appear: begin, blow
up, break, come,
figure, form, ghost,
happen, look, loom,
materialize, occur,
peep, perform,
report, present,

result, rise, show,
show up, sound,
surface, turn out
appearance:
attendance,
beginning, cast,
colour, complexion,
description, entrance,
entry, façade, face,
fashion, garb, image,
jib, likeness, look,
manifestation,
manner, occurrence,
onset, performance,
publication,
semblance, shape,
show, sight
appease: compose,
mollify, pacify,
placate, quench,
quieten, relieve,
satisfy, soften
appeasing:
conciliatory
appellation: name,
term
append: attach, join,
tack
appendage: limb,
member, tail
appertain: belong,
relate
appetite: gusto,
hunger, lust, relish,
stomach, swallow,
taste, want, zest
appetizer: relish
appetizing: delicious,
luscious, palatable,
savoury, tasty
applaud: clap,
commend, hail, praise
applause: clap,
jubilation, ovation,
praise, rave
appliance:
convenience, device,
gadget, implement,
instrument, machine,
mechanism
appliances: furniture
applicability:
reference
applicable: material,
pertinent, relevant,
suitable, viable
applicant: candidate,
client
applicants: field
application:
concentration,
diligence,
expenditure, form,
imposition, industry,
instance, lotion,
order, pack, practice,

request, run, use,
bearing, petition
applied: practical
apply: ask, doctor,
coat, concern,
convert, exercise, go
in for, impose,
invoke, lay, order,
practise, pursue,
refer, regard, relate,
request, rub, set,
study, tackle, treat,
use
appoint: assign,
attach, call, cast,
commission,
designate, elect, fix,
furnish, make,
nominate, ordain,
place, schedule, set,
slate
appointed: made
appointment:
assignation,
assignment, capacity,
commission,
engagement, job,
office, place, post,
station
apportion: assign,
dole, dispense, parcel,
partition, ration,
share, weigh
apportioning:
assignation, partition
apportionment:
assignment,
distribution
apposite (to):
germane
appraisal: judgement,
valuation
appraise: assess,
judge, rate, value, vet
appraiser: judge
appreciable:
conceive, respectable
appreciate: criticize,
devour, dig, enjoy,
follow, like, love,
prize, realize,
recognize, relish,
respect, see, sense,
understand, value
appreciated:
understood, welcome
appreciation:
awareness,
conception, criticism,
eye, gratitude, liking,
premium, relish,
respect, sense,
sensibility, thanks,
understanding
appreciative: aware,
complimentary,

grateful, obliged,
sympathetic, thankful
appreciator:
connoisseur
apprehend: capture,
catch, collar,
conceive, divine, fear,
know, nab, perceive,
pick up, pinch,
realize, see, seize,
sense, understand
apprehension:
capture, concern,
dread, fear,
foreboding, fright,
misgiving,
perception,
premonition, reason,
seizure, suspense,
tension, worry
apprehensive:
expectant, fearful,
tense, uptight,
worried
apprentice: beginner,
novice, student,
recruit, trainee
apprise: inform,
instruct, tell
apprised (of): aware
apprising:
understanding
approach: attitude,
avenue, channel,
come, compare,
contact, draw,
imminence, lead up
to, light, line,
manner, method,
near, overture, pass,
policy, principle,
style, tack, way
approachable:
human, outgoing,
receptive, sociable
approach (at sea):
lift
approach (in age):
push
approaching: close,
coming, impending,
near, towards
approbation: favour,
sanction
appropriate (to):
germane
appropriate: assume,
becoming, borrow,
commandeer,
commensurate,
confiscate, due,
fitting, happy, just,
liberate, lift, likely,
logical, meet,
pertinent, pirate,
pocket, proper,

relevant, requisition, right, seize, steal, suitable, whip
appropriated: poached
appropriately: duly, happily, right
appropriateness: fit, fitness, propriety
appropriation: assumption, conquest, requisition, seizure
approval: blessing, confirmation, consent, credit, favour, liking, okay, permission, sanction, assent, vogue
approve: assent, authorize, confirm, favour, like, okay, pass, ratify, recognize, recommend, sanction, sustain, underwrite
approved: formal, hot, orthodox, popular, regular
approving: favourable
approvingly: well
approximate: compare, comparative, imprecise, rough
approximately: much, nearly, roughly
approximation: contact
appurtenant: relevant
apron: flap
apropos: concerning, regarding
apt: capable, clever, fitting, happy, just, liable, opportune, pertinent, prone, proper, ready, sharp, skilful, smart, suitable
aptitude: capacity, fit, fitness, flair, head, knack, leaning, potential, promise, skill, talent, turn
aptly: right, sharply
aptness: propriety
aquamarine: blue
aqueous: fluid, liquid, watery
aquiline: haggard
arable: fertile, cultivated
arbiter: judge, mediator, umpire

arbitrarily: haphazardly
arbitrary: random, summary, unreasoning, wild
arbitrate: compromise, decide, intercede, judge, mediate, moderate, officiate, referee, umpire
arbitration: decision, judgement, truce
arbitrator: judge, mediator, referee, umpire
arbitrators: jury
arboriculture: forestry
arc-lamp: torch
arc: sweep, turn
arcadian: idyllic, pastoral, Utopian
arcane: secret
arch: coy, foot, hog, hoop, hump, hunch, span, vault, wicked
archaeological site: dig
archaic: historical, obsolete, old, old-fashioned, outdated, quaint
arched: vaulted
archetypal: classic, representative
archetype: copy, model, original, pattern, picture, prototype, representative, paragon
architect: founder, originator, artist
architecture: design
archive: book
archives: history, papers, record, register
arctic: cold, cutting, freezing, frigid, glacial, icy, piercing, wintry
ardent: avid, devoted, devout, earnest, fervent, fiery, hot, impassioned, keen, passionate, spirited, warm, zealous
ardour: emotion, fervour, fire, flame, glow, love, passion, soul, spirit, warmth, zeal
arduous: difficult, formidable, gruelling,

hard, killing, laborious, murderous, painful, punishing, rough, rugged, severe, stiff, strenuous, tough
arduously: roughly
area: bay, breadth, circle, clearing, compass(es), country, discipline, field, grounds, jurisdiction, kingdom, locality, parcel, part, patch, place, plot, preserve, province, quarter, range, realm, region, room, scene, scope, terrain, territory, tract, vicinity, walk, world, zone
arears: deficit
arena: board, clearing, floor, ground, ring, scene, stage, terrain, venue
argot: cant, jargon, language, slang
arguable: inconclusive, open, tenable
argue: beef, contend, contest, debate, disagree, dispute, plead, protest, quarrel, reason, row, spar, submit, wrangle
argument: beef, brief, debate, dispute, hassle, issue, matter, plea, polemic, premise, quarrel, reason, reasoning, remonstration, theme, words, wrangle
argumentation: dialectic
argumentative: contentious, obstreperous, pugnacious, quarrelsome
argy-bargy: wrangle
aria: number
arid: baking, dry, infertile, jejune, parched, thirsty
aridity: drought, poverty
arise: blow up, get up, grow, happen, issue, materialize, occur, originate, proceed, result, rise, stem, well
arising: beginning
aristocracy: blood,

nobility, quality, peerage
aristocrat: noble, patrician, peer
aristocratic: gentle, jaunty, lordly, noble, well-bred
arm: boom, branch, fuel, gird, index, limb
armada: fleet, navy
armament: battery, armature (in an electrical circuit): whip
armature (of a magnet): keeper
armed: forcible
armed forces: military
armistice: peace, truce
armour: mail, protection
armoured vehicle: tank
arms: flag, seal, sword
army: crowd, force, host, legion, military, multitude, swarm
army camp: barracks
aroma: bouquet, breath, emanation, fragrance, incense, nose, odour, perfume, scent, smell, whiff
aromatic: fragrant, heady, pungent, redolent, spicy, sweet
around: round, through
arouse: call, challenge, fan, fire, ginger, inspire, jog, kindle, pique, quicken, raise, stimulate, stir, turn on, wake, whet, work up
aroused: awake
arousing: erotic, provocative, sexy, titillating
arraign: denounce
arrange: classify, comb, compose, contract, contrive, dispose, divide, do, drape, dress, fix, form, get, group, lay, list, marshal, mastermind, orchestrate, order, organize, place, plan, plot, point, pose, position, programme, provide, put, range,

rank, ready, regulate, rig, schedule, score, see to, set, set out, set up, size, sort, spread, stage, structure, work
arranged: assorted, prepared, ready, set, straight
arrangement: assortment, bargain, composition, contract, deal, disposal, distribution, formation, harmony, lay, layout, lie, manipulation, medley, order, organization, pact, pattern, presentation, provision, regulation, scheme, series, set-up, structure, system
arrangements: facilities
arranger: musician
arrant: flagrant, outright, thorough, utter
array: bank, deck, display, marshal, parade, position, range, rank, robe, spread, stock, trim
arrears: debt
arrest: bust, capture, catch, check, get, halt, hold, keep, knock, lift, nab, nick, paralyse, pick up, pinch, pull, retard, seize, seizure, stop, stoppage, take
arrested: attached, bust
arresting: outstanding, salient
arrhythmia: palpitation
arrival: coming, entrance
arrive: attain, come, disembark, gain, get, land, make, materialize, reach, return, strike, touch
arrogance: conceit, disdain, pride, vanity,
arrogant: big, cavalier, cocky, conceited, high, jaunty, lofty, lordly, overbearing, proud, snobbish, supercilious, uppish, vain

arrogate: assume, hog
arrogation: assumption
arrow: bolt, quarrel
arrow-case: quiver
arrow-holder: quiver
arse: behind, bottom
arse-licking: obsequious
arsenal: depot, magazine
arsonist: pyromaniac
art: craft, knack, science, technique
arterial: through
artful: cunning, deep, designing, devious, foxy, politic, scheming, sharp, shrewd, sly, subtle, vulpine, wily
artfulness: artifice
article: clause, essay, feature, item, object, paper, piece, property, report, story, thing, throw
articulate: coherent, fluent, hinge, joint, phrase, pronounce, sound, speak, state, voice, voluble
articulated: vocal
articulation: diction, fluency, gab, hinge, joint, speech
artifice: deception, device, guile, machination, pretence, quibble
artificial: camp, contrived, dummy, false, hollow, imitation, laboured, mock, plastic, precious, sham, spurious, stilted, synthetic, unnatural, unreal, unrealistic, strained
artillery: battery
artillery piece: cannon
artisan: worker
artisanship: handicraft
artist: drawer, painter, professional
artiste: player
artistic: ornamental, craft, dexterity, finesse, hand, handicraft
artistic ruin: folly
artistry: touch,

workmanship
artless: careless, innocent, naive, natural, rude, simple, sincere
artlessly: naturally
artlessness: innocence, simplicity, sincerity
arts: culture
artwork: diagram, figure, graphic, illustration, picture
ascend: climb, get on, get up, jump, lift, mount, rise, scale, soar
ascendancy: domination, influence, leverage, prerogative, reign, sway
ascending: uphill
ascent: climb, pull, rise
ascertain: certify, determine, discover, gauge, learn, see
ascertaining: discovery
ascetic: austere, continent, severe, spartan, monastic
asceticism: austerity
ascribe: assign, attach, attribute, credit, impute, lay
ascription: assignation, assignment
aseptic: hygienic
asexual: neuter
ash: dust
ashamed: guilty, remorseful, repentant
ashen: cadaverous, deadly, ghastly, grey, livid, lurid, pale, wan, white
aside: away, by, note, off, parenthesis, remark, wide
asinine: crazy, fatuous, foolish, idiotic, lunatic, mad, mindless
asininity: idiocy, stupidity
ask: beg, bid, consult, indent, interrogate, invite, petition, plead, query, question, quiz, request, seek, solicit, touch
askew: crooked, lopsided, skew,

wrong, wry
aslant: wry
aspect: complexion, face, feature, lie, light, look, outlook, point, regard, respect, semblance, shape, side, tone, view, way
asperity: warmth
asperse: smear
aspersion: disgrace, vilification
asphalted: paved
asphyxiate: choke, strangle, stifle
aspirant: nominee
aspiration: desire, dream, end, longing, objective, purpose, wish
aspirations: pretensions
aspire: desire, hope, pretend, purpose, pursue
aspiring: coming
ass: dunce, fool, idiot, jackass, lunatic, monkey, wally
assail: assault, attack, charge, pelt, ply, press, set about, storm, strike, visit
assailable: vulnerable
assassin: killer
assassinate: execute, hit, kill, knock off, murder, remove, slay, waste
assassination: hit, killing, murder
assault: assail, attack, batter, charge, invade, invasion, onset, onslaught, push, raid, rush, storm, strike, turn on, violate, violation
assay: prove
assemblage: cluster
assemble: band, build, bunch, call, cluster, collect, congregate, crowd, fabricate, flock, gather, group, herd, manufacture, mass, meet, organize, package, raise, rally, round up, set up, structure, summon, construct
assembled: collected
assembly: build-up, cabinet, chamber, circle, collection,

company,
congregation,
congress, council,
flock, government,
huddle, knot, lodge,
manufacture,
organization,
parliament,
production, senate,
session

assembly line:
factory

assent: concession,
concur, concurrence,
confirmation,
consent, nod, okay,
permission

assert: aver, claim,
confess, contend,
declare, have,
maintain, make out,
plead, profess,
pronounce, protest,
say, state, submit,
swear, testify

assertion: claim,
declaration,
profession, remark

assertions:
pretensions

assertive: dogmatic

assess: balance,
criticize, gauge,
judge, mark, overrate,
put, quantify, rate,
reckon, review, test,
value, vet

assessment:
criticism, judgement,
opinion, tax, test,
valuation

assessor: judge

assessors: jury

asset: find, strength

assets: capital, estate,
finance, money,
possession, principal,
property, resources,
substance, treasury,
wherewithal

asseveration: vow

assiduous: close,
painstaking,
persistent, studious

assiduously: hard

assiduousness:
diligence

assign: attach,
attribute, cast,
delegate, designate,
dispense, grant,
impute, lay, leave,
nominate, place, post,
put, set, share, station

assignation: date,
meeting

assigned (in law):
limited

assignment:
business,
consignment,
delegation, disposal,
duty, job, mission,
post, project, task,
work

assimilable:
digestible

assimilate: digest,
incorporate,
integrate, soak, take
in

assimilation:
digestion, orientation

assist: back, back up,
befriend, bolster,
cooperate, further,
hand, help, lubricate,
promote, relieve,
second, serve,
support, sustain

assistance: backing,
cooperation, hand,
help, facilities, relief,
service, support

assistant: auxiliary,
companion, deputy,
help, junior, mate,
second, secretary,
subordinate, waiter

assizes: court

associate: assistant,
auxiliary, band,
collaborator,
colleague, combine,
companion, comrade,
connect, connection,
consort, friend,
group, mate, member,
mingle, pal, partner,
relate, unite

associated: federal,
related, relative

associate with:
attach, befriend,
cultivate, identify,
join, mix, see, side

association: club,
coalition,
combination,
company, connection,
connotation, contact,
federation,
fellowship, fraternity,
friendship,
implication, league,
order, organization,
overtone, party,
relationship, ring,
society, union

assort: group, sort

assorted:
miscellaneous, mixed,

several, sundry,
various

assortment:
collection, diversity,
hash, medley, mix,
range, selection, set,
stock, variety

assuage: comfort,
compose, dull,
lighten, mitigate,
quieten, satisfy

assuagement:
consolation

assume: bear,
conclude, imagine,
let, postulate,
presume, put on,
reckon, say, sham,
suppose, take, take
on, think, understand

assume again:
resume

assume control of:
take over

assumed: artificial,
fake, fictitious,
phoney, putative,
supposed,
understood,
unnatural

assuming: if

assumption: premise,
presumption,
presupposition,
surmise, theory,
understanding

assurance:
commitment,
confidence,
conviction, guarantee,
insurance, pledge,
poise, promise, safety,
security, word

assure: certify, clinch,
confirm, convince,
promise, satisfy,
warrant

assured: certain,
confident, positive,
sanguine, secure, sure

assuredly: really

asterisk: star

asthmatic: breathless

astonish: confound,
flabbergast, rock,
stagger, surprise

astonishing:
incredible,
marvellous, striking

astonishment:
surprise

astound: astonish,
confound,
flabbergast, rock,
shock, stagger,
stupefy, surprise

astounding:
astonishing,
incredible,
marvellous,
portentous,
prodigious,
sensational, startling,
stupendous

astral: psychic

astray: lost, wide,
wrong

astride: straddling

astringent: bitter,
harsh, severe

astrologer: prophet

astronomical:
heavenly, vast

astute: bright, clever,
discerning, judicious,
keen, knowing,
knowledgeable,
penetrating,
perceptive,
perspicacious, politic,
quick-witted, ready,
sharp, smart

asylum: harbour,
home, hostel, refuge,
reserve, sanctuary,
security

asymmetrical:
irregular, lopsided,
shapeless, uneven,
crazy

ataxia: paralysis

atheist: heathen,
pagan

atheistic: heathen

athlete: runner

athletic: fit, light,
muscular, robust,
stout, strong, sturdy

athleticism: fitness

athwart: straddling

atmosphere: feeling,
medium, odour,
semblance, sense, sky,
spirit, undertone

atmospheric:
climatic, meteoric

**atmospheric
conditions:** weather

atom: grain, jot,
particle, rap, spark,
speck

atomizer: jet

atone: compensate,
make up, redeem,
satisfy

atonement:
compensation,
redress, penance

atop: on, over

atrium: foyer, lobby

atrocious: diabolical,
fearful, outrageous,

rank, scandalous, shameful, shocking
atrocity: enormity, obscenity, outrage
atrophied: vestigial
atrophy: consumption, decay, wane, waste
attach: belong, bind, cement, cling, clip, fasten, fix, graft, hitch, hook, lash, link, nail, peg, pin, suspend, tack, tether, yoke
attaché: diplomat
attached: attendant, close, constant, friendly, loyal
attachment: bond, connection, fitting, friendship, link, love, loyalty, regard
attack: assail, assault, campaign, charge, fit, invade, invasion, mug, offensive, onset, onslaught, push, raid, rush, savage, seizure, set about, slam, storm, strike, stroke, tackle, turn on, turn, visit, waylay, worry
attacking: martial, offensive
attain: come, fulfil, gain, hit, land, obtain, reach, touch, win
attainable: manageable
attainment: feat, qualification, scholarship
attar: perfume
attempt: bid, bite, cause, crack, effort, essay, go, seek, shot, stab, strive, throw, trial, undertake, venture, wait
attend church: worship
attend: await, chaperon, conduct, fix, go, hear, listen, look after, mark, mind, minister, regard, see to, serve, tend, turn out
attendance: being, crowd, gate, presence
attendant: companion, custodian, follower, janitor, keeper, lackey, man, page,

satellite, servant, subordinate, usher, waiter
attendants: court, suite, care
attention: concern, consideration, ear, heed, interest, mind, notice, regard, remark, study
attentions: suit
attentive: careful, concerned, considerate, courteous, jealous, observant, solicitous, studious, watchful
attentiveness: diligence
attenuate: dilute, thin
attenuated: dilute, narrow, spindly, thin
attest: support, swear, testify, warrant, witness
attestation: seal
attested: historical
attic: garret
attire: clothe, clothes, clothing, dress, garb, gear, robe, wardrobe
attitude: aspect, bearing, conduct, demeanour, manner, mentality, mind, outlook, philosophy, pose, position, posture, principle, sentiment, set, spirit, stance, stand, state, trim, vein, view, viewpoint, will
attorney: lawyer, solicitor
attract: captivate, charm, court, draw, fascinate, invite, lure, pull, tempt, turn on
attraction: bait, charm, draw, fascination, feature, lure, pull, temptation
attractive: becoming, charming, dreamy, engaging, fetching, fine, good-looking, handsome, inviting, lovable, lovely, magnetic, pretty, sweet, winning
attractiveness: beauty, grace, personality
attribute: assign, characteristic, credit, feature, gift, impute,

lay, point, property, qualification, quality, refer, thing
attributes: character
attribution: assignation, assignment
attrition: erosion, friction, wash, wear
attune: key
atypical: different, exceptional, uncharacteristic, unusual
auburn: brown
audacious: assured, bold, daring, gallant, heroic, high-spirited, intrepid, presumptuous, rash, shameless, valiant
audacity: assurance, courage, daring, face, gallantry, heroism, insolence, nerve, presumption, prowess, temerity, valour
audible: clear
audience: attendance, hearing, interview, public
auditorium: floor, hall
auditory perception: hearing
au fait: up to date
auger: drill
augment: build, grow, increase, let out, pad out, raise, recruit, reinforce, swell, whet
augmentation: build-up, enlargement, growth, increase
augur: forecast, foretell, predict, promise, prophesy, prophet, seer
augury: divination, forerunner, omen, oracle, portent, warning
august: dignified, exalted, grand, great, majestic, princely, proud, regal, solemn, stately, venerable
aumbry: bay, niche
au naturel: nude
aura: feeling, glory, halo, nimbus, nuance, odour, sense, undertone

aureola: halo
aurora: sunrise
auspice: sign
auspices: supervision
auspicious: hopeful, lucky, promising, propitious, ripe, rosy
austere: ascetic, bare, dour, frigid, harsh, monastic, plain, puritanical, rigorous, rough, rugged, severe, stern, stiff, strict, tight
austerely: barely
austerity: frigidity
authentic: authoritative, factual, faithful, genuine, good, historical, honest, legitimate, official, original, pure, real, realistic, right, true, valid
authentically: truly
authenticate: certify, confirm, seal, support, witness
authentication: confirmation, proof, seal
authenticity: faithfulness, honesty
author: dramatist, father, founder, ghost, narrator, originator, source, write, writer, parent
authoritarian: bossy, dictatorial, totalitarian, tyrant
authoritarianism: repression, tyranny
authoritative: dogmatic, imperative, magisterial, official, potent, powerful, responsible, weighty
authority: chair, clout, command, connoisseur, control, critic, domination, government, influence, judge, jurisdiction, leadership, licence, mastery, oracle, power, precedent, qualification, quarter, right, rule, sage, sanction, say, source, specialist, sway, warrant, weight
authorization: certificate, faculty, franchise, leave,

liberty, licence,
mandate, okay, pass,
permission, permit,
power, remit,
sanction, warrant
authorize: charter,
commission, delegate,
deputize, enfranchise,
invest, legalize, let,
license, okay, pass,
permit, ratify,
sanction
authorized: lawful,
legitimate, official
authorizing:
mandatory
authorship: writing
autistic: withdrawn
autobiography:
history, life, memoirs
autochthon: savage
autocracy: tyranny
autocrat:
authoritarian, despot,
dictator, sovereign,
tyrant
autocratic:
authoritarian, bossy,
dictatorial,
overbearing,
totalitarian
autograph: inscribe,
sign
autoharp: zither
automated:
mechanical
automatic: inevitable,
involuntary,
mechanical, mindless
perfunctory,
unconscious
automaton: machine,
robot
automobile: car
autonomous: free,
independent, separate
autonomy: freedom,
independence,
liberty, self-
government
autopsy: postmortem
auxiliary: assistant,
extra, fresh, other,
secondary,

subordinate,
supplementary
avail: boot, help,
purpose, service, use
availability:
convenience
available: disposable,
free, handy, on,
present, vacant
avail oneself of:
resort
avalanche: landslide,
slide
avant-garde:
progressive,
revolutionary,
underground
avaricious: covetous,
grasping, mercenary,
miserly, narrow,
niggardly, rapacious,
ravenous, selfish,
sordid, worldly
avenge: repay,
revenge
avenging: vengeance
avenging angel:
scourge
avenue: channel,
drive, entrance, entry,
outlet, passage, road,
route, street, walk,
way
aver: assert, attest,
avow, maintain,
profess
average: common,
fair, folksy, mean,
mediocre, medium,
middling, moderate,
norm, normal,
ordinary, par,
satisfactory, standard
averageness:
normality
averse: reluctant,
unwilling
aversion: disgust,
dislike, loathing,
phobia, repugnance,
revulsion
avert: deflect, fend off,
forestall, obviate,

prevent
avian: bird
aviation: flight
aviator: pilot
avid: keen, longing,
thirsty, wild, wishful,
wishful, zealous
avocation: hobby
avoid: bypass, dodge,
duck, forestall, fudge,
help, jump, ostracize,
parry, prevent, resist,
shirk, sidestep, skirt
avoidance: evasion,
omission
avoided: shunned,
unpopular
avow: own
avowed: known
await: look forward to
awaited: due
awaiting: expectant,
pending
awake: attentive,
conscious, live,
responsive
awaken: kindle,
quicken, revive,
rouse, wake, whet
awakening:
renaissance
award: confer,
decoration,
distinction, give,
grant, maintenance,
present, presentation,
prize, purse, trophy
award-winning:
prize
aware: awake,
conscious, knowing,
knowledgeable,
mindful, responsive,
sensible, sentient,
wise
awareness: attention,
conscious, intuition,
knowledge, light,
perception, sensation,
sense, sensibility
away: aside, by, forth,
gone, off, out
awe-inspiring:

breathtaking
awe: dazzle, dread,
terrify, terror, wonder
awesome:
breathtaking, dread,
formidable, holy,
monumental, wonder,
wonderful
awestricken:
overcome
awful: beastly,
deplorable, dire,
dreadful, fearful,
frightful, hideous,
horrible, horrid,
painful, terrible,
woeful
awfully: beastly,
terribly
awkward: clumsy,
contrary, difficult,
gauche, halting,
heavy, inept,
lumbering,
ponderous, sensitive,
sticky, stiff, strained,
strange, uncouth,
ungainly, unhappy,
unwieldy, wooden
awkwardly: heavily,
unhappily
awkwardness:
embarrassment
awn: beard
awned: hairy
awning: canopy, fly,
screen, roof
awry: crooked,
lopsided, skew, wrong
axe: chop, cut,
dismiss, pick, sack
axed: cut
axiom: law, maxim,
precept, principle,
proverb, rule, saying,
theorem, verity
axiomatic:
proverbial,
understood
axis: backbone, stem
axle-guard: pedestal
axle: hub, pin, pivot
azure: blue

B

babble: babel, bubble, chatter, drivel, gabble, gibberish, gurgle, noise, prattle, ramble, warble, rave
babbling: delirious, maundering, murmuring
babe: baby, infant
babel: pandemonium, uproar
babes: young
babied: pampered
babies: young
baby: babyish, child, indulge, infant, mother, pet, tot
babyish: infantile, juvenile, puerile
bacchanal: orgy, revel
bacchanalian: drunken
bacillus: bacterium, microbe
back: assist, champion, finance, flat, patronize, promote, rear, reverse, sanction, second, sponsor, stand by, support, underwrite, urge
back away: retreat
backbite: slander
backbiter: gossip
backbiting: calumny, slander
backbone: grit, guts, pluck, spine, spirit, strength, support
backbreaking: gruelling, hard, onerous, punishing
backchat: mouth, sauce
backdrop: flat, scene
back down: yield
back end: rear
backer: assistant, benefactor, guarantor, patron, punter, second, sponsor, support
backfire: rebound, recoil
background: context,

environment, foil, form, past, qualification, record, scene, setting, upbringing
back-handed: sarcastic
backhander: bribe,
backing: assistance, behind, blessing, finance, mount, offices, patronage, promotion, reassurance, sanction, support
backlash: kickback, recoil, repercussion
backpack: knapsack
backpacking: hiking
backs: defence
backside: behind, bottom, buttocks, rear, tail
backslide: fall, relapse, revert
backsliding: relapse
back-stabber: bitch
back-street: side-street, sordid
bactericide: disinfectant
bacterium: bug, microbe
back to front: reverse
backtrack: reverse
back-up: assistant, auxiliary, bear out
backward: godforsaken, retrograde, reverse
backwardness: diffidence
backwash: wake
backwoods: provincial, wild
bad: awful, baneful, evil, hard, ill, nasty, naughty, off, poor, putrid, rancid, rank, reprehensible, rigorous, rotten, sad, sour, terrible, villainous, wicked, wrong, unfavourable
baddie: villain
badge: device, mark, plaque, plate, sign,

symbol, token
badger: besiege, harass, hassle, hound, lobby, molest, nag, persecute, pester, plague, worry
badgering: demanding, harassment, importunate, teasing
badinage: banter, repartee
badly: hard, ill, poorly, seriously, terribly, unhappily, wrong
badness: evil
baffle: cheat, confound, confuse, defy, foil, fox, frustrate, nonplus, perplex, puzzle, stump
baffled: bewildered, lost, puzzled, stuck
bafflement: frustration
baffling: impenetrable, inexplicable, tough
bag: capture, drop, pot, sack, shoot, thing
bagatelles: knick-knacks
bagful: sack
baggage: cargo, hussy, luggage, piece
baggy: full, loose, slack, pendulous
bags: luggage
bail: pledge, scoop
bailiff: factor
bairn: baby, kid
bait: badger, bribe, decoy, incentive, lure, needle, temptation
baiting: teasing
bake: cake, fire, roast
balance: compensate, composition, coordination, difference, equalize, equate, harmony, juggle, keep up, par, parallel, parity, poise, redress, remainder, remnant, square,

steady, surplus, trim, weigh
balanced: equal, even, level, offset, rational, regular, right, sane, steady
balancing: audit
bald: unconfirmed
balderdash: bunk, drivel, rot, rubbish, stuff
bale: bundle, pack
baleful: baneful, ominous
balk: baffle, foil, jib, shy
ball: bead, bowl, bullet, dance, fling, globe, nut, orb, pill, roll
ballad: song
ballast: weight
ballcock: float
ballet: dance
ball game: situation
ballista: catapult
balloon: bag, inflate, swell
ballot: poll, vote
ballpoint: pen
balls-up: bungle
ballyhoo: hype, racket
balm: help, ointment, salve
balmy: bland, temperate
balusters: banisters
balustrade: banisters, rail, railing
bamboo: cane
bamboozle: cheat, deceive, fool, hoax, kid, swindle
ban: banish, bar, boycott, forbid, outlaw, proscribe, reject, restraint, sanction, veto
banal: hackneyed, insipid, mundane, stale, stock
banality: tedium, platitude
bananas: crazy, lunatic, mad
band: bar, belt, body, bunch, circle, clan,

company, crew, gang,
group, hoop, knot,
pack, party, ring, set,
sling, squad, tape,
team, vein, zone,
band-aid: bandage
bandage: bind, dress,
plaster
banded: striped
bandit: gangster,
outlaw
bandleader:
conductor
bandolier: magazine
bandsman: musician
bandy: hawk, quarrel,
spar, swap
bane: scourge, trial,
venom
baneful: harmful,
venomous
bang: bark, beat,
blast, blow, box,
bump, clap, clash,
crack, crash, flap,
hammer, hit, impact,
rattle, report, right,
slam, slap, strike
banger: bus, cracker,
crate, sausage
banging: flap
banish: ban, dismiss,
exile, outlaw,
proscribe, resolve,
transport
banishment: ban,
exile, expulsion
banister: rail
bank: bar, bargain,
beach, brink, deposit,
drift, embankment,
grade, mound, row,
treasury
banker: gnome
banking: finance
banknote: bill, cash
bankroll: finance,
fund
bankrupt: beggar,
bust, defaulter,
exhaust, miserable,
reduce, ruin,
penniless
bankruptcy: failure,
finish, ruin
banned: black,
forbidden,
inadmissible,
prohibited
banner: flag, pennant,
standard
banquet: blow-out,
dine, dinner, do,
feast, meal, repast
bant: diet
banter: joke, kid,

quip, ridicule, roast,
repartee
baptise: christen,
convert, immerse,
name, wash, wet
baptized: named
bar: ban, bank,
barrage, barrier,
beam, block, bolt,
boom, cake, canteen,
check, choke, close,
counter, court, dock,
except, inn, lever,
line, loaf, local, lock,
oasis, obstruct,
obstruction, oppose,
outlaw, perch, pin,
prevent, pub, rail,
reject, rod, saloon,
shut, stop, table
barb: gaff, hook,
shaft, spine
barbarian: boorish,
brute, heathen,
heathen, lout,
philistine, primitive,
savage
barbaric: atrocious,
inhuman, outrageous
barbarism: outrage
barbarity: atrocity,
barbaric, cruelty,
barbarous: cruel,
inhuman, murderous,
savage, wild
barbecue: fire, grill
barbed: cutting,
jagged, pointed,
prickly, thorny
barbel: barb, beard
barbican: bastion,
battlements,
fortification, tower
bard: dramatist, poet
bare: bald, blank,
bleak, desolate, hard,
nude, open, plain,
poor, reveal, scanty,
strip, unconfirmed,
void, waste
barefaced: flagrant
barely: hardly, ill,
just, little, narrowly,
scarcely
bargain: barter,
cheap, compact, deal,
find, haggle,
negotiate, pact, treat,
bargaining:
negotiation
barge: burst, scrum,
shove
bark: bay, cork,
cough, hack, peel,
skin, snap, yap
barm: ferment

barmy: crazy, foolish,
insane, lunatic, mad
barn: stable
barney: disturbance,
wrangle
baron: magnate
baroque: quaint
barrack: heckle
barracking: bird,
jeering
barracks:
headquarters,
quarters
barrage: dam, shell,
shower, volley
barred: inadmissible,
prohibited, striped
barrel: bore, cask,
drum, keg, vat, wood
barren: bald, bare,
bleak, dead, desolate,
fruitless, infertile,
inhospitable, jejune,
lean, lifeless, meagre,
poor, sterile,
uninhabited, waste
barrenness: poverty,
barricade: bar,
barrier, blockade,
dam, defence, defend,
fence, obstruct,
obstruction, wall
barrier: bar, barrage,
block, blockade,
bumper, dam, fence,
gate, hedge,
hindrance, hurdle,
obstacle, obstruction,
partition, preventive,
protection, rail,
railing, wall
barring: besides,
except
barrister: counsel,
lawyer
barrow: mound, tomb
bars: enclosure, grate,
grill
bartender: drawer
barter: bargain,
change, swap
bartizan: battlements
base: basis, block,
bottom, build,
contemptible, depot,
floor, foot, footing,
found, foundation,
ground, haunt,
headquarters, home,
knavish, lair, low,
mean, menial,
miserable, mount,
pedestal, plate, rest,
root, rotten, seat,
servile, small, sordid,
sorry, stand, vile

baseless: unfounded
basement: cellar
bash: attempt, bang,
bite, club, crack,
cudgel, effort, fling,
go, hit, party, punch,
throw, wallop
bashful: ashamed,
coy, demure, modest,
retiring, self-
conscious, shy
bashfulness:
embarrassment,
modesty, shyness
basic: bare, base,
elemental,
elementary, first,
fundamental,
inherent, integral,
key, primary, prime,
radical, raw, rough,
simple, standard,
stock, ultimate,
underlying
basically: roughly,
primarily
basics: rudiments
basin: bowl, crater,
depression, dock,
hollow, pan, sink,
valley
basis: backbone, base,
bottom, cause,
derivation, die,
footing, foundation,
grounds, leg, origin,
platform, reason,
score
bask: bathe, indulge,
revel, wallow
basket: pot, skip,
hamper
bass: deep
bassinet: cradle, crib
bastard: devil,
illegitimate
bastion: battlements,
defence, fort,
rampart, tower
bat: club, flutter,
knock
batch: bunch, bundle,
cluster, consignment,
lot, lump, pack,
package, parcel, set
bath: immerse, scrub,
rub, wash
bathe: dip, immerse,
splash, wash
bathrobe: robe
bathroom: lavatory,
toilet
baton: bar, rod, stick,
wand, warder
bats: crazy, insane,
lunatic, mad

batsman: batter
batten: bar
batter: assault, beat, club, cudgel, maul, punish
battered: decrepit, dilapidated
battery: assault, farm, pile
battle: combat, conflict, contest, engagement, fight, scrap, skirmish, struggle, war
battleaxe: dragon, harridan, nag
batty: wild
batwitted: foolish, mindless, thick
bauble: bead, decoration, knick-knack
bawdiness: coarseness, impropriety, lewdness, obscenity
bawdy: blue, coarse, fruity, immodest, improper, lewd, obscene, racy, raunchy, suggestive
bawl: bark, bellow, cry, roar, shout, sob, yell
bawling: vociferous
bay: bark, chestnut, gulf, recess, red, roar, trumpet
bazaar: boutique, fair, market
be: do, fall, fare, go, keep, lie, live, obtain, occur, represent
beach: coast, strand, shore
beacon: blaze, fire, flare, guide, light, pylon, signal, torch, warning
bead: ball, bubble, drop, globule
beak: bill, judge, ram
beaker: cup, mug
beam: boom, breadth, emanation, flare, illumination, pile, shaft, shine, sparkle
beaming: radiant, shining, splendid, sunny
beams: timber
beano: blow-out, feast
bear: brook, carry, cart, deliver, digest, endure, go through, have, hold, meet,

mother, produce, put up with, run, stand for, stand, stomach, suffer, support, sustain, take, tolerate, undergo, withstand, yield
bearable: digestible, tolerable
beard: beaver
bearded: hairy
bearer: custodian, messenger, runner
bearing: aspect, attitude, carriage, concern, conduct, course, demeanour, direction, heading, look, pose, posture, purport, regard, respect, set, stance, tack
bearings: orientation, position
beast: brute, creature, devil, monster, pig, savage
beastly: horrible, horrid, savage
beasts: cattle
beat: assault, bang, batter, belt, best, better, birch, break, cane, cap, castigate, churn, click, club, conquer, defeat, flail, flap, flog, flutter, hammer, hit, jacket, lambast, lash, lather, lay on, leather, lick, mash, maul, measure, movement, outdo, overcome, pass, paste, post, pulse, punish, puzzle, quarter, rhythm, round, rout, route, scour, scourge, strap, stress, strike, surpass, tan, time, wallop, whip, whisk, worst
beaten: battered, puzzled
beater: whisk
beatific: divine, happy, heavenly, joyous, Utopian
beatification: glory
beatify: glorify
beating: assault, battery, defeat, drubbing, flap, hiding, licking, palpitation, pulse, punishment, rout
beatitude: happiness

beau: cavalier, gallant, lover, swell
beautiful: artistic, attractive, divine, fair, fairytale, fine, fragrant, glorious, gorgeous, heavenly, lovely, stunning
beautify: deck, glorify, jewel
beautifying: cosmetic
beauty: cracker, doll, dream, fragrance, glory, knockout
beaver: beard
because: as, since
beck: stream
beckon: gesticulate, gesture, sign, signal, wave
become: be, befit, fall, flatter, get, go, grow, suit, turn, wax
becoming: decent, fetching, handsome, proper, right, suitable
bed: base, berth, bunk, cot, couch, floor, layer, litter, measure
bedaub: smear
bedclothes: linen
bedeck: festoon, garland, garnish, grace, trim
bedecked: ornate
bedfellow: partner
bedlam: babel, chaos, pandemonium, uproar
bedraggled: dishevelled, scruffy
bedridden: disabled, invalid, unwell
bedrock: backbone, base, basis, shelf
bedstead: cot
beef: bitch, brawn, difficulty, grievance, moan, niggle, whine
beefeater: warder
beefy: burly, meaty, rugged, stout, strong
beer-belly: paunch
beer: brew, stout, wallop
beeswax: wax
beetle: bug, project
beetling: prominent, protuberant
beezer: wizard
befall: be, chance, happen, occur, pass
befit: suit
befitting: like, suitable

befog: obfuscate
before: by, previously, prior
beforehand: first, previously
befoul: blacken, dirty
befuddle: fox
befuddled: dazed
befuddlement: confusion
beg: invoke, petition, plead, press, ask, implore, pray
beget: breed, father, procreate
begetter: father
beggar: bankrupt, devil, vagrant
beggared: poverty-stricken
beggarly: mean, niggardly, paltry
beggary: poverty, penury
begin: cause, dawn, develop, get, inaugurate, initiate, launch, lead, open, originate, preface, set about, start
beginner: initiate, novice, recruit
beginning: baptism, birth, conception, fountain, genesis, germ, head, incipient, initial, kick-off, launch, onset, opening, origin, outset, preliminary, prime, seed, source, start, threshold
beginnings: root, rudiments
begrimed: filthy
begrudge: deny, resent
begrudging: ungrateful, unhelpful
beguile: captivate, charm, cheat, coax, seduce
beguiling: seductive, wily
behalf: part, sake
behave: bear, conduct, do, go on
behaviour: carriage, conduct, demeanour, form, manner, manners, performance
behead: decapitate
behest: command, dictate
behind: bottom,

buttocks, down, end,
rear, slow, tail,
beyond, tardy
behindhand:
delinquent, late,
tardy,
behold: look,
perceive, regard, see,
witness, view
beholden: obliged,
thankful
beholder: spectator,
witness
behove: become
beige: buff, fawn, tan
being: body, creature,
existence, fibre,
individual, life, living,
organism, soul
bejewel: jewel
belabour: batter,
overdo, set about
belatedly: late
beleaguer: besiege,
harass
belfry: tower
belief: assumption,
bet, confidence,
conviction, credit,
faith, idea, notion,
opinion, persuasion,
principle,
understanding
beliefs: lore,
philosophy
believability:
credibility
believable: likely,
reasonable, plausible
believe: assume, buy,
consider, credit,
fancy, hold, imagine,
presume, reckon,
suppose, suspect,
swallow, take, think,
understand
believer: faithful,
follower
believing: gullible
belittle: knock, lessen,
lower, run down,
scoff
belittling: detraction
bell: bay, flare
belles-lettres:
writing
bellicose: hostile,
martial, pugnacious,
quarrelsome, warlike
belligerence: fight
belligerent: hawk,
hostile, martial,
militant,
obstreperous,
offensive, pugnacious,
quarrelsome,

unfriendly, warlike
bellow: bawl, cry,
roar, shout, thunder,
trumpet, yell
bellpush: button
belly: balloon,
stomach
bellyache: whine
belongings: gear,
goods, property, stuff
beloved: darling,
dear, familiar,
inamorata, love,
precious, sweet,
sweetheart
below: beneath, down,
lower, under, under,
underneath
belt: band, blow,
circle, corset, gird,
girdle, hit, hoop,
strap, strip, zone
belting: hiding
bemoan: complain,
lament, regret,
sorrow, wail
bemuse: confuse,
fuddle, spellbind
bemused: distracted
bench: bank, bar,
chair, couch, court,
form, judge, seat
benchmark:
criterion, measure,
yardstick
bend: bow, buckle,
corner, crook, curl,
dent, distort, flex,
give, hinge, hook,
hump, hunch, incline,
kink, loop, slant,
stoop, submit,
swerve, thumb, turn,
warp, wind, yield
bendable: pliable, soft
bending: inclination
beneath: below,
lower, under,
underneath
benediction: blessing,
grace
benefactor: donor,
patron
beneficence:
generosity, goodwill,
kindness,
magnanimity,
munificence,
patronage
beneficent:
benevolent, bountiful,
generous, good, kind,
liberal, philanthropic
beneficial: benign,
convenient, desirable,
fruitful, good,

healthy, helpful,
nourishing,
nutritious, positive,
profitable, salutary,
serviceable,
therapeutic, useful,
valuable, wholesome,
worth while,
favourable
beneficially: right
benefit: asset, beauty,
blessing, fruit, gain,
good, help, interest,
pay, pension, profit,
purpose, return,
reward, sake, use,
value, welfare, worth
benevolence:
goodwill, grace,
humanity, kindness,
kindliness
benevolent: big,
charitable, friendly,
good, kind, kindly,
benevolent: good-
natured, paternal,
philanthropic,
propitious,
benevolently: kindly
benign: benevolent,
friendly, gentle,
gracious, humane,
kind, propitious,
white
benignity: kindness
benignly: kindly
benison: blessing
bent: corrupt,
criminal, crooked,
curved, dishonest,
gay, homosexual,
inclination, kinky,
knack, leaning,
mangled, rotten, set,
skew, twisted, venal
benumb: paralyse
benumbed:
insensible, silly
bequeath: devise,
donate, endow, will
bequeathed:
hereditary
bequest: disposal,
gift, heritage,
inheritance, legacy
berate: censure,
lecture, scold, slang,
slate
bereave: deprive
bereavement: death,
deprivation, loss,
mourning
bereft: bereaved,
desolate, forlorn,
bonnet
beribbon: festoon

berk: wally
berry: fruit
berserk: crazy,
lunatic, mad,
possessed, rabid,
raving, violent, wild
berth: bed, bunk,
cabin, compartment,
dock, mooring, space
beseech: ask, beg,
conjure, exhort,
implore, petition,
plead, pray, solicit,
sue, urge
beset: assail,
beleaguered, besiege,
bombard, haunt,
invest, ply, press,
storm
beside: by
besides: beyond, else,
further, moreover,
then, yet
besiege: blockade,
bombard, invest,
press, surround,
swamp
besieged: beleaguered
besmirch: defile, soil
besom: brush
bespangle: star, stud
bespatter: muddy,
spatter
bespattered: muddy
besprinkle: baptise
best-selling:
successful
best: beat, choice,
classic, cream,
favourite, flower, fox,
gold(en), king,
maximum, optimum,
pride, prime, upset,
victor, victorious,
worst
bestial: beastly,
brutal, inhuman,
monstrous, savage
bestir: kindle, rouse
bestow: heap, do,
award, cast, confer,
contribute, endow,
give, grant, impart,
lend, pay, rain, spend,
show
bestowal:
contribution
bestride: strid
bet: dare, flutter,
gamble, hazard, put
on, stake, wager, stake
beta rhythm:
brainwave
betide: befall, chance
betoken: import,
indicate, mean,

promise, symbolize
betray: display,
expose, finger, give
away, knife, let out,
reveal, squeal
betrayal: exposure,
indiscretion,
revelation
betrayer: Judas
betrothal:
engagement
betrothed: fiancé(e)
better: break, cap,
improve, mend,
preferable, punter,
reform, superior,
whole
betterment:
improvement,
progress
betwixt: between
beverage: drink,
squash
bevy: swarm
bewail: keen, lament,
mourn
beware: warning
bewhiskered: hairy
bewilder: baffle,
confound, confuse,
nonplus, obfuscate,
perplex, puzzle,
stump, surprise
bewildered:
bemused, blank,
distracted, lost,
muddled, puzzled,
strange
bewildering:
inexplicable
bewilderment:
confusion, fog,
surprise
bewitch: conjure,
entrance, fascinate,
possess
bewitched: possessed
bewitching: lovely,
beautiful, ravishing
beyond: behind, by,
outside, past, without
bhang: marijuana
bias: bent, favour,
favouritism, injustice,
leaning, liking, load,
slant, warp, weight
biased: bigoted,
jaundiced, loaded,
narrow, narrow-
minded, one-sided,
opinionated, partial,
partisan, prejudiced,
unfair, unreasoning
bib: napkin
bibelots: knick-
knacks

bible: manual
biblical: scriptural
bicker: disagree, fight,
jar, quarrel, scrap,
spar, wrangle
bickering:
contentious,
recrimination, strife
bicoloured: pied
bid: attempt, call,
charge, command,
invite, offer, require,
summon, tender,
wish
biddable: easy,
gentle, obedient
bidding: command,
wish
bidet: basin
bifurcate: diverge,
fork
big-headed: boastful,
opinionated
big: bulky, burly,
great, large, stout, tall
bigger: major
bighead: egoist
bigheaded: conceited,
vain
bigheadedness:
vanity
bight: bay, gulf
bigoted: narrow-
minded, officious,
opinionated, rabid
bigwig: celebrity,
somebody
bijouterie: knick-
knacks
bike: cycle
bikini: bathing
costume
bile: gall, nausea
bilge: flannel
bilious: jaundiced,
liverish, sallow, sickly
biliousness: nausea
bilk: take
bill: beak, legislation,
measure, poster,
price, programme,
score, tab
billet: board, lodge,
log, quarter
billets: kindling
billow: cloud, heave,
roll, surge, swell,
wave, well
billowing: roll,
voluminous
bills: papers
bin: crib
bind: brace, cement,
chain, combine,
commit, fasten, knit,
knot, lash, link, ratify,

rope, shackle, stick,
strap, tape, tether,
wrap
binder: cement
binding: band, bond,
compelling,
compulsory, mordant,
obligatory, tape, valid
binge: bat, drunk,
kick, orgy, overeat
biodegradable:
disposable
biography: life,
history, profile
biological: organic
biosphere: life
biotic: organic
birch: cane, lash, whip
bird: doll, girl, woman
birdsong: warble
biro: pen
birth: beginning,
blood, dawn,
delivery, labour
birthplace: cradle
birthright: heritage,
inheritance
biscuit: cracker
bisect: divide
bisected: split
bisection: division
bishop: patriarch
bishopric: see
bistre: buff, brown
bit: bridle, crumb,
drill, fraction,
fragment, grain, jot,
lick, little, lump,
parcel, part, particle,
patch, piece, pinch,
portion, remnant,
routine, scrap, shred,
snatch, speck, spot,
strip
bitchiness: spite
bite: bit, chew, chill,
knap, little, meal,
nibble, nip, prick,
punch, snap, taste,
teeth, titbit, worry
biting: bitter, caustic,
chill, cold, cutting,
icy, keen, mordant,
nippy, penetrating,
peppery, piercing,
pointed, pungent,
raw, sarcastic,
scathing, sharp,
strong, vitriolic,
bits and pieces: offal
bits: wreckage
bitter: cold, fiery,
freezing, hard, harsh,
icy, jaundiced, keen,
piercing, pungent,
raw, sardonic, severe,

sharp, sour, virulent
bitterly: sharply
bitterness: regret,
resentment, gall
bitty: patchy, scrappy
bivouac: camp
bizarre: crazy,
curious, freak,
grotesque, kinky,
odd, peculiar, quaint,
strange, unnatural,
unusual, weird
blab: blurt, inform,
squeal, talk, tell
black: boycott, credit,
dark, funereal,
gloomy, inauspicious,
jet, mourning, murky,
oily, satanic, sick,
ugly
blackboard: slate
blacken: darken,
scorch, smear, stain
blackened: filthy,
tainted
blackening:
incriminatory
blackguard: dog,
knave, rogue,
scoundrel, villain,
wretch
blackhearted: wicked
blacking: boycott
blacklist: ban,
ostracize
blackmail: extortion,
ransom, threat
blackmailer: bully
blackness: oblivion
blackout: censorship,
faint
blacksmith's: forge
blade: blood, float,
knife, leaf, oar, sword
blah-blah: etcetera
blame: charge, check,
condemn, fault, rap,
scold, stick
blameless: innocent,
pure, unimpeachable
blamelessness:
innocence, purity
blameworthiness:
guilt
blaming:
recrimination
blanch: bleach, fade,
flinch, pale, wince,
quail
blanched: cadaverous
blancmange: dessert,
mould
bland: digestible,
gentle, insipid, mild,
light
blandish: wheedle

blandness: mildness
blank: bare, dull,
  fishy, glassy, hiatus,
  space, vacant, void,
  wooden
blanket:
  comprehensive,
  envelop, general,
  mantle, rug, sheet,
  universal
blankness: void
blare: blast, blaze,
  blow, trumpet
blaring: loud
blarney: claptrap,
  flannel
blasé: casual,
  nonchalant,
  sophisticated,
  unimpressed
blaspheme: curse
blasphemous: evil,
  foul, impious, profane,
  sacrilegious, unholy
blasphemy: evil,
  heresy, swearing
blast: blow up, blow,
  boom, bother, burst,
  detonate, discharge,
  gust, puff, report,
  shatter, shoot,
  thunder, wither, zap
blasted: bleeding,
  flaming, shattered
blasting: withering
blastomere: seed
blatant: brazen,
  conspicuous, flagrant,
  glaring, gross, loud,
  open, overt, palpable,
  patent, rank
blatantly: openly
blather: natter,
  nonsense, waffle,
  wind
blaze: burn, fire,
  flame, flare, flash,
  glare, heat, light,
  trumpet, warmth
blazer: jacket
blazing: bright, fierce,
  fiery, glaring, torrid
blazon: splash
bleach: blue,
  discolour, fade
bleached: pale
bleak: austere, chill,
  cold, dark, desolate,
  dismal, gaunt,
  godforsaken, harsh,
  inhospitable, raw,
  rigorous, spartan,
  unfriendly, wintry
bleakness: austerity,
  sadness
blear: blur

bleb: blister
bleed: flow, milk, sap,
  squeeze
bleeding: flow,
  haemorrhage
bleeper: reminder
blemish: blot, blur,
  defect, disfigurement,
  fault, mar, mark, scar,
  speck, spoil, spot,
  stain, vice
blemished: faulty,
  marked, tainted
blench: flinch, gulp,
  pale, quail, wince
blend: combination,
  combine, compound,
  fuse, knead, mingle,
  mix, solution, weave
blended: composite,
  mixed
bless: glorify
blessed: happy,
  heavenly, holy, lucky,
  sacred, saintly
blessedness:
  beatitude, bliss,
  happiness
blessing: beatitude,
  glory, godsend,
  mercy, miracle,
  support
blether: gibberish,
  prattle
blethering: prattle
blight: cancer, curse,
  dash, disease, infect,
  mar, overshadow,
  pest, plague, rot, rust,
  shadow, wither
blighted: shattered,
  tainted
blighting: withering
blind: camouflage,
  cloak, dazzle,
  insensible, shade,
  unreasoning,
  unshakable
blindfold: hood
blink: bat, twinkling,
  twitch
blinker: hood
blinkered:
  unreasoning
blinking: twinkling
bliss: beatitude,
  happiness, heaven,
  joy, paradise, rapture
blissful: happy,
  joyful, radiant, rapt
blister: bubble, bulge,
  corn, pustule, scorch,
  swelling
blithe: carefree,
  cheerful, happy, light,
  light-hearted, merry,

  oblivious
blithely: happily
blitz: bomb, bombard,
  shell, storm
blizzard: storm
bloat: balloon, blow
  up, distend, gorge,
  inflate, swell
bloated: turgid,
  pompous
bloating: filling
blob: bead
bloc: coalition, faction
block: bar, building,
  cake, choke, chunk,
  clog, close, frustrate,
  halt, head, jam, keep,
  loaf, mass, obstruct,
  pad, parry, plate,
  plug, prevent,
  preventive, spike,
  stall, stop, tablet,
  tackle, warp
blockage: barrier,
  block, jam, obstacle,
  obstruction, stoppage
blockbuster:
  knockout
blockhead: ass,
  dummy, dunce, fool,
  idiot, nincompoop,
  oaf, simpleton
blockheaded: dense,
  idiotic
blockhouse: fort
blocking: choke,
  frustration,
  opposition,
  preventive
blockish: oafish
bloke: bird, boy, chap,
  fellow, guy, man,
  punter
blond: fair, gold(en),
  light
blonde: fair, gold(en)
blood-thirsty: savage
blood: birth, family,
  gore, kin, race
bloodbath: butchery,
  massacre
bloodcurdling: hair-
  raising, macabre
bloodless: grey, white
bloodletting:
  bleeding
bloodshed: bleeding,
  butchery, slaughter,
  violence
bloodshot: red
bloodstained: red
bloodsucker: leech,
  parasite
bloodthirstiness:
  cruelty, ferocity
bloodthirsty: cruel,

  ferocious, murderous
bloody: atrocious,
  grisly, gruesome,
  lurid, murderous,
  raw, underdone,
  violent
bloom: blossom,
  blush, colour,
  flourish, flower,
  mature, maturity
bloomer: error, slip
bloomers: knickers,
  pants
blooming: fresh,
  green, out, red, rosy,
  thriving
blossom: boom,
  flourish, flower,
  mature, progress
blossoming: bloom,
  maturity, thriving
blot: blemish, blur,
  disfigurement, mar,
  mark, mess, shame,
  slur, smear, speck,
  spot, stain
blotch: blemish, blot,
  disfigurement, mess,
  smear
blotchy: messy,
  mottled
blotto: drunk,
  inebriated, tight
blouson: blouse
blow: bang, blast, box,
  breathe, bump,
  catastrophe, check,
  clip, crack, cut,
  disaster, distress, fan,
  flurry, hit, impact,
  jab, knock, lash,
  mishap, pant,
  percussion, pity,
  punch, rage, rap,
  reverse, shock, slap,
  smack, sorrow,
  squander, strike,
  stroke, switch,
  wallop, waste, wind
blower: fan, telephone
blowy: chilly
blub: weep, whimper
blubber: bawl, cry,
  fat, snivel, sob, weep,
  whimper
blubbering: bawl
blubbery: fat
blubbing: tearful
bludgeon: club,
  cudgel
blue: bawdy, broad,
  dejected, dirty, flat,
  foul, fruity, gloomy,
  glum, immodest,
  lewd, low, miserable,
  obscene,

pornographic, racy, raunchy, sad, suggestive
blueprint: chart, design, plan, projection, scheme
bluff: blunt, rough, strut
bluffing: bluster
blunder: err, fault, gaffe, mistake, oversight, slip
blundering: awkward, clumsy, uncouth, ungainly
blunt: bald, bluff, brusque, candid, curt, direct, dull, forthright, frank, obtuse, outspoken, plain, raw, rough, round, rude, rugged, straight
bluntly: directly, frankly, roughly
blur: dim, film, flash, muddy, obfuscate, obscure, smear
blurred: cloudy, dim, foggy, ghostly, indistinct, muddy, obscure, vague, woolly
blurry: filmy
blush: bloom, colour, flame, flush, glow
blushing: red, rosy
bluster: bluff, wind
blustery: boisterous, choppy, foul, stormy, tempestuous, violent, wild
boar: hog, male, pig
board: authority, commission, committee, council, get on, keep, leaf, lodge, lodgings, management, panel, put up, quarter, shelf, sign, table
boarder: guest, lodger
boarding: lodgings
boards: timber
boast: bluster, display, pride, show off, strut
boastful: big, proud, pompous
boastfulness: bluff
boasting: bluster, mouth, strut
boat: craft, gig, launch, ship, vessel
bob: bow, float, nod
bobber: float

bobbin: roll
bobwhite: quail
bodge up: fudge
bodice: blouse, corset
bodily: sensual, sensuous, corporal, physical
body: assembly, band, bodily, bulk, company, contingent, corpse, density, fat, figure, flesh, floor, force, form, frame, mass, object, organization, party, soul, substance, trunk
bodywork: chassis
bog: fen, lavatory, mire, swamp, toilet, quagmire
bogey: ogre
boggle: muddy, sodden, watery, wonder
bogus: artificial, mock, phoney, sham, spurious
boil: bubble, ferment, jug, pustule, seethe, sore
boiled: poached
boiler: copper
boiling: baking, furious, hot, smouldering
boisterous: blustery, furious, heavy, mischievous, obstreperous, robust, rough, rowdy, tempestuous, undisciplined, uproarious, violent, wild
boisterously: roughly
boisterousness: mischief, riot, violence
bold: assured, brazen, chivalrous, confident, cool, daring, defiant, familiar, fearless, forward, fresh, gallant, hardy, heroic, high-spirited, immodest, intrepid, pert, presumptuous, resolute, spartan, spirited, stout, strong, valiant
boldness: assurance, confidence, courage, daring, familiarity, forwardness, gallantry, heroism,

presumption, prowess, resolution, resolve, valour
bole: trunk
bolero: blouse, jacket
bollock: nut
bolshie: unhelpful
bolster: back up, buttress, prop, reinforce, shore up, support
bolstering: reassurance
bolt: bar, career, catch, clinch, devour, eat, fastener, flee, fly, gorge, gulp, key, lock, make off, peg, quarrel, run, secure, shoot, sieve, sift, bundle, wolf
bomb: bombard, fortune, killing, mine, mint, pile, pelt
bombard: bomb, cannon, pepper, plaster, ply, shell
bombardment: barrage, fire, hail, volley
bombast: bluster, claptrap
bombastic: pompous, pretentious, turgid
bombshell: surprise
bon mot: witticism
bona fide: genuine, good, honest, official, sincere, sincerity
bonce: block, head, nut
bond: bail, bridge, cement, chain, charter, compact, connection, cord, engagement, fasten, fix, knot, liaison, link, oath, pawn, pledge, promise, relationship, seal, shackle, tack, tenacity, treaty, unify, union, unite, unity, weld, yoke
bondage: yoke, servitude, slavery
bonds: papers, restraint
boneheaded: obtuse
bones: remains
bonkers: crazy, insane, lunatic, mad
bonnet: hood
bonny: fair, fine, good-looking, pretty, winning
bonus: gratuity,

reward, tip, windfall, premium
bony: gaunt, lean, meagre, scrawny, skeletal, thin
boo: barrack, catcall
boob: blunder, breast, error, fluff, mistake, slip
boogie: dance
booing: bird, jeering
book-keeping: clerical
book-learning: scholarship
book: bag, block, novel, order, programme, publication, reserve, schedule, take, volume, writing
bookcase: press
booking: order
bookish: intellectual, literary, pedantic, studious
booklet: tract
bookstall: kiosk
bookworm: scholar
boom: chime, bang, bar, barrage, barrier, bellow, crane, gate, jib, pole, report, roll, thunder
boomerang: backfire, rebound, recoil
booming: hollow, resounding, successful, thriving, thunderous
boon: asset, barbarian, blessing, godsend
boor: barbarian, brute, clown, hog, lout, philistine, savage
boorish: barbarian, bovine, churlish, coarse, gross, ignorant, impolite, philistine, rude, rustic, tactless, uncouth, ungracious, vulgar
boorishness: coarseness
boos: jeering
boost: augment, bolster, flip, intensify, jack, jump, kick, lift, promote, push, raise, reassurance, speed, tonic
booster: pylon
boosting: promotion
boot: hack, kick

booth: boutique, compartment, kiosk, stand
bootleg: illegal, run
bootless: fruitless, futile, ineffectual, senseless, unprofitable, vain
bootlicker: creep, yes-man
bootlicking: grovelling, ingratiating, obsequious
boots: footwear
booty: haul, loot, pillage, plunder, prize, winnings
booze: carouse, drink, fuddle, tipple
boozed up: drunk, inebriated
boozer: inn, pub
bop: dance
borborygmus: gurgle
bordello: brothel
border: bank, bed, bind, binding, bound, boundary, divide, fringe, hedge, hem, junction, limb, limit, line, march, margin, neighbour, periphery, rim, side, skirt, touch, trim, verge
bordering: beside, marginal
borderland: march
borders: outskirts
bore: bind, bit, calibre, drag, drill, gauge, nuisance, pain, pall, perforate, pest, pill, sink, weary, well
bored: blasé, jaded, sick, unimpressed, weary
boredom: tedium
borer: drill
boring: barren, dead, deadly, dismal, dull, flat, interminable, lacklustre, menial, monotonous, routine, trying, unimaginative, wearisome
born: destined
borough: municipal
borrowed: derivative
bosh: flannel, rot
bosom: breast, bust
boss: button, captain, chief, contractor, director, gaffer, head, knob, master, oracle,

overseer, stud, superior
bossy: overbearing, peremptory
botch: bungle, butcher, fluff, miscarriage, ruin
botched: jerry-built
bother: badger, bind, bite, bore, concern, distress, disturb, disturbance, drag, fret, fuss, hassle, inconvenience, irritate, kerfuffle, molest, nuisance, pain, persecute, perturb, pest, pester, plague, put out, state, trial, trouble, upset, vex, worry
bothered: concerned, flustered, upset, worried
bothering: inconvenience
bothersome: importunate, nagging, trying, vexatious
bothy: cabin
bottle: backbone, courage, flask, guts, heart, pluck
bottled-up: pent-up
bottleneck: congestion, throttle
bottom: base, basis, beam, bed, behind, buttocks, dell, end, floor, foot, minimum, nadir, rear, tail
bottomless: profound, yawning
boudoir: cabinet
bough: branch, limb, log, spray
boulder: rock
boulevard: avenue, street
bounce: bob, bound, bump, caper, jerk, jog, jump, put out, rattle, rebound, skip, spring
bouncy: bumpy, resilient
bound: border, bounce, certain, circumscribe, compass(es), end, hop, jump, leap, liable, limit, lunge, march, obliged, responsible, restrict, spring, sure
boundaries: confines

boundary: barrier, border, end, hedge, limit, line, march, margin, outskirts, side, paling
bounded: finite, limited
boundless: incalculable, indefinite, infinite, unbounded, vast
boundlessness: immensity
bounds: circle, confines, field, range
bounteous: liberal
bounteousness: munificence
bountiful: copious, fruitful, generous, handsome, hearty, lavish, liberal, prodigal, round
bounty: bonus, generosity, largess, munificence
bouquet: bunch, buttonhole, fragrance, nose, odour, perfume, scent, smell
bourgeois: conventional
bourgeoisie: yuppies
bourse: finance
bout: attack, dose, fight, fit, match, round, spell, tournament, turn
bovine: dense, lumbering, oafish
bovines: cattle
bow: beak, bend, bob, buckle, dip, distort, flex, fore, inclination, incline, knot, nod, yield
bowdlerize: censor
bowed: bent, crooked, curved, round, untrue
bowels: guts, inside, intestines
bowl: basin, crater, delivery, depression, dish, flare, hollow, pot
bows: prow
box: bang, booth, canister, carton, case, casket, clip, clout, crate, crib, drawer, knock, package, panel, punch, smack, spar, trunk
boxer: pugilist
boxing-match: fight, spar

boy: juvenile, kid, lad, male, page, youngster, youth
boycott: ban, ostracize, sanction
boycotted: black
boyfriend: date, flame, lover, man
boyhood: youth
boyish: babyish
bra: cup
brace: bolster, buttress, clamp, couple, fortify, harden, immobilize, lag, leg, nerve, pair, plate, prop, shore up, stake, steady, strut, support
bracelet(s): cuff, handcuff
bracelet: bangle, jewellery
bracer: tonic
bracing: brisk, crisp, fresh, healthy, invigorating, refreshing
bracken: brake, undergrowth
bracket: brace, clamp, fish, link, pair, range, yoke
brackish: salty, stagnant
bract: leaf
brag: bluster, boast, show off
braggadocio: bluster
bragging: boastful, mouth
braid: lace, loop, twine, weave
braids: tresses
brain: genius, loaf, mind, nut
brainchild: invention
brainless: fatuous, foolish, silly, simple
brainlessness: stupidity
brains: capacity, head, intelligence, mastermind, wits
brainteaser: puzzle
brainwash: indoctrinate, notion
brainy: intelligent
brake: curb, pull up
bramble: lawyer
branch: bough, discipline, diverge, fork, limb, lodge, log, perch, section, shoot, spray, split
branches: wood

brand-new: mint
brand: burn,
characterize,
impression, kind,
label, line, make,
mark, scar, slur, sort,
stamp, variety
branded: marked,
tainted
brandish: dangle,
flourish, hold up,
parade, shake, wave,
wield
brandishing: pass
brandy: cognac
brash: bold, cocky,
loud, meretricious,
overconfident, pushy,
rash, shameless
brashness: temerity
brass: brazen, money,
sauce
brassica: cabbage
brassicas: greens
brassière: bra
brassy: brazen,
garish, loud
brat: child
bravado: bluff,
bluster, panache
brave: beard, bold,
challenge, chivalrous,
daring, defy, face,
gallant, game, heroic,
intrepid, manfully,
stout, strong, valiant,
warrior
bravery: bottle,
courage, daring,
gallantry, guts,
heroism, manliness,
nerve, pluck,
prowess, valour
brawl: fight, fracas,
row, scrap, scuffle,
wrangle
brawn: beef, flesh,
meat, muscle,
strength, power
brawny: beefy, burly,
lusty, meaty, mighty,
muscular, powerful,
robust, rugged, stout,
sturdy, tough
brazen: assured,
blatant, cool, flagrant,
forward, fresh,
impertinent,
shameless
brazenness:
forwardness, nerve
brazier: blaze, fire,
hearth
breach: break, burst,
chasm, disaffection,
fracture, leak, rift,

rupture, schism, split,
violation
breached: burst
bread: money
breadth: beam,
depth, width
break: breach, burst,
bust, cashier, change,
crack, crash, crumple,
dawn, decipher,
degrade, divorce,
domesticate, falter,
fracture, gap, hiatus,
holiday, infringe,
interlude, interval,
jump, kick, master,
opening, opportunity,
pause, puncture,
quaver, recess,
release, relief, relieve,
rent, respite, rest, rift,
ruin, rupture, schism,
secession, separation,
shatter, shivers,
smash, snack, snap,
split, start, stop,
violate
breakable: fragile
breakaway: rogue
breakdown: collapse,
decomposition,
dissolution, failure,
ruin, shock,
malfunction
breaker: wave
breakneck:
precipitate
breakwater: jetty,
pier
breast: bosom, bust,
mound
breath: life, puff,
spirit, waft, whiff,
whisper, wind
breathe: live, puff,
waft, whisper
breather: break,
pause, relief, respite
breathing: live
breathtaking:
spectacular,
stupendous, superb
breed: develop, farm,
generate, grow, kind,
mate, multiply, order,
pedigree, proliferate,
race, raise, rear,
reproduce, sort,
species, stamp, stock,
variety
breeder: farmer
breeding:
background, birth,
propagation,
reproduction
breeze: breath,

draught, waft, wind
breezy: buoyant,
jaunty, chilly
brethren:
congregation
brew: concoct, drink,
ferment, potion
briar: pipe
briars: undergrowth
bribe: buy, corrupt,
kickback, lubricate,
nobble, payoff, rake-
off, square
bribery: graft,
kickback
bric-à-brac: jumble,
junk, knick-knacks
brick: block
brickwork: wall
bridal: conjugal
bride: bar, wife,
woman
bridegroom: groom
bridge: cross, span,
traverse
bridging: temporary
bridle-path: track
bridle: bristle, master,
rein
brief: compact,
concise, crisp, file,
laconic, momentary,
passing, post, prime,
quick, remit,
succinct, short,
spastic
briefly: quickly,
shortly
briefs: pants
brig: jail
brigade: force, legion,
team
brigand: bandit,
gangster, outlaw,
pirate
bright: astute, bold,
brilliant, buoyant,
clear, clever,
colourful, fair, festive,
fine, florid, fresh,
gaudy, gay, glaring,
gleaming, glorious,
intelligent, intense,
irrepressible, light,
liquid, lively, lucid,
promising, quick-
witted, ready,
resourceful, rich,
rosy, scintillating,
sharp, shining, shiny,
smart, strong, sunny,
vivid, white
brighten: cheer up,
clear, dawn,
illuminate, kindle,
light, lighten, smarten

brightly: gaily,
sharply
brightness: brilliance,
fire, glare, glory,
glow, light, lucidity,
magnitude, polish,
serenity, sheen, shine,
splendour
brilliance: blaze,
colour, fire, genius,
glare, glory, light,
lucidity, lustre,
sparkle, splendour,
virtuosity
brilliant: bright,
colourful, fine, gaudy,
gifted, gleaming,
glorious, jewel, light,
lucid, luminous,
masterly, meteoric,
radiant, scintillating,
shining, splendid,
star, vivid, wonder,
wonderful
brilliants: jewellery
brim: brink, lip, rim,
verge
brimming: teeming,
full
brindle: mottled
brindled: speckled
bring: bear, carry,
deliver, fetch, get,
give, move, put,
reduce, see, take,
transport
bringer: bearer
brink: bank, border,
brim, rim, threshold,
verge
briny: drink, sea
brio: life, panache, zip
brisk: chilly, crisp,
fast, fresh, lively,
nimble, perky, quick,
rousing, smart, spry,
stiff, vigorous
briskly: fast, quickly
briskness: rapidity
bristle: barb, bridle
bristles: brush, beard
bristling: teeming,
thick
bristly: rough, wiry
brittle: crisp, fragile
broach: bring up,
introduce, lead up to,
raise, tap
broad: capacious,
comprehensive, deep,
expansive, fat, full,
heavy, liberal,
spacious, sweeping,
thick, wide
broadcast: beam,
carry, cry, disclose,

disperse, emanation, emit, herald, issue, project, publicize, publish, put out, relay, report, scatter, screen, seed, send, transmit, trumpet
broadcaster: journalist
broadcasting: propagation, publication, revelation
broaden: liberalize, spread, thicken, widen
broadening: bulge, dilation, enlargement
broads: fen
broadsheet: bill
brochure: publication
broil: disturbance, grill
broilery: grill
broke: bankrupt, bust, hard up, penniless
broken: battered, burst, bust, cushioned, defective, faltering, faulty, imperfect, kaput, mangled, ragged, rough, rugged, shattered, split, uneven
brokenhearted: heartbroken, wretched
brokerage: commission
bronze: brazen, sculpture
bronzed: brown
brooch: clasp
brooches: jewellery
brood: fret, hatch, litter, mope, muse, nest, ponder, puzzle, think, worry, young
brooding: morbid
broody: moody
brook: bear, digest, endure, river, stream, take
broom: brush
broth: liquor, soup
brotherhood: fellowship, fraternity, order, union
browbeat: bully, intimidate, push
browbeaten: hangdog, overawed
brown: toast
brownie: elf, fairy
bruin: bear

bruise: batter, hurt, swelling
bruised: battered, hurt, livid
bruiser: pugilist, rough, ruffian
bruising: battery, haemorrhage
brunette: brown, dark
brunt: impact
brush: clash, dust, graze, groom, kiss, mop, scrub, scuff, shave, struggle, sweep, touch, undergrowth, whisk, wipe
brushoff: snub
brushwood: scrub
brusque: brief, churlish, crisp, curt, hasty, peremptory, rough, rude, short, surly
brusquely: roughly
brusqueness: asperity
brut: dry
brutal: barbaric, beastly, bestial, cold-blooded, cruel, ferocious, harsh, heartless, inhuman, monstrous, raw, ruthless, sadistic, savage, scathing, violent, vicious
brutality: atrocity, cruelty, ferocity, violence
brutalize: harden
brute: barbarian, beast, coarse, creature, fiend, lout, monster, pig, ruffian, savage
brutish: barbarian, beastly, bestial, monstrous, rude, savage, unnatural, wild
bubble: balloon, bead, blister, boil, ferment, gurgle, seethe, sparkle, yeast
bubbles: foam, lather
bubbling: irrepressible, vivacious
buccaneer: pirate
buck: blade, blood, deer, gallant, male
bucket: bale, kit, skip
buckle: bend, clasp, dent, distort, fasten, fastener, strap
buckled: bent

buckler: shield
bucolic: idyllic, pastoral
bud: bulb, button, germ, germinate, graft, leaf, shoot, sprout
budding: potential
buddy: comrade, friend, mate, pal
budge: move, shift, stir
budget: ration
budgetary: economic
buff: connoisseur, fan, fawn, fiend, freak, nut, tan, zealot
buffer: bumper, guard, pad
buffet: batter, beat, blow, box, crack, hit, knock, punch, wallop
buffoon: clown, joker, zany
buffoonery: farce, fun, slapstick
bug: harass, passion, pester, sickness, tap
bugger: bastard, devil, gay, homosexual
bugle: horn, trumpet
build: base, body, constitution, construct, erect, fashion, figure, form, found, frame, knock off, make, manufacture, mould, physique, put up, raise, rear, shape
builder: founder
building: block, fabric, formation, house, pile
building: construction, premises, property, structure
buildings: facilities
built: made
bulb: globe, light
bulbous: rotund, round
bulge: bag, blister, bump, distend, hump, jut, knot, lump, projection, prominence, stick, swell
bulging: convex, protuberant
bulk: body, density, gross, immensity, majority, mass, quantity, size, volume, width

bulky: corpulent, fat, great, gross, heavy, hulking, massive, overweight, ponderous, stout, ungainly, unwieldy, voluminous
bull: male
bulldoze: bully, compel, demolish, level
bulldozing: demolition
bullet: ball, round, shot
bulletin: communiqué, information, news, report,
bullion: cash
bullock: calf
bullseye: blank, bull, target
bullshit: drivel
bully: bluster, brute, intimidate, lout, maltreat, menace, oppressor, prey on, rough, ruffian, tyrant, yob
bullying: obstreperous
bulwark: bastion, battlements, defence, fortification, rampart, rock, shield, wall
bum: behind, bottom, buttocks, end, false, rear, tail, vagrant
bumbling: inept
bump: brush, bulge, collision, hit, hump, jar, jerk, jostle, knob, knot, lump, percussion, shake, swelling
bumper: drink, guard
bumpkin: lout, peasant, yokel
bumptious: pushy
bumpy: rough, rugged, uneven
bunch: batch, bouquet, bundle, cluster, contingent, crew, crowd, group, knot, lot, lump, pack, parcel, party, press, switch
bundle: bale, bunch, pack, parcel
bung: block, cork, fill, plug, tap, throw, tip, spill
bungalow: chalet
bungle: blunder, mess

bungling: clumsy
bunk: bed, berth, cot,
nonsense
bunker: cellar,
hazard, pocket
bunkum: bull, drivel,
rot, rubbish, stuff
bunny: rabbit
buoy: mooring
buoyancy:
exuberance, spring,
trim
buoyant: carefree,
cheerful, exuberant,
irrepressible,
optimistic, resilient,
sanguine, sunny
burble: babel
burden: charge,
chore, cross, curse,
difficulty,
disadvantage, drag,
drone, exercise,
hardship, impact,
imposition, labour,
lay, liability, load,
misery, obligation,
onus, oppress,
overwork, pack,
penance, pig, prey on,
refrain, saddle, strain,
substance, tax, weary,
weigh, weight, woe,
yoke
burdened: heavy,
laden, loaded
burdensome:
difficult, heavy,
onerous, oppressive,
wearisome, weighty
bureau: department,
desk, ministry, office,
secretary
bureaucratic:
impersonal
burgee: banner, flag,

pennant
burgeon: bloom,
blossom, bud,
flourish, flower,
mushroom,
proliferate, shoot,
spring
burger: cutlet
burgher: citizen
burglar: intruder,
thief
burglary: larceny,
robbery
burgle: rob
burial: funeral
buried: sunken,
underground
burlesque: caricature,
farce, lampoon, mock,
parody, satire, skit
burly: beefy,
corpulent, meaty,
rugged, stout, strong
burn: blaze, brook,
colour, cremate,
flame, flush, glow,
ignite, roast, scorch,
set fire to, smart, tan,
torch
burning: caustic,
excruciating,
fanatical, feverish,
fiery, flaming, hot,
instant, intense, live,
sharp, sore, torrid,
zealous
burnish: furbish,
polish, scour
burnished: shiny
burro: ass
burrow: dig, hole,
tunnel
bursar: cashier
bursary: scholarship
burst: blaze, blow up,
boom, bust, deflate,

flash, flat, flurry,
frenzy, gale, gust,
outbreak, rupture,
shattered, spasm,
splash, split, spurt,
volley
bury: hide, inter
bus: coach, omnibus
bush: hedge
bushes: brush
bushman: pygmy
business: clientele,
commerce,
commercial,
company, concern,
department, firm,
function, game,
house, industry,
interest, job, line,
lookout, patronage,
pigeon, profession,
province, racket,
right, scene, subject,
traffic, work
businesslike:
efficient, impersonal,
methodical, orderly,
practical, pragmatic,
realistic, systematic
buss: kiss
bust: bankrupt,
bosom, breast,
through
bustle: commotion,
confusion, fuss, hum,
kerfuffle, press, whirl
bustling: brisk, lively,
restless
busy: brisk, florid,
fussy, lively,
occupied, working
busybody: gossip
busyness: load
but: except, however,
just, still, yet
butch: male

butcher: joint, kill,
killer, massacre,
mutilate, slaughter
butchery:
assassination,
bloodshed, carnage,
massacre
butt: barrel, fool,
head, joke, nut,
object, ram, target,
victim
butter: fat
buttercup: yellow
buttery: creamy
buttocks: beam, stern
button: fasten,
fastener, knob
buttress: bolster,
brace, fortification,
fortify, pier, prop,
reinforce, shore up,
support
buxom: feminine,
full, voluptuous,
womanly
buy: bribe, credit, pick
up, purchase,
swallow, take, wear
buyer: bull, client,
consumer, customer
buyers: public
buzz: bang, hum, kick,
ring, rumour, sing,
telephone, whisper
by: past
bygone: former, past
bypass: get round,
roundabout, sidestep
bypass: skirt
bystander: passer-by,
witness
byword: maxim,
precept, saying

C

cab: carriage
cabal: ring
cabalistic: mystical
cabbages: greens
cabin: berth, booth,
  box, chalet, cottage,
  hut, lodge, shack
cabinet: booth, case,
  closet, cupboard
cable: flex, line, main,
  rope
cache: hide, hoard,
  stock, store, supply,
  treasury
cachet: kudos,
  prestige
cachinnation:
  laughter
cackle: chuckle,
  laugh, quack
cackling: laughter
cacophonous: noisy,
  rough
cacophony: babel,
  discord, jangle
cadaver: body
cadaverous: gaunt
caddy: canister
cadence: measure,
  rhythm
cadger: scrounger
caduceus: wand
café: canteen
cafeteria: café
cage: crib, enclosure,
  muzzle, pen, shut up,
  skip
caged: captive, pet
cagey: cautious
cahoots: league
cajole: charm, coax,
  get round, wheedle
cajolery: persuasion
cake: bar, bun, dainty,
  delicacy, harden,
  loaf, pastry, pat,
  plug
calamitous: dire,
  disastrous, evil, fatal,
  sad, tragic
calamity: blow,
  calamity, casualty,
  catastrophe, curse,
  disaster, distress, evil,
  tragedy,
calamus: barrel
calcification:

ossification
calcified: concrete
calcine: roast
calculate: balance,
  cast, cipher, count,
  determine, find out,
  plot, quantify,
  reckon, value, work
  out
calculated: conscious,
  deliberate,
  premeditated,
  strategic
calculating: devious,
  scheming, self-
  seeking, shrewd
calculation: count,
  deliberation,
  valuation
calculator: teller
caldron: copper
calendar: schedule
calibrate: measure,
  zero
calibration:
  measurement, scale
calibre: bore,
  character, gauge,
  mould, quality
caliper: brace
call: bay, bid, brand,
  buzz, christen, cite,
  claim, contact, cry,
  demand, designate,
  hail, hold, invitation,
  invite, knell, name,
  nickname, request,
  style, telephone,
  term, visit
callbox: kiosk
called: by, known,
  named
caller: guest
callers: company,
  visitors
calligraphy: hand,
  script, writing
calling: career, craft,
  job, niche, profession,
  station, vocation
callous: brutal, cold-
  blooded, cruel,
  heartless, insensitive,
  merciless, ruthless,
  thick-skinned,
  unnatural,
  unrepentant

callousness: cruelty
callow: fresh, green,
  immature,
  inexperienced, jejune,
  juvenile, mere, naive,
  raw, tender
calm: bland,
  collected, compose,
  cool, even, gentle,
  glassy, halcyon,
  idyllic,
  imperturbable, lull,
  moderate, mollify,
  nonchalance,
  nonchalant, order,
  orderly, pacify,
  patient, peaceful,
  placate, placid, quell,
  quiescent, quiet,
  quieten, relieve, rest,
  restful, sedate, serene,
  settle, silence,
  smooth, sober, soften,
  steady, still, stoical,
  temperate, peace,
  philosophical,
  restrained
calming: dreamy, lull,
  sedative
calmness: calm, cool,
  deliberation, patience,
  serenity, sobriety
calumniate: blacken,
  libel, run down,
  slander, smear, wrong
calumnious:
  defamatory, libellous
calumny: attack,
  libel, mud, vilification
camaraderie:
  companionship
camber: bank, slant
cameo: brooch,
  profile, sculpture
camiknickers:
  knickers
camise: blouse
camisole: blouse
camouflage: cloak,
  conceal, cover,
  disguise, hide, mask,
  secret, whitewash
camp: base, faction,
  gay, headquarters,
  homosexual,
  precious, quarters,
  side

campaign: canvass,
  crusade, drive, lobby,
  move, movement,
  operation, war
campus: college
can: canister
canal: channel, vessel
canary: yellow
cancel: axe, delete,
  dissolve, end, kill, lift,
  nullify, remit, repeal,
  rescind, reverse,
  revoke, rub out,
  scrub, undo, void,
  write off
cancellation: end,
  killing, repeal
cancelled: undone
cancer: growth,
  plague, tumour
cancerous: malignant
candid: direct,
  forthright, frank,
  honest, open,
  outspoken, plain, raw,
  round, transparent,
  unguarded
candidate: entry,
  nominee
candidates: field
candidly: directly,
  frankly, freely, openly
candle: light
candour: honesty,
  simplicity, sincerity
cane: beat, birch,
  castigate, lather,
  punish, rod, scourge,
  staff, stick, wand,
  whip
canines: teeth
caning: hiding,
  punishment
canister: can, case
canker: cancer, rot
cannabis: grass,
  marijuana, pot, weed
canned: drunk,
  inebriated
cannon: battery,
  glance, graze, gun, hit
cannonade: barrage,
  cannon
canny: astute,
  calculating,
  circumspect, clever,
  crafty, cunning, deep,

fly, foxy, keen, sage, sensible, shrewd, smart, tactful, tactical, vulpine, wily
canoe: boat, ship
canon: law, rule, vicar
canonical: dogmatic, scriptural
canopy: awning, blind, cover, roof, screen, shade
cant: bank, hypocrisy, jargon, list, slang, terminology, tip
cantabile: melodious
cantankerous: contrary, mean, peevish, perverse, prickly, querulous
canteen: bar, bottle, flask
canter: jog, trip
canticle: gradual, song
canting: sanctimonious, sententious
canvass: poll
canvasser: solicitor
canyon: defile, gorge, pass, precipice, ravine, valley
cap: better, bonnet, clinch, complement, complete, cover, crown, head, lid, roof, seal, tip
capability: capacity, faculty, potential, power, promise, qualification, wherewithal
capable: clever, competent, proficient, resourceful, self-reliant
capacious: broad, full, roomy, spacious, voluminous, wide
capacitate: enable
capacity: calibre, complement, content, faculty, head, knack, magnitude, office, position, potency, potential, power, qualification, quantity, reach, role, room, scope, space, sphere, volume, wherewithal
cape: cloak, mantle, point, promontory, robe, wrap, head, headland
caper: gambol, lark,

leap, skip, trip
capering: frisky, prancing
capital: cardinal, chief, finance, fund, good, high, means, money, primary, principal, property, reserve, resources, stock, treasury, wherewithal
capitulate: kowtow, lose, submit, succumb, surrender, yield
capitulator: loser
caprice: crank, eccentricity, fancy, freak, humour, quirk, whim
capricious: changeable, fanciful, moody, quirky, unreasonable, wayward, whimsical
capsicum: pepper
capsize: invert, keel, overturn, swamp
capsized: upset, upside down
capstan: mooring
capstone: key, roof
capsule: cartridge, case, medicine, module, pill, tablet
captain: head, leader, master, pilot, sail, skipper
captaincy: leadership
caption: key, legend, motto, narrative
captions: words
captious: fractious, petulant
captivate: catch, charm, delight, enslave, entrance, fascinate, mesmerize, spellbind, transport
captivated: enamoured, bewitched, rapt
captivating: attractive, beguiling, catchy, charming, delightful, inviting, lovable, lovely, magnetic, seductive, winning
captivation: conquest, fascination
captive: hostage, powerless
captivity: restraint, slavery
capture: bag, catch,

collar, gain, grab, hijack, net, nick, seize, seizure, take
car: bus, machine, motor
carafe: flask, jug
caravan: train
carbohydrate: fat
carbonated: bubbly
carbuncle: boil, monstrosity
carcass: corpse, remains
carcinoma: cancer, tumour
card: board, laugh, line, ticket
cardiac muscle: heart
cardigan: jersey, woolly
cardinal: capital, chief, first, main, primary, principal, strategic, supreme, vital
carding: teasing
cardiopulmonary: vital
care: caution, charge, custody, diligence, heed, keeping, maintenance, mind, oversight, protection, prudence, supervision, treatment, trouble, ward, worry
careen: overhaul, keel
career: calling, job, life, pelt, plunge, practice, race, run, rush, speed, sweep
carefree: easy, gay, jaunty, jolly, light, light-hearted, merry, unconcerned
careful: cag(e)y, cautious, circumspect, close, conscientious, frugal, guarded, judicious, meticulous, nice, painstaking, sparing, thorough, thoughtful, wary
carefully: exactly, gingerly, narrowly, warily, well
careless: carefree, heedless, imprecise, inadvertent, lackadaisical, lax, loose, mindless, mischievous, reckless, remiss, short-sighted,

slapdash, slovenly, unbusinesslike, unguarded, unthinking
carelessly: badly
carelessness: negligence, oversight
caress: brush, endearment, feel, fondle, handle, kiss, massage, pat, pet, rub, stroke, touch
caretaker: attendant, custodian, janitor, keeper, warden
cargo: bulk, burden, fetish, freight, load
caricature: cartoon, guy, imitate, imitation, lampoon, mimic, mock, parody, ridicule, satire, send up, take off
caries: decay
carillon: peal
caring: concerned, devoted, solicitous, sympathetic, thoughtful
carmine: red
carnage: bloodshed, butchery, killing, massacre, murder, slaughter
carnal: bawdy, bestial, brutal, erotic, flesh, lecherous, physical, sensual, worldly
carnality: lewdness, lust
carnival: fair, gala
carnivore: predator
carnivorous: predatory
carol: chant, sing, song
carom: plane
carousal: bat, blind, orgy
carouse: drink, revel, riot, tipple
carousel: roundabout
carp: cavil, complain, moan, niggle, quarrel
carpet: blanket, lambast, mat, pull up, rug, upbraid
carpeting: carpet, rebuke, reprimand
carping: fuddy-duddy, nit-picking
carriage: bearing, car, coach, compartment,

freight, poise, presence, stance, transit, transport
carrier: bag, bearer, messenger
carrot: bait, bribe, fiery, incentive, lure, temptation
carry: bear, bring, cart, conduct, deliver, fetch, haul, have, hold, hump, keep, move, run, sustain, transmit, transport
cart: float, haul
carte blanche: liberty, licence
cartel: combination, league, ring
carton: box, case, pack, package, parcel
cartoon: caricature
cartoonist: artist
cartridge: bullet, case, round
carve: butcher, cut, engrave, inscribe, joint, sculpture, slice
carved: cut
carving: etching, sculpture
Casanova: wolf
cascade: cataract, fall, flash, flow, lash, rain, run, stream, waterfall
cascading: gushing
case: box, brief, cabinet, capsule, carton, cartridge, casket, chest, crate, frame, instance, jacket, litigation, matter, patient, process, reasoning, sheath, shell, subject, suit
cased: bound
casern: barracks
cases: luggage
cash: bread, capital, coin, honour, liquidate, monetary, money, wherewithal
cashbox: till
cashier: degrade, discharge, dismiss, fire, teller
casing: bark, binding, bullet, case, frame, jacket, pod
cask: barrel, keg, vat, wood
casket: case, chest
casserole: hash
cassette: cartridge
cassock: gown, frock

cast: look, mint, mould, pitch, precipitate, sculpture, shed, sling, stamp, throw, turn
castanet: rattle,
caste: class, estate, order, position, rank, tribe
castigate: censure, lash, pull up, punish, rebuke, scold, slam, slate
castigation: censure, punishment, row
casting: sculpture, sling
castle: bastion, fort, keep
cast-off: reject
castrate: neuter
casual: blasé, careless, chance, contingent, easy, free, happy, informal, laid-back, lax, mindless, nonchalant, odd, passing, promiscuous, random, scratch, superficial, temporary, throwaway, unenthusiastic
casually: happily
casuals: jeans
casualty: victim
casuistical: evasive
casuistry: sophistry
cat: bitch, scourge
cataclysm: disaster, earthquake
cataclysmic: disastrous
catacomb: tomb, vault
catalogue: canon, classify, detail, identify, list, order, range, recite, register, roll, schedule, table, pigeonhole
cataloguing: breakdown, recital,
catalyse: precipitate
catamite: gay, homosexual, queer
cataract: waterfall
catarrh: cold
catastrophe: blow, calamity, casualty, debacle, disaster, doom, evil, fiasco, tragedy
catastrophic: dire, disastrous, evil, fatal, tragic

catcalling: jeering
catcalls: jeering
catch: bag, bolt, buckle, bust, capture, clutch, collar, conquest, contract, draught, field, find, fire, fish, get, glee, grab, grasp, haul, hear, hitch, hook, jingle, keeper, lodge, make, nab, nail, net, obtain, pitfall, pull, rub, snag, snap, snare, take, trap, trip
catching: contagious
catchword: slogan
catchy: memorable, melodious
categorical: dogmatic, flat, peremptory, positive, unqualified
categorically: flat, flatly, really, positively
categorization: order
categorize: class, classify, grade, label, sort, stamp
categorized: numbered
category: class, compartment, denomination, grade, group, kind, label, league, manner, nature, pigeonhole, run, sort, species, style, variety
catering: board, provision
caterpillar: grub
caterwaul: bawl
caterwauling: bawling
cathartic: laxative, purge
cathedral: basilica, church, dome
catheterize: bleed
catholic: general, liberal, universal
cathouse: brothel
catnap: doze, snooze, sleep
cattle: stock
cattleman: farmer
catwalk: bridge
Caucasian: white
caucus: cell, movement
caught: bust, made
causative: effective
cause: breed, call, create, derivation, do, effect, fountain,

generate, give, grounds, impel, induce, kindle, lead, part, produce, prompt, provoke, raise, reason, root, sake, source, spring
causeless: needless
causeway: embankment
caustic: biting, bitter, corrosive, cutting, devastating, mordant, peppery, pungent, sarcastic, scathing, severe, sharp, vitriolic
cauterize: fire, scour
caution: calculation, care, forewarn, heed, precaution, providence, prudence, warn, warning
cautionary: warning
cautious: cag(e)y, calculating, careful, circumspect, conservative, discreet, far-sighted, guarded, judicious, noncommittal, safe, tentative, wary
cautiously: gingerly, warily
cavalcade: column, parade, procession
cavalier: gallant
cave: pot, tomb, tunnel
caveat: qualification
cavern: cave, grotto
cavernous: profound, yawning
cavil: carp, niggle, prevaricate, quarrel, quibble
cavity: cave, cell, chamber, corner, hole, lacuna, pocket, recess
cavort: caper, dance, gambol, lark, leap
cavorting: prancing
cavy: guinea-pig
caw: croak
cayenne: pepper
cease: close, conclude, discontinue, drop, end, fail, finish, halt, lay off, leave, pass, quit, rest, stop, suspend, wind up
ceasefire: truce
ceaseless: constant, incessant, nonstop,

steady, perennial
ceaselessly: nonstop
cede: concede, give,
leave, render, yield
ceding: delivery
ceiling: limit,
maximum, vault
celebrate:
commemorate,
glorify, honour, keep,
lionize, observe
celebrated:
distinguished,
famous, glorious,
great, illustrious,
known, leading,
legendary, noted,
prestigious,
prominent, public,
star
celebrating: rejoicing
celebration: carnival,
do, feast, festival,
gala, jubilation,
jubilee, keeping,
party, rave, revel,
rejoicing
celebratory: festive
celebrity: distinction,
eminence, fame,
figure, god, hero,
legend, name,
personage,
personality, prestige,
prominence,
somebody, star,
renown, worthy
celerity: rapidity,
speed
celestial: divine,
heavenly, seraphic
celibate: ascetic,
continent, monastic
cell: battery, egg,
enclosure, ring, seed
cellar: basement,
vault
cells: jug, nick, tissue
celluloid: film, wax
cembalom: zither
cement: bond, cake,
concrete, consolidate,
fasten, fix, glue, join,
knit, paste
cemented: stuck
cenobite: hermit
cenobitic: monastic
cense: fumigate
censor: hush up,
mutilate, muzzle,
suppress
censorious: fuddy-
duddy, vituperative
censorship: blackout,
repression
censure: blame, carp,

castigate, criticism,
criticize, denounce,
deprecate, jaw, knock,
lash, lecture, pan, rap,
rebuke, reprimand,
reproach, scold,
upbraid
census: poll, roll
central: base, basic,
capital, middle
centralization:
concentration
centre: base, basis,
bosom, concentrate,
core, foreground,
heart, hub, interior,
middle, mission,
nucleus, pivot, seat,
thick
ceramics: china,
pottery
cereals: grain
cerebral: intellectual
cerebrate: ponder
cerebrum: brain
ceremonial:
ceremony, formal,
occasional, ritual,
solemnity
ceremonious: ritual,
solemn, stately
ceremony:
ceremonial, formality,
rite, ritual, service
cert: favourite, nap,
natural, selection
certain: clear,
confident, dead,
definite, known,
positive, safe, secure,
special
certainly: indeed,
naturally, necessarily,
positively, really,
undeniably,
undoubtedly, yes
certainty: breeze,
conviction, favourite,
knowledge, natural,
security, selection
certifiable: crazy,
insane, mad,
psychotic
certificate: diploma,
licence, paper, patent,
qualification,
certified: official
certify: license,
warrant
certitude: assurance
cerulean: blue
cessation: end,
respite, rest, stop
chador: veil
chafe: fret, fume, gall,
graze, irritate, pain,

pinch, rub, sore,
sweat
chaff: banter, joke,
ridicule, roast
chaffer: haggle
chaffing: banter
chafing: friction
chagrin: confusion,
crush, disappoint,
disappointment,
dismay,
embarrassment,
mortification,
mortify, shame
chagrined: ashamed
chain: bond, cable,
curb, fasten, leash,
range, run, secure,
shackle, sling, string,
tissue, train
chained: bound,
powerless
chains: irons
chair: chairperson,
moderate, place,
preside over, seat,
umpire
chairperson: chair,
principal
chalet: booth, cabin,
cottage, hotel, lodge
chalice: cup
chalky: white
challenge: chicken,
compete, contest,
dare, defy, dispute,
query, question, run
challenger:
champion,
competitor,
opponent, rival
challengers:
competition
challenging: defiant,
demanding,
formidable, rigorous
chamber: barrel,
cabinet, chamber,
cell, compartment,
council, hall, lock,
room, tomb,
champagne: bubbly
champion: befriend,
best, conqueror,
defend, hero,
immortal, maintain,
patron, prize,
promote, support,
uphold, urge, victor,
victorious, warrior
championship:
crown, competition
chance: break, casual,
coincidental,
convenience, fortune,
gamble, hazard,

incidental, light, lot,
lottery, luck, opening,
opportunity,
prospect, random,
resort, risk, room,
stake, start, stray,
time, unpredictable,
venture, wager
chancellor: premier
chances: odds
chancy: speculative,
hairy, precarious
change: break, coin,
convert, departure,
difference,
differentiate, doctor,
dress, falsify,
innovation, juggle,
metamorphosis,
modification, modify,
modulation,
mutation, rearrange,
reverse, shift,
substitute, transit,
transition, trim, turn,
variation, variety,
vary
changeable: fickle,
fluid, giddy,
inconsistent, mobile,
moody, mutable,
unpredictable,
unsettled, variable,
volatile, wayward
changed: different
changeless: timeless,
transition
changeover:
transition,
transposition
changing: chequered,
variable
channel: band,
conductor, course,
cutting, ditch, dock,
feed, funnel, gate,
groove, harness,
hollow, instrument,
lane, main, medium,
outlet, pipe, slide,
slot, strait(s), trench,
vehicle, vessel, way
chant: intone, lay,
sing, song, ululate
chaos: babel,
confusion, disarray,
disorder, havoc,
hubbub, maelstrom,
mayhem, mess,
misrule, shambles,
void
chaotic: disorganized,
muddled,
promiscuous, upset
chap: bird, boy, devil,
fellow, guy, lad, man,

scout
chapel: church
chaperon: attend,
attendant,
companion, guide
chaplain: clergyman,
padre, vicar
chaplet: crown,
garland
chapter: clause,
episode, lodge, phase
char: burn, daily,
maid, scorch, woman
charabanc: bus
character: backbone,
card, chap, cipher,
complexion,
constitution,
customer,
description, face,
figure, fish, flavour,
form, grain,
individual, initial,
key, kind, letter, lot,
make-up, mould,
nature, original, part,
personality, quality,
reputation, role, sort,
stamp, temperament,
tone, worthy
characterful:
colourful
characteristic:
attribute, classic,
demonstrative,
distinction, idiomatic,
idiosyncratic,
individual,
mannerism, natural,
peculiar, point,
proper, property,
quality,
representative,
respect, special,
specific, style, unique,
unusual
characterization:
description
characterize:
describe, label,
qualify
characterless: grey,
insipid, mousy
characters: writing
charade: masquerade,
pretence
charge: assignment,
attack, attribute,
bearing, bill, blame,
care, cartridge,
command,
commission, control,
cost, count, custody,
demand, duty, fee,
fuel, function, hire,
imposition, job,

keeping, lay, levy,
libel, load, lunge,
management,
mission, obligation,
onset, onslaught,
price, prime,
protection, push, rate,
rush, saddle, score,
storm, sue,
supervision, task, toll,
ward, weight
charged: electric,
explosive, fateful,
loaded, pregnant
charily: gingerly,
warily
chariness: distrust
charisma: glamour,
magic, personality
charitable:
benevolent, generous,
good, humane, kind,
kindly, liberal,
philanthropic,
understanding, soft-
hearted
charity: compassion,
generosity, grace,
hand-out, kindliness,
kindness, largess
charlatan: cheat,
fake, fraud, hypocrite,
rogue, swindler,
quack
charlie: sap
charm: attract,
attraction, beauty,
captivate, catch,
conjure, delight,
entrance, fascination,
grace, lure, medicine,
melt, personality,
please, sorcery, spell,
spellbind, take,
talisman, wheedle,
win
charmed: lucky,
pleased, rapt
charmer: beauty
charming: attractive,
delightful, disarming,
engaging, fetching,
idyllic, lovable,
lovely, magnetic,
nice, personable,
pleasant, pretty,
ravishing, romantic,
suave, sweet, winning
chart: diagram,
graphic, grid,
illustration, plan,
plot, profile, scheme,
table
charter: booking,
constitution, diploma,
franchise, hire, lease,

legislation, licence,
rent
chartered:
constitutional
chary: wary
chase: badger, course,
engrave, game,
hound, hunt, pursue,
pursuit, quest, race,
rout, woo
chasm: defile, drop,
gorge, gulf, pit,
precipice, ravine
chaste: celibate, clean,
continent,
immaculate, innocent,
modest, pure, severe,
virgin, virtuous
chasten: deflate,
humble, mortify,
punish, upbraid
chastened: repentant,
subdued
chastening:
punishment
chastise: castigate,
discipline, punish,
strike
chastisement:
discipline,
punishment
chastity: honour,
innocence, modesty,
purity, virtue
chat: chatter,
conversation, gossip,
jaw, natter, talk, tête-
à-tête, word
chateau: castle
chattels: goods
chatter: chat, gab, go
on, hubbub, jaw, keep
on, mouth, natter,
prattle, rabbit,
ramble, rattle, talk,
yap
chatterbox: gossip
chatterer: chatterbox
chattering: babel,
maundering
chattiness: jaw
chatty: garrulous
chauffeur: driver,
ferry
chauvinism:
intolerance
chauvinist:
intolerant,
xenophobic
cheap: economic,
flashy, jerry-built,
low, petty, pulp,
shabby, petty, vulgar
cheapen: degrade,
depress, devalue,
prostitute

cheapening:
prostitution
cheat: charlatan,
deceive, do, fiddle,
fleece, have, outwit,
rob, rogue, screw,
swindle, swindler,
take in, take,
victimize, wrong
cheating: deception
check: audit, barrier,
block, bottleneck,
brake, bridle, cheat,
control, curb, delay,
go through, govern,
halt, hitch, hindrance,
inhibit, interrupt,
keep, leash, lid, limit,
look into, nip,
obstacle, obstruct,
obstruction, probe,
quell, rein, repress,
restraint, restriction,
retard, reverse, run
over, scan, service,
setback, slow, stem,
stifle, stop, stoppage,
suppress, temper
cheek: face,
forwardness, gall,
impertinence,
insolence, lip, mouth,
nerve, presumption
cheekiness: sauce
cheeky: bold, cool,
disrespectful,
forward, fresh,
impertinent,
irrepressible,
irreverent,
presumptuous, saucy
cheep: peep, warble
cheer: clap, comfort,
hail, lighten, please,
rejoicing, revive,
whoop
cheered: pleased
cheerful: bright,
carefree, exuberant,
gay, glad, happy,
jocular, jolly, joyous,
light, light-hearted,
optimistic, pleasant,
rosy, smiling
cheerfully: gaily,
happily
cheerfulness:
exuberance,
happiness
cheering: auspicious,
glad, heart-warming,
jubilation, satisfying
cheerless: bleak,
desolate, dismal,
inhospitable, sad
cheerlessness:

sadness
cheers: thanks
cheery: buoyant,
cheerful, genial,
irrepressible, sunny
chef: cook
chemise: blouse
cheque: draft
chequered:
changeable
cherish: foster, love,
mother, support,
value
cherished: dear, fond,
pet, precious,
valuable
chest: bosom, box,
breast, bust, case,
casket, drawer, trunk
chestnut: bay, brown,
maroon, red, wheeze
chevalier: cavalier
chevron: bar, tab
chew: bite, mouth
chic: exclusive,
fashionable, natty,
sharp, smart, style
chicanery: artifice,
deception, fraud,
machination
chick: bird, doll, girl,
woman
chicken: hen, layer,
yellow
chide: boss, check,
lecture, rebuke,
reprimand, reproach,
scold, upbraid
chief: capital, captain,
cardinal, director,
first, foremost, great,
head, high, leader,
leading, main, master,
operator, oracle,
overseer, paramount,
predominant, pre-
eminent, primary,
principal, ruling,
senior, sovereign,
special, superior,
supreme, trunk
chiefly: mainly,
primarily
chieftain: chief
chieftaincy:
leadership
chiffon: filmy, flimsy,
lace
child: baby, issue,
junior, juvenile, kid,
offspring, youngster
childbirth: delivery,
labour
childish: baby,
babyish, frivolous,
immature, infantile,

puerile, juvenile
childless: barren
childlike: babyish,
naive, primitive,
simple
children: brood,
descendants, family,
issue, litter, offspring,
posterity, young
chill: cold, cool,
cough, cutting, damp,
freeze, freezing, frost,
nip
chilled: cool
chilling: cool
chilly: bleak, chill,
cold, frigid, frosty,
nippy, raw, stiff,
unfriendly, wintry
chime: jangle, jingle,
knell, peal, ring, toll
chimerical: fanciful,
fantastic, romantic,
Utopian
chiming: jangle,
jingle, knell, peal
chimney: funnel
chin: jowls
china: friend, mate
chine: defile, gorge,
precipice, ravine
chink: crack, cleft,
gap, jangle, jingle,
rift, rent
chinking: jangle,
jingle
chinwag: tête-à-tête
chip: bit, carve,
counter, crack, flake,
fraction, fragment,
knap, nick, splinter
chipping: flake
chippings: ballast,
grit
chippolata: sausage
chirp: peep, sing,
warble, peep
chirpy: bubbly, lively
chirrup: peep, warble
chisel: carve, chip,
cut, engrave
chiselling: sculpture
chitchat: gossip,
natter, chat
chivalrous: gallant
chivalry: gallantry,
manliness
chivvy: badger,
harass, nag
chivvying:
harassment
chock-a-block: full
choice: bet, cream,
decision, favourite,
lot, nominee, option,
pick, pleasure,

preference, pride,
prime, select,
selection, superb,
superior, vote, will
choicest: optimum,
pick
choir: chorus
choirboy: girlish
choke: block, stifle,
strangle, throttle
choked: overcrowded,
smothered
choky: prison
choler: bile, wrath
choleric:
cantankerous,
quarrelsome, quick-
tempered, wrathful
chomp: bite, eat,
nibble
choose: cast, decide,
draw, elect, nominate,
opt for, pick, please,
prefer, return, select,
single, sort, take, will
choosing: draw
choosy: dainty, fussy,
particular
chop: cut, cutlet, hack,
knap, log, mince
chopped: cut
chopper: axe
choppily: roughly
choppy: bumpy,
rough, spastic, wild
chops: mouth
chore: bore, drag,
grind, labour, pig,
sweat, task, work
choristers: choir,
chorus
chortle: chuckle,
giggle, gurgle, laugh
chortling: laughter
chorus: chant, choir,
refrain
chosen: elect,
representative
chow: food, grub,
meat
christen: baptize, call,
name, term
christened: named
christening: baptism
Christmastide: Yule
chromosomal:
genetic
chronic: habitual
chronicle: book, log,
record, register,
relate, roll, narrate,
story
chronicled: historical
chronicler: journalist,
narrator
chronicles: history

chronological:
consecutive, temporal
chronometer: clock,
watch
chubby: obese,
plump, rotund,
overweight
chuck: cast, fling,
pitch, sling, throw,
tip
chuckle: giggle,
gurgle, laugh
chuckling: laughter
chum: friend,
intimate, pal, mate
chummy: friendly
chump: ass, fool,
idiot, sap
chunder: waffle
chunk: lump, mass,
piece
church: basilica, faith,
faithful, mission,
sanctuary, sect
churchman: divine,
priest
churchyard:
cemetery
churl: lout
churlish: boorish,
disagreeable, rough,
rude, rugged, sour,
sulky, surly
churn: boil, shake
chute: shoot, slide
chutney: relish
cicatrix: scar
cigar: weed
cigarette: weed
ciggy: cigarette
cinch: breeze,
favourite, picnic
cincture: belt, girdle,
hoop
cinematography:
projection
cipher: character,
figurehead, formula,
language, zero
circadian: daily,
quotidian
circle: clique, club,
company,
compass(es), crease,
cycle, disc, knot, lap,
loop, orbit,
revolution, revolve,
ring, round, school,
set, society, sphere,
wheel, whirl
circlet: hoop
circling: circulation
circuit: beat, circle,
compass(es), course,
lap, revolution, ring,
round, route, tour

circuitous: complex, devious, oblique, rambling, roundabout, wandering, winding
circuitously: indirectly
circuitry: network
circular: bill, handout, memo, round, spiral
circulate: broadcast, float, flow, issue, proclaim, put out, release, rumour, run, spread
circulating: current
circulation: currency, flow
circumference: circle, compass(es), confines, periphery
circumnavigate: bypass, circle, detour, orbit
circumnavigation: bypass, detour, orbit
circumscribe: define, enclose, limit
circumscribed: finite, limited
circumscribing: definition
circumspect: careful, cautious, judicious, noncommittal, safe, wary, watchful
circumspection: calculation, care, caution, prudence
circumspectly: warily
circumstance: case, development, fact, fortune, incident, matter, occurrence, particular, phenomenon, posture, way,
circumstances: background, condition, context, position, situation, state
circumstantial: detailed
circumvent: foil, get round
circumvention: evasion
circus: ring
cissy: drip
cistern: tank
citadel: bastion, castle, fort, tower
citation: mention

cite: extract, instance, mention, name, quote, specify
cited: named
citing: quotation
citizen: customer, national, native, nobody, resident, subject
citizens: public, people
citrus peel: zest
city: urban
civic: civil, municipal, public, urban
civil: attentive, fair, genteel, gracious, national, obliging, polite, public, temporal
civility: refinement
civilization: culture
civilize: cultivate, educate
civilized: cultivated, cultured, polite, refined, urbane
civilizing: education
clack: click
clad: face
claim: demand, interest, maintain, make out, plea, plead, profess, profession, purport, right, say, stake
claimant: candidate, litigant
clairvoyance: divination
clairvoyant: prophet, prophetic, psychic, seer
clamber: climb, scramble, scale
clamminess: damp, wet
clammy: damp, fishy, moist, slimy, sticky, wet
clamorous: blatant, demanding, importunate, loud, noisy, vocal, vociferous
clamour: babel, bawl, noise, roar, uproar, wail, yell
clamp: clinch, muzzle
clan: family, folk, house, kin, race, tribe
clandestine: hidden, secret, sneak, stealthy, surreptitious
clang: chime, jangle, jingle, peal, ring, toll

clanger: mistake
clangour: peal
clank: clash, jangle, jingle
clanking: jangle, jingle
clap: bang, boom, hand, knock, slap, smack
clapper: hammer
clapping: jubilation, ovation
claptrap: bunk, nonsense, rot, rubbish, stuff
claret: blood
clarification: definition, explanation, illumination, refinement, solution
clarified: clean, refined
clarify: clear, explain, filter, focus, illuminate, light, spell out, solve
clarino: trumpet
clarion: trumpet
clarity: definition, focus, legibility, lucidity, purity, simplicity, water
clash: bang, battle, collide, collision, conflict, crash, difference, disagree, discord, fight, incident, jangle, jar, quarrel, scream, shock, showdown, skirmish, strife, strike, struggle, wrangle
clashing: contrary, different, gaudy, jangle, strident
clasp: brooch, buckle, catch, clutch, couple, embrace, fastener, gather, grasp, grip, hold, hook, hug, keeper, lock, press, seize, squeeze
class: brand, breed, breeding, caste, category, condition, degree, denomination, estate, family, form, grade, group, kind, league, order, polish, position, quality, run, school, sect, sort, species, variety, water
classes: course

classic: ideal, monumental, simple
classification: assortment, category, class, denomination, kingdom, label, method, nomenclature, order, rank, system, theory
classified: assorted, confidential, numbered, secret, undisclosed
classify: catalogue, class, grade, group, identify, label, number, order, organize, pigeonhole, place, range, rank, rate, seed, size, sort
classy: exclusive, sharp
clatter: bang, clash, rattle, noise
clause: chapter, passage, provision, stipulation, member, sentence
claw: maul, rake, scratch
clay: earth, soil, till, wax
clean: bath, brush, clear, dust, fresh, groom, hygienic, immaculate, polish, pure, purify, rub, sanitary, scrub, simple, sweep, vacuum, wash, white, wholesome
cleaner: daily, detergent
cleanly: freely
cleanness: purity
cleanse: bathe, clarify, clean, fumigate, purge, purify, wash
cleansing: catharsis, refinement, wash
clear: articulate, bright, broad, conspicuous, definite, discharge, distinct, dust, elementary, fair, fine, glassy, graphic, honour, hurdle, jump, justify, leap, light, liquid, liquidate, lucid, luminous, manifest, marked, net, noticeable, obvious, open, patent, pay, plain, rid, serene, settle, simple, sunny,

sure, sweep, transparent, turn out, vindicate, vivid, void, weed

clearance: disposal

clearly: decidedly

clearness: clarity, lucidity, purity, serenity

cleavage: rift

cleave: fracture, joint, rupture

cleaver: axe, bill

cleft: breach, break, chasm, chink, crack, cut, gulf, rift

cleg: fly

clemency: grace, mercy, pity, quarter

clement: favourable, lenient, merciful, temperate

clench: bite, bunch, tense

clenched: tenacious, tight

clergyman: divine, minister, parson, pastor, priest

cleric: clergyman, divine, minister, parson, priest

clerical: pastoral

clerk: secretary, teller

clever: astute, bright, cunning, gifted, good, handy, intelligent, keen, knowing, knowledgeable, mean, quick, quick-witted, ready, sly, wise, witty

cliché: chestnut, corn, platitude, vulgarity,

cliché: hackneyed, old ordinary, tired

click: snap

client: buyer, customer, patient, patron, punter, satellite

clientele: custom, goodwill, public

clients: clientele

cliff: bluff, ravine, wall, precipice

clifftop: brink

climactic: critical, dramatic

climatal: climatic

climate: atmosphere, sky, weather

climatical: climatic

climax: crisis, head, height, highlight, payoff, peak, zenith

climb: ascend, ascent,

get up, mount, pull, rise, run, scale, scramble

climbing: uphill

clime: climate

clinch: clamp, confirm, contract, embrace, hug

cling: hang, stick

clinging: sticky, tenacious

clinic: ward

clink: jail, prison

clip: blow, box, brooch, catch, clasp, crack, crop, cuff, cut, excerpt, fastener, fleece, grip, knock, lick, magazine, nip, prune, shear, trim

clipped: cut

clipper: yacht

clipping: cutting, trim

clique: circle, clan, club, crowd, faction, gang, knot, outfit, party, ring, school

cloak: blanket, camouflage, cape, cover, eclipse, envelop, mantle, mask, muffle, pall, pretext, veil, wrap

cloaked: hidden

cloakroom: lavatory

clobber: club, hammer, hit, strike

clobbering: drubbing

clock: face, mug, time

clockwork: robot

clod: earth, fool, idiot, lump, oaf

clodhopping: boorish, bovine, hulking, rustic, uncouth, ungainly

clog: ball, block, close, foul, jam, retard, stick

clogging: choke, congestion

cloister: court, monastery

cloistered: monastic, secluded, sheltered, solitary

clomp: stump

clone: double

close: bosom, choke, conclusion, dear, end, fast, finish, frowsty, halt, hard, hot, intimate, last, lock, muggy, narrow, near, oppressive, ready, shut, side-street, terminate,

tight, uncommunicative, warm

closed: over, shut

closely: heavily, narrowly, nearly, well

closeness: communion, familiarity, fidelity, imminence, presence, proximity, resemblance

closest: immediate, next

closet: cabinet, cupboard, secret, toilet, wardrobe

closing: final, last, net

closure: end, seam, stoppage

clot: coagulate, silly, thicken

cloth: drape, fabric, linen, mat, material, ministry, mop, napkin, pall, rag, stuff

clothe: cover, dress, garb, gird, robe, turn out

clothes: dress, garb, gear, outfit, wardrobe

clothier: tailor

clothing: dress, garb, gear, wardrobe

cloud: blur, dull, dust, film, fog, muddy, nebulosity, nimbus, obfuscate, obscure, overshadow, puff

cloudburst: rain

clouded: milky, obscure, opaque, overcast, unclear

cloudiness: bloom, nebulosity

cloudless: bright, clear, fair, serene

cloudlike: nebulous

cloudy: dim, dull, filmy, foggy, gloomy, grey, muddy, opaque, overcast, turbid, woolly

clout: blow, box, clip, club, credit, effect, hit, influence, leverage, muscle, power, pull, punch, slap, strike, weight

clown: comedian, fool, joker, laugh, wally, zany

clowning: fun

clownish: zany

cloy: pall

cloying: sugary, sweet

club: association, bat, cudgel, fellowship, fraternity, lodge, mace, society

clue: conception, hint, idea, index, key, lead, light, line, wind

clueless: lost

clump: blow, bunch knot, stump

clumsily: heavily

clumsy: awkward, gauche, halting, heavy, hulking, inept, lumbering, oafish, ponderous, slapdash, stiff, tactless, uncouth, ungainly, unwieldy, wooden

cluster: bunch, centre, collect, concentrate, conglomerate, crowd, group, huddle, knot, press

clustered: conglomerate

clutch: brood, catch, clasp, clinch, cling, grab, grasp, grip, hold, lock, seize, snatch, squeeze

clutches: grip

clutter: confusion, jumble, junk, litter, mess

cluttered: messy

coach: bus, car, carriage, educate, groom, instruct, instructor, omnibus, prepare, prime, teach, school, teacher

coaching: education, instruction, lesson

coachman: whip

coagulate: cake, thicken

coalesce: mingle

coalition: combination, pact, party, union

coals: fire

coarse: barbaric, bawdy, beastly, boorish, broad, brutal, common, foul, gross, heavy, immodest, loud, low, obscene, plebeian, profane, rank, raunchy, raw, robust, rough, rude, rustic, scurrilous, uncouth, vile, vulgar

coarsely: roughly

coarseness:
obscenity, vulgarity
coast: cruise, drift,
glide, shore, slide,
strand
coastal: maritime
coaster: mat
coastline: coast,
coat: blanket, cloak,
cover, face, finish,
fleece, glaze, jacket,
lacquer, layer, paint,
plaster, plate, sheet,
wash
coating: coat, cover,
crust, film, lacquer,
layer, skin, wash
coax: jolly, persuade,
wheedle
cobble: darn
coccus: bacterium
cock: male, prick
cockateel: parrot
cockatoo: parrot
cockerel: cock
cockeyed: crazy, mad
cockiness: vanity
cocksure:
opinionated,
overconfident
cocktail: brew, drink
cocky: conceited, vain
cocoon: bandage
cocooned: smothered
coda: epilogue, tail
coddle: baby, pet
coddled: pampered
code: cipher, formula,
language, notation,
policy, principle
codification: order,
nomenclature,
scheme
codify: class, classify,
formulate, frame,
organize
codswallop: drivel,
rot, rubbish
coerce: compel, lean,
push, screw
coercion: compulsion,
extortion, force,
pressure, repression,
restraint
coexisting:
contemporary
coffer: casket, chest,
safe, trunk
coffers: treasury
cog: gear, module,
trip, wheel
cogent: forceful,
logical, pithy, potent,
strong, valid
cogitate: consider,
muse, ponder, reflect,

speculate, think
cogitation: reasoning
cognate:
homogeneous, kin,
related
cognitive:
psychological,
rational
cognizance:
knowledge
cognomen: name
cogs: mechanism,
teeth
cogwheel: gear
coherence:
coordination, logic,
lucidity
coherent: articulate,
clear, consistent,
logical
cohesion: solidarity
coiffeur: barber
coiffeuse: barber
coil: bun, circle, curl,
element, kink, loop,
roll, spiral, tangle,
turn, twine, wind,
coiled: kinky, spiral,
wound
coiled: labyrinthine
coiling: serpentine
coin: bit, create, mint,
piece
coinage: cash, tender
coincide: concur, tally
coincidence: chance,
concurrence
coincident:
coincidental,
simultaneous
coincidental:
incidental
coition: sexual
intercourse,
coitus: intercourse,
sexual intercourse
col: pass
colander: sieve
cold: austere, bare,
bleak, blue, callous,
catarrh, chill, dead,
distant, exposure,
fishy, frigid, frosty,
glacial, hard, harsh,
heartless, icy,
impersonal, lifeless,
phlegmatic, raw,
remote, severe,
undemonstrative,
unfriendly, wintry,
coldness: asperity,
austerity, cold,
distance, frigidity,
frost
collaborate:
cooperate

collaboration:
assistance,
cooperation, help,
league
collaborator:
assistant, associate,
partner
collapse: breakdown,
crack, crash, crumble,
crumple, deflate,
disintegration,
eclipse, failure, fall,
fizzle out, flop, fold,
founder, keel, ruin,
shock, slump, smash,
subside
collapsed: flat
collar: get
collateral: earnest,
guarantee, pawn,
security
collation:
comparison, repast
colleague: associate,
collaborator,
companion, comrade,
fellow, friend, mate,
partner
collect: assemble,
build, compile,
concentrate, flock,
garner, gather, group,
harvest, herd, lay in,
levy, mass, pick up,
rake, round up, save,
take
collected: calm, cool,
placid, philosophical
collection: assembly,
batch, battery, body
build-up, bunch,
bundle, compilation,
concentration,
donation, flight, flock,
group, hash, heap,
herd, knot, levy, lot,
mass, medley, pack,
selection, set
collective: communal,
general, joint,
multiple, pool
collectively: bodily,
together
college: institute,
school, seminary
collide: cannon,
conflict, impinge,
smash, skirmish
collision: bump,
clash, concussion,
conflict, crash, hit,
shock, smash
colloquial: informal
colloquialism: slang
colloquy: tête-à-tête,
word

collude: collaborate,
plot, scheme
cologne: perfume
colonize: settle
colonizer: settler,
pioneer
colonnaded: vaulted
colony: flock,
possession, province
colophon: brand,
device, seal
colorant: dye
coloration: colour
colorative: grain
colossal: big, giant,
huge, immense,
jumbo, large,
massive, mighty,
monster, monstrous,
monumental,
prodigious, vast
colossus: giant,
monster
colour: blush, dye,
glow, paint, shade,
stain, tint, tone
colourful: festive,
florid, gaudy, gay,
juicy, lively, pictorial,
salty, vivid
colourfully: gaily
colouring:
complexion, dye
colourless: bleak,
cadaverous, flat, grey,
insipid, lifeless,
mousy, negative,
neutral, toneless,
unimaginative, wan,
white
colours: banner,
decoration, flag, jack,
standard
coltish: frisky, young
column: caravan, file,
line, obelisk, pier,
pile, pillar, post, rank,
row, train
columnar:
monolithic,
monumental
columnist: journalist,
writer
columnists: press
coma: trance
comatose:
unconscious
comb: dress, rake,
ransack, search, scour
combat: battle,
conflict, contest,
fight, resist, skirmish,
war
combatant: militant,
warrior
combative: militant,

pugnacious,
quarrelsome, warlike
combe: dell, valley
combination:
association, blend,
coalition, compost,
compound,
federation, mix,
package, system,
union, wedding
combine: associate,
blend, cement,
compound, concur,
connect, consolidate,
conspire, fuse, join,
lump, mix, organize,
unite, weave, weld
combined:
composite, concerted,
federal, joint, mixed
combing out: teasing
combustion: fire
come: draw, originate,
show up, turn out
comeback: reply,
response, return
comedian: clown,
joker, laugh, wag, wit
comedown: bathos
comedy: farce,
humour, play
comely: pretty
comeuppance:
reward
comfort: cheer up,
cherish, consolation,
content, convenience,
luxury, nourish,
reassurance, relief,
relieve, revive, style
comfortable:
capacious,
considerable, content,
easy, homely,
leisurely, luxurious,
restful, snug, soft,
wealthy
comfortably:
leisurely, well
comforter: dummy
comforting: healing
comfy: cosy,
comic: comedian,
farcical, fool, funny,
joker, laugh
comical: humorous,
jocular, ludicrous
coming: future,
unborn
command: authority,
bid, bring, charge,
control, dictate,
direct, directive,
disposal, edict,
govern, government,
head, headquarters,

instruct, instruction,
jurisdiction, lead,
leadership, mandate,
manipulation,
manoeuvre, master,
mastery, order,
overlook, power,
prowess, reign,
require, rule, tell,
touch, will, word
commandeer:
confiscate, hijack,
requisition
commandeering:
requisition
commander: captain,
chief, head,
instructor, leader,
lord, master, ruler
commanding:
authoritative,
imperative,
impressive,
magisterial, potent,
powerful, ruling
commandment:
command, law,
precept
commandments:
teachings
commands: direction
commemorate:
celebrate, keep,
observe
**commemoration
programme:** festival
commemoration:
celebration,
ceremony, keeping,
memory
commemorative:
monumental
commence: begin,
develop, inaugurate,
initiate, launch, lead,
open, start
commencement:
beginning, kick-off,
launch, onset,
opening, origin, start
commencing:
opening
commend: celebrate,
compliment, eulogize,
favour, honour,
praise, recommend
commendable: good,
laudable, worthy
commendation:
bouquet, compliment,
credit, honour, praise,
puff, testimonial
commendatory:
complimentary, rave
commensurate:
equal, level

comment: criticize,
note, observation,
observe, parenthesis,
remark, word
commentary:
comment, criticism,
review
commentator: critic,
journalist, narrator
commerce: business,
finance, industry,
traffic
**commercial
traveller:**
representative
commercial:
economic, financial,
mercantile, profitable
commiserate:
comfort, pity,
sympathize
commiseration:
compassion, pity,
sympathy
commission:
assignment,
authorize, bonus,
charter, contract,
delegate, delegation,
deputize,
engagement,
inaugurate, kickback,
license, mandate,
place, rake-off, retain,
warrant, work
commissioners:
commission
commissioning:
delegation,
mandatory
commit: delegate,
bequeath, charge,
commend, consign,
fall, foul, leave,
offend, perpetrate,
purpose, put, refer,
resign, send up,
submit, undertake
commitment:
interest, obligation,
promise, zeal
committal:
consignment
committed:
dedicated, devoted,
resigned,
wholehearted,
zealous,
**committee
member:** councillor
committee: board,
commission, council,
senate, jury
commode: cabinet
commodious:
convenient, roomy,

spacious, wide
commodities: goods,
merchandise, stock,
wares
common sense:
brain, judgement,
loaf, maturity,
prudence, sanity
common: barbarian,
cheap, conventional,
customary, epidemic,
everyday, familiar,
general, green,
humble, known, low,
lowly, mean, mutual,
natural, normal,
ordinary, pervasive,
plain, plebeian,
popular, rife, social,
stale, unanimous,
universal, usual,
vulgar, widespread
commoners: rabble
commonly: generally,
often, ordinarily
commonness:
normality
commonplace:
average, banal,
common,
conventional,
everyday, folksy,
hackneyed, humble,
inconspicuous,
known, mediocre,
mundane,
nondescript,
ordinary, platitude,
prevalent, quotidian,
regular, vulgar,
vulgarity
commonplaces:
minutiae
commonsense:
realistic
commonwealth:
community
commotion: bother,
bustle, confusion,
convulsion,
disturbance, dust,
excitement, ferment,
flap, flurry, furore,
fuss, hell, hurry,
incident, kerfuffle,
noise, outcry,
pandemonium,
racket, riot, row,
scene, scramble,
sensation, stir, storm,
tempest, trouble,
unrest, upheaval,
uproar, whirl
communal: civic,
common, joint,
mutual, public, social,

unanimous
communicants:
faithful
communicate:
carry, commune,
contact, impart,
promulgate, publish,
reflect, relay, report,
say, signify, tell,
transmit
communication:
commerce,
connection, contact,
conversation,
intercourse, letter,
liaison, note, relay
communicative:
expansive
communion:
denomination, faith,
fellowship, mass, rite
communiqué:
message, news
community: civic,
civilization, common,
communal,
commune, hamlet,
local, nation,
monastery, people,
population, public,
society
compact: bargain,
close, concise,
condense, contract,
crush, dense, firm,
hard, impact, league,
pack, pocket, solid,
succinct, summary,
snug, telescope, thick
compactness:
density, firmness
companion:
associate, attendant,
chaperon, colleague,
complement,
comrade, consort,
fellow, friend, mate,
partner
companionable:
friendly, social
companionship:
association,
fellowship,
friendship, society
company: assembly,
association, band,
business, cast, circle,
collection, concern,
crew, firm, fleet,
flock, fraternity,
group, house,
internal, knot,
number, order,
organization, outfit,
parcel, party,
presence, set, society,

team, visitors
comparability:
comparison,
correspondence,
resemblance,
similarity
comparable:
equivalent, similar
comparative: relative
compare: beside,
balance, check,
contrast, correspond,
juggle, match, rival,
touch
comparison:
contrast, illustration,
parallel
compartment: bay,
booth, pigeonhole,
quarter, stall, well
compass-point:
bearing, direction,
heading, quarter
compass: breadth,
capacity, circle,
comprehension,
jurisdiction, latitude,
orbit, range, reach,
room, round, scope,
sweep, width
compassion: feeling,
humanity, kindliness,
kindness, mercy, pity,
sympathy, tenderness
compassionate:
gentle, humane, kind,
kindly, lenient,
merciful, soft, soft-
hearted, sorry,
sympathetic, tender,
understanding,
warm-hearted
compassionately:
kindly
compatibility:
harmony
compatible:
becoming,
commensurate,
consistent,
harmonious, parallel,
sympathetic
compatriot: national
compeer: comrade,
contemporary, equal,
peer, rival,
compel: bring, bind,
command, drive,
force, impel, oblige,
press, require, whip
compelled: bound,
obliged
compelling: effective,
forceful, forcible,
gripping, interesting,
irresistible,

overpowering,
overriding,
peremptory, potent,
powerful, strong,
urgent
compendious:
succinct, summary
compendium:
compilation, manual,
set, summary
compensate:
remunerate, reward,
satisfy
compensate for:
atone, balance,
cancel, make up,
redeem, redress,
repair, right
compensation:
commission,
indemnity, justice,
price, redress,
restitution,
retribution, return,
reward
compere: host
compete: contend,
contest, play, rival,
struggle
competence: skill,
power
competent: capable,
decent, effective,
efficient, experienced,
fit, good, knowing,
knowledgeable,
professional,
proficient,
satisfactory, skilful,
sufficient
competing: rival
competition:
competitor, contest,
game, match,
opposition, race,
tournament, war
competitive: rival
competitor: athlete,
candidate, enemy,
entry, match, player
competitors: field
compilation:
collection,
composition,
formation, writing
compiled: collected
compiling:
compilation
complacency: conceit
complacent:
imperturbable, self-
satisfied, smug,
yielding
complacently:
quietly
complain: beef, carp,

cavil, croak, kick,
libel, moan, protest,
squeal, storm, whine,
complaining:
lamentation,
querulous
complaint: beef,
bitch, condition,
difficulty, disease,
grievance, grudge,
illness, indisposition,
lament, libel, moan,
niggle, outcry,
protest,
remonstration,
sickness, stink,
trouble
complaisant: tolerant
compleat: ideal
complement: crew,
match, mate, parallel
complementary:
matching, parallel,
supplementary
complete: cap, clean,
close, complement,
comprehensive,
conclude, congenital,
consummate, dead,
do, execute, finish,
fulfil, full, great,
implicit, intact,
integral, knock off,
make out, make up,
outright, overall,
perfect, positive,
pure, radical, realize,
right, ripe, round,
settle, sheer, solid,
sound, strict,
terminate, thorough,
total, unabridged,
unconditional,
unqualified,
unshakable, utter,
whole
completed: over,
past, through
completely:
backwards, bodily,
full, fully, hard,
heavily, hollow, out,
outright, quite, right,
unreservedly, utterly,
wholly
completeness:
integrity, perfection
completion:
complement,
conclusion, end,
execution, finish,
perfection,
performance, term
complex:
complicated,
composite,

compound, elaborate, fixation, hang-up, hard, heavy, intricate, involved, labyrinthine, maze, network
complexion: character, look
complexities: ramifications
complexity: depth, knot, obscurity
compliance: obedience
compliant: deferential, flexible, manageable, obedient, passive, plastic, pliable, yielding
complicate: compound, elaborate, involve, obfuscate, perplex, snarl
complicated: complex, difficult, elaborate, hard, intricate, involved, labyrinthine, prickly, sophisticated
complication: difficulty, hurdle, kink, problem, snag
complications: ramifications
complicity: collusion, connivance
compliment: attention, bouquet, commend, congratulate, eulogize, honour, greeting, regard, praise
complimentary: attentive, free, honorary
compliments: congratulations, praise, respect
complot: intrigue
comply: consent, keep, meet, mind, obey, observe, perform, respect, satisfy, submit, take, yield
component: constituent, detail, element, factor, ingredient, integral, item, member, module, part, unit
comportment: behaviour, demeanour, manner

compose: dictate, steady, comprise, devise, frame, make up, organize, write
composed: calm, collected, cool, even, imperturbable, made, nonchalant, patient, philosophical, placid, sedate, serene, sober, temperate
composer: musician
composing: component
composite: combination, complex, compound, conglomerate, hybrid, mixed
composition: constitution, construction, essay, fabric, formation, habit, make-up, opus, organization, piece, texture, work, writing
compost: fertilizer
composure: balance, cool, nonchalance, patience, poise, serenity, sobriety, temper
compound: blend, combination, combine, complex, compose, composite, compromise, mingle, mix, multiple, preparation
comprehend: catch on, comprise, conceive, cover, embrace, enclose, fathom, follow, get, grasp, have, imagine, include, know, make out, penetrate, perceive, read, realize, see, take in, understand
comprehended: understood
comprehensible: clear, coherent, intelligible, lucid, plain
comprehension: conception, grasp, grip, insight, knowledge, light, reason, understanding, wit
comprehensive: blanket, broad, capacious, catholic, detailed, exhaustive,

expansive, full, general, overall, thorough, total, universal, wide
comprehensively: fully
compress: bandage, compact, contract, crush, ointment, pack, press, screw, squash, squeeze, stuff, telescope
compressed: compact, concise, concrete, dense, short
compression: concentration, pressure
compressor: motor, pump
comprise: compose, consist of, contain, include, make up
compromise: concession, endanger, medium
compromising: awkward
compulsion: force, necessity, restraint, urge
compulsive: gripping, insistent, irresistible, neurotic, obsessive, overpowering, urgent
compulsory: binding, imperative, mandatory, necessary, obligatory
compunction: compassion, penitence, regret, remorse
computation: calculation, count, valuation
compute: balance, calculate, cast, cipher, count, gauge, plot, quantify, value
comrade: colleague, companion, fellow, friend, mate, partner
comradeship: companionship, friendship
con: cheat, criminal, deceive, do, fiddle, fleece, fraud, hoax, peruse, ramp, rip off, rob, screw, swindle, take in, take, victimize
con artist: bandit, fraud

concave: bay, cavernous
concavity: bay, dent, depression, dip, hollow, pan
conceal: bury, camouflage, cover, envelop, harbour, hide, mask, muffle, obscure, palm, protect, screen, secrete, slip, slur, suppress, veil, whitewash
concealed: hidden, invisible, mysterious, obscure, private, secret, smothered, ulterior, underlying, veiled
concealing: cosmetic
concealment: camouflage, censorship, cover, hide, veil
concede: cede, compromise, consent, grant, own, recognize, surrender, yield
conceded: lost
conceit: narcissism, pride, vanity, whim
conceited: big, boastful, cocky, pretentious, proud, smug, uppish, vain
conceivable: plausible, possible
conceivably: perhaps
conceive: coin, discover, dream, hatch, invent, picture, realize, suppose, think, visualize
concentrate: bunch, centre, condense, congregate, fasten, focus, intensify, mass, thicken
concentrated: intense, meaty, thick
concentrating: intent
concentration: attention, mind
concept: conception, idea, intention, notion, vision
conception: comprehension, discovery, genesis, idea, image, imagination, opinion, reading, view, vision
conceptual: ideal, notional
conceptualize:

imagine
concern: attention,
business, care,
company,
consideration,
importance, interest,
involve, issue, job,
lookout, matter,
moment,
organization, part,
pigeon, place, regard,
touch, worry
concerned: attentive,
careful, considerate,
involved, solicitous,
sympathetic, worried
concerning:
regarding, towards
concert: chorus,
cooperation, gig
concerted:
harmonious, joint,
unanimous
concertina: telescope
concession:
compromise, consent,
discount, franchise,
monopoly
concierge: caretaker,
janitor
conciliate: mediate,
pacify, placate
conciliator: mediator
conciliatory:
peaceable
concise: brief,
compact, curt,
laconic, pithy, pocket,
sententious, short,
succinct, summary
concisely: shortly
conclave: council,
meeting
conclude: cease,
clinch, close,
complete,
consummate, decide,
deduce, determine,
dissolve, do, end,
finish, fulfil, gather,
infer, judge, knock
off, make, perceive,
reason, resolve, seal,
settle, stop, suppose,
surmise, terminate,
think, understand,
wind up
concluded: closed,
complete, over
concluding: final,
last, terminal
conclusion:
catastrophe, clinch,
decision, deduction,
dissolution, end,
finding, finish,

implication,
inference, issue,
judgement, last,
outcome, resolve,
result, stop, surmise,
tail, understanding,
upshot, verdict
conclusive: certain,
clean, compelling,
decisive, final,
positive, ultimate,
unanswerable,
unquestioned, valid
conclusively: finally,
positively
concoct: brew,
compound, fabricate,
invent, make up,
manufacture, plot,
prepare, spin
concoction: brew,
potion, preparation
concomitant:
attendant, incidental
concord: communion,
composition,
friendship, harmony,
peace, unity
concordance:
concert, similarity,
solidarity
concordant:
harmonious
concourse: meeting
concrete: material,
tangible
concretion: concrete,
knot
concupiscence: lust,
lecherous
concur: assent,
coincide, nod, tally
concurrence: assent
concurrent:
coincidental,
contemporary,
simultaneous, then
concurrently:
meanwhile
concussion: impact,
percussion
condemn: blame,
doom, censure,
convict, denounce,
disapprove of, knock,
rap, reproach
condemnation:
censure,
disapprobation, doom
condemnatory:
damning, hard-
hitting, incriminatory
condemned: doomed
condensation:
compression, digest,
mist, wet

condense: compact,
consolidate, contract,
digest, precipitate,
press, set, telescope,
thicken
condensed: compact,
concise, laconic,
succinct, summary,
thick
condescend: lower,
stoop
condescending:
cavalier, officious,
snobbish,
supercilious, superior
condiment: relish
condition:
circumstance,
determine, dispose,
disease, estate, form,
health, phase,
prerequisite,
provision, proviso,
qualification,
restriction, repair,
rule, shape, state,
status, trim, way
conditional:
contingent,
dependent,
provisional, subject
conditioned:
habituated
conditions:
atmosphere, medium,
proposal, set-up
condole: sympathize
condolence:
compassion,
sympathy
condom: preventive
condominium: tower
condone: tolerate
conduce: contribute
conduct: bear,
behave, behaviour,
bring, carriage,
channel, control,
demeanour, direct,
do, form, guide, hold,
keep, lead, manners,
marshal, part,
performance,
procedure, steer, take,
usher, wage
conductor: guide,
lead, leader, musician
conduit: channel,
drain, gutter, pipe
cone: funnel, pot
confab: tête-à-tête
confabulate: talk
confabulation:
natter, talk
confectionary: sweet
confederacy:

coalition, conspiracy,
federation, league,
party, union
confederate:
assistant, associate,
collaborator,
colleague, comrade,
conspire, federal,
partner, unify, unite
confederation:
association,
combination, league,
union
confer: award,
commune, discuss,
do, endow, give,
grant, impart, lend,
show, talk, vouchsafe
conference: congress,
consultation, council,
discussion, huddle,
meeting, talk
conferral: award,
presentation
confess: own, believe,
concede, disclose,
profess
confession: belief,
profession, testimony
confessor: father
confidant: friend,
intimate
confidante: friend,
intimate
confide: commit,
confess
confidence:
assurance, conviction,
credit, faith, morale,
secret, self-esteem
confident: assured,
authoritative, certain,
optimistic, positive,
sanguine, secure, self-
assured, sure
confidential: inside,
intimate, private,
privileged,
undisclosed
confidentially:
quietly
confiding:
unsuspecting
configuration:
composition, design,
form, formation, line,
mould
confine: bind, bound,
box, cage, chain,
circumscribe,
commit, cramp, crib,
gate, hold, impound,
imprison, jail, limit,
pen, pinch, restrict,
shut up, stall
confined: captive,

limited, local, narrow, secure, shut
confinement: custody, restraint, restriction
confines: field, limit, range, restraint, scope
confirm: ascertain, attest, authorize, back up, bear out, certify, clinch, confess, ensure, prove, ratify, sanction, settle, support, sustain
confirmation: backing, clinch, proof, sanction
confirmed: authoritative, inveterate, true
confiscate: commandeer, impound, seize
confiscation: deprivation, seizure, sequestration
conflagration: blaze, fire
conflict: battle, clash, collide, collision, combat, confrontation, contest, difference, disagree, discord, dispute, diverge, engagement, faction, feud, fight, friction, interfere, jar, scream, skirmish, strife, struggle, war
conflicting: contradictory, different, incompatible, inconsistent, opposing, rival
confluence: meeting
conform: correspond, fit, follow, suit, square
conformability: obedience
conformable: obedient
conformation: organization, structure
conformism: orthodoxy
conformist: orthodox
conformity: correspondence, keeping, orthodoxy, parity, resemblance
confound: baffle, bedevil, confuse,

dash, defeat, demolish, flabbergast, floor, get, nonplus, perplex, put out, shame, stump, stupefy, throw
confounded: blank, flaming
confounding: tough, wreck
confront: beard, breast, challenge, defy, face, meet, oppose, run into, take on
confrontation: brush, challenge, clash, collision, scene, showdown
confronting: opposing
confuse: cloud, complicate, confound, fuddle, garble, jumble, muddy, obfuscate, perplex, perturb, scramble, stump, upset
confused: bewildered, chaotic, cloudy, dazed, deranged, dim, disorganized, distracted, foggy, incoherent, muddled, muddy, pied, turbid, upset, woolly
confusing: inexplicable, misleading
confusion: babel, chaos, disarray, disorder, doubt, flutter, fog, garble, jumble, kerfuffle, maelstrom, mayhem, mess, riot, shambles, wilderness
congeal: cake, coagulate, fix, harden, set, thicken
congenial: compatible, genial, good, kind, kindly, pleasant, sympathetic
congeniality: kindliness
congenially: kindly
congenital: constitutional, genetic, temperamental
congenitally: naturally
congest: choke, clog, crowd, jam
congested: close,

crowded, overcrowded, packed
congestion: bottleneck, choke, jam, squeeze
conglomerate: composite, compound, lump
congratulate: compliment, praise
congratulation: praise
congratulations: compliment
congratulatory: complimentary
congregate: assemble, audience, bunch, collect, concentrate, crowd, flock, herd, mass, meet, swarm
congregation: assembly, church, collection, faithful, flock, fold, rally
congress: conference, council, government, legislative, parliament, senate
congressional: legislative
congressman: councillor
congruency: similarity
congruent: identical
congruity: correspondence, parity
congruous: compatible, consistent, similar
conjectural: hypothetical, speculative, tentative
conjecture: assumption, believe, divine, fancy, guess, hypothesis, imagine, presume, reckon, say, shot, speculate, suppose, supposition, surmise, suspect, suspicion, theorize, theory, wonder
conjugal: marital, married, matrimonial
conjunction: meeting
conjuration: spell
conjure: invoke, juggle
conjuring: magic
conjuror: magician
conk out: fail, malfunction

conker-tree: chestnut
con man: charlatan, cheat, quack, rogue, swindler
connect: articulate, assemble, associate, attach, bridge, clasp, close, combine, couple, fasten, gear, hitch, integrate, involve, join, joint, knit, link, loop, meet, mesh, piece, switch, unite, yoke
connected: attached, germane, implicated, live, related
connecting: between
connection: assembly, association, bearing, bridge, communication, contact, context, flex, hitch, implication, joint, junction, kinship, lead, liaison, link, logic, reference, regard, relationship, respect
connections: influence, kin
connivance: collusion
connive: intrigue
conniving: designing, scheming, sly
connoisseur: authority, critic, lover, specialist
connotation: meaning, overtone
connote: imply, mean, signify, suggest, symbolize
connubial: conjugal, marital, married, matrimonial
conquer: beat, best, crush, lick, overcome, quell, rout, suppress, whip, worst
conquering: victorious, winning
conqueror: champion, hero, victor
conquest: occupation, victory
consanguine: kin
consanguineous: related
consanguinity: kin, kinship
conscience: breast, ethics, principle
conscience-stricken: ashamed, remorseful,

rueful, sorry
conscientious:
careful, close,
painstaking,
punctilious, religious,
responsible, rigorous,
scrupulous, thorough
conscious: awake,
aware, deliberate,
knowing, mindful,
rational, sensible,
sentient, wilful, wise
consciousness:
attention, awareness,
feeling, knowledge,
mind, perception,
wits
conscript: levy
conscription: levy
consecrate: bless,
enshrine, invest,
ordain
consecrated:
dedicated, devoted,
holy, sacred,
scriptural
consecration:
blessing
consensus: feeling,
unity
consent: assent,
concur, concurrence,
leave, okay,
permission
consent to: comply,
grant, permit, ratify
consequence:
conclusion, effect,
fruit, gravity, import,
importance,
magnitude, mark,
matter, moment,
outcome,
repercussion, result,
significance, upshot
consequences:
impact, price,
ramifications
consequent:
attendant, next
consequential:
effective, historic,
momentous, weighty
consequently:
subsequently, then,
therefore, thus
conservation:
maintenance
conservatism:
orthodoxy, reaction
conservative: fuddy-
duddy, reactionary,
right, safe
conserve: husband,
jam, keep, maintain,
preserve, reserve,

save
consider: believe,
calculate, call,
cogitate, consult, feel,
count, debate,
deliberate, digest,
figure, have, heed,
hold, judge, juggle,
reckon, regard,
revolve, see, suppose,
surmise, suspect,
take, think, weigh,
considerable: good,
great, much,
respectable, round
considerably: dear,
far, materially, much,
way, well
considerate:
attentive, benevolent,
charitable, helpful,
kind, kindly, obliging,
thoughtful,
understanding
considerately: kindly
consideration:
attention, care, cause,
concern, debate,
deliberation,
digestion, factor,
judgement,
kindliness, kindness,
notice, regard,
remark, sake, view
considered:
deliberate, judicious,
premeditated
consign: doom,
commend, commit,
put, refer, send
consignment: cargo,
delivery, freight, load
consist: comprise, lie
consistency: density,
keeping, temper,
texture
consistent:
commensurate,
compatible,
homogeneous,
lasting, logical,
regular, same, steady,
uniform
consistently:
invariably
consolation: comfort
console: comfort,
relieve
consolidate: cake, fix,
knit
consolidated:
concrete
consolidation:
compression,
concentration
consommé: soup

consonance: harmony
consonant:
harmonious
consort: associate,
cultivate, mingle,
partner, queen
consortium:
combination,
organization, pool
conspicuous: blatant,
bold, clear,
distinguished,
glaring, marked,
notable, noticeable,
obvious, ostentatious,
outstanding, plain,
prominent,
pronounced,
remarkable, salient,
signal, singular
conspicuously:
notably
conspicuousness:
prominence
conspiracy: collusion,
intrigue, league,
machination, plot,
scheme
conspire: collaborate,
intrigue, scheme, plot
conspiring:
connivance, designing
constabulary: police
constancy: diligence,
faith, faithfulness,
fidelity, loyalty
constant: certain,
consistent, continual,
continuous, even,
frequent, habitual,
incessant, loyal,
mechanical,
monotonous,
nonstop, obsessive,
perpetual, persistent,
regular, same, stable,
static, steady, tireless,
unbroken
constantly: ever,
nonstop
consternation: panic,
shock, terror
constipate: bind
constituency: seat
constituent:
component, element,
factor, ingredient,
integral, member,
part, unit
constituents:
material, recipe
constitute: compose,
comprise, create,
make up
constituted: made
constitution: being,

creation, habit,
legislation, make,
make-up, nature,
physique
constitutional:
congenital, lawful,
organic, promenade,
quintessential,
radical, saunter,
stroll, temperamental,
turn, walk
constrain: bind,
brake, control, cramp,
curb, drive, force,
impel, inhibit, keep,
oblige, press, put,
require, screw,
shackle, urge
constrained:
pent-up, stiff, stilted,
strained
constraint: brake,
compulsion,
diffidence, pressure,
repression, reserve,
restriction, urgency
constrict: choke,
contract, narrow, thin
constricted: narrow,
tight
constriction:
bottleneck, choke,
compression, throttle
construct: base,
build, compose,
contrive, erect,
fabricate, form,
frame, invent, knock
off, make,
manufacture, model,
organize, produce,
put up, raise, rear, set
up, turn
constructed: made
construction:
building, fabric,
form, formation,
invention, make-up,
manufacture,
organization,
production, structure
constructive: helpful,
inventive, positive,
productive,
worthwhile
constructor: founder
construe: read, render
consuetude: habit
consul: diplomat,
minister
consular: diplomatic
consulate: embassy,
legation
consult: confer,
discuss, talk
consultant: counsel,

counsellor, doctor,
specialist
consultation:
audience, discussion,
huddle, interview,
talk, word
consume: burn,
devour, eat, exhaust,
go through, polish
off, spend, swallow,
take, use
consumed: obsessed,
possessed, spent
consumers: market,
sale
consuming:
consumption, intense,
obsessive
consummate: carry
out, complete, crown,
ideal, masterly,
perfect, positive,
realize, seal
consummation:
crown, perfection
consumption:
exhaustion,
expenditure
consumptive: hectic
contact: brush, call,
communication,
connection, exposure,
get, impact,
intercourse, junction,
kiss, liaison, link,
reach, touch
contagion: disease,
plague
contain: comprise,
consist of, cover,
embrace, enclose,
govern, have, hold,
house, include,
incorporate, involve,
record, restrict, seat,
stem, take in, take
contained:
undemonstrative,
implicit
container: bag, bowl,
carton, case, jar, pot,
reservoir, tank, vessel
contaminate:
corrupt, defile, foul,
infect, pollute,
profane, poison
contaminated:
corrupt, foul,
insanitary, tainted
contamination:
poison
contemn: scorn
contemplate: brood,
cogitate, commune,
consider, digest,
expect, eye, look,

meditate, muse,
ponder, reflect,
speculate, study,
survey, think, weigh
contemplation:
consideration,
digestion, gaze,
scrutiny, study
contemplative:
meditative, monastic,
pensive, wistful
contemporaneous:
being, live,
simultaneous,
contemporaneously:
meanwhile, while
contemporary:
current, effective,
latest, living, modern,
new, present, recent,
then, topical
contempt: disdain,
scorn, shame
contemptible: base,
cheap, derisory,
despicable, dirty,
disgraceful,
laughable, low, mean,
petty, pitiful,
ridiculous, rotten,
unworthy, vile,
worthless, wretched
contemptuous:
derisory, sarcastic,
scornful, supercilious
contemptuousness:
scorn
contend: assert,
battle, combat,
compete, conflict,
contest, debate,
maintain, protest,
rival, run, strive,
struggle, submit
contended:
controversial
contender: athlete,
candidate, litigant,
rival
contend with: differ,
dispute, resist, tangle,
wrestle
content: please,
satisfy, willing
contented: cheerful,
comfortable, happy,
pleased
contentedly: happily,
quietly
contention: brief,
competition, conflict,
debate, difference,
discord, dispute,
feud, friction, query,
question, resistance,
strife, thesis, war

contentious:
different, pugnacious
contentment:
content, happiness,
pleasure
contents: filling,
inside, interior,
matter, text
contest: battle, bout,
combat, compete,
competition, conflict,
confrontation,
contend, fight, game,
match, race, struggle,
tournament
contestant: athlete,
candidate,
competitor, entry,
field, nominee,
opposing, player,
rival
context: background,
backing, case,
connection,
environment, light,
setting
contiguity: contact
contiguous: beside
continence:
temperance
continent: temperate
continental: overseas
contingency: case,
casualty, chance,
circumstance, joker
contingent:
dependent, casual,
chance, conditional,
faction, provisional,
relative, secondary,
subject
continual: constant,
frequent, incessant,
lasting, monotonous,
perennial, perpetual,
persistent, tireless,
unbroken
continually: ever,
forever, long
continuance:
duration,
maintenance
continuation:
duration
continue: be, carry
on, dwell, endure, go
on, hold, keep, keep
on, keep up, last,
linger, live, maintain,
persist, proceed,
prolong, prosecute,
pursue, remain,
resume, run, stand,
stay, sustain
continued:
continuous

continuing: being,
lingering, living
continuous: constant,
continual, gradual,
incessant, lasting,
nagging, narrative,
nonstop, persistent,
progressive, straight,
unbroken
continuously: away,
nonstop, together
contort: screw
contorted:
misshapen, twisted,
wry
contortion:
convulsion
contour: line, outline,
profile, shape
contract: bargain,
bond, bunch, catch,
charter, commission,
compact, condense,
deal, deed, develop,
engagement, flex,
form, get, instrument,
lease, lessen, let, let
out, make, order,
pact, pledge, promise,
pump, reduce, sicken,
take in, telescope,
tense, treaty
contraction:
convulsion, spasm
contractions: labour
contractor: farmer,
operator, party
contradict: deny,
disagree, dispute,
negate, rebut, oppose
contradiction:
negative, paradox,
reverse
contradictory:
counter,
incompatible,
incongruous,
inconsistent,
negative, opposite
contraption: device,
gadget
contrarily: counter
contrariness: irony
contrary: converse,
counter, incongruous,
inconsistent,
negative, opposing,
opposite, reverse,
wayward,
unfavourable
contrast: compare,
comparison, differ,
difference,
differentiate,
distinction, foil,
highlight, oppose

contrasted: offset
contrasting: counter, different, other
contravene: contradict, infringe, violate
contravention: violation
contretemps: difference, mishap
contribute: conspire, cooperate, donate, give, go, make, provide, render, supply
contribution: collection, donation, gift, offering, share, tax
contributor: benefactor, donor, participant
contributory: elemental, instrumental
con trick: swindle
contrite: guilty, penitent, remorseful, repentant, rueful, sorry
contrition: penitence, regret, remorse
contrivance: artifice, calculation, device, dodge, gadget, manipulation, scheme, shift, wangle
contrive: brew, compose, conceive, concoct, conspire, design, devise, fabricate, get, hatch, improvise, lay, manage, manoeuvre, plan, prepare, scheme, wangle, work, work out
contrived: artificial, laboured, overwrought, spurious, unnatural, unrealistic
contriving: calculating, shifty
control: authority, bridle, check, command, compose, conduct, curb, determine, direct, direction, discipline, dominate, domination, drive, fly, govern, government, grasp, grip, guide, handle, harness, head,

influence, initiative, jurisdiction, leadership, leash, manage, management, manipulation, manoeuvre, manage, master, mastery, moderate, mould, order, pilot, police, possess, possession, power, preside over, ration, regulate, regulation, rein, repress, repression, restraint, restriction, ride, rule, run, steer, superintend, supervision, sway, wield, work
controllable: manageable
controlled: orderly, restrained,
controller: director, ruler
controlling: capital, key, ruling
controls: helm
controversial: contentious, emotive, sensitive
controversialist: polemic
controversy: issue, polemic, quarrel, query, question, row, strife
contumacious: defiant
contumely: disdain, insolence, mockery
contuse: bruise
contused: livid
contusion: bruise, bump
conundrum: enigma, problem, puzzle, riddle
conurbation: city
convalesce: recover
convalescence: recovery
convalescent: invalid
convene: assemble, call, collect, congregate, gather, hold, meet, rally, summon
convener: foreman
convenience: bog, lavatory, toilet
convenient: comfortable, fortunate, handy, manageable, nearby,

opportune, serviceable, suitable
conveniently: fortuitously
convent: cloister
convention: assembly, committee, conference, congress, custom, etiquette, fashion, formality, meeting, rally, ritual, rule, tradition, treaty, usage
conventional: conservative, customary, everyday, formal, general, orthodox, popular, proper, ritual, routine, set, slavish, square, stock, straight, stuffy, traditional
conventionalities: propriety
conventionality: orthodoxy
conventionally: generally
conventions: protocol
conventual: monastic, veil
converge: centre, collect, concentrate, congregate, focus, huddle, join, meet, touch
convergence: concentration, focus, junction, meeting
conversant: familiar, knowledgeable
conversation: communication, dialogue, discussion, jaw, natter, speech, talk, tête-à-tête, word
converse: discuss, commune, confer, opposite, reverse, speak, talk
conversion: change, transit, transition
convert: turn, sell, change, make, modify, recruit, resolve, sell, trim, turn, win
convertible: mutable
convey: bear, bring, carry, channel, communicate, conduct, deliver, ferry, fetch, funnel, grant, haul, impart, import, lead, move,

pass, pipe, plant, purport, return, route, say, send, signify, take, transmit, transport
conveyance: carriage, delivery, transport, vehicle
conveyor: bearer
convict: captive, condemn, criminal, villain
conviction: assurance, belief, cause, conclusion, faith, idea, impression, rap, persuasion
convince: convert, persuade, satisfy, sell
convinced: certain, confident, positive
convincing: cogent, compelling, powerful, satisfying
convivial: festive, genial, good, jolly, merry, sociable
conviviality: merriment
convocation: meeting
convoke: hold
convolute: coil
convoluted: labyrinthine, meandering, rambling, voluminous, wandering, winding
convolution: coil, loop
convoy: train
convulse: heave, quake, thresh, twitch
convulsion: fit, frenzy, heave, quake, seizure, shake, start, twitch
convulsive: spasmodic, work
cook: bake, boil, chef, concoct, do, doctor, fix, invent, juggle, plot, falsify, fudge, heat, plot, roast
cooker: oven
cookie: biscuit
cooking: baking, food
cool: brittle, calm, chill, collected, distant, even, imperturbable, lukewarm, nonchalance, nonchalant, patience, patient,

philosophical, placid, poise, quench, shady, steady, sober, stoical, temper, temperate, tepid

cooling: refreshing

coolness: deliberation, distance, chill, philosophy, reserve, sobriety

coop: pen, run

coop up: cage, crib, pen, shut up

cooperate: assist, collaborate, concur, conspire, help, team

cooperation: assistance, concurrence, help, liaison

cooperative: helpful

cooperatively: together

coordinate: cooperate, mesh, orchestrate, organize, relate, set

coordinated: concerted

coordinates: grid

coordinating: matching

coordination: organization, system

cop: bust

cope: get on, hood, make do, make out, manage

cope with: deal, field, handle, manage, reckon, stand, withstand

copied: derivative, fake

coping: roof

copious: bountiful, exuberant, fruitful, full, generous, heavy, lavish, liberal, luxuriant, much, numerous, prodigal, profuse, prolific, rich

copiously: freely, heavily

copiousness: exuberance, plenty, wealth

copper: coin

coppery: auburn

coppice: wood, woods

cops: police

copse: wood, woods

copulate: couple, mate

copulation: intercourse, sexual

intercourse

copy: borrow, edition, facsimile, fake, follow, forge, forgery, imitate, imitation, lift, likeness, match, matter, mimic, mirror, model, number, parrot, pirate, replica, reproduce, reproduction, script, specimen, transcribe, Xerox

copycat: parrot

copying: forgery

copyright: patent

coquetry: flirtation

coquette: minx, flirt

coquettish: coy, demure, girlish

coral: red

cord: bond, cable, familiar, flex, friendly, gracious, hearty, kind, kindly, lace, line, rope, sociable, string, tonic, warm, warm-hearted, wholehearted

cordiality: kindliness, warmth

cordon: circle

core: base, basic, basis, body, bottom, focus, framework, heart, interior, kernel, marrow, nucleus, pivot, point, root

corinthian: gallant

cork: close, fill, float, plug

corker: beauty, cracker, doll

corkscrew: spiral

corm: bulb, germ

corn: grain

corner: bay, bend, hog, nook, predicament, trap, turn, wind

cornerstone: rock

cornucopia: glut, profusion

corny: banal, tired

corollary: deduction, implication, inference

corona: crown, garland, halo, nimbus

coronet: bonnet, crown

corporal: bodily

corporation: belly, bulge, company, concern, organization, society

corporeal: bodily, material, mortal, physical

corporeally: bodily

corps: force

corpse: body, remains

corpselike: cadaverous

corpulent: fat, gross, obese, plump, rotund, stout, overweight

correct: better, castigate, cure, discipline, fitting, fix, formal, improve, just, legitimate, meet, mend, okay, perfect, proper, punish, rectify, redress, reform, regular, remedy, revise, right, true

correction: discipline, improvement, justice, punishment, redress, reform

corrective: remedy, therapy, therapeutic

correctly: okay, truly, well

correctness: formality, precision

correlate: correspond, parallel, relate

correlation: comparison, connection, correspondence, parallel

correspond: balance, coincide, equate, fit, interact, reciprocate, represent, parallel, tally, write

correspondence: communication, connection, fidelity, fitness, harmony, keeping, kinship, likeness, line, mail, parity, resemblance, sympathy

correspondent: commentator, journalist, reporter

correspondents: press

corresponding: attendant, equal, identical, like, matching, relative, same

corridor: hall, lobby, passage, tunnel

corrigendum: insert

corroborate: attest, back up, bear out, certify, confirm, prove, ratify, support, witness

corroboration: backing, confirmation, proof, witness

corrode: bite, decay, eat, rot, rust, waste

corroded: rotten, rusty

corrosion: erosion, rot, rust

corrosive: biting, caustic, mordant, poisonous

corrosiveness: bite

corrugate: wrinkle

corrugated: uneven

corrugation: crease, wrinkle

corrupt: bastard, degenerate, dirty, dishonest, garble, immoral, libertine, pervert, poison, pollute, putrid, rot, rotten, sinful, stain, venal, wicked

corrupting: unhealthy, unwholesome

corruption: bribery, cancer, garble, graft, immorality, mortification, poison

corsage: bouquet

corsair: buccaneer, pirate

cortege: caravan, court, procession, train

cortex: bark, outside

cortical: outer

coruscate: glitter

coruscating: brilliant, gleaming

coruscation: brilliance, glitter

coryza: cold

cosh: club, cudgel

cosiness: comfort

cosmetic: make-up, paint, superficial

cosmic: mundane

cosmopolitan: broad-minded, cool, sophisticated, worldly

cosmos: creation, nature, universe, world

cosset: baby, cherish, indulge, pet, spoil

cosseted: pampered
cost specification: budget
cost: budget, charge, damage, expense, fee, figure, loss, outlay, premium, price, quotation, quote, rate, toll, value, worth
costly: dear, expensive, extravagant, luxurious, precious, rich, splendid, valuable
costs: expenditure
costume: clothes, clothing, disguise, dress, garb, habit, outfit, robe, suit, uniform
cosy: comfortable, homely, intimate, snug
cot: bunk, crib
coterie: clan, clique, ring
cottage: cabin, chalet, cot, lodge
cotton: thread
couch: formulate, frame, litter, phrase, word
couchette: berth
cough: bark, hack, pay, stump, wheeze
council: authority, board, cabinet, chamber, committee, consultation, municipal, parliament, senate
councillor: representative
counsel: barrister, caution, consultant, guide, instruct, instruction, instructor, lawyer, recommend, urge
count: bank, bargain, calculate, gauge, matter, number, poll, rate, reckon, score, signify, tally, tell, weigh
countenance: complexion, face, sanction, stand, support
counter: bar, bench, booth, bureau, contrary, converse, desk, frustrate, oppose, refute, rejoinder, reply,

table, teller, traverse
counteract: compensate, contradict, neutralize, offset, resist
counteraction: opposition, resistance
counteractive: negative, preventive
counterargument: objection
counterbalance: ballast, cancel, cover, neutralize, offset, oppose
counterblast: backlash
counterfeit: base, bastard, bogus, copy, dummy, fake, false, fictitious, forge, forgery, fraud, fraudulent, imitation, mock, phoney, quack, queer, sham, spurious
counterfeiting: forgery
counterfoil: receipt, tally
countering: frustration
countermand: cancel, lift, negate, overrule, overturn, repeal, rescind, revoke
countermeasure: remedy
counterpart: companion, complement, equal, equivalent, fellow, like, match, mate, parallel
counterpoise: balance, weight
countersign: initial, underwrite, witness, word
counterstrike: backlash
counterstroke: reprisal
counterweight: balance, ballast
count in: include
counting on: confident
countless: incalculable, infinite, many, myriad, numerous, umpteen
count on: depend, presume, reckon, rely on
countrified: rustic

country: domicile, land, nation, nature, realm, rustic, soil, state, territory
countryman: peasant, yokel
countryside: country, environment, land, nature
countrywide: nationwide
count up: figure, tot
coup: insurrection, killing, transaction
coup d'état: revolution
coup de grâce: kill, knockout
couple: attach, brace, dock, few, hitch, hook, join, joint, link, match, mate, pair, unite, yoke
coupled with: plus
coupler: hook
coupling: chain, hitch, junction, link, sexual intercourse, union, yoke
coupon: ticket
courage: assurance, backbone, bottle, confidence, daring, fortitude, gallantry, guts, heart, heroism, manliness, nerve, pluck, prowess, resolve, soul, spirit, valour
courageous: assured, bold, daring, heroic, spartan, strong, valiant
courageously: manfully
courgette: zucchini
courier: messenger, runner
course: beat, career, channel, cycle, direction, dish, flow, lane, layer, line, measure, orbit, passage, path, pour, procedure, procession, resort, road, round, route, rule, run, sequence, series, stream, tack, tour, track, way
course of action: bet, process, scheme, way
court: bar, cultivate, invite, judicial, pursue, trial, woo
courteous: attentive,

chivalrous, civil, fair, gallant, genteel, gracious, kind, kindly, ladylike, nice, obliging, polite, suave
courtesan: whore
courtesies: protocol
courtesy: attention, breeding, compliment, complimentary, etiquette, gallantry, kindliness, manners, refinement
courtly: chivalrous, gracious, well-bred
courtroom: bar
courtship: suit
couturier: dressmaker, tailor
cove: bay
covenant: bond, contract
cover: bandage, bank, bathe, bind, binding, blanket, blind, bonnet, bury, camouflage, cap, carpet, case, cloak, clothe, coat, conceal, defence, defend, disguise, do, drape, envelop, face, fill, flap, fleece, hedge, hide, hood, house, hush up, include, insurance, inter, involve, jacket, lay, lid, line, log, mantle, mask, muffle, obscure, patch, plaster, plate, plug, pretence, pretext, protect, protection, rake, roof, screen, seal, shade, shadow, shed, shelter, shield, slate, smear, spread, stretch, suppress, traverse, veil, veneer, whitewash, wrap
covered: bound, shrouded, thick, veiled, wreathed
covering: bark, binding, blanket, canopy, coat, crust, defensive, fleece, jacket, layer, mantle, sheet
coverlet: blanket, rug
covert: hidden, mysterious, secret, sidelong, stealthy, surreptitious, ulterior,

underground, veiled
cover-up: whitewash
covet: fancy
covetous: envious,
jealous, longing,
possessive, ravenous,
sordid
covetousness: greed,
jealousy, longing
cow: frighten,
intimidate, neat
coward: chicken
cowardly: dirty,
fearful,
pusillanimous, weak,
yellow
cowboy: driver
cowed: hangdog,
overawed
cower: quail, shrink,
sneak
cowl: bonnet, hood
cowling: hood
cowpat: mess
cows: cattle
coxswain: pilot
coy: bashful, demure,
playful, retiring, shy,
tongue-in-cheek
crabby: cantankerous,
ill-humoured
crack: attempt,
breach, break, cleft,
decipher, first-class,
fling, fracture, gap,
go, hole, leak,
masterly, pick, rent,
resolve, rift, sally,
say, shatter, shiver,
shot, smack, snap,
solve, split, stab,
thunder
crackbrained: lunatic
cracked: crazy, leaky,
mad, split
cracker: beauty,
biscuit, knockout
crackers: crazy,
insane, lunatic, mad
crackle: snap
crackling: crisp,
sizzling
cradle: cot, crib,
frame, seat
craft: boat, business,
finesse, occupation,
shift, technique,
vessel, work,
workmanship
craftiness: guile
craftsman: artist,
worker
craftsmanship:
workmanship
crafty: calculating,
cunning, deceitful,

foxy, politic, sharp,
shrewd, slippery, sly,
subtle, underhand,
vulpine, wily
crag: cliff, height,
mountain,
prominence
craggy: mountainous,
rough, rugged
cram: coach,
compact, cramp,
crowd, devour, fill,
glut, gorge, jam, load,
pack, ram, squeeze,
stuff, surfeit
crammed: full,
loaded, overcrowded,
packed,
uncomfortable
cramp: kink, pinch,
restrict
cramped: close,
crowded, limited,
tight, uncomfortable
crane: hoist, lift
cranium: crown,
dome, head
crank: card, grind,
lunatic, nut, oddity
cranky: kinky, lunatic
cranny: chink, corner,
crack, nook, rift
crap: drivel
crash: bang, blast,
boom, bump, clash,
collide, collision,
concussion, crack,
failure, fold,
fulminate, impact,
report, roar, ruin,
slam, slump, smash,
thunder, total, write
off
crashing: thunderous
crash into: barge,
bump, hit, ram, run
down, run into, run
over
crass: gross, ignorant,
immodest, loud,
philistine
crate: box, case, chest,
crib
crater: cavity, chasm,
hollow, pit
crave: desire, fancy,
hunger, itch, long,
lust, solicit, want,
yearn
craven: cowardly,
fearful,
pusillanimous, yellow
craving: desire,
hunger, itch, longing,
lust, passion, want,
yearning

craw: crop
crawl: bristle, creep,
drag, scramble,
swarm, wriggle
crawler: creep,
yes-man
crawling: grovelling,
ingratiating, teeming,
thick
craze: bug, fad,
fashion, kick, mania,
passion, rage, rave,
sensation, vogue
crazed: berserk,
deranged, possessed,
rabid, wild
crazily: madly
craziness: lunacy,
madness
crazy: asinine, insane,
irrational, ludicrous,
lunatic, mad,
nonsensical, queer,
raving, screwy,
senseless, wild, zany,
creaking: rusty
cream: dessert, filling,
flower, ointment,
white
creamy: rich, soft
crease: crumple, dent,
fold, hollow, knit,
laugh, line, wrinkle
creased: wreathed
create: begin, breed,
build, cause, coin,
compose, conceive,
construct, do, effect,
fashion, form,
generate, give,
imagine, invent, make
up, make, mint,
mould, originate,
produce, raise, start,
take on, weave
creation: beginning,
birth, composition,
discovery, existence,
fashion, formation,
generation, genesis,
innovation, invention,
opus, origin, piece,
production, work,
world
creations: works
creative: artistic,
imaginative,
inventive, original,
pregnant, productive
creativity: fire,
imagination,
inspiration,
invention, muse
creator: artist, author,
cause, father,
originator, parent

creature: beast,
being, individual,
organism, thing
creatures: life
crèche: nursery
credentials:
background,
certificate, reference
credible: likely,
plausible, possible,
reasonable
credit: attribute,
believe, buy,
distinction, honour,
impute, kudos, loan,
merit, rebate, refer,
reputation, standing,
wear
creditable:
honourable, laudable,
reputable, worthy
credo: belief
credulous: green,
gullible, innocent,
naive, unsuspecting
credulousness:
innocence
creed: belief,
conviction, faith,
persuasion, principle,
school
creel: basket
creep: crawl, drag,
drip, lurk, run, skulk,
slope, steal
creeping: insidious,
slimy, slow
creepy: frightening,
hair-raising, macabre,
weird
cremate: burn
cremation: funeral
crème de la crème:
pick
crenellation:
battlements
creole: jargon
crepuscular: dusky,
shadowy
crest: banner, crown,
head, height,
maximum, peak,
pinnacle, tip
crestfallen: ashamed
cretin: dunce, fool,
idiot, wally
cretinous: foolish,
idiotic, unintelligent
crevasse: chasm,
cleft, gap, nook, rift
crevice: chink, crack
crew: band, following,
gang, man, mob,
outfit, parcel, set,
squad, team
crewman: hand

crib: cot, cradle, text
crick: cramp, kink
crier: herald, enormity, impropriety, incident, misdemeanour
crime: offence, sin, misdeed
criminal: bent, convict, crook, delinquent, illegal, lawless, malefactor, offender, outlaw, scoundrel, villain, villainous, wrong
crimp: kink
crimped: kinky
crimson: blush, flush, red
cringe: cower, flinch, quail
cringing: hangdog, servile, slavish
crinkle: crease, curl, wrinkle
cripple: disable, hamstring, immobilize, lame, mutilate, paralyse, sabotage
crippled: crooked, disabled, halt, lame, misshapen
crisis: emergency, head, juncture, pinch, showdown
crisp: brittle, chilly, fresh, sharp
crispbread: biscuit
crispness: chill
criss-cross: weave
criterion: canon, gauge, mark, measure, precedent, rule, standard, yardstick
critic: commentator
critical: climactic, crucial, decisive, delicate, desperate, fatal, fateful, fine, grave, great, hard-hitting, judicial, main, querulous, scathing, serious, severe, significant, sore, vital
critically: desperately, seriously
criticism: attack, censure, comment, complaint, knock, niggle, review, stick, stink
criticize: attack, carp, castigate, censure,

comment, jaw, knock, lash, pan, rap, review, roast, slate
critique: criticism, notice
croak: die
croaking: hoarse, rusty
crochet: freak
crochetwork: lace
crock: hack, jar, jug
crockery: china
crocodile: file, line, procession, queue, train
croft: farm
crofter: farmer
crone: bag, harridan, prune
crony: companion, comrade, friend, intimate, mate, sidekick
crook: bandit, criminal, flex, fraud, hook, knave, malefactor, rogue, scoundrel
crooked: bent, corrupt, criminal, delinquent, dishonest, fraudulent, irregular, knavish, lopsided, mangled, misshapen, rotten, shady, skew, twisted, underhand, venal, winding, wrong, wry
croon: sing
crop: browse, clip, feed, fruit, gather, harvest, mow, produce, shave, trim, whip, yield
crop up: happen, materialize, occur, rise, surface
crosier: crook
cross: contentious, disagreeable, hybrid, ill-humoured, liverish, peevish, quarrelsome, querulous, transit, traverse, waspish
crossbar: yoke
crossbred: mixed
crossbreed: hybrid
crosshatch: score, cross
crossing: intersection, junction, passage, meeting
crossover: bridge, transverse
crossroads:

intersection, junction
crossways: transverse
crotch: crutch
crotchet: kink
crotchety: cantankerous, capricious, moody
crouch: cower, stoop
crouched: motionless
crow: boast
crowbar: lever
crowd: assembly, attendance, audience, beseige, bunch, collection, cramp, crew, crush, fill, flock, horde, huddle, hustle, jostle, lot, mass, mill, mob, multitude, pack, pile, pour, press, rabble, scrum, shove, squeeze, swarm
crowded: full, lively, packed, thick
crowds: score
crown: cap, complement, garland, head, height, tip
crowned: wreathed
crow's foot: line, wrinkle
crow's nest: lookout
crucial: climactic, critical, decisive, great, imperative, indispensable, key, momentous, operative, principal, serious, strategic, urgent, vital
crucifix: cross
crucify: blister, rack, torture
crude: barbarian, barbaric, coarse, gross, immature, primary, primitive, profane, ragged, raw, rough, rude, rugged, rustic, sketchy, stiff, uncouth, unfinished, vulgar
crudely: roughly
crudeness: vulgarity
crudity: vulgarity
cruel: barbaric, brutal, cold-blooded, fell, ferocious, flinty, harsh, heartless, inhuman, merciless, monstrous, murderous, rough, ruthless, sadistic, savage, stiff, unkind, unnatural, vicious, villainous, violent,

wicked
cruelty: atrocity, ferocity, torture, violence
cruise: coast, prowl, range, sail, voyage
cruiser: boat
crumb: bit, grain, jot, nibble, particle, scrap
crumble: collapse, crush, decay, dissolve, rot, waste
crumbling: dilapidated, disintegration, ramshackle, rotten
crumbly: dusty
crumbs: remains
crummy: rotten
crumple: buckle, crease, crush, fold, screw up, wrinkle
crunch: chew, crisis, crossroads, emergency
crunchy: crisp
cruor: blood
crusade: drive, quest
crusader: pilgrim
crush: batter, bow, break, bruise, conquer, crumble, defeat, grind, infatuation, jam, mash, mill, overcome, pile, pinch, powder, press, prostrate, pulp, pulverize, quash, quell, repress, rout, ruin, scotch, scrum, smash, squash, squeeze, stamp, suppress, telescope, trample, tread, wither
crushed: battered, fine, ground, heartbroken, mangled
crusher: flail, mill
crushing: compression, pressure, withering
crust: rind, skin
crusty: cantankerous, peevish, surly
crux: centre, crisis, emergency, heart, juice, juncture, marrow, point, root
cry: bawl, bay, call, exclamation, greet, roar, scream, shout, shriek, snivel, sob, trumpet, wail, weep, whimper, whoop, yell
crying: bawl, lacrimose,

lamentation, sob,
tearful
crypt: cellar, grave,
tomb, vault
cryptic: dark, deep,
hidden, mysterious,
obscure, opaque,
secret
cryptograph: cipher
crystal: flake
crystal-gazer: oracle,
prophet
crystalline: clear
crystallization:
ossification
crystallize: polarize,
set
cub: pup, youngster
cubbyhole: booth,
pigeonhole
cube: block, cake
cubicle: cell,
chamber,
compartment
cubs: litter, young
cuckoo: crazy, insane,
lunatic, mad
cuddle: caress, clinch,
embrace, fondle,
huddle, pet, snuggle,
squeeze
cuddly: sexy
cudgel: club
cudgelling: drubbing
cue: feed, key, prod,
prompt, signal
cuff: bang, clip,
crown, hit, knock,
slap
cuisine: cookery, food
cuisinier: chef, cook
cull: extract, gather,
killing, pluck, pull
culled: cut
culminate in: finish,
result
culminate: cease,
climax
culminating:
supreme
culmination:
catastrophe, climax,
conclusion, crisis,
finish, head, height,
issue, peak, summit,
term, zenith
culpability: blame,
fault, guilt
culpable: guilty,
reprehensible,
responsible, remiss
culprit: convict,
convict, offender,
principal
cult: fad, persuasion
cultivable: fertile,

breed
cultivate: develop,
educate, farm, form,
foster, grow, nourish,
nurse, nurture,
perfect, raise, rear,
till, woo, work
cultivated: literate,
sophisticated, urbane
cultivation: breeding,
civilization, culture,
gardening, growth,
refinement
cultural: liberal
culture: background,
breeding, civilization,
education, finish,
learning, taste
cultured: artistic,
civilized, cultivated,
genteel, learned,
literate, nice, polite,
refined, well-bred
culvert: drain
cumbersome:
awkward, bulky,
ponderous, unwieldy,
weighty
cummerbund: belt,
girdle
cunning: astute,
calculating, crafty,
deceitful, deep,
devious, foxy, guile,
knowing,
machination, policy,
scheming, serpentine,
sharp, shrewd,
slippery, sly, subtle,
tactical, vulpine, wily,
cunningly: sharply
cup: drink, mug, plate,
pot, trophy
cupboard: cabinet,
closet, press,
wardrobe
cupidity: avarice,
greed, lust
cupola: dome
cur: dog, pariah
curate: clergyman,
priest
curative: healing,
medicinal,
therapeutic
curator: caretaker,
custodian, guardian,
keeper, warden
curb: bit, brake,
bridle, check, contain,
control, gag, govern,
halt, keep, leash, lid,
master, moderate,
muzzle, obstruct,
quell, rein, repress,
resist, restraint,

restriction, slow,
stem, stifle, suppress,
temper
curbed: pent-up
curdle: coagulate,
spoil
cure: break, heal,
help, panacea,
redress, relief,
remedy, therapy
cured: better, whole
curfew: gate
curing: healing
curiosity: interest,
novelty, rarity,
spectacle, wonder
curious: funny,
inquisitive,
interesting, nosy,
odd, peculiar, queer,
singular, strange,
uncommon, unusual
curiously:
uncommonly
curl: coil, kink, lock,
loop, roll, wind
curled: kinky, twisted,
wound
curlicue: flourish
curling: winding
curls: tresses
curly: kinky
currency: cash,
circulation, money,
tender, vogue
current:
contemporary,
draught, drift,
effective, fashionable,
flow, immediate,
juice, latest, live,
living, modern,
movement, new,
present, prevalent,
recent, rife, rip, river,
ruling, run, shoot,
stream, tide, topical,
up to date, watt, wave
curriculum: course
curriculum vitae:
record
curried: hot
curry: comb, groom
curse: ban, blast,
imprecation, jinx,
oath, plague, scourge,
swear
curse: pest
cursed: bleeding,
execrable
cursing: imprecation,
swearing
cursorily: quickly
cursory: careless,
casual, facile, hasty,
passing, perfunctory,

quick, rough, sketchy,
summary, superficial
curt: brief, brusque,
laconic, rough, rude,
ungracious,
peremptory, short
curtail: condense, cut,
dock, lower, reduce,
shorten, telescope
curtailed: cut, short
curtailment:
restraint, stoppage
curtain: awning,
catastrophe, drape,
mantle, pall, shade,
veil
curtly: roughly,
shortly
curtness: warmth,
asperity
curtsey: bob, dip
curvaceous:
feminine, full,
voluptuous, womanly
curve: bend, bow,
contour, crook, curl,
hook, hump, hunch,
kink, loop, sweep,
turn, turn, warp,
wind
curved: bent,
crooked, kinky, round
curvet: gambol, vault
cushion: bolster,
break, pad
cushioning: bolster,
insulation
cushy: easy, luxurious
cusp: horn
cuss: customer
custard: sauce
custodian: attendant,
caretaker, guard,
guardian, janitor,
keeper, warden
custody: care, charge,
goodwill, keeping,
possession,
protection, ward
custom: etiquette,
fashion, formality,
habit, manner,
patronage, policy,
practice, rite, ritual,
routine, rule, style,
tradition, usage, use,
vogue, way
customarily:
generally
customary: common,
conventional,
frequent, general,
habitual, old,
ordinary, orthodox,
prevalent, proverbial,
regular, regulation,

ritual, routine, set,
standard, stock,
traditional, usual,
wonted
customer: buyer,
chap, client,
consumer, fellow,
patron, punter
customers: clientele,
sale
customs: civilization,
tax
cut: barb, bite, carve,
censor, chop, clip,
commission, crop,
dilute, discount,
engrave, fashion,
gash, hack, incision,
indent, joint, knife,
lacerate, laceration,
lot, lower, machine,

mow, mutilate, pare,
proportion, quota,
reap, rebuff, record,
reduce, rip, score,
scotch, sculpture,
shaft, shear, shred,
slash, slice, slit, stab,
style, tip, trim,
weaken, wound
cut back: axe,
economize,
rationalize, prune,
run down
cut dead: disregard,
ignore, ostracize,
snub
cut down: butcher,
fell, reduce, shorten
cute: pretty
cutlass: sword
cut off: blockade,

disconnect, dock,
interrupt, secluded,
silence, terminate
cut short: curtail,
dock, interrupt, stop,
suspend
cutter: barge, boat,
gig, knife, launch,
cutthroat: killer
cutting: biting,
caustic, corrosive,
corrosive, excerpt,
fine, groove, keen,
mordant, plant,
pointed, pungent,
sarcastic, scathing,
section, severe, sharp,
trench
cuttingly: sharply
cut up: butcher,
dismember, joint, log,

mince, partition
cyan: blue
cycle: circle, orbit,
period, revolution,
roll, round, run,
sequence, procession
cyclone: low, gale,
hurricane, storm,
tempest, whirlwind
cylinder: barrel,
beam, can, canister,
cartridge, drum,
funnel, pipe, roll
cylindrical: round
cynic: sceptic
cynical: jaundiced,
sarcastic, sardonic,
sceptical, sour
cynicism: pessimism
cyst: bulge, blister,
gall

D

da: dad
dab: dot, little, lick, pat
dabble: paddle
dad: father
daemonic: infernal
daft: asinine, foolish, idiotic, insane, lunatic, mad, soft
daftness: madness
dagga: marijuana
dagger: knife
daily: common, everyday, maid, paper, quotidian
daintily: gingerly
daintiness: delicacy
dainty: choice, delicacy, delicate, fine, nice, pretty, savoury, titbit
dairyman: farmer
dais: base, pedestal, platform, podium, stage, stand
dale: valley
dales: highlands
dally: delay, saunter
dam: barrage, choke, lake, mother, reservoir, stem
damage: bruise, cost, cripple, harm, havoc, hit, hurt, impair, loss, maltreat, mischief, mutilate, nick, price, ravage, ruin, sabotage, scar, spoil, trauma, wound
damaged: bad, battered, hurt, incapacitated, imperfect
damages: compensation
damaging: bad, battery, defamatory, harmful, ill, libellous, pernicious, traumatic
dame: woman
damn: condemn, curse, slam
damnable: diabolical
damned: execrable, doomed, flaming
damning: hard-hitting

damp: humid, moist, moisture, musty, soak, steep, water, watery, wet
dampen: bathe, chill, cool, dull, mute, water, chill, wet
dampish: musty
dampness: moisture, wet
damsel: girl, maid, maiden, virgin
dance: ball, do, hop, measure, trip, promenade
dancing: twinkling
dandy: blade, gallant, swell, wizard
danger: difficulty, emergency, exposure, fire, hazard, jeopardy, menace, peril, pitfall, threat, woods
dangerous: awkward, bad, chancy, desperate, ferocious, fierce, grave, lethal, malignant, mean, nasty, serious, severe, ugly, unsafe, vicious, violent, warm
dangerously: desperately, seriously
dangle: flop, hang, loll, sling, suspend, swing
dangling: pendulous
dank: damp, moist, wet
dankness: damp, moisture
dapper: dashing, crisp, jaunty, natty, trim
dappled: chequered, mottled, pied, speckled
dare: challenge, chicken, risk, tempt
daredevil: gallant, reckless
daring: courage, defiant, desperate, fearless, gallant, gallantry, hardy, heroic, heroism, high-spirited, intrepid,

prowess, spartan, valiant, valour
dark-skinned: dusky
dark: black, brown, deep, dim, dingy, dismal, dusky, foggy,
dark: forbidding, frightening, funereal, gloomy, grey, grim, hidden, murky, night, ominous, sad, shadowy, sober, sombre, thunderous, turbid, ugly, unknown, wintry
darken: blacken, cloud, dim, eclipse, obfuscate, overshadow, shade, shadow, veil
darkening: discolour, eclipse
darkness: depth, fog, gloom, night, oblivion, pall
darling: dear, inamorata, love, pet, sweet, sweetheart
darn: patch, tack
darnel: weed
dart: dance, dash, dive, fly, lick, pounce, quarrel, race, run, rush, shaft, shoot, whip, zap, zip
dash: bustle, career, course, disappoint, fire, flair, flash, fly, gallop, hint, hurry, knap, line, little, panache, pelt, pinch, plunge, race, run, rush, shade, shoot, slam, smack, smattering, splash, sprinkling, style, touch, whip, zap, zip
dashboard: panel
dashing: gallant, high-spirited, saucy
dastardly: shameful
data: information, intelligence, material, output
data-bank: memory
date: court, day, engagement, see, time

dated: obsolete, old-fashioned, out, unfashionable
daub: dabble, paint, plaster, slap, smear, spot
daughter: girl
daunt: awe, depress, dismay, frighten, intimidate, scare
daunted: overawed
daunting: awesome, depressing, discouraging, forbidding, formidable, frightening, tall, uninviting, uphill
dauntless: confident, daring, fearless, gallant, intrepid, spartan, stout, valiant
dauntlessness: daring, prowess, spirit, valour
dawdle: crawl, creep, delay, drag, idle, lag, linger, loaf, lounge, loiter
dawdler: laggard
dawdling: slow
dawn: beginning, birth, light, start, sunrise, threshold
day: date, generation, time
daybook: journal
daybreak: dawn, sunrise
daydream: fancy, fantasy, illusion, vision
daydreaming: bemused
daylight: light, sunrise
daytime: light
daze: knock, numbness, rock, whirl
dazed: bemused, glassy, groggy, numb, silly
dazzle: captivate, glare, lustre, sparkle, splendour
dazzling: bright,

brilliant, glaring,
gorgeous, meteoric,
ostentatious,
ravishing,
scintillating,
spectacular, striking,
strong, stunning
dead: cold, defunct,
extinct, flat, gone,
inanimate, inert,
insensible, kaput,
late, lifeless, lost,
marked, numb,
obsolete, old, out,
void
deaden: drown,
muffle, mute, quieten,
silence
deadened: cushioned,
muffled, senseless
deadly: baneful,
devastating, fatal, fell,
killing, lethal, mortal,
murderous,
pernicious,
poisonous, tragic,
virulent, withering
deadness: numbness
deadpan: blank, dry,
wooden
deadweight: ballast,
lump
deaf: insensible
deafening: loud,
noisy, thunderous
deal: bargain,
compact, contract,
deliver, give, lot,
negotiate, operation,
package, pact, sale,
transaction, treaty
dealer: distributor,
merchant, seller
deal in: handle, job,
run, sell, stock, traffic
dealing: commerce,
negotiation, traffic
dealings: intercourse
deal out: dispense,
dole, measure, parcel,
ration
deals: business
deal with: do, field,
handle, process, treat
dean: principal, vicar
dear: expensive, high,
intimate, love, near,
sweet, sweetheart,
valuable
dearest: darling, love,
pet, precious
dearth: lack, scarcity,
shortage, want
death: departure,
dissolution, doom,
end, fall, finish, kill,

passing, tragedy
deathless: timeless,
immortal
deathly: cadaverous,
deadly, killing, mortal
debacle: catastrophe,
fiasco, flop, rout
debar: ban, preclude,
prevent
debase: cheapen,
corrupt, degrade,
depress, devalue,
lower, pervert,
prostitute, shame,
weaken
debased: base,
bastard, corrupt,
degenerate, vile,
vulgar, wicked
debasement:
prostitution
debatable:
controversial,
doubtful,
inconclusive, open,
undecided, unsettled
debate: reason,
consult, contest,
deliberate,
deliberation,
dialectic, discuss,
discussion, dispute,
negotiate,
negotiation, polemic,
query, question
debauch: corrupt,
orgy, pervert, revel,
violate
debauched:
degenerate, depraved,
dissipated, dissolute,
drunken, immoral,
lewd, libertine,
promiscuous, sordid
debauchee: pervert,
rake, libertine
debauchery:
depravity,
immorality, lewdness,
licence,
licentiousness
debauching: violation
debilitate: disable,
impair, paralyse, run
down
debilitated: decrepit,
disabled, feeble,
infirm, limp, low,
powerless, spent,
weak
debilitating: killing
debilitation:
exhaustion
debility: fatigue
debit: debt,
deduction, liability,

loss, withdraw
debonair: dashing
debris: garbage, junk,
leavings, litter, refuse,
remains, rubbish,
waste, wreckage
debt: debit, liability,
loss, obligation, score
debtor: bankrupt,
defaulter
debunked:
discredited
debut: baptism,
introduction, launch,
presentation
decadence: decay
decadent: degenerate,
libertine
decamp: go off, take
off
decant: pour
decanter: carafe, flask
decapitate: head
decay: consume,
corrupt, decadence,
decline,
decomposition,
degenerate,
disintegration, perish,
putrefy, rot, ruin,
rust, spoil, squalor,
stagnate, wane, waste,
wither
decayed: bad,
corrupt, dilapidated,
moth-eaten, putrid
decaying: corrupt,
rotten
decease: death,
departure, end,
passing
deceased: gone, late,
lifeless, dead, defunct
deceit: cheat,
collusion, falsehood,
fraud, lying, pretence
deceitful: crafty,
crooked, dishonest,
evasive, false,
fraudulent, lying,
perfidious, perjured,
unfaithful, untruthful
deceive: betray, cheat,
fool, have, have on,
hoax, kid, lie, outwit,
stab, swindle
deceiver: knave, liar,
rogue
deceiving: false
decelerate: retard,
throttle
decency: honesty,
honour, modesty,
morality, propriety
decent: chaste, clean,
fitting, honest,

honourable, just, law-
abiding, modest,
moral, proper,
respectable, savoury,
solid, square,
wholesome, worthy
deception: artifice,
betrayal, cheat,
deception, fraud,
guile, hoax,
imposition, lie, lying,
shave, swindle
deceptive: beguiling,
deceitful, false,
fraudulent, illusory,
knavish, meretricious,
misleading, specious,
underhand,
unreliable, untrue
decide: conclude,
determine, govern,
judge, resolve, rule,
think
decided: certain,
clear, closed, great,
sure
decidedly:
particularly
deciding: key
decipher: crack,
interpret, make out,
read, solve
decipherable:
intelligible
decipherment:
interpretation
decision: clinch,
finding, judgement,
option, pick,
resolution, resolve,
result, ruling,
sentence, verdict,
voice, vote, will
decisive:
authoritative, clean,
climactic, critical,
crucial, fatal, fateful,
final, key, landslide,
momentous,
peremptory, positive,
strategic
decisively: finally,
heavily
deck: hang, jewel,
pack
deckhouse: cabin
declaim: mouth,
quote, recite, speak
declaration:
notification,
profession,
publication,
resolution, word
declare: assert, aver,
avow, call, confess,
find, have, intimate,

judge, maintain,
manifest, pass,
proclaim, profess,
promulgate,
pronounce, protest,
say, state, swear,
testify, voice
decline: decadence,
decay, decrease,
degenerate,
depression,
deterioration, die,
dip, drop, eclipse,
fade, fail, fall, forbear,
languish, lapse, pine,
recede, recession,
refuse, rot, set, settle,
sink, slide, slope,
slump, subside, wane,
wither
declining: dying,
obsolescent,
retrograde
declivity: decline,
descent, gradient
decode: decipher,
interpret
decoding:
interpretation
decompose: crumble,
decay, degenerate,
degrade, dissolve,
perish, putrefy, rot
decomposed: off,
putrid, rotten
decomposition:
breakdown, decay,
disintegration,
dissolution, rot
decompressor: pod
decontaminate:
purify
decontaminated:
clean
decor: furniture, trim
decorate: figure,
furnish, garnish,
grace, hang, honour,
jewel, ornament,
paint, pattern,
rearrange, trim,
varnish
decorated: fancy
decorating: cosmetic
decoration: decor,
fitting, flourish,
furniture, garnish,
honour, ornament,
pattern, varnish
decorations: frills
decorative: festive,
ornamental
decorator: painter
decorous: chaste,
decent, dignified,
formal, proper,

respectable, sedate,
tactful, reverent
decorousness: tact
decorum: ceremony,
dignity, etiquette,
formality, manners,
propriety, protocol
decoy: bait, lure,
tempt, temptation
decrease:
consumption, cut,
decline, deduction,
degenerate, descend,
descent, dilute, drop,
fall, impair, lessen,
loss, lower, lull,
minimize, narrow,
pale, reduce, remit,
run down, shrink,
subside, wane,
weaken
decreased: cut,
dilute, lower
decree: bull, call,
dictate, directive,
doom, edict, institute,
judge, judgement,
law, mandate, ordain,
order, precept,
prescribe, pronounce,
regulation, rule,
ruling, word
decree nisi: divorce
decrepit: frail, infirm,
senile, worn out
decrepitude: dotage,
frailty
decry: quarrel
dedicate: enshrine,
inaugurate, inscribe,
invest
dedicated: devoted,
resolute, strong, true,
wholehearted, zealous
dedication:
commitment,
resolution, zeal
deduce: conclude,
divine, draw, gather,
induce, infer, judge,
perceive, reason,
reconstruct, surmise,
work out
deduced: logical
deduct: knock off,
subtract, take,
withhold
deduction:
conclusion, inference,
judgement, logic,
reasoning, rebate,
surmise
deed: charter, feat,
gesture, instrument,
job, paper, step,
thing, turn

deeds: works,
deem: believe,
consider, count, hold,
imagine, judge,
reckon, see, think
deemster: judge
deep: dark, far, full,
heavy, hollow,
intense, low,
profound, rich, sea,
thick, unbroken,
yawning
deepen: intensify,
thicken
deeply: badly, heavily,
very, well
deep-rooted: stable,
strong
deep-seated: chronic
deep-set: cavernous,
hollow
deep-sounding:
sonorous
deface: score
defamation:
calumny, detraction,
libel, mud, slander,
smear, vilification
defamatory:
libellous, scandalous
defame: blacken,
libel, slander
defamer: backbiter
default: neglect,
negligence, want
defaulter: bankrupt,
delinquent, loser
defeat: baffle, beat,
best, better, conquer,
conquest, debacle,
defy, demolish,
failure, fall, finish,
floor, foil, fox,
frustrate, hammer,
kill, knockout, lick,
licking, loss,
overcome, overthrow,
quell, reverse, rout,
ruin, sink, smash,
undo, upset, wallop,
whip, worst
defeated: hangdog,
undone
defeater: conqueror
defeating: frustration
defeatist: resigned
defecate: pass
defecation: motion
defect: bug, crack,
deformity, desert,
failing, fault, frailty,
handicap,
malfunction, revolt,
speck, vice, warp
defection: desertion,
revolt

defective: bad, faulty,
imperfect, inaccurate,
incorrect, jerry-built,
lacking, lame, rogue,
wrong
defector: deserter
defence: barrier,
bastion, counter,
justification,
maintenance,
operation, parade,
plea, rampart, reason,
screen, security,
shield, vindication,
wall
defenceless: helpless,
insecure, powerless,
prostrate, unguarded,
vulnerable, weak
defences:
fortification,
protection
defend: champion,
cover, guard, justify,
keep, maintain,
protect, secure,
shelter, shield, stand
by, support, uphold
defendant: party
defended: secure
defender: champion,
guard, keeper, patron,
saviour
defensible: tenable
defensive: martial
defer: comply, delay,
kowtow, postpone,
procrastinate, put off,
remit, reserve, retard,
stay, submit,
suspend, waive
deference: duty,
homage, humility,
respect
deferential: humble,
meek, reverent
deferment: delay,
reprieve
deferral: moratorium
deferred: off, shelved
defer to: respect,
revere
defiance: challenge,
mutiny, resistance
defiant:
insubordinate,
rebellious,
recalcitrant, scornful
deficiency: drought,
failure, fault, lack,
scarcity, shortage,
want
deficient: bad,
bankrupt, faulty,
imperfect,
inadequate, lacking,

low, meagre, poor,
scanty, short
deficiently: badly
deficit: deficiency,
lack
defile: blacken,
corrupt, dirty, foul,
gorge, outrage, pass,
poison, pollute,
profane, shame, soil,
stain, violate
defiled: corrupt, foul
defilement: filth,
nastiness, rape,
violation
define: formulate,
frame, prescribe,
shape, specify,
defined: limited
definite:
authoritative, certain,
clear, decisive,
outright, pronounced,
secure, set, specific,
sure, unquestioned
definitely: decidedly,
far, indeed,
positively, quite,
undoubtedly, yes
definition: clarity,
focus
definitive: classic,
decisive, final,
positive, precise
definitively: finally,
positively
deflate: mortify,
puncture, shrink
deflated: flat
deflect: divert, field,
sidetrack, swerve,
turn, ward
deflection: rebound,
turn
defloration: rape,
violation
deflower: seduce,
violate, wrong
deform: creep,
distort, mutilate
deformation: creep
deformed: crooked,
imperfect, mangled,
misshapen,
monstrous, twisted
deformity:
disfigurement,
malformation
defraud: cheat, fleece,
outwit, rob, screw,
swindle, victimize,
wrong
deft: cunning,
delicate, efficient,
handy, neat, quick,
ready, slick

deftness: artifice,
dexterity, hand,
neatness
defunct: dead,
extinct, flat,
inanimate, lifeless
defy: beard, challenge,
face, flout, oppose,
rebel, resist
degeneracy:
decadence, decay,
depravity, immorality
degenerate: corrupt,
decay, decline,
depraved, descend,
dissolute, immoral,
kinky, libertine,
mean, regress,
relapse, rot, rotten,
villainous
degeneration:
decadence, decay,
decline, descent,
deterioration,
disgrace, prostitution
degrade: break,
cheapen, devalue,
humble, lower,
prostitute, reduce
degraded: base,
bestial, low, mean,
vulgar
degrading:
humiliating, shameful
degree: deal, diploma,
elevation, grade,
level, measure, peg,
pitch, plane, point,
rate, scale, shade,
step, unit
degrees: scale
dehydrate: dry
dehydrated: dry,
parched, thirsty
dehydration: drought
deification: idolatry
deify: idolize, worship
deign: lower, stoop
deity: god, idol,
immortal
deject: damp, chill
dejected: flat, gloomy,
glum, low,
melancholy,
miserable, prostrate,
subdued, unhappy,
woeful, wretched
dejectedly: unhappily
dejection: depression,
disappointment,
down, gloom,
melancholy, misery,
pessimism, woe
dekko: glance, look,
peek
delay: linger, check,

hamper, hesitate,
hitch, hold up, keep,
linger, loiter,
moratorium, obstruct,
pause, procrastinate,
postpone, put off,
remit, reserve,
respite, retard, slow,
stall, stay, suspend,
wait
delayed: slow
delectable: charming,
dainty, delicious,
pleasant, savoury
delectation:
diversion, pleasure
delegate: assign,
commission,
deputize, deputy,
proxy, representative
delegated:
representative
delegates:
assignment,
commission,
committee, congress,
legation
delete: cancel, censor,
kill, obliterate, omit,
remove, rub out,
scratch
deleterious: harmful,
mischievous,
undesirable,
unwholesome
deletion: cancellation
deliberate:
circumspect, cogitate,
confer, conscious,
consider, consult,
debate, judicious,
knowing, leisurely,
meditate, ponder,
premeditated, reflect,
revolve, sedate, see,
speculate, study,
think, wilful
deliberately:
leisurely
deliberation:
calculation, caution,
consideration,
consultation, debate
deliberative:
thoughtful
delicacy: dainty,
finesse, nicety,
propriety, refinement,
sensibility, tact,
tenderness, titbit
delicate: feeble,
feminine, fine, flimsy,
fragile, frail, fussy,
ladylike, light, nice,
pretty, sensitive,
sickly, slight, soft,

squeamish, subtle,
tactful, tender,
tenuous, unhealthy,
weak
delicately: gingerly
delicious: dainty,
luscious, palatable,
savoury, tasty
delight: catch,
content, divert, feast,
glee, gratify,
happiness, joy, please,
pleasure, pride, treat
delighted: glad,
happy, joyful,
pleased, radiant, rapt,
overjoyed
delightedly: happily
delightful: delicious,
enjoyable, fetching,
jolly, joyful, lovable,
lovely, nice, pleasant,
ravishing, sweet
delineate:
circumscribe, define,
describe, draw,
outline, sketch
delineation:
definition, drawing,
outline, sketch
delinquent: hooligan,
malefactor, problem,
remiss, scoundrel,
yob
deliquesce: dissolve,
melt
delirious: feverish,
funny, light, raving
delirium: fever,
frenzy, intoxication
deliver: bring,
commend, commit,
consign, execute,
fetch, give, hand,
have, issue, liberate,
mount, plant,
produce, read, recite,
redeem, relieve,
rescue, return, rid,
save, say, serve, turn
in, yield
deliverance:
liberation, release,
relief, salvation
deliverer: saviour
delivery: birth,
carriage,
consignment, diction,
distribution, issue,
execution, surrender
dell: depression, dip,
hollow, valley
delta: basin
delude: kid
deluded: misguided,
paranoid

deluge: avalanche, barrage, besiege, cataract, cloudburst, flash, flood, flow, glut, inundate, lavish, ply, rain, shower, spate, swamp
delusion: dream
delve: dig
demand: ask, insist, call, challenge, claim, command, compulsion, condition, expect, indent, market, necessitate, necessity, need, press, request, require, requirement, requisition, run, sale, take, want, warrant
demanding: difficult, gruelling, importunate, insistent, rigorous, rugged, severe, strenuous, tall, tough, weighty
demands: pressure
demarcate: circumscribe, detach, limit, restrict
demarcation: detachment, restriction
demean: cheapen, degrade, humble, lower, prostitute
demeaning: humiliating, prostitution
demeanour: aspect, attitude, bearing, carriage, cast, conduct, jib, look, manner, poise, presence, quality
demented: berserk, crazy, deranged, distracted, insane, lunatic, mad, maddened, possessed, psychotic, wild
dementedly: madly
dementia: insanity, lunacy, madness
demigod: hero
demise: death, departure, end, passing
demo: march
demobilization: discharge
demobilize: discharge
democratic: free
démodée:

unfashionable
demolish: blast, confound, consume, destroy, overthrow, pulverize, ravage, ruin, sack, shatter, smash, take down, wreck, write off
demolition: destruction, finish
demon: devil, fiend, monster, ogre
demoniac: satanic
demonic: infernal, monstrous, satanic
demonstrate: teach, barrack, attest, display, give, illustrate, manifest, present, produce, prove, reflect, show, show off
demonstration: gesture, illustration, manifestation, march, show, testimony, unrest
demonstrator: malcontent, teacher
demoralize: confuse, unnerved
demoralizing: unhealthy, unwholesome
demote: break, degrade, reduce, relegate
demur: coy, differ, ladylike, modest, obedient, object, objection, prim, protest, quarrel, question, retiring, scruple, self-effacing
demurely: quietly
demureness: modesty, obedience
den: burrow, cave, cloister, garret, haunt, hole, lair, lodge, nest, retreat
denature: treat
dendrology: forestry
denial: defence, negative, retraction
denigrate: attack, run down
denigrating: attack, calumny, defamatory, detraction, vilification
denims: jeans
denizen: citizen, inhabitant, occupant, resident
denizens: population
denominate: name

denominated: named
denomination: church, name, persuasion, school, sect
denominator: term
denote: designate, imply, indicate, mean, represent, stand for, symbolize
denoting: significant
dénouement: end, head, payoff
denounce: condemn, expose
dense: close, compact, dim, dull, firm, rank, solid, thick, tough, turbid, unintelligent, impenetrable, intense
densely-growing: lush, luxuriant
densely: heavily
density: firmness, temper
dent: bruise, cavity, chip, impression, indent, mark, nick, pit, scrape
dental: oral
dented: battered, marked
dentition: bite, teeth
denture: plate
dentures: teeth
denude: bare
denuded: bare
denunciation: diatribe, exposure, invective
deny: contradict, disclaim, negate, rebut, repudiate, renounce, withhold
depart: die, go, go off, leave, move, pass, pull out, quit, remove, retire, retreat, run, set off, vacate, withdraw
departed: dead, gone, late
departing: outgoing
department: bureau, category, class, compartment, desk, faculty, field, lookout, office, realm, school, section
departure: death, disappearance, exodus, leave, recession, retreat, secession, withdrawal
depend: bank, bargain, lean, rest

depend on: hinge, pivot, presume, reckon, rely on, turn on
dependability: faithfulness, fidelity, infallible, loyalty
dependable: certain, consistent, faithful, loyal, regular, reliable, responsible, safe, serviceable, solid, steady, sure
dependant: satellite, subject, ward
dependence: habit
dependency: colony, province
dependent: contingent, conditional, relative, satellite, subject
depict: describe, draw, mirror, paint, perform, picture, render, represent, sketch, tell
depiction: description, picture
depilated: bald
deplete: consume, drain, sap
depleted: low, poor
depletion: consumption, exhaustion, loss
deplorable: awful, criminal, despicable, execrable, lamentable, miserable, rotten, sad, sorry, unfortunate, woeful
deplorably: regrettably, unfortunately
deplore: complain, disapprove of, lament, manoeuvre, mourn, regret
deploy: marshal
deployment: manoeuvre
depone: declare, witness
deponent: witness
deport: ban, banish, exile
deportation: ban, exile
deportee: exile
deportment: bearing, carriage
depose: oust, overthrow, remove, overturn, testify
deposing: overthrow

deposit: bank, cast, commit, consign, drop, lay, lodge, pawn, payment, place, plaque, pledge, put, sediment, store
deposition: declaration, testimony
depository: bank, barn, store, vault
depot: factory, station, stop
deprave: corrupt, pervert, poison, pollute, stain
depraved: bestial, corrupt, degenerate, dissolute, depraved: immoral, kinky, libertine, lost, low, perverse, shameless, sinful, villainous, wicked
depraving: unwholesome
depravity: dissolution, enormity, immorality, lewdness, vice
deprecate: disapprove of, minimize
deprecating: pejorative
deprecation: disapprobation
depreciate: deflate, devalue, wear
depreciating: pejorative
depreciation: rape, robbery, sack, wear
depress: damp, darken, dull, lower, oppress
depressed: dejected, flat, gloomy, glum, low, melancholy, miserable, prostrate, sad, sorrowful, sunken, unhappy, woeful
depressing: black, desolate, dim, discouraging, dismal, gloomy, sad, uninviting
depression: crash, decline, dell, dent, despair, dip, down, gloom, hollow, lacuna, low, melancholy, misery, pan, pessimism, recess, recession, sadness, scrape,

slump, valley, woe
deprivation: lack, loss, need
deprive: cheat, divest, rob, shear, strip
deprived: bereaved, needy, underprivileged
depth: dead, fall, nadir, tread, width
deputation: contingent, delegation, mission
deputize: substitute, understudy
deputy: assistant, auxiliary, substitute
derange: disturb
deranged: berserk, crazy, dishevelled, distracted, insane, lunatic, mad, mental, psychotic
derangement: disarray, disorder
deregulate: liberalize
derelict: ramshackle, remiss, wreck, wreckage
dereliction: desertion, neglect
derestrict: liberalize
deride: catcall, despise, flout, mock, ridicule, scoff, scorn, sneer, taunt
deriding: jeering
derision: contempt, jeering, mockery, ridicule, sarcastic, scorn, shame, sneer
derisive: sardonic, scornful
derisory: laughable, paltry, ridiculous
derivation: descent, emanation, extraction, fountain, origin, parent, root, source
derivative: secondary, unimaginative
derive: base, deduce, induce, infer, originate, proceed, reap, result, spring, stem
derogate: cheapen
derogation: calumny
derogatory: critical, defamatory, vituperative
derrick: crane
derring-do: valour
descant: chant

descend: decline, dip, drop, fall, get off, gravitate, settle, sink, spring, swoop
descendant: offspring
descendants: offspring, posterity, seed
descent: derivation, dip, down, extraction, fall, family, genealogy, pedigree, slope, stock, strain, swoop
describe: cover, define, detail, label, narrate, picture, portray, qualify, quantify, relate, report, represent, set out, tell
description: definition, fashion, form, kind, label, picture, quality, report, sort
descriptive: pictorial, poetic
descry: spot
desecrate: defile, pollute, profane, violate
desecrating: sacrilegious
desecration: blasphemy, violation
desert: barren, betray, defect, drop, forsake, leave, lifeless, maroon, quit, repudiate, waste, wild, wilderness
deserted: derelict, forlorn, godforsaken, lonely, uninhabited, unsettled, void
desertion: betrayal, disappearance
deserts: due
deserve: merit, rate
deserved: due, just, right
deservedly: fairly
deserving of: worth, worthy
deserving: fit
déshabillé: dishevelled, disarray, undress
desiccate: evaporate, roast, wither
desiccated: parched, shrivelled
design: calculate, composition, conceive, conception,

concoct, construct, contrive, devise, draw, figure, goal, idea, intention, lay, layout, make, mean, meaning, model, motive, object, objective, organization, organize, pattern, plan, plot, project, purpose, resolve, scheme, structure, style
designate: call, choose, class, define, detach, detail, label, name, nominate, number, represent, term
designated: detailed, named, numbered
designation: definition, denomination, detachment, label, name, term
designed: made
designer: artist, engineer, founder, originator
designing: calculating, scheming
desirable: fitting, lovable, lovely, welcome
desire: choose, craving, fancy, greed, hankering, hope, hunger, itch, longing, lust, notion, passion, pleasure, prize, purpose, sex, urge, want, way, will, wish, yearning
desirous: longing, wishful
desist: halt, lay off, leave
desk: bureau
desk-bound: sedentary
desolate: barren, depress, forlorn, gaunt, godforsaken, inhospitable, lonely, miserable, ravage, solitary, uninhabited, waste, wild
desolation: depression, loneliness, ravage, wilderness
despair: depression, gloom, misery, pessimism

despairing: hopeless
despatch: launch,
letter
desperado: bandit,
gangster, outlaw
desperate: dire,
forlorn, hopeless,
hunted, last-ditch
desperately: badly,
madly, terribly
despicable: base,
cheap, contemptible,
damnable, nasty,
paltry, pitiful, rotten,
shabby, vile,
worthless, wretched
despise:
notwithstanding,
scoff
despoil: loot, pillage,
plunder, raid,
ransack, rape, sack
despoiling: predatory
despoliation: pillage,
rape, sack
despondency:
depression, gloom,
melancholy,
pessimism, sadness
despondent: dejected,
desolate, gloomy,
glum, low,
melancholy,
miserable, unhappy
despondently:
unhappily
despot: authoritarian,
dictator, oppressor,
tyrant
despotic:
authoritarian,
dictatorial, oppressive
despotism: tyranny
dessert: sweet
destination:
direction, stop
destine: intend,
doom, mean, ordain,
preordain
destined: certain,
doomed, fated, future
destiny: doom, fate,
fortune, lot, luck,
providence, portion
destitute: bankrupt,
hard up, miserable,
poor, poverty-
stricken
destitution:
deprivation, misery,
penury, poverty, ruin
destroy: blast,
confound, consume,
demolish, devour,
end, finish, kill,
obliterate, overthrow,

pulverize, ravage,
rout, sabotage, sack,
shatter, sink, slay,
smash, undo, wreck,
write off, zap
destroyed: kaput,
lost, shattered,
undone
destroyer: killer
destruction:
assassination,
damage, death,
demolition,
disintegration,
dissolution, doom,
end, fall, finish,
havoc, kill, killing,
overthrow, ravage,
sabotage, sack,
sacrifice, waste, wreck
destructive: baneful,
corrosive, deadly,
disruptive, harmful,
killing, malignant,
mischievous,
murderous,
pernicious, predatory,
subversive
desultory: occasional,
scatterbrained,
superficial
detach: detail,
disconnect, isolate,
loose, part, second,
separate
detached: detailed,
disinterested,
distinct, impersonal,
loose, nonchalant,
objective, remote,
separate, thick-
skinned,
unconcerned,
undemonstrative,
withdrawn
detachment:
contingent, detail,
indifference,
isolation, party,
section, separation,
unit
detail: circumstance,
cover, describe,
formulate, item,
itemize, jot, narrate,
particular, point,
recite, regard, relate,
report, respect,
specify
detailed: close,
elaborate, factual,
faithful, full, graphic,
intimate, minute,
particular
details: minutiae,
specifications

detain: buttonhole,
delay, gate, hold, hold
up, jail, keep, lift,
retain, slow, withhold
detained: attached
detainee: captive
detect: catch,
discover, find, locate,
make out, notice,
scent, spot
detectable: audible
detected: found
detection: discovery,
finding
detector: monitor
detention: custody,
restraint
deter: dissuade, keep
deteriorate: decay,
decline, degenerate,
descend, fail, go off,
impair, putrefy,
regress, relapse, rot,
rust, sink, slump,
stagnate, suffer, wear
deterioration:
decadence, decay,
decline, descent,
drop, failure, relapse,
wear
determination:
backbone, diagnosis,
fortitude, heart,
nerve, purpose, push,
resolution, resolve,
self-assertion,
tenacity, willpower
determine: assign,
calculate, clinch,
conclude, decide, fix,
gauge, govern, judge,
learn, measure,
provide, purpose,
resolve, rule, set, will
determined:
constant, desperate,
dogged, earnest,
resolute, serious, set,
strenuous, strong,
tenacious, wilful
determinedly: hard,
manfully
determining:
overriding
deterrent: bar,
preventive
detest: hate, loathe
detestable:
contemptible,
damnable,
disgraceful,
disgusting, execrable,
obnoxious, odious
detestation: disgust,
revulsion
dethrone: eject, oust,

overthrow, remove
dethronement:
overthrow
detonate: bang, blast,
crash, discharge, fire,
fulminate, let off, set
off
detonation: bang,
blast, crack, crash,
discharge
detonations: thunder
detonator: cap
detour: bypass,
diversion, skirt
detract: subtract
detractor: backbiter,
critic
detriment:
deterioration,
disadvantage,
disservice, harm
detrimental:
damaging, harmful,
ill, mischievous,
pernicious
detritus: debris,
leavings, refuse
deuce: hell
devalue: deflate,
depress, lower
devastate: consume,
hit, pulverize, ruin,
sack, shatter, wither
devastated: waste
devastating:
disastrous, lethal,
murderous, stunning,
withering
devastation:
catastrophe, damage,
havoc, ravage, ruin,
sack, waste, wreck
develop: become,
bud, build, catch,
conceive, contract,
cultivate, dawn,
evolve, follow, form,
go, grow, improve,
increase, perfect,
pioneer, progress,
raise, result, turn out,
wax, work out
developed: cultivated
developing:
progressive, viable
development: build-
up, enlargement,
evolution, formation,
growth,
improvement,
increase, march,
metamorphosis,
movement,
occurrence, phase,
progress, variant,
variation

developments:
ramifications
deviant: bent,
homosexual, perverse
deviate: detour,
depart, digress,
diverge, sidetrack,
stray, swerve, switch,
turn off, turn, wander
deviation: departure,
detour, diversion,
eccentricity,
inequality, turn,
variation
deviationist:
subversive
device: artifice,
bearing, cipher,
convenience, figure,
gadget, implement,
instrument, legend,
machine, mark,
mechanism, pretext,
scheme, sign, thing,
wangle, wrinkle
devil: fiend, mischief,
monster, terror,
villain, wolf
devilish: diabolical,
infernal, satanic,
savage, wicked
devilment: mischief
devious: calculating,
circuitous, crafty,
cunning, deep, funny,
lying, shifty, slippery,
sly, subtle,
underhand, vulpine,
wily
deviously: indirectly
devise: brew,
compose, conspire,
contrive, create,
design, discover,
fabricate, hatch,
imagine, improvise,
invent, lay, make up,
make, manoeuvre,
manufacture, mint,
model, pioneer, plan,
plot, produce,
project, scheme,
shape, work out
devised: made
deviser: originator,
pioneer
devising: invention
devoid (of): destitute
devolve: formulate
devote: give, invest,
spend
devoted: attached,
attentive, close,
constant, dedicated,
devout, doting,
earnest, faithful,

fanatical, fond, keen,
loyal, unselfish,
wholehearted, zealous
devotedly: madly,
truly
devotee: believer,
connoisseur, fan,
fanatic, follower,
freak, lover, partisan
devotees: faithful,
following, school
devotion:
commitment,
faithfulness, fervour,
fondness, idolatry,
love, loyalty, piety,
prayer, sanctity,
worship, zeal
devotional: solemn,
spiritual
devour: consume,
demolish, eat, feed,
prey on, swallow
devouring: ravenous,
voracious
devout: fervent,
godly, monastic,
pious, religious,
reverent, saintly
devoutness: piety
dew: damp
dewlap: jowls
dewy: damp
dexterity: craft,
facility, hand, knack,
mastery, neatness,
skill
dexterous: clever,
cunning, efficient,
good, handy, neat,
nimble, quick, ready,
skilful
diabolic: satanic
diabolical: atrocious,
dark, infernal,
inhuman, monstrous,
savage, vicious,
villainous
diadem: crown
diagnose: identify
diagnosis:
interpretation
diagnostic: critical
diagonal: oblique,
bias, transverse
diagram: chart,
figure, graphic,
pattern, plan, profile,
scheme, table
diagrammatic:
graphic
dial: clock, face,
gauge, instrument,
mug, telephone
dialect: language,
speech, terminology

dialectal: idiomatic
dialectics: logic
dialogue:
consultation,
conversation, debate,
discussion, jaw,
script, speech, talk,
tête-à-tête, truce
diameter: width
diamonds: jewellery
diaper: napkin
diaphanous: filmy,
fine, flimsy, thin
diaphoresis: sweat
diaries: papers
diary: chronicle,
journal, log
diatribe: onslaught
dice: cut, die, mince
dicey: hairy, thorny
dickens: hell
dicker: haggle
dictate: canon,
determine,
necessitate, ordain,
regulation
dictator:
authoritarian, despot,
oppressor, tyrant
dictatorial:
authoritarian, lordly,
overbearing,
totalitarian
dictatorship: tyranny
diction: language,
speech, style
dictionary:
vocabulary
dictum: saying
didactic: pedantic
die: croak, disappear,
end, fade, fail, fall,
go, mortify, mould,
pass, perish, punch,
sink
die away: fizzle out,
lessen, wane
die down: quench
die out: peter out
die-hard:
conservative,
reactionary, square
diet: food,
government,
legislative,
parliament, senate,
slim
differ: deviate,
disagree, diverge,
quarrel, vary
difference: balance,
breach, break,
change, contrast,
departure,
distinction, diversity,
gap, inequality, odds,

rift, variation, variety
different: distinct,
distinctive, diverse,
fresh, incongruous,
inconsistent, more,
new, novel, opposite,
other, otherwise,
revolutionary,
several, unequal,
unfamiliar, unlike,
various
differentiate:
contrast,
discriminate,
distinguish, judge,
key, know, tell
differentiation:
distinction
differently: otherwise
differing: diverse,
various
difficult: awkward,
cantankerous,
complicated,
contrary, delicate,
demanding,
disagreeable,
formidable, fussy,
hard, heavy,
laborious, murderous,
painful, prickly,
problem, profound,
rebellious,
recalcitrant,
refractory, serious,
sticky, strained,
thorny, tight, tough,
unpopular, uphill
difficulty: barrier,
distress,
embarrassment, fix,
handful, handicap,
hang-up, hardship,
hassle, hindrance,
hitch, hoop, hurdle,
kink, matter, obstacle,
obstruction, pitfall,
problem, puzzle,
quagmire, rub,
strait(s), trouble,
wrinkle
diffidence: humility,
modesty
diffident: bashful,
faltering, hesitant,
insecure, modest,
self-conscious,
tentative,
uncomfortable,
unsure
diffuse: permeate,
disperse, emit, loose,
mix, radiate,
redundant, scatter,
shed, soft, verbose,
winnow

diffuser: hood
diffusing: pervasive
diffusion: enlargement, propagation
dig: barb, burrow, bury, ferret, grub, mine, nudge, poke, prod, quarry, rake, scoop, taunt, till, tunnel, undercut
digest: assimilate, summary, synopsis
digestible: edible, light
digging up: discovery
digit: cipher, figure, finger, number, numeral
dignified: august, exalted, grand, lofty, majestic, noble, princely, **dignified:** solemn, stately
dignify: grace, honour
dignitary: celebrity, official, personage, worthy
dignity: gravity, honour, majesty, nobility, self-respect
digress: detour, deviate, pad, ramble, wander
digression: aside, detour, diversion
digressive: rambling
digs: garret, lodgings, quarters
dig up: discover, exhume, fork, pull up
dilapidated: battered, decrepit, derelict, elderly
dilapidated: motheaten, ramshackle, seedy, shabby
dilate: bulge, distend, inflate, swell, widen
dilated: wide
dilating: expansive
dilation: bulge, swelling
dilatory: late, remiss, slow, tardy
dilemma: bind, jam, plight, predicament, puzzle, quandary
diligence: industry, patience
diligent: conscientious, persevering, tireless
diligently: hard
dilute: degrade, doctor, lower, reduce,

thin, water, weaken
diluted: watery, weak
dim: cloudy, dark, darken, dense, dull, dusky, fade, faint, foggy, gloomy, grey, indistinct, murky, obscure, pale, shadowy, shady, slow, sombre, thick, vague
diminish: decline, decrease, drop, fall, lessen, lower, lull, minimize, narrow, recede, reduce, relax, remit, shorten, slacken, subside, wane, waste, weaken
diminished: limited, lower, rusty
diminution: decline, decrease, loss
diminutive: baby, dwarf, little, nickname, pygmy, small, stunted
dimly: vaguely
dimmed: soft
dimness: gloom, shade, shadow, stupidity
dimple: cleft, hollow
dimwit: dummy, dunce, idiot, nincompoop
dimwitted: idiotic
din: babel, hubbub, jangle, noise, pandemonium, racket, thunder, uproar
dine: eat
dinghy: gig, launch
dingle: dell, hollow, valley
dingy: dark, dim, dirty, muddy
dining-room: canteen, grill, mess, saloon
dinner: dance, meal
diocese: see
dip: bath, bathe, decline, depression, duck, fall, immerse, paddle, plunge, scoop, wet
diploma: certificate
diplomacy: finesse, negotiation, tact
diplomat: minister
diplomatic: discreet, judicious, politic, suave, tactful
dipper: scoop
dipping: baptism

dipsomaniac: drunkard
dire: critical, desperate, disastrous, dread, sinister
direct: channel, conduct, control, dictate, drive, focus, govern, guide, head, immediate, instruct, lead, manage, navigate, nonstop, order, outright, outspoken, point, prescribe, refer, regulate, route, run, short, simple, straight, tell, turn, work
direction: bearing, course, drift, government, heading, instruction, jurisdiction, leadership, line, orientation, path, prescription, quarter, road, route
directive: command, mandate, order
directly: immediately, right, straight, straight away, through
directness: simplicity
director: conductor, head, instructor, leader, master, principal
directorate: executive
directory: catalogue, guide, roll
direly: desperately
dirge: lament
dirigible: balloon
dirt: dung, dust, filth, grime, mud, ordure
dirty: bawdy, black, defile, dingy, dusty, filthy, foul, insanitary, lewd, messy, muddy, nasty, obscene, pornographic, rotten, shabby, sordid, tainted, unhealthy
disability: handicap, trouble
disable: cripple, hamstring, immobilize, nobble, paralyse
disadvantage: catch, detraction, handicap, liability, penalty, snag

disagree: diverge, conflict, jar, protest, quarrel, wrangle
disagreeable: cantankerous, horrible, horrid, illhumoured, liverish, mean, nasty, objectionable, obnoxious, rotten, sour, unfriendly, unpleasant
disagreement: clash, conflict, difference, discord, dispute, hassle, quarrel, rift, wrangle
disallow: ban, overrule
disappear: depart, evaporate, fade, fail, vanish
disappearance: loss
disappoint: dash, disillusion, let down
disappointment: check, dismay, regret, reverse, setback, washout
disapproval: censure, disapprobation
disarming: conciliatory, winning
disarrange: confuse, jumble, litter, perturb, ruffle, shuffle
disarray: disorder, jumble, mess, shambles
disaster: calamity, catastrophe, crash, debacle, doom, failure, fiasco, flop, tragedy, washout
disastrous: bad, baleful, dire, evil, fatal
disbelief: astonishment
disbelieve: discount, question
disburse: dispense, spend
disbursement: expense, outlay,
disc: bat, button, circle, counter, record, round, wheel
discard: ditch, jettison, junk, reject, repudiate, scrap, shed
discern: catch, detect, discover, distinguish, divine, identify, know, make out, notice, perceive,

scent, see, taste, tell, understand

discernible: audible, noticeable, visible

discerning: astute, deep, intelligent, judicious, penetrating, perceptive, refined, sage, shrewd, wise

discernment: comprehension, distinction, insight, intelligence, judgement, knowledge, perception, sense, wisdom, wit

discharge: burst, carry out, complete, comply, dismiss, eject, emanation, emission, emit, execute, exhaust, fire, implement, launch, lay off, leak, let off, ooze, outburst, overflow, pardon, perform, redeem, release, relieve, remove, report, sack, satisfy, secrete, shoot, spill, unload

disciple: believer, convert, follower, pupil, scholar, student

disciplinarian: despot, dictatorial, ogre

discipline: castigate, control, drill, exercise, faculty, field, govern, order, punish, school

disclaim: deny, renounce, revoke, take back

disclose: bare, communicate, confess, display, expose, impart, leak, let on, let out, publish, reveal, say

disclosure: betrayal, communication, confession, exposure, indiscretion, news, publication, revelation

discolour: bruise, fade, fox, stain

discomfit: chagrin, defeat, discompose, floor, mortify, nonplus

discomfited: ashamed

discomfort: distress, pain

discommode: inconvenience

disconcert: confuse, nonplus, perturb, put out, rattle, ruffle, surprise, throw

disconcerting: off-putting

disconnect: break, cut off, detach, dislocate, divide, loose, separate

disconsolate: dejected, desolate, heartbroken, mournful, sad, unhappy, woeful, wretched

discontent: dissatisfied

discontinuance: stoppage

discontinue: break, cease, close, cut off, dissolve, interrupt, quit, stop, terminate, wind up

discontinued: lapsed, withdrawn

discontinuity: gap, hiatus

discord: conflict, contest, dispute, friction, quarrel, schism, split, strife

discordant: harsh, rough, strident

discount: disregard, rebate, reduce

discounted: underrated

discourage: deter, dissuade, frustrate, inhibit, put off, rebuff

discouragement: disappointment, dismay, frustration, rebuff

discouraging: depressing, dim, dismal

discourse: conversation, dialogue, dissertation, lecture, oration, speech

discourteous: disrespectful, impolite, offensive, rough, short, tactless, ungracious

discover: ascertain, catch, detect, determine, find, find

out, learn, locate, look up, pioneer, read, see, surprise

discovered: found

discovery: find, finding, invention, revelation

discredit: cheapen, compromise, disgrace, refute, shame, slur

discreet: cagey, careful, cautious, circumspect, delicate, diplomatic, guarded, noncommittal, politic, restrained, tactful

discrepancy: difference, hole

discrete: distinct, individual

discretion: calculation, caution, finesse, judgement, policy, prudence, tact, will

discretionary: judicial, optional, voluntary

discriminate: differentiate, discern, distinguish

discriminating: cultivated, discerning, fine, fussy, judicious, keen, refined, searching

discrimination: distinction, eye, indication, injustice, intolerance, judgement, refinement, taste

discriminatory: one-sided, partial, partisan, prejudiced, unfair, unreasoning

discursive: wordy

discuss: commune, debate, negotiate, review, talk

discussion: conference, conversation, debate, deliberation, huddle, session, speech, talk, tête-à-tête, word

disdain: contempt, despise, disregard, scorn, slight, sneer

disdainful: cavalier, condescending, lofty, lordly, scornful

disease: complaint, illness, plague, sickness

disembark: get off, land

disenchant: sour, turn off

disengage: clear, detach, disconnect, loose, release, withdraw

disengagement: detachment, withdrawal

disentangle: clear, free, resolve, simplify, solve, unravel

disfavour: disapprobation, dislike

disfigure: deface, mar, mutilate, scar

disfigured: crooked, deformed, mangled

disgrace: humble, lower, opprobrium, reproach, shame, slur

disgraced: discredited, ignominious, tainted

disgraceful: deplorable, reprehensible, scandalous, shameful, shocking, vile

disgruntled: dissatisfied, sulky

disguise: camouflage, cloak, conceal, cover, hide, mask, obscure, varnish, veil

disgust: horrify, horror, loathing, nauseate, offend, repel, repugnance, revolt, revulsion, scandalize

dish: beauty, disc, knockout, plate, pot

disharmony: discord

dishearten: chill, dismay, frustrate, intimidate, put off

disheartened: low, unnerved

disheartening: discouraging

dishevelled: bedraggled, messy, rough, wild

dishonest: bent, corrupt, crooked, deceitful, false, fraudulent, knavish, lying, perfidious, rotten, underhand, unethical, untrue, untruthful, venal

dishonesty:

falsehood,
immorality,
insincerity
dishonour: defile,
degrade, disgrace,
stain, violate
dishonourable: base,
disgraceful, foul,
ignominious,
infamous, unethical
disillusion:
disappointment,
dismay, let down,
puncture
disinclined:
reluctant, unwilling
disinfect: clean,
fumigate, purify
disinfected: sterile
disinformation:
propaganda
disintegrate:
crumble, decay,
fragment, rot, splinter
disintegration:
breakdown, collapse,
decay, decomposition,
erosion, failure
disinter: exhume
disinterest: frigidity,
indifference
disinterested:
impersonal, liberal,
neutral, objective
disjointed:
incoherent, scrappy,
separate, spastic
dislike:
disapprobation,
disapprove of, hate,
loathe, loathing,
repugnance, resent
dislodge: budge,
remove, shake off
disloyal: false, rotten,
unfaithful, unreliable,
untrue
disloyalty: betrayal
dismal: desolate,
funereal, gloomy,
lugubrious,
miserable, overcast,
uninviting
dismantle: destroy,
dissolve, strip, take
down
dismantling:
breakdown,
destruction,
dissolution
dismay: dread, scare
dismember: dissolve,
joint
dismiss: axe, banish,
discharge, fire, forget,
ignore, lay off,

remove, sack
dismissal: chop,
discharge, expulsion,
notice, sack
dismount: descend,
descent, get off
disobedience:
mischief, misconduct,
mutiny, naughtiness
disobedient: bad,
insubordinate,
mischievous,
naughty, rebellious,
recalcitrant,
undisciplined,
wayward
disobey: defy, rebel,
violate
disorder: babel,
confusion, disarray,
disease, disturbance,
havoc, illness, jumble,
kerfuffle, litter,
maelstrom, mayhem,
riot, shambles,
sickness, trouble,
upheaval, upset
disordered: chaotic,
deranged,
dishevelled,
disorganized,
muddled, unsettled,
upset
disorderly:
disruptive, lawless,
obstreperous, rowdy
disorganization:
chaos, disarray,
disorder
disorganize: jumble,
mess, upset
disorient: cloud,
confuse
disoriented: dazed,
lost, muddled
disown: cut off, deny,
disclaim, drop,
forsake, renounce,
repudiate
disparage: criticize,
knock, lessen, run
down, slander, slight
disparagement:
detraction, scorn,
vilification
disparate: different,
distant, diverse,
unequal
disparity: contrast,
difference, gap,
inequality, odds
dispassionate: calm,
disinterested,
impersonal, objective,
unconcerned
dispatch:

communication,
communiqué,
consignment,
delivery, forward,
haste, kill, mail,
message, news, post,
rapidity, relay, remit,
report, route, send
dispel: banish,
dismiss, disperse,
resolve, rout, scatter
dispensation:
disposal, dole,
exemption, leave,
liberty, licence,
permission, waiver
dispense: deal,
deliver, divide,
release
disperse: broadcast,
dissolve, dot,
fragment, lift, scatter
dispersed: dissipated
dispersion:
distribution, spread
dispiriting:
depressing,
discouraging, gloomy,
off-putting
displace: shift,
supersede, supplant
display: carry,
demonstrate,
demonstration,
expose, flash, flourish,
glitter, hold up,
indicate, indication,
layout, look, manifest,
mirror, model,
parade, present,
presentation, reflect,
reveal, riot, run,
scene, set out, show,
sight, spectacle, wear,
write
displeased:
discontent, uptight
displeasing:
objectionable,
vexatious
displeasure: chagrin,
disapprobation,
offence
dispose: form, lay,
marshal, place, range
disposed: liable,
prepared, susceptible,
willing
disposition: attitude,
character, climate,
constitution,
distribution,
formation, heart,
inclination, lie,
make-up, mentality,
mood, nature, part,

pattern, personality,
spirit, temperament,
tendency, will
dispossess: deprive,
oust, rob, turn out
disproportionate:
inappropriate,
inordinate, lopsided,
unreasonable
disprove: refute
disputable:
controversial
disputatious:
pugnacious,
quarrelsome
dispute: battle, beef,
case, challenge,
contend, contest,
contradict, debate,
difference, disagree,
fight, hassle, oppose,
quarrel, query,
question, rebut, row
disqualified:
disabled, ineligible,
out
disquiet: chagrin,
concern, perturb,
qualm, trouble,
unrest
disquisition:
dissertation, lecture,
speech, thesis
disregard: condone,
discount, ignore,
leave out, neglect,
overlook, pass over,
waive, write off
disreputable:
doubtful, infamous,
loose, low, notorious,
scandalous, scruffy,
seamy, sordid
disrepute: notoriety,
opprobrium, shame
disrespect: contempt,
disregard, insolence
disrespectful:
flippant, irreverent
disrobe: strip,
undress
disrupt: dislocate,
disturb, divide,
inconvenience,
sabotage
disrupted:
disorganized
disruption:
breakdown, disorder,
division, havoc,
paralysis, rupture,
sabotage, split,
upheaval, wreck
dissatisfied:
discontent, fed up
dissect: dismember,

joint
dissemble: pretend
dissembling: evasive,
  lying
disseminate:
  broadcast, disperse,
  plant, promulgate,
  scatter, sow
dissemination:
  diffusion,
  distribution, issue,
  propagation
dissension: conflict,
  discord, dispute,
  feud, friction,
  polemic, quarrel,
  unrest
dissent: disagree,
  dispute, protest,
  quarrel, rebel
dissention: split
dissertation: essay,
  paper, talk, thesis,
  tract
disservice:
  disadvantage, harm
dissident: malcontent,
  subversive
dissimilar: other,
  unequal, unfaithful,
  unlike
dissimulating:
  deceitful, dishonest
dissimulation:
  deception, hoax,
  insincerity, lying
dissipate: disperse,
  evaporate, scatter,
  spend, squander,
  waste
dissipation:
  consumption,
  licentiousness, waste
dissociate: distance,
  divorce
dissolute: degenerate,
  depraved, dissipated,
  fast, immoral, loose
dissoluteness:
  immorality,
  licentiousness
dissolution: end,
  solution
dissolve: disperse, eat,
  evaporate, liquidate,
  melt, vanish
dissonance: discord,
  jangle
dissuade: deter, put
  off
distance: background,
  detachment, gulf,
  interval, length,
  space, span, stretch
distant: away, back,
  cold, disinterested,

faint, far, faraway,
  icy, outside, overseas,
  remote, taciturn,
  withdrawn
distantly: far, long,
  wide
distaste: disgust,
  dislike, repugnance
distasteful:
  disagreeable,
  objectionable,
  repulsive, revolting,
  sickening, ungrateful,
  unpleasant
distend: balloon,
  bulge, flex, inflate
distended: puffy,
  turgid, untrue, wide
distension: bulge,
  dilation, enlargement
distil: extract, rectify
distillation:
  extraction, refinement
distilled: refined
distinct: different,
  individual, known,
  marked, obvious,
  particular,
  pronounced, thick,
  visible, vivid
distinction: calibre,
  comparison,
  consequence,
  difference, eminence,
  fame, glory, honour,
  importance, mark,
  note, prestige,
  prominence,
  reputation, status
distinctive:
  characteristic,
  colourful, different,
  individual, particular,
  peculiar, racy,
  unusual
distinctly: clearly,
  measurably, notably,
  particularly
distinguish:
  characterize, contrast,
  detect, differentiate,
  discern, discriminate,
  judge, know, make
  out, perceive, qualify,
  see, taste, tell
distinguishable:
  distinctive, visible
distinguished:
  conspicuous, famous,
  great, illustrious,
  notable, noted,
  prominent,
  remarkable, shining,
  special
distinguishing:
  characteristic,

indication, specific
distort: buckle,
  colour, garble,
  misinterpret,
  mutilate, pervert,
  warp
distorted: crooked,
  deformed, mangled,
  twisted, unfaithful,
  untrue, wry
distortion: deformity,
  garble, malformation,
  mannerism, warp
distract: disturb,
  divert, sidetrack, turn
distracted: flustered,
  frantic, hysterical,
  preoccupied, wild
distracting:
  disruptive,
  disturbance, relief,
  sidetrack
distress: concern,
  difficulty, discomfort,
  disturb, fret, grieve,
  hurt, misery, pain,
  prick, sorrow, sweat,
  trouble, unrest, upset,
  vex, woe, worry
distressed:
  concerned, hurt,
  sorry, uncomfortable,
  upset
distressing: awful,
  bad, depressing, hard,
  lamentable, nagging,
  painful, pathetic,
  pitiful, sad, sore,
  sorrowful, traumatic
distressingly:
  piteously, regrettably
distribute: assign,
  cast, deal, deliver,
  dispense, divide,
  issue, ration, release,
  serve, share, sort,
  split, spread, trim
distribution:
  assignment,
  circulation, deal,
  delivery, diffusion,
  disposal, division,
  dole, issue, partition,
  propagation,
  proportion
district: domicile,
  grounds, jurisdiction,
  land, local, locality,
  part, place, precinct,
  quarter, region,
  section, territory,
  vicinity, ward, zone
distrust: doubt,
  jealousy, mistrust,
  suspect, suspicion
distrustful: cynical,

doubtful, unsure
disturb: bug, concern,
  dislocate, distress,
  fret, inconvenience,
  interrupt, jar,
  perturb, pester, rattle,
  rouse, ruffle, shake,
  stir, touch, trouble,
  upset, vex, worry
disturbance:
  commotion, furore,
  incident, racket, riot,
  row, stir, storm,
  trouble, unrest,
  upheaval, upset
disturbed: flustered,
  maladjusted,
  unsettled, upset
disturbing:
  provocative,
  traumatic, vexatious
ditch: barrier, discard,
  drain, gutter, trench
dither: flutter,
  hesitate, waver, whirl
dive: drop, duck, fall,
  hole, joint, launch,
  pitch, plunge, swoop
diverge: depart,
  deviate, differ,
  disagree, fork,
  radiate, separate,
  split, stray, swerve,
  wander
divergence: break,
  contrast, departure,
  difference,
  eccentricity, fork,
  gap, split
divergent: different,
  various
diverse: assorted,
  different, manifold,
  miscellaneous, other,
  several, unlike,
  various
diversion: change,
  detour, fun, game,
  pastime, play,
  recreation, relief
diversity: assortment,
  variation, variety
divert: delight,
  sidetrack, switch
diverting: beguiling,
  comical, delightful,
  interesting
divest: deprive, take
  off
divide: break, cut,
  deal, dismember,
  fork, fragment, part,
  quarter, rend,
  separate, sever, share,
  sort, space
divided: cut, separate,

split
divider: distributor,
  partition, screen, wall
divination: oracle,
  sorcery
divine: celestial,
  fathom, glorious,
  heavenly, holy,
  miraculous, parson
divinity: deity, god
division: breach,
  break, category, class,
  degree, department,
  discord, faction, fork,
  fraction, grade,
  movement, panel,
  partition, piece, rank,
  region, rent, round,
  scene, schism, season,
  section, separation,
  split, stage, ward
divorce: disaffection,
  division, isolate,
  secession, separation
divulge: betray,
  communicate,
  confess, disclose,
  expose, give away,
  impart, leak, let on,
  publish, reveal, say,
  tell
dizzy: dazed, faint,
  frivolous, giddy,
  queer
do: cheat, commit,
  complete, discharge,
  execute, fare, finish,
  function, give,
  imitate, manage,
  party, pass, perform,
  perpetrate, practise,
  produce, put on, rave,
  realize, reception,
  render, satisfy, say,
  see to, serve, stage,
  suit, take
docile: easy, facile,
  flexible, gentle,
  manageable, meek,
  obedient, passive,
  plastic, yielding
dock: bar, basin,
  berth, curtail, cut,
  jetty, land, quay, trim
doctor: cook, corrupt,
  counsellor, falsify,
  juggle, neuter, rig
doctrinaire:
  authoritarian,
  dogmatic
doctrinal: dogmatic,
  religious, scriptural
doctrine: belief,
  institute, principle,
  teachings
document: charter,

diploma, file, form,
  paper, record, report
doddle: breeze,
  picnic, pushover
dodge: device, duck,
  evasion, fudge, hedge,
  jump, lose,
  machination,
  manoeuvre, parry,
  scheme, shift, shirk,
  shuffle, sidestep,
  wriggle
dodgy: chancy,
  precarious
doff: divest, remove,
  salute
dog: follow, fox,
  hound, male, pariah,
  sausage, shadow, tail,
  track
dogged: close,
  constant, determined,
  durable, obdurate,
  persevering,
  persistent, resolute,
  stubborn
doggedness: grit,
  resolution
dogma: principle
dogmatic: assertive,
  authoritative,
  intolerant, narrow,
  peremptory, positive
dogsbody: hack,
  lackey, menial
dole: benefit, ration,
  welfare
dole out: assign,
  dispense, give,
  measure, portion,
  ration, split
doleful: dark,
  dejected, gloomy,
  glum, melancholy,
  miserable, rueful, sad,
  sombre, woeful,
  wretched
doll: bird, effigy, girl,
  puppet, titivate,
  woman
dolt: ass, fool, jackass,
  oaf, wally
domain: department,
  environment, estate,
  field, grounds,
  kingdom, land,
  preserve, range,
  realm, region, sphere,
  territory, world
domestic: civil, daily,
  familiar, homely,
  household, interior,
  internal, maid,
  national, native,
  servant, woman
domicile: habitat,

home, house,
  residence
domiciliary:
  domestic, home
dominance: hold,
  power, prominence
dominant: leading,
  magisterial,
  overriding,
  paramount, powerful,
  predominant,
  rampant, ruling,
  sovereign
dominate: command,
  dwarf, master,
  overshadow, possess,
  prey on, ride, rule,
  sway
domination:
  command, influence,
  mastery, occupation,
  repression, rule
domineering: high,
  lordly, macho,
  magisterial,
  obstreperous,
  opinionated,
  overbearing,
  peremptory
dominion: authority,
  colony, jurisdiction,
  kingdom, mastery,
  possession, province,
  realm, reign
don: assume, put on
donate: contribute,
  give, present
donated:
  complimentary
donation:
  contribution, dole,
  gift, hand-out,
  largess, offering,
  present, grant
done: gone, kaput,
  over, past, right,
  through
done in: tired, weary,
  worn out
donjon: castle, keep
doom: condemn,
  destiny, preordain
doomed: destined,
  fated, luckless,
  marked, predestined
door: entrance, entry,
  port, threshold
doorhandle: knob
doorkeeper: janitor
doorstep: step,
  threshold
doorway: entrance,
  entry, gate, hatch,
  passage, port,
  threshold
dope: drug, nobble,

simpleton
dormant: asleep,
  fallow, inactive,
  potential, quiescent,
  torpid
dormitory: hostel,
  ward
dose: draught, drench,
  drug, fix, quantity
dossier: file, paper
dot: pepper, period,
  point, speck, spot
doting: fond
dotty: lunatic, mad
double: fold, image,
  mirror, picture
doubling: loop
doubt: diffidence,
  distrust, indecision,
  qualm, query,
  question, suspense,
  suspicion
doubtful:
  implausible,
  improbable, remote,
  sceptical, suspect,
  uncertain, vague
doubtfully: askance,
  vaguely
doubting:
  disbelieving,
  sceptical, incredulous
doubtless: likely,
  probably
douche: bath, flush
dough: cash, crust,
  money, paste, pastry
dour: harsh, rugged,
  severe
douse: bath, plunge,
  put out, quench,
  saturate, water, wet
dousing: bath
dove: pigeon
dowdy: frumpish,
  unfashionable
dowel: rod, screw
down: below,
  dejected, depressed,
  destitute, drink, fluff,
  hair, hill, low,
  miserable, nap, polish
  off, quaff, sad,
  swallow, under
downcast: gloomy,
  glum, morbid, sad,
  subdued
downer: drug,
  sedative
downfall: calamity,
  collapse, end,
  overthrow, ruin,
  shower
downgrade: depress,
  reduce, relegate
downpour: cataract,

rain, shower
downright:
decidedly, outright,
rank
downturn: decline,
deterioration, drop
downy: fluffy, hairy,
soft
dowser: psychic, seer
dowsing: divination
doze: nap, nod, rest,
sleep, snooze
dozing: asleep,
slumbering
drab: dark, dingy,
dowdy, dull, grey,
lacklustre, sombre
draconian: harsh,
severe
draft: design, layout,
make out, outline,
plan, plot, project,
recruit, rough,
scheme, skeleton,
sketch, write
drag: bind, draw,
grind, haul, heave,
pain, pill, puff, pull,
shuffle
drain: consume,
ditch, exhaust,
fatigue, gutter, milk,
ooze, prostrate, sap,
sink, spend, tax,
trench, void, valley
drained: prostrate,
spent, tired, weary
dram: drink, nip, peg,
snort, tot
drama: play
dramatic: lurid,
scenic, sensational,
spectacular, vivid
drape: clothe, dress,
festoon, hang, pall,
robe
drapery: linen
drastic: desperate,
dire, revolutionary,
rough, stiff, strong
draught: breeze,
current, drink, nip,
potion, puff, pull,
traction, wind
draw: attract,
attraction, cartoon,
describe, design,
drag, extract, haul,
lead, line, lottery,
lure, paint, picture,
plot, portray, puff,
pull, sketch, tempt
drawback: catch,
detraction, handicap,
hindrance, hitch,
liability, pitfall, rub,

shortcoming, snag
drawing: cartoon,
design, extraction,
figure, graphic,
illustration, picture,
plan, profile, sketch,
study, traction
drawn: even, haggard,
pinched, sunken,
worn
dread: awe, fear,
fright, horror, phobia,
terror
dreadful: awesome,
awful, diabolical,
dire, fearful,
formidable,
frightening, frightful,
ghastly, hideous,
holy, horrible,
painful, shocking,
terrible, unholy
dream: aspire, create,
devise, fancy, hope,
imagine, make up,
knockout, muse,
trance, unreal,
Utopian, vision
dreamy: faraway,
inattentive,
lackadaisical, pensive,
romantic, wistful
dreariness: tedium
dreary: dismal, dull,
lugubrious,
ponderous, stuffy,
uninviting
dredge: drag, rake,
shovel
dregs: deposit,
grounds, leavings,
lees, offal, residue,
scum, sediment
drench: bathe, flood,
saturate, soak, steep,
water, wet
drenched:
bedraggled, sodden,
wet
dress: bandage, bind,
butcher, clothe,
clothes, comb, cover,
deck, fertilize, frock,
garb, get up, gown,
groom, habit, outfit,
robe, suit, turn out,
uniform
dresser: cabinet,
cupboard, maid
dressing: bandage,
plaster, sauce
dribbling: leaky
drift: coast, cruise,
current, float, flow,
gist, glide, heading,
hover, idle, import,

meaning, movement,
purport, roam, run,
sail, stray, tendency,
tide, waft, wander
drill: bit, bull, coach,
discipline, educate,
education, exercise,
groom, indoctrinate,
instruct, instruction,
perforate, pierce,
practise, rehearse,
school, teach
drink: beverage,
bumper, carouse,
devour, down,
draught, peg, pledge,
quaff, swig, take,
tipple, toast, wet
drip: drop, filter, flow,
leak, ooze, perspire,
weep, wet
dripping: damp, flow,
leaky, wet
drive: campaign,
carry, compel,
compulsion, crusade,
energy, flog, force,
hammer, impel,
impulse, initiative,
journey, manoeuvre,
momentum, move,
movement, pilot,
prod, propel,
propulsion, pump,
push, reduce, ride,
round up, run, spin,
spur, strike, turn,
urge, wheel, whip
drivel: claptrap,
gibberish, nonsense,
rot, rubbish, slaver
driver: chauffeur,
operator, whip
driving: dynamic,
manipulation, motive
drizzle: cloudburst,
mist, rain, spray, wet
droll: comical,
facetious, humorous,
jocular, ludicrous,
merry, queer, witty
drollery: comedy,
humour, merriment
drone: buzz, hum,
parasite, prattle,
whine
droning: maundering,
murmuring
drool: drivel, slaver
droop: dangle, drop,
flag, flop, hang,
languish, loll, nod,
pine, sag, slump,
stoop, wilt, wither
drooping: flagging,
lank, limp,

pendulous, tired
drop: bead, bubble,
cast, decrease,
deposit, depth,
descend, descent,
discard, discontinue,
ditch, dive, down,
drip, fall, globule,
lower, lunge, lurch,
omit, plunge, quit,
rain, release, scrap,
shed, sink, subside
droppings: dung,
manure
dross: debris, dregs,
garbage, leavings,
rubbish, scum, waste
drove: herd, swarm
drover: driver
drown: drench, drink,
flood, inundate,
overflow, quench,
sink
drowse: doze, nap,
sleep
drowsy: comatose,
lethargic, sleepy,
yawning
drub: beat, demolish,
hammer, jacket,
lambast, lather,
leather, lick, murder,
rout, whip
drubbing: licking,
rout
drudge: hack,
hammer, labour,
menial, plug, slave,
work
drudgery: grind,
labour, sweat, work
drug: hypnotic, lace,
load, medicine,
narcotic, sedate
drugged: comatose,
loaded
drum: barrel, beat,
cylinder, hammer
drumming: beat, roll
drunk: drunkard,
inebriated, loaded,
tight
drunkenness:
intoxication
drupe: fruit, nut, seed
dry: bake, baking,
cake, cure, evaporate,
fair, fine, jejune,
parched, sardonic,
shrivelled, stale,
sterile, thirsty,
wither, wring, wry
dub: baptise, call,
christen, create,
designate, name,
style, term, transcribe

dubious: disbelieving, doubtful, fishy, implausible, incredulous, queer, sceptical, shady, shaky, suspect, tenuous, uncertain

duck: dip, dodge, hedge, jink, nil, nod, parry, shirk, sidestep, stoop

duct: canal, channel, feed, funnel, main, outlet, pipe, vessel

dud: failure, flop, loser

due: coming, debt, just, outstanding, owing, payable, prerogative, right, rightful, share, unpaid, unsettled

duffer: dunce

dulcet: harmonious, liquid, lyric, rich

dull: barren, bland, cloudy, dead, dim, dismal, dry, faint, glaze, grey, heavy, hollow, insensitive, insipid, lacklustre, lethargic, lifeless, mousy, muddy, muffle, nondescript, oafish, obscure, obtuse, overcast, pale, pedestrian, ponderous, routine, slack, sleepy, slow, sluggish, sombre, stolid, stuffy, thick

dullard: dunce

dulled: jaded, muffled

dullness: narcosis, numbness, tedium

dumb: inarticulate, mute, oafish, obtuse, quiet, silent, simple, slow

dumbfound: astonish, confound, flabbergast, nonplus, perplex, rock, shatter,

stagger, stupefy

dumbfounded: blank

dumbness: silence

dummy: effigy, model

dump: depot, discard, ditch, dive, hole, jettison, park, shack, tip, unload

dumping: disposal

dumpy: short

dunce: dummy, fool, nincompoop, oaf, simpleton

dung: filth, manure, ordure

dungeon: cell

dunk: bathe, dip, duck, immerse, plunge

duo: couple, pair

dupe: cheat, deceive, do, flat, fool, hoax, mark, mug, outwit, pawn, pigeon, swindle, take, take in, trap, victim

duplicate: copy, double, facsimile, imitate, imitation, match, mimic, parallel, picture, repeat, replica, reproduce, reproduction

duplicated: double, identical

duplication: imitation, repetition

duplicitous: deceitful, fraudulent, scheming, wily

duplicity: artifice, betrayal, deception, fraud, hypocrisy, insincerity

durable: indestructible, lasting, strong, sturdy, tough

duration: course, length, life, quantity, space, span, term, time, while

duress: compulsion, force

during: as, on, pending, through, while

dusk: gloom, nightfall, shade, shadow

dust: brush, clean, fluff, fuss, grime, mould, powder, seed, soil

dutiful: good, law-abiding, loyal, obedient

duty: assignment, business, charge, chore, commission, commitment, function, imposition, job, levy, mission, obligation, part, rate, role, service, task, tax, toll, work

duvet: quilt

dwarf: gnome, midget, overshadow, pygmy, runt

dwarfed: stunted

dwell: inhabit, live, lodge, remain, settle, sojourn

dwelling: domicile, home, house, living, lodgings, place, residence

dwindle: die, fade, lessen, pass, peter out, recede, remit, shrink, subside, taper, wane, weaken, wilt

dye: colour, grain, paint, stain, tint

dying: moribund, obsolescent

dyke: dam, ditch, embankment

dynamic: forceful, live, moving, potent, progressive, vibrant, vigorous, vital

dynamism: drive, force, go, initiative, punch, push, vigour

E

each: every, everybody

eager: avid, earnest, expectant, hungry, impatient, impetuous, keen, longing, obliging, passionate, ready, solicitous, strenuous, strong, studious, thirsty, wild, willing, wishful,

eagerly: readily, willingly

eagerness: fire, impatience, passion

eagle-eyed: observant

earlier: before, back, former, formerly, old, past, preceding, previous, previously, prior

earliest: first, premier, primary, primitive

early: fast, forward, inchoate, infantile, initial, original, premature, primitive

earmark (for): intend

earn: bring, clear, fetch, gain, get, gross, incur, make, merit, net, realize, return, win, work, yield

earned: made

earnest: close, devout, fervent, intense, serious, sincere, solemn, warm, wholehearted, zealous

earnestly: seriously

earnestness: fervour, gravity, solemnity, zeal

earnings: gain, income, pay, proceeds, profit, salary, takings, yield

earshot: hearing, sound

earth-shattering: historic, sensational

ear-splitting: deafening, loud, noisy, piercing, thunderous

earth: conductor, dirt, dust, globe, ground, hole, mould, nature, soil, world

earthenware: ceramics, crockery, pottery

earthing: ground

earthly: mundane, worldly

earthquake: tremor, quake

earthwork: embankment, mound, rampart

earthy: coarse, robust, worldly

ease: comfort, consolation, content, convenience, decrease, fluency, freedom, grace, lessen, liberalize, lighten, mollify, relax, relieve, remedy, simplicity

easement: relief

easily: freely, leisurely, readily, well

easy-going: carefree, genial, indulgent, liberal, mild, permissive, slack, soft, tolerant

easing: decrease, relaxation

easy: elementary, familiar, fluent, free, gentle, informal, jaunty, leisurely, light, manageable, outgoing, painless, slow, smooth, soft

eat: dine, fare, feed, live, nibble, partake, take

eatable: edible

eats: grub

eaves: verge

ebb: die, disappear, fade, flag, ooze, pass, peter out, recede, regress, retire, retreat, sink, subside, tide, wane

ebbing: flagging

ebony: black, dark, jet

ebullience: exuberance, vivacity

ebullient: exuberant, hearty, high-spirited, irrepressible, scintillating, vivacious

eccentric: character, crank, crazy, freak, funny, idiosyncratic, irregular, kinky, lunatic, nut, oddity, original, quaint, quirky, rebel, singular, uncharacteristic, unconventional, whimsical

eccentricity: failing, figure, kink, oddity, quirk, whim

ecclesiastical: clerical

ecclestiastic: pastor

echo: imitate, imitation, mimic, mirror, parrot, rebound, reflect, repeat, repetition, resemble, reverberate, sound

echoing: cavernous, resounding

eclectic: catholic

eclipse: cloud, darken, disappearance, dominate, obfuscate, obscure, outweigh, overshadow, transit

eclipsing: variable

economic: financial

economical: austere, cheap, frugal, low, spare, sparing

economics: finance

economize: cut, pinch, save

economy: cut, prudence

ecstasy: beatitude, bliss, elevation, happiness, heaven, high, joy, paradise, rapture, transport

ecstatic: delirious, exalted, happy, joyful, joyous, lyrical, overcome, overjoyed,

poetic, radiant, rave, unique,

ectoplasm: emanation

ecumenical: catholic, universal

eddy: maelstrom, surge, whirlwind

edge: bound, bank, bind, blade, border, boundary, brim, brink, creep, deflect, end, face, fringe, glance, handicap, hedge, hem, junction, limb, limit, line, lip, march, margin, nick, outskirts, periphery, purchase, rim, side, skirt, threshold, verge

edged: keen

edgeways: sideways

edginess: nervousness, tension

edging: binding, border, fringe, trim

edgy: brittle, nervous, prickly, restless, tense

edict: bull, command, law, mandate, precept, regulation, word

edifice: building, construction, house, pile, structure

edifying: wholesome

edit: cut, delete, revise

edited: cut

edition: impression, issue, number

editor: journalist

editorial: leader

educate: breed, bring up, discipline, groom, ground, instruct, school, teach

educated: knowledgeable, learned, literate

education: culture, instruction, knowledge, learning, reading, scholarship, upbringing

eerie: creepy, forbidding, frightening, ghostly, macabre, queer,

weird
efface: cancel,
obliterate
effect: carry out,
carry, cause,
conclude,
consequence,
contrive, do, execute,
fruit, harvest,
impression, induce,
influence, legacy,
manage, perfect,
perform, perpetrate,
procure, produce,
purpose, realize,
result, sensation,
splash, take, tone,
touch, value, work
effecting: execution
effective: cogent,
efficient, forceful,
influential, operative,
potent, productive,
useful, valid
effectiveness: duty,
force, potency, virtue
effector: motor
effects: belongings,
estate, gear, goods,
impact, kit,
possessions, property,
stuff, things
effectual: forceful,
powerful, productive,
sovereign
effectually: virtually
effectuate:
consummate
effeminate: camp,
feminine, gay, girlish,
homosexual, ladylike,
soft, womanly
effervesce: bubble,
sparkle
effervescent: brisk,
bubbly, irrepressible,
vivacious
effete: feeble, weak,
wet
efficacious: effective,
influential, positive,
potent, productive,
successful
efficacy: force,
potency, strength,
virtue
efficiency: capacity,
facility, performance
efficient: businesslike,
capable, good,
methodical, operative,
practical, practised,
pragmatic, proficient,
regular, sovereign,
systematic, thorough
efficiently:

practically, well
effigy: image
effloresce: flower
efflorescence: flower
effluent: emanation
effluvium: emanation
efflux: surge
effort: attempt, back,
bid, drag, drive,
exercise, grind,
handful, industry,
labour, push, strain,
struggle, sweat, trial,
trouble, work
effortful: laborious
effortless: easy, facile,
light, smooth
effortlessness: facility
effrontery: crust,
face, gall,
impertinence,
insolence, nerve,
presumption
effulgence: brilliance,
light
effulgent: bright,
brilliant, luminous,
radiant, shining
effusion: emanation,
flow
effusive:
demonstrative,
expansive, garrulous,
gushing, hearty,
lavish, lyrical
egalitarian:
democratic
egg: germ
egg on: urge, prod,
push
egg-shaped: oval
ego: conscious, self-
esteem
egotism: conceit,
narcissism, pride,
vanity
egotistic:
opinionated, self-
centred
egotistical: boastful,
bossy, conceited, vain
egress: door
eiderdown: quilt
ejaculate: blurt, emit
ejaculation: emission,
exclamation
eject: bale, banish,
bounce, discharge,
emit, jettison, oust,
overthrow, remove,
spit
ejection: discharge,
expulsion, overthrow
eke out: pad out
elaborate: develop,
complicated, fancy,

florid, heroic,
intricate, involved,
luxuriant, ornate,
rich, set out,
sophisticated
elaboration:
decoration,
enlargement
elapse: fly, go, pass,
roll
elapsed: gone
elapsing: course
elastic: expansive,
flexible, resilient, soft,
supple, yielding
elasticity: bounce,
give, spring
elastoplast: bandage
elate: lift, lighten
elated: exalted,
exultant, happy, high,
joyful, jubilant,
overcome, overjoyed,
rejoicing
elating: joyous
elation: excitement,
glee, joy, jubilation,
mania, rejoicing
elbow: crowd, jostle,
nudge, poke, prod,
push, scrum, shove
elbow-room: room,
scope, space
elder: big, councillor,
father, major,
patriarch, sage, senior
elderly: grey, old
elect: decide,
designate, make, opt
for, ordain, pick,
select, will
elected: made,
representative
election: poll,
selection
electioneer: canvass
elective: discretionary
elector: constituent
electorate: public
electors: country
electric: explosive,
fateful
electricity: juice
electrify: fire,
galvanize, ginger
electrifying:
dramatic, exciting,
rousing
electrode: element,
pole
electroplate: plate
elegance: delicacy,
flair, grace, style
elegant: artistic,
becoming, chic, clean,
dainty, dashing,

delicate, fine, fluid,
genteel, graceful,
natty, polite, smart,
womanly
elegiac: mournful,
poetic
elegy: lament
element: component,
constituent, detail,
factor, ingredient,
material, member,
part, unit
elemental:
constituent, primary
elementary: basic,
first, fundamental,
primary, primitive,
simple, underlying
elements: rudiments,
smattering, weather
elephantine: jumbo,
lumbering, uncouth,
ungainly
elevate: bring up,
cultivate, dignify,
jack, lift, prefer,
promote, raise
elevated: exalted,
grand, high, lofty,
mellow
elevation: design,
eminence, height,
level, lift, plan,
preferment,
promotion, rise
elevator: lift
elevenses: snack
elf: gnome, sprite
elfin: pygmy
elicit: draw, extract,
fetch, prompt,
provoke
eligibility: fitness,
qualification
eligible: preferable
eliminate: cancel,
censor, extinguish,
kill, liquidate,
obliterate, omit,
polish off, reject,
remove, scratch, slay,
void
eliminated: extinct,
out
elimination:
assassination,
cancellation,
disqualification, kill,
killing
eliminator: heat
élite: best, choice,
cream, elect, flower,
pick, pride,
privileged, select,
society,
elixir: panacea,

potion, restorative
elliptical: oval,
 roundabout
elocution: delivery,
 diction
elongate: lengthen,
 produce, stretch
elongated: long,
 protracted
elongation:
 enlargement
eloquent: expressive,
 knowing, literary,
 lyrical, meaning,
 vocal
else: besides
elsewhere: away, off,
 out
elucidate: clarify,
 comment, explain,
 illuminate, interpret,
 rationalize, resolve,
 spell out, solve
elucidation:
 definition,
 explanation,
 interpretation, light
elude: baffle, dodge,
 duck, jink, lose,
 sidestep, slip
eluded: shunned
elusive: evasive
elysian: celestial,
 heaven, paradise
emaciate: macerate
emaciated:
 cadaverous, haggard,
 scrawny, skeletal,
 skinny, thin
emanate: come, emit,
 flow, issue, originate,
 proceed, result, rise,
 spring, stem
emanation: emission,
 flow
emancipate:
 enfranchise, free,
 liberate, redeem,
 release
emancipated: free
emancipation:
 freedom, liberation,
 liberty, release
emasculate: neuter
embank: bank
embankment: bank,
 dam, rampart
embargo: ban, bar,
 boycott, proscribe,
 restraint, sanction,
 veto
embargoed: black,
 prohibited
embark: begin,
 undertake, launch,
 sail, set out

embarrass:
 compromise, confuse,
 discomfort,
 discompose, mortify,
 put out, show up
embarrassed:
 ashamed, bashful,
 red, self-conscious,
 sensitive, sheepish
embarrassing:
 awkward,
 humiliating, sensitive,
 shameful, sticky,
 undignified
embarrassment:
 chagrin, confusion,
 mortification, shame,
 strait(s)
embassy: legation,
 mission
embattled: militant
embed: bury, found,
 implant, lodge, plant
embellish: elaborate,
 exaggerate, figure,
 garnish, grace,
 ornament, trim,
 varnish
embellished: fancy,
 florid
embellishing:
 ornamental
embellishment:
 decoration,
 exaggeration,
 flourish, garnish,
 ornament, varnish
embellishments:
 finery, frills
embers: fire
embezzle: steal
embezzlement: job,
 robbery
embezzler: defaulter,
 thief
embitter: poison,
 sour
embittered: sour
emblem: character,
 device, mark, sign,
 symbol
embodiment: height,
 ideal, picture,
 representative, soul
embody: include,
 personify, represent,
 typify
embolden: fortify
emboss: impress
embouchure: lip,
 caress, clasp, clinch
embrace: cling,
 clutch, cover, crush,
 cuddle, enclose,
 gather, hug, include,
 lock, press, squeeze

embraceable: cuddly
embrasure: bay, port
embrocation: lotion
embroider: colour,
 elaborate
embroil: involve,
 snarl, tangle
embroiled:
 implicated
embryonic: incipient,
 unborn
emend: rectify,
 reform, revise
emendation:
 improvement
emerge: begin, break,
 come, dawn, flow,
 form, hatch, issue,
 loom, originate, rise,
 spring, surface
emergence:
 beginning, birth,
 emanation, origin
emergency: auxiliary,
 crisis, critical,
 juncture, rush,
 scramble, urgent,
 pinch, spare
emetic: purge
émigré: exile
eminence: bulge,
 consequence, dignity,
 distinction, fame,
 glory, height,
 importance,
 magnitude, mark,
 prestige, prominence,
 status
eminent:
 conspicuous,
 distinguished,
 exalted, famous,
 glorious, great, high,
 illustrious, noble,
 notable, noted,
 outstanding,
 prestigious,
 prominent, proud,
 shining, signal
emissary: messenger
emission: beam,
 bleeding, burst,
 discharge, emanation,
 exhaust, flow, leak
emit: beam, cast,
 discharge, eject, give,
 issue, leak, let off, let
 out, ooze, radiate,
 secrete, shed, shine,
 utter, vent, void,
 vomit
emolument: fee,
 gain, pay, payment,
 wage
emotion: feeling,
 passion, sensation,

sensibility, sentiment,
 warmth
emotional:
 demonstrative,
 impassioned, lyrical,
 maudlin, mawkish,
 passionate,
 psychological,
 sensitive, sentimental,
 temperamental,
 tempestuous, tender,
 thin-skinned, torrid,
 warm
emotionless:
 mechanical, wooden
emotions: bosom
emotive: fateful,
 heart-rending,
 memorable, moving,
 stirring
empathize with:
 identify, pity
empathy: feeling,
 identity, pity,
 sympathy
emperor: king
emphasis:
 exaggeration, force,
 slant, stress, tone,
 weight
emphasize: impress,
 exaggerate, feature,
 highlight, pronounce,
 punctuate, stress,
 underline, voice
emphatic: assertive,
 dogmatic, effective,
 insistent, marked,
 positive, pronounced,
 weighty
emphatically:
 positively
employ: exercise,
 harness, hire, ply,
 requisition, retain,
 take on, turn, use,
 wield
employed:
 professional, working
employee: hand,
 man, operative,
 professional, worker
employees: labour,
 office, people,
 personnel, staff
employer: boss,
 master
employment:
 commission, disposal,
 engagement, exercise,
 function, job,
 livelihood, living,
 occupation, office,
 place, province,
 service, situation, use,
 work

emporium: store,
empower: authorize,
commission, delegate,
enable, invest, license
empowered:
privileged
empress: queen
emptied: void
emptiness: blank,
hunger, solitude,
vacancy, vanity, void
emptor: buyer
empty: bare, barren,
blank, clear, dead,
destitute, discharge,
do, drain, evacuate,
exhaust, flat, free,
frothy, hollow,
hungry, jejune,
lifeless, meaningless,
old, ransack, shallow,
spend, strip, turn out,
uninhabited,
unsettled, vacant,
vacate, vain, void,
waste, wild
emptying: discharge
empty out: pump, tip
emulate: compete,
copy, follow, imitate,
mirror, reproduce,
rival
emulating: rival
emulation: imitation
emulator: competitor
emulsion: cream,
paint, solution
en masse: bodily,
together
en route: bound,
destined
enable: let
enact: legislate, make,
pass, perpetrate
enacted: made
enactment:
legislation, passage
enamel: paint
enamour: captivate,
charm
encampment: camp
encase: crate, wrap
encash: liquidate
encashable: liquid
enchant: attract,
captivate, catch,
charm, conjure,
delight, enslave,
entrance, fascinate,
possess, take,
transport
enchanted:
bewitched, rapt,
possessed
enchanter: magician,
wizard

enchanting:
attractive, beautiful,
compelling,
delightful,
irresistible, lovable,
lovely, magnetic,
ravishing, winning
enchantment:
attraction, charm,
conquest, fascination,
glamour, magic, spell,
witchcraft
enchantress:
magician
encincture: gird
encircle: besiege,
blockade, circle,
circumscribe, enclose,
gird, girdle, loop,
orbit, ring, round,
surround, wind, zone
encircled: wreathed
encirclement:
blockade
encircling: orbit,
roundabout
enclose: bank, box,
circle, circumscribe,
embrace, envelop,
gird, hedge, hem,
impound, include,
incorporate, jacket,
lock, pen, rail, ring,
surround, wall, wrap
enclosed: shut
enclosure: booth,
cage, chamber, circle,
pen, railing, run, walk
encode: key, scramble
encompass: besiege,
circumscribe, cover,
embrace, enclose,
girdle, include,
incorporate, ring,
surround, take in
encounter: battle,
bout, brush, collision,
combat, conflict,
confrontation,
engagement,
experience, face, find,
hit, light, meet,
meeting, run into,
see, skirmish,
struggle, taste
encourage: back,
boost, cheer up,
cherish, foster, fuel,
nerve, nourish,
promote, push,
second, stimulate
encouragement:
backing, blessing,
boost, consolation,
fuel, reassurance,
support

encouraging:
auspicious, bright,
favourable, hopeful,
promising,
propitious, rosy
encroach: infringe,
invade, impinge
encroached: poached
encroaching:
intrusive
encroachment:
imposition, invasion
encrust: cake
encumber: burden,
hamper, handicap,
load, retard, saddle,
shackle
encumbered: heavy,
laden, loaded
encumbrance:
burden, detraction,
handicap, hardship,
hindrance, liability,
load
encyclopaedic:
broad, exhaustive,
wide
end: back,
catastrophe, cause,
cease, conclusion,
death, design,
destination,
determine,
disappearance,
dissolution, dissolve,
doom, finish, foot,
goal, halt, idea,
intent, kill, last, lift,
limit, object,
objective, outcome,
passing, point,
purpose, quarry,
quench, quit, reason,
result, run out, sake,
stop, tail, term,
terminate, tip,
upshot, wind up
endanger: chance,
expose, hazard,
imperil, risk, venture,
endearing: lovable
endeavour: attempt,
bid, effort, pursuit,
seek, stab, strain,
strive, undertake,
venture
ending: finish, killing,
last
endless: constant,
continual, incessant,
infinite, interminable,
nonstop, perpetual,
unbounded
endlessly: nonstop
endmost: terminal
endorse: back, back

up, bear out, certify,
confirm, execute,
initial, permit, ratify,
sanction, second,
sign, support, sustain,
underwrite, uphold,
witness, write
endorsed: official
endorsement:
backing,
confirmation,
reference, sanction
endoscope: probe
endow: present,
award, bequeath,
fund, invest, supply,
will
endowed: competent
endowment: award,
calibre, grant,
heritage, largess,
legacy, present
endurable: tolerable
endurance: bearing,
bent, patience
endure: bear, brook,
continue, digest, go
through, have, hold
up, keep on, keep,
languish, last, live,
lump
endure: meet, put up
with, stand, stand for,
stick, stomach, suffer,
support, survive,
sustain, take, tolerate,
undergo, wear,
withstand
enduring: classic,
lasting, long-
suffering, patient,
stable
enemy: bandit, foe,
opponent
energetic: athletic,
brisk, dynamic,
effective, exuberant,
fresh, hearty, live,
lively, lusty,
powerful, quick,
spirited, strenuous,
tireless, vigorous,
vital, vivacious
energetically: hard
energize: pump
energizer: pump
energy-source: food
energy: back, bounce,
drive, effort,
exuberance, force, go,
heart, impetus, life,
momentum, motor,
potency, power,
punch, push, snap,
soul, spirit, stamina,
strength, vigour,

vivacity, zip
enervate: sap
enervated: lethargic,
listless
enervation: malaise
enfold: drape,
embrace, envelop,
gather, hug, jacket,
press, roll, wrap
enforce: compel,
impose, press
enforcement:
imposition
enfranchise: liberate
enfranchisement:
liberation, liberty
engage: book,
contract, fight, hire,
lock, mesh, promise,
recruit, reserve,
retain, take, take on,
undertake, wage
engage in: go in for,
immerse, participate,
partake, practise,
prosecute, pursue
engaged: busy,
occupied
engagement: battle,
booking, combat,
contract, fight, gig
engaging: charming,
lovable, lovely,
pleasant, sweet,
winning
engender: bear,
father, generate,
mother, procreate
engendering:
generation, genesis
engine: machine,
motor
engineer: construct,
contrive, jockey,
manage, manoeuvre,
mastermind, stage
engineering:
manipulation,
research
engirdle: belt
engrave: carve, cut,
inscribe, stamp
engraved: cut
engraving: etching,
graphic, picture,
print, sculpture
engross: bury, grip,
immerse, interest,
involve
engrossed: busy,
deep, intent, lost,
preoccupied
engrossing: gripping,
interesting
engulf: cover, drown,
flood, overtake,

swamp
engulfing: voracious
enhance: augment,
better, flatter, grace,
improve, increase,
lift, set off, swell,
touch up
enhancement:
improvement,
increase
enigma: difficulty,
mystery, paradox,
problem, puzzle,
riddle, secret,
unknown
enigmatic: dark,
imponderable,
mysterious, obscure,
opaque
enjoin: charge,
command, exhort,
enjoy: devour, dig,
have, lap, like, love,
possess, relish
enjoyable: fun, good,
pleasant
enjoyment: comfort,
diversion, fun, gusto,
happiness, kick,
pleasure, recreation,
relaxation, relish, zest
enkindle: inspire
enlarge: elaborate,
blow up, boost,
exaggerate, gain,
grow, increase, let
out, magnify, raise,
swell, wax, widen
enlargement:
dilation,
exaggeration, gain,
growth, increase,
swelling
enlighten: educate,
inform, teach
enlightened:
civilized, cultured,
judicious, knowing,
knowledgeable,
progressive, wise
enlightening:
luminous
enlightenment:
civilization, culture,
education,
illumination,
knowledge, light,
wisdom
enlist: enter, join,
recruit, register
enliven: cheer up,
comfort, ginger, wake
enmesh: involve, net,
snarl
enmity: feud, ill
feeling, war

ennoble: dignify,
honour
ennui: boredom,
languor, tedium
enormity: atrocity,
outrage
enormous: big, fat,
giant, huge, immense,
jumbo, large,
massive, mighty,
monster, monstrous,
monumental,
mountainous, outsize,
stupendous, terrific,
vast
enough: due,
sufficient
enounce: articulate
enquire: query,
question, ask
enquiring: curious,
inquisitive
enquire into: check,
explore, investigate
enquiry: postmortem
enrage: incense,
inflame, infuriate,
provoke
enraged: furious,
livid, maddened,
wrathful
enraging: offensive
enrapture: charm,
entrance, fascinate,
joy, transport
enraptured:
enamoured, joyful,
enrich: cultivate,
fortify
enrol: enter, join, list,
record, recruit,
register, take on
ensemble: band,
whole
enshroud: cover
ensign: banner, flag,
jack, sign, standard
enslave: chain, ride,
yoke
enslaved: captive
ensnare: betray,
catch, decoy, hook,
lure, mesh, net, trap
ensue: follow,
proceed, result,
succeed
ensuing: eventual,
following, next
ensure: mind,
procure, see
entail: ball, demand,
involve, imply, mean,
necessitate
entangle: catch,
complicate, foul,
involve, jumble, knot,

mesh, perplex, snarl
entangled:
implicated,
labyrinthine
entanglement:
implication, liaison,
quagmire
entente: compact,
pact, protocol, treaty,
understanding
enter: board, book,
chronicle, come, file,
go in for, include,
inscribe, join, list,
penetrate, record,
register
enterprise:
transaction, cause,
concern, design,
drive, initiative, job,
leap, package, ploy,
project, push, quest,
venture
enterprising:
progressive
entertain: bear,
cherish, delight,
divert, foster,
harbour, have, host,
interest, put up,
receive, socialize
entertainer: artist,
player
entertaining:
beguiling, comical,
delightful, enjoyable,
fun, interesting, light,
racy
entertainment:
diversion, fun,
pastime, play,
recreation, relaxation,
show, welcome,
hobby
enthral: captivate,
enslave, entrance,
fascinate, grip,
spellbind
enthralled: rapt
enthralling:
compelling, gripping
enthralment:
conquest
enthuse (about): rave
enthusiasm: fervour,
fire, gusto, heart,
passion, spirit,
warmth, zeal, zest
enthusiast: buff, fan,
fanatic, fiend, freak,
nut, zealot
enthusiastic: avid,
cheerful, fervent,
great, gushing,
hearty, keen, lyrical,
passionate, rave,

receptive, warm,
wholehearted, wild,
willing, zealous
enthusiastically:
willingly
entice: attract, coax,
decoy, draw, lure,
persuade, pull,
seduce, tantalize,
tempt, wheedle
enticement:
attraction, bait, bribe,
conquest, decoy,
draw, incentive, lure,
persuasion,
temptation
enticing: attractive,
beckoning, inviting,
seductive, enticing:
voluptuous
entire: clean,
complete, full, intact,
integral, perfect,
radical, sound, total,
whole
entirely: bodily,
completely, full, fully,
just, quite, right,
utterly, wholly
entirety: complement,
gross, mass, whole
entitle: authorize,
baptize, designate,
name, style, term,
warrant
entitled: named
entitlement: licence,
prerogative
entity: being, piece,
substance, unit
entourage: court,
following, suite, train
entrails: guts, inside,
intestines, offal
entrance: door, drive,
entry, fascinate, gate,
grip, hall, lobby,
mesmerize, mouth,
passage, possess,
threshold, transport
entranced: bewitched
lost, possessed
entrance-hall: foyer
entrancing: beguiling
entrant: candidate,
entry, nominee
entrants: field
entrap: betray, catch,
decoy, get, snare, take
entrapment: betrayal
entreat: ask, beg,
conjure, desire,
exhort, implore,
petition, plead, pray,
request, seek, solicit,
sue, urge

entreaty: petition,
plea, prayer, request,
suit, supplication,
wish
entrée: entry
entrench: root
entrenched: set
entrust: bequeath,
charge, commend,
commit, consign,
delegate
entrusting:
consignment
entry: door, entrance,
hall, item, record
entwine: coil, curl,
lace, lock, roll, snarl,
weave, entwined:
wreathed
enumerate: detail,
itemize, list, recite,
specify, state
enumeration: list,
recital, mouth
enunciate: proclaim,
pronounce, sound,
utter
enunciation:
delivery, diction
envelop: fold, blanket,
circle, cover, jacket,
mantle, muffle, wrap,
envelope: bag, case,
cover, jacket
enveloped: shrouded,
wreathed
envious: covetous,
discontent, green,
grudging, jaundiced,
jealous
enviousness: jealousy
environment:
atmosphere,
background, habitat,
medium, nature,
scene, surroundings
environmental:
background, green
environmentalist:
green
environs: locality,
precincts, vicinity
envisage: see, think,
visualize
envision: see
envoi: epilogue
envoi: moral
envoy: delegate,
diplomat, messenger,
minister
envy: begrudge,
grudge, resentment
enzyme: juice
epaulette: tab
ephemeral: fleet,
fugitive, passing

epic: heroic, last-
ditch, legendary
epicarp: rind
epicentre: centre,
earthquake
epicurean: luxurious
epidemic: contagion,
contagious, outbreak,
plague, rampant,
rash, wave
epigrammatic:
sententious
episode: chapter,
experience,
happening, incident,
leg, occurrence, scene
epistle: letter
epithet: name,
nickname
epitome: height,
ideal, paragon,
picture,
representative,
summary
epitomize: condense,
personify, represent,
typify
epoch: page, period,
time
epoch-making:
historic, monumental,
sensational
equable: calm, level,
moderate, smooth,
temperate
equal: balance, be,
compare, equivalent,
even, fellow,
identical, keep up,
level, like, match,
parallel, peer,
reciprocate, rival,
touch, uniform
equality: balance,
identity, par, parity
equalize: balance,
level
equally: as
equanimity: balance,
philosophy, poise,
temper
equate: compare,
equal
equation: function
equestrian: cavalier
equilateral: square
equilibrium: balance,
par, parity, poise
equip: fit, gear,
provide, clothe,
furnish, kit, outfit,
prepare, provision,
qualify, ready, rig,
stock
equipment: facilities,
furniture, gear, kit,

plant, rig, stuff
equipoise: balance
equipoised: offset
equipotential: level
equipped: fit
equipping: provision
equitable:
disinterested, fair,
honest, honourable,
just, objective,
reasonable, right,
rightful, square,
straight
equitably: fairly
equity: honesty,
justice, right
equivalence: balance,
parity
equivalent:
commensurate, equal,
identical, level, like,
match, parallel, rival,
same
equivocal: imprecise
equivocate: fence, fib,
flannel, fudge, lie,
prevaricate, quibble
equivocating: evasive
equivocation:
evasion, fib, quibble
era: date, day,
generation, page,
period, time, world
eradicate: extinguish,
kill, obliterate, scotch
eradicated: extinct
eradication:
destruction
erase: cancel, clear,
delete, obliterate,
omit, quash, rub out,
wipe
erect: build,
construct, pitch, put
up, raise, rampant,
rear, set up, standing,
straight, upright,
vertical
erection: building,
construction,
structure
eremite: hermit
ergo: hence
erica: heath
erode: degrade, bite,
eat, lessen, sap, scuff,
undercut, wash,
waste, wear
eroded: ground
erogenous: erotic
erosion: friction,
ulcer, wash, wear
erosive: corrosive
erotic: bawdy, blue,
fruity, lascivious,
lewd, passionate,

pornographic,
provocative, raunchy,
seductive, sensual,
sexy, titillating
err: deviate, sin, stray,
wander
errand: commission
erratic: capricious,
changeable, devious,
fitful, irregular,
moody,
temperamental,
uncertain,
unpredictable,
unreasonable,
unreliable, volatile,
wayward
erratum: error
erring: sinful
erroneous: bad, false,
illusory, improper,
inaccurate, incorrect,
untrue, wrong
erroneously: wrong
error: defect, fallacy,
fault, heresy, lapse,
misapprehension,
miscarriage, mistake,
oversight, sin, slip
ersatz: false, imitation
erstwhile: former,
late, old, once, past,
previous
erudite: cultured,
deep, knowledgeable,
learned, literary,
literate, pedantic,
profound, wise
erudition: culture,
depth, knowledge,
learning, reading,
scholarship
erupt: burst, flare,
sally, spurt
eruption: blast, blaze,
blow-out, burst, gust,
outbreak, outburst,
rash, spasm
escalade: scale
escalate: increase,
intensify, jump, leap,
mount, raise, soar,
spread
escalation: increase,
leap, spread
escapade: caper, lark,
ploy, prank, sally
escape: bale,
disappear,
disappearance,
emission, exhaust,
flee, flight, flow, leak,
loophole, lose,
puncture, run,
salvation, shave, vent
escapee: deserter,

fugitive, runner
escaping: fugitive
eschew: ostracize, skip
escort: attend,
attendant, bring,
cavalier, chaperon,
companion, conduct,
ferry, fetch, gallant,
guard, guardian,
guide, lead, marshal,
see, show, take, take
back, take over, take
to, usher, walk
escritoire: bureau,
desk
escutcheon: banner,
shield
esoteric: deep,
mystical, obscure,
technical
ESP: divination,
paranormal, psychic
especial: chief, special
especially: notably,
particularly
esplanade: parade,
promenade
espouse: embrace,
wed
espy: glimpse,
observe, remark, see
essay: composition,
paper, tract
essayist: writer
essence: base, basis,
being, body
concentrate, content,
flavour, form, heart,
idea, juice, kernel,
marrow, meat,
nature, picture, point,
quality, root, sap,
soul, spirit, stuff,
summary
essential: base, basic,
cardinal, constituent,
fundamental,
imperative,
indispensable,
integral, invaluable,
key, main, material,
must, necessary,
necessity, obligatory,
prerequisite, primary,
principal, priority,
requirement, urgent,
vital
essentially: basically,
naturally, primarily,
virtually
essentials: basis,
rudiments
establish: ascertain,
base, build, create,
determine, develop,
erect, father, fix, float,

form, found, ground,
impose, install,
institute, introduce,
locate, place, plant,
post, prove, rule, set,
set up
established: certain,
customary, habitual,
inveterate, known,
orthodox, proper,
regular, set, sound,
stable, traditional,
unquestioned
establishing:
creation, definition,
launch
establishment:
constitution
formation,
foundation, house,
household,
imposition,
introduction, regime,
footing
estate: grounds, land,
park, possession,
property, substance
esteem: credit,
favour, honour,
kudos, like, liking,
prize, regard, respect,
value, venerate
esteemed: dear,
prestigious, venerable
estimable: good,
honourable, laudable,
reputable,
respectable, valuable,
worthy
estimate: assess,
balance, budget,
calculate, calculation,
call, gauge, guess,
judge, price, project,
projection, quotation,
quote, say, theorize,
theory, valuation,
value
estimated: rough
estimation:
calculation,
judgement, kudos,
opinion, standing
estrange: divide,
separate
estrangement:
breach, break,
disaffection, division,
divorce, rift, rupture,
separation, split
estranging: divisive
estuary: mouth
esurience: greed
etch: carve, engrave,
inscribe, scratch
etching: engaging,

graphic
eternal: celestial,
immortal, infinite,
perennial, perpetual,
timeless
eternally: ever,
forever
ethereal: celestial,
spiritual, unworldly
ethic: principle
ethical: honest,
honourable, moral,
right, square, upright,
virtuous
ethics: honesty,
morality, standard
ethnic: racial
ethnological: racial
etiolate: bleach,
discolour, fade
etiquette: ceremony,
form, formality,
manners, propriety,
protocol
etymology: base,
derivation
Eucharist:
communion, mass
eulogies: praise
eulogize: celebrate,
commend, glorify,
praise
eulogy: compliment,
glory
euphonic: sweet
euphonious:
harmonious, musical
euphony: harmony
euphoria: buzz, high,
intoxication,
jubilation, mania,
transport, trip
euphoric: high,
jubilant, overjoyed
evacuate: discharge,
drain, leave, pass,
purge, vacate, void
evacuation:
discharge,
exhaustion, exodus,
motion, retreat
evade: beg, bypass,
dodge, duck, fudge,
get round, hedge,
jink, jump, lose,
neglect, shuffle,
sidestep, skirt, slip
evaluate: reckon,
assess, balance,
gauge, judge, mark,
price, quantify, rate,
review, value, weigh
evaluation:
judgement, price,
review, test,
valuation, value

evaluator: judge
evanesce: disappear, vanish
evanescence: disappearance
evanescent: fleet
evangelist: missionary
evaporate: boil, dissolve, dissolution, vanish, volatile
evaporation: disappearance
evasion: oblique, quibble, shift, shifty, slippery,
even out: flatten, level
even: constant, equal, flush, homogeneous, if, level, plain, plane, redress, regular, retaliate, roll, smooth, square, still, temperate, tight, toneless, uniform, yet
evening: eve, night, nightfall
evenly: equally, even, flush
evenness: balance
event: case, circumstance, competition, development, do, episode, experience, fact, fortune, happening, incident, landmark, matter, occurrence, phenomenon, result, spectacle, thing, tournament, transaction
eventful: lively
eventide: dusk, eve
eventual: future
eventually: finally
eventuate: befall, happen, occur, result, turn out
eventuation: occurrence
everlasting: constant, immortal, infinite, interminable, perennial, perpetual
evermore: forever
every: each
everybody: world
everyday: banal, daily, familiar, folksy, general, homely, idiomatic, inconspicuous, mundane, ordinary, plain, prevalent,

quotidian, regular, routine, unspoilt, usual
everyone: everybody, world
everywhere: galore, universally
evict: banish, eject, oust, turn out
eviction: expulsion
evidence: cite, demonstration, designate, give, indication, manifestation, material, proof, record, sign, testimony, token, vestige, witness
evident: clear, conspicuous, distinct, manifest, notable, noticeable, obvious, ostensible, outward, overt, palpable, patent, plain, pronounced, superficial, tangible, undisguised, visible
evidential: incriminatory
evidently: clearly, undeniably
evil: atrocious, bad, baleful, baneful, black, cancer, crime, dark, enormity, ill, immoral, immorality, impropriety, infernal, mischievous, monstrous, pernicious, satanic, sin, ugly, unholy, vice, vile, villainous, wicked, wrong
evildoer: malefactor, villain
evil eye: curse, jinx
evilly: badly
evince: attest, demonstrate, display, look, manifest
eviscerate: draw
evocative: reminiscent, representative, suggestive
evoke: extract, incur, paint, prompt, provoke, suggest, wake
evolution: development, formation, growth, mutation, transition
evolve: develop, form,

originate, work out
ewer: jug
exacerbate: compound, inflame, intensify, sour
exacerbated: embittered
exacerbating: inflammatory
exact: claim, close, compel, conscientious, definite, demand, enforce, faithful, impeccable, just, levy, particular, perfect, precise, proper, refined, religious, right, rigid, specific, strict, true, very
exacting: busy, demanding, fussy, nice, onerous, rigorous, rugged, severe, stiff, tough, weighty, judicious
exactitude: faithfulness, fidelity, precision
exactly: bang, even, just, literally, quite, right, sharp, smack, truly, unerringly
exactness: perfection
exaggerate: blow up, colour, inflate, lay on, magnify, overdo, overrate
exaggerated: extravagant, heroic, lavish, lurid, melodramatic, pretentious, romantic, sweeping
exaggeratedly: unduly
exalt: celebrate, dignify, glorify, honour, lift, lionize, promote, raise, revere
exaltation: elevation, excitement, intoxication, joy, rapture
exalted: dignified, grand, high, joyful, joyous, lofty, magnificent, majestic, prestigious, rejoicing
examination: audit, check, check-up, consideration, consultation, interview, look, overhaul, paper,

postmortem, probe, question, quiz, reading, review, scrutiny, search, survey, test
examine: audit, canvass, check, consider, explore, go through, hear, inspect, interrogate, interview, investigate, look, look into, overhaul, probe, prove, quiz, rake, research, scan, screen, search, sift, sound, study, survey, test, treat, vet, view
examiners: jury
example: authority, case, gauge, guide, ideal, illustration, instance, lead, lesson, light, manifestation, model, paradigm, pattern, piece, precedent, sample, specimen, standard
exasperate: bedevil, displease, gall, harass, irritate, nark, provoke, put out, sour, vex, wear, weary
exasperated: fed up, indignant, stung, uptight, weary
exasperating: trying, vexatious, wearing
exasperation: gall, indignation
excavate: burrow, dig, ditch, mine, quarry, scoop, scrape, sink, tunnel
excavation: cutting, dig, hole, mine, quarry, scrape, working
exceed: break, cap, overrun, overshoot, surpass, transcend
exceeding: over
exceedingly: mightily, much, very
excel: cap, head, lead, lick, outdo, pass, shine, surpass, transcend,
excellence: merit, nobility, perfection, prowess, rarity, worth
excellent: brilliant, bumper, capital, exceptional, fantastic, fine, first-class,

glorious, gold(en), great, masterly, noble, outstanding, perfect, prime, rare, rave, sensational, splendid, superior, terrific, wonder, wonderful

except: bar, leave out, unless, without

excepting: besides

exception: difference, exemption, objection, phenomenon, prodigy, qualification

exceptional: different, first-class, freak, irregular, noteworthy, odd, outstanding, prodigious, rare, sensational, singular, special, splendid, uncommon, unusual

exceptionally: uncommonly

excerpt: passage, quotation

excess: embarrassment, extra, glut, licence, overindulgence, redundant, residue, rest, riot, superfluous, surfeit, surplus

excessive: extravagant, fulsome, heavy, inordinate, lavish, luxuriant, profuse, prohibitive, radical, rank, steep, superfluous, unconscionable

excessively: heavily, unduly

exchange: bargain, barter, bazaar, change, commerce, currency, reciprocate, redeem, relationship, render, substitute, swap, switch, take back, traffic, transposition

exchanging: barter

exchequer: budget, fund, purse

excise: cut off, duty, tax

excitability: temperament

excitable: quick, skittish, temperamental

excite: fan, ferment, heat, inflame, inspire,

key, kindle, move, pique, provoke, pump, quicken, raise, rouse, send, spark, stir, touch up, turn on, wake, warm, wind, wind up, work up

excited: bubbly, exuberant, flustered, hectic, mad, passionate, tempestuous, warm, wild, wound

excitedly: madly

excitement: commotion, drama, exuberance, ferment, fire, fun, furore, heat, kick, madness, sensation, stir, warmth, zest

exciting: breathtaking, dramatic, dreamy, erotic, fun, gripping, heady, lively, moving, provocative, racy, romantic, rousing, sensational, stirring, titillating,

exclaim: blurt

exclude: banish, bar, except, leave out, omit, ostracize, outlaw, preclude, proscribe, reject

excluded: shut

excluding: bar, except

exclusion: disqualification, expulsion, omission

exclusive: choice, closed, inside, monopoly, narrow, patent, private, scoop, select, single, superior

excommunicate: ban, curse, ostracize, proscribe

excommunication: ban

excoriate: gall

excrement: dirt, dung, filth, ordure, waste

excrescence: tumour

excreta: filth, waste

excrete: pass

excruciating: diabolical, painful, piercing, sharp, violent

exculpate: justify, pardon, vindicate

exculpation:

vindication

excursion: detour, drive, jaunt, jog, journey, outing, picnic, ramble, run, sally, stroll, tour, turn, visit, voyage

excusable: venial

excuse: condone, defence, explain, explanation, grounds, justification, justify, let off, palliate, pardon, plea, pretext, rationalize, reason, release, vindicate, vindication, warrant

execrable: deplorable, odious

execration: curse, invective

execute: commit, complete, discharge, dispense, do, enforce, fill, fulfil, implement, kill, manage, obey, perform, perpetrate, remove, take, turn, work

execution: bloodshed, discharge, government, implementation, killing, performance, technique

executioner: killer

executive: officer, official, operative, responsible

exegesis: dissertation, interpretation, lecture

exemplar: gauge, ideal, light, model, paradigm, representative, specimen

exemplary: classic, faultless, ideal, model, representative, virtuous

exemplify: mark, personify, represent, stand for, symbolize, typify

exempt: except, immune, let off, release, relieve

exempting: except

exemption: franchise, freedom, indemnity, liberty, licence, release

exercise: bear, composition, discipline, drill, flex, lesson, limber,

manoeuvre, movement, operation, play, ply, practice, practise, resort, use, walk, wield, work out

exert: exercise, lobby, strain, strive, struggle, trouble

exertion: effort, exercise, handful, labour, strain, struggle, work

exhalation: breath

exhale: blow, breathe, emit, puff

exhaust: blow, blue, consume, do, drain, fatigue, go through, lose, overwork, prostrate, run down, run out, sap, spend, tax

exhausted: faint, gone, limp, out, poor, prostrate, shattered, spent, through, tired, weary, worn out

exhausting: gruelling, killing, onerous, punishing, strenuous, tough, wearisome

exhaustion: breakdown, collapse, fatigue, lassitude

exhaustive: comprehensive, detailed, full, minute, thorough

exhibit: boast, brandish, demonstrate, display, expose, hold up, illustrate, look, manifest, model, present, produce, reflect, render, reveal, set out, show, specimen, wear, write

exhibited: vaunted

exhibition: demonstration, display, exposure, fair, manifestation, parade, performance, scene, scholarship, show, view

exhilarate: rouse

exhilarated: exalted, high

exhilarating: brisk, exciting, heady, invigorating, racy, rousing, stirring

exhilaration: intoxication

exhort: charge, press,

urge
exhortation: charge,
persuasion
exigency: crisis,
emergency, juncture,
need, urgency
exigent: critical,
imperative, onerous,
pressing, urgent,
weighty
exiguous: scanty
exile: ban, banish,
fugitive, outcast,
proscribe, refugee,
transport
exist: be, hold, live,
obtain, occur, stand
existence: being,
duration, life, living,
standing, world
existent: being, real
existing: immediate,
living, present, then
exit: depart,
departure, door, gate,
leave, passage, quit,
retire
exodus: withdrawal
exonerate: clear,
discharge, release,
vindicate
exoneration:
discharge, pardon,
release, vindication
exorbitance:
extortion, expensive,
extravagant,
inordinate,
outrageous
exorcism: spell
exorcize: lay
exotic: external,
foreign
expand: balloon, blow
up, boom, boost,
branch, build, bulge,
bulk, distend, gather,
grow, increase,
inflate, magnify,
multiply, mushroom,
open, spread, stretch,
swell, wax, widen
expanding: dilation
expanse: immensity,
room, sea, sheet,
space, stretch, tract
expansion: boom,
boost, build-up,
bulge, enlargement,
growth, increase,
spread
expansive: capacious,
demonstrative, great,
large, mellow,
spacious, wide
expansively: wide

expatriate: exile
expatriation: exile
expect: look forward
to, reckon, suppose,
think
expectancy: hope
expectant: hopeful,
pregnant
expectation: hope,
prospect, suspense,
view
expectations: outlook
expected: due, likely,
unborn
expectorate: spit
expediency:
convenience,
opportunism
expedient: judicious,
politic, pragmatic,
resort, step,
substitute
expedite: forward,
further, hasten,
hurry, lubricate,
precipitate, quicken,
speed
expedition:
campaign, foray,
haste, jaunt, journey,
outing, ploy, quest,
speed
expeditionary:
exploratory
expeditious: rapid,
speedy
expel: banish, cashier,
chase, discharge,
dismiss, eject, exile,
ostracize, overthrow,
put out, remove, turn
out
expend: burn,
consume, lavish, lose,
spend, use
expendable:
disposable
expended: spent
expenditure: charge,
consumption,
expense, loss, outlay,
price, upkeep
expense: charge, cost,
damage, luxury,
outlay, price
expenses:
expenditure, upkeep
expensive: dear,
extravagant, high,
luxurious, precious,
rich, valuable
experience:
background, bear,
endure, enjoy, face,
feel, happening, have,
know, knowledge,

lead, lore, meet, past,
practice, qualification,
sample, standing,
suffer, sustain, taste,
undergo
experienced: capable,
knowledgeable, old,
practical, practised,
professional,
proficient, seasoned,
worldly
experiences: memoirs
experiment: prove,
research, trial
experimental:
exploratory, pilot,
revolutionary, trial
experimentation:
research
expert: artist,
authority, brain,
brilliant, connoisseur,
critic, delicate,
experienced, genius,
gifted, good, great,
knowing,
knowledgeable,
learned, magician,
marvel, master,
masterly, perfect,
professional, sage,
skilful, specialist,
wizard
expertise: craft,
dexterity, learning,
mastery, prowess,
skill, virtuosity,
workmanship
expertly: well
expiate: purge
expiation: penance
expiration: death
expire: croak, die,
end, go, go off, lapse,
pass, perish,
terminate
expired: defunct,
lapsed, out
expiring: dying
expiry: end
explain: clarify,
comment, define,
illuminate, interpret,
justify, render,
resolve, set out, show,
solve, state, unravel
explanation:
comment,
construction, defence,
definition,
interpretation,
justification, key,
light, plea, reason,
solution, theory,
vindication
explanatory:

defensive
expletive: curse,
imprecation, oath,
obscenity
explicit: blunt, clear,
concrete, definite,
direct, graphic, lucid,
outspoken, specific
explicitly: barely,
outright, particularly
explicitness: clarity,
lucidity
explode: bang, blast,
blaze, blow up, boom,
burst, crash,
detonate, fire,
fulminate, go off, let
off, set off, thunder,
zap
exploded: burst,
shattered
exploit: deed, feat,
harness, milk,
overwork,
performance, prey on,
profit by, tap, use,
victimize
exploitation:
opportunism
exploited: commercial
exploiter: bandit
exploration:
research, search
exploratory:
preliminary
explore: investigate,
look into, probe,
prospect, range,
reconnoitre
explorer: pioneer
explosion: bang,
blast, blow-out,
boom, burst, crash,
gale, gust, outbreak,
outburst, report
explosive:
inflammatory, volatile
explosive device:
bomb, mine
expose: bare, catch,
compromise, disclose,
disgrace, find out,
flash, light, show up,
subject, unmask,
weather
exposé: revelation
scoop, showdown
exposed: bald, bare,
bleak, discredited,
helpless, insecure,
liable, open, out,
public, subject,
unsafe, vaunted,
vulnerable, weak
exposition: comment,
demonstration,

dissertation,
presentation,
reasoning, show
expositor:
commentator
expostulate: protest,
reason
expostulation:
remonstration
exposure: confession,
currency, flash,
revelation
expound: lecture,
preach, present,
solve, state
express: articulate,
certain, couch,
definite, extract,
formulate, frame,
indicate, mean, milk,
phrase, positive,
precise, put, quick,
rapid, reflect, register,
represent, say,
signify, sound, speak,
specific, speedy, state,
vent, voice, wish,
word
expression: diction,
face, idiom,
indication, language,
letter, look, phrase,
phraseology, style,
term, token, voice,
word
expressionless:
blank, fishy, glassy,
neutral, vacant,
wooden
expressive: articulate,
dramatic, knowing,
lyric, lyrical,
meaning, mobile,
pithy, pregnant,
significant
expressly: especially,
particularly
expropriate: assume,
hijack
expropriation:
assumption, hijack
expulsion: dismissal,
disqualification, exile,
overthrow
expunge: cancel,
delete, extinguish,
quash, wipe
expurgate: censor
exquisite: artistic,
beautiful, choice,
delicate, delicious,
excruciating, fine,
gorgeous, heavenly,
impeccable, lovely,
piercing, rare, rich,
superb

exquisiteness: rarity
extant: immediate,
living
extemporaneous:
impromptu,
unprepared
extemporaneously:
impromptu
extempore: blind
extemporize: hack,
improvise
extend: augment,
build, continue, fill,
grow, increase, jut,
lengthen, liberalize,
lie, pay, produce,
prolong, range, run,
strain, stretch, sweep,
swell
extended: continuous,
lengthy, long,
protracted
extendedly: long
extension: build-up,
dilation, enlargement,
growth, increase,
limb, projection,
reach, traction
extensions:
ramifications
extensive: broad,
capacious,
comprehensive,
copious, exhaustive,
expansive, full, good,
great, large, long,
main, pervasive,
profound, roomy,
spacious, sweeping,
wide, widespread
extensively:
generally, long, wide
extensiveness: length
extensor: muscle
extent: breadth,
capacity, compass(es),
deal, degree, distance,
distribution, latitude,
length, limit,
magnitude, measure,
measurement, point,
quantity, range,
reach, room, scale,
scope, size, space,
span, spread, stretch,
width
extenuate: mitigate,
palliate, rationalize,
smooth
exterior: external,
façade, face, outer,
outside, outward,
superficial, surface
exterminate: destroy,
kill, liquidate,
massacre, slaughter,

slay
extermination:
death, destruction,
killing, massacre
exterminator: killer
external: exterior,
outer, outside,
outward, superficial,
surface
externally: outwardly
extinct: dead,
defunct, obsolete,
past
extinction: death,
destruction, eclipse,
end, oblivion
extinguish: bank,
end, put out, quash,
quell, quench, stifle,
suppress
extinguished: extinct
extirpate: destroy,
extinguish, kill,
obliterate
extirpation:
assassination,
destruction, killing
extol: bless, celebrate,
commend,
compliment, eulogize,
glorify, praise
extort: blackmail,
shave, squeeze, wring
extortion: blackmail,
kickback
extortionate:
expensive,
extravagant,
rapacious, steep
extortioner: bandit
extra: bonus, further,
interpolation, luxury,
more, new, nonentity,
optional, ornamental,
other, plus, residue,
second, spare,
superfluous,
supplementary,
surplus, tip,
unwanted, waste
extract: cite,
concentrate, draw,
excerpt, juice, milk,
passage, pull, pull
out, quarry,
quotation, remove,
summary, withdraw,
wring
extraction: blood,
derivation, descent,
genealogy, origin,
pedigree, stock,
strain, withdrawal
extramural: outside
extraneous: foreign,
incongruous,

insignificant,
irrelevant, outside,
remote
extraordinarily:
uncommonly
extraordinary:
bizarre, curious,
distinctive,
distinguished,
exceptional, irregular,
memorable,
miraculous, odd,
peculiar, prodigious,
queer, remarkable,
signal, singular,
special, strange,
striking,
unaccountable,
uncharacteristic,
uncommon,
unnatural, unusual,
phenomenal,
portentous
extrapolate: deduce
extras: frills
extrasensory:
psychic
extraterrestrial:
unworldly
extravagance:
luxury, profusion,
waste
extravagant:
expensive, fanciful,
fancy, flamboyant,
grandiose, heroic,
high, inordinate,
lavish, lush,
luxuriant,
ostentatious,
pretentious, prodigal,
profuse, romantic,
spendthrift, wasteful,
wild
extravaganza: riot,
spectacle, spectacular
extreme: critical,
deep, dire,
extravagant, fanatical,
fantastic, great, high,
intense, last, marked,
outside, profound,
rabid, radical, rare,
rigorous, rough, sore,
spartan, stiff, strong,
supreme, terrific,
ultimate
extremely: badly,
desperately, jolly,
mightily, most,
roughly, terribly,
truly, unutterably,
very
extremist: fanatic,
radical, revolutionary,
zealot

extremity: boundary, crisis, digit, emergency, end, limb, necessity, pole, strait(s), tail
extricate: clear, free, redeem, release, rescue
extrication: rescue
extrinsic: remote
extrovert: demonstrative, outgoing
extrude: draw
exuberance: profusion
exuberant: boisterous, gushing, high-spirited, profuse, rampant, rich
exudation: emission, ooze, sweat
exude: discharge, drain, emit, fume, leak, let off, ooze, perspire, secrete, weep
exuding: leaky
exult: glory, joy
exultant: happy, joyful, jubilant, rejoicing
exultation: glee, joy, jubilation, rejoicing
eye-catching: lovely, ostentatious, outstanding, prominent
eye: lamp, view, watch
eyeball: orb
eyeful: look
eyelet: loop
eyelid: lid
eyes: vision
eyeshot: sight
eyesight: sight, vision
eyesore: fright, monstrosity, sight

F

fable: legend, myth, parable, tale
fabric: cloth, material, stuff, texture, tissue
fabricate: coin, concoct, construct, contrive, invent, lie, make up, make, manufacture
fabrication: construction, fable, falsehood, fiction, invention, lie, lying, pretence
fabricator: liar
fabulous: knockout, legendary, marvellous, stupendous
façade: blind, colour, disguise, display, face, outside, pose, pretence, semblance, veneer
face: cliff, clock, defy, experience, façade, finish, jib, line, look, make-up, meet, mop, mug, oppose, pan, run into, take on, veneer
facet: aspect, attribute, face, respect, side
facetious: flippant, humorous, jocular, tongue-in-cheek
facetiousness: comedy, levity
facile: light
facilitate: enable, help, simplify, smooth, speed
facilitation: help
facility: dexterity, faculty, fluency, knack, prowess, touch
facing: opposing, opposite, towards
facsimile: likeness, model, replica, reproduction, Xerox
fact: circumstance, deed, object, phenomenon, thing, verity
faction: clique, party,

persuasion, school, sect, set, side
factor: bailiff, circumstance, constituent, detail, element, fact, fraction, ingredient, instrument
factory: mill, plant, works
facts: data, information, intelligence
factual: authoritative, concrete, down-to-earth, faithful, historical, known, practical, real, right, true
factually: practically, right, truly
faculties: wits
faculty: calibre, capacity, function, genius, gift, head, power, school, sense, talent
fad: bug, fashion, kick, mania, rage, sensation, vogue
fade away: melt, dissolve, evaporate, go off, peter out
fade out: dim, disappear, fizzle out, quench
fade: bleach, die, discolour, fail, flag, languish, pale, pass, pine, relapse, sink, tail, taper, vanish, wane, waste, weaken, wilt, wither
faded: dingy, dull, faint, pale, seedy, shabby
fading: dying, flagging, moribund, obsolescent, recession, wane
faecal: filthy
faeces: filth, waste
fag: cigarette, weary
fagged: tired, weary
faggots: kindling
fail: cease, collapse, disappoint,

disillusion, fade, flag, flop, fold, go, lack, languish, lapse, let down, lose, malfunction, pack up, relapse, weaken
failed: bankrupt
failing: deficiency, derelict, disease, feeble, flagging, frailty, moribund, senile, vice, without
failure: breakdown, collapse, crash, defeat, down, eclipse, fatigue, flop, frost, lapse, loser, malfunction, miscarriage, miss, reverse, ruin, slump, smash, washout
faint-hearted: cowardly, pusillanimous, spineless
faint: blackout, collapse, delicate, distant, dizzy, feeble, illegible, imperceptible, indistinct, keel, languid, languish, light, muffled, obscure, pale, queer, remote, shadowy, sickly, slim, soft, unlikely, wan, weak
fainting: unconscious
faintly: vaguely
faintness: dizziness, lassitude, nausea, vertigo
fair: bazaar, beautiful, bright, carnival, decent, fine, gala, good, good-looking, honest, honourable, judicial, just, large, legitimate, light, likely, lovely, moderate, modest, objective, palatable, reasonable, respectable, right, rightful, satisfactory, show, sound, square, straight, temperate,

tolerable, valid, white
fairly: equally, passably, pretty, quite, rather, right
fairness: honesty, justice
fairy: elf, gay, homosexual, queer, sprite
fairytale: fanciful
faith: belief, confidence, conviction, credit, persuasion, piety, school
faithful: confidential, constant, factual, loyal, reliable, religious, steady, true, unselfish
faithfully: exactly, literally, truly
faithfulness: fidelity, honesty, loyalty
faithless: disloyal, false
fake: artificial, base, bastard, bogus, deception, false, forge, forgery, fraud, fudge, imitation, mock, phoney, pretend, quack, queer, rig, sham, spurious
faker: hypocrite
faking: forgery
falcon: hawk
fall: autumn, come, decadence, descend, descent, deterioration, die, dip, dive, down, drop, lower, lunge, lurch, plunge, rain, relapse, sin, sink, slip, slope, slump, spill, stumble, throw, tumble, wane
fallacious: bad, deceptive, false, illogical, illusory, invalid, misleading, specious, wrong
fallacy: hole, sophistry
fall apart: crumble
fall back: lag, lapse,

retire, withdraw
fall behind: lag
fallen: lost
fall guy: mug, victim
fallible: human,
 unreliable
fall ill: sicken
falling apart:
 dilapidated,
 disintegration
falling off: decline,
 decrease, wane
fall off: decline,
 decrease, wane
fall out: go, happen,
 occur, quarrel, spar,
 wrangle
fallow: dormant,
falls: cataract,
fall upon: assail,
 assault, attack, strike
false: artificial,
 bastard, bogus,
 deceitful, dishonest,
 dummy, faithless,
 fake, hollow, illusory,
 improper, invalid,
 libellous, lying,
 misleading, mock,
 perfidious, perjured,
 plastic,
 sanctimonious, sham,
 slippery, spurious,
 titular, unfounded,
 unnatural, unreal,
 unrealistic, untrue,
 untruthful, wrong
falsehood: fallacy,
 invention, lie,
 pretence
falsehoods: lying
falsely: hollow
falsetto: warble
falsification: lie,
 lying
falsified: twisted
falsifier: liar
falsify: colour, cook,
 disguise, doctor,
 fudge, juggle, lie,
 misinterpret, rig,
 pervert
falter: crack, hesitate,
 pause, quail, reel,
 stagger, stammer,
 stumble, waver, wilt
faltering: faint,
 flagging, halting,
 inarticulate, shaky,
 stammer
fame: celebrity,
 distinction, eminence,
 honour, kudos, lustre,
 memory, prestige,
 prominence, renown,
 report, reputation

famed: proverbial
familiar: close,
 common, dear,
 everyday, forward,
 free, frequent, fresh,
 friendly, habitual,
 home, homely,
 informal, intimate,
 knowledgeable,
 known, near, old,
 ordinary, routine,
 usual, wonted
familiarity:
 experience, exposure,
 forwardness,
 freedom, knowledge,
 liberty
familiarization:
 orientation
familiarized:
 habituated
family: birth, blood,
 breed, breeding,
 brood, clan, domestic,
 dynasty, folk,
 hereditary, house,
 household, kin, kind,
 litter, order, paternal,
 people, pet, tribe
famine: lack
famished: hungry,
 ravenous, starving
famous: conspicuous,
 distinguished,
 historic, illustrious,
 known, leading,
 legendary, notable,
 popular, prominent,
 vaunted
fan: blow, buff,
 conquest, follower,
 lover, stimulate
fanatic: fiend, freak,
 hothead, militant,
 radical, zealot
fanatical: crazy, mad,
 intense, intolerant,
 obsessive, rabid, wild,
 zealous
fanaticism:
 intolerance,
 obsession, zeal
fan out: spread, string
fanciful: capricious,
 dreamy, extravagant,
 imaginative,
 romantic, whimsical
fancy: conceit,
 conceive, desire,
 elaborate, fantasy,
 favour, freak, guess,
 humour, idea,
 imagine, impulse,
 like, liking, love,
 mind, notion, relish,
 taste, whim

fanfare: flourish
fangs: teeth
fans: audience,
 following
fantasize: dream
fantastic: bizarre,
 dreamy, extravagant,
 fanciful, grotesque,
 marvellous,
 phenomenal,
 prodigious, quaint,
 sensational,
 spectacular, splendid,
 strange, stupendous,
 terrific, weird, wild,
 wonder, wonderful
fantastical: fancy,
 whimsical
fantasy: dream, fancy,
 fiction, hallucination,
 invention, myth,
 mythical, vision
far: away, way, wide
faraway: distant,
 dreamy, overseas,
 preoccupied, remote
farce: caricature,
 comedy, mockery,
 slapstick
farcical: comical,
 funny, hysterical,
 ludicrous, ridiculous
fardel: burden
fare: diet, food, go,
 make out, manage,
 passenger, table
farewell: leave
far-fetched:
 improbable, tall
far-flung: distant,
 widespread
farm: breed, cultivate,
 grow, work
farming: breeding,
 culture
farmland: country
farmstead: hamlet
farrago: jumble
far-reaching: long,
 profound
farrier's: forge
far-sighted: shrewd
far-sightedness:
 foresight vision
farther: beyond,
 behind, far, past
fascia: dashboard
fascinate: attract,
 captivate, catch,
 charm, conjure,
 enslave, entrance,
 grip, interest,
 intrigue, mesmerize,
 spellbind
fascinated:
 enamoured,

bewitched, rapt
fascinating:
 attractive, gripping,
 interesting,
 intriguing,
 irresistible, killing,
 lovable, lovely,
 magnetic, romantic,
 winning
fascination:
 attraction, charm,
 glamour, magic, spell,
 wonder
fashion: beat, build,
 carve, custom, cut,
 design, fad, forge,
 form, frame, habit,
 hammer, kind, make,
 manner, method,
 model, mould, rave,
 sculpture, shape,
 style, turn, vogue,
 way, work
fashionability: vogue
fashionable: chic,
 exclusive, genteel,
 latest, natty, popular,
 smart, up to date,
 vogue
fashioned: made
fashioning:
 composition,
 formation
fast: diet, firm, fleet,
 hard, loose, nippy,
 painless,
 promiscuous, quick,
 quickly, rapid,
 speedy, tenacious,
 through, tight,
 unbroken,
 unwholesome
fasten: attach, belt,
 bind, bolt, bond,
 buckle, clamp, clasp,
 clinch, cling, clip, fix,
 hook, join, joint, key,
 lace, lash, leash, link,
 lock, nail, peg, pin,
 root, rope, seal,
 secure, shut, stick,
 strap, unite, zip
fastened: attached,
 secure, stuck
fastener: catch,
 clamp, clasp, clinch,
 clip
fastening: bend,
 bond, lock, seal
fastidious: careful,
 dainty, delicate,
 difficult, fine,
 meticulous, neat,
 nice, particular,
 precise, prim,
 punctilious, refined,

religious, scrupulous, squeamish
fastidiousness: delicacy, neatness, nicety, refinement
fastness: bastion, castle, keep
fat: flesh, grease, gross, obese, overweight, rotund, thick
fatal: baneful, damning, deadly, fateful, incurable, killing, lethal, morbid, mortal, murderous, poisonous, terminal, tragic, venomous
fatalistic: resigned
fatality: killing, victim
fate: chance, destiny, doom, fortune, judgement, lot, luck, mean, portion, preordain, providence
fated: bound, destined, doomed, predestined
fateful: decisive, fatal, momentous
fathead: ass, fool
fatheaded: foolish
father: clergyman, dad, parent, patriarch
fatherless: bereaved
fatherly: paternal
fathom: follow, penetrate, resolve, see, sound, understand
fathomless: yawning
fatigue: bore, exhaust, exhaustion, lassitude, overwork, strain, wear, weary
fatigued: faint, jaded, tired, weary, worn
fatiguing: killing, punishing, wearing
fatty: greasy, milky, rich
fatuity: folly, idiocy, nonsense
fatuous: asinine, foolish, idiotic, senseless, silly
faucet: tap
fault: blame, blemish, blot, bug, defect, error, failing, hole, lapse, malfunction, mistake, oversight, shortcoming, slip, speck, vice

fault-finder: censor, critic
fault-finding: complaint, nit-picking, querulous
faultless: immaculate, impeccable, innocent, perfect
faultlessly: exactly
faultlessness: purity, perfection
faulty: bad, defective, imperfect, inaccurate, incorrect, jerry-built, poor, wrong
faux pas: gaffe, impropriety
favour: back, backing, blessing, goodwill, grace, kindness, lean, oblige, prefer, side, vogue
favourable: auspicious, benign, bright, charitable, fair, fortunate, gold(en), good, happy, propitious, ripe, rosy
favourably: right, well
favoured: fortunate, pet, preferable
favourite: best, darling, fond, idol, like, likely, pet, popular, precious, preference,
favouritism: leaning
fawn: creep, kowtow
fawning: flattery, fulsome, greasy, grovelling, ingratiating, obsequious, oily, servile
fay: fairy
fazed: disconcerted
fealty: homage, loyalty, nationalism
fear: awe, diffidence, dread, foreboding, fright, misgiving, panic, terror, worry
fearful: awesome, dread, faint, uptight, worried
fearless: bold, gallant, game, heroic, intrepid
fearlessness: heroism, valour
fearsome: frightening
feasible: attainable, likely, logical, perhaps, possible, practicable, practical,

viable
feast: banquet, blow-out, dine, dinner, do, festival, holiday, meal, repast, spread
feat: attainment, coup, deed, job, performance, stroke, thing
feathering: flight
feathers: down
feature: aspect, attribute, characteristic, figure, film, highlight, landmark, point, property, quality, run, story, way
featureless: bare
features: face, pan
feature-writer: journalist
feckless: irresponsible
feculent: filthy
fecund: fertile, fruitful, luxuriant, pregnant, productive, prolific, rich, teeming
fed up: dissatisfied, sick
federate: band, consolidate
federation: association, league, state
fee: commission, consideration, fare, fine, hire, pay, payment, premium, price, rate, remittance, rent, toll, wage
feeble: decrepit, faint, flimsy, frail, helpless, ineffectual, inefficient, lame, languid, low, pale, pathetic, powerless, puny, pusillanimous, slender, slight, spineless, thin, unhealthy, wan, weak
feeble-minded: fatuous, idiotic, simple, soft
feeble-mindedness: stupidity
feebleness: debility, frailty
feed: board, dine, eat, fare, fatten, food, fuel, gorge, live, nourish, nurture, tend
feedback: reaction, response

feel: finger, flair, flavour, grope, handle, have, know, paw, sense, taste, tone, touch
feeling: atmosphere, belief, blood, climate, emotion, heart, hunch, idea, impression, intuition, pity, sensation, sense, sensibility, sensitive, sensuous, sentient, sentiment, soul, spirit, touch, undertone, warmth, will
feign: assume, fake, make out, pretend, put on, sham
feigned: artificial, fake, false, fictitious, simulated
feigning: assumption
feint: blind, bluff, deception, dodge, jink
felicitate: compliment, congratulate
felicitous: fortunate, happy, opportune
felicitously: happily
felicity: beatitude, bliss, joy
feline: cat
fell: axe, chop, down, fierce, flatten, floor, height, hill, mountain, pelt, skin, tackle, take, throw
fellow: boy, chap, character, comrade, equal, guy, lad, like, mate, rival, scout
fellowship: association, companionship, familiarity, fraternity, scholarship, society
felon: convict, criminal, crook, malefactor
felonious: criminal, delinquent, illegal, wrong
felony: crime, job
female: feminine, girl, girlish, hen, woman, womanly
feminine: girlish, ladylike, womanly
fen: bog
fence: barrier, cage, enclosure, hazard, hedge, hurdle, jump, paling, partition, pen,

rail, railing, screen, wall
fencing: paling, panel
fend off: avert, deflect, divert, forestall, head off, parry
fend: ward
fender: bumper
feral: fierce, savage, untamed, wild
fermata: hold
ferment: brew, fever, flurry, seethe, work, yeast
fermentation: working
fermented: sour
fermenting: working
ferns: brake
ferocious: fierce, hard-hitting, rapacious, ravenous, savage, untamed, vicious, violent, wild
ferocity: cruelty, fury, lash, passion, violence, warmth
ferrule: tip
ferry: boat, take, transport
fertile: creative, fat, fruitful, luxuriant, productive, prolific, rich, teeming
fertilization: conception
fertilizer: manure
fervency: flame
fervent: avid, devout, earnest, fanatical, fiery, flaming, hot, impassioned, intense, keen, passionate, rabid, strong, violent, warm, zealous
fervid: fiery, impassioned
fervour: emotion, feeling, fire, force, glow, heat, passion, soul, violence, warmth, zeal
festal: festive
fester: mortify, rot, stagnate
festering: rotten, septic, smouldering
festival: carnival, celebration, feast, gala, holiday, jubilee
festive: gay, joyous, special
festive season: Yule
festivity: celebration, jolly, jubilation, jubilee, party, revel

festoon: crown, deck, garland, ornament
festooned: wreathed,
fetch: bear, bring, get, give, move, realize, take, transport
fetching: charming, lovable, winning
fête: bazaar, carnival
fetid: rotten, stale, stuffy
fetish: charm, deity, god, idol, talisman
fetor: smell, stench, stink
fetter: bond, chain, chain, shackle
fetters: irons, restraint
fettle: condition, shape, repair
feud: quarrel
feudal: dependent
fever: excitement, heat, lather, madness
fevered: hectic
feverish: fiery, fragile, frantic, hectic, tempestuous
few: couple, handful, scattering, sprinkling
fewest: least
fiancé: lover
fiancée: lover
fiasco: catastrophe, crash, debacle, failure, flop, washout
fib: falsehood, fudge, lie, story, tale
fibber: liar
fibbing: lying
fibre: cartilage, nap, pile, strand, string, thread, yarn
fickle: capricious, changeable, faithless, giddy, inconsistent, mutable, skittish, variable, volatile
fickleness: levity
fiction: fable, falsehood, fib, invention, lie, myth, romance, story
fictitious: imaginary, legendary, mythical, nonexistent, romantic, unreal
fiddle: cook, fidget, mess, wangle
fiddle with: finger, monkey, rig, tamper
fiddling: footling
fidelity: faith, faithfulness, honesty, loyalty, precision

fidget: fiddle, fuss, shuffle
fidgeting: restless
fidgety: jittery, jumpy, nervous, skittish
field: compass(es), competition, comprehension, concern, discipline, element, enclosure, ground, jurisdiction, kingdom, line, meadow, paddock, province, realm, region, sphere, terrain, venue, walk, world, zone
fields: farm
fiend: beast, devil, monster, savage, terror, wolf, zealot
fiendish: atrocious, beastly, diabolical, inhuman, infernal, monstrous, sadistic, satanic, vicious, villainous, wicked
fiendishness: cruelty
fierce: barbaric, bitter, cruel, fell, ferocious, furious, grim, hard, hard-hitting, hot, intense, relentless, savage, severe, sharp, untamed, vicious, violent, wild
fiercely: sharply
fierceness: ferocity, violence
fiery: diabolical, explosive, fierce, flaming, hasty, hot, impassioned, inflammatory, lurid, passionate, peppery, quick-tempered, short-tempered
fiesta: carnival
fife: flute, pipe
fight: battle, bout, box, champion, clash, combat, conflict, contest, engagement, fracas, oppose, repel, resist, row, scrap, scuffle, spar, struggle, take on, war, wrangle, wrestle
fighter: militant, pugilist, warrior
fighting: battle, boxing, war
figment: fantasy, hallucination, illusion

figmentary: illusory
figurative: metaphorical
figure: body, build, calculate, cast, character, cipher, design, dummy, effigy, form, frame, icon, illustration, image, line, number, numeral, physique, profile, reckon, shape, unit
figurehead: puppet
figure out: cipher, decipher, do, find out, penetrate, puzzle
figures: data, poll
figuring: calculation
filament: barb, element, fibre, hair, line, thread, yarn
filch: knock off, nick, pinch
filching: robbery
file: bank, catalogue, classify, grate, grind, list, lodge, papers, pigeonhole, planc, prefer, procession, queue, range, rasp, record, register, row, scrape, tail, train, whet
filed down: ground
filigree: open
filing: friction, scrape
fill: charge, flood, glut, gorge, line, load, make up, pack, pad, pass, permeate, prime, satisfy, spend, steep, stuff, top up
filled: full, loaded
filler: key
fillet: strip
fill in: brief, post, prime, understudy
filling: padding, satisfying
fillip: flip, kick, lift, snap, tonic
fill out: make out, pad, pad out
fill up: fuel, take in
filly: doll, girl
film: blanket, layer, photograph, picture, sheet, tape, veil, wash
films: cinema
filmy: thin
filter: drip, funnel, infiltrate, permeate, screen, sift, strain
filtered: refined
filtering: refinement

filth: dirt, grime, nastiness, ordure, squalor
filthiness: obscenity
filthy: bawdy, black, dirty, foul, insanitary, nasty, obscene, pornographic, rank, rotten, scatological, sordid
finagle: jockey
final: decisive, dying, eventual, last, last-ditch, net, overriding, peremptory, terminal, ultimate
finale: catastrophe, end, epilogue, issue, tail
finality: decision
finalize: complete, seal, wind up
finally: last
finance: back, economy, fund, set up, sponsor, underwrite,
finances: budget, capital, fund, money, treasury
financial: economic, monetary
financing: backing
find: detect, discover, hear, jewel, judge, locate, look up, meet, rarity, reach, recover, rule, search, see, strike, windfall, work out
find fault: blame, carp, criticize, complain, jaw, niggle, quarrel, scold
finding: discovery, judgement, observation, resolution, ruling, verdict
find out: ascertain, catch, catch on, detect, determine, dig, discover, learn
fine: capital, clear, delicate, fair, forfeit, fragile, glorious, good, graceful, handsome, imperceptible, magnificent, masterly, minute, narrow, okay, penalty, rare, sheer, splendid, tenuous, terrific, thin, well
fineness: purity, rarity
finer: better

finery: jewellery
finesse: artifice, delicacy, dexterity, grace, polish, refinement, skill, sophistication, tact
finest: best, classic
finger: digit, feel, fondle, nip, paw, thumb, tot, touch
fingerprint: print
finicky: fussy, niggling, nit-picking, particular, precise, punctilious, squeamish
finish: cap, cease, close, complete, conclude, conclusion, consummate, determine, discontinue, dissolution, dissolve, do, end, exhaust, glaze, knock off, machine, pack up, polish, quench, run out, sink, stop, terminate, wind up
finished: closed, complete, consummate, gone, kaput, off, out, over, past, perfect, ripe, spent, through
finish off: polish off, touch up
finish up: polish off, wind up
finite: ultimate
fire: axe, bark, beacon, blaze, discharge, dismiss, electrify, energy, flame, flare, galvanize, go off, heat, hell, ignite, inflame, inspire, kindle, launch, let off, light, magic, oven, passion, quicken, sack, send, shoot, volley, wake, warmth
firearm: gun,
firebrand: hothead, torch
fireplace: grate, hearth
fireside: hearth, home
firewood: fuel, kindling
firework: cracker
firing: burn, crack, discharge
firkin: barrel
firm: assertive, business, compact,

company, concern, concrete, decisive, fast, hard, house, obdurate, obstinate, positive, rigorous, set, solid, stable, steady, stiff, strict, strong, sturdy, tight, true, unshakeable
firmament: heaven, sky
firmly: decidedly, fast, hard, positively
firmness: backbone, body, conviction, decision, nerve, purpose, resolution, resolve, strength, tenacity
first: base, basic, basically, beginning, best, cardinal, foremost, forward, initial, leader, leading, maiden, opening, original, originally, outset, paramount, preliminary, premier, primary, primitive, senior, victor
first-hand: intimate, original
first-rate: capital, classic, first-class, good, masterly, prime, prize
fiscal: economic, financial
fishy: queer, screwy, unusual
fission: disintegration
fissure: breach, break, chasm, chink, cleft, crack, defile, gorge, hole, leak, opening, orifice, rift, rupture, slit
fisticuffs: boxing
fistula: opening
fit: athletic, attack, becoming, competent, convulsion, frenzy, healthy, kit, orgy, qualify, ready, reasonable, reconcile, regulate, right, robust, seizure, sound, spasm, square, stroke, trim, well
fitch: ferret
fitful: intermittent, irregular, moody, spasmodic, spastic, uncertain, variable
fitness: condition,

health
fit out: clothe, furnish, outfit, prepare, ready, rig, stock, turnout
fitting: assembly, becoming, commensurate, decent, due, just, likely, meet, pertinent, proper, relevant, right
fittingly: duly, right
fittings: furniture, rig
fit together: articulate, assemble, joint
fix: ascertain, assign, attach, clamp, clinch, clip, conclude, confirm, cook, corrupt, difficulty, do, freeze, get, hole, jam, juggle, limit, load, locate, mend, mess, nail, peg, pin, place, put, quagmire, rectify, remedy, repair, resolve, rig, right, root, scrape, secure, set, settle, square, station, stick, work
fixated: obsessed, obsessive
fixation: complex, fetish, hang-up, infatuation, mania, obsession, preoccupation, thing
fixative: mordant
fixed: assured, certain, constant, definite, earnest, fast, firm, flat, immobile, limited, loaded, motionless, permanent, regular, resolute, rigid, secure, set, stable, standing, static, steady, stuck, tight, unshakeable
fixedly: fast
fixing: definition
fixity: firmness
fix on: choose, hook, impose, mount, single
fix together: bond, piece
fixtures: rig
fix up: patch, prepare
fizz: bubble, gurgle, sparkle
fizzle out: die
fizzy: bubbly
flab: fat
flabbergast: astonish,

confound, stagger
flabbergasted: overcome
flabbergasting: astonishing
flabby: fat, lank, lax, limp, soft, unfit
flaccid: lank, limp
flag: banner, fade, fall, falter, fizzle out, Jack, languish, pennant, pin, standard, weaken, wilt
flagellate: lash, whip
flagellation: mortification
flagging: faltering, jaded, languid
flagon: carafe, jar
flagrant: blatant, glaring, gross, open, patent, rank, shameless
flagrantly: openly
flail: flap
flailing: flap
flair: dash, genius, gift, head, knack, panache, promise, style, talent, turn virtuosity
flak: criticism, stick
flake: chip, knap, scale, splinter
flaky: scaly
flambé: set fire to
flamboyance: ostentation, panache
flamboyant: dashing, extravagant, gay, ostentatious
flamboyantly: gaily
flame: blaze, flare, heat, light, torch, warmth
flames: blaze, fire
flaming: fiery, hot, lurid, red
flange: bead, lip
flank: round
flanking: side
flap: door, flip, flurry, flutter, fly, furore, fuss, kerfuffle, lather, lid, state, tab, wave
flare: beacon, blaze, fire, flame, flash, glare, light, spark, widen
flaring: glaring
flare up: ignite
flare-up: blaze, blow-out, bristle, outbreak, tantrum
flash: blaze, blur, flake, flame, flare,

garish, gaudy, gay, glance, glimpse, glitter, instant, light, minute, ostentatious, snap, spark, sparkle, speed, twinkling, whip
flashing: meteoric, twinkling
flashlight: lamp, torch
flashy: conspicuous, extravagant, glaring, loud, meretricious
flask: bottle, canteen, carafe, magazine
flat: barren, bland, blunt, boring, burst, dead, dull, even, flush, jejune, lacklustre, level, lifeless, mawkish, muddy, pad, plain, plane, prone, prostrate, regular, shallow, smooth, stale, toneless
flatfish: sole
flatlands: lowland
flats: basin, lowland, table, valley
flatten: deflate, demolish, fell, floor, level, lodge, press, pulverize, roll, smooth, trample, tread
flattened: blue
flatter: boast, court, flannel, humour, jolly, pride, wheedle
flatterer: creep, lackey
flattering: complimentary, grovelling
flattery: compliment, jolly, salve, flannel
flatulence: wind
flatus: wind
flaunt: brandish, dangle, display, parade, promenade, show off, splash
flaunted: flagrant, vaunted
flaunting: ostentation, parade
flavour: garnish, pepper, principle, relish, season, smack, taste, zest
flavoured: spicy
flavoursome: fruity
flaw: blemish, blot,

chink, crack, defect, disadvantage, failing, fallacy, fault, frailty, hole, rent, rift, shortcoming, speck, spot
flawed: faulty, imperfect, incorrect
flawless: clean, faultless, immaculate, impeccable, pure, perfect
flawlessness: purity
flaxen: fair, gold(en)
flay: bark, blast, castigate, flog, pan, skin
fleck: dot, pepper, speck, spot
flecked: dappled
fledgling: young
flee: bolt, disappear, make off, run
fleece: cheat, coat, pluck, shear
fleecy: fluffy, hairy, soft, woolly
fleeing: flight
fleet: fast, marine, navy, quick
fleeting: brief, fugitive, hasty, momentary, passing, short
fleetness: speed
flesh: meat, pulp, quick
fleshly: physical, sensual, sensuous, worldly
fleshy: fat, round
flex: bend, cable, limber, telescope, tense, yield
flexed: taut
flexibility: give, spring
flexible: easy, liberal, limber, limp, lithe, loose, plastic, pliable, resilient, slack, soft, universal, versatile, yielding
flexion: bent
flexor: muscle
flick: brush, flip, snap, whisk
flicker: dance, flare, flash, gutter, lick, spark, sparkle, twinkling, waver
flickering: fitful, twinkling
flight: ascent, disappearance, exodus, flock, retreat

flightiness: dizziness, levity
flighty: dizzy, fickle, frivolous, giddy, irresponsible, scatterbrained, volatile, wayward
flimsiness: frailty
flimsy: feeble, filmy, frail, hollow, insecure, jerry-built, lame, ramshackle, shallow, slender, tenuous, thin, weak
flinch: cower, falter, quail, recoil, shrink, shy, start, wince
fling: bowl, cast, dash, heave, hurl, launch, pitch, precipitate, project, scatter, send, shoot, slam, sling, throw, venture
flip: leaf
flippancy: levity
flippant: facetious, jocular, saucy, tongue-in-cheek
flirt: minx
flirtatious: bold, coy, playful
flit: dance, ghost
float: drift, finance, fund, glide, hang, hover, sail, till, waft
floating: buoyant, launch
floats: pageant
flocculent: hairy, woolly
flock: assemble, assembly, bank, cluster, congregate, congregation, crowd, flight, fold, herd, mass, mob, press, walk
floe: pan
flog: beat, belt, birch, cane, castigate, lash, lather, lay on, leather, lick, mortify, peddle, punish, scourge, strap, tan, whip
flogging: hiding, licking, punishment
flood: avalanche, besiege, blizzard, burst, cover, drench, drown, flash, flow, flush, glut, inundate, irrigate, overflow, pile, rain, rash, spate, water, wave, wet
floodgate: hatch
flooding: gushing

floor: base, basis, bed, bottom, deck, down, ground, level
floozy: hussy
flop: collapse, crash, dangle, fail, failure, frost, loll, loser, lounge, relax, sprawl, washout
floppy: disc, limp
florid: flamboyant gaudy, luxuriant, ornate, sanguine, overwrought
flotation: launch
flotilla: fleet, navy
flotsam: wreckage
flounce: storm
flounced: frilly
flounces: frills
flounder: blunder. grope, pitch, stumble, wallow
flour: meal
flourish: bloom, blossom, brandish, dangle, decoration, display, fanfare, flower, grow, live, prosper, quirk, wave, wield
flourishes: frills
flourishing: green, growth, healthy, lush, luxuriant, thriving, vigorous
floury: white
flout: defy, scoff, scorn
flow: bleeding, circulation, come, course, current, drain, drift, flood, go, issue, movement, passage, pour, river, roll, run, spate, stream, tide, well
flower: best, bloom, blossom, buttonhole, flourish, gem, ornament, pick, plant, pride
flowering: bloom
flowers: blossom
flowery: florid, lush, luxuriant
flowing: fluid, graceful, liquid, smooth
flu: cold
flub: fail
fluctuate: change, oscillate, range, seesaw, shake, shift, vary, waver
fluctuating: fitful,

fluid, irregular, undulating, uneven, variable, weak
fluctuation: bulge, shift
fluency: diction, facility, gab
fluent: articulate, facile, glib, idiomatic, smooth, voluble
fluff: down, dust, hair
fluffy: puffy
fluid: juice, liquid, moisture, watery, wet
fluke: hit
flummox: baffle
flummoxed: puzzled
flunk: fail
flunkey: attendant, groom, lackey, menial
flurried: disconcerted, unsettled
flurry: bustle, excitement, flutter, fuss, gust, hurry, puff, stir, whirl
flush: bloom, blush, colour, even, fever, flame, glow, level, plane, smooth
flushed: feverish, florid, hectic, red
fluster: confuse, confusion, discompose, disturb, flap, flurry, flutter, fuss, lather, ruffle, upset, perturb
flustered: disconcerted, distracted, jittery, jumpy, nervous, upset
flute: groove
flutter: breath, flap, flickering, flurry, fly, gamble, quake, quiver, twitch, wag, wager, wave, winnow
fluttering: flap, palpitation
flux: discharge
fly: ascend, bolt, bomb, dash, disappear, flee, gallop, hare, hop, hurry, jet, leap, make off, pilot, race, rush, sail, shoot, soar, whip, wily
flying: flight
flyover: bridge
foam: boil, churn, ferment, lather, scum, seethe, soup, yeast

foaming: frothy
foamy: frothy
focal: base, basic
focal point: base, basis, focus, highlight, pivot
focus on: fasten, concentrate, turn on
focus: centre, concentrate, definition, fix, foreground, hub, kernel, key, knot, level, nucleus, object
fodder: food, fuel
foe: enemy, opponent
foetid: bad, putrid, rancid, rank
fog: blur, damp, mist
foggy: damp, rough
fogy: stick
foible: eccentricity, failing, kink, mannerism, quirk
foil: baffle, cheat, contrast, cross, dash, defeat, defy, disappoint, dish, fox, frustrate, hamstring, obstruct, prevent, scotch, spike, stump, queer
foiled: disconcerted
foiling: frustration
foist: wish
fold: bend, buckle, collapse, crease, double, drape, flap, flop, gather, loop, telescope, wind, wrinkle
folded: bent, wound
folder: brochure, case, file, jacket
fold up: crease, crash, fizzle out, flop
folio: leaf, page
folklore: legend, tradition
folkloric: mythical, traditional
folks: family, household, kin, people,
follow: attend, catch, comply, copy, dangle, dog, get, hunt, look into, mind, obey, observe, practise, proceed, pursue, result, shadow, tail, track, understand
followed: dogged
follower: man, partisan, satellite
followers: faithful,

school, train
following: behind, consecutive, later, rear, school, second
folly: indiscretion, insanity, lunacy, madness, monstrosity, nonsense, stupidity
foment: ferment, incite, inflame, instigate, kindle, raise, stimulate, work up
fond: doting, friendly, tender
fondle: caress, cuddle, feel, finger, handle, manhandle, massage, molest, pet, stroke, touch
fondling: caress
fondness: endearment, fancy, feeling, friendship, inclination, liking, love, passion, penchant, predilection, relish, taste, tenderness
font: face, print
food: board, bread, diet, fare, flesh, fuel, grub, meat, nourishment, repast, table
fool: ass, clown, deceive, dessert, have, have on, hoax, idiot, jackass, kid, lunatic, monkey, nincompoop, oaf, sap, take in, tamper, wally, zany
foolhardiness: idiocy, stupidity, temerity
foolhardy: imprudent, overconfident, rash, reckless, silly
foolish: babyish, insane, lunatic, ridiculous, soft, unwise
foolishness: folly, lunacy
foot: base, measure, paw, pay, pedestal, plate, walk
footfall: tread
foothold: purchase
footing: basis, foundation, grip, hold, purchase, standing

footloose: restless
footman: lackey
footnote: parenthesis
footpad: bandit
footpath: track
footprint: mark
footprints: track
footslogger:
  pedestrian
footstep: step, tread
footsteps: track
footway: path
for: now
forage: grub, hunt
foraging trip: foray
foray: flight, raid
forbear: withhold
forbearance:
  patience, tolerance
forbearing: indulgent
  lenient, long-
  suffering, patient,
  permissive, tolerant,
  understanding
forbid: ban, bar,
  deny, proscribe, veto
forbidden:
  prohibited,
  unmentionable
forbidding: austere,
  ban, dark, dour,
  frigid, gaunt, grim,
  inhospitable, severe,
  stern
force: calibre, drive,
  effect, effort, energy,
  fire, fleet, gravity,
  hustle, impact, impel,
  impulse, influence,
  jam, kick, lash,
  legion, lever, load,
  meaning, momentum,
  muscle, oblige, pick,
  police, potency,
  power, press,
  pressure, propel,
  pump, punch, rack,
  ram, reduce, screw,
  spirit, squad, squeeze,
  stamina, strain,
  strength, strike, teeth,
  value, vengeance,
  vigour, violence,
  wallop, waterfall,
  weight, weld, whip,
  work, wrench, wring,
  zap
forced: contrived, far-
  fetched, laboured,
  obliged, stilted,
  strained, unnatural
forceful: assertive,
  blunt, bold, cogent,
  compelling, decisive,
  dramatic, dynamic,
  effective, expressive,

forcible, hard, hard-
  hitting, mighty,
  pithy, positive,
  potent, powerful,
  strong, vigorous,
  violent, weighty
forcefully: hard,
  mightily
forcible: cogent
ford: cross, wade
fore: bow, head, prow
forebear: forerunner,
  predecessor,
  precursor
forebears: stock
foreboding: black,
  fear, premonition,
  sign
forecast: calculation,
  cast, expect, fate,
  foresee, foretell,
  outlook, predict,
  project, projection,
  prophesy
forecaster: prophet
forefather: forebear,
  predecessor
forefinger: index
forefront:
  foreground, head
forego: sacrifice
foreground: forefront
foreign: barbarian,
  external, overseas,
  strange,
  uncharacteristic,
foreigner: barbarian
foreigners: visitors
foreland: bluff, head,
  headland,
  promontory
foreleg: calf
foreman: boss,
  contractor, gaffer,
  overseer
foremast-sail: jib
foremost: best,
  capital, cardinal,
  chief, first, forward,
  leading, master,
  paramount, pre-
  eminent, premier,
  principal
foreordain: doom,
  mean, preordain
foreordained:
  destined, doomed,
  fated, predestined
forerunner: herald,
  leader, predecessor,
  precursor
foresee: expect,
  forecast, foretell,
  predict, prophesy
foreseeing: far-
  sighted

foresight: calculation,
  precaution,
  preparation,
  providence, vision
forest: bush, timber,
  wood, woods
forestall: avert, fend
  off, frustrate, obviate,
  preclude, stop
forestalling:
  frustration
foretell: divine,
  expect, forecast,
  foresee, predict,
  preordain, project,
  prophesy
foreteller: seer
forethought: care,
  caution, calculation,
  deliberation,
  foresight, precaution,
  providence, prudence
forewarning: notice,
  portent
foreword:
  introduction, preface,
  prelude
forfeit: fine, lose,
  penalty, sacrifice
forfeited: lost
forfeiture: loss
forge: beat, coin, fake,
  falsify, form,
  hammer, weld
forged: base, fake,
  false, imitation,
  phoney
forger: fraud
forgery: fake, fraud,
  imitation, phoney,
  sham
forget: leave out, lose,
  neglect, overlook,
  pass over
forgetful: careless,
  mindless, oblivious,
  remiss
forgetfulness:
  neglect, negligence,
  oblivion
forgetting: loss
forgivable: human,
  venial
forgive: let off,
  pardon, purge
forgiveness: grace,
  mercy, pardon
forgiving: humane,
  long-suffering,
  merciful,
  understanding
forgo: decline, miss,
  pass up, renounce,
  resist, waive
forgotten: forlorn
fork: branch, dig,

diverge, split
forlorn: desolate,
  desperate, forgotten,
  low, wistful, wretched
forlornly: desperately
form: bench, body,
  build, cast, ceremony,
  compose,
  composition,
  comprise,
  constitution, contour,
  create, custom,
  design, develop,
  dummy, evolve,
  fabricate, fashion,
  figure, forge,
  formation, frame,
  idea, knead, knock
  off, likeness, make,
  make up, manner,
  materialize, method,
  model, mould,
  organize, outline,
  physique, raise,
  repair, sculpture,
  shape, stamp,
  structure, style, trim,
  turn, usage, version,
  work, work out
formal: brittle,
  ceremonial,
  conventional,
  dignified, distant,
  dry, genteel,
  honorary, impersonal,
  nominal, occasional,
  official, orderly,
  proper, regular,
  ritual, set, stiff,
  unbending,
  undemonstrative
formalities:
  propriety, protocol,
  solemnity
formality:
  ceremonial, etiquette,
  reserve, rite, ritual
formation: build-up,
  conception,
  constitution, creation,
  evolution, make-up,
  organization, rank
formed: made
former: back, lapsed,
  late, old, once,
  outgoing, past,
  previous, preceding
formerly: once,
  previously
formidable:
  awesome, dreadful,
  grim, hard, nerve-
  racking, stiff, strong,
  tall, uninviting, uphill
forming: incipient
formless: shapeless

formula: prescription, recipe, routine, rule, secret, theorem

formulate: coin, conceive, construct, frame, invent, phrase, plan, work out

formulation: composition, invention, phraseology

fornicate: whore

forsake: betray, desert, drop, quit, renounce, repudiate

forsaken: derelict, forgotten, forlorn, lonely

forsakenness: loneliness

forsaking: betrayal

forswear: disclaim, forsake

forsworn: perjured

forte: line, loud, talent

forthcoming: coming, impending, responsive

forthright: bald, blunt, brusque, candid, frank, outspoken, plain, straight

forthrightly: frankly, openly

fortification: barrier, bastion, defence, rampart, wall, work

fortifications: battlements

fortify: blockade, confirm, consolidate, defend, fence, gird, harden, lace, nerve, reinforce, secure, wall

fortissimo: loud

fortitude: backbone, grit, guts, heart, heroism, patience, resolution, tolerance

fortress: bastion, castle, keep, tower

fortuitous: chance, coincidental, incidental, lucky, passing, random

fortuitously: indirectly

fortuitousness: luck

fortuity: chance

fortunate: happy, lucky, opportune, well

fortunately: fortuitously, happily

fortune-teller: oracle, seer

fortune: bomb, destiny, killing, mint, pile, portion, wealth

forum: organ

forward: assured, better, bold, brazen, bring, familiar, forth, further, hasten, immodest, obtrusive, on, presumptuous, promote, remit, route, saucy, second, send, transmit, pert, precocious

forwardness: familiarity, presumption, temerity

fosse: ditch, trench

fossil: fuddy-duddy

fossilization: ossification

fossilized: petrified

foster: boost, bring up, cultivate, develop, father, feed, further, harbour, keep, maintain, mother, nourish, nurse, promote, raise, rear

fostered: cultivated

fostering: maintenance, upbringing

foul up: bungle, fluff, mess

foul: beastly, black, dark, defile, dirty, disgusting, evil, filthy, mess, muddy, nasty, obnoxious, pollute, profane, putrid, rancid, rank, repulsive, rotten, screw, sickening, smelly, soil, sordid, tainted, vile

foulness: filth, nastiness, squalor

found: base, begin, build, cast, construct, create, erect, father, form, institute, locate, plant, set up, settle, start

foundation: backbone, base, basis, bed, beginning, bottom, creation, derivation, footing, formation, framework, institute, origin, preliminary, rock, root, start

founder: author, collapse, father, flop, keel, originator, pioneer, sink

foundry: forge, plant

fount: cradle, origin, print, well

fountain: jet, rain, waterworks

fountainhead: beginning

fourth: quarter

fowl: bird, chicken

foxlike: vulpine

foxy: cunning, scheming, vulpine, wily

foyer: hall, lobby

fracas: conflict, disturbance, fight, kerfuffle, row, skirmish

fraction: fragment, hair, jot, little, part, piece, proportion

fractious: difficult, perverse, quarrelsome

fracture: breach, break, crack, crash, knap, rift, rupture, splinter

fractured: split

fragile: brittle, delicate, fine, slight, tender

fragility: delicacy, tenderness

fragment: bit, break, chip, crumble, fraction, knap, part, patch, piece, remnant, scrap, shivers, shred, snatch

fragmentation: disintegration

fragments: debris, remains, shivers, wreckage

fragrance: bloom, incense, odour, perfume, scent, smell, nose

fragrant: feminine, redolent, spicy

frail: delicate, feeble, flimsy, infirm, invalid, low, poorly, powerless, puny, tender, unhealthy, weak

frailty: debility, delicacy, shortcoming, tenderness

frame: bench, body brace, build, chassis, couch, devise, figure, form, formulate, gate, grid, habit, make, mount, organize, panel, phrase, physique, plot, project, rack, reel, setting, shape, shell, still, stud, yoke,

frame of mind: outlook, state, temper, temperament, posture

framework: context, cradle, crib, fabric, form, gate, grid, organization, outline

franchise: charter, lease, liberty, monopoly

frank: bluff, blunt, candid, direct, forthright, honest, naive, open, outspoken, plain, raw, round, simple, straight, transparent, undisguised, unguarded

frankfurter: sausage

frankly: directly, freely, openly, straight

frankness: freedom, honesty, sincerity

frantic: desperate, hectic, mad, precipitate, rabid, raving

frantically: madly

fraternal: harmonious

fraternity: circle, clan, club, companionship, fellowship, order, society, union

fraternize: associate, collaborate

fraternizer: collaborator

fraud: charlatan, cheat, deception, defaulter, fake, fiddle, hoax, hypocrite, imposition, job, liar, lying, phoney, quack, racket, ramp, robbery, rogue, sham, thief

fraudulence: deception

fraudulent: base, bent, crooked, deceitful, dirty, knavish, lying, quack

fray: battle, rag, riot, scuffle, wear
frayed: ragged, worn, worn out
freak: buff, deviant, fan, fiend, humour, monster, monstrosity, nut, prodigy, stray
freaked out: high
freakish: bizarre, capricious, grotesque, monstrous, odd, peculiar, unnatural, weird, whimsical
freakishness: oddity
freckled: speckled
freckly: dappled
freak out: trip, turn on
free: available, broad, clear, complimentary, detach, discharge, disconnect, dispose, enfranchise, generous, gratuitous, immune, independent, leisure, let out, liberal, liberate, loose, love, off, outspoken, pardon, quit, redeem, rescue, rid, save, single, spare, uninhibited, unpaid, unravel, unsolicited, vacant, void, voluntary, welcome
freebie: hand-out
freebooter: pirate
freedom: independence, latitude, leave, leisure, liberation, liberty, licence, scope
free-for-all: fight, fracas
freehold: tenure
freeholder: proprietor
freeing: discharge, liberation
freelance: mercenary
freely: barely, unreservedly, wild, willingly
freestyle: crawl
freethinker: libertine
freewheel: coast, cruise, glide
freeze: chill, cool, harden, immobilize, moratorium, peg
freezing: biting, bitter, chill, cold, frost, glacial, icy, piercing, raw, wintry

freight: burden, cargo, carriage, forward, load, traffic
frenetic: feverish, frantic, hectic, hysterical, zany
frenzied: berserk, delirious, fanatical, feverish, frantic, furious, hectic, possessed, rabid, raving, wild
frenziedly: madly
frenzy: ferment, fever, fury, hysteria, lather, madness, orgy, passion, spasm
frequency: incidence
frequent: attend, common, continual, familiar, habitual, haunt, patronize, prevalent, resort
frequently: often
fresh: brand-new, chilly, clean, crisp, extra, forward, impertinent, invigorating, late, lively, maiden, mint, more, new, novel, original, raw, refreshing, virgin, warm
freshly: lately
freshness: bloom, flush, forwardness, novelty
fret: chafe, fume, fuss, gall, plague, trouble, vex, worry
fretful: fractious, impatient, peevish, petulant, querulous, restless, worried
fretfulness: impatience
fretting: friction, gnawing
friable: brittle, dusty, light
friary: monastery
friction: brush, conflict, discord, dispute, drag, strife, wear
friend: associate, connection, date, intimate, lover, pal, saviour
friendless: lonely, needy, unpopular
friendliness: consideration, kindliness, kindness
friendly: benign,

cordial, decent, familiar, folksy, genial, good-natured, harmonious, hearty, homely, intimate, kind, kindly, nice, obliging, outgoing, peaceable, peaceful, pleasant, receptive, sociable, social, thick, warm
friendship: association, familiarity, goodwill, harmony, kindness, love
frigate: ship
fright: dread, fear, horror, monstrosity, panic, scare, terror, turn,
frighten: awe, intimidate, menace, panic, scare, terrify
frightened: fearful, petrified, worried
frightening: awesome, dread, dreadful, forbidding, hair-raising, macabre, nerve-racking
frightful: ghastly, grim, hideous, horrible, monstrous, terrible, ugly
frightfully: beastly
frigid: chilly, cold, dead, frosty, glacial, icy, phlegmatic,
frigidity: cold, frost
frill: decoration, ornament, trim
fringe: border, boundary, hem, line, skirt, trim, verge
frippery: finery, frills
frisk: caper, leap, search
frisking: prancing
frisky: playful
fritter away: consume, idle, kill, spend, squander, waste
frittered away: dissipated
frivolity: levity, vanity
frivolous: dizzy, flippant, frothy, futile, giddy, idle, light, shallow, silly
frivolousness: dizziness
frizz: curl
frizzled: kinky

frizzling: sizzling
frizzy: kinky
frock: dress, gown
frolic: caper, gambol, lark, play, prank, riot, sally
frolicsome: frisky, gay, jolly, playful
from: hence, henceforth, immediately, off, since, sometimes
frond: leaf
front: blind, border, bow, camouflage, cloak, disguise, façade, face, fore, forefront, foreground, head, lead, mask, nose, outside, pose, prow, veneer
frontage: façade
frontier: border, boundary, limit, march
frontiersman: pioneer
frost: freeze, nip
frostbite: exposure
frostiness: cold, frigidity
frosty: cold, freezing, frigid, glacial, icy, wintry
froth: churn, foam, head, lather, residue, scum, seethe, soup, yeast
frown: face, glare, grimace, scowl
frowzy: dowdy
frozen: blue, frigid, frosty, glacial, motionless, numb, wintry
fructiferous: fruitful
frug: dance
frugal: light, parsimonious, spare, sparing
frugality: economy, prudence
fruitful: fat, fertile, lucrative, luxuriant, pregnant, productive, rich, teeming
fruitfulness: plenty
fruitless: barren, futile, sterile, unavailing, unprofitable, vain
fruits: crop, harvest
frumpish: ugly, unfashionable
frumpy: dowdy
frustrate: baffle,

cheat, cross, dash,
defy, disappoint,
dish, foil, hamstring,
obstruct, prevent,
scotch, spike, stop,
tantalize
frustrated:
disconcerted,
dissatisfied
frustration: check,
disappointment
fry: brown, grill
fry-up: grill
fuck: screw
fucker: bastard
fuddled: maudlin,
merry
fuddy-duddy: old-
fashioned, square,
stick, unfashionable
fuel: feed, fire, food,
kindling, prime
fuggy: stuffy
fugitive: deserter,
outcast, outlaw,
refugee, runner
fulcrum: centre, pivot
fulfil: attain, carry
out, crown, discharge,
execute, fill, honour,
keep, meet, obey,
perfect, realize,
redeem, satisfy, serve
fulfilled: content
fulfilment:
attainment, crown,
discharge, execution,
implementation,
perfection
full: big, broad, busy,
complete, crowded,
exhaustive, fruity,
generous, laden,
mellow, occupied,
overcrowded, packed,
rich, rife, rotund,
round, thorough,
total, unconditional,
unquestioned, volley,
whole, wide
fullness: body, fat
fully: backwards,
completely, even,
hard, quite,
unreservedly, utterly,
well, wholly, wide
fulminate: boil
fulsome: hard-
hitting, luscious,

profuse
fumble: flounder,
grope, maul
fume: boil, chafe,
rage, rave, seethe,
storm
fumes: dust, incense
fumigate: purify
fuming: furious, livid,
simmering,
smouldering
fun: frivolity, game,
lark, merriment,
merry, play
function: business,
capacity, ceremony,
commission, do, duty,
faculty, go, job, office,
operate, part,
perform, place,
position, province,
reception, role, run,
sphere, work
functional: dynamic,
serviceable, operative,
practical
functionary: officer,
official,
functioning:
mechanism, on,
operation, operative,
performance, working
functionless: otiose
fund: finance, mine,
patronize, reserve,
reservoir, savings,
sponsor, stock,
underwrite
fundamental:
axiomatic, basic,
bottom, cardinal,
elemental,
elementary, integral,
key, primary, prime,
quintessential,
radical, revolutionary,
ultimate, underlying,
vital
fundamentally:
basically, materially,
primarily
fundamentals: basis,
preparation,
rudiments
funding: backing,
finance
funds: bank, bread,
budget, capital, cash,
means, money, pool,

purse, resources,
stock, treasury,
wherewithal
funeral: burial
funereal: black,
lugubrious, sombre
funfair: circus, fair,
park
fungus: mould, rust
funk: quail
fun-loving: frivolous,
gay
funny: comical,
facetious, fishy,
humorous,
interesting, jocular,
light, ludicrous, odd,
peculiar, queer, rich,
whimsical, witty
fur: coat, hair, pelt,
wrap
furbish: dress
furfuraceous: scaly
furious: fierce, livid,
mad, rabid,
tempestuous,
wrathful
furl: roll
furlough: holiday
furnace: forge,
hearth, oven
furnish: cater, find,
gird, give, hang, kit,
lay on, produce,
provide, render, rig,
stock, yield
furnishing: provision
furnishings: décor
furore: excitement,
flurry, fuss, kerfuffle,
tempest, uproar
furrow: channel,
crease, fold, groove,
knit, line, rut, seam,
trench, wrinkle
furrowed: rugged
furry: fluffy, hairy,
soft
further: assist,
benefit, beside,
besides, better, boost,
forward, fresh,
hasten, lower, more,
moreover, on, other,
precipitate, promote,
second, speed, yet
furtherance:
assistance, boost,
promotion

furthermore: beside,
besides, moreover,
plus, yes
furtive: hidden,
insidious, mysterious,
secret, shifty, sneak,
stealthy, underhand
furtively: quietly
furuncle: boil
fury: fume, outrage,
rage, temper,
vengeance, wrath
fuse: blend, bond,
combine, compound,
consolidate,
incorporate,
integrate, link, match,
melt, mix, run, unify,
unite
fused: mixed
fuselage: body,
chassis
fusillade: barrage,
fire, shower, volley
fusion: blend,
coalition, composite,
compound, union
fuss: bother, bustle,
commotion, dust,
flurry, furore,
kerfuffle,
performance, racket,
row, scene, stir, work
fussy: busy, dainty,
difficult, elaborate,
florid, niggling,
particular, pedantic,
prim, punctilious,
overwrought
fusty: frowsty, rank,
old-fashioned, stale
futile: fruitless,
hopeless, idle,
ineffectual, nugatory,
otiose, pointless,
senseless, unavailing,
unprofitable, vain
futile: worthless
futility: despair,
nullity, vanity
future: coming, fate,
potential, unborn
fuzz: fluff, police
fuzzily: vaguely
fuzzy: dim, fluffy,
indistinct, opaque,
rough, vague, woolly

G

gab: chatter, drivel, mouth, talk
gabble: natter, prattle, rabbit, rattle, yap
gabbling: jargon
gabby: garrulous
gadabout: flirt
gadget: device, instrument, machine, mechanism
gaffe: impropriety, indiscretion, mistake
gaffer: boss, foreman, overseer
gag: crack, censor, heave, joke, muzzle, quip, silence, strangle, throttle, wheeze
gaga: insane, lunatic, mad
gaily: happily
gain: benefit, carry, clear, find, get, good, have, hit, improvement, increase, incur, interest, killing, land, make, net, obtain, procure, profit, progress, purchase, purpose, put on, reap, receipt, return, revenue, reward, sake, score, secure, win, yield
gained: made
gainful: beneficial, lucrative, worthwhile
gains: income, proceeds, profit, winnings
gainsay: deny, negate
gait: carriage, pace, rate, skip, step, stride, walk
gal: doll, girl, woman
gala: festival, special
gale: blow, gust, hurricane, storm, tempest, wind
gall: bile, crust, displease, face, insolence, pain, presumption, provoke, spite
gallant: attentive, blade, cavalier, chivalrous, courteous, dashing, heroic, stout
gallantly: manfully
gallantry: attention, courage, heroism, manliness
galled: peeved
gallery: audience, balcony, burrow, mine, tunnel
galley: proof, ship
galling: bitter, provocative
gallivant: gad
gallop: race, run
galvanize: electrify, fire, ginger, wake
galvanizing: exciting, sensational
gambit: device, gimmick, machination, manoeuvre, move, ploy, tactic
gamble: bet, chance, flutter, hazard, lottery, risk, speculate, stake, venture, wager
gamble on: back, play
gambler: punter
gambling: play
gambol: caper, leap, play, skip, trip
gambolling: prancing
game: bag, contest, kill, killing, lame, match, prey, quarry, racket, ready, scheme, willing
gameness: fight
gamete: germ
gamine: youngster
gaming: play
gammy: lame
gamut: range, scale
gamy: high
gander: glance, look, peek
gang: band, bunch, crew, group, knot, mob, pack, parcel, ring, set, team
gangland: underworld
gangling: lanky

gangrene: mortification
gangster: bandit, hood
gangway: path
ganja: grass, marijuana
gantry: bridge, cradle, jib
gaol: prison
gaoler: keeper
gap: blank, breach, break, cavity, chink, distance, gulf, hiatus, hole, interval, jump, lacuna, leap, omission, opening, pass, pause, rift, separation, space, split, vacancy, vacuum, void
gape: gaze, marvel, stare
gaping: beckoning, open, yawning
garage: depot
garb: clothe, clothes/clothing, dress, habit, robe
garbage: litter, offal, refuse, rubbish, waste
garble: colour, misinterpret
garbled: mangled, meaningless, twisted
garden: bed, grounds, nurse, nursery, park
garderobe: wardrobe
gargantuan: giant, huge
gargle: hawk
garish: blatant, conspicuous, extravagant, fancy, flamboyant, flashy, gaudy, glaring, loud, lurid
garishness: glare
garland: crown, deck, festoon
garment: habit
garments: clothes/clothing, dress, gear
garner: gather, harvest, husband, hoard
garnish: decoration, dress, ornament, trim
garotte: throttle
garret: hovel
garrison: barracks, man, station
garrulous: expansive, verbose, voluble, wordy
gas: emanation, fluid, fume, wind
gasbag: chatterbox
gaseous: fluid
gash: chip, cut, incision, lacerate, laceration, rent, rip, scotch, slash, slit, stab, wound
gasp: breath, breathe, gulp, pant, puff, sob, wheeze, whoop
gasper: cigarette
gasping: breathless
gastronomy: cookery
gat: gun
gate: attendance, audience, crowd, door, entrance, takings, port
gatehouse: lodge, pylon
gateway: pylon, threshold
gather: assemble, bank, brew, call, cluster, collect, compile, concentrate, conclude, congregate, deduce, extract, flock, garner, group, harvest, hear, herd, huddle, imagine, infer, learn, levy, meet, perceive, pick up, pile, pluck, press, raise, rake, rally, reap, recruit, round up, summon, think, turn out, understand
gathered: collected
gathering: assembly, build-up, cluster, collection, group, harvest, huddle, levy, meeting, rally
gatherings: frills
gauche: inept
gaucherie:

impropriety
gaudiness: glare
gaudy: blatant,
extravagant, fancy,
flamboyant, flashy,
florid, garish, glaring,
loud, lurid,
meretricious,
ostentatious, vulgar
gauge: assess,
calculate, calibre,
clock, criterion, essay,
fathom, measure,
monitor, probe,
quantify, standard,
test, tread, yardstick
gauging:
measurement
gaunt: bleak,
cadaverous, drawn,
haggard, lank, lean,
meagre, pinched,
scrawny, skeletal,
spare, underweight
gauze: bandage, filter,
tissue
gauzy: filmy, fine,
flimsy
gavel: hammer
gawk: stare
gawky: awkward,
clumsy, gauche,
ungainly, wooden,
gawp: look
gay: bent, buoyant,
fairy, festive,
homosexual, jocular,
jolly, light-hearted
gaze: glare, look, peer,
regard, stare
gear: belongings,
clothes/clothing,
goods, harness, kit,
outfit, plant, rig, stuff,
tack, tackle, trim
geezer: fellow, guy,
man
Gehenna: hell
geld: neuter
gell: harden
gelt: money
gem: bead, delight,
dream, jewel, rarity
gemma: bud
gems: jewellery
gemstone: jewel
gemstones: jewellery
gen: information,
intelligence, news
gender: sex
genealogy: blood,
derivation, descent,
family, pedigree
general: blanket,
catholic, common,
communal,

customary,
nationwide, overall,
popular, rough,
tactician, universal,
usual, widespread,
worldwide
generalize: widen
generally: mainly,
ordinarily, roughly,
often, universally,
**general
practitioner:** doctor
general public:
community, people
general-purpose:
useful
generate: breed,
cause, create,
develop, father,
germinate, make,
procreate, produce,
provoke, reproduce,
work up, yield
generated: made
generation: creation,
day, production,
reproduction, time
generative: prolific
generator: author,
machine, motor,
parent, pile
generosity:
hospitality, humanity,
kindness, largess,
magnanimity,
munificence,
patronage
generous: benevolent,
big, bountiful, broad,
capacious, charitable,
copious, decent, free,
friendly, handsome,
hospitable, kind,
lavish, liberal,
obliging, open,
philanthropic,
princely, profuse,
round, selfless, soft-
hearted, unselfish,
warm-hearted,
wholehearted
genesis: birth, cause,
dawn, generation,
origin
genetic: hereditary
genial: benign, easy,
engaging, friendly,
hearty, jocular, jolly,
kindly, sociable,
sunny
geniality: kindliness
genially: kindly
genital(s): private
genius: brain,
brilliance, flair, gift,
immortal, inspiration,

invention, magician,
marvel, mastermind,
mind, natural,
prodigy
genocide: killing,
massacre
genre: class, family,
order, style
genteel: cultivated,
cultured, decent,
ladylike, polite,
proper, refined
gentility: kindliness,
refinement, propriety
gentle: bland, easy,
fair, gradual,
harmless, humane,
kind, kindly, ladylike,
lenient, light, low,
lowly, meek, mild,
milky, peaceable,
quiet, soft, sweet,
tender
gentleman: cavalier,
gallant, man,
gentlemanliness:
gallantry, manliness
gentlemanly: gallant,
genteel
gentleness: humanity,
mildness, tenderness
gently: low, quietly
gentry: society
Gents: bog, lavatory,
toilet
genuine: authentic,
cordial, good, hearty,
honest, legitimate,
natural, original,
pure, real, right,
rightful, serious,
sincere, solid, square,
true, undisguised,
unspoilt, valid
genuinely: naturally,
really, right, truly
genuineness:
honesty, purity,
sincerity
genus: kind, sort
geography: country,
layout, lie, terrain
geology: terrain
geriatric: elderly
germ: bacterium, bug,
kernel, microbe, seed
germane (to):
material
germ-free: hygienic,
sanitary, sterile
germicide:
disinfectant
germinate: bud,
grow, spear, sprout
germination:
conception, growth

gestating: unborn
gesticulate: flail,
gesture, signal, wave
gesticulation:
flourish, gesture,
motion, pass, wave
gesture: motion,
movement, ploy, sign,
sweep, turn, wave
gestures: language
gewgaws: knick-
knacks
geyser: jet
ghastly: awful,
cadaverous, deadly,
dreadful, fearful,
frightening, frightful,
grim, grisly,
gruesome, horrible,
lurid, macabre,
morbid, nerve-
racking, shocking,
wan, white
ghetto: jungle
ghost: hack, presence,
shade, shadow,
spectre, spirit
ghostly: creepy,
ghastly, macabre,
shadowy, spiritual,
weird
ghoulish: creepy,
macabre, morbid
giant: heavy, jumbo,
large, monster,
monstrous,
monumental,
mountainous, ogre,
outsize
gibber: drivel, gabble,
waffle
gibbering: prattle
gibberish: drivel,
jargon, nonsense,
rubbish, waffle
gibbet: gallows
gibe: barb, catcall,
crack, cut, dig,
ridicule, scoff, sneer,
taunt
gibes: jeering,
mockery, teasing
gibing: jeering
giblets: offal
giddiness: dizziness,
levity, vertigo, whirl
giddy: dizzy, faint,
light, irresponsible
gift: attainment,
award, blessing,
contribution, dole,
donate, donation,
faculty, flair, genius,
knack, largess,
offering, present,
purse, talent, treat,

turn
gifted: capable, clever, promising
gifts: calibre
gig: barge, engagement, performance
gigantic: big, huge, immense, jumbo, large, massive, mighty, outsize, vast
giggle: chuckle, gurgle, laugh, titter
giggling: laughter
gild: plate
gilded: gold(en)
gill: brook
gilt: gold(en)
gimcrack: knick-knacks
gimlet: drill
gimmick: novelty, wrinkle
gin: trap
ginger: fiery, flaming
gingerly: warily
gird: circle
girder: beam, keel, principal
girdering: frame
girdle: belt, corset, gird, hoop, ring
girl: bird, hen, juvenile, kid, maid, maiden, woman, youngster
girlfriend: bird, date, flame, lover, woman
girlhood: youth
girlish: babyish, feminine
girn: face, grimace
girth: width
gist: content, core, idea, import, kernel, marrow, matter, meaning, plot, point, purport, sense, spirit, substance
give: award, bounce, carry, cast, commit, confer, contribute, delegate, do, donate, flex, grant, hand, impart, lend, pass, pay, present, provide, put up, render, spare, spring, supply, tender, utter, yield
giveaway: bargain, revelation
give away: betray, finger, leak, reveal
give back: refund, return, render
give birth to: bear,

drop, have, mother
give evidence: witness
give in: bow, capitulate, cave in, defer, kowtow, submit, turn in, yield
given: axiomatic, provided,
give notice: forewarn, warn
give off: discharge, emit, let off, radiate, secrete
give out: assign, bear out, deal, deliver, dole, emit, fail, proclaim, ration, run out,
giver: donor
give rise to: produce, provoke, raise
give up: cough, despair, discontinue, drop, fail, forgo, jettison, kick, lay off, leave, lose, pack up, quit, raise, relinquish, render, renounce, sacrifice, scrub, surrender, yield
give way: defer, budge, collapse, crack, crumple, go, kowtow, retire, snap, split, succumb, surrender, weaken, yield
gizmo: gadget
glabrous: bald
glacial: freezing, icy
glad: happy, joyful, ready, rejoicing, willing
gladden: feast, gratify, joy, lighten, please
gladdened: pleased
gladdening: joyful, joyous
glade: clearing
gladiator: warrior
gladly: happily, readily, willingly
gladness: happiness, joy, rejoicing
gladsome: joyous
glamorous: brilliant, romantic
glamour: brilliance, glitter
glance (into): dip,
glance: bounce, brush, deflect, glimpse, graze, kiss, look, nick, peek, peep,

scan, tip
gland: node
glare: blaze, flare, frown, shine
glaring: blatant, flagrant, garish, gaudy, gross, lurid, strong
glass: barometer, cup, drink, glaze, mirror, mug, telescope,
glassy: clear, fishy, icy, lucid
glaucescence: bloom
glaze: lacquer, lustre, shine, size, varnish
glazed: dead, glassy
gleam: beam, flare, flash, glance, glitter, glow, light, lustre, radiate, sheen, shine, sparkle
gleaming: lucid, shimmering, radiant
glean: extract, gain, harvest, reap, salvage
gleaning: harvest
glee: chuckle
gleeful: exultant
glen: dell, valley
glengarry: bonnet
glib: facile, plausible, slick, smooth, voluble
glide: cruise, float, fly, plane, run, sail, slide, slip, sweep
glimmer: ghost, glance, glitter, glow, suspicion, twinkling, vestige
glimmering: gleaming, twinkling
glimpse: glance, look, peek, spy, peep, whiff
glint: flash, light, spark, sparkle
glisten: flash, glitter
glistening: flash, gleaming, glitter, lustre, shimmering, shiny, twinkling
glitter: brilliance, lustre, radiate, sheen, shine, sparkle, twinkling
glittering: bright, brilliant, gorgeous, radiant, scintillating, shining, splendid, twinkling
glitz: glitter
gloaming: dusk
gloat: revel
global: catholic, worldwide
globe: ball, bulb,

earth, orb, round, sphere
globular: rotund, round
globule: ball, bead, bubble, drop, sphere
gloom: cloud, damp, dusk, fog, obscurity, pessimism, shade, shadow, woe
gloomily: heavily, unhappily
gloominess: sadness
gloomy: bad, bleak, cloudy, dark, desolate, dim, dingy, dire, dismal, dull, dusky, foggy, forbidding, funereal, glum, grey, grim, heavy, lugubrious, miserable, moody, morbid, murky, negative, sad, shadowy, sombre, unhappy, woeful, wretched
glorification: honour, idolatry, worship
glorify: bless, distinguish, hail, honour, lionize, worship
glorious: bright, brilliant, gold(en), gorgeous, grand, illustrious, magnificent, proud, splendid
glory: celebrity, honour, kudos, lustre, magnificence, majesty, ornament, ostentation, palm, pride, splendour, state, wallow
gloss: glamour, glaze, lacquer, lustre, nuance, polish, shine, varnish
glossary: vocabulary
glosses: notes
gloss over: play down, whitewash
glossy: gleaming, shiny, sleek, slick, smooth
glow: beam, blaze, blush, burn, colour, flame, flare, flash, light, nimbus, sweat
glower: frown, glare, pout, scowl
glowering: dark, lurid, ominous, thunderous

glowing: bright, fiery, fresh, light, live, luminous, radiant, red, rosy
glowingly: well
glue: attach, bind, bond, cement, fasten, fix, paste, tack
glued: stuck
gluey: tenacious
glueyness: tack
glum: blue, dejected, gloomy, low, lugubrious, melancholy, sad, solemn
glumness: sullenness
glut: flood, surfeit
gluteus maximus: buttocks
glutinous: sticky
glutted: jaded, satiated
glutton: hog, pig
gluttonous: ravenous
gluttony: greed
glyphs: writing
gnash: grind, grit
gnat: fly
gnaw: bite, chew, nibble
gnawing: biting, niggle
gnome: dwarf
gnomon: index, needle
go: attempt, bat, be, bear, bite, crack, depart, disappear, do, drive, effort, fare, fling, function, get, head, journey, leave, log, move, operate, push, quit, range, repair, ride, run, shot, snap, stab, throw, transit, trial, turn, turn out, walk, work, work out
goad: egg, hasten, nag, prod, spur, stimulate, urge, whip
goal: basket, design, destination, end, intent, mark, motivation, needle, object, objective, point, prize, purpose, quarry, quest, reason, target
goat-leather: kid
gob: cough, mouth, hawk
gobbet: lump, nibble
gobble: demolish, bolt, consume,

devour, gulp, stuff, wolf
gobbledegook: gibberish, jargon, waffle
gobbling: guzzling
goblet: cup
goblin: dwarf, gnome, sprite
God-fearing: godly, pious, religious, saintly
God: trinity
god: deity, idol, immortal
goddess: beauty, deity, immortal
godforsaken: remote
godless: heathen, impious, pagan, profane
godlike: divine
godliness: piety, sanctity
godly: devout, divine, holy, saintly
godsend: blessing, mercy, miracle, windfall
gofer: hack, menial
goggle: gape, look, stare
going: departure, disappearance, dying, leave, withdrawal, working
gold: yellow
gold-digging: opportunism
golden: yellow
golden rule: principle
gondola: basket
gone: away, lapsed, lost, mislaid, obsolete, past, spent
gonfalon: banner, flag
good: benefit, clean, desirable, favourable, fine, friendly, honest, honourable, just, kind, kindly, moral, okay, proficient, profit, right, sake, upright, use, useful, valid, virtuous, welfare, wholesome, worth while
goodbye: farewell, leave
good-for-nothing: layabout, wastrel
good-humoured: jocular, pleasant
good-looker: beauty
good-looking: handsome, pretty

goodly: considerable, respectable
good-natured: folksy, humane, obliging
goodness: honesty, kindliness, kindness, morality, virtue, worth
goods: cargo, freight, kind, luggage, merchandise, property, wares
goodwill: custom, favour, friendship, grace
goody-goody: pious, priggish, sanctimonious
goody: titbit
gooey: sticky
goof: mistake
goose pimples: tingling
gore: blood, stab
gorge: bolt, chasm, cutting, defile, glut, overeat, precipice, ravine, surfeit, valley
gorged: full, jaded, satiated
gorge on: devour, feast
gorgeous: attractive, beautiful, glorious, good-looking, lovely, ravishing, splendid, stunning, superb
gorging: guzzling
gormless: asinine, unintelligent
gory: grisly, gruesome, red
gossamer: filmy, fine, flimsy
gossip: backbiter, buzz, chat, chatterbox, conversation, dirt, gab, jaw, natter, news, rabbit, rattle, rumour, talk, tête-à-tête, whisper
got: made
gothic: quaint
gouge: dent, gash, pit, rut, scoop, score
gourd: squash, zucchini
govern: bridle, command, determine, direct, head, lead, preside over, rule, steer
governing: direction, prevalent

governing: ruling
government: authority, command, executive, legislative, management, parliament, regime, regulation, rule
governmental: diplomatic, national
governor: director, foreman, lord, patriarch, ruler
gown: dress, frock, robe
goy: atheist, heathen
grab: catch, clutch, collar, get, grasp, nab, nobble, paw, seize, snap, snatch, tackle
grabbing: clutch, rapacious
grace: beauty, become, blessing, dignify, favour, forgiveness, honour, mercy, ornament, pardon, poise, sanctity, taste
graceful: artistic, beautiful, becoming, dainty, delicate, feminine, fluid, light, liquid, lyric
graceless: gauche, lumbering, stiff
gracious: courteous, gallant, hospitable, kind, princely, propitious, refined
graciousness: gallantry, refinement
gradation: degree, scale
grade: caste, category, class, classify, condition, degree, denomination, form, level, mark, order, place, range, rank, rate, score, sort, station, status, unit, water
graded: assorted
gradient: ascent, hill, inclination, incline, pitch, rake, ramp, slope
grading: assortment
gradual: gentle, imperceptible, slow
graduate: pass
graduation: scale
graft: beaver, bribery, fiddle, implant
grain: corn, fruit, jot, particle, seed, shred,

speck, texture
grains: dust
granary: barn
grand: august,
brilliant, exalted,
gallant, gorgeous,
great, high, large,
lofty, lordly,
luxurious,
magnificent, majestic,
master, palatial,
princely, proud,
regal, solemn, stately
grandchildren:
descendants
grandee: magnate
grandeur: brilliance,
dignity, elevation,
height, luxury,
magnificence,
majesty, ostentation,
solemnity, splendour,
state, style
grandiloquent:
pretentious, rotund,
turgid
grandiose:
flamboyant, heroic,
magnificent, palatial,
pompous, pretentious
grandstand: stand
grange: barn
grant: award, benefit,
buy, cede, concession,
confer, confess,
contribution, do,
dole, give, impart, let,
maintenance, own,
permit, recognize,
remittance, reprieve,
show, supply,
vouchsafe, yield
granted: axiomatic
granulate: grind,
mill, pulverize
granule: grain
grapey: fruity
graph: chart, profile,
table
graphic: diagram,
illustration, pictorial,
vivid
graphics: design
grapple: clash, clasp,
close, contend, lock,
struggle, tackle,
wrestle
grasp: bite, catch on,
catch, clasp, clinch,
clutch, command,
comprehension,
conceive, fathom,
feel, follow, grab,
grip, handle, hold,
know, knowledge,
learn, lock, make out,

master, mastery, nab,
perceive, perception,
pick up, purchase,
reach, reading,
realize, retain, see,
seize, sense, snatch,
take, take in, tenacity,
understanding
grasping: avaricious,
avid, covetous,
miserly, possessive,
rapacious, ravenous,
sordid, tenacious,
tight, worldly
grass: inform,
marijuana, meadow,
nark, pasture, sing,
sneak, split, squeal,
talk, tell, weed
grassy: green, pastoral
grate: chafe, creak,
fire, grid, grill, grind,
grit, hearth, jangle,
jar, rub, scrape
grateful: obliged,
thankful
gratefulness: thanks
grater: file, rasp
gratification: delight,
diversion, jolly, kick,
luxury, pleasure,
pride
gratified: complacent,
glad, happy, joyful,
obliged, pleased,
proud, self-satisfied
gratify: content,
delight, divert, feast,
humour, indulge,
jolly, oblige, pander
to, please, satisfy
gratifying: delightful,
enjoyable, glad, good,
heart-warming,
joyful, pleasant,
proud, satisfying,
sensuous, welcome
grating: creak, grid,
harsh, hoarse, jangle,
jar, rasp, raucous,
rough, strident
gratis: free
gratitude: thanks
gratuitous:
complimentary, free,
mindless, needless,
unasked, uncalled-
for, unsolicited
gratuitously: unasked
gratuity: bonus, box,
dole, donation, gift,
present, tip
grave: bad, carve,
critical, demure,
dignified, earnest,
great, heavy, high,

sedate, serious,
solemn, sombre,
subdued, terrible,
tomb
gravel: ballast, grit
gravelly: hoarse
gravely: badly,
desperately, seriously,
terribly
graveyard: cemetery
gravid: expectant,
pregnant
gravitate (towards):
tend
gravity: earnest,
sobriety, solemnity
gravy: liquor, sauce
graze: browse, brush,
crease, crop, feed,
gall, kiss, rake, score,
scrape, scratch, scuff,
shave, skin, wound
grazed: frayed, raw
grazing: pasture,
pastoral
grease: bribe, fat,
lubricate
grease-paint:
make-up
greasy: fat, oily
great: big, deep,
enjoyable, fantastic,
fat, glorious, good,
high, historic,
illustrious, intense,
large, main, major,
marked, much,
outstanding,
prestigious, princely,
profound, splendid,
stunning, terrific,
wide, wonder,
wonderful
greater: better, major,
superior
greatest: best, king,
maximum, prime,
supreme, ultimate
greatly: badly,
materially, mightily,
much, very, well
greatness: brilliance,
majesty, nobility
greed: avarice, lust
greedy: avaricious,
avid, covetous,
grasping, hog,
hungry, mercenary,
possessive, rapacious,
ravenous, selfish,
thirsty, voracious,
worldly
greedyguts: pig
green: common,
envious, fresh,
ignorant, immature,

inexperienced, lush,
mere, naive, raw,
simple, tender,
unripe, unsuspecting,
young
greenery: grass
greenhorn: beginner,
mark, mug, rabbit
green light: okay,
permission, signal,
word
greenness: tenderness
greet: bid, cry, hail,
kiss, meet, salute,
weep, welcome
greeting: hail, kiss,
reception, regard,
salute, welcome
greetings:
congratulations, hail,
respect
gregarious: outgoing,
sociable
gremlin: bug,
malfunction
grey: dim, foggy,
frosty, livid, mousy,
murky, overcast
greybeard: gaffer
grid: grill, hearth,
lattice, network,
screen
griddle: grate, grid,
grill, rack
gridiron: grill
grief: cross, distress,
misery, mourning,
pain, regret, remorse,
sadness, sorrow, woe
grief-stricken:
lacrimose, miserable,
mournful
grievance: beef,
bitch, complaint,
grudge, score, wrong
grieve: depress,
distress, regret,
sorrow, suffer, wound
grieved: sad, sorry
grieving: bereaved,
lamentation,
mourning
grievous: bitter, hard,
sad, sore, sorrowful
grievously: seriously
grill: cooker, gate,
grate, grid,
interrogate, pump,
question, quiz,
screen, toast
grille: grate, lattice,
network, rack
grilse: peal
grim: austere, bad,
dark, deadly, difficult,
dire, dour, fearful,

forbidding, frightful,
funereal, gaunt,
ghastly, grave,
gruesome, hard,
harsh, horrible,
morbid, nerve-
racking, relentless,
severe, stern
grimace: face, mop,
mouth, pout, scowl
grimalkin: cat
grime: dirt, filth
grimness: austerity,
gravity
grimy: black, dingy,
dirty, dusty, filthy
grin: beam
grind: bite, chew,
creak, crumble,
crush, grate, grit,
mill, mince, powder,
pulp, pulverize, rasp,
routine, scrape,
struggle, wear, whet
grinder: mill
grinding: creak,
gruelling, laborious,
oppressive,
punishing, rasp,
severe, smiling
grip: bite, catch,
clamp, clasp, cling,
clutch, fastener,
footing, grab, grasp,
handle, hold, hug,
involve, nip,
purchase, restraint,
retain, ride, snap,
snatch, spellbind,
squeeze, take,
tenacity, traction
gripe: beef, grievance,
kick, moan, pang,
qualm, whine
gripes: hump, nausea
gripped: obsessed,
rapt
gripping: compelling,
interesting, nerve-
racking, tenacious
grisly: atrocious,
gruesome
grist: powder
gristle: cartilage, flesh
grit: backbone,
courage, daring, dust,
fortitude, grind,
nerve, pluck, spirit,
stamina
gritty: daring, dusty
grizzle: whine
grizzly: bear
groan: complain,
creak, moan
groceries: produce
groggy: dazed, silly

groin: crutch
groom: comb, dress,
prepare, prime
grooming: toilet
groove: channel,
crease, flute, gutter,
hollow, line, nick, rut,
slide, slot
grope: cuddle, feel,
flounder, fondle,
handle, manhandle,
maul, molest, paw
gross: bawdy, boorish,
brutal, deformed,
foul, glaring,
ignorant, immodest,
low, lump, nasty,
obese, obscene,
overweight, rank,
rude, scurrilous,
turgid, uncouth
grossness: obscenity
grotesque: bizarre,
hideous, monstrous,
quaint, weird
grotto: cave
grotty: fleabitten
grouch: malcontent
grouchy: querulous
ground: base, bottom,
conductor, dust,
floor, found, land,
patch, pitch, reason,
refrain, root, score,
site, soil, terrain
grounding: base,
basis, foundation
groundless: baseless,
idle, needless,
unfounded
grounds: basis, call,
cause, dregs,
justification, land,
lees, ooze, park,
premises,
presumption,
property, rationale,
reason, residue,
sediment
groundwork: basis,
preliminary,
preparation
group: assembly,
association, band,
batch, block, body
bunch, bundle, cell,
circle, clan, class,
clique, club, cluster,
collection, company,
contingent, crowd,
dispose, faction,
family, flock, gang,
gather, grade, knot,
league, lot, lump,
marshal, mob,
module, organization,

organize, outfit, pack,
party, place, range,
rank, ring, school,
sect, section, set,
social, society,
species, squad, unit
grouped: assorted
grouping: assortment,
basket, battery,
category,
distribution,
formation, order,
organization, party
grouse: bitch, croak,
growl, moan, whine
grove: wood, woods
grovel: cower, crawl,
creep, kowtow
grovelling: servile,
slavish, slimy
grow: boom, cultivate,
develop, evolve,
flourish, gain, gather,
germinate, get,
improve, increase,
mount, progress,
proliferate, raise, rear,
rise, spring, sprout,
wax
grower: farmer
growing: gardening,
young
growl: complain, snarl
grown: cultivated
grown-up: big,
mature
growth: boom, build-
up, cancer, culture,
development,
enlargement,
evolution, gain,
improvement,
increase, lump,
nodule, progress,
tumour
groyne: jetty, pier
grub: food, meat
grubby: dirty, dusty,
filthy, fleabitten
grudge: feud, resent,
resentment, score,
spite
grudging: covetous,
discontent, envious,
jealous, niggardly,
petty, reluctant,
small, sour
gruelling: killing,
punishing, uphill
gruesome: atrocious,
ghastly, grim, grisly,
hideous, horrible,
macabre, monstrous,
morbid
gruff: coarse, hoarse,
rough, rugged, short,

surly
gruffly: roughly
grumble: beef,
complain, complaint,
croak, growl, kick,
moan, roll, snarl,
whine
grumbler:
malcontent
grumpy:
cantankerous, cross,
ill-humoured,
liverish, peevish,
prickly
grunt: croak
guano: dung
guarantee: assurance,
bail, bond, certify,
commitment, cover,
earnest, ensure,
finance, hedge,
indemnity, insurance,
pledge, secure,
security, sponsor,
underwrite, warrant,
word
guaranteed: assured,
foolproof, sure
guarantor: principal,
sponsor
guard: attend,
attendant, custodian,
defence, defend,
guardian, hug, keep,
keeper, look after,
lookout, muzzle, pad,
patrol, police,
protection, save,
screen, sentry,
shelter, shield, tend,
ward, warder, watch
guarded: cag(e)y,
cautious,
circumspect, discreet,
noncommittal, safe,
uncommunicative,
wary, watchful
guardedly: warily
guardian: custodian,
keeper, parent,
patron, saviour,
warden
guardianship: care,
custody, keeping,
patronage, protection,
ward
guarding: defensive
guerrilla: insurgent,
partisan,
guess: assume,
believe, bet, fancy,
figure, gauge, reckon,
shot, supposition,
surmise, suspicion,
theorize, theory,
think, venture

guest: lodger
guest-house: boarding-house, hotel, pension
guests: company, visitors
guffaw: laugh, roar
guffawing: laughter
guidance: control, counsel, direction, lead, leadership, manipulation, supervision
guide: bring, channel, conduct, conductor, direct, fetch, lead, leader, manoeuvre, marshal, master, mould, navigate, pattern, pilot, refer, shepherd, show, standard, steer, sway, take, usher
guidebook: itinerary, manual
guideline: gauge, maxim, parameter, precept, remit, rule
guild: club, fraternity, order, society
guile: artifice, craft, finesse, machination

guileful: foxy, sly
guileless: candid, naive, open, simple
guilelessness: sincerity
guillotine: blade
guilt: blame, fault, remorse
guiltless: immaculate, innocent
guiltlessness: innocence
guilty: ashamed, bad, responsible
guinea pig: subject
guise: camouflage, colour, complexion, form, garb, likeness, pretence, semblance, shape
gulch: dip, valley
gulf: bay
gull: flat, fool, hoax, mark, mug, victim
gullet: swallow
gullibility: innocence
gullible: green, impressionable, innocent, naive, unsuspecting, vulnerable
gully: ditch, ravine

gulp: down, drink, swallow
gulping: guzzling
gum: bond, cement, glue, paste, tack
gumless: used
gummy: sticky
gumption: initiative
gun: piece
gunman: bandit, hood, killer
gunmetal: blue
gurgle: bubble
guru: master, oracle, sage, teacher
gush: burst, flood, flow, jet, pour, run, spurt, stream, surge, well
gushing: demonstrative, garrulous
gust: blast, blow, breeze, burst, draught, flurry, puff, storm, wind
gusto: relish, zest
gusty: blustery, boisterous, stormy, tempestuous
gut: belly, ransack
gutless: cowardly,

spineless, yellow
guts: bottle, courage, daring, fortitude, heart, inside, intestines, nerve, offal, pluck, spirit, works
gutsy: daring
gutter: channel, sensational, trench, valley, waver
guttering: flickering
guttural: thick
guv'ner: dad, father, gaffer
guy: bird, boy, chap, character, effigy, fellow, lad, lover, man, punter
guzzle: bolt, consume, drink, gorge, gulp, overeat, pig, quaff, stuff
gybe: jib
gymnast: athlete
gypsum: plaster
gyrate: revolve, roll, rotate, spin, turn, wheel, whirl
gyration: revolution, roll, spin, turn, whirl
gyratory: rotary

H

haar: drizzle, mist
habit: custom, frock, gown, manner, mannerism, practice, robe, rule, way
habitat: domicile, element, haunt, home, environment
habitation: domicile, habitat, home, occupation, residence
habitual: automatic, common, constant, conventional, everyday, frequent, general, inveterate, mechanical, old, ordinary, regular, ritual, steady, usual, wonted
habitually: generally, ordinarily
habituate: harden
habituating: narcotic
habitué: buyer, customer
hack: chop, cough, cut, journalist, kick, mow, nag, reporter, slash, writer
hackneyed: banal, common, conventional, old, ordinary, routine, stale, stock, tired, unimaginative, worn
Hades: hell
haemorrhage: bleeding
haemorrhoid: pile
haft: grip, handle
hag: bag, harridan, prune
haggard: cadaverous, drawn, gaunt, pinched, worn
haggle: bargain, negotiate
haggling: negotiation
hagiography: legend
hail: barrage, call, flag, greet, greeting, salute, volley
hailing: flagging
hair: bristle, brush, coat, down, pile, tresses

haircutter: barber
hairdresser: barber
hairless: bald
hair-raising: creepy
hairsplitting: footling, nit-picking, pedantic
hair stylist: barber
hairy: critical, dangerous, fluffy, rough, shaggy, woolly
hajji: pilgrim
halcyon: calm, clear, good, serene
hale: fit, hardy, hearty, robust, sound, strong, well
half cut: inebriated,
half-baked: crazy, foolish, mad
half-breed: cross, mongrel
halfhearted: faint, lukewarm, tepid, unenthusiastic
halfpint: midget, runt
halftone: illustration, photograph
halfwit: fool, idiot, natural, oaf
halfwitted: asinine, idiotic, senseless, simple
hall: auditorium, court, hostel, lobby, passage, residence
hallmark: attribute, brand, stamp
halloo: whoop, yell
hallow: bless, honour, venerate
hallowed: divine, holy, sacred, venerable
hallucinating: delirious
hallucination: delusion, vision
halo: glory, nimbus, ring
halt: block, brake, break, cease, check, end, immobilize, interlude, jam, kill, lame, moratorium, paralyse, pause, quit, remit, respite, rest,

stand, stay, stop, tackle, wait, wind up
halting: hesitant, inarticulate, killing
halve: divide, split
halving: division
hammer: bang, beat, drive, knock, monkey, murder, nail, pick, ram, sledge, whip
hammering: drubbing
hammock: cot
hamper: basket, clog, cramp, handicap, keep, restrict, shackle
hampered: limited
hamstring: disable, obstruct
hamstrung: disabled
hand: employee, index, man, operative, palm, pass, paw, reach, script, touch, worker, writing
handbook: guide, manual
handcuff: chain, cuff, irons, shackle
hand down: bequeath
handed down: hereditary
handful: bunch, few, scattering, sprinkling
handicap: burden, detraction, disable, disadvantage, hamper, hindrance, liability, penalize, penalty, restrict, restriction, retard, weight
handicapped: disabled, halt, lame
handiman: painter
hand in: turn in
handiness: convenience, neatness
handing out: distribution
handing over: consignment
handiwork: craft, touch
handkerchief: kerchief, napkin

handle: bar, behave, conduct, crank, crop, feel, field, finger, fondle, grip, guide, knead, knob, lever, manage, manoeuvre, name, operate, pilot, ply, process, regulate, ride, shaft, stand, stock, touch, treat, wield, work
handler: operator
handling: behaviour, distribution, management, manipulation, operation, treatment, usage
handmaiden: maid
hand on: relay, will
hand over: bequeath, cede, commend, commit, concede, consign, delegate, deliver, give, refer, render
handout: bill
handrail: banisters
hands: crew, labour
handset: telephone
handsome: attractive, beautiful, fair, good-looking, lovely
handwriting: hand, script
handy: close, convenient, nearby, neat, skilful, versatile
hang: dangle, drape, execute, hinge, hover, loll, poise, rest, sling, string
hang about: hover, loiter
hang around: mope, linger, mingle, stay
hang-dog: guilty, lugubrious
hanger-on: follower, leech, parasite, satellite
hanging: drape, execution, loose, rope
hangout: haunt
hang-up: fixation, obsession, preoccupation, thing

hanker: pine, wish, yearn
hankering: fancy, wish
haphazard: contingent, irregular, purposeless, random, slapdash, blindly
hapless: luckless, poor, unfortunate, unhappy, wretched
happen: be, befall, chance, come, fall, go, go off, go on, light, occur, pass, result, rise, turn out, work out
happening: development, episode, fact, incident, landmark, occurrence, on
happenstance: luck
happily: gaily, willingly
happiness: bliss, delight, joy, pleasure, rapture, rejoicing
happy: bright, cheerful, comfortable, fairytale, festive, gay, glad, gold(en), halcyon, idyllic, joyful, mellow, merry, opportune, pleased, rejoicing, willing
harangue: diatribe, onslaught, preach, sermon, speak, speech
harass: badger, bait, bedevil, bombard, distress, disturb, gall, hassle, hound, molest, nag, needle, pain, persecute, pester, plague, press, ruffle, scourge, weary, worry
harassed: beleaguered, distracted, hunted
harassment: gall
harbinger: herald, portent, precursor
harbour: basin, bear, cherish, dock, foster, house, lair, lodge, lodgings, port, protect, shelter
hard: austere, bang, bare, difficult, dour, erect, firm, flinty, formidable, harsh, heavy, ill, obdurate, onerous, painful, punishing, rigorous,

rough, rugged, severe, smart, stiff, strenuous, tall, tough, uncomfortable, uphill
hardback: bound
harden: bake, cake, consolidate, erect, fix, impact, knot, polarize, reinforce, season, temper, weather
hardened: habitual, insensitive, inveterate, seasoned, set, stiff
hardening: baking, ossification
hardhearted: callous
hardihood: fortitude, grit, manliness
hardly: barely, ill, just, little, roughly, scarcely
hardness: austerity, firmness
hardship: calamity, care, deprivation, difficulty, disadvantage, discomfort, distress, fire, grievance, imposition, misery, penance, pig, pinch, sorrow, strait(s), trial, woe
hardy: durable, hearty, resilient, robust, rugged, spartan, strong, sturdy, tough
hare: rabbit
harebrained: rash
harlequin: clown
harlot: bitch, prostitute, whore
harlotry: prostitution
harm: cost, damage, disservice, hurt, impair, mischief, offence, spite, spoil, trauma, violence, wound, wrong
harmed: hurt
harmful: bad, baleful, baneful, damaging, ill, mischievous, pernicious, traumatic, venomous, violent, virulent
harmless: edible, innocent, inoffensive, safe
harmonic: vertical
harmonious: compatible, consistent, musical,

peaceful
harmoniously: happily
harmonization: blend
harmonize: blend, coincide, correspond, go, integrate, match, salve
harmony: chorus, communion, composition, concert, correspondence, keeping, peace, solidarity, unity
harness: gear, hitch, tack, yoke
harp: dwell, stress
harpoon: gig
harpy: harridan, nag
harridan: dragon
harrier: runner
harrow: rack, rake
harrowed: drawn
harrowing: excruciating, heart-rending, murderous, nerve-racking, traumatic
harry: badger, bombard, harass, hassle, hound, hunt, molest, scourge, worry
harrying: harassment
harsh: austere, barbaric, bitter, brutal, churlish, cruel, flinty, gaunt, grim, hard, heartless, merciless, obdurate, raucous, raw, relentless, rigid, rigorous, rough, rude, rugged, scabrous, scathing, severe, sharp, stern, stiff, strict, strident, uncharitable, unkind
harshly: hard, roughly, sharply
harshness: asperity, austerity, cruelty
hart: deer
harvest: crop, fruit, gather, haul, lift, produce, reap, till, yield
harvested: cut
hash: marijuana, mash, mess
hashish: hash, marijuana
hasp: buckle
hassle: harass, pester, plague, press,

pressure, scramble, stress, worry
hassling: harassment
haste: hurry, rapidity
hasten: hurry, hustle, leap, quicken, run
hastily: fast, quickly, roughly
hastiness: impatience
hasty: facile, fast, heady, impatient, impetuous, passing, premature, quick, rapid, rash, rough, rush, speedy, unguarded, whirlwind
hat: bonnet, lid
hatch: brew, brood, concoct, line, make up
hatchel: comb
hatchery: nest
hatchet: axe
hate: loathe, loathing
hateful: damnable, execrable, odious
hatred: feud, loathing, phobia
haughtiness: disdain, pride, vanity
haughty: bossy, cavalier, erect, high, lofty, lordly, overbearing, proud, scornful, unbending, vain
haul: carry, cart, drag, draught, draw, heave, hump, loot, manhandle, march, prize, pull, take, transport, warp, winnings
haulage: traction
haunt: frequent, lodge, nest, prey on, resort, retreat, ride
haunted: hunted, intense, obsessed, possessed
haunting: catchy, obsessive, memorable
hauteur: dignity, disdain, frost
have: be, bear, boast, borrow, enjoy, foster, hold, keep, own, possess, receive, take
haven: basin, harbour, lair, oasis, port, refuge, rest, sanctuary, shelter
haversack: knapsack, pack
havoc: carnage,

mayhem, ravage, ruin, shambles, waste
hawk: cough, cry, flog, hustle, market, militant, peddle, push, sell, vend
hawking: traffic
hawkish: militant, warlike
hawser: cable, mooring, rope
hayfield: meadow
hayseed: provincial
hazard: chance, danger, endanger, guess, imperil, jeopardy, lot, lottery, luck, menace, peril, pitfall, risk, speculate, venture, wager
hazardous: awkward, chancy, dangerous, desperate, hairy, precarious, speculative, tight, unsafe, warm
haze: blur, cloud, film
hazel: brown
hazily: roughly, vaguely
haziness: obscurity
hazy: cloudy, dim, faint, filmy, foggy, indistinct, murky, obscure, opaque, rough, uncertain, vague, woolly
head: block, chef, chief, climax, command, director, first, foam, fore, forefront, general, lead, leader, loaf, master, nut, principal, prow, run,
headdress: bonnet
header: dive
heading: category, clause, course, orientation, tack, tendency
headland: bluff, cape, point, prominence, promontory
headlight: lamp
headline: heading, motto
headlong: bang, frantic, impetuous, precipitate, speedy, unreasoning, whirlwind
headmaster: principal
headmistress: principal

headquarters: barracks, base, seat, station
heads: lavatory
headscarf: kerchief
headstone: grave
headstrong: obstinate, rash, stubborn, wayward, wilful
headway: gain, progress
heady: strong
heal: cure, knit, mend, mesh, recover, remedy, repair
healed: whole
healing: medicinal, recovery, therapeutic, therapy
health: condition, constitution, fitness, form, pledge, shape, tone, trim, vigour, welfare
healthful: beneficial, nourishing, nutritious, wholesome
healthier: better
healthy: fit, fresh, good, lusty, red, right, salutary, sound, therapeutic, thriving, vigorous, well, whole
heap: bank, bus, collect, collection, crate, drift, hoard, keep, lavish, load, lot, mass, mound, mountain, pile, shovel
heaped: loaded
heaps: plenty
hear: catch, get, judge, learn, listen, sense
hearing: ear, sound, trial
hearken: hear, listen
hearsay: gossip, news, rumour
heart: base, basis, bosom, bottom, breast, core, focus, hub, interior, kernel, life, marrow, meat, morale, pivot, quick, root
heartache: grief, sorrow, wrench
heartbeat: pulse
heartbreak: grief, woe
heartbroken: miserable, mournful, sorrowful

hearten: comfort, fortify, lighten
heartening: heart-warming, hopeful, invigorating, joyous
heartfelt: cordial, genuine, passionate, profound, real, sincere, wholehearted
hearth: home
heartily: well
heartiness: warmth
heartland: interior
heartless: callous, cold-blooded, cruel, inhuman, merciless, ruthless, unnatural
heartlessness: cruelty
heart-rending: bitter, deplorable, depressing, pathetic, pitiful, plaintive, poignant, sad, tragic
heart-rendingly: piteously
heart-stopping: nerve-racking
heart-to-heart: chat
hearty: bluff, cordial, genial, lusty, robust, sturdy, warm, warm-hearted, wholehearted
heat: excitement, ferment, fever, fire, fume, glow, machine, radiate, rage, temper, toast, warm, warmth
heated: fiery, frayed, hot, impassioned, vociferous
heater: oven
heath: common, forest, green, plain, scrub
heathen: atheist, pagan, savage
heather: heath
heave: cart, catapult, fling, gag, haul, hump, manhandle, pant, pitch, pull, push, put, raise, sling, throw, vomit, wallow, warp, wheeze, wrench
heaven: paradise
heavenly: celestial, divine, glorious, seraphic, Utopian,
heavens: sky
heaviness: weight
heaving: earthquake
heavy: beefy, bulky, close, filling, florid, great, laborious, lethargic, lifeless, lumbering, onerous,

oppressive, overweight, phlegmatic, ponderous, rich, sleepy, stolid, stuffy, weighty
heavyweight: somebody
heavyweights: top brass
hebdomadal: weekly
hebdomadally: weekly
hecatomb: sacrifice
heck: hell
heckle: barrack, comb
heckling: jeering
hectic: feverish, frantic, mad
hectically: madly
hector: barrack, bluster, worry
hedge: bush, enclose, enclosure, fence, flannel, fudge, indemnity, pen, prevaricate, stall
hedonistic: voluptuous
heed: attention, care, caution, concern, hear, listen, mind, note, notice, obey, observe, regard, remark, respect
heedful: attentive, mindful, observant, watchful
heedless: careless, headstrong, inadvertent, oblivious, precipitate, precipitous, rash, reckless, scatterbrained, slovenly
heedlessly: blindly
heedlessness: disregard, negligence, temerity
heel: foot, hook, inclination, incline, lean, list
hefty: burly, heavy, massive, overweight, ponderous, unwieldy, weighty
hegemony: reign
heifer: calf, neat
height: drop, elevation, eminence, fall, level, maximum, mountain, pinnacle, pitch, precipice, prime, prominence, zenith

heighten: augment, intensify, magnify, raise
heinous: infamous, villainous, wicked
heir: offspring
heirloom: legacy
heirs: descendants, offspring, posterity, seed
helical: spiral, winding
heliport: pad
helix: corkscrew, spiral
hell: murder
hellish: dark, diabolical, infernal, satanic
helm: wheel
helmsman: navigator, pilot
help: asset, assist, assistance, back, back up, backing, bale, befriend, benefit, blessing, boost, comfort, consolation, contribute, cooperate, daily, hand, maid, offices, profit, promote, redress, relief, relieve, second, servant, serve, service, speed, use, value
helper: assistant, attendant
helpful: beneficial, constructive, convenient, decent, favourable, friendly, good, good-natured, handy, instrumental, kindly, obliging, positive, productive, salutary, thoughtful, useful, valuable, worthwhile
helpfully: kindly
helpfulness: cooperation, kindliness
helping: portion, quantity, quota, ration, serving, slice
helpless: impotent, incapable, powerless, weak
helplessness: impotence, inability
helpmeet: partner
hem: border, fringe
hem in: hedge, besiege, circumscribe, enclose, rail, restrict,

ring
he-man: macho
hemiplegic: cripple
hemisphere: dome
hemp: grass, marijuana
hen: chicken
hence: away, consequently, therefore, thus
henchman: assistant, follower, mate
henpeck: nag
herald: fanfare, forerunner, knell, precursor, spell
herbage: grass
herd: assembly, crowd, drive, flock, mob, multitude, pack, round up, shepherd, wrangle
herder: driver
herdsman: driver
here: present
hereafter: below, future, henceforth
hereditary: genetic, paternal
heretic: rebel
heretical: disbelieving, sacrilegious
heritage: inheritance, legacy
hermetic: tight
hermit: ascetic
hermitical: solitary
hernia: rupture
herniate: rupture, throttle
hero: conqueror, gallant, god, icon, idol, immortal, legend
heroic: fairytale, fearless, gallant, hardy, intrepid, legendary, selfless, spartan, valiant
heroism: gallantry, valour
heron: crane
hero-worship: idolatry, lionize
hesitancy: diffidence, doubt, indecision
hesitant: disinclined, doubtful, faltering, reluctant, shy
hesitate: falter, pause, stammer, waver
hesitating: sceptical
hesitation: diffidence, indecision, pause, qualm, scruple
heterodoxy: heresy

heterogeneous: complex, conglomerate
hew: chop, curse, cut, hack, jinx
heyday: prime, time, youth
hiatus: blank, chasm, gap, interval, jump, lacuna, omission, parenthesis, respite, vacuum, void, wait
hibernating: asleep, dormant
hick: provincial, yokel
hidden: blind, close, invisible, mysterious, obscure, secret, ulterior, veiled
hide: camouflage, cloak, coat, conceal, cover, disguise, envelop, lurk, obscure, leather, pelt, protect, screen, secrete, shelter, skin, slip, veil
hideaway: den, lair, nest, retreat
hideous: deformed, ghastly, grim, horrible, monstrous, repulsive, shocking, ugly
hideout: den
hiding: cosmetic, rout
hierarch: priest
hierarchical: feudal
hierarchy: order, scale
hieroglyph: character, writing
high: buzz, exalted, great, lofty, merry, tall
highborn: well-bred, brain, cultured, intellectual, noble, princely
higher: better, major
highest: best, chief, first, grand, maximum, prime, ultimate
high-handed: overbearing, peremptory
high jinks: caper, fun, riot
highland: mountainous
highlight: climax, emphasize, feature, publicize, show up, underline
highlighted: offset

highly: very, well
highly-strung: jumpy, sensitive, temperamental, thin-skinned
high-minded: conscientious
high-mindedness: magnanimity
high-pitched: piercing, shrill
high society: fashion, nobility, society
high-spirited: frisky, spirited
hight: climax
highway: road
highwayman: bandit
hijack: commandeer, kidnap, seize, seizure, take
hijacker: bandit
hike: boost, jack, jump, leap, march, ramble, walk
hiker: pedestrian
hilarious: comical, funny, hysterical, killing, priceless, rich, ridiculous, uproarious, zany
hilarity: comedy, glee, laughter, merriment
hill: down, elevation, eminence, height
hillock: knoll, mound, rise
hills: highlands
hilt: handle
hind: back, deer
hinder: check, clog, cramp, depress, disadvantage, far, further, hamper, handcuff, handicap, hold up, impair, inhibit, keep, limit, obstruct, oppose, resist, retard, save, stop, traverse
hindered: limited
hindmost: back, rear
hindquarters: back
hindrance: barrier, bottleneck, check, handicap, hitch, let, liability, obstacle, obstruction, resistance, restraint, rub, stop
hinge: articulate, depend, joint, pivot, rest, turn on
hint: breath, clue, dash, flavour, ghost,

idea, imply,
innuendo, intimate,
key, lead, light, line,
nuance, overtone,
prompt, shade,
shadow, sign, spark,
tip, touch, vestige,
whiff, whisper, wind,
wrinkle
hinted: veiled
hips: beam
hire: charter, fee,
lease, let, let out, pay,
payment, rent, retain,
take, take on,
hired: hack,
mercenary
hirer: contractor
hiring: lease
hirsute: hairy, shaggy
hiss: barrack, catcall,
wheeze
hisses: jeering
hissing: jeering
historic: memorable,
momentous,
monumental,
traditional
historical: temporal
historicity: moment
history: background,
chronicle, form, life,
memoirs, past,
qualification, story
histrionic:
melodramatic
histrionics: drama
hit: assault, bang, bat,
beat, clout, crown,
cut, dawn, dawn on,
dot, drive, get,
hammer, impact,
impinge, knap, knock,
knockout, lash, lay
on, murder, paste,
pull, punch, run into,
sky, slap, smack,
strike, stroke, take,
venue, wallop, zap
hitch: bind, catch,
couple, kink, obstacle,
rope, rub, setback,
snag, thumb
hitched: married
hitchhike: thumb
hitherto: previously,
yet
hitman: killer
hoar: frost
hoard: bank, collect,
collection, conserve,
garner, gather, heap,
husband, lay in, mine,
pile, reserve, save,
stock, store, treasury
hoarder: miser,

gnome
hoarse: raucous,
rusty, thick
hoarseness: cough
hoary: elderly, frosty,
grey
hoax: bluff, cheat,
deceive, deception,
fraud, have,
imposition, jest, kid,
sham, shave, spoof
hob: cooker, fire, oven
hobble: limp, shackle
hobbling: lame
hobby: interest,
pastime, pursuit,
thing
hobbyhorse:
preoccupation
hobnob: mingle
hobo: vagrant
hock: pawn
hocus-pocus: magic
hodgepodge: jumble
hoe: dig, rake
hog: pig
hogan: hut
hogshead: barrel
hogwash: rot
hoi polloi: mob,
rabble
hoist: boost, bring up,
crane, fly, heave, jack,
lift, pick up, raise,
warp, weigh
hoisting: lift
hoity-toity: snobbish,
uppish
hold: bear, believe,
bolster, brandish,
bulk, clasp, clip,
contain, contend,
embrace, enclose, fall,
grasp, grip, handle,
hang, harbour, have,
hug, impound,
influence, involve,
keep, lever, lock,
maintain, own, peg,
possess, possession,
purchase, reckon,
regard, rein, reserve,
restraint, save,
squeeze, tackle, take,
think, touch, wield
holder: bearer, case,
clip, container
holding: caretaker
holdings: asset, estate,
property, resources
hole: bore, breach,
break, burrow, cavity,
crater, den, dive, fix,
gap, hollow, hovel,
jam, lacuna, leak,
opening, orifice, pit,

plight, pocket, pot,
puncture, rent, rip,
scrape, tunnel, well
holed: burst, leaky
holiday: carnival,
festive, leave, leisure,
recess
holiness: piety,
sanctity
holler: bawl, bellow,
cry, scream, shout,
whoop, yell
hollow: artificial, cave,
cavernous, cavity,
chamber, chasm,
depression, dip, hole,
lacuna, low,
meaningless, niche,
pan, pocket, scoop,
scrape, vain, valley,
well
hollowness: vanity
holocaust: carnage
holy: devout, divine,
godly, monastic,
pious, sacred,
scriptural
homage: court, duty,
glory, honour,
incense, praise,
worship
home: base, civil,
domicile, habitat,
headquarters, hearth,
house, household,
interior, internal, lair,
nest, place, residence
homecoming: return
homeless: itinerant,
needy
homely: comfortable,
cosy, domestic, plain,
rustic, simple, snug
homestead: farm
homesteader: farmer
homework:
preparation
homicide:
assassination, killing,
murder
homily: oration,
reading, sermon, tract
homoerotic: gay,
homosexual
homogeneity:
density, diffusion,
integrity, temper,
unity
homogeneous:
integral, monolithic,
unbroken, uniform
homosexual: bent,
gay, lesbian, queer,
queen
homspun: coarse
homunculus: dwarf,

midget, pygmy
hone: grind, whet
honed: keen
honest: direct, fair,
frank, genuine,
honourable, just, law-
abiding, moral, open,
reasonable, reputable,
respectable, savoury,
simple, sincere,
square, straight,
upright, white
honestly: directly,
fairly, frankly, right,
straight, truly
honesty: honour,
integrity, justice,
morality
honeycomb:
perforate
honk: blast, quack,
whiff
honorarium: bonus,
testimonial
honorary: unpaid,
voluntary
honour: celebrate,
character,
commemorate,
compliment, credit,
degree, dignify,
dignity, diploma,
distinction, glorify,
glory, grace, hail,
homage, honesty,
integrity, keep,
kudos, lustre,
morality, nobility,
ornament, pay,
praise, pride,
principle, recognize,
respect, revere,
reward, right, salute,
venerate, worship
honourable:
chivalrous,
conscientious, good,
honest, just, moral,
noble, reputable,
right, upright,
virtuous, worthy
honoured: glorious,
proud, venerable
honouring:
celebration
hoo-ha: hype
hooch: drink
hood: gangster,
mantle, muffle
hoodlum: gangster,
hood, ruffian
hoodoo: jinx
hoodwink: cheat, fool,
hoax, kid, take in
hooey: bunk
hoof: foot, kick

hook: barb, catch, clasp, crook, crowbar, fastener, fish, gaff, peg, pick, probe, tab
hooked: crooked, curved
hooker: prostitute, whore
hooligan: barbarian, insurgent, ruffian, yob
hoop: bangle, link, loop, ring
hooray: whoop
hoosegow: jail
hoot: barrack, blast, blow, laugh, roar, scream, ululate, whoop
hooter: horn, nose
hooting: jeering
hoover: vacuum
hop: dance, jump, leap, skip, spring
hope: aspire, desire, dream, look, wish
hopeful: auspicious, buoyant, expectant, idealistic, optimistic, promising, rosy, sanguine, unrealistic, wishful, wistful
hopeless: black, desperate, forlorn, futile, pathetic, terrible, unavailing, wretched
hopelessly: desperately, impossible
hopelessness: depression, despair, gloom, impracticality, pessimism,
horde: cloud, concentration, crew, herd, host, legion, mass, mob, multitude
hordes: millions
horizontal: flat, level, prone, prostrate, straight
horizontality: trim
horn: hooter, magazine, nail, trumpet
horoscope: fate
horrendous: fearful, frightening, ghastly
horrible: awful, frightful, ghastly, grim, grisly, gruesome, hideous, monstrous, obscene, ugly, unpleasant
horrid: obnoxious,

odious, revolting
horrific: atrocious, dire, grisly, gruesome, nerve-racking
horrified: overcome
horrify: nauseate, scandalize, terrify
horrifying: hair-raising, sensational, terrible
horror: atrocity, enormity, fear, monstrosity, phobia
horse: hack, mount, nag
horseplay: fun, mischief, slapstick
horsepower: soup
horses: stock
horticulture: gardening
hose: irrigate, line, pipe, scour, water
hospice: hotel, inn, pub
hospitality: invitation, kindness, welcome
host: conductor, congregation, crowd, horde, landlord, legion, load, lot, mass, mob, multitude, proprietor, sea
hostage: captive
hostel: boarding-house, hotel, inn
hostelry: inn, local, pub
hostess: conductor
hostile: baleful, bitter, black, chilly, hard, icy, ill, inhospitable, malignant, opposing, quarrelsome, unfavourable, unfriendly, venomous, virulent, warlike
hostilities: war
hostility: aversion, conflict, disaffection, feud, friction, gall, ill feeling, opposition, rancour, stick, war
hosts: millions, score
hot: feverish, fierce, fiery, flaming, lecherous, live, passionate, peppery, sensitive, soup, strong, warm
hotbed: nest
hotchpotch: hash,

jumble, medley
hotel: boarding-house
hotfoot: run
hound: badger, chase, dog, harass, hassle, hunt, molest, persecute, pursue
hounded: dogged
hounding: harassment
hour: time
house: attendance, audience, brothel, building, clan, company, cover, domestic, domicile, dynasty, family, lodge, place, put up, quarter
houseboat: barge
housebreaker: burglar, thief
housebreaking: burglary
household: domestic, family, home, ordinary, people, residence
housekeeper: woman
housemaid: maid
houseman: doctor
housing: pod
hovel: cabin, shack
hover: drift, flickering, float, flutter, fly, hang, loom, poise, soar
hovering: impending
however: but, notwithstanding, still, though, yet
howl: barrack, bawl, bay, bellow, bewail, gale, outcry, roar, shriek, sob, ululate, wail, yell
howler: blunder, gaffe, mistake
howling: wild
hoyden: minx
hoydenish: girlish
hub: centre, focus, heart, key, pivot, wheel
hubbub: disturbance, noise, pandemonium, racket, storm
hubby: husband
hubristic: overconfident
huddle: crowd
hue: colour, complexion, shade, tint, tone
huff: pet
hug: caress, clasp, clinch, crush, cuddle,

embrace, endearment, gather, lock, press, squeeze
huge: big, fat, giant, immense, jumbo, large, massive, mighty, monolithic, monster, monstrous, monumental, mountainous, stupendous, vast
hugely: mightily
hugeness: size
huggable: cuddly
hulk: derelict, remains, wreck, wreckage
hulking: beefy, big, bulky, burly, gross, lumbering, massive, meaty, stout
hull: bottom, shell
hullabaloo: commotion, hubbub, outcry, racket, uproar
hum: buzz, drone, sing
human: body, fallible, life, man, mortal, mundane
humane: benevolent, charitable, civilized, gentle, good, kind, kindly, merciful
humanitarian: kind, kindly, liberal
humanitarianism: kindliness, kindness
humanity: compassion, flesh, kindliness, kindness, man, mercy, society, world
humankind: flesh, man, world
humans: flesh
humble: base, conquer, deflate, low, lower, lowly, mean, meek, menial, modest, obscure, ordinary, poor, puncture, reduce, reverent, self-effacing, shame, small, snub, wither
humbled: ashamed
humbly: low
humbug: bunk, cant, claptrap, fudge, sham, spoof, stuff
humdrum: boring, common, monotonous, mundane, ordinary, routine

humid: damp, moist, muggy, sticky, watery, wet
humidity: damp, moisture, wet
humiliate: chagrin, crush, degrade, disgrace, humble, lower, mortify, ridicule, shame, snub, squash, wither
humiliating: ignominious, shameful, undignified, withering
humiliation: chagrin, disgrace, embarrassment, indignity, mortification, shame
humility: modesty
humming: murmuring
hummock: hill, knoll, prominence
humorist: joker, wag, wit
humorous: funny, jocular, playful, rich, salty, twinkling
humour: baby, comedy, content, fancy, fit, gratify, indulge, jolly, mood, pander to, please, spirit, temper, temperament, vein, whim, wit
humouring: jolly
hump: haul, hog, hunch, knoll
humped: curved
humus: compost
hunch: bow, hump, intuition, slump, stoop
hunched: bent,

crooked, misshapen
hundred: ward
hundreds: score
hunger: craving, desire, long, longing, lust, pant, pine, want, yearn, yearning
hungover: fragile, jagged
hungry: avid, longing, ravenous, starving, thirsty, voracious,
hunk: chunk, lump
hunker: hunch
hunt: chase, comb, course, flush, go through, grub, gun, hawk, look up, persecute, prey on, pursue, pursuit, quest, scour, scout, search, seek, track
hunted: defensive, quarry
hunter: predator, wolf
hurdle: barrier, difficulty, fence, flight, hazard, hindrance, jump, obstacle, panel
hurl: bowl, cast, catapult, dash, fling, heave, loose, precipitate, project, put, send, shoot, slam, sling, throw
hurling: sling
hurly-burly: bedlam, bustle, unrest, whirl
hurrah: whoop
hurricane: gale, storm, tempest
hurried: fast, flustered, precipitous, pushed, quick, rush
hurriedly: fast, quickly
hurry: breeze, bundle,

bustle, gallop, hasten, hustle, leap, push, run, rush, speed, whisk
hurrying: haste
hurt: burn, damage, grieve, harm, ill, incapacitated, lesion, maltreat, mischief, offence, pain, punish, smart, sore, spite, stung, torture, trauma, upset, wound
hurtful: harmful, sharp, traumatic
hurting: painful
hurtle: barrel, bomb, career, catapult, flee, plunge, race, shoot, zap, zip
husband: garner, groom, man, mate, partner, save
husbandry: prudence
hush: calm, lull, mute, peace, quiet, quieten, shut up, silence, stifle, still
hushed: low, noiseless, peaceful, quiet, silent, still
husk: bark, pod, rind, shell, skin, wreck, wreckage
huskiness: cough
husky: hoarse, raucous, robust, rough, rugged, thick
hussy: minx
hustle: bundle, compel, haste, hum, hurry, jostle, quicken
hustler: prostitute, whore
hut: booth, box, cabin, chalet, cot, cottage, hovel, lodge, shack, shed

hutch: pen
hybrid: cross, mixed, mongrel
hybridize: cross
hydrophobic: rabid
hygienic: clean, healthy, sanitary, wholesome
hymn: glorify, lay, psalm, song
hype: fanfare, market, plug, propaganda, publicize, puff
hypnotic: magnetic, narcotic, sedative, sleepy, soporific
hypnotize: dazzle, entrance, mesmerize
hypocrisy: cant, insincerity
hypocritical: pious, sanctimonious
hypothermia: exposure
hypothesis: guess, idea, premise, presumption, reasoning, theory, thesis
hypothesize: guess, postulate, speculate, theorize
hypothetical: ideal, imaginary, nonexistent, notional, possible, pure, speculative, tentative
hysteria: panic
hysterical: crazy, delirious, mad, maladjusted, neurotic, paranoid, raving, uproarious, wild
hysterically: madly
hythe: jetty, quay

I

Iberian: peninsular
ice: freeze, hail
iceberg: automaton
icefall: avalanche
iciness: frigidity
icing: filling
icon: idol, freezing, frigid, frosty, glacial, glassy, wintry
idea: assumption, baby, conceit, conception, fancy, feeling, gist, image, impression, intention, muse, notion, plan, point, purport, purpose, sound, supposition, theme, thing, view, vision
ideal: cause, classic, idyllic, model, moral, optimum, paragon, perfect, perfection, right, ripe, Utopian
idealism: impracticality
idealistic: exalted, great, impractical, romantic, unrealistic, unworldly, Utopian
ideals: morality, standard
ideas: opinion
identical: homogeneous, like, same, uniform, very
identicality: identity
identically: equally
identification: association, diagnosis, pass
identified: marked, named
identify: associate, characterize, detect, finger, key, know, label, name, place, recognize, spot, stamp, tell
identity: parity, personality
ideograms: writing
ideology: philosophy
idiocy: folly, lunacy
idiom: jargon, language, phraseology, speech,

usage
idiomatic: fluent, informal
idiosyncracy: feature, characteristic, distinction, eccentricity, figure of speech, habit, mannerism, oddity, property, way
idiosyncratic: characteristic, individual, peculiar, quirky, temperamental, unique
idiot: fool, jackass, nincompoop, lunatic, wally, zombie
idiotic: crazy, fatuous, foolish, insane, lunatic, mad, mindless, senseless, silly, zany
idiotically: madly
idle: fallow, free, inactive, ineffectual, inert, lackadaisical, lazy, light, loaf, loiter, lounge, otiose, rest, slack, stagnate, unemployed, vacant, vain
idleness: inertia, laziness, sloth
idler: laggard, layabout, wastrel
idol: deity, fetish, god, hero, icon, queen, star
idolize: lionize, love, worship
idolizer: lover
idyllic: romantic
if: once, proviso, so, though
iffy: unpredictable
ignite: burn, detonate, fire, inflame, kindle, light, set fire to, torch, turn on,
ignited: live
ignoble: base, low, lowly, menial, unworthy, vulgar, worthless
ignominious: contemptible,

disgraceful, humiliating, shameful
ignominy: disgrace, shame
ignoramus: dunce, philistine, silly
ignorance: innocence
ignorant: dark, gross, illiterate, raw
ignore: cut, discount, disregard, leave out, neglect, overlook, pass, pass over, pass up, think nothing of
ilk: kind, order, sort
ill: bad, fragile, green, harm, invalid, liverish, low, morbid, off colour, poorly, queer, rough, seedy, sick, unwell
ill-advised: foolish, imprudent, irresponsible, misguided, mistaken, rash, unwise
ill-bred: gauche, low, vulgar
ill-considered: premature, short-sighted, unprepared
ill-defined: general, indistinct, loose, vague
illegal: criminal, dirty, foul, illegitimate, prohibited, unauthorized, wrong
illegality: foul
illegible: unintelligible
illegitimate: bastard
ill-fated: doomed, luckless, marked, poor
ill-favoured: plain, ugly
ill-fitting: uncomfortable
ill-founded: false
ill-humoured: cantankerous, cross, moody, petulant
illiberal: bigoted, intolerant, narrow-minded

illiberality: intolerance
illicit: illegal, wrong
illimitable: infinite
illiterate: barbarian
ill-judged: impolitic, indiscreet, irresponsible, mistaken, unwise
ill-mannered: impolite, rough, rude
ill-natured: disagreeable, surly
illness: complaint, disease, indisposition, sickness
illogical: illegitimate, irrational, unfounded, unreasonable
ill-omened: inauspicious
ill-starred: disastrous, luckless, tragic
ill-tempered: churlish, peevish, perverse, quarrelsome, sour
ill-timed: inopportune, premature
ill-treat: harm, maltreat, persecute, wrong
illuminate: glorify, inform, kindle, light, lighten
illumination: light, torch
illumine: light
ill-use: harm, wrong
illusion: dream, hallucination, myth, vision
illusionist: magician
illusory: deceptive, fantastic, imaginary, meretricious, nonexistent, shadowy, unreal, Utopian
illustrate: demonstrate, explain, mark, picture, portray, represent
illustrated: pictorial
illustration:

demonstration, drawing, explanation, figure, instance, picture, plate, sample
illustrative: demonstrative, sample
illustrious: bright, brilliant, distinguished, famous, glorious, great, historic, legendary, lofty, noted, prestigious, shining, splendid
illustriousness: eminence, fame, glory, lustre, nobility, renown
illwish: jinx
image: face, fantasy, god, icon, idol, likeness, mirror, picture, semblance, shadow, vision
imaginable: possible
imaginary: fanciful, fictitious, ideal, illusory, mythical, nonexistent, notional, romantic, unreal
imagination: fancy, fantasy, fiction, invention, mind, sense, vision
imaginative: bright, creative, fanciful, inventive, lyrical, original, pregnant, resourceful
imaginatively: originally
imagine: assume, believe, conceive, dream, fancy, figure, guess, invent, reckon, say, scheme, suppose, surmise, think, visualize
imagined: fictitious, imaginary, nonexistent
imbecile: dunce, fatuous, fool, foolish, idiot, jackass, lunatic, oaf, simpleton, unintelligent, wally, zombie
imbecilic: lunatic
imbecility: density, idiocy, lunacy, stupidity
imbibe: assimilate, carouse, drink, quaff, tipple
imbroglio: quagmire,

tangle
imbue: saturate
imitate: borrow, copy, follow, impersonate, mimic, parrot, reflect, reproduce, sham, take off
imitating: simulated
imitation: bogus, copy, dummy, fake, false, mock, model, phoney, replica, reproduction, sham, spurious
imitative: derivative, slavish
imitator: mimic, parrot
immaculate: clean, faultless, innocent, pure, unimpeachable, virgin, white
immaterial: inadmissible, irrelevant, remote, spiritual, unreal
immature: babyish, childish, green, inexperienced, jejune, juvenile, minor, premature, puerile, raw, tender, unripe, young
immaturity: childhood, tenderness, youth
immeasurable: imponderable, inestimable, infinite, priceless, vast
immediacy: presence
immediate: direct, instant, intimate, present, prompt, quick, snap, speedy
immediate: unhesitating
immediately: directly, forthwith, hot, now, outright, promptly, quick, quickly, readily, right, straight, straight away
immense: big, bulky, bumper, giant, great, huge, incalculable, infinite, jumbo, large, massive, mighty, monster, monstrous, monumental, mountainous, prodigious, profound, vast
immensely: mightily

immensity: bulk, enormity, magnitude, size
immerse: baptize, bath, bathe, bury, cover, dip, drown, duck, flood, inundate, overflow, plunge, soak, steep
immersed: deep, sunken
immersion: baptism, bath, dip, flood, plunge
immigrant: foreigner, import
imminent: close, coming, impending, near
immobile: becalmed, inactive, inert, motionless, sedentary, static
immobility: firmness, inertia, paralysis
immobilization: numbness
immobilize: paralyze, pin
immobilized: incapacitated, numb
immoderate: extravagant, fulsome, lavish, outrageous, prodigal, profuse, unconscionable, unreasonable
immoderation: licence, overindulgence
immodest: brazen, conceited, indelicate, racy, shameless, unseemly
immolate: sacrifice
immolation: sacrifice
immoral: bad, degenerate, dissolute, evil, libertine, loose, obscene, perverse, promiscuous, rotten, sinful, unethical, unholy, unmentionable, vile, wicked, wrong
immorality: dissolution, evil, licentiousness, misconduct, obscenity, vice
immorally: badly
immortal: celestial, classic, deity, indestructible, timeless
immortalize:

perpetuate
immovable: firm, obstinate, persistent, secure
immunity: exemption, franchise, impunity, indemnity, liberty, licence, safety
immunization: vaccination
immunize: inject
immure: cage, imprison, jail, wall
immutable: permanent
imp: elf, knave, monkey, sprite
impact: bind, bump, concussion, effect, hit, impression, percussion, punch, shock, splash, weight
impair: blemish, cloud, cripple, damage, deface, harm, hurt, mar, queer, reduce, shake, shatter, spoil
impaired: hurt, imperfect, incapacitated, rusty, shattered
impairing: harmful
impairment: damage, deterioration, handicap, harm, loss, trauma
impale: break, fork, gore, hook, knife, skewer, spike
impart: give, lend, provide, publish, relate, reveal, teach, transmit
impartial: candid, disinterested, fair, independent, judicial, just, neutral, nonaligned, objective, open
impartiality: detachment, independence, justice
impartially: equally, fairly
impassable: impenetrable
impasse: cul-de-sac, halt, quandary
impassioned: fervent, feverish, flaming, intense, keen, lyrical, tempestuous, zealous
impassive: blank, calm, listless,

phlegmatic, stoical,
thick-skinned,
undemonstrative,
unimpressed
impassivity: frigidity
impatience:
intolerance,
temperament
impatient: cross,
hasty, intolerant,
temperamental
impeach: charge,
denounce
impeachment:
indictment
impeccable: faultless,
perfect,
unimpeachable
impecunious: hard
up, needy, penniless,
poverty-stricken
impede: block, check,
clog, cross,
disadvantage,
hamper, handcuff,
handicap, keep,
obstruct, restrict,
retard, shackle, stop
impediment: bar,
barrier, block,
bottleneck, check,
clog, detraction,
difficulty,
disadvantage,
handicap, hindrance,
hurdle, let, liability,
obstacle, obstruction,
preventive,
resistance, rub, stop
impedimenta: kit,
luggage
impel: carry, compel,
drive, hustle, induce,
oblige, propel, push,
spur
impend: brew, loom
impending: close,
coming, near
impenetrable: close,
impassable,
impregnable, thick
impenitent:
unrepentant
imperative:
authoritative,
compelling,
compulsory, instant,
must, necessary,
obligatory,
overpowering,
prerequisite,
pressing, urgent
imperceptible:
gentle, invisible,
negligible
imperfect: bad,

defective, faulty,
immature, inchoate,
lame, marked,
unfaithful, unfinished
imperfection:
blemish, defect, fault,
frailty, vice
imperfectly: badly,
roughly
imperial: majestic
imperil: endanger,
expose, hazard, risk,
stake, venture
imperious:
authoritative, bossy,
dictatorial, dogmatic,
imperative, lordly,
magisterial,
peremptory,
supercilious
imperishable:
immortal,
indestructible,
perennial, permanent,
timeless
impermanent:
mortal, mutable,
temporary
impermeable:
impenetrable,
impervious
impermissible:
unacceptable
impersonal:
disinterested,
mechanical, objective
impersonate: imitate,
mimic, play
impersonation:
imitation
impersonator: mimic
impertinence:
discourtesy,
insolence, liberty, lip,
sauce
impertinent: cool,
disrespectful,
flippant, irreverent,
rude, saucy, smart
imperturbability:
nonchalance
imperturbable:
calm, nonchalant,
philosophical, placid,
serene, stoical
impervious:
insensitive, tight
impetuosity: haste,
impatience,
indiscretion
impetuous:
foolhardy, hasty,
headstrong, heady,
hot, impatient,
precipitate,
precipitous, rash,

whirlwind
impetus: bang, drift,
impulse, momentum,
spur, weight
impiety: blasphemy,
heresy
impinge: impact,
infringe
impious: irreverent,
profane, wicked
impish: knavish,
mischievous, playful,
sly, wicked
implacable: cruel,
deadly, grim, hard,
merciless, obdurate,
relentless
implant: bed, fix,
graft, insert, lodge,
root, sow
implausible:
fantastic, far-fetched,
flimsy, improbable,
remote, tall, unlikely,
unrealistic
implement: carry
out, dispense,
enforce, execute,
gadget, instrument,
invoke, material,
organ, thing, work
implementation:
effect, execution
implements: gear, kit
implicate:
compromise, involve
implicated:
concerned, involved
implicating:
damning,
incriminatory
implication:
connotation, drift,
hint, import,
indication, innuendo,
meaning, overtone,
sense, significance
implicit: roundabout,
understood, unspoken
implied: oblique,
silent, subtle,
understood,
unspoken, veiled
implode: burst
implore: beg,
conjure, plead, pray,
press, seek, solicit,
urge
imploring: urgent
imply: hint, indicate,
intimate, involve,
mean, say, signify,
spell, suggest
impolite: improper,
rough, tactless,
uncouth, ungracious

impolitely: roughly
impoliteness:
discourtesy
impolitic: imprudent,
indiscreet,
unguarded, unwise
imponderable:
philosophical
import: bearing, idea,
meaning, message,
purport, sense,
significance,
substance
importance: concern,
consequence, dignity,
effect, eminence,
gravity, import,
interest, magnitude,
matter, moment,
position, prestige,
prominence,
significance, thing,
weight, worth
important: big,
capital, cardinal,
effective, high,
historic, influential,
leading, main, major,
material, memorable,
momentous,
noteworthy,
portentous, pressing,
prominent, public,
salient, serious,
significant, special,
valuable, weighty
imported: foreign
importunate:
demanding, insistent,
intrusive, obtrusive,
urgent
importune: badger,
besiege, buttonhole,
conjure, molest, ply,
solicit, worry
importunity:
urgency
impose: clamp,
dictate, enforce, lay,
levy, prescribe,
quarter, set
imposing: august,
awesome, dignified,
gallant, grand,
grandiose,
impressive,
magnificent, majestic,
monolithic, palatial,
solemn, sonorous,
stately
imposition: levy
impossibility:
impracticality
impossible: hopeless,
inconceivable,
insufferable,

unattainable
impost: duty, levy, tax
impostor: bastard, charlatan, cheat, fake, fraud, hypocrite, liar, phoney, quack, sham, swindler
imposture: deception, disguise, display, fiction, hoax, lying, masquerade
impotence: inability
impotent: barren, helpless, powerless, prostrate, weak
impound: cage, confiscate, seize
impoverish: bankrupt, bust, reduce, ruin
impoverished: bankrupt, bust, destitute, hard up, miserable, penniless, poor, poverty-stricken
impracticable: hopeless, idealistic, impossible, impractical, unrealistic, wild
impractical: bookish, dreamy, idealistic, unrealistic, Utopian
imprecate: swear
imprecation: oath, swearing
imprecise: general, inaccurate, indefinite, lax, loose, nebulous
impregnability: safety
impregnable: safe, secure, tenable
impregnate: fertilize, saturate
impress: penetrate, score, stamp, touch
impression: belief, conception, edition, feeling, hunch, idea, impact, indent, issue, notion, opinion, perception, picture, print, sensation, sense, sound, suspicion, view
impressionable: pliable, sensitive, susceptible
impressionist: mimic
impressions: notes
impressive: awesome, breathtaking, effective, grand,

grandiose, great, memorable, noble, portentous, potent, powerful, prestigious, prodigious, remarkable, spectacular, splendid, stately, striking
imprint: dent, engrave, impress, impression, print, punch, stamp
imprison: commit, convict, hold, jail, jug, nick, shut up
imprisoned: captive
imprisonment: capture, restraint
improbable: far-fetched, farcical, unlikely, unrealistic
impromptu: scratch
improper: coarse, gross, illegitimate, indelicate, obscene, spicy, suggestive, unseemly, wrong
improperly: badly
impropriety: indiscretion, liberty, misconduct
improve: better, boom, boost, cultivate, gain, help, look up, mend, perfect, pick up, profit, progress, rally, recover, rise, work up, up
improved: cultivated, new
improvement: benefit, boom, boost, gain, help, progress, rally, recovery, reform, rise
improvident: imprudent, lavish, spendthrift, wasteful
improvise: contrive, jam
improvised: impromptu, scratch, unprepared
imprudence: indiscretion
imprudent: foolish, impolitic, indiscreet, misguided, mistaken, reckless, short-sighted, silly, tactless, unguarded, unwise
impudence: crust, forwardness, gall, impertinence, insolence, liberty, lip,

nerve, presumption, sauce
impudent: bold, cool, disrespectful, flippant, forward, fresh, immodest, impertinent, impolite, irrepressible, irreverent, pert, presumptuous, rude, saucy, shameless
impulse: excitement, force, impetus, spur, urge, whim
impulsion: propulsion
impulsive: capricious, hasty, heady, impetuous, motive, precipitate, precipitous, premature, rash, unthinking, whimsical, whirlwind
impure: base, muddy,
impurities: scum
impurity: dirt
imputation: brand
impute: lay, refer
in: current, fashionable, inside, latest, on, popular, through, vogue, within
in abeyance: inactive
inability (to): failure,
inability to be wrong: infallible,
inability: impotence,
in abundance: galore
inaccessible: unattainable
inaccuracy: defect, error, fault, miss, mistake
inaccurate: careless, false, faulty, imprecise, incorrect, misleading, mistaken, unfaithful, untrue, wide, wrong
inaccurately: wide, wrong
inaction: omission
inactive: dead, extinct, fallow, idle, inanimate, inert, lazy, otiose, passive, quiescent, sedentary, slack, slow, sluggish, supine, torpid
inactivity: idleness, inertia, laziness, rest, sloth
inadequacy: defect, deficiency, drought,

impotence, need, poverty
inadequate: awful, bad, feeble, impotent, ineffectual, lacking, lame, lean, limited, low, poor, rotten, scanty, slender, small, thin, unacceptable, unfit, weak
inadequately: badly, poorly
in addition: beside, besides, else, moreover
inadmissible: irrelevant, unacceptable
inadvertent: unconscious, unintentional, unthinking
inadvertently: unwittingly
inadvisable: unwise
in agreement: similar
inane: fatuous, lunatic, nonsensical, pointless, silly, vacant,
inanimate: dead, inert, lifeless
inanity: idiocy, nonsense, platitude, vanity
inapplicability: impracticality
inapplicable: impractical, irrelevant
inapposite: improper, inappropriate
inappropriate: unfit, impractical, improper, inadmissible, incongruous, inept, irrelevant, unseemly, wrong
inapt: inappropriate, incongruous, wrong
inarticulate: dumb, incoherent, maundering, unintelligible
inasmuch as: since
inattention: indifference, neglect, negligence
inattentive: blind, forgetful, inadvertent, loose, oblivious, remiss
inattentiveness: preoccupation
inaudible: noiseless, unintelligible

inaugural: beginning, initial, maiden, opening, premier

inaugurate: baptize, begin, found, initiate, install, introduce, launch, open

inauguration: baptism, beginning, birth, introduction, launch, opening, start

inauspicious: ill, ominous, unfortunate, unfriendly, unfavourable

inauspiciously: unfortunately

inborn: inherent, instinctive, native, natural, temperamental

inbred: congenital, native

inbuilt: inherent

incalculable: imponderable, inestimable, priceless

incandescence: light

incandescent: radiant

incantation: sorcery, spell

incapable: helpless, inefficient, powerless, unable

incapacitate: cripple, disable, hamstring, nobble, sabotage

incapacitated: disabled, impotent, powerless

incapacitation: disqualification

incapacity: inability

incarcerate: cage, imprison, jail, jug, shut up

incarcerated: captive

incautious: careless, foolhardy, imprudent, indiscreet, reckless, tactless, unguarded

incendiary: inflammatory, pyromaniac

incense: chafe, inflame, infuriate, outrage, provoke

incensed: furious, livid, mad, maddened, stung, wrathful

incentive: cause, impetus, motivation, motive, reason, spur

inception: conception, genesis, outset

incessant: chronic, constant, continual, nonstop, perennial, perpetual, persistent, relentless, unbroken

incessantly: away, ever, forever, nonstop

inchoate: incipient

incident: circumstance, episode, experience, fact, happening, matter, occurrence, phenomenon, scene, skirmish, thing

incidental: background, casual, chance, mindless, odd, passing, side

incidentally: fortuitously, indirectly

incinerate: burn, cremate

incipient: beginning, inchoate

incise: carve, cut, gash, scratch

incised: cut

incision: cut, gash, laceration, section, slit, stab, wound

incisive: biting, corrosive, crisp, devastating, keen, mordant, penetrating, pointed, pungent

incisors: teeth

incite: cause, kindle, persuade, prod, provoke, push, put up, raise, rouse, spur, stimulate, urge, whip, work up

incitement: fuel

incivility: discourtesy, indignity, insult

inclemency: cold

inclement: unfavourable, unfriendly

inclination: bent, bow, fancy, impulse, leaning, liking, notion, pleasure, slope, stomach, taste, tendency, will, wish

incline: bank, bow, cant, fall, grade, gradient, hill, influence, lean, list, pitch, rake, ramp,

rise, slant, slope, stoop, sway, swerve, tip

inclined: liable, oblique, predisposed, prepared, prone, ready, susceptible

include: comprise, consist of, contain, cover, embrace, enclose, have, involve, take in

included: implicit

inclusive: comprehensive, overall

incoherent: delirious, inarticulate, rambling, unintelligible, wild

income: livelihood, living, means, pay, proceeds, revenue, salary, takings, yield

incomer: outsider

incommode: trouble

incommoding: inconvenience

incomparable: matchless, peerless, rare, unique

incompatible: contradictory, incongruous, inconsistent, opposing, repulsive, unlike

incompetence: inability

incompetent: failure, helpless, hopeless, inadequate, incapable, inefficient, ineligible, ineffectual, unqualified

incompetently: defectively, inadequately, inchoately, incomplete

imperfect: partial, poorly, premature, rough, sketchy, undone, unfinished

incompletely: partly

incompleteness: deficiency

incomprehending: vacant

incomprehensibility: obscurity

incomprehensible: impenetrable, inarticulate, inaudible, inexplicable,

meaningless, mysterious, unaccountable

inconceivable: implausible, imponderable, impossible, unattainable, unheard-of

inconclusive: undecided

incongruity: oddity

incongruous: inappropriate, inconsistent

inconsequential: insignificant, light, lightweight, minor, puny

inconsiderate: tactless, unkind, unthinking

inconsistency: fallacy, hypocrisy, paradox

inconsistent: contradictory, illegitimate, illogical, incompatible, incongruous, patchy, unreasonable

inconsolable: heartbroken, mournful

inconspicuous: invisible

inconstancy: levity

inconstant: capricious, changeable, faithless, fickle, giddy, inconsistent, mutable, restless, uncertain, unpredictable, unreasonable, unsettled, variable, volatile, wayward

incontestable: unanswerable, unquestioned

incontestably: undeniably

incontrovertible: unanswerable, unquestioned

incontrovertibly: undeniably

inconvenience: bother, disadvantage, discomfort, disturb, nuisance, put out, trouble

inconvenient: awkward, inopportune

incorporate:

combine, cover,
include, integrate,
involve, receive
incorporation:
digestion
incorrect: bad, false,
faulty, improper,
inaccurate, invalid,
illegitimate, mistaken,
out, untrue, wrong
incorrectly: badly,
wrong
incorrigible:
incurable, inveterate,
irrepressible,
unrepentant, wicked
incorruptibility:
integrity
incorruptible:
conscientious,
indestructible
increase: augment,
boom, boost, branch,
build, build-up,
climb, development,
double, enlargement,
flourish, fortify, gain,
gather, grow, growth,
improve,
improvement,
intensify, jack, jump,
leap, lengthen,
magnify, mount,
multiply, progress,
proliferate, put on,
raise, rise, spread,
swell, wax, whet
increasing:
progressive
incredible: fantastic,
far-fetched,
implausible,
inconceivable,
marvellous,
miraculous,
preposterous, tall,
unlikely, wonder,
wonderful
incredulity: surprise
incredulous:
disbelieving, sceptical
increment: gain,
increase, rise
incriminate: charge
incriminated:
implicated
incriminating:
damning
incubate: brood,
hatch
inculcate: implant,
teach
incumbency:
occupation, seat
incumbent: occupant
incurable: chronic,

fatal, inveterate,
terminal
incurious:
unconcerned, vacant
incurring: liable
incursion: foray,
invasion, raid, sally
indebted: bankrupt,
obliged, thankful
indebtedness:
liability
indecency: filth,
immorality,
impropriety,
lewdness, nastiness
indecent: bawdy,
blue, broad, dirty,
filthy, foul, fruity,
gross, immodest,
immoral, improper,
indelicate, lewd,
nasty, obscene,
pornographic, racy,
rank, salacious,
suggestive,
unmentionable
indecipherable:
illegible, insoluble,
unintelligible
indecision: doubt,
suspense
indecisive: feeble,
inconclusive, infirm
indecorous:
ignominious,
indelicate,
undignified, unseemly
indecorum: vulgarity
indeed: even, much,
quite, really
indefatigability:
stamina
indefatigable:
dogged, persevering,
persistent, tireless
indefensible:
inexcusable,
untenable
indefinable:
imponderable
indefinite: general,
imprecise, lax, loose,
uncertain, uncertain,
undecided
indelible: binding,
lasting, memorable,
permanent
indelicacy:
coarseness, vulgarity
indelicate: bawdy,
broad, coarse, gross,
immodest, improper,
rough, scabrous,
spicy, tactless,
unseemly, vulgar
in demand:

commercial, popular
indemnify:
compensate, cover,
satisfy, underwrite
indemnity:
compensation, cover,
insurance, restitution
indent: carve, pit,
punch, score
indentation: bay,
bruise, depression,
impression, pit, recess
indented: hollow
independence:
freedom, liberty,
licence, projection,
self-government
independent:
autonomous, free,
private, self-reliant,
separate, unpopular,
voluntary
independently:
unaided
indescribable:
nameless,
unmentionable
indescribably:
unutterably
indestructible:
immortal, indelible,
invincible, permanent
indeterminate:
doubtful, imprecise,
inconclusive,
indefinite, indistinct,
shapeless, uncertain,
vague
index: catalogue, roll,
table
indicate: characterize,
designate, intimate,
mean, nod, read,
record, reflect,
register, show, signal,
signify, specify, spell,
suggest, wave
indicated: marked
indication: clue,
direction, index, line,
manifestation, nod,
sample, sign, signal,
suggestion, symptom,
testimony, token,
vestige
indications: language
indicative:
demonstrative,
expressive,
significant, suggestive
indicator: barometer,
beacon, gauge, index,
key, landmark
indict: charge,
denounce, prosecute,
sue

indicting: damning,
incriminatory
indictment: charge
indifference:
disregard, languor,
neglect, negligence,
nonchalance,
indifferent: blasé,
blind, callous, cold,
cool, dead, deaf, dull,
insensitive,
lackadaisical, listless,
lukewarm, mediocre,
middling, mindless,
moderate, ordinary,
remiss, remote, thick-
skinned,
unconcerned,
unenthusiastic,
ungrateful, unhelpful,
unimpressed,
unrepentant
indigene: savage
indigenous: domestic,
native
indigent: needy,
penniless, poverty-
stricken
indignant: dirty
indignation: offence,
outrage, resentment
indigo: blue
indirect: circuitous,
devious, oblique,
roundabout,
secondary, sidelong
indiscernible:
imperceptible,
indistinct, invisible
indiscreet: careless,
foolish, impolitic,
misguided,
precipitate, rash,
reckless, tactless,
unguarded, unwise
indiscretion: lapse,
slip, stupidity
indiscriminate:
promiscuous,
random, sweeping
indiscriminately:
haphazardly
in disguise: incognito
indispensability:
necessity
indispensable:
fundamental,
imperative, integral,
invaluable, necessary,
prerequisite, vital
indisposed: averse,
disinclined, ill,
incapacitated, poorly,
sick, sickly, unwell,
unwilling
indisposition:

aversion, complaint,
illness, sickness, upset
indisputable: hard,
obvious, patent,
positive, sure,
unanswerable
indisputably:
undeniably
indissoluble:
indestructible
indistinct: dim,
distant, dull, faint,
foggy, grey, light,
muffled, nebulous,
neutral, uncertain,
unclear,
unintelligible, vague,
woolly,
indistinctly: vaguely
indistinguishable:
identical, same
individual: being,
chap, character,
characteristic,
different, distinct,
distinctive, fish, head,
human, man, mortal,
own, party, peculiar,
private, proper,
rarity, single, soul,
special,
temperamental,
unconventional
individuality:
character, distinction,
identity
individualize:
distinguish
individually: each,
particularly, singly
indivisible: prime
indoctrinate:
educate, school
indoctrination:
education
indolence: idleness,
inertia, laziness, sloth
indolent: inactive,
idle, lazy, listless,
otiose, sluggish,
supine, torpid
indomitability:
valour
indomitable: fearless,
invincible, valiant
indoors: inside,
within
indrawn: introverted
indubitably:
undeniably
induce: attract, bring,
cause, draw, get,
impel, influence,
kindle, lead, motivate,
move, persuade,
prompt, provoke,

sway, urge, win
inducement:
attraction, bait, bribe,
cause, incentive,
invitation, lure,
motivation, motive,
persuasion, reason
induct: inaugurate,
initiate, invest, ordain
indulge: baby, gratify,
humour, oblige,
pander to, please,
satisfy, spoil
indulged: pampered
indulgence:
kindliness, kindness,
licence, luxury,
tolerance
indulgent: broad-
minded, easy, fond,
gracious, kind,
kindly, lenient,
liberal, permissive,
tolerant
industrial: mercantile
industrious: busy,
tireless
industriously: hard
industry: business,
diligence, labour,
work
inebriate: drunk,
fuddle
inebriated: drunk,
drunken, high,
loaded, tight
inebriating: heady
inebriety:
intoxication
ineffable: nameless
ineffably: unutterably
ineffective: nugatory,
spineless
ineffectual: feeble,
fruitless, futile,
incapable, powerless,
unavailing, vain, void,
weak, wet, worthless
ineffectualness:
nullity
inefficient: incapable,
shiftless,
unbusinesslike
inelegant: awkward,
gauche, lumbering,
undignified, wooden
ineligibility:
disqualification
ineligible: unfit,
unqualified,
unworthy
inept: awkward,
clumsy, gauche,
impractical,
incapable, inefficient,
tactless, unhappy

ineptitude: stupidity
inequality: injustice
inequitable:
iniquitous, one-sided,
unfair, unsporting
inequity: injustice
ineradicable:
chronic, indelible
inert: dormant,
fallow, inactive,
inanimate, languid,
lazy, lifeless,
motionless, passive,
quiescent, sluggish,
static, still, supine,
torpid
inertia: idleness,
languor, sloth
inescapable:
automatic, certain,
destined, inevitable,
irresistible, sure
inescapably:
necessarily
inessential:
expendable,
ornamental,
redundant,
unnecessary
inestimable:
imponderable
incalculable, infinite,
priceless
inevitable: automatic,
certain, destined,
necessary, sure
inevitably:
necessarily
inexact: general,
imprecise, inaccurate,
indefinite, loose,
rough
inexactly: roughly
inexhaustible:
infinite
inexorable: certain,
implacable,
incvitable,
irresistible, obdurate,
relentless
inexorably:
necessarily
inexpensive: cheap,
economic, low,
reasonable
inexperience:
ignorance, innocence
inexperienced: fresh,
green, ignorant,
immature, innocent,
juvenile, raw,
unskilled, unworldly,
virgin, young
inexplicable:
impenetrable,
insoluble, miraculous,

mysterious,
unaccountable
inexpressible:
nameless
invariable:
permanent
infallible: foolproof,
sure, unimpeachable
infallibly: unerringly
infamous: despicable,
disgraceful, famous,
flagrant, iniquitous,
notorious,
outrageous,
scandalous,
scurrilous, shameful,
vaunted, villainous
infamy: atrocity,
fame, notoriety,
opprobrium, shame,
stain
infancy: childhood
infant: baby, child,
kid, tot, young
infantile: baby,
babyish, childish,
juvenile, puerile
infantry: foot
infantrymen: foot
infants: young
infatuate: captivate,
enslave, entrance,
fascinate
infatuated:
enamoured, obsessed,
stuck
infatuation: dotage,
fascination, love,
obsession, passion
infect: invade, pollute
infected: morbid,
septic, tainted
infection: bug,
disease, pest, plague
infectious: contagious
infective: virulent
infecund: infertile,
sterile
infelicitous:
improper,
inappropriate, inept,
unfortunate,
unhappy, wrong
infelicitously:
unfortunately,
unhappily
infer: assume,
conclude, deduce,
divine, draw, gather,
imagine, induce,
reason, surmise
inference:
assumption,
construction,
deduction,
implication,

innuendo, logic,
surmise
inferior: bad, base,
below, cheap,
common, hopeless,
junior, less, lesser,
low, lower, mean,
petty, poor, rotten,
second, secondary,
shoddy, subject,
subordinate, under,
worse
infernal: dark,
profound, satanic
inferno: fire,
underworld
inferred: implicit
infertile: barren,
impotent, meagre,
poor
infertility:
impotence, poverty
infest: invade
infestation: disease,
invasion, plague
infested: fleabitten
infidel: atheist,
heathen, pagan
infiltrate: leak,
penetrate, permeate,
work
infiltrating: pervasive
infiltration: diffusion
infinite:
imponderable,
incalculable,
interminable,
unbounded
infinitesimal:
imperceptible,
invisible, little,
microscopic, minimal
infinity: immensity
infirm: decrepit, frail,
ill
infirmity: debility,
delicacy, frailty,
illness, indisposition
inflame: chafe,
ferment, fire, heat,
incense, incite,
infuriate, irritate,
kindle, light, provoke,
stimulate, work up
inflamed: feverish,
fiery, red, sore, tender
inflammation:
catarrh, rash, rousing,
sore, subversive,
swelling, tenderness
inflate: balloon, blow
up, devalue, distend,
exaggerate, fill,
magnify, pad out,
pump, widen
inflated: bloated,

heroic, pretentious,
pompous, puffy,
turgid
inflater: pump
inflation:
exaggeration
inflection: tone
inflexibility: firmness
inflexible: firm, hard,
obdurate, obstinate,
relentless, resolute,
rigid, set, stiff, tough,
unbending,
uncharitable, wooden
inflict: deliver,
impose, visit
inflicting on:
imposition
influence: authority,
bend, bias, carry,
clout, credit, effect,
get, govern, grip,
hand, hit, hold,
impact, importance,
impress, impression,
induce, interest, lead,
leverage, mould,
persuade, power,
pressure, prestige,
pull, purchase, push,
reach, say, sway,
touch, weight
influenced:
prejudiced
influential: big,
effective,
instrumental,
operative, potent,
powerful, prestigious,
weighty, winning
influenza: cold
info: information
inform: betray, brief,
communicate,
educate, finger, grass,
instruct, leak, mould,
notify, prime, report,
sing, sneak, split,
squeal, teach, tell,
warn
informal: casual,
easy, everyday,
familiar, free, homely,
intimate,
unauthorized,
informality:
familiarity, freedom
informant: leak,
source
information:
counsel, data,
instruction,
intelligence,
knowledge, material,
news, notification,
word

informed: aware,
judicious, wise
informer: leak, nark,
plant, sneak
informing: education
infract: break
infraction: breach
infrastructural:
skeletal
infrastructure:
fabric, machine
infrequency: rarity
infrequent:
occasional, rare,
uncommon
infrequently:
occasionally, seldom,
uncommonly
infringe: breach,
break, impinge,
invade, violate
infringement:
breach, invasion,
misdemeanour,
violation
infuriate: incense,
inflame, outrage,
provoke
infuriated: livid,
maddened, wrathful
infuriating: offensive,
provocative
infuse: breathe, draw,
flavour, inject, mash,
steep
infusion: brew, drink,
liquor
ingenious: bright,
creative, cunning,
inventive, original,
practical, resourceful,
smart, subtle, witty
ingeniously:
originally, practically
ingenuity: brilliance,
imagination,
invention, wit, wits
ingenuous: candid,
innocent, naive,
natural, unsuspecting
ingenuously:
naturally
ingenuousness:
innocence
ingest: assimilate, take
ingestible: edible
inglorious:
ignominious
ingot: bar, block, pig
ingraft: implant
ingrafting: implant
ingrained: chronic,
habitual
ingratiating:
fulsome, greasy,
smooth

ingredient:
component,
constituent, element,
factor, part
ingredients: mix,
recipe
ingress: entrance,
entry
inhabit: live, people,
populate
inhabitant: citizen,
local, lodger, national,
native, occupant,
resident
inhabitants: people,
population
inhabited: occupied
inhalation: breath,
drag, pull
inhale: breathe, draw,
puff, pull
inharmonious:
divisive,
incompatible, rough
inherent: basic,
component,
congenital,
constitutional,
implicit, instinctive,
natural, organic,
potential
inherently: basically,
naturally
inherit: get, take over
inheritable:
hereditary
inheritance:
derivation, heritage,
legacy
inherited: genetic,
hereditary
inheritors:
descendants
inhibit: cramp, curb,
damp, deter, keep,
obstruct, prevent,
repress, restrict,
shackle, strangle
inhibited: pent-up
inhibition: hang-up,
repression, restraint,
restriction, scruple
inhospitable:
churlish, rigorous,
unfriendly
inhuman: atrocious,
barbaric, beastly,
brutal, cruel,
impersonal,
monstrous, ruthless,
savage, unnatural,
villainous, wicked
inhumane: merciless
inhumanity: atrocity,
cruelty, outrage
inhume: bury

inimical: averse, contrary, hostile, icy, ill, malignant, unfriendly, warlike

inimitable: matchless

iniquitous: evil, foul, infamous, outrageous, satanic, sinful, unholy, wicked, wrong

iniquity: evil, vice

initial: beginning, first, incipient, opening, original, pilot, preliminary, premier, primary, underwrite

initially: first, originally, primarily

initiate: baptize, begin, blood, create, generate, ground, inaugurate, institute, launch, lead, originate, pioneer, recruit, set up, start

initiation: baptism, beginning, kick-off, preliminary, start

initiative: drive, move

initiator: founder

inject: interpose

injection: fix, interpolation, jab

injudicious: foolish, impolitic, indiscreet, misguided, rash, short-sighted, unhappy, unwise

injudiciously: unhappily

injunction: caution, charge, command, order

injure: batter, bruise, damage, harm, hurt, impair, lame, maltreat, outrage, punish, ruin, strain, wound, wrong

injured: battered, hurt, lame, victim

injurious: bad, baneful, damaging, evil, harmful, mischievous, pernicious, sinister, traumatic, violent, virulent

injury: battery, cost, damage, disservice, evil, harm, hurt, ill, lesion, mayhem, mischief, outrage, punishment, scar,

score, strain, trauma, wound, wrong, violence

injustice: disservice, score, wrong

inkling: clue, conception, idea, indication, notion, wind

inky: black, oily

inland: rustic

inlet: bay, mouth

inmate: inhabitant, occupant

inn: bar, hotel, local, pub

innards: inside, intestines

innate: congenital, inherent, instinctive, intuitive, native, radical, temperamental

innately: naturally

inner: blank, bull, inside, interior, internal, target, white, wrong

innermost self: psyche

innings: bat, knock

innkeeper: host, landlord

innocence: ignorance, purity

innocent: chaste, cherubic, clean, clear, green, idyllic, ignorant, mark, mug, naive, pure, unsuspecting, white

innocently: unwittingly

innocuous: harmless, innocent, inoffensive, safe

innovative: brainwave, change, departure, invention, inventive, novel, novelty, revolution, revolutionary

innovatively: originally

innovator: pioneer

innovatory: original

innuendo: hint, nuance, overtone, slur

innumerable: incalculable, many, myriad

inoculate: immunize, inject

inoculation: jab, vaccination

inoffensive: harmless,

innocent, peaceable, quiet

inoffensively: quietly

inoperable: impractical, incurable

inoperative: dead, defective, defunct, idle, inactive, invalid, nugatory, void

inopportune: awkward, premature, unfavourable, unfortunate, unpopular

inordinate: extravagant, fulsome, redundant, unconscionable

inordinately: unduly

inquest: probe

inquiline: guest

inquire: search, wonder

inquiry: hearing, probe, query, question, study, survey,

inquisitive: curious, nosy, prying

insane: berserk, crazy, deranged, distracted, idiotic, irrational, lunatic, mad, mental, preposterous, psychotic, screwy

insanitary: unhealthy

insanity: idiocy, lunacy, madness

insatiability: greed

insatiable: rapacious, voracious

inscribe: line, sign, stamp, write

inscription: etching, legend, motto

inscrutable: impenetrable

insect: bug, fly

insecure: brittle, precarious, self-conscious, shaky, unsettled, unsure

insecurity: diffidence, jeopardy, woods

inseminate: fertilize, sow

insemination: conception

insensibility: narcosis, numbness, oblivion

insensible: lifeless, numb, senseless, unconscious

insensitive: blind, callous, dull, gauche,

gross, inconsiderate, numb, obtuse, tactless, thick-skinned, unkind, unthinking

insensitivity: numbness

inseparable: thick

insert: bed, book, boot, box, enclose, file, fudge, graft, implant, include, incorporate, inject, interpose, introduce, lag, slot, stick, weigh

insertion: import, interpolation, introduction

insertion: enclosure, implant

inset: box, fudge, insert, panel

inshore: maritime

inside: interior, internal, privileged, within

insider: nark

insides: filling, guts, offal, works

insight: depth, illumination, imagination, inspiration, light, understanding, vision, wisdom

insightful: observant, profound, understanding

insignia: banner, seal

insignificance: indifference, obscurity

insignificant: feeble, footling, humble, light, lightweight, little, low, marginal, mere, minor, minute, negligible, niggling, nominal, paltry, petty, puny, slight, small, small-time, venial, worthless

insincere: double, hollow, unreal

insincerely: hollow

insincerity: hypocrisy

insinuate: hint, imply, intimate, mean, slur, suggest, work

insinuation: hint, innuendo, meaning, slur, suggestion

insipid: bland, boring, dilute, flat, lifeless, mawkish, mousy, negative, stale, thin, unappetizing, unimaginative, watery

insist: claim, demand, maintain

insistence: self-assertion

insistent: assertive, bent, demanding, imperative, importunate, positive, urgent

insolence: gall, impertinence, lip, mouth, presumption, sauce

insolent: cavalier, disrespectful, impertinent, impolite, offensive, presumptuous, rude, saucy, scornful, shameless, supercilious

insoluble: impossible, impossible, inexplicable, mysterious, unanswerable

insolvency: poverty, ruin

insolvent: bankrupt, destitute, hard up

insomniac: sleepless

insouciance: nonchalance

insouciant: nonchalant

inspect: audit, check, look, look into, overhaul, patrol, reconnoitre, sample, survey, view, walk

inspection: audit, check-up, look, observation, overhaul, review, search, survey

inspiration: brainwave, fire, guide, lesson, motivation, muse, soul

inspire: fire, impel, inhale, kindle, motivate, move, prompt, put up, spark, stir

inspired: exalted, lyrical

inspiring: moving, rousing

inspirit: ginger

instability: levity

install: inaugurate, initiate, invest, lay on,

make, mount, ordain, seat, set, set up, site, station

installed: made

instalment: batch, episode, issue, premium

instance: case, illustration, manifestation, occurrence, piece, point, precedent, quote, sample, specimen

instant: flash, immediate, minute, moment, point, prompt, second, shake, snap, twinkling, unhesitating, unwholesome, whirlwind

instantaneous: momentary, prompt

instantaneously: immediately, outright

instantly: directly, forthwith, immediately, now, outright, promptly, quickly, right, straight, straight away

instead: else, rather

instep: foot

instigate: impel, incite, motivate, pick, pioneer, prompt, provoke, put up, raise, rouse, start, stimulate, stir

instigation: motivation

instil: drum, charge, implant

instinct: intuition

instinctive: intuitive, natural, unconscious

instinctively: naturally

instinctual: automatic, intuitive, involuntary, unreasoning

institute: begin, college, erect, father, found, impose, install, introduce, plant, school, society, start

institution: beginning, foundation, home, imposition, introduction, organization, school,

tradition

instruct: brief, charge, coach, direct, drill, educate, ground, indoctrinate, lecture, order, require, school, show, teach, tell

instruction: command, direction, directive, education, knowledge, lesson, mandate, precept, prescription

instructions: pattern, recipe, remit, teachings

instructor: coach, master, teacher

instrument: deed, device, means, medium, organ, paper, pawn, protocol, thing

instrumentalist: player

instrumentality: means

instruments: gear, kit

insubordinate: defiant, rebellious, recalcitrant

insubordination: disobedience

insubstantial: flimsy, light, lightweight, tenuous, unreal

insufferable: frightful, obnoxious, unbearable

insufficiency: deficiency, need, scarcity, want

insufficient: inadequate, lame, lean, limited, poor, scanty, slender, small, short

insufficiently: ill, poorly

insular: narrow-minded, provincial, xenophobic

insularity: isolation

insulate: lag

insult: attack, barb, calumny, liberty, mock, name, offence, offend, outrage, slight, slur, snub, taunt

insulting: derisory, impolite, offensive, scornful

insults: mockery

insupportable:

insufferable, unacceptable, unbearable, untenable

insurance: assurance, cover, indemnity

insure: cover, guarantee, secure, underwrite

insurgency: revolt, revolution

insurgent: lawless, rebel, rebellious, revolutionary

insurmountable: impassable, overpowering

insurrection: coup, mutiny, revolt, uprising

insurrectionary: subversive

insurrectionist: revolutionary

insusceptible: immune

intact: full, safe, sound, unbroken, unharmed, unspoilt, whole

intaglio: cameo, sculpture

intangible: dreamy, shadowy, unreal

integer: number, unit

integral: complete, constituent, organic, whole

integrate: combine, incorporate

integrated: organic

integration: coalition, coordination, unity

integrity: breadth, character, credibility, ethics, honesty, honour, justice, mentality, morality, nobility, principle, right, virtue

integument: bark, film

intellect: brain, genius, intelligence, mentality, mind, reason,

intellectual: bookish, exalted, liberal, mental, moral, scholar

intelligence: brain, common sense, communication, comprehension, espionage, head, information, knowledge, loaf,

mentality, mind,
news, notice,
notification, nut, wit,
wits, word
intelligent: bright,
clever, discerning,
knowing,
knowledgeable,
quick, quick-witted,
rational, reasonable,
sage, sensible,
shrewd, wise
intelligentsia:
yuppies
intelligibility: clarity,
lucidity
intelligible: clear,
coherent, lucid,
luminous, simple
intemperance:
overindulgence
intemperate:
dissipated, fast,
lavish, prodigal,
rabid, unbridled
intend: calculate,
design, mean, plan,
propose, purpose,
think, vow, will
intend: resolve
intended: destined,
fiancé(e), knowing
intense: avid, bitter,
bright, brilliant,
close, colourful, deep,
excruciating, fierce,
hot, impassioned,
keen, lurid,
passionate, piercing,
profound, rich,
strong, tempestuous,
terrific, violent,
warm, wild
intensely: badly,
hard, madly
intensification:
concentration,
increase, surge
intensify: augment,
compound, fuel,
increase, inflame,
magnify, mount,
raise, swell
intensifying:
inflammatory,
progressive
intensity: brilliance,
degree, depth, fire,
flame, force, heat,
passion, violence,
warmth
intensive: exhaustive,
thorough
intent: bent, close,
earnest, rapt,
searching, spirit, set

intention: design,
drift, end, goal, idea,
meaning, motive,
object, objective,
point, purport,
purpose, resolution,
target, will
intentional:
conscious, deliberate,
knowing,
premeditated,
voluntary, wilful
intently: hard
inter: bury
interbreed: cross
intercede: interpose,
mediate
intercept: obviate,
stop, waylay
intercession: offices,
plea
intercessor: mediator
interchange: liaison,
reciprocate, rotate,
swap, transposition
interchangeable:
same
intercity: through
**intercommu-
nication:** intercourse
intercourse:
commerce,
connection, liaison
interdict: ban, forbid,
veto
interdicted:
forbidden, prohibited
interdiction: ban
interest: bag,
concern, importance,
intrigue, kickback,
line, part, pursuit,
return, revenue,
right, sake, warm,
zest
interested: concerned
interesting:
beguiling, intriguing
interface: joint,
junction
interfere: conflict,
snoop
interference:
disturbance, let, static
interfering: busy,
impertinent,
intrusive, obtrusive,
officious, prying
interfere with:
corrupt, disturb,
falsify, interrupt,
mess, molest,
obstruct, tamper
interim: caretaker,
interval, provisional,
temporary

interior: inside,
internal
interjection:
exclamation,
interpolation
interlace: knit, tangle,
weave
interlaced:
complicated
interlock: mesh
interloper: intruder,
outsider
interlude: pause, rest
intermediary:
liaison, mediator
intermediate:
average, between,
mean, medium,
middle
interment: burial,
funeral
interminable:
compound, constant,
incessant, lengthy,
long, perpetual
intermingle: fuse,
mix
intermission: break,
gap, interlude,
interval, pause,
recess,
intermittent: fitful,
flickering, irregular,
occasional, patchy,
spasmodic
intermittently:
occasionally
intermix: mingle
intermixing:
diffusion
intern: imprison, shut
up
internal: domestic,
inside, interior,
mental, national
international:
overseas, worldwide
internee: captive
internment: jail
interpolate: break,
insert, introduce,
weigh
interpolation:
import, insert,
interpolation,
introduction,
outburst, parenthesis
interpose: break,
comment, divide,
insert, intercede
interposing: divisive
interpret: comment,
decipher, define,
explain, read, render,
solve, take,
transcribe,

understand
interpretation:
construction,
definition, diagnosis,
explanation, key,
light, meaning,
performance, reading,
reasoning, version
interpreter:
commentator
interred:
underground
interrogate: grill,
interview, pump,
query, question, quiz
interrogation:
interview, question,
quiz
interrupt: break, cut
off, disturb, heckle,
obstruct, obtrude,
punctuate, relieve,
suspend
interrupted:
uncertain
interruption:
breakdown,
disturbance, division,
outburst, pause,
respite, sidetrack
interruptive:
discouraging, divisive
intersect: cross,
traverse
intersection: cross,
crossroads, joint,
junction
interstice: gap
interstice: hiatus,
lacuna
intertwine: knit,
tangle, weave
interval: break, delay,
distance, gap, grace,
hiatus, interim, jump,
lacuna, lapse, leap,
lull, omission,
parenthesis, pause,
period, recess,
respite, rest, season,
space, spell, time,
vacuum, wait
intervene: intercede,
interfere, interpose,
mediate
intervening:
intermediate
intervention: offices
interview: audience,
consultation, poll, see
interweave: lace
intestines: guts
intimacy: familiarity,
fellowship,
knowledge, liaison
intimate: bosom,

close, confidential,
cosy, dear, familiar,
friend, friendly,
imply, lead up to,
near, private, signify,
suggest, thick
intimately:
particularly
intimation: clue,
hint, suggestion, wind
intimidate: awe,
blackmail, buzz,
domineer, frighten,
lean, menace, nobble,
prey on, scare, shake,
terrify
intimidated: fearful,
overawed, unnerved
intimidating:
awesome, formidable,
off-putting
intimidation:
blackmail, threat
intimidator: bully
intimidatory:
frightening
into: inside
intolerable:
insufferable,
unacceptable,
unbearable
intolerance:
impatience
intolerant: bigoted,
narrow-minded,
quick-tempered,
rabid
intonation: delivery,
tone
intone: chant
intoxicate: fox,
fuddle, light, send
intoxicated: drunk,
drunken, high,
inebriated, loaded,
tight
intoxicating: heady,
strong
intoxication:
madness
intractability:
disobedience
intractable: fractious,
headstrong,
implacable,
intransigent,
obstinate, perverse,
pig-headed,
rebellious,
recalcitrant,
stubborn, unbending,
wilful
intransigence:
resistance
intransigent: rigid,
wilful

intrepid: bold,
chivalrous, daring,
fearless, gallant,
game, hardy, heroic,
spartan, stout, valiant
intrepidity: daring,
fortitude, heroism,
manliness, nerve,
prowess, valour
intricacies:
ramifications
intricacy: depth,
difficulty
intricate: complex,
complicated,
compound, difficult,
elaborate, hard,
involved,
labyrinthine, prickly,
sophisticated
intrigue: collusion,
conspiracy, conspire,
design, fascinate,
interest, liaison,
machination, plot,
scheme
intriguing: beguiling,
designing,
interesting, politic,
subtle
intrinsic: basic,
component,
constitutional,
inherent, integral,
native, quintessential,
real
intrinsically:
basically, lick,
prelude
introduce: baptize,
blood, bring up,
broach, host, import,
inject, insert, install,
institute, lead up to,
preface, present,
propose, raise,
seduce, table
introduction:
baptism, build-up,
discovery, entrance,
entry, fanfare,
import, innovation,
overture, preface,
preliminary, prelude,
presentation, start
introductory: initial,
opening, pilot,
preliminary, primary
introspective:
introverted,
thoughtful
introverted: insular,
remote, thoughtful,
withdrawn
intrude: barge,
disturb, impose,

infringe, interfere,
interrupt, obtrude
intruder: burglar
intrusion:
disturbance,
imposition, invasion,
outburst
intrusive:
impertinent,
inquisitive, nosy,
obtrusive, offensive,
officious, prying
intuition: divination,
hunch, premonition,
sense
intuitive: immediate
inundate: besiege,
drench, drown, flood,
flow, glut, overflow,
overrun, shower,
swamp
inundated:
smothered
inundation:
avalanche, flood, flow,
overflow
inure: harden
inured: callous,
habituated
invade: attack,
overrun, raid, violate
invader: boarder,
intruder
invalid: bad, false,
faulty, illegitimate,
illogical, lapsed,
patient, void, weak,
weakling
invalidate: disable,
nullify, overrule,
overturn, quash,
repeal, rescind,
reverse, revoke, undo,
void
invalidated: disabled,
undone
invalidation:
dissolution
invalidity: nullity
invaluable:
inestimable, precious,
priceless, rare
invariable: constant,
same
invasion: attack,
conquest, foray,
occupation, offensive,
raid, violation
invasive: intrusive
invective:
imprecation, insult
inveigh: denounce,
fulminate, slang
inveigle: jockey, lure,
tempt, wheedle, work
invent: coin, compose,

concoct, create,
design, develop,
devise, discover,
fabricate, formulate,
frame, imagine, lie,
make, make up, mint,
pioneer, produce,
spin
invented: fictitious,
imaginary, made,
mythical, nonexistent
invention: baby,
bright, composition,
conception, creation,
discovery, fable,
falsehood, fantasy,
fiction, imagination,
innovation, lie
inventive: creative,
imaginative, original,
practical, pregnant,
productive,
resourceful
inventively:
originally, practically
inventor: author,
engineer, father,
founder, originator,
pioneer
inventory: bill,
catalogue, list, list,
roll, schedule, stock
invert: capsize,
reverse
inverted: reverse,
upside down
invest: besiege,
crown, ordain, place,
put up
investigate: canvass,
explore, look into,
probe, reconnoitre,
research, search, see,
sound, study, test,
scan
investigation:
canvass, check, probe,
postmortem,
research, scrutiny,
study, test
investigative:
exploratory,
inquisitive
investigator:
detective
investiture:
presentation
investment: capital,
backing, blockade,
finance, stake, stock
investor: creditor
inveterate: habitual,
incurable
invigilate: officiate
invigilation: scrutiny
invigilator: monitor

invigorate: comfort, revive
invigorated: fresh
invigorating: brisk, cordial, fresh, healthy, lively, refreshing
invincible: impregnable
inviolability: sanctity
invisible: imperceptible, implicit, minimal
invitation: call, overture, temptation
invite: bid, call, court, draw, host, lure, propose, summon
inviter: host
inviting: beckoning, seductive, sexy
invocation: blessing, prayer
invoice: bill
invoke: conjure, incur
involuntarily: unwittingly
involuntary: automatic, instinctive, intuitive, unconscious, unintentional, unreasoning
involve: complicate, concern, consist of, contain, cover, demand, immerse, imply, interest, mean, tangle
involved: complex, complicated, concerned, difficult, hard, implicated, intricate, prickly
involvement: commitment, concern, depth, experience, implication, interest, part, stake
invulnerable: immune, impervious, impregnable, invincible, sacred, secure, tenable
inward: interior
inwardly: within
iota: jot, particle, shred, speck
IQ: mentality
irascibility: bile
irascible: cantankerous, fiery, hasty, ill-humoured, liverish, passionate, peevish, peppery,

quarrelsome, querulous, quick, quick-tempered, short-tempered, warm, waspish
irate: flaming, livid
ire: fury, passion, rage, wrath
irk: bug, chagrin, displease, fret, gall, jar, needle, provoke, put out, rasp, wear, weary
irked: peeved, sore, uptight, weary
irksome: ungrateful, unpleasant, wearing, wearisome
iron: press, smooth, tough
ironic: cutting, cynical, wry
ironical: facetious, sarcastic, sardonic
irony: satire
irradiate: light, lighten
irrational: deranged, insane, illogical, invalid, mad, nonsensical, rabid, raving, unfounded, unreasonable, wild
irrationality: madness
irrationally: madly
irreconcilable: contradictory, incompatible, inconsistent, opposing, opposite
irrefutable: certain, compelling, peremptory, unquestioned
irregular: bastard, casual, changeable, chequered, flickering, occasional, patchy, ragged, rambling, rugged, shapeless, spastic, unconventional, unequal, uneven, wayward
irregularity: inequality
irregularly: occasionally, roughly
irrelevance: quibble, foreign
irrelevant: idle, insignificant, pointless, remote
irreligious: heathen, impious, irreverent,

pagan, unholy, wicked
irremediable: incurable
irreparable: hopeless
irreplaceable: priceless
irrepressible: resilient
irreproachable: faultless, impeccable, unimpeachable
irresistable: charming, cogent, compelling, disarming, killing, overpowering
irresolute: doubtful, faltering, hesitant, infirm, restless, spineless, uncertain, undecided, unsure, weak
irresolution: doubt, indecision
irresponsibility: frivolity, insanity, licence, stupidity
irresponsible: careless, crazy, frivolous, imprudent, mad, promiscuous, silly, unreliable, unwise, wild
irresponsibly: madly
irreverence: blasphemy
irreverent: disrespectful, flippant, impious, profane, sacrilegious
irreversible: hopeless
irrevocable: binding, final, sure
irrevocably: finally
irrigate: ditch, water
irrigation channel: canal
irritable: cantankerous, fractious, liverish, passionate, peppery, petulant, prickly, quarrelsome, querulous
irritate: bait, bother, chafe, chagrin, discomfort, displease, get, itch, jar, molest, nag, nark, niggle, offend, pain, provoke, put out, rasp, ruffle
irritated: sore
irritating: beastly, nagging, niggling, trying

irritation: bother, chagrin, discomfort, itch, niggle, nuisance, pest, resentment
island: pocket
isolate: blockade, cut off, maroon, segregate
isolated: desolate, insular, lonely, private, remote, secluded, sequestered, sheltered, solitary, unique, withdrawn
isolation: desert, loneliness, seclusion, solitude
isolationist: xenophobic
issue: business, child, coin, come, conclusion, consequence, consideration, descendants, edition, emission, emit, family, flow, follow, fruit, give, impression, jet, leak, number, offspring, posterity, proceed, promulgate, publication, publish, put out, question, release, result, rise, run, sally, seed, stem, subject, vent, young
isthmian: peninsular
italicize: underline
itch: hankering, irritate, longing, scab
itching: tingling
itchy: prickly
item: clause, count, detail, element, entry, feature, number, object, piece, point, regard, thing, throw unit
itemize: detail, formulate, list, programme, specify
itemized: detailed, particular
items: specifications, supply
iterate: repeat
iteration: repetition
itinerant: mobile, vagrant, wandering
itinerary: schedule
ivories: notes
ivory: key, white

J

jab: dig, inject, lunge, poke, prick, prod, punch, stick, stab
jabber: chatter, gabble, natter, prattle, rabbit, waffle, yap
jabbering: babel
jack: flag, knave, male, mark
jackanapes: pup
jackass: simpleton
jacket: bark, binding, case, cover, roundabout
jackpot: pool, prize
jackrabbit: hare
Jack Tar: sailor
jacuzzi: bath
jade: hack, minx, nag, screw, weary
jaded: satiated, weary
jag: barb
jagged: ragged, rough, rugged
jail: imprison, jug, nick, prison, send up
jailbird: criminal
jailer: custodian, guard, keeper, warder
jam: bottleneck, clog, congestion, cramp, crush, difficulty, filling, fix, foul, gig, hole, lock, mess, pack, pile, plight, predicament, preserve, press, ram, scrape, seize, squeeze, stick, stuff, quagmire
jamboree: carnival
jammed: full, packed, thick, tight
jangle: jar, jingle, rattle
Janissary: warrior
janitor: caretaker, custodian, warden
jape: caper, crack, giggle, jest, joke, lark, prank, rag, wheeze
japes: fun
jar: bottle, bump, clash, grate, jangle, jerk, jog, jostle, jug, pot, rock, scream, shake, shock, start

jargon: cant, idiom, language, slang, speech, terminology, vocabulary
jarring: concussion, harsh, jangle, rough
jars: crockery
jaundiced: prejudiced, yellow
jaunt: drive, journey, outing, ride, sally, tour, trip, turn
jauntiness: vivacity
jaunty: buoyant, carefree, cheerful, dashing, perky, pert, saucy, vivacious
javelin: spear
jaw: chat, jowls, natter
jaws: mouth
jealous: covetous, envious, green, jaundiced, possessive
jeer: barrack, catcall, flout, heckle, mock, ridicule, scoff, sneer, taunt
jeered: ragged
jeering: derisory, sardonic, scornful
jejune: barren, immature, naive, puerile
jelly: dessert, mould, preserve
jemmy: crowbar, lever, lever, pick
jennet: ass
jeopardize: chance, compromise, endanger, expose, hazard, imperil, queer, risk, stake, venture
jeopardy: chance, danger, difficulty, exposure, hazard, peril, risk
jerk: bob, flip, galvanize, hitch, jar, jog, jump, kick, pluck, pull, recoil, sap, shake, start, switch, twitch, whip, wrench, wriggle
jerky: bumpy, spasmodic, stiff

jersey: woolly,
jest: banter, caper, clown, joke, quip, sally
jester: clown, comedian, fool, joker, wag, zany
jesting: banter
jet: black, blast, fountain, plane, spurt
jetsetting: fashionable
jetting: gushing
jettison: discard, ditch
jettisoning: disposal
jetty: mooring, pier, projection, quay, stage
jewel: brooch, gem, ornament, pet
jibe: barb
jiffy: instant, minute, second, shake
jig: dance, reel, trip
jiggle: jog, jostle, rattle, wriggle
jihad: crusade
jilt: desert
jingle: chime, jangle, slogan
jingoist: patriotic
jinx: curse
jinxed: luckless
jittery: jumpy, nervous, tense
jive: dance
job: assignment, berth, business, chore, engagement, function, labour, line, livelihood, living, mission, occupation, place, ploy, position, post, project, role, situation, task, work
jobless: idle, unemployed
joblessness: idleness
jock: box
jockey-shorts: briefs
jocose: humorous, jocular
jocular: tongue-in-cheek
jocularity: fun, humour, laughter
jocund: jocular, jolly

jog: jostle, nudge, run
joggle: jog, jostle, shake
john: bog, flat, fool, lavatory, pigeon, punter, victim
join: attach, associate, band, bridge, cement, close, collaborate, connect, couple, dock, enter, fasten, focus, fuse, hitch, junction, knead, knit, lash, link, loop, marry, meet, nail, organize, pal, participate, peg, relate, stick, team, unify, unite, wed, weld, yoke
joined: attached, one, stuck
joiner: carpenter
joining: assembly, between, union, wedding
joint: articulate, butcher, communal, concerted, corner, cut, dive, hole, junction, knot, link, mutual, node, related, seam, weld
jointed: articulate
jointly: together
joist: beam, board
joists: timber
joke: banter, crack, farce, gag, game, giggle, jest, kid, lark, laugh, quip, sally, spoof, wheeze
joker: clown, comedian, wag, zany
jokes: banter
jokey: jocular, playful, tongue-in-cheek
joking: banter, comedy, humour, jocular
jollification: celebration, jolly, riot
jollity: fun, merriment
jolly good: wizard
jolly: bright, cheerful, festive, jocular, light-hearted, mellow,

merry
jolt: bump, electrify, galvanize, ginger, impact, jar, jerk, jog, jump, kick, percussion, rattle, shake, shock
jolting: bumpy, concussion
Jonah: jinx
jostle: contend, crowd, hustle, jockey, jog, mob, push, scramble, scrum, shove, squeeze
jot: dot, particle, rap, scrawl, shred, spark
jot down: note, pen, take down, write
jotter: pad
jotting: notation, note
jottings: notes
jounce: jog; shake
journal: chronicle, log, magazine, organ, paper, periodical, review
journalism: press
journalist: hack, reporter, writer
journalists: press
journey: ascent, do, haul, leap, migrate, passage, progress, ride, route, tour, voyage, way
joust: tournament
jovial: gay, genial, jocular, jolly, light-hearted
joy: boast, delight, dream, glee, happiness, heaven, jubilation, paradise, pride, rapture
joyful: happy, joyous, radiant, rejoicing, sunny
joyfully: happily
joyfulness: happiness
joyless: gloomy, glum
joyous: exultant,

festive, gay, happy, jubilant, rejoicing
joyously: gaily
joyousness: happiness
jubilant: exultant, joyful, joyous, overjoyed, rejoicing
jubilation: happiness, rejoicing
jubilee: carnival, celebration
judder: tremble
judge: assess, calculate, connoisseur, consider, count, discern, gauge, hear, hold, justice, officiate, reckon, referee, review, rule, say, see, think, umpire
judgement: calculation, conclusion, decision, doom, finding, logic, mind, opinion, prudence, review, ruling, sentence, tact, taste, verdict, view, wisdom, wit
judges: jury
judicial: legislative
judiciary: bench, judicial, justice, legislative
judicious: cautious, discreet, rational, sage, sane, sensible, tactful, wise
judiciousness: prudence, sanity
jug: carafe, jail, jar, mug, prison
juggle: conjure
juice: blood, liquor, milk, marrow
juicy: fluid, liquid, luscious, lush, mellow, rich, tasty
jumble: mess, bazaar, confusion, disarray, dislocate, garble,

garble, hash, huddle, jungle, litter, medley, mess, perplex, scramble, shuffle, upset, wilderness
jumbled: deranged, disorganized, incoherent, messy, miscellaneous, muddled, pied, unintelligible, upset
jumbo: bumper, fat, heavy, jet, monster, monstrous, monumental, outsize
jump: bale, bound, caper, clear, dive, flight, hop, hurdle, kick, launch, leap, lunge, miss, mug, omission, omit, pounce, scramble, skip, spring, start, twitch, vault
jumped-up: pretentious
jumper: jersey, woolly,
jumpy: fearful, jittery, nervous, nervousness, restless, skittish, tense, thin-skinned
junction: connection, contact, cross, crossroads, intersection, join, joint, juncture, meeting
juncture: concurrence, moment, phase, point, stage, time
jungle: bush, undergrowth, wilderness
junior: inferior, minor, subordinate, under, young
junk: belongings, bunk, garbage, knick-knacks, rubbish, scrap, unwholesome

juridical: judicial
jurisdiction: authority, reach, sway
jurisdictive: legislative
jurisprudence: law
jury: panel
just: barely, but, conscientious, due, fair, hardly, honest, honourable, narrowly, objective, only, reasonable, right, rightful, sound, square, valid
just about: nearly, practically
just as: even, like,
justice: honesty, redress, retribution
justifiable: legitimate, reasonable, tenable
justification: call, defence, explanation, grounds, reason, vindication
justificatory: defensive
justify: bear out, defend, deserve, explain, rationalize, uphold, vindicate, warrant,
justly: equally, fairly, right
jut: overhang, obtrude, poke, project, stick
jutting: obtrusive, prominent
juvenile: babyish, child, childish, frivolous, immature, infantile, junior, minor, puerile, young
juveniles: young
juvenility: youth
juxtapose: compare
juxtaposition: comparison, proximity

K

kale: cabbage, greens
kangaroo: jump,
  unauthorized
karma: destiny
keek: peek
keel: back, bottom
keel over: capsize,
  faint, fall, fold,
  overturn
keelson: back
keen: astute, avid,
  brisk, clever, close,
  fine, fresh, great,
  lament, moan,
  penetrating, piercing,
  profound, pungent,
  quick, ready,
  receptive, searching,
  sensitive, shrewd,
  smart, spicy, strong,
  stuck, ululate, wail,
  warm, willing,
  wishful, zealous
keening: lamentation
keen on: sweet
keen over: bewail
keenly: hard
keenness: zeal
keep: castle,
  commemorate,
  conserve, follow,
  fortification, fulfil,
  garner, have, hold,
  honour, house,
  maintain,
  maintenance, mount,
  obey, preserve,
  redeem, rest, retain,
  stock, store, support,
  tend, ward, watch,
  withhold
keep alive:
  perpetuate, sustain
keep an eye on:
  mind, observe,
keep apart: screen,
  separate,
keep back: reserve,
  withhold
keeper: caretaker,
  custodian, guardian,
  warder
keep going: carry on,
  last, perpetuate,
  persist
keeping: custody,
  ward

keep safe: defend,
  protect, save
keepsake: favour,
  memento, reminder,
  souvenir
keep secret: conceal,
  hide, hush up,
  protect, suppress,
keep up: maintain,
  perpetuate, persist,
  preserve, sustain
keg: barrel, cask,
  magazine, vat, wood
kenning: nickname
keratin: horn, nail
kerb: path
kerchief: favour, veil
kern: flourish
kernel: core, grain,
  heart, marrow,
  nucleus, nut, seed
ketch: boat, yacht
ketchup: sauce
key: bar, basic, button,
  cardinal, chief,
  fundamental, guide,
  indispensable, legend,
  material, operative,
  panel, peg, pin,
  principal, punch,
  secret, solution, table,
  vital, wind, wind up
keyboard: manual
key-change:
  modulation
keyed up:
  overwrought, tense,
  wound
keying: writing
keys: notes
khaki: tan
kibbutz: commune
kick: bang, bite, boot,
  excitement, hack,
  pass, paw
kickback: backlash,
  bribe
kicker: punter
kickoff: opening, start
kick off: open, start
kick out: boot,
  bounce, sack, turn out
kickshaws: knick-
  knacks
kick the bucket:
  croak, die
kick up a fuss:

complain, squeal
kid: banter, child, jest,
  joke, jolly, youngster
kidding: banter
kidnap: seize, take
kidnapper: bandit
kidnapping: seizure
kidney: mould
kids: young
kif: marijuana
kill: bag, blast,
  butcher, death,
  destroy, end, execute,
  knock off, knockout,
  liquidate, massacre,
  murder, quarry,
  slaughter, take, waste,
  zap
killer: butcher, wolf
killing: assassination,
  bloodshed,
  destruction, funny,
  hilarious, hysterical,
  murder, priceless,
  slaughter, uproarious,
kiln: oven, pottery
kilt: skirt
kin: connection
kind: brand, breed,
  class, considerate,
  decent,
  denomination, family,
  fashion, friendly,
  generous, good-
  natured, helpful,
  liberal, make,
  manner, model,
  mould, nature,
  obliging, order,
  pattern, quality,
  range, run, smiling,
  soft-hearted, sort,
  species, stamp, style,
  sweet, tender,
  thoughtful, unselfish,
  variety, version,
  warm
kindle: burn, fan, fire,
  ignite, inflame,
  instigate, light,
  quicken, spark, wake,
  whet
kindliness: goodwill,
  humanity, warmth
kindling: fuel
kindly: benevolent,
  benign, charitable,

friendly, good, good-
  natured, gracious,
  human, humane,
  sympathetic,
  understanding, warm,
  warm-hearted, well
kindness:
  compassion,
  consideration, favour,
  generosity, grace,
  hospitality, humanity,
  magnanimity,
  tenderness
kindred: blood,
  connection, family,
  related
kinfolk: people
king: crown, lord
kingdom: country
kink: buckle, buckle,
  curl, eccentricity,
  quirk, warp
kinked: twisted
kinky: bent, wiry,
kinship: relationship
kinsman: relative
kinsmen: family
kinswoman: relative
kiosk: boutique, desk
kip: doze, doze, nap
kirk: chapel, church
kismet: destiny, lot
kiss: caress, cuddle,
  graze, pet, salute
kisser: clock, face,
  mouth, mug
kit: gear, pack, set,
  stuff, wardrobe
kitbag: knapsack
kitchen: grill
kite: bus, crate
kith: kin
kittenish: coy
kittens: litter
kitty: bank, fund,
  pool, pot
kleptomaniac: thief
knack: faculty, flair,
  genius, hang, skill,
  talent, technique,
  turn
knackered: spent,
  tired, weary, worn out
knapsack: pack
knave: jack, scoundrel
knead: fashion,
  massage, rub, work

kneading: rub
knell: ring
knew: made
knick-knack: novelty
knickers: pants
knife: blade, slit, stab,
knife-edged: sharp
knight: cavalier
knightly: chivalrous
knit: heal, join, knot,
mend, mesh
knitting: healing
knob: boss, bump,
button, fastener,
handle, knot, node,
nodule, nut, pat, stud
knobbly: protuberant
knobkerrie: cudgel,
mace
knock: bang, bat,
blow, carp, clip,
criticize, cut, hit, jar,
jog, knap, pan, pull,
punch, rap, rattle, run
down, scoff, strike,

stroke, tap,
percussion, run down
knock about:
manhandle, maul,
punish
knock back: down,
drink, flatten, gulp,
quaff
knock down: down,
fell, floor, run down,
run over
knocked out:
senseless,
unconscious
knocker: critic
knocking: criticism,
rattle
knocking-shop:
brothel
knock into: barge,
bump
knock off: clock, kill,
rest
knock out: drug,
sedate

knock over: overturn,
upset
knoll: down, hill,
mound
knop: button
knot: bend, bun,
bunch, bundle,
cluster, hitch, kink,
knob, loop, node,
reminder, tangle,
twine
knotty: complex,
difficult, hard, prickly
knout: whip
know: experience,
identify, make, place,
recognize, see, taste,
understand
knowhow: craft,
technique
knowing: deep,
discerning, foxy,
worldly
knowledge:
awareness,

experience,
intelligence, learning,
lore, mastery, notion,
reading, scholarship,
understanding,
wisdom
knowledgeable:
aware, clever,
experienced, literate,
wise
known: familiar,
public, unquestioned
knuckle under:
kowtow, submit,
succumb
knuckle: knead
KO: knockout
koala: bear
kopje: hill
kowtow: bow
kowtowing:
grovelling
kudos: honour,
prestige

L

label: brand, call, distinguish, flag, identify, mark, name, number, pigeonhole, stamp, tab, term, ticket
labelled: marked, named
labelling: flagging
labile: changeable
labium: lip
lable: style
laborious: difficult, gruelling, hard, heavy, onerous, tough, uphill
laboriously: hard, heavily
laborous: rugged
labour: birth, delivery, difficulty, grind, hardship, industry, ordeal, trouble, work, wrestle
laboured: halting, stiff, stilted, strained, unnatural, unrealistic
labourer: hand, worker
labouring: busy
labour-saving: convenient
labyrinth: maze, network, tangle
labyrinthine: complex, complicated, intricate, involved
lace: buckle, fasten, fastener
laced: seamy
lacerate: claw, cut, gash, knife, maul, savage, scratch, slash, wound
lacerated: cut
laceration: cut, gash, scratch, slash, wound
lacework: net
lachrymose: tearful, watery
lack: defect, deficiency, deprivation, failure, need, poverty, require, scarcity, shortage, void, want

lackadaisical: careless, casual, remiss
lackey: attendant, menial, satellite, servant, yes-man
lacking: bankrupt, bare, defective, less, missing, short, weak, without
lacklustre: half-hearted, lifeless, sickly
laconic: compact, concise, dry, sententious, short, succinct
lacquer: finish, glaze, varnish
lacrimate: water
lactation: milk
lacuna: gap, hiatus, space
lacy: open
lad: boy, guy, male, youngster, youth
ladder: run, scale
laden: loaded
ladies: bog, lavatory, toilet
ladle: bale, scoop, shovel
lady: girl, hen, woman
lady-killer: wolf
ladylike: feminine, genteel, womanly
lag: criminal, drag, jacket, linger, slow
lager: brew
laggard: slow
lagging: insulation, jacket
laic: lay, secular, temporal
laid-back: free
laid off: unemployed
lair: burrow, den, haunt, hole, lodge, nest
laity: people
lake: lagoon, pool, sea, tank, water
lambast: lash, set about, slam, slate
lambency: glow
lame duck: failure, flop, loser

lame: cripple, feeble, halt, hamstring, ineffectual, mutilate, paralyse, thin, weak
lamed: mangled
lameness: limp
lament: bewail, grieve, keen, lamentation, moan, mourn, regret, ululate
lamentable: deplorable, pathetic, sad
lamentation: mourning
lamina: leaf, plate, scale, sheet
laminate: face, glaze, plate
lamp-glass: globe
lamp: beacon, bulb, light
lampoon: caricature, cartoon, mock, parody, ridicule, satire, take off
lance: spear
land: bag, country, disembark, ground, grounds, light, patch, property, realm, settle, soil, state, terrain, territory
landing-stage: quay
landlord: host, owner, proprietor
landmark: beacon, guide
landmass: continent
landowner: proprietor
lands: estate
landscape: environment, scene
landscaping: gardening
landslide: avalanche, slide
landslip: avalanche, landslide
landwards: ashore
lane: passage, road, street, track, walk, way
language: phraseology, speech, terminology, usage,

vocabulary
languid: lackadaisical, lethargic, listless, restful, sickly, supine
languish: mope, pine, rot, wither
languor: fatigue, lassitude
languorous: fluid, lackadaisical, torpid
lank: mousy, spare
lanky: gangling, tall, thin
lanolin: grease
lantern: lamp, light
lap: circle, course, leg, lick, round, stage
lapdog: yes-man
lappet: flap
lapse: degenerate, die, err, fall, fault, go, oversight, regress, relapse, revert, sin, sink, terminate, wander
lapsed: disbelieving, lost
larboard: port
larceny: burglary, robbery
lard: fat, grease
large: big, broad, bulky, burly, considerable, corpulent, good, great, handsome, main, outsize, princely, roomy, round, spacious, voluminous, wide
largely: generally, mainly
larger: major
largest: maximum
lark: caper, crack, fool, fun, game, jest, joke, laugh, prank, rag, wheeze
larruping: hiding
larva: grub
lascar: sailor
lascivious: bawdy, depraved, lecherous, lewd, salacious, sensual
lasciviousness: depravity, lewdness,

licentiousness, lust
lash: batter, beat,
bind, castigate, flog,
scourge, strap,
switch, tether, whip
lashing: heap,
mooring
lass: girl, maid,
maiden, woman
lassie: girl, woman,
youngster
lassitude: inertia,
languor
lasso: rope
last: be, continue,
dying, endure, final,
go on, hold, hold up,
keep, keep on, late,
linger, live, old,
persist, rear, remain,
run, runt, survive,
terminal, ultimate,
wear, weather
lasting: classic,
durable, monumental,
perennial, permanent,
stable, standing
lastly: finally
latch: fasten,
latch: bar, bolt,
buckle, catch,
fastener, grip, lock,
trip
latchkey: key
late: behind, night,
overdue, recent, slow,
tardy
lately: just
latent: dormant,
fallow, inactive,
incipient, potential,
quiescent,
unconscious,
underlying
later: below,
following, future,
next, since,
subsequently, then
lateral: side
laterally: sideways
latest: contemporary,
fashionable, fresh,
high, last, modern,
new, news, rage
lath: bat, board, leaf,
panel
lather: foam
latitude: breadth,
freedom, licence,
margin, room, scope,
width
latrine: bog, toilet
lattermost: last
lattice: grid, grill,
mesh, net
laud: celebrate,

compliment, eulogize,
glorify, magnify,
worship
laudable: worthy
laudatory:
complimentary, rave
laugh: chuckle,
comedian, crack,
disregard, flout,
giggle, mock, scoff,
scream, sneer, titter
laughable: derisory,
farcical, ludicrous,
preposterous,
ridiculous
laughing-stock: joke,
monkey, spectacle
laughing: laughter,
twinkling
laughter: chuckle
launch: baptise,
barge, begin,
beginning, boat,
burn, cast, float, hurl,
inaugurate, initiate,
institute, introduce,
mount, open,
opening, pioneer,
pitch, project,
projection,
publication, publish,
release, send, start,
throw
launching: baptism,
conception,
introduction, pad,
presentation
launder: clean, wash
laundered: clean
laundering: wash
laurel: bay
laurels: palm, victory
lava: slag
lava-ball: bomb
lavatory: bog, head,
pot, toilet
lavish: charitable,
considerable,
consume, copious,
extravagant,
exuberant, free,
generous, high,
liberal, lush,
luxuriant, luxurious,
magnificent, opulent,
ornate, plush,
princely, prodigal,
profuse, rain, rich,
shower, spend,
splendid, squander
lavishly: freely
lavishness:
exuberance,
magnificence,
profusion
law-abiding: honest,

honourable, obedient,
orderly, reputable,
straight, upright
law-breaker:
offender
law: bill, directive,
edict, institute,
justice, legality,
legislation, measure,
police, precept,
principle, regulation,
rule, verity
lawbreaker: criminal,
delinquent,
malefactor
lawbreaking: crime
lawcourt: court
lawful: just, law-
abiding, legitimate,
right, true
lawfulness: legality
lawless: delinquent,
wild
lawlessness: chaos,
disorder,
licentiousness,
misrule, riot
lawmaking:
legislation, legislative
lawn: grass, green
laws: teachings
lawsuit: case,
litigation, suit
lawyer: barrister,
counsel, solicitor,
writer
lawyers: bar
lax: delinquent,
derelict, limp, loose,
permissive, remiss,
slack, soft
laxative: purge
laxity: freedom,
latitude, licence,
neglect, negligence
lay: deposit, drop,
lodge, melody, place,
profane, put, rest,
secular, set, sink,
spread, stick, wager,
worldly
layabout: laggard,
wastrel, yob
layer: bed, belt,
blanket, course, film,
flake, fleece, level,
plane, plate, scale,
seam, sheet, wash
layered: voluminous
laying-on: imposition
lay-off: stoppage
layout: composition,
diagram, grid,
make-up, outline,
plan, scheme
lazar: leper

laze: idle, lounge, rest
laziness: idleness
lazy: idle, inactive,
lackadaisical,
lethargic, otiose,
shiftless, slack, slow,
supine, torpid
lea: field, meadow
leach: filter
lead: bring, cause,
clue, conduct, direct,
direction, divert,
dominate, egg, fetch,
fore, forefront, give,
go, guide, head, hero,
induce, influence,
initiative, introduce,
key, leash, line, live,
lure, marshal, mean,
move, pervert, pipe,
preface, preside over,
principal, provoke,
rule, seduce, shot,
show, star, start,
suggest, take,
tantalize, tempt, tend,
usher, walk, weight
leaden: cloudy, heavy,
livid, overcast, slow
leader: boss, captain,
chief, director,
general, guide, head,
lord, pillar, pioneer,
ruler
leadership: conduct,
executive, initiative,
lead, regime, rule, top
brass
leading: beginning,
best, capital, cardinal,
chief, first, foremost,
forward, great,
loaded, main, major,
predominant,
premier, primary,
prime, principal,
prominent, ruling,
shining, star, supreme
leaf: blade, browse,
foil, glance, page,
sheet, soon, thumb
leaflet: bill, brochure,
hand-out,
publication, tract
leafy: green, shady
league: associate,
association, band,
coalition, federation,
fellowship, order,
society, union
leak: bleed, discharge,
disclose, drip,
emission, flow, give
away, indiscretion, let
out, ooze, publish,
puncture, reveal,

revelation, run, weep

lean: bank, gaunt, haggard, inclination, lank, lanky, lie, list, loll, meagre, pinched, recline, rest, scrawny, slant, slender, slim, slope, stoop, sway, tip, underweight, wiry

leaning: bent, bias, predilection, slant, tendency

leap: bounce, bound, caper, clear, dance, dive, hurdle, jump, lunge, pounce, scramble, skip, spring, spring, vault

leaping: frisky, prancing

learn: ascertain, assimilate, determine, discover, find out, get, hear, know, master, pick up, see, take

learned: bookish, deep, knowledgeable, literary, literate, philosophical, profound, wise

learner: beginner, initiate, novice, pupil, scholar, trainee

learning: depth, discovery, education, knowledge, lore, reading, scholarship, wisdom

lease-holder: landlord, lessee

lease: charter, hire, let out, let, rent, take

leasehold: tenure

leash: lead, strap

least: base, basic, minimum, nadir, worst

leather: whip

leave: bequeath, break, cease, delete, depart, desert, devise, disappear, discontinue, dismissal, ditch, donate, endow, evacuate, except, forget, forsake, get, go off, go, holiday, jump, kick, lay off, liberty, licence, litter, maroon, miss, move, omit, park, part, pass over, pass, permission, pull out,

quit, relegate, render, renounce, resign, resist, retire, retreat, set off, skip, start, stop, take off, vacate, will, withdraw

leaven: ferment, yeast

leavening: ferment

leaves: greens

leave-taking: farewell

leaving: departure, disappearance, exodus, scrap, waste, withdrawal

lecher: rake, libertine

lecherous: bawdy, lascivious, lewd, salacious, sensual

lechery: desire, lewdness, licentiousness

lectern: desk

lecture: jaw, lesson, oration, preach, reading, rebuke, reprimand, row, scold, scolding, speak, speech, talk, teach, upbraid

lecture-hall: auditorium

lecturer: orator, teacher

lectures: course

led astray: misguided

ledge: projection, shelf

ledger: book

leech: bleed, parasite, scrounger

leer at: eye

leerily: warily

leery: wary

lees: deposit, dregs, grounds, ooze, residue, sediment

leeway: berth, freedom, latitude, margin, play, room, slack, space, tolerance

left: forgotten, superfluous

left-hand: port,

leftover: end, odd, remnant, scrap, waste

leftovers: leavings, remains, rest

leg: foot, hop, limb, peg, pin, run, stage

legacy: gift, heritage, inheritance

legal: just, law, lawful, legislation, legitimate, litigation, rightful, valid

legality: honesty,

right

legate: delegate, diplomat

legation: embassy, mission

legato: slur

legend: fable, key, motto, myth, romance, story, tale

legendary: famous, heroic, mythical, nonexistent, proverbial, romantic

legends: lore

legerdemain: deception, magic

legger: bunk

legible: fair, intelligible, plain

legion: multitude

legions: score

legislate: pass

legislation: passage

legislator: deputy

legislature: congress, chamber

legitimacy: legality

legitimate: genuine, good, just, lawful, legalize, official, proper, real, rightful, valid

legitimize: justify, legalize

legless: drunk, high, inebriated, loaded, tight

leg-over: screw

leg-pulling: banter

legume: pulse, pod

lei: garland

leisure: game, hobby, liberty, pastime, play, recreation, relaxation, rest

leisure-time: holiday

leisurely: easy

lemon: yellow

lend: give, help, loan, provide, second

lender: creditor

length: duration, quantity, strand, way

lengthen: continue, draw out, prolong

lengthways: out, vertical

lengthy: long, protracted

lenience: grace

leniency: forbearance, generosity, humanity, mercy, quarter

lenient: charitable, generous, gentle, humane, indulgent,

lax, liberal, merciful, patient, soft, tolerant

leper: outcast, pariah

leprechaun: elf, fairy, gnome, sprite

lesbian: homosexual

lesion: hurt, ulcer, wound

less: light

lessee: occupant

lessen: contract, cool, decline, decrease, descend, dilute, fall, impair, lighten, lower, mitigate, modify, pale, palliate, qualify, recede, reduce, shorten, shrink, slacken, soften, subside, wane, weaken

lessened: dilute, lower

lessening: decrease, descent, fall, modification, wane

lesser: below, incidental, inferior, junior, lower, second, secondary, side, small, subordinate, under

lesson: lecture, moral, reading

lessor: contractor

let: hire, job, lease, rent, suffer

let-down: bathos, disappointment

let-off: release

let-out: loophole

let-up: lull, relaxation

lethal: baneful, deadly, fatal, killing, mortal, murderous, poisonous, terminal, venomous, virulent, withering

lethargic: comatose, inactive, lackadaisical, languid, listless, phlegmatic, sleepy, sluggish, torpid

lethargy: fatigue, inertia, lassitude, narcosis, languor

letter: character, initial, key, line, note, scrawl, write

lettered: cultivated, cultured, learned, literary, literate, writing

letters: correspondence, learning, mail, papers, script, writing

leukaemia: cancer
level: balance, deck,
degree, demolish,
direct, elevation,
equal, equalize, even,
fell, flat, flatten, floor,
flush, grade, mark,
par, parity, pitch,
plain, plane, point,
range, rank, regular,
roll, round, smooth,
square, stage, step,
straight, subside, take
down, toneless
level-headed: cool,
down-to-earth,
realistic, responsible,
sane, sober, solid,
sound, steady
level-headedness:
common sense,
sanity, sobriety
levelling-off: plateau
levelling: demolition
lever: bar, beam,
crank, crowbar,
handle, hoist, key,
pin, switch
leverage: footing,
grip, hold, influence,
pull, purchase,
traction
levitate: float
levy: assess, raise,
recruit, tax, toll
lewd: bawdy,
immodest, immoral,
lascivious, loose,
nasty, obscene,
salacious, titillating
lewdness: immorality,
licentiousness, lust,
obscenity
lexicon: vocabulary
liability: blame,
commitment, debit,
debt, disadvantage,
obligation, onus
liable: fallible, open,
prone, ready,
responsible, subject,
susceptible,
vulnerable
liaise: link
liaison: intrigue,
relationship, romance
libel: calumny, lie,
lying, mud, slander,
smear
libeller: backbiter,
liar
libellous: defamatory,
scandalous
liberal: big, bountiful,
broad, broad-minded,
catholic, easy, free,

generous, handsome,
hospitable, indulgent,
kind, lavish, left,
open, permissive,
princely, progressive,
tolerant
liberality: breadth,
generosity,
hospitality, kindness,
largess, munificence
liberally: freely
liberate: clear,
deliver, discharge,
enfranchise, free, let
out, loose, ransom,
redeem, release, save,
take
liberated:
independent,
uninhibited
liberation:
deliverance, delivery,
discharge, release,
rescue
liberator: saviour
libertine: dissolute,
promiscuous, rake,
villain
liberty: freedom,
independence,
latitude, leave,
leisure, licence,
release, right, scope
libidinous: bawdy,
lascivious, lewd,
lecherous
libido: desire, lust, sex
library: study
librettist: dramatist
libretto: book, script,
words
licence: authority,
certificate, charter,
faculty, franchise,
freedom, impunity,
latitude, liberty,
patent, permission,
permit, power,
warrant
license: authorize,
invest, legalize, right,
enfranchise
licensed: privileged
licentious: bawdy,
depraved, dissolute,
fast, immoral, lewd,
libertine, obscene
licentiousness:
depravity,
immorality,
impropriety,
lewdness, nastiness,
obscenity
licit: lawful, legitimate
lick: lap, little, rout,
whip, wipe

licking: drubbing,
rout
lickspittle: sycophant
lid: bonnet, cap, cover,
flap, hood, seal
lie: bed, deception,
falsehood, fib, fiction,
fudge, hide,
invention, lurk,
recline, repose, rest,
run, story, wallow
lie-down: rest
liefer: first
liege: dependent,
feudal, lord
lieutenant: deputy,
minister
life: being, breath,
career, creation,
energy, existence,
fire, force, go, living,
magic, memoirs, past,
soul, sparkle, spirit,
time, vocation, world,
zip
lifeblood: life, sap
life force: spirit
lifeless: blank, dead,
dull, fishy, flat,
glassy, inanimate,
inert, insensible,
insipid, lacklustre,
listless, unimaginative
lifelike: living,
realistic, vivid
lifeline: salvation
lifelong: perennial
life-span: time
life-story: memoirs
life-style: culture,
living
lifetime: life, time
lift: boost, bring up,
capture, carry, heave,
hoist, jack, lighten,
pick up, pirate,
pocket, pull up, raise,
ride, rise, run, steal
lift up: hold up, rear
lift-off: ascend,
ascent, burn, take off
ligament: muscle
ligature: knot
light: beacon, burn,
clear, delicate,
detonate, easy,
emanation, faint, fair,
fine, fire, flame, flare,
flimsy, frothy, gentle,
glow, highlight,
ignite, illuminate,
illumination, kindle,
lamp, lyric, match,
radiate, set fire to, set
off, torch, white
light-buoy: beacon,

lighten: bleach, dawn,
discolour, lessen,
mitigate, mollify,
unload
lighter: barge, light,
taper
light-headed: dizzy,
faint, giddy, queer
light-headedness:
dizziness
light-hearted:
buoyant, carefree,
gay, sunny
light-heartedly: gaily
light-heartedness:
happiness, levity
lighthouse: beacon,
light
lighting: illumination
lightly-built: slight
lightly: gingerly
lightness: delicacy
lightning-rod:
conductor
lightning: whirlwind
lights: illumination
lightweight:
mediocrity, nobody,
nonentity, pygmy,
superficial
ligneous: wooden,
xyloid
like: as, care, dig,
enjoy, equal, fellow,
identical, please,
relish, take to
likeable: disarming,
engaging, lovable,
nice, pleasant
likelihood: chance,
liability, odds,
presumption,
prospect
likely: fair, liable,
logical, moral,
plausible, probable,
promising, prone,
ready
like-minded:
compatible,
sympathetic
like-mindedness:
solidarity
liken: compare
likeness: community,
image, mirror,
parallel, parity,
picture, resemblance,
semblance, shape,
show, similarity
likewise: besides,
moreover, so
liking: fancy,
fondness, inclination,
love, penchant,
predilection, relish,

taste
lily-livered:
cowardly, spineless
limb: branch, leg,
member, part
limber: athletic,
flexible, lithe, nimble,
pliable, supple, warm
limbo: oblivion
limelight:
foreground,
limit: border,
boundary, check,
circumscribe, control,
define, end, handicap,
height, keep, line,
margin, narrow, peg,
qualify, ration,
restrict, side
limitation: check,
condition, control,
handicap, hindrance,
parameter, proviso,
qualification,
restraint, restriction
limited: finite, inside,
insular, local,
numbered, provincial,
select, small
limiting: ultimate
limitless:
incalculable,
indefinite, infinite,
vast
limitlessness:
immensity
limits:
comprehension,
confines, field, fringe,
range
limp-wristed:
homosexual
limp: insipid, languid,
lank, listless, mousy
limpid: liquid, lucid,
transparent
limping: lame
linctus: medicine
line: back, bag, band,
bank, boundary,
business, cable,
calling, column, cord,
course, craft, crease,
department,
direction, dynasty,
face, family, fashion,
field, file, flex, game,
genealogy, horizon,
house, leash, mark,
measure, occupation,
order, pad, path,
pedigree, pitch,
policy, procession,
profession, province,
queue, racket, rail,
range, rank, rope,

routine, row, seam,
string, tactic, tail,
telephone, track,
work, wrinkle
lineage: birth, blood,
breed, breeding,
caste, extraction,
family, genealogy,
house, origin,
pedigree, stock, strain
lined: drawn, rugged,
worn, wreathed
line-drawing:
graphic, illustration
liner: boat
lines: dialogue, script,
track
linesman: umpire
line up: book, file,
marshal, organize,
programme, queue,
rank
line-up: programme,
queue, selection
ling: heath
linger: delay, lag,
loiter, saunter, stay,
stick
lingerer: laggard
lingerie: underwear
lingering: slow
lingo: cant, language
liniment: lotion
lining: backing,
basement, mantle
link: associate,
association, attach,
bond, bridge, chain,
combine,
communication,
connect, connection,
cord, couple, dock,
fasten, gear, join,
joint, knit, liaison,
lock, marry, relate,
span, string, team,
unite, yoke
linkage: gear, lock,
union
linked: related
linking: basket,
between, junction,
through
links: course
lint: bandage, fluff
lion-hearted: valiant
lip: brim, mouth, rim,
sauce, verge
lip service: cant
liquefaction:
dissolution
liquefy: dissolve, fuse,
melt, run
liquid: beverage,
drink, fluid, juice,
moisture, watery, wet

liquidate: bankrupt,
kill, knock off, polish
off, remove, settle,
square, wind up
liquidation:
assassination, finish,
slaughter
liquidator: killer
liquidity: money
liquor: brew, drink,
fluid, juice, liquid,
tipple
lissome: lithe
list: bill, canon,
catalogue, category,
detail, enter,
inclination, incline,
itemize, lean,
programme, recite,
register, roll, slant,
table, tip
listen: attend, bug,
hear, heed, mind,
regard, tap
listing: breakdown,
recital
listless: lackadaisical,
languid, murmuring,
sluggish, supine,
unsettled
listlessness: boredom,
languor, malaise
lit: luminous, score
literacy: learning
literal: bare, close,
error, letter, verbal
literary: bookish,
writing
literate: learned
literature: brochure,
tract, writing
lithe: athletic, flexible,
light, limber, loose,
nimble, supple, wiry
litigant: party
litigate: prosecute
litter: bed, debris,
garbage, junk, refuse,
rubbish, scatter,
waste, young
littérateur: writer
little: baby, bit,
handful, lick, low,
petty, small, spot
littoral: beach,
maritime, shore
liturgical: ceremonial
liturgy: rite, ritual
live: be, dwell,
electric, lead, living,
remain, settle, survive
lived-in: occupied
livelihood: bread, job,
keep, living, support,
sustenance, work
liveliness: bounce,

energy, exuberance,
life, snap, vigour,
vivacity, zip
lively: bold, bright,
brisk, bubbly,
colourful, dynamic,
expressive,
exuberant, fresh,
frisky, high-spirited,
imaginative, jaunty,
juicy, nimble, nippy,
pert, piquant, playful,
quick, racy, rousing,
salty, scintillating,
smart, spicy, stirring,
vibrant, vigorous,
vital, vivacious,
warm, witty
liven: juice
liverish: fragile
livery: uniform
livestock: cattle, stock
livid: furious, lurid
living: being, keep,
life, live, livelihood,
maintenance, organic,
quick, vital
lizard: dragon
load: burden, cargo,
charge, freight, fuel,
heap, mass, oppress,
pack, prime, saddle,
stuff, tax, weigh,
weight
loaded: full, heavy,
laden, rich, wealthy
loaf: bread, cake, hang
around, head, idle,
loiter, loll, lounge
loafer: drone, laggard,
layabout, wastrel
loafing: idle, idleness
loam: earth, mould
loan: lend
loath: disinclined,
reluctant, unwilling
loathe: hate
loathing: disgust,
hate, phobia,
repugnance, revulsion
loathsome:
disgusting, execrable,
monstrous, nasty,
odious, repulsive,
revolting, shocking,
sickening, vile
lob: cast, put, shot,
throw
lobby: buttonhole,
faction, foyer, hall,
passage
local: civic, home, inn,
native, neighbour,
pub, resident, topical
locale: habitat,
position

locality: place, quarter, region, scene, situation, vicinity
locate: base, find, lay, manoeuvre, place, set
located: found
location: finding, fix, locality, place, point, position, spot, station, surroundings, venue
loch: lake
lock: cage, bar, bolt, close, fastener, gate, imprison, jail, key, seal, secure
locked: captive, closed
locker: cabinet, closet, trunk
locks: hair, tresses
lockup: jail, prison
locomotion: propulsion
locomotive: train
locum: substitute
lode: lead, ledge, vein
lodge: bed, board, box, cabin, club, deposit, dwell, harbour, hostel, install, live, order, prefer, put up, quarter, stay, stop
lodger: guest, resident
lodging: living, residence
lodgings: quarters
loess: deposit, sediment
loft: attic, garret
loftiness: condescending, dignity, elevation, majesty, pride
lofty: cavalier, dignified, exalted, grand, great, high, majestic, stately, supercilious, superior, tall
log-cabin: lodge
log: book, enter, itinerary, journal, minute, notes, protocol, record, tally, wooden
logged: noted
logic: dialectic, philosophy, rationale, reason, reasoning, sense
logical: consistent, legitimate, natural, rational, reasonable, sound, valid
logo: brand, character,

cipher, device, mark, motto, seal, sign, symbol
logs: kindling, wood
loiter: hang about, hover, lag, linger, lounge, lurk, saunter, skulk
loll: hang, loaf, lounge, recline, slump
lolly: money
lone: only, solitary
loneliness: isolation, seclusion, solitude
lonely: forlorn, godforsaken, remote, secluded, solitary
lonesome: solitary
long: aspire, desire, die, good, great, hope, hunger, itch, lanky, lengthy, look forward to, lust, miss, pant, pine, want, wish, yearn
long-drawn-out: interminable, lengthy, lingering, protracted, slow
longer: more
long-established: old
longhand: hand
longing: thirsty, craving, desire, greed, hankering, hunger, itch, lust, want, wish, wishful, yearning
long-lasting: durable
long-serving: veteran
long-standing: inveterate, indestructible, lasting, passive, patience, patient, persevering, resigned, stoical, thick-skinned, tolerant
long-term: overall
long-winded: interminable, pedestrian, ponderous, rambling, verbose, wordy
loo: bog, lavatory, toilet
look: aspect, attend, browse, cast, check, clock, complexion, description, do, eye, face, frown, gaze, glance, glimpse, hunt, observe, peek, peep, peer, peruse, prospect, read, regard, research, scan, scout, scowl,

search, see, semblance, sound, view, watch, witness
look after: attend, cradle, do, keep, maintain, mind, nurse, protect, run, save, superintend, support, tend, watch
lookalike: double, match
look down on: despise, disdain, patronize, scorn
looker: cracker, doll
look for: await, expect, follow, invite, seek
look forward to: hope, face, await
looking after: maintenance
looking-glass: mirror
look into: explore, investigate, probe, study
look like: favour, mimic, promise, resemble
look lively: stir
lookout: guard, scout, sentry, watch
look out for: watch, mind
look over: inspect, overlook, survey
look up to: lionize, respect, revere
loom: bulk, dominate, menace, overhang, rear, tower
looming: impending, near
loony: crazy, insane, lunatic, mad
loony bin: asylum
loop: circle, coil, crook, curl, flourish, hook, kink, knit, knot, lap, link, ring, sling, string, tab, turn, twine, warp, wheel, wind
looped: crooked, wound
looping: curved, winding
loopy: insane, mad
loose: deliver, dissolute, dissolve, fast, free, imprecise, indefinite, lax, liberal, liberate, light, limp, open, promiscuous, relinquish, scrappy, slack, slovenly, undo,

unsettled, vague, wide
loose-fitting: comfortable
loose-limbed: flexible, lithe
loosely: vaguely
loosely-built: gangling
loosen: clear, detach, disconnect, key, liberalize, relax, undo, yield
loosened: undone
looseness: dissolution, slack
loosing: liberation
loot: haul, money, pillage, plunder, prize, ransack, rape, ravage, rip off, rob, sack, strip, winnings
looting: pillage, rape, rapine, sack
lop: chop, crop, curtail, cut, head, prune, trim
lope: jog
lopped: cut
lopsided: crooked, irregular, unequal, uneven, expansive
loquacious: garrulous, verbose, vocal, voluble, wordy
lord: husband, master, patriarch, peer
lordly: dignified, grand, lofty
lords: peerage
lordship: patronage
lore: learning, scholarship
lose: blow, forfeit, misplace, miss, pass up, sacrifice, shake off
loser: failure, flop
lose weight: diet, reduce, slim
loss: casualty, consumption, cost, death, deprivation, disadvantage, disappearance, failure, forfeit, sacrifice, toll, waste
loss-leader: bait, temptation
loss-making: uneconomic, unprofitable
lost: dissipated, forlorn, gone, missing, strange, stray, mislaid
lot: barrel, batch,

bundle, crew, doom,
fate, heap, load, luck,
lump, many, mass,
parcel, pile, plot,
portion, range, share,
umpteen, whole
Lothario: wolf
lotion: ointment, wash
lots: many, much,
plenty, score,
umpteen
lottery: gamble
loud: big, blatant,
boisterous, bold,
flamboyant, flashy,
full, garish, glaring,
meretricious, noisy,
obstreperous,
ostentatious, raucous,
sonorous, strong,
uproarious,
vociferous
loudmouthed:
blatant
loudness: glare,
volume
lounge: hearth, living-
room, loaf, loll,
recline, sprawl
lounger: drone,
laggard, layabout
louse: jerk
lousy: fleabitten,
rotten
lout: barbarian, brute,
oaf, yob
loutish: churlish,
coarse, oafish,
philistine, rough,
rowdy, rude, rustic,
uncouth, ungracious
louvres: blind
lovable: cherubic,
cuddly, lovely
love: darling, dear,
duck, endearment,
flame, fondness,
friendship, heart,
idolize, inamorata,
kindliness, kindness,
lap, like, liking, nil,
passion, regard,
romance, sweetheart,
tenderness, warmth,
worship
love-child: bastard
loved: familiar
loveliness: beauty
lovely: attractive,
beautiful, beauty,
divine, fair, gorgeous,
heavenly, stunning
lover: inamorata,
man, mate
lovey-dovey:
romantic

loving: close, devoted,
fond, kind, kindly,
passionate, tender,
warm, warm-hearted
low: barbarian, base,
common,
contemptible, deep,
despicable, dirty,
faint, fleabitten,
gentle, humble,
lamentable, mean,
miserable, quiet, sad,
shabby, short, slavish,
slump, soft, vile,
vulgar, weak,
wretched
low-born: mean
lowbrow: barbarian,
philistine
low-cost: cheap
low-down: dirt
lower: below,
beneath, cheapen,
depress, descend, dip,
fall, glare, inferior,
junior, less, let down,
modify, petty, reduce,
relax, slash,
subordinate, take
down, under,
underneath, wane
lower-class: plebeian
lowering: black, dirty,
dismal, drop, fall,
heavy, modification,
ominous, overcast,
pout, thunderous,
wane
lowest: base, basic,
bottom, least,
minimum, nadir, zero
low-grade: rotten
low-key: subdued,
underdone
lowland: flat
lowliness: humility,
obscurity
lowly: base, humble,
menial, obscure
low-priced: economic
loyal: devoted,
faithful, fast,
patriotic, true,
unselfish
loyalist: patriotic
loyally: fast, truly
loyalty: commitment,
duty, faith,
faithfulness, fidelity,
nationalism
lozenge: capsule,
tablet
LSD: money
lubberly: boorish,
hulking, oafish,
uncouth

lubricant: grease
lubricate: grease
lubricious: lecherous
lubricity: lewdness,
licentiousness
lucid: articulate,
coherent, intelligible,
luminous, rational,
sane, simple
lucidity: clarity
lucifer: devil, match
luck: chance, fortune,
hit, lot, lottery,
portion, windfall
luckily: fortuitously,
happily
luckless: doomed,
unfortunate, unhappy
lucky: fairytale,
fortunate, happy,
opportune,
successful, well
lucrative: economic,
fruitful, profitable,
successful
lucre: money, wealth
ludicrous: comical,
crazy, derisory,
farcical, laughable,
mad, nonsensical,
preposterous, rich,
ridiculous, senseless,
tall, undignified
ludicrousness:
nonsense, stupidity
lug-hole: ear
lug: carry, cart, haul,
hump, manhandle,
take
**luggage
compartment:** boot
lugubrious: baleful,
dismal, lachrymose,
rueful, sad, sorrowful
lukewarm: cool,
halfhearted, tepid,
unenthusiastic
lull: pause, respite,
rest, silence, still
lulling: dreamy
lumbar: back
lumber: roll, saddle,
stump, timber
lumbered: laden
lumbering: awkward,
clumsy, heavy,
ponderous, ungainly
luminary: celebrity,
worthy
luminescence:
glamour, light
luminosity:
brilliance, light,
lucidity, shine
luminous: bright,
brilliant, light, lucid,

radiant, shining,
sunny
lummox: oaf
lump: bat, bulge,
bump, chunk,
growth, hump,
hunch, knob, knot,
loaf, mass, nodule,
nut, pat, prominence,
put up with, swelling,
tumour
lumpen: ignorant
lumpish: hulking,
rustic
lumpy: bumpy,
irregular,
uncomfortable,
uneven
lunacy: folly, idiocy,
insanity, madness,
stupidity
lunatic: asinine,
crazy, fatuous, idiot,
idiotic, insane, mad,
nut, psychotic,
screwy
lunch: dinner, meal
lunchroom: caf
lunge: jab, pass,
swoop, venue
lurch: founder, jerk,
jump, limp, lunge,
pitch, plunge, reel,
rock, roll, stagger,
stumble, wallow
lurching: halting, roll,
tottering
lure: attract,
attraction, bait,
captivate, decoy,
draw, incentive, pull,
seduce, tempt,
temptation
lurid: frightful, juicy,
loud, pulp
luring: attractive,
beckoning
lurk: hover, prowl,
skulk, sneak
luscious: delicious,
rich, savoury, tasty
lush: drunkard, fat,
juicy, luxuriant, rank,
rich
lust: craving, desire,
fancy, hunger, itch,
long, longing,
passion, pine, sex,
yearn, yearning
lustful: bawdy, hot,
lascivious, lecherous,
lewd, longing,
passionate, salacious,
sensual
lustration: catharsis
lustre: brilliance,

finish, fire, glaze,
polish, sheen, shine,
splendour, water
lustrous: brilliant,
gleaming, shiny,
splendid
lusty: hardy, hearty,
muscular, vigorous,
virile

luxate: dislocate
luxuriance:
exuberance,
profusion, wealth
luxuriant: exuberant,
fertile, lush, prodigal
luxuriate: indulge,
wallow
luxurious: grand,

lush, magnificent,
palatial, plush,
splendid
luxury: magnificence,
plenty, style
lying: dishonest, false,
perjured, prone,
untrue, untruthful
lynch: hang

lynching: rope
lyre: harp
lyric: lay
lyrical: lyric, poetic
lyricist: dramatist,
poet
lyrics: words

M

ma: mother
macabre: creepy, forbidding, frightening, grisly, gruesome, morbid, sick
macaw: parrot
mace: rod
Machiavellian: scheming, subtle
machinate: conspire, plot, scheme
machination: artifice, conspiracy, design, intrigue, manoeuvre, plot, scheme
machine: automaton, car, gadget, mechanism, motor, robot, thing
machine-like: mechanical
machine-operated: mechanical
machinery: gear, guts, mechanism, plant, rig, works
machismo: manliness
macho: male, virile
mackinaw: rug
macrocosm: universe
mad: crazy, distracted, foolish, insane, ludicrous, psychotic, rabid, screwy, stuck, unreasoning, wild, zany
madcap: foolhardy, hothead, precipitate, rash, reckless, scatterbrained, wild
madden: incense, infuriate, outrage, provoke
maddened: berserk, furious, rabid
made: rich
made-up: fictitious, imaginary, romantic
madhouse: asylum, bedlam
madman: lunatic
madness: insanity, lunacy
madonna: virgin
madrigal: glee

madwoman: lunatic
maestro: conductor, wizard
magazine: cartridge, journal, review, periodical
maggot: grub
magic: fairytale, fascination, glamour, medicine, miracle, miraculous, spell, unique, witchcraft
magical: fairytale, miraculous
magician: wizard
magisterial: dictatorial, judicial
magistracy: bench
magistrate: beak, judge, justice
magnanimity: forbearance, generosity, kindness, mercy
magnanimous: big, charitable, generous, handsome, liberal, merciful, noble, patient, selfless, thick-skinned, understanding, unselfish
magnate: king
magnetic: attractive
magnetism: attraction, charm, fascination, glamour, magic, personality, pull
magnetize: mesmerize
magnification: enlargement
magnificence: brilliance, glory, luxury, majesty, splendour
magnificent: beautiful, breathtaking, bright, brilliant, fine, gallant, glorious, gorgeous, grand, grandiose, lordly, luxurious, majestic, princely, spectacular, splendid, superb, terrific,

wonder, wonderful
magnify: blow up, compound, exaggerate, glorify
magnitude: bulk, enormity, gauge, immensity, mass, measure, measurement, quantity, size
magnum opus: masterpiece
magus: prophet, wizard
maid: daily, girl, maiden, servant, woman
maiden: girl, virgin, woman
maidenly: virgin
maidservant: woman
mail: post, remit, send
maim: cripple, lame, mutilate
maimed: lame, mangled, misshapen
maiming: mayhem
main: base, basic, body, capital, cardinal, channel, chief, grand, great, headquarters, high, leading, major, master, paramount, predominant, premier, primary, prime, principal, prominent, ruling, sea, special, trunk
mainland: continent
mainline: inject
mainly: basically, especially, generally, primarily
mainspring: cause, root
mainstay: backbone, bastion, pillar, rock, strength, support
maintain: assert, aver, avow, bolster, carry, carry on, claim, contend, continue, have, insist, keep, keep up, make out, perpetuate, plead, preserve, profess,

protest, retain, say, service, support, sustain, tend, wield
maintenance: keep, overhaul, service, support, sustenance, upkeep
maize: corn
majestic: august, grand, grandiose, lofty, magnificent, palatial, regal
majesty: dignity, glory
major: bulk, key, special, star, through
majority: body bulk, mass, maturity
make: brand, brew, build, clear, compel, compose, construct, create, discover, do, draw, drive, effect, fabricate, fashion, fetch, form, frame, gain, get, give, gross, hammer, kind, knock off, line, lodge, machine, manufacture, model, mount, net, package, prepare, produce, quality, reach, realize, render, return, score, shape, sort, take, turn, turn out, variety, weave, win
make-believe: fictitious, pretence, unreal
maker: author, cause, father
makers': factory
makeshift: rude
make-up: composition, constitution, habit, nature, organization, paint, personality, structure, temperament
making: composition, creation
making for: bound, destined
makings: potential
maladjusted:

neurotic
maladministration:
misrule
maladroit: clumsy,
gauche, impractical,
inept, rustic
maladroitness:
impracticality
malady: condition,
disease, illness
malaise: discomfort
male: macho, man,
virile
malediction: curse,
imprecation
malefactor: culprit,
offender, outlaw,
villain
maleness: manliness
malevolence: malice,
nastiness, spite,
venom
malevolent: baleful,
horrid, ill, malignant,
satanic, sinister, ugly,
venomous, vicious,
virulent, vitriolic,
waspish, wicked
malfeasance: crime
malformation:
deformity,
disfigurement, freak
malformed:
deformed, misshapen,
monstrous
malfunctioning:
faulty
malice: nastiness,
rancour, spite, venom
malicious: evil,
malevolent,
malignant,
pernicious,
poisonous, sardonic,
unkind, vexatious,
vicious, virulent,
vitriolic, wicked
malign: blacken, libel,
malevolent,
mischievous, slander,
smear, ugly,
venomous, wicked,
wrong
malignancy: cancer,
poison, tumour
malignant: baleful,
black, evil, harmful,
horrid, malevolent,
morbid, pernicious,
sardonic, satanic,
sinister, vicious,
virulent, vitriolic,
waspish
maligning: libellous
malignity: malice,
nastiness, venom

malison: imprecation
malleable: plastic,
pliable, soft, yielding
mallet: hammer, mace
malnourished:
skeletal, underweight
malodorous: smelly
malpractice:
misconduct
malt: mash
maltreat: harm,
molest, outrage,
persecute
maltreated: battered
maltreatment:
battery, rape
mama: mother
mammal: brute
mammary gland:
breast
mammoth: bumper,
giant, huge, immense,
jumbo, massive,
monster, monstrous,
monumental,
mountainous, vast
**man (in chess,
draughts):** piece,
man: fellow, guy,
human, husband,
lover, male, nobody,
passer-by, piece,
punter, scout, world
manacle: bond,
chain, handcuff,
shackle
manacled: powerless
manacles: irons,
restraint
manage: carry on,
command, conduct,
contrive, control,
direct, do, get on, go
on, govern, handle,
head, husband,
jockey, keep, lead,
make do, make out,
manoeuvre, operate,
organize, preside
over, regulate, ride,
rule, run, see to,
spare, superintend,
work
manageable: gentle,
light, pliable, viable
management: care,
command, conduct,
control, direction,
executive,
government,
leadership,
manipulation,
operation, oracle,
oversight, regulation,
supervision,
treatment, upkeep,

usage
manager: boss, chief,
director, executive,
gaffer, head, overseer,
superior
managerial:
professional
man-at-arms:
warrior
mandate: charge,
commission, edict,
jurisdiction, order
mandatory:
compulsory,
necessary, obligatory,
prerequisite
mandible: beak, jaw
mane: hair
manes: shade
mange: scab
manger: crib
mangle: batter, claw,
crush, hack, maul,
murder, mutilate,
press, ruin, savage
mangled: battered,
deformed
mangling: battery
manhandle: knead,
maul, molest, paw
manhood: maturity
mania: fetish,
fixation, lunacy,
obsession, passion
maniac: lunatic,
zealot
maniacal: berserk,
violent, wild
manic: obsessed,
obsessive
manifest: attest,
betray, clear,
conspicuous,
demonstrate, distinct,
form, give, gross, let
on, look, marked,
materialize, notable,
noticeable, obvious,
overt, patent, reflect,
register, render,
reveal, tangible,
transparent,
undisguised, visible
manifestation:
demonstration,
formation, garb,
indication,
occurrence, presence,
testimony, token
manifestly: notably,
undeniably
manifesto: platform
manifold: complex,
multiple
manikin: doll, dwarf,
midget

manipulate: finger,
handle, jockey,
juggle, knead,
manage, manoeuvre,
ply, rig, wangle, work
manipulation:
management,
massage, operation,
therapy, wangle
manipulative:
calculating,
manipulator:
operator
mankind: flesh,
humanity, people,
society, world
manly: gallant, hardy,
lusty, male, virile
man-made: artificial,
synthetic
manna: windfall
mannequin: model
manner: attitude,
bearing, carriage,
cast, course,
demeanour,
description,
execution, fashion,
form, kind, look,
method, quality,
strain, style,
technique, way
mannered: camp,
idiosyncratic
mannerism: habit
mannerly: decent,
genteel, good, polite,
proper, urbane, well-
bred
manners: behaviour,
breeding, conduct,
etiquette, form,
propriety
mannish: male
manoeuvering:
manipulation
manoeuvre: artifice,
device, finesse, guide,
handle, jockey,
manhandle, measure,
move, movement,
navigate, operate,
ploy, run, scheme,
tactic
manoeuvring:
operation
manor: court, patch,
place, residence, seat,
territory
manor-house: hall
manorial: feudal
manservant: groom,
lackey
mansion: hall,
residence
mantle: cloak, crust,

frock, layer, pall,
robe, veil, wrap
mantled: veiled
manual: bank, guide
manufacture:
construct, machine,
make, package,
produce, production,
synthesize, turn out
manufactured:
artificial, made,
synthetic
manufacturing:
business, industry
manumission:
liberation
manumit: liberate
manure: dung,
fertilize, ordure
many: manifold,
numerous, several,
umpteen, various
many-sided: versatile
map: draw,
illustration, plan, plot
map-reader:
navigator
maquis: underground
mar: blemish, blot,
deface, impair,
overshadow, poison,
pollute, queer, ruin,
score
maracca: rattle
maraud: forage,
pillage, raid, sack
marauder: bandit,
boarder, buccaneer,
outlaw, predator
marauding: foray,
predatory
marbles: mind
march: border,
demonstrate,
demonstration,
fringe, pace, walk
marching: hiking
marching orders:
dismissal
march-past: parade,
review
mare's nest: knot
margarine: fat
margin: border,
boundary, brim,
divide, fringe, lip,
march, parameter,
periphery, play, rim,
room, side, skirt,
space, verge
marginal: outside,
side
margins: precincts
marijuana: grass,
hash, pot, weed
marina: basin,

harbour, mooring,
port
marine: jolly,
maritime, nautical
mariner: navigator,
sailor
marionette: puppet
marital: conjugal,
married, matrimonial
maritime: marine,
nautical, navy
mark: blemish, blot,
brand, characterize,
define, degree,
disfigurement, dot,
feature, flag, fool,
goal, grade, heed,
importance,
impression, indicate,
indication, key, label,
line, measure, mind,
mug, nick, note, pace,
point, prey, punter,
remark, scar, score,
scratch, seal, speck,
spot, stain, stamp,
symptom, tally,
target, thumb, token,
track, vestige, wand,
watch
mark down:
discount, reduce
marked: chequered,
distinct, notable,
obvious, salient,
sharp, strong, thick
markedly: especially,
notably, particularly,
clearly
marker: label,
landmark, pen, tab
market: audience,
bazaar, clientele, fair,
hawk, outlet,
promote, public,
publicize, publish,
push, sale, sell, vend
marketable:
commercial
marketing: business,
mercantile,
production,
promotion,
propaganda,
publication
marketplace: bazaar
marking: flagging
mark out:
circumscribe,
differentiate,
describe, designate,
distinguish, key, stake
marksman: shot
mark up: key,
punctuate
marmalade: preserve

maroon: beach,
desert, ditch, red
marque: make, model
marquee: roof
marriage: match,
matrimonial,
matrimony, union,
wedding
married: conjugal,
marital
marrow: heart,
kernel, meat, pulp,
zucchini
marry: couple, hitch,
match, mate, pair,
take, unify, unite,
wed
marsh: bog, fen, flat,
quagmire, sink,
swamp
marshal: compile,
dispose, group, order,
organize, rank, round
up, shepherd
marshy: muddy,
sodden, watery
mart: bazaar, market
martial: warlike
martin: swallow
martinet:
authoritarian, ogre,
oppressor, tyrant,
despot
martyr: victim
martyrdom: hell
marvel: jewel,
phenomenon,
prodigy, spectacle,
wonder
marvellous:
enjoyable, glorious,
great, prodigious,
sensational, splendid,
stunning, wonder,
wonderful
marzipan: filling
mascot: talisman
masculine: male,
virile
masculinity:
manliness
mash: crush, pulp,
squash
mask: blanket, blind
camouflage, cloak,
conceal, cover,
disguise, façade, hide,
mantle, muffle,
obscure, pretext,
screen, veil, veneer
masked: hidden,
veiled
masked ball:
masquerade
masonry: fabric
masquerade:

impersonate, pose
mass: bank, bloom,
body, bulk, bundle,
cake, collection,
communion,
concentration,
congregate, crowd,
flock, heap, hoard,
host, immensity,
jungle, load, lot,
lump, mat, mob,
mountain, multitude,
pipe, quantity, raise,
rally, size, swarm,
tangle, volume,
weight
massacre:
assassination,
butchery, carnage,
destruction, kill,
killing, murder,
slaughter, slay, sword
massage: knead, rub,
therapy
massed:
conglomerate, crowd,
herd, millions, mob,
people, plenty,
proletariat, rabble,
score
massif: highlands,
plateau
massive: big, bulky,
fat, gross, heavy,
huge, immense,
jumbo, large, mighty,
monolithic, monster,
monstrous,
monumental,
mountainous,
overweight,
ponderous,
prodigious, vast,
weighty
mass-produce:
manufacture
mass-production:
manufacture
mast: pole, pylon
master: artist,
authority, boss,
bridle, captain, chief,
classic, conquer,
control, genius,
govern, guide, head,
learn, lord, original,
owner, pick up,
professional, repress,
sage, skipper,
specialist, teacher,
wizard, worst
masterful:
authoritative
masterfulness: self-
assertion
masterly: brilliant,

classic, gifted, perfect
mastermind: brain,
genius, orchestrate,
run, tactician
masterpiece: classic,
gem
masters: top brass
masterstroke: coup
mastery: dexterity,
domination, grip,
prowess, virtuosity
masthead rope: lift
masticate: bite
mat: rug, tangle
match: balance,
coincide, companion,
compare, contest,
equal, even, fellow,
fidelity, fit, fitness,
game, keep up, light,
like, marry, mate,
meet, pair, parallel,
pit, reciprocate,
reconcile, rival,
square, suit, tally,
touch, tournament
matching: identical,
like
matchless: peerless
mate: associate,
companion, comrade,
couple, fellow, friend,
intimate, pair, pal,
partner, tally
matelot: sailor
mater: mother,
material: germane,
bodily, cloth,
concrete, corporeal,
fabric, matter,
pertinent, physical,
relevant, significant,
stuff, substance,
tangible
materialistic:
worldly
materialization:
formation,
manifestation,
occurrence
materialize: come,
form, happen, occur
materializing: onset
materially:
measurably
materials: kit, supply
materiel: fuel
matey: friendly
mating: sexual
intercourse
matrimonial:
conjugal
matrimony: wedding
matrix: mould
matron: mother
matronly: womanly

matted: messy
matter-of-fact:
down-to-earth,
practical, pragmatic,
realistic, sensible,
unspoilt
matter: body,
business, concern,
count, hassle,
interest, issue, item,
mass, material,
regard, respect,
significance, signify,
stuff, subject, text,
thing, transaction,
weigh
mattress: bed
maturation:
development
mature: blossom,
develop, experienced,
flower, mellow,
payable, ready,
responsible, ripe,
season, seasoned
maturity: autumn,
majority, perfection
maudlin: drunk,
drunken, lachrymose,
mawkish, sentimental
maul: batter, claw,
handle, manhandle,
paw, savage
mauled: battered
mauling: battery
maunder: drivel,
ramble
mauve: maroon
maverick: oddity,
rogue
mawkish: oafish,
sickly, wet
maxilla: jaw
maxim: motto,
principle, proverb,
rule, saying, theorem
maximum: ceiling,
full, height, limit,
peak, zenith
maybe: perchance,
perhaps, possibly
mayhem: havoc
maze-like:
labyrinthine
maze: network,
puzzle, tangle,
wilderness
mazuma: money
meadow: field,
paddock, pasture
meagre: few, frugal,
inadequate, jejune,
lamentable, lean,
little, low, narrow,
niggardly, paltry,
poor, remote, scanty,

skimpy, slender,
small, spare, sparse:
thin
meal: banquet,
dinner, feast, powder,
repast
meals: board
mealy-mouthed:
pusillanimous
mean: avaricious,
average, bare, base,
beastly, cheap,
churlish, close,
contemptible, design,
despicable, dirty,
fleabitten, grasping,
hard, horrible, horrid,
humble, imply,
import, intend,
involve, lean, little,
low, mangy, menial,
middle, miserable,
miserly, narrow,
nasty, near,
niggardly, norm,
paltry, parsimonious,
petty, plan, poor,
propose, purpose,
represent, rotten,
selfish, servile,
shabby, shameful,
signify, skimpy,
small, sorry, stand
for, symbolize, tight,
uncharitable, unkind,
vicious, vile,
villainous, will,
wretched
meander: coil,
ramble, roam, stray,
thread, wander, wind
meandering:
circuitous, crooked,
maundering,
rambling, serpentine,
wandering, winding
meanest: least
meaning: content,
definition, drift,
effect, gist, idea,
implication, import,
interpretation,
message, point, sense,
significance, spirit,
substance, value
meaningful:
articulate, coherent,
expressive, knowing,
meaty, pregnant,
significant,
worthwhile
meaningless: hollow,
illogical, insignificant,
nonsensical,
pointless, senseless,
shallow, silly

meanly: low, poorly
meanness: avarice,
misery, nastiness
means: capital, card,
channel, facilities,
instrument,
livelihood, living,
manner, mechanism,
medium, process,
resources, step,
substance, technique,
vehicle, way, wealth,
wherewithal
meant: destined,
predestined,
supposed
meantime: interim,
interval, while
meanwhile: interim,
interval
measly: petty
measure: bar, beat,
bill, breadth, calibre,
dance, degree,
dispense, divide,
dose, draught,
fathom, gauge,
legislation, length,
level, magnitude,
meet, pace, process,
quantify, quantity,
rhythm, rival, ruler,
standard, step, test,
tot, unit, weigh,
yardstick
measured: deliberate
measureless:
imponderable,
incalculable, infinite,
unbounded,
measurement:
fitting, proportion,
size, unit
measures: manner
measuring:
distribution, division
meat: flesh
mechanic: engineer,
worker
mechanical:
automatic, mindless,
perfunctory,
unthinking
mechanism: gear,
instrument, machine,
movement, trip,
vehicle, works
medal: decoration
meddle: interfere,
mess, monkey, nose,
obtrude, tamper
meddlesome: busy,
intrusive, nosy,
prying
meddling: curious,
obtrusive, officious

median: mean, medium, middle
mediate: intercede, judge, moderate
mediation: offices
mediator: diplomat
medical: medicinal
medical centre: clinic
medicament: dose, medicine, remedy
medicate: drug
medication: dose, drug, medicine, treatment, wash
medicinal: healing
medicine: cordial, cure, dose, drug, preparation, restorative, remedy, treatment
mediocre: low, middling, moderate, ordinary, poor
mediocrity: nonentity
meditate: brood, cogitate, commune, consider, deliberate, debate, digest, muse, reflect, revolve, speculate, study, think, wonder
meditation: debate, digestion
meditative: contemplative, pensive, studious, thoughtful, wistful
medium-sized: moderate
medium: average, conductor, element, instrument, intermediate, mean, means, mediocre, middle, middling, moderate, psychic, vehicle, vessel, voice
medley: assortment, compound, diversity, hash, mix, selection, variety
meek: gentle, lowly, mild, modest, quiet, retiring, reverent, self-effacing
meekly: quietly
meekness: diffidence, humility, mildness, modesty
meet: becoming, breast, collide, compromise, cross, experience, find, focus, greet, have,

join, pay, receive, redeem, run into, satisfy, see, touch
meeting house: chapel, church
meeting-place: hall, lodge
meeting: assignation, conference, congress, consultation, crossroads, date, engagement, interview, session
megastar: celebrity
melancholia: depression
melancholy: bad, blue, deplorable, depressing, desolate, funereal, lachrymose, lugubrious, miserable, misery, mood, moody, morbid, mournful, pessimism, plaintive, rueful, sad, sadness, sombre, sorrowful, sorry, woe, woeful
melanoma: tumour
melee: fight, fracas, scramble
mellifluent: lyrical
mellifluous: fluent, fluid, harmonious, liquid, lyric, mellow, rich, round
mellifluousness: harmony
mellow: fruity, mature, merry, rich, ripe, smooth, soft, sweet
mellowness: maturity
melodic: lyric, musical
melodious: harmonious, lyric, musical, soft
melody: chant, song, strain, theme, warble
melt: disappear, dissolve, fuse, run, soften, vanish, warm, weld
melted: fluid, liquid
melting: dissolution, solution
member: element, fellow, leg, limb, organ, part, participant, prick, unit
members: personnel
membership: seat
membrane: film, wall
memento: keepsake,

novelty, reminder, souvenir, token
memo: entry, message, note, reminder
memoir: reminiscence
memoirs: life
memorable: catchy, proud, signal, special
memoranda: notes
memorandum: minute, note, record, register, reminder
memorial: funeral, memory, monumental, testimonial, token, wake
memorize: learn, retain, revise
memory: impression, mind, recall, reminiscence
menace: danger, frighten, imminence, intimidate, loom, peril, threat
menacing: baleful, black, dangerous, forbidding, frightening, grim, impending, lurid, ominous, sinister, thunderous, ugly, portentous
ménage: household
mend: cure, darn, doctor, fix, fudge, heal, improve, knit, make up, patch, pick up, recover, rectify, redress, reform, refurbish, repair
mendacious: dishonest, false, lying, perjured, untruthful
mendacity: falsehood, insincerity, lying
mendicant: beggar
mending: healing, renewal, recovery
menial: attendant, base, lackey, mean, slavish
menstrual period: curse
menstruation: curse, period
mental defective: idiot
mental derangement: insanity, madness
mental health: sanity

mental illness: insanity
mental institution: asylum
mental picture: fantasy, image, vision
mental powers: paranormal
mental: crazy, insane, intellectual, interior, mad, moral, psychic, psychological, psychotic
mentality: head, reason
mentally disordered: insane, mad
mentally unbalanced: deranged
mention: bring up, broach, cite, comment, glance, hint, instance, name, note, observe, plug, puff, remark, say, specify, tell, thanks
mentioned: named
mentor: instructor, teacher
menu: food, formula
mephitic: smelly
mercantile: commercial, economic
mercenary: commercial, hack, rotten, selfish, self-seeking, sordid, venal
merchandise: cargo, goods, stock, wares
merchandising: mercantile
merchant: dealer, seller
merciful: gentle, humane, lenient, tender
merciless: brutal, cruel, ferocious, flinty, grim, heartless, implacable, relentless, ruthless, savage
mercilessness: ferocity
mercurial: fickle, fluid, moody, quick-tempered, temperamental, variable, volatile
mercury coating: foil
mercy: compassion, forbearance, forgiveness, grace,

humanity, pardon, pity, quarter, tenderness
mere: bare, lake, main, pure, very
merely: but, just, only
meretricious: artificial
merge: band, blend, combine, fuse, incorporate, integrate, meet, mingle, mix, pool, sink, touch, unify, unite
merger: coalition, combination, union, wedding
merging: blend, junction, meeting
merit: calibre, credit, deserve, good, quality, rate, reward, value, virtue, worth
merited: due, just, worth
meriting: worth
meritorious: laudable, worth, worthy
meritoriously: fairly
merits: due
merrily: gaily
merrimaking: revel
merriment: glee, jolly
merry-go-round: roundabout
merry-making: celebration, riot
merry: cheerful, festive, gay, high, inebriated, jocular, jolly, joyous, light-hearted, mellow, playful
merrymaking: carnival
merryman: fool
mesa: plateau, table
mesh: filter, gear, grate, grill, integrate, lattice, lock, maze, net, network, screen, tangle, tissue, weave
mesmeric: attractive, compelling
mesmerize: captivate, entrance, fascinate, spellbind, possess
mesmerizing: hypnotic, magnetic
mess: bungle, canteen, clown, confusion, difficulty,

dirty, disarray, dish, dislocate, fiddle, fidget, fix, fluff, fool, fright, hash, hole, huddle, jumble, knot, litter, mat, monkey, predicament, quagmire, ruffle, scramble, scrape, screw, spoil, shambles, sight, spot, strait, tangle
message: communication, information, letter, moral, note, notification, relay, report, scrawl
messenger: bearer, herald, precursor
messy: scruffy
metabolism: digestion
metabolize: digest
metal socket: chair
metamorphose: disguise, evolve
metamorphosis: evolution, mutation, revolution, transition
metaphysical: mystical, philosophical, unworldly
metaphysics: philosophy
metastatic: malignant
mete out: dispense, dole, give, measure, parcel, ration
metempsychosis: reincarnation
meteoric: quick
meteorological: climatic
meter: clock, gauge, instrument, measure, monitor
method: drill, form, line, manner, means, mechanism, medium, plan, policy, procedure, process, recipe, routine, rule, system, tack, tactic, technique, touch, way
methodical: businesslike, deliberate, neat, orderly, regular, systematic
methodological: technical
methodology: means
meticulous: conscientious,

minute, nice, painstaking, particular, precise, punctilious, religious, rigorous, scrupulous, strict, thorough
meticulously: exactly
meticulousness: care, nicety, precision
métier: bag, business, game, job, profession, work
metre: beat, measure, movement, rhythm, time
metrical: poetic
metro: underground
metropolis: city
metropolitan: urban
mettle: backbone, fight, nerve, pluck, spirit
mettlesome: frisky, high-spirited, spirited
Micawberish: optimistic
microbe: bacterium, germ
microorganism: bacterium, bug, germ, microbe
microscopic: imperceptible, invisible, minute
microwave: heat, oven, warm
micturate: urinate
middle: average, centre, heart, hub, intermediate, mean, medium
middling: average, medium, moderate, tolerable
middle-man: liaison, mediator
middle-of-the-road: conservative
midge: bug, fly
midget: baby, dwarf, pygmy, runt
midpoint: medium, middle
midriff: middle
midshipman: youngster
midst: bosom, depth, middle, thick
midwinter: Yule
mien: aspect, attitude, bearing, carriage, demeanour, description, look, manner
miff: offend
miffed: hurt

might: main, potency, power, strength
mighty: formidable, potent, powerful
migrant: refugee
migrate: move
migration: exodus
mild: benign, bland, calm, gentle, good-natured, harmless, inoffensive, lenient, light, lowly, meek, moderate, quiet, smooth, temperate
mildew: mould, rust
mildewed: musty
mileage: wear
milestone: landmark
milieu: background, environment, medium, scene, surroundings
militancy: fight, zeal
militant: fanatic, fanatical, hawk, radical, zealot, zealous
military: martial, warlike
milk: drain, tap
milk-fat: cream
milkiness: bloom
milksop: weakling, weed
milky: creamy, white
mill: crush, grind, plant, press, pulp, pulverize, works
milled: ground
millions: myriad, score
millstone: burden, liability, load, weight
milometer: clock
mime: gesticulate
mimic: caricature, copy, imitate, impersonate, lampoon, parrot, send up, take off
mimicry: camouflage, caricature, imitation
minaret: tower
mince: grate
mind: attention, brain, breast, care, conscious, grudge, guard, head, heart, heed, intelligence, keep, listen, look after, mark, notice, nut, obey, psyche, reason, regard, see, soul, stomach, watch, will
mind-blowing:

astonishing,
inconceivable
mind-boggling:
incredible,
stupendous
minded: predisposed,
ready
mindful: attentive,
aware, careful,
considerate,
observant, sensible,
watchful
mindless: fatuous,
heedless, irrational,
mechanical,
monotonous, reckless,
senseless
mine: bomb, bore,
dig, lift, pit, store,
tap, tunnel, well, win,
working
mingle: assimilate,
blend, confuse,
consort, integrate,
mix
mingled: complex,
miscellaneous, mixed
miniature: baby,
dwarf, little, midget,
model, pygmy, runt,
small
minicab: cab
minimal: least,
limited, marginal,
nominal
minimally: least
minimize: lessen,
play down, slur
minimum: base,
basic, least, low,
nadir, threshold, zero
minion: lackey,
menial, satellite,
yes-man
minister: clergyman,
divine, padre, parson,
pastor, priest,
secretary, vicar
minister to: pander
to, serve, treat
ministration: care
ministry: cabinet,
embassy
minor: child,
frivolous, incidental,
insignificant, junior,
juvenile, less, lesser,
little, lower, niggling,
obscure, secondary,
slight, small, small-
time, subordinate,
under, venial,
youngster
minority: childhood
minster: basilica,
church

mint: bomb, coin,
fortune, pile
minus: debit,
disadvantage, less,
light, under
minuscule:
microscopic, minimal,
minute, pygmy
minute(s):
transaction
minute: baby, bit,
close, date, detailed,
elaborate, entry,
imperceptible, little,
microscopic, minimal,
negligible, note,
particular, record,
searching, small, take
down, transaction
minuted: noted
minutes: notes
minx: flirt, hussy
miracle:
phenomenon, wonder
miracle-worker:
magician
miraculous:
phenomenal,
supernatural, wonder,
wonderful
mirage: illusion
mire: mud, swamp
mirror-image:
imitation
mirror: imitate,
reflect, reproduce,
resemble
mirth: glee, laughter,
merriment
mirthful: jolly
miry: muddy
misadventure:
calamity, casualty,
reverse
misanthrope: cynic
misanthropic:
cynical
misapplied: lost
misapprehend:
misinterpret
misapprehension:
delusion, fallacy,
illusion
misappropriate:
steal, take
misappropriation:
larceny
misattribute:
misplace
misbehave: carry on
misbehaving:
mischievous, naughty
misbehaviour:
mischief, misconduct,
naughtiness
misbelief: delusion

miscalculate:
mistake, slip
miscalculation:
mistake
miscarry: backfire,
fail
miscellaneity:
diversity
miscellaneous:
different, diverse,
mixed, odd, sundry,
various
miscellany:
compilation, medley,
variety
mischance:
catastrophe,
misadventure, mishap
mischief: caper,
harm, hurt, ill,
mayhem, misrule
mischief-maker:
malcontent
mischievous:
harmful, jocular,
naughty, playful,
rogue, sly, wicked
mischievousness:
disobedience,
naughtiness
misconceived: false
misconception:
delusion, illusion,
misapprehension,
mistake
misconduct: crime,
guilt
misconstruction:
misapprehension
misconstrue:
misinterpret
miscreant: culprit,
knave, knavish,
offender, outlaw,
ruffian, sinner, villain,
wretch
misdeed: crime,
misdemeanour, sin,
wrong
misdemeanour:
crime, foul, misdeed,
offence
miserable: dejected,
desolate, fleabitten,
lamentable, low,
melancholy,
mournful, niggardly,
paltry, pitiful, poor,
sad, sorry, unhappy,
woeful, wretched
miserably: unhappily
misère: nil
miserliness: avarice
miserly: avaricious,
churlish, close,
grasping, mean, near,

niggardly,
parsimonious, tight
misery: despair,
distress, grief,
sadness, trial, woe
misfire: backfire
misfit: deviant
misfits: dregs
misfortune: calamity,
casualty, catastrophe,
chance, curse,
disappointment,
disaster, distress, evil,
ill, misadventure,
misery, pity, reverse,
scourge, sorrow, woe
misgiving: doubt,
fear, foreboding,
premonition, qualm,
scruple, suspicion,
worry
misguided: mistaken
mishap: calamity,
casualty, catastrophe,
reverse
mishmash: hash,
jumble, medley, mess
misinformed:
mistaken
misinterpret: garble,
mistake, pervert,
warp
misjudge: err,
miscalculate, mistake
misjudged:
underrated
mislaid: lost, missing
mislay: lose, misplace
mislaying: loss
mislead: have on, lie
misleading:
deceptive, evasive,
false, illusory,
sophistry, specious,
untrue
misled: misguided
mismanagement:
miscarriage, misrule
misogynist: celibate
misplace: lose
misplaced: lost,
misguided, mislaid,
missing
misplacing: loss
misread: misinterpret
misrepresent:
colour, distort, falsify,
fudge, garble, lie,
misinterpret, pervert,
warp, wrong
misrepresentation:
calumny, fallacy,
slander, lying
misrepresented:
mangled, twisted
miss: blow, clear, girl,

jump, lack, lose, mourn, need, omit, overlook, pass, pass over, pass up, require, shave, skip, want, woman

missal: gradual

misshapen: crooked, deformed, imperfect, shapeless

misshapenness: malformation

missing: gone, lacking, lost, mislaid, without

mission: assignment, calling, chapel, church, concern, delegation, duty, embassy, function, quest, task, vocation

missive: letter

misspent: lost

missus: wife

mist: blur, cloud, damp, drizzle, film, fog

mistake: confuse, defect, error, fault, gaffe, lapse, miscalculate, slip

mistaken: incorrect, misguided, wrong

mistakenly: wrong

mistimed: inopportune

mistiness: nebulosity

mistranslation: garble

mistress: inamorata, lover, queen, teacher, woman

mistrust: doubt, ill feeling, jealousy, suspect, suspicion

mistrustful: disbelieving, jealous, sceptical

misty: damp, dreamy, filmy, foggy, grey, indistinct, murky, nebulous

misunderstand: misinterpret, mistake

misunderstanding: misapprehension, mistake

misuse: pervert, squander, waste

misused: lost

mite: jot, particle, speck, tot

mitigate: dilute, dull, lighten, moderate, palliate, qualify, relax, remit, smooth,

soften

mitigated: dilute

mitigation: relief

mitt: hand, tab, paw

mix: assimilate, associate, blend, compound, consort, cross, fuse, jumble, knead, mash, mingle, run, shake up, shuffle, socialize, solution, temper, whip, whisk

mixed: assorted, composite, concerned, involved, miscellaneous, mongrel, muddled, pied, upset

mixer: whisk,

mixture: assortment, blend, choke, combination, compound, cross, hash, hybrid, jumble, medley, mix, preparation, soup, variety

mix up: confound, confuse, fuddle, garble, perplex, scramble, tangle, upset

moan: complaint, croak, grievance, groan, lament, lamentation, snivel, sorrow, wail, whimper, whine

moaning: lamentation

moat: fortification

mob: besiege, bunch, clique, crew, crowd, herd, horde, host, mass, multitude, pack, people, press, proletariat, rabble, ring

mob-cap: bonnet

mobile: changeable, loose, moving

mobile home: caravan

mobilization: levy

mobilize: levy, rally, recruit

mobster: gangster

mock-up: dummy, model, prototype

mock: artificial, banter, caricature, dummy, jest, lampoon, ridicule, scoff, sham, sneer, spurious, synthetic, taunt

mocked: ragged

mockery: banter, contempt, jeering, parody, ridicule, scorn, sneer, spoof, teasing

mocking: derisory, jeering, sacrilegious, sarcastic, sardonic, scornful, tongue-in-cheek

mode: course, creation, cut, execution, fad, fashion, form, manner, means, medium, method, posture, practice, process, rage, style, usage, vein, vogue, way

model: cast, classic, dummy, effigy, follow, form, frame, gauge, ideal, impression, lead, lesson, make, mark, master, mould, norm, original, paradigm, paragon, pattern, pose, precedent, prototype, queen, sample, sculpture, shape, specimen, standard, version

modelling: formation, sculpture

modelling clay: wax

moderate: conservative, cool, fair, gentle, good-natured, lessen, liberalize, loosen, lower, lull, mediate, middling, mild, mince, mitigate, modest, modify, mollify, qualify, reasonable, regulate, restrained, sane, season, sober, temper, temperate, umpire, weaken

moderately: fairly, passably, pretty, quite

moderation: measure, mildness, modesty, modification, reason, restraint, sobriety, temperance

moderator: judge, mediator

modern: contemporary, fresh, late, latest, new, up to

date

modernization: renewal, renovation

modest: chaste, coy, decent, demure, humble, low, lowly, meek, plain, poor, quiet, reasonable, retiring, self-effacing, simple, small, spare

modestly: quietly

modesty: honour, humility

modicum: little, smattering, speck

modification: change, condition, difference, modulation, mutation, qualification, shift, variation

modified form: variant, variation

modify: change, convert, differentiate, juggle, qualify, revise, shape, soften, tailor, vary

modish: fashionable, latest, new, smart, up to date, vogue

modiste: dressmaker

modulate: modify

modulation: modification, pitch, regulation, tone

module: fitting, part, unit

modus operandi: procedure

moggy: cat

mogul: magnate

moist: damp, fluid, humid, liquid, watery, wet

moisten: bathe, damp, irrigate, soak, steep, wash, water, wet

moisture: damp, liquid, spray, wet

moistureless: dry

moke: ass

molars: teeth

mole: jetty, leak, pier, quay, spy

molecular force: bond

molecule: grain, particle

molest: maul, paw, persecute

molestation: harassment

mollify: calm, mitigate, placate, quell, quieten, relieve, satisfy, smooth
mollifying: conciliatory
mollycoddle: baby, mother, spoil
mollycoddled: pampered
molten: liquid
moment: bit, flash, gravity, import, importance, instant, interest, juncture, matter, minute, point, second, time, twinkling, weight
momentary: brief, fugitive, meteoric, passing, short
momentous: great, historic, portentous, serious, significant, solemn, special, weighty
momentousness: solemnity
momentum: drift, force, impact, impetus, impulse, pace, speed
monarch: crown, king, lord, queen, ruler, sovereign
monarchal: sovereign
monarchy: kingdom
monastery: cloister
monetary: commercial, economic, financial
money: bank, bread, capital, cash, coin, currency, draft, finance, loot, principal, purse, resources, tender, treasury, wealth, wherewithal
moneybox: bank, till
moneyed: jet, loaded, rich, wealthy
money-grubbing: mercenary
money-making: profitable
mongrel: cross, hybrid, mixed
moniker: name, nickname
monitor: censor, observe, police, regulate
monitoring: observation

monk: celibate, hermit
monkey: knave, villain
monogram: cipher
monograph: paper, thesis, tract
monolith: obelisk
monolithic: monumental
monologue: oration
monomaniac: egoist
monomaniacal: bossy, self-centred
monopolize: dominate, hog
monopolized: obsessed
monotonous: boring, deadly, drone, dry, dull, mechanical, menial, unbroken, wearisome
monotony: boredom, tedium
monsoon: cloudburst
monster: beast, devil, fiend, freak, horror, ogre, prodigy, savage, terror
monstrosity: prodigy, sight
monstrous: beastly, hideous, outrageous, preposterous, scandalous, unnatural
monstrousness: enormity
monthly: journal, magazine, periodical
monument: landmark
monumental: huge, immense, large, massive, monolithic, vast
moo: low
mood: atmosphere, attitude, climate, current, down, emotion, feeling, fit, frame, humour, state, temper, tone, vein
moodiness: sullenness
moods: temperament
moody: sulky, temperamental
moolah: money
moon: satellite, world
moonlight: night
moonshine: rot, rubbish
moor: dock, forest, heath, plain, root, rope, tether
mooring: berth,

harbour, painter, port
moorland: heath
moose: bull
moot: undecided, unsettled
mop: clean, hair, wipe
mope: pout
moral: clean, conscience, epilogue, ethics, honourable, idealistic, lesson, message, right, standard, virtuous, wholesome
morale: self-respect
moralistic: sententious
morality: ethics, good, honesty, honour, principle, right, virtue
moralize: censor, preach
morally: right
morass: bog, fen, quagmire, swamp
moratorium: respite, truce, waiver
morbid: dark, macabre, sick
mordant: caustic, sarcastic, scathing, sardonic
more: better, beyond, extra, further, on, other, over, preferable, rather, senior, superior, worse
moreover: beside, besides, further, plus, yes
mores: civilization, manners
morning: dawn, light
moron: dunce, fool, idiot, jackass, lunatic, oaf, simpleton, wally, zombie
moronic: asinine, dense, fatuous, foolish, idiotic, lunatic, mindless, simple, thick, unintelligent
morose: black, churlish, dejected, discontent, flat, gloomy, glum, ill-humoured, low, lugubrious, moody, sulky, surly
moroseness: mood, sullenness
morphology: frame
morsel: bit, bite,

crumb, dainty, grain, jot, little, nibble, piece, portion, scrap, spot, taste, titbit
mortal: baneful, body, deadly, fallible, fatal, human, incurable, individual, killing, lethal, mundane, soul, terminal
mortality: death
mortar: bond, cannon, concrete, plaster
mortgage: loan, pledge
mortgagee: creditor
mortification: chagrin, decay, disappointment, embarrassment, shame
mortified: ashamed, sheepish
mortify: chagrin, confuse, crush, decay, deflate, disgrace, humble, shame, show up, snub, wither, wound
mortifying: humiliating, ignominious, shameful, undignified, withering
mosey: saunter, stroll
moss: bog
most: best, bulk, last, latest, least, maximum, optimum, outside, pre-eminent, preponderant, quintessential, ultimate, worst
mostly: basically, generally, mainly, primarily
motel: hotel
motes: grit
moth-eaten: musty
mother: ferment, native, parent
motherless: bereaved
motherly: womanly
motif: design, device, pattern, text, theme
motion: gesticulate, gesture, momentum, move, movement, pace, proposal, proposition, question, resolution, run, signal, suggestion, way

motioning:
beckoning
motionless:
becalmed, immobile,
inert, quiescent,
quiet, still
motivate: carry,
cause, prod, raise
motivating: moving
motivation: cause,
drive, impetus,
impulse, incentive,
lease, rationale, spirit
motive: grounds,
point, reason, spur
motiveless:
purposeless
motley: colourful,
pied
motor: car, drive,
machine
motorbike: machine
motorcade:
procession
motorcar: car
motorman: driver
motorway: road
motte: embankment,
mound
mottle: spot
mottled: dappled,
speckled
motto: legend, phrase,
slogan
moue: pout
mould: bend, build,
carve, coin, decay,
die, earth, fashion,
forge, form, fungus,
impression, knead,
master, model,
pattern, pig, plate,
rot, rust, sculpture,
shape, stamp, temper,
turn, work
mouldable: flexible
moulder: decay, rot
mouldering: musty,
rotten
moulding: formation,
sculpture
mouldy: bad, musty,
off
moult: shed
mound: bank, breast,
down, drift,
embankment, heap,
hill, hump, knoll,
pile, prominence
mount: ascend, board,
climb, do, frame, get
on, get up, jump,
produce, put on, rise,
soar, stand, swell
mountain: elevation,
height

mountains: highlands
mountebank:
charlatan, clown,
fake, fraud, hypocrite,
quack, rogue
mounting: cradle,
frame, production
mourn: bewail,
grieve, keen, lament,
regret, sorrow,
ululate, weep
mournful: baleful,
black, dark, funereal,
lachrymose,
lugubrious,
melancholy, plaintive,
rueful, sad, sombre,
sorrowful, unhappy,
wistful, woeful
mournfully:
unhappily
mournfulness:
sadness
mourning: bereaved,
grief, lamentation,
sorrow
mouse: weakling
mouser: cat
mousy: frumpish,
nondescript
mouth: crater,
entrance, gab,
muzzle, oral, orifice
mouthful: bite, drink,
drop, gulp, nip, piece,
swallow, taste
mouthpiece: bit,
figurehead, medium,
muzzle, organ,
prophet, puppet,
vessel
mouthwatering:
delicious, luscious,
savoury
movable: mobile
movable joint: hinge
movables: furniture
move: ascend, bear,
breeze, budge, buzz,
carry, come, crawl,
creep, depart,
dispose, evacuate,
gambit, go, go on,
haul, head, hum,
impel, impress,
induce, influence,
join, journey, leave,
machination,
manoeuvre, migrate,
pass, phase, pierce,
progress, prompt,
pull, rearrange,
remove, reorganize,
repair, ride, rip, rise,
rouse, run, settle,
shift, step, stir,

submit, suggest,
table, tactic, tend,
touch, transit,
transport, traverse,
wag, walk, work,
work up
moved: sorry
movement:
campaign, cause,
crusade, drift,
exercise, motion,
operation, play,
progress, rhythm,
stroke, sweep,
tendency, tide, wave,
way
movie: feature, film,
picture
movies: cinema
moving: departure,
dramatic, emotive,
expressive, heart-
rending, impressive,
influential,
memorable, pathetic,
poetic, poignant,
rousing, sad, stirring,
tender
movingly: piteously
mow: crop, cut,
harvest, reap
mow down: massacre
mown: cut
muck: dirt, dung,
filth, litter, manure,
mess, misbehave,
ordure
mucker: friend, mate,
pal
mucking about:
mischief, mischievous
muckrake: slander
mucky: dirty, filthy
mucous: slimy
mucus: catarrh
mud-slinger:
backbiter
mud-slinging: smear
mud: dirt, filth, grime,
mire, ooze, quagmire
muddied: messy
muddle: cloud,
complicate, confuse,
confusion, disarray,
fluff, fuddle, hash,
huddle, jumble, mess,
perturb, shambles,
snarl
muddled:
disorganized, messy
muddy: bedraggled,
cloudy, dirty, filthy,
messy, slimy,
turbid
muff: bungle
muffin: bun

muffle: baffle, blunt,
drown, mumble,
mute, quieten,
repress, silence,
soften, stifle,
suppress
muffled: faint,
inaudible, indistinct,
smothered, weak,
wooden
mug: assault, cup,
drink, face, fool, hold
up, jug, pigeon,
pushover
mugger: hooligan,
thief
mugging: assault
muggy: damp, humid,
sticky
mulch: compost,
fertilize, litter,
manure
mulct: fine
mule: hybrid
mulish: obstinate,
perverse, pig-headed,
wayward, wilful
mull: brood, chew,
cogitate, consider,
deliberate, meditate,
ponder, puzzle,
reflect, revolve, think,
weigh
multicoloured:
colourful
multifaceted:
sophisticated
multifarious:
manifold, versatile
multinational:
conglomerate
multiple: complex,
compound, manifold
multiplicand: factor,
fraction
multiplication:
growth, increase,
propagation,
reproduction
multiplicity:
diversity, variety
multiply: breed,
double, grow,
increase, proliferate,
reproduce, spread
multiplying: teeming
multipurpose:
versatile
multitude: cloud,
congregation, crowd,
herd, horde, host,
legion, load, lot,
mass, mob, number,
press, profusion, sea,
swarm
multitudes:

numerous, score
mum: mother, mute,
reticent, silent
mumble: snarl
mumbled:
inarticulate
mumbling: inaudible
mumbo-jumbo:
gibberish
mummy: mother
munch: bite, chew,
eat, nibble
mundane: banal,
boring, down-to-
earth, everyday,
familiar, matter-of-
fact, practical,
worldly
municipal: civic,
civil, urban
municipality: city
munificence:
generosity, kindness,
largess
munificent:
bountiful, free,
generous, kind,
liberal, philanthropic,
open
murder:
assassination, blood,
butchery, execute,
hit, kill, killing, knock
off, liquidate, polish
off, remove,
slaughter, slay, waste
murderer: killer
murderous: fierce,
killing, lethal, savage,
violent, withering
murderousness:
cruelty
murine: mousy
murk: cloud, dusk,
fog, gloom

murkiness: obscurity
murky: black, cloudy,
dark, dirty, dull,
dusky, foggy, gloomy,
grey, obscure,
opaque, shadowy
murmur: babel,
breathe, bubble,
gurgle, hubbub, hum,
mumble, snarl,
undertone, warble,
whisper
murmured: soft
muscle: beef, brawn,
flesh, meat, power
muscular: athletic,
beefy, burly, macho,
meaty, mighty,
powerful, robust,
rugged, stout, strong,
sturdy
muscularity: brawn,
manliness
muse: cogitate,
commune,
inspiration, meditate,
ponder, puzzle, think
mush: face, mug, pulp
mushroom: fungus,
proliferate, spread,
spring
mushy: maudlin,
mawkish, romantic
music-hall: gaff
musical: harmonious,
lyric, melodious
musicality: ear,
harmony
musician: artist,
player
musing:
contemplative,
meditative, pensive,
wistful
must: obligation,

prerequisite,
requirement
muster: assemble,
call, congregate,
crowd, gather, herd,
levy, mass, meet,
mobilize, raise, rally,
recruit, round up,
summon
mustering: assembly,
levy
musty: frowsty, old-
fashioned, stale, stuffy
mutant: freak,
monster, monstrosity,
monstrous, mutation,
prodigy, rogue
mute: dumb, lower,
muffle, quiet, quieten,
uncommunicative
muted: delicate,
gentle, low, muffled,
noiseless, restrained,
silent, subdued
mutedly: low
mutilate: butcher,
cripple, damage,
deface, hack
mutilated: mangled
mutilation:
deformity,
disfigurement
mutineer: insurgent,
rebel, revolutionary
mutinous: defiant,
insubordinate,
quarrelsome,
rebellious,
revolutionary,
ungovernable
mutiny: defy,
disobedience,
insurrection, rebel,
revolt, revolution,
rise, unrest, uprising

mutt: dog
mutter: mumble,
undertone
muttering:
maundering,
murmuring
mutual: joint
mutually: together
muzzle: censor, curb,
gag, throttle
muzzy: faint, groggy
myopic: cross-eyed,
short-sighted
myriad: legion, score,
swarm
mysterious: dark,
deep, impenetrable,
obscure, odd, queer,
romantic, secret,
unknown, weird
mysteriousness:
obscurity
mystery: enigma,
puzzle, riddle, rite,
secret, unknown
mystic: divine,
supernatural
mystified:
bewildered, puzzled
mystify: baffle,
confuse, get, nonplus,
puzzle, stump
mystifying:
inexplicable,
insoluble
myth: fable, legend,
romance
mythical: legendary,
nonexistent
mythological: heroic
myths: lore

N

nab: grab, knock off, net, nick, whip
nabob: magnate
nadir: minimum, zero
naff: precious
nag: badger, carp, discomfort, fret, hack, keep on, mount, needle, niggle, pester, scold, screw, vex
nagging: gnawing, niggling, vexatious
nail: claw, clinch, fasten, fix, impale, pin, skewer, skewer, tack
naive: green, gullible, idealistic, ignorant, innocent, jejune, primitive, simple, unsuspecting, unworldly
naivety: innocence, simplicity, stupidity
naked: bald, bare, nude, raw, simple
nakedness: undress
namby-pamby: soft
name: baptise, call, celebrity, christen, Christian-name, cite, denomination, designate, fame, fix, handle, identify, label, mention, nomenclature, nominate, propose, reputation, specify, star, style, term
named: known
nameless: obscure, unidentified, unknown
namely: like
name-tag: label
naming: baptism, nomenclature
nancy-boy: fairy, gay, homosexual
nap: doze, fibre, flock, fluff, pile, rest, selection, sleep, snooze
napkins: linen
napped: plush
napping: asleep, slumbering

nappy: napkin
narcissism: conceit, vanity
narcissist: egoist
narcissistic: opinionated, self-centred, vain
narcotic: drug, hypnotic, sedative, soporific
narcotics: junk
narrate: detail, recite, relate, tell
narration: description, yarn
narrative: chronicle, fiction, novel, recital, saga, story
narrator: teller
narrow: contract, limited, scanty, slender, slim, small, taper, thin
narrow-boat: barge
narrow-minded: bigoted, insular, intolerant, little, prejudiced, priggish, provincial
narrow-mindedness: intolerance
narrows: bottleneck, strait(s)
nasal timbre: whine
nascent: incipient
nasty: awful, beastly, dangerous, disagreeable, disgusting, horrible, horrid, obnoxious, painful, revolting, rotten, rough, sticky, thorny, ugly, unkind, unpleasant
nation: country, folk, kingdom, land, people, public, race, seed, state
national: domestic, home, nationwide, native, public, racial, subject
nationalist: partisan, patriotic
nationwide: national
native: barbarian,

idiomatic, inhabitant, inherent, local, national, natural, savage, vulgar
natives: population
nativity: birth
natter: chat, chatter, gab, jaw, talk, tête-à-tête
natty: saucy, sharp, smart, trim
natural: bastard, easy, fluent, fresh, genius, genuine, graceful, habitual, homely, human, idiomatic, illegitimate, inherent, instinctive, intuitive, live, naive, normal, organic, physical, pure, radical, raw, simple, temperamental, true, uninhibited, unspoilt, wild
naturalistic: realistic
naturally: undoubtedly
naturalness: normality, simplicity
nature: being, character, complexion, constitution, creation, environment, fibre, habit, heart, kind, make-up, manner, personality, quality, sort, temper, temperament, world
nature reserve: forest, park, sanctuary
naughtily: badly
naughtiness: disobedience, mischief, misconduct
naughty: bad, knavish, mischievous, racy, rebellious, sexy, undisciplined, wicked
nausea: disgust, horror, sickness
nauseate: disgust, horrify, offend, repel, revolt, sicken
nauseated: liverish,

queasy, satiated, sick
nauseating: disgusting, fulsome, nasty, offensive, repulsive, revolting, sickening, sickly, vile
nauseous: fragile, green, squeamish
nautical: marine, maritime
naval: marine, maritime, nautical
nave: auditorium, basilica, body, hall
navigate: manoeuvre, pilot, sail
navigation light: beacon
navigation office: bridge
navigator: driver, pilot, sailor
navy: fleet, marine
nay: even
ne'er-do-well: layabout, rogue
neanderthal: barbarian, barbaric
near: by, close, come, coming, fast, hard, impending, indelicate, intimate, mean, present, ready, war
nearby: convenient, handy
nearest: immediate, next
nearly: much, practically, towards, virtually
nearly all: most
nearly-new: used
nearness: imminence, proximity
near-sighted: short-sighted
neat: becoming, clean, crisp, dainty, efficient, natty, nice, orderly, pretty, smart, snug, straight, taut, tight, trim
neb: bill
nebula: cloud
nebulous: cloudy, shadowy, shapeless,

tenuous, unreal
necessary:
imperative,
indispensable,
inevitable, invaluable,
obligatory,
prerequisite, urgent,
vital
necessitate: bind,
demand, involve,
need, require, supply,
warrant
necessity: must,
prerequisite,
requirement
neck: kiss, pet
necromancy: sorcery
necropolis: cemetery
necrose: mortify
necrosis:
mortification
necrotic: morbid
nectar: juice
need: compulsion,
demand, deprivation,
hunger, lack,
necessity, require,
requirement, take,
urgency, want
needful: money
needle: bait, index,
obelisk, pin
needless: superfluous,
uncalled-for,
unnecessary
needling: teasing
needy: destitute, poor,
underprivileged
nefarious: knavish,
lawless, villainous,
wicked
negate: contradict,
deny, neutralize,
nullify, refuse, refute,
reverse, revoke, veto
negation: veto
negative: dusty,
exposure,
unfavourable, veto
neglect: disregard,
fail, forget, ignore,
leave out, miss, omit,
slack
neglected:
dilapidated,
forgotten, forlorn,
godforsaken, shabby,
undone
neglectful: careless,
delinquent, forgetful,
heedless, remiss
neglecting: failure,
without
negligence: disregard,
failure, indifference,
oblivion, omission,

oversight
negligent: careless,
delinquent, derelict,
loose, mindless,
oblivious, reckless,
slack
negligible:
insignificant,
marginal, minor,
minute, outside,
petty, remote, slight
negotiate: bargain,
contract, haggle, talk,
treat
negotiation:
discussion,
transaction, truce
negotiator: diplomat,
mediator
negroid: black
neigh: snort
neighbourhood:
communal, local,
locality, place,
precincts, proximity,
quarter, resident,
surroundings, vicinity
neighbouring: close,
nearby
neighbourly: folksy,
friendly, helpful,
sociable, social
nemesis: destiny,
scourge
neon light: bulb
neonate: baby, infant
neophyte: beginner,
novice, pupil
neoplasm: tumour
nerve: backbone,
bottle, confidence,
courage, crust,
daring, face, gall,
guts, harden, heart,
impertinence, key,
pluck, presumption,
ready, sauce
nerve centre: hub
nerveless: daring,
imperturbable,
intrepid
nerve-racking: tense
nervous: bashful,
brittle, fearful,
flustered, hysterical,
impatient, jittery,
jumpy, neurotic,
restless, self-
conscious, sensitive,
skittish, tense, thin-
skinned, uptight,
worried, wound
nervousness:
hysteria, impatience,
shyness, tension
nervy: jumpy

ness: headland
nest: burrow, den,
domicile, home, lair
nest egg: savings
nestle: cuddle,
huddle, snuggle
net: basket, bring,
fish, gain, get, goal,
let, make, mesh,
realize, return, snare,
win, yield
nether: infernal
nether regions:
underworld
nether world: hell
netted: made
netting: lace
nettle: gall, jar,
needle, pique, put
out, ruffle, spite,
vex
nettled: peeved, stung
nettling: vexatious
network: complex,
grid, lattice, mesh,
tissue
neural tract: nerve
neurosis: hang-up,
hysteria
neurotic: hysterical,
maladjusted, paranoid
neutral: disinterested,
grey, impersonal,
neuter, nonaligned,
noncommittal
neutrality:
detachment
neutralize: cancel,
kill, neuter, obviate
neutralizer: killer
never-ending:
constant, perpetual,
protracted
**never-to-be-
repeated:** unique,
unrepeatable
nevertheless: but,
however,
notwithstanding, still,
though, yet
New Testament:
scriptural
new: brand-new,
different, extra, fresh,
green, late, maiden,
modern, more, novel,
original, raw, recent,
strange, tender,
unfamiliar, unknown,
unripe, untried, up to
date, virgin, young
newborn: baby
newcomer: outsider
newest: latest
newfangled:
contemporary

newly: lately
newness: novelty,
news: communication,
communiqué, flash,
information,
intelligence, message,
notice, revelation,
story, word
newscaster:
journalist, reporter
newshound: reporter
newsmedia: press
newsmen: press
newspaper: daily,
journal, paper
newspaper article:
cutting
newspaperman:
journalist
newspapers: press
newsstand: kiosk
next: beside, coming,
following, later,
second, then,
underneath
nib: beak, pen
nibble: bite, browse,
knap, nip, pare, pick,
snack, taste
nibbling: gnawing
nice: decent, fussy,
neat, personable,
pleasant, precise,
pretty, refined,
rigorous, subtle,
wholesome
niceties: ceremony,
minutiae
nicety: detail, quibble,
refinement
niche: bay, booth,
compartment, corner,
grotto, indent, nook,
pigeonhole, recess,
slot, well
nick: chip, cut, indent,
jail, knock off, mark,
nobble, pick up,
pinch, pit, prison,
score, steal, take,
whip
nicked: marked
nickname: handle,
name, term
niff: whiff
niffy: high
niggard: miser
niggardly: churlish,
close, grasping,
miserly, narrow,
parsimonious, poor,
skimpy, sordid
niggle: quibble
nigh: nigh, towards
night: nocturnal
nightfall: dusk

nightie: gown
nightly: nocturnal
nightmare: fantasy, hell, ordeal
nightmarish: creepy
nightstick: cudgel
night-time: dark, night, nocturnal
nil: cipher, duck, love, nothing, zero
nimble: athletic, fleet, flexible, handy, light, limber, lithe, neat, nippy, quick, smart, spry
nimbleness: neatness
nimble-witted: smart
nimbus: halo
nincompoop: ass, fool, oaf, sap, simpleton
ninny: sap
nip: belt, bite, chill, drop, pinch, prevent, scotch, snap, snort, taste, tot, tweak
nipper: child, claw, youngster
nipple: breast
nippy: chilly, cool, fast
nit-pick: quibble
nit-picking: niggling
nitwit: ass, fool, nincompoop, sap
no: nay, negative, none
nob: swell
nobble: cook, corrupt, doctor, lace, lame
nobility: blood, dignity, magnanimity, peerage, quality
noble: august, big, dignified, exalted, gallant, gentle, great, high, honourable, lofty, lord, lordly, patrician, peer, princely, proud, regal, sedate, selfless, unselfish, well-bred
nobleman: lord, patrician, peer
nobles: nobility
nobly: manfully
nobody: cipher, none, nonentity, nothing, pygmy, unknown, upstart
nobs: society, top brass
nocturnal: dark, night
nod off: sleep, snooze
nod: bob, bow, inclination, incline

nodding: superficial
noddle: head
noddy: sap
node: bundle, gate, joint, junction, knot
nodule: bump, knob
no-hoper: derelict, failure, loser
noise: babel, racket, report, sound, volume, whine
noise abroad: broadcast, say
noiseless: quiet
noiselessly: quietly
noise level: hubbub
noisily: bang
noisome: foul, smelly
noisy: bedlam, blatant, boisterous, loud, obstreperous, raucous, rowdy, uproarious, vocal, vociferous, wild
nomad: vagrant
nomadic: fugitive, itinerant, mobile, restless, wandering
nominal: figurehead, honorary, minimal, notional, titular
nominate: assign, commission, designate, name, ordain, propose, put up, slate
nominated: named
nomination: assignation, assignment
nominee: candidate
non-aligned: independent, neutral
non-amateur: professional
nonbelligerent: peaceable
nonce: occasional
nonchalant: blasé, careless, casual, unconcerned
nonclerical: lay
noncommittal: cag(e)y, neutral
noncompliance: disobedience
noncompulsory: optional
nonconformist: heretic, independent, individual, libertine, rebel, unconventional
nonconformity: eccentricity
none: nil, nobody
nonentity: cipher,

mediocrity, nobody, nothing, pygmy, unknown, upstart
non-essential: expendable
nonetheless: however, nevertheless, notwithstanding, though, yet
nonexecutive: honorary
nonexistence: nothing, nullity
nonexistent: illusory, imaginary
nonfunctional: vestigial,
non-incorporated: private
non-involvement: detachment
non-irritant: bland
non-malignant: benign
non-material: spiritual
nonmember: outsider,
non-military: peaceful
no-nonsense: down-to-earth, sensible, sincere, strict
nonpareil: champion,
non-party MP: independent
nonplus: baffle, floor, put off, puzzle
nonplussed: blank, disconcerted, stuck
nonpoisonous: edible, safe
nonprofessional: lay
non-profit-making: uneconomic
non-returnable: disposable
nonsense: bull, bunk, claptrap, drivel, farce, frivolity, fudge, gibberish, joke, junk, rot, rubbish, slaver, stuff, waffle
nonsensical: crazy, farcical, frivolous, irrational, laughable, ludicrous, mad, pointless, preposterous, senseless, unreasonable
nonsensically: madly
nonspecific: lax
non-starter: failure, flop, loser

nonstop: constant, direct, straight, through, together
nontoxic: safe
nonviability: impracticality
nonvocal: silent
noodle: ass, jackass, nincompoop, sap, wally
nook: bay, booth, corner, grotto, indent, niche, recess
noose: gallows, loop, rope, snare
norm: average, criterion, mark, mean, measure, par, pattern, standard
normal: average, conventional, customary, habitual, home, legitimate, mean, natural, norm, ordinary, quotidian, regular, regulation, right, routine, sane, standard, weather, wonted
normality: sanity
normally: generally, naturally, ordinarily
nose: beak, ferret, flush, hooter, prow, scent, trunk
nose-dive: plunge
nosegay: bouquet, buttonhole
nosh: food, grub, meal
nostalgic: romantic, sentimental
nosy: curious, inquisitive, intrusive, prying
notability: celebrity, eminence, renown
notable: figure, great, major, memorable, remarkable, worthy
notably: especially, particularly
notation: notes
notch: chip, dent, indent, nick, pit, poll, score, ward
notched: jagged
note: bill, check, comment, consequence, distinction, eminence, enter, entry, fame, find, importance, jot, key, letter, line, list, log, magnitude, mark, memo, mind, minute, notice, observation,

observe, parenthesis, record, regard, register, scrawl, take down, tone, watch
noted: distinguished, famous, glorious, illustrious, known, leading
notepad: pad, tablet
notes: crib, money
noteworthy: considerable, outstanding, remarkable, signal, singular
nothing: love, nil, none, zero
nothingness: nullity, oblivion, vacuum
notice: attention, call, criticism, detect, discover, dismissal, ear, feel, find, heed, interest, item, knowledge, note, notification, observe, perceive, poster, regard, remark, review, sign, spy, warning
noticeable: considerable, conspicuous, distinct, notable, obvious, prominent, pronounced, salient, striking, visible
noticeably: rather
noticing: discovery
notification: intelligence, notice, warning
notify: certify, inform, instruct, post, report, tell, warn
notion: assumption, conceit, conception, fancy, feeling, idea, image, impression, perception,

supposition, surmise, suspicion, view, whim
notional: ideal, mental, speculative
notoriety: fame
notorious: famous, infamous, vaunted
notwithstanding: despite, nevertheless, still, though
nought: cipher, love, nil, nothing, zero
nourish: fatten, feed, nurse, nurture, sustain
nourishing: healthy, meaty, nutritious, wholesome
nourishment: bread, diet, food, fuel, meat, sustenance
nous: brain, common sense, intelligence, loaf, maturity, sense
nouveau-riche: upstart
novel: curious, fresh, modern, new, original, refreshing, revolutionary, romance, story, strange, uncommon, unfamiliar, unheard-of
novelist: narrator, writer
novelty: change, departure, innovation, invention, sensation
novice: beginner, initiate, pupil, recruit
now: date, immediately, straight away, yet
nowadays: now
noxious: baneful, evil, harmful, pernicious, rank, unwholesome, venomous, virulent

nozzle: gun, jet
nuance: overtone, refinement, shade
nub: centre, core, gist, idea, juice, kernel, marrow, meat, nucleus, root
nubbing-cheat: gallows
nucleus: cell, centre, germ, heart, kernel, root
nude: bare, buff
nudge: jab, jar, jockey, jog, nose, poke, prod
nudity: undress
nugatory: futile, insignificant
nuisance: bind, bore, bother, drag, inconvenience, menace, mischief, pain, pest, pill, plague, trial
null: invalid
nullification: frustration
nullify: cancel, frustrate, negate, neutralize, quash, repeal, revoke, void
nullity: nothing
numb: blue, dead, freeze, petrified, sedate, senseless, shock, torpid
numbed: asleep, cold, insensible
number: battery, count, digit, figure, huddle, index, integral, itemize, numeral, quantity, reckon
numberless: incalculable, infinite
numbing: boring, freezing, piercing
numbness: narcosis,

paralysis
numbskull: dunce, fool, dummy
numeral: cipher, figure, number, term
numerous: manifold, many, multiple, rife
numinous: divine
nun: celibate
nuncio: delegate
nuptial: conjugal, matrimonial
nuptials: matrimony, wedding
nurse: attend, conserve, cradle, harbour, hug, look after, rear, tend, treat
nurture: bring up, cherish, cradle, foster, keep, maintain, mother, nourish, nurse, promote, raise, rear, sustain
nurtured: cultivated
nurturing: maintenance
nut: biscuit, fastener, fruit, head
nutcase: lunatic
nuthouse: asylum
nutmeg: mace
nutriment: diet, nourishment
nutrition: nourishment
nutritious: edible, nourishing, wholesome
nutritive: nourishing
nuts: crazy, insane, lunatic, mad, wild
nutter: lunatic
nutty: lunatic
nuzzle: caress, snuggle
nylon: plastic, tissue
nymph: sprite

O

oaf: lout
oafish: boorish, bovine, churlish, rude, uncouth
oar: blade, paddle
oarsmen: crew
oasis: inn
oath: assurance, curse, engagement, imprecation, pledge, promise, vow, word
obduracy: firmness, tenacity
obdurate: callous, firm, hard, intransigent, persistent, perverse, pig-headed, positive, tenacious, tough, unrepentant, wayward, wilful
obedience: duty, piety, servitude
obedient: deferential, good, law-abiding, subject
obeisance: salute
obelisk: column, needle, pinnacle
obese: fat, overweight, rotund, stout
obey: follow, keep, mind, observe, respect, take
obfuscate: camouflage, obscure, overshadow
obfuscated: opaque
obituary: knell
object to: contest, deprecate, resent
object: cause, cavil, challenge, design, destination, disapprove of, dislike, goal, idea, intent, item, meaning, mind, motive, point, protest, purpose, reason, subject, thing, use
objection: difficulty, protest, query, question, remonstration, scruple
objectionable: nasty,

offensive, reprehensible, unpleasant
objective: design, destination, end, factual, goal, idea, independent, intent, intention, judicial, mark, open, purport, purpose, quarry, quest, resolve, sake, target
objectivity: detachment, independence
oblation: gift, offering, presentation, sacrifice
obligate: commit
obligation: commitment, compulsion, debt, duty, gratitude, liability, necessity, onus, pressure, score
obligatory: binding, compulsory, imperative, mandatory, necessary, prerequisite
oblige: bind, bring, compel, drive, favour, force, have, impel, push, put, require
obliged: bound, grateful, liable, supposed, thankful
obliging: attentive, civil, considerate, decent, good-natured, kind, suave
oblique: bias, cross, diagonal, roundabout, sideways, transverse
obliquely: askance, indirectly, sideways
obliterate: cancel, deface, delete, drown, kill, rub out
obliteration: killing
oblivion: preoccupation
oblivious: asleep, blind, deaf, forgetful, insensible, preoccupied, unsuspecting

oblong: panel
obloquy: detraction, jeering, slander
obnoxious: disagreeable, nasty, objectionable, odious, offensive, repulsive, revolting, undesirable, unpleasant
obscene: bawdy, bestial, blue, dirty, filthy, foul, immodest, immoral, lewd, monstrous, nasty, pornographic, profane, rank, raunchy, rude, salacious, scatological, scurrilous
obscenity: curse, dirt, filth, immorality, lewdness, monster, monstrosity, nastiness
obscurantist: reactionary
obscure: blanket, blur, camouflage, cloud, cloudy, conceal, cover, dark, deep, dim, distant, doubtful, dull, eclipse, envelop, foggy, gloomy, hidden, humble, illegible, imponderable, indistinct, low, lowly, muddy, murky, mysterious, nameless, nebulous, obfuscate, obstruct, opaque, overshadow, unclear, unheard-of, unknown, vague, veil, veiled, woolly
obscured: blind
obscurely: vaguely
obscuring: eclipse
obscurity: background, fog, gloom, humility, mystery, nebulosity, pall, retirement
obsequies: burial, funeral

obsequious: grovelling, humble, ingratiating
obsequiousness: flattery
obsequy: humility
observance: celebration, ceremony, custom, discharge, formality, keeping, rite, ritual, service, solemnity
observant: circumspect, mindful, perceptive, perspicacious, watchful
observation: attention, comment, experience, look, note, perception, remark, scrutiny, watch
observation post: lookout
observe: celebrate, commemorate, comment, comply, discern, discharge, experience, find, find out, follow, fulfil, keep, look, monitor, note, notice, obey, perceive, practise, reconnoitre, regard, remark, respect, see, view, watch, witness
observer: spectator, student
observing: onlooking
obsess: haunt, possess
obsessed: possessed, stuck
obsession: complex, compulsion, fetish, fixation, hang-up, infatuation, mania, passion, phobia, preoccupation, rage, thing
obsessive: crank, neurotic
obsolesce: date
obsolescent: old-fashioned
obsolete: dead, defunct, old, old-

fashioned
obstacle: bar, barrier, block, difficulty, hazard, hindrance, hurdle, jump, preventive, rub, wall
obstinacy: resolution
obstinate: contrary, dour, headstrong, intransigent, obdurate, persistent, perverse, pig-headed, rebellious, recalcitrant, refractory, resolute, stubborn, tough, wayward, wilful, wooden
obstreperous: difficult, disruptive, undisciplined
obstruct: bar, block, blockade, check, choke, clog, cut off, foul, halt, hamper, hold up, interrupt, jam, keep, oppose, prevent, retard, shackle, stall
obstruction: bar, barrier, block, blockade, bottleneck, check, choke, clog, hindrance, jam, let, obstacle, opposition, preventive, stoppage, wall
obstructive: discouraging, preventive, unhelpful
obtain: attain, collect, fetch, find, gain, get, have, land, pander to, pick up, prevail, procure, purchase, raise, reap, receive, recruit, secure, take, win
obtainable: attainable
obtained: found
obtrude: impinge
obtrusive: loud, officious
obtuse: dense, dim, insensitive, mindless, oafish, slow, stolid, thick, unintelligent
obtuseness: density
obverse: face
obviate: preclude, prevent, save
obvious: blatant, clear, conspicuous, glaring, known, logical, manifest, marked, natural,

noticeable, overt, palpable, patent, plain, prominent, pronounced, transparent, undisguised, visible
obviously: clearly, undeniably
obviousness: simplicity
occasion: breed, call, case, cause, chance, do, happening, incident, induce, opportunity, prompt, provoke, raise, reason, root, thing
occasional: casual, odd
occasionally: sometimes, uncommonly
occlusion: bite, teeth
occult: dark, hidden, mystical, paranormal, supernatural
occultation: eclipse, transit
occupancy: possession, presence, residence
occupant: inhabitant, lodger, resident
occupation: business, calling, career, conquest, craft, interest, invasion, job, line, livelihood, living, office, profession, pursuit, task, tenure, work
occupied: busy, involved, working
occupier: inhabitant, occupant
occupy: conquer, fill, hold, inhabit, invade, live, overrun, pass, people, populate, requisition, spend
occupying: living
occur: be, befall, chance, coincide, come, dawn on, fall, go off, go on, happen, pass, rise, strike
occurrence: case, circumstance, development, episode, experience, fact, fortune, happening, incidence, incident, matter, phenomenon, piece, thing, transaction
occurring: on

ocean: drink, main, sea, water
ocean-going: marine
oceanographic: marine, maritime, nautical
ochre: buff, yellow
octave: key
odd: crazy, curious, fishy, funny, grotesque, idiosyncratic, interesting, irregular, kinky, memorable, occasional, peculiar, quaint, queer, quirky, screwy, strange, stray, surplus, unaccountable, uncommon, unconventional, unnatural, unusual, weird
oddball: freak
oddity: character, crank, eccentricity, novelty, original, paradox, quirk
oddly: uncommonly
odd man out: outsider
oddments: remains
oddness: eccentricity, oddity
odds: chance, handicap, price
odds and ends: junk
odds-on: probable
odious: invidious, nasty, obnoxious, repulsive, scandalous
odium: disapprobation, disgrace, loathing
odometer: clock
odoriferous: redolent
odour: breath, scent, smell, whiff
odyssey: journey
oestrus: heat
oeuvre: opus, works
of: by
off: aside, asleep, astray, away, bad, false, from, putrid, rank, untrue, wide
offal: garbage, refuse, waste
offbeat: unconventional
off colour: ill, peaky, poorly, rotten, rough, seedy
offence: crime, fault, insult, misdeed, misdemeanour,

obscenity, outrage, pique, sin, wound, wrong
offend: chafe, disgust, displease, err, insult, irritate, nauseate, outrage, pique, provoke, repel, revolt, scandalize, shock, sin, spite, turn off, wound, wrong
offended: dirty, hurt
offender: criminal, culprit, delinquent, malefactor
offensive: assault, attack, bad, campaign, coarse, disagreeable, disgusting, evil, foul, fulsome, gross, horrid, invidious, mawkish, nasty, objectionable, obnoxious, odious, onslaught, provocative, push, rank, repulsive, revolting, sally, scurrilous, sickening, storm, ugly, unpleasant, vile
offensiveness: coarseness, nastiness
offer: bid, present, produce, proposal, sacrifice, tender, vend
offering: collection, contribution, donation, gift, presentation
offhand: blasé, careless, casual, cavalier, nonchalant, perfunctory, rude, throwaway, ungracious
offhandedness: nonchalance
office: booth, branch, bureau, capacity, chair, clerical, department, desk, duty, function, job, place, position, post, room, service, situation, tenure
officer: captain, general, marshal, official
offices: headquarters
official: authoritative, diplomatic, dry, executive, formal, legitimate, minister, officer, orthodox,

regular, regulation,
secretary, usher, valid
officialdom:
bureaucracy
officiate: preside over,
serve
officious: busy,
forward, overbearing,
upstart, wordy
officiousness:
forwardness
offing: wind
off-putting:
depressing,
discouraging,
uninviting
offset: balance, cancel,
compensate,
highlight, neutralize,
redeem
offshoot: bough,
branch, derivative,
limb, plant, runner,
shoot
offshoots:
ramifications
offshore: marine
offspring: brood,
child, descendants,
family, fruit, increase,
issue, litter, posterity,
young
off-target: wide
off the cuff: blind,
impromptu
off-white: cream,
creamy
ogle: eye, leer
ogre: beast, devil,
fiend, giant,
oppressor
oil: fat, grease,
lubricate
oil-painting: canvas
oilrig: platform
oilskin: mackintosh
oily: creamy, fat,
greasy, ingratiating,
slimy
ointment: cream,
salve
okay: fair, fine,
middling, underwrite,
well, yes
old: back, elderly,
former, grey, late,
past, seedy, square,
stale, traditional,
veteran
old age: dotage
Old Bill: police
old boy: gaffer
olden days: history
older: senior
old-fashioned:
fuddy-duddy,

historical, obsolete,
out, quaint, square,
unfashionable
old fogy: fuddy-
duddy
old-fogyish: fuddy-
duddy, stuffy
old girl: wife
old hand: veteran
old hat: obsolete,
unfashionable
old joke: wheeze
old lady: mother, wife
old lag: villain
old-maidish: prudish
old man: dad, father,
gaffer, husband
Old Nick: devil
Old Testament:
scriptural
old woman: wife
old-world: quaint
oleaginous: fat
omen: forerunner,
portent, sign, warning
ominous: baleful,
black, dark, dire,
forbidding, ill,
inauspicious,
portentous, ugly,
uninviting, warning
omission: failure,
fault, lacuna,
negligence, oversight,
skip, surcharge
omit: delete, drop,
except, forget, jump,
leave out, miss,
neglect, overlook,
pass, pass over, skip
omitted: forgotten,
undone
omitting: except
omniscience:
infallible
on: by, forward, live,
operative, over, past,
possible, through,
working
once: formerly, now,
previously,
sometimes
one: individual, single,
sole, somebody
onerous: heavy,
oppressive, weighty
ongoing: current,
lasting, living,
progressive
onlooker: passer-by,
spectator, witness
onlookers: audience
only: barely, but,
hardly, just, little,
merely, narrowly,
single, sole

onrush: onset
onset: attack,
beginning, opening,
raid, start
onslaught: assault,
attack, barrage,
charge, offensive,
push, raid, rush,
storm
onus: burden,
liability, load, weight
onward: forth,
forward
oodles: plenty
ooze: bleed, discharge,
drain, drip, filter,
flow, leak, mire, mud,
quagmire, weep
oozing: discharge,
flow, leak, leaky
oozy: slimy
opacity: body,
cataract, obscurity,
purity
opaque: dim, milky,
obscure, thick,
turbid, unclear
open: bare, beckoning,
begin, bleak, bloom,
brazen, broach,
broad, candid, clear,
colonize, direct,
discretionary, fair,
familiar, flagrant,
flower, frank, free,
gape, give, honest,
inaugurate, initiate,
innocent, launch,
lead, liable, liberal,
loose, loosen, naive,
outgoing, permissive,
pioneer, plain,
preface, progressive,
public, raw,
responsive, rip,
sincere, subject,
susceptible, tap,
transparent,
undecided,
undisguised, undo,
unguarded,
uninhibited, unsafe,
vulnerable, warm-
hearted, widen,
yawning
opened: undone
opener: key
opening: beginning,
bloom, chance, door,
entrance, first,
gambit, gap, hatch,
hole, initial,
introduction, kick-off,
leak, mouth,
opportunity, orifice,
outlet, outset,

overture, preliminary,
prime, rift, start,
threshold, vent, void
openly: barely,
directly, frankly,
freely
openness: breadth,
familiarity, freedom,
honesty, simplicity
operate: behave, carry
on, drive, fly,
function, go, hold,
keep, manage,
perform, pilot, run,
take, work
operating costs:
overheads
operation: behaviour,
campaign, effect,
function, manoeuvre,
mechanism,
movement,
performance,
practice, process,
section, use, working
operational: working
operations: duty
operative: effective,
hand, living, motive,
on, valid, working
operator: jockey,
motor
opiate: hypnotic,
narcotic, soporific
opinion: belief, bet,
conceit, conclusion,
conviction, feeling,
idea, impression,
judgement, mind,
notion, observation,
persuasion,
sentiment, side,
stand, verdict, view
opinionated: bigoted,
narrow-minded,
prejudiced,
unreasoning
opponent:
competitor,
opposition, rival
opportune:
convenient,
favourable, fortunate,
good, happy,
propitious, right, ripe
opportunely:
fortuitously
opportunistic: self-
seeking
opportunities:
facilities
opportunity: break,
chance, convenience,
freedom, opening,
room, scope, start,
time

oppose: breast, combat, contest, contradict, contrast, cross, fight, match, pit, resist, rival, traverse

opposed: averse, counter, different, hostile, repulsive, rival

opposing: counter, cross, negative, rival

opposite: contradictory, contrary, converse, different, inversion, reverse

opposite number: equivalent

opposition: aversion, competition, conflict, contrast, enemy, kick, objection, resistance

oppress: bow, bully, burden, crush, flog, grind, load, persecute, pinch, prey on, rack, ride, surcharge, wrong, yoke

oppressed: ground, laden, loaded, overloaded

oppression: domination, hardship, tyranny, yoke

oppressive: close, dictatorial, muggy, severe, sticky, stiff, stuffy, sultry, wearisome

oppressor: bully, despot, ogre, tyrant

opprobrious: disgraceful, infamous, reprehensible, scandalous, vituperative

opprobrium: disgrace, notoriety, shame

opt: choose, elect, pick, plump, prefer, select, vote, will

optic: eye, measure

optimal: ideal

optimism: hope

optimistic: auspicious, bright, buoyant, hopeful, idealistic, promising, rosy, sanguine, sunny, wishful

optimum: best

option: choice, pick, preference, selection

optional: discretionary, voluntary

opulence: comfort, luxury, magnificence, plenty, wealth

opulent: gorgeous, grand, lush, luxurious, magnificent, palatial, rich, wealthy

opus: composition, work

oracle: prophet

oracular: prophetic

oral: verbal, vocal

oral contraceptive: pill

orate: mouth, preach, say

oration: speech, talk

oratorical: literary

oratory: chapel, language

orb: ball, bulb, circle, eye, globe, round, sphere

orbicular: round

orbit: circle, cycle, lap, range, revolution, revolve, scope, track

orchard: nursery

orchestra: band

orchestral: musical

orchestra-member: musician

orchestrate: manage, manoeuvre, mastermind, organize, score, stage

orchestration: manipulation

orchestrator: tactician

ordain: call, dictate, impose, invest, legislate, make, order, will

ordained: made

ordeal: fire, hell

order: bid, call, charge, class, club, command, commission, decoration, demand, dictate, direct, directive, discipline, dispose, divide, edict, estate, fellowship, form, grade, group, hand, indent, instruct, instruction, law, mandate, marshal, method, pattern, place, programme,

programme, range, rank, regulation, sequence, series, sort, tell, train, trim, variety, word

ordered: organic, regular

ordering: division

orderliness: neatness, pattern, system

orderly: law-abiding, methodical, neat, regular, straight, taut, trim

orders: direction, remit

ordinance: edict, imposition, law, order, regulation, ritual, rule

ordinarily: daily, generally

ordinariness: mediocrity, normality

ordinary: average, banal, boring, common, customary, daily, everyday, familiar, folksy, general, habitual, homely, humble, idiomatic, inconspicuous, lowly, mean, mediocre, moderate, mundane, natural, nondescript, normal, orthodox, plain, quotidian, regular, routine, unspoilt, usual

ordure: dung, filth

organ: medium, member, paper, part, vehicle

organic: living, natural, radical, raw

organically: naturally

organism: being, creature

organisms: life

organization: business, complex, composition, concern, conduct, coordination, fabric, firm, form, formation, house, leadership, machine, manipulation, movement, network, order, outfit, ring, set-up, society, staff, structure, system

organize: compile, construct, do, form, get, hold,

mastermind, mount, orchestrate, plan, plot, programme, rally, ready, regulate, schedule, see to, set up, stage

organized: businesslike, ready, straight, systematic

organized crime: underworld

organizer: director, mastermind

organs: offal

orgiast: pervert

orgiastic: drunken

orientation: direction

orifice: hole, opening, vent

origin: base, basis, cradle, dawn, derivation, descent, fountain, genesis, head, mint, source, spring

original: authentic, base, basic, beginning, character, creative, distinctive, first, forerunner, genuine, imaginative, individual, inventive, master, model, new, novel, old, pregnant, prime, prototype, refreshing, unconventional, witty

originality: fantasy, imagination, invention, novelty

originally: basically, primarily

originate: begin, create, date, dawn, descend, develop, discover, father, formulate, found, generate, hail, initiate, institute, invent, make, proceed, raise, spring, start, stem

originated: made

origination: beginning, birth, creation, discovery, foundation, generation, germ, invention, production

originator: author, cause, founder, parent, precursor, source

origins: root

orison: prayer

ornament: bead,

boss, deck,
decoration, elaborate,
figure, garnish, grace,
jewel, pattern, stud,
trim
ornamental: fancy
ornamentation:
decoration, flourish
ornamented: gaudy,
ornate
ornaments: jewellery
ornate: elaborate,
fancy, flamboyant,
florid, lush, luxuriant
ornery: mean
orotund: pompous,
rotund
orphaned: bereaved
orthodox: regular,
standard, straight
orthopedic support:
brace
oscillate: fluctuate,
hover, quiver, seesaw,
shake, sway, swing,
tremble, vibrate, wag,
waver
oscillating: flickering,
irregular, swing,
undulating, vibrant,
wave, wriggle
osculate: kiss
osculation: kiss
ossify: cake
osteal: skeletal
ostensible: nominal,
outward, superficial
ostensibly: outwardly
ostentation: display,
parade, vanity
ostentatious: blatant,
camp, elaborate,
extravagant,
flamboyant, flashy,
loud, meretricious,
pompous,
pretentious, vain
osteopathy: massage
osteotherapy:
massage
ostler: groom
ostracize: boycott,
cut, ignore, proscribe
ostracized: cut,
unpopular
other: different,
enemy, except, far,
more, opposing,
opposite, opposition,
reverse, second
others: rest
otherwise: besides,
else
otherworldly:
spiritual
ought: have, must,

supposed
ounce: grain
oust: banish, eject,
overthrow, remove,
supersede, supplant
ouster: overthrow
out: away, extinct,
forbidden, forth,
forward, inaccurate,
incorrect, obsolete,
off, unconscious
outback: bush, desert,
waste, wild
outbreak: epidemic,
fit, onset, rash, wave
outburst: blast, blaze,
gale, spasm, storm,
tantrum, volley
outcast: leper, outlaw,
pariah, refugee,
rogue, unwanted,
wretch
outcasts: dregs
outcome: conclusion,
consequence, effect,
fruit, issue, purpose,
resolution, result,
score, upshot
outcry: furore, noise,
protest, storm, uproar
outcurved: convex
outdistance: overtake
outdo: beat, best,
better, break, cap,
head, lead, lick,
overtake, pass,
surpass, transcend
outdoor: outside
outer: exterior,
external, outside,
outward, utter
outer layer: rind, peel
outermost: outside
outfit: cater, clothe,
clothes/clothing,
dress, firm, garb, kit,
prepare, provide, set,
suit, tackle, uniform
outfit: wardrobe
outfitter: tailor
outflow: vent, beak
outfox: outwit
outgoings:
expenditure, outlay
outgrowth: derivative
outing: drive, jaunt,
jog, journey, picnic,
run, tour, trip, turn
outlander: foreigner
outlandish: bizarre,
foreign, grotesque,
odd, peculiar, queer,
unnatural, weird
outlandishness:
eccentricity
outlaw: ban, bandit,

banish, forbid,
proscribe
outlawed: forbidden,
lawless, prohibited
outlawry: ban
outlay: cost,
expenditure, expense,
payment, price
outlet: beak, drain,
hole, port, sale, store,
vent
outline: brief, chart,
contour, describe,
design, diagram,
draft, draw, drawing,
figure, form, layout,
line, plan, plot,
profile, project,
projection, rough,
scenario, scheme,
shape, skeleton,
sketch, stake,
summary
outlook: aspect,
attitude, future,
lookout, mentality,
nature, position,
posture, prospect,
school, scope,
sentiment, spirit,
temperament, view
outlying: back,
distant, far, faraway,
outer
outmanoeuvre: jink,
outdo, outwit
outmoded: historical,
kaput, obsolete, old-
fashioned,
unfashionable
outpost: colony
outpouring: burst,
outburst, spate
output: job, load,
works, yield
outrage: atrocity,
disgust, enormity,
horrify, insult,
obscenity, offend,
rape, scandalize,
shock, violate,
violation
outrageous:
atrocious, crazy,
criminal, damnable,
deplorable, derisory,
diabolical,
disgraceful, gross,
impossible, infamous,
offensive,
preposterous,
prohibitive, rank,
ridiculous,
scandalous,
sensational, shameful,
shocking, unheard-of,

unholy, zany
outrageously: badly
outrider: scout
outright: straight,
unqualified
outrun: distance
outset: beginning,
conception, dawn,
kick-off, origin,
threshold
outshine: dominate,
surpass
outside: beyond, face,
jacket, marginal, out,
outer, outward, past,
remote, skin, surface,
without
outsized: jumbo
outskirts: border,
periphery, skirt,
precincts
outsmart: fox, outwit
outspoken: bluff,
blunt, candid, direct,
forthright, frank,
plain, round
outspokenly: frankly
outspread: wide
outstanding:
conspicuous,
distinguished, due,
exceptional, first-
class, great, knockout,
major, monumental,
notable, noteworthy,
overdue, owing,
payable, phenomenal,
pre-eminent, prize,
prominent,
remarkable, salient,
shining, signal,
singular, splendid,
striking, terrific,
uncommon, undone,
unpaid, unsettled,
wonder, wonderful
outstandingly:
especially, notably,
particularly,
uncommonly
outstretched: wide,
widespread
outstrip: beat,
distance, head, lead,
outdo, transcend
outward: exterior,
external, face, façade,
ostensible, outside,
superficial, surface,
varnish, veneer
outwardly: without
outwit: best, foil, fox,
have, slip
ovation: hand,
jubilation
oven: cooker, fire

over: beyond, by, closed, gone, hog, lapsed, lost, past, spare, straddling, waste
overact: mug, overdo
overall: eventual, nationwide, panorama
overalls: jeans
overawe: dazzle, intimidate
overbearing: bossy, dogmatic, high, lordly, magisterial, opinionated, oppressive, peremptory, supercilious
overblown: pompous
overburden: surcharge
overcast: cloud, cloudy, dark, dim, dull, grey
overcharge: surcharge, swindle
overcharged: overloaded
overcharging: extortion
overcome: beat, conquer, face, kill, outdo, quell, repress, upset, whip, worst
overconfident: self-satisfied
overcrowding: congestion
over-detailed: busy, fussy
overdo: labour, lay on, magnify, overshoot
overdone: contrived, elaborate, laboured, lavish, melodramatic, overwrought
overdraft: debit, deficit, loan
overdue: behind, delinquent, late, unpaid
over-eager: impatient
over-elaborate: labour, laboured, florid, fussy
overestimate: overrate
over-exact: meticulous
overexcited: overwrought
overfall: rip
overfeed: surfeit
overflow: burst, flood,

inundate, run over, spill
overflowing: bumper, copious, flush, teeming
overgrow: overrun
overgrowth: jungle
overhang: bulge, cliff, jut, loom, project, projection, shadow, verge
overhanging: impending
overhaul: renewal, renovation, repair, service
overhead: over
overheads: upkeep
overindulge: spoil, stuff
overindulged: soft
overindulgent: lax, soft
overjoyed: happy
overlap: impinge, join, stagger, touch
overlay: coat, grid, patch, plaster, plate, sheet
overload: glut, surcharge, swamp
overloaded: packed
overlook: condone, face, forget, forgive, ignore, leave out, miss, neglect, omit, pardon, pass, pass over
overlooked: forgotten
overlord: king
overly: unduly
overnice: precious
overpass: bridge
overpopulated: overcrowded
overpower: crush, dazzle, master, overcome, rout, whip, worst
overpowering: devastating, irresistible, oppressive
overpriced: expensive, steep
overprotective: possessive
overreact: panic
overreaction: furore
over-refined: sugary
override: overrule
overriding: compelling
overrule: reverse
overruling: capital,

overriding
overrun: invade, overshoot
over-salted: salty
oversee: control, direct, govern, manage, monitor, officiate, run, superintend
overseer: boss, foreman, keeper, master, monitor
over-sensitive: thin-skinned
overshadow: dominate, dwarf, loom, menace, surpass
overshadowing: impending
overshoot: overrun
oversight: blunder, control, mistake, neglect, negligence, omission, slip, supervision
oversimplified: facile
overstate: blow up, exaggerate, magnify, overdo
overstatement: exaggeration
overt: blatant, brazen, flagrant, glaring, known, obvious, open, ostensible, outward, public
overtake: beat, overhaul
overtax: overwork
overtaxed: overloaded
overthrow: confound, conquest, defeat, fall, prostrate, quash, quell, reverse, rout, ruin, smash, supplant, suppress
overtly: openly, outright, outwardly
overtone: innuendo, nuance, undertone
overture: introduction, pass, prelude
overturn: capsize, demolish, invert, keel over, overrule, overthrow, rescind, ruin, spill, throw, undo, upset
overturned: undone, upset, upside down
overturning: inversion

overuse: overdo, overwork
overused: stock
overweening: lofty, vain
overweight: corpulent, fat, obese, stout
overwhelm: beat, break, crush, dazzle, drown, flabbergast, glut, hit, kill, overrun, overtake, prostrate, sink, stagger, surcharge, swamp
overwhelmed: numb, overcome, prostrate, smothered
overwhelming: devastating, fantastic, irresistible, knockout, landslide, obsessive, overpowering
overwhelmingly: unutterably
overwork: flog, overdo, strain
overworked: hackneyed
overwrought: distracted, frantic, hysterical, neurotic
overzealous: officious
ovoid: oval
ovum: egg, germ
owed: due, payable
owing: outstanding, overdue, thanks, through, unpaid
own: boast, concede, confess, enjoy, have, home, keep, peculiar, possess, private, profess, proper, receive, recognize
owner: custodian, keeper, landlord, lord, master, proprietor
ownership: custody, possession
ox: beef, bull, neat
ox-hide: buff
ox-leather: buff
ox-like: bovine
oxidation: rust
oxidize: burn, rust
oxidized: rusty
oxyacetylene welder: torch
ozalid: proof

P

pa: dad, father
PA: secretary
pace: bat, clock, foot, gait, lick, movement, rate, speed, step, time, walk
pacific: calm, conciliatory, peaceable
pacify: compose, lull, placate, quell, quiet, quieten, satisfy, sedate, settle
pacify: mollify
pack: bale, batch, box, bunch, bundle, carton, clique, cramp, crate, crew, crowd, deck, fill, group, horde, hunt, jam, lag, load, malfunction, overeat, package, parcel, pile, plug, press, ram, squeeze, wolf, wrap
package: bale, box, bundle, parcel, wrap
packed: close, crowded, full, loaded, overcrowded, thick
packet: carton, fortune, mint, pack, package, parcel, pile, unwholesome
packing-case: crate
packing: padding
pact: bargain, compact, treaty, understanding
pad: block, bolster, button, drum, guard, patch, paw, place, stuff, tablet, waffle, widen
padded: cushioned, plush, quilted
padding: bolster, filling, insulation, waffle
paddle: blade, dabble, float, oar, row, splash, wade
paddock: meadow, pasture
paddy: tantrum
padlock: lock, secure
padre: clergyman,

minister, parson, pastor, vicar
paean: hymn, psalm
pagan: atheist, heathen
page-width: measure
page: leaf
pageant: parade, scene, show, spectacle
pageantry: ostentation
paid: mercenary
pail: kit
pain: bore, cramp, discomfort, distress, drag, evil, grieve, hurt, menace, pang, pest, pierce, pill, plague, stick, torture, trauma, trouble, wound, wrench, wring
pained: hurt, uncomfortable
painful: awkward, bad, bitter, evil, hard, nagging, smart, tender, traumatic, uncomfortable, vicious
painfully: hard
painfulness: tenderness
painkiller: narcotic
painkilling: narcotic
painless: easy
pains: care, effort, trouble
painstaking: careful, close, conscientious, difficult, laborious, meticulous, particular, scrupulous, thorough
painstakingly: narrowly
paint: brush, colour, picture, portray, whitewash
painter: artist
painting: panel, picture
pair: brace, couple, match, mate, team, yoke
paired: double, matching

pairing: match
pal: comrade, friend, intimate, mate
palace: basilica, castle, residence
palanquin: litter
palatable: dainty, digestible, savoury, tasty
palate: taste
palatial: grand, luxurious
palaver: performance
pale: cadaverous, dim, discolour, fade, ghostly, grey, light, livid, lurid, sallow, soft, unwholesome, wan, watery, white
paling: bar, barrier, panel, pole, post, stake
palings: fence, railing
palisade: barrier, fence, wall
pallet: bed
palliasse: bed, litter
palliate: dull, mitigate, mollify, quieten, relieve, remedy, smooth, soften
palliative: painkiller
pallid: cadaverous, deadly, ghastly, green, grey, livid, lurid, pale, sallow, sickly, unwholesome, wan, white
palm: hollow, victory
palmer: pilgrim
palpable: clear, material, obvious, physical, tangible
palpate: touch
palpation: touch
palpitate: flutter, quake
palpitation: flutter, quiver
palsy: paralysis
paltry: base, cheap, frivolous, insignificant, light, lightweight, little, low, meagre, niggardly, petty,

poor, puny, slight, small, sorry, worthless
pamper: baby, indulge, mother, pet, spoil
pampered: luxurious, soft
pamphlet: brochure, hand-out, publication
pan: blast, blister, criticize, crucify, lambast, pot, prospect, rubbish, sift
panacea: remedy
panache: dash, finesse, flair, grace, polish, sparkle, style, virtuosity
panda: bear
pandemic: plague
pandemonium: babel, bedlam, chaos, kerfuffle, noise, racket, uproar
pander to: humour, indulge
panegyrical: complimentary
panegyrics: praise
panel: board, committee, council, jury, plaque, plate, screen, sheet, wall
pang: pain, prick, qualm, smart, stab
pangs: nausea
panic: fear, flap, flip, flurry, fret, fright, hysteria, scare, state, terror
pannier: basket
panorama: outlook, prospect, scene, view
pansy: fairy, gay, homosexual, queer
pant: blow, breath, breathe, heave, puff, yearn
panties: knickers, pants
panting: breathless
pants: briefs, knickers
pap: breast, pulp
papa: dad, father
paper: daily, essay, filter, magazine,

organ, periodical,
thesis
papers: memoirs,
permit
paprika: pepper
par: average, mean,
norm, parity, weather
parable: fable, myth
parables: teachings
parachute: bale
parade: ceremony,
demonstration,
display, flourish,
march, pageant,
procession,
promenade, review,
show, show off, strut
paraded: vaunted
paradigm: classic,
guide, ideal, original,
paragon, precedent
paradise: heaven
paradisial: heavenly,
ideal, Utopian
paradox: puzzle,
irony
paradoxical:
contradictory,
contrary
paraffin wax: wax
paragon: ideal, jewel,
perfection
paragraph: clause
parakeet: parrot
parallel: balance,
compare, equal,
equate, equivalent,
even, flush, keep up,
level, like, line,
match, par, parity,
relationship,
reproduce
paralyse: cripple,
disable, immobilize
paralysed: dead,
disabled, impotent,
incontinent,
motionless, numb,
powerless, prostrate,
torpid
paralysis: impotence,
numbness
paralytic: drunk,
inebriated
paramount: capital,
cardinal, chief,
climactic, overriding,
predominant, pre-
eminent,
preponderant,
primary, principal,
sovereign, supreme
paramour: lover
paranoid: obsessive
paranormal: magic,
mystical, supernatural

parapet: battlements,
rampart
paraphernalia:
belongings, gear,
goods, kit, luggage,
stuff
paraphrase: digest,
recapitulate
paraplegic: cripple
parapsychology:
psychic
parasite: drone,
leech, satellite,
scrounger, sycophant
parasol: awning
parcel: bale, bunch,
bundle, package,
portion, wrap
parch: dry, scorch
parched: baking, dry,
thirsty
parching: torrid
parclose: screen
pardon: condone,
forgive, forgiveness,
grace, let off, purge,
reprieve, spare
pardonable: venial
pare: clip, peel, prune,
shave, trim
parent: author, father,
mother
parentage: birth,
descent, extraction,
family, stock
parental: fatherly,
paternal
parenthesis: aside
parents: people
paresis: paralysis
pariah: leper, outcast
paring: chip, splinter
parings: refuse
parish: fold, local
parishioners:
congregation
parity: balance,
resemblance
park: ground, reserve
parking fine: ticket
parkland: forest
parlance: idiom,
speech
parley: commune,
confer, negotiate,
talk, treat
parleying:
negotiation
parliament:
congress,
government,
legislative, senate
parliamentary:
legislative
parlour: living-room,
lounge

parochial: insular,
local, provincial
parodist: mimic
parody: caricature,
cartoon, imitate,
imitation, lampoon,
mimic, ridicule,
satire, send up, skit,
spoof, take off
paroxysm: attack,
frenzy, spasm,
tantrum
parry: counter,
deflect, divert, fend
off, field, forestall,
obstruct, repel, ward
parsimonious: close,
frugal, mean, miserly,
near, niggardly,
skimpy, tight
parson: clergyman,
minister, pastor,
priest, vicar
part: behalf, bit,
branch, break,
character, clause,
component,
constituent, divide,
divorce, element,
episode, factor,
fraction, fragment,
hand, lap, leg, lot,
member, organ,
parcel, portion,
proportion, quantity,
quota, region, role,
scene, scrap, section,
separate, sever, side,
split, unit, voice
partake: drink,
sample, share
partaker: participant
partial: attached,
narrow, one-sided,
partisan, prejudiced,
unfair
partiality: bias,
fancy, favour,
favouritism,
fondness, inclination,
leaning, like, liking,
penchant, relish,
taste, tendency
partially: partly
participant: player,
subject
participate:
collaborate, feature,
go in for, partake,
play, share, worship
participation:
cooperation
particle: fraction,
fragment, grain, jot,
shred, speck
particles: dust

particular: careful,
certain, circumstance,
conscientious, dainty,
detail, detailed,
different, distinctive,
fussy, individual,
item, meticulous,
peculiar, pedantic,
pet, point, precise,
prim, proper,
punctilious, regard,
requirement, respect,
separate, single,
special, specific,
squeamish, strict
particularity:
difference,
distinction, identity
particularly:
especially, notably
particulars: identity,
past, specifications
parting: break,
division, divorce,
leave, separation
partisan: insurgent,
partial, prejudiced,
zealot
partisanship:
favouritism
partition: divide,
screen, split, wall,
zone
partner: assistant,
associate, auxiliary,
collaborator,
colleague, companion,
comrade, consort,
fellow, friend, match,
mate, pal, participant,
sidekick, wife
partnership:
association, company,
friendship, league,
match
partridge: quail
parts: kit, locality
parturition: birth
party: attached, band,
bunch, celebration,
company, dance,
detachment, detail,
do, faction, festival,
function, gang,
group, individual,
movement, people,
persuasion, rave,
reception, sect, shoot,
side
parvenu: upstart
pass: breeze, cross,
defile, die, elapse,
enter, funnel, go, go
on, hand, happen,
honour, jink, lapse,
lead, live, lunge,

make, migrate, move, occur, okay, outdated, overhaul, overtake, permit, position, reach, roll, run, spend, state, strait(s), ticket
passable: fair, middling, moderate, okay, satisfactory, tolerable
passably: fairly, okay
passage: burrow, canal, career, channel, excerpt, gate, lane, motion, path, progress, quotation, route, run, text, transit, tunnel, voyage, way
passageway: hall
passé: obsolete, old-fashioned, unfashionable
passed: lapsed, made
passenger: fare
passenger-list: manifest
passengers: traffic
passer-by: pedestrian
passing: course, death, disappearance, dying, fugitive, passage, superficial, temporary
passing away: moribund
passing over: skip
passion: blood, emotion, excitement, feeling, fervour, fever, fire, flame, frenzy, fume, fury, glow, heat, impulse, infatuation, love, lust, madness, mania, rage, temper, violence, warmth, wrath, zeal
passionate: avid, devout, earnest, fanatical, feverish, fiery, hot, intense, keen, madly, obsessive, romantic, sultry, temperamental, torrid, violent, warm, wild, zealous
passive: inactive, inert, supine, torpid
passivity: frigidity, inertia
past: back, background, beyond, by, dead, former, gone, history, lapsed,

late, lost, outgoing, over, previous, qualification
paste: batter, cement, cream, glue, mix, ointment, plaster, stick, tack
pastel: soft
pastime: game, hobby, interest, play, pursuit, recreation, thing
pastor: clergyman, padre, parson, shepherd, vicar
pastoral: clerical, fatherly, idyllic
pastry: bun, crust, waffle
pasturage: grass
pasture: field, meadow, paddock
pasty: wan, white
pat: caress, clap, endearment, pet, smack, stroke, tap, touch
patch: bed, doctor, fix, fudge, haunt, heal, mend, piece, plot, reconcile, repair, touch up
patchwork: medley
patchy: irregular, mottled, scrappy, uneven
pate: crown, dome
patent: distinct, glaring, known, manifest, marked, obvious, overt, public, transparent, visible
patently: undeniably
pater: dad, father
paternal: fatherly
path: career, channel, course, lead, line, orbit, passage, run, track, walk, way
pathetic: lame, lamentable, moving, pitiful, plaintive, poignant, poor, sad, sentimental, sorry, tearful, weak, wretch
pathetically: piteously
pathology: medicine
pathway: avenue, drive, road, walk, way
patience: forbearance, tolerance
patient: client, invalid, long-suffering, passive,

persevering, resigned, subject, thick-skinned, tolerant
patina: finish
patois: jargon, language
patriarch: founder
patrician: gentle, noble, well-bred
patrimonial: hereditary, paternal
patrimony: heritage, inheritance, legacy
patriotic: loyal, national
patriotism: loyalty, nationalism
patrol: beat, force, guard, pace, police, prowl, reconnoitre
patrolman: scout
patron: benefactor, buyer, champion, customer, founder, sponsor
patronage: backing, favour, offices, support
patronize: frequent, sponsor
patronizing: condescending, lofty, lordly, snobbish, supercilious, superior
patrons: custom, public
patsy: mark, mug, victim
patter: jargon, pitch
pattern: design, fashion, form, gauge, ideal, master, model, mould, norm, original, paradigm, prototype, rhythm, routine, rut, sample, scheme, shape, specimen, standard, tread
paucity: need, poverty, rarity, scarcity, want
paunch: belly, pot, stomach
paunchy: obese
pauper: beggar
pause: break, gap, halt, hesitate, hold, interlude, interval, lull, respite, rest, stammer, stand, stay, wait
pavement: path
paw: feel, finger, hand, handle, manhandle, maul,

pad, palm
pawn: hostage, instrument, pledge, puppet
pay: atone, bribe, buy, deposit, discharge, foot, fund, give, honour, income, remunerate, render, repay, return, salary, screw, settle, spend, square, treat, wage, yield
payable: due, mature, outstanding, unpaid, unsettled
paying: lucrative
paying guest: lodger, boarder
payload: freight
payment: charge, compensation, discharge, expenditure, expense, fee, hire, ransom, remittance, rent, reward, tender, toll, wage
paynim: heathen, pagan
payoff: ransom
payola: bribery
peace: calm, order, quiet, serenity, still, truce
peaceable: gentle, inoffensive, law-abiding, meek, mild, moderate
peaceful: calm, easy, halcyon, idyllic, placid, quiet, quietly, restful, smooth, sound, still
peacemaker: mediator
peach: beauty, inform, knockout
peak: ceiling, climactic, climax, head, height, high, highlight, maximum, mountain, optimum, pinnacle, prime, summit, tip, zenith
peal: blast, chime, course, gale, knell, ring, thunder, toll
pealing: thunderous
peals: thunder
pearl: bead, globule, jewel
pearls: jewellery
pearly: white
peasant: clown, yokel
peccadillo:

indiscretion
peck: kiss, nibble
pecking order: scale
peckish: hungry
peculator: defaulter
peculiar: crazy,
curious, distinctive,
fishy, funny,
idiosyncratic,
individual, irregular,
kinky, odd, quaint,
queer, quirky,
screwy, singular,
special, specific,
strange, uncommon,
unnatural, unusual,
weird
peculiarity:
characteristic,
distinction,
eccentricity, failing,
oddity, point,
property, quirk
peculiarly: especially,
particularly,
uncommonly
pecuniary:
commercial,
economic, monetary
pedagogic: pedantic
pedantic: difficult,
meticulous, nit-
picking, officious,
ponderous,
punctilious,
scrupulous, stilted
pedantry: nicety,
quibble
peddle: flog, hawk,
hustle, market, push,
sell, vend
peddler: dealer, seller
peddling: traffic
pedestal: base,
podium
pedestrian: banal,
common,
conventional,
hackneyed, mediocre,
ordinary, passer-by,
ponderous,
unimaginative
pedestrianism:
mediocrity
pedigree: blood,
breed, breeding,
extraction, family,
genealogy, origin,
stock, strain, well-
bred
peduncle: stem
pee: urinate
peek: glance, glimpse
peek: look, peep
peel: bark, castle,
flake, outside, pare,

rind, skin, take off,
undress
peeled: bare
peep: glance, glimpse,
peek, peer, squeak
peeper: eye
peer: equal, lord,
noble, rival
peerless: matchless
peers: peerage
peeve: chagrin, fret,
gall, nark, pique,
ruffle, vex
peeved: cross, sore
peeving: vexatious
peevish:
cantankerous,
contentious,
disagreeable, liverish,
perverse, petulant,
prickly, quarrelsome,
querulous, sour,
waspish
peevishness: bile
peg: bolt, drink,
freeze, nail, perch,
pin, plug, skewer
pejorative:
vituperative
pelf: money, wealth
pellet: ball, bullet,
pill, shot
pellucid: bright, clear,
lucid, transparent
pellucidity: lucidity
pelt: batter, hail,
pepper, skin
pen: box, cage, crib,
enclosure, fence,
ghost, impound, jot,
run, walk, write
penal institution:
prison
penalize: burden,
fine, punish
penalty: cost, fine,
forfeit, handicap,
penance, price,
punishment, sanction,
scourge
penchant: bent,
leaning, liking,
predilection, relish
pencil sketch:
drawing
pendant: brooch,
jewellery
pendulum: bob,
weight
penetrate: bore,
broach, enter, indent,
infiltrate, invade,
knife, perforate,
permeate, pierce,
puncture, soak, spear
penetrating: astute,

biting, chilly, cutting,
deafening, deep,
intelligent, intimate,
keen, perspicacious,
piercing, poignant,
pointed, profound,
pungent, searching,
shrill, subtle, wise
penetration: depth,
insight, invasion,
judgement, wisdom,
wit
penetrative: hard,
intuitive, observant,
pervasive
peninsula: cape,
headland,
promontory
penis: prick
penitence: remorse
penitent: remorseful,
repentant, sorry
penitentiary: jail,
prison
pennant: banner, flag,
standard
penniless: destitute,
hard up, miserable,
poverty-stricken
pennilessness:
misery, poverty
penning: writing
pennon: banner,
pennant
penny-pincher:
miser
penny-pinching:
grasping, mean,
miserly, parsimonious
penny-whistle: pipe
penpusher: writer
pension: boarding-
house
pensioner: boarder
pensioners: old
pensive:
contemplative,
serious, thoughtful,
wistful
pentacle: star
penurious: hard up,
niggardly, penniless,
poor, poverty-
stricken
penury: misery,
necessity, need,
poverty
people: civilization,
community, family,
folk, household,
humanity, inhabit,
man, nation,
personnel, populate,
population, public,
race, settle, society
pep: bounce, drive,

season, vigour,
vivacity, zap, zip
pepper: pelt, plaster,
punctuate
peppery: hot,
pungent, quick-
tempered, short-
tempered, waspish
per annum: yearly
per capita: each
per person: each
perambulate:
promenade, ramble,
walk, wander
perambulation:
ramble, walk, wander
perceive: catch,
detect, discern,
discover, distinguish,
divine, feel, find, find
out, get, know, make
out, note, notice,
observe, read,
recognize, remark,
see, sense, take,
understand
perceiving: discovery
percentage:
commission, cut,
proportion, rate
perceptible:
conspicuous,
noticeable, obvious,
audible
perceptibly:
measurably
perception:
awareness,
comprehension,
conscious, depth,
dexterity, eye, feeling,
grasp, grip,
illumination, image,
insight, intelligence,
knowledge, sensation,
sensibility,
understanding, wit
perceptive: astute,
discerning,
intelligent, keen,
knowing, observant,
penetrating,
perspicacious,
piercing, quick,
quick-witted, ready,
responsive, sensitive,
sensuous, sentient,
sharp, shrewd,
understanding
perch: light
perchance: maybe
percipience:
judgement, wisdom,
wit, wits
percipient:
discerning, intuitive,

observant, perceptive, perspicacious, wise
percolate: filter, infiltrate, leak, permeate, strain
percolating: pervasive
percolation: leak
percussion: beat, drum, jar
peregrinate: wander
peregrination: journey, wander
peremptory: authoritative, compelling, dogmatic, imperative, magisterial, rude, overbearing
perennial: lasting
perfect: clean, complete, consummate, crown, divine, faultless, finish, fluent, ideal, idyllic, immaculate, impeccable, intact, matchless, mint, model, optimum, paragon, prime, pure, ripe, sound, total, touch up, unimpeachable, Utopian, whole
perfection: bloom, crown, ideal, optimum, prime, purity
perfectionist: idealistic
perfectly: full, fully, just, quite
perfidious: dishonest, disloyal, double, faithless, false, lying, perjured, rotten, unfaithful, untrue
perfidy: betrayal, insincerity
perforate: penetrate, prick, puncture
perforated: leaky
perforation: opening, prick, ulcer
perforce: necessarily
perform: behave, commit, consummate, discharge, do, effect, execute, fulfil, give, go, honour, implement, keep, manage, obey, operate, perfect, perpetrate, play, produce, prosecute, pursue, realize, recite,

render, run, say, serve, stage, star, take, work
performance: behaviour, execution, gig, hearing, implementation, interpretation, keeping, mechanism, operation, play, presentation, production, programme, recital, record, routine, spectacle, turn, work
performer: artist, musician, player
performing: on, operative
perfume: bouquet, breath, fragrance, incense, odour, scent
perfumed: fragrant, sweet
perfunctorily: quickly
perfunctory: careless, casual, halfhearted, hasty, mechanical, quick, slapdash, summary, superficial
perhaps: maybe, perchance, possibly
pericarp: capsule
peril: danger, difficulty, hazard, jeopardy, threat
perilous: awkward, dangerous, grave, unsafe, warm
perilousness: gravity
perimeter: circle, limit, margin, periphery
period: bout, chapter, cycle, date, day, duration, generation, interval, lapse, length, life, page, patch, phase, point, round, run, season, space, span, spell, spread, stretch, term, time, watch, while
periodic: intermittent, regular
periodical: journal, magazine, organ, paper, publication, review, temporal
periodically: occasionally
peripatetic: mobile, wandering
peripheral: marginal, outer, superficial

periphery: fringe, limit, margin, outskirts, side, skirts
periphrastic: rambling, verbose
perish: die, fall, go, rot
perished: dead
perjure: lie
perjurer: liar
perjuring: lying
perjury: falsehood, lie, lying
perk up: cheer up, cock, look up, pick up, rally
perk: bonus, gratuity, premium
perks: kickback
perky: jaunty, lively, saucy
perm: curl, wave
permanent: constant, durable, fast, forever, indelible, indestructible, lasting, perennial, stable, standing
permeable: leaky
permeate: inform, invade, overrun, penetrate, soak, steep
permeating: pervasive
permeation: invasion
permissibility: legality
permissible: lawful, on, venial
permission: assent, authority, consent, leave, liberty, licence, okay, right, warrant
permissive: broad, broad-minded, indulgent, slack, soft, tolerant
permit: authorize, bear, charter, concession, consent, enable, have, legalize, let, licence, license, okay, pass, sanction, suffer, tolerate, warrant
permitted: free, lawful
permutation: change
pernicious: baleful, baneful, damnable, deadly, divisive, harmful, malevolent, mischievous, poisonous
perniciousness: malice

pernickety: fussy
peroxide: bleach
perpendicular: erect, precipitous, standing, straight, upright, vertical
perpetrate: commit
perpetual: continual, immortal, incessant, infinite, interminable, lasting, permanent, persistent, standing
perpetually: ever, forever
perpetuate: carry on, preserve
perplex: baffle, confound, confuse, floor, intrigue, nonplus, obfuscate, puzzle, stump
perplexed: bemused, bewildered, lost, muddled, puzzled
perplexing: complicated, intriguing, mysterious, strange, tough
perplexity: confusion, doubt, fog, puzzle
perquisite: consideration, gratuity, premium
persecute: bait, oppress, plague, torture, victimize
persecuted: beleaguered, hunted
persecution: harassment
persecutor: bully, oppressor
perseverance: diligence, fortitude, grit, heroism, industry, patience, resolution
persevere: carry on, continue, keep, keep on, keep up, persist, prosecute
persevering: constant, determined, dogged, durable, indestructible, patient, resolute, tireless
persist: be, carry on, continue, endure, go on, hold, keep, keep on, last, linger, live, persevere, pursue, recur, remain
persistence: duration,

patience, purpose,
tenacity
persistent: chronic,
consistent, constant,
determined, dŏgged,
frequent, game,
habitual, incessant,
insistent, nagging,
niggling, obsessive,
obstinate, patient,
perennial, permanent,
perpetual,
persevering,
relentless, steady,
strenuous, stubborn,
tenacious, tireless
persisting: lingering,
living
person: bird, body,
fish, head, human,
individual, life, man,
mortal, party, punter,
soul, thing
persona: psyche
persona non grata:
outcast
personable:
handsome, pretty
personage: celebrity,
figure, personality,
worthy
personal: emotive,
idiosyncratic,
individual, interior,
intimate, own,
private, proper,
unauthorized
personality:
celebrity, character,
figure, name,
personage, presence,
temperament
personification:
picture,
representative, soul
personify: represent,
typify
personnel: crew,
internal, staff
persons: people
perspective: attitude,
viewpoint
perspicacious:
discerning, keen, sage
perspicacity: insight,
sagacity
perspicuity: lucidity
perspicuous: lucid,
luminous
perspiration: grease,
sweat
perspire: sweat
persuadable:
vulnerable,
persuade: bend,
bring, coax, convince,

educate, get, get
round, incline,
induce, influence,
lead, push, satisfy,
sway, turn, win
persuasion: belief,
conviction,
denomination, school,
sentiment, influential,
potent, smooth,
strong, winning
pert: flippant,
forward, fresh,
impertinent, perky,
saucy
pertain: belong,
concern, refer,
regard, relate
pertinacious:
dogged, importunate,
obstinate,
persevering,
persistent
pertinence: germane,
interest, live,
material, pointed,
relevant, suitable
pertness: forwardness
perturb: concern,
discompose, disturb,
put off, rattle, worry
perturbation:
commotion, upheaval,
worry
perturbed: flustered,
worried
perusal: reading,
scrutiny
peruse: browse, read,
study
pervade: infiltrate,
permeate, steep
pervasive:
penetrating
pervasiveness:
diffusion
perverse: awkward,
headstrong,
opinionated, sadistic,
unnatural, wayward,
wilful, wry
perversion:
depravity, garble,
miscarriage,
obscenity, warp
perversive:
subversive
pervert: colour,
corrupt, deviant,
distort, garble,
misinterpret, poison,
warp
perverted: bent,
bestial, degenerate,
depraved, kinky,
obscene, sadistic,

unhealthy, unnatural,
vile
perverting:
unwholesome
pessimist: bear, cynic
pessimistic: cynical,
gloomy, glum,
morbid, negative
pest: bore, gall,
menace, mischief,
nuisance, pain, pill,
plague, trial, worry
pester: badger,
besiege, bombard,
bother, bug, disturb,
gall, harass, hassle,
hound, irritate,
molest, nag, needle,
persecute, plague,
weary, worry
pestering:
harassment, plague
pestilence: pest
pestle: powder,
pulverize
pet: baby, caress,
cuddle, darling,
domestic, duck,
familiar, fond, fondle,
indulge, stroke, sweet
petal: blade, leaf
peter out: die,
disappear, fail, fizzle
out, run out, stop,
subside
petering out:
disappearance
petite: dainty, little,
short, small
petition: ask, beg,
buttonhole, claim,
cry, desire, invoke,
lobby, plea, plead,
press, request, seek,
solicit, sue, suit,
supplication, urge
petrifaction:
ossification
petrify: frighten,
terrify
petrifying:
frightening, hair-
raising
petrol: juice
petticoat: frock
pettish: fractious,
prickly
petty: footling,
insignificant, light,
lightweight, little,
minor, narrow-
minded, negligible,
niggling, paltry,
pathetic, puerile,
puny, small, small-
time

petty cash: float
petulant: fractious,
moody, peevish,
querulous, sulky
pew: bench, seat
phallus: prick
phantasmagorical:
fantastic
phantom: ghost,
shade, spectre, spirit
pharisaical:
sanctimonious
phase: chapter,
instance, kick, page,
posture, quarter,
stage, step
phases: cycle
phenomenal:
astonishing,
marvellous,
miraculous,
portentous,
prodigious,
stupendous, wonder,
wonderful
phenomenon:
marvel, miracle,
object, prodigy,
spectacle, thing,
wonder
philanderer: flirt,
wolf
philandering:
flirtation
philanthropic:
benevolent,
charitable, kind,
liberal, unselfish
philanthropist:
benefactor, donor
philanthropy:
kindness, largess,
munificence
philistine: barbarian,
boorish, heathen
philosopher:
intellectual
philosophical:
intellectual, profound
philosophy: rationale,
sect, theory
philtre: potion
phizog: clock, face,
mug
phlegmatic: cold,
sluggish, stoical
phobia: complex, fear,
obsession
phobic: obsessive,
paranoid
phone: call, contact,
ring, telephone
phoney: artificial,
bogus, charlatan,
fake, forgery, fraud,
fraudulent, mock,

plastic, quack, sham,
spurious
phosphorescence:
glow
photo: illustration,
likeness
photocopy: copy,
facsimile, Xerox
photograph:
exposure, film,
picture, print, slide,
still, take
photographers: press
phrase: couch, idiom,
put, term, word
phraseology:
language, style,
terminology
phrasing: diction,
language, phraseology
phthisis: consumption
physical: bodily,
check-up, corporal,
flesh, hard, material,
sensual, sensuous,
tangible, worldly
physically: bodily,
measurably
physician: doctor,
leech
physicist: engineer
physiognomy: face
physique: body,
build, constitution,
figure, form, frame
pick: axe, best, bill,
cast, choice, choose,
cream, designate,
draw, favourite,
flower, gather,
harvest, pluck, prefer,
preference, probe,
pull, pull up, return,
selection, single, take
picked: named
picket: demonstrate,
sentry, stake
picking: draw
pickings: prize
pickle: corner, cure,
difficulty, fix, jam,
mess, plight,
predicament, trouble
pickled: drunk,
inebriated, tight
pickpocket: dip, thief
picky: fussy
picnic: pushover
pictorial: graphic
pictorialize: illustrate
picture: canvas,
cinema, figure,
graphic, illustration,
image, imagine,
likeness, paint, panel,
photograph, portray,

represent, see, still,
tableau, view,
visualize
picturesque:
colourful,
ornamental, scenic
piddle: urinate
pidgin: jargon
pie: pastry
piece: assemble, bar,
bit, block, chunk,
composition,
creation, essay,
excerpt, feature, item,
length, lot, lump,
man, mass, opus,
part, passage, play,
portion, reconstruct,
remnant, report,
routine, scrap,
section, shred, snatch,
strip, unit, work
pieces: kit, remains,
works, wreckage
pie-crust: pastry
pied: dappled
pie-eyed: drunk
pier: buttress, jetty,
pedestal, pile, pillar,
projection,
promenade, quay,
stage
pierce: bite, bore,
broach, drill, enter,
gore, impale, knife,
penetrate, perforate,
prick, puncture,
spear, stab, stick,
wound, wring
piercing: biting,
bitter, cutting,
deafening,
excruciating, high,
keen, loud, noisy,
penetrating, poignant,
pungent, raw, sharp,
smart, wintry
piercingly: sharply
pierrot: clown
pietistic:
sanctimonious
piety: purity, sanctity
piffle: bunk, rubbish
pig: hog, overeat
pigeonhole:
compartment, slot
piggery: farm
pig-headed:
headstrong, obdurate,
obstinate,
opinionated,
perverse, stubborn,
wilful
piglet: hog
pigment: colour, dye,
paint

pigmentation:
complexion
pigtail: queue
pigtails: tresses
pike: spear
pilaster: column,
pillar
pile: bank, bulk,
bunch, bundle,
crowd, drift, fibre,
flock, gather, heap,
hoard, keep, load,
mass, mound, mount,
mountain, nap, pier
piled: loaded, plenty
pile-driver: monkey
pile-up: collision,
crash, smash
pilfer: borrow, crib,
knock off, nick,
nobble, pinch,
pocket, steal
pilgrimage: journey,
quest
pill: capsule,
medicine, painkiller,
tablet
pillage: loot, plunder,
raid, ransack, rape,
rapine, ravage, rob,
robbery, sack, strip
pillar: column,
obelisk, pier, pile,
post, support
pillion: seat
pillion rider:
passenger
pillory: lampoon,
slam
pillow: bolster
pillow-block:
pedestal
pilot: captain, driver,
fly, govern, guide,
lead, manoeuvre,
navigate, navigator,
preliminary, sail,
sample, steer, trial
piloting:
manipulation
pimp for: prostitute
pimple: boil, pustule,
spot
pin: axle, bolt, brooch,
clasp, clip, fasten,
fastener, fix, impale,
key, leg, locate, nail,
peg, skewer, stud,
tack
pincer: claw, jaw
pincers: forceps
pinch: dash, drop,
kink, knock off, little,
nibble, nick, nip,
nobble, squeeze,
steal, take, touch,

tweak
pinched: drawn,
gaunt, haggard, peaky
pine: hunger, itch,
languish, long, miss,
pant, want, yearn
pinhole: prick
pinion: pin, rope,
shackle
pinioned: bound
pinions: restraint
pink: knock, red, rosy
pinking: knock, rattle
pinna: ear
pinnacle: crown,
height, maximum,
peak, summit, zenith
pinpoint: identify,
locate, show up
pinprick: niggle
pins and needles:
tingling
pint-glass: jar
pint-mug: jar
pint-sized: puny,
small
pioneer: colonize,
initiate, introduce,
originate, originator,
precursor, settler,
start
pioneering:
introduction
pious: devout, godly,
holy, monastic,
religious, reverent,
saintly,
sanctimonious
pip: seed
pipe: blow, cylinder,
feed, flute, gutter,
main, squeak
pipeline: wind
pipes: waterworks
piping: trim
pipistrelle: bat
piquancy: bite,
flavour, juice, relish,
zest
piquant: brisk,
peppery, poignant,
pungent, racy, salty,
sharp, spicy, strong
pique: indignation,
offence, provoke,
resentment, spite,
whet
piqued: hurt, peeved,
stung
piracy: hijack
pirate: bandit,
borrow, buccaneer,
crib, lift, steal, thief,
wolf
pirouette: dance,
rotate, spin, whirl

piscatorial: fishy
piss: urinate
pissed: drunk, high, inebriated
pistol: gun
piston: ram
pit: cavity, dent, hole, hollow, lacuna, mine, quarry, scrape, well, working
pitch: bank, bowl, cast, crash, delivery, erect, fling, ground, heave, hurl, labour, lurch, plunge, put, reel, slant, slope, terrain, tone, venue
pitcher: jar, jug, carafe
piteous: heart-rending, mournful, moving, pitiful, plaintive, sorrowful, sorry
pitfall: difficulty, hazard, obstacle, peril, snare, trap
pith: core, gist, heart, kernel, marrow, meat, pulp, substance
pithy: compact, concise, laconic, meaty, sententious, short, succinct, summary, xyloid
pitiable: lamentable, miserable, pathetic, tearful, wretched
pitiful: lamentable, rueful, sad, woeful, wretched
pitifully: piteously
pitiless: cold-blooded, cruel, hard, harsh, heartless, implacable, merciless, relentless, ruthless, stiff
pit-prop: punch
pitted: bumpy
pitter-pattering: twinkling
pit-top: bank
pity: mercy, sympathize, sympathy
pitying: sorry
pivot: axle, centre, hinge, hub, key, roll, rotate, wheel
pivotal: critical, crucial, key
pixie: elf, fairy, sprite
pizzazz: hype
placard: poster, sign
placate: calm, compose, content,

mitigate, pacify
placatory: conciliatory
place: attach, base, berth, deposit, dispose, fix, grade, home, identify, install, locality, locate, lodge, manoeuvre, mount, plant, point, position, post, put, quarter, recognize, scene, seat, set, site, situation, slot, space, spot, stand, station, stick
placid: calm, collected, cool, even, gentle, halcyon, mild, peaceful, phlegmatic, quiescent, quiet, restful, serene, still, undisturbed
placidity: mildness, serenity
placidly: quietly
placing on: imposition
plagiarism: crib
plagiarist: pirate
plagiaristic: unimaginative
plagiarize: borrow, crib, lift, pirate, steal
plagiarized: derivative
plagiarizer: thief
plague: badger, bedevil, besiege, bombard, bother, bug, curse, disturb, epidemic, harass, molest, nag, nuisance, pest, pester, press, rash, scourge, trouble, weary, worry
plagued: beleaguered, weary
plain: austere, bald, bare, blank, certain, clear, common, direct, distinct, dull, elementary, flat, frumpish, gross, hard, homely, known, level, lowland, lowly, lucid, luminous, manifest, mere, mousy, natural, noticeable, obvious, open, ordinary, overt, patent, plateau, public, quiet, raw, round, rustic, severe, simple, spartan, table, ugly, undisguised, unidentified, visible

plainly: barely, directly, openly, quietly
plainness: legibility, lucidity, simplicity
plaintiff: litigant, party
plaintive: lugubrious, mournful, woeful
plaintiveness: pathos
plait: double, twine, weave
plaits: tresses,
plan: baby, budget, calculate, card, chart, conception, contrive, design, devise, diagram, draft, elevation, form, framework, game, grid, idea, imagine, intention, lay, layout, mastermind, model, move, organization, organize, outline, pattern, plot, procedure, programme, project, projection, proposal, propose, proposition, provision, purpose, schedule, scheme, shape, sketch, tactic, think
plane: crate, face, file, flat, glide, jet, level
planet: earth, globe, world
plank: bat, beam, board, panel
planking: deck, wood, wooden
planks: timber
planned: concerted, contrived, methodical, premeditated, strategic
planner: engineer, mastermind
planning: calculation, method, organization
plant: bed, bury, cultivate, factory, fix, implant, mill, pitch, pot, sow, works
plantation: farm, nursery
planted: cultivated
planter: farmer, settler
planting: gardening
plash: gurgle
plasma: blood
plaster: bandage, cement, dress, slick

plastered: drunk, inebriated, tight
plastic: flexible, pliable, soft, supple, yielding
plasticene: wax
plate: dish, fish, illustration, plaque, scale, sheet
plateau: highlands, lowland, plain, table
plates: crockery
platform: bay, bench, block, board, podium, stage, stand
platinum blonde: white
platitude: chestnut
platitudinous: banal, stale
platter: dish, plate, record
plaudits: ovation
plausibility: credibility
plausible: glib, likely, logical, probable, reasonable, slick, tenable
play: blow, do, drama, lark, latitude, margin, move, perform, pipe, portray, render, room, stage, tolerance, tour
playboy: rake
played down: underdone
played out: worn out
player: athlete, entry, jockey, musician
players: cast
playful: frisky, humorous, jocular, jolly, light-hearted
playfulness: fun
playground: park
playing: flirtation, hearing
playing card: card
playing-field: park, pitch
play-room: nursery
playwright: dramatist, writer
plea: call, entry, instance, petition, prayer, supplication, vindication
plead: beg, implore, intercede, petition, press, solicit, speak, sue, whimper
pleasant: comfortable, delightful, engaging,

enjoyable, good, halcyon, jolly, kindly, mild, nice, personable, smiling, sunny, temperate
pleasantries: banter, humour, repartee
pleasantry: jest, quip
please: charm, content, delight, gratify, joy, oblige, satisfy, take
pleased: complacent, glad, happy, joyful, obliged, proud, self-satisfied, smiling, willing
pleasing: charming, delicious, delightful, glad, good, heart-warming, interesting, joyful, joyous, light, likely, lovable, lovely, pretty, proud, welcome, winning
pleasurable: delicious, delightful, enjoyable, fun, pleasant, satisfying, sensuous, welcome
pleasurably: happily
pleasure: content, delight, diversion, feast, fun, happiness, joy, kick, liking, luxury, recreation, treat
pleasure-boat: barge, yacht
pleasure-flight: flip
pleasure-trip: cruise
pleat: drape, fold, gather
pleated: frilly, voluminous
pleats: frills
plebeian: humble, low, lowly, mean, vulgar
plebiscite: poll, vote
plebs: crowd, proletariat
pledge: assurance, bail, bet, bond, commit, commitment, contract, earnest, engagement, guarantee, oath, pawn, promise, put up, security, stake, vow, wager, warrant, word
pledged: devoted
plenitude: lot, profusion, wealth

plenteous: bountiful, much
plentiful: bountiful, considerable, copious, fruitful, full, lavish, liberal, luxuriant, numerous, opulent, profuse, rich
plenty: prosperity
pleonastic: verbose
plethora: flood, glut, lot, profusion, surfeit, wealth
plexus: mesh, network
pliable: flexible, green, limp, lithe, plastic, resilient, soft, supple, yielding
pliancy: facility
pliant: easy, flexible, limber, lithe, pliable
pliers: forceps
plight: case, condition, crisis, difficulty, pass, pinch, position, predicament, promise, scrape, situation, spot, state, strait(s)
plinth: base, mount, pedestal
plod: crawl, tread, wade
plodder: zombie
plodding: ponderous, slow
plonk: drink
plot: bed, brew, chart, concoct, conspiracy, conspire, intrigue, lay, line, lot, machination, navigate, parcel, plan, scheme, site, sketch, thread, tract
plough: crash, till, wade
ploy: blind, bluff, device, dodge, gambit, game, gimmick, machination, manoeuvre, measure, move, pretext, scheme, tactic, wangle, wheeze, wrinkle
pluck: bottle, courage, extract. gather, guts, harvest, nerve, pull, pull up, snatch, twitch
plucky: spirited, stout, strong
plug: block, close,

cork, electrify, fill, hammer, jack, market, labour, mention, peg, publicize, puff, push, seal, switch, tap
plugging: promotion
plumb: bob, fathom
plumbing: waterworks
plummet: descend, dive, drop, lurch, plunge, sink, slump
plump: chubby, fat, obese, overweight, rotund, round
plunder: forage, liberate, loot, pillage, prize, raid, ransack, rape, ravage, rob, robbery, sack, strip, winnings
plunderer: predator
plundering: pillage, predatory, rape, rapine
plunge: bathe, catapult, descend, descent, dip, dive, drive, drop, duck, fall, lunge, lurch, pitch, quench, slump, swoop, tumble
plunger: ram
plural: manifold
plus: virtue
plush: luxurious, swell
plutocracy: rich
plutonium: fuel
ply: layer, practise, pursue, run, use, veneer, wield, work
pneuma: psyche
pneumatic: womanly
poach: boil, pirate, steal
pocket-lamp: torch
pocket: midget, pot
pod: capsule, fruit, shell
podgy: chubby, obese, overweight, plump, rotund, soft
podium: base, foot, mount, platform
poem: lay
poet: writer
poetic: fanciful, lyrical
pogrom: purge
poignancy: pathos, venom
poignant: emotive, expressive, moving, pungent, tearful
point: attribute, beam, brink, cape, clause,

consideration, degree, direct, dot, gist, headland, issue, item, juncture, level, mark, matter, meaning, message, moment, moral, needle, object, peak, period, pitch, promontory, purpose, range, refer, regard, respect, sense, significance, spike, spot, stage, step, subject, thing, time, tip, turn, use
point-blank: smack, straight
pointed: barb, compact, cutting, expressive, jagged, keen, pithy, pregnant, pungent, sharp, witty
pointedly: sharply
pointer: beacon, guide, hint, index, indication, key, landmark, line, needle
pointing: indication
pointless: footling, futile, hollow, hopeless, idle, meaningless, needless, purposeless, senseless, silly, unnecessary, vain, worthless
pointlessness: vanity
points: score
poise: assurance, balance, cool, grace, presence, sophistication
poised: assured, collected, self-assured
poison: drink, infect, tipple, venom
poisoned: tainted
poisoning: intoxication
poisonous: deadly, lethal, pernicious, venomous, virulent
poke: dig, grub, jab, lunge, nudge, prod, stick
poker: prod
polar: freezing
polarization: ossification
pole: bar, barrier, boom, gaff, oar, paling, perch, post, rod, spar, staff, stake
polecat: ferret
polemic: dialectic
police: guard, law,

patrol
policeman: copper
police station: nick
policing: patrol
policy: course,
  insurance, line,
  platform, procedure,
  rule, tactic
polish: breeding, buff,
  consume, culture,
  devour, dust, finish,
  furbish, glaze, grace,
  improve, perfect,
  refinement, rub,
  scour, shine, smooth,
  touch up, varnish,
  wax
polished:
  consummate,
  cultivated, cultured,
  fine, perfect, polite,
  professional, refined,
  shiny, slick, urbane,
  well-bred
polishing:
  improvement
polite: bland, civil,
  civilized, courteous,
  decent, fair, good,
  proper, suave, well-
  bred
politeness: etiquette,
  propriety
politic: diplomatic,
  discreet, judicious,
  pragmatic, sensible,
  tactful, tactical
politic: wise, worldly
political: civil,
  strategic
politician: orator
poll: canvass, count,
  head, vote
pollinate: fertilize
pollute: defile, foul,
  infect, mess, poison,
  profane, soil
polluted: corrupt,
  dirty, filthy, foul,
  insanitary, messy,
  tainted
pollution: filth
polymer: plastic
polymeric: plastic
polytechnic: college
polyunsaturates: fat
pome: fruit
pommes frites: chips
pomp: ceremony,
  glory, magnificence,
  majesty, ostentation,
  splendour, state
pompous: big,
  grandiose,
  ostentatious,
  portentous,

pretentious,
  sententious, stately,
  stiff, stilted, turgid,
  upstart, wordy
pond: lagoon, lake,
  pool
ponder: brood, chew,
  cogitate, commune,
  consider, deliberate,
  digest, juggle,
  meditate, puzzle,
  reflect, revolve, study,
  think, weigh, wonder
pondering: digestion,
  meditative
ponderous: bulky,
  heavy, laborious,
  lumbering, slow,
  unwieldy, weighty
ponderously: heavily
pong: smell, stench,
  stink, whiff
pongy: smelly
pontiff: patriarch
pontifical: portentous
pontoon: float
pooch: dog
poof: fairy, gay,
  homosexual
poofter: fairy, gay,
  homosexual, queer
pooh-pooh: ridicule,
  scoff
pool: bank, basin,
  bath, fund, lagoon,
  lake, lump, pot, sink,
  tank, unite, well
poor: awful, bad,
  bankrupt, bare, base,
  destitute, feeble,
  humble, inferior,
  lame, lamentable,
  lean, low, lowly,
  meagre, miserable,
  needy, poverty-
  stricken, remote,
  rotten, scanty,
  shoddy, slim, terrible,
  thin, underprivileged,
  unfavourable, weak,
  wretched
poorest: least
poorly: badly, barely,
  ill, off colour, rotten,
  rough, seedy, sick,
  unwell
pop: bang, deflate,
  father, snap
pope: patriarch, vicar
popinjay: pup
poppycock: drivel,
  rot, rubbish, stuff
populace: country,
  crowd, herd, people,
  public, rabble
popular: catchy,

commercial, common,
  current, fashionable,
  general, hot, known,
  public, standard,
  vogue, widespread,
popularity: currency,
  goodwill, vogue
popularize: promote,
  widen
popularly: generally
populate: colonize,
  inhabit, people, settle
population: nation,
  people, public
populist: democratic
porcelain: ceramics,
  china
pore: orifice, read
porker: pig
pornographic: dirty,
  filthy, immoral,
  improper, lewd,
  nasty, obscene
pornography: dirt,
  filth, immorality,
  lewdness, nastiness,
  obscenity
porous: leaky, open
porridge: bird
port: door, entrance,
  harbour, hatch
portable: light,
  mobile, moving,
  pocket
portage: transit
portal: gate
portend: import,
  signify, spell
portent: consequence,
  forerunner, omen,
  sign
portentous: fatal,
  fateful, ominous,
  pompous, solemn,
  weighty
portentousness:
  solemnity
porter: bearer, janitor
porter's room: lodge
porticoed: vaulted
portion: chunk, cut,
  deal, dole, fate,
  length, lot, parcel,
  part, partition, pat,
  piece, quantity,
  quota, rake-off,
  ration, section,
  serving, share, slice
portly: chubby,
  corpulent, fat, heavy,
  obese, overweight,
  plump, rotund, stout
portmanteau: trunk
portrait: likeness,
  picture, profile
portray: describe,

draw, paint, picture,
  play, render,
  represent
portrayal: character,
  description,
  performance, role
pose: assign, attitude,
  impersonate, mince,
  pretence, position,
  posture, put
poser: model
posh: exclusive, swell
posit: put, postulate
position: attitude,
  berth, capacity,
  circumstance,
  condition, credit,
  degree, estate,
  exposure, fix, footing,
  grade, install, job, lay,
  level, mount, niche,
  order, place, point,
  pose, post, posture,
  put, quality, rank,
  role, scene, set, side,
  site, situation, spot,
  stance, stand, state,
  station, status, stick,
  vacancy, viewpoint
positioning: disposal,
  lay, lie, pattern
positive: assertive,
  assured, certain,
  clear, confident,
  decisive, definite,
  dogmatic, favourable,
  flat, great, optimistic,
  plus, print, real, sure,
  worthwhile
positively: decidedly,
  far, flat, flatly, indeed,
  just, quite, really, yes
positivity: assurance,
  security, self-
  assertion
possess: bear, boast,
  enjoy, have, hold,
  keep, obtain, own,
  receive, spellbind
possessed: obsessed,
  wild
possession: asset,
  blessing, custody,
  grasp, grip, keeping,
  occupation, tenure,
  thing
possessions:
  belongings, estate,
  goods, property, stuff
possessive: jealous
possessiveness:
  jealousy
possessor: custodian,
  keeper, owner,
  proprietor
possibility: chance,

hypothesis, liability, prospect, resort, risk, surmise
possible: attainable, feasible, manageable, plausible, potential, practicable, viable
possibly: maybe, perchance, perhaps, reputedly
post: base, berth, book, capacity, column, correspondence, direct, engagement, function, headquarters, job, mail, office, place, plant, pole, position, quarter, quarters, remit, role, send, situation, stake, station, support, upright, vacancy
postage: transport
postal service: post
postbag: correspondence
postcard: line
poster: bill, notice
posterior: back, behind, bottom, buttocks, end, rear, tail
posterity: descendants
posthaste: swiftly
postmark: frank
postmarked: used
postpone: defer, delay, pigeonhole, procrastinate, put off, remit, reserve, suspend
postponed: off, shelved
postponement: delay, moratorium, reprieve, respite, stay
postscript: epilogue
postulant: beginner, initiate, pupil
postulate: hypothesis, premise, presume, suppose, thesis
postulated: hypothetical
posture: attitude, bearing, carriage, mince, pose, set, stance
posy: bouquet, bunch, buttonhole
pot: belly, bowl, grass, jar, jug, marijuana, mug, pan, paunch,

plug, weed
potato slice: crisp
potbelly: pot, paunch
potency: kick, strength, virtue, zap
potent: cogent, forceful, forcible, strong, virile
potentate: ruler
potential: attainable, possible, power, promise
potentially: reputedly
potion: brew
pots and pans: crockery
pottery: ceramics, china
potty: crazy, lunatic, mad, wild
pouch: bag, pocket, purse
poultice: bandage, ointment
pounce: descend, descent, jump, lunge, mug, swoop, tackle, turn on, waylay
pound: bang, batter, beat, bombard, bruise, cage, cannon, crush, mash, pace, powder, pulverize, ram, squash, strike
poundage: weight
pounding: palpitation
pounds: notes
pour: flow, hail, lash, lavish, overflow, pelt, perspire, rain, run, shed, shower, tip, vent, well
pourboire: gratuity
pouring: teeming
pout: face, grimace, mouth, scowl
pouting: petulant
poverty-stricken: destitute, hard up, needy, penniless, poor
poverty: humility, misery, need, want
powder: break, dust, film, meal, mill, pulp, seed
powdered: ground
powdery: bloom, dusty, fine
power: authority, back, capacity, clout, command, domination, drive, effect, effort, electric, energy, faculty, force, grip, hold, impact,

index, influence, jurisdiction, kick, leverage, liberty, licence, life, load, magic, main, manliness, motor, move, muscle, potency, potential, propulsion, pull, qualification, reach, reign, right, rule, say, sway, teeth, throttle, vigour, violence, wallop, wherewithal, zap
powerful: athletic, big, brilliant, burly, cogent, compelling, dramatic, effective, forceful, forcible, formidable, hard, hard-hitting, heady, high, impressive, influential, intense, lusty, macho, mighty, muscular, potent, resounding, stiff, vigorous, violent, vivid, weighty
powerfully: hard, mightily
powering: moving
powerless: helpless, impotent, incapable, ineffectual, unable, weak
powerlessness: impotence, inability
practicability: sense
practicable: attainable, feasible, possible, practical, viable
practical: bright, constructive, down-to-earth, handy, hard, helpful, inventive, mature, positive, pragmatic, realistic, reasonable, robust, salutary, self-reliant, sensible, serviceable, useful, working
practicality: common sense, maturity, sense, wit, wits
practically: virtually
practice: custom, discipline, exercise, experience, habit, manner, method, performance, policy, procedure, process, rite, ritual, routine, rule, system, tradition, usage, use,

way
practise: exercise, go in for, ply, prosecute, pursue, rehearse, work out
practised: experienced, habitual, old, seasoned
pragmatic: down-to-earth, practical
pragmatism: opportunism
prairie: plain
praise: bless, bouquet, celebrate, commend, compliment, eulogize, glorify, glory, honour, incense, kudos, magnify, rave, recommend, salve, worship
praiseworthy: good, laudable, worthy
prance: dance, gambol, skip, strut
prancing: strut
prank: caper, hoax, jest, joke, lark, rag
prankster: clown, joker
prat: wally
prate: gab, natter
prattle: babel, chatter, gabble, gossip, natter, rabbit, rattle, talk, waffle, yap
pray: implore, invoke, worship
prayer: cry, grace
prayers: worship
pre-eminence: celebrity, priority
pre-eminent: capital, cardinal, chief, foremost, leading, main, major, outstanding, principal, prominent, remarkable, ruling, supreme
pre-med: sedative
pre-publicity: build-up
preacher: minister, missionary
preamble: introduction, preface, prelude
prearranged: concerted, set
precarious: critical, dangerous, insecure, shaky, tight, uncertain, unpredictable, unsafe

precariousness:
jeopardy
precaution:
calculation,
preparation,
preventive, prudence
precautionary:
defensive, preventive
precede: herald, lead
precedence: lead,
place, preference,
priority, prominence
precedent: authority,
instance
preceding: former,
late, past, previous
precept: axiom, basis,
canon, charge,
command, dictate,
institute, law, motto,
principle, rule, verity
precepts: teachings
preceptual:
understood
precinct: ward
precincts: confines
precious: choice,
darling, dear,
invaluable,
opinionated,
priceless, rare, rich,
sweet, valuable
preciousness: rarity
precipice: cliff, drop,
ravine, wall
precipitate: cause,
condense, deposit,
hasty, heady,
impetuous,
precipitous,
premature, previous,
provoke, reckless,
spark, speedy,
unreasoning
precipitation: fall,
residue, speed
precipitous: dizzy,
mountainous, sheer,
steep
précis: brief, memo
precise: careful,
certain, close, deadly,
definite, delicate,
faithful, fine,
impeccable, just,
minute, neat, nice,
pedantic, perfect,
prim, proper,
punctilious, refined,
right, rigorous,
scrupulous, specific,
strict, sure,
systematic, true, very
precisely: bang,
exactly, just, literally,
quite, right, truly,

unerringly
preciseness: neatness
precision: clarity,
delicacy, faithfulness,
fidelity, nicety,
perfection
preclude: avert, bar,
obviate, prevent
precluded: prohibited
precocious: forward,
opinionated
preconceived:
jaundiced
preconception:
presupposition
precondition:
prerequisite,
stipulation
precursor:
forerunner, herald,
predecessor
precursory:
preliminary
predator: wolf
predatory: ferocious,
fierce, rapacious
predecessor:
forebear, forerunner,
precursor
predestination: fate,
providence
predestine: ordain,
preordain
predestined: fated
predetermine:
ordain, preordain
predetermined:
predestined
predicament: bind,
case, condition,
corner, crisis,
difficulty,
embarrassment, fix,
jam, juncture, mess,
pass, pinch, plight,
position, problem,
quagmire, quandary,
scrape, spot, state,
strait(s), trouble
predict: divine,
expect, forecast,
foresee, foretell,
project, prophesy
predictable: reliable
prediction: forecast,
oracle, projection
predilection: bias,
fancy, fondness,
leaning, like, liking,
relish, taste
predispose: bias,
influence
predisposed: prone
predisposition: bias
predominance: sway
predominant: chief,

overriding, pre-
eminent,
preponderant,
prevalent, prime,
ruling, sovereign,
superior, supreme
predominantly:
generally, mainly
predominate:
outweigh, prevail,
reign, rule
preface: introduce,
introduction, lead up
to, preliminary,
prelude
prefect: monitor
prefer: choose, fancy,
favour, lean, like, opt
for, will
preferable: better,
desirable
preferably: instead
preference: bent,
choice, fancy,
favourite,
favouritism, leaning,
like, liking, option,
pick, pleasure,
predilection, priority,
taste, will
preferred: pet,
superior
prefine: roast
prefix: particle,
preface
pregnable: unsafe
pregnant: big,
expectant, expressive,
heavy, meaning,
ominous
prehistoric: primitive
prehistorically:
originally
prejudgement:
presupposition
prejudice: bias,
colour, compromise,
injustice, intolerance,
load, slant
prejudiced: bigoted,
intolerant, jaundiced,
narrow, narrow-
minded, partial,
partisan, unfair,
unreasoning
preliminary: prelude
prelude: introduction,
overture, preface
premature: forward,
precocious, previous,
rash
premeditated:
deliberate
premise: basis,
hypothesis,
presupposition, thesis

premises: property
premium: bonus,
deposit, insurance,
payment, price,
reward
premolars: teeth
premonition:
foreboding, hunch,
portent, sense,
warning
preoccupation:
complex, compulsion,
hang-up, obsession,
thing
preoccupied:
bemused, busy,
dreamy, faraway,
inattentive, intent,
lost, pensive
preoccupy: bury,
exercise
preordained: fated,
predestined,
preliminary,
production, provision
prepare: condition,
cook, do, lead up to,
practise, prime,
process, provide,
qualify, ready,
rehearse, school, set,
shape, spread
prepared: game,
ready, ripe, willing
preparedness:
foresight
preponderance:
majority, weight
preponderant:
predominant, ruling,
crazy
preposterous:
fantastic, laughable,
ludicrous, mad,
outrageous,
prohibitive,
ridiculous, silly, tall,
unheard-of, wild
prerequisite:
condition, must,
necessity, priority,
requirement,
stipulation
prerogative:
authority, charter,
franchise, place,
power, right
presage: herald,
warning
prescience: foresight,
vision
prescient: far-
sighted, prophetic
prescribe: dictate,
ordain, order
prescribed: formal

prescription: formula, recipe
presence: attendance, being, company, figure, spectre
present: award, being, blessing, bring, confer, current, deliver, display, do, donate, donation, expose, face, feature, furnish, gift, give, hold up, host, immediate, introduce, largess, offer, offering, pay, perform, pose, produce, propose, purse, put, put on, relate, release, render, screen, set out, stage, state, tender, treat
presentable: decent, fair, personable
presentation: award, demonstration, display, exposure, introduction, layout, performance, production, programme, proposal, show
present-day: contemporary, current, modern, recent
presenter: bearer, host, jockey
presentiment: feeling, foreboding, intuition, portent, premonition, sense
presently: shortly, soon, then
preservation: cure, keeping, maintenance, protection, salvation, upkeep
preserve: conserve, defend, jam, keep, keep up, maintain, reserve, retain, save
preserved: unspoilt
preserver: keeper, saviour
preserving: defensive
preside: conduct, lead, moderate, officiate, umpire
president: principal
presider: chairperson
press: assert, bear, clasp, crowd, crush, cupboard, depress, exhort, hasten,

implore, jam, jostle, knead, lock, mill, mob, pack, prefer, print, proceed, push, scrum, shove, smooth, speed, spur, squash, squeeze, touch, urge
pressed: mangled, pushed
pressing: compelling, demanding, importunate, insistent, instant, live, serious, sore, urgent
pressure: care, compression, compulsion, force, heat, impulse, influence, load, press, run, strain, stress, tension, touch, urgency, weight
pressure-gauge: barometer
pressure-wave: blast
pressurize: force, lean, lobby, press, screw, squeeze
pressurizer: pump
prestidigitator: magician
prestige: clout, credit, face, honour, kudos, note, position, prominence, status
presumably: probably
presume: assume, believe, gather, impose, infer, say, suppose, surmise, take, think
presumed: putative, supposed
presumption: assumption, familiarity, forwardness, freedom, impertinence, imposition, inference, liberty, presupposition, pride, supposition, surmise
presumptive: putative
presumptuous: familiar, forward, fresh, impertinent, overconfident, proud, pushy, saucy, ungrateful, uppish, upstart
presumptuousness: presumption

presuppose: imply
presupposed: axiomatic, supposed
presupposition: premise, presumption
pretence: blind, bluff, colour, deception, display, insincerity, masquerade, pose, pretext, sham, show, veneer
pretend: bluff, kid, let on, make out, purport, represent, suppose
pretended: artificial, fake, quack, simulated
pretender: charlatan, phoney, sham
pretense: stall
pretension: claim, ostentation, pride, vanity
pretentious: big, grandiose, officious, ostentatious, pompous, snobbish, stilted, superior, vain
pretentiousness: cant
preternatural: mystical
pretext: blind, cloak, colour, evasion, grounds, loophole, pretence, stall
prettiness: beauty
pretty: fair, fairly, good-looking, lovely, rather
prevail: conquer, obtain, reign, remain, rule, win
prevailing: chief, common, general, immediate, overriding, popular, preponderant, regular, ruling, superior
prevalence: incidence
prevalent: epidemic, pervasive, rife, widespread
prevaricate: fence, fib, flannel, lie, niggle, pad, quibble, shuffle, stall, waffle
prevaricating: evasive, lying
prevarication: evasion, fib, flannel, lie, lying, nicety, padding, quibble, stall, waffle,

whitewash
prevaricator: liar
prevent: avert, bar, cheat, deter, foil, forestall, frustrate, inhibit, keep, obstruct, obviate, preclude, save, scotch, stop
prevented: prohibited
prevention: frustration
preventive: prohibitive
previous: back, former, late, old, past, preceding, precocious, prior
previously: before, formerly, once, prior
prey: bag, game, kill, killing, quarry, quest, target, victim
price: charge, cost, damage, fare, fee, figure, fine, hire, premium, quotation, quote, ransom, rate, remittance, value, worth
priceless: invaluable, precious, rare, rich
prick: bite, needle, pang, pierce, prod, puncture, spur, stab, whip
prickle: barb, bristle, prick
prickling: tingling
prickly: awkward, thin-skinned, thorny
pride: boast, dignity, morale, narcissism, ornament, pick, self-esteem, self-respect, vanity
priest: clergyman, father, minister, parson, pastor
priesthood: ministry
priestly: fatherly, pastoral
prig: stick
priggish: pompous, prim, prudish, smug, stuffy
prim: demure, fuddy duddy, precise, priggish, prudish, puritanical, stiff, stuffy
prima donna: queen
primacy: lead
primal: primary
primarily: basically, mainly

primary: base, basic, beginning, chief, elemental, elementary, first, fundamental, incipient, infantile, initial, leading, main, paramount, prime, principal, special, ultimate, underlying
primate: monkey
prime: bloom, brief, capital, cardinal, choice, first, flush, fuel, groom, load, master, overriding, paramount, predominant, prepare, principal, school, select, supreme, youth
primed: loaded
primeval: old, primary, primitive
primitive: barbarian, barbaric, low, primary, rude, savage, wild
primordial: old, primitive
primordially: originally
primp: mince
primrose: yellow
prince: king, lord
princeling: magnate
princely: august, big, lordly, magnificent, majestic, regal
principal: base, basic, capital, cardinal, chief, first, foremost, grand, great, head, key, lead, leader, leading, main, master, paramount, predominant, premier, primary, prime, ruling, sovereign, star, superior, supreme, trunk
principally: basically, especially, mainly, most, primarily
principle: axiom, basis, canon, dictate, ideal, institute, integrity, law, maxim, moral, precept, rationale, rule, theorem, verity
principled: honourable, idealistic, moral, upright
principles:

conscience, ethics, morality, philosophy, teachings
print: engrave, enlargement, etching, face, facsimile, illustration, impress, impression, machine, photograph, picture, plate, publish, reproduce, reproduction, run, write, writing
printing: edition, impression, publication
printout: information, output
prior: before, by, father, former, once, preceding
prioress: mother
priority: lead, preference, prerogative, urgent
priory: monastery
prise: lever
prison: jail, jug, nick, pen
prisoner: captive, convict
prissy: prudish
pristine: blank, brand-new, immaculate, maiden, new, pure, virgin
privacy: close, confidential, domestic, exclusive, home, inside, interior, internal, intimate, own, peculiar, quiet, retirement, retreat, seclusion, secret, solitude, unauthorized, undisclosed
privateer: buccaneer
privately: aside, quietly
privation: deprivation, distress, hardship, necessity, need, poverty, want
privatization: enclosure
privilege: charter, claim, concession, due, faculty, franchise, honour, licence, prerogative, right
privileged: select
privy: bog, lavatory, toilet
prize: award, bonus,

cherish, choice, conquest, crown, delight, distinction, gem, jewel, loot, lottery, love, pride, purse, trophy, value, victory, winnings
prized: precious, valuable
prizewinner: victor
prizewinning: victorious
pro: sympathetic
probability: chance, odds, presumption
probable: likely, moral
probably: likely
probationary: untried
probationer: initiate, novice
probe: check, dig, explore, grub, investigate, look into, research, search, sound
probing: exploratory, piercing, searching
probity: good, honesty, honour, integrity, sincerity, virtue
problem: bother, condition, difficulty, embarrassment, exercise, handful, hang-up, hassle, hitch, issue, matter, nut, pig, puzzle, query, question, riddle, rub, snag, worry, wrinkle
problematic: chancy, complicated, thorny
problematical: difficult, doubtful
proboscis: beak, nose, trunk
procedural: ritual
procedure: career, course, drill, line, manner, means, mechanism, method, operation, policy, programme, recipe, regulation, rite, ritual, routine, rule, step, system, tack, technique, usage, way
proceed: continue, do, fare, follow, go, journey, move, pass, progress, receipt, resume, run
proceeding:

operation, suit, transaction
proceedings: case, solemnity, thing
proceeds: income, profit, return, revenue, takings, winnings
process: case, manner, manufacture, means, medium, method, parade, procedure, treat, work
processing: refinement,
procession: column, line, march, pageant, parade, review
processional: gradual
proclaim: assert, broadcast, call, celebrate, cry, declare, deliver, find, herald, knell, profess, promulgate, pronounce, reveal, tell, trumpet, utter
proclamation: cry, declaration, edict, publication, release, revelation
proclivity: habit, leaning, tendency
procreate: breed, reproduce
procreation: generation, reproduction
procreator: parent
procure: buy, find, get, obtain, pander to, purchase, recruit, secure, take
procured: found
prod: dig, drive, jab, jog, needle, nudge, poke, probe, prompt, spur, stick, whip
prodigal: exuberant, lavish, profuse, spendthrift, wasteful, wastrel
prodigality: exuberance, waste
prodigious: exceptional, huge, immense, legendary, marvellous, phenomenal, portentous, singular, stupendous
prodigy: brain, legend, marvel, phenomenon, wonder
produce: bear, breed,

compose, conceive,
create, crop, do,
effect, fetch, fruit,
generate, grow,
harvest, lead, make,
manufacture, mint,
mother, mount,
perform, present,
prolong, publish, put
on, raise, stage,
supply, synthesize,
turn out, yield
produced: made
producer: author,
cause, farmer
product: fruit,
harvest, job,
manufacture,
number, output,
package, upshot,
work, yield
production:
composition,
creation, generation,
manufacture, output,
performance, piece,
presentation,
programme, show,
work
productions: works
productive:
constructive, creative,
effective, efficient,
fertile, fruitful,
helpful, lucrative,
pregnant, profitable,
prolific, rank, rich,
worthwhile
productivity: output
products:
merchandise,
produce, wares
profanation: outrage,
violation
profane: defile,
impious, physical,
pollute, prostitute,
sacrilegious,
scurrilous, secular,
temporal, uncouth,
unholy, worldly
profanity:
blasphemy, invective,
oath, obscenity,
prostitution, swearing
profess: avow, claim,
confess, protest,
purport
professed: ostensible,
supposed
profession: business,
calling, job, line,
occupation, practice,
vocation, work
professional:
businesslike,

technical, veteran
professor: teacher
proffer: bring, offer,
pay, present, propose,
submit, tender
proficiency:
dexterity, skill,
technique
proficient: capable,
competent, efficient,
good, nimble,
practical, practised,
professional, skilful
proficiently: well
profile: outline
profit: benefit, boot,
fruit, gain, good,
interest, killing,
proceeds, purpose,
receipt, return,
reward, sake, use,
value, yield
profitable: beneficial,
commercial,
desirable, economic,
fruitful, helpful,
lucrative, productive,
salutary, serviceable,
successful, useful,
valuable
profits: revenue,
takings, winnings
profligacy:
immorality, licence,
licentiousness, waste
profligate: dissipated,
extravagant, immoral,
libertine, prodigal,
rake, shameless,
spendthrift, wasteful,
wastrel
profound: deep,
heavy, heavily,
intense, radical,
subtle, unbroken,
very, well
profundity: depth
profundo: depth
profuse: copious,
exuberant, heavy,
lavish, liberal,
luxuriant, numerous,
prodigal, prolific,
rampant, rank
profusely: heavily
profusion:
exuberance, flood,
plenty, wealth
progenitor: father,
forebear, parent
progeny: brood,
descendants, family,
fruit, increase, issue,
litter, offspring,
posterity, seed, young
prognosis: forecast,

projection
prognosticate:
foresee, foretell,
prophesy
prognostication:
omen, oracle
programme: bill,
broadcast, brochure,
course, edition,
itinerary, plan,
project, proposal,
schedule, scheme
progress: career,
civilization, course,
develop,
development,
evolution, evolve,
gain, grow, growth,
improve,
improvement,
journey, lift, look up,
march, motion, move,
movement, passage,
ride, rise, way
progressing: better
progression: chain,
climb, course,
evolution, movement,
order, queue,
sequence, step, train,
transition
progressive: broad,
broad-minded,
gradual, liberal,
positive,
revolutionary
prohibit: ban, bar,
deter, forbid,
preclude, proscribe,
veto
prohibited:
forbidden, illegal
prohibition: ban, bar,
veto
project: bulge,
concoct, design,
hatch, jut, launch,
obtrude, overhang,
plan, prolong,
proposal, proposition,
scheme, screen,
venture
projectile: shot
projecting: obtrusive,
proud
projection: forecast,
knob, limb, overhang,
prominence
projections: teeth
proletarian: plebeian
proletariat: crowd,
multitude, rabble
proliferate: branch,
multiply, mushroom,
reproduce, spread
proliferation:

growth, propagation,
reproduction, spread
prolific: bountiful,
fertile, fruitful, lavish,
liberal, lush,
luxuriant, pregnant,
productive, profuse,
rich, voluminous
prolix: garrulous,
lengthy, verbose,
wordy
prolixity: length
prologue:
introduction, prelude,
preface
prolong: continue,
increase, lengthen,
procrastinate
prolonged:
continuous, lingering,
long, protracted, slow
promenade: jaunt,
parade, ramble,
saunter, stroll, walk,
wander
prominence:
celebrity, distinction,
eminence
prominent: big,
conspicuous, great,
high, noted,
obtrusive,
outstanding,
predominant,
prestigious,
protuberant, public,
remarkable, salient,
star
promiscuity:
licentiousness
promiscuous: fast,
lascivious, loose, lost,
unfaithful
promise: assurance,
bond, guarantee,
hope, oath,
obligation, pledge,
spell, swear,
undertake, vouchsafe,
vow, word
promising:
auspicious, bright,
coming, fair,
gold(en), happy,
hopeful, likely,
propitious, rosy
promontorial:
peninsular
promontory: bluff,
cape, head, headland,
point, prominence
promote: boost,
develop, forward,
foster, further, hype,
launch, lift, market,
nourish, plug, prefer,

provoke, publicize, puff, push, raise, recommend, sell, set up, speed, sponsor, support, uphold
promoter: sponsor
promotion: build-up, elevation, fanfare, hype, preferment, progress, propaganda, propagation, rise
prompt: dispose, impel, induce, instant, instigate, jog, lead, motivate, move, prod, provoke, punctual, quick, rapid, ready, speedy, spur, unhesitating
prompting: instance
promptitude: rapidity
promptly: directly, immediately, now, quickly, readily, right, sharp, soon, swiftly
promulgate: proclaim, publish, spread, utter
promulgation: publication
prone: flat, grovelling, liable, low, predisposed, prostrate, ready, subject, susceptible, vulnerable
prong: barb, fork, needle, spike
prongs: teeth
pronounce: articulate, declare, dictate, find, pass, proclaim, rule, say, speak, stamp, utter
pronounced: blatant, clear, great, marked, obvious, prominent, salient, thick
pronouncement: declaration, diagnosis
pronunciation: diction
proof: confirmation, demonstration, immune, impregnable, pull, receipt, sign, specimen, test, testimony, tight, token, trial
prop: bastion, bolster, brace, buttress, cradle, crutch, flat, fortify, hold up, keep

up, leg, pillar, reinforce, rest, shore up, stake, support
propaganda: hype
propagate: breed, grow, increase, multiply, raise, reproduce, spread
propagation: generation, growth, increase, reproduction
propagator: distributor
propel: catapult, drive, impel, launch, move, project, push, send, throw
propeller: screw
propelling: motive, moving
propensity: bent, inclination, knack, leaning, penchant, tendency, turn
proper: conventional, decent, fitting, good, honourable, just, legitimate, logical, meet, moral, official, prim, prudish, puritanical, reasonable, regular, relevant, respectable, right, sound, suitable
properly: duly, fairly, right, well
property: attribute, capital, estate, feature, goods, grounds, land, lot, means, place, possession, premises, purchase, quality, resources, stock, thing, wealth
prophecy: divination, forecast, oracle
prophesier: seer
prophesy: forecast, foresee, foretell, predict, preordain
prophet: mouth, oracle, seer
prophetic: scriptural
prophylactic: preventive
propinquity: imminence, presence, proximity
propitiate: pacify, placate
propitiative: conciliatory
propitious: auspicious, benign,

favourable, gold(en), good, hopeful, lucky, opportune, promising, right
proportion: composition, deal, keeping, measure, quota, rate, scale
proportional: relative
proportionate: commensurate, relative
proportionately: equally
proportions: magnitude, measurement, mix, size
proposal: bill, motion, move, nominee. offer, overture, plan, project, proposition, scheme, suggestion, tender
propose: design, intend, mean, move, nominate, offer, plan, postulate, premise, purpose, put, put up, recommend, submit, suggest, table, venture, vote
proposed: hypothetical
proposition: bid, hypothesis, motion, offer, overture, plan, premise, project, proposal, question, resolution, suggestion, theorem, thesis, venture
propound: pose, propose, submit
proprieties: manners
proprietor: host, keeper, landlord, owner
proprietorship: patronage, possession
propriety: morality, order, protocol, reason, right
propulsion: projection
prosaic: matter-of-fact, mundane, ordinary, pedestrian
proscribe: ban, boycott, forbid, outlaw
proscribed: forbidden, illegal, prohibited
proscription: ban,

bar, boycott
prosecute: enforce, sue, wage
prosecution: litigation, suit
proselyte: believer, convert, novice, recruit
proselytiser: missionary
proselytize: convert
prospect: chance, lease, lookout, outlook, panorama, scene, view
prospective: future
prosper: bloom, boom, flourish, flower, make out, rise, succeed
prosperity: fortune, plenty, wealth, welfare
prosperous: comfortable, gold(en), opulent, rich, successful, thriving, wealthy
prostitute: whore
prostitution: game, vice
prostrate: flat, flatten, kowtow, low, prone, worship
prostration: exhaustion, lassitude
protagonist: hero
protect: chaperon, conserve, cover, defend, guard, harbour, keep, look after, preserve, save, screen, shade, shelter, shield, tend, watch
protected: cushioned, sacred, safe, secure, sheltered
protection: barrier, care, cover, custody, defence, hedge, insulation, keeping, maintenance, pad, patronage, preventive, rock, safety, sanctuary, security, shadow, shield, support, ward
protective: defensive, jealous, paternal, preventive
protectiveness: jealousy
protector: box, bumper, champion, guardian, patron, saviour

protectorate:
patronage, possession
protectress: mother
protest: barrack, beef,
demonstration,
difficulty, kick,
object, objection,
outcry,
remonstration,
scruple, squeal
protester: malcontent
protesting: querulous
protocol: ceremony,
etiquette, form,
formality, manners,
policy, propriety,
ritual
prototype: classic,
forerunner, model,
original, parent,
precedent
protract: lengthen,
pad out, produce,
prolong, sustain
protracted: great,
interminable, lengthy,
lingering, long, slow
protractedness:
length
protrude: bulge, jut,
obtrude, overhang,
project, stick, swell
protruding:
obtrusive, prominent,
protuberant, salient
protrusion: bulge,
knob, lump,
overhang, projection,
prominence
protuberance: bulge,
hump, knob, lump,
prominence, swelling
protuberant: convex,
prominent
proud: erect, high,
lofty, lordly, vain
prove: bear out,
confess, show
proven: logical, sound
provenance: origin
provender: food
proverb: maxim,
phrase, saying
provide: cater,
contribute, deliver,
dispense, find,
furnish, invest, kit,
lay on, render, serve,
supply, yield
provided: if
providence: chance,
destiny, fate, fortune
provident: far-
sighted, thoughtful
providential: happy,
miraculous

providentially:
happily
province: calling,
department, field,
jurisdiction,
kingdom, range,
realm, world
provinces: country
provincial: insular,
local
provision: cater,
clause, condition,
feed, furnish, kit,
maintenance,
preparation, ration,
rig, stipulation, stock,
store
provisional:
conditional,
contingent, interim,
tentative, trial
provisions: board,
bread, fare, food,
groceries, meat,
supply, sustenance
proviso: qualification
provocation:
challenge, fuel,
inflammatory,
invidious, juicy,
offensive, piquant,
seductive, sexy,
suggestive, sultry,
taunt, teasing,
titillating, vexatious
provoke: bait, cause,
chafe, challenge,
court, fan, ferment,
fuel, hound, incite,
incur, instigate,
invite, irritate, kindle,
nag, needle, offend,
pick, prompt, put out,
raise, rouse,
stimulate, stir,
tantalize, taunt, wake,
whip, wind up
provoking: titillating
prow: beak, bow, fore
prowl: lurk, roam,
skulk
prowler: intruder
proximity:
imminence, presence
proxy: deputy,
substitute
prudence: care,
caution, judgement,
maturity, policy,
providence, wisdom
prudent: careful,
circumspect,
deliberate,
diplomatic, discreet,
far-sighted, judicious,
mature, politic,

pragmatic, safe, sage,
sensible, sound,
sparing, tactful,
thoughtful, well, wise
prudish: delicate,
demure, priggish,
prim, puritanical
prune: axe, clip, thin,
trim
pry: nose, obtrude,
poke, snoop
prying: busy, curious,
inquisitive, nosy
psalm: chant, hymn,
song
psephologist: teller
pseudo: sham,
spurious
psyche: mind, soul,
spirit
psychedelic:
colourful,
psychological
psychic: paranormal,
supernatural
psycho: lunatic
psychoanalyst:
psychiatrist
psychological:
critical, crucial,
mental, psychic
psychologist:
psychiatrist
psychopath: lunatic
psychopathic: insane,
mad, psychotic
psychopathy:
madness
psychosis: lunacy,
madness
psychosomatic:
psychological
psychotherapist:
psychiatrist
psychotic: insane,
lunatic, mad, mental
pub: bar, inn, local
pubescent: young
public: audience,
common, communal,
crowd, following,
municipal, national,
open, out, overt,
popular, social
publication: book,
issue, organ, release,
revelation, writing
publicity: exposure,
fanfare, hype,
promotion,
propaganda
publicize: hype, plug,
post, promote,
publish, puff, push,
splash, spread,
vaunted

publicly: openly
publish: broadcast,
communicate, cry,
deliver, disclose, float,
herald, issue, launch,
post, proclaim,
promulgate, put out,
release, report,
rumour, run, tell,
trumpet, utter, write
publishing: literary
pucker: purse, screw,
wrinkle
pudding: dessert,
sweet
puddle: pool
puerile: babyish,
childish, infantile,
juvenile, shallow
puff: balloon, blow,
breath, breathe,
breeze, distend, fluff,
gust, inflate, pant,
plug, swell, waft,
whiff, wind
puffiness: swelling
puffing: breathless
pugilism: boxing
pugnacious:
contentious, militant,
quarrelsome, warlike
puke: vomit
puking: sick
pulchritude: beauty
pull: attract,
attraction, clout,
drag, draught, draw,
haul, heave,
hitch, hold,
influence, jerk,
leverage, manhandle,
pluck, proof, puff,
rack, snatch, stretch,
temptation, tweak,
whip, wrench
pulled: twisted
pulley: block, hoist,
whip
pulling: extraction,
traction
pullover: jersey,
woolly
pulp: mash, squash
pulpit: desk, dock
pulpy: soft
pulsate: beat, vibrate
pulsating: variable,
vibrant
pulsation: shake
pulse: beat, rhythm
pulsing: palpitation
pulverize: grind, mill,
powder, shatter
pulverized: fine,
ground, devastating
pummel: bang,

batter, club
pump: grill,
  interrogate, question,
  ram
pun: gag, joke, quip,
  witticism
punch: assault, bang,
  belt, bite, blow, box,
  brew, clip, force, hit,
  jab, kick, knock, mill,
  mint, vigour, wallop
punctilio: formality
punctilious: careful,
  conscientious, formal,
  meticulous, minute,
  painstaking, pedantic,
  proper, refined,
  religious, rigorous,
  stiff
punctiliousness:
  propriety
punctual: prompt
punctually: duly,
  promptly, sharp
punctuate: interrupt
puncture: bite, blow-
  out, broach, burst,
  deflate, hole, leak,
  perforate, pierce,
  prick, rupture, stab,
  stick
punctured: burst,
  flat, leaky
pundit: critic, sage
pungency: kick, zest
pungent: caustic,
  fiery, harsh,
  penetrating, peppery,
  piquant, poignant,
  rank, salty, sharp,
  spicy
puniest: runt
punish: discipline,
  flog, penalize
punishing: gruelling,
  killing, relentless,
  severe
punishment:
  discipline, judgement,
  medicine, penalty,
  penance, rap,
  retribution, scourge,
  vengeance
punnet: basket
punster: wit
punt: bet, boot, kick
punters: public
puny: feeble, paltry,
  peaky, small,
  unhealthy, weak

pup: dog, youngster
pupil: novice, scholar,
  student, trainee
pupils: school
puppet: doll, effigy,
  figurehead,
  instrument, nominal,
  pawn, satellite, titular
pups: litter, young
purchase: buy,
  footing, grip, hold,
  leverage, pick up,
  procure, take, traction
purchaser: buyer,
  consumer, customer
purchasers: market,
  sale
pure: chaste, clean,
  clear, fine, fresh,
  genuine, hygienic,
  immaculate, innocent,
  lucid, main, mere,
  natural, neat, refined,
  safe, seraphic, sheer,
  simple, solid, straight,
  strong, true, very,
  virgin, virtuous,
  white
purebred: pedigree
purée: cream
purely: merely, only
purest: quintessential
purgative: laxative
purgatory: hell
purge: drench,
  remove, rid
purging: catharsis
purification:
  baptism, catharsis,
  refinement
purified: clean,
  refined
purify: baptize,
  clarify, clean, clear,
  filter, fumigate,
  purge, rarefy, rectify,
  retort, treat
puritanical: austere,
  precise
puritanism: austerity
purity: honour,
  innocence, lucidity,
  sanctity, simplicity,
  virtue
purlieus: outskirts
purloin: knock off,
  lift, pinch, pocket,
  steal, take
purloining: larceny
purple: livid, prune

purport: matter,
  meaning, pretend,
  sense, significance,
  spirit
purported: ostensible
purpose: cause,
  design, destination,
  determine, end,
  function, goal, idea,
  intend, intent,
  intention, mean,
  meaning, motivation,
  motive, object,
  objective, point,
  purport, reason,
  resolution, resolve,
  sake, will
purposeful: resolute
purposeless: chaotic,
  meaningless, random,
  vague
purposelessly:
  blindly, vaguely
purr: buzz, hum, sing
purring: murmuring
purse: prize
purser: cashier
pursue: badger, chase,
  continue, course, dog,
  follow, go in for,
  hound, hunt,
  persecute, ply,
  practise, prosecute,
  seek, track, wage, woo
pursued: dogged
pursuit: calling,
  career, chase, hobby,
  hunt, interest,
  occupation, quest
purvey: cater, supply
purview: scope
pus: matter
push: barge, bear,
  bully, bundle,
  campaign, crank,
  crowd, dent, depress,
  drive, egg, fasten,
  hurry, hustle, impel,
  impetus, impulse,
  jam, jog, jostle,
  launch, manhandle,
  market, move, nose,
  nudge, offensive,
  pass, plug, poke,
  press, prod, promote,
  propel, propulsion,
  publicize, puff, put,
  scramble, scrum,
  shove, sprout, urge
pusher: dealer, seller

pushiness:
  forwardness, self-
  assertion
pushover: picnic
pushy: assured,
  forward, immodest,
  officious,
  presumptuous
pusillanimous:
  cowardly, fearful
pussyfoot: shuffle
pustule: boil
put: attach, deposit,
  dispose, lay, locate,
  lodge, phrase, place,
  position, post, set,
  stand, state, stick,
  submit, throw, word
putative:
  hypothetical, titular
putrefaction: decay,
  decomposition, rot
putrefy: corrupt,
  decay, rot
putresce: decay
putrescence: decay,
  decomposition
putrescent: bad,
  corrupt, evil, foul,
  high, rancid, rotten
putrid: corrupt,
  rancid, rotten, septic,
  smelly
putsch: coup,
  insurrection, uprising
puzzle: baffle,
  confuse, enigma,
  floor, intrigue, maze,
  mystery, nonplus,
  paradox, perplex,
  ponder, problem,
  quandary, riddle,
  stump, unknown,
  wonder, work out
puzzled: lost
puzzlement:
  confusion, fog
puzzling:
  complicated,
  imponderable,
  intriguing,
  mysterious, tough,
  unaccountable
pygmy: baby, dwarf,
  midget
pyramid: tomb
pyrotechnics:
  fireworks

Q

quack: fraud
quadrangle: court
quadriplegic: cripple
quaff: carouse, down, drink
quaggy: soft
quagmire: bog, swamp
quail: cower, dread, flinch, quake, quiver, recoil, wince
quaint: curious, odd, peculiar, queer
quake: cower, quail, quaver, quiver, shake, shudder, tremble, tremor
quaking: shake
qualification: condition, degree, proviso, requirement
qualifications: background
qualified: capable, competent, conditional, experienced, finite, fit, knowing, knowledgeable, professional, proficient
qualifier: heat
qualify: pass, satisfy
qualifying: preliminary
quality: attribute, calibre, character, characteristic, degree, flavour, grade, idea, merit, mould, nature, odour, property, rank, texture, thing, water, worth
qualm: doubt, misgiving, pang, scruple, suspicion
qualmish: squeamish
quandary: bind, difficulty, fix, jam, predicament, problem, puzzle, quagmire, spot
quantifiably: measurably
quantification: valuation
quantify: measure,

value
quantifying: measurement
quantitatively: measurably
quantities: plenty
quantity: batch, degree, dose, length, load, lot, magnitude, mass, matter, measure, number, pile, sum, volume
quarantine: isolate
quarrel: bolt, clash, disagree, dispute, feud, hassle, jar, rift, riot, row, rupture, scrap, words, wrangle
quarrelsome: cantankerous, contentious, quick-tempered, obstreperous, pugnacious
quarry: bag, dig, game, hare, kill, killing, mine, prey, quest, target, victim, working
quarter: board, lodge, mercy
quarterly: periodical
quarters: barracks, cabin, lodgings, residence
quash: cancel, censor, kill, nullify, quell, repress, rescind, reverse, revoke, squash, suppress, undo
quashed: undone
quashing: cancellation, killing
quaver: quiver, warble
quavering: warble
quay: berth, dock, harbour, jetty, pier, stage
quayside: mooring
queasiness: sickness, upset
queasy: queer, sick, squeamish, upset
queen: crown, fairy, homosexual

queer: fairy, funny, gay, homosexual, irregular, kinky, singular, squeamish, strange, unusual
quell: compose, conquer, crush, kill, quash, repress, settle, soften, squash
quench: extinguish, glut, put out, satisfy, suppress
quenched: extinct
querulous: fractious, sulky
query: doubt, probe, question, wonder
quest: hunt, mission, pursuit, search
question: challenge, consult, dispute, doubt, interrogate, interview, issue, matter, poll, pump, puzzle, query, quiz, subject, wonder
questionable: doubtful, improbable, queer, shaky, suspect
questioning: curious, sceptical
queue: bottleneck, caravan, column, file, jam, line, procession, row, string, tail
quibble: carp, cavil, niggle, prevaricate, shuffle, sophistry
quibbling: niggling, nit-picking
quick: facile, fast, hasty, keen, lively, momentary, nimble, nippy, observant, painless, passionate, penetrating, perceptive, precipitate, prompt, rapid, responsive, rough, rush, smart, speedy, spry, sudden
quicken: hurry, resuscitate, revive, whet
quickly: fast, forthwith, promptly, readily, right,

roughly, soon
quickness: rapidity, speed, vivacity
quicksand: mire, quagmire
quick-tempered: hasty, passionate, short-tempered
quick-witted: bright, clever, intelligent, ready, resourceful, sharp, smart
quid: plug
quiescence: silence, dormant
quiescent: inert
quiet: calm, compose, conservative, cool, gentle, halcyon, idyllic, inoffensive, low, lull, noiseless, off, order, orderly, pacify, peace, peaceful, placid, quell, restful, restrained, reticent, retiring, satisfy, self-effacing, sequestered, silent, sleepy, slow, sober, still, subdued, uncommunicative, weak, withdrawn
quieten: calm, lower, lull, muffle, settle, silence, still, subside
quietly: low, still
quietness: languor, serenity
quill: barrel, float, pen, spine
quintessence: paragon, soul, stuff
quintessential: classic, ideal
quip: banter, crack, jest, joke, sally, witticism
quipping: merriment
quips: banter, wit
quirk: eccentricity, freak, kink, mannerism, oddity, whim
quirky: capricious, funny, kinky, whimsical
quisling: collaborator

quit: bale out, desert, discontinue, drop, evacuate, forsake, go off, kick, lay off, leave, part, pull out, remove, renounce, resign, stop, surrender, vacate

quite: bang, completely, even, fairly, just, passably, pretty, rather, right, utterly, yes

quittance: redress

quiver: bob, flutter, quake, quaver, shudder, stir, tremble, tremor, vibrate

quivering: flickering, flutter, palpitation, vibrant

quivers: shivers

quixotic: dreamy, Utopian

quiz: ask, competition, grill, interrogate, interview, pump, question

quiz team: panel, quizzical: sceptical

quizzical: sceptical

quoit: disc

quondam: former, once, past, previous

quota: complement, dole, lot, measure, portion, proportion, ration, share

quotation: passage, quote

quotation mark: quote

quote: cite, extract, quotation, repeat

quoted: direct

quotidian: daily

R

rabbi: clergyman
rabbinical: scriptural
rabbit: chat, gab, go on, jaw, natter, prattle, ramble, rattle, talk, waffle, yap
rabbiting: maundering
rabble: crowd, herd, mob, multitude, proletariat, riffraff, scum
rabid: fanatical, raving, wild, zealous
race: barrel, bat, bomb, breed, brood, career, chase, clan, course, dash, flee, fly, folk, gallop, gun, hare, hurry, kind, nation, pelt, run, rush, scramble, seed, speed, tribe, whisk, zap, zip
racialist: xenophobic
racist: xenophobic,
rack: crib, grid, grill, stand, stretch, wring
racket: babel, commotion, hubbub, jangle, noise, pandemonium, rattle, row, swindle, uproar
racketeer: gangster
racking: excruciating, piercing
raconteur: narrator
racy: juicy, salty
raddle: screen
radiance: beam, blaze, bloom, brilliance, fire, fragrance, glamour, glory, glow, light, lucidity, lustre, sheen, warmth
radiant: beautiful, brilliant, carefree, fragrant, gleaming, glorious, lucid, luminous, ravishing, shining, splendid, sunny
radiate: beam, cast, emit, glow, project, send, shed, shine
radiating: warm

radiation: emanation, emission, projection, warmth
radical: left, liberal, progressive, revolutionary, root, sweeping, underground
radio: broadcast, transmit
radius: range
radix: root
raffish: garish
raffle: lottery
raft: float
rafter: principal
rafters: attic
rag: banter, kid, mop
rage: backlash, bluster, boil, bug, fad, fashion, fume, fury, madness, passion, pet, rampage, rave, seethe, storm, style, tantrum, temper, vogue, wrath
ragged: frayed, jagged, moth-eaten, worn, worn out
ragging: banter, jeering, teasing
raging: fierce, flaming, furious, rabid, rampant, tempestuous, wild, wrathful
raid: attack, bust, do, forage, foray, invade, invasion, pillage, ransack, rob, robbery, sack, sally
raided: bust
raider: boarder, burglar, intruder, pirate
raiding: predatory
rail: banisters, bar, barrier, line, slide, train
railing: screen
railings: fence
raillery: banter, jeering, ridicule, satire
rails: track
railway: track
raiment: dress, garb

rain: barrage, fall, hail, water, wet
raincoat: mackintosh
rainfall: cloudburst
rainy: dirty, moist, watery, wet
raise: breed, bring up, collect, construct, crane, cock, erect, farm, fly, foster, hoist, jack, lift, mother, pick up, present, promote, put up, rear, recruit, set up, sky, stir, yeast
raising: breeding, lift, upbringing
rake: comb, flirt, fork, libertine, villain
rakish: saucy
rally: assemble, call, cheer up, collect, congregate, demonstrate, herd, improve, improvement, mass, meeting, mobilize, pick up, raise, recover, revive, round up, summon
rallying: assembly
ram: beak, drive, jam, male, pack, push, run into, squeeze, stuff
ramble: digress, drivel, jaunt, journey, range, roam, saunter, sprawl, stray, stroll, walk, wander
rambling: circuitous, delirious, devious, hiking, incoherent, maundering, verbose, wandering
ramification: branch, fork, implication
ramify: branch, fork
ramp: ascent, buttress, fiddle, incline, racket, slant, slope
rampage: rage
rampaging: obstreperous
rampant: epidemic, prevalent, rank, unbridled
rampart: bank,

barrier, embankment, fortification, mound, shield, wall
ramparts: battlements
ramshackle: decrepit
ranch: farm
rancher: farmer
rancid: bad, high, off, putrid, rank, sour
rancorous: bitter, grudging, hard, venomous, virulent
rancour: bile, gall, grudge, ill feeling, resentment, spite
random: casual, chance, contingent, incidental, odd, promiscuous, purposeless, stray, unpredictable, vague
randomly: blindly, haphazardly, vaguely
randy: fruity, lecherous, sensual
range: assortment, breadth, capacity, circle, compass(es), comprehension, distance, distribution, field, grade, grasp, hearing, incidence, jurisdiction, latitude, line, measure, orbit, play, prowl, quarter, rank, reach, region, roam, room, row, run, scale, scope, size, sound, sphere, stock, sweep, traverse, variety, wander, width
ranged: assorted
ranger: warden
ranging: wandering
rangy: gangling,
rank: bank, caste, category, class, classify, column, commit, condition, degree, dignity, elevation, estate, file, footing, fulsome, grade, level, line, number, order, place,

position, quality, range, rate, rotten, situation, sort, standing, station, step

ranking: scale

rankle: niggle

ransack: comb, forage, loot, pillage, plunder, rape, ravage, rob, strip

ransacking: rape, rapine

ransom: deliverance, redeem

rant: bluster, boil, create, rail, rampage, rave, storm

ranting: railing

rap: bang, bat, hit, knap, knock, reprimand, stroke, tap

rapacious: avaricious, covetous, predatory, ravenous, venal, voracious

rapacity: avarice, ferocity, greed

rape: outrage, sack, violate, violation

rapid: fast, fleet, instant, precipitate, quick, rush, speedy, sudden, whirlwind

rapidity: speed

rapidly: fast, quick, quickly, swiftly

rapids: cataract, shoot, waterfall

rapier: sword

rapine: pillage, robbery, sack

rapport: communion, companionship, friendship, harmony, identity, relationship, sympathy, touch

rapscallion: knave, rogue, villain

rapt: contemplative, deep, faraway, happy, intent, lost, preoccupied

raptor: predator

rapture: bliss, delight, heaven, joy, paradise, transport

rapturous: exalted, happy, joyous, lyrical, radiant

rare: choice, novel, occasional, odd, singular, strange, uncommon, underdone, unusual

rarefied: thin

rarefy: thin

rarely: little, seldom, uncommonly

rareness: scarcity

rarity: jewel, oddity, phenomenon, wonder

rascal: devil, knave, monkey, rogue, ruffian, scab, scoundrel, swindler, terror

rascally: knavish

rash: epidemic, fast, foolhardy, hasty, heady, impatient, impetuous, imprudent, outbreak, precipitate, precipitous, reckless, sudden, unguarded, unthinking, unwise, wave, wild

rashness: idiocy, stupidity, temerity

rasp: buzz, creak, file, grate, hack, jar, plane, rattle, scrape, wheeze

raspberry: catcall, bird

rasping: friction, harsh, hoarse, raucous, rough, scrape, strident

rat: desert, jerk, maroon, run out, sing

ratchet: rack

rate: assess, bat, calculate, charge, class, clip, clock, consider, degree, deserve, gait, judge, lick, merit, pace, price, quotation, quote, regard, scold, seed, tax, time, value

rather: fairly, first, instead, passably, pretty, quite, vaguely

ratification: confirmation, passage, sanction

ratify: authorize, confirm, pass, sanction, seal, sustain

rating: valuation, value

ratio: index, mix, proportion, rate, scale

ratiocination: dialectic, logic

ration: cut, dole, limit, lot, measure, partition, portion, proportion, quantity, quota, share

rational: coherent,

conscious, intellectual, logical, lucid, normal, philosophical, realistic, reasonable, responsible, right, sane, sober, tenable

rationale: basis, justification, motive, reason

rationalism: philosophy

rationality: lucidity, mentality, mind, normality, reason, sanity

rationalization: explanation, justification

rationalize: explain

rationally: practically

rations: fare, food, meat, supply, sustenance

rattan: cane

ratting: betrayal

rattle: bump, clash, confuse, jangle, jar, jerk, ruffle, shake

rattled: disconcerted, flustered, unnerved

ratty: liverish, prickly, short-tempered

raucous: harsh, hoarse, loud, obstreperous, rough, strident

raucously: roughly

ravage: consume, destroy, devour, loot, pillage, ransack, sack, waste, wreck

ravaged: waste

ravages: havoc

ravaging: predatory

rave: create, rage, rampage, revel

ravel: snarl

raven: black

ravening: hunger, hungry, savage, voracious

ravenous: avid, rapacious, starving

ravine: chasm, defile, gorge, precipice

raving: delirious, distracted, incoherent, insane, lunatic, mad, wild

ravish: delight, fascinate, outrage, rape, violate

ravished: rapt

ravishing: beautiful,

good-looking, gorgeous, heavenly, irresistible, joyful, lovely, stunning

ravishment: rape, rapture, violation

raw: bleak, chill, cold, cutting, fresh, fiery, green, hoarse, icy, inexperienced, painful, piercing, primary, robust, rough, sore, tender, underdone, unfinished, unripe, wintry, young

rawhide: whip

rawness: chill, tenderness

ray: beam, emanation, flare, illumination, light, shaft, spine

raze: demolish, destroy, fell, flatten, floor, level, ravage, ruin, take down, overthrow

razor: blade

razzamatazz: glitter, hype

reach: attain, come, compass(es), comprehension, distance, get, grasp, hit, impress, incidence, join, latitude, length, make, penetrate, range, run, scale, scope, span, stretch, strike, touch, width, win

reached: made

react: behave, bite, counter, interact, interfere, recoil, reply

reaction: backlash, behaviour, bite, impression, kickback, response, result

reactivate: quicken

reactive: sensitive, sensuous

reactionary: right

reactor: pile

read: decipher, deliver, indicate, interpret, make out, mug, record, review, say, study

readability: legibility

readies: money

readily: freely, soon, well, willingly

readiness: obedience,

preparation, zeal
reading: diagnosis,
interpretation, lesson,
observation, passage,
recital, version
ready: condition,
facile, game, gird,
glib, mature,
obedient, prepare,
prepared, present,
qualify, quick, quick-
witted, ripe, smart,
unhesitating,
wherewithal, willing
real: authentic,
concrete, factual,
genuine, good, hard,
honest, legitimate,
live, palpable,
physical, positive,
pure, rightful, solid,
tangible, true,
unspoilt, very
realign: rearrange,
reorganize
realistic: down-to-
earth, practical,
pragmatic, rational,
raw, safe, sensible,
vivid
realistically:
practically
reality: deed,
existence, fact, object,
substance, verity
realizable: attainable,
disposable, feasible,
possible, liquid
realization:
attainment,
awareness,
comprehension,
discovery, execution,
grasp, insight,
perfection
realize: attain, carry
out, complete,
discover, execute,
find, find out, fulfil,
get, grasp, imagine,
know, liquidate,
make, net, perceive,
recognize, see, sense,
understand, visualize
really: indeed,
literally, quite, truly,
very, yes
realm: kingdom, land,
preserve, territory,
world
reanimate: quicken,
resuscitate, wake
reap: clear, cut,
extract, gather,
harvest, lift, mow
reappearance:

renaissance, return
rear: back, behind,
bottom, breed, bring
up, develop, educate,
end, farm, foster,
mother, nurture,
raise, reverse, shy,
stern, tail, terminal,
tower
rearing: breeding,
rampant, upbringing
rearrange:
reorganize, shift,
switch
reason: basis, call,
cause, explanation,
grounds, infer,
intelligence,
judgement, justice,
justification, logic,
mind, motivation,
motive, normality,
point, purpose,
rationale, right, sake,
sanity, score, sense,
soul
reasonable: cheap,
decent, economic,
fair, likely, logical,
moderate, modest,
normal, plausible,
rational, respectable,
restrained, right,
sane, sensible, sober,
sound
reasonably: fairly,
passably, practically,
pretty, quite
reasoned: coherent,
logical
reasoning: conscious,
deduction, dialectic,
idea, inference,
intelligent,
judgement, logic,
lucid, motivation,
motive, philosophy,
rational, reason
reassemble: rally,
reconstruct
reassure: comfort,
satisfy, settle
reassuring:
promising, rosy
rebate: discount,
refund
rebel: defy, hothead,
insurgent, kick, lad,
mutiny, revolt,
revolutionary, rise
rebellion:
insurrection, mutiny,
revolt, revolution,
sedition, unrest,
uprising
rebellious: defiant,

insubordinate,
lawless, refractory,
ungovernable
rebirth:
reincarnation,
renaissance
rebound: backfire,
bounce, recoil,
reverberate, spring
rebuff: check, defeat,
deny, knock, reject,
repel, setback, slap,
slight, snub
rebuke: blame, carpet,
castigate, censure,
check, lash, lecture,
lesson, rap,
reprimand, reproach,
scold, scolding, slate,
upbraid
recalcitrant: defiant,
fractious,
insubordinate,
obstinate, rebellious,
refractory, reluctant,
stubborn, unhelpful
recall: lure, memory,
mind, recognize,
remember, retain,
retraction, review,
think, withdraw,
withdrawal
recant: renounce,
revoke
recapitulate: repeat,
review
recapitulation:
repeat, repetition,
review
recapture: recover,
recovery, retrieve,
take back
recede: cave in,
regress, retire, retreat,
subside
receipts: income,
papers, takings
receive: embrace,
gain, get, have, make,
partake, see, take,
take in, welcome, win
received: made,
orthodox
receiver: fence,
telephone
recent: fresh, late,
modern, new
recently: just, lately
receptacle: basket,
box, capsule, case,
container, pocket,
vessel
reception: audience,
function, hospitality,
lodge, party, receipt,
treatment, welcome

receptive: hospitable,
pliable, susceptible
recess: bay, booth,
break, corner, gap,
grotto, indent, niche,
nook, pigeonhole,
respite
recessed: bay, sunken
recession: decline,
depression, slump
recipe: dish, formula,
prescription
reciprocal: mutual,
relative
reciprocate: interact,
repay, retaliate,
return
reciprocating:
mutual, return
recital: history,
quotation, reading,
repetition, story
recite: chant, intone,
narrate, parrot, quote,
rattle, read, relate,
repeat, say
reckless: fast,
foolhardy, heady,
imprudent,
irresponsible, lunatic,
precipitate,
precipitous, prodigal,
rash, unthinking,
unwise, wild
recklessness: folly,
idiocy, lunacy,
madness, temerity
reckon: believe,
calculate, cast,
conclude, count,
depend, fancy, figure,
guess, hold, include,
rate, tally, theorize,
think, tot, total, value
reckoning: bill,
calculation, count,
retribution, score,
sum, tab, valuation
reclaim: recover,
redeem
recline: lie, loll,
lounge, repose, rest
reclusive: retiring,
self-effacing,
sheltered, solitary
recognition:
awareness, honour,
knowledge,
perception, reception,
remark, respect,
salute, thanks
recognizable: clear,
distinct, obvious
recognize: discern,
distinguish, identify,
know, make, perceive,

place, realize, salute, scent, see, spot
recognized: familiar, known, made, public, sound, understood
recoil: backlash, bounce, bridle, bristle, falter, flinch, gulp, jib, kick, kickback, quail, reaction, rebel, rebound, return, reverberate, shrink, shy, spring, start, turn, wince
recollect: recall, remember, review, think
recollection: impression, memory, mind, recall, reminiscence
recommend: commend, counsel, move, nominate, promote, propose, put up, refer, suggest, urge, vote
recommendation: counsel, promotion, proposition, reference, suggestion
recompense: compensate, justice, pay, premium, price, redress, remunerate, restitution, retribution, return, reward, satisfy
reconcile: compose, heal, square
recondite: obscure, profound, secret
reconditioning: overhaul, renovation
reconnoitre: explore, scout, survey
reconsider: review, think better of
record: background, book, catalogue, chronicle, cutting, disc, entry, file, form, journal, list, lodge, log, memo, minute, monitor, notation, note, notes, past, protocol, qualification, read, register, report, roll, score, take down, tally, tape, transaction, write
recorded: historical, noted
records: history,

memoirs, papers
recount: chronicle, cover, detail, narrate, recite, report, spin, tell
recoup: recover, retrieve
recover: fetch, find, improve, mend, pick up, rally, rescue, retrieve, revive, salvage, take back, tot
recovery: finding, improvement, rally, rescue, restoration
recreate: reconstruct, reproduce
recreation: diversion, fun, game, leisure, pastime, play, relaxation, renewal
rectangle: box, panel
rectification: improvement, redress, reform
rectify: better, improve, mend, reconcile, redress, reform, remedy, repair, right
rectitude: character, justice, right, virtue
rector: clergyman, parson, pastor, priest, principal, vicar
recumbent: flat, prone, supine
recuperate: improve, recover
recur: return, revert
recurrence: cycle, relapse, repetition, return
recurrent: frequent, habitual, perennial, perpetual
red: fiery, flaming, lurid, rosy, sanguine, tender, underdone
redden: blush, colour, glow
reddening: blush, flush, glow
redeem: free, justify, liberate, ransom, rescue, salvage, save
redemption: deliverance, justification, liberation, ransom, salvation
redispose: rearrange, reorganize
redolence: bouquet, odour, perfume, scent, smell

redolent: reminiscent, sweet
redress: justice, redeem, remedy
reduce: condense, contract, curtail, cut, decrease, degrade, depress, descend, digest, dilute, discount, dock, impair, kill, lessen, lighten, lower, minimize, modify, narrow, palliate, prune, qualify, relax, remit, resolve, run down, shorten, shred, slacken, slash, slim, slow
reduced: cut, dilute, limited, low, lower, poor, prostrate
reduction: cut, decline, decrease, deduction, descent, discount, drop, fall, loss, modification, rebate, relaxation
redundant: extra, idle, superfluous, unemployed, unnecessary
reef: bank, bar, shelf
reek: smell, stench
reel: fish, lurch, rattle, rock, roll, rotate, spin, stagger, stumble, waver, whirl, wind, wind up
reeling: retraction, tottering
refectory: canteen, mess
refer: consult, go, mean, mention, quote, relate, submit
referee: judge, mediate, mediator, officiate, umpire
reference: bearing, concern, connection, glance, mention, quotation, quote, regard, respect, testimonial
referendum: poll, vote
refine: clarify, clear, cultivate, elaborate, filter, finish, modify, process, rarefy, rectify, thin, treat
refined: chaste, civil, courteous, cultivated, cultured, decent, delicate, fine, genteel,

gentle, ladylike, proper, sophisticated, subtle, thin, urbane, well-bred
refinement: civilization, culture, delicacy, finish, manners, modification, modulation, polish, propriety, taste
refit: refurbish, renewal, renovation
reflect: chew, cogitate, commune, consider, glance, mirror, muse, register, revolve, think
reflection: consideration, deliberation, glance, highlight, image, mirror, observation
reflective: contemplative, meditative, pensive, studious, thoughtful, wistful
reflex: automatic, instinctive, intuitive, involuntary, mechanical, unconscious, unintentional
reform: change, improve, rally, redress
reformation: improvement, metamorphosis, rally, revolution
reformist: liberal, progressive
refractory: defiant, difficult, insubordinate, naughty, perverse, rebellious, recalcitrant, tough, ungovernable, wayward, wilful
refrain: cease, chorus, fast, forbear, keep, leave, resist, spare, stop, withhold
refreshing: cool, invigorating, lively, pleasant
refreshments: snack, sustenance
refrigerate: cool, chill, freeze
refuge: asylum, burrow, den, harbour, haunt,

home, lair, nest, oasis,
protection, rest,
safety, sanctuary,
shelter
refugee: exile,
fugitive, outcast
refund: compensate,
pay back, rebate,
repay, restitution,
return
refurbishing:
renewal, renovation,
restoration
refusal: negative,
rebuff, veto
refuse: deny, filth,
garbage, jib, junk,
leavings, litter, offal,
rubbish, spoil, veto,
waste
refute: confound,
deny, negate, rebut
regain: find, recover,
redeem, retrieve, take
back
regal: august, lordly,
majestic, princely,
sovereign
regalia: finery,
jewellery, uniform
regard: attention, call,
care, concern,
consider,
consideration, count,
credit, eye,
friendship, gaze,
greeting, heed,
interest, look, love,
notice, observe,
reckon, reference,
remark, respect, sake,
take, venerate, view
regarding:
concerning, towards
regardless: despite,
nevertheless
regardlessly: blindly
regards: respect
regenerate: convert,
heal
regeneration:
healing, rebirth
regime: government,
rule, set-up
regimen: diet,
discipline
region: circle, climate,
country, domicile,
land, locality, part,
place, province,
quarter, realm, soil,
territory, vicinity,
zone
regional: local
register: book,
catalogue, chronicle,

dawn on, definition,
enter, file, focus,
indicate, journal, key,
list, lodge, log, mark,
minute, poll, read,
record, roll, scale,
score, strike, tally, tell
registered: noted
regress: back,
degenerate, recede,
relapse, revert
regression: descent,
deterioration, relapse
regressive:
degenerate,
deterioration
regret: lament,
mourn, penitence,
qualm, remorse
regretful: penitent,
remorseful
regrettable:
lamentable, rotten,
sad, unfortunate
regrettably:
unfortunately
regroup: rally
regrouping: rally
regular: classic,
consistent, constant,
conventional,
customary, customer,
daily, even, general,
habitual, methodical,
normal, orderly,
ordinary, reliable, set,
smooth, standard,
steady, stock,
uniform, usual,
wonted
regularity: normality,
order, system
regularly: daily,
equally, generally,
invariably
regulars: clientele
regulate: attune,
conduct, determine,
discipline, order,
police, restrict, rule,
run, scale, set, shape,
square
regulation: canon,
dictate, discipline,
edict, law, leadership,
legislation,
modulation, precept,
restriction, rule
regulator: baffle,
balance
rehabilitate: redeem,
reform
rehabilitation:
recovery, reform,
therapy
rehabilitative:

therapeutic
rehash: paraphrase
rehearsal: practice
rehearse: drill,
practise, repeat, run
over, say
reheat: warm
reign: kingdom,
regime, rule
reigning: ruling
reimburse:
compensate, pay, pay
back, refund,
remunerate, repay,
return
reimbursement:
compensation,
indemnity, pay,
refund, restitution
rein in: pull up
rein: brake, curb, lead,
leash, restraint
reincarnation:
rebirth
reinforce: back, back
up, bolster, brace,
confirm, consolidate,
fortify, lag, line,
recruit, support
reinforced: strong
reinforcement:
backing, fortification,
patch
reinforcing:
basement
reinstate: redeem,
return
reinstatement:
restoration, return
reinstitute: resume
reissued: new
reiterate: keep on,
recapitulate, repeat
reiteration: repeat,
repetition
reject: decline,
disclaim, drop,
jettison, junk, kill,
leave out, pass up,
rebuff, refuse, repel,
repudiate, veto
rejected: disowned,
old, unwanted, waste
rejecting: negative,
disapprobation,
rebuff, veto
rejoice: celebrate,
glory, joy, revel
rejoicing: jubilant,
jubilation
rejoin: retort, return
rejoinder: reply,
response, return
rejuvenating:
invigorating,
reincarnation,

restoration
rekindle: quicken,
revive
relapser: backslider
relate: associate,
cover, describe,
identify, impart, link,
narrate, present,
recite, refer, regard,
spin, tell
related: attendant,
germane, kin,
matching, relative,
relevant
relating: concerning,
association,
connection, kinship
relation: bearing,
recital, reference,
regard, relative,
respect
relations: blood,
commerce, family,
kin
relationship:
association,
connection, kin,
kinship, link,
proportion
relative: comparative,
connection
relatively: quite,
rather
relatives: blood,
family, kin
relax: calm, knock off,
liberalize, lift, loose,
loosen, remit, repose,
rest, slacken,
soften
relaxation: leisure,
recreation, relief,
repose, rest
relaxed: calm,
comfortable, easy,
familiar, free, laid-
back, leisurely, loose,
restful, slack,
unconcerned
relaxedly: leisurely
relaxing: dreamy,
sedative
relay: broadcast,
carry, report,
transmit
release: carry,
catharsis, death,
deliver, deliverance,
delivery, discharge,
disconnect, dismissal,
dispense, enfranchise,
free, freedom, issue,
let off, let out,
liberate, liberation,
loose, news, pardon,
put out, record, relief,

relieve, relinquish,
rescue
releasing: liberation
relegate: degrade,
remove
relegating: pejorative
relent: capitulate
relentless: brutal,
constant, cruel,
deadly, harsh,
implacable,
monotonous,
nonstop, obdurate,
persistent, resolute,
ruthless, unbroken
relentlessly: away,
nonstop
relentlessness:
resolution
relevance: bearing,
concern, connection,
interest, regard,
significance
relevant: germane,
material, operative,
pertinent, suitable
reliability:
faithfulness, fidelity,
infallible
reliable:
authoritative, certain,
faithful, honest,
honourable,
reputable,
responsible, safe,
secure, solid, sound,
stable, steady,
straight, sure, true,
white
reliance: belief,
confidence,
conviction, faith
reliant: dependent
relic: keepsake
relics: remains
relict: bereaved
relief: comfort,
consolation, contour,
help, mercy, redress,
relay, release, rescue,
respite, rest,
secondary, substitute,
support
relieve: comfort, free,
lighten, mollify, raise,
redress, relax,
remedy, rid
religion: faith, sect
religious: devout,
divine, godly, holy,
monastic, pious,
spiritual, unworldly
religiousness:
sanctity
relinquish: cede,
concede, disclaim,

drop, forgo, forsake,
give, leave, render,
renounce, resign,
surrender, waive,
yield
relinquishment:
surrender
relish: enjoy, garnish,
gusto, like, love, lust,
revel, sauce, taste,
zest
relive: remember
relocate: move,
rearrange, remove,
reorganize
relocation: move,
transposition
reluctance: aversion,
diffidence,
indisposition,
repugnance, reserve,
scruple
reluctant: averse,
disinclined, grudging,
hesitant, involuntary,
unwilling
rely: bank, bargain,
depend, expect, lean,
presume, reckon, rest
remain: be, continue,
endure, hold, keep,
last, lie, linger, live,
obtain, persist, rest,
stay, stick, survive,
wait
remainder: balance,
difference, end,
remains, residue, rest,
surplus
remaining: lingering,
living, odd, other,
outstanding, over,
surplus
remains: corpse,
debris, leavings,
remnant, rest, vestige,
wreckage
remand: custody
remanent: lasting
remark: comment,
note, observe, phrase,
say, word
remarkable:
conspicuous, great,
memorable, notable,
noteworthy,
particular,
phenomenal,
prodigious, salient,
singular, splendid,
uncommon, unusual,
wonder, wonderful
remarkably: notably,
uncommonly
remedial: healing,
medicinal,

therapeutic
remedy: cure, heal,
help, panacea, rectify,
redress, relief,
restorative, treatment
remedying: healing
remember:
commemorate,
consider, mind, place,
recall, recognize,
retain, think
remembrance:
celebration, keepsake,
memory, recall,
record, reminiscence,
token
remind: prompt
reminder: keepsake,
memento, memo,
note, prod, prompt,
souvenir
reminisce: remember
reminiscence:
memory
reminiscences:
memoirs
reminiscent:
redolent, suggestive
remiss: careless,
delinquent, derelict
remission: discharge,
forgiveness, pardon,
reprieve, stay
remissness: neglect
remit: discharge,
forgive, forward,
mitigate, pardon,
quit, return, waive
remittance: payment
remnant: end, rag,
remainder, residue
remnants: leavings
remodel: reorganize
remodelling:
renovation
remonstrance:
complaint
remonstrate: protest
remonstration:
objection, protest
remorse: penitence,
regret
remorseful: ashamed,
bad, guilty, penitent,
repentant, rueful,
sorry
remorsefully:
regretfully
remorseless:
implacable, ruthless
remote: back,
desolate,
disinterested, distant,
far, faraway,
godforsaken, insular,
lonely, long, obscure,

overseas, provincial,
secluded,
sequestered, slender,
slim, solitary,
unbending, unlikely,
withdrawn
remotely: far, long,
wide
remoteness: desert,
detachment, seclusion
remoter: further
removal: deprivation,
dismissal, disposal,
expulsion, extraction,
overthrow,
withdrawal
remove: banish,
budge, change, cut
off, deduct, discharge,
dismiss, distance,
divest, eject, get off,
overthrow, rend,
resolve, retire, rub
out, shift, subtract,
supersede, take,
weed, withdraw
removed: remote
remunerate:
compensate, pay,
repay, reward, satisfy
remuneration:
compensation,
consideration, fee,
pay, payment,
premium, restitution,
reward, salary, wage
remunerative:
lucrative, profitable
renaissance: rebirth,
reincarnation
rename: nickname
rend: bite, breach,
break, fracture, part,
perforate, rip,
scratch, slash, split,
wring
render: bear, do, give,
interpret, paraphrase,
pay, perform, picture,
produce, provide,
represent, return, say,
turn, yield
rendering:
breakdown,
construction,
paraphrase, recital
rendezvous:
assignation, date,
engagement, meeting,
venue
rending: biting
rendition: execution,
hearing,
interpretation,
presentation, reading,
version

renegade: black sheep, rebel
renege: trim
renew: recall, repair, repeat
renewal: rally, rebirth, renaissance, renovation, repetition, restoration
renounce: cede, deny, disclaim, drop, forgo, forsake, quit, relinquish, repudiate, revoke, surrender, take back, waive
renouncement: retraction
renovate: furbish, mend, modernize, rearrange, reconstruct, reform, refurbish, repair
renovation: reincarnation, renewal, restoration
renown: celebrity, fame, glory, kudos, lustre, memory, note, prestige, reputation, splendour
renowned: distinguished, famous, illustrious, legendary, noted, prestigious, prominent, splendid
rent: break, charter, fracture, gap, hire, hole, job, laceration, lease, let, let out, rip, rupture, slit, split, take, ulcer
rental: hire, rent
renting: lease
renunciation: sacrifice, surrender, waiver
reoccupy: resume
reopen: resume
reorder: rearrange, vary
reordering: transposition
reorganization: rally
reorganize: change, convert, rally, rearrange, reconstruct, reform, shake up
rep: representative
repair: darn, doctor, fix, go, make up, mend, overhaul, patch, rectify, redress, reform, remedy, renewal,

renovation, restoration, resort, right, service
reparation: compensation, indemnity, justice, penance, redress, restitution, return
repartee: banter, wit
repast: banquet, dinner, feast, meal, spread
repay: avenge, compensate, pay, pay back, quit, refund, remunerate, return, revenge, reward
repayment: rebate, refund, restitution, return
repeal: cancel, cancellation, negate, nullify, overrule, overturn, quash, recall, remit, rescind, retraction, reverse, revoke
repeat: copy, imitate, keep on, multiply, parrot, recapitulate, recite, recur, repetition, say, stress
repeated: frequent, multiple, standing
repeatedly: away, often
repeater: clock
repel: disgust, nauseate, offend, resist, revolt, turn off
repellent: disagreeable, disgusting, nasty, obnoxious, revolting, uninviting, unpleasant, vile
repent: regret
repentance: penitence, regret, remorse
repentant: penitent, remorseful, rueful, sorry
repentantly: regretfully
repercussion: backlash, consequence, kickback
repercussions: impact
repertoire: vocabulary
repetition: quotation, quote, refrain, repeat
repetitious:

monotonous, redundant
repetitive: continual, monotonous
rephrase: paraphrase
rephrasing: paraphrase
replace: mend, replenish, return, substitute, supersede, supplant, understudy
replacement: patch, substitute, understudy
replant: pot
replay: repeat
replenish: fill, recruit, stock, supply, top up
replenishment: renewal
replete: full, rife
replica: copy, double, facsimile, imitation, likeness, match, model, picture, reproduction
replicate: reproduce
reply: counter, reaction, response, retort, return, say
report: bang, chronicle, communicate, communication, crack, description, information, item, log, narrate, narrative, news, record, relate, return, review, rumour, sound, story
reporter: commentator, journalist, narrator
reporters: press
repose: calm, lie, peace, quiet, recline, rest
reposing: slumbering
reposition: rearrange
repository: bank, barn, depot, safe, treasury, well
repossess: impound, redeem, seize, take back
repossession: recovery, seizure
reprehend: carpet, censure, condemn, upbraid
reprehensible: deplorable, shameful, wrong
reprehension: censure

represent: be, characterize, describe, paint, personify, picture, portray, reproduce, signify, sketch, stand for, symbolize
representation: description, diagram, drawing, effigy, image, likeness, model, performance, picture, presentation, role, scene, shadow, token
representative: commission, councillor, deputy, diplomat, member, officer, official, operator, proxy, sample, scout
representatives: congress
repress: contain, curb, moderate, quash, quell, suppress, swallow, withhold
repressed: pent-up, unconscious
repression: domination, yoke
repressive: brutal, oppressive, prohibitive
reprieve: let off, pardon, respite, stay
reprimand: carpet, castigate, censure, check, lecture, lesson, pull up, rebuke, reproach, row, scold, upbraid
reprisal: retribution, revenge, vengeance
reproach: blemish, carp, censure, condemn, disgrace, opprobrium, rebuke, reprimand, scold, shame, slur, upbraid
reprobate: dissipated, immoral, knave, knavish, libertine, rogue, shameless, sinner
reproduce: breed, copy, fake, multiply, procreate, render, transcribe, Xerox
reproduction: copy, facsimile, fake, imitation, model, picture, print, propagation, replica,

Xerox
reproof: lesson, rap, rebuke, reprimand, reproach
reprove: censure, lecture, rap, rebuke, reprimand, roast, upbraid
reptile: dragon
repudiate: cancel, deny, disclaim, forsake, refuse, renounce, revoke
repudiated: disowned
repudiation: retraction
repugnance: disgust, hate, horror, loathing, revulsion
repugnant: disgusting, horrible, nasty, objectionable, obnoxious, revolting, ugly, uninviting, unpleasant, vile
repulse: defeat, parry, rebuff, reject, repel, reverse, revolt
repulsion: loathing, revulsion
repulsive: disagreeable, hideous, horrible, obnoxious, odious, revolting, shocking, sickening, ugly, unpleasant, vile
reputable: honest, honourable, respectable, savoury, sound
reputation: character, eminence, fame, memory, name, prominence, report, standing
repute: celebrity, consequence, credit, fame, honour, report, reputation
reputed: famous, putative, supposed
request: ask, call, claim, demand, desire, instance, invitation, invite, order, petition, plea, plead, prayer, seek, suit, supplication, wish
requiem: funeral
require: bind, challenge, charge, claim, command, demand, impel, necessitate, need, oblige, order,

prescribe, provide, take, want, warrant
required: mandatory, necessary, obligatory, obliged, regulation
requirement: claim, command, condition, demand, dictate, must, necessity, need, obligation, prerequisite, priority, regulation, stipulation, want
requirements: specifications
requisite: compulsory, obligatory, vital
requisition: commandeer, demand, hijack, indent, request, seize
requisitioning: seizure
requital: restitution, revenge, reward
requite: compensate, reciprocate, repay, retort, return, revenge, reward, satisfy
rerun: repeat
reschedule: put off, rearrange, reorganize
rescind: lift, negate, nullify, overrule, quash, repeal
rescue: bale, deliverance, delivery, free, liberate, liberation, ransom, redeem, resuscitate, retrieve, salvage, salvation, save
rescuer: saviour
research: explore, look into, look up, study, survey
resemblance: comparison, kinship, like, likeness, parallel, parity, similarity
resemble: favour
resembling: like, similar
resent: begrudge, grudge
resentful: bitter, black, dirty, embittered, grudging, jaundiced, jealous, petulant, sore, vengeful, virulent, wrathful
resentment: backlash, grudge,

ill feeling, indignation, jealousy, offence, outrage, passion, pique, rancour
reservation: booking, doubt, keeping, misgiving, order, place, preserve, proviso, qualification, query, question, reserve
reserve: asset, auxiliary, bag, bank, book, deliberation, diffidence, distance, fund, keep, modesty, order, retain, save, secondary, store, substitute, supply, take, understudy, withhold
reserved: bashful, cool, coy, distant, evasive, guarded, introverted, modest, noncommittal, quiet, remote, reticent, retiring, self-effacing, shy, taciturn, uncommunicative, undemonstrative, unfriendly, withdrawn
reserves: resources, savings
reservist: irregular
reservoir: bank, dam, lake, quarry, reserve, supply, tank
reset: rearrange, reorganize, wind up
reshow: repeat
reshowing: repeat
reside: dwell, live, settle, sojourn
residence: domicile, hall, headquarters, home, hostel, house, lodgings, occupation, place, presence, quarters, seat, tenure
resident: boarder, citizen, inhabitant, local, lodger, national, native, occupant
residential: domestic, home, living
residents: community, population
residing: living
residual: background, basic
residually: basically
residuary: superfluous

residue: balance, dregs, leavings, remainder, remains, remnant, rest, surplus
resign: cede, quit, relinquish, surrender, withdraw, yield
resignation: forbearance, lassitude, philosophy, secession, surrender, withdrawal
resigned: long-suffering, passive, patient, philosophical, stoical
resilience: bounce, give, kick, spring, stamina, tolerance
resilient: strong, tough
resist: combat, counter, defy, fend off, help, oppose, rebel, repel, revolt, rise, stem
resistance: baffle, drag, element, give, kick, opposition, partisan, protest, pull, tolerance, underground
resistant: durable, immune, tough
resisting: negative
resolute: constant, decisive, determined, earnest, firm, persevering, persistent, positive, serious, stout, strenuous, tenacious, tough, unhesitating
resolutely: manfully
resoluteness: resolve
resolution: backbone, conclusion, decision, end, explanation, fortitude, heart, measure, nerve, pluck, resolve, ruling, solution, spirit, willpower
resolve: backbone, bottle, clarify, compose, crack, decide, decision, determine, do, explain, firmness, purpose, rationalize, reconcile, rule, set, settle, tenacity, unravel, vow, will, willpower
resolved: clear
resonance: roll,

sound, thunder
resonant: cavernous,
full, hollow,
resounding, rich,
rotund, round,
sonorous, vibrant
resonantly: hollow
resonate: peal, sound,
vibrate, voice
resort: oasis, retreat,
stoop
resound: bang, boom,
peal, rebound,
reverberate, ring,
sound, thunder
resounding:
deafening, loud,
thunderous, vibrant
resource: asset,
finance, fund
resourceful: clever,
inventive, practical,
ready, strong,
versatile
resourcefully:
practically
resourcefulness:
imagination, initiative
resources: budget,
capital, cash,
facilities, means,
potential, property,
purse, savings,
substance, treasury,
wealth, wherewithal
respect: attention,
awe, comply,
consideration,
consult, fear,
greeting, homage,
keep, rate, regard,
revere, sake, value,
way
respectability:
propriety
respectable: clean,
decent, nice,
reputable, savoury,
wholesome, worthy
respected: dear,
respectable, venerable
respectful: attentive,
courteous,
deferential, humble,
reverent
respectfulness:
humility
respecting: regarding
respective:
individual, relative
respiration: breath,
wind
respirator: muzzle
respire: breathe
respite: interlude,
lull, moratorium,

pause, recess, relief,
repose
resplendence:
brilliance, glory,
lustre, magnificence,
splendour
resplendent: bright,
brilliant, glorious,
gorgeous,
magnificent, radiant,
shining
respond: bite,
counter, retort, say
response: backlash,
bite, chorus, reaction,
reception, rejoinder,
reply
responsibility: baby,
blame, burden,
business, care,
charge, commitment,
concern, department,
duty, fault, function,
job, liability,
obligation, onus,
pigeon, place,
province
responsible:
conscious, guilty,
liable
responsive:
conscious, flexible,
impressionable,
receptive, sensitive,
sensuous, sentient,
susceptible, thin-
skinned
responsivity:
behaviour
rest: balance, base,
break, difference,
dwell, interlude,
knock off, lean,
leisure, lie, nap,
pause, perch, place,
put, quiet, recess,
relax, relief,
remainder, remnant,
repose, residue,
respite, set, sit, sleep,
sojourn, stand, wait
restart: resume
restate: paraphrase,
repeat
restatement:
paraphrase, repetition
restaurant: café,
canteen, grill
restful: calm,
comfortable,
leisurely, peaceful,
quiet, still
restfully: leisurely
restfulness: peace
resting: quiescent,
unemployed

restitution:
compensation,
indemnity, redress,
restoration
restive: murmuring,
restless, unsettled
restless: busy,
discontent, impatient,
jumpy, murmuring,
sleepless, tense,
uncomfortable,
unsettled, uptight
restlessness:
impatience, malaise
restock: fill, replace,
replenish
restoration: healing,
rebirth, recovery,
renaissance, renewal,
renovation, repair,
restitution, return,
salvation
restorative: cordial,
healing, therapeutic,
tonic
restore: cure, heal,
mend, reconstruct,
recover, recruit,
reform, refund,
remedy, render,
repair, replenish,
resuscitate, retrieve,
return, revive
restored: new
restrain: bind,
bound, bridle, cage,
check, compel,
contain, control, dam,
damp, govern,
handcuff, handicap,
hold, inhibit, keep,
leash, moderate, pin,
repress, restrict, stem,
stifle, stop, suppress,
temper, withhold
restrained: distant,
moderate, orderly,
plain, quiet, reticent,
severe, subdued
restraint: bound,
bridle, check, control,
curb, damp, distance,
forbearance, leash,
lid, measure, rein,
repression, reserve,
restriction, self-
control, simplicity,
sobriety, temperance
restrict: bind,
circumscribe, cramp,
curb, dam, gate,
handcuff, handicap,
limit, muzzle,
obstruct, qualify,
ration, shackle, slow
restricted: captive,

closed, exclusive,
finite, inside, limited,
local, narrow, scanty
restriction: barrier,
condition, detraction,
handicap, hindrance,
limit, parameter,
qualification, rein,
restraint, stipulation
restrictive:
prohibitive
restructure:
reorganize
result: come,
conclusion,
consequence, effect,
finding, follow, fruit,
go, harvest, issue,
legacy, outcome,
proceed, purpose,
repercussion, score,
upshot, work out
resultantly: therefore
resulting: next
results: ramifications
résumé: digest, draft,
paraphrase, revert,
scenario, summary
resupply: replace,
replenish
resurgence: rally,
rebirth, renaissance
resurrect: quicken
resurrection: rebirth
resuscitate: revive
ret: macerate, water,
wet
retail: hawk, sell
retailer: merchant,
seller
retain: foster,
harbour, have, hold,
impound, keep, keep
up, maintain, own,
possess, remember,
reserve, wield,
withhold
retainer: deposit,
follower, man, owner,
satellite, servant
retaining: tenacious
retaliate: avenge,
counter, pay back,
repay, reply, revenge
retaliation: backlash,
payoff, reprisal,
retribution, return,
revenge, vengeance,
vengeful
retape: transcribe
retard: delay, depress,
dwarf, handicap, hold
up, keep,
procrastinate
retarded: defective
retarding: depressing

retch: gag, heave
retching: nausea
retention: keeping,
  maintenance, tenacity
retentive: possessive,
  tenacious
rethink: review
reticence: modesty,
  reserve, shyness,
  silence
reticent: bashful,
  close, distant, evasive,
  guarded, restrained,
  retiring, self-effacing,
  shy, taciturn,
  uncommunicative,
  undemonstrative
reticulation: mesh
reticulum: net
retinue: court,
  following, suite, train
retire from: leave
retire: depart, lay off,
  quit, recede, repair,
  retreat, turn in,
  withdraw
retirement:
  secession, withdrawal
retiring: bashful, coy,
  demure, departure,
  modest, mousy,
  outgoing, quiet, self-
  effacing, withdrawn
retort: blurt, flask,
  rejoinder, reply,
  response, return,
  sally, snap
retouch: touch up
retract: negate, recall,
  rescind, reverse,
  revoke, take back,
  withdraw
retraction: recall,
  withdrawal
retreat: asylum, back,
  burrow, cloister, den,
  grotto, harbour,
  haunt, lair, lodge,
  nest, pull out, recede,
  refuge, regress,
  resort, rest, retire,
  retirement, return,
  reverse, sanctuary,
  seclusion, take to,
  withdraw, withdrawal
retreating: retrograde
retrench: economise
retribution:
  judgement, reprisal,
  revenge, reward,
  vengeance
retributive: vengeful
retrieval: finding,
  recall, recovery,
  seizure
retrieve: fetch, field,

find, recover, redeem,
  repair, salvage, tot
retrogress: regress,
  sink
retrogression:
  decadence, relapse
retrogressive:
  degenerate
retrogressively:
  back, backwards
retrospect: review
retrospection:
  reminiscence
retrospectively: back
return: fruit, gain,
  give, harvest, haunt,
  pay, profit, purpose,
  rebound, recede,
  reciprocate, recur,
  refund, rejoinder,
  render, repetition,
  reply, restitution,
  restoration, revert,
  reward, turn in, yield
returns: poll,
  proceeds, revenue,
  takings
rev: gun, throttle
revamp: modernize,
  refurbish, revise
revamping:
  renovation
reveal: bare, betray,
  blow, blurt, break,
  communicate,
  confess, disclose,
  discover, display,
  expose, find, find out,
  give away, impart,
  indicate, leak, let on,
  let out, level,
  manifest, open,
  reflect, register, say,
  show, show up,
  unmask
revealed: open
revealing: pregnant
revel: caper, enjoy,
  glory, live, play,
  relish, riot, wallow
revelation:
  confession, exposure,
  illumination,
  indication,
  manifestation,
  production, scoop,
  surprise, titbit, vision
revelatory: prophetic
reveller: lad
revelry: carnival,
  celebration,
  merriment, misrule,
  orgy, riot
revenge: avenge,
  payoff, repay,
  reprisal, retribution,

vengeance
revenue: income,
  proceeds, profit,
  return, takings, yield
reverberant: boom,
  buzz, cavernous,
  hum, jangle, peal,
  rebound, ring, sound,
  thunder, vibrate
reverberating:
  resounding,
  thunderous
reverberation:
  boom, hum, jangle,
  peal, rebound,
  repercussion, roll,
  sound, thunder
revere: enshrine, fear,
  glorify, honour,
  respect, venerate
revered: sacred,
  venerable
reverence: awe,
  celebrate, fear, glory,
  homage, honour,
  idolize, piety, respect,
  revere, venerate,
  worship
reverend: clergyman,
  divine, padre, parson
reverent: pious,
  religious
reverential:
  deferential, reverent,
  solemn
reverie: dream, muse,
  preoccupation, trance
reversal: debacle,
  down, inversion,
  knock, switch, upset
reverse: back, back
  up, calamity,
  catastrophe, check,
  converse, defeat,
  disaster, flop, invert,
  mishap, opposite,
  overturn, repeal,
  retraction, revoke,
  setback, slump, turn,
  undo, upset, wrong
reversed: converse,
  retrograde, undone
reversible: versatile
reversion: relapse,
  return
revert: regress,
  relapse, return
reverting: retrograde
review: audit,
  criticism, criticize,
  look, notice, puff,
  revise, run over,
  summary, survey, vet
reviewer: critic
revile: scoff, slang
revilement: calumny

reviling: vituperative
revise: convert,
  modify, review
revised: variation
revision: preparation,
  review
revitalization:
  renewal
revitalize: quicken,
  resuscitate, revive
revitalizing:
  invigorating
revival: rally, rebirth,
  recovery, renaissance,
  restoration
revive: quicken, rally,
  recall, recover,
  resuscitate, wake
revived: fresh
reviving: cordial
revocation:
  cancellation, repeal,
  withdrawal
revoke: cancel, lift,
  negate, nullify, quash
revoking: retraction
revolt: coup, disgust,
  disobedience, horrify,
  insurrection, mutiny,
  rebel, repel,
  revolution, rise,
  uprising
revolting: disgusting,
  foul, obnoxious,
  odious, offensive,
  repulsive, shocking,
  sickening, sickly,
  ugly, vile
revolution: change,
  circle, coup, cycle,
  disobedience,
  insurrection, orbit,
  period, revolt, roll,
  sedition, spin, turn,
  upheaval, uprising,
  whirl
revolutionary:
  insurgent,
  progressive, radical,
  rebel, rebellious,
  underground
revolutionist:
  revolutionary
revolve: circle, orbit,
  pivot, reel, roll,
  rotate, spin, turn,
  whirl
revolver: gun
revolving: rotary
revs: throttle
revulsion: disgust,
  hate, horror, loathing,
  phobia, repugnance
reward: bonus,
  compensation,
  consideration, crown,

gratuity, premium, price, prize, purse, remunerate, return, satisfy, tip, treat
rewarding: fruitful, productive, profitable
rewards: revenue
rework: reorganize
reworking: falsify, revise, transcribe, variation
rhapsodize: rave
rhetoric: language
rhetorical: literary
rhetorician: orator
rheum: cold
rheumy: watery
rhizome: root
rhyme: jingle
rhymer: poet
rhyming: poetic
rhythm: beat, measure, movement, pulse, time
rhythmic: regular, smooth, steady
rhythmical: poetic
rib-tickling: funny
rib: banter, cutlet
ribald: bawdy, coarse, gross, naughty, obscene, suggestive
ribaldry: coarseness, naughtiness, vulgarity
ribbing: banter
ribbon: band, decoration, favour, tape
rich: colourful, deep, exuberant, fat, fertile, flush, full, generous, gold(en), high, jet, loaded, luscious, lush, luxuriant, luxurious, meaty, mellow, ornate, plush, princely, prolific, round, savoury, splendid, vivid, warm, wealthy
riches: fortune, money, prosperity, wealth
richness: depth, exuberance, fat, luxury, rarity
rick: wrench
ricked: twisted
rickety: decrepit, dilapidated, flimsy, frail, insecure, jerry-built, ramshackle, shaky
ricochet: bounce, deflect, glance, kickback, rebound

rid: clear, dispose, free, quit
riddle: enigma, mystery, poke, problem, puzzle, sieve
riddled: leaky
ride: flip, hack, jaunt, journey, lift, mount, promenade, run, turn, weather
rider: jockey, passenger, proviso
ridge: bank, bar, drill, keel, ledge, projection, seam, shed, wrinkle
ridged: bumpy, jagged, uneven
ridicule: caricature, jeering, lampoon, mock, mockery, roast, satire, scoff, shame, sneer, teasing
ridiculing: jeering
ridiculous: comical, derisory, farcical, laughable, ludicrous, nonsensical, preposterous, rich, senseless, silly, tall, undignified
rife: epidemic, pervasive, prevalent, rampant, widespread
riff: lick
riffle: thumb, leaf
riffraff: mob, rabble, scum
rifle: groove, gun, plunder, raid, rip, rob, sack, search
rift: breach, chasm, chink, crack, gap, gorge, groove, gulf, ravine, rent, rupture, schism, separation, split
rig: clothe, dress, fake, fit, furnish, garb, gear, kit, square, tackle, turn out
rigged: loaded
rigging: gear
right: bang, charter, claim, due, even, fit, fitting, honourable, just, liberty, licence, logical, meet, power, prerogative, proper, ripe, reasonable, rectify, smack, sound, suitable
righteous: just, right, saintly, virtuous,
righteousness: good,

sanctity, virtue
rightful: due, lawful, legitimate, real, right, true
rightist: reactionary
rightly: duly, well
rightness: fit, justice
right-winger: conservative, reactionary
rigid: brittle, erect, firm, frigid, hard, immobile, religious, rigorous, set, severe, stern, stiff, tight, unbending, uncharitable, wooden
rigidity: firmness, frigidity, tension
rigidly: invariably
rigmarole: tale, yarn
rigorous: ascetic, austere, brutal, close, dour, hard, rigid, rugged, severe, spartan, stiff, strict, tight
rigorousness: austerity
rigour: austerity
rile: incense, inflame, infuriate, nark, offend, provoke, vex
riling: offensive, vexatious
rill: brook
rim: bank, border, brim, fringe, lip, side
rime: frost
rind: peel, skin
ring: bangle, basket, buzz, call, chime, circle, communicate, disc, gang, gird, girdle, hoop, jangle, jingle, knell, link, loop, peal, reverberate, ringcraft: round, surround, telephone, toll
ringer: double, match
ringing: jangle, jingle, knell, peal, resounding
ringleader: principal, chief
ringlet: bangle, curl, lock
rings: jewellery
rink: ring
rinse: bath, bathe, clean, dip, flush, tint, wash, wet
riot: fight, fracas, hubbub, profusion, scream, tempest,

uproar
rioter: insurgent
riotous: boisterous, chaotic, funny, lawless, mad, mischievous, obstreperous, priceless, rampant, subversive, unbridled, uproarious, wild
riotously: madly
riotousness: unrest
rip: break, claw, cut, lacerate, laceration, rent, run, scratch, slash, slit, snag, split, wrench
ripe: mature, mellow, ready
ripen: flower, mature, mellow
ripened: ripe
ripeness: maturity
rip off: cheat, fiddle, fleece, rob
rip-off: cheat, fiddle, robbery, swindle
riposte: quip, reply, rejoinder, response, return, sally, witticism
ripostes: repartee
ripped: cut, mangled
ripple: bubble, curl, gurgle, lap, warble
rippling: murmuring
rise: ascend, ascent, bank, bristle, bulge, cant, climb, dawn, elevation, eminence, ferment, fountain, gain, gather, get up, grade, gradient, harden, head, heave, hill, improve, improvement, increase, issue, jump, leap, lift, preferment, prominence, promotion, ramp, rear, revolt, rouse, slope, soar, surface, surge, swell, tower, well
rise up: mutiny, rebel
risible: derisory, ludicrous, undignified
rising: lift, mutiny, promising, revolt
risk: bet, chance, danger, dare, gamble, hazard, imperil, jeopardy, lottery, peril, speculate, stake, threat, venture, wager

risking: liable,
riskless: safe,
risky: chancy,
dangerous, desperate,
hairy, precarious,
speculative, unsafe
risqué: bawdy,
indelicate, juicy, racy,
scabrous, suggestive
rite: ceremonial,
formula, mystery,
ritual, solemnity
ritual: ceremonial,
mystery, mystical,
rite, solemn
rival: compete,
competitor, enemy,
equal, keep up,
match, opponent,
opposing, opposition,
touch
rivalry: competition,
feud, war
rivals: competition
river: stream, water
riverbank: brink
riverside: bank,
embankment
rivet: button, clinch,
fasten, fastener, grip,
involve, secure, stud
riveting: interesting
rivulet: brook, stream
road: avenue, lane,
passage, route, street,
track, way
road-race: rally
roads: port
roadside: verge
roadstead: road
roam: journey, prowl,
quarter, ramble,
range, saunter, stray,
traverse, wander
roaming: stray,
wandering
roar: bawl, beat,
bellow, belt, boom,
fulminate, growl,
laugh, rave, roll,
shout, thunder, yell
roaring: thunderous
roast: bake, brown,
fire, grill, joint,
scorch, toast
roasting: baking, hot,
torrid
rob: deprive, do,
fleece, hold up,
liberate, lift, loot,
mug, pillage, pluck,
plunder, strip
robber: bandit,
burglar, thief
robbery: burglary,
larceny, pillage,

rapine
robe: clothe, dress,
frock, gown
robot: automatic,
automaton, machine
robust: beefy, bluff,
fit, hardy, healthy,
hearty, lusty,
muscular, powerful,
rugged, sound, stout,
strong, sturdy,
vigorous, virile, well
robustness: brawn,
strength, vigour
rock: bastion, cradle,
dance, jar, jewel, jog,
reel, roll, shake, sway,
swing, wag
rocker: cradle
rocket: bomb, flare,
leap, soar
rockfall: landslide
rocking: roll, tottering
rocklike: petrified
rocks: jewellery
rocky: insecure,
mountainous, rough,
rugged
picturesque: quaint
rod: axle, bar, bolt,
gun, pin, pole, probe,
shaft, staff, stick,
wand
roger: yes
rogue: cheat, devil,
hound, knave,
mischief, monkey,
ruffian, scoundrel,
swindler, terror,
villain
roguish: jocular,
knavish, naughty,
playful, sly, wicked
roguishness:
naughtiness
roister: carouse, revel,
riot
roisterer: lad
roisterous: robust
role: cameo, capacity,
character, duty,
function, hand, job,
office, part, pose,
position, province
roll: bolt, bowl, bun,
bundle, catalogue,
flatten, glide, labour,
list, lurch,
manhandle, reel,
register, rock, run,
spin, tumble, wall
roll about: wallow
roll by: elapse
roller: beam, cylinder,
reel, wave
rollick: lark

rollicking: boisterous,
hilarious, robust, row,
uproarious
rolling: roll,
undulating
roll up: bundle, wrap
roly-poly: fat, obese,
plump, rotund, round
romance: intrigue,
liaison, novel, story
romantic: fairytale,
fanciful, idealistic,
impractical, lyric,
lyrical, tender,
unrealistic,
unworldly, Utopian
romanticism:
impracticality
Romany: gypsy
romp: caper, game,
lark, play, riot
romping: frisky,
prancing
rood: cross
roof-space: attic,
garret
roof: ceiling, slate,
vault
roofing plate: slate
roofing-slate: rag
rook: fleece
rookery: flock
room: berth, cabin,
capacity, chamber,
flat, latitude, lodge,
lodgings, margin,
pad, place, play,
scope, slack, space,
vacancy, ward, way
roomer: lodger
rooming-house:
hotel
rooms: facilities,
lodgings, quarters,
suite
roomy: broad,
capacious, spacious,
voluminous, wide
roost: perch
rooster: chicken, cock
root: beginning, base,
basic, basis, bottom,
cause, derivation, dig,
ferret, genesis, heart,
implant, spring,
underlying
rooted: firm
rootle: grub
root out: obliterate
roots: origin
rope: bind, bond,
cable, cord, line,
mooring, painter,
shackle, strand, tether
roped: bound
ropy: rotten, rough

rose-coloured: rosy
rose: jet
rosiness: bloom,
blush
roster: catalogue,
register, rota
rostrum: beak,
platform, podium
rosy: fresh, hectic,
promising,
propitious, red
rot: cancer, corrupt,
decay, decomposition,
go off, nonsense,
perish, putrefy,
rubbish, spoil,
stagnate, stuff
rotate: circle, pivot,
revolve, roll, spin,
turn, wheel, whirl
rotating: circulation,
cycle, orbit,
revolution, roll, rota,
rotary, turn, wheel,
whirl
rotational: rotary
rotgut: drink
rotor arm:
distributor
rotten: bad, beastly,
corrupt, off, poor,
putrid, rancid, rough,
shabby, terrible
rotting: corrupt,
decay, decomposition
rotund: chubby,
corpulent, fat, obese,
plump, round, stout
roué: libertine, villain
rough: barbaric,
boisterous, bumpy,
choppy, coarse, draft,
foul, harsh,
imprecise, jagged,
low, mischievous,
ragged, raucous, raw,
robust, rotten, rowdy,
rude, rugged, savage,
scabrous, scratch,
shaggy, sketchy,
stormy, tough,
uncomfortable,
uneven, unfinished,
violent, wild, woolly
roughly: hard, nearly
roughneck: ruffian,
savage
roughness: asperity,
coarseness, violence
round: beat, bout,
cartridge, lap, plump,
ring, rota, rotund,
route, run, turn, whirl
roundabout:
circuitous, detour,
devious, side,

winding
rounded: curved, full,
    mellow, obtuse,
    rotund, round
roundel: button
round off: complete,
    conclude, crown,
    finish
round on: turn on
round robin: memo
rounds: patrol
round trip: tour,
    voyage
round up: assemble,
    rally, recruit
round-up: assembly
rouse: call, ferment,
    fire, ginger, heat,
    incite, inflame,
    kindle, provoke,
    quicken, revive,
    shake, stimulate,
    whet, work up
rousing: emotive,
    exciting, impassioned
rout: conquer,
    conquest, crush,
    debacle, defeat,
    fiasco, flight, lick,
    licking, overrun,
    overthrow, whip
route: bet, channel,
    course, direct,
    itinerary, line,
    passage, path, road,
    way
routine: automatic,
    common,
    conventional, custom,
    customary, daily,
    drill, everyday,
    familiar, groove,
    habit, habitual,
    manner, mechanical,
    menial, method,
    perfunctory, practice,
    procedure, regular,
    ritual, rota, round,
    rule, rut, set, stock,
    system, usual
routinely: daily
rove: journey, ramble,
    roam, stray, wander
rover: buccaneer,
    gypsy
roving: fugitive,
    itinerant, restless
row: babel, bank, bed,
    block, column, dust,
    fight, file, layer, line,
    oar, paddle, pull,
    quarrel, racket, range,
    rank, riot, scene,
    scrap, scuffle, storm,
    trouble, words,
    wrangle

rowdiness: mayhem
rowdy: boisterous,
    hooligan, loud,
    obstreperous,
    vociferous,
    wild
rowel: spur
royal: majestic,
    princely, regal
royalist: cavalier
rub: bark, chafe, fret,
    gall, grate, irritate,
    massage, rasp, scour,
    scrape, scuff, wear,
    wipe
rubbed: frayed
rubber: preventive
rubberneck: stare
rubbing: friction
rubbish: bull, bunk,
    claptrap, drivel, filth,
    fudge, garbage, junk,
    litter, nonsense, offal,
    refuse, rot, stuff,
    waste
rubbishy: pathetic,
    poor, shoddy,
    worthless
rubble: ballast,
    debris, wreckage
rubicund: florid, red,
    rosy
rub out: delete, kill,
    knock off, murder
rubric: formula,
    heading
ruby: red
ruched: frills, frilly
ruck: maul, scrum,
    tackle, wrinkle
ruckle: wrinkle
rucksack: knapsack,
    pack
ruckus: disturbance,
    uproar
ruction: disturbance
rudder: helm
ruddiness: flush
ruddy: red, rosy,
    sanguine
rude: barbaric,
    bawdy, brutal,
    churlish, coarse,
    disrespectful, gross,
    immodest, impolite,
    improper, low, mean,
    offensive, robust,
    rough, rugged, saucy,
    suggestive, tactless,
    uncouth, ungracious,
    unmentionable, wild
rudely: roughly
rudeness:
    discourtesy, insult,
    misconduct, sauce
rudiment: element

rudimentary:
    beginning, elemental,
    elementary,
    immature, inchoate,
    initial, primary,
    primitive, rough,
    vestigial
rudiments:
    smattering
rue: bewail, regret
rueful: guilty,
    penitent, remorseful
ruefulness: regret
ruffed: frilly
ruffian: barbarian,
    brute, bully,
    hooligan, rough, yob
ruffianly: villainous
ruffle: chafe,
    discompose, disturb,
    flutter, gather, needle,
    perturb
ruffled: choppy,
    disconcerted,
    dishevelled, frilly
ruffles: frills
ruffs: frills
rug: blanket, carpet,
    mat
rugged: hardy,
    robust, rough, savage,
    tough
ruin: bankrupt, blast,
    break, bust, calamity,
    confound, damage,
    destroy, destruction,
    dish, dissolution,
    failure, fall, fiasco,
    finish, kill, loss,
    murder, overshadow,
    overthrow, queer,
    ravage, reduce, sack,
    shatter, sink, smash,
    spoil, undo, waste,
    wreck, wreckage
ruination: death,
    debacle, disaster,
    doom, havoc, ruin
ruined: bankrupt,
    bust, derelict,
    dilapidated, kaput,
    lost, shattered,
    tainted, undone,
    waste
ruinous: bad, baneful,
    damaging, dire,
    disastrous, evil,
    harmful
ruins: debris, remains
rule: authority,
    command, control,
    custom, determine,
    dictate, direct,
    directive, dominate,
    edict, govern,
    government, habit,

head, institute, judge,
    jurisdiction, law,
    leadership, legislate,
    line, master, mastery,
    maxim, measure,
    norm, ordain, order,
    policy, practice,
    prescribe, principle,
    regime, regulate,
    regulation, reign,
    restriction, ruler,
    standard, sway,
    theorem, usage
ruler: chief, king,
    leader, lord, measure,
    monarch, patriarch,
    queen, sovereign
ruling: decision,
    direction, high,
    judgement, leading,
    legislation,
    overriding, precept,
    predominant,
    privileged, rule,
    sentence, sovereign,
    verdict
rumble: boom, find
    out, growl, gurgle,
    hum, roar, roll,
    thunder
rumbling:
    murmuring, thunder,
    thunderous
rumbustious:
    boisterous
ruminant: bovine
ruminate: chew,
    cogitate, consider,
    meditate, muse,
    ponder, reflect
    revolve, think
ruminative:
    meditative, pensive,
    thoughtful
rummage: comb,
    grub, junk, jumble,
    knick-knacks, ransack
rumour: buzz, news,
    report, say, tale,
    whisper, wind
rumoured: supposed
rump: bottom, stern,
    tail
rumple: crease,
    crumple, ruffle,
    wrinkle
rumpled: dishevelled
rumpus: commotion,
    disturbance, fracas,
    kerfuffle, row, scuffle,
    storm, uproar
run: carry on, dash,
    direct, drive,
    enclosure, ferry, flow,
    function, gallop, go,
    hare, hasten, head,

hold, hurry, keep,
leap, manage,
operate, organize,
pour, preside over,
regulate, roll, route,
rush, stream, stretch,
superintend, trip,
walk, well, work
runaway: deserter,
fugitive, landslide
rundown: scenario,
summary
rune: character
rung: degree
runner: athlete,
bearer, bolt,
candidate, nominee
runners: field
running: conduct,

consecutive,
direction, fugitive,
management,
operation, operative,
upkeep, working
runny: fluid, liquid,
watery
runt: scrub, weed
runtish: puny
rupture: break, burst,
bust, divorce,
fracture, opening,
puncture, rent,
schism
ruptured: burst, bust,
split
rural: idyllic, pastoral,
rustic
ruse: artifice, blind,

bluff, deception,
dodge, hoax,
machination, scheme,
trap, wheeze
rush: burst, bustle,
career, charge, drift,
flood, flurry, haste,
hasten, hurry, hustle,
jet, leap, pelt, pile,
press, run, sally,
scramble, shoot,
spate, speed, spurt,
storm, surge, swoop,
whisk
rushed: pushed
rust: fungus, stagnate
rustic: idyllic,
pastoral, peasant,
simple, yokel

rustle: stir, whisper
rustling: murmuring
rut: groove
ruthless: barbaric,
brutal, cold-blooded,
cruel, deadly, fell,
ferocious, flinty,
grim, hard, harsh,
inhuman, merciless,
relentless, sadistic,
savage
ruthlessness: cruelty,
ferocity
rutted: bumpy
rutting: lecherous

S

sable: black
sabot: clog
saboteur: subversive
sabre: sword
saccharine: sugary,
  sweet
sacerdotal: clerical
sack: axe, bag,
  discharge, dismiss,
  loot, pillage, plunder,
  raid, ravage, rob
sacking: chop,
  dismissal
sacrament:
  communion, mystery,
  rite
sacred: divine, holy,
  scriptural, solemn,
  spiritual
sacredness: sanctity
sacrifice: cost,
  expense, forgo, gift,
  offering
sacrilege: blasphemy,
  evil, violation
sacrilegious:
  disrespectful, evil,
  impious, irreverent,
  profane
sacrosanct: holy,
  sacred
sad: bad, baleful,
  forlorn, funereal,
  lachrymose, low,
  lugubrious,
  melancholy,
  mournful, pathetic,
  pitiful, plaintive,
  sombre, sorrowful,
  sorry, subdued,
  tearful, tragic,
  unhappy
sadden: darken,
  depress, distress,
  grieve, hurt
saddened: hurt
saddening:
  depressing,
  deplorable
saddle: harness, seat,
  tack
sadism: cruelty,
  torture
sadist: brute, butcher,
  fiend
sadistic: cruel, savage
sadly: regretfully,

unhappily
sadness: depression,
  grief, melancholy,
  misery, pain, pathos,
  shadow, sorrow
safe: foolproof,
  harmless, hygienic,
  reliable, secure,
  sound, sure, vault
safeguard: chaperon,
  insurance, precaution,
  preserve, preventive,
  protect, save, shelter,
  shield
safeguarding: patrol
safekeeping: security
safety: protection,
  security, shelter
saffron: yellow
sag: bag, dangle, flag,
  flop, hang, loll, sink,
  stoop, wilt
saga: legend,
  romance, tale
sagacious: deep,
  judicious, profound,
  sage, wise
sagacity: depth,
  prudence, wisdom
sage: wise
sagging: flagging,
  pendulous
sail: coast, cruise, fly,
  glide, navigate, put
  out, sweep
sailcloth: canvas
sailor: hand, jack
sainted: saintly
saintly: holy, pious
salacious: bawdy,
  fruity, lecherous,
  lewd, obscene,
  scurrilous, spicy
salaciousness:
  lewdness,
  licentiousness
salad: greens
salami: sausage
salaried: professional
salary: pay, payment,
  screw, wage
sale: cheap
salesman:
  representative
salience: prominence
saline: salty
saliva: catarrh, lick,

slaver, spit, water
salivate: water
sallies: repartee
sallow: grey, livid,
  lurid, pale, yellow
sally: flight, jest, raid
salon: hall
saloon: bar, living-
  room, lounge
salt: cellar, cure,
  sailor, salty
salted: salty
salubrious: benign,
  good, salutary,
  sanitary
salutary: benign,
  beneficial
salutation: greeting,
  hail, kiss, salute,
  welcome
salute: commemorate,
  compliment, flag,
  greet, greeting, hail,
  kiss, recognize, toast
saluting: flagging
salvage: rescue,
  retrieve, save
salvation: grace,
  saviour
salve: cream,
  disinfectant,
  ointment, relieve
salvo: barrage, burst,
  flight, volley
same: image, very
sameness: identity,
  similarity
sample: dummy,
  excerpt, experience,
  gauge, lick, pattern,
  piece, sip, specimen,
  taste
sanatorium: home,
  hostel, ward
sanctified: sacred,
  venerable
sanctify: bless,
  enshrine
sanctimonious: cant,
  pious, sententious
sanction: authority,
  authorize, blessing,
  charter, confirm,
  confirmation,
  consent, leave,
  legalize, let, liberty,
  licence, okay, pass,

permission, permit,
  ratify, warrant
sanctioned:
  authoritative, lawful,
  legitimate, official,
  privileged
sanctitude: sanctity
sanctity: solemnity,
  piety
sanctuary: asylum,
  den, harbour, lair,
  preserve, refuge,
  reserve, retreat,
  safety, security,
  shelter
sanctum: haunt,
  sanctuary
sand: ballast, beach,
  desert, file, grind,
  grit, rasp
sandbags: ballast
sandbank: bar,
  shallow, shelf, shoal
sands: beach, shore
sandy: red, yellow
sane: lucid, rational,
  right
saneness: sanity
sangfroid:
  nonchalance
sanguinary:
  murderous
sanguine: hopeful,
  red
sanitary: clean,
  healthy, hygienic,
  pure
sanitize: fumigate,
  purify
sanity: lucidity, mind,
  reason
sans: less
sap: blood, drain,
  exhaust, juice, milk,
  prostrate, run down,
  tax, wally, weaken
sapped: prostrate
sapphic: homosexual
sapphist: lesbian
sappy: juicy
sarcasm: hit,
  invective, irony,
  ridicule, satire, scorn
sarcastic: biting,
  caustic, cutting,
  cynical, derisory,
  mordant, peppery,

pungent, sardonic,
scathing, scornful,
sharp
sarcophagus: tomb
sardonic: cynical,
devastating, dry,
keen, sarcastic,
scornful, sharp, wry
sash: belt, girdle
Satan: devil
satanic: dark,
diabolical, infernal,
monstrous, wicked
sate: fill, satisfy
sated: blasé, full,
jaded, satiated
satellite: subject,
world
satiate: fill, glut,
indulge, quench,
satisfy
satiated: full, jaded
satiety: surfeit
satiny: shiny
satire: caricature,
lampoon, parody,
ridicule
satirical: keen,
sarcastic, severe
satirize: caricature,
lampoon, parody,
ridicule, send up
satisfaction:
compensation,
content, joy, liking,
luxury, pleasure,
pride, redress
satisfactorily:
enough, fair, fairly,
okay
satisfactory: decent,
good, okay, palatable,
right, satisfying,
sufficient, suitable
satisfied: certain,
complacent, content,
full, joyful, pleased,
satiated, sure
satisfy: compensate,
comply, content, fill,
fulfil, glut, gratify,
hold, indulge, meet,
please, quench,
redeem, square,
suit
satisfying: heart-
warming, pleasant
saturate: drench, fill,
flood, glut, soak,
steep
saturated:
bedraggled, sodden,
wet
saturation: glut
saturnalia: revel
saturnalian: drunken

sauce: impertinence,
insolence, lip, mouth,
relish
saucer: disc, dish
saucers: crockery
saucy: bold, brazen,
flippant, fresh,
impertinent,
irreverent, perky,
pert, smart
saunter: jaunt, loaf,
lounge, promenade,
ramble, stroll, walk
saut: brown
savage: atrocious,
barbarian, barbaric,
beast, beastly, brutal,
brute, cold-blooded,
cruel, devastating,
devil, fell, ferocious,
fiend, fierce, heathen,
monster, monstrous,
murderous, primitive,
rogue, untamed,
vicious, violent,
worry
savagery: cruelty,
ferocity, violence
savant: scholar
save: bank, bar,
besides, conserve,
deliver, economise,
except, garner,
husband, liberate,
preserve, redeem,
rescue, reserve,
resuscitate, retain,
salvage, store
saving: cut, economy,
except, rescue,
salvation, scriptural
savings: bank, reserve
savour: flavour, gusto,
love, relish, taste, zest
savoury: biscuit,
delicacy, palatable,
piquant, rich, spicy,
tasty
saw: cut, machine,
proverb, saying
say: aver, bid, choice,
comment, mean, part,
phrase, pronounce,
record, remark,
rumour, speak, utter,
voice, word
saying: maxim,
phrase, precept,
proverb
sayings: lore,
teachings
scab: crust
scabby: fleabitten,
mangy
scabies: scab
scabrous:

unrepeatable, scaly
scaffold: stage,
gallows
scalding: hot
scale: ascend, breadth,
climb, degree,
enormity, flake,
index, key,
magnitude, mass,
measure, mount,
munificence, rate
scales: balance
scallywag: knave
scalpel: knife
scaly: fishy
scamp: knave,
mischief, monkey,
rogue, terror, villain
scamper: run
scan: canvass, inspect,
look, monitor, pan,
peruse, rake,
reconnoitre, screen,
survey, vet, view
scandal: buzz, dirt,
gossip, indiscretion,
notoriety,
opprobrium, shame,
slander, tale
scandalize: shock
scandalmonger:
backbiter, gossip
scandalous: criminal,
deplorable,
disgraceful, foul,
indiscreet, infamous,
outrageous,
sensational, shocking
scanner: monitor
scant: defective, little,
low, scanty
scantily: barely
scanty: few,
inadequate, jejune,
lean, meagre, narrow,
niggardly, poor,
slender, small, spare
scapegoat: victim
scapegrace: knave,
monkey
scar: blemish,
disfigurement, lesion,
mar, mark, nick, pit
scarce: few, rare, thin,
tight, short
scarcely: barely,
hardly, ill, just, little
scarcity: deficiency,
drought, lack,
poverty, rarity,
shortage, want
scare: fright, frighten,
intimidate, panic,
rattle
scarecrow: fright
scarf: bonnet, hood,

kerchief, veil, wrap
scarlet: red
scarp: cliff, slope
scarper: flee, run
scarred: marked,
misshapen
scarring: traumatic
scary: creepy,
frightening, hair-
raising, macabre
scatheless: unharmed
scathing: biting,
caustic, cutting,
mordant, poisonous,
pungent, scornful,
severe, sharp,
vitriolic
scatological: foul
scatter: broadcast,
cast, disperse, dot,
dust, emit, litter,
plant, radiate, rout,
scattering, seed, shed,
sow, spatter, spill,
spray, spread,
sprinkling, stud
scatterbrained:
crazy, dizzy, giddy,
mad
scattered: dissipated,
distant, widespread
scattering: diffusion,
distribution, few,
flight
scenario:
background, habitat,
layout, plan, plot,
tableau
scene: circle, drama,
excerpt, happening,
incident, locality,
outlook, panorama,
prospect, set, setting,
sight, spectacle,
tableau, view
scenery: background,
nature, set
scenic: ornamental,
pictorial
scent: bouquet,
breath, detect, drag,
emanation, fragrance,
incense, odour,
perfume, sense, smell,
track, whiff, wind
scented: fragrant
sceptic: atheist, cynic
sceptical: cynical,
disbelieving,
incredulous,
jaundiced, unsure
sceptically: askance
scepticism: distrust,
suspicion
sceptre: rod
schedule: bill, book,

catalogue, form,
itinerary, list, memo,
programme, register,
roll, round, scheme,
set, table, time
scheduled: due
schema: material,
plan, plot
scheme: baby, brew,
complex, conspire,
contrive, design,
game, idea, intrigue,
key, machination,
manoeuvre, plan,
plot, procedure,
programme, project,
proposal, proposition,
scenario, speculate,
system, tactic,
wangle, wheeze
schemer: tactician
scheming:
calculating, crafty,
designing, devious,
politic, shifty, sly,
subtle
schism: heresy, rent,
rift, rupture, split
schismatic:
disbelieving, heretic,
rebel
schizomycete:
bacterium
schnitzel: cutlet
scholar: brain,
intellectual, student,
trainee
scholarly: bookish,
cultured, intellectual,
knowledgeable,
learned, literary,
literate
scholarship: depth,
knowledge, learning,
reading
school: educate,
faculty, indoctrinate,
institute, instruct,
qualify, seminary,
teach
schoolboy: pupil
schooldays: youth
schoolgirl: pupil
schooling: education,
instruction,
knowledge
schoolmarmish:
prim
schoolmaster: beak
schoolwork:
preparation
schooner: yacht
science: knowledge
scimitar: sword
scintilla: jot
scintillate: flash,

glitter, shine, sparkle
scintillating: bright,
brilliant, gleaming,
piquant, shimmering,
vivacious
scintillation:
brilliance, fire, flash,
glitter, light
scion: cutting, graft
scions: descendants
sclerosis: ossification
scoff: eat, ridicule,
sneer, wolf
scoffer: sceptic
scoffing: derisory,
jeering, sceptical,
scornful
scoffs: jeering
scold: castigate, check,
dragon, jaw, lash,
lecture, nag, rag,
rebuke, reprimand,
reproach, slate,
storm, upbraid
scolding: jaw, lecture,
lesson, nagging,
reprimand
sconce: torch
scone: bun
scoop: bale, coup, dig,
grab, measure,
sensation, shovel
scope: breadth,
calibre, capacity,
chance, compass(es),
comprehension,
distribution, field,
grasp, latitude,
measure, orbit, play,
range, reach, region,
room, scale, space,
sphere, sweep, width
scorch: bake, burn,
wither
scorched: parched
scorching: baking,
hot, torrid, withering
score: bill, count,
groove, grudge, line,
make, nick,
orchestrate, point,
rut, scotch, scratch,
slash, sum, tally
scorer: umpire
scores: many
scoria: slag
scorn: contempt,
despise, disdain,
mockery,
opprobrium, ridicule,
scoff, slight, sneer
scornful: cynical,
derisory, scathing,
withering
scornfulness: scorn
Scotch mist: drizzle

scotch: kill
scotching: killing
scoundrel: black
sheep, devil, dog,
hound, knave, rogue,
ruffian, scab, terror,
villain, wretch
scoundrelly: knavish
scour: comb, rake,
ransack, rasp, rub,
scan, scrape, scrub,
search
scourge: flog, lash,
plague, whip
scouring: scrape
scout: explore
scow: barge
scowl: face, frown,
glare, grimace
scrabble: grope,
scramble
scraggly: scabrous
scraggy: scrawny,
skinny, thin
scram: flee, get off
scramble: rush,
scrum, struggle
scrambled: muddled
scrap: bit, crumb,
end, fight, fraction,
fragment, grain,
jettison, jot, junk,
nibble, part, particle,
patch, piece, rag,
refuse, reject,
remnant, rubbish,
shred, waste, wrangle
scrape: bark, brush,
claw, file, gall, grate,
graze, hole, jam,
plight, predicament,
rake, rasp, rub, scoop,
score, scratch, scuffle,
wound
scraper: file, plane
scrapping: end
scraps: garbage,
leavings, offal,
remains
scratch: chip, claw,
grate, graze, mark,
nick, rake, score,
scrape, scrawl,
withdraw
scratched: marked,
raw
scrawl: jot, scratch,
writing
scrawny: gaunt, lank,
lanky, meagre, thin,
underweight
scream: cry, laugh,
shout, shriek, squeal,
wail, yell
screaming: hysterical
scree: filter, till

screech: cry, outcry,
scrape, scream,
shriek, squeal,
ululate, whoop, yell
screeching: shrill,
strident
screen: awning, blind,
camouflage, cloak,
conceal, cover,
disguise, grate, hedge,
hide, mantle, mask,
obscure, partition,
protection, shade,
shadow, shelter,
shield, sift, veil, wall,
winnow
screened: sheltered,
veiled
screening: projection
screw: fastener,
guard, throw, warder,
wring
scribble: jot, scrawl,
write, writing
scribbler: writer
scribe: engrave,
journalist, secretary,
writer
scrimmage: down,
fight, scramble, scrap,
scrum, scuffle,
skirmish
scrimp: pinch, scrape
scrimping:
parsimonious
script: book, hand,
notation, scrawl,
writing
scripture: writing
scriptwriter:
dramatist
scroll: roll
scrolled: spiral
Scrooge-like: miserly
Scrooge: miser
scrounger: drone,
parasite
scrub: bath, brush,
bush, clean, desert,
forest, heath, scour
scrape, undergrowth,
wash
scrubber: hussy
scrubbing: bath
scrubby: bare
scruffy: fleabitten,
mangy, seedy,
shabby, wild
scrum: scuffle, wrestle
scrummage: down,
scrum
scrumple: crease,
crumple
scrumptious:
delicious, savoury,
tasty

scruple: qualm, pang
scruples: conscience, ethics
scrupulous: careful, conscientious, dainty, meticulous, minute, nice, painstaking, pedantic, precise, punctilious, religious, rigorous, squeamish, strict, thorough
scrupulously: exactly
scrupulousness: precision
scrutinize: canvass, check, inspect, look, look into, peruse, probe, rake, reconnoitre, regard, research, review, scan, sift, survey, vet, view
scrutiny: check, consideration, observation, reading, regard, review, study, survey
scud: course
scuff: scrape
scuffed: frayed
scuffle: fight, fracas, scrap, shuffle, struggle, wrestle
scull: blade, oar, paddle, pull, row
sculpt: carve, cut, engrave, mould
sculpted: cut
sculptor: artist
scum: dregs, foam, mob, residue, riffraff
scurfy: scabrous, scaly
scurrility: insult
scurrilous: rank, rotten, rude, scandalous
scurry: bustle, course, hasten, run, rush
scurvy: cheap
sea: drink, marine, maritime, multitude, water
seafarer: sailor
seafaring: nautical
seagoing: marine, nautical
seal: bull, cap, cement, clinch, close, fill, join, junction, lid, lock, shut
sealant: cement
sealed: bound, closed, impervious, tight
seam: join, joint, junction, layer, vein, weld

seaman: sailor
seamstress: dressmaker, tailor
seamy: sordid
sear: bake, scorch, wither
search: comb, explore, go through, grope, hunt, look, prospect, pursuit, quest, rake, ransack, scan
searching: close, curious, penetrating, piercing
searing: baking, excruciating, hot, scathing, torrid, withering
seashore: shore
seaside: beach, coast
season: dress, festival, flavour, harden, mature, pepper, period, run, spell, time, weather
seasonal: temporal
seasoned: experienced, habituated, mature, piquant, tough, veteran
seat: behind, bench, berth, bottom, buttocks, chair, contain, couch, feed, form, hold, locate, perch, place, rear, residence, tail
sebaceous: oily
secessionist: rebel
seclude: segregate
secluded: close, lonely, monastic, private, quiet, remote, secret, sequestered, sheltered, solitary, withdrawn
seclusion: isolation, loneliness, retirement, retreat, sequestration, solitude
second: assist, assistant, back, back up, bit, flash, instant, minute, moment, reject, shake, side, subordinate, support
secondary: background, inferior, less, lesser, side, subordinate, supplementary
seconding: backing

secrecy: mystery
secret: confidential, enigma, gaff, hidden, insidious, internal, mysterious, mystery, private, quiet, sneak, surreptitious, tale, undisclosed, unmentionable, underground
secretaire: secretary
secretarial: clerical
secretary: bureau, desk
secrete: conceal, discharge, emit, perspire
secretion: discharge, emission, juice
secretive: close, evasive, furtive, mysterious, reticent, stealthy, uncommunicative
secretively: quietly
secretly: quietly
sect: church, denomination, persuasion, school
sectarian: religious
section: bit, branch, category, chapter, clause, compartment, contingent, department, excerpt, faction, fraction, fragment, head, heading, joint, lap, leg, length, locality, office, part, passage, piece, pigeonhole, region, unit, zone
sector: fraction, part, region, section, zone
secular: lay, mundane, physical, profane, temporal, worldly
secure: assured, attach, bar, blockade, bolt, buy, capture, clamp, clinch, close, collect, confident, cosy, fast, fasten, fence, firm, fix, gain, get, guard, have, knit, knot, land, lash, leash, lock, nail, obtain, peg, pin, pot, preserve, procure, purchase, reserve, sacred, safe, shackle, shut, sound, stable, steady, strap, sturdy, sure, take, tape, tether, tight, win

secured: bound
securely: fast
security: bail, bond, defence, earnest, firmness, guarantee, hostage, insurance, pawn, pledge, principal, protection, safety
sedan: chair, saloon
sedate: demure, grave, quiet, settle, sober
sedately: quietly
sedation: narcosis
sedative: drug, hypnotic, narcotic, painkiller, soporific
sedentary: inactive
sediment: deposit, dregs, grounds, lees
sedition: revolt, unrest
seditionary: subversive
seditious: disloyal, lawless, rebellious, revolutionary, subversive
seduce: betray, decoy, draw, lure, tempt, wrong
seducer: libertine, wolf
seduction: betrayal, temptation
seductive: attractive, charming, desirable, inviting, lovable, provocative, sexy, sultry, voluptuous
sedulous: painstaking
sedulousness: diligence
see: catch on, clock, discern, discover, distinguish, get, grasp, know, look, make out, note, notice, observe, perceive, picture, read, recognize, remark, sense, sight, spot, take, tell, tour, understand, view, witness
seed: broadcast, fruit, germ, grain, kernel, nut, offspring, plant, sow
seedy: dingy, mangy, mean, scruffy, seamy, shabby, sordid
seeing: discovery, onlooking, vision
seek: ask, aspire, hunt,

pursue, request,
solicit, want, woo
seeker: pilgrim
seem: look, purport,
sound
seeming: ostensible,
putative, superficial
seemingly: clearly,
outwardly,
presumably
seemliness: propriety
seemly: becoming,
decent, fitting, meet,
right, suitable
seep: bleed, discharge,
leak, ooze, penetrate,
well
seepage: discharge,
leak, ooze
seeping: leaky
seer: oracle, prophet
seesaw: bob,
fluctuate, waver
seesawing:
undulating
seethe: boil, bubble,
churn, ferment, fume,
press, rage, rave
seething: packed,
simmering,
smouldering
seethrough: sheer
segment: bit, excerpt,
fraction, joint, length,
part, partition, piece,
portion, section, zone
segmented: articulate
segregate: divide,
isolate, separate
segregation: division,
isolation, partition
seize: assume, bite,
capture, catch, collar,
commandeer,
confiscate, conquer,
get, grab, grasp, grip,
hijack, kidnap, nail,
possess, snare, snatch,
take, whip
seizure: assumption,
attack, capture,
convulsion, fit,
frenzy, grab, hijack,
requisition,
sequestration, spasm,
stroke
seldom: little,
uncommonly
select: assign, cast,
draw, elect, exclusive,
like, narrow,
nominate, opt for,
prefer, pick, single,
sort, take
selected: detailed
selection: assignation,

assignment,
assortment, choice,
compilation,
detachment, draw,
lot, medley, option,
pick, preference,
range
selective: fussy
self: psyche
selfish: bossy,
inconsiderate, self-
centred, self-seeking,
small, sordid,
undisciplined,
ungrateful, worldly
selfishness: greed,
self-assertion
selfless: unselfish
selflessness:
magnanimity
selfsame: same, very
sell: flog, hawk,
market, peddle,
promote, prostitute,
publish, stab, stock,
vend
seller: merchant
selling: sale, traffic
semantics: language
semblance: cast,
colour, disguise,
likeness, look,
pretence,
resemblance, shade,
shape, show
semen: seed
semester: term
semicircular: bay
seminal: historic
seminar: clinic,
conference
seminary: college,
school
senate: government,
legislative, parliament
senator: councillor,
father
senatorial: legislative
send: attach,
commission, direct,
drive, forward, mail,
post, relay, route,
transmit
sending: consignment
senile: old
senility: dotage
senior: major,
superior
seniority: majority,
priority
seniors: top brass
sennet: fanfare
sensation: emotion,
feeling, hit, knockout,
phenomenon,
prodigy, perception,

scoop
sensational:
astonishing,
breathtaking,
dramatic, exciting,
fantastic, juicy,
knockout, lurid,
melodramatic,
phenomenal, pulp,
spectacular, stunning,
wonder, wonderful
sensationalize: hype
sense: catch, discern,
faculty, feel, feeling,
gist, import,
intuition, judgement,
loaf, logic, matter,
meaning, message,
perception, reason,
respect, sanity, scent,
sensation, spirit, tact,
taste, way, wisdom,
wit, wits
senseless: asinine,
crazy, foolish,
illogical, insane,
insensible, irrational,
mad, purposeless,
silly, unreasonable
senselessly: madly
senselessness:
insanity, stupidity
senses: wits
sensibility:
awareness, delicacy,
sentiment
sensible: discreet,
down-to-earth,
judicious, logical,
lucid, politic,
practical, pragmatic,
rational, realistic,
reasonable,
responsible, robust,
sage, sane, solid,
sound, steady, wise
sensibly: practically
sensitive: artistic,
delicate, discerning,
emotive, fine,
impressionable,
jagged, keen, poetic,
psychic, receptive,
sentient, soft,
susceptible, tender,
thin-skinned,
understanding,
vulnerable, warm
sensitivity: ear, nose,
sensibility, tact,
tenderness
sensory: sensuous
sensual: brutal, erotic,
passionate, poetic,
provocative, sexy,
sultry, voluptuous

sensuality:
licentiousness, lust
sensuality: sex
sentence: condemn,
convict, judge,
judgement, period,
send up
sententious: laconic,
wordy
sentiment: emotion,
heart, notion,
sensibility, tenderness
sentimental:
emotive, lyric, lyrical,
maudlin, mawkish,
romantic, soft-
hearted, tender,
unrealistic,
unworldly, wet
sentimentality:
bathos, feeling
sentiments: bosom,
opinion
sentinel: guard,
lookout, patrol,
warder
sentry: guard,
lookout, warder
separate: break, cut
off, detach, different,
differentiate,
disconnect, disperse,
dissolve, distant,
distinct, distinguish,
diverge, diverse,
divide, divorce,
fragment, individual,
isolate, open, other,
part, partition,
resolve, scatter,
screen, segregate,
sever, sieve, sift,
single, singular, snap,
sort, split, strain,
various, wall, winnow
separately: aside,
through
separation: breach,
break, breakdown,
detachment,
disaffection,
dissolution, distance,
distinction, division,
divorce, extraction,
isolation, partition,
rift, schism,
secession,
sequestration,
withdrawal
sepia: brown
septum: partition
sepulchral: hollow
sepulchrally: hollow
sepulchre: tomb
sequel: ramifications,
result

sequence: battery, chain, course, line, pattern, procession, programme, round, row, run, scale, series, string, train
sequential: narrative
sequester: hijack, impound, seize
sequestrate: commandeer, confiscate
sequestration: grab, seizure
sequins: glitter
seraphic: celestial, cherubic, heavenly
serendipitous: lucky
serendipity: luck
serene: calm, even, gentle, halcyon, idyllic, imperturbable, mild, peaceful, placid, quiescent, quiet, smooth, unconcerned, undisturbed
serenely: quietly
serenity: calm, mildness, peace, quiet, repose
serf: peasant, yes-man, slave
serfdom: servitude, slavery, yoke
serge: flannel
serial: narrative, secondary
serialize: list
series: battery, chain, cycle, line, list, procession, queue, range, rank, rash, round, row, run, scale, set, string, suite, tournament, train, whirl
serious: bad, earnest, grave, great, heavy, high, nasty, pensive, pressing, profound, sad, sedate, significant, sincere, sober, solemn, stern, studious, subdued, terrible, terrific, weighty
seriously: badly, desperately, materially, terribly
seriousness: earnest, gravity, sobriety, solemnity
sermon: dissertation, oration, reading, talk
serpent: bitch

serpentine: meandering, winding
serrate: indent, mill
serrated: jagged, mountainous, ragged, sharp
serrations: teeth
serum: blood, juice
servant: attendant, bearer, lackey, man, page, slave
serve: assist, attend, benefit, do, execute, help, minister, obey, oblige, please, profit, satisfy, tend
service: bureau, capacity, ceremony, china, convenience, duty, favour, force, function, kindness, meeting, military, office, overhaul, rite, ritual, use, wear
serviceable: handy, helpful, operative, practical, useful
services: facilities, military
servicing: service
serviette: napkin
servile: base, grovelling, low, mean, obsequious, slavish, slimy
servility: flattery, humility
serving: portion
servitude: slavery, yoke
session: bout, consultation, dose, round, term
set: assign, batch, battery, block, body, cast, chain, circle, clan, class, clique, club, coagulate, collection, company, contingent, crowd, cycle, deck, deposit, dispose, dress, faction, fix, formal, frame, gang, ground, group, harden, kit, layout, limit, locate, lot, mob, module, mount, outfit, pack, party, peg, place, polarize, pose, position, posture, prepared, prescribe, put, ready, regular, resolute, rigid, root, scene, school, score, seat, setting, stand,

standard, station, stick, stock, suite, tableau, team, thicken, unit, wind, wind up
setback: blow, debacle, defeat, disappointment, down, knock, mishap, rebuff, relapse, reverse, upset
sett: hole
settee: couch, seat
setting: background, backing, environment, exposure, foil, frame, medium, mount, scene, situation, surroundings
settings: crockery
settle: balance, bank, bed, choose, clinch, colonize, complete, compose, compromise, conclude, couch, decide, deposit, determine, discharge, fix, foot, form, gravitate, heal, install, judge, light, liquidate, pay, people, perch, plant, populate, put, quit, reconcile, resolve, right, rule, satisfy, seal, seat, set, sit, square, stay, still, subside
settled: assured, certain, closed, definite, over, resident, set, steady
settlement: clinch, colony, compromise, conclusion, decision, discharge, judgement, payment, payoff, resolution
settler: pioneer
settlings: dregs, residue, lees
setup: system
sever: break, chop, cut, cut off, detach, divide, divorce, fracture, fragment, part, separate, slice
several: sundry, various
severance: break, separation
severe: ascetic, austere, bad, bare, brutal, dour, grave, harsh, heavy, intense,

nasty, oppressive, puritanical, radical, rigorous, rough, serious, spartan, stern, stiff, strong, terrible, terrific, tight, unbending, uncharitable, unflattering, vicious, violent, warm
severed: cut
severely: badly, barely, desperately, roughly, seriously, terribly, way
severing: division
severity: asperity, austerity, gravity, vengeance, violence
sew: machine
sewage: filth
sewer: drain, sink
sewn: seamy
sex: intercourse
sexless: neuter
sexual: sensual
sexuality: sex
sexy: desirable, erotic, fruity, passionate, provocative, raunchy, seductive, sultry
sgian dhu: knife
shabbily: poorly
shabbiness: misery
shabby: base, dilapidated, dingy, dirty, dowdy, fleabitten, frumpish, jerry-built, mangy, mean, miserable, moth-eaten, petty, pitiful, poor, ragged, ramshackle, scruffy, seedy, sordid, sorry, undesirable, wretched
shack: cabin, cot, cottage, hovel, hut
shackle: bond, chain, clog, handcuff
shackled: powerless
shackles: irons
shade: awning, blind, canopy, cloud, colour, darken, eclipse, nuance, obscure, screen, shadow, tint, tone
shaded: soft
shadiness: dusk, notoriety, shade
shading: blend, eclipse
shadow: background, cloud, darken, dog, dusk, eclipse, follow, ghost, gloom,

imminence, nebulosity, spy, suspicion, tail, track, whisper

shadower: tail

shadows: obscurity, shade

shadowy: dim, dusky, ghostly, gloomy, indistinct, nebulous, shady, sombre, vague

shady: doubtful, dusky, lawless, murky, notorious, obscure, shadowy, sombre, unethical

shaft: axle, bar, barrel, beam, blade, bore, column, hole, mine, pit, pole, rod, upright, well, working

shag: nap, pile, screw

shaggy: hairy, rough, woolly

shake: bump, disturb, jar, jerk, jog, quake, quaver, quiver, rack, rattle, rock, shudder, stagger, stir, vibrate, wag, wave, wriggle

shaken: disconcerted, shivers, unnerved

shakiness: dizziness

shaking: earthquake, quake

shaky: dilapidated, dizzy, flimsy, groggy, infirm, insecure, jittery, nervous, tenuous, unsettled, untenable

shallop: launch

shallow: flat, flimsy, frivolous, low, passing, shoal, superficial

shallowness: levity

shallows: bank, bar, ford, lagoon

sham: artificial, bastard, bogus, cant, charlatan, dishonest, fake, false, fictitious, forgery, fraud, fraudulent, hypocrite, imitation, mock, phoney, plastic, pretence, pretend, quack, queer, spurious

shaman: magician, oracle, wizard

shamble: shuffle

shambles: carnage, confusion, disarray,

hash, havoc, mess, rout

shame: black sheep, blemish, crush, degrade, disgrace, embarrassment, guilt, humble, mortification, mortify, pity, stain, wither

shamefaced: hangdog, red, sheepish

shameful: contemptible, despicable, disgraceful, humiliating, ignominious, mean, miserable, reprehensible, scandalous, unworthy, wretched

shamefully: badly

shameless: bold, brazen, flagrant, immodest, unrepentant

shaming: humiliating, withering

shampoo: wash,

shank: beam, calf

shanty: cabin, hovel, hut, shack, song

shape: bend, cast, condition, construction, contour, cut, fashion, figure, fit, fitness, forge, form, frame, hammer, health, knead, make, model, mould, outline, pattern, physique, prune, repair, sculpture, structure, way, work

shaped: made

shapeless: irregular, lax, nebulous

shaping: formation

shard: fragment

share: cut, deal, divide, dole, hand, lot, measure, part, partake, partition, pool, portion, proportion, quantity, quota, rake-off, ration, stake

shared: joint, mutual

shareholder: participant

sharing: division

shark: cheat, swindler, wolf

sharp: astute, bitter, brief, brisk, brusque, calculating, chill, chilly, cunning, curt, cutting, dry, fine, fly, harsh, high, keen, nippy, penetrating, peppery, perceptive, piercing, poignant, pointed, pungent, quick, quick-witted, ready, resourceful, responsive, rough, rude, sarcastic, short, shrill, slick, smart, sore, unripe, venomous, violent, vitriolic, vivid, vulpine, wily

sharpen: grind, intensify, point, whet

sharply: roughly

sharpness: asperity, chill, definition, focus, venom, warmth

shatter: blast, break, burst, bust, crash, dash, destroy, fracture, fragment, knap, ravage, ruin, shivers, smash, wreck

shattered: burst, bust, dead, spent, tired, worn out

shattering: destruction, devastating, disintegration, piercing

shave: graze, pare, scrape

shaver: plane

shaving: chip, shave, splinter

shawl: veil, wrap

sheaf: bunch

shear: clip, crop, cut, fleece, mow, reap, shave

sheath: capsule, case, cover, jacket

sheathe: envelop, face, house, jacket, wrap

sheathing: retraction

shed: cabin, cast, draw, emit, hovel, hut, spill, spread, stable, stream

sheen: brilliance, lacquer, lustre, polish, shine

sheep: stock

sheepish: ashamed, bashful

sheepminder: shepherd

sheer: bare, bluff, filmy, fine, flimsy, main, mere, mountainous, precipitous, pure, rank, steep, thin, thorough, transparent, utter, very

sheet: blanket, leaf, mooring, page, plate, tablet

sheeted: shrouded

shekels: money

shelf: bank, drawer, ledge, projection, shallow, shoal

shell: bomb, bombard, cannon, capsule, cartridge, frame, framework, horn, mine, pod, remains

shellac: lacquer, varnish

shelling: fire

shelter: asylum, awning, cover, defence, defend, harbour, house, keep, lair, lodge, lodgings, preserve, protect, protection, refuge, rest, safety, sanctuary, screen, shadow, shed, shield

sheltered: snug, secluded

sheltering: defensive

shelve: defer, dismiss, pigeonhole, postpone, suspend, write off

shenanigans: mischief

shepherd: driver, farmer, guide, herd, pastor

sherd: fragment, piece

shield: cloak, counter, cover, defence, defend, fence, guard, harbour, hood, keep, pad, protect, protection, save, screen, shade, shadow, shelter

shielded: defensive, insulation, sheltered

shift: budge, change, evasion, frock, hedge, move, movement, relay, revolution, scheme, shovel, shuffle, swerve,

switch, vary
shifting: changeable, fugitive, shift, variable
shiftless: lazy, lackadaisical
shifty: evasive, furtive, shady, slippery, sly
shillelagh: cudgel
shillyshally: hesitate
shimmer: glance, glitter, lustre, shine
shimmering: bright, gleaming, glitter
shimmy: dance
shine: beam, finish, flame, glaze, glow, lustre, polish, rub, sheen, sparkle
shingle: beach
shining: brand-new, bright, brilliant, clear, glaring, gleaming, lucid, luminous, radiant
shiny: sleek, smooth
ship: boat, craft, ferry, forward, transport, vessel, yacht
shipment: cargo, consignment, freight, load, transit, transport
shipshape: neat, orderly, straight, taut
shirk: dodge, idle, loaf, neglect, slack
shirking: idle, idleness
shirt: blouse
shirts: linentowels
shit: dirt, dung, filth, mess, ordure
shitty: filthy
shiver: crash, dash, flutter, fragment, quake, quiver, shake, shudder, splinter, vibrate, wince, wriggle
shivered: shattered
shivering: flutter, palpitation, vibrant
shivery: cold
shoal: bank, bar, flat, shallow
shock: astonishment, bump, concussion, electrify, fright, galvanize, horrify, impact, jar, mop, numbness, outrage, revolt, rock, scandalize, scare, shake, stagger, stroke,

stupefy, surprise, terror, trauma, upset, wound, wrench
shocked: numb
shocking: atrocious, diabolical, disgraceful, dreadful, fearful, gross, infamous, lurid, outrageous, revolting, scandalous, sensational, startling, tragic, traumatic, unnatural, vile, woeful
shoddily: badly
shoddy: awful, cheap, inferior, low, poor, ramshackle, raunchy, shabby
shoe: boot
shoes: footwear
shoot: bag, bough, branch, bud, catapult, cutting, discharge, drop, film, fire, flash, fly, germinate, get, graft, grow, growth, inject, jet, loose, photograph, plug, pot, propel, sail, send, spear, spray, sprout, take, wand, zap, zip
shooter: shot
shooting: discharge
shop: boutique, outlet, store
shopfloorman: operative
shopkeeper: merchant, seller
shoplift: knock off
shoplifter: thief
shopper: client, consumer, customer, patron
shopping: groceries
shore: bank, beach, coast, strand
shorn: bare, cut
short: brief, brusque, close, curt, defective, hasty, lacking, laconic, light, limited, little, low, meagre, momentary, under
shortage: deficiency, deficit, drought, lack, need, poverty, scarcity, want
shortcoming: deficiency, failing, vice
shorten: clip, condense, crop, curtail, cut, digest,

take in, telescope
shortened: cut
shortfall: deficit, lack, shortage
shortlived: meteoric, momentary, volatile
shortly: soon
shorts: briefs, pants
shot: attempt, ball, bang, bullet, crack, effort, fix, fling, go, hit, photograph, pot, round, tot
shotgun: gun
should: must
shoulder: assume, carry, push, shove
shouldering: assumption
shout: bark, bawl, bellow, call, cry, hail, roar, scream, squeal, thunder, yell
shouting: railing, vociferous
shove: barge, bundle, crowd, jam, jostle, manhandle, nose, nudge, poke, prod, propel, push, scrum, stuff
shovel: scoop
show: attest, ceremony, demonstrate, designate, disclose, display, expose, fair, flash, flourish, gala, gig, give, glitter, hold up, indication, lead, let on, look, manifest, manifestation, mark, mirror, pageant, parade, present, presentation, pretence, programme, prove, read, record, register, render, represent, reveal, riot, scene, sight, spectacle, spectacular, usher, varnish, veneer, view, write
showdown: confrontation
shower: bath, burst, cloudburst, hail, lavish, pepper, rain, scatter, spray, volley, wash
showered: smothered
showery: wet
showiness: glare
showing: exposure
showman: artist
showy: bold,

conspicuous, flamboyant, flashy, florid, garish, gay, glaring, loud, meretricious, ornate, ostentatious, spicy
shred: crumb, fraction, fragment, grate, jot, particle, patch, rag, remnant, scrap, speck, strip
shredding: teasing
shrew: bitch, nag, scold
shrewd: astute, bright, cag(e)y, calculating, clever, cunning, deep, discerning, fly, foxy, judicious, keen, knowing, mean, penetrating, perceptive, perspicacious, piercing, quick, quick-witted, searching, sensible, sharp, smart, subtle, tactical, wily, wise
shrewdly: sharply
shrewdness: dexterity, judgement, policy, sagacity
shrewish: nagging
shriek: bawl, cry, scream, squeal, yell
shrill: high, penetrating, piercing, squeak, squeal, strident
shrimp: midget, runt, weakling, weed
shrine: icon, sanctuary, tomb
shrink: contract, decline, decrease, jib, lessen, minimize, psychiatrist, quail, recede, wane, wince, wither
shrinkage: loss
shrinking: bashful, decrease, wane
shrive: purify
shrivel: blast, scorch, shrink, wilt, wither
shrivelled: parched
shroud: eclipse, hide, mantle, obscure, veil, wrap
shrouded: hidden, veiled
shrub: bush
shrunken: haggard, shrivelled
shuck: shell

shudder: quail, quake, quiver, shake, wince, wriggle
shuffle: crawl, jumble, mix, scramble, scuff, scuffle
shun: ignore, ostracize, parry, shirk
shunned: unpopular
shunt: bypass, switch
shut: close, closed, closet, lock
shutdown: paralysis, stoppage
shutter: blind, board, port
shy: ashamed, bashful, demure, modest, mousy, pot, quiet, retiring, self-conscious, self-effacing, throw, withdrawn
shyly: quietly
shyness: diffidence, reserve
shyster: quack
sibilance: buzz
sibyl: prophet
sibylline: prophetic
sick: bad, fragile, green, ill, invalid, liverish, morbid, queer, rotten, squeamish, unhealthy, unwell, upset
sicken: disgust, horrify, nauseate, offend, pall, pine, revolt
sickening: disgusting, fulsome, grisly, gruesome, hideous, nasty, nerve-racking, obnoxious, obscene, repulsive, revolting, shocking, vile
sickle: hook
sickliness: debility
sickly: delicate, feeble, invalid, mawkish, morbid, peaky, poorly, puny, sallow, seedy, unhealthy, unwell, unwholesome, wan
sickness: complaint, disease, illness, indisposition, upset
side: aspect, bank, beam, behalf, leaf, page, party, people, persuasion, quarter, team, verge
sidefoot: kick

sidekick: follower, satellite
sidelight: lamp
sideline: hobby
sidelong: oblique, sideways
sideshow: gaff
sidesman: usher
sidestep: dodge, duck, hedge, parry
sidestreet: lane
sidetrack: divert
sidewalk: path
sidewards: sideways
sideways: askance, sidelong
siding: sidetrack
sidle: sneak
siege: blockade, doze, nap, rest, snooze
sieve: filter, screen, sift, strain
sift: comb, pan, probe, screen, sieve, strain, thresh, winnow
sifter: sieve
sigh: breathe, groan, whisper
sighing: whisper
sight: fright, glimpse, look, prospect, scene, spectacle, spot
sightless: blind
sightsee: explore, lionize, tour, visit
sightseer: tourist
sign: attribute, beacon, brand, character, clue, execute, forerunner, frank, guide, index, indication, initial, inscribe, join, key, letter, manifestation, mark, nod, note, omen, portent, sample, signal, symbol, symptom, token, underwrite, vestige, warning, write
signal: beacon, call, flare, gesture, guide, indicate, indication, key, motion, nod, output, prod, sign, sound, warning, wave, word
signalling: beckoning
signalpost: pylon
signature: mark
significance: bearing, consequence, drift, effect, gist, gravity, idea, impact, implication, import,

importance, interest, magnitude, matter, meaning, moment, purport, sense, stress, substance, thing
significant: considerable, effective, expressive, great, historic, influential, knowing, leading, major, material, meaning, momentous, monumental, noteworthy, operative, pregnant, relevant, serious, signal, special, weighty, worthwhile
significantly: rather
signification: significance
signify: count, imply, import, indicate, matter, mean, purport, spell, stand for, symbolize
signpost: beacon, guide, landmark
signs: notation, notes
silence: blackout, censor, gag, hiatus, lull, muffle, mute, muzzle, peace, quiet, quieten, squash, still, stop, suppress, throttle
silencer: baffle, gag
silent: dumb, inarticulate, inaudible, mute, noiseless, peaceful, quiescent, quiet, still, taciturn, uncommunicative, unspoken
silently: quietly
silhouette: contour, outline, profile
silky: silken, smooth, soft
sill: ledge, projection
silliness: dizziness, folly, frivolity, levity, stupidity
silly: babyish, dizzy, farcical, frivolous, irrational, ridiculous, sheepish, simple, soft, unreasonable, unwise
silo: barn
silt: deposit, ooze, residue, sediment
silver: coin, plate
silvering: foil
silvery: lyric, sweet

silviculture: forestry
simian: monkey
similar: like
similarity: community, comparison, correspondence, kinship, likeness, parallel, parity, relationship
similitude: parity, resemblance, similarity
simmer: seethe
simmering: smouldering
simpering: sentimental
simple: bald, bare, childish, clean, easy, elementary, facile, folksy, homely, humble, innocent, intelligible, lowly, mere, naive, natural, ordinary, painless, plain, primary, primitive, pure, rude, rustic, severe
simpleton: ass, fool, idiot, mug, natural, nincompoop, oaf, sap, zany
simplicity: austerity, clarity, innocence, purity
simplified: facile
simplify: clarify, narrow
simply: barely, but, just, merely, naturally
simulate: assume, copy, fake, imitate, let on, mimic, mirror, put on, sham
simulated: dummy, fake, false, fictitious, imitation, spurious
simulation: assumption, disguise, fake, fiction, imitation, likeness, masquerade
simultaneous: coincidental
simultaneously: meanwhile, together
sin: crime, err, evil, fall, fault, impropriety, misdeed, vice, wrong
since: as, because, now
sincere: candid, cordial, devout, direct, earnest, frank,

genuine, hearty,
honest, open,
profound, real,
serious, simple,
wholehearted
sincerely: directly,
earnest, frankly,
freely, seriously
sincerity: honesty,
integrity, purity
sinew: cartilage,
muscle, nerve
sinewy: athletic,
robust, wiry
sinful: bad, evil,
immoral, unholy, vile,
wicked, wrong
sinfully: badly
sinfulness: evil,
immorality, wrong
sing: chant, intone,
talk
singe: burn, scorch
singer: musician,
voice
singers: choir, chorus
single: individual,
lonely, odd, only,
record, separate,
singular, sole, unique
singular:
characteristic,
curious, different,
distinctive,
exceptional,
idiosyncratic,
individual, novel,
odd, particular,
peculiar, phenomenal,
quaint, queer, quirky,
rare, remarkable,
single, strange,
uncommon, unheard-
of, unusual,
whimsical
singularity:
difference,
distinction, identity,
quirk
singularly: especially,
particularly,
uncommonly
sinister: baleful,
creepy, dark,
forbidding,
frightening, grim, ill,
ominous, portentous,
ugly, uninviting
sink: bath, bury, cave
in, decline,
degenerate, descend,
die, dip, drop, fail,
founder, gravitate,
hole, lower, lurch,
plunge, relapse, sag,
set, settle, slump,

stoop, subside,
swamp, wane
sinker: bob, weight
sinking: dying,
flagging, wane
sinless: immaculate
sinner: backslider,
malefactor, offender
sinter: weld
sinuous: curved, fluid,
labyrinthine,
meandering,
rambling, serpentine,
wandering, winding
sip: drink, drop, lap,
lick, nip, taste
siphon: pipe, pump
sire: father, parent,
procreate
siren: hooter, horn
sissy: chicken
sit: seat
site: block, lay, lie,
locality, locate, lot,
parcel, place, plot,
point, position,
premises, scene, seat,
setting, situation,
spot, venue
siting: fix
sitter: model
sitting: session
situate: locate, place,
put, set, site
situated: found
situation: berth, case,
circumstance,
condition, context,
crisis, development,
engagement, job,
matter, office, pass,
plight, position, post,
posture, predicament,
scene, state, station,
vacancy
sizable: big,
capacious,
considerable,
handsome, hearty,
respectable, roomy,
spacious
size: breadth, bulk,
capacity, content,
denomination,
enormity, fit,
immensity,
magnitude, mass,
measure,
measurement, prime,
quantity
sizzling: baking
skald: poet
skate: glide, plane
skein: flock
skeletal: derelict,
scrawny, skinny, thin

skeleton: chassis,
derelict, frame,
framework, remains,
shell, wreck,
wreckage
sketch: cartoon, chart,
design, draft, draw,
graphic, notes,
outline, paint,
picture, plan, portray,
profile, represent,
scenario, skit, study
sketcher: artist,
painter
sketchily: roughly
sketchy: patchy,
perfunctory, rough,
superficial
skid: slip
skiddy: slippery
skiff: yacht
skilful: capable,
clever, handy,
knowing,
knowledgeable,
learned, neat, perfect,
quick, ready, slick
skilfully: well
skilfulness: neatness,
skill
skill: artifice,
attainment, craft,
dexterity, finesse,
hand, handicraft,
knack, learning,
mastery, prowess,
qualification, science,
technique, touch,
virtuosity,
workmanship
skilled: consummate,
efficient, good, great,
learned, master,
masterly, practical,
practised,
professional,
proficient, skilful
skim: glide, graze,
leaf, plane, run, sail,
slide, sweep
skimp: neglect
skimpy: little,
niggardly, poor,
scanty, thin
skin: bark, coat, crust,
film, jacket, outside,
peel, pelt, rind,
sheath, surface
skinflint: miser
skinny: feeble, gaunt,
lank, lanky, lean,
meagre, scrawny,
thin, underweight
skint: bankrupt, hard
up, penniless
skip: bound, caper,

gambol, hop, jump,
leap, miss, omission,
omit, overlook, pass,
pass over, sidestep
skipper: captain,
master, navigate, sail
skipping: prancing
skirmish: battle,
brush, collision,
combat, contend,
engagement, fight,
scrap, scuffle, struggle
skirt: doll, fringe,
frock, get round, girl,
hug, line, round,
shave
skit: lampoon
skittish: coy, demure
skittle: pin
skive: idle, loaf, shirk,
slack
skiver: layabout
skiving: idle, idleness
skivvy: menial
skulk: cower, creep,
loiter, lurk, prowl,
slope, sneak
skulking: furtive,
stealthy
skull: head
sky: heaven
skyjack: kidnap
skylarking: fun
skyline: horizon
skyscraper: tower
slab: cake, loaf,
plaque, tablet
slack: delinquent,
idle, languid, lax,
limp, loaf, loose, off,
remiss, scrappy,
shirk, slovenly
slacken: decrease,
languish, liberalize,
loose, loosen, lull,
relax, relieve, remit,
slack, subside, yield
slackened: loose
slackening: decrease,
recession, relaxation
slacker: laggard,
layabout
slacking: idleness
slackness: laziness,
neglect, negligence,
sloth
slacks: jeans
slag: bag, spoil, whore
slake: quench, satisfy
slam: bang, knockout,
punch, shut
slander: blacken,
blemish, calumny,
detraction, libel, lie,
lying, mud, smear,
vilification

slanderer: backbiter, liar
slanderous: defamatory, libellous, scandalous
slang: jargon
slanging match: quarrel
slant: bank, bias, cant, colour, descent, distort, fall, gradient, inclination, incline, lean, light, list, load, pitch, rake, side, slope, tip, viewpoint
slanted: loaded, oblique, prejudiced, sideways
slanting: crooked, diagonal, skew
slap: clap, hit, lap, smack, strike
slapstick: comedy, farce
slash: cut, gash, hack, incision, knife, lacerate, laceration, lower, reduce, rent, score, slit, split, wound
slashed: lower
slat: board, leaf
slate: bill, blast, blister, criticize, crucify, lambast, pan, roof, rubbish, slam, tally
slats: blind
slatted: wooden
slattern: slut
slaughter: assassination, bloodshed, butcher, carnage, destruction, kill, killing, massacre, murder, slay
slaughterer: butcher, killer
slaughterhouse: butchery
slave: beaver, captive, hack, labour, menial, work
slave-driver: oppressor
slave merchant: slaver
slavery: servitude, yoke
slavish: hack, obsequious, servile
slay: butcher, kill, murder, slaughter
slayer: butcher, killer
slaying: assassination, bloodshed, killing,

slaughter
sleaziness: squalor
sleazy: fleabitten, seamy, seedy, sordid
sled: sledge
sleek: slick
sleep: bed, flop, nap, repose, rest
sleeping: dormant, honorary
sleeping pill: sedative
sleeping-place: berth, bunk
sleepy: comatose, lethargic, restful, slow, slumbering
sleight: artifice, magic
slender: fine, gangling, lank, lean, remote, scanty, slim, spare, spindly, thin
slew: deflect
slice: bit, carve, cut, dainty, knife, lacerate, pastry, piece, quota
sliced: cut
slicing: incision
slick: facile, glassy, glib, greasy, smooth
slide: bolt, deterioration, float, glide, mount, photograph, shoot, slip
sliding: slide
slight: contempt, cut, discourtesy, faint, feeble, fine, flimsy, fragile, frail, gentle, indignity, insult, light, lightweight, marginal, meagre, minor, offence, offend, outside, petty, rebuff, remote, scorn, sketchy, slender, slim, snub, subtle, superficial, unlikely, weak, wound
slighted: cut
slighter: less
slightest: least, minimum
slighting: scornful
slightly: just, little, rather, somewhat
slim: diet, lank, lean, narrow, outside, reduce, remote, slender, spare, tenuous, thin
slime: dirt, filth, mire, mud, ooze, quagmire
slimy: dirty, filthy, greasy, muddy
sling: cast, catapult,

dash, fling, hurl, pitch, send, throw
slink: creep, lurk
slinking: furtive
slip: cutting, dip, error, fall, fault, form, gaffe, glaze, glide, lapse, mistake, oversight, slide, slope, sneak, steal, strip, stumble, ticket
slippers: footwear
slippery: evasive, glassy, greasy, icy, oily, precarious, scheming, shady, shifty
slippy: icy, slippery
slipshod: careless, jerry-built, lax, remiss, shoddy, slapdash, slovenly
slit: cut, gash, loophole, puncture, slash, slot, split
slither: crawl, creep, slide, slip
slitting: incision
sliver: chip, flake, fraction, fragment, scrap, shred, slice, spill, splinter
slob: pig
slobber: drivel, slaver
slog: beaver, slave, work
slogan: cry, motto, phrase, propaganda
sloop: boat, launch
slop: splash
slope: ascent, bank, cant, climb, decline, descend, descent, dip, fall, grade, gradient, hill, inclination, incline, lean, list, pitch, rake, ramp, slant, slide
sloping: oblique
sloppy: careless, imprecise, inefficient, loose, remiss, romantic, sentimental, slapdash, unbusinesslike
slops: garbage
slot: loophole, niche, opening, pigeonhole
sloth: idleness, inertia, laziness
slothful: idle, lazy, torpid
slouch: loll, lounge, slump, sprawl, stoop
slough: bog, mire, quagmire, shed,

swamp
sloven: slut
slovenly: messy, slapdash
slow: behind, brake, delay, dense, depress, dim, dull, funereal, gentle, gradual, heavy, hold up, laborious, laid-back, late, leisurely, lessen, lethargic, lingering, long, obtuse, pedestrian, simple, sleepy, sluggish, stolid, tardy, thick, unintelligent
slowcoach: laggard, zombie
slowing: flagging
slowly: hard, leisurely
slowness: density, stupidity
sludge: mud
slug: ball, belt, bullet
sluggard: laggard
sluggish: comatose, dull, heavy, inactive, lazy, lethargic, lifeless, phlegmatic, slack, sleepy, slow, stagnant, tardy
sluggishly: heavily
sluggishness: idleness, laziness, sloth
sluice: gate, hatch
slum: hovel
slumber: repose, rest, sleep
slumbering: asleep, dormant, sleepy
slump: depression
slump: dip, dive, drop, fall, flag, loll, lounge, lurch, recession, sink, sprawl, stoop
slumping: flagging
slums: jungle
slur: brand, disgrace, slander, stain
slurp: lick
slush: mud
slushy: muddy
slut: bag, bitch, hussy, whore
sly: calculating, crafty, deceitful, designing, devious, foxy, insidious, politic, scheming, sharp, shrewd, slick, stealthy, subtle, surreptitious, tongue-

in-cheek, underhand, vulpine, wicked, wily
slyboots: fox
smack: bang, bat, blow, clip, cuff, dash, dot, flavour, hit, knock, relish, slap, strike, wallop, yacht
smacker: kiss
small: baby, dwarf, inside, little, low, meagre, niggardly, outside, pygmy, short, slender, slight, stunted
smaller: less, lower
smallest: least, minimum, runt
smallholder: farmer
smallholding: farm
smalls: knickers, underwear
smarmy: fulsome, greasy, ingratiating, slimy, smooth
smart: becoming, burn, chic, clever, cunning, dashing, fine, fly, intelligent, jaunty, natty, neat, pain, prick, sharp, shrewd, spicy, swell
smarting: pain, painful, prickly, simmering, smart, sore
smartish: quickly
smartly: sharply
smartness: neatness, style
smash: blast, cave in, collision, crash, dash, destroy, hit, impact, knockout, mash, pulverize, punch, ruin, shatter, shivers, slam, squash, wreck
smashed: inebriated, kaput, shattered, tight
smashing: destruction, stunning
smatter: smattering
smattering: scattering, snatch, sprinkling, touch
smear: blacken, blur, calumny, coat, foul, grease, libel, mess, muddy, rub, shame, slander, slur, spatter, vilification
smeared: messy
smell: emanation, nose, odour, perfume, scent, whiff, wind
smelly: rancid

smidgeon: handful, jot
smile: beam
smiling: genial
smirk: grimace, leer
smite: strike
smithereen: piece
smithereens: shivers
smithy: forge
smock: blouse, frock
smog: fog, mist
smoke: burn, cigarette, cure, fume, gutter, marijuana
smokescreen: fable
smooch: kiss, pet
smooth: bland, calm, clear, creamy, easy, facile, file, fluent, fluid, glassy, glib, graceful, level, liquid, lubricate, mellow, milky, oily, pacify, plain, plane, plaster, plausible, press, regular, roll, rub, silken, sleek, slick, slippery, soft, still, suave, uniform
smoothe: salve
smoother: plane
smoothly: freely, readily
smoothness: facility, fluency
smother: choke, hush up, kill, quench, repress, stifle, strangle, suppress
smoulder: fume, glow
smudge: blemish, blot, blur, mess, smear, spot
smudged: messy
smug: complacent, priggish, sanctimonious, self-satisfied
smuggle: run, sneak
smut: coarseness, dirt, filth, lewdness, obscenity
smutty: blue, coarse, dirty, filthy, immoral, improper, lewd, obscene, pornographic, salacious, suggestive
snack: bite, meal, nibble, titbit
snaffle: bit
snag: bug, catch, disadvantage, hindrance, hitch, hurdle, obstacle, obstruction, pitfall,

problem, rub, run, stick
snail: laggard
snake: coil, wind, wriggle
snap: bark, break, clasp, crack, flip, fracture, knap, nip, photograph, split, take, vigour, yap
snappily: quickly, cross, fractious, impatient, peevish, peppery, petulant, prickly, waspish
snappishness: impatience
snappy: natty, quick, salty, sharp, smart
snapshot: photograph
snare: catch, hook, mesh, pitfall, trap
snarl: growl, knot, scowl, snap, tangle
snatch: catch, clutch, grab, pinch, pluck, seize, snap, taste, whip
snazzy: natty
sneak: backbiter, cower, creep, leak, nark, prowl, run, skulk, slip, steal
sneaking: furtive, insidious, surreptitious
sneaky: slippery, stealthy, underhand
sneck: catch
sneer: crack, dig, grimace, ridicule, scoff, scorn
sneering: jeering, sarcastic, scornful
sneers: jeering
snib: lock
snick: nick, tip
snicker: giggle, titter
sniff: scent, smell, snort, whiff, wind
sniffle: snivel
snigger: chuckle, giggle, sneer, snort, titter
snip: bargain, crop
sniping: fire
snippet: crumb, shred, snatch
snivel: weep, whimper
snivelling: sob
snobbish: pompous, pretentious, proud, superior, uppish
snog: cuddle, kiss, pet
snood: hood, nose
snooping: inquisitive,

nosy, prying
snooty: condescending, lofty, proud, snobbish, supercilious
snooze: doze, nap, rest, sleep
snoozing: asleep, slumbering
snort: drink
snout: beak, hooter, muzzle, nose
snowball: conglomerate, proliferate
snowslip: avalanche
snowstorm: blizzard
snowy: white, wintry
snub: cut, discourtesy, disregard, offence, offend, ostracize, rebuff, slap, slight
snubbed: cut
snuff: put out
snuffle: snivel
snug: comfortable, cosy, intimate
snuggle: cuddle, huddle
snugness: comfort
so: therefore, thus
soak: bath, bathe, dip, drench, drunkard, flood, immerse, macerate, saturate, steep, water, wet
soaked: bedraggled, sodden, wet
soaking: dip, wet
soap: bath, detergent, lather, scrub
soaping: scrub
soapsuds: lather
soar: ascend, climb, fly, leap, rear, sail, tower
soaring: high, lofty, mountainous
sob: bawl, moan, wail, weep, whimper
sobbing: bawl
sober: conservative, demure, grave, lucid, matter-of-fact, quiet, responsible, sane, solemn, solid, steady, subdued, temperate
soberly: quietly
soberness: sobriety
sobriety: gravity, lucidity, temperance
sobriquet: name, nickname
sociability: fellowship
sociable: easy, folksy,

friendly, outgoing, social

social: common, dance

socialist: left

socialize: mingle

society: circle, civilization, club, community, culture, fellowship, institute, league, lodge, nation, order, population, public

sock: blow, clout, smack

socket: jack, pod, stud

socks: footwear

sod: bastard, devil, earth

sodden: bedraggled, damp, moist, wet

sodomite: gay, homosexual, queer

sofa: couch, seat

soft: babyish, bland, creamy, cuddly, delicate, faint, feminine, fluid, gentle, ladylike, lax, light, limp, liquid, low, mellow, milky, puffy, quiet, slick, smooth, spineless, subdued, sweet, temperate, weak, wet, yielding

soften: blunt, blur, dull, liberalize, loosen, lower, macerate, mellow, melt, mince, mitigate, moderate, mollify, mute, qualify, relieve, remit, smooth, temper

softened: cushioned

softly: gingerly, low, quietly

softness: languor

softy: drip, weakling

soggy: damp, moist, sodden, watery, wet

soil: blacken, defile, dirt, dirty, discolour, dust, earth, foul, ground, land, mess, mould, muddy, pollute, spot, stain

soiled: bedraggled, black, dingy, dirty, foul, messy, tainted

soirée: party, reception

sojourn: residence, stay, stop, visit

solace: relief

solder: cement, fuse, wipe

soldier: man, militant, warrior

soldierly: military

sole: exclusive, foot, only, pad, single, singular, solitary, unique

solecism: discourtesy, gaffe, impropriety, lapse

solecistic: unrepeatable

solely: just, merely

solemn: austere, ceremonial, devout, dignified, earnest, formal, funereal, grave, great, pensive, portentous, sacred, sedate, serious, stately, subdued

solemnities: ceremony

solemnity: austerity, ceremonial, dignity, earnest, formality, gravity, ritual, sanctity, sobriety, splendour

solemnization: celebration

solicit: ask, court, desire, hustle, lobby, petition, proposition, request, sue, whore

solicitant: candidate

solicitation: request, supplication

solicitor: lawyer

solicitous: careful, concerned, jealous, paternal, thoughtful

solicitousness: jealousy

solid: compact, concrete, dense, firm, good, hard, hearty, impenetrable, palpable, physical, precipitate, round, stiff, straight, sure, tangible, tenable, tough, unbroken

solidarity: unity

solidify: cake, coagulate, consolidate, fix, harden, precipitate, set

solidifying: ossification

solidity: body density, firmness

solidly: completely,

hard

solidus: diagonal, oblique

solitariness: loneliness

solitary: desolate, hermit, lonely, odd, private, secluded, sole, withdrawn

solitude: desert, isolation, loneliness, seclusion

Solomon: sage

solution: explanation, insight, key, liquor, lotion, remedy, resolution

solve: crack, do, remedy, resolve, unravel, work out

solvent: detergent, economic, solution, sound

solving: solution

somatic: genetic

sombre: black, bleak, cloudy, dark, dim, dismal, dull, funereal, gloomy, grave, lugubrious, morbid, obscure, sad, sober

some: several, sundry

somebody: one, personage

someone: somebody

sometime: once, previous

sometimes: occasionally

somewhat: passably, pretty, quite, rather, vaguely

somnolent: lethargic, sleepy, soporific, torpid

son: boy, lad

sonde: balloon

song: chant, lay, melody, number

sonorous: loud, resounding, rotund, round

soon: quickly, shortly, then

sooner: before, first, rather

soot: grime

soothe: calm, comfort, compose, lull, massage, mollify, placate, quell, quiet, quieten, relieve, remedy, settle, soften, still

soothing: bland, dreamy, healing,

idyllic, mild, restful, smooth, soft

soothsayer: oracle, prophet, seer

sophistic: specious

sophistical: slick

sophisticated: civilized, cool, experienced, refined, suave, subtle, urbane, worldly

sophistication: civilization, finesse, finish, refinement, style

sophistry: evasion, fallacy, quibble

soporific: boring, hypnotic, monotonous, narcotic, sedative, sleepy

soporose: comatose

sopping: damp, wet

soppy: maudlin, mawkish, wet

soprano: high

sorcerer: magician, wizard

sorcery: magic, spell, witchcraft

sordid: base, bestial, despicable, fleabitten, low, lurid, mean, miserable, scruffy, seamy, seedy, unappetizing

sordidness: misery

sore: gall, hurt, lesion, painful, raw, sharp, tender, ulcer

soreness: discomfort, pain, tenderness

sorority: fellowship

sorrow: dismay, evil, grief, grieve, lament, melancholy, misery, woe

sorrowful: lugubrious, miserable, mournful, sorry, woeful

sorrowfully: regretfully

sorrowfulness: sadness

sorrowing: lamentation, mourning

sorry: ashamed, bad, guilty, ignominious, miserable, penitent, pitiful, poor, remorseful, repentant, rotten, rueful, sad, sorrowful,

woeful, wretched
sort: brand, breed,
character, class,
classify,
denomination, divide,
fashion, form, grade,
group, kind, make,
manner, model,
nature, order,
pattern, place,
quality, range, rank,
run, species, stamp,
style, variety
sorted: assorted
sortie: charge, foray,
raid, sally
sorting: assortment,
division
sot: drunk, drunkard
souk: bazaar, market
soul: body, breast,
fibre, head, heart,
human, individual,
life, psyche, spirit
soulless: dead,
inanimate
sound: bay, blow,
chime, durable, fast,
fathom, genuine,
good, hardy, healthy,
knell, let out, level,
logical, lucid, noise,
peal, practical,
rational, reasonable,
reliable, report, right,
ring, robust, safe,
sane, sensible, sober,
solid, stable, strait(s),
strong, toll,
unbroken, valid,
vigorous, voice,
volume, well, whole,
wind
sounding: peal,
resounding
soundless: noiseless,
quiet, silent
soundlessly: quietly
soundly: heavily
soundness: health,
reason
sour: bad, bitter,
dour, harsh, mean,
poison, querulous,
rancid, rotten,
rugged, sharp, stale
source: base, basis,
beginning, bottom,
cause, cradle,
derivation, fountain,
genesis, head, mint,
oracle, origin, parent,
quarry, quarter, root,
seed, spring, supply,
text, well
soured: embittered

souse: saturate, water,
wet
souvenir: keepsake,
memento, novelty,
reminder, token
sovereign:
autonomous, crown,
independent, king,
lord, monarch, queen,
regal, ruler
sovereignty:
independence,
kingdom, reign, self-
government, sway
sow: broadcast, hog,
implant, pig, plant,
seed
sowing: gardening
sozzled: inebriated,
merry
space: atmosphere,
bay, berth, blank,
capacity, distance,
gap, gulf, hiatus,
interval, jump,
lacuna, latitude,
parenthesis, place,
play, room, scope,
slot, stretch, time,
vacancy, vacuum,
void, wait, way
spaceship: craft
spacious: broad,
capacious, open,
roomy, wide
spade: shovel
span: breadth, bridge,
cross, gauge, length,
life, period, scope,
space, spread, sweep,
team, time, vault,
width
spangle: stud
spank: lick, punish,
slap, smack
spanking: brand-new,
fresh, hiding, licking,
punishment, smart
spanner: key, wrench
spanning: straddling
spar: beam, box, gaff
spare: austere,
auxiliary, crazy, extra,
free, gaunt, lean,
leisure, let off, mad,
odd, other, over, save,
superfluous, surplus,
unwanted, wiry
sparing: frugal,
niggardly,
parsimonious, scanty,
spare
spark: blood, flake,
flash, impulse, magic,
sparkle
sparkle: fire, flash,

glitter, light, lustre,
polish, shine, spirit,
vivacity
sparkler: jewel
sparklers: jewellery
sparkling: bubbly,
cheerful, electric,
gleaming, radiant,
scintillating,
shimmering, shining,
vibrant
sparks: fire
sparring: boxing
sparse: few,
inadequate, lean,
little, low, meagre,
poor, rare, scanty,
short, thin
sparseness: rarity
spartan: ascetic,
austere, harsh, plain,
rough, severe
spasm: attack, cramp,
fit, jerk, kink, quake,
quiver, seizure,
shudder, start,
wriggle
spasmodic: fitful,
flickering,
intermittent, irregular
spate: flood, flow,
rush, spurt
spatter: dabble,
pepper, soil, splash,
spot
spattering: splash
spatula: float
spawn: reproduce
spay: neuter
speak: articulate,
preach, say, talk,
understand, utter
speakeasy: dive
speaker: chairperson,
narrator, orator
speaking: meaning
spear: gore, spike
special: choice,
distinctive,
exceptional,
individual, particular,
pet, specific,
uncommon, unique,
unusual
specialism: discipline
specialist: authority,
connoisseur,
consultant,
counsellor, doctor,
professional,
technical
speciality: discipline,
feature, field, line
specially:
uncommonly
species: breed, class,

kind, sort, variety
specific: certain,
characteristic,
concrete, cure,
dedicated, detailed,
particular, peculiar,
precise, proper,
special
specifically:
especially, exactly,
particularly,
unerringly
specification: clause,
definition, parameter,
prescription,
provision,
requirement,
standard, stipulation
specified: named
specify: cite, define,
detail, fix, formulate,
instance, itemize,
limit, name,
prescribe, provide,
set, spell out, state
specimen:
illustration, pattern,
piece, sample
specious: artificial,
deceptive, hollow,
illegitimate,
meretricious,
misleading, plausible,
pretentious, slick
speciousness:
hypocrisy
speck: dot, hint, jot,
lick, particle, pinch,
point, spot
speckle: speck, stud
speckled: mottled
spectacle: display,
drama, pageant,
scene, show, sight,
spectacular,
splendour, vision,
wonder
spectacular:
meteoric, sensational,
stunning
spectator: witness
spectators: audience,
crowd, gate
spectral: ghastly,
ghostly, shadowy,
supernatural
spectre: ghost,
presence, shade,
shadow, spirit
spectrum: scale
speculate: surmise,
suspect, theorize,
wonder
speculation: bet,
flutter, gamble, guess,
risk, supposition,

surmise, theory, venture
speculative: hypothetical, notional, pure, tentative, uncertain
speculator: bull
speech: diction, gab, language, oration, talk, word
speechless: dumb, inarticulate, mute, overcome, silent
speechlessness: astonishment, silence
speed: barrel, bat, bomb, career, clip, dash, flash, flee, fly, further, gait, gallop, hare, hasten, hurry, lick, pace, pelt, race, rapidity, rate, run, rush, shoot, time, whisk, zap, zip
speedily: fast, promptly, quick, quickly, swiftly
speedometer: clock
speedy: fleet, prompt, quick, rapid, whirlwind
spell: bout, charm, fascination, fit, flurry, glamour, influence, jinx, medicine, period, run, snatch, sorcery, span, stretch, term, time, trance, write
spellbind: entrance, fascinate, mesmerize
spellbinding: hypnotic
spellbound: bewitched, rapt
spells: magic, witchcraft
spend: blow, blue, consume, exhaust, invest, kill, lead, pass, squander, take, use
spendthrift: prodigal, wasteful, wastrel
spent: dead, gone, jaded, limp, prostrate, through, tired, weary, worn
spew: eject, jet, pour, spit, spurt, void, vomit
sphere: ball, bead, bulb, capacity, circle, compass(es), department, field, globe, jurisdiction, kingdom, orb, orbit,

preserve, province, range, realm, region, round, scope, walk, world, zone
spherical: ball, orifice, rotund
spice: bite, flavour, garnish, pepper, season, zest
spicule: needle
spicy: hot, juicy, peppery, piquant, pungent, racy, salty, savoury, strong, suggestive
spiel: pitch, tale
spiffing: wizard
spigot: plug, spill
spike: barb, doctor, gore, impale, needle, paling, pick, pierce, pin, point, spine, stake
spiked: jagged
spiky: jagged, pointed, sharp, thorny, wiry
spill: leak, run, shed, taper, upset
spillage: leak, spill
spilt: upset
spin: corkscrew, dance, drive, flip, jaunt, outing, pivot, reel, revolution, revolve, ride, roll, rotate, screw, throw, weave, wheel, whirl
spindle: axle, hub, pin, pivot, spill
spindling: spindly
spindly: gangling, scrawny, thin
spine: back, backbone, bristle, keel, spike
spineless: cowardly, meek, pusillanimous, weak, wet
spinning: rotary
spinster: maiden, virgin
spiny: prickly, thorny
spiral: coil, corkscrew, curl, loop, wind, winding
spiralled: wound
spire: pinnacle, roof, tower
spirit: atmosphere, daring, fibre, fight, fire, ghost, go, grit, heart, impulse, life, marrow, morale, odour, passion, pluck, presence, psyche, shade, sneak, soul, sparkle, spectre, style,

tone, valour, vigour, vivacity, warmth, zeal, zest, zip
spirited: bold, daring, fiery, game, high-spirited, lively, passionate, piquant, racy, rousing, sanguine, smart, spicy, stirring, vibrant, vigorous, vital, vivacious, zealous
spiritist: medium
spiritless: inanimate, jejune, lackadaisical, languid, listless
spirits: drink, form, humour, liquor
spiritual: celestial, divine, religious, unworldly
spiritualist: medium
spirituality: sanctity
spirochaete: bacterium
spit: hawk, impale, skewer
spite: malice, venom
spiteful: horrid, malevolent, malignant, mischievous, nasty, unkind, venomous, vicious, virulent, waspish, wicked
spitefulness: malice, nastiness, spite
spitting: sizzling
spittle: spit
splash: dabble, drip, fanfare, feature, riot, spatter
splatter: spatter
spleen: attack, chagrin, spite
splendid: breathtaking, brilliant, capital, fine, gallant, glorious, grand, magnificent, noble, proud, rich, spectacular, superb, wizard
splendour: brilliance, glory, lustre, magnificence, majesty, ostentation, state
splice: graft
spliced: married
splint: brace, immobilize
splinter: fracture, fragment, knap, shivers, spill, split

splintering: schism
splinters: shivers
split: breach, break, burst, cleft, crack, cut, diverge, flee, fork, fracture, gulf, knap, open, part, rend, rent, rift, rip, rupture, schism, separate, separation, share, shattered, slit, splinter, ulcer
splitting: divorce
splodge: blot, blur, mark, mess, splash, spot
splodged: marked
splotch: smear
splurge: blot, orgy, splash
splutter: blurt, fizzle out, gabble, rave, spit, stammer
spoil: baby, blemish, blot, corrupt, cripple, damage, dash, deface, dish, harm, impair, indulge, kill, leavings, mar, murder, mutilate, overshadow, pet, queer, ruin, sack, strip, wreck
spoiled: babyish, bad, corrupt, putrid
spoiling: wreck
spoils: haul, loot, pillage, plunder, winnings
spoilt: pampered
spoken: oral, verbal, vocal
spokesman: foreman, representative
spokesperson: mouth, prophet, vessel, voice
sponge: clean, mop, wipe
sponger: drone, leech, parasite, scrounger
sponging: bath
spongy: open, soft, yielding
sponsor: back, benefactor, connection, finance, guarantor, patron, patronize, promote, subsidize
sponsorship: backing, patronage, promotion
spontaneous: automatic, gratuitous, impromptu, instinctive, intuitive,

involuntary, natural, unasked, uninhibited, unprepared, unsolicited, voluntary
spontaneously: freely, impromptu, naturally, unasked
spoof: lampoon, satire
spook: ghost, spirit
spooky: frightening, weird
spool: reel, roll
spoon: scoop
spoonfeed: baby
spoonful: nibble
spoor: scent, track
sporadic: fitful, intermittent, irregular, occasional, rare, spasmodic
sporadically: occasionally
spore: germ, seed
sport: caper, diversion, freak, fun, game, mutation, pastime, play, rogue, variant, wear
sportive: frisky, gay, playful
sportively: gaily
sportscaster: commentator
sportsman: athlete
sportswoman: athlete
sporty: saucy
spot: bind, blot, boil, detect, discover, disfigurement, dot, find, fix, glimpse, hole, jam, lick, little, locality, mark, mess, notice, observe, perceive, place, plight, point, predicament, pustule, random, recognize, resort, scene, see, sight, site, situation, speck, spy, stain, stud, touch
spotless: clean, faultless, immaculate, innocent, pure, white
spotlessness: purity
spotlight: publicize
spotted: dappled, found, marked, pied, speckled
spotting: discovery
spotty: fleabitten, speckled
spouse: consort, husband, man, mate, partner, wife
spout: beak, burst,

eject, fountain, gab, jet, mouth, stream, tap, well
spouting: gushing
sprain: strain, wrench
sprawl: loll, lounge, recline, spread
sprawling: rambling
spray: atomizer, bouquet, bunch dabble, fountain, gun, irrigate, jet, mist, powder, rain, shower, splash, water, wet
spread: breadth, broadcast, cast, circulation, coat, communicate, diffusion, dilation, dinner, disperse, distribution, dot, feast, grow, growth, incidence, increase, multiply, mushroom, plaster, propagation, publish, radiate, reach, repast, roll, rub, run, scale, scatter, slap, span, sprawl, stretch, widen
spreading: contagion, distribution, flare, pervasive, spread
spree: fling, orgy, revel
sprig: runner, shoot, spray, wand
sprightliness: vivacity
sprightly: brisk, cheerful, jaunty, lively, nimble, playful, spirited, spry, vivacious
spring: begin, bound, fountain, gambol, hop, issue, jump, leap, originate, pounce, prime, result, skip, source, sprout, vault, well
springe: snare
springiness: bounce
springy: flexible, resilient, yielding
sprinkle: dabble, dust, irrigate, pepper, powder, punctuate, rain, scatter, shower, splash, spray, sprinkling, water, wet
sprinkler: jet, spray
sprinkling: baptism, handful, scattering
sprint: bolt, burst, dash, flash, flee, fly,

gallop, hare, race, run
sprite: dwarf, fairy, gnome, spirit
sprout: bud, cabbage, germinate, grow, growth, runner, shoot, spear
spruce: crisp, jaunty, natty
spry: brisk, fresh, lively, nippy, quick
spumante: bubbly
spume: foam
spunk: guts
spur: barb, carry, drive, gaff, impel, inspire, limb, needle, prod, prominence, promontory, prompt, spine, stimulate, whip, work up
spurious: artificial, bad, fraudulent, illegitimate, illogical, meretricious, mock, sham, unfounded, untrue
spurn: despise, disdain, flout, rebuff, refuse, reject, renounce, repudiate, scorn
spurt: burst, flash, flow, run, well
spurting: gushing
sputnik: satellite
sputter: gabble
sputtering: sizzling
spy: detect, nark, plant, scout, snoop
spyglass: telescope
spying: espionage, prying
squab: pigeon
squabble: difference, fight, hassle, quarrel, row, spar, wrangle
squabbling: recrimination, strife
squad: crew, detachment, detail, fleet, force, gang, knot, outfit, party, section, team
squaddie: private
squadron: flight
squalid: dirty, fleabitten, foul, lurid, mangy, mean, miserable, scruffy, seamy, seedy, sordid, undesirable
squalidness: squalor
squall: bawl, blast, flurry, gust
squalling: bawl

squally: blustery, boisterous, choppy, dirty
squalor: misery, nastiness
squamous: scaly
squamulose: scaly
squander: blow, blue, consume, lavish, lose, spend, waste
squandered: dissipated, lost, prodigal, spendthrift, wastrel
squandering: loss, waste
square: balance, block, buy, consort, corrupt, court, equalize, equate, fair, flush, immobile, liquidate, pay back, reconcile, rectify, repay, tally
squarely: bang, equally, fairly, right, smack
squash: cordial, crush, deflate, pulp, squeeze, telescope, trample, zucchini
squashed: battered
squashing: battery
squashy: soft
squat: hunch, low, occupation, stoop
squatter: occupant
squawk: croak, quack
squeak: creak, peep, scrape
squeal: creak, shriek, sing, squeak, talk, tell
squeamish: delicate, fussy, mawkish, queasy, spineless
squeamishness: scruple
squeegee: mop
squeeze: bleed, clasp, clinch, cramp, crush, embrace, hug, jam, jostle, knead, nip, pinch, press, push, stuff, thread, wring
squeezing: compression, pressure
squiffy: inebriated
squiggle: scrawl
squiggling: scrawl
squinny: glance, glimpse, peek
squint: glance, glimpse, look
squinting: cross-eyed
squire: page

squirm: creep, thresh, wriggle
squirt: jet, splash, spurt
stab: drive, effort, fling, fork, go, jab, knife, lunge, pang, pierce, prick, shot, spear, stick
stabbing: piercing, sharp
stability: balance, firmness, sanity, solidarity
stabilize: consolidate, shore up
stabilizer: ballast
stable: certain, constant, durable, even, firm, immobile, level, reliable, responsible, solid, sound, steady, sure, temperate
stableboy: groom
stablegirl: groom
stack: bale, bank, bundle, funnel, heap, keep, load, lot, mound, mountain, pile
stacked: loaded
stacks: plenty
staff: cane, crew, following, internal, mace, man, office, personnel, quarter, rod, stick, wand
stag: deer
stage: board, chapter, instance, lap, leg, mount, page, perform, period, phase, platform, podium, point, produce, put on, round, scene, stand, time
stagecraft: drama
stagger: astonish, flabbergast, lurch, reel, rock, roll, shock, stumble, stupefy, wallow
staggered: bemused
staggering: astonishing, groggy, prodigious, sensational, startling, stupendous, tottering, wonder, wonderful
staging: presentation, production
stagnant: moribund, slow, stale
stagnating: moribund

stagnation: depression, slump
stagy: melodramatic
staid: demure
stain: blacken, blemish, blot, colour, dirty, discolour, disfigurement, disgrace, dye, foul, fox, mar, mark, shame, slur, smear, soil, spatter, speck, spot, tint, wash
stained: foul, marked
stainless: clear, immaculate
stair: step
staircase: flight
stake: bar, bet, chance, dare, deposit, fund, gamble, hazard, interest, lay, paling, pawn, peg, post, put on, security, skewer, stick, venture, wager
stakes: pool, pot
stale: banal, barren, boring, close, common, flat, frowsty, insipid, mawkish, musty, rancid, rank, stagnant, tired
stalemate: draw
stalk: follow, hunt, shadow, stem, storm, strut, track
stalker: tail
stalking: prancing
stall: bay, booth, boutique, cell, crib, desk, enclosure, fudge, keep, kill, kiosk, malfunction, obstruct, prevaricate, procrastinate, retard, stable, stand, stop
stalling: stall
stallion: stud
stalwart: hardy, lusty, mighty, muscular, powerful, strong, sturdy
stamina: energy, muscle, resolution, strength, tolerance
stammer: falter, gabble, hum, jerk, mumble, stumble
stammering: faltering, halting, inarticulate, incoherent, stammer
stamp: brand, cast, characterize, complexion, dent,

die, flavour, frank, impress, impression, kind, label, mill, mint, mould, print, punch, quality, school, seal, temperament
stampede: flight
stance: attitude, pose, position, posture, stand, viewpoint
stanchion: brace, buttress, foot, prop, support
stand: base, boutique, brook, carry, cradle, desk, digest, dispose, endure, get up, hold, kiosk, lump, mount, obtain, pedestal, pier, place, put up with, rack, rally, remain, rest, run, side, stick, table, take, tolerate, undergo
standard: average, banner, base, basic, basis, canon, classic, common, conventional, criterion, degree, flag, gauge, level, mean, measure, norm, normal, ordinary, par, popular, prototype, regular, regulation, routine, rule, stock, usual, yardstick
standardized: regular, systematic
standards: ethics, morality
standing: clout, consequence, credit, degree, dignity, erect, estate, footing, importance, level, mark, perpendicular, position, prestige, prominence, quality, rank, reputation, stagnant, station, status
standoffish: cold
standpoint: outlook, position, stance, stand
standstill: halt, rest, stall, stand, stop, stoppage
staple: clip, standard, stock
star: feature, hero, lead, leader, personality, queen, world
starchy: priggish,

prudish, stiff
stardom: fame
stare: gape, gaze, leer, look, look, regard
stark: austere, bald, bare, mere, plain
starkers: nude
starkly: barely
starkness: austerity
stars: fate
start: begin, beginning, develop, found, genesis, get, head, initiate, institute, jar, jerk, jump, kick-off, kindle, launch, onset, open, opening, origin, originate, outset, pick, preliminary, prelude, produce, raise, scare, seed, set about, shy, spark, spring, wince
started: away
starter: beginner
starting: base, basic, incipient, original
startle: astonish, frighten, galvanize, pull up, rouse, scare, surprise
startlement: astonishment
startling: astonishing, frightening, lurid, rude, unexpected
starvation: hunger
starved: hungry, ravenous, starving
starving: hungry, underweight
stash: secrete
stasis: paralysis
state: assert, aver, case, country, declare, diplomatic, domestic, domicile, flap, fret, kingdom, lather, maintain, majesty, nation, national, observe, phase, position, posture, present, profess, public, put, repair, report, say, shape, speak, submit, way
stateliness: dignity, majesty, splendour
stately: august, ceremonial, dignified, funereal, grand, grandiose, lofty, lordly, majestic, palatial, princely, regal, sedate, solemn

statement: brief, comment, communication, declaration, narrative, news, notification, period, profession, remark, report, return, sentence, testimony, word
statements: papers
statesman: diplomat
static: immobile, inanimate, inert, lifeless, motionless
station: base, bay, caste, depot, estate, headquarters, lay, mission, office, park, pitch, place, plant, post, quarter, quarters, rank, situation, standing, stop, terminal
stationary: idle, immobile, motionless, sedentary, static
statistics: data
statuary: monumental, sculpture
statue: bust, image, sculpture
statuette: image
stature: calibre, prestige, reputation
status: caste, class, condition, consequence, degree, dignity, elevation, estate, face, footing, kudos, level, place, position, prestige, quality, rank, situation, standing, station
statute: canon, constitution edict, law, legislation, measure, precept, regulation
statutory: constitutional, judicial, lawful, legitimate
staunch: constant, loyal, resolute, robust, strong, sturdy, unshakable
staunchness: loyalty
stave: staff, stake
stay: be, brace, buttress, cease, delay, dwell, fish, keep, keep on, linger, live, lodge, moratorium, prop, quarter,

remain, residence, respite, rest, sojourn, stand, stick, stop, support, suspend, visit, wait
stays: corset
stead: place
steadfast: determined, dogged, faithful, fast, firm, implicit, loyal, obstinate, permanent, persevering, persistent, resolute, steady, strong, sturdy, tenacious, unhesitating, unshakable
steadfastly: fast
steadfastness: firmness, loyalty, purpose, resolution, resolve, tenacity
steadily: nonstop
steadiness: balance, firmness, sobriety
steady: certain, consistent, constant, date, earnest, even, firm, gradual, immobile, level, nonstop, regular, restrained, sober, stable, sure
steak: cut, cutlet
steal: bargain, creep, crib, kidnap, knock off, liberate, lift, lurk, nab, nick, nobble, palm, pinch, plunder, take, whip
stealing: larceny, robbery
stealthy: furtive, insidious, secret, sly, sneak, surreptitious
steam: boil, jug, press
steamer: hooligan
steamy: humid
steed: mount
steel: harden, knife, nerve, screw
steely: flinty
steep: bath, bathe, bluff, dizzy, drench, expensive, extravagant, high, immerse, macerate, precipitous, saturate, sheer, wash, water, wet
steeping: bath
steeple: pinnacle, roof, tower
steer: beef, bring, calf, conduct, drive,

govern, guide, lead, manoeuvre, navigate, neat, pilot, pull, rein, sail, shepherd,
steering: manipulation
steersman: driver, navigator, pilot
stem: bough, branch, cane, cutting, dam, issue, mop, runner, shaft, spring, stop
stench: odour, smell, stink, whiff
stencil: mould, pattern, plate
stenographer: clerical, secretary
stentorian: deafening, loud
step: dance, degree, gait, grade, hop, ledge, measure, pace, peg, stride, walk
steppe: plain
steps: manner, scale
stereotyped: banal, conventional, hackneyed, ritual, stale, stock
sterile: barren, dead, hygienic, impotent, infertile, lifeless, pure
sterility: impotence, poverty
sterilized: clean, sterile
sterilizer: disinfectant
sterling: genuine, money
stern: ascetic, austere, back, behind, brutal, end, hard, harsh, rear, rigid, rugged, severe, strict, tail, tough
sternness: austerity
stew: ferment, fret, hash, jug
steward: bailiff, factor, lackey, waiter
stewed: drunk
stick: attach, bar, bat, cane, cling, club, crutch, fix, glue, hang, lodge, paste, pole, prod, rod, root, set, spike, stab, stake, switch, tack, wash
sticker: poster
stickiness: bond
sticky: awkward, humid, muggy, oily, sultry, tenacious, tight
stiff: brittle, erect,

firm, frigid, gruelling, hard, high, immobile, lifeless, prim, rigid, rusty, steep, stilted, strained, tight, tough, unbending, unnatural, wiry, wooden
stiffen: erect, fortify, freeze, harden, size, tense, whisk
stiffening: ossification
stiffling: sultry
stiffness: cramp, firmness
stifle: choke, contain, damp, drown, extinguish, gag, kill, muffle, quell, quench, repress, silence, strangle, throttle
stifled: close, muggy, oppressive, pent-up, smothered, stuffy
stigma: brand, disgrace, slur, stain
stigmatized: discredited, tainted
stiletto: knife
still: but, calm, dead, even, halcyon, however, immobile, inanimate, inert, kill, lull, motionless, nevertheless, notwithstanding, peaceful, quiescent, quiet, quieten, silent, stagnant, static, yet
stillbirth: miscarriage
stillness: calm, languor, lull, paralysis, peace, quiet, serenity, silence, still
stilted: brittle, laboured, unnatural, unrealistic
stiltedness: mannerism
stimulant: drug, electrify, foster, get, ginger, heat, impel, inspire, jog, key, kindle, quicken, rouse, spur, tonic, wake, warm, whet
stimulated: warm
stimulating: colourful, cordial, electric, erotic, exciting, interesting, invigorating, lively, moving, piquant, racy, refreshing, rousing, scintillating,

stirring, titillating
stimulation:
excitement, kick
stimulus: bang,
impetus, impulse,
incentive, inspiration,
kick, motivation,
motive, spur,
sting: barb, bite, burn,
hurt, needle, pierce,
prick, shaft, smart,
venom, wound
stinginess: avarice
stinging: biting,
bitter, caustic,
peppery, poignant,
prickly, pungent,
sharp, smart,
venomous, waspish
stingy: avaricious,
close, grasping, hard,
mean, miserly, near,
parsimonious, petty,
tight
stink: odour, smell,
stench, whiff
stinking: foul, smelly,
rank
stint: bout, spell,
stretch
stipend: pay,
payment, remittance,
salary, wage
stipple: dot
stippled: speckled
stipulate: prescribe,
provide, specify
stipulation: clause,
condition, provision,
proviso, restriction
stipulations:
specifications
stir: budge, bustle,
electrify, fire, flurry,
fuss, hum, inspire,
jail, jog, kindle, move,
pique, prison, prod,
rouse, ruffle, send,
sensation, shake,
spark, splash, touch,
wake, wave, whet,
whip, whirl
stirring: electric,
emotive, impassioned,
impressive, lively,
movement, rousing
stitch: cramp, pang
stock: banal, bank,
blood, breed, capital,
carry, common, fund,
furnish, genealogy,
goods, hackneyed,
handle, have, keep,
kin, liquor,
merchandise, mine,
origin, outfit,

pedigree, popular,
provision, race,
reservoir, set,
standard, stem, store,
strain, supply, usual,
vocabulary, wares
stockade: barrier,
fence, fort, paling
stockings: footwear
stockpile: collect,
collection, gather,
hoard, lay in, reserve,
stock, supply
stodgy: stuffy
stoep: balcony
stoic: stoical
stoical:
imperturbable, long-
suffering, patient,
philosophical,
phlegmatic, resigned,
thick-skinned
stoicism: philosophy
stoke: fuel
stole: wrap
stolen: poached
stolid: beefy, bovine,
dense, dull, obtuse,
phlegmatic
stoma: mouth, orifice
stomach: bear, belly,
digest, digestion,
endure, middle, put
up with, stand, stick,
take, tolerate
stomaching: bearing
stomp: stump
stone: bead, gem, nut,
rock, seed
stoned: drunk, high,
inebriated, loaded,
tight
stony: cold, flinty, icy,
rough
stooge: pawn, puppet
stook: bale
stool: seat
stools: waste
stoop: bend, hunch,
incline, lower, sink,
swoop
stooping: bent
stop: block, brake,
break, cease, check,
choke, defeat, delay,
destination, deter,
die, discontinue, dot,
dwell, end, fail, fill,
finish, fix, foil, halt,
hold, immobilize,
inhibit, interrupt,
jam, kill, lapse, lay
off, leave, limit,
lodge, obstruction,
park, plug, prevent,
pull up, quench,

quieten, quit, remain,
remit, rest, seal,
sojourn, stall, stand,
stay, stem, stick,
stifle, tackle, terminal,
terminate, visit, wait,
wind up
stopcock: tap
stopgap: interim,
provisional
stopover: sojourn,
stand, stay, stop
stoppage: block,
breakdown, choke,
delay, hitch,
interlude, paralysis,
pause, stop, strike
stopped: lapsed,
motionless,
prohibited
stopper: cork, plug,
spill, tap
stopping: filling,
killing
store up: stock
store: bank, boutique,
collection, depot,
fund, garner, have,
heap, hoard,
husband, keep, lake,
mine, outlet, pack,
pile, preserve,
reserve, reservoir,
save, savings, stock,
supply, vocabulary,
well
storehouse: barn
storeroom: store
stores: supply
storey: deck, flat,
floor, level
stories: lore
storm: assault, attack,
barrage, blast,
bluster, charge,
frenzy, gale, gust,
hurricane, orgy,
outburst, passion,
rage, rampage, rush,
tantrum, tempest, wet
storminess: fury,
violence
storming: assault
stormy: blustery,
dirty, explosive, foul,
furious, heavy, hot,
passionate, rough,
tempestuous,
unfavourable,
unfriendly, violent
story: description,
fable, falsehood, fib,
fiction, history,
invention, legend, lie,
line, myth, narrative,
news, novel, plot,

recital, report, tale,
yarn
storybook: fairytale
storyteller: liar,
narrator
storytelling: lying
stout: chubby,
corpulent, fat, hardy,
heavy, lusty, obese,
overweight, plump,
robust, rotund, tough
stoutly: manfully
stove: cooker, fire,
oven
stow: pack
strabismal: cross-
eyed
strabismic: cross-
eyed
straddle: bridge,
stride
strafe: bombard,
plaster
straggle: drag, lag,
range, sprawl, stray,
wander
straggler: laggard
straggling: lank,
maundering,
rambling
straggly: bedraggled
straight: bang, direct,
directly, full, honest,
neat, perpendicular,
pure, regular, short,
smack, square,
upright
straightaway: right
straighten: dress,
unravel
straightforward:
blunt, candid, direct,
elementary,
forthright, frank,
obvious, outright,
plain, robust, round,
sensible, simple,
sincere, transparent
straightforwardly:
directly, frankly,
freely
**straightforward-
ness:** honesty,
simplicity, sincerity
strain: blood, burden,
chorus, drain, effort,
filter, kind, labour,
manner, melody,
overwork, press,
pressure, pull, sieve,
stress, strive,
struggle, suspicion,
sweat, tax, tension,
variety, vein, weight,
wrench
strained: contrived,

drawn, frayed,
intense, laboured,
overloaded, taut,
tense, unnatural
strainer: filter, sieve
strait: channel,
juncture
straiten: narrow
straitened: difficult,
poor
straitjacket: restraint
straitlaced: austere,
prim, prudish,
puritanical
straits: bottleneck,
crisis
stramash:
disturbance, scrum
strand: beach, coast,
desert, fibre, hair,
line, lock, maroon,
rope, string, thread,
wreck, yarn
stranded: becalmed
strange: bizarre,
curious, exceptional,
fishy, foreign, funny,
grotesque,
interesting, kinky,
memorable,
mysterious, novel,
odd, peculiar, quaint,
queer, screwy,
singular, uncommon,
unfamiliar, unknown,
unnatural, unusual,
weird
strangely:
uncommonly
strangeness:
eccentricity, novelty,
oddity
stranger: foreigner,
outsider
strangle: choke, stifle,
throttle
strangled: smothered
strangulate: strangle,
throttle
strap: band, bind,
brace, curb, leash,
scourge, sling, tab,
whip
strapping: beefy,
burly, hiding, lusty,
meaty, mighty,
muscular, powerful,
robust, stout, strong,
tough
stratagem: artifice,
blind, deception,
device, dodge, finesse,
game, gimmick,
intrigue, machination,
manoeuvre, ploy,
scheme, shift, tactic

strategic: martial,
tactical
strategist: tactician
strategy: device,
move, plan,
procedure, scheme,
tactic
strath: valley
stratified:
voluminous
stratify: bed
stratigraphy: terrain
stratum: bed, belt,
course, horizon, layer,
level, plane, seam,
sphere, vein
stray: depart, deviate,
digress, diverge, gad,
ramble, range, roam,
swerve, wander
straying: departure
streak: band, blur,
flash, line, shaft, vein,
zap, zip
stream: beam, brook,
course, current, drift,
flow, funnel, jet,
pour, river, run,
swarm, tide, wave,
well
streamer: pennant
streaming: gushing
streamline:
rationalize, simplify
street: avenue, lane,
road, way
streetwalker:
prostitute, whore
streetwalking:
prostitution
strength: beef, brawn,
capacity, depth,
energy, firmness,
force, kick, main,
manliness, muscle,
potency, power, tone,
vigour, violence,
virtue, wallop, zap
strengthen: augment,
back, comfort,
confirm, consolidate,
feed, fortify, gird,
harden, intensify,
raise, recruit,
reinforce, support
strengthening:
backing, cordial,
fortification
strenuous: busy,
difficult, hard, killing,
laborious, murderous,
punishing, rugged,
tough, uphill,
vigorous, warm
strenuously: hard
strenuousness:

difficulty
stress: beat, burden,
care, effort,
emphasize, fatigue,
highlight, overwork,
press, pressure,
pronounce,
punctuate, rack,
strain, tax, tension,
tone, underline, voice
stressed: pronounced,
taut
stressful: nerve-
racking, tense
stretch: belt, bird,
crane, distance, grow,
length, lengthen, pad
out, patch, period,
plot, prolong, pull,
rack, range, reach,
run, sheet, span,
spell, spread, strain,
string, sweep, tract,
widen
stretched: long, taut,
tense, tenuous, tight
stretcher: litter
stretching:
enlargement,
expansive, growth,
pull, traction
strew: disperse, litter,
scatter
striated: striped
stricken: hunted
strict: austere, brutal,
conscientious, dour,
hard, harsh,
merciless, precise,
punctilious,
puritanical, rigid,
scrupulous, set,
severe, spartan, stern,
stiff, tight,
unbending,
uncharitable
strictly: literally
strictness: austerity,
discipline, precision
stricture: censure
strictures: criticism
stride: gait, pace, step,
walk
strident: harsh, loud,
noisy, vocal,
vociferous
stridulant: strident
strife: competition,
conflict, discord,
faction, feud, riot,
storm, struggle, war
strike: assault, attack,
awe, bang, bat, beat,
bump, chime, clout,
club, dawn, dawn on,
deliver, drive, get,

hammer, hit, impact,
impinge, knap, knock
lay on, mint,
overtake, paste,
pierce, plant, pull,
punch, rap, shell,
splash, switch, touch,
zap
striking: awesome,
bizarre, bold,
dramatic, effective,
fine, impressive,
marked, memorable,
notable, noticeable,
out, outstanding,
percussion,
prodigious,
prominent,
pronounced,
remarkable, salient,
spectacular, stunning
strikingly: notably
strim: mow
string: chain, cord,
lace, leash, line,
queue, range, row,
run, series, sling,
stable, strand, thread,
yarn
stringent: rigid,
severe, spartan, stiff,
strict, tight
stringer: journalist
strip: band, bar, bare,
belt, deprive, divest,
panel, pillage, pull,
rape, rip, rob, shear,
tape, undress
stripe: band, bar, lash,
line, tab, vein
stripling: boy, youth
stripped: bare, nude
stripping: rape
stripy: striped
strive: compete,
contend, contest,
labour, seek, strain,
struggle
stroke: brush, caress,
drive, feat, feel,
fondle, hit, knead,
lash, line, massage,
move, pat, piece, pull,
rub, sweep, swing,
switch, touch
stroll: constitutional,
jaunt, loiter,
promenade, ramble,
range, roam, saunter,
walk
strong: athletic, beefy,
burly, cogent,
decisive, durable,
fierce, firm, great,
hard, hard-hitting,
heady, healthy,

hearty, living, lusty, macho, main, mighty, muscular, potent, powerful, pronounced, pungent, racy, resilient, rich, robust, solid, stiff, strenuous, thick, tough, vigorous, violent, virile, vivid, warm
strongbox: chest, safe
stronger: better
stronghold: bastion, castle, fort, keep, lair
strongly: hard, mightily
strongroom: vault
strop: whet
structural: elemental, organic
structure: building, complex, composition, construction, form, framework, habit, make-up, method, network, organization, organize, pile, rack, shell, skeleton, system, texture, tissue
structured: organic
structuring: organization
struggle: battle, combat, compete, conflict, contend, contest, effort, fight, flounder, handful, limp, scramble, scuffle, strain, strive, war
strum: pluck
strumpet: whore
strut: boom, keel, posture
struts: frame
strutting: jaunty, prancing
stub: tally
stubble: beard
stubbly: hairy
stubborn: dour, fractious, headstrong, intransigent, obdurate, obstinate, opinionated, persistent, perverse, pig-headed, positive, recalcitrant, refractory, resolute, tenacious, tough, wayward, wilful
stubbornness: resolution, tenacity

stucco: plaster
stuck: puzzled, tight
stud: boss, button, dot, farm, knob, stable
student: beginner, pupil, scholar, trainee
studfarm: stud
studied: deliberate
studies: course
studious: attentive, bookish, thoughtful
study: composition, consider, deliberation, den, eye, garret, grind, investigate, learn, lesson, look, look into, observation, observe, paper, preparation, profile, read, reading, research, review, revise, scrutiny, search, study, survey, take
stuff: belongings, bolt, compact, fatten, feast, fill, gear, glut, gorge, jam, line, load, luggage, pack, pad, plug, substance, surfeit, wolf
stuffed:loaded,satiated
stuffing: filling, guzzling, padding
stuffy: close, frowsty, fuddy-duddy, priggish, prudish, square, sultry
stultifying: boring
stumble: blunder, falter, flounder, founder, light, lurch, reel, stammer, wallow
stumbling: halting, maundering, tottering
stump: baffle, dock, floor, get, log, perplex, puzzle
stumped: puzzled
stun: astonish, flabbergast, knock, shock, stagger, stupefy, surprise
stunned: bemused, bewildered, dazed, numb, silly, unconscious
stunner: beauty
stunning: astonishing, beautiful, devastating, gorgeous, knockout, lovely, ravishing, spectacular, striking, stupendous

stunt: caper, dwarf, gimmick, wheeze
stunted: dwarf, low, pygmy
stupefaction: astonishment, narcosis
stupefied: bemused, silly
stupefy: fuddle, shock, stagger
stupefying: narcotic
stupendous: sensational, wonder, wonderful
stupid: asinine, bovine, dense, dim, foolish, idiotic, inane, oafish, obtuse, senseless, silly, slow, thick, unintelligent, unwise
stupidity: density, folly, idiocy, inanity, lunacy
stupor: comatose, narcosis, shock, trance
stupport: rock
sturdiness: firmness, strength
sturdy: burly, firm, hardy, healthy, lusty, powerful, robust, rugged, solid, sound, stout, strong, tough
stutter: falter, gabble, hum, jerk, mumble, stammer, stumble
stuttering: faltering, halting, inarticulate, incoherent
sty: enclosure, pen
stygian: black, infernal
style: bond, call, cast, christen, creation, cut, dash, date, denomination, designate, fashion, flair, form, grace, kind, language, make, manner, model, mould, name, nature, panache, pattern, phraseology, polish, refinement, sort, state, strain, tailor, term, touch, version, vogue, way
styled: named
stylish: artistic, chic, dashing, fashionable, fine, jaunty, natty, neat, pert, sharp, smart, swell, up to

date
stylishly: sharply
stylishness: neatness, style
stylus: needle
stymie: frustrate
suave: bland, glib, laid-back, smooth, urbane
subaltern: subordinate
subconscious: mind, psychological
subcontractor: farmer
subdivide: partition
subdivision: branch, compartment
subdivisions: ramifications
subdue: bow, break, conquer, control, crush, humble, lower, lull, master, overcome, overthrow, quash, quell, quieten, reduce, repress, silence, soften, suppress
subdued: delicate, faint, low, quiet, resigned, sober, soft
subeditor: journalist
subhuman: inhuman
subject: guinea-pig, head, host, issue, item, lesson, liable, matter, model, motion, national, question, subordinate, substance, term, text, theme, thing, under, underneath
subjection: conquest, domination
subjugate: conquer, enslave, master, mortify, oppress, overthrow, repress, subordinate
subjugated: captive, subject
subjugation: mortification, occupation, overthrow, repression, servitude
subjugator: conqueror, oppressor
sublime: celestial, heavenly, idyllic, lofty, perfect, poetic, seraphic, splendid
subliminal: unconscious
sublimity: perfection

submerge: cover, dive, drown, duck, flood, immerse, inundate, lower, overflow, plunge, sink, steep, swamp
submerged: sunken
submersion: flood
submission: capitulation, entry, motion, obedience, surrender, testimony
submissive: deferential, easy, facile, manageable, meek, obedient, passive, resigned, reverent, spineless, yielding
submissiveness: obedience
submit: capitulate, cave in, comply, enter, kowtow, lodge, nominate, obey, offer, present, propose, put, put up, render, return, subject, succumb, support, surrender, tender, yield
subnormal: defective, imperfect
suborbinate: assistant, inferior, junior, less, lesser, lower, minister, minor, petty, satellite, second, secondary, subject, under
suborn: bribe, corrupt, nobble
subornation: bribery
subpoena: cite
subscription: contribution
subsequent: below, following, future, later, next, unborn
subsequently: behind, consequently, later, next, since, then
subservience: humility, obedience
subservient: base, humble, menial, obedient, subordinate
subsidary: inferior
subside: cave in, collapse, decrease, descend, die, dip, founder, lull, quench, recede, settle, sink, wane
subsidence: collapse, decrease

subsidiary: auxiliary, branch, side, subordinate
subsiding: lull, wane
subsidize: back, set up, support
subsidizer: benefactor
subsidizing: backing
subsidy: grant
subsist: be, live, survive
subsistence: diet, keep, living, meat, support, sustenance, upkeep
subsisting: living
subspecies: variety
substance: basis, being, body, content, fat, form, import, importance, kernel, marrow, mass, material, matter, meaning, means, meat, sense, spirit, stuff, wealth, weight
substandard: inferior, off, rotten, weak
substantial: big, capacious, concrete, considerable, dense, durable, filling, good, hearty, large, monolithic, much, palpable, respectable, round, solid, sound, strong, tangible, thick, weighty
substantially: mainly, materially, well
substantiate: back up, bear out, confirm, prove, support
substantiation: backing, confirmation, proof
substitute: auxiliary, change, deputy, dummy, false, proxy, replace, switch, temporary, understudy
substitution: change, switch
substratum: bed
substructure: chassis
subterfuge: bluff, camouflage, craft, deception, evasion, quibble, scheme, trap
subterranean: infernal, underground
subtle: astute, crafty,

cunning, delicate, diplomatic, imperceptible, insidious, nice, profound, refined, searching, sharp, sophisticated, subdued, tactful, underdone
subtleties: minutiae
subtlety: craft, delicacy, finesse, nicety, quibble, refinement
subtly: sharply
subtract: deduct, knock off, take
subtracting: deduction, less
suburban: local
suburbs: outskirts, periphery
subversion: disloyal, rebellious, revolutionary, sabotage, sedition
subvert: corrupt, mine, pervert, sabotage
subway: underground
succeed: bloom, follow, get on, make out, prosper, replace, win
succeeding: consecutive, following, later, next, second
success: bomb, fortune, hit, knockout, palm, prosperity, victory, win
successful: gold(en), happy, thriving, victorious, winning
successfully: happily
succession: chain, course, dynasty, line, procession, queue, rash, sequence, series, string, train, whirl
successive: consecutive, following, later
successors: descendants, offspring, seed
succinct: brief, crisp, curt, laconic
succour: assistance, comfort, help, relief, relieve, support, strength
succulent: juicy, luscious, lush, rich,

tasty
succumb: capitulate, submit, sink, surrender
suck: pull
sucker: fool, mark, mug, pigeon, pushover, runner, shoot, victim
sudden: meteoric, precipitate, quick, rude, sharp, snap, spastic, unexpected
suddenly: bang, quickly, sharply, short
suds: lather
sudsy: frothy
sue: press, prosecute
suffer: bear, endure, experience, go through, have, languish, stand for, stomach, support, sustain, tolerate, undergo
sufferance: patience, tolerance
sufferer: casualty, loser, patient, victim
suffering: distress, evil, hardship, ill, miserable, misery, pain, patient, torture, woe
suffice: content, do, last, pass, satisfy, serve
sufficient: commensurate, competent, due, enough, satisfactory
sufficiently: enough, fully
suffix: particle
suffocate: choke, stifle
suffocated: smothered
suffocating: close, oppressive, stuffy
suffocation: choke
suffrage: franchise, vote
suffuse: blush, charge, fill, flame, flush, penetrate, saturate, steep
suffused: red
suffusion: blush, wash
sugarless: dry
sugary: sweet
suggest: hint, imply, indicate, intimate, make out, mean, move, offer, postulate, present, promise, propose,

raise, recommend, say, signify, spell, submit, venture, vote
suggestibility: trance
suggestible: impressionable, susceptible
suggestion: breath, connotation, dash, flavour, ghost, hint, hypothesis, idea, indication, innuendo, invitation, lead, meaning, move, nominee, nuance, offer, overtone, proposal, shade, shadow, sign, smack, strain, suspicion, tip, touch, whisper, wind
suggestions: counsel
suggestive: bawdy, juicy, obscene, provocative, racy, reminiscent, sexy, significant, titillating
suggestiveness: obscenity
suicidal: desperate
suicidally: desperately
suit: become, befit, case, fit, litigation, match, offer, outfit, petition, please, process, reconcile, request, serve, square, supplication, uniform
suitability: convenience, fit, fitness, propriety
suitable: becoming, compatible, competent, convenient, favourable, fine, fit, fitting, just, likely, meet, pertinent, proper, right, ripe
suitably: happily, right, well
suitcase: case
suitcases: luggage
suite: battery, court, following, train
suited: suitable
suitor: gallant, lover, sweetheart
sulk: mope, pout
sulkiness: mood, sullenness
sulks: hump, sullenness
sulky: bitter, black, dark, dour, gig,

grudging, ill-humoured, moody, peevish, petulant, taciturn
sullen: black, cross, dark, dour, grim, ill-humoured, moody, perverse, sulky, surly, taciturn
sullied: tainted
sully: disgrace, dull, mar, pollute, smear, stain
sulphur: yellow
sultry: hot, humid, muggy
sum: count, damage, figure, mass, number, quantity, total, whole
summarize: brief, condense, digest, outline, paraphrase, recapitulate
summary: brief, concise, curt, digest, memo, outline, report, return, scenario, short, speedy, succinct, synopsis
summit: ceiling, climax, crown, head, height, high, maximum, mountain, peak, pinnacle, point, zenith
summon: call, carpet, challenge, cite, invite, knell, rally, recall, sue
summons: brief, call, prosecute, recall
sumptuous: florid, gorgeous, grand, lush, luxurious, magnificent, ornate, palatial, plush, rich, splendid
sumptuousness: luxury, magnificence
sun: light, star, world
sunburn: tan
sunder: divide, divorce, rip
sundering: divorce
sundown: nightfall
sundry: assorted, diverse, many, miscellaneous, multiple, odd, several, various
sung: vocal
sunken: cavernous, hollow, low
sunlit: sunny
sunny: bright, buoyant, carefree,

cheerful, clear, fair, fairytale, fine, gay, good, happy, light, light-hearted, rosy
sunrise: dawn
sunset: nightfall
sunshade: awning, light, warmth
sunup: dawn
sup: drink, lap
super: bumper, enjoyable, fantastic, wonder, wonderful
superabundance: embarrassment, glut
superabundant: luxuriant
superannuation: pension
superb: capital, consummate, fantastic, first-class, gifted, glorious, magnificent, perfect, rare, rich, sensational, splendid, stupendous, terrific, wonder, wonderful
supercilious: cavalier, condescending, lofty, lordly, overbearing, proud, scornful, superior, unrepentant
superciliousness: disdain
superficial: facile, hasty, light, outer, outward, passing, perfunctory, plastic, shallow, sketchy, slight, surface, thin, topical
superficially: outwardly
superfluity: glut, profusion, surfeit, surplus
superfluous: extra, intrusive, lavish, needless, otiose
superfluously: unduly
superhuman: inhuman
superintend: direct, manage, officiate, watch
superintendent: caretaker, chief, foreman, keeper, warden
superintending: direction
superior: better, choice, exalted, high,

leader, leading, lofty, lord, major, matchless, mother, overbearing, preferable, prevalent, prime, select, senior, superb
superiority: disdain, perfection, priority, quality
superlative: first-class, optimum, outstanding, peerless, rare, supreme, ultimate
supermarket: store
supernal: heavenly
supernatural: celestial, ghostly, magic, miraculous, mystical, paranormal, psychic
supernumerary: superfluous
supersede: follow, replace, supplant
superstar: celebrity, hero, idol
superstition: myth
superstitious: mythical
supervise: command, conduct, control, look after, manage, monitor, police, preside over, regulate, run, superintend, watch
supervision: care, command, control, direction, jurisdiction, management, oversight, regulation, scrutiny, upkeep
supervisor: boss, director, foreman, gaffer, monitor, overseer, superior
supinated: supine
supine: flat, listless, prone
supper: dinner
supplant: replace, supersede
supple: flexible, green, limber, lithe, pliable, resilient, soft, spry
supplement: complement, reinforce
supplementary: auxiliary, extra, fresh, further, more, new, optional, ornamental,

other, plus,
subordinate
supplicant: beggar
supplicate: conjure,
invoke, petition, pray,
press, request, solicit,
sue
supplication: call,
cry, petition, plea,
prayer, request
supplier: buyer
supplies: gear,
groceries,
wherewithal
supply: cater, deliver,
delivery, dispense,
feed, fill, find,
furnish, give, invest,
kit, lay on, nourish,
outfit, prepare,
produce, production,
provision, put up,
recruit, render,
reserve, reservoir, rig,
serve, service, stock,
store, yield
supplying: issue,
provision
support: assist,
assistance, back, back
up, backbone,
backing, base, bear,
bear out, befriend,
blessing, block,
bolster, boost, brace,
buttress, carry,
champion, comfort,
consolation, cradle,
crutch, cup, defend,
favour, finance,
fortify, forward,
found, frame, fuel,
hand, help, hold, hold
up, keep, keep up,
leg, lift, livelihood,
living, maintenance,
patronage, patronize,
pedestal, pier, pile,
pillar, post, promote,
promotion, prop,
protect, reassurance,
reinforce, relief,
relieve, rest, sanction,
second, shore up,
side, stake, stand,
stand by, steady,
stick, strut, stud,
subsidize, sustain,
uphold
supportable:
tolerable
supporter: assistant,
benefactor, conquest,
fan, follower,
partisan, second,
support

supporters:
following, lobby,
public
suppose: assume,
believe, conceive,
conclude, fancy,
figure, judge, let,
postulate, presume,
reckon, say, surmise,
suspect, think,
understand
supposed:
hypothetical,
imaginary, nominal,
nonexistent,
ostensible, putative,
titular
supposedly:
reputedly
supposing: if
supposition:
assumption, guess,
hypothesis, idea,
opinion,
presumption,
presupposition,
surmise, suspicion,
theory, understanding
supposition: bet
suppress: ban, censor,
choke, crush, curb,
extinguish, gag, hide,
hush up, kill, muffle,
muzzle, oppress,
overthrow, quash,
quell, repress, silence,
stifle, strangle,
withhold
suppressed: muffled,
pent-up, smothered,
unconscious
suppression:
blackout, censorship,
killing, overthrow,
repression, restraint
suppurate: discharge,
flow, weep
suppuration:
discharge, flow
supremacy:
authority,
domination,
leadership, mastery,
power, prerogative,
priority, reign, rule,
victory
supreme: best, chief,
grand, ideal,
overriding,
paramount, pre-
eminent,
predominant, ruling,
sovereign, ultimate
supremely: best
supremo: king
surcharge: kickback

sure: assured, certain,
clear, confident, dead,
definite, foolproof,
known, positive, safe,
secure, stable
surely: presumably,
probably,
undoubtedly, yes
surety: bail, bond,
earnest, guarantor,
ransom, security
surf: beach, wash
surface: board,
counter, crust,
exterior, external,
face, fleece, floor,
horizon, jacket,
outside, outward,
plane, rise, sheet,
side, table, texture,
veneer
surfaced: paved
surfeit: congestion,
embarrassment, glut,
overindulgence,
satisfy, surplus
surfeited: blasé,
jaded, satiated
surge: burst, course,
crowd, crush, flood,
flow, gust, heave,
increase, jump, leap,
outburst, rage, sally,
sea, splash, spurt,
swell, wallow, wash,
wave, well
surgery: clinic
surly: cross, peevish,
perverse, rugged,
short, taciturn, ugly,
unfriendly
surmise: assume,
assumption, fancy,
gather, guess,
imagine, infer,
inference,
presumption, reckon,
say, speculate,
suppose, suspect,
suspicion, think
surmount: conquer,
hurdle, overcome,
pass, scale, weather
surpass: beat, best,
cap, lead, lick, outdo,
pass, transcend
surpassing: superior,
supreme
surplus:
embarrassment, extra,
glut, margin, odd,
over, overflow,
profusion, redundant,
remainder, residue,
rest, spare,
superfluous,

unnecessary,
unwanted
surprise: catch,
confound, jump,
rock, stagger,
unexpected, waylay
surprising: marked,
startling, uncommon,
unexpected, unusual
surprisingly: even,
uncommonly
surrender: capitulate,
capitulation,
concession, delivery,
fall, forfeit, give,
kowtow, leave, lose,
quit, relinquish,
render, resign,
sacrifice, submit,
succumb, yield
surrendering: forfeit
surreptitious:
furtive, insidious,
stealthy
surrey: jingle
surrogate: proxy,
substitute
surround: bank,
bathe, besiege, circle,
circumscribe, frame,
gird, girdle, hedge,
invest, line, mob,
neighbour, ring, wall,
wrap
surrounded:
wreathed
surrounding:
background,
roundabout
surroundings:
atmosphere,
background,
environment, setting
surveillance:
observation,
oversight,
supervision, watch
survey: canvass,
inspect, look, poll,
profile, reconnoitre,
review, scan, study,
view, watch
survival: vital
survive: be, continue,
endure, keep, last,
linger, live, manage,
overcome, remain,
weather
surviving: bereaved,
lingering
susceptibility:
liability
susceptible: capable,
gullible,
impressionable,
liable, predisposed,

prone, responsive, subject, vulnerable
suspect: distrust, doubt, doubtful, implausible, mistrust, shaky, think
suspected: marked
suspend: cut off, defer, delay, discontinue, dissolve, freeze, hang, interrupt, poise, postpone, quit, remit, stay, stop, string, supersede, swing
suspended: pendulous, withdrawn
suspense: tension
suspension: delay, dissolution, liquor, moratorium, paste, pause, respite, solution
suspicion: breath, clue, distrust, doubt, feeling, hint, hunch, idea, ill feeling, jealousy, misgiving, suggestion, vestige
suspicious: disbelieving, doubtful, fishy, funny, implausible, interesting, jaundiced, jealous, queer, screwy, shady, unsure, unusual
suspiciously: askance
sustain: bear, buttress, carry, cherish, continue, have, hold, hold up, keep, keep up, maintain, nourish, nurture, perpetuate, preserve, prop, receive, relieve, stand, suffer, support, uphold
sustained: constant, long, relentless, straight
sustaining: maintenance, nourishing, nutritious
sustenance: bread, fare, food, nourishment, relief, support
susurrate: whisper
susurration: whisper
suture: join, junction, seam, union, unite
svelte: suave
swab: mop, wipe

swag: haul, loot, plunder, prize
swagger: bluster, conceit, posture, roll, show off, strut
swaggering: cocky, flamboyant, jaunty, prancing, vain
swallow: credit, devour, draught, drink, eat, endure, gulp, pull, put up with, repress, take, taste, tolerate
swallowing: guzzling, voracious
swami: master
swamp: bog, drown, fen, flat, flood, overflow, overrun, quagmire
swampy: muddy
swap: bargain, barter, change, reciprocate, render, substitute, switch
swapping: barter
sward: grass
swarm: cloud, crowd, flight, herd, horde, multitude, pour, press, scrum, seethe
swarming: crowded, packed, thick
swarms: score
swart: black
swarthy: dark, dusky
swashbuckling: dashing
swat: bat, whisk
swathe: bandage, bind, envelop, festoon, muffle, strip, wrap
swathed: shrouded
sway: bend, command, convince, dance, hold, influence, jurisdiction, lobby, power, pressure, reel, reign, rock, roll, rule, run, say, stagger, swing, waver
swayed: prejudiced
swear: avow, curse, testify, vow
swearing: imprecation
swearword: oath
sweat: grease, lather, perspire, secrete, work
sweater: cardigan, jersey, woolly
sweaty: moist

sweep: blow, breadth, breeze, brush, clean, comb, flourish, lash, paddle, pan, rake, range, sail, scan, spread, swoop, whisk, width
sweeping: broad, comprehensive, exhaustive, general, open, radical, wide, widespread
sweepings: garbage, waste
sweepstake: lottery
sweet: cherubic, dainty, delicacy, dessert, duck, fetching, liquid, lovable, lovely, luscious, lyric, mellow, rich, winning
sweeten: mellow
sweetheart: darling, dear, flame, inamorata, love, lover
sweetness: fragrance
swell: augment, bag, balloon, blister, blow up, bulge, distend, grow, heave, inflate, rise, sea, surge, wash, wave, wax
swelling: blister, bulb, bulge, bump, dilation, enlargement, gall, growth, hump, knob, knot, lump, node, nodule, prominence, proud
swelter: perspire
sweltering: baking, hot, sticky
swerve: bend, deflect, dodge, jink, sheer, shift, shy
swift: fast, fleet, precipitate, prompt, quick, rapid, speedy, sudden, swallow, whirlwind
swiftly: fast, quick, quickly
swiftness: speed
swig: draught, drink, gulp, pull
swigging: guzzling
swill: gulp, swallow
swilling: guzzling
swim: bathe, dip, spin
swimsuit: bathing costume
swindle: cheat, deceive, deception, do, fiddle, fleece, fraud, have, outwit,

racket, ramp, rob, robbery, screw, spoof, take, take in, victimize
swindler: bandit, charlatan, crook, fraud, quack, rogue, thief
swindling: deception, fraudulent
swine: hog, jerk, pig
swing: brandish, dance, dangle, flap, fluctuate, hang, lash, lunge, oscillate, rock, roll, seesaw, sling, suspend, sway, sweep, swerve, switch, tolerance, wave, wheel, work
swinging: flap
swipe: hit, lunge, take
swirl: churn, corkscrew, lash, maelstrom, reel, surge, whirl
swish: flourish, switch, whisper
switch: handle, lever, rotate, shift, substitute, swap, transposition, whip
switchboard: panel
swivel: pivot, roll, rotate, wheel
swollen: bloated, protuberant, puffy
swoon: blackout, dive, faint, plunge, pounce
swordsman: blade
sworn: dedicated
swotting: study
sybaritic: luxurious
sycophancy: flattery
sycophant: creep, lackey, satellite, yes-man
sycophantic: fulsome, ingratiating, obsequious, slavish, slimy
syllabus: programme
sylph: sprite
sylphlike: slender, slim
symbol: attribute, brand, character, cipher, icon, letter, mark, note, sign, token
symbolic: metaphorical, mystical, nominal, representative
symbolize: personify, represent, signify,

stand for
symbols: notation,
notes, writing
symmetrical:
graceful, regular
symmetrically:
equally
symmetry:
composition, order
sympathetic: benign,
charitable, friendly,
humane, kind, kindly,
receptive, responsive,
soft, soft-hearted,
sorry, tender,
understanding,
warm-hearted
sympathetically:
kindly
sympathies:
understanding
sympathy:
communion,
compassion, feeling,
harmony, heart,

humanity, identity,
kindliness, kindness,
pity, regard,
tenderness
symphonic:
harmonious, musical
symposium:
conference, garland,
omnibus
symptom: indication,
manifestation
symptomatic:
characteristic,
demonstrative
synagogue: church
synchronization:
coordination
synchronize:
coincide, phase, set
synchronous:
coincidental,
contemporary,
simultaneous
syncope: faint
syndicate:

association,
combination,
company, federation,
organization, pool,
ring
syndicated: federal
syndication:
federation
syndrome: symptom
synod: council
synonymous: same
synopsis: brief,
digest, outline,
scenario, summary
syntax: diction,
phraseology, usage
synthesis: blend,
composite, union
synthesize: blend,
combine
synthesized:
composite
synthetic: artificial,
false, imitation,
plastic, sham

syringe: gun, inject,
pump, scour
syrupy: sickly, sweet
system: complex,
form, frame, grid,
language, machine,
maze, mechanism,
method, network,
pattern, scheme,
technique, theory,
tissue, way
systematic:
businesslike,
methodical, neat,
orderly, organic,
regular
systematization:
system
systematize: classify,
regulate
systematized:
systematic

T

ta: thanks
tab: flag, flap, label, ticket
tabbing: flagging
tabby: cat, mottled
table: block, board, chart, counter, profile, roll
tableau: scene
tablecloths: linen
tableland: plain, plateau
tablet: capsule, medicine, painkiller, pill, plaque
tableware: china
tabloid: paper
taboo: fetish, forbidden, restraint, unmentionable
tabulate: list, table
tabulation: list, parameter, table
tachycardia: palpitation
tacit: implicit, silent
taciturn: close, reticent, silent, uncommunicative, withdrawn
taciturnity: reserve, silence
tack: fasten, fix, glue, harness, nail, pin, tenacity, turn
tackiness: bond
tackle: down, gear, hoist, kit, rig, set about, stuff, take, take on, trip, undertake
tacky: sticky
tact: consideration, finesse
tactful: considerate, delicate, diplomatic, discreet, politic
tactic: artifice, game, machination, manoeuvre, ploy
tactics: scheme
tactile: tangible
tactless: gauche, indiscreet, unhappy, unthinking
tactlessness: indiscretion
tag: identify, label,

mark, phrase, tab, ticket
tagged: marked
tail: back, dog, pursue, rear, shadow, spy, stern, track
tailback: jam, queue
tailor: square, style
taint: blacken, blemish, brand, colour, defile, infect, mar, poison, pollute, spot, stain
tainted: corrupt
take-off: ascent, imitation, lampoon, skit
take: bag, bear, bring, brook, carry, catch, choose, endure, fetch, film, gain, get, gross, have, hold, liberate, lift, move, nick, nobble, obtain, opt for, pocket, put up with, receive, require, seat, seize, stand, stick, stomach, tolerate, transport, walk, wheel, withstand
taken: occupied
takeover: assumption, conquest, coup, grab, hijack, occupation, requisition, seizure
taking: fetching, sweet, winning
takings: haul, pay, proceeds, profit, receipt, return, revenue, winnings, yield
talc: powder
tale: fable, fiction, legend, narrative, novel, recital, story, yarn
talent: attainment, brilliance, calibre, faculty, flair, genius, gift, knack, promise, skill, turn
talented: clever, gifted, promising, resourceful
tales: lore

talisman: charm, fetish
talk: articulate, chat, conversation, debate, discussion, gab, interview, jaw, lecture, mouth, natter, preach, rumour, speech, tête-à-tête, word
talkative: expansive, garrulous, voluble
talkativeness: jaw
talker: orator
talking-to: lecture, sermon
talking: hubbub
talks: discussion, truce
tall: gangling, high, lanky, lofty
tallness: height
tally: balance, bill, canvass, coincide, consort, correspond, count, equate, fit, list, log, poll, reckon, reconcile, score, square, suit, sum, tab
talon: claw
tambour: drum
tame: break, domesticate, familiar, feeble, gentle, govern, half-hearted, insipid, master, meek, moderate, pet, unimaginative
tamp: ram
tamper: cook, corrupt, doctor, falsify, fiddle, juggle, monkey, rig
tan: brown, whip
tang: flavour, relish, taste, zest
tangible: bodily, concrete, material, palpable, physical
tangle: confuse, confusion, jumble, jungle, kink, knot, mat, maze, mesh, mop, perplex, twine, wilderness
tangled: complex, intricate, involved,

messy, muddled, rough, twisted
tangy: piquant, poignant, racy, salty, savoury, spicy
tank: reservoir, vat, vessel
tankard: jar, jug, mug
tanned: brown
tannin: tan
tanning: hiding, punishment
tantalization: temptation
tantalize: tempt
tantalizing: provocative
tantamount: equivalent
tantrum: fireworks, outburst, pet, scene, temper
tap: broach, bug, drain, hit, knap, massage, milk, pat, rap, smack, touch
tape: band, fastener, film, fix, measure, record
taper: disappear, flag, go off, light, peter out, point, tail, thin, wane
tapering: batter, disappearance, flagging, pointed, wane
taproom: bar
tapster: drawer
tar: sailor
tardily: late
tardy: late, remiss, slack, slow
tare: weed
target: bull, design, destination, focus, goal, intention, joke, mark, object, objective, prey, purpose, reason, victim, zero
tariff: rate, rent, tax, toll
tarn: lake, pool
tarnish: blacken, blemish, blot, dim, discolour, dull, mar,

rust, smear, soil, spot, stain
tarnished: dim, dirty, dusty, tainted
tarpaulin: canvas
tarred: paved
tarry: delay, lag, oily, saunter, sojourn, stay, stop, wait
tart: bitch, bitter, curt, dainty, hussy, keen, pastry, piquant, prostitute, pungent, sour, whore
tartar: dragon, nag, plaque
task: assignment, chore, commission, concern, duty, exercise, function, job, labour, mission, onus, part, project, role, saddle, work
taskforce: labour
tassel: fringe
taste: culture, delicacy, drop, experience, flavour, fondness, grace, hint, judgement, leaning, lick, liking, little, nibble, nip, penchant, pinch, predilection, refinement, relish, sample, sense, sensibility, sip, smack, stomach, style, zest
tasteful: artistic
tasteless: barbaric, dilute, flashy, insipid, loud, unseemly, vulgar
tastelessness: vulgarity
tasty: dainty, delicious, mean, palatable, piquant, racy, rich, savoury
tatter: rag, shred
tattered: frayed, moth-eaten, ragged, worn, worn out
tatting: lace
tattle: gossip
tattoo: drum
tatty: cheap, shabby, shoddy
taunt: barrack, dig, heckle, mock, ridicule, scoff
taunting: jeering, ridicule, sarcastic
taunts: jeering, teasing
taut: brittle, drawn,

explosive, stiff, tense, tight
tauten: tense
tautness: tension
tautological: redundant
tautology: repetition
tavern: bar, inn, local, pub, saloon
tawdriness: vulgarity
tawdry: vulgar
tawny: auburn, brown
tax: assess, challenge, duty, imposition, levy, rate, saddle, strain, toll, weary
taxed: weary
taxi: cab, coast
taxicab: cab
taxing: difficult, gruelling, heavy, laborious, onerous, punishing, rugged, strenuous, uphill, wearing, weighty
taxonomy: nomenclature
tea-chest: crate
tea: brew, dinner
teach: bring up, demonstrate, drill, educate, ground, impart, indoctrinate, instruct, lecture, take
teacher: instructor, master
teaching: education, instruction, lesson
teachings: lore
teacup: cup
team: bunch, crew, fleet, gang, outfit, party, people, pool, section, side, squad, staff
teamwork: cooperation
tear: bite, break, career, fly, gash, hole, lacerate, laceration, part, pelt, perforate, race, rack, rampage, rend, rent, rip, run, scratch, shoot, shred, slit, snag, speed, split, sweep, ulcer, whip, wrench, zip
tearaway: hooligan, hothead
tearful: lachrymose, maudlin, sad, sentimental, watery
tearing: biting
tearoom: café
tears: water
tease: badger, banter,

comb, flirt, have on, jest, joke, jolly, kid, plague, rag, tantalize, taunt, tempt, wind up, worry
teased: ragged
teasing: banter, flirtation, fun, jocular
teat: breast, dummy
teazle: comb
technicality: detail
technician: engineer, worker
technique: execution, hang, knack, mechanism, method, recipe, science, style, system, touch, way, wrinkle
technologist: engineer
tedious: boring, deadly, dismal, dry, dull, interminable, jejune, lengthy, monotonous, painful, pedestrian, ponderous, routine, slow, trying, wearisome
tediousness: boredom
tedium: boredom
teem: flow, rain, seethe
teeming: crowded, fertile, lush, luxuriant, pregnant, prodigal, prolific, thick
teenager: kid, youngster, youth
teenagers: youth
teens: youth
teepee: lodge
teeter: seesaw, waver
teetering: tottering
teetotal: dry, temperate
teetotalism: temperance
telecast: transmit
telegram: cable
telekinetic: psychic
telepathic: psychic
telepathy: projection
telephone: buzz
televise: broadcast, transmit
tell: blow, break, describe, discern, disclose, grass, inform, instruct, knoll, know, leak, narrate, notify, prime, recite, relate, report, reveal, rumour, say,

speak, spin, weigh
teller: cashier
telling: effective, expressive, forceful, graphic, influential, pregnant, recital, revelation, strong, vivid
telling-off: lecture, rebuke, row, scolding
telltale: leak, sneak
temerarious: daring, immodest
temerity: daring, nerve
temp: substitute
temper: blood, climate, cool, dilute, frame, grain, harden, humour, mitigate, mood, nature, overshadow, personality, qualify, season, spirit, strain, tantrum, tone, vein, weaken, wrath
temperament: blood, character, constitution, heart, make-up, mentality, nature, part, personality, spirit
temperamental: moody, quick-tempered, variable
temperance: sobriety
temperate: bland, gentle, good-natured, mild, moderate, restrained, sober, soft
temperateness: mildness
temperature: climate, heat, warmth
tempered: dilute
tempest: gale, hurricane, storm
tempestuous: blustery, boisterous, choppy, fierce, furious, heavy, passionate, rough, stormy, violent, wild
tempestuousness: fury
template: design, die, form, jack, mould, pattern
temple: basilica, church, sanctuary
tempo: movement, pace, rhythm, time
temporal: mortal, mundane, physical, profane, secular, worldly

temporary: caretaker, fugitive, interim, irregular, provisional, substitute
tempt: draw, invite, lure, seduce, tantalize
temptation: bait, invitation, lure
tempting: beckoning, desirable, inviting, seductive
tenable: plausible, reasonable
tenacious: determined, dogged, intransigent, obstinate, persevering, persistent, possessive, resolute, sticky, strong, stubborn
tenacity: backbone, grit, purpose, resolution
tenancy: lease, occupation, residence,
tenant: inhabitant, lessee, lodger, occupant, resident
tend: attend, bear, conspire, contribute, cradle, cultivate, farm, guard, keep, lean, look after, mother, nourish, nurse, nurture, treat
tended: cultivated
tendency: bent, climate, current, habit, inclination, leaning, liability, liking, movement, run, strain, tide
tendentious: invidious, partisan
tender-hearted: warm-hearted
tender: bid, enter, feminine, fluid, gentle, green, kind, kindly, lush, lyric, mild, offer, present, proposal, propose, quotation, quote, raw, render, romantic, sensitive, sentimental, soft, soft-hearted, sore, submit, sweet, vulnerable, warm, womanly
tenderly: kindly
tenderness: bruise, compassion, kindliness, kindness, languor, love,

mildness, sentiment, warmth
tending: liable, prone
tendon: muscle, nerve
tendril: runner
tenebrous: dusky, shadowy
tenet: belief, persuasion, principle, rule
tenets: philosophy, teachings
tenor: drift, purport, sound, spirit, style, tone, vein
tense: brittle, dramatic, electric, explosive, hunch, jumpy, nervous, overwrought, simmering, stiff, strained, taut, thin-skinned, tight, unsettled, uptight, wound up
tensed: motionless
tensile: flexible
tension: friction, frustration, nervousness, strain, stress, suspense, weight
tent-door: fly
tent-peg: skewer
tentative: cautious, faltering, noncommittal, provisional, speculative, undecided
tents: camp
tenuous: fine
tenure: lease, occupation, possession
tepid: lukewarm
term: call, christen, course, designate, duration, interval, length, life, name, period, phrase, season, session, spell, stipulation, style, time, word
termagant: bitch, dragon, harridan, nag, scold
termed: named
terminal: fatal, incurable, last, morbid, mortal, pole, ultimate
terminate: bound, close, determine, discontinue, dissolve, end, finish, halt, kill,

knock off, lapse, lift, liquidate, result, stop, wind up
terminated: lapsed
terminating: final, last
termination: boundary, catastrophe, dissolution, end, finish, halt, killing, last, limit, result
terminology: language, nomenclature, phraseology, vocabulary
terminus: end, limit, stop, terminal
terms: condition, proposal
terrace: promenade, street
terracotta: ceramics
terrain: country, land, lie
terrible: atrocious, awful, dreadful, fearful, fell, frightful, grim, grisly, gruesome, hideous, painful, woeful
terribly: very
terrific: great, wonder, wonderful
terrifically: very
terrified: overawed, overcome, petrified
terrify: frighten, intimidate, scare
terrifying: dread, formidable, frightening, ghastly, hair-raising, nerve-racking
territory: colony, country, field, grounds, haunt, kingdom, land, part, possession, property, province, quarter, realm, region, sphere
terror-stricken: petrified
terror: fear, fright, phobia, scare, scourge
terrorist: insurgent, militant, subversive
terrorize: bully, intimidate, menace, scare, scourge, terrify
terse: brief, brusque, compact, concise, crisp, curt, laconic, short, succinct
terseness: asperity

test: challenge, check, essay, feel, ordeal, probe, quiz, sample, screen, sound, tempt, trial
testament: will
tester: canopy, monitor
testicle: ball, nut
testificatory: incriminatory
testifier: witness
testify: attest, certify, declare, protest, swear, witness
testimonial: reference
testimony: authority, demonstration, profession, proof, record, witness
testy: cantankerous, cross, ill-humoured, liverish, peevish, querulous, quick-tempered, surly, waspish
tetchy: liverish
tether: chain, knot, leash, rope, shackle, stake
text: lyric, matter, narrative, passage, script, words
textbook: manual
textile: cloth, fabric, stuff
texture: fabric, fibre, finish, substance, tissue
thallophyte: fungus
thankful: grateful, obliged
thankfulness: gratitude
thanks: credit, gratitude
thanksgiving: blessing, grace
thatch: mop, roof
thaumaturge: wizard
thaumaturgic: miraculous
thaumaturgy: miracle
thaw: dissolve, melt, warm
theatre: auditorium, floor, gaff, stage, terrain
theatrical: dramatic, flamboyant, melodramatic
theatricality: panache
theft: burglary,

larceny, robbery
thematic: topical
theme: melody,
message, motion,
point, strain, subject,
substance, text, thing
theologian: divine,
doctor
theological:
dogmatic, religious
theology: faith
theorem: maxim
theoretical:
hypothetical, ideal,
imaginary, nominal,
notional, possible,
pure, speculative,
tentative, titular
theorize: postulate,
speculate, wonder
theory: assumption,
fancy, guess,
hypothesis, idea,
opinion,
presupposition,
rationale, scheme,
supposition, system,
thesis
theosophy: faith
therapeutic: healing,
medicinal
therapist: counsellor
therapy: medicine,
treatment
thereafter: later,
next, then
therefore:
consequently, hence,
so, thus
thereupon: next
thesis: dissertation,
paper, principle,
theme
thick: bovine, broad,
close, compact, dense,
dim, dull, gross,
heavy, impenetrable,
oafish, obtuse, simple,
slow, teeming, tough,
turbid, unintelligent,
wide
thicken: bulk, cake,
coagulate, condense,
consolidate, fix,
gather, set
thickening: bulge
thicket: brake, brush,
bush, forest, hedge,
jungle
thickness: density,
gauge, layer, width
thicko: dunce
thief: bandit, crook
thieve: palm, steal,
whip
thievery: larceny

thimbleful: sip
thin: degrade, dilute,
feeble, fine, flimsy,
haggard, jejune, lank,
lanky, lean, light,
meagre, narrow, pale,
pinched, rarefy,
scanty, scrawny,
sheer, skinny,
slender, slim, spindly,
tenuous, unhealthy,
water, watery, weak,
weaken
thing: fixation,
hang-up, infatuation,
item, matter, object,
obsession, phobia
things: belongings,
gear, goods, luggage
think: assume,
believe, brood, call,
cipher, cogitate, coin,
conceive, concoct,
consider, count,
deliberate, devise,
dream, fancy, feel,
figure, hatch, hold,
imagine, invent,
judge, manufacture,
meditate, mint, muse,
plan, presume,
reason, reckon,
reflect, regard,
remember, review,
see, suppose, suspect,
understand, weigh,
wonder
thinker: intellectual,
mind
thinking: intelligent,
motive, philosophy,
rational, reasoning
third-world: non-
aligned,
underprivileged
thirst-quenching:
refreshing
thirst: craving,
longing, lust, want,
yearn, yearning
thirsty: parched
thong: lace, leash,
whip
thorax: chest, trunk
thorn: barb, bristle
thorny: awkward,
difficult, hard,
prickly, scabrous,
sticky, tight, tough
thorough: clean,
close, complete,
comprehensive,
congenital,
conscientious,
detailed, elaborate,
exhaustive, full,

intimate, meticulous,
outright, painstaking,
particular, positive,
radical, right,
rigorous, searching,
total
thoroughbred:
pedigree
thoroughfare:
avenue, passage, road,
street
thoroughgoing:
radical, revolutionary,
sweeping
thoroughly:
backwards,
completely. full, fully,
heavily, hollow, out,
outright, right,
utterly, well, wholly
though: as, if,
notwithstanding
thought-provoking:
interesting
thought: conceit,
consideration,
deliberation, fancy,
heed, idea, logic,
notion, observation,
philosophy,
reasoning, regard,
remark, sentence,
surmise, thing
thoughtful: attentive,
careful, considerate,
contemplative,
judicious, kind,
kindly, meditative,
profound, serious,
solemn, studious,
wistful
thoughtfully: kindly
thoughtfulness:
attention,
consideration,
gravity, kindliness,
kindness, sympathy
thoughtless: careless,
hasty, heedless,
inadvertent,
inconsiderate, loose,
rash, reckless, remiss,
scatterbrained,
tactless, unguarded,
unthinking
thoughtlessness:
levity, negligence
thoughts: content,
mind, opinion
thousands: many,
myriad
thraldom: servitude,
slavery
thrall: yes-man
thrash: beat, belt,
birch, cane, cudgel,

defeat, demolish, do,
flail, flog, flounder,
function, hammer,
jacket, lace, lambast,
lash, lather, lay on,
leather, lick, maul,
party, paste, rave,
rout, scourge, tan,
thresh, whip
thrashing: debacle
[débâcle], defeat,
drubbing, hiding,
licking, rout
thread: fibre, hair,
lace, line, plot, screw,
strand, string, tap,
twine, yarn
threadbare: feeble,
frayed, hackneyed,
moth-eaten, ragged,
worn, worn out
threat: danger,
imminence, lever,
menace, warning
threaten: brew,
frighten, intimidate,
loom, menace,
overhang
threatened: marked
threatening: black,
dangerous, dark,
frightening, grave,
grim, impending,
lurid, near, ominous,
overcast, sinister,
thunderous, ugly,
warning
threnody: lament
thresh: flail, flap,
flounder, kick
thresher: flail
threshing: flap
threshold: brink,
verge
thrift: economy,
prudence
thriftless: wasteful
thrifty: careful,
frugal, sparing
thrill: bang, buzz,
electrify, excitement,
gratify, kick, pierce,
send, sensation, stir,
treat, vibrate
thrilled: happy,
jubilant, overjoyed,
pleased
thrilling:
breathtaking,
dramatic, electric,
exciting, heady,
sensational, stirring,
vibrant
thrive: bloom, boom,
flourish, flower, live,
prosper, succeed

thriving: luxuriant, successful
throat: swallow
throaty: hoarse, thick
throb: beat, drum, hurt, pain, pulse, quake, smart, vibrate
throbbing: painful, palpitation, pulse, vibrant
throne: chair
throng: assembly, besiege, cloud, congregate, crowd, crush, flock, herd, horde, jam, jostle, mass, mill, mob, multitude, number, pack, pour, press, rabble, scrum, swarm
throttle: choke, gun, strangle
through: by, direct, long, on, trunk
throughout: during, round, through
throw: bowl, cast, dash, deliver, fall, fling, floor, heave, hurl, launch, loose, pass, pitch, pot, precipitate, project, put, send, shed, sky, slam, sling
thrown: disconcerted
thrum: hum, pluck
thrust: bear, bundle, burn, cast, clap, dig, hit, hustle, impact, impulse, jab, lunge, meaning, momentum, nudge, pass, poke, propel, propulsion, push, ram, sally, shaft, shove, squeeze, stab, strike
thud: bang, bounce, crash
thug: barbarian, brute, bully, hooligan, rough, ruffian, yob
thuggery: violence
thuggish: violent
thumb: leaf
thumbnail: brief
thump: assault, bang, belt, blow, bounce, box, bump, clip, clout, crack, crown, cudgel, hit, knock, percussion, punch, slam, strike, stroke, wallop
thunder: bang, beat, bellow, crash,

fulminate, rave, roar, roll, storm
thunderflash: bolt
thunderous: deafening, loud
thus: consequently, therefore
thwack: blow, clap, hit
thwart: baffle, cheat, check, cross, dash, defeat, defy, disappoint, dish, foil, fox, frustrate, hamstring, nip, obstruct, prevent, resist, scotch, spike, traverse
thwarted: disconcerted
thwarting: frustration
tiara: crown, jewellery
tic: flutter, jerk, quiver, tremor, twitch
tick: click, minute, run, second, work
ticket: fare, label
tickling: awkward, delicate, difficult, itch, thorny, tight, tingling
tiddly: merry
tiddlywink: counter
tide: current, flood, flow, run, sea, water
tidiness: neatness, news, order, rumour
tidy: clean, clear, considerable, crisp, efficient, groom, methodical, neat, nice, orderly, pack up, respectable, straight, taut, trim
tie: attach, bind, bond, buckle, bundle, connection, cord, dock, draw, equal, fasten, fix, hitch, join, knit, knot, lace, lash, leash, link, reconcile, rope, secure, seize, shackle, stake, strap, tape, tether, yoke
tied: bound, even, kin, occupied, pushed
tier: bank, floor, row
tiff: quarrel, row, wrangle
tigerish: fierce
tight: avaricious, close, drunk, fast, hard, mean, miserly, narrow, near, secure, stiff, taut, tenacious, tense

tighten: contract, key, knot, narrow, purse, screw, strain, stretch, take in, tense
tightfisted: grasping, parsimonious
tight-lipped: evasive, reticent, severe, taciturn, uncommunicative
tightly: fast, hard
tightness: avarice, tension
tightwad: miser
tigress: bitch
tile: roof
till: cultivate, dig, farm, work, yet
tillage: culture
tilled: cultivated
tiller: helm
tilt: bank, cant, incline, lean, list, pitch, rhythm, slant, slope, tip
tilted: oblique
tilting: lopsided
timber: beam, board, wood, wooden
timbre: quality, tone, voice
time: beat, bird, bout, clock, course, date, day, duration, generation, instance, instant, interval, juncture, length, life, moment, opportunity, page, patch, period, phase, point, rate, rhythm, schedule, slot, space, spell, stretch, temporal, term, turn, while
timed: temporal
timeless: immortal
timely: fortunate, happy, helpful, opportune, prompt, punctual, ripe, salutary
timepiece: clock, watch
timetable: programme, schedule
timid: bashful, cowardly, faint, faltering, fearful, hesitant, mousy, self-effacing, shy, tentative, yellow
timidity: diffidence, fear, shyness
timidly: gingerly
timorous: bashful, cowardly, faint,

fearful, pusillanimous, retiring, self-effacing, sheepish
timorousness: diffidence
tin: can
tincellant: bubbly
tincture: colour, preparation, restorative
tinder: fuel, kindling
tine: barb, fork, needle, point
tines: teeth
tinge: cast, colour, flavour, hint, nuance, smack, stain, suspicion, tint, touch
tingle: glow, itch, prick, smart
tingling: itch, prickly
tiniest: least
tinker: gypsy, mess, tamper, vagrant
tinkle: jangle, jingle
tinkling: jangle, jingle
tinsel: decoration, glitter, ostentation
tint: colour, dye, paint, shade, stain, tone
tintinnabulate: jangle, jingle
tintinnabulation: jangle, jingle
tiny: baby, dwarf, imperceptible, little, marginal, microscopic, midget, minimal, minute, small, stunted
tip: bank, beak, box, capsize, caution, clue, consideration, end, favourite, filter, gift, glance, gratuity, head, hint, horn, incline, lean, list, peak, warning
tipple: drink, fuddle
tipster: prophet
tipsy: high, inebriated, maudlin
tiptoe: steal
tiptop: first-class
tirade: diatribe, onslaught
tire: bore, exhaust, falter, fatigue, flag, prostrate, run down, strain, wear, weary
tired: banal, hackneyed, jaded, sick, spent, weary, worn, worn out

tiredness: exhaustion, fatigue, overwork
tireless: determined, persistent
tiresome: boring, difficult, dull, routine, trying
tiresomeness: boredom
tiring: faltering, flagging, killing, wearing
tissue: film, flesh, napkin, sheath
tit: breast
titanic: giant, massive
titbit: dainty, delicacy, nibble
titch: midget, pygmy, runt, weakling
tithe: levy
titian: red
titillate: turn on
titillating: erotic, fruity, provocative, raunchy, sexy, suggestive
titivate: touch up
titivation: toilet
title-holder: proprietor
title: deed, denomination, handle, heading, honour, monopoly, name, nomenclature, patent, possession, term
titled: noble
titter: chuckle, giggle, laugh
tittering: laughter
tittle-tattle: gossip
titular: honorary, nominal
tizzy: flap, state
to: towards
to-do: bother, commotion, dust, kerfuffle, performance, scene, stir
toadstool: fungus, mushroom
toady: crawl, creep, flatter, lackey, sycophant, yes-man
toadying: flattery, grovelling, ingratiating, obsequious, slimy
toast: bumper, celebrate, grill, pledge, wet
toastmaster:

chairperson
toboggan: sledge
toddle: stroll
toddler: child, infant, tot
toddy: flip
toe: digit, kick
toehold: purchase
toes: foot
toffee-nosed: condescending, snobbish, supercilious
toga: gown
togetherness: communion, companionship
toggle: pin
toil: difficulty, industry, labour, slave, strive, struggle, work, wrestle
toilet: bog, head, lavatory, pot
toilette: toilet
toils: mesh
toilsome: laborious
token: counter, favour, figurehead, forerunner, herald, index, indication, keepsake, mark, memento, minimal, nominal, note, signal, souvenir, symbol, talisman, vestige
tolerable: digestible, middling, moderate, okay, respectable
tolerably: fairly, passably
tolerance: patience
tolerant: broad-minded, easy, indulgent, lenient, liberal, long-suffering, patient, permissive, understanding
tolerate: bear, brook, digest, endure, have, live, permit, put up with, stand, stand for, stick, stomach, submit, support, take, withstand
toleration: bearing, humanity
toll: chime, duty, fee, fine, imposition, knell, levy, peal, price, rate, ring, tax
tolling: knell, peal
tom: male
tomb: grave, vault
tombola: lottery

tome: book, volume
tommy: private
tone: atmosphere, buzz, cast, drone, flavour, hum, manner, pitch, quality, shade, sound, spirit, strain, style, tint, vein, voice, whine
toneless: neutral
tones: notes
tongs: forceps
tongue: language, lick, speech
tongue-in-cheek: facetious, jocular
tongue-lashing: rebuke, scolding
tongue-tied: dumb, silent
tonic: prime, restorative
tonnage: cargo, weight
tonnish: fashionable
too: beside, besides, moreover
tool: device, gadget, implement, instrument, kit, lackey, machine, material, pawn, thing
tools: gear, kit
toothed: jagged
toothsome: palatable, savoury, sweet, tasty
top: back, best, better, cap, ceiling, climb, counter, cover, crater, crown, face, first, head, height, hood, lid, maximum, optimum, peak, premier, primary, prominent, roof, seal, successful, summit, supreme, surface, surpass, tip, zenith
tope: drink, tipple
topic: business, head, item, motion, question, subject, text, theme, thing
topical: latest, live, local, new, witty
topknot: bob
topping: sauce
topple: fall, keel, overthrow, overturn, pitch
toppled: upset
toppling: tottering
topside: outside
topsy-turvy: chaotic
tor: hill

torch: lamp, light
torment: bait, bedevil, crucify, curse, distress, harass, hell, ordeal, pain, persecute, rack, scourge, torture
torn: mangled, ragged
tornado: storm, whirlwind
torpid: callous, comatose, heavy, inactive, languid, lazy, lethargic, lifeless, listless, sleepy, sluggish
torpor: idleness, inertia, narcosis, numbness, sloth
torque: bent, tension, traction
torrent: barrage, cataract, flood, rain, shower, stream
torrid: baking, dry, hot
torridity: heat
torso: body, trunk
tortuous: complex, crooked, curved, intricate, labyrinthine, meandering, rambling, serpentine, twisted, wandering, winding
torture: crucify, murder, rack
torturer: butcher, fiend
tory: conservative, right
tosh: bunk, drivel, rot, cast, catapult, fling, flip, heave, hurl, pitch, put, rock, roll, shovel, sling, throw, tumble
tossing: roll
tot: belt, child, drink, figure, infant, kid, nip, peg, snort, total
total: balance, cast, clean, complement, complete, consummate, count, dead, equal, finding, general, great, implicit, make, number, outright, overall, pure, quantity, rank, reckon, score, sheer, sum, thorough, unconditional, unqualified,

unshakable, utter,
whole, write off
totalitarian:
dictatorial
totalitarianism:
tyranny
totality: breadth,
complement,
integrity, mass, whole
totalled: made,
numbered
totally: bodily,
completely, fully,
hollow, quite, right,
unreservedly, utterly,
wholly
tote: juggle
totter: lurch, paddle,
reel, shake, stagger,
waver
tottering: ramshackle,
shaky
touch: brush, dash,
disturb, feel, finger,
flavour, graze, handle,
hit, impinge, involve,
join, kiss, knack, lick,
little, meet, move,
pat, penetrate, reach,
smack, splash, stir,
suspicion, tap
touched: crazy,
lunatic, mad, queer
touching: concerning,
emotive, heart-
rending, moving,
pathetic, poignant,
tender
touchpaper: fuse
touchstone: criterion,
gauge, measure,
yardstick
touchy: delicate,
fractious, moody,
peevish, peppery,
prickly, querulous,
quick, quick-
tempered, sensitive,
short-tempered, thin-
skinned, warm,
waspish
tough: demanding,
durable, hard, hard-
hitting, hardy,
insensitive, macho,
resilient, rigorous,
robust, rough,
rugged, severe, stiff,
stout, strenuous,
strong, thorny, yob
toughen: harden,
reinforce, season,
weather
toughly: roughly
toughness: manliness,
strength

tour: clock, do,
explore, jaunt,
journey, lap, lionize,
passage, trip, visit
tourists: visitors
tournament:
competition, contest,
game
tourney: tournament
tousle: ruffle
tousled: dishevelled,
rough, wild
tout: hawk, splash
tow: drag, draw, haul,
heave, pull
towelling: flannel
tower: bastion,
battlements, castle,
fortification, keep,
lookout, rear, soar
tower above:
dominate,
overshadow
towering: high, lofty,
mountainous, tall
town: place, urban
towpath: bank
toxic: poisonous,
septic, venomous,
virulent, venom
toxin: poison
toy: fiddle, fidget,
finger, flirt, fool,
play
toying: flirtation
trace: clue, drop, hint,
jot, little, locate, look
up, mark, record,
relish, shade, shadow,
shred, sign, smack,
spark, step, strain,
suggestion, suspicion,
tail, touch, track,
vestige, whiff,
whisper
tracery: lattice
track: band, chase,
course, detect, dog,
find, follow, hunt,
lane, line, locate, pan,
path, pursue, road,
rut, scent, slide, step,
tail, vestige, wake,
way
tracker: tail
tract: land, plot,
stretch, territory
tractability:
obedience
tractable: easy,
flexible, gentle,
manageable,
obedient, plastic,
pliable, yielding
traction: draught
trade: bargain, barter,

business, calling,
change, clientele,
commerce, craft,
custom, deal,
economic, handle,
industry, job, line,
mercantile,
occupation,
patronage, peddle,
public, redeem,
render, sell, stock,
swap, switch,
technical, traffic,
work
trademark: attribute,
device, label
trader: dealer,
merchant, operator
tradesman:
merchant, seller,
worker
trading: barter,
business, commercial,
mercantile
tradition: heritage,
legacy, legend, myth,
practice, usage
traditional:
conservative,
conventional,
legendary, mythical,
old, orthodox,
proverbial, regular,
set, straight
traditionalism:
orthodoxy
traditionalist:
conservative
traditionally:
reputedly
traditions: lore
traduce: libel
traducing: libellous
traffic: bargain,
commerce, deal,
intercourse, swap,
trade
tragedy: calamity,
catastrophe, disaster,
play
tragic: disastrous,
dreadful, heart-
rending, lamentable,
sad, woeful
trail: dangle, dog,
follow, hang, haul,
lag, path, run, sack,
scent, spy, tail, track,
wake, walk
trailed: dogged
trailer: caravan,
excerpt
trailing: rambling
train: breed, bring up,
caravan, chain, coach,
column, condition,

cultivate, direct,
discipline, drill,
educate, exercise,
groom, harden,
indoctrinate, instruct,
level, practise,
prepare, prime,
range, rear, rehearse,
school, season, series,
suite, tail, teach, work
out
trained: cultivated,
domestic,
experienced,
habituated, pet,
practised,
professional,
proficient
trainee: beginner,
junior, recruit
trainer: coach,
instructor, teacher
training: discipline,
drill, education,
exercise, instruction,
practice
traipse: march, walk
trait: attribute,
characteristic, feature,
habit, mannerism,
point, property,
quality, strain, way
traitor: collaborator,
Judas, subversive
traitorous: disloyal,
faithless, false,
perfidious, unfaithful
trajectory: course,
line, track
tram: bus
trammel: chain,
shackle
tramp: beggar, bitch,
derelict, hussy,
march, tread, vagrant,
walk, whore
trample: flatten,
squash, stamp,
suppress, tread
trance: rapture, spell
tranquil: calm, easy,
even, halcyon,
imperturbable, mild,
peaceful,
philosophical, placid,
quiescent, quiet,
restful, smooth, still,
undisturbed
tranquillity:
mildness, peace,
quiet, repose, rest,
serenity, still
tranquillize: lull,
mollify, pacify,
quieten, sedate, still
tranquillizer:

narcotic, sedative, soporific

tranquillizing: sedative, soporific

tranquilly: quietly

transact: perform

transaction: bargain, deal, package, sale

transactions: business, memoirs

transatlantic: overseas

transcend: cap, outdo, pass, surpass

transcendental: divine, mystical, unworldly

transcribe: copy, record, render, write

transcription: copy, notation

transfer: cede, delegate, deliver, grant, move, pass, refer, remove, shift, transcribe, transport, transposition

transference: delegation, projection

transfix: freeze, gore, immobilize, impale, paralyse, pierce, skewer, spellbind, stab, stick

transfixed: motionless

transform: change, convert, evolve, process, resolve, turn, vary

transformation: evolution, metamorphosis, mutation, renewal, revolution

transgress: breach, break, err, fall, infringe, offend, sin, violate

transgression: breach, crime, fall, fault, misdeed, misdemeanour, offence, sin, violation, wrong

transgressor: criminal, culprit, malefactor, offender, sinner

transient: fleet, fugitive, meteoric, mortal, restless, temporary, volatile

transients: visitors

transit: eclipse

transition: change,

passage, transit

transitional: intermediate, provisional

transitory: brief, momentary, passing, temporary

translate: decipher, interpret, render, transcribe, turn, understand

translation: crib, interpretation, key, version

transliterate: transcribe

translucency: lucidity

translucent: bright, liquid, lucid, transparent

transmissible: contagious, hereditary

transmission: beam, broadcast, burst, circulation, contagion, delivery, drive, emanation, emission, gear, output, projection, propagation, relay

transmit: beam, broadcast, communicate, consign, emit, give, pass, project, relay, remit, return, screen, send, spread

transmittal: consignment, delivery

transmitter: medium, vessel

transmutation: transition

transmute: resolve

transparency: lucidity, photograph

transparent: bright, clear, glassy, lucid, thin, undisguised, white

transpire: be, befall, happen, occur, surface, turn out

transplant: graft

transplantation: graft

transport: banish, bear, bring, carriage, carry, deliver, ferry, haul, import, lift, move, rapture, remove, run, spellbind, take, traffic, transmit, waft,

wheel

transportation: distribution, freight, traffic, transit, transport

transported: exalted, exultant, joyful, rapt

transporting: import

transpose: invert, move, reverse

transposition: inversion

transverse: cross

trap: bag, bay, catch, corner, decoy, door, entrance, filter, gig, mouth, net, pitfall, snare, trip

trapdoor: hatch

trapping: capture

trappings: finery, furniture, gear, harness, kit, outfit, stuff, tackle, trim

trash: garbage, junk, litter, nonsense, refuse, rubbish, scum, waste

trashy: pulp, worthless

trauma: haemorrhage, hurt, shock, stress, wound

traumatize: scar, shock

travail: effort, labour, work

travel: ascend, cover, cruise, do, drive, explore, gad, go, go on, head, journey, migrate, motion, move, progress, ride, tour, transit, walk, wander

traveller: fare, gypsy, passenger, pilgrim, tourist, vagrant

travelling: itinerant, mobile, wandering

travels: journey, voyage

traverse: cross, ford, span, transit

travestied: mangled

travesty: butcher, caricature, farce, garble, misinterpret, mockery, parody, satire, skit, take off

travois: litter

trawl: drag, draught, fish, net

tray: case, waiter

treacherous: crooked, deceitful,

dirty, dishonest, disloyal, double, lying, perfidious, perjured, rotten, serpentine, unfaithful, unreliable, unsafe, untrue

treachery: betrayal, deception, sabotage

tread: march, pace, step, trample

treason: betrayal, conspiracy, sabotage

treasonable: disloyal

treasonous: subversive

treasure: boast, cherish, darling, dear, delight, dream, enshrine, find, fortune, garner, gem, jewel, love, ornament, pet, pride, prize, rarity, save, value

treasured: dear, precious, valuable

treasurer: cashier

treasure-trove: hoard

treasury: fund, purse

treat: bomb, doctor, drug, feast, handle, luxury, nurse, patch, process, subject, synthesize, use

treated: proof

treatise: dissertation, paper, tract

treatment: cure, dose, medicine, reading, usage, use

treaty: bargain, compact, contract, pact, peace, truce

trebuchet: catapult

treeless: bald, bare

trees: timber, wood

trek: jaunt, journey, march, migrate, passage, walk

trekking: hiking

trellis: grid, lattice

tremble: dread, falter, fear, flutter, jerk, quail, quake, quiver, shake, shudder, vibrate, waver

trembles: shivers

trembling: quaver, shudder, tremor, vibrant

tremendous: fantastic, great, prodigious, stupendous, terrific, wonder, wonderful

tremolo: warble
tremor: convulsion, earthquake, flutter, quake, quaver, quiver, shake, shudder
tremulous: faltering
tremulousness: quaver, quiver
trench: ditch, groove, gutter, pit
trenchant: caustic, corrosive, cutting, keen, pointed, pungent, scathing, sharp, vitriolic, withering
trench-coat: mackintosh
trend: bent, current, fad, fashion, movement, run, style, tendency, tide, vogue, wave
trendy: current, fashionable, latest, up to date, vogue
trepidation: dread, fear, fright
trespass: fault, impose, misdeed, offence, offend, sin, wrong
trespasser: burglar, intruder, malefactor
tress: lock, strand
tresses: hair
trestle: bench, cradle, crib, frame, grid, rack, rest
triad: trinity
trial: calamity, case, catastrophe, challenge, contest, cross, distress, dummy, experience, exploratory, fire, hardship, hearing, hoop, ill, misery, ordeal, penance, pest, pilot, plague, preliminary, process, sample, scramble, sorrow, suit, woe, worry
tribade: lesbian
tribal: racial
tribe: clan, family, folk, kin, nation, people
tribesman: warrior
tribulation: care, fire, hardship, hoop, ill, misery, ordeal, sorrow, trial, trouble, woe, woods

tribunal: bar, bench, council, court, jury, trial
tributary: satellite, stream
tribute: compliment, mention, praise, salute
trice: flash, instant, second, shake, twinkling
trick: artifice, catch, cheat, deceive, deception, fool, fraud, gimmick, have, have on, hoax, imposition, intrigue, kid, knack, phoney, quirk, shave, shift, spoof, swindle, take in, trap, wangle
trickery: cheat, craft, deception, fraud, guile, magic, pretence, swindle
trickle: bleed, drip, flow, leak, well
trickling: drip, flow, murmuring
trickster: cheat, joker, knave, quack, swindler
tricksy: knavish
tricky: funny, knavish, mean, precarious, prickly, quirky, scheming, shifty, slick, slippery, sticky, thorny, tight, unpredictable, wily
trident: fork
trifle: dabble, dessert, fidget, flirt, fool, jot, little, novelty, play
trifles: minutiae
trifling: flirtation, footling, frivolous, frothy, futile, insignificant, light, lightweight, little, low, mere, minor, minute, negligible, niggling, nugatory, paltry, puny, small, worthless
trigger: precipitate, spark, touch, trip
trike: cycle
trill: pipe, quaver, sing, warble
trilling: warble
trim: bind, clip, condition, crop, cut, face, fit, form, garnish, jaunty, natty, neat, nice, orderly, ornament, pare,

pretty, prune, rationalize, reap, run down, shave, shorten, slim, smart, snug, taut, thin, tight
trimmed: cut
trimmer: backslider
trimming: binding, border, decoration, fringe, garnish, hem, opportunism, ornament, self-seeking
trimmings: frills
trimness: neatness
trinket: charm, novelty, ornament
trinkets: jewellery, knick-knacks
trio: trinity
trip: down, drive, fall, founder, hallucination, haul, high, jaunt, journey, outing, passage, ride, run, sally, slip, stumble, tour, tumble, turn on, visit, voyage
tripe: stuff
tripes: guts, intestines, offal
triplet: trinity
tripulation: calamity
trite: banal, barren, hackneyed, insipid, pedestrian, stale, stock, tired, worn
triturate: crumble
triumph: attainment, conquest, glee, hit, jubilation, knockout, mastery, ovation, palm, prevail, rejoicing, score, victory, win
triumphal: jubilant
triumphant: exultant, glorious, jubilant, knockout, rejoicing, self-satisfied, victorious, winning
triumvirate: trinity
trivia: minutiae
trivial: banal, flimsy, footling, frivolous, frothy, futile, idle, insignificant, light, lightweight, little, mere, minor, minute, negligible, paltry, petty, poor, puny, shallow, slight, small, superficial, venial, worthless

triviality: frivolity, levity, platitude, vanity
trivium: detail
troll: gnome
trolley: cradle, waiter
trollop: hussy, prostitute, slut, whore
trombone: horn
troop: band, company, force, legion, pack, parade, squad, team, unit
trooping: parade
trophy: award, crown, cup, palm, plate, pot, prize, victory
tropical: jungle
trot: jog, trip
troubadour: poet
trouble: care, catastrophe, concern, disadvantage, disaster, distress, disturb, fireworks, fret, handful, harass, hardship, hassle, ill, load, matter, mischief, nuisance, plague, press, prey on, prick, problem, put out, row, ruffle, sorrow, spot, visit, work, worry
troubled: concerned, loaded, restless, solicitous, worried
troublemaker: bully, malcontent, yob
troublesome: awkward, difficult, disruptive, mischievous, niggling, prickly, sore
trough: dell, gutter, hollow, rut, trench, valley
trounce: crush, defeat, demolish, hammer, lick, murder, rout, wallop, whip
trouncing: defeat, drubbing, licking, rout
troupe: cast, team
trousers: flannels, jeans
trowel: float, shovel
truancy: desertion
truant: deserter
truce: peace
truck: caravan
truckle: flatter, kowtow, obey
truculent: defiant

trudge: stump, tread, walk

true: authentic, certain, chivalrous, constant, devoted, faithful, genuine, good, honest, just, legitimate, loyal, original, pure, real, reliable, right, sincere, sound, very

truelove: sweetheart

true-to-life: realistic, vivid

truism: axiom, platitude, verity

truly: just, literally, quite, really, right, very

trump: fabricate, fanfare, rig

trumped-up: false, unfounded

trumpet: cry, herald, horn, proclaim, splash, thunder

truncate: chop, curtail, cut, reduce, telescope

truncated: cut

truncheon: club, cudgel

trunk: beam, body, boot, box, case, log, nose, stem

trunks: bathing costume, luggage

truss: bind, corset, strap, tether

trust: belief, believe, charge, confidence, credit, faith, hope, lean, obligation, rely on

trusted: confidential, unquestioned

trustee: guardian

trustees: board

trustiness: loyalty

trusting: gullible, naive, unsuspecting

trustworthiness: credibility, fidelity, honesty, loyalty

trustworthy: authoritative, certain, constant, confidential, honest, honourable, loyal, reliable, reputable, responsible, safe, straight, true, unfailing, upright, white

trusty: faithful, loyal, solid, sure

truth: axiom, deed, fact, faithfulness, justice, right, verity

truthful: faithful, honest

truthfulness: honesty

try: attempt, bid, bite, crack, effort, essay, experience, feel, fish, fling, go, hear, judge, prove, push, rehearse, sample, seek, shot, stab, strive, taste, tax, test, throw, trial, turn, undertake, wear

trying: awkward, demanding, difficult, fitting, painful, rugged, stiff, thorny, wearing, wearisome

tryst: assignation, date, engagement, meeting

trysting-place: venue

tub: bath, kit, sink

tubby: chubby, corpulent, fat, obese, overweight, plump, rotund, stout

tube: barrel, can, canal, cylinder, funnel, line, pipe, tunnel, underground, vessel

tuber: bulb, root

tuberculosis: consumption

tuck: crease, fold, food, gather, grub, insert

tucket: fanfare, flourish

tucks: frills

tuft: beard, bunch, flock

tufted: hairy

tug: drag, haul, heave, hitch, jerk, pluck, pull, wrench

tuition: education, knowledge, lesson

tumble-down: dilapidated

tumble: drop, fall, lurch, overturn, pitch, plunge, roll, spill

tumbledown: ramshackle

tumbril: cart

tumesce: erect, touch up

tumescent: erect

tumid: puffy

tummy: belly, stomach

tumour: cancer, growth, lump, nodule

tump: hump, knoll, mound

tumult: bedlam, chaos, convulsion, disturbance, fuss, noise, pandemonium, racket, riot, tempest, unrest

tumultuous: chaotic, furious, noisy, uproarious

tumulus: knoll, mound

tun: barrel, cask, keg

tundra: desert

tune: key, melody, number, song, strain, temper, theme

tuneful: mellow, melodious, musical, sweet

tunefulness: melody

tuner: key

tunic: frock

tuning: temperament

tunnel: bore, burrow, dig, mine, undercut

turbid: muddy, opaque

turbulence: fury, maelstrom, tempest, violence

turbulent: boisterous, bumpy, furious, heavy, rough, stormy, tempestuous, violent, wild

turbulently: roughly

turd: mess

turf: grass, green

turgid: pompous

turmoil: commotion, confusion, ferment, kerfuffle, riot, storm, unrest, uproar

turn: avert, back, bear, become, bend, bring, convert, crank, curl, deflect, deviate, diverge, divert, double, fall, field, fold, get, go, grind, grow, haul, head, hinge, jink, key, leaf, loop, machine, make, move, pan, pivot, relay, return, revolution, roll, rotate, round, saunter, screw, send, set, sheer, shock, spell, spin, spoil, swerve, swing, thing, throw, tweak, wax,

wheel, whirl, wind, wriggle

turnaround: transition

turncoat: black sheep, collaborator

turned: sour, twisted, wound

turning: rotary

turnout: attendance, audience

turnover: economy, output, takings

turntable: roundabout

turquoise: blue

turret: battlements, fortification, garret, tower

tusks: teeth

tussle: brush, fight, hassle, scramble, scrum, scuffle, skirmish, struggle

tutelage: education

tutor: coach, educate, ground, master, school, teach, teacher

tutorial: clinic

twaddle: bull, bunk, chatter, gibberish, nonsense, rot, rubbish, stuff

twang: pluck

tweak: jerk, kink, nip, pinch

twee: precious

tweet: pipe, warble

twentieth-century: modern

twerp: simpleton

twice: double

twiddle: tweak

twig: bough, branch, stick, take in, understand, wand

twilight: dusk, nightfall

twilit: dusky

twill: flannel

twin: companion, double, fellow, identical, match, mate, mirror, picture, same, tally

twine: cling, cord, string, wind

twined: twisted, wound

twinge: pang, qualm, stab, tweak

twinkle: brilliance, dance, glitter, shine, sparkle

twinkling: brilliant, flickering, moment,

shimmering
twinned: matching
twirl: corkscrew, curl,
pivot, reel, roll, spin,
whirl
twist: coil, corkscrew,
curl, distort, flip, jerk,
jink, kink, knot, loop,
pervert, quirk,
revolve, roll, screw,
slant, spin, strain,
tangle, turn, tweak,
twine, warp, weave,
wind, wrench,
wriggle, wring
twisted: bent,
deformed, kinky,
misshapen, quirky,
skew, wound,
twisted: wry
twisting: devious,
winding

twit: ass, banter, fool,
idiot, jackass, sap,
scoff, silly, wally
twitch: hop, jerk, pull,
spasm, start, switch
twitter: peep, pipe
twittering: jargon
two-faced: lying,
slippery
two-timing:
unfaithful
twofold: double
twosome: couple, pair
tycoon: king, magnate
typanum: drum
type: brand, breed,
brood, category,
chap, character, class,
denomination,
description, face,
fashion, fish, kind,
letter, make, manner,

mark, model, mould,
nature, order,
pattern, print, punch,
quality, rank,
representative, run,
sort, soul, species,
specimen, stamp,
standard, style,
symbol, variety,
version, writing
typecast: stamp
typeface: print
typhoon: gale,
hurricane, tempest
typical: average,
characteristic, classic,
general, natural,
ordinary, regular,
representative,
routine, standard,
usual
typically: generally,

naturally
typify: characterize,
personify, represent,
symbolize, writing
tyrannical:
authoritarian, brutal,
dictatorial, lordly,
oppressive,
totalitarian
tyrannize: domineer,
enslave, oppress
tyranny: domination,
repression
tyrant: authoritarian,
despot, dictator, ogre,
oppressor
tyre: wheel
tyro: beginner,
initiate, novice,
trainee

U

ubiquitous:
pervasive, popular
udder: breast
ugliness: deformity
ugly: awful,
dangerous, deformed,
hard, hideous
ulcer: corn, lesion,
pustule, sore
ulcerate: perforate
ulterior: hidden,
underlying
ultimate: bottom,
consummate,
eventual, final,
height, last, limit,
primary, supreme,
terminal
ultimately: finally,
last
ultimatum:
challenge, command
ultramarine: blue
umber: brown
umbrage: offence,
pique, resentment
umbrageous: shady
umpire: judge,
mediate, mediator,
officiate, referee
unabashed:
shameless
unabated: relentless
unable: impotent
unabridged:
complete
unaccented:
idiomatic, toneless
unacceptable:
impossible,
inadmissible,
ineligible, offensive,
out, unbearable,
undesirable, unheard-
of
unaccountable:
inexplicable,
miraculous,
unanswerable
unaccustomed:
uncharacteristic
unachievable:
impractical
unacknowledged:
disowned
unadorned: plain
unadulterated: clean,

fine, mere, neat,
perfect, sheer
unadventurous: safe
unaffected: chaste,
naive, plain, sincere,
unspoilt
unaffiliated:
independent, private,
voluntary
unafraid: fearless
unalloyed: fine, pure,
simple, solid
unalluring: plain
unaltered: same
unambiguous: clear,
direct, plain, specific
unambiguously:
directly
unanimity: concert,
concurrence,
harmony, identity,
solidarity, unity
unanimous: solid
unanswerable:
imponderable,
impossible
unappealing:
unappetizing,
uninviting
unappeasable:
insatiable
unappetizing:
uninviting
unappreciative:
ungrateful
unapproachability:
frigidity
unapproachable:
frosty, inaccessible,
remote
unapproved:
unauthorized
unashamedly:
decidedly
unasked-for:
gratuitous
unasked: unexpected,
unwanted
unassailable:
impregnable,
invincible, secure,
tenable,
unanswerable,
unshakable
unassertive: self-
effacing
unassisted: unaided

unassuming: homely,
humble, meek,
retiring, unspoilt
unattached: separate,
single
unattainable: ideal,
impossible,
impractical,
inaccessible, Utopian
unattended: unaided
unattractive: plain,
ugly, unappetizing,
undesirable,
uninviting,
unpleasant
unauthorized: illegal,
illegitimate,
inadmissible,
irregular,
unconfirmed
unavailable: off,
occupied
unavailing: fruitless,
ineffectual, vain
unavoidable:
automatic, destined,
inevitable, necessary,
obligatory
unavoidably:
necessarily
unaware: ignorant,
innocent, insensible,
short, unconscious,
unsuspecting
unawareness:
ignorance, innocence,
oblivion
unbalanced: crazy,
insane, mad,
maddened,
maladjusted, mental,
one-sided, unequal,
uneven
unbearable:
insufferable
unbeatable:
invincible
unbecoming:
improper,
inappropriate,
undignified, unseemly
unbelievable:
fantastic, farcical,
implausible,
inconceivable,
incredible, knockout,
marvellous,

miraculous, unlikely
unbeliever: atheist,
heathen, pagan
unbelieving: heathen,
incredulous, pagan,
sceptical
unbend: relax
unbending: frigid,
severe, uncharitable
unbiased: candid,
disinterested, fair,
judicial, just, liberal,
neutral, objective
unbigoted: catholic
unbind: liberate
unbinding: liberation
unblemished: clean,
clear, faultless,
immaculate,
impeccable, innocent,
perfect,
unimpeachable,
unspoilt
unblended: simple,
single
unblock: clear
unborn: future
unbounded:
indefinite, infinite,
open-ended, vast
unbowed: unbroken
unbreakable:
indestructible
unbridled:
unbounded
unbroken: constant,
even, integral,
smooth, solid, sound,
uniform, untamed
unburden: discharge,
relieve, unload
unburdening:
discharge
uncalled for:
improper, gratuitous,
intrusive, needless
uncanny: macabre,
mysterious, odd,
queer, supernatural
uncaring: callous,
insensitive, oblivious
unceasing:
continuous, incessant,
perennial, perpetual
unceasingly: ever
unceremonious:
familiar, informal

uncertain: chancy,
changeable, doubtful,
hesitant, improbable,
nebulous, tentative,
unclear, undecided,
unreliable, unsettled,
unsure, vague
uncertainly: vaguely
uncertainty: chance,
doubt, nebulosity,
puzzle, query,
question, suspense
unchain: release
unchallenged: freely
unchanged: same
unchanging:
mechanical,
permanent
uncharacteristic:
unworthy
uncharitable:
intolerant
unchaste: light
unchecked: rampant,
unbounded,
unbridled,
uninhibited
unchic: unfashionable
unchristian: heathen,
pagan
uncivil: churlish,
coarse, short, surly,
tactless
uncivilized:
primitive, savage,
uncouth
unclean: insanitary,
unsafe
uncleanliness:
nastiness
unclear: opaque,
uncertain, vague
unclosed: open
unclouded: clear,
serene, sunny
uncluttered: clean,
simple
uncomfortable:
awkward, queasy
uncommercial:
unbusinesslike
uncommitted: free,
neutral, open
uncommon: choice,
different, exceptional,
queer, rare,
remarkable,
unaccustomed,
unusual
uncommonly:
notably, particularly
uncommonness:
rarity
uncommunicative:
reticent, taciturn
uncompleted:

unfinished
uncomplicated:
facile, simple
uncomplimentary:
unflattering
uncomprehending:
blank, ignorant,
obtuse, unaware
uncompromising:
dour, intransigent,
relentless, unbending
unconcealed: open,
undisguised
unconcern:
detachment,
indifference, neglect,
nonchalance
unconcerned:
careless, casual,
complacent, cool,
insensitive,
nonchalant, oblivious
unconditional: total,
unqualified
unconditionally:
unreservedly
unconfined:
unbounded
unconfirmed:
tentative
uncongenial:
inhospitable,
unfriendly
unconnected:
distinct, irrelevant
unconscionable:
unholy
unconscious:
automatic, comatose,
ignorant, inanimate,
inert, insensible,
lifeless, senseless,
unaware, unthinking
unconsciously:
unwittingly
unconsciousness:
narcosis, oblivion
unconstitutional:
unauthorized
unconstrained:
uninhibited
uncontaminated:
pure
uncontrollable:
berserk, irrepressible,
overpowering,
rampant,
undisciplined,
ungovernable,
untamed
uncontrolled:
chaotic, incontinent,
involuntary, lawless,
obstreperous,
tempestuous,
unbounded,

unbridled,
uninhibited
unconventional:
fringe, kinky, queer,
unusual
unconventionality:
eccentricity, oddity
unconversant:
unfamiliar
unconvinced:
doubtful, sceptical
unconvincing: far-
fetched, flimsy,
implausible, lame,
thin, unlikely,
unreliable
uncooked: raw,
underdone
uncooperative:
clumsy, scrappy,
unhelpful
uncork: open
uncorroborated:
unconfirmed
uncorrupted: pure
uncouple: disconnect
uncouth: clumsy,
vulgar
uncouthness:
coarseness, vulgarity
uncover: detect,
disclose, discover,
expose, find, open,
reveal, unmask
uncovered: nude
uncovering:
exposure, revelation
unctuous: greasy,
ingratiating, oily,
pious, sanctimonious,
slimy, smooth
uncultivated:
philistine, savage
uncured: fresh
uncut: blank,
unabridged
undamaged: intact,
mint, unharmed,
unspoilt
undaunted: intrepid,
resolute
undeceive: disillusion
undeception:
disillusion
undecided: open,
uncertain, unsettled,
unsure
undecipherable:
illegible
undefended: open,
unguarded
undefiled: clean,
clear, immaculate,
intact, maiden, virgin
undefined: neutral,
open-ended

undemanding: easy,
facile, light, soft
undemonstrative:
phlegmatic,
restrained
undeniable: certain,
obvious, peremptory,
simple, sure,
unanswerable,
unquestioned
undeniably: clearly
undependable:
irresponsible
under: below,
beneath, underneath
underclothes:
underwear
undercoat: primer
undercover: secret,
underground
undercurrent:
overtone, undertone
underdeveloped:
imperfect
underestimated:
underrated
undergo: endure,
experience, go
through, have, know,
lead, meet, receive,
see, suffer, support,
sustain
underground:
partisan, subversive
undergrowth: brake,
brush, forest
underhand: crooked,
deceitful, devious,
foul, funny, hidden,
scheming, shifty, sly,
surreptitious,
unethical
underline:
emphasize, highlight
underling: menial,
yes-man
underlying:
fundamental, prime,
ulterior
undermine: break,
knife, poison,
sabotage, sap, shake,
supplant, undercut
undermined:
discredited
underneath: below,
beneath, bottom
undernourished:
skinny, underweight
underpants: pants
underpin: shore up,
support
underpinning:
support
underrate:
underestimate

underscore:
punctuate, underline
underside: bottom
undersized: dwarf,
puny, pygmy, small
understand: catch on,
conceive, deduce, dig,
digest, divine,
fathom, grasp, hear,
infer, interpret, know,
make out, perceive,
realize, recognize, see,
sympathize, take in,
tell
understandable:
human, intelligible
understandably:
thus
understanding:
awareness, belief,
charitable, compact,
comprehension,
conception, contract,
deal, engagement,
experience, feeling,
grasp, grip, harmony,
head, human,
humane, humanity,
illumination,
indulgent, inference,
insight,
interpretation,
judgement, kind,
kindliness, kindly,
kindness, knowledge,
learning, light,
mastery, notion,
obligation, pact,
patient, perception,
protocol, reading,
reason, sense,
sympathetic,
sympathy, vision
understated: soft,
subtle, underdone
understood:
axiomatic, implicit,
silent, unspoken
understudy: deputy
undersupply: scarcity
undertake: assume,
do, pledge, promise,
resolve, tackle, take
on, venture, vow
undertaking:
assumption, cause,
commitment, job,
leap, mission,
operation, pledge,
ploy, project,
promise, resolve,
venture
undertone: innuendo,
mumble, nuance
undervalue:
underestimate

undervalued:
underrated
underwear: knickers
underweight: light,
scrawny
underworld: hell
underwrite: finance,
subsidize, support
underwriter:
guarantor
undeserving:
unworthy
undesignated:
nameless
undesirable: pariah
undetectable:
imperceptible
undetermined:
uncertain
undeveloped: fallow,
immature, inchoate,
juvenile, potential,
premature, vestigial
undeviating:
consistent, direct
undies: knickers,
underwear
undignified:
ignominious
undiluted: neat
undiplomatic:
indiscreet, tactless,
unthinking
undisclosed: secret,
ulterior
undiscovered:
unheard-of
undiscriminating:
promiscuous
undisguised: flagrant
undissolvable:
insoluble
undistinguished:
common, humble,
mediocre,
nondescript, obscure
undisturbed: calm,
peaceful, quiet,
restful, sound
undivided: complete,
integral, single, total,
unbroken
undo: betray,
demolish, disconnect,
overthrow, quash,
release, reverse,
unravel, upset, zip
undoing: death,
destruction,
dissolution,
overthrow
undomesticated:
unbroken
undoubted: sure
undoubtedly: indeed,
really, undeniably

undreamed-of:
unheard-of
undress: divest
undressed: nude
undue: unreasonable
undulate: coil,
fluctuate, oscillate,
surge
undulating: uneven
undying: immortal,
lasting, perennial,
perpetual, timeless
unearth: discover,
exhume, reveal
unearthing:
discovery, revelation
unearthly: holy,
macabre,
supernatural, unholy
unease: fear, malaise
uneasiness:
nervousness, qualm,
scruple, unrest
uneasy: concerned,
discontent, nervous,
queasy, restless,
uncomfortable,
unsettled, uptight
uneconomic:
unprofitable
uneducated:
ignorant, illiterate,
philistine
unembellished: raw,
severe
unemotional: calm,
cold-blooded, cool,
laid-back, matter-of-
fact, phlegmatic,
undemonstrative
unemphasized:
toneless
unemployed: idle
unemployment:
idleness
unenclosed: open
unending: perpetual
unendurable:
excruciating,
impossible,
insufferable,
unbearable
unengaged: free,
open, vacant
unenlightened: dark
unenlightenment:
ignorance
unenthused: languid
unenthusiastic: half-
hearted, negative,
reluctant, tepid
unequal: irregular,
one-sided, uneven,
unlike
unequalled:
matchless, peerless,

pre-eminent, unique
unequivocal: certain,
direct, flat, patent,
positive
unequivocally:
directly, flat, flatly,
positively
unerring: deadly,
perfect, true
unerringly: exactly
unethical: immoral,
unconscionable,
unfair, unsporting
uneven: bumpy,
crooked, irregular,
jagged, odd, patchy,
ragged, unequal
unevenness:
inequality
uneventful: slow
unexamined:
unquestioned, untried
unexceptionable:
unimpeachable
unexceptional:
average, everyday,
ordinary
unexcitable:
imperturbable, placid
unexcited: blasé, calm
unexpected: casual,
freak, marked, new,
precipitate, unasked,
uncharacteristic .
unexpectedly: sharp,
unasked
unexperienced: new
unexplained:
paranormal
unexplored:
unknown
unexpurgated:
unabridged
unfading: fast
unfailing: same
unfailingly:
invariably
unfair: foul,
iniquitous, one-sided,
partial, prejudiced,
unequal, uneven,
unreasonable,
unsporting
unfairness: injustice
unfaithful: disloyal,
faithless, false, fickle,
untrue
unfaltering: firm,
relentless,
unhesitating
unfamiliar: foreign,
new, unheard-of,
unknown, untried
unfamiliarity:
novelty
unfashionable: old,

old-fashioned,
outdated
unfasten: detach,
undo, zip
unfastened: undone
unfastening:
detachment
unfathomable:
impenetrable,
imponderable,
inexplicable,
insoluble, opaque
unfavourable: foul,
ill, unfortunate,
unfriendly
unfavourably: ill
unfeeling: brutal,
callous, cruel, gross,
hard, harsh, heartless,
inhuman, insensitive,
mechanical, numb,
numbness, thick-
skinned, uncharitable,
unkind, unnatural
unfeigned: real,
undisguised
unfenced: open
unfinished:
imperfect,
inconclusive, partial,
ragged, sketchy,
undone, unprepared
unfit: incapable,
unqualified,
unworthy
unfitted: inadequate
unfitting:
inappropriate
unflagging:
determined, tireless
unflappable: calm,
imperturbable
unflinching: fearless,
firm, resolute,
spartan, valiant
unflinchingly: fast
unfocus: blur
unfold: communicate,
open, solve, spin,
spread
unfolded: open,
unsolicited, voluntary
unforeseeable:
improbable,
unpredictable
unforeseen: casual,
chance, unexpected
unforgettable:
memorable
unforgetting:
tenacious
unforgivable:
inexcusable
unforgiving:
implacable, merciless,
tough

unformed: blank,
immature, nebulous
unforseen: sudden
unforthcoming:
close, evasive,
reticent,
uncommunicative
unfortified: open
unfortunate: devil,
inauspicious,
lamentable, poor, sad,
unhappy, unpopular
unfortunately:
regrettably,
unhappily
unfrequented: quiet,
secret, sequestered,
solitary
unfriendly:
disagreeable, frosty,
hostile, ill,
inhospitable,
uncharitable, unkind,
unpopular
unfulfilled:
dissatisfied
unfurl: break
unfussy: lax
ungainly: awkward,
clumsy, hulking,
lanky, unwieldy
ungenerous: close
ungentlemanly:
impolite
ungetatable:
inaccessible
ungodliness: evil
ungodly: evil,
heathen, impious,
pagan, unholy
ungovernable:
lawless
ungraceful: ungainly
ungracious: curt,
impolite, unkind
unguarded:
inadvertent
unguent: salve
unguis: claw
unhandy: unwieldy
unhappily:
regrettably,
unfortunately
unhappiness:
melancholy, misery,
sadness
unhappy: desolate,
discontent,
dissatisfied, forlorn,
miserable, mournful,
sad, sorrowful
unharmed: intact,
safe
unhealthy: green,
insanitary, morbid,
sallow, sickly, unfit,

unwholesome
unheard-of: freak,
nameless, obscure,
unaccountable,
unknown
unheard: inaudible
unhelpful: awkward,
inopportune
unhindered: clear
unhinge: dislocate
unhinged: crazy,
insane, mad,
maddened
unhitch: detach
unhoned: dull
unhurried:
deliberate, easy, laid-
back, leisurely, slow
unhurriedly:
leisurely
unhurt: unharmed
unhygienic:
fleabitten, insanitary,
unhealthy, unsafe
unidentified:
unknown
uniform: equal, even,
flat, homogeneous,
level, monolithic,
monotonous, parallel,
plane, unbroken
uniformly: equally,
universally
unify: combine,
integrate
unimaginable:
imponderable,
inconceivable,
incredible,
unattainable,
unutterably
unimaginative: dull,
matter-of-fact,
pedestrian, slavish
unimpaired: clean,
intact, sound,
unbroken, unharmed,
unspoilt
unimpeachable:
impeccable
unimpeded: clear,
free
unimportance:
indifference,
obscurity
unimportant:
footling, frivolous,
frothy, humble,
insignificant, light,
lightweight, mere,
minor, minute,
negligible, nugatory,
obscure, petty, slight,
small-time
uninflected: toneless
uninformed:

ignorant, provincial,
unaware
uninhabitable:
inhospitable
uninhabited:
desolate, free,
unsettled
uninhibited: broad,
frank, free, libertine
uninhibitedly:
frankly, freely
uninjured: intact,
unharmed
uninspired:
lacklustre, mediocre,
slavish,
unimaginative
unintelligence:
ignorance
unintelligent: foolish,
limited, obtuse,
shallow
unintelligible:
inarticulate,
incoherent,
meaningless
unintended:
involuntary,
unintentional
unintentional:
casual, chance,
coincidental,
inadvertent,
involuntary,
unconscious
unintentionally:
unwittingly
uninterested: cool,
unconcerned,
unimpressed
uninteresting: bland,
boring, dead, deadly,
dull, jejune, mousy,
nondescript
uninterruptedly:
consecutive, constant,
continual,
continuous, nonstop,
perpetual, smooth,
unbroken,
undisturbed
uninvited: intrusive,
unasked, uncalled-
for, unexpected,
unwanted
uninviting:
inhospitable,
unappetizing
uninvolved:
disinterested, neutral,
objective, remote,
unconcerned
union: association,
chain, club, coalition,
combination,
connection, contact,

fraternity, join, joint,
junction, league,
liaison, society,
sympathy
unique: different,
distinctive,
individual, matchless,
only, peculiar,
phenomenal, single,
singular, special,
unrepeatable
uniqueness:
distinction, identity
unisex: mixed
unison: concert,
concurrence
unit: cell, component,
constituent, count,
degree, element,
factor, individual,
integral, item, mark,
measure, module,
number, numeral,
organ, outfit, package,
part, party, point,
throw
unite: associate,
attach, chain,
compound, connect,
consolidate, couple,
fasten, join, joint,
knit, marry, organize,
rally, team, unify,
yoke
united: concerted,
federal, joint, one,
solid, unanimous
unity: communion,
harmony, identity,
integrity, parity,
piece, solidarity
universal: blanket,
broad, catholic,
common, mixed,
nationwide, public
universe: creation,
nature
university: college
unjust: iniquitous,
unfair, unreasonable,
unsporting
unjustifiable:
inexcusable,
unfounded
unjustified:
gratuitous, uncalled-
for, unfounded
unkempt: bedraggled,
dishevelled, messy,
ragged, scruffy,
shaggy, slovenly
unkind: horrible,
tactless, uncharitable
unkindness:
disservice, ill
unknowing:

ignorance
unknowingly:
unwittingly
unknown: incognito,
nameless, obscure,
undisclosed,
unfamiliar, unheard-
of, unidentified
unladylike: impolite
unlawful: criminal,
illegal
unlearned: ignorant
unleash: free
unless: but
unlettered: ignorant,
illiterate
unlifelike: unrealistic
unlikable:
disagreeable,
obnoxious,
unpleasant
unlike: unequal
unlikely: far-fetched,
implausible,
improbable, outside,
remote
unlimited: indefinite,
open-ended,
unconditional,
universal, vast
unlit: dark
unload: clear,
discharge, lighten, tip
unloading: discharge
unlock: open
unlocked: open
unloving: frigid
unluckily:
unfortunately,
unhappily
unlucky: disastrous,
evil, inauspicious,
jinx, tough,
unfavourable,
unfortunate, unhappy
unmaking:
dissolution
unmanageable:
awkward, difficult,
insubordinate,
obstreperous,
problem, recalcitrant,
refractory,
undisciplined
unmanned: unnerved
unmannerly:
impertinent, impolite,
ungracious, vulgar
unmarked: blank,
unidentified
unmarried: celibate,
maiden, single
unmask: betray,
expose, find out
unmasking: betrayal,
exposure

unmatched:
incongruous, unique
unmentionable:
nameless,
unrepeatable
unmerited:
gratuitous
unmindful: careless,
forgetful, heedless,
insensible, mindless,
oblivious, unaware,
unconscious
unmistakable:
certain, clear,
distinct, obvious,
patent, positively,
prominent, sure,
undisguised,
undoutedly, visible
unmitigated: mere,
positive, rank,
thorough, utter
unmixed: pure,
simple, solid
unmoved: cold, cold-
blooded,
imperturbable,
unconcerned,
unimpressed
unmoving: immobile,
inanimate, inert,
lifeless, motionless,
quiescent
unnamed: nameless,
unidentified,
unknown
unnatural: artificial,
cruel, far-fetched,
kinky, monstrous,
perverse, queer,
supernatural,
uncharacteristic,
unrealistic
unnavigable:
impassable
unnecessarily:
unduly
unnecessary: idle,
intrusive, needless,
purposeless,
redundant,
superfluous, uncalled-
for
unneeded: extra
unnerve: discompose,
dismay, frighten,
panic, shake
unnerving:
frightening, off-
putting
unnoticeable:
imperceptible,
inconspicuous
unobservant:
oblivious
unobstructed: clear,

fair, free
unobtrusive:
inconspicuous,
inoffensive, quiet,
restrained
unobtrusively:
quietly
unoccupied: idle,
inactive, leisure,
open, otiose, spare,
uninhabited,
unsettled, vacant,
void
unofficial: honorary,
informal, irregular,
unauthorized,
unconfirmed
unoriginal:
derivative,
hackneyed,
unimaginative
unorthodox: curious,
fringe, irregular,
queer,
unconventional
unostentatious:
inconspicuous
unpack: unload
unpaid: delinquent,
honorary,
outstanding, owing,
unsettled, voluntary
unpalatable:
unpleasant
unparalleled: freak,
phenomenal, unique
unpardonable:
inexcusable
unpatriotic: disloyal
unperson: pariah
unperturbed:
collected,
unconcerned,
unimpressed
unpleasant: awful,
fearful, frightful,
hard, harsh, horrid,
nasty, objectionable,
obnoxious, odious,
painful, undesirable,
ungrateful,
uninviting, unkind
unpolished: coarse,
dusty, unfinished,
unprepared
unpolluted: clean,
pure, safe, sanitary
unpopulated:
uninhabited,
unsettled
unpractised: green,
inexperienced
unprecedented:
original, unheard-of
unpredictable:
awkward, capricious,

changeable,
explosive, fickle,
inconsistent, moody,
speculative,
temperamental,
uncertain
unprejudiced:
candid, disinterested,
fair, judicial, just,
liberal, objective
unpremeditated:
random, unconscious,
unintentional
unprepared: raw,
unfit, unripe
unprepossessing:
frumpish, homely,
plain, ugly
unpretentious: easy,
folksy, homely,
humble, modest,
naive, natural,
ordinary, plain, quiet,
simple, unspoilt
unpretentiously:
naturally, quietly
unpretentiousness:
modesty
unprincipled:
corrupt, immoral,
knavish,
unconscionable,
unethical, unfair
unprocessed: fresh,
unfinished
unproductive: dead,
fruitless, idle,
infertile, lean,
meagre, pointless,
poor, unavailing,
unprofitable, vain
unprofessional:
unbusinesslike
unprofitable: futile,
lean, uneconomic,
vain
unpromising: blue,
ominous,
inauspicious,
unfavourable
unpropitious:
ominous,
unfavourable,
unfortunate,
unfriendly
unprotected:
helpless, insecure,
open, unguarded,
vulnerable
unprovocative:
inoffensive
unprovoked:
gratuitous, uncalled-
for
unpunctual: late,
overdue, slow, tardy

unpunctually: late
unputdownable:
gripping
unqualified:
consummate, flat,
implicit, outright,
pure, sweeping,
unable,
unconditional, unfit,
unskilled
unquenchable:
insatiable, voracious
unquestionable:
certain, unquestioned
unquestionably:
decidedly, positively,
undeniably,
undoubtedly
unquiet: murmuring
unravel: decipher,
penetrate, resolve,
solve
unravelling:
resolution, solution
unreachable:
inaccessible,
unattainable
unreadable: illegible,
unintelligible
unready: unprepared,
unripe
unreal: dreamy,
fanciful, fictitious,
illusory, imaginary,
nonexistent, notional,
shadowy
unrealistic:
impractical
unreality:
impracticality
unreasonable:
extravagant,
implausible,
inconsiderate,
irrational,
preposterous,
senseless,
unconscionable,
unholy
unreasoning: blind,
mindless
unreasoningly:
blindly
unreceptive:
impervious,
inhospitable
unrecognizable:
incognito
unrecognizably:
incognito
unrecognized:
disowned, unknown
unrefined: boorish,
coarse, natural,
philistine, plebeian,
primitive, raw

unrehearsed:
impromptu
unrelated: foreign,
irrelevant, remote,
unlike
unrelenting: austere,
constant, flinty, grim,
harsh, implacable,
incessant, obdurate,
persistent, relentless,
unbending
unreliable: deceptive,
faithless, fallible,
false, inaccurate,
insecure,
irresponsible, shaky,
slippery, uncertain,
unfaithful,
unpredictable
unremarkable:
nondescript, ordinary
unremitting:
incessant, nonstop,
perpetual, persistent,
relentless, unbroken
unremittingly:
nonstop
unremunerative:
unprofitable
unrepeatable: freak,
unique
unrepresentative:
misleading
unrepressed:
uninhibited
unrequired:
superfluous
unreserved: implicit,
unqualified, zealous
unreservedly:
openly, out
unresisting: passive
unresolved:
uncertain, undecided,
unsettled
unresponsive: chilly,
deaf, frigid, inert,
quiet, sluggish,
undemonstrative
unresponsiveness:
inertia
unrest: trouble
unrestrained: broad,
demonstrative,
furious, immodest,
impetuous,
incontinent,
inordinate, lavish,
lawless, libertine,
rampant, unbounded,
unbridled
unrestrainedly:
freely, unreservedly
unrestricted: free,
libertine, open-ended,
public, unconditional,

uninhibited,
universal, unqualified
unrestrictedly: freely
unrevealed:
undisclosed
unrewarding:
unprofitable
unrighteous: sinful
unrighteousness: sin
unripe: green,
immature, tender
unripeness:
tenderness
unrivalled:
matchless, peerless,
pre-eminent, unique
unruffled: calm,
collected, cool, even,
imperturbable,
peaceful,
philosophical, placid,
serene, smooth,
sober, unconcerned,
undisturbed,
unimpressed,
unrepentant
unruliness: licence,
licentiousness
unruly: boisterous,
disruptive, fractious,
lawless, obstreperous,
problem, recalcitrant,
unbridled,
undisciplined,
ungovernable
unsalaried: unpaid
unsatisfactorily:
poorly
unsatisfactory:
inadequate, limited,
sad, unacceptable
unsatisfied:
murmuring
unsatisfying: jejune
unsavoury:
unappetizing,
undesirable
unscalable:
impassable
unscathed: safe,
unharmed
unschooled:
inexperienced,
undisciplined
unscripted:
impromptu
unscrupulous: bent,
corrupt, crooked,
dishonest, foul,
knavish, shady, sharp,
unconscionable,
unethical
unscrutinized:
unquestioned
unseal: open
unseasoned: green

unseat: oust, remove, supplant, throw
unsectarian: catholic
unseeing: blind
unseemly: improper, inappropriate, indelicate, objectionable, scandalous, undignified
unseen: blind, invisible
unselfconscious: uninhibited
unselfish: considerate, selfless
unselfishness: magnanimity
unsentimental: realistic
unserviceable: kaput
unsettle: disturb, perturb, put off, shake up, turn
unsettled: changeable, disconcerted, inconclusive, open, outstanding, owing, pending, queasy, restless, undecided, volatile
unsettling: divisive, off-putting
unshackle: release
unshakable: firm, implicit, obdurate
unshaped: blank
unshared: exclusive, single
unshaven: hairy
unsheathe: draw
unshorn: shaggy
unsightly: hideous, ugly
unskilful: clumsy, menial, raw
unsociable: inhospitable, solitary, unfriendly
unsoiled: clean
unsolicited: unwanted
unsolvable: unanswerable
unsophisticated: green, gross, innocent, juvenile, naive, natural, primitive, provincial, simple, unworldly
unsophistication: innocence
unsought: unasked, uncalled-for, unexpected,

unsolicited
unsound: illogical, shaky, specious, unreliable, unsafe, untenable
unsparing: free, hard, hard-hitting, severe
unspeakable: nameless, outrageous, shocking, unbearable, unmentionable
unspeakably: unutterably
unspecified: vague
unspiritual: physical
unspoilt: savage
unspoken: implicit, mute, silent, understood
unsporting: unfair
unsportsmanlike: foul
unstable: brittle, changeable, chequered, dazed, explosive, maladjusted, mutable, neurotic, precarious, shaky, slippery, unsafe, unsettled, variable, volatile
unstated: unspoken
unsteadiness: frailty
unsteady: dazed, flimsy, frail, groggy, insecure, irregular, precarious, ramshackle, restless, slippery, unsettled
unstinting: bountiful, profuse, zealous
unstoppable: irrepressible, relentless
unstretched: untried
unsuccessful: failure, fruitless, futile, unavailing, vain
unsuitability: impracticality
unsuitable: impractical, improper, inappropriate, ineligible, inept, undesirable, unfit, unseemly
unsuited: inappropriate, incongruous, unequal
unsullied: virgin
unsung: unheard-of, unknown
unsupported: unaided, unconfirmed
unsure: doubtful,

insecure, tentative, uncertain
unsurpassed: peerless
unsurprised: unimpressed
unsusceptible: callous
unsuspecting: gullible
unsustainable: untenable
unswept: dusty
unswerving: firm, religious, unhesitating, unshakable
unsympathetic: callous, cold, incompatible, uncharitable
unsystematic: unbusinesslike
unsystematically: haphazardly
untainted: good, pure
untamable: ungovernable
untamed: fierce, savage, unbroken
untangle: comb, unravel
untarnished: clear, immaculate, perfect
untaught: dark, ignorant, illiterate, unaware
untenanted: uninhabited
untested: untried
unthinkable: impossible, inconceivable, preposterous, unattainable, unheard-of
unthinking: blind, careless, impetuous, inadvertent, inconsiderate, mechanical, perfunctory, rash, short-sighted, unguarded, unintelligent, unintentional, vacant
unthinkingly: blindly
untidiness: disorder, mess
untidy: dishevelled, disorganized, scruffy, slovenly, unbusinesslike, upset
untie: free, liberate, release, undo
untied: undone

until: pending
untilled: fallow
untimely: awkward, impolitic, inappropriate, inopportune, premature, previous, unfavourable, unpopular
untiring: tireless
untitled: nameless
untold: incalculable, infinite, myriad
untouchable: leper, outcast, pariah
untouched: intact, undisturbed, unspoilt, virgin
untoward: fishy, improbable, uncommon
untraced: mislaid
untrained: fresh, green, ignorant, primitive, raw, undisciplined, unskilled
untreated: raw
untried: inexperienced, new
untroubled: carefree, unconcerned
untrue: false, fictitious, illusory, invalid, legendary, libellous, scandalous
untrustworthy: deceitful, deceptive, dishonest, faithless, fallible, false, irresponsible, perfidious, shady, shifty, slippery, unreliable, untrue
untruth: falsehood, fib, fiction, fudge, invention, lie
untruthful: dishonest, false, perjured
untruthfulness: falsehood, insincerity
untying: liberation
untypical: uncharacteristic
unusable: inadmissible
unused: blank, extra, fallow, free, idle, inactive, maiden, mint, new, unaccustomed, virgin
unusual: colourful, curious, exceptional, interesting, irregular, notable, novel, odd,

original, particular,
peculiar, quaint,
queer, rare,
remarkable,
unaccustomed,
uncharacteristic,
uncommon,
unconventional,
unnatural
unusually: especially,
particularly
unuttered: unspoken
unvarnished: hard,
unfinished
unvarying: constant,
homogeneous,
monotonous, same,
uniform
unveil: reveal, unmask
unventilated: close
unverified:
unconfirmed
unversed:
inexperienced
unvetted:
unquestioned
unviable:
uneconomic,
unprofitable
unviolated: intact
unvoiced: unspoken
unwanted: needless,
unasked, undesirable,
unpopular
unwarrantable:
inexcusable
unwarranted:
gratuitous,
illegitimate,
improper, inordinate,
unauthorized,
uncalled-for,
unfounded,
unreasonable
unwary: unsuspecting
unwavering:
constant, even, flinty,
resolute,
unhesitating,
unshakable
unwed: maiden
unwelcome:
inopportune,
intrusive, uncalled-
for, undesirable,
unpopular,
unsolicited, unwanted
unwelcoming: chilly,
inhospitable
unwell: ill, off colour,
peaky, poorly, seedy
unwieldy: awkward,
bulky, hulking
unwilling: averse,
disinclined, grudging,
hesitant, involuntary,

negative, reluctant,
unhelpful
unwillingness:
aversion,
indisposition
unwind: relax,
unravel
unwitting: happy,
ignorant, inadvertent,
unconscious,
unintentional,
unsuspecting
unwittingly: blindly,
happily
unwonted:
unaccustomed,
uncharacteristic
unworkability:
impracticality
unworkable: crazy,
impossible,
impractical, mad,
unrealistic
unworkmanlike:
inept
unworldliness:
innocence
unworldly: bookish,
innocent, naive
unworthy: below,
beneath, disgraceful,
reprehensible,
shameful, unseemly
unwrap: open
unwrinkled: smooth
unwritten: traditional
unyielding: dogged,
dour, flinty, hard,
intransigent,
obdurate, relentless,
tough, unbending
upbraid: censure,
condemn, lash, nag,
rebuke, reprimand,
reproach, scold
upcountry: provincial
update: modernize,
revise
upend: overturn,
reverse
upgrade: lift, prefer,
promote, raise
upgrading: elevation,
preferment,
promotion
upheaval: confusion,
convulsion,
maelstrom, revolution
uphill: difficult, hard,
ordeal, tough
uphold: assert, carry,
champion, claim,
defend, justify,
maintain, preserve,
ratify, support,
sustain, vindicate

upholder: pillar
upholstery: trim
upkeep: maintenance
upland: highlands,
mountainous
uplift: lift
upper: drug, senior
uppermost: chief
uppish:
presumptuous,
snobbish
upraise: lift
upright: clean,
column,
conscientious, erect,
good, honest,
honourable, just, law-
abiding, leg, noble,
perpendicular, pier,
pile, pillar, post,
quarter, rampant,
reliable, reputable,
respectable, shaft,
solid, true, vertical,
virtuous
uprightness:
character, honesty,
honour, nobility
uprising:
insurrection, mutiny,
revolt, revolution
uproar: bedlam,
commotion,
disturbance, furore,
hell, hubbub,
kerfuffle, noise,
outcry, racket, rattle,
tempest
uproarious: hilarious,
hysterical, killing,
noisy
uproot: extract, pull
up
uprooting: extraction
upset: blow, capsize,
concerned, confuse,
dislocate, displease,
distress, disturbance,
ferment, flustered,
inconvenience, invert,
keel over, offend,
peeved, perturb, put
out, rattle, shake up,
shatter, spill, spoil,
swamp, trauma,
trouble, turn,
unnerved, upheaval,
upside down, vex
upsetting: disruptive,
divisive, poignant,
sad, traumatic,
vexatious
upshot: conclusion,
issue, outcome,
ramifications
upstage: dominate

upstanding: moral
upsurge: boom,
increase, leap,
outbreak, surge
uptight: nervous,
overwrought,
simmering
upturn: boom, jump,
recovery
urban: municipal
urbane: bland,
civilized, cool,
imperturbable,
refined, sophisticated,
suave
urbanity:
sophistication
urchin: youngster
urge: call, carry,
caution, compel,
compulsion, counsel,
egg, excitement,
exhort, hankering,
hasten, impel,
implore, impulse, jog,
mind, petition, press,
prod, push, put up,
recommend, spur
urgency: emergency,
haste, hurry, need,
press
urgent: cogent,
compelling, critical,
desperate, dire, grave,
immediate,
imperative, pressing,
sore
urgently: desperately
urination: leak
urn: jar, jug, pot, vat
usable: available,
disposable, operative,
viable
usage: custom,
etiquette, fashion,
habit, idiom, jargon,
manner, practice,
system, tradition,
treatment, use, vogue
use: benefit, borrow,
burn, consume,
convenience, enjoy,
exercise, finish, go
through, good,
handle, help, manage,
management,
manipulation,
operate, operation,
ply, practice, profit,
profit by, purpose,
requisition, resort,
sense, service, take,
tap, touch, usage,
value
used: gone
useful: beneficial,

constructive,
convenient, desirable,
effective, good,
handy, helpful,
instrumental,
positive, productive,
profitable, salutary,
serviceable, valuable
usefulness:
convenience, good,
importance, value
useless: dead,
dreadful, fruitless,
futile, hollow,
hopeless, idle,
impotent, ineffectual,
kaput, meaningless,
needless, nugatory,
otiose, pathetic,
pointless,
purposeless,
redundant, terrible,

unavailing, unfit,
unhelpful,
unnecessary,
unprofitable, vain,
void
uselessness:
impotence,
impracticality,
nullity, vanity
user: operator
usher: attend,
attendant, conduct,
direct, guide, guide,
herald, inaugurate,
introduce, lead,
marshal, see,
shepherd, take
using: consumption
usual: average,
common,
conventional,
customary, habitual,

home, natural,
normal, ordinary,
orthodox, par,
prevalent, quotidian,
regular, regulation
usually: mainly,
ordinarily
usualness: normality
usurp: assume,
commandeer, possess,
supersede
usurpation:
assumption, seizure
usurped: poached
utensil: implement,
instrument
utensils: kit
utilitarian: down-to-
earth, practical,
pragmatic
utility: disposal, duty,
service

utilization: exercise
utilize: borrow,
exercise, harness, ply,
profit by, requisition,
tap, turn, use
utmost: best, last,
supreme
utopian: ideal
utter: complete,
congenital,
consummate, gross,
heave, outright,
perfect, pure, rank,
say, sheer, speak,
thorough, total, vent
utterance: remark
uttered: vocal
utterly: completely,
flat, flatly, fully,
heavily, hollow,
unreservedly

V

vacancy: opening
vacant: available,
bare, fishy, free,
hollow, listless, open,
uninhabited,
unsettled, unthinking,
void
vacate: desert,
evacuate, leave,
remove, resign
vacation: leave,
leisure, rest
vaccinate: immunize
vaccination: jab
vacillate: change,
doubt, falter,
fluctuate, hesitate,
hover, oscillate,
stagger, vary, waver
vacillating: faltering,
fickle, hesitant,
infirm, spineless,
tottering, uncertain,
undecided, variable
vacillation:
indecision
vacuity: blank
vacuous: blank,
fatuous, vacant
vacuum: blank, gap,
oblivion, vacancy,
void
vagabond: scoundrel,
vagrant, wretch
vagary: freak,
humour, kink, quirk,
whim
vagrant: beggar,
derelict, gypsy,
itinerant, outcast,
wandering
vague: dim, doubtful,
dreamy, faint, foggy,
general, ghostly, grey,
imprecise, inattentive,
indefinite, indistinct,
lax, loose, muddled,
muddy, nebulous,
noncommittal,
nondescript, obscure,
rough, shadowy,
sketchy, uncertain,
unclear, woolly
vaguely: roughly
vagueness: blur,
obscurity
vain: cocky, fruitless,

futile, hopeless, idle,
ineffectual, pointless,
proud
vainglorious:
conceited, pompous,
supercilious
vale: valley
valentine: sweetheart
valet: man
Valhalla: heaven
valiant: bold,
chivalrous, gallant,
hardy, heroic,
intrepid, stout
valiantly: manfully
valid: authentic,
authoritative,
available, certain,
good, legitimate,
logical, real, right,
sound, true
validate: certify,
execute, justify,
legalize, pass, ratify,
seal, sustain
validation:
confirmation
validity: legality, life,
meaning
valley: basin, dell, dip
valour: courage,
gallantry, heroism,
manliness, prowess
valuable: beneficial,
big, choice, good,
precious, profitable,
rich, salutary, useful,
worthwhile
valuation: judgement,
measurement, worth
value: assess,
calculate, class,
consequence,
denomination, figure,
gauge, ideal,
importance, judge,
meaning, measure,
merit, premium,
price, prize, profit,
quality, rarity, rate,
respect, use, weight,
worth
valued: dear, precious
valueless: otiose,
unprofitable,
worthless
values: philosophy

valve: gate
vamoose: get off
van: car, caravan, fore,
forefront, head
vandal: barbarian,
hooligan, yob
vandalize: damage,
deface, sabotage
vane: fan
vanguard: leader,
precursor
vanish: consume,
depart, disappear,
dissolve, evaporate,
fade, flee, fly, melt,
pass, perish, set, take
off
vanished: extinct,
gone, lost, mislaid
vanishing:
disappearance
vanity: conceit, levity,
narcissism
vanquish: beat,
conquer, overcome,
reduce, worst
vanquisher:
conqueror, victor,
victorious
vantage point:
viewpoint
vapid: banal, barren,
bland, flat, insipid,
lacklustre, mousy,
unimaginative, watery
vaporize: boil,
evaporate
vaporizing: volatile
vapour: cloud, damp,
fume, mist
variability: inequality
variable: changeable,
fickle, flexible,
inconsistent,
irregular, mutable,
patchy, uncertain,
uneven,
unpredictable,
unsettled, volatile
variance: breach,
diversity, modulation
variant: derivative,
mutation, other,
rogue, version
variation: difference,
diversity, inequality,
tolerance

varied: chequered,
different, diverse,
sundry
variegated:
chequered, colourful,
dappled, mottled,
pied
variety: assortment,
brand, breed, change,
choice, description,
diversity, hash, kind,
make, medley, mix,
nature, pattern,
range, run, sort,
species, stock
various: assorted,
different, diverse,
manifold, many,
miscellaneous, mixed,
multiple, odd,
several, sundry,
unequal
varnish: glaze,
lacquer, polish
vary: change, deviate,
differ, fluctuate,
oscillate, range,
relieve, shift, swing,
waver
varying: irregular,
scrappy, uncertain,
uneven
vase: cup, jar
vases: crockery
vassal: satellite, slave,
subject
vassalage: servitude,
slavery
vast: bumper, fat,
giant, great, huge,
immense,
incalculable, infinite,
large, massive,
mighty, monster,
monstrous,
monumental,
mountainous,
prodigious, profound,
spacious, stupendous,
wide
vastness: enormity,
immensity, wild
vat: barrel, keg
vault: basement,
cellar, dome, grave,
jump, leap, safe,
spring, tomb,

treasury
vaunt: boast, display, flourish, parade
vaunting: boastful
veer: back, bear, bend, change, deflect, depart, haul, hook, jerk, jink, lurch, shift, slide, swerve, swing, tack, turn, wander
veering: shift
vegetable: plant
vegetables: greens
vegetate: idle, stagnate
vegetation: plant
vehemence: emotion, fervour, force, heat, passion, strength, vengeance, violence
vehement: earnest, fervent, flaming, hot, impassioned, intense, passionate, strong, violent, vociferous
vehicle: car, carriage, cart, coach, instrument, machine, medium, transport, voice
vehicles: traffic
veil: blanket, cloak, cloud, cover, disguise, envelop, hide, mantle, mask, obscure, pall, shade, veneer
veiled: hidden, obscure, shrouded, ulterior
vein: band, bed, fund, ledge, manner, pipe, seam, strain, style
veldt: bush, desert, scrub, waste, wild
velocity: clip, lick, pace, rate, speed
velum: veil
velvety: fluffy, plush, silken, smooth, soft
venal: commercial, mercenary, rotten, sordid
vend: hawk, market, peddle, sell
vendetta: feud, quarrel
vending: sale
vendor: seller
veneer: façade, face, lacquer, sheet, surface
venerable: holy, sacred, solemn
venerate: fear, glorify, honour, idolize, respect, revere, worship

veneration: awe, fear, glory, homage, honour, piety
vengeance: reprisal, retribution, revenge
venom: gall, poison, spite
venomous: baleful, baneful, deadly, pernicious, poisonous, vicious, virulent
vent: give, opening, outlet, pipe, utter
ventilate: fan
venture: attempt, chance, dare, gamble, hazard, job, presume, project, risk, speculate, stake, throw, wager
venturesome: daring
venue: place
veracious: honest
veracity: honesty
verandah: balcony
verb-form: voice
verbal: oral
verbatim: direct, literally
verbiage: gab, padding, stuff, waffle
verbose: garrulous, ponderous, redundant, wordy
verdant: fresh, green, lush, luxuriant
verdict: decision, diagnosis, doom, finding, judgement, resolution, ruling, sentence, vote
verdure: grass
verge: brink, ditch, margin, rim, side, threshold
verification: backing, clinch, confirmation, proof, testimony, witness
verified: historical
verify: ascertain, attest, back up, certify, check, clinch, confirm, prove, support, sustain, test, witness
veritable: authentic, genuine, real, true
veritably: even, indeed, truly
vernacular: cant, idiom, idiomatic, native, terminology, usage, vulgar
versatile: changeable,

quick, universal, useful
verse: school, text
versifier: poet
version: interpretation, model, reading, variant, variation
verso: reverse
versus: counter
vertebrae: back, backbone, spine
vertex: pinnacle, zenith
vertical: bluff, erect, perpendicular, standing, straight, upright
vertiginous: dizzy, giddy
vertigo: dizziness
verve: energy, fire, go, kick, life, vigour, zeal, zip
very: beastly, desperately, full, jolly, mightily, rather, same, so, truly
vesicatory: blister
vesicle: blister, bubble
vessel: boat, bowl, capsule, container, craft, jar, launch, pan, pipe, pot, reservoir, ship, tank, vat
vest: blouse
vestal: chaste
vested: constitutional
vestibule: foyer, hall, lobby, passage
vestige: mark, shadow, spark, whiff
vestiges: remains
vestigial: elemental, elementary
vestment: pall, robe, clothes/clothing
vet: censor, inspect, screen
veteran: experienced, old, seasoned
veto: ban, forbid, kill, miss, negative, overrule, refuse, reject
vetoed: forbidden
vetoing: killing
vetting: censorship
vex: bother, chafe, chagrin, discomfort, displease, fret, gall, harass, molest, nag, nark, offend, pain, pique, press, ruffle, spite, wear

vexation: bother, care, chagrin, discomfort, gall, mischievous, nagging, nuisance, resentment, trouble, wearisome
vexed: peeved, sore, sulky, uptight
vexing: wearing
via: by, through
viable: economic, feasible, possible, practicable, tenable, working
viaduct: bridge
viands: meat
vibrance: depth, vivacity
vibrant: colourful, resounding, rich, vital, vivacious
vibrate: beat, flutter, jangle, jar, jerk, jog, oscillate, pulse, quake, quiver, rattle, reverberate, swing, tremble, wag
vibration: beat, flutter, jar, pulse, quake, quaver, quiver, shake, swing, tremor
vicar: clergyman, father, minister, parson, pastor, priest
vice: clamp, depravity, disease, evil, frailty, immorality
vice-: assistant
vicinity: locality, part, patch, place, proximity, region
vicious: cruel, ferocious, iniquitous, malevolent, malignant, monstrous, nasty, poisonous, rotten, sadistic, savage, villainous, virulent, wicked
viciousness: cruelty, ferocity, malice, nastiness
vicissitude: reverse
victim: casualty, guinea-pig, patient, pigeon, prey, quarry, target
victimize: persecute, prey on
victor: best, champion, conqueror, hero
victorious: best, winning

victory: attainment, conquest, gain, knockout, mastery, palm, win
victual: cater, feed, provision, ration, supply
victualling: provision
victuals: food, groceries, meat, ration, repast, sustenance
video: film, tape
video-tape: record
vie: play, rival, take on
view: belief, conviction, elevation, exposure, feeling, glimpse, idea, judgement, light, look, observe, opinion, outlook, panorama, persuasion, prospect, regard, scene, see, sentiment, side, sight, survey, thesis, understanding, vision, voice, watch, witness
viewer: audience, spectator, witness
viewing: onlooking
viewpoint: aspect, attitude, idea, light, philosophy, sentiment, slant, stance
vigil: eve, lookout, wake, watch
vigilance: care, caution, guard, jealousy, prudence
vigilant: awake, careful, cautious, circumspect, jealous, observant, sleepless, wary, watchful
vigilantly: warily
vignette: profile
vigorous: athletic, beefy, brisk, dynamic, effective, exuberant, hard-hitting, hearty, live, lively, living, lusty, mighty, muscular, potent, powerful, productive, racy, rank, robust, rousing, sound, stiff, strenuous, sturdy, virile, warm
vigorously: hard, mightily
vigour: bang, beef,

brawn, drive, energy, exuberance, fire, force, go, kick, life, potency, power, push, snap, spirit, stamina, strength, tone, warmth, zip
vile: beastly, contemptible, despicable, disgusting, evil, nasty, obscene, odious, offensive, repulsive, rotten, sickening, sordid
vile: villainous
vileness: nastiness, obscenity
vilification: attack, calumny, invective, libel, smear
vilificatory: defamatory, vituperative
vilify: attack, blast, libel, slam, slander, smear
vilifying: libellous
villa: chalet, lodge
village: hamlet, place
villager: yokel
villain: black sheep, criminal, crook, dog, hound, jerk, knave, malefactor, rogue, ruffian, scoundrel, terror, wretch
villainous: black, knavish, wicked
villainy: crime, foul
villein: slave
villus: hair
vim: sparkle, vigour, zip
vindicate: assert, bear out, clear, defend, justify, rationalize, revenge, right, salve, uphold
vindication: defence, justification, plea, reason
vindicator: champion
vindictive: malevolent, malignant, vengeful, venomous, vicious, virulent
vindictiveness: malice, revenge
vinegary: sharp
vino: drink
vinyl: plastic
violate: breach, break, infringe, outrage, profane, rape

violating: sacrilegious
violation: betrayal, breach, outrage, rape
violence: force, fury, sword, vengeance
violent: blustery, boisterous, explosive, fierce, flaming, forcible, furious, hard, heavy, passionate, precipitate, rabid, rough, tempestuous, torrid, tough, unbridled, vicious, wild
violently: bang, hard, roughly
violet: maroon
violin: fiddle
VIP: personage, somebody, top brass
virago: bag, bitch, dragon, harridan, nag
virgin: immaculate, innocent, intact, maiden, new, pure, wild
virginal: celibate, maiden, pure
virginity: honour, innocence, purity
virgule: diagonal
virile: lusty, macho, male, strong, vigorous
virility: manliness, vigour
virtually: literally, nearly, practically
virtue: good, honesty, honour, innocence, integrity, merit, morality, principle, propriety, purity, right, worth
virtuosity: flair, mastery
virtuoso: artist, genius, magician, marvel, master, masterly, player, professional, wizard
virtuous: chaste, clean, good, honest, honourable, immaculate, moral, pure, right, saintly, upright, wholesome, worthy
virtuously: right
virulence: venom
virulent: bitter, caustic, corrosive, lethal, malignant, poisonous, venomous, vitriolic, waspish

virus: bug, microbe
visa: permit
viscera: guts, insides, intestines
viscous: slimy, sticky
visibility: prominence, sight
visible: conspicuous, external, manifest, obvious, ostensible, outward, overt, physical, transparent
visibly: measurably, outwardly
vision: dream, eye, fantasy, hallucination, imagination, insight, knockout, sight, spectre, spirit
visionary: impractical, prophetic, romantic, Utopian
visit: attend, call, clock, do, haunt, inflict, lionize, look up, see, sojourn, stay, stop, tour
visitor: guest
visitors: company
visor: mask
vista: outlook, panorama, prospect, scene, sight, sweep, view
visual: graphic
visualize: imagine, picture, see
vital: basic, capital, chief, critical, crucial, imperative, indispensable, invaluable, key, live, main, material, necessary, prerequisite, pressing, principal, significant, strategic, urgent
vitality: life, soul, vigour, zap, zip
vitriolic: sharp
vituperate: scold, slang
vituperation: attack, calumny, imprecation, insult, invective, vilification
vivacious: bright, dynamic, exuberant, high-spirited, lively, playful, quick, spirited, vibrant, vital
vivacity: bounce, energy, exuberance, fire, go, life, sparkle

vivid: bold, bright, colourful, dramatic, expressive, gaudy, glaring, graphic, imaginative, juicy, living, lurid, pictorial, poetic, rich, warm

vividness: colour

vixen: bitch, fox

vocable: word

vocabulary: diction, language, nomenclature, notation, terminology, usage

vocalists: choir

vocation: calling, career, craft, job, niche, occupation, practice, profession

vocational: professional

vociferate: bawl, roar

vociferation: bawl

vociferous: noisy, vocal

vogue: currency, fad, fashion, kick, rage, rave, style

voice: let out, part, say, speak, state, utter, vent, vote

voiced: vocal

voiceless: mute, silent

voice-over: narrative, narrator

void: bare, blank, chasm, evacuate, exhaust, gap, gulf, immensity, invalid, nothing, oblivion, vacancy, vacuum

volatile: changeable, explosive, fiery, fluid, giddy, moody, mutable, quick, quick-tempered, temperamental

volatility: temperament

volition: will

volitional: wilful

volley: barrage, burst, cannon, flight, hail, shower

voltaic cell: battery

voluble: gushing, wordy

volume: book, bulk, capacity, content, edition, magnitude, novel, quantity, room, size, space

voluminous: capacious, full

voluntarily: freely, readily, unasked, willingly

voluntary: deliberate, discretionary, gratuitous, interlude, optional, unpaid, unsolicited, wilful, willing

volunteer: irregular, offer, tender, venture

volunteered: unsolicited

voluptuary: libertine

voluptuous: erotic, luscious, sensual, sexy, sultry

volute: spiral

voluted: spiral

vomit: bring up, cough, eject, void

voodoo: jinx

voracious: insatiable, predatory, rapacious, ravenous

voracity: greed, passion

vortex: maelstrom, whirlwind

vote: elect, franchise, plump, poll, say, voice

vote-counter: teller

voter: constituent

voters: country, people, public

vouch: attest, authorize, certify, guarantee, pledge, promise, recommend, sanction, warrant

voucher: certificate, pass, ticket

vouchsafe: grant

vow: engagement, oath, pledge, promise, swear, word

voyage: cruise, journey, migrate, passage, sail, trip

voyager: tourist

vulgar: barbarian, barbaric, base, boorish, broad, cheap, churlish, coarse, common, flashy, gross, immodest, improper, indelicate, loud, low, naughty, plebeian, profane, rank, raunchy, rude, scurrilous, uncouth, unseemly, upstart, vile

vulgarity: impropriety, naughtiness

vulnerability: exposure, frailty, jeopardy

vulnerable: helpless, human, insecure, liable, open, powerless, subject, susceptible, unguarded, unsafe, untenable, weak

vulture: predator

vulturine: predatory

W

wad: pad, plug
wadding: padding
waddle: roll
wade: dabble, ford,
paddle, splash,
wallow
wadi: oasis
wafer: chip, cracker
waffle: drivel, evasion,
flannel, gab, go on,
nonsense, padding
waft: blow, breath,
drift, ooze
wag: joker, laugh,
wave, wit
wager: bet, chance,
dare, flutter, gamble,
hazard, lay, play, put
on, stake, venture
wages: hire, pay,
payment, reward,
screw
waggish: funny,
humorous, jocular,
merry, playful, witty
waggishness:
merriment
waggle: wriggle
wagon: caravan, cart,
skip
wail: bawl, blast, keen,
lament, moan,
scream, shriek,
squeal, ululate,
whine, yell
wailing: bawl,
lamentation
waist: middle
wait: attend, await,
delay, hesitate, linger,
remain, stand by
waiter: attendant
waive: forgo,
surrender
wake: track
wakeful: sleepless
waken: call
walk: avenue,
constitutional, foot,
gait, march, pace,
path, ramble, roam,
saunter, step, stroll,
tread, turn
walker: pedestrian
walking: hiking,
pedestrian
walkover: pushover,

whitewash
walkway: path
wall: barrier, dam,
embankment,
enclosure, face,
fortification,
partition, rampart
wallop: bang, batter,
blow, box, clap, clip,
clout, hit, punch,
slap, strike
walloping: drubbing,
hiding
wallow: blunder.
wallow: flounder,
indulge, pitch, revel,
roll, splash
wallowing: roll
walrus: bull
wan: cadaverous, grey,
livid, lurid, pale,
sallow, seedy,
unwholesome
wand: mace, rod, staff,
stick
wander: digress,
diverge, gad, journey,
ramble, range, roam,
saunter, stray, stroll,
traverse
wanderer: stray,
vagrant
wandering: delirious,
itinerant,
maundering,
meandering, restless
wanderings: journey
wane: decrease, die,
disappear, fade, fail,
fizzle out, flag, lull,
pass, recede, regress,
remit, subside, taper,
weaken, wilt
wangle: contrive, get,
manoeuvre
waning: decrease,
disappearance,
flagging, moribund,
obsolescent, recession
want: care, desire,
lack, necessity, need,
please, require,
requirement, scarcity,
shortage, void, will,
wish
wanting: lacking,
short, wishful

wanton: dissolute,
lascivious, libertine,
loose, lost,
promiscuous,
shameless
wantonness:
dissolution, licence,
licentiousness, lust
wapentake: ward
war: battle, clash,
feud, fight, sword
warble: intone, pipe,
sing
ward: avert, bay, care,
charge, custody,
deflect, head, repel
warden: attendant,
caretaker, custodian,
guardian, janitor,
keeper, monitor
warder: guard,
guardian, keeper,
screw
wardrobe: clothes/
clothing
wardship: patronage
ware: cargo
warehouse: depot,
factory, store
wares: goods,
merchandise
warfare: battle,
combat, conflict
warily: gingerly
wariness: distrust,
guard, jealousy,
precaution, prudence,
suspicion
warlike: martial,
militant
warlock: magician,
wizard
warm-hearted:
genial
warm: cordial, cosy,
cuddly, hearty, heat,
intimate, kindly,
mild, snug, sociable,
wholehearted
warmish: tepid
warmly: kindly, well
warmonger: hawk,
militant
warmth: feeling,
glow, heat, kindliness,
love, mildness,
sympathy

warn: caution,
intimate, notify
warning: beacon,
caution, lesson,
notice, notification,
omen, sign, symptom,
threat
warp: bend, bow,
buckle, distort,
eccentricity, flex,
mooring, pervert,
poison
warpaint: make-up
warpath: offensive
warped: bent,
crooked, deformed,
kinky, misshapen,
twisted, unhealthy,
unnatural, untrue
warrant: authority,
authorize, certificate,
commission, deserve,
guarantee,
justification, justify,
licence, license,
mandate, merit, pass,
permit, power,
sanction, swear
warranted: legitimate
warranty: bail,
guarantee, insurance
warren: burrow
warrior: champion
warships: navy
wary: cag(e)y, careful,
cautious, defensive,
discreet, guarded,
jealous, judicious,
observant, shy,
watchful
wash: bath, bathe,
clean, fade, flush, lick,
lotion, paint, pan,
purge, purify, scrub,
splash, tint, wake
washbasin: basin
washbowl: basin
washed: clean
washout: failure
washroom: lavatory,
toilet
washstand: basin
washtub: bath
waspish: cross, ill-
humoured, peevish,
peppery, petulant,
prickly, quick-

tempered, sour
wastage: loss
waste: barren,
consume,
consumption, decay,
desert, exhaust,
garbage, junk, kill,
knock off, languish,
lavish, leavings, lose,
loss, murder, perish,
pine, ravage, refuse,
rubbish, sack, scrap,
slag, solitude, spend,
squander, swallow,
uninhabited, wild,
wilderness, wither
wasted: barren,
hectic, lost, vain
wasteful: extravagant,
inefficient, lavish,
spendthrift,
unnecessary
wasteland: desert,
heath, wild,
wilderness
waster: spendthrift
wasting: decay
wastrel: layabout,
prodigal
watch: clock, eye,
look, lookout, mark,
observation, observe,
patrol, police, regard,
see, sentry, spy, view,
wake, witness
watched: marked
watcher: spectator,
tail, witness
watchful: awake,
cautious,
circumspect,
expectant, jealous,
observant, sleepless,
wary
watchfully: warily
watchfulness: guard,
jealousy
watching: onlooking
watchman: guard,
lookout, patrol,
warden, warder
watchtower: beacon,
lookout
watchword: cry,
motto
water: damp, irrigate,
wet
watercourse: canal,
river
waterfall: cataract
waterfowl: duck
waterlog: saturate,
swamp
waterlogged: sodden,
wet
waterproof:

mackintosh, seal
watershed: divide,
shed
waterside: shore
watersplash: ford
waterway: river
watery: dilute, flat,
fluid, insipid, juicy,
liquid, moist, thin,
weak, wet
wattle: jowls
wave: dangle,
epidemic, flag, flap,
flourish, fly, hold up,
motion, pass, shake,
sign, signal, surge,
sway, swell, swing,
switch, vehicle, wag
waver: doubt, falter,
fluctuate, hesitate,
hover, oscillate,
pause, quaver,
stagger, vary, wilt
wavering:
changeable, doubt,
flickering, hesitant,
suspense, tottering,
undecided, variable
waving: flagging
wavy: undulating
wax: finish, polish,
rise
waxen: livid, wan,
white
way: channel, course,
fashion, form, habit,
manner, means,
medium, method,
motion, passage,
path, practice,
progress, route,
routine, rule, scale,
style, tack, tactic,
technique, thread, use
wayfarer: pilgrim
wayfaring: itinerant,
wandering
waylay: buttonhole,
hold up
ways: conduct
wayward: capricious,
contrary, naughty,
perverse, problem,
recalcitrant,
undisciplined, wild
waywardness:
naughtiness
weak: bland,
cowardly, decrepit,
delicate, dim, faint,
feeble, flimsy, fragile,
frail, helpless,
impotent, indistinct,
ineffectual, inefficient,
infirm, insipid,
jejune, lame, languid,

lazy, lean, light, limp,
low, meek, pale,
pathetic, powerless,
sickly, slender, soft,
spineless, tender,
tenuous, thin,
unhealthy, untenable,
vulnerable, wan,
watery, wet
weaken: blunt,
decline, degrade,
depress, devalue,
dilute, exhaust,
fatigue, impair,
languish, loosen,
rarefy, reduce,
relapse, sap, shake,
sink, tax, thin,
undercut, water, wilt
weakened: dilute
weakening: decline,
depressing, relaxation
weakest: runt
weakling: drip,
rabbit, sap, weed, wet
weakly: puny
weakness: crack,
debility, defect,
deficiency,
disadvantage, disease,
failing, fatigue,
fondness, frailty,
impotence, languor,
lassitude, love,
shortcoming,
tenderness
weal: lash
wealth: capital, estate,
fortune, means, mine,
money, plenty,
profusion, property,
prosperity, resources
wealthy: fashionable,
flush, jet, loaded,
opulent, rich, warm
wear: assume,
clothes/clothing,
erosion, get on, have
on, put on, thumb,
wash
wearied: jaded,
languid, worn
weariness: fatigue,
languor, lassitude
wearing: gnawing,
punishing
wearisome: boring,
interminable,
monotonous, slow,
trying
weary: bore, flag,
languish, pall, sick,
spent, tired, wear
wearying: flagging,
wearing
weather: climate,

overcome, resist, sky,
withstand
weatherbeaten:
battered, elderly
weathered: rugged,
seasoned
weave: bob, fabric,
grain, knit, knot,
texture, tissue
web: mat, maze, mesh,
net, network, tissue
webbing: mesh
wed: hitch, married,
marry, mate, pair,
take, unify, unite
wedded: conjugal,
marital, married,
matrimonial
wedding: matrimony
wedge: jam, key, slice,
squeeze, stuff
wedlock: matrimony,
union
wee: little, urinate
weed: drip, marijuana,
weakling, wet
weedy: lanky
weekly: journal,
magazine, periodical
weep: bewail, cry,
greet, grieve, ooze,
sob, wail, whimper
weeping: lamentation,
mourning, ooze,
pendulous, sob,
tearful
weepy: lachrymose,
tearful
weigh: balance, bring
up, calculate, chew,
consider, gauge, lean,
quantify, rate, review
weight: ballast, bias,
bob, burden, clout,
consequence, effect,
force, gravity, impact,
impetus, importance,
influence, interest,
leverage, load,
magnitude, main,
moment, muscle,
pressure, prestige,
pull, say, significance,
slant, stress, tax
weighted: loaded
weightily: heavily
weighting: bias
weighty: bulky,
cogent, compelling,
forceful, grave, heavy,
influential, major,
momentous, onerous,
ponderous, pregnant,
serious, significant,
strong
weir: waterfall

weird: bizarre, crazy, creepy, fantastic, fate, funny, grotesque, kinky, lunatic, macabre, mysterious, odd, peculiar, queer, strange, unnatural
weirdness: eccentricity
weirdo: card, crank, deviant, freak, lunatic, oddity, original, pervert, rebel
welcome: desirable, greet, greeting, hospitality, invitation, invite, meet, pleasant, receive, reception, salute, take in
welcoming: favourable, homely, hospitable, inviting, receptive
weld: cement, fasten, fuse, seal, unify, union, unite
welfare: benefit, dole, hand-out, sake
well: fit, healthy, now, quarry, right, robust, so, spring
wellbeing: comfort, good, health, prosperity, sake, welfare
wellie: boot
wellington: boot
well-off: comfortable
well-read: cultured
well-versed: cultured
welsher: defaulter
welt: lip, scourge
wen: bulge, gall
wench: girl, maid, maiden
wend: journey
wet: bathe, damp, drip, irrigate, juicy, liquid, lubricate, moist, mud, muddy, pathetic, sap, soak, splash, wash, watery, weakling, weed
whack: bang, bat, beat, belt, blow, cane, clap, clip, crack, crown, fatigue, hit, knock, punch, quota, share, slap, wallop,
whacked: through, tired, weary
whale: bull
wham: clout
wharf: berth, dock, harbour, jetty,

mooring, pier, quay
wheedle: coax, flatter, get round, jolly
wheedling: persuasion
wheel: helm, revolve, roll, rotate, swing, turn, whirl
wheelmark: rut
wheeze: cough, croak, heave, pant, puff, whoop
wheezing: breathless
whelp: pup
when: as, on, once
whenever: once
whereabouts: position, scene
whereas: while
wherewithal: capital, cash, means, money, resources
whet: grind, pique, point
whether: if
whiff: breeze, gust, hint, puff, smell, whisper
whiffy: high
while: as, bit, idle, on, period, term, though, time
whim: conceit, crank, fancy, freak, humour, idea, impulse, kink, quirk, wish
whimper: snivel
whimsical: capricious, fanciful, jocular, kinky, quaint, quirky, romantic
whine: buzz, complain, moan, snivel, wail, whimper
whinge: whimper, whine
whining: querulous
whinny: snort
whip: beat, belt, birch, cane, castigate, dessert, flog, lash, mash, nick, punish, rouse, scourge, strap, switch, tan, whisk
whiplash: rebound
whippersnapper: pup
whipping: hiding, punishment
whir: buzz
whirl: blow, brandish, circle, fling, go, maelstrom, reel, revolution, revolve, ride, roll, spin, turn
whirlpool: gulf,

maelstrom, storm
whirring: buzz
whisk: blow, shoot, switch, whip
whisker: bristle, hair
whiskers: beard
whisper: breath, breathe, buzz, hint, jot, rumour, wind
whispered: soft
whispering: murmuring
whistle: blow, catcall, flute, pipe, sing, wheeze
whit: jot, rap, shred, speck
white: blank, bright, deadly, frosty, livid, milky, wan
whiten: bleach, pale
whiteness: brilliance
whitewash: prime
whiting: whitewash
whitish: light, pale
whittle: carve, chip, cut
whittled: cut
whizz: wizard, zip
whizkid: prodigy
whole: catholic, clean, complete, gross, intact, integral, lump, mass, natural, package, perfect, piece, round, sound, sum, total, unbroken, unit
wholehearted: dedicated, hearty
wholeheartedly: unreservedly
wholeheartedness: sincerity
wholeness: integrity
wholesale: sweeping, widespread
wholesaler: dealer, distributor, merchant
wholesome: fresh, good, healthy, nourishing, pure, safe, sanitary, savoury
wholly: bodily, completely, quite
whoop: call, cry, yell
whopper: monster
whopping: monster, monstrous, monumental
whore: bitch, prostitute
whoredom: prostitution
whorehouse: brothel
whorl: curl, loop,

spiral
whorled: spiral
wick: fuse
wicked: atrocious, bad, black, damnable, dark, depraved, evil, foul, ill, immoral, iniquitous, mischievous, naughty, pernicious, satanic, shameful, sinful, unholy, vile, villainous, wrong
wickedly: badly
wickedness: atrocity, crime, depravity, enormity, evil, immorality, impropriety, vice, wrong
wicket: gate
widdle: urinate
wide: broad, capacious, comprehensive, deep, fat, roomy, thick, untrue
widely: generally
widen: flare, gape, spread, thicken
widening: dilation, enlargement, flare
widespread: common, epidemic, general, pervasive, popular, prevalent, public, rampant, rife
widowed: bereaved
width: beam, breadth, depth, gauge, latitude
wield: brandish, flourish, handle, manage, manoeuvre, operate, ply, use, work
wielder: operator
wielding: management, manipulation, operation
wife: mate, partner, woman
wiggle: wag, wind, wriggle
wigwam: lodge
wild: barbaric, boisterous, delirious, desperate, dissolute, extravagant, fanciful, fantastic, fast, ferocious, fierce, foul, furious, incoherent, insubordinate, irresponsible, lawless, lunatic, mad, passionate, rampant,

rogue, romantic,
rough, rowdy, savage,
tempestuous,
unbridled, unbroken,
undisciplined,
ungovernable,
unreasoning,
unspoilt, untamed,
violent, waste, weird
wildcat: unauthorized
wilderness: desert,
forest, jungle,
solitude,
undergrowth, waste
wildly: madly,
roughly
wildness: dissolution,
fury, lunacy,
madness, violence
wilds: bush, waste,
wilderness
wile: artifice, device,
dodge, shift
wilful: conscious,
defiant, fractious,
headstrong, obstinate,
perverse, pig-headed,
premeditated,
rebellious,
recalcitrant,
refractory, stubborn,
undisciplined,
wayward
wiliness: guile,
machination
will: endow, nerve,
ordain, pleasure,
purpose, way, wish
willed: voluntary
willing: game, glad,
obedient, obliging,
predisposed,
prepared, prompt,
ready, voluntary
willingly: happily,
readily, soon
willingness:
obedience
willow: bat
willowy: slender
willpower: backbone,
resolution, resolve,
self-control, spirit
wilt: die, fade, flag,
languish, pine, wither
wilting: flagging
wily: astute, cag(e)y,
crafty, cunning,
designing, devious,
foxy, insidious,
scheming, sharp,
shrewd, sly, subtle,
vulpine
wimp: rabbit,
weakling, weed, wet
wimpish: wet

wimple: veil
win: attain,
attainment, captivate,
carry, conquer, gain,
get, land, obtain, pot,
prevail, score, take,
victory
wince: flinch, shrink
winch: crane, hoist,
jack, warp, wind,
wind up
wind: blast, blow,
breeze, coil, crank,
curl, draught, ramble,
reel, roll, screw,
swerve, terminate,
thread, twine
windbag: chatterbox
windblown: wild
windbreak: awning,
screen
winded: breathless
winder: key
windfall: bonus,
godsend
winding: circuitous,
crooked, curved,
devious, labyrinthine,
meandering,
rambling, spiral,
wandering
windless: calm
windmill: flail, thresh
window: light, port
windswept: bleak,
wild
windy: bleak,
blustery, boisterous,
stormy
wine: sack
wing: flight, limb, sail,
soar, wound
wink: bat, flutter,
sparkle, twinkling
winnable: attainable
winner: best,
champion, hit, nap,
victor
winning: best,
charming, disarming,
engaging, inviting,
lovable, lovely,
victorious
winnings: bonus,
gain, loot, prize
winnow: single,
thresh
wino: drunkard
winsome: fetching,
lovable, sweet
wintry: chill, cold,
frosty
wipe: clean, clear,
dust, mop, rub, whisk
wire: cable, element,
enclosure, fence, flex,

lead, line, snare
wiry: spare
wisdom: depth,
insight, judgement,
knowledge, learning,
lore, maturity,
prudence, reason,
tact, teachings, wit
wise: deep, discerning,
judicious, mature,
profound, reasonable,
sage, sensible
wisecrack: dig, gag,
jest, joke, quip, sally
wisecracking:
comedy
wisecracks: banter
wish: aspire, bid, care,
choose, desire, dream,
hankering, hope,
impulse, long,
longing, mind,
notion, pine, please,
pleasure, purpose,
require, urge, want,
way, will, yearn,
yearning
wishful:
impracticality,
longing, unrealistic,
wistful
wispy: thin
wistful: longing,
pensive, plaintive, sad
wit: brain, comedian,
common sense,
humour, imagination,
intelligence, joker,
laugh, satire, wag
witch: bag, harridan,
magician, prune
witchcraft: magic,
sorcery
with: on, plus,
through
withdraw: cave in,
deduct, depart, go,
leave, part, pull out,
recall, recede, repeal,
retire, retreat, revoke,
scratch, subtract, take
back, walk
withdrawal:
deduction, departure,
deprivation, exodus,
leave, recall, repeal,
retirement, retraction,
retreat, secession,
seclusion,
sequestration
withdrawn: distant,
introverted, lonely,
remote, sheltered,
taciturn,
uncommunicative,
undemonstrative

wither: blast, decay,
die, fade, flag,
languish, perish, pine,
rot, scorch, shrink,
wane, waste, wilt
withered: parched,
shrivelled
withering: biting,
decay, devastating,
flagging, murderous,
scathing, scornful,
wane
withhold: refrain,
refuse, reserve,
suppress, suspend
within: under
without: less
withstand: combat,
endure, resist, stand,
stem, sustain, take,
weather
witless: fatuous,
idiotic, silly
witness: observe,
passer-by, see,
testimony, view
witnessing: onlooking
wits: mind
witter: natter, prattle,
rabbit, rattle, talk,
waffle
witticism: hit, jest,
quip, sally
witticisms: humour,
repartee
witty: facetious,
humorous,
imaginative, jocular,
light, salty,
scintillating, smart
wizard: magician,
oracle
wizardry: sorcery
wizen: wither
wobble: bob, reel,
rock, shake, stagger,
tremble, tremor,
waver
wobbly: dizzy,
groggy, infirm,
insecure, loose, shaky
woe: calamity,
distress, misery, pain,
sorrow
woebegone:
lugubrious, rueful,
sad, wretched
woeful: plaintive,
rueful, wretched
wolf: bolt, gorge, gulp
wolfing: guzzling
woman: daily, girl,
hen, lover, maid,
piece, wife
womanhood:
maturity

womaniser: libertine
womanish: feminine
womanize: whore
womanizer: wolf
womanly: feminine, girlish
wonder: awe, jewel, marvel, miracle, phenomenon, query
wonderful: divine, enjoyable, fantastic, glorious, great, heavenly, marvellous, sensational, splendid, terrific
wonderment: astonishment
wondrous: awesome, miraculous
wont: custom, habit, routine, rule, way
wonted: habitual, routine
woo: court, pursue
wood: bowl, kindling, timber
woodcraft: forestry
wooden: dead, heavy, laboured, lifeless
woodenly: heavily
woodland: forest, park, woods
woods: forest, timber
woodwork: trim
woody: xyloid
woof: bark
woofter: fairy, gay, homosexual
wool: coat, fleece, flock
woollen: woolly
woolly: cardigan, hairy, jersey, muddled, muddy, vague
woozy: dazed, dizzy, faint, groggy, merry
word: assurance, authority, commitment, couch, hint, information, intelligence, message, news, oath, phrase, put, remark, rumour, term, warning, whisper
worded: verbal
wording: language, legend, letter, phraseology, style
wordless: inarticulate, mute, silent
wordplay: wit
words: dialogue, language, lyric, talk, teachings, text,

vocabulary
wordsmith: writer
wordy: rambling, verbose
work: beat, behave, book, business, calling, composition, craft, creation, cultivate, effort, exercise, farm, fashion, ferment, forge, function, go, grind, hammer, job, knead, labour, livelihood, living, novel, occupation, operate, opus, perform, practice, run, serve, service, settle, struggle, take, task, temper, till, volume, wash, weave, writing
workable: feasible, operative, practicable, practical, viable
workaholic: beaver, machine
worked: cultivated
worker: employee, hand, help, man, operative, operator
workers: labour, office, personnel
workforce: labour
working: mechanism, occupied, on, operation, operative, performance, practical
workmanship: craft, handicraft
workmate: colleague
works: factory, farm, guts, mechanism, motor, movement, plant
workshop: forge
workshy: lazy
world: creation, earth, globe, orb, realm, scene, universe
worldly: mundane, profane, secular, temporal
worldwide: universal
worm: jockey, wind, work, wretch, wriggle
worn: bare, dead, decrepit, drawn, frayed, limp, motheaten, pinched, seedy, used
worried: concerned, jittery, jumpy, loaded, restless,

solicitous, upset, uptight
worrisome: nagging, vexatious
worry: badger, burden, care, chafe, concern, distress, disturb, fret, fuss, harass, load, lookout, misgiving, molest, pain, persecute, perturb, pester, pigeon, plague, press, ruffle, sorrow, stress, sweat, trouble, unrest, vex
worrying: gnawing, thorny, vexatious
worse: inferior
worsen: compound, decline, degenerate, impair, inflame, relapse, sink
worsening: decline, deterioration, progressive, relapse
worship: bless, glorify, glory, honour, idolatry, idolize, love, magnify, praise, revere, service
worshipper: conquest, follower, lover
worshipping: doting
worst: end
worsted: flannel
worth: calibre, distinction, merit, quality, rarity, value
worthily: fairly
worthiness: virtue
worthless: bad, base, dreadful, futile, hopeless, idle, meaningless, nugatory, otiose, pathetic, pitiful, pointless, poor, vain, vile, void, wretched
worthlessness: nullity, vanity
worthwhile: productive, profitable, useful, valuable
worthy: good, respectable, saintly, solid, virtuous
wound: bruise, distress, grieve, haemorrhage, hurt, incision, knife, lacerate, laceration, lame, lesion, pain, pierce, prick, trauma,

twisted, wring
wounded: hurt, lame, stung
wounding: mayhem, traumatic
wraith: ghost, presence, spectre
wraithlike: ghostly
wrangle: beef, clash, disagree, dispute, fight, fracas, haggle, hassle, jar, quarrel, row, scrap, scuffle, spar
wrangling: contentious, strife
wrap: bandage, cloak, cover, envelop, fold, jacket, package, parcel, roll, twine, wind
wrapped: bound, wound
wrapper: cover, jacket, robe
wrapping: case, insulation, jacket, paper
wrath: bile, passion, rage
wreak: inflict
wreath: garland
wreathe: wind
wreck: blast, bus, crash, damage, derelict, destroy, dish, loss, pulverize, queer, ravage, ruin, sabotage, shatter, smash, spoil, total, undo, write off
wreckage: debris, destruction, remains, ruin
wrecked: derelict, lost, undone
wrecking: demolition, sabotage
wrench: jar, jerk, rack, rend, rip, snatch, strain, wring
wrenched: twisted
wrest: rip, snatch, squeeze, wrench, wring
wrestle: fight, scuffle, tackle
wretch: ruffian
wretched: awful, bad, base, desolate, desperate, forlorn, hangdog, lamentable, luckless, mean, melancholy, miserable, mournful, pitiful, poor, sad,

sorry, unhappy, vile,
woeful
wretchedly:
desperately,
piteously, unhappily
wretchedness:
despair, distress,
grief, melancholy,
misery, woe
wriggle: crawl, creep,
work
wring: force, milk,
squeeze
wringing: wet
wrinkle: crease,

crumple, dodge, fold,
hint, knit, line, ruffle,
tip
wrinkled: haggard,
rugged
wristband: cuff
writ: brief, instrument
write: book, compose,
devise, inscribe, jot,
make out, make up,
mark, pen, record,
reply, scrawl, take
down, transcribe
writer: author, hack,
narrator

writhe: thresh, wind,
wriggle
writhing: serpentine
writing: composition,
hand, notation,
scrawl, script
writings: works
written: fated
wrong: bad, crime,
disservice, false,
faulty, grievance,
guilty, hurt, ill,
illegal, immoral,
impractical,
improper, inaccurate,

inappropriate,
incorrect, injustice,
mistaken, offence,
out, score, untrue,
wicked
wrongdoer:
delinquent, offender,
sinner
wrongdoing: evil,
guilt, sin
wrung: mangled
wry: sardonic, tongue-
in-cheek
wunderkind: prodigy

X

Xmas: Yule
xylem: wood

Y

Y-fronts: briefs
yacht: boat, ship
yahoo: clown, lout, philistine
yak: yap
yammer: gab
yank: jerk, pluck, pull, twitch, wrench
yap: bark
yard: court, enclosure
yardstick: canon, criterion, gauge, mark, measure, norm, ruler, standard
yarn: fable, fiction, story, tale, thread, twine
yawl: boat, yacht
yawn: gape
yawning: beckoning, deep, profound
year: form
year's: yearly
year-long: yearly
yearn: aspire, burn, desire, fancy, hunger, itch, long, look forward to, lust, miss, pant, pine, want, wish

yearning: craving, desire, hunger, itch, longing, thirsty, want, wish, wishful, wistful
yeast: ferment, fungus
yell: bark, bawl, bellow, call, cry, hail, outcry, rail, roar, scream, shout, shriek, squeal, thunder, trumpet, whoop
yelling: railing, vociferous
yellow: chicken, discolour, fair, gold(en), spineless
yellow-bellied: cowardly
yellowish: buff, cream, creamy, fawn, jaundiced, lurid, sallow
yelp: bark, squeal, yap
yen: hankering, impulse, longing, want
yeoman: warder
yes-man: creep, lackey

yesterday: history
yet: but, even, however, nevertheless, notwithstanding, still, though
yield: bear, bow, budge, capitulate, cave in, cede, concede, consent, crack, crop, crumple, defer, deliver, fall, fruit, gain, give, grant, harvest, haul, kowtow, lose, output, pay, produce, profit, provide, quit, render, resign, return, revenue, submit, succumb, surrender
yielder: loser
yielding: capitulation, concession, deferential, facile, pliable, servile, soft
yip: whoop, yap
yobbo: brute, hooligan, lout, savage, yob

yodel: sing, warble
yoke: couple, harness, hitch, join, link, pair, team
yokel: clown, peasant
yomp: march, walk
yomping: hiking
young: baby, brood, childish, fresh, fruit, girlish, immature, juvenile, litter, mere, pup, tender, youth
younger: junior, minor
youngster: child, juvenile, kid, lad, youth
younker: youngster
youth: boy, childhood, juvenile, lad, tenderness, young, youngster
youthful: fresh, juvenile, young
youthfulness: youth
yowl: wail, whine

Z

zany: dizzy
zap: blast, shoot
zeal: fervour, fire, industry, passion, warmth, zest
zealot: fanatic
zealous: dedicated, devout, earnest, fanatical, fervent, jealous, keen, passionate, rabid, solicitous, strenuous, strong, wholehearted
zealousness: jealousy
zenith: climax, crown, height, high, maximum, peak, pinnacle, summit
zeppelin: ship
zero: cipher, duck, love, nil, nothing
zest: bang, energy, gusto, kick, life, relish, spirit, zip

zestful: salty
zigzag: fork, indent, ramble, stagger, tack, turn, weave, wriggle
zilch: nil, nothing
zing: zest, zip
zip: bounce, drive, energy, fasten, fastener, flash, fly, race, snap, sparkle, vigour, vivacity, zap
zip-fastener: zip

zombie: automaton
zone: belt, compass(es), country, grounds, jurisdiction, locality, province, quarter, region, section, territory, ward
zoologist: vet
zoom: race, speed, sweep, zap, zip